Exploring Autodesk Revit 2018 for Architecture

(14th Revised and Updated Edition)

Sham Tickoo
Professor
Purdue University Northwest
Hammond, Indiana, USA

Contributing Authors
Bhawna Kathpalia
Sr. Civil Engineer
Tickoo Institute of Emerging Technologies (TIET)

CADCIM Technologies, USA
Tickoo Institute of Emerging Technologies (TIET), India

ISBN: 978-93-86551-72-6
14th Revised and Updated Edition
(For distribution in SAARC countries only)

Limits of Liability and Disclaimer of Warranty

Distributors

BPB PUBLICATIONS
20, Ansari Road, Darya Ganj
New Delhi-110002
Ph: 23254990/23254991

BPB BOOK CENTRE
376 Old Lajpat Rai Market
DELHI-110006
Ph: 23861747

DECCAN AGENCIES
4-3-329, Bank Street
HYDERABAD-500195
Ph: 24756967/24756400

COMPUTER BOOK CENTRE
12, Shrungar Shopping Centre
M.G. Road
BENGALURU–560001
Ph: 25587923/25584641

MICRO MEDIA
Shop No. 5, Mahendra Chambers
150 DN Rd. Next to Capital Cinema
V.T (C.S.T.) Station
MUMBAI-400001
Ph: 22078296/22078297

Published by Manish Jain for BPB Publications, 20 Ansari Road, Darya Ganj
New Delhi-110002 and Printed by Repro India Pvt. Ltd, Mumbai

DEDICATION

To teachers, who make it possible to disseminate knowledge to enlighten the young and curious minds of our future generations

To students, who are dedicated to learning new technologies and making the world a better place to live in

SPECIAL RECOGNITION

A special thanks to Mr. Denis Cadu and the ADN team of Autodesk Inc. for their valuable support and professional guidance to procure the software for writing this textbook

THANKS

To employees at CADCIM Technologies and Tickoo Institute of Emerging Technologies (TIET) for their valuable help

To Ayushi Dang for technical editing this manuscript

To Rajendra Badola, Anju Jethwani, and Kusha Gupta for copy editing this manuscript

Note

If you are a faculty member, you can register by clicking on the following link to access the teaching resources: ***www.cadcim.com/Registration.aspx***. The student resources are available at ***www.cadcim.com***.

Table of Contents

Chapter 2: Starting an Architectural Project

Chapter 3: Creating Walls

Chapter 4: Using Basic Building Components-I

Chapter 5: Using the Editing Tools

Chapter 6: Working with Datum Plane and Creating Standard Views

Chapter 7: Using Basic Building Components-II

Chapter 8: Using Basic Building Components-III

Chapter 9: Adding Site Features

Chapter 10: Using Massing Tools

Chapter 11: Adding Annotations and Dimensions

Chapter 12: Creating Project Details and Schedules

Chapter 13: Creating and Plotting Drawing Sheets

Chapter 14: Creating 3D Views

Preface

Autodesk Revit 2018

Autodesk Revit 2018 is a Building Information Modeling software developed by Autodesk. This software helps architects and designers to develop high quality and accurate architectural designs.

The **Autodesk Revit 2018 for Architecture** textbook introduces the users to the spectacular realm of one of the most powerful software in the architectural quiver. This textbook is a gateway to power, skill, and competence in the field of architectural and interior presentations, drawings, and documentations.

This textbook is specially meant for professionals and students of architecture and interior design, facilities planners, and CAD professionals who are associated with the building construction and allied fields in the construction industry.

Special emphasis has been laid to explain new concepts, procedures, and methods in Revit by using sufficient text and graphical examples.The accompanying tutorials and exercises, which relate to the real-world projects, help you understand the usage and abilities of the tools available in Autodesk Revit.

The main features of this textbook are as follows:

- **Project-based Approach**
  The author has adopted the project-based approach and the learn-by-doing approach throughout the textbook. This approach helps the users learn the concepts and procedures easily.

- **Real-World Designs as Projects**
  The author has used real-world building designs and architectural examples as projects in this textbook so that the users can correlate them to the real-time designs.

- **Tips and Notes**
  Additional information related to various topics is provided to the users in the form of tips and notes.

- **Learning Objectives**
  The first page of every chapter summarizes the topics that will be covered in that chapter. This will help the users to easily refer to a topic.

- **Self-Evaluation Test, Review Questions, and Exercises**
  Every chapters ends with Self-Evaluation test so that the users can assess their knowledge of the chapter. The answers to Self-Evaluation Test are given at the end of the chapters. Also, the Review Questions and Exercises are given at the end of the chapters and they can be used by the instructors as test questions and exercises.

- **Heavily Illustrated Text**
  The text in this book is heavily illustrated with around 900 line diagrams and screen capture images that support the command sections and tutorials.

Symbols Used in the Textbook

Note

The author has provided additional information to the users about the topic being discussed in the form of notes.

Tip

Special information and techniques are provided in the form of tips that helps in increasing the efficiency of the users.

New

This symbol indicates that the command or tool being discussed is new in the current release of Autodesk Revit.

Enhanced

This symbol indicates that the command or tool being discussed is enhanced in the current release of Autodesk Revit.

Formatting Conventions Used in the Textbook

Please refer to the following list for the formatting conventions used in this textbook.

- Names of tools, buttons, options, browser, palette, panels, and tabs are written in boldface.
  Example: The **Wall: Architecture** tool, the **Modify** button, the **Build** panel, the **Architecture** tab, the **Properties** palette, the **Project Browser**, and so on.

- Names of dialog boxes, drop-downs, drop-down lists, list boxes, areas, edit boxes, check boxes, and radio buttons are written in boldface.
  Example: The **Options** dialog box, the **Wall** drop-down of the **Build** panel in the **Architecture** tab, the **Name** edit box of the **Name** dialog box, the **Chain** check box in the **Options Bar**, and so on.

- Values entered in edit boxes are written in boldface.
  Example: Enter **Brick Wall** in the **Name** edit box.

- Names of the files are italicized.
  Example: *c14_Club_tut2.rvt*

- The methods of invoking a tool/option from the ribbon, **File** menu, or the shortcut keys are given in a shaded box.

> **Ribbon:** Home > Build > Wall drop-down > Wall
> **File menu:** New
> **Shortcut Keys:** CTRL+N

- When you select an element or a component, a contextual tab is displayed depending upon the entity selected. In this textbook, this contextual tab is referred to as **Modify | (Elements / Components)**.

> **Ribbon:** Modify | (Elements / Components) > Modify > Move
> **Shortcut Key:** MV

Naming Conventions Used in the Textbook

Please refer to the following list for the naming conventions used in this textbook.

Tool

If you click on an item in a panel of the ribbon and a command is invoked to create/edit an object or perform some action, then that item is termed as **tool**.

For example:
Wall: Architectural tool, **Window** tool, **Railing** tool
Filled Region tool, **Trim/Extend to Corner** tool, **Rotate** tool
Link Revit tool, **Detail Line** tool

If you click on an item in a panel of the ribbon and a dialog box is invoked wherein you can set the properties to create/edit an object, then that item is also termed as **tool**, refer to Figure 1.
For example:
Load Family tool, **Materials** tool, **Project Units** tool
Design Options tool, **Visibility/Graphics** tool

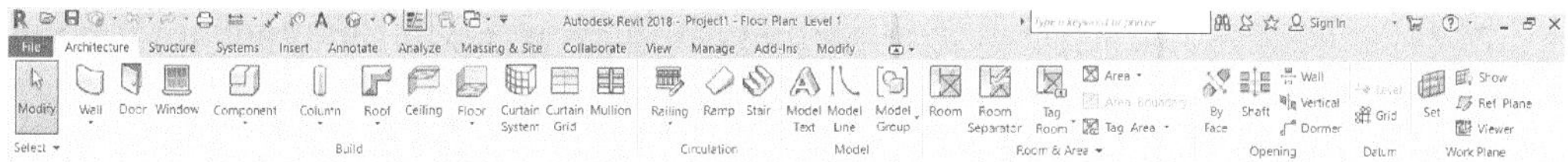

Figure 1 Tools in the ribbon

Button

The item in a dialog box that has a 3d shape is termed as **button**. For example, **OK** button, **Cancel** button, **Apply** button, and so on. If an item in a ribbon is used to exit a tool or a mode then that item is also termed as a button. For example, **Modify** button, **Finish Edit Mode** button, **Cancel Edit Mode** button, and so on; refer to Figure 2.

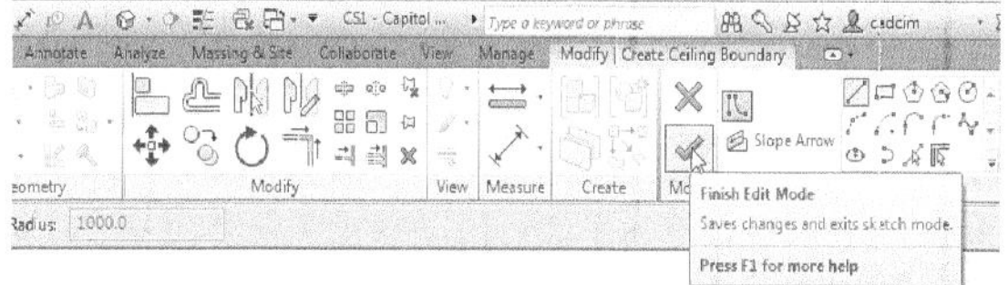

*Figure 2 Choosing the **Finish Edit Mode** button*

Dialog Box

In this textbook, different terms are used for referring to the components of a dialog box. Refer to Figure 3 for the terminology used.

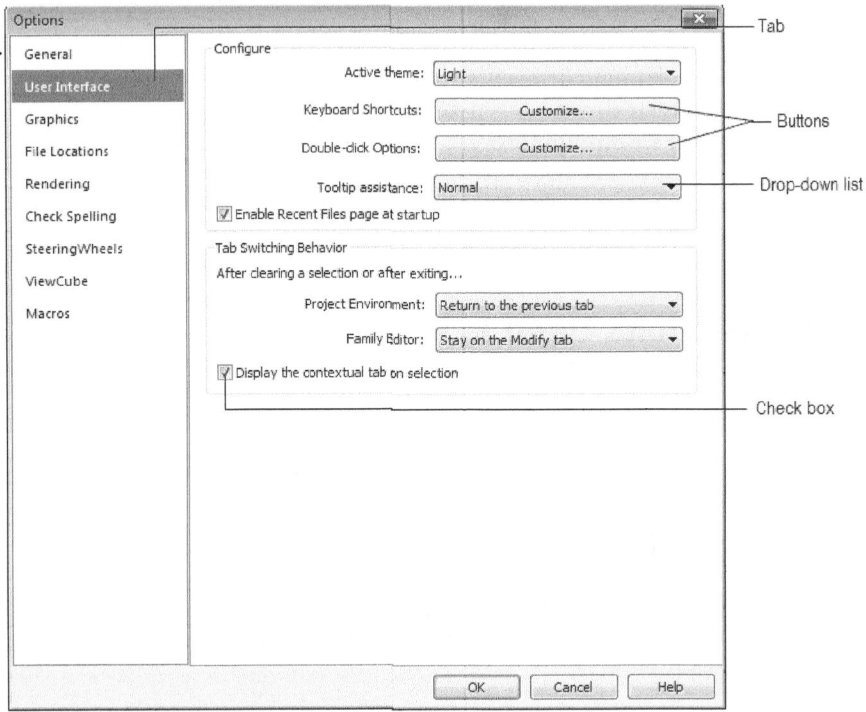

Figure 3 Different components of a dialog box

Drop-down

A drop-down is the one in which a set of common tools are grouped together for performing an action. You can identify a drop-down with a down arrow on it. The drop-downs are given a name based on the tools grouped in them. For example, **Wall** drop-down, **Component** drop-down, **Region** drop-down, and so on, refer to Figure 4.

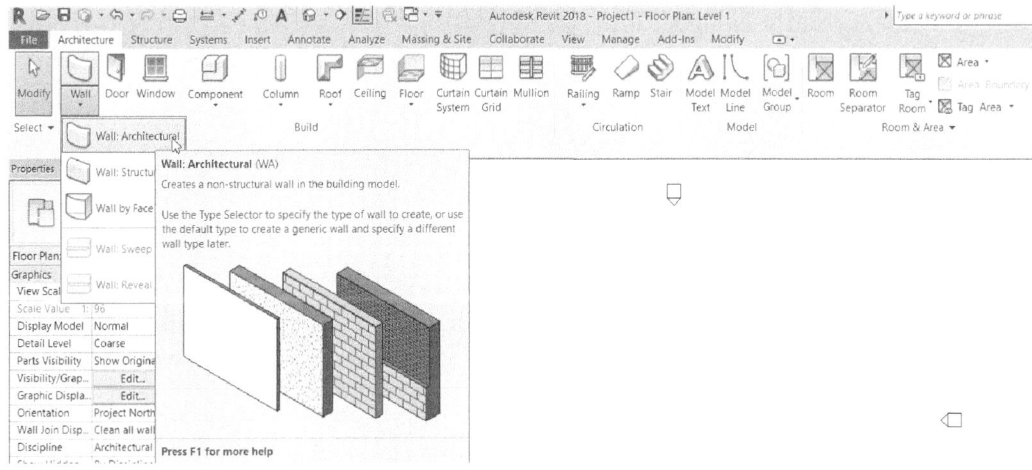

Figure 4 Choosing a tool from a drop-down

Drop-down List

A drop-down list is the one in which a set of options are grouped together. You can set a parameter using an option from this drop-down list. You can identify a drop-down list with a down arrow on it. For example, **Type Selector** drop-down list, **Units** drop-down list, and so on; refer to Figure 5.

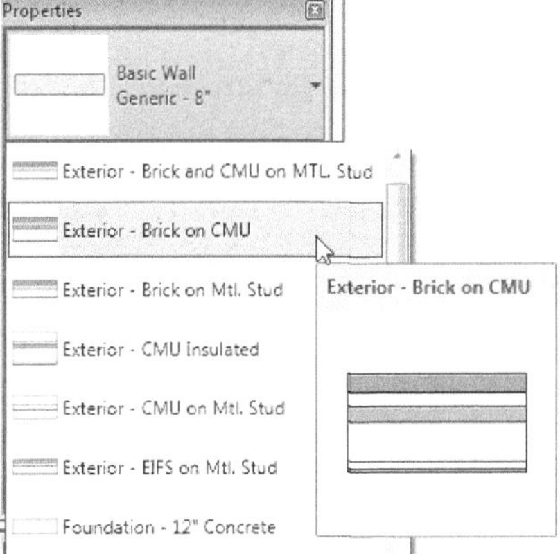

Figure 5 Selecting an option from the ***Type Selector*** *drop-down list*

Options

Options are the items that are available in shortcut menus, drop-down lists, dialog boxes, flyouts, and so on. For example, choose the **Zoom In Region** option from the shortcut menu displayed on right-clicking in the drawing area; refer to Figure 6.

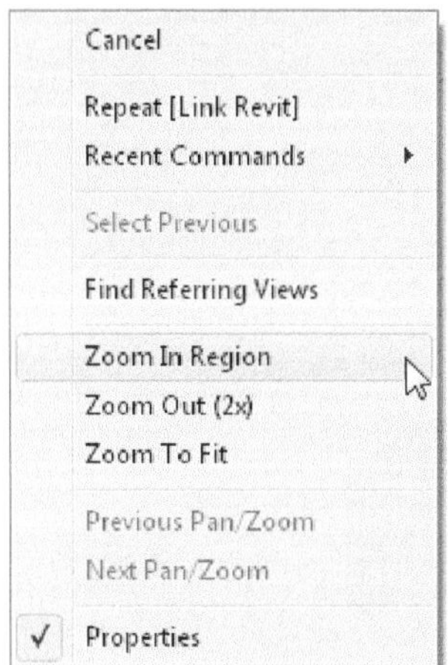

Figure 6 *Choosing an option from the shortcut menu*

Free Companion Website

It has been our constant endeavor to provide you the best textbooks and services at affordable price. In this endeavor, we have come out with a free Companion website that will facilitate the process of teaching and learning of Autodesk Revit 2018. If you purchase this textbook, you will get access to the files on the Companion website.
The following resources are available for the faculty and students in this website:

Faculty Resources

- **Technical Support**
  You can get online technical support by contacting ***techsupport@cadcim.com***.

- **Instructor Guide**
  Solutions to all review questions and exercises in the textbook are provided in this guide to help the faculty members test the skills of the students.

- **PowerPoint Presentations**
  The contents of the book are arranged in PowerPoint slides that can be used by the faculty for their lectures.

- **Revit Files**
  The Revit files used in illustration, tutorials, and exercises are available for free download.

- **Learning Resources**
  You can access additional learning resources by visiting ***http:/revitxperts.blogspot.com*** and ***http:/youtube.com/cadcimtech***.

Student Resources

- **Technical Support**
  You can get online technical support by contacting ***techsupport@cadcim.com***.

- **Revit Files**
  The revit files used in illustrations and tutorials are available for free download.

- **Free Download Chapter**
  Chapter 16 of this textbook is available for free download at *www.cadcim.com*.

If you face any problem in accessing these files, please contact the publisher at *sales@cadcim.com* or the author at *stickoo@pnw.edu* or *tickoo525@gmail.com*.

Stay Connected

You can now stay connected with us through Facebook and Twitter to get the latest information about our textbooks, videos, and teaching/learning resources. To get such updates, follow us on Facebook (***www.facebook.com/cadcim***) and Twitter (**@cadcimtech**). You can also subscribe to our YouTube channel (***www.youtube.com/cadcimtech***) to get the information about our latest video tutorials.

Chapter 1

Introduction to Autodesk Revit 2018 for Architecture

Learning Objectives

After completing this chapter, you will be able to:

- *Understand the basic concepts and principles of Revit 2018 for Architecture*
- *Understand different terms used in Revit*
- *Know the parametric behavior of Revit*
- *Use different components of the User Interface screen of Revit*
- *Access the Revit 2018 Help*
- *Know Worksharing using Revit Server*

INTRODUCTION

Welcome to the realm of Revit, a powerful building modeler that has changed the outlook of the building industry about computer aided designs. Autodesk Revit is a design and documentation platform that enables you to use a single, integrated building information model to conceptualize, design, and finally document a project. Its integrated parametric modeling technology is used to create the information model of a project, and to collect and coordinate information across all its representations. In Autodesk Revit, drawing sheets, 2D views, 3D views, and schedules are a direct representation of the same building information model. Using its parametric change engine, you can modify a design at any stage of a project. The change in the project is automatically made and represented in all its views, resulting in the development of better designs, along with an improved coordination. The use of Revit provides a competitive advantage and a higher profitability to architects and building industry professionals.

Autodesk Revit AS A BUILDING INFORMATION MODELER

The history of computer aided design and documentation dates back to the early 1980s when architects began using this technology for documenting their projects. Realizing its advantages, information sharing capabilities were developed, especially to share data with other consultants. This led to the development of object-based CAD systems in the early 1990s. Before the development of these systems, objects such as walls, doors, windows were stored as a non-graphical data with the assigned graphics. These systems arranged the information logically, but were unable to optimize its usage in a building project. Realizing the advantages of the solid modeling tools, the mechanical and manufacturing industry professionals began using the information modeling CAD technology. This technology enabled them to extract data based on the relationship between model elements.

In 1997, a group of mechanical CAD technologists began working on a new software for the building industry. The Building Information Modeling (BIM) provided an alternative approach to building design, construction, and management. This approach, however, required a suitable technology to implement and reap its benefits. In such a situation, the use of parametric technology with the Building Information Modeling approach was envisaged as an ideal combination. They developed a software that was suitable for creating building projects. This software was earlier known as Autodesk Revit Architecture, and has now been changed to Autodesk Revit.

Autodesk Revit is a building design and documentation platform in which a digital building model is created using the parametric elements such as walls, doors, windows, and so on. All the building elements have inherent relationship with one another, which can be tracked, managed, and maintained by the computer.

BASIC CONCEPTS AND PRINCIPLES

Autodesk Revit enables you to envisage and develop a building model with actual 3D parametric building elements. It provides a new approach to the architectural thought and the implementation process. In a way, it replicates the way architects conceive a building. For example, 2D CAD platforms mostly use lines to represent all elements, as shown in Figure 1-1. However, in Autodesk Revit, you can create a building model using 3D elements such as walls, floors, doors, and windows, as shown in Figure 1-2.

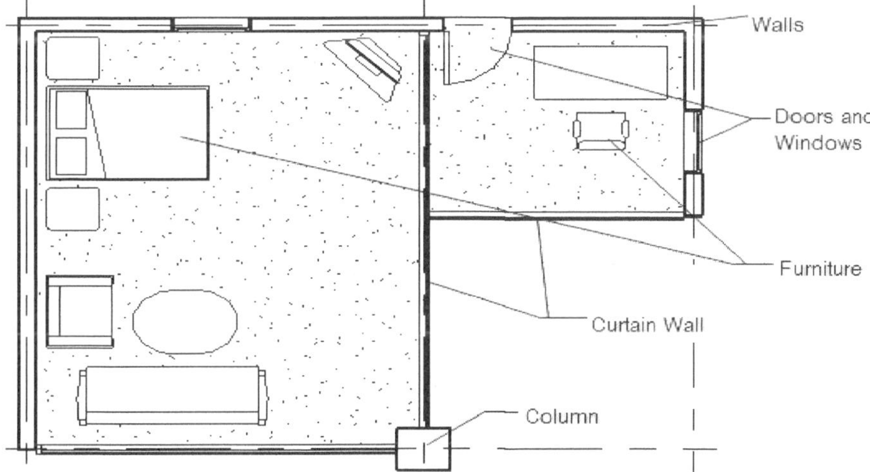

Figure 1-1 *CAD project created using 2D lines and curves*

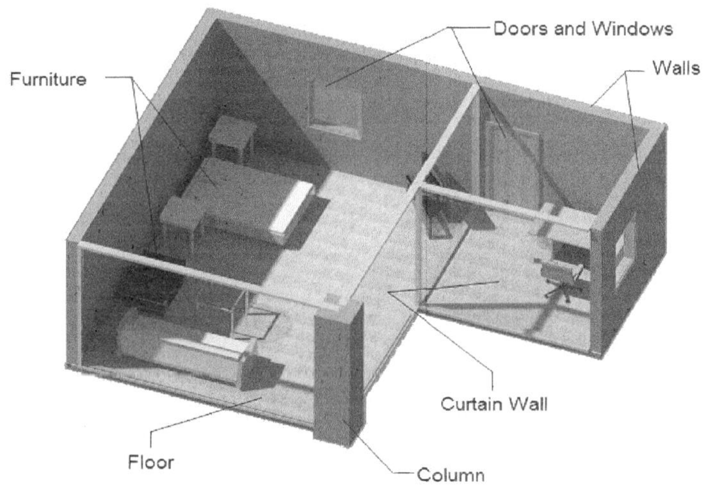

Figure 1-2 *Autodesk Revit project created using parametric building model*

Using these 3D elements, you can visualize the architectural or interior project with respect to its scale, volume, and proportions. This enables you to study design alternatives and develop superior quality design solutions. Autodesk Revit automates routine drafting and coordination tasks and assists in reducing errors in documentation. This, in turn, saves time, improves the speed of documentation, and lowers the cost for users.

Understanding the Parametric Building Modeling Technology

A project in Autodesk Revit is created using the in-built parametric building elements. The term parametric refers to the relationship parameters between various building elements. Some relations are applied automatically to building elements whie creating them, and some are user defined. For example, doors, which have an inherent parametric relationship with walls cannot be created without first creating a host wall. A door always moves with the host wall. Similarly, floors too are parametrically linked to walls. When you move walls, the floor extents are also modified automatically. Each building element has in-built bidirectional associativity with many other elements in the project.

A building information model is created using different interdependent parametric building elements such as walls, floors, roof, ceiling, stairs, ramps, curtain walls, and so on. As they are bidirectionally associated elements, any change made in one element is automatically adopted by others. The integrated building information model thus created contains all the data for a project. You can then create project presentation views such as plans, sections, elevations, and so on for documentation. As you modify the model while working in certain views, Autodesk Revit's parametric change engine automatically updates other views. This capability is, therefore, the underlying concept in Autodesk Revit.

Autodesk Revit's parametric change engine enables you to modify design elements at any stage of the project development. As changes are made immediately and automatically, it saves the time and effort in coordinating them in all other associated views which for most projects is an inevitable part of the design process. Revit's capability to coordinate between various aspects of the building design provides immense flexibility in the design and development process along with an error-free documentation.

Revit also provides a variety of in-built parametric element libraries that can be selected and used to create a building model. It also provides you with the flexibility of modifying properties of these elements or create your own parametric elements based on the project requirement.

Terms Used in Autodesk Revit

Before using Revit, it is important to understand the basic terms used for creating a building model. Various terms in Revit such as project, level, category, family, type, and instance are described next.

Autodesk Revit Project

A project in Revit is similar to an actual architectural or interior project. In an actual project, the entire documentation such as drawings, 3D views, specifications, schedules, cost estimates, and so on are inherently linked and read together. Similarly, in Revit, a project not only includes the digital 3D building model but also its parametrically associated documentation. Thus, all the components such as the building model, its standard views, architectural drawings, and schedules combine together to form a complete project. A project file contains all the project information such as building elements used in a project, drawing sheets, schedules, cost estimates, 3D views, renderings, walkthroughs, and so on. A project file also stores various settings such as environment, lighting, and so on. As data is stored in the same file, it becomes easier for Revit to coordinate the entire database.

Levels in a Building Model

In Autodesk Revit, a building model is divided into different levels. These levels may be understood as infinite horizontal planes that act as hosts for different elements such as roof, floor, ceiling, and so on. The defined levels in a building model in most cases relate to different floor levels, or stories of the building project. Each element that you create belongs to a particular level.

Subdivisions of Elements into Categories and Subcategories

Apart from building elements, an Autodesk Revit project also contains other associated elements such as annotations, imported files, links, and so on. These elements have been divided into following categories:

Model Category : Consists of various building elements used in creating a building model such as wall, floor, ceiling, roof, door, window, furniture, stairs, curtain systems, ramps, and so on

Annotation Category : Consists of annotations such as dimensions, text notes, tags, symbols, and so on

Datum Category : Consists of datums such as levels, grids, reference planes, and so on

View Category : Consists of interactive project views such as floor plans, ceiling plans, elevations, sections, 3D views, renderings, and walkthroughs

In addition to these four categories, other categories such as **Imported**, **Workset**, **Filter**, and **Revit Categories** can also exist if the project has imported files, enabled worksets, or linked Revit projects, respectively.

Families in Autodesk Revit

Another powerful concept in Autodesk Revit is family. Family in Revit is described as a set of elements of the same category that can be grouped together based on certain common parameters or characteristics. Elements of the same family may have different properties, but they all have common characteristics. For example, **Double Hung** is a single window family, but it contains different sizes of double hung windows. Family files have a *.rfa* extension. You can load additional building component families from the libraries provided in Revit package.

Families are further divided into certain types. Type or family type, as it is called, is a specific size or style of a family. For example, **Double Hung : 36" x 48"** is a window type. All uses of the same family type in a project have same properties. Family and family types can also be used to create new families using the **Family Editor**.

Instances are the actual usage of model elements in a building model or annotations in a drawing sheet. A family type created in a new location is identified as an instance of the family type. All instances of the same family type have same properties. Therefore, when you modify the properties of a family type, the properties of all its instances also get modified. The family categorization of Revit elements is given below:

Model Category : Wall
Family : Basic Wall
Family type : Brick on Mtl. Studs
Instance : Particular usage of a family type

The hierarchy of building elements in Revit plays an important role in providing the flexibility and ease of managing a change in the building model. Figure 1-3 shows the hierarchy of categories and families in a typical Revit project. The following is another example of the terms described in this section.

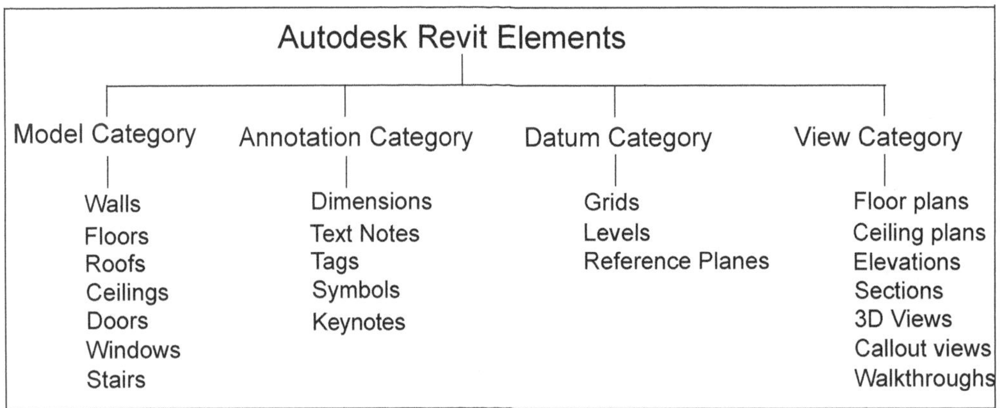

***Figure 1-3** Hierarchy of Autodesk Revit categories and families*

Creating a Building Model Using Parametric Building Elements

Another classification of categories of elements followed in Revit is based on their usage. Revit uses five classes of elements: host, component, annotation, view, and datum. Hosts are the element categories that form the basic structure of a building model and include model elements such as walls, floor, roof, and ceiling. Components are the elements that are added to host elements or act as stand-alone elements such as doors, windows, and furniture. Annotations are the 2D, view-specific elements that add content to the project documentation such as dimensions, tags, text notes, and so on. Views represent various orientations of a building model such as plans, elevations, sections, 3D views, and so on. Datum refers to the reference elements that assist you in creating a building model, which include grids, levels, reference planes, and so on.

There is no specific methodology available for creating a building model in Revit. It provides you with the flexibility of generating building geometry based on the project requirement, design complexity, and other factors. However, the following steps describe a general procedure that may be followed for creating an architectural building model using the in-built parametric elements provided in Revit.

The first step is to create the exterior walls of a building at the predefined lowest level (level 1). Next, create interior walls at that level and add components to the building model. Then, define the upper levels based on the story height of the building. You can also link the control height of the walls to the levels and extend the exterior walls to their full height. Next, create floors and roof using the defined levels. Add the site topography to the building model and then add site components to complete the building project. You can then create drawing sheets with the desired views for its presentation. Revit also provides tools to create rendered 3D views and walkthroughs. Figure 1-4 shows an example of a building section with various building elements and annotations.

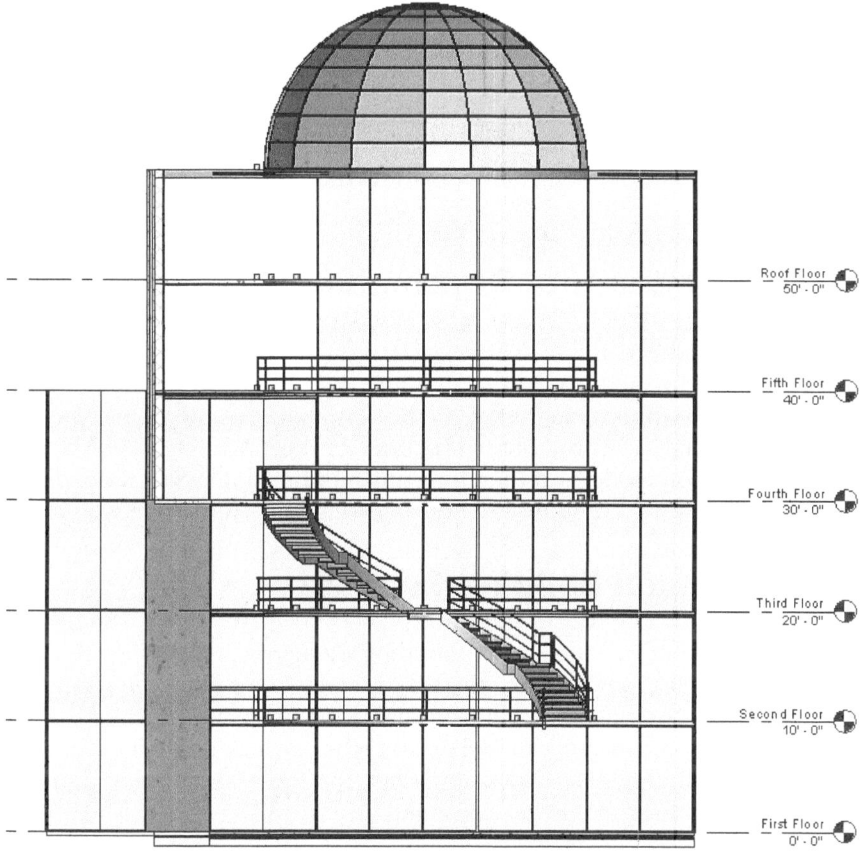

Figure 1-4 *Building section showing building elements and levels*

Visibility/Graphics Overrides, Scale, and Detail Level

Revit enables you to control the display and graphic representation of a single element or the element category of various elements in project views by using the visibility and graphics overrides tools. You can select a model category and modify its linetype and detail level. This can also be done for various annotation category elements and imported files. These settings can be done for each project view based on its desired representation. You can also hide an element or an element category in a view using the **Hide in View** and **Isolate** tools. You can override the graphic representation of an element or an element category in any view using the **Visibility/Graphics** tool.

The scale is another important concept in a Revit project. You can set the scale for each project view by selecting it from the available list of standard scales such as 1/16"=1'0", 1/4"=1'0",

1"=1'0", 1/2"=1'0", and so on. As you set a scale, Revit automatically sets the detail level appropriate for it. There are three detail levels provided in an Revit project: **Coarse**, **Medium**, and **Fine**. You can also set the detail level manually for each project view. Each detail level has an associated linetype and the detail lines associated with it. The details of annotations such as dimensions, tags, and so on are also defined by the selected scale.

Extracting the Project Information

A single integrated building information is used to create and represent a building project. You can extract project information from a building model and create area schemes, schedule, and cost estimates, and then add them to the project presentation.

Revit also enables you to export the extracted database to the industry standard Open Database Connectivity (ODBC) compliant relational database tables. The use of the building information model to extract database information eliminates the error-prone method of measuring building spaces individually.

Creating an Architectural Drawing Set

After creating the building model, you can easily arrange the project views by plotting them on drawing sheets. Drawing sheets can also be organized in a project file based on the established CAD standards followed by the firm. In this manner, the project documentation can easily be transformed from the conceptual design stage to the design development stage and finally to the construction document stage. The project view on a drawing sheet is only a graphical representation of the building information model and therefore, any modification in it is immediately made in all the associated project views, keeping the drawings set always updated.

Creating an Unusual Building Geometry

Revit also helps you conceptualize a building project in terms of its volume, shape, and proportions before working with the actual building elements. This is possible by using the **Massing** tool, which enables you to create quick 3D models of buildings and conduct volumetric and proportion study on overall masses. It also enables you to visualize and create an unusual building geometry. The same massing model can then be converted into a building model with individual parametric building elements. It provides continuity in the generation of building model right from sketch design to its development.

Flexibility of Creating Special Elements

Revit provides a large number of in-built family types of various model elements and annotations. Each parametric element has the associated properties that can be modified based on the project requirement.

Revit also enables you to create the elements that are designed specifically for a particular location. The in-built family editor enables you to create new elements using family templates. This provides you with the flexibility of using in-built elements for creating your own elements. For example, using the furniture template, you can create a reception desk that is suitable for a particular location in the design.

Creating Structural Layouts

Revit's structural tools enable you to add structural elements to a building model. An extensive in-built library of structural elements has been provided in Revit. You can add structural columns, beams, walls, braces, and so on to the project. Thus, structural consultants can also incorporate their elements in the basic architectural building model and check for inconsistency, if any.

Working on Large Projects

In Revit, you can work on large projects by linking different building projects together. For a large project that consists of a number of buildings, you can create individual buildings as separate projects and then link all of them into a single base file. The database recognizes the linked projects and includes them in the project representation of the base file.

For example, while working on a large campus of an educational institution, you can create separate project files for academic building, administration area, gymnasium, cafeteria, computer centre, and so on, and then link them into the base site plan file. In this manner, large projects can be subdivided and worked upon simultaneously.

Working in Large Teams and Coordinating with Consultants

Worksets in Revit enable the division of the building model into small editable set of elements. The worksets can be assigned to different teams working on the same project and then their work can easily be coordinated in the central file location. The effort required to coordinate, collaborate, and communicate the changes between various worksets is taken care of by computer. Various consultants working on a project can be assigned a workset with a set of editable elements. They can then incorporate their services and modify the associated elements.

For example, a high rise commercial building project can be divided into different worksets with independent teams working on exterior skin, interior walls, building core, toilet details, finishes, and so on. The structural consultants can be assigned the exterior skin and the core workset in which they can incorporate structural elements. Similarly, the rest of the teams can work independently on different worksets.

STARTING Autodesk Revit 2018

You can start Autodesk Revit 2018 by double-clicking on it's shortcut icon located on the desktop. Alternatively, choose **Start > All Programs > Autodesk > Revit 2018 > Revit 2018** from the taskbar, as shown in Figure 1-5; the user interface of Revit 2018 will be displayed, as shown in Figure 1-6.

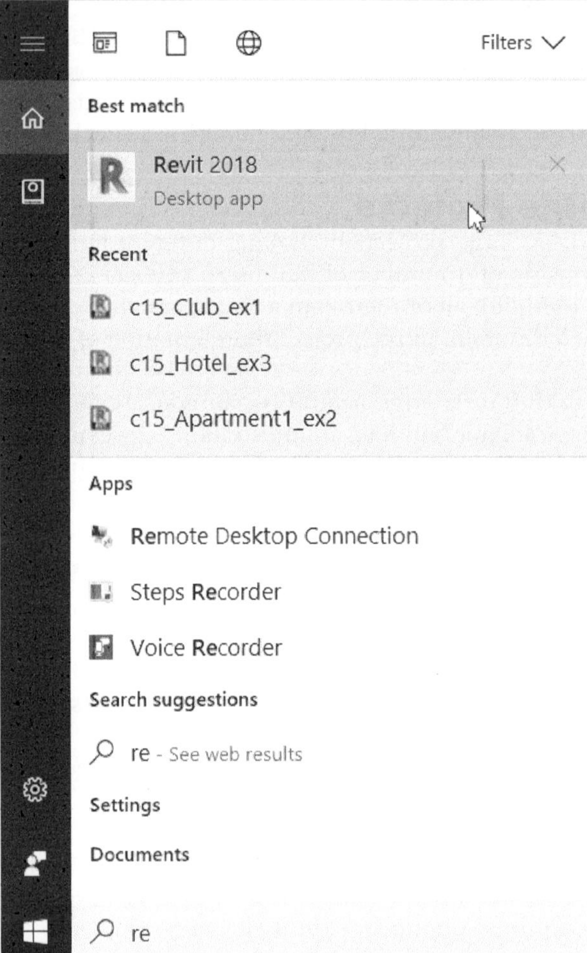

Figure 1-5 Starting Revit 2018 using the taskbar

Note

The path for starting Revit depends on the operating system being used.

The interface screen has three sections: **Projects**, **Families**, and **Resources**. The options in the **Projects** section are used to open an existing project, a new project, and an existing template. The options in the **Families** section are used to open a new or an existing family. You can also invoke the Conceptual Mass environment from this section to create a conceptual mass model.

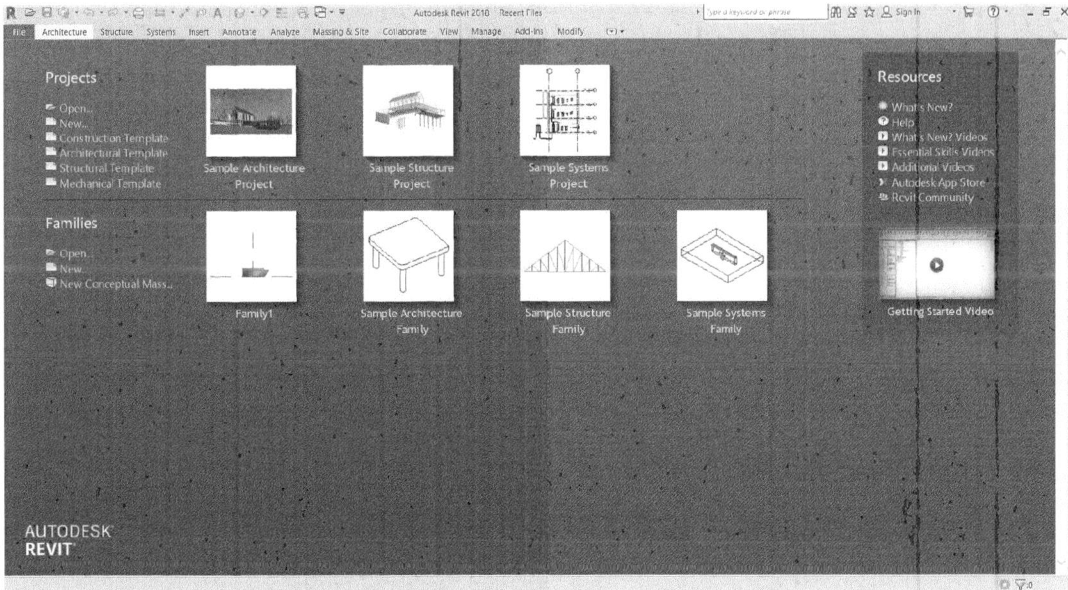

Figure 1-6 *The interface of Autodesk Revit 2018*

In the **Resources** section, you can choose the **What's New?** option to get information about the new tools and features in Revit 2018. In addition, you can choose the **Help** option from the **Resources** section to get help on various tools. When you choose this option, you will be directed to ***http://help.autodesk.com/view/RVT/2018/ENU/***. Also, the **Autodesk Revit 2018** page with the **Welcome to Revit 2018 Learning** area will be displayed. To access information related to additions and enhancements in Revit 2018 release, you can expand the **What's New** node from the left pane and then click on the **What's New in Autodesk Revit 2018** link. On doing so, the **What's New in Autodesk Revit 2018** page will be displayed with various links. You will learn about various enhancements in Revit 2018 by accessing these links.

The **What's New? Videos** option in the **Resources** section is an enhancement in Revit 2018. When you click on this option, you are directed to the **Autodesk Revit 2018** page that has a list of videos of newly added features in Revit. You can click on a link to view the corresponding video.

You can choose the **Essential Skills Videos** option to view the videos related to basic and advance concepts in Revit 2018. These videos and their associated information help you to learn about the complete software. Moreover, you can choose the **Autodesk App Store** option to access various add-ons that can be used to enhance the productivity of Revit. On choosing this option, the **AUTODESK APP STORE** page will be displayed. In this page, various links are available as add-ons which can be used in Revit applications. In the **Revit Community** option of the **Resources** section, you can access information related to various communities and their contribution in the form of articles, tutorials, and videos.

In the **Projects** section, choose the **Open** option; the **Open** dialog box will be displayed. Browse to the desired location in the dialog box and select the file. Now, choose the **Open** button to open the file.

To open a new project file, choose the **New** option from the **Projects** section. Alternatively, choose **New > Project** from the **File** menu; the **New Project** dialog box will be displayed. In this dialog box, you can select the desired template from the **Template file** drop-down or you can browse the other template files by choosing the **Browse** button from the **Choose Template** dialog box. In this dialog box, make sure that the **Project** radio button is selected, and then choose the **OK** button; a new project file will open and the interface screen will be activated.

USER INTERFACE

Autodesk Revit has ribbon interface. The ribbon which contains task-based tabs and panels, streamlines the architectural workflow and optimizes the project delivery time. In Revit, when you select an element in the drawing area, the ribbon displays a contextual tab that comprises of tools corresponding to the selected element. The interface of Autodesk Revit is similar to the interfaces of many other Microsoft Windows based programs. The main parts in the Revit interface are **Ribbon**, **Options Bar**, **Project Browser**, Drawing Area, **Status Bar**, and **View Control Bar**, as shown in Figure 1-7.

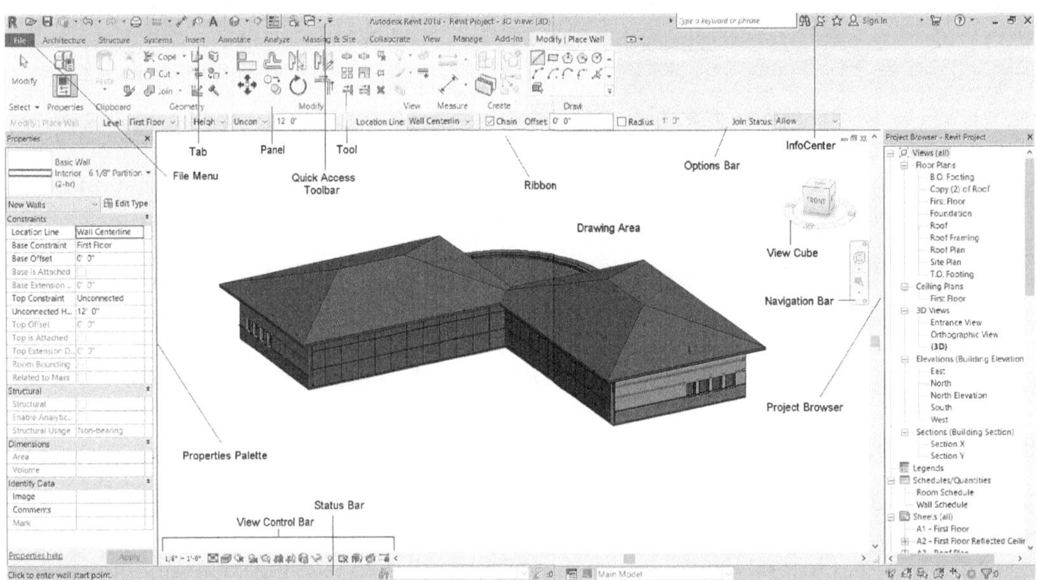

Figure 1-7 The Autodesk Revit 2018 user interface screen

Invoking Tools

To perform an operation, you can invoke the required tools by using any one of the following two options:

Ribbon: You can invoke all necessary tools from the ribbon.

Shortcut Keys: Some tools can also be invoked by using the keys on the keyboard.

Title Bar

The Title bar, docked on the top portion of the user interface, displays the program's logo, program's name, name of the current project, and the view opened in the viewing area. **Project 1- Floor Plan: Level 1** is the default project and view.

Ribbon

The ribbon, as shown in Figure 1-8, is an interface that is used to invoke tools. When you open a file, the ribbon is displayed at the top in the screen. It comprises of task-based tabs and panels, refer to Figure 1-8, which provide all the tools necessary for creating a project. The tabs and panels in the ribbon can be customized according to the need of the user. This can be done by moving the panels and changing the view states of the ribbon (changing the ribbon view state is discussed later in this chapter). The ribbon has three types of buttons: general button, drop-down button, and split button. These buttons can be invoked from the panels.

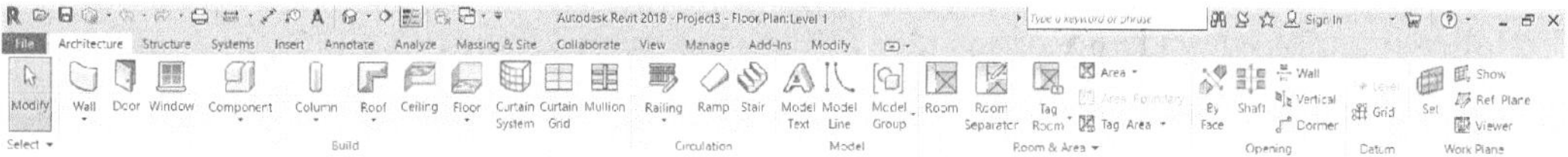

Figure 1-8 Different components of a ribbon

Moving the Panels

In the ribbon, you can move a panel and place it anywhere on the screen. To do so, press and hold the left mouse button on the panel label in the ribbon and drag it to some desired place on the screen. Next, use the tools of the moved panel and place the panel back to the ribbon. To do so, place the cursor on the moved panel and choose the **Return Panels to Ribbon** button from the upper right corner of this panel, as shown in Figure 1-9; the panel will return to the ribbon.

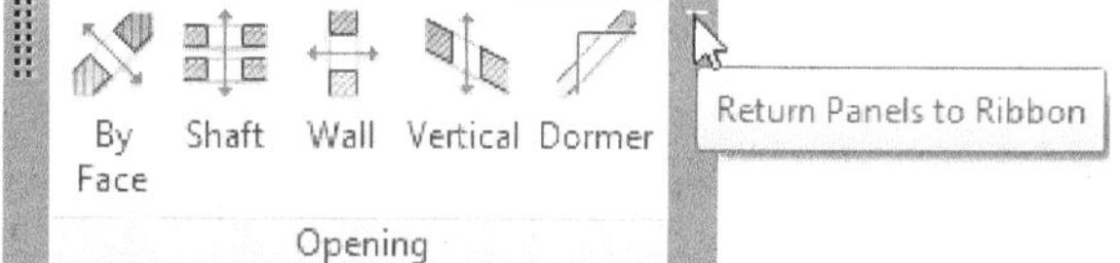

*Figure 1-9 Choosing the **Return Panels to Ribbon** button*

Changing the View States of the Ribbon

The ribbon can be displayed in three view states by selecting any of the following four options: **Minimize to Tabs**, **Minimize to Panel Titles**, **Minimize to Panel Buttons**, and **Cycle through All**. To use these options, move the cursor and place it over the second arrow on the right of the **Modify** tab, refer to Figure 1-10 in the ribbon; the arrow will be highlighted. Now, click on the down arrow; a flyout will be displayed, as shown in Figure 1-10. In this flyout, you can choose the **Minimize to Tabs** option to display only the tabs in the ribbon. If you choose the **Minimize to Panel Titles** option, the ribbon will display the titles of the panels along with the tabs. You can choose the **Minimize to Panel Buttons** option to display the panels as buttons in the ribbon along with tabs.

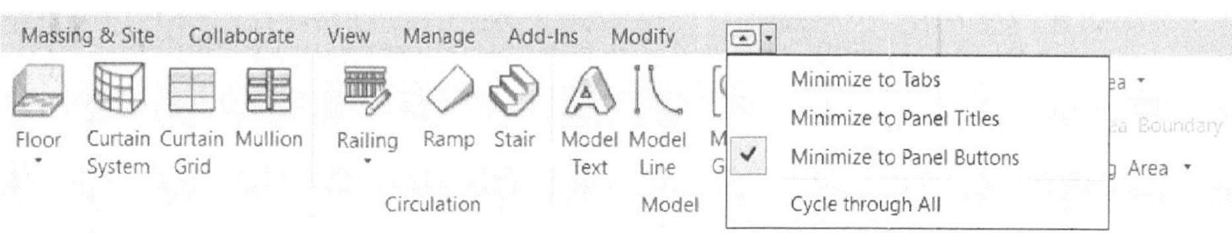

Figure 1-10 Various options in the flyout for changing the view state of the ribbon

Tip

Tooltips appear when you rest the cursor over any of the tool icons in the ribbon. The name of the tool appears in the box helping you to identify each tool icon.

Note

If the view state of the ribbon is changed, place the cursor over the first arrow at the right of the ***Modify*** *tab, the* ***Show Full Ribbon*** *tooltip will be displayed. Click on the arrow; full ribbon will be displayed.*

The following table describes various tabs in the ribbon and their functions:

Tab	Description
Architecture	Contains tools for creating architectural elements for a project
Structure	Contains tools for creating structural elements in a project
Systems	Contains tools for creating mechanical elements in a project
Create	This tab is available in family editor. It contains tools that are used to create a family
Insert	Contains tools to insert or manage secondary files such as raster image files or CAD files
Annotate	Contains tools for documenting a building model such as adding texts and dimensions
Massing & Site	Contains tools for modeling and modifying conceptual mass and site elements
Analyze	Contains tools for energy analysis of the project
Collaborate	Contains tools for collaborating the project with other team members (internal and external)
View	Contains tools used for managing and modifying the current view and also for switching views
Manage	Contains tools for specifying the project and system parameters and project settings
Modify	Contains tools for editing elements in the model

Contextual Tabs in the Ribbon

These tabs are displayed when you choose certain tools or select elements. These tabs contain a set of tools or buttons that relate only to a particular tool or element. For example, when you invoke the **Window** tool, the **Modify | Place Window** contextual tab is displayed. This tab shows ten panels: **Select**, **Properties**, **View**, **Measure**, **Geometry**, **Clipboard**, **Create**, **Modify**, **Mode**, and **Tag**. The **Select** panel contains the **Modify** tool. The **Properties** panel contains the

Properties button and the **Type Properties** tool. The **Mode** panel has some necessary tools that are used to load model families or to create the model of a window in a drawing. The other panels, apart from those discussed above, contain the tools that are contextual and are used to edit elements when they are placed in a drawing or selected from a drawing for modification.

File Menu

This menu is displayed on choosing the **File** button from the ribbon, refer to Figure 1-11. It contains tools that provide access to many common file actions such as **Open**, **Close**, and **Save**. You can also invoke this menu by using the keyboard shortcut ALT+F.

*Figure 1-11 The **File** menu*

Quick Access Toolbar

The **Quick Access Toolbar**, as shown in Figure 1-12, contains the options to undo and redo changes, open and save a file, create a new file, and so on.

By default, the **Quick Access Toolbar** contains the following options: **Open**, **Save**, **Redo**, **Undo**, and others. You can customize the display of the **Quick Access Toolbar** by adding more tools and removing the unwanted tools. To add a tool or a button from the panel of the ribbon to the **Quick Access Toolbar**, place the cursor over the button; the button will be highlighted. Next, right-click; a flyout will be displayed. Choose the **Add to Quick Access Toolbar** from the flyout displayed; the highlighted button will be added to **Quick Access Toolbar**. The **Quick Access Toolbar** can be customized to re-order the tools displayed in it. To do so, choose the down arrow next to the **Switch Windows** drop-down, refer to Figure 1-12; a flyout will be displayed. Choose the **Customize Quick Access Toolbar** option located at the bottom of the flyout; the **Customize Quick Access Toolbar** dialog box will be displayed. Use various options in this dialog box and choose the **OK** button; the **Customize Quick Access Toolbar** dialog box will close and the tools in the **Quick Access Toolbar** will be re-ordered.

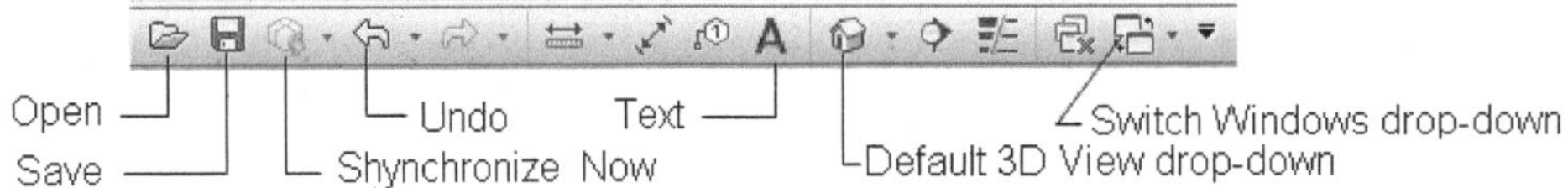

*Figure 1-12 The **Quick Access Toolbar***

InfoCenter

You can use the **InfoCenter** to search the information related to Revit Help, display the **Communication Center** panel for subscription services and product updates, and display the **Favorites** panel to access saved topics. Also in the **InfoCenter**, you can use the **Autodesk 360** and the **Autodesk App Store** options to log-in to **Autodesk 360** and **Autodesk Exchange Apps** pages. Figure 1-13 displays various tools in the **InfoCenter**.

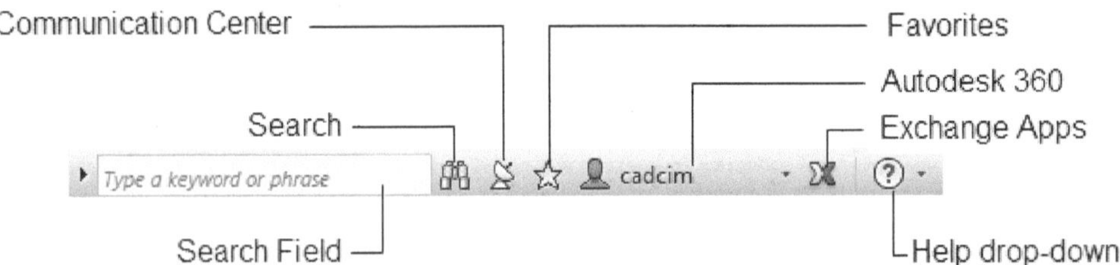

*Figure 1-13 The **InfoCenter***

Status Bar

The **Status Bar** is located at the bottom of the interface screen. When the cursor is placed over an element or component, the **Status Bar** displays the name of the family and type of the corresponding element or components. It also displays prompts and messages to help you use the selected tools.

View Control Bar

The **View Control Bar** is located at the lower left corner of the drawing window, as shown in Figure 1-14. It can be used to access various view-related tools. The **Scale** button shows the scale of the current view. You can choose this button to display a flyout that contains standard drawing scales. From this flyout, you can then select the scale for the current view. The **Detail Level** button is used to set the detail level of a view. You can select the required detail level as **Coarse**, **Medium**, and **Fine**. Similarly, the **Visual Style** button enables you to set the display style. The options for setting the display style are: **Wireframe**, **Hidden Line**, **Shaded**, **Consistent Colors**, **Realistic**, and **Raytrace**.

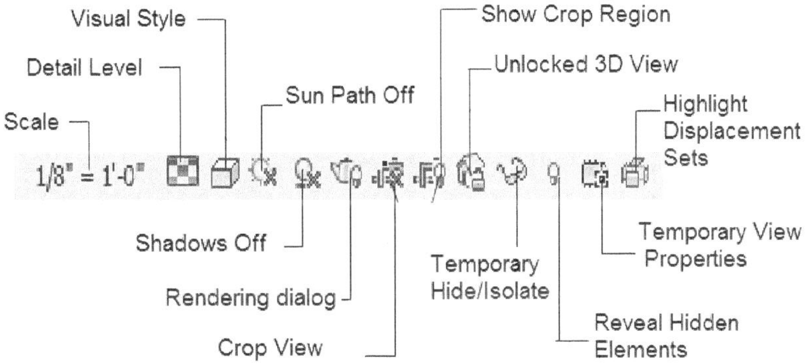

Figure 1-14 The View Control Bar

Options Bar

The **Options Bar** provides information about the common parameters of component type and the options for creating or editing of building elements. The **Options Bar** changes its appearance based on the type of component selected or being created. You can also modify the properties of the component by entering a new value in the edit box for the corresponding parameter in the **Options Bar**. For example, the **Options Bar** for the **Wall** tool displays various options to create a wall, as shown in Figure 1-15.

*Figure 1-15 The **Options Bar** with different options to create a wall*

Type Selector

The **Type Selector** drop-down list is located in the **Properties** palette of the currently invoked tool. For example, if you invoke the **Wall** tool, all the properties of the wall will be displayed in the **Properties** palette. In the **Properties** palette, you can use the **Type Selector** drop-down list to select the required type of the wall. The options in the **Type Selector** drop-down list keep on changing based on the current function of the tool or the elements selected. When you place an element or a component in a drawing, you can use the **Type Selector** drop-down list to specify the type of element or component. You can also use this drop-down list to change the existing type of a selected element to a different type. In Revit, you can add the **Type Selector** drop-down list to the **Quick Access Toolbar**. To do so, right-click on the **Type Selector** drop-down list in the **Properties** palette and choose the **Quick Access Toolbar** option from the flyout displayed.

Drawing Area

The Drawing Area is the actual modeling area where you can create and view the building model. It covers the major portion of the interface screen. You can draw various building components in this area using the pointing device. The position of the pointing device is represented by the cursor. The Drawing Area also has the standard Microsoft Windows functions and buttons such as close, minimize, maximize, scroll bar, and so on. These buttons have the same function as that of the other Microsoft Windows-based programs.

Project Browser

The **Project Browser** is located below the ribbon. It displays project views, schedules, sheets, families, and groups in a logical, tree-like structure, as shown in Figure 1-16, and helps you open and manage them. To open a view, double-click on the name of the view; the corresponding view will be displayed in the drawing area. You can close the **Project Browser** or dock it anywhere in the drawing area.

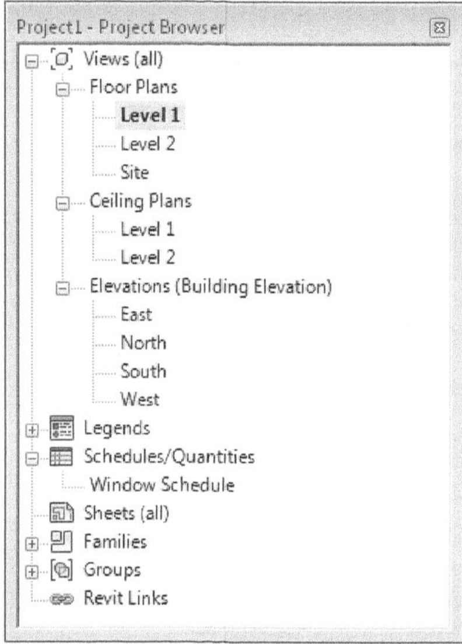

Figure 1-16** The **Project Browser

Note

*If the **Project Browser** is not displayed on the screen, choose the **View** tab from the ribbon and then click on the **User Interface** drop-down from the **Windows** panel. Next, select the **Project Browser** check box from the flyout displayed.*

The **Project Browser** can be organized to group the views and sheets based on the project requirement. For example, while working on a large project with a number of sheets, you can organize the **Project Browser** to view and access specific sheets.

Note

*In the **Project Browser**, you can expand or collapse the view listing by selecting the '+' or '-' sign, respectively. The current view in the drawing window is highlighted in bold letters. The default project file has a set of preloaded views.*

Keyboard Accelerators

In Revit, accelerator keys have been assigned to some of the frequently used tools. These keys are shortcuts that you can type through the keyboard to invoke the corresponding tool. Accelerator keys corresponding to a tool appear as a tooltip when you move the cursor over the tool. In Revit 2018, you can export all commands (even if they do not have shortcut keys assigned) to a XML file. You can further edit the XML file to assign shortcut keys to commands, and then import them back to be used in Revit.

Tip

*As you become accustomed to using Revit, you will find these **Keyboard Accelerators** quite useful because they save the effort of browsing through the menus.*

Properties Palette

The **Properties** palette, as shown in Figure 1-17, is a modeless interface, which displays the type and element properties of various elements and views in a drawing. The **Properties** palette is dockable and resizable, and it supports multiple monitor configurations. The **Properties** palette is displayed in the Revit interface by default and it shows the instance properties of an active view. When you select an element from a drawing, the **Properties** palette displays its instance properties. You can also access the **Type Properties** of the selected element from the **Properties** palette. To do so, choose the **Edit Type** button from the palette; the **Type Properties** dialog box will be displayed. In this dialog box, you can change the **Type Properties** of the selected element. In the **Properties** palette, you can assign a type to a selected element in a drawing from the **Type Selector** drop-down list. In Revit, you can toggle the display of the **Properties** palette in its interface. Choose the **Properties** button in the **Properties** panel of the **Modify** tab to hide it. Similarly, you can choose the **Properties** button to display the palette if it is not visible in the interface.

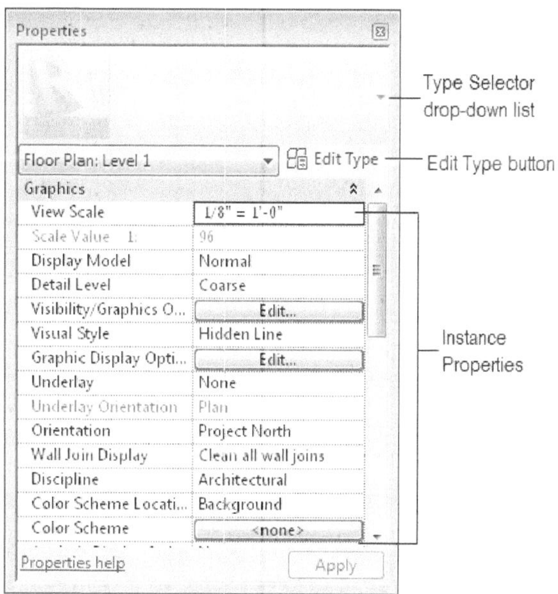

*Figure 1-17 The **Properties** palette*

DIALOG BOXES

Certain Revit tools when invoked display a dialog box. A dialog box is a convenient method of accessing and modifying the parameters related to that tool. For example, when you choose **Save As > Project** from the **File** menu, the **Save As** dialog box will be displayed, as shown in Figure 1-18. A dialog box consists of various parts such as dialog label, radio buttons, text or edit boxes, check boxes, slider bars, image box, and tool buttons, which are similar to other windows-based programs. Some dialog boxes contain the [**...**] button. On choosing such buttons, another related dialog box will be displayed. There are certain buttons such as **OK**, **Cancel**, and **Help**, which appear at the bottom of most of the dialog boxes. The names of the buttons imply their respective functions. The button with a dark border is the default button.

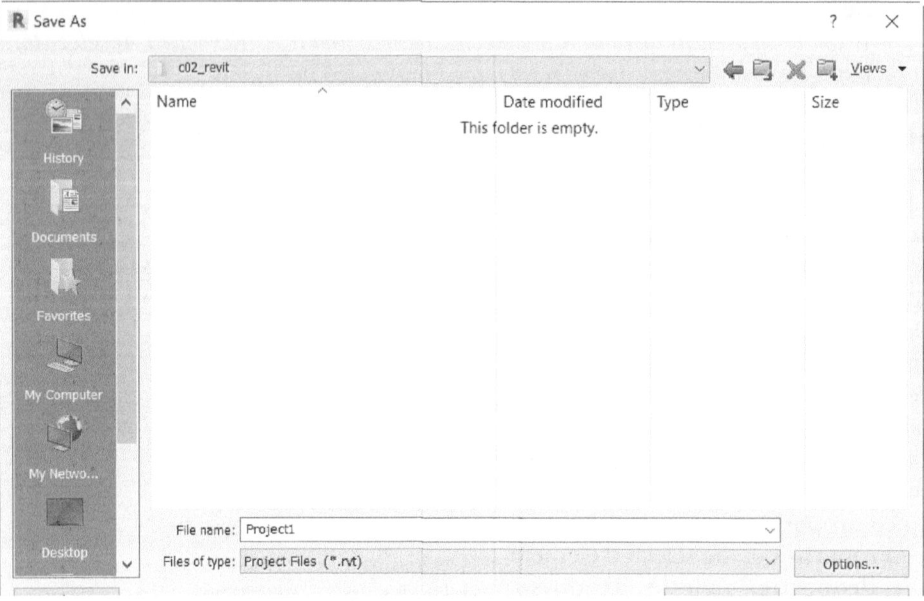

*Figure 1-18 The **Save As** dialog box*

MULTIPLE DOCUMENT ENVIRONMENT

The multiple document environment feature allows you to open more than one project at a time in a single Revit session. This is very useful when you want to work on different projects simultaneously and make changes with reference to each other.

Sometimes you may need to incorporate certain features from one project into the other. With the help of multiple document environments, you can open multiple projects and then use the **Cut**, **Copy**, and **Paste** tools from the **Clipboard** panel of the **Modify (type of element)** tab to transfer the required components from one project to another. These editing tools can also be invoked by using the CTRL+C and CTRL+V keyboard shortcuts.

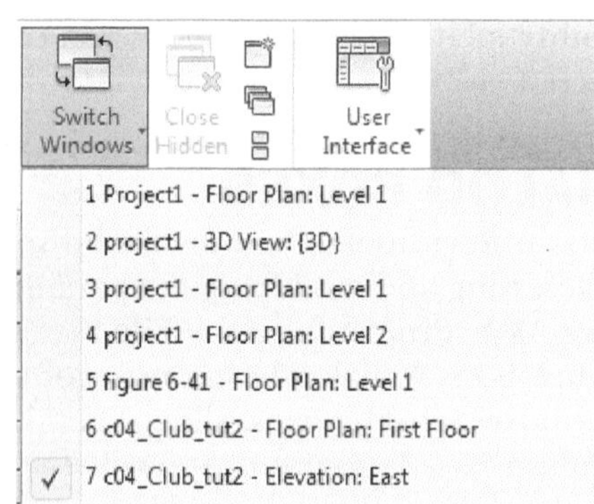

*Figure 1-19 Selecting an option from the **Switch Windows** drop-down*

To access the opened projects, choose the **Switch Windows** drop-down from the **Windows** panel of the **View** tab; a menu will be displayed showing the name of different project files opened, as shown in Figure 1-19. Like other Microsoft Windows-based programs, you can select and view the opened projects using the **Cascade** and **Tile** tools from the **Windows** panel of the **View** tab. Figure 1-20 shows the cascaded view of projects.

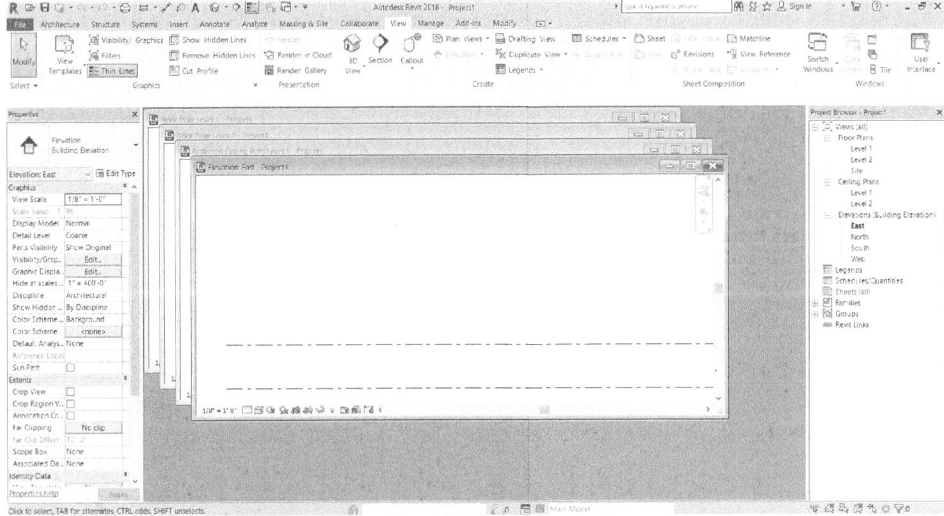

Figure 1-20 The cascaded view of the projects

INTEROPERABILITY OF Autodesk Revit

The models or geometries created in Revit can easily be exported to AutoCAD based programs, such as 3ds Max and Max Design in the DWG file format. This enables you to visualize and create photorealistic exterior and interior renderings for your project designs. You can also transfer drawings from Revit to Google SketchUp to visualize your projects in a better way.

Revit follows a wide range of industry standards and supports various CAD file formats such as DWG, DXF, DWF, DGN, FBX, and SAT. For image files, it supports JPG, TIFF, BMP, PNG, AVI, PAN, IVR, and TGA file formats. Besides these, the formats that are supported by Revit include ODBC, HTML, TXT, gbXML, XLS, and MDB. Revit is compatible with any CAD system that supports the DWG, DXF, or DGN file format. Revit can import the models and geometries as ACIS solids. This enables designers to import models from AutoCAD Architecture and AutoCAD MEP (Mechanical, Electrical, and Plumbing) software and to link and import 3D information to Revit. This feature makes Revit an efficient, user-friendly, and compatible software.

In Revit, you can directly link the files into 3ds Max Design and load selected views in it. You can also override material in 3ds Max Design and retain its settings when you reload Revit link file. Also, in 3ds Max Design, you can add high level of details to the curved objects to make them smooth. V8 Microstation is interoperable with Revit. Therefore, the V8 Microstation files can be imported to the Revit project. In addition to this, mapping functionality for levels, lines, line weights, patterns, and texts and fonts is added to export DGN workflow.

BUILDING INFORMATION MODELING AND Autodesk Revit

Building Information Modeling (BIM) is defined as a design technology that involves creation and use of coordinated, internally consistent, and computable information about a building project in design and construction. BIM covers spatial relationships, geographic information, quantities, and properties of building components. Using this technology, you can demonstrate the entire life cycle of a building project starting from the process of construction, facility operation, and information about quantities and shared properties of elements. BIM enables the circulation of virtual information model from the design team to contractors and then to the owner, thereby adding changes and their knowledge to update the model at each stage of transfer. The ability to keep information up-to-date and make it available in an integrated digital environment enables the architects, owners, builders, and engineers to have clear vision of the project before the commencement of actual construction. It enables them to make better and faster decisions as well as to improve the quality and profitability of projects. Autodesk Revit is a specially designed platform based on BIM. Revit is the best example of the BIM technology. Revit's parametric model represents a building as an integrated database of coordinated information. In Revit, change anywhere is change everywhere. Any change made in your project at any stage is reflected in the entire project, and also, due to the parametric behavior of elements, the project is updated automatically according to the changes made anywhere in the project. Also, the integration of Revit with the available in-built commercial tools such as solar studies, material takeoffs, greatly simplifies the project design and reduces the time consumed by these analyses, thereby enabling faster decision making.

Autodesk Revit 2018 HELP

Autodesk Revit provides help to easily understand various tools and methods used in it. In Autodesk Revit 2018, you can access online help documentation. To access the help feature, click on the down arrow on the right of the **InfoCenter**; a flyout will be displayed. Next, choose the **Help** option, as shown in Figure 1-21. Various options to access the help are discussed next.

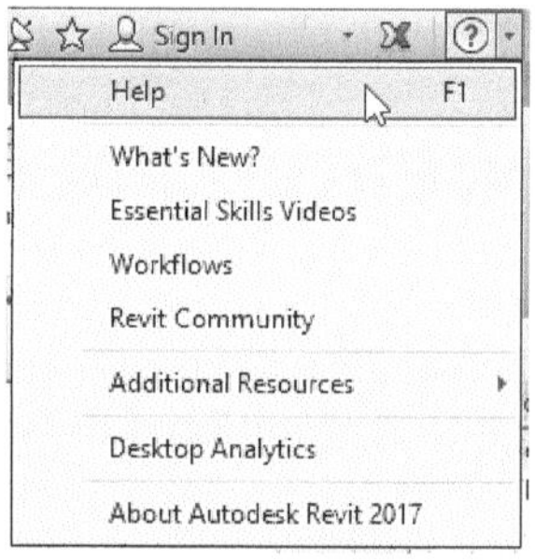

Figure 1-21 A drop-down menu displaying help options

Using the Revit 2018 Help

You can access Autodesk Revit 2018 help when you are online. To do so, choose the **Help** tool from the **InfoCenter**; the **Autodesk Revit 2018** page will be displayed, as shown in Figure 1-22. In this page, there are several tabs that contain information of help topics. These tabs are discussed next.

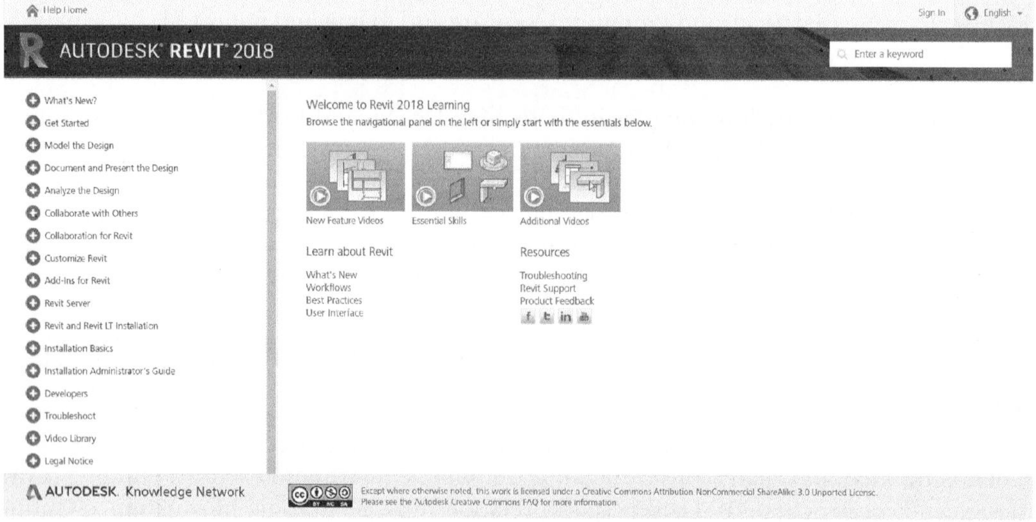

*Figure 1-22 The **Revit Help** page*

WORKSHARING USING REVIT SERVER

Worksharing is a method of distributing work among team involved in a project, and accomplishing it within the stipulated period of time. In worksharing, each person involved in the project is assigned a task that has to be accomplished by proper planning and by coordinating with the other members of the team.

In a large scale building project, worksharing helps in finishing a project in time and meeting the quality requirements that are set during the process. Generally, in a large scale building project, worksharing is based on the specialization of work. The professionals such as structural engineers, architects, interior architects, and MEP engineers are involved in their respective fields to accomplish the project. So, the distribution of work at the primary stage is made on the basis of the area of specialization. Each professional has his own set of work to perform for the accomplishment of the project.

You can apply server-based worksharing with the help of Revit Server as it is a server based application. Revit Server uses a central server and multiple local servers for collaborating across a Wide Area Network (WAN). The central server hosts the central model of a workshared project and remain accessible to all the team members over the Wide Area Network. Similarly, the local server is accessible to all team members in a Local Area Network (LAN). The local server hosts a local updated copy of the central model. In the Worksharing environment, the team members are not aware of the local server, as it is transparent in their daily operations. Refer to Figure 1-23 for the network model of Revit Server.

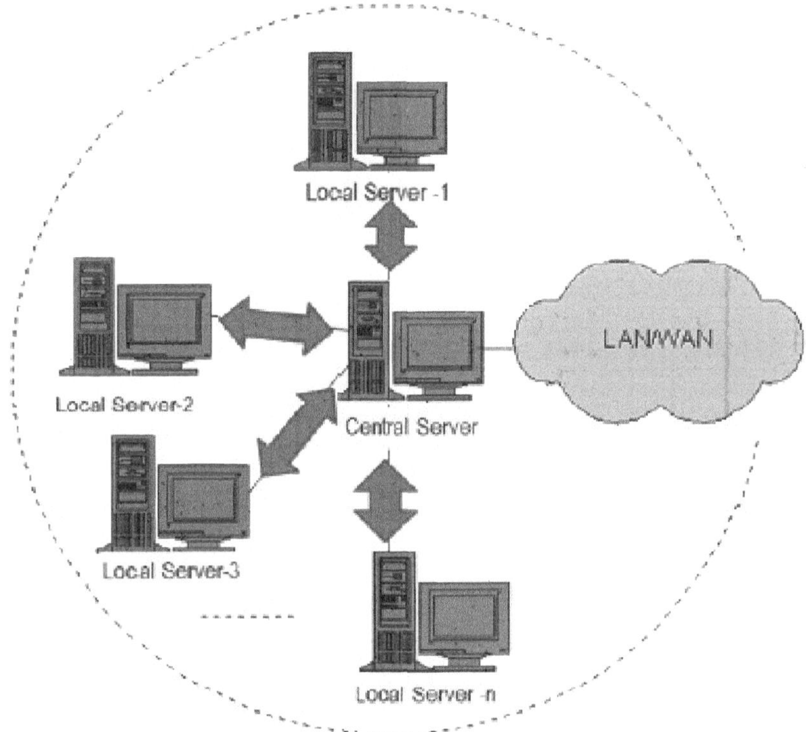

***Figure 1-23** The network model of Revit Server*

In Worksharing environment, a team member starts working on the local model of the central model. The local model will be saved in the computer of the team member. As the team member works, the local server requests updated information from the central model on the central server using available network capacity to transfer the data over the WAN. The updated version of the model is stored on the local server, so the updates are readily available when a team member requests them.

Self-Evaluation Test

Answer the following questions and then compare them to those given at the end of this chapter:

1. In Revit, you can access offline help only. (T/F)

2. You cannot import 3ds Max file into Revit. (T/F)

3. You can do parametric modeling in Revit. (T/F)

4. You can control the display of the elements in Revit. (T/F)

Answers to Self-Evaluation Test

1. F, 2. F, 3. T, 4. T

Chapter 2

Starting an Architectural Project

Learning Objectives

After completing this chapter, you will be able to:

- *Start a new architectural project*
- *Set units of various measurement parameters of a project*
- *Understand the concept of snaps, dimensions, and object snaps*
- *Save a project*
- *Modify parameters and settings of a project*
- *Close a project and exit Revit 2018*
- *Open an existing project*
- *Explore the building model using viewing tools*
- *Use the navigation tools*

INTRODUCTION

In Revit, you can work on structural, architectural, and MEP (Mechanical, Electrical and Plumbing) projects on a single platform. The chapters in this textbook are specially written for professionals in architectural and space design field. In this chapter, you will learn about the tools and the processes involved in starting up a new architectural project

STARTING A NEW ARCHITECTURAL PROJECT

Shortcut Key: CTRL+N
File menu: New > Project

In Revit, a project is considered as a single database that contains all information related to building design. Starting from geometry to construction data, each project file contains complete information of the building design. In a building design, the three dimensional models drawn using this software are called BIM (Building Information Model). BIM is a process involving the generation and management of digital representation of physical and functional features of different infastructure elements.

To start an architectural project, choose **New > Project** from the **File** menu, as shown in Figure 2-1. On doing so, the **New Project** dialog box will be displayed, as shown in Figure 2-2. Using this dialog box, select an existing *.rte* template file format that can be used in the new project.

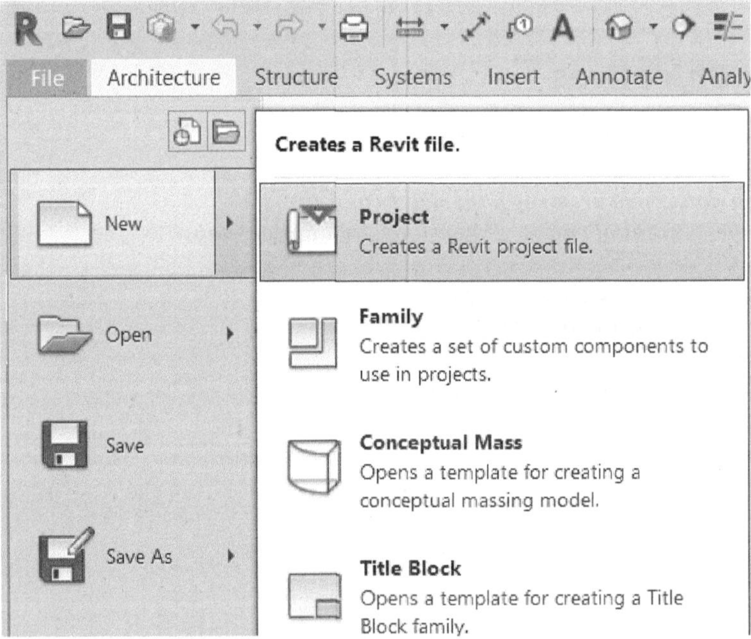

Figure 2-1 *Choosing the **Project** option*

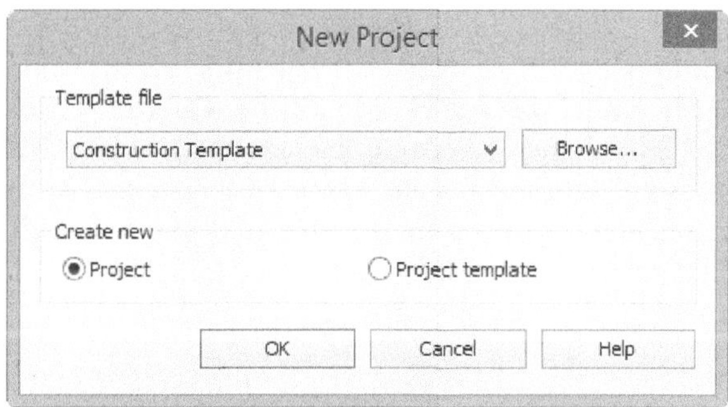

Figure 2-2 *The **New Project** dialog box*

A template file can be defined as a template which has various project parameters such as units and views, already saved in it. On using the template file, the new project file will adopt the same parameters as the template file. The difference between a template file and a project file is that the template file has a *.rte* extension, whereas the project file has a *.rvt* extension. You can either select any of the template files provided in Revit or create your own file. Any project file can be saved as a template file.

In the **New Project** dialog box, select the desired template file from the drop-down list in the **Template file** area. By default, the **Construction Template** option is selected. To select a different template file which is not available in the drop-down list, choose the **Browse** button. On doing so, the **Choose Template** dialog box will be displayed. In this dialog box, browse to the **US Imperial** or **US Metric** folder, select a template file, and then choose the **Open** button; the selected template file will be added to the drop-down list in the **Template file** area.

In the **Create new** area of the **New Project** dialog box, two radio buttons will be displayed: **Project** and **Project template**. The **Project** radio button is selected by default. As a result, you will work on a new project. Alternatively, if you select the **Project template** radio button, you will work on a new project template.

Note

*If you select the **None** option from the drop-down list in the **New Project** dialog box, a new project file will be created without a template file but with the default settings of Revit.*

PROJECT UNITS

Ribbon: Manage > Settings > Project Units
Shortcut Key: UN

Project Units Units are important parameters in a project. While installing Revit, you are prompted to set the default unit as Imperial (feet and inches) or Metric (meter). The default selection of units helps you open project with the specified/selected unit system. However, you can change the default unit set system. To set units, choose the **Project Units** tool from the **Settings** panel of the **Manage** tab; the **Project Units** dialog box will be displayed, as shown in Figure 2-3. Project units are grouped into six disciplines: **Common**, **Structural**, **HVAC**,

Electrical, **Piping**, and **Energy**. Each discipline has a set of measurement parameters. You can select any of these disciplines from the **Discipline** drop-down list of this dialog box. In this drop-down list, the **Common** option is selected by default. As a result, various measurement parameters such as **Length**, **Area**, **Volume**, **Angle**, **Slope**, **Currency**, and **Mass Density** will be displayed in the **Project Units** dialog box. The **Format** column in the dialog box displays the current unit format for the corresponding parameter. You can preview and select the possible digit grouping and decimal separators from the **Decimal symbol/digit grouping** drop-down list located at the lower left corner of the dialog box, refer to Figure 2-3. The options for settings various measurement units are discussed next.

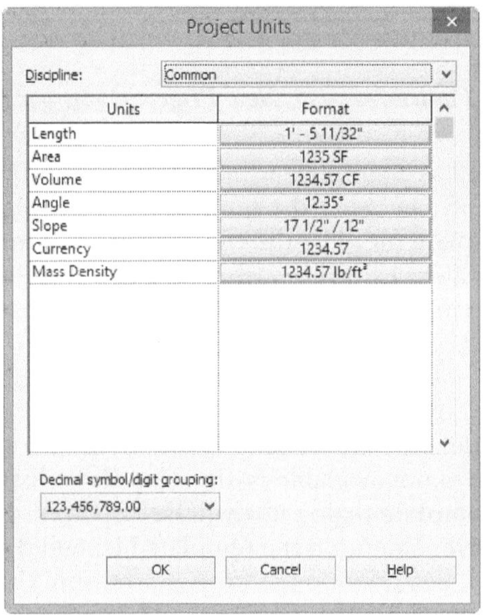

*Figure 2-3 The **Project Units** dialog box*

Length Unit

To assign a unit for measuring the lengths of building elements in your project, click on the **Format** column corresponding to the **Length** parameter; the **Format** dialog box will be displayed, as shown in Figure 2-4. This dialog box displays different units of length and their settings. You can select the desired unit from the **Units** drop-down list in the dialog box. After selecting the desired unit, you can specify the rounding value for the selected unit. To do so, select the desired option from the **Rounding** drop-down list in the **Format** dialog box. Note that by default, the **Rounding increment** edit box in the **Format** dialog box is inactive. To make it active, select the **Decimal feet** or **Decimal inches** option from the **Units** drop-down list and then select the **Custom** option from the **Rounding** drop-down list. The default value in the **Rounding increment** edit box is 1. You can change this value by entering a value in this edit box. Similarly, the **Unit symbol** drop-down list will be inactive for the **Feet and fractional inches**, **Fractional inches**, and **Meters and Centimeters** options of the **Units** drop-down list. From the **Unit symbol** drop-down list, you can select the measurement symbol that will be added to the unit of length. For example, you can select '**m**' as the measurement symbol after all metric length measurement. In case, you select **Feet and fractional inches** from the **Units** drop-down list in the **Format** dialog box, then you need to select the **Suppress spaces** check box to remove spaces in the dash when a length string is expressed in feet and fractional inches to denote a particular measurement.

Tip

*While selecting a rounding value from the **Rounding** drop-down list in the **Format** dialog box, you should consider the extent of detailing that may be required for the project. For projects that require too much detailing, a lower rounding value may be set. This parameter, however, can be modified at any stage during the project development.*

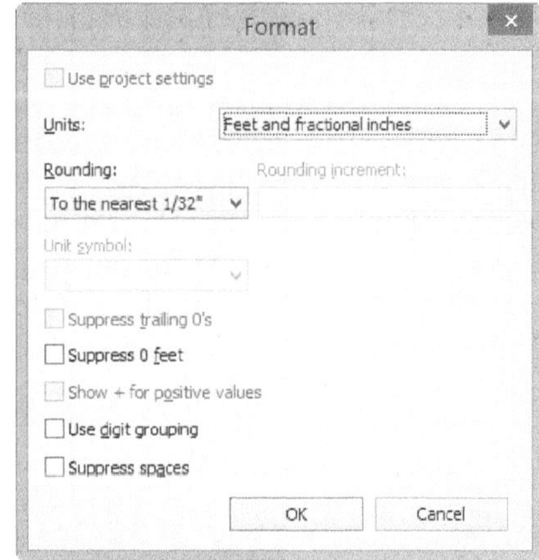

Figure 2-4 *The **Format** dialog box*

Area Unit

To assign a unit for measuring the areas of building elements, click on the **Format** column for the **Area** parameter; the **Format** dialog box will be displayed. In this dialog box, you can set the unit for measuring an area by selecting an option from the **Units** drop-down list. This drop-down list contains various options such as **Square feet**, **Square meters**, **acres**, and so on. By default, the **Square feet** option is selected in this drop-down list. The settings for rounding, rounding increment, and units can be done by selecting the desired option from the respective drop-down list and edit boxes.

Volume Unit

The units for volume can be set similar to that of the length and area. You can set the unit for the volume measurement by selecting any of the options from the **Units** drop-down list in the **Format** dialog box of the **Volume** parameter.

Angle Unit

The units for angle can be set by using the **Units** drop-down list in the **Format** dialog box of the **Angle** parameter.

Slope Unit

To specify the unit for the slope measurement, click in the **Format** column for the **Slope** parameter; the **Format** dialog box will be displayed. In this dialog box, you can specify the desired unit settings by selecting the required option from the **Units** drop-down list. The default option for the Imperial unit setting in the drop-down list is **Rise /12"**.

Currency Unit

The currency unit is used to set the unit of currency for its usage in the cost and estimation schedules. To set the unit of currency, invoke the **Project Units** dialog box and then choose the button displayed in the **Format** column corresponding to the **Currency** parameter; the **Format** dialog box will be displayed. From this dialog box, you can select the required type of currency symbol from the **Unit symbol** drop-down list.

Mass Density Unit

The mass density of building elements is required for structural analysis. In Revit, you can assign a unit for measuring mass density. To assign the unit of mass density, invoke the **Project Units** dialog box. In the **Format** column of this dialog box, choose the button corresponding to the **Mass Density** parameter; the **Format** dialog box will be displayed. In this dialog box, you can select different units from the **Units** drop-down list. Also, you can assign a unit symbol for the selected unit. To do so, click on the **Unit symbol** drop-down list and then select any of the options displayed.

Tip

*As soon as you change the units and choose the **OK** button to close the **Format** dialog box, the numbers and units shown for each measurement parameter in the **Project Units** dialog box are modified to the new settings. You can modify these settings and format them as per your requirement.*

Note

*You can format the display of units represented on the screen using the **Project Units** dialog box. The actual values for these units in the project may be different. For example, if you set the wall length rounding to the nearest 1', the wall may show this rounded value, but the actual length of the wall might be in fractional feet.*

SNAPS TOOL

Ribbon:	Manage > Settings > Snaps

The **Snaps** tool is one of the most productive tools available while creating and editing elements in a building model. This tool represents the ability of the cursor to snap or jump to the preset increments or specific object properties of various elements such as endpoint, midpoint, and so on. Invoke the **Snaps** tool from the **Settings** panel of the **Manage** tab; the **Snaps** dialog box will be displayed, as shown in Figure 2-5. This dialog box has three areas: **Dimension Snaps**, **Object Snaps**, and **Temporary Overrides**. These areas are discussed next.

Note

*The settings in the **Snaps** dialog box are applied to all the projects opened in the session but are saved in the project you are working on.*

Tip

The values that you will enter for dimension snapping should be set based on the scale and the amount of detailing required for the project. You may set smaller increments for working on a detail or a small portion of a building.

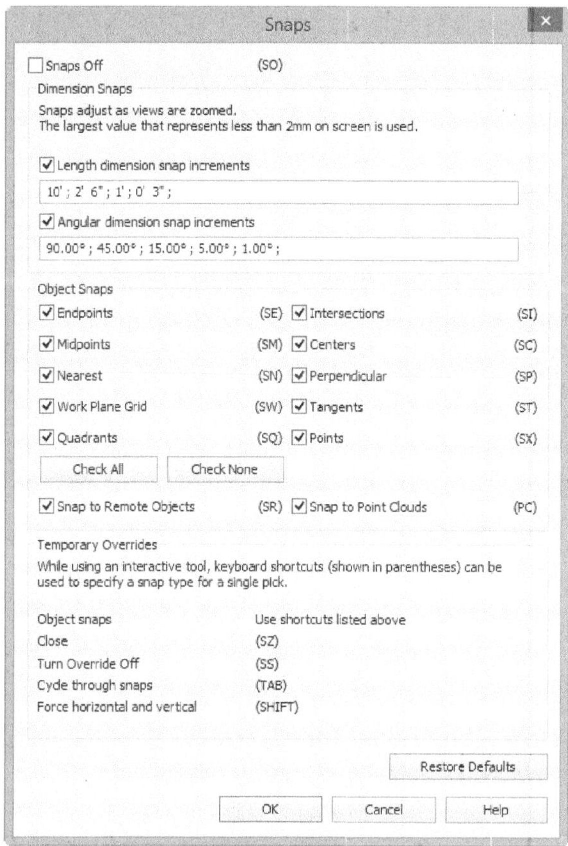

*Figure 2-5 The **Snaps** dialog box*

Dimension Snaps Area

In this area, you can set increments for placing elements or components in a project view. You can set increments for the length and angle dimensions. To set the increment of length dimension, select the **Length dimension snap increments** check box, if it is not selected by default, and then enter the increment values in the edit box below it. The default values entered in this edit box are: **4'**; **0'6";0'1"**; **0'1/4"**; for Imperial (**1000** ; **100** ; **20** ; **5** ; for Metric). Note that every incremental value is separated by a semicolon (;). You can also set increments by typing the values separated by a semicolon. For example, to create an interior layout plan in which the length of the partitions is in 5'(1524 mm) modules, counter top width is 2'(609.6 mm), and the thickness of partitions is 4"(101.6 mm), you can enter the values for the dimension snaps as 5'; 2';4" for Imperial (1524; 609.6;101.6 for Metric). This will enable the cursor to move in these increments and help create the layout with relative ease.

In the **Dimension Snaps** area, snap increments for angular dimensions can be set by selecting the **Angular dimension snap increments** check box and then entering suitable values in the edit box below this check box. This setting is quite useful for projects that have radial geometry.

Tip

*The **Snaps** tool is frequently used not only while creating various building elements but also while editing and placing them. By efficiently using this feature, you can improve the performance and accuracy of your project besides making modeling much simpler.*

Object Snaps Area

In the **Object Snaps** area, you can specify various object snaps for using them in a project. Object snapping refers to the cursor's ability to snap to geometric points on an element such as endpoints, midpoint, perpendicular, and so on. It is useful for creating and editing elements. The advantage of using object snapping is that you can locate the appropriate point on a drawing object. When enabled, the appropriate object snap is displayed as soon as the cursor is near to an element. For example, it is virtually impossible to pick the exact endpoint to start a wall from an endpoint of an already drawn wall. But when you enable the **Endpoints** object snap, the cursor automatically jumps or snaps to the endpoint of this wall. This helps to start the new wall from the endpoint. This, besides making the drawing accurate, later helps in adding dimensions to the project.

Note

The object snapping works only with the objects that are visible on the screen. A tooltip, with the same name as the object snap, is also displayed when you bring the cursor close to the snap point.

Various object snaps modes available in the **Object Snaps** area are: **Endpoints**, **Midpoints**, **Nearest**, **Work Plane Grid**, **Quadrants**, **Intersections**, **Centers**, **Perpendicular**, **Tangents**, **Points**, **Snap to Remote Objects,** and **Snap to Point Clouds**.

The use of each object snap corresponds to its respective name. The **Work Plane Grid** snap option enables you to snap to a point on a reference plane already defined in the model. For example, you can place a furniture component exactly on the floor by snapping to the floor level reference plane. You can snap to the object that is closest to the cursor using the **Snap to Remote Objects** option. You can also snap points of a point cloud data object by selecting the **Snap to Point Clouds** check box. Each object snap mode has a geometrical shaped marker to identify it from the other object snaps. For example, the endpoint object snap is indicated by a square, midpoint by a triangle, nearest by a cross, and so on. To use an object snap mode, move the cursor over the object. You will notice a marker that appears as you move it close to the snap point. To select the appropriate snap point, click when the corresponding marker or tooltip is displayed.

In Revit, all the enabled object snaps work simultaneously. You can turn off all the snap options including the dimension snaps and object snaps by clearing the **Snaps Off** check box located at the top of the **Snaps** dialog box. Alternatively, you can type **SO** on the keyboard to turn them off and on while using a tool. The **Check All** and **Check None** buttons can be used to enable or disable the object snaps, respectively.

Temporary Overrides Area

The options in the **Temporary Overrides** area provide you the alternative of overriding snaps setting for a single use only. For example, if you have not selected the **Endpoints** object snap in the **Snaps** dialog box and you want to use this option while working with a tool, you need not open the **Snaps** dialog box and set this option. You can instead type the shortcut, **SE** to temporarily activate the endpoint object snap. Once you have used this object snap option, snapping to the endpoint is automatically turned off.

You can toggle between various object snap options available at the same location using the TAB key on the keyboard. Hold down the SHIFT key to create the elements vertically or horizontally. This restricts the movement of the cursor in the orthogonal directions only. Once you release the SHIFT key, the cursor resumes its movement in all directions. You can select the **Snaps Off** check box to disable all types of snapping.

SAVING A PROJECT

You must save your work before closing a project or exiting the Revit 2018 session. You have the option of saving the project file in a permanent storage device, which may be a hard disk or a removable disk. Also, you must save your work at regular intervals to avoid loss due to any error in the computer's hardware or software.

Saving the Project File

File menu:	Save As > Project
Shortcut Key:	CTRL+S

To save the project file to the desired location, choose **Save As > Project** from the **File** menu; the **Save As** dialog box will be displayed, as shown in Figure 2-6. Alternatively, you can save the project file by choosing the **Save** button from the **Quick Access Toolbar**. In the **Save As** dialog box, the **Save in** drop-down list displays the current drive and path in which the project file will be saved. The list box below the **Save in** drop-down list shows all the folders available in the current directory. The **File name** edit box can be used to enter the name of the file to be assigned to the project. The **Places List** area on the left of the **Save As** dialog box contains shortcuts for the folders that are frequently used.

*Figure 2-6 The **Save As** dialog box*

Tip

The selection of a large number of backup files for storing may lead to consumption of resources in the hard disk.

Using the Options Button

You can use different features for saving a file by choosing the **Options** button from the **Save As** dialog box. On choosing this button, the **File Save Options** dialog box will be displayed, as shown in Figure 2-7. Using the **Maximum backups** edit box from this dialog box, you can specify the maximum number of backup files that you need to store for the project. In Revit, by default the non-workshared projects have three backup files and the workshared projects have twenty backup files. The options in the **Thumbnail Preview** area enable you to specify the image to be used as the preview of the project file that can be used at the time of opening a project file. You can specify the view of the model to be used as a preview image by selecting an option from the **Source** drop-down list. The **Active view/sheet** is the default option for previewing a project file. For example, to make the **Floor Plan: Level 1** the preview image, select it from the drop-down list. Whenever you select this project file, the preview will always show the **Floor Plan: Level 1**, irrespective of the last active view.

Select the **Regenerate if view/sheet is not up-to-date** check box to see the preview with the latest modifications. Selecting this check box will update the preview image on closing the project file.

Note

Revit updates the preview image continuously. Therefore, selecting the ***Regenerate if view/sheet is not up-to-date*** *check box can consume considerable resources.*

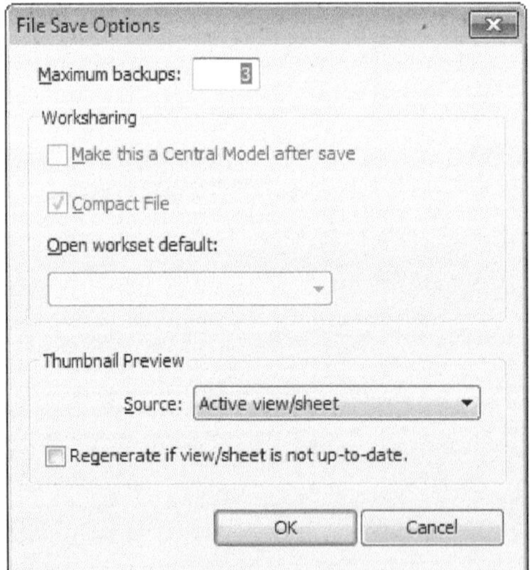

Figure 2-7 The ***File Save Options*** *dialog box*

Using the Save Tool

Once the project is saved using the **Save As** tool, you do not need to re-enter the file parameters to save it again. To save a project to a location, choose the **Save** tool from the **File** menu, as shown in Figure 2-8. While saving the project for the first time, the **Save As** dialog box is displayed, even if you invoke the **Save** tool. Alternatively, you can save your project by choosing the **Save** button from the **Quick Access Toolbar**. As you save your project file, Revit 2018 updates it automatically without prompting you to re-enter the file name and path.

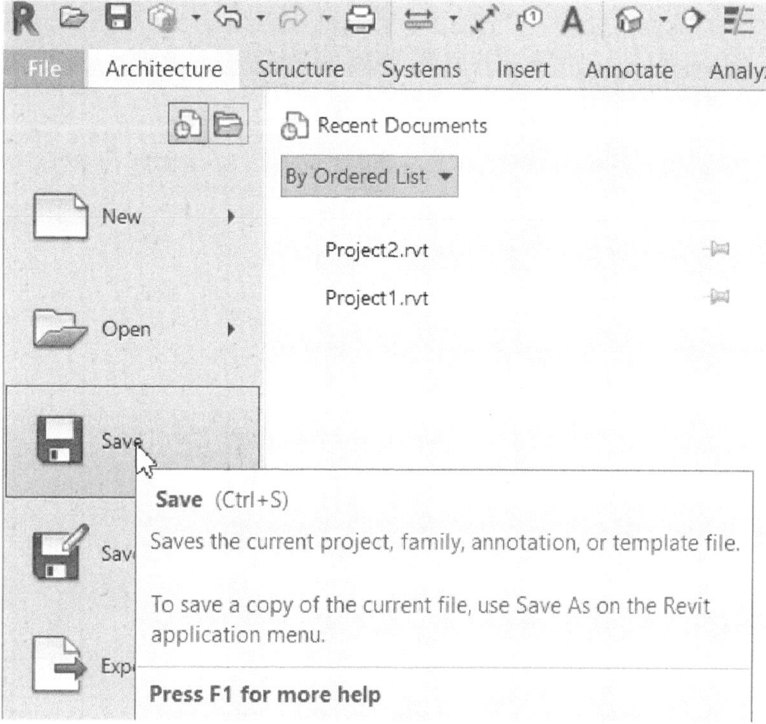

***Figure 2-8** Choosing the **Save** tool from the **File** menu*

CONFIGURING GLOBAL SETTINGS

In Revit 2018, you can configure global settings by using the **Options** dialog box. This dialog box can be invoked by choosing the **Options** button from the **File** menu. The **Options** dialog box, as shown in Figure 2-9, contains nine tabs: **General**, **User Interface**, **Graphics**, **File Locations**, **Rendering**, **Check Spelling**, **SteeringWheels**, **ViewCube**, and **Macros**. The options in these tabs are discussed next.

General Tab

The **General** tab is chosen by default in the **Options** dialog box. This tab contains the following areas: **Notifications**, **Username**, **Journal File Cleanup**, **Worksharing Update Frequency**, and **View Options**, refer to Figure 2-9. These areas are discussed next.

Notifications Area

The **Notifications** area provides you the option for setting reminders to save work at regular intervals. In this area, you can set the time interval at which Revit will remind you to save the project file. The default value for the **Save reminder interval** parameter is **30 minutes**. You can specify the time interval by selecting the interval option from the drop-down list corresponding to the **Save reminder interval** parameter. If you do not want a reminder, you can select the **No reminders** option from the drop-down list. Similarly, you can set the value for the **Synchronize with Central reminder interval** parameter.

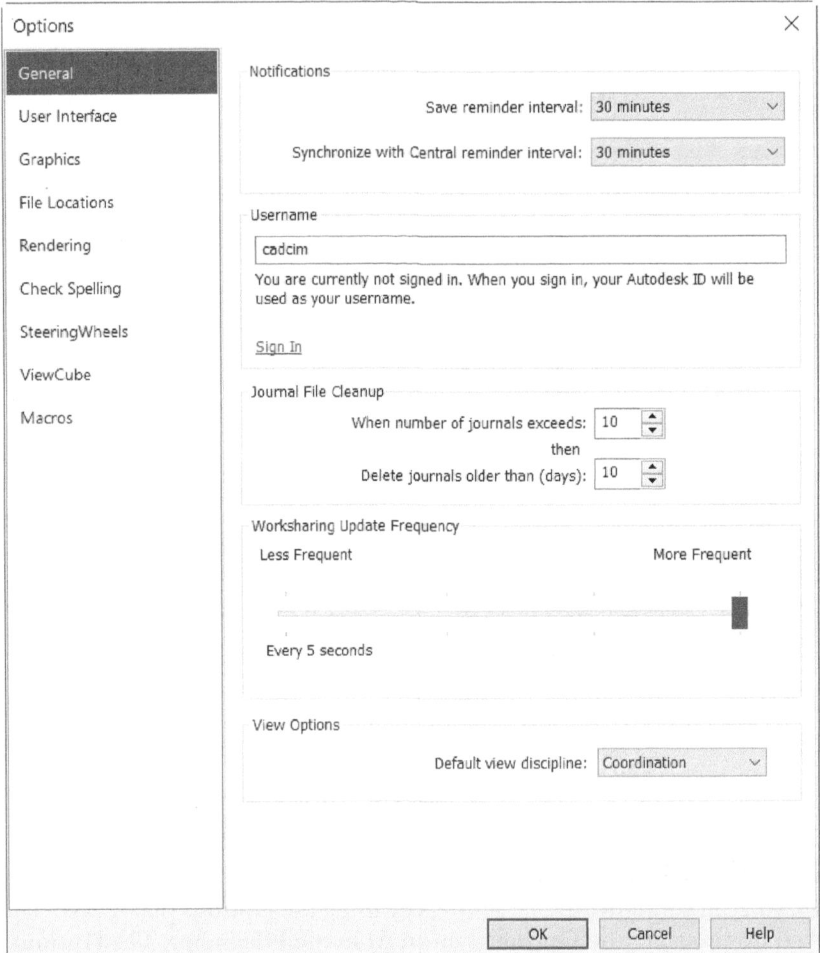

*Figure 2-9 Various areas in the **General** tab*

Username Area

In Revit, if you are not signed in as a user of Autodesk Account, then the system default username will be displayed. To enter a name in the **Username** area, you need to sign in to Autodesk 360. When you sign in, your autodesk ID will be used as a username.

Tip

If you are not logged into an Autodesk account, you can directly enter a username.

Journal File Cleanup Area

Journal files are the text files that are used to resolve technical problems that may occur during the Revit session and they record every step during the session. Whenever you encounter any technical problem with the software, you can run this file to detect the problem as well as to recover the lost files or steps that had caused the problem. In Revit, these files are saved at the following default location: *C:\Users\<Username>\AppData\Local\Autodesk\Revit\Autodesk Revit 2018\Journals* for Windows 7/8 and for Window Vista users *C:\Documents and Settings\<Username>\Local Settings\Application* for Windows XP users. These files are saved each time you close the Revit 2018 session. As such the quantity of these files keeps on increasing until you remove these files from their location. To retain certain files and clean others, you can use the **Journal File Cleanup** area in the **General** tab of the **Options** dialog box. This area contains two spinners: **When number of journals exceeds then** and **Delete journals older than (days)**. You can set the required values in these spinners to retain the files that are recently created. For example, if you need to delete journal files if their number exceeds 15, then set the value in the **When number of journal exceeds** spinner to **15** and to delete journals older than 30 days, then set the value in the **Delete journals older than (days)** spinner to **30**.

Worksharing Update Frequency Area

In this area, you can set the time interval for updating the project in a worksharing environment. To set the update frequency for worksharing, you can set the slider between **Less Frequent** and **More Frequent**.

View Options Area

In this area, you can set the default view discipline for the project. To do so, select an option from the **Default view discipline** drop-down list. The list of options available in this drop-down list are: **Architectural**, **Structural**, **Mechanical**, **Electrical**, **Plumbing**, and **Coordination**.

User Interface Tab

The **User Interface** tab contains two areas: **Configure** and **Tab Switching Behavior**. You can specify the options for the display of Revit user interface. You can do so by selecting the **Dark** or **Light** option from the **Active theme** drop-down list in this area. To customize the use of shortcut keys in a project, you can choose the **Customize** button corresponding to the **Keyboard Shortcuts** parameter. You can also choose the **Customize** button corresponding to the **Double-click Options** parameter, the **Customize Double-click Settings** dialog box will be displayed, as shown in Figure 2-10.

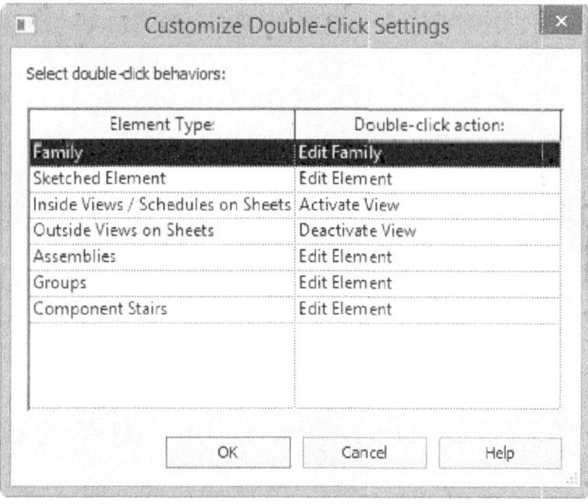

Figure 2-10 The ***Customize Double-click Settings*** *dialog box*

In the **Configure** area of the **Options** dialog box, you can select an option from the **Tooltip assistance** drop-down list to set the extent of the tip that will be displayed with the cursor when it is close to a tool. The options in this drop-down list are **None**, **Minimal**, **Normal**, and **High**. By default, the **None** option is selected in this drop-down list. Note that the tooltip will appear more frequently in your drawing if you select **High** in the **Tooltip assistance** drop-down list. In the **Configure** area, the **Enable Recent Files page at startup** check box is selected by default. As a result, the recent files will be displayed on starting the Revit software. You can clear this check box if you do not want to display the recent files at the startup. In the **Tab Switching Behavior** area, you can specify the tab to be displayed once you clear a selection or exit a tool. In this area, the **Project Environment** drop-down list contains two options: **Stay on the Modify tab** and **Return to the previous tab** options. Select the **Stay on the Modify tab** option to display the options in the **Modify** tab after exiting a tool or clearing a selection. Alternatively, you can select the **Return to the previous tab** option to display the last used tab after exiting a tool or clearing a selection. In the **Tab Switching Behavior** area, the **Display the contextual tab on selection** check box is selected by default. As a result, the contextual tab is displayed once you select a tool from the Revit interface.

Tip

When you rest the cursor on the project file name, a tooltip appears which provides you the information regarding the type and size of the project file.

Graphics Tab

The options in the **Graphics** tab enable you to configure the display card of your computer to improve the display performance. You can also use this tab to assign colors to selections, highlights and alerts, and enable anti-aliasing for 3D views. In the **Graphics Mode** area of this tab, the **Use Hardware Acceleration (Direct 3D)** check box is selected by default. As a result, the hardware accelerators are enabled. Hardware accelerators help display the larger models faster on refreshing the views. In addition, the hardware accelerators help you speed up the process of switching between the windows of views. The selection of the check box will result in the improvement of the performance of the display while navigating a 2D view or a 3D view using the following methods of navigation. Using the tools in the **Navigation Bar**, you can navigate by scrolling the mouse wheel.

In the **Graphics Mode** area, the **Smooth lines with anti-aliasing** check box is selected to display the views as aliased. On selecting this check box, the **Allow control for each view in the Graphics Display Options dialog** and **Use for all views (control for each view is disabled)** options will be enabled. The selection of the **Allow control for each view in the Graphics Display Options dialog** check box will allow you to control the aliasing using the **Graphic Display Options** dialog box for each view. The **Graphic Display Options** dialog box can be invoked using the options in the **Visual Styles** menu of the **Status Bar**, refer to Table 2-1. On selecting the **Use for all view (control for each view is disabled)** option, you can observe the sketched lines as smooth lines in all views.

Table 2-1 The list of features barred for Visual Styles

Feature	Visual Styles			
	Hidden Line	Shaded	Consistent Colors	Realistic
Edges	-----------	Barred	Barred	Barred
Fill Patterns	Barred	Barred	Barred	Barred
Shadows	Barred	Barred	Barred	Barred
Structural Hidden Lines	Barred	Barred	Barred	Barred
Mechanical Hidden Lines	Barred	Barred	Barred	Barred

Note
*While navigating a camera view in the **Wireframe** view style, the fill patterns are not displayed in the model.*

In the **Colors** area of the **Graphics** tab, choose the button corresponding to the **Background** parameter to change the color of the background. The **Selection** parameter specifies a color that an element acquires when it is selected. The default color is **RGB 000-059-189**. To use any other color, click the button on the right of the **Selection** parameter to display the **Color** dialog box and then select the desired color. The **Pre-selection** parameter specifies the color of the highlighted elements. To use any other color for highlighting the element, click the button on the right of the **Selection** parameter and select the desired color from the **Color** dialog box displayed. Revit uses the **Alert** button to highlight elements when an error occurs. In the **Colors** area, the **Semi-transparent** check box is selected by default. As a result, you can make the selected elements semi-transparent and you can view the elements behind the selection. In the **Temporary Dimension Text Appearance** area, you can select an option from the **Size** drop-down list to specify the size of the text to be used in temporary dimensions. In this area, you can set the background of the text in the temporary dimensions. To do so, select the **Opaque** or **Transparent** option from the **Background** drop-down list.

File Locations Tab

The options in the **File Locations** tab can be used to display the link of the default template files present in the project. The options in this tab can also be used to set the path for the template files, user files, family template files that are accessed frequently, and the root path for the point clouds. Figure 2-11 shows various options in this tab.

The path for these files is set at the time of installing Revit. However, you can modify the location by choosing the corresponding **Browse** button and specifying a new path. The default template file location can be changed, in case you wish to use a custom made template file for your projects. Revit uses the default path for user files for saving or opening a project. You can also specify the default path for family template files and for the point clouds by using the corresponding **Browse** button.

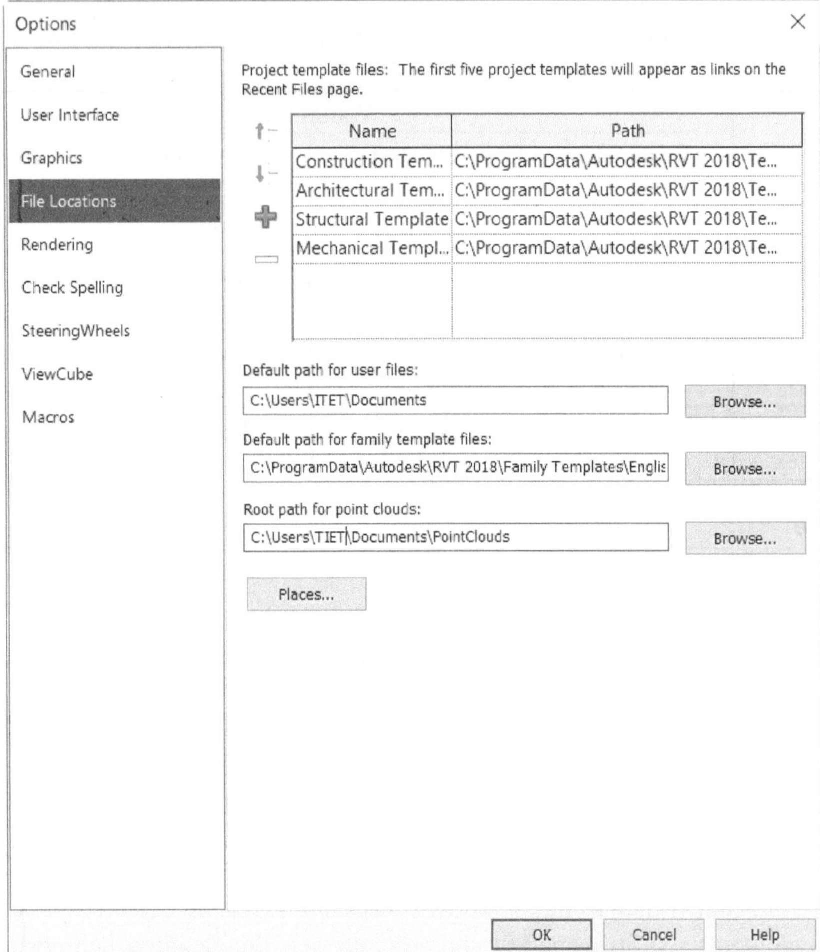

***Figure 2-11** Options in the **File Locations** tab*

Rendering Tab

The **Additional Render Appearance Paths** section in the **Options** dialog box specifies the path for the additional image files that defines texture, bump map, custom color for the render appearance which can be used in the project. These image files are not present in the software and therefore, you need to specify their paths to use them. To do so, choose the **Add Value** button in the **Additional Render Appearance Paths** area and specify the required path in the displayed field or choose the **Browse** button; the **Browse for Folder** dialog box will be displayed. In this dialog box, select the desired path and choose the **Open** button to add the path to the field. In the **ArchVision Content Manager Location** area of the **Rendering** tab, you can specify the location of the licensed additional RPC content from Archvision. In this area, the **Network** radio button is selected by default. As a result, you can provide the address of the licensed Archvision content in a network so that more than one user can access the content. To provide the network location of the RPC content, you can specify the IP address or the machine name in the **Address** edit box. Also, you can specify the port used by the Archvision Content Manger in the edit box next to the **Address** edit box. By default, the value entered in the edit box for the port is **14931**. Alternatively, you can select the **Local** radio button in the **ArchVision Content**

Manager Location area of the **Rendering** tab, if the additional RPC content is available in the local drive of the computer. On selecting the **Local** radio button, you can specify the location of the local ACM executable file (*rcpACMapp.exe*) in the **Executable Location** edit box. To browse to the local ACM executable file, you can choose the **Browse** button; the **Browse for Template File** dialog box will be displayed. Select the desired executable file and then choose the **Open** button; the path of the file will be added and displayed in the **Executable Location** edit box. In the **Archvision Content Manager** area, you can choose the **Get More RPC** button to connect to *http://www.archvision.com* page and get additional RPC required for the project.

Check Spelling Tab

This tab provides you with the option to run spell check in the text and then rectify the errors. You can choose the **Check Spelling** from the **Options** dialog box to display its options. Various self-explanatory settings can be selected from the **Settings** list. You can choose the **Restore Defaults** button available below the **Settings** list to revert back to the default settings. In the **Main Dictionary** area of this tab, you can select the type of dictionary to be used as main dictionary for the spelling check from the **Autodesk Revit** drop-down list. Apart from the main dictionary, you can also use additional dictionaries such as the personal and building industry dictionaries. This facilitates the use of various personal and industry related terms in the text matter of the project. There are many words that are not included in the main dictionaries but are frequently used in the building industry. For example, the abbreviation for architecture 'archi' is not available in the main dictionaries. The additional building industry dictionary has many such words and abbreviations that can be used in the text matter of the project without being prompted for errors while checking spellings. You can also add or remove words from your personal and building industry dictionary. Choose any of the **Edit** buttons available in the **Additional Dictionaries** area to view the list of words. You can enter or remove any word from these lists using the cursor and keyboard. To run spell check in your drawing, choose the **Check Spelling** tool from the **Text** panel in the **Annotate** tab; the **Check Spelling** dialog box will be displayed, as shown in Figure 2-12, wherein you can rectify the spelling errors in the text by selecting the correct spelling and then choosing the **Change** button in the dialog box, refer to Figure 2-12. Alternatively, you can press the F7 key to display the **Check Spelling** dialog box, refer to Figure 2-12, and then make necessary corrections in the text.

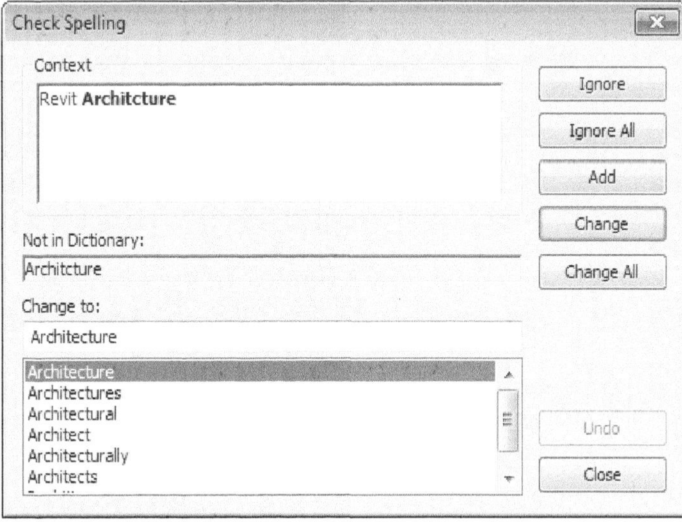

Figure 2-12 *The **Check Spelling** dialog box*

SteeringWheels Tab

The options in the **SteeringWheels** tab in the **Options** dialog box are used to control the visibility, appearance, and operational tools of different types of SteeringWheels. This tab has seven different areas of control to use the SteeringWheels, as shown in Figure 2-13. These areas are discussed next.

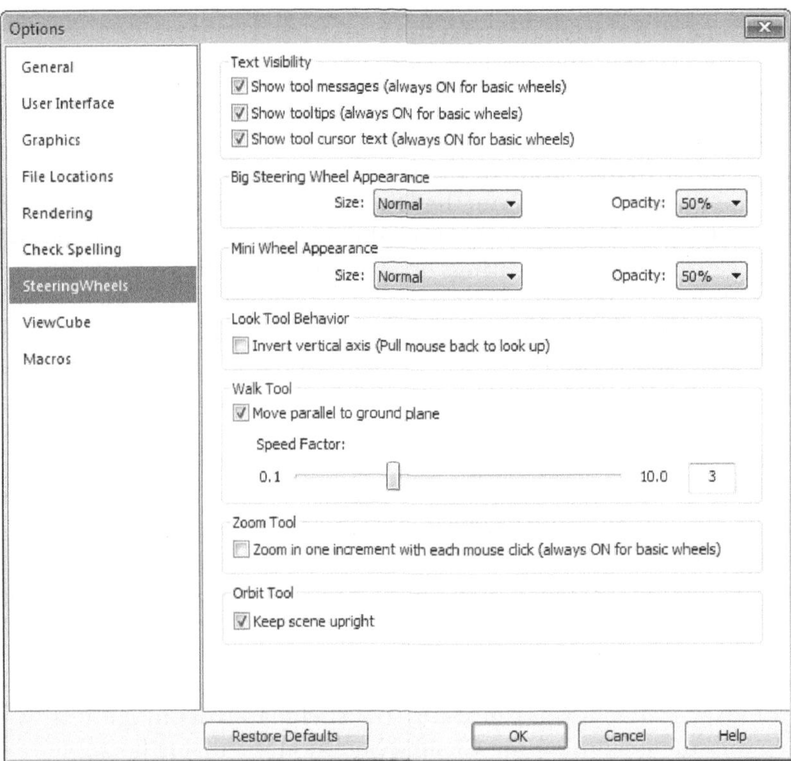

*Figure 2-13 The **SteeringWheels** tab of the **Options** dialog box*

Text Visibility Area

You can control the display of tool messages, tooltips, and tool cursor of the SteeringWheels. You can do so by using the options in the **Text Visibility** area of the **SteeringWheels** tab. In this area, the **Show tool messages** check box is selected by default. As a result, the visibility of tool messages in the SteeringWheels is enabled. To display the tooltips along with the SteeringWheels, select the **Show tooltips** check box in this area. Similarly, to control the display of the cursor text when a tool is active, use the **Show tool cursor text** check box. Select this check box to display the cursor text when the tool is active.

Big Steering Wheel Appearance and Mini Wheel Appearance Areas

To set the size of the SteeringWheels, select the required option from the **Size** drop-down list in the corresponding areas and set its size to small, normal, or large. Similarly, you can set the transparency of the SteeringWheels by selecting the required option from the **Opacity** drop-down list.

Look Tool Behavior and Walk Tool Areas

In the **Look Tool Behavior** area of the **SteeringWheels** tab, select the **Invert vertical axis** check box to change the movement of the view along the vertical axis while using the **Look** tool. Note that on selecting the check box, the view will move in the same direction as that of the cursor. In the **Walk Tool** area of the **SteeringWheels** tab, use the **Speed Factor** slider to change the speed of the walk while using the **Walk** tool of the SteeringWheels. Select the **Move parallel to ground plane** check box, if it is not selected by default, to constrain the walk movement angle to ground plane.

Zoom Tool and Orbit Tool Areas

Select the **Zoom in one increment with each mouse click** check box in the **Zoom Tool** area to enable the zooming operation with a single click. In the **Orbit Tool** area, ensure that the **Keep scene upright** check box is selected. This helps maintaining the perpendicularity between the sides of the model and the ground plane while using the **Orbit** tool.

ViewCube Tab

The options in the **ViewCube** tab in the **Options** dialog box are used to edit various settings of the ViewCube. It has four different areas to modify the ViewCube: **ViewCube Appearance**, **When Dragging the ViewCube**, **When Clicking on the ViewCube**, and **Compass**, as shown in Figure 2-14. These areas are discussed next.

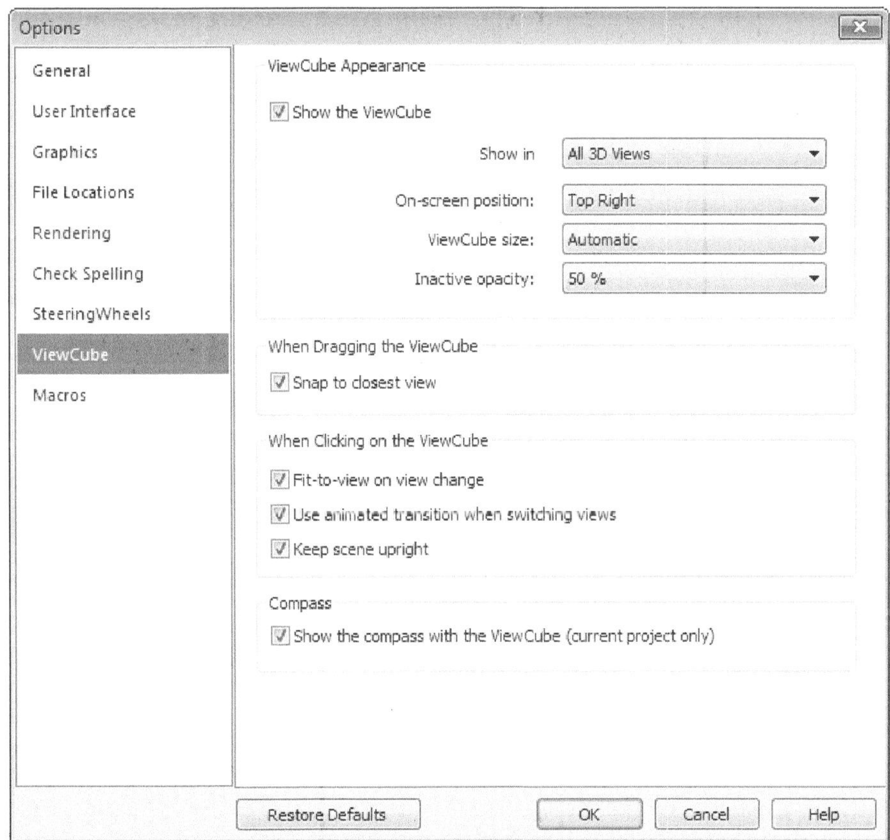

Figure 2-14 The ***ViewCube*** *tab of the* ***Options*** *dialog box*

ViewCube Appearance Area

The appearance and display of the ViewCube can be controlled by the **ViewCube Appearance** area in the **ViewCube** tab.

In the **ViewCube Appearance** area, the **Show the ViewCube** check box is selected by default, so the ViewCube will be visible. If you clear this check box, the ViewCube will disappear and all options of the **ViewCube** in the **ViewCube Appearance** area will be deactivated.

In the **ViewCube Appearance** area, you can use various drop-down lists to align, resize, and change the transparency of the ViewCube. You can select an option from the **Show in** drop-down list to specify whether the ViewCube will be displayed in all 3D views or only in the active view. The **On-screen position** drop-down list is used to position the ViewCube on the screen. Similarly, you can resize the ViewCube by selecting the required option from the **ViewCube size** drop-down list. You can also set the opacity of the inactive ViewCube by selecting various options from the **Inactive opacity** drop-down list.

When Dragging the ViewCube Area

In this area, the **Snap to closest view** check box is selected by default. As a result, the closest ViewCube view orientation will be snapped.

When Clicking on the ViewCube Area

Select the **Fit-to-view on view change** check box in the **When Clicking on the ViewCube** area to fit the view on screen while changing the viewing direction. The **Use animated transition when switching views** check box is selected by default in this area. As a result the view will change with animation. Clearing this check box will result in the change of view without any animation. Select the **Keep scene upright** check box to keep the sides of the ViewCube and the sides of the view perpendicular to the ground plane. Clear the check box to turn around the model in full 360-degree swing. Clearing this check box can be useful when you are editing a family.

Compass Area

The **Show the compass with the ViewCube** check box in the **Compass** area is selected by default. As a result, the compass along with the ViewCube will be visible in the drawing.

In the **ViewCube** tab, you can choose the **Restore Defaults** button to restore the default settings that were changed in its different areas.

Macros Tab

The options in the **Macros** tab can be used to set the security level for the **Macros** used in the project. The options in this tab are available in two areas: **Application Macro Security Settings** and **Document Macro Security Settings**. The various options in these areas are discussed next.

Application Macro Security Settings Area

In this area, the **Enable application macros** radio button is selected by default. As a result, the application macros in the project are enabled. To disable the application macros, select the **Disable application macros** radio button.

Document Macro Security Settings Area

In this area, the **Ask before enabling document macros** radio button is selected by default. As a result, the document macros are disabled, but you will be prompted to enable them whenever you open a project that contains a macro. To enable the document macros, select the **Enable document** macros radio button. Similarly, to disable a document macros in the project, select the **Disable document macros** radio button.

Tip

*If you disable the macros by selecting the **Disable application macros** radio button in the **Macros** tab of the **Options** dialog box, you will still be able to modify the code, although the modifications in the code will not change the current status of the macros.*

CLOSING A PROJECT

To close a project, choose the **Close** option from the **File** menu displayed, as shown in Figure 2-15. If you have already saved the latest changes, the project file will be closed. Otherwise, Revit will prompt you to save the changes through the **Save File** confirmation box. You can save the changes by choosing the **Yes** button or discard them by choosing the **No** button. You can also choose the **Cancel** button to return to the interface and continue working on the project file. You can also use the **Close** button (**X**) in the drawing window to close the project.

***Figure 2-15** Choosing the **Close** option*

EXITING REVIT

To exit the Autodesk Revit session, choose the **Exit Revit** button from the **File** menu. Even if the project is open, you can still choose the **Exit Revit** button to close the file and exit Revit 2018. In case, the project has not been saved, it enables you to save the work through the **Save File** message box, as shown in Figure 2-16. If you choose the **No** button, all the changes that were not saved will be lost. You can also use the **Close** button (**X**) in the main Revit window (in the title bar) to end the Revit 2018 session.

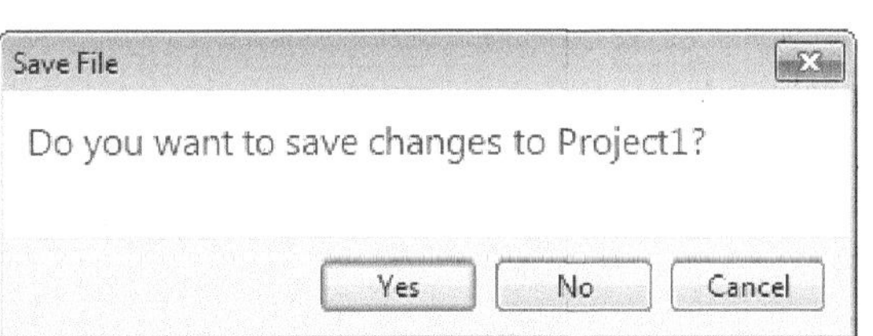

***Figure 2-16** The **Save File** message box*

OPENING AN EXISTING PROJECT

To open an existing project, you can use various options, such as the **Open** tool or the Windows explorer. These options are discussed in detail in the next section.

Opening an Existing Project Using the Open Tool

To open an existing project file, choose **Open > Project** from the **File** menu, as shown in Figure 2-17. Alternatively, you can open a project by choosing the **Open** button from the **Quick Access Toolbar** or by pressing CTRL+O. On doing so, the **Open** dialog box will be displayed, as shown in Figure 2-18. In this dialog box, you can open a particular project file by accessing the appropriate folder using the **Look in** drop-down list.

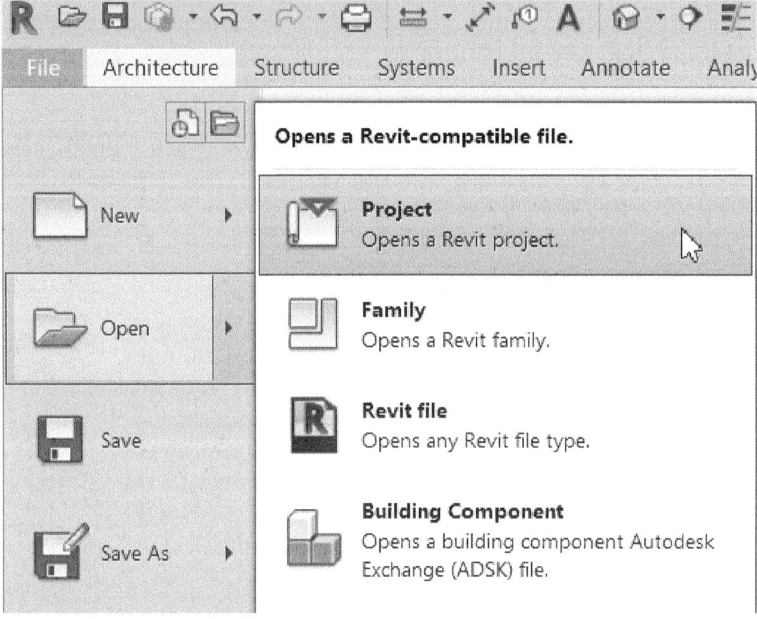

*Figure 2-17 Choosing the **Project** option from the **File** menu*

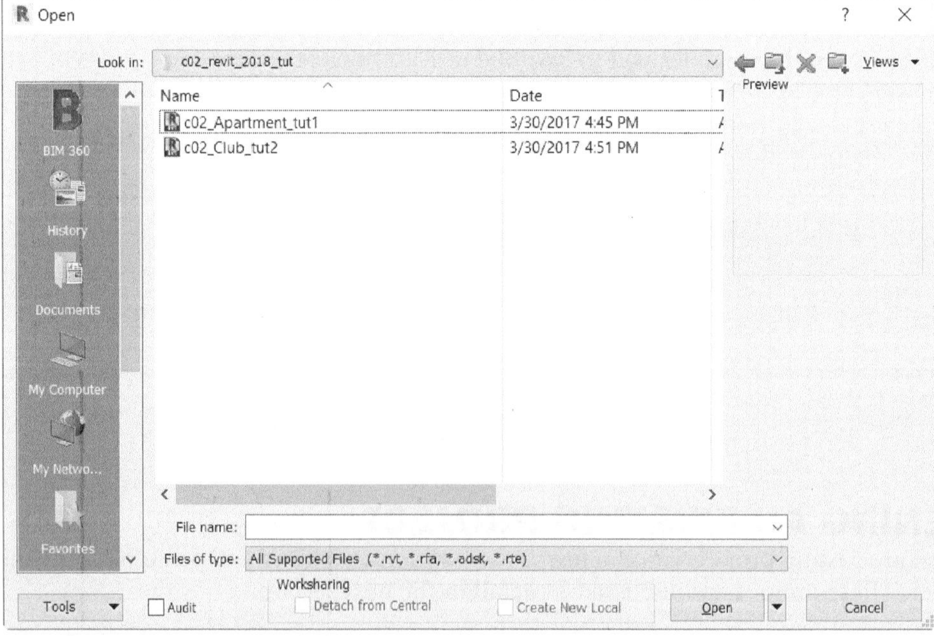

*Figure 2-18 The **Open** dialog box*

Tip

*The **Preview** image acts as a thumbnail to identify a project file. You must select the view that will help you identify the project file easily.*

The **Preview** area of the **Open** dialog box shows the preview of the selected project file. It helps you select a particular file by viewing its contents, even if you are not sure about the file name. The window icons such as the **Views** menu placed along with the **Look in** drop-down list, help you select a project file based on its size, type, and the date when it was last saved. On choosing the **Thumbnails** option from the **Views** menu, you can preview the contents of the project files inside the selected folder in the file list area, refer to Figure 2-19.

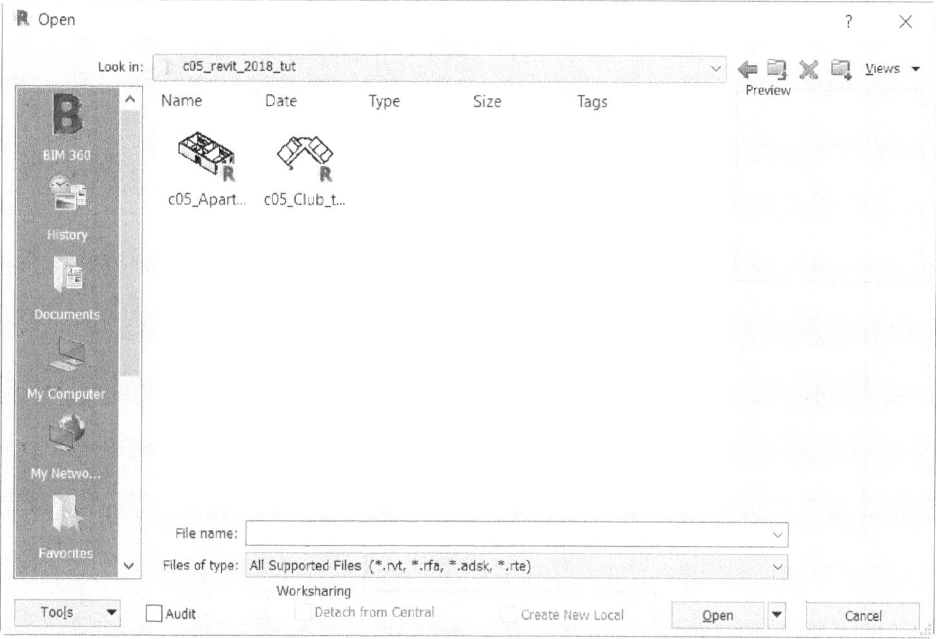

***Figure 2-19** Previewing the files in the **Open** dialog box*

The **Places** list is located on the left in the **Open** dialog box. You can add or remove folders from the **Places** list by choosing the **Options** button from the **File** menu. On doing so, the **Options** dialog box will be displayed. Choose the **File Locations** tab from the dialog box, and then choose the **Places** button from it; the **Places** dialog box will be displayed, as shown in Figure 2-20.

The **Places** dialog box contains two columns: **Library Name** and **Library Path**. You can add or remove folders in the libraries list to create a list of frequently accessed folders. The four buttons on the left in the **Places** dialog box can be used to create or delete a library, or move it up and down in the list. To create a new library, choose the **Add Value** button which is third button from the top; a new library will be added to the defined path. By default, the name of the new library in the **Library Name** section will be **NewLibrary2**. Change the name of the new library and then click in the **Library Path** column to display the browse button. Choose the browse button and select the folder to be added in the libraries list using the **Browse For Folder** dialog box. Choose the **Open** button after selecting the folder; the new folder gets added to the list. If required, choose the upward arrow button in the **Places** dialog box to move the folder up to the top of the list.

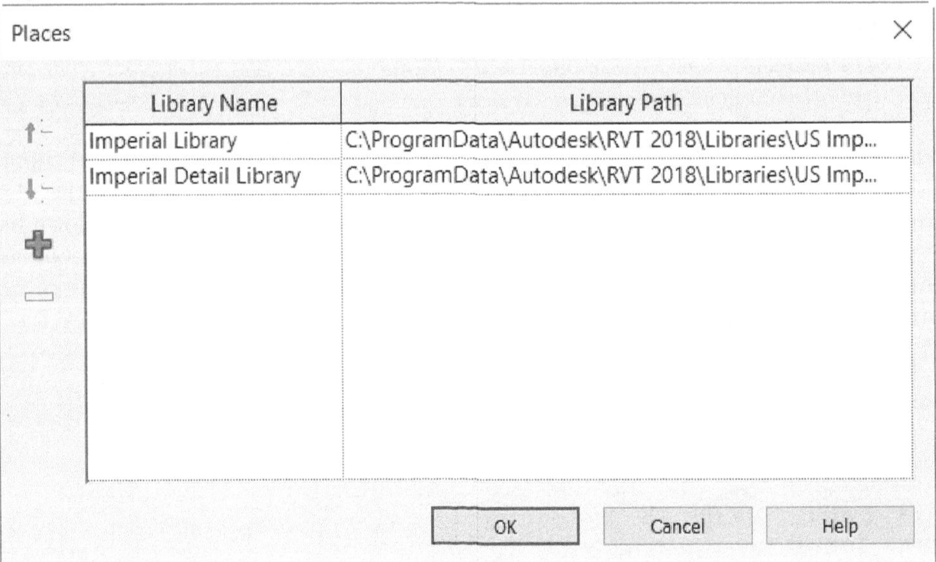

*Figure 2-20 The **Places** dialog box*

Similarly, you can choose the down arrow button to move it down. To delete any library, select the library and choose the **Remove Value** button. Choose the **OK** button in the **Places** dialog box to exit, and then close the **Options** dialog box. When you invoke the **Open** tool next time, the new folder icon will be displayed in the places list.

Once the file to be opened has been selected, its name will be displayed in the **File Name** edit box of the **Open** dialog box and its preview will be displayed in the **Preview** area.

Note

*If you try opening an already opened file, which has been modified in the Revit session, a message box appears, prompting you to close the file first and reopen it. In case you open a file that has been created using an older version of Revit, the **Program Upgrade** message box will be displayed. It mentions that the file is being upgraded to the latest file format and that this is a onetime process. Once the file is opened, it gets upgraded to Revit 2018 version.*

Tip

*The names of the recently opened files are displayed in the **File** menu. On starting Revit, you can click on the name of the project file that you wish to open.*

Using the Windows Explorer to Open an Existing Project

Apart from using the **Open** tool from the Revit interface, you can also open files directly from the **Windows Explorer** by using the methods discussed next.

A file can be opened by double-clicking on its icon in the **Windows Explorer**. It opens the project file in the latest Revit session. If Revit is not running, double-click on the file icon to start Revit and then open the file. Another method of opening a project file is by dragging the project file icon from the **Windows Explorer** and dropping it into the drawing window of the

Revit interface. You can also select, drag, and drop more than one file in the drawing window. In this case, Revit prompts you to open the files in separate windows. Choose the **OK** button to open all the files in the same Revit session.

Tip

*By default, the preview of a file is the last active view or sheet at the time it was last saved. You can set the preview to a particular view by using the **Options** button in the **Save As** dialog box.*

MODEL DISPLAY TOOLS

As described earlier, in Revit, you can create the building model using the 3D parametric elements. Various tools are provided to view the building model. Based on the requirement, you can use these tools to navigate and edit elements in the building model.

Using the Zoom Tools

The **Zoom** tools are used to enlarge or reduce a project view in the viewing area. To use these tools, you need to display the **Navigation Bar** in your drawing. Generally, the **Navigation Bar** is displayed by default. If it is not displayed, click on the down arrow on the **User Interface** drop-down in the **Windows** panel of the **View** tab; a drop-down list will be displayed, as shown in Figure 2-21. From the drop-down list, select the **Navigation Bar** check box if it is not selected; the **Navigation Bar** will be displayed in the viewing area. In the **Navigation Bar**, click on the down arrow below the **Zoom All to Fit** tool; a cascading menu will be displayed, as shown in Figure 2-22. This cascading menu displays different zooming options which are discussed next.

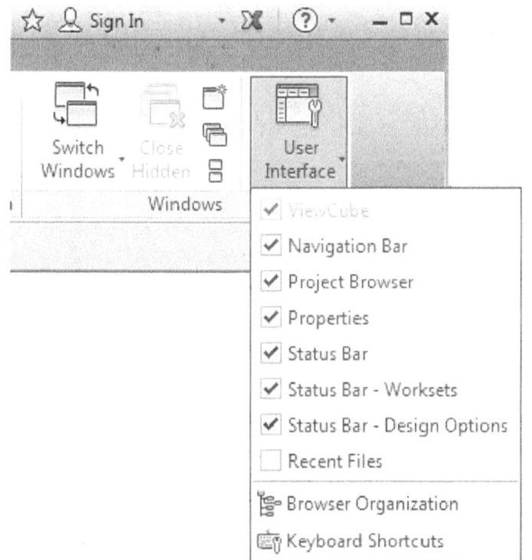

*Figure 2-21 A drop-down list displayed on clicking the **User Interface** drop-down*

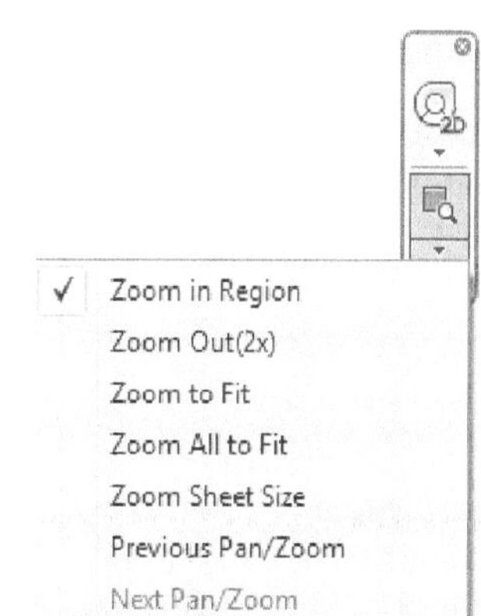

Figure 2-22 Different zooming options in the cascading menu

Zoom In Region

This tool is used to zoom in a specified area or window. When you invoke the **Zoom In Region** tool from the **Navigation Bar**, the cursor is replaced by a magnifying glass. To zoom into an area, you need to define a rectangular window by picking its diagonally opposite corners. You can click at a point to specify the start point of the window. When you move the cursor, a dynamic rectangular window is created whose one corner is the specified point and the other corner is attached to the cursor. Move the cursor across the area you want to enlarge. When the area is enclosed in the rectangle, click to specify the diagonally opposite corners of the zoom window. The specified portion of the current view is enlarged. For example, to work on the stairs of a building plan, you can invoke the **Zoom In Region** tool and click to specify the two opposite corners of the window, as shown in Figure 2-23. The resulting enlarged view is shown in Figure 2-24.

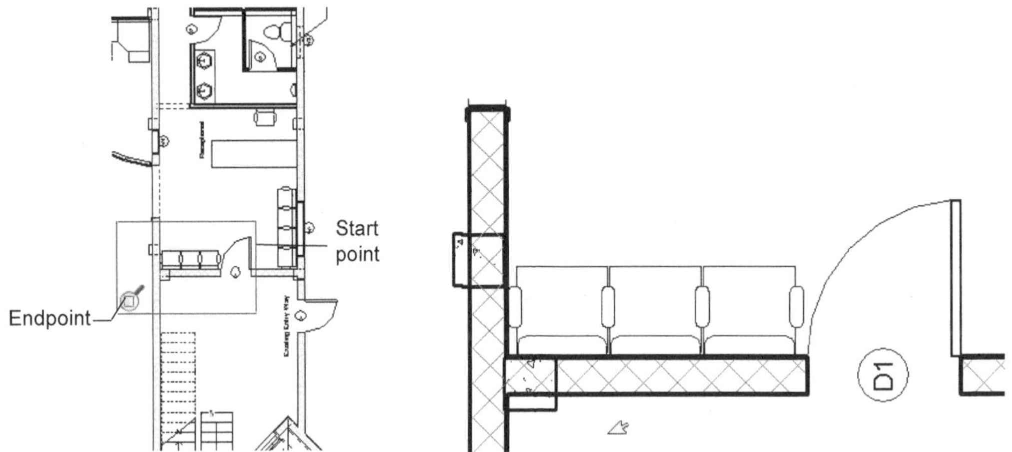

Figure 2-23 *Specifying the corners of the zoom window*

Figure 2-24 *The resulting enlarged view*

Zoom Out(2X)m

This tool is used to zoom out of the existing view by twice the size of the current view. This means, when you invoke this tool, the new view will show twice the length and width of the original view.

Zoom to Fit and Zoom All to Fit

The **Zoom To Fit** tool is used to display all the contents of the project in the current view. On invoking this tool, the drawing window will adjust to show all the elements that have been created in a view. If there are multiple windows open with different zoom factors, invoke the **Zoom All to Fit** tool to perform **Zoom to Fit** in all the windows.

Zoom Sheet Size

The **Zoom Sheet Size** tool is used to fit the drawings in the default sheet size displayed in the **Paper** tab of the printer's **PDF Report Writer's Properties** dialog box. This dialog box will be displayed on choosing the **Properties** button in the **Print** dialog box. To invoke the **Print** dialog box, choose the **Print** option from the **File** menu or enter a shortcut key CTRL+P.

Previous Pan/Zoom and Next Pan/Zoom

The **Previous Pan/Zoom** tool reverts back to the last displayed view using zoom or pan, whereas the **Next Pan/Zoom** tool is a toggle tool to show the next displayed view.

Using the Orient Options

In Revit, you can view a building model in 3D from the preset viewpoints using the **Orient** options.

To use the **Orient** options, activate the 3D view by choosing the **Default 3D View** tool from **View > Create > 3D View** drop-down. Alternatively, you can activate the 3D view by double-clicking on **{3D}** under the **3D Views** head in the **Project Browser**. On doing so, the current view will orient to the default 3D view along with the ViewCube displayed at the upper-right corner of the drawing area. Now, place the cursor over the ViewCube and right-click; a shortcut menu will be displayed, as shown in Figure 2-25. Now, in the shortcut menu, click on the **Orient to a Direction** option; a cascading menu will be displayed, as shown in Figure 2-26. From this cascading menu, select the appropriate view that will be displayed in the drawing window.

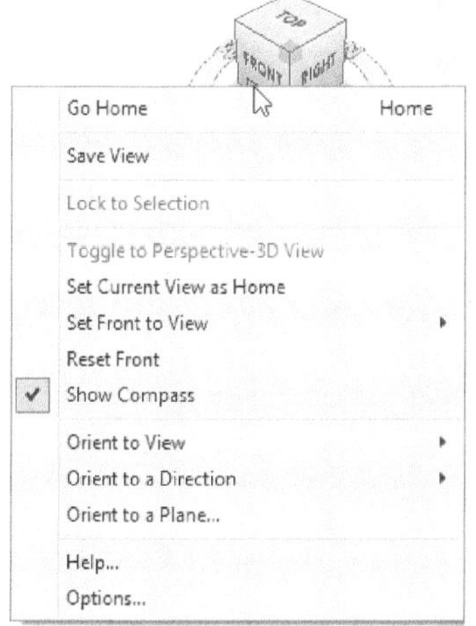

*Figure 2-25 Options in the shortcut menu of the **ViewCube***

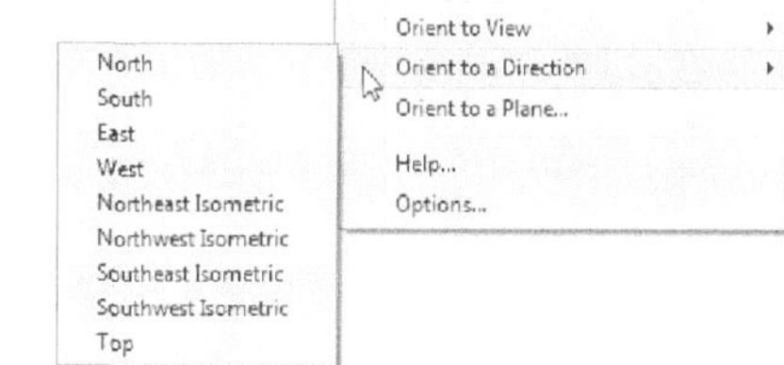

*Figure 2-26 Options in the cascading menu of the **Orient to a Direction** option*

Navigation Tools

Navigation tools in Revit help you navigate and maneuver into your model in different directions and views. The two navigation tools, **SteeringWheels** and **ViewCube**, are discussed next.

ViewCube

The **ViewCube** tool is an interactive 3D navigation tool that appears in all 3D views of a Revit project. By default, the **ViewCube** tool is visible at the top right corner of your drawing area.

The **ViewCube** navigation tool comprises of a cube, a compass ring at the base with various directions marked on it, and a home icon that helps you set the default view, as shown in Figure 2-27. The **ViewCube** navigation tool is displayed in your drawing area either in an active or an inactive state, as shown in Figures 2-28 and 2-29. By default, the ViewCube is in its inactive state and it appears partially transparent over your drawing area. Therefore it prevents the obstruction of the view of your model. Whereas, in its active state, the ViewCube appears opaque and distinct and obstructs the view of your model. You can change the size, on-screen placement, visibility of the compass, and the inactive opacity of the ViewCube as per your requirement. To do so, choose the **ViewCube** tab from the **Options** dialog box as discussed earlier. In the

ViewCube tool, there are twenty-six defined areas comprising faces, edges, and corners. The twenty-six defined areas can be divided into three categories; corner, edge, and face, as shown in Figure 2-30. Out of the twenty-six defined areas, six areas represent the standard orthographic views of a model such as top, bottom, front, back, left, and right. The standard orthographic views are set by clicking on one of the faces on the ViewCube. The other twenty areas are defined to access the angular views of a model.

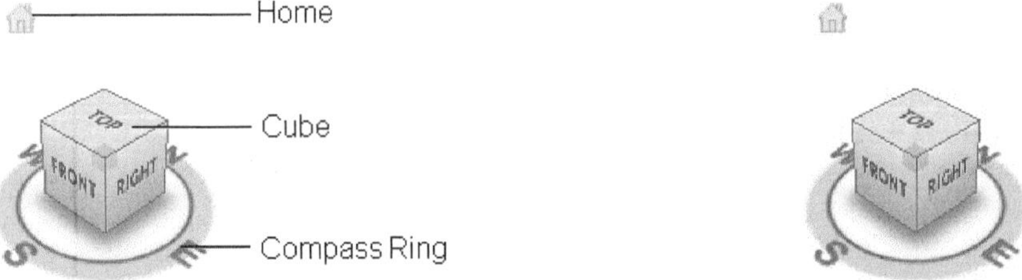

Figure 2-27 *The ViewCube and its components*

Figure 2-28 *The ViewCube in active state*

Figure 2-29 *The ViewCube in the inactive state*

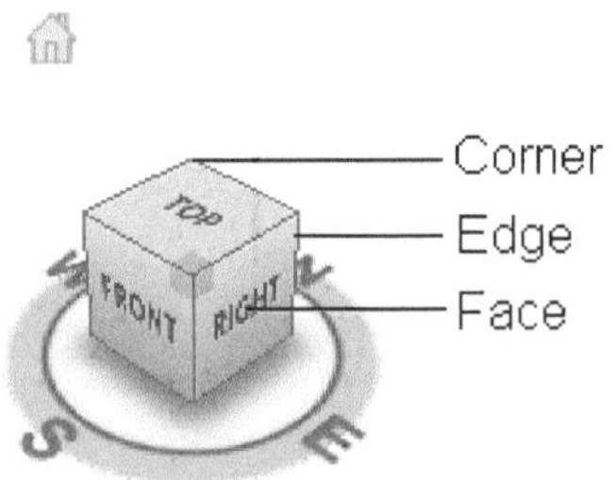

Figure 2-30 *Different areas on the ViewCube*

When you move the cursor on the faces, edges, or vertices of an active ViewCube, the corresponding area gets highlighted in dark-gray color. These highlighted regions are called hotspots. While using the ViewCube, you can click on these hotspots to orient your view as per your requirement.

Tip

*You can link the **Navigation Bar** to the ViewCube. To do so, choose the **Customize** button located at the bottom of the **Navigation Bar**; a flyout will be displayed. Choose the **Docking positions** option in the flyout; a cascading menu will be displayed. From the cascading menu, choose the **Link to ViewCube** option; the **Navigation Bar** will get linked to the ViewCube displayed.*

SteeringWheels

The **SteeringWheels** navigation tools are tracking menus that comprise of multiple navigation features in a single interface. Using the features in these tools, you can pan, zoom, walk, look, and adjust the view of your model as per your requirement. The **SteeringWheels** tool is divided into different sections known as wedges. Each wedge represents a unique function for navigation.

To activate the **SteeringWheels** navigation tool in your model, press the F8 key. The **SteeringWheels** tool will appear according to the state of view in which you are working. If you are currently working in a 2D view, you can use the **2D SteeringWheels** tool. Similarly, you can use the **3D SteeringWheels** tool when you are working in the 3D view.

In Revit, you can access various types of SteeringWheels from the **Navigation Bar**. In the **Navigation Bar**, click on the down arrow below the default **Full Navigation Wheel** tool; a shortcut menu with various types of Steering Wheels will be displayed, as shown in Figure 2-31. To navigate the 2D view, you can use the 2D navigation wheel, as shown in Figure 2-32. The 2D navigation wheel has three navigation tools, **Zoom**, **Pan**, and **Rewind**. **Zoom** is a common navigation tool for enlarging or reducing the viewing scale of the model. You can use the **Pan** tool for traversing across the model view. The **Rewind** tool can be used to see the views of the previous zooming states which are saved temporarily.

Figure 2-31 *Shortcut menu displaying various types of SteeringWheels*

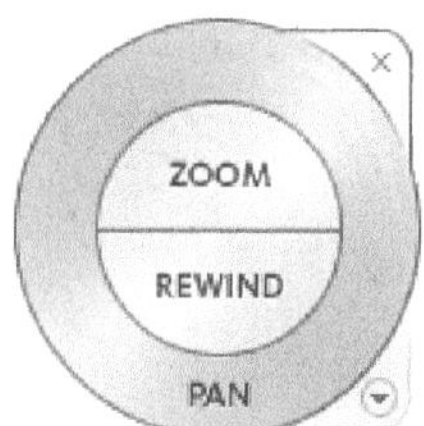

Figure 2-32 *The 2D **Steering Wheels** navigation tool*

The **3D SteeringWheels** navigation tools help you navigate through your 3D views. Based on the size and appearance, the 3D SteeringWheels is categorized into two groups, Mini Steering Wheels and Big SteeringWheels.

The Mini SteeringWheels are classified into three types, **Mini Tour Building Wheel**, **Mini View Object Wheel**, and **Mini Full Navigation Wheel**, as shown in Figure 2-33. The **Mini View Object Wheel** has four distinct navigation tools, **Pan**, **Zoom**, **Rewind**, and **Orbit**. Similarly, the **Mini Tour Building Wheel** comprises of four unique navigation options,**Up/Down**, **Look**, **Walk**, and **Rewind**. The **Full Navigation Wheel** comprises of eight wedges with each wedge defining a unique navigation function. The **Mini Full Navigation Wheel** combines all the functions of the **Mini View Object Wheel** and the **Mini Tour Building Wheel**. The Big SteeringWheels has similar classification as that of the Mini SteeringWheels, as shown in Figure 2-34, and it has same navigation tools as that in the Mini SteeringWheels with the only difference in their appearances on screen.

As you put your cursor over any of the navigation tools, the tooltips and messages are displayed, as shown in Figure 2-35. The tooltips inform you regarding the tool that you want to use and provide instruction for using it. You can control the visibility of the tooltips and the tool messages while using the SteeringWheels by using the **Options** dialog box, as discussed earlier in this chapter.

While using the **SteeringWheels** navigation tool, you can activate the available navigation tools by clicking and holding the left mouse button over any one of the wedges. After holding the left mouse button and dragging it over the drawing area, you can use the selected navigation tool for reorienting your view. Now, to exit the selected navigation tool, release the left mouse button.

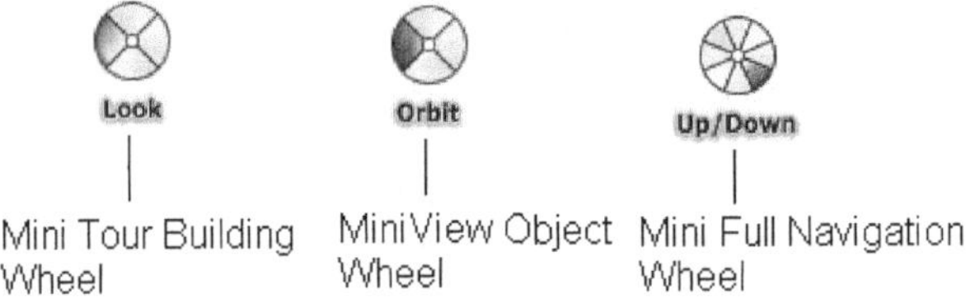

Figure 2-33 *Types of Mini SteeringWheels for 3D Views*

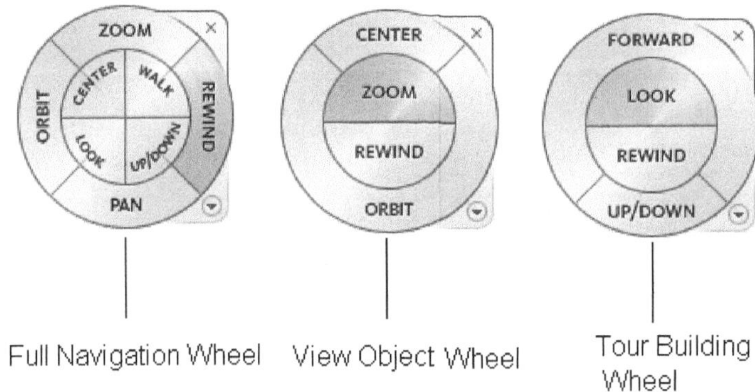

Figure 2-34 *Appearance of Big SteeringWheels*

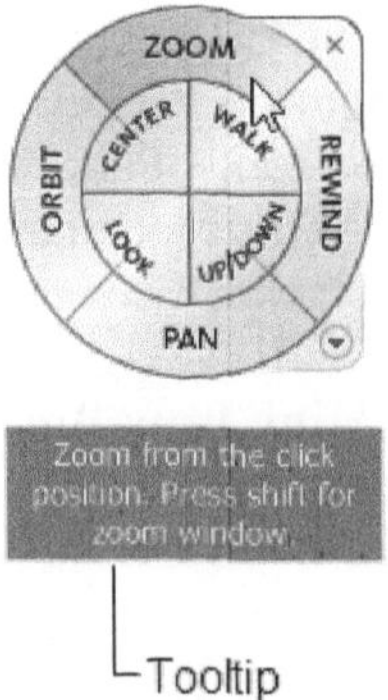

Figure 2-35 *Appearance of the tooltip displayed with the* ***SteeringWheels***

Other Display Options

Revit provides five options to view the building model in different modes of shading. You can select these options by choosing the **Visual Style** button from the **View Control Bar** and then selecting the desired option from the shortcut menu that will be displayed. There are six options that are available in the shortcut menu and are discussed next.

Wireframe : Displays the model with all the lines and edges without surfaces.

Hidden Line : Displays the model with lines and edges that are visible.

Shaded : Displays the building model with the surfaces shaded with respect to the material shading and default lighting effect.

Consistent Colors : Displays the building model in different consistent colors, making the model more aesthetic.

Realistic : Displays the realistic view of the model with textures visible in the elements. In this view style, you can specify and visualize the effect of artificial lights and photographic exposure lighting schemes in the project. The use of this style is helpful for quick presentation, where you do not want to render the image using mental ray.

Ray Trace : Displays the real time ray trace render view. As you select, an option from the **View Control Bar**, Autodesk Revit starts rendering the model in a photorealistic Style. Initially, the render quality is low, but it improves after sometime.

Note

By default, these options affect the current view only. However, you can save the shading effects by saving the shaded view in the project file.

TUTORIALS

In the tutorials of this chapter, you will work on three projects: an apartment complex, a club building and a residential building. However, some portions of these three projects will be completed in the tutorials and the rest will be given as exercises that need to be completed by the students themselves. The tutorials and exercises form a sequence, and therefore, to complete these projects, you need to complete both the tutorials and exercises in the previous chapters. The following tutorials will familiarize you with the tools and concepts discussed in this chapter such as starting Revit, opening a new project, setting units, setting snaps, saving, and closing a project.

Tutorial 1 Apartment 1

In this tutorial, you will create a new project file for the *Apartment 1* project with the following parameters. **(Expected time: 15 min)**

1. Template file-
   For Imperial *default.rte*
   For Metric *DefaultMetric.rte*
2. Project Units-
   For Imperial **Feet and fractional inches** Rounding- **To the nearest 1/2"**
   For Metric **Millimeters** Rounding- **0 decimal places**
3. Length dimension snap increment-
   For Imperial **5' ; 2'6"; 3"; 0'1/2"**
   For Metric **1500 ; 750 ; 75 ; 10**
4. File name to be assigned-
   For Imperial *c02_Apartment1_tut1.rvt*
   For Metric *M_c02_Apartment1_tut1.rvt*

The following steps are required to complete this tutorial:

a. Start Revit 2018 session.
b. Use the template file for the project.
   For Imperial *default.rte*
   For Metric *DefaultMetric.rte*
c. Set the project units using the **Format** dialog box.
   For Imperial **Feet and fractional inches**
   For Metric **Millimeters**
d. Set the length dimension snap increment using the **Snaps** dialog box.
   For Imperial **5'; 2'6"; 3"; 0'1/2"**
   For Metric **1500 ; 750 ; 75 ; 10**
e. Set **Endpoint**, **Midpoint**, **Nearest**, **Perpendicular**, **Work Plane Grid**, **Snap to Remote Objects**, and **Intersection** as the object snaps in the **Snaps** dialog box.
f. Save the project using the **Save As** tool.
   For Imperial *c02_Apartment1_tut1.rvt*
   For Metric *M_c02_Apartment1_tut1.rvt*
g. Close the project.

Starting Revit 2018

1. Start Revit 2018 by choosing **All Programs > Autodesk > Revit 2018 > Revit 2018** from the **Start** menu (for Windows 7). Alternatively, double-click on the Revit 2018 icon on the desktop. As a result, the program is loaded and the user interface screen is displayed.

2. Choose **New > Project** from the **File** menu; the **New Project** dialog box is displayed.

Using the Template File

To use the template file for the project, you need to access the appropriate folder and then select the required template file.

1. In the **New Project** dialog box, choose the **Browse** button from the **Template file** area; the **Choose Template** dialog box is displayed showing a list of the template files available in the **US Imperial** folder.

2. In the **Choose Template** dialog box, select the **default** template file from the **US Imperial Folder** (**DefaultMetric** template file from the **US Metric** folder), refer to Figure 2-36 and then choose the **Open** button; the **Choose Template** dialog box closes and the selected template file is applied to the new project.

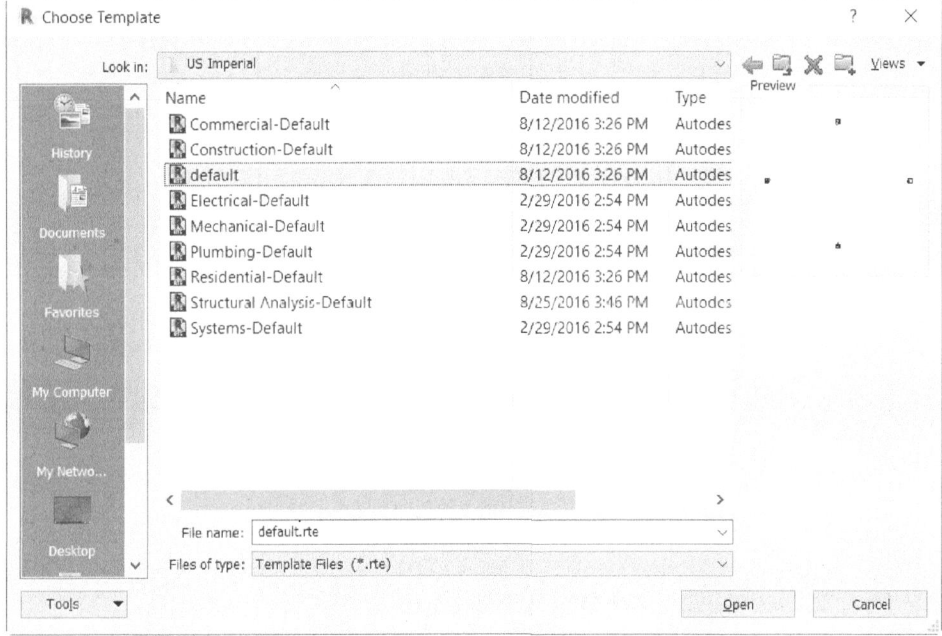

*Figure 2-36 The **Choose Template** dialog box with the **default.rte** file selected*

3. Ensure that the **Project** radio button is selected in the **New Project** dialog box. Next, choose the **OK** button from the dialog box; the *default.rte* (for Metric *DefaultMetric.rte*) template file is loaded. Notice that the **Project Browser** now shows different levels and views that have already been created in the selected template.

Setting Units

To set units for the project,

1. Choose the **Project Units** tool from the **Settings** panel of the **Manage** tab; the **Project Units** dialog box is displayed.

2. Click on the **Format** column next to the **Length** parameter; the **Format** dialog box is displayed.

3. In the **Format** dialog box, select the required option from the **Units** drop-down list, if not selected by default.

   For Imperial **Feet and fractional inches**
   For Metric **Millimeters**

4. Click on the **Rounding** drop-down list in this dialog box and select the required option, as shown in Figure 2-37.
   For Imperial **To the nearest 1/2"**
   For Metric **1 decimal place**

5. Choose the **OK** button; the **Project Units** dialog box is displayed. Choose the **OK** button; the specified units are applied and the dialog box is closed.

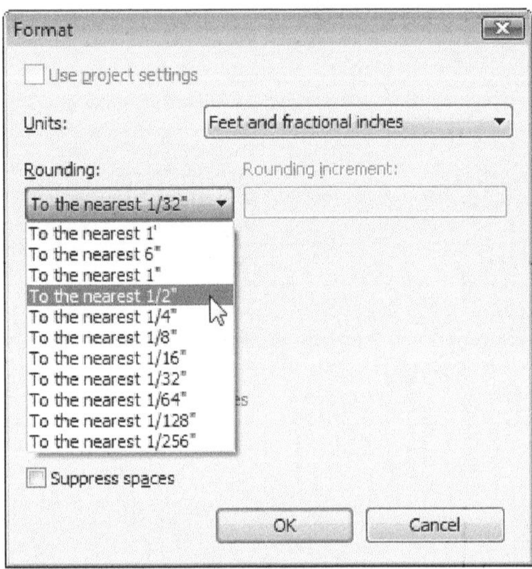

*Figure 2-37 Selecting the **To the nearest 1/2"** option in the **Format** dialog box*

Setting the Dimension and Object Snaps

To set the dimension and object snaps, use the **Snaps** tool. These settings are based on the type of the project and the amount of detailing required.

1. Choose the **Snaps** tool from the **Settings** panel of the **Manage** tab; the **Snaps** dialog box is displayed. In the **Length dimension snap increments** edit box, enter the following values.
   For Imperial **5'; 2'6"; 3"; 0'1/2";**
   For Metric **1500 ; 750 ; 75 ; 10;**

2. In the **Object Snaps** area, clear the **Quadrants**, **Centers**, **Tangents**, and **Points** check boxes. Leave other check boxes selected. Choose the **OK** button; the settings are applied and the **Snaps** dialog box is closed.

3. Select the **Temporary Dimensions** option from **Manage > Settings > Additional Settings** drop-down list; the **Temporary Dimension Properties** dialog box is displayed. In this dialog box, ensure that the **Centerlines** radio button is selected in the **Walls** and **Doors and Windows** areas.

4. Choose the **OK** button; the **Temporary Dimension Properties** dialog box is closed.

Saving the Project

The project parameters set in the previous steps are an integral part of the project file. To save this project file with these settings, use the **Save** tool.

1. Choose the **Save** tool from the **File** menu; the **Save As** dialog box is displayed.

2. In this dialog box, browse to the *C* drive and then create a folder with the name **rvt_2018**.

3. Open the *rvt_2018* folder and then create a sub-folder with the name *c02_revit_2018_tut*. Next, open the created folder and save the file with the following name, refer to Figure 2-38.
   For Imperial *c02_Apartment1_tut1*
   For Metric *M_c02_Apartment1_tut1*
   Notice that the **Files of type** drop-down list shows **Project Files (*.rvt)** as the default option.

4. Choose the **Save** button to save the project with the name *c02_Apartment1_tut1.rvt*. The project is saved at the specified location.

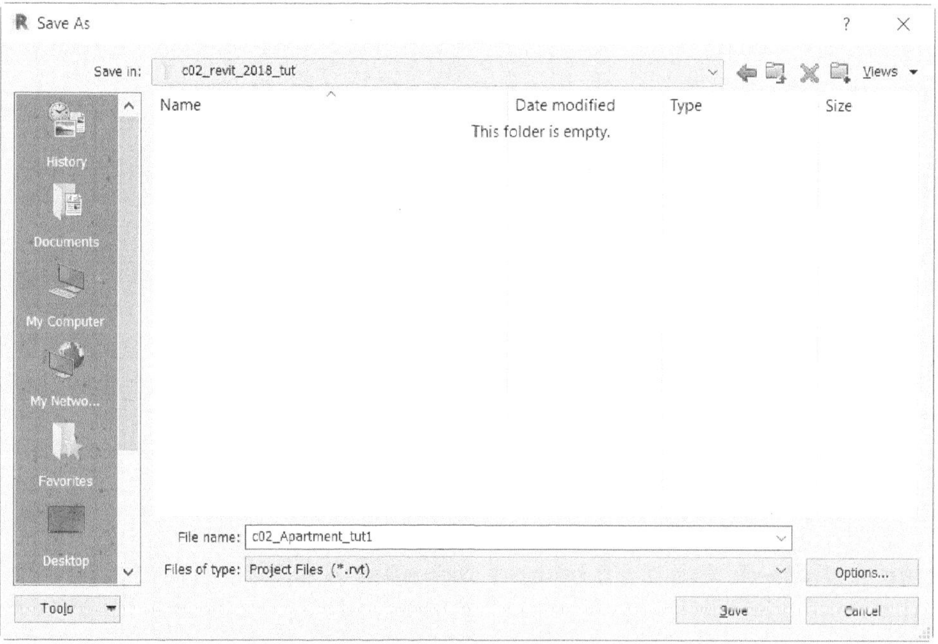

Figure 2-38 *Saving the project using the* ***Save As*** *dialog box*

Closing the Project

1. To close the project, choose the **Close** option from the **File** menu.

Tutorial 2 Club

In this tutorial, you will create a new project file for the *Club* project using the following project parameters. **(Expected time: 15 min)**

1. Template file-
   For Imperial *Commercial-Default.rte*
   For Metric *DefaultMetric.rte*
2. Project Units-
   For Imperial **Feet and fractional inches**
   For Metric **Millimeters**
3. Length dimension snap increment-
   For Imperial **10';2'6";1'; 0'3"**
   For Metric **3000; 750; 300; 75**
4. Object snaps to be set- all available object snaps
5. File name to be assigned-
   For Imperial *c02_Club_tut2.rvt*
   For Metric *M_c02_Club_tut2.rvt*

The following steps are required to complete this tutorial:

a. Start Revit 2018 session.
b. Use the template file by accessing the **US Imperial** templates folder.
   For Imperial *Commercial-Default.rte*
   For Metric *Construction-DefaultMetric.rte*
c. Set the project units using the **Project Units** dialog box.
   For Imperial **Feet and fractional inches**
   For Metric **Millimeters**
d. Set the length dimension snap increment in the **Snaps** dialog box.
   For Imperial **10';2'6";1'; 0'3"**
   For Metric **3000 ; 750 ; 300 ; 75**
e. Select the option for rounding.
   For Imperial **To the nearest 1/4"**
   For Metric **2 decimal places**
f. Enable all the object snaps using the **Snaps** dialog box.
g. Save the project using the **Save As** tool.
   For Imperial *c02_Club_tut2.rvt*
   For Metric *M_c02_Club_tut2.rvt*
h. Close the project.

Starting Autodesk Revit 2018 and Opening a New Project

1. Start a new Autodesk Revit 2018 session by double-clicking on the Revit 2018 shortcut icon on the desktop. On doing so, the user interface screen is displayed. In case, the Revit 2018 session is already running, this step can be ignored and the project file can be opened directly.

2. Choose **New > Project** from the **File** menu; the **New Project** dialog box is displayed.

Using the Template File

As given in the project parameters, you need to use the *Commercial-Default.rte* template file for Imperial and *DefaultMetric.rte* in this project.

1. In the **New Project** dialog box, choose the **Browse** button; the **Choose Template** dialog box is displayed. In this dialog box, select the **Commercial-Default** template file from the **US**

Imperial templates folder (**DefaultMetric** from US Metric folder) and then choose **Open**; the selected template file is assigned to the project. Next, choose **OK**; the template file is loaded.

Notice that the **Project Browser** now shows several levels that are preloaded in the template file.

Setting Units

You can set units for various measurement parameters using the **Project Units** dialog box.

1. Choose the **Project Units** tool from the **Settings** panel of the **Manage** tab; the **Project Units** dialog box is displayed, as shown in Figure 2-39.

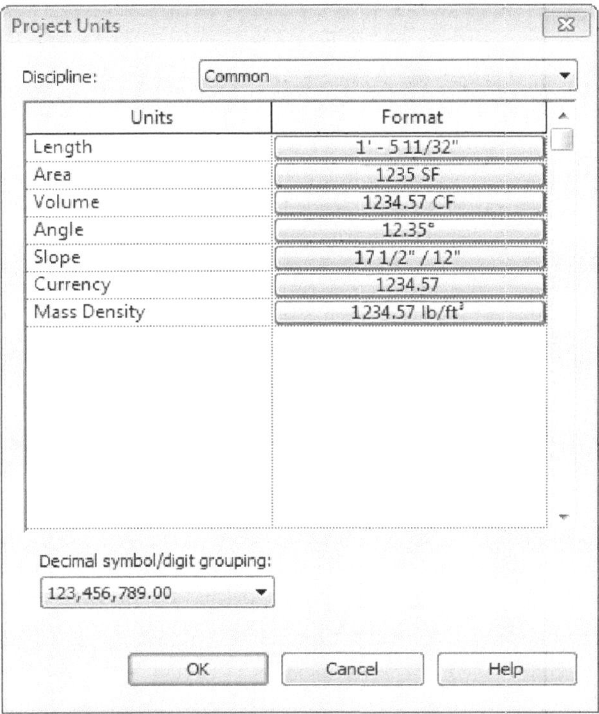

*Figure 2-39 The **Project Units** dialog box*

2. Click on the **Format** column next to the **Length** unit; the **Format** dialog box is displayed. In this dialog box, make sure that the **Feet and fractional inches** option for Imperial or **Millimeters** option for Metric (default option) is selected in the **Units** drop-down list.

3. Next, select the required option from the **Rounding** drop-down list.
   For Imperial **To the nearest 1/4"**
   For Metric **2 decimal places**

4. Choose **OK** to return to the **Project Units** dialog box. Next, choose the **OK** button to apply the settings and return to the user interface screen.

Setting Dimensions and Object Snaps

In this section of the tutorial, you need to access and modify the settings in the **Snaps** dialog box. Further, you need to specify the dimension snap increment and enable all the object snap options.

1. Choose the **Snaps** tool from the **Settings** panel of the **Manage** tab; the **Snaps** dialog box is displayed, as shown in Figure 2-40.

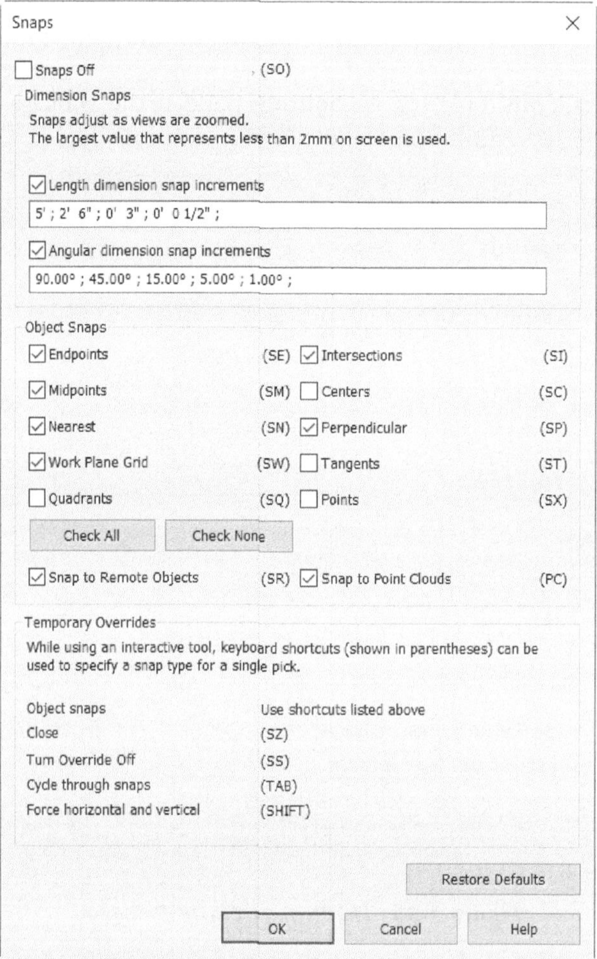

***Figure 2-40** The **Snaps** dialog box*

2. In the **Object Snaps** area, ensure that all the check boxes for snapping are selected.

3. In the **Length dimension snap increments** edit box, enter the following values.
   For Imperial **10'; 2'6"; 1'; 0'3";**
   For Metric **3000 ; 750 ; 300 ; 75**
   Choose the **OK** button; the settings are applied and the **Snaps** dialog box is closed.

4. Choose the **Temporary Dimension** option from **Manage > Settings > Additional Settings** drop-down list; the **Temporary Dimension Properties** dialog box is displayed. In this dialog box, ensure that the **Centrelines** radio button is selected in the **Walls** and **Doors and Windows** areas.

5. Choose the **OK** button; the **Temporary Dimension Properties** dialog box is closed.

Saving the Project

In this section, you will save the project and the settings using the **Save** dialog box.

1. Choose **Save As > Project** from the **File** menu; the **Save As** dialog box is displayed.

2. Browse to the *c02_revit_2018_tut* sub-folder in the *rvt_2018* folder and enter the required file name in the **File name** edit box. Notice that the **Files of type** drop-down list shows **Project Files (*.rvt)** as the default option.
   For Imperial **c02_Club_tut2**
   For Metric **M_c02_Club_tut2**

3. Choose the **Save** button to save the project. The project is saved at the specified location.

Closing the Project

1. Choose the **Close** option from the **File** menu.

Self-Evaluation Test

Answer the following questions and then compare them to those given at the end of this chapter:

1. The keyboard shortcut for the **Save** tool is __________.

2. You can use the __________ tab of the **Options** dialog box to specify the location of the default template file.

3. The __________ button in the **Save As** dialog box can be used to specify the maximum number of backup(s) for a project file.

4. The __________ option of Revit enables you to override the snap settings for a single pick only.

5. You can add folders to the __________ list in the **Save As** dialog box to access the frequently used folders directly.

6. You can open only one Revit project at a time. (T/F)

7. In Revit, all the enabled object snaps work together. (T/F)

8. While saving a project file for the first time, the **Save As** dialog box is displayed on choosing the **Save** tool from the **File** menu. (T/F)

9. A project file can be opened by double-clicking on the file name in the **Windows Explorer**. (T/F)

10. You can save any project file as a template file. (T/F)

Review Questions

Answer the following questions:

1. Which of the following options cannot be used for object snapping?

   (a) **Endpoint** (b) **Work Plane Grid**
   (c) **Dimension** (d) **Centers**

2. Which of the following keys can be used to toggle between the object snap options available at the same point?

   (a) TAB (b) CTRL
   (c) ALT (d) F3

3. Which of the following shortcut keys is used to activate the SteeringWheels?

   (a) F2 (b) F6
   (c) CTRL (d) F8

4. Which of the following conditions are inherited from the new projects of the project template?

   (a) Levels (b) Workflow Settings
   (c) Families (d) Library Structure

5. Which of the following dialog boxes helps to set the units of project?

   (a) **Format** (b) **Snaps**
   (c) **Options** (d) **Project Information**

6. You can modify the project unit settings anytime while the project is in progress. (T/F)

7. The file name and path of a project have to be specified each time you save a project. (T/F)

8. You cannot control the visibility of the tooltip assistant. (T/F)

9. The **Save reminder interval** drop-down list available in the **General** tab of the **Options** dialog box is used to specify the time interval between the reminder prompts to save a project file. (T/F)

10. If changes made to a project file have not been saved, Revit prompts you to save the changes when you choose the **Close** tool from the **File** menu. (T/F)

11. You cannot control the display of tooltips, and tool cursor of the SteeringWheels. (T/F)

12. You can add words to revit dictionaries for checking spellings. (T/F)

EXERCISES

Exercise 1 Apartment 2

Create a new project file for the Apartment 2 project with the following parameters:
(Expected time: 15 min)

1. Template file-
   For Imperial **default.rte**
   For Metric **DefaultMetric.rte**
2. Project Units-
   For Imperial **Feet and fractional inches**
   For Metric **Millimeters**
3. Length dimension snap increment-
   For Imperial **5'; 2'6"; 3"; 0'1/2"**
   For Metric **1500 ; 750 ; 75 ; 10**
4. File name to be assigned-
   For Imperial *c02_Apartment2_ex1.rvt*
   For Metric *M_c02_Apartment2_ex1.rvt*

Exercise 2 Elevator and Stair Lobby

Create a new project file for the *Elevator and Stair Lobby* project with the following parameters:
(Expected time: 15 min)

1. Template file-
   For Imperial **default.rte**
   For Metric **DefaultMetric.rte**
2. Project Units-
   For Imperial **Feet and fractional inches**
   For Metric **Millimeters**
3. Length dimension snap increment-
   For Imperial **5'; 1'; 3"; 0'1"**
   For Metric **1500 ; 300 ; 75 ; 25**
4. File name to be assigned-
   For Imperial *c02_ElevatorandStairLobby_ex2.rvt*
   For Metric *M_c02_ElevatorandStairLobby_ex2.rvt*

Exercise 3 Residential Building

Create a new project file for the project with the following parameters:
(Expected time: 15 min)

1. Template file-
   For Imperial default.rte
   For Metric **DefaultMetric.rte**

2. Project Units-
   For Imperial **Feet and fractional inches**
   For Metric **Millimeters**
3. Length dimension snap increment-
   For Imperial **4' ; 0' 6" ; 0' 1" ; 0' 0 1/4" ;**
   For Metric **1200 ; 150 ; 25 ; 5**
4. Name for saving the file-
   For Imperial **c02_residential_ex3.rvt**
   For Metric **M_c02_residential_ex3.rvt**

Answers to Self-Evaluation Test

1. CTRL+S, **2**. **File Locations**, **3**. **Options**, **4**. **Temporary Overrides**, **5**. **Places**, **6**. F, **7**. T, **8**. T, **9**. T, **10**. T

Chapter 3

Creating Walls

Learning Objectives

After completing this chapter, you will be able to:

- *Understand the concept of walls*
- *Understand the properties of walls*
- *Use the sketching tools to create walls*
- *Create stacked walls*
- *Create exterior and interior walls based on the given parameters*
- *Create wall sweeps and wall reveals*

INTRODUCTION

In the previous chapter, you learned about various tools and options to start, open and save an architectural project in Revit. In this chapter, you will learn about various tools and options to create different types of walls. You will also learn about the functions and parameters of different types of walls. Moreover, you will learn various options to modify the properties of an architectural wall and its type properties will be discussed in detail. Also, you will learn about various tools that are used to add modifiers in a wall, such as sweep and reveal.

CREATING A BUILDING PROJECT

In Revit, the term 'project' comprises not only the physical building model but also its associated documentation such as drawings, views, schedules, areas, and so on. The first step in creating a project is to create the building model. In Autodesk Revit, you can create it using the following two methods:

Method 1: Create a building model using individual building elements such as walls, windows, doors, floors, roofs, and so on.

Method 2: Create a conceptual mass of a building model using the massing tools and conceptualize the overall building shape and volume before working with individual elements.

Tip

You can also use a combination of above two methods. You can generate a building mass using the massing tools and then convert it into a building model with individual building elements using the building maker tools.

The selection of method depends on different project parameters such as project magnitude, building shape, building technology, current documentation stage of a project, industry parameters, and so on. The use of the massing tools to create a building geometry and the usage of individual building components to develop a building model will be described later.

Autodesk Revit provides you with several tools to add individual building elements such as wall, floor, roof, and so on for creating a building model. Several predesigned element types have been provided for each building element in Autodesk Revit libraries. You have the flexibility to either use the predesigned element types or create your own element type to create a building model.

Sequence of Creating a Building Model

The sequence of using building elements for creating a building model depends on various parameters such as building type, building volume, building shape, and so on. For most of the building projects, the sequence given below may be adopted.

Step 1: Start the model by creating the exterior walls of the building at Level 1 (lowest level).

Step 2: Create interior walls at the desired locations.

Step 3: Add doors and windows to the exterior and interior walls at the desired location.

Step 4: Add the floor to the building model.

Step 5: Add the roof to the building model.

Step 6: Add the structural or architectural grid and structural elements.

Step 7: Add stand-alone components such as furniture items and plumbing fixtures.

Step 8: Add text and annotations to different spaces.

Step 9: Create dimensions for different parameters of the project.

Step 10: Create project details and documentation.

Step 11: Create the rendered 3D views and walkthrough.

In Revit, each building element is considered a three-dimensional parametric entity. This means, on adding elements to the model, you also add the related information and specification about the elements. One of the most important elements in a building model is the wall. It defines the basic spatial arrangement of the building that acts as the host for doors and windows.

Understanding Wall Types

Autodesk Revit provides you with several predefined wall types such as **Exterior**, **Interior**, **Retaining**, **Foundation**, **Curtain**, and **Stacked Wall**, based on their usage.

Exterior Wall Type

This category constitutes the wall types that are primarily used for generating the exterior skin of the building model. It has predefined wall types such as **Brick on CMU**, **Brick on Mtl. Stud**, **CMU Insulated**, and so on.

Interior Wall Type

The interior walls are used as the interior partitions in a building project. These walls are non-bearing in character. The predefined interior walls provided in Autodesk Revit have a dry wall construction with a metal stud frame and varying thickness.

Retaining Wall Type

As the name suggests, the primary function of the retaining walls is to retain the earth. You can either use the retaining walls provided in the program or set the function of any wall type as retaining. For example, you can select a wall from the drawing and select **Retaining - 12" Concrete** for Imperial (**Retaining 300mm Concrete** for Metric) from the **Properties** palette. On doing so, the current wall type will be changed to retaining wall.

Foundation Wall Type

The walls that form the foundation or substrate of the main building structure belong to this category. To create a foundation wall, the **Foundation - 12" Concrete** option for Imperial (**Foundation- 300mm Concrete** for Metric) is provided as the predefined foundation wall type in the **Properties** palette.

Curtain Wall Type

These wall types have predefined curtain walls or screen walls that consist of panels and mullions.

Stacked Wall Type

A stacked wall is a wall that is made of different types of walls stacked vertically on top of each other.

This software provides you with the flexibility of creating your own wall type. The walls that you will create can have different parameters which can be modified, depending on their usage. In Revit, you can create both architectural and structural walls. An architectural wall does not contain analytical properties like the structural walls. In the next section, various techniques to create and modify architectural walls are discussed.

Creating Architectural Walls

Ribbon:	Architecture > Build > Wall drop-down > Wall: Architectural
Shortcut Key:	WA

In this section, you will learn the method of creating and editing architectural walls. In Autodesk Revit, each wall type has specific predefined properties such as its usage, composition, material, characteristics, finish, height, and so on. You can select the wall type based on its specific usage in the project. Walls, like most other model elements, can be created in a plan view or a 3D view.

To create an architectural wall, first you need to invoke the **Wall: Architectural** tool and then select the appropriate wall type and specify various properties. To do so, choose the **Wall: Architectural** tool from the **Build** panel of the **Architecture** tab, refer to Figure 3-1; the **Modify | Place Wall** tab with the **Options Bar** will be displayed. In the **Options Bar**, you can define the direction of the wall by choosing either the **Height** or **Depth** option from the **Height** drop-down list. You can select the desired level upto which the wall is to be created from the **Unconnected** drop-down list. If you select the **Unconnected** option from the drop-down list then the edit box next to it will be activated. Enter the desired height upto which you want the wall to be raised. Select the reference line for sketching the wall from the **Location Line** drop-down list.

Select an exterior or interior wall type from the **Type Selector** drop-down list in the **Properties** palette, as shown in Figure 3-2. Next, from the **Properties** palette, specify and edit various properties of the wall to be created. Various wall properties and the process to specify them are discussed next.

Tip

*Besides the **Properties** palette, wall types are also listed under the **Families** head in the **Project Browser**. Left-click on the arrow sign next to the **Families** head to view the families available in Autodesk Revit. Click the arrow symbol next to the **Walls** subhead and then the one next to the **Basic Wall** subhead to display various basic wall types. Select and right-click on any wall type to display a shortcut menu with the options that can be used for editing.*

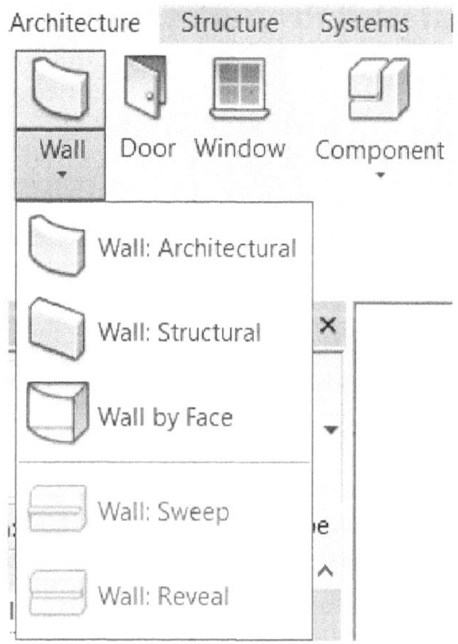

Figure 3-1 Invoking the ***Wall: Architectural*** *tool from the* ***Build*** *panel*

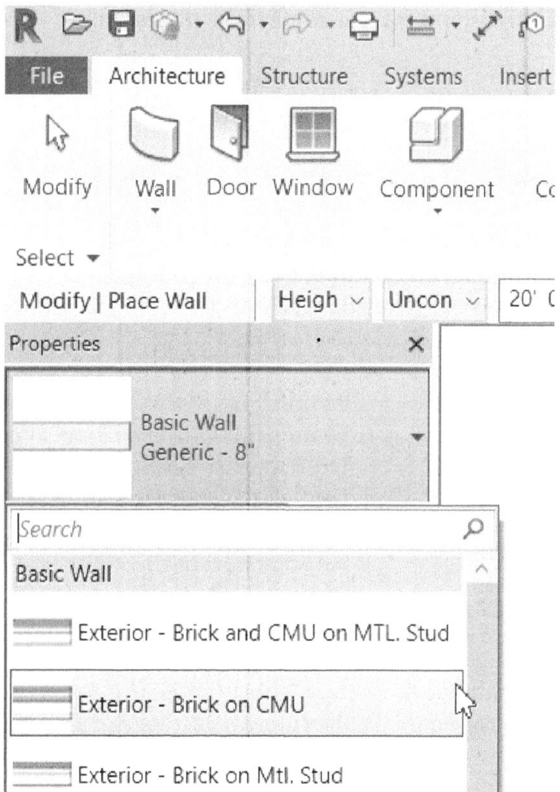

Figure 3-2 Selecting the wall type from the ***Type Selector*** *drop-down list*

Specifying Architectural Wall Properties

In Autodesk Revit, wall has two sets of properties, type and instance. These set of properties control the appearance and the behavior of the element concerned.

Specifying Instance Properties

After invoking the **Wall: Architectural** tool, the instance properties of the wall will be displayed in the **Properties** palette, as shown in Figure 3-3.

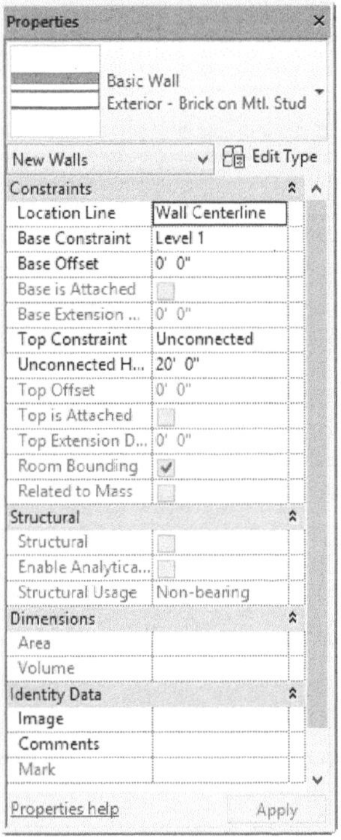

The **Properties** palette contains the **Type Selector** drop-down list. You can select the family and the type of the proposed wall from this drop-down list. This palette shows various instance properties and their corresponding values for the specified instance of the element. The options in this palette depend on the type and instance of the selected element or the elements created based on the options selected in the **Type Selector** drop-down list. The properties of exterior walls are displayed in different categories such as **Constraints**, **Structural**, **Dimensions**, and **Identity Data** each representing a set of properties corresponding to the title. You can use the twin arrows on the extreme right of the title to collapse the table of properties for each title. Some of the important parameters are discussed next.

*Figure 3-3 The **Properties** palette for the **Exterior - Brick on Mtl. Stud** wall type*

In the **Properties** palette, the **Location Line** parameter indicates the reference line used for creating a wall. In 3D environment, the location line in a wall refers to a plane that does not get modified even if the wall parameters are changed. To assign a value to the **Location Line** parameter, click in the value field corresponding to this parameter; a drop-down list will be displayed. Click on the drop-down list to view the available options. The options in the drop-down list are given next.

Wall Centerline	-	Center line of the entire composite wall
Core Centerline	-	Center line of the structural core of the wall
Finish Face: Exterior	-	Exterior face of the wall as the location line
Finish Face: Interior	-	Interior face of the wall as the location line
Core Face: Exterior	-	Exterior face of the core
Core Face: Interior	-	Interior face of the core

The location line is indicated by a dashed line, which appears while sketching a wall segment. For example, on selecting the **Wall Centerline** option as the location line, you will notice a dashed line in the middle of the wall, as shown in Figure 3-4. When you select the **Finish Face: Interior** option, it appears on the interior face of the wall, refer to Figure 3-5.

Figure 3-4 Wall on selecting the ***Wall Centerline*** *option*

Figure 3-5 Wall on selecting the ***Finish Face: Interior*** *option*

Note

When a design is developed, you may need to modify certain parameters of the exterior wall such as its thickness and composition, based on the final selection of materials and their specifications. Considering this flexibility, the ***Location Line*** *parameter enables you to create walls.*

In Autodesk Revit, you can specify the height of walls by applying the base and top constraints with respect to the levels defined in the project. This means, if you set the base and height parameters of a top storey and apply these constraints, all walls will be sketched with the same base and the top. To create a wall segment that is not related to these components and levels, you can type the desired height in the column of the **Unconnected Height** instance parameter. The default value for the unconnected height is 20' 0".

The various instance parameters for walls and their usage are given next. The values of some of the instance parameters will be available only after an instance is created. The instance parameters of the wall are given in the table below.

Instance Parameter	Description
Location Line	Line or reference plane for sketching the wall
Base Constraint	Level or reference plane of the base of a wall
Base is Attached	Check box showing whether or not the base of the wall is attached to any other element
Base Offset	Height of a wall from its base constraint
Base Extension Distance	Distance of the base of the layers in a wall
Top Constraint	Specifies whether the wall height is defined by specified levels or is unconnected
Unconnected Height	Explicit height of a wall
Top Offset	Distance of the top of a wall from the top constraint
Top is Attached	Check box showing whether the top of the wall is attached to any upper element or not
Top Extension Distance	Distance of the top of a layer on a wall
Room Bounding	Specifies whether the wall constitutes the boundary of a room
Related to Mass	Specifies whether the wall relates to a massing geometry
Structural Usage	Defines the specific structural usage of a wall
Length	Indicates the value of the length of a wall
Area	Indicates the value of the surface area of a wall

Volume	Indicates the value of the volume of a wall
Image	Specifies the image file corresponding to a wall instance. This parameter can be used in the wall schedule to display the image of the wall instance.
Comments	Specific comments that give description of a wall
Mark	To add a unique value or label to each wall

Tip

The selection for the ***Location Line*** *parameter should be based on your design intent. For example, to create walls defined by exact interior dimensions, you can select the* ***Finish Face: Interior*** *option as the location line value. Once this parameter is selected, any addition or reduction of wall thickness in the project will be made toward its outer face.*

Specifying Type Properties

The type properties of a wall specify the common parameters shared by certain elements in a family. Any changes made in the type properties of a wall element will affect all individual elements of that family in the project. To modify the type properties of an element, invoke the **Wall: Architectural** tool; the **Modify | Place Wall** tab will be displayed. In this tab, choose the **Edit Type** tool from the **Properties** panel; the **Type Properties** dialog box will be displayed, as shown in Figure 3-6.

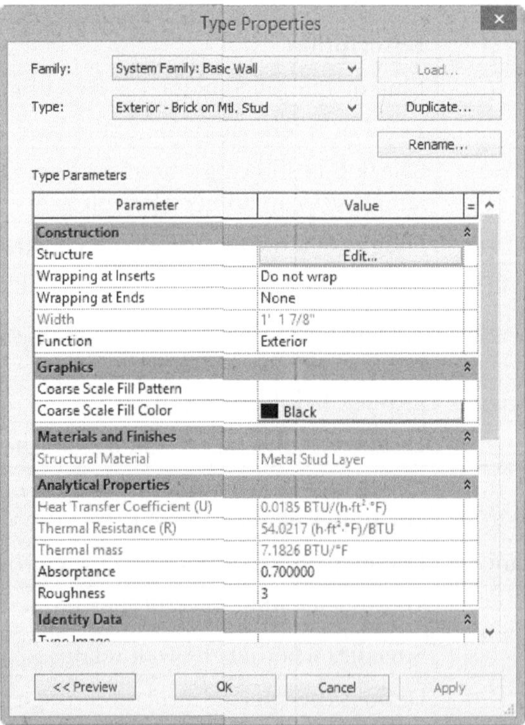

Figure 3-6 *The* ***Type Properties*** *dialog box with the* ***Exterior-Brick on Mtl. Stud*** *wall type*

Using this dialog box, you can modify the type properties of the selected wall type such as **Structure**, **Function**, **Coarse Scale Fill Pattern**, and so on. In Autodesk Revit, in the **Type Properties** dialog box, you can view the Analytical Properties of the wall such as the **Thermal Mass**, **Thermal Resistance**, and **Heat Transfer Coefficient**. The Analytical Properties that you can edit are: **Absorptance** and **Roughness**. In the **Type Properties** dialog box, you can also define the composition of the wall type. To do so, choose the **Edit** button in the **Value** column of the **Structure** parameter; the **Edit Assembly** dialog box will be displayed. In the **Edit Assembly** dialog box, choose the **Preview** button; a preview box will be displayed. The preview box will display sectional detail of the selected wall type, as shown in Figure 3-7.

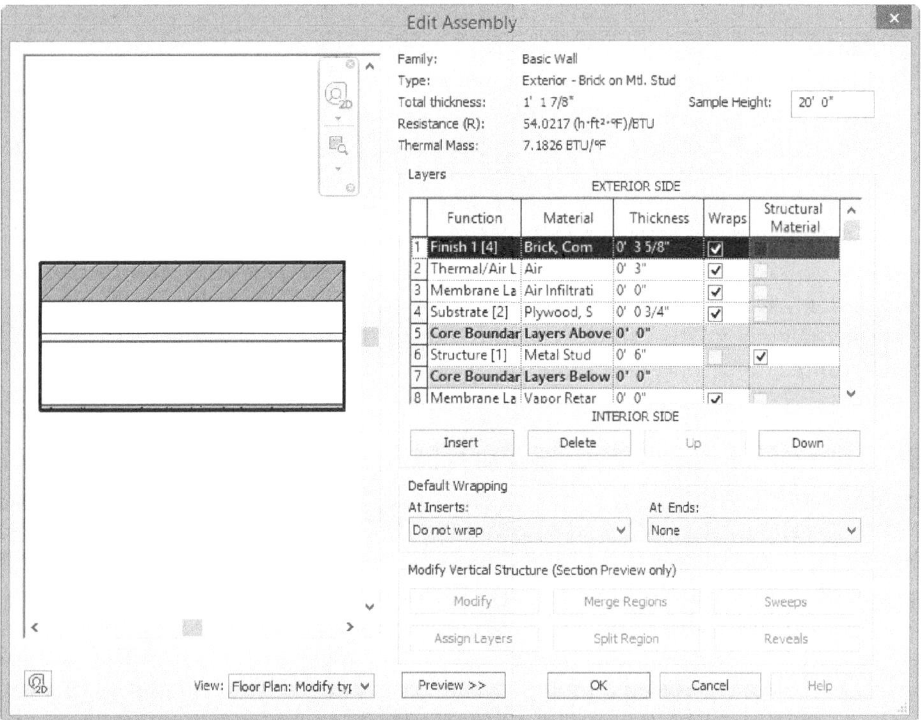

*Figure 3-7 The **Edit Assembly** dialog box with the **Preview** button chosen*

In Autodesk Revit, a wall is a composite building element and can consist of several layers. The **Layers** area in the **Edit Assembly** dialog box displays multiple layers of the selected wall, each with a specific function, material, and thickness. The layer on the top of the table represents the exterior side of a wall and the last layer represents the interior face. The **Layers** area, refer to Figure 3-7, displays the layers of the selected wall type. In this case, it is **Exterior- Brick on Mtl. Stud**. This wall type has nine layers. Each layer of the composite wall is assigned a specific function and priority based on its usage. The layers available in Autodesk Revit can be broadly classified into the categories given next.

Structure [1] - Consists of main supporting element of the structure such as concrete, brick, wood, metal stud, and so on.

Substrate [2] - Consists of material that functions as substructure, such as foundation and plywood.

Thermal/Air Layer - Indicates the air cavity or the thermal insulation layer.

Membrane Layer - A zero thickness layer primarily for the prevention against water vapor penetration.

Finish 1 [4] - Exterior finish such as metal, brick, and stone.

Finish 2 [5] - Interior finish such as paint, gypsum wall board, and so on.

Note

The numbers placed next to certain layers show the priority set of the layer and enable Autodesk Revit to work out the joinery detail of wall segments at corners and intersections according to the priority. When joined, a higher priority layer takes precedence over a lower priority layer.

In the **Edit Assembly** dialog box, the **Material** column displays the material specification, whereas the **Thickness** column displays the thickness of each layer. The total thickness of this composite wall is the sum of thickness of all layers. In the present case, the total thickness of wall is **1'1 7/8" (350 mm)** which is given beside the **Total thickness** parameter on the top of the dialog box. You can click on the **View** drop-down list and select **Section: Modify type attributes** to view the section of the wall.

Note

*The **View** drop-down list will only be visible if you choose the **Preview** button in the **Edit Assembly** dialog box.*

Autodesk Revit enables you to add and remove layers by using the **Insert** and **Delete** buttons, respectively, provided in the **Layers** area in the **Edit Assembly** dialog box. To shift the layers, choose the **Up** and **Down** buttons. You can also create your own layers. You will learn more about materials, layers, and composite walls in the later chapters. The **Default Wrapping** area in the **Edit Assembly** dialog box has two drop-down lists namely, **At Inserts** and **At Ends**. The options in these drop-down lists allow wrapping of a compound wall at the end and at the inserts (for doors and windows). From the **At Inserts** drop-down list, you can select any of the following options: **Exterior**, **Interior**, **Both**, or **Do not wrap**. Similarly, from the **At Ends** drop-down list, you can select any of the following options: **Exterior**, **Interior**, or **None**. The wrapping in the walls can be viewed in a plan view. Figures 3-8 through 3-11 illustrate the effects of different types of wrapping options on the wall.

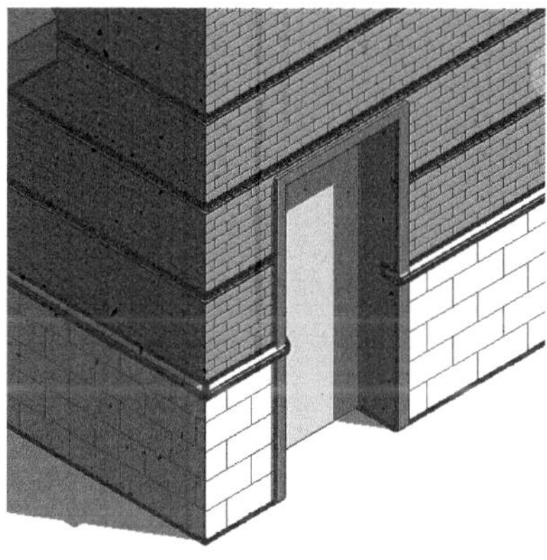

*Figure 3-8 The wall created with the **Do not wrap** option selected from the **At Inserts** drop-down list in the **Default Wrapping** area*

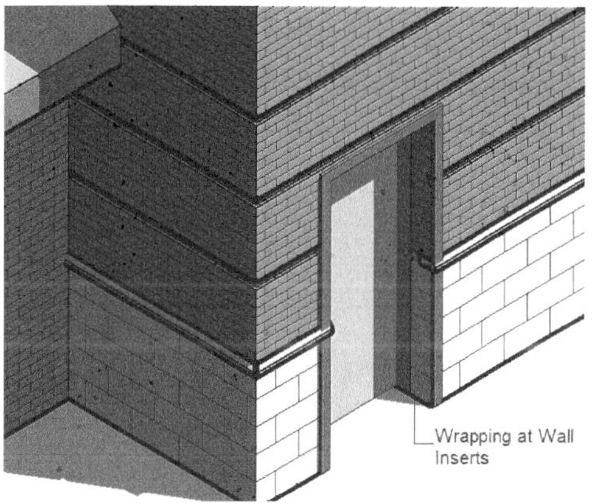

*Figure 3-9 The wall created with the **Exterior** option selected from the **At Inserts** drop-down list in the **Default Wrapping** area*

Tip

*While creating a new wall type, you can specify whether a wall is an exterior or interior wall. To do so, invoke the **Type Properties** dialog box of the wall to be created and click in the **Value** field of the **Function** parameter; a drop-down list will be displayed. From this drop-down list, you can select the **Exterior** option to assign exterior wall type function to the selected wall. Similarly, you can select the **Interior** option to assign the interior wall type function to the wall.*

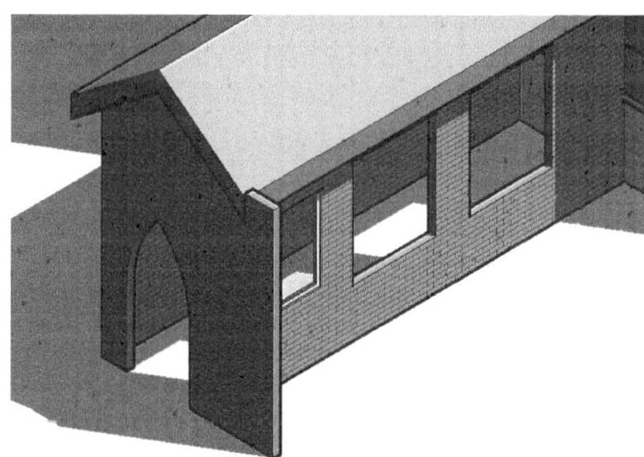

*Figure 3-10 The wall created with the **None** option selected from the **At Ends** drop-down list in the **Default Wrapping** area*

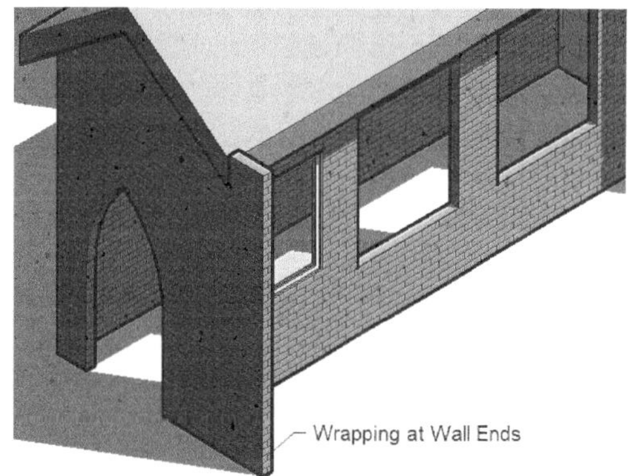

*Figure 3-11 The wall created with the **Exterior** option selected from the **At Ends** drop-down list in the **Default Wrapping** area*

Sketching Walls

The next step after selecting the wall type from the **Properties** palette is to select the sketching tool. Autodesk Revit provides several sketching tools, such as **Line**, **Rectangle**, and others to sketch the walls of different shapes. These tools, along with the **Options Bar**, can be invoked from the **Draw** panel in the **Modify | Place Wall** tab, as shown in Figure 3-12.

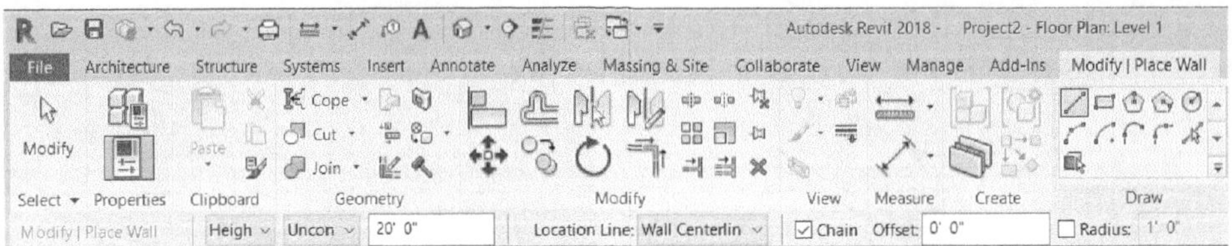

*Figure 3-12 Wall sketching tools available in the **Draw** panel*

Using Sketching Tools

In Autodesk Revit, you can access different sketching tools from the **Draw** panel and the **Options Bar** in the **Modify | Place Wall** tab. On invoking these tools, you can sketch different wall profiles. The procedure to do so is discussed next.

Sketching Straight Wall Profiles. You can sketch straight walls using the **Line** sketching tool by specifying the start point and the endpoint of the wall segment. To specify the location of the start point, click anywhere in the drawing area. Now, move the cursor in the drawing area, you will notice that a wall segment is starting from the specified point and the dimension that changes dynamically appears on it. This dimension is called the temporary dimension or listening dimension, and it shows the length and angle of the wall segment at any given location of the cursor, as shown in Figure 3-13. Also, notice that the cursor moves in increments by the value set in the **Dimension Snaps** area of the **Snaps** dialog box (See Snaps tool topic, Chapter 2). The angle subtended by the wall on the horizontal axis is also displayed and it keeps changing dynamically as you move the cursor to modify the inclination of the wall. Also notice that on bringing the cursor near the horizontal or the vertical axis, a dashed line will appear on the wall segment. This is called the alignment line and it helps you sketch the components with respect to the already created components. You will also notice that a tooltip is displayed indicating that the wall segment being sketched is horizontal, as shown in Figure 3-14.

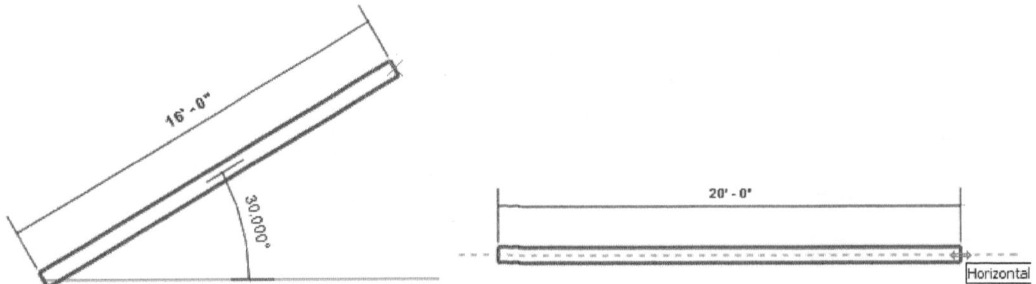

Figure 3-13 Length and angle of the wall segment

Figure 3-14 Sketching a horizontal wall

Autodesk Revit provides you the flexibility of specifying the length of the walls in different ways. The first option is to specify the starting point of the wall, move the cursor in the desired direction, and click when the angle and the temporary dimension attain the required values. The second option is to sketch the wall and then modify its length and angle to the exact value. For example, to sketch a 18'0"(5486 mm) long horizontal wall after specifying the starting point, you can move the cursor to the right until you see a dashed horizontal line parallel to the sketched wall. Click when the temporary dimension shows 20'0"(6096 mm) approximately. Note that the length of the wall may not be exactly 18'0"(5486 mm). You can now use the wall controls to modify the dimensions of the wall to its exact value.

To modify the wall, select the wall segment and view its control and properties. As you select the wall segment, it gets highlighted in blue and the symbols appear in blue above the wall segment, as shown in Figure 3-15.

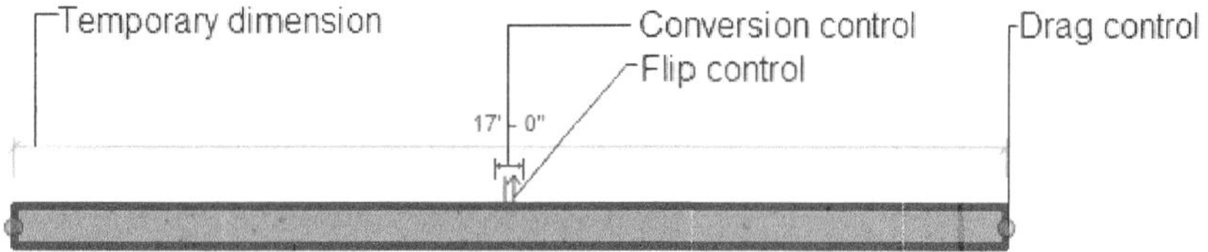

Figure 3-15 *Highlighted wall displaying its various controls*

The exact dimension of the sketched wall is visible in the dimension text of the temporary dimension. The conversion control symbol, which appears below the dimension value, is used to convert the temporary dimension into a permanent dimension. The two blue arrows which also appear on the upper face of the wall, indicate the flip control symbol for the sketched walls. They appear on the side interpreted as the exterior face of the wall. By default, the walls drawn from the left to right have the external face on the upper side and the walls drawn from the top to bottom have the external face on the right side. You can flip the orientation of the wall by clicking on the arrows symbol. Alternatively, you can place the cursor over the flip control symbol and notice the change in its color. After the color of the flip control changes, press SPACEBAR to flip the wall. The two blue dots that appear at the two ends of the wall segments are the drag control symbols. You can use them to stretch and resize the walls. To set the wall to the exact length, click on the temporary dimension; an edit box will appear showing the current dimension of the wall segment. Now, you can change the length of the wall by entering the desired value in the edit box. For example, you can enter **14' 8"(4470 mm)** in the edit box, as shown in Figure 3-16. Next, press ENTER; the length of the wall will be modified to 14' 8"(4470 mm).

Alternatively, you can create a straight wall by typing the dimension of the length before choosing the endpoint. As soon as you start typing the length, an edit box appears above the dimension line. Enter the value of the length and press ENTER to create a wall segment of the specified length. To sketch a wall at a given angle, sketch it at any angle and then click on the angular dimension symbol; an edit box will appear. In the edit box, you can enter the exact angular dimension from the horizontal axis to which the wall will be inclined.

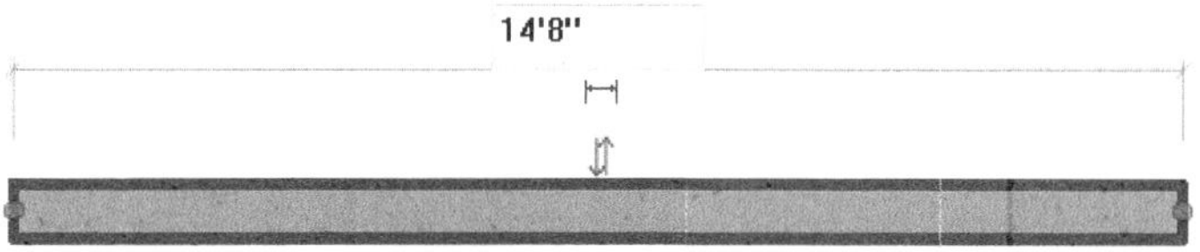

Figure 3-16 *Specifying the length of the wall*

Note

*The **Project Browser** shows **Level 1** in bold letters. This indicates that the wall has been sketched in that level.*

Sketching Rectangular Wall Profiles. You can invoke the **Rectangle** tool from the **Draw** panel in the **Modify | Place Wall** tab to sketch a rectangular wall profile. After you invoke the **Rectangle** tool, click on the screen to specify the location of one corner of the rectangular wall to be drawn. Next, move the cursor away from the point; a rectangular wall profile will be displayed along with the temporary dimension between the two parallel walls. Now, move the cursor to the desired location and when the temporary dimension attains the desired value, click to specify the diagonally opposite corner of the profile; the rectangular wall will be created along with the temporary dimensions displayed. Alternatively, you can also create a rectangular wall profile by sketching it using some rough dimension and then modifying its size. This can be done by clicking on the temporary dimension of the sketched profile and entering the exact distance in the edit box, as shown in Figure 3-17. The size of the rectangle will be modified to the exact values.

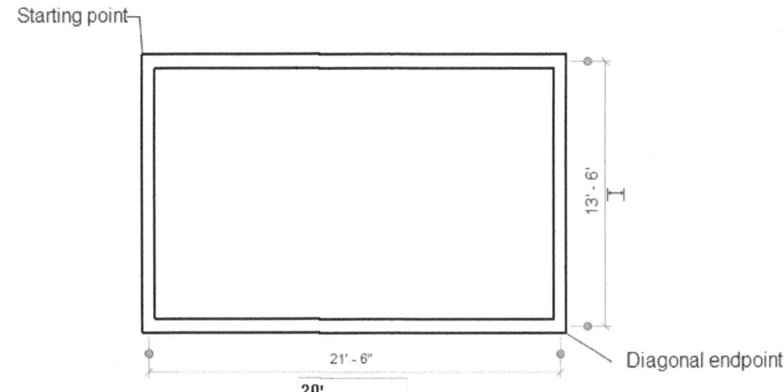

Figure 3-17 Creating and modifying a rectangular wall profile

Sketching Polygonal Wall Profiles. You can sketch a polygonal wall profile using either the **Inscribed Polygon** or **Circumscribed Polygon** tool from the **Draw** panel in the **Modify | Place Wall** tab. To draw an inscribed polygon, invoke the **Inscribed Polygon** tool or to draw a circumscribed polygon, invoke the **Circumscribed Polygon** tool. When you invoke any of these tools, various options for polygon creation are displayed in the **Options Bar**. In the **Options Bar**, you can specify the number of sides of the polygon in the **Sides** edit box. The polygonal profile can be created by specifying the radius of the inscribed or circumscribed circle. To draw an inscribed polygon, choose the **Inscribed Polygon** tool from the **Draw** panel in the **Modify | Place Wall** tab and then specify the desired number of sides, height (if unconnected), and offset value in the respective edit boxes in the **Options Bar**. Next, click in the drawing area to specify the center of the polygon. Then, drag the cursor and click again to get the desired radius; the inscribed polygon will be created. Similarly, a circumscribed polygon can also be created by choosing the **Circumscribed Polygon** tool from the **Draw** panel in the **Modify | Place Wall** tab.

Sketching Circular Wall Profiles. The **Circle** tool in the list box can be used to sketch circular wall profile. To sketch a circular wall profile, invoke the **Circle** tool from the **Draw** panel of the **Modify | Place Wall** tab and click in the drawing area to specify the center point of the circular wall. You will notice that a circular wall profile is extending dynamically with the specified point as the center and the other end attached to the cursor, as shown in Figure 3-18. The temporary radial dimension will also be displayed. Click when the desired value for the radius is displayed. Alternatively, before clicking on the second point, type the value for the radius of the circular profile. As you type, the value will be displayed in the edit box. Press ENTER to complete the profile. Notice that the dimension that you entered is the distance of the center point to the location line of the profile.

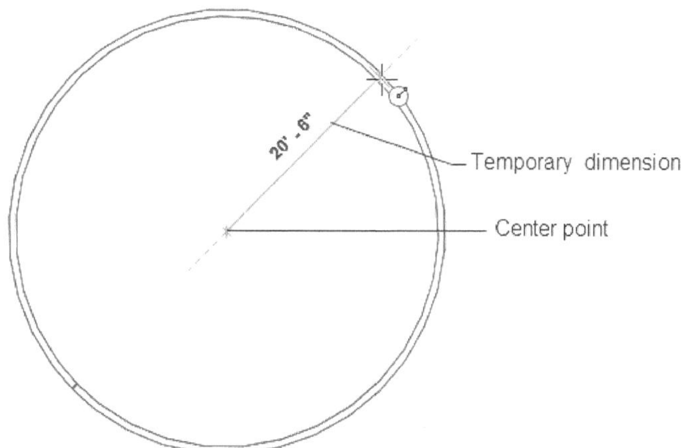

Figure 3-18 *Sketching the Circular wall profile*

Sketching Start-End-Radius Arc Profiles. The **Start-End-Radius Arc** tool in the **Draw** panel of the **Modify | Place Wall** tab enables you to sketch an arc wall by specifying the start point, end point, and the intermediate point that determines the radius of the arc. To create an arc wall, invoke the **Start-End-Radius Arc** tool from the **Draw** panel of the **Modify | Place Wall** tab; you will be prompted to specify the start point of the proposed arc wall. Specify the start point by clicking in the drawing area. Now, you will be prompted to specify the endpoint of the curved wall. Specify the endpoint of the curved wall; a curved wall with a variable radius stretches dynamically between the two specified points. Specify the location of the third point between the two specified points to specify the subtended angle or the radius of the arc. As you specify the third point, the angular and radial temporary dimensions are displayed along with the curve on the screen. Next, click in the drawing area to specify the third point; the curved wall will be sketched. You can also modify the sketched wall to the desired curvature parameters such as radius, angle subtended, orientation, and so on. To modify the curvature, select the sketched wall, click on the parameter such as the angular dimension and enter the new value, as shown in Figure 3-19. You can also use the drag controls to increase or decrease the extent of the wall. The central blue dot can be used to stretch the wall, keeping the subtended angle constant.

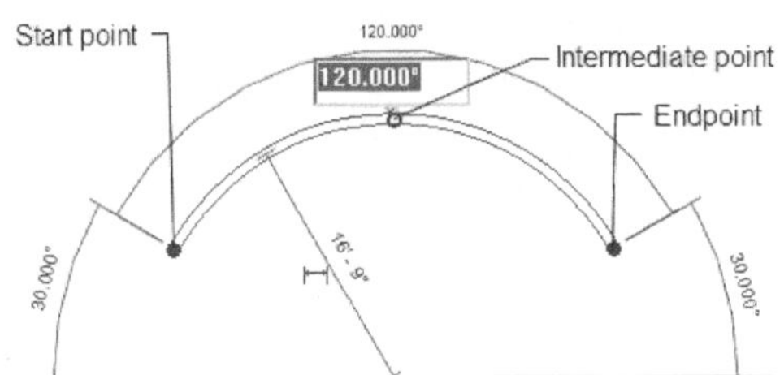

Figure 3-19 Sketching and modifying a curved wall profile

Sketching Center-ends Arc Wall Profiles. You can sketch a curved wall by specifying its center point and two endpoints. To do so, choose the **Center-ends Arc** tool from the **Draw** panel in the **Modify | Place Wall** tab. Next, click in the drawing area to specify the location of the center point and then move the cursor. Click when the desired value of the radius is displayed. You can also type the radius value and then press ENTER. The point that you specify will be taken as the start point of the wall. Next, click in the drawing area again to specify the endpoint of the arc wall. Note that the curved wall segment can be extended up to 180-degree. When the angle exceeds 180-degree, the wall will flip the side. Once the wall is sketched, you can select it and modify its parameters such as its subtended angle and radius. You can also modify the curvature keeping the radius fixed by using the drag controls, refer to Figure 3-20.

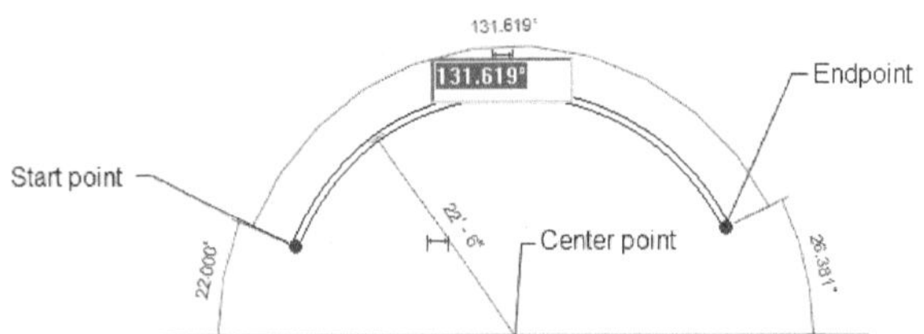

*Figure 3-20 Sketching a curved wall profile using the **Center-ends Arc** sketching tool*

Sketching Tangent End Arcs Wall Profiles. To sketch a curved wall profile that starts tangentially from an existing wall, invoke the **Tangent End Arc** tool from the **Draw** panel in the **Modify | Place Wall** tab and click at the endpoint of an existing wall to specify the start point. After specifying the start point, move the cursor to the desired distance and click to define the curved wall profile.

Sketching Fillet Arc Wall Profiles. To create a curved fillet wall between the two existing walls, choose the **Fillet Arc** tool in the **Draw** panel of the **Modify | Place Wall** tab. Now, one by one, click on the two walls to create a fillet close to the desired fillet end. On doing so, a fillet wall will appear, showing its possible locations, as shown in Figure 3-21. Click to specify the location of the fillet. Once the fillet wall is sketched, you can modify its radius by clicking on it and typing its value. Notice that the walls are automatically trimmed after placing the fillet arc.

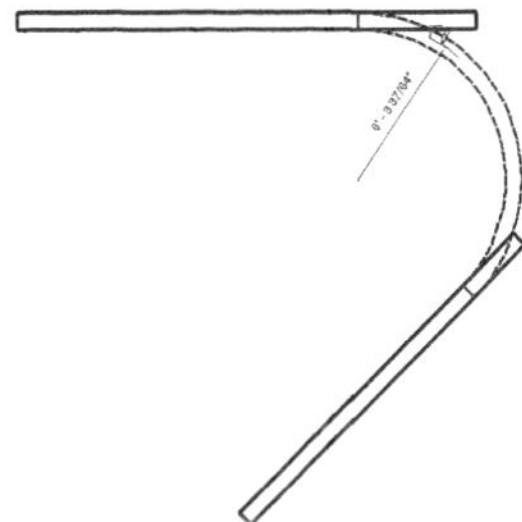

Figure 3-21 Sketching a fillet arc wall profile using the ***Fillet Arc*** *tool*

Using the Chain Option. Select the **Chain** check box in the **Options Bar** to create a continuous wall profile with a number of wall segments. It enables you to create a continuous wall with wall segments connected end to end. The end point of the previous wall becomes the start point of the next wall. To enable the **Chain** option, select the check box before or while sketching the wall profile. You can also use this option while using different sketching tools.

Using the Offset Option. The **Offset** edit box can be used to create a wall that starts at a specified offset distance from a point defined in an existing element. You can enter the offset distance value in the **Offset** edit box provided in the **Options Bar**. However, the shape of the resulting wall depends on the sketching tool selected. After entering the offset value and selecting the sketching option, click near the element to define the offset distance. When you move the cursor, the wall will start at the specified distance from the selected point. For example, this option can be used for creating boundary walls that are placed at a specific distance from the building profile.

Using the Radius Option. The **Radius** edit box in the **Options Bar** is used to specify the radius while sketching a circular, curved, or a fillet wall. You can type the value of the radius in the **Radius** edit box before or after invoking the desired sketching tool.

Tip

An appropriate sketching option should be selected based on the desired wall profile. You can also sketch walls using a combination of available sketching tools.

WORKING WITH STACKED WALLS

In Autodesk Revit, besides basic wall and curtain wall there is a special kind of wall called a stacked wall. A stacked wall is a wall created using two or more basic walls that are stacked on top of another to form a complex design. These walls are assembled in such a way that the entire facade acts as a single wall. In the next section, you will learn about various options that are used to create a stacked wall and then add it to the project.

Creating a Stacked Wall

To create a stacked wall, choose the **Wall: Architectural** tool from **Architecture > Build > Wall** drop-down; the **Modify | Place Wall** tab with the instance parameters in the **Properties** palette will be displayed. In the **Properties** palette, select the stacked wall type from the **Type-Selector** drop-down list. After selecting the stacked wall type, choose the **Edit Type** button from the **Properties** palette; the **Type Properties** dialog box will be displayed.

In the **Type Properties** dialog box, choose the **Duplicate** button to create a new type of stacked wall; the **Name** dialog box will be displayed. In this dialog box, enter a desired name and choose the **OK** button; the **Type Properties** dialog box will be displayed and the created type will be updated in the **Type** drop-down list. Now, you are required to edit the structural properties to form a new type. Choose the **Edit** button corresponding to the **Structure** parameter; the **Edit Assembly** dialog box will be displayed. In this dialog box, select the type of wall from the **Name** column. In the **Height** column, you need to specify the height of the walls. By default, the height of first wall is **Variable**. If you want to make other wall types as variable, select the desired wall type; the **Variable** button will be activated. Choose the **Variable** button to change the wall to variable. If you want to insert a row then choose the **Insert** button and to delete a row, choose the **Delete** button. You can use the **Preview** button to preview the stacked wall. Next, choose the **OK** button twice; the **Edit Assembly** and the **Type Properties** dialog boxes will be closed and will be selected in the **Type Selector** drop-down list. Now, you can use the stacked wall to create the building.

ADDING INTERIOR WALLS

In Autodesk Revit, interior walls form a separate family of wall types. They differ from the exterior wall types based on their usage, material specifications, and non load-bearing character. Several predefined interior wall types are provided in the Autodesk Revit libraries.

To view the interior wall types, choose the **Wall: Architectural** tool from **Architecture > Build > Wall** drop-down; the instance parameters of the wall will be displayed in the **Properties** palette. From this palette, you can select different types of walls available in Revit. The wall types that may be used as interior walls have been assigned the prefix **Interior**. Based on the project requirement, you can select the appropriate interior wall type from the drop-down list. For example, **Interior- 5" Partition (2-hr)** is a type of interior wall for Imperial (**Interior- 135 mm Partition (2-hr)** for Metric) with a 2-hour fire rating and can be selected from the **Properties** palette, as shown in Figure 3-22.

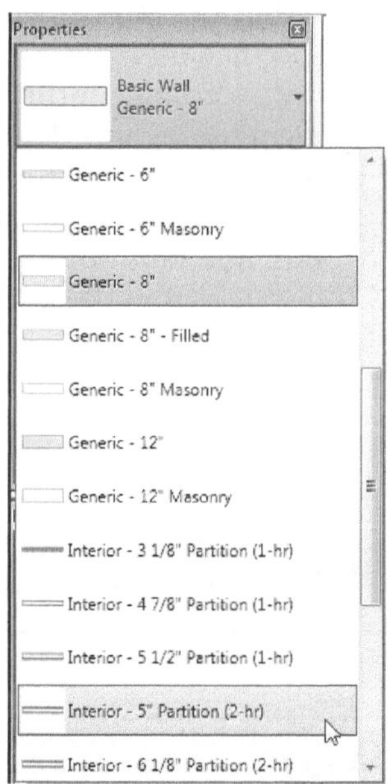

***Figure 3-22** Selecting the interior wall type from the **Properties** palette*

To view and specify the properties of an interior wall type, you can use the **Properties** palette, as shown in Figure 3-23. This palette shows various parameters of the selected wall such as **Unconnected Height**, **Location Line**, **Structural Usage**, **Top Constraint**, and so on. You can modify these parameters by entering a new value or selecting the required value from the corresponding value field in the **Properties** palette.

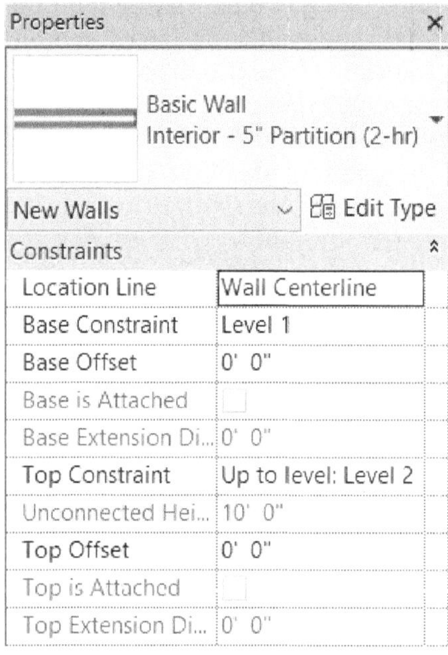

***Figure 3-23** The **Properties** palette for the **Interior - 5" Partition (2-hr)** wall type*

Tip

*After creating a wall, right-click on any end of the wall; a shortcut menu will be displayed. Choose the **Disallow Join** option from the shortcut menu to prevent the wall end from joining with other walls.*

The sketching tools explained earlier (for exterior walls) can also be used for sketching interior walls. When you sketch the interior walls, the top constraint of the interior walls is automatically set to a level above the current level.

Tip

*The **Location Line** parameter in the **Properties** palette of the selected walls is useful for creating interior walls. You can create interior walls at some specified distance from another existing wall using the **Finish Face: Interior** option.*

Note

The interior walls do not create a neat junction with the exterior walls as they have different composition and characteristics.

Walls are the host elements for other building elements such as doors and windows. Therefore, deleting walls will delete all their dependent elements as well.

The basic composition of an interior wall type can be viewed by choosing the **Type Properties** tool from the **Properties** panel in the **Modify | Place Wall** tab. On doing so, the **Type Properties** dialog box will be displayed, showing different type parameters of the selected wall type.

To view the structural composition of a wall type, choose the **Edit** button in the **Structure** type parameter; the **Edit Assembly** dialog box will be displayed, showing layers for the corresponding wall type. For example, the **Interior-5" Partition (2-hr)** for Imperial or (**Interior-135 mm Partition (2-hr)** for Metric) wall type comprises of seven layers with different materials and thickness. You can use the **Insert** and **Delete** buttons to modify the wall type. You can choose the **Preview** button to display the graphic view of the **Interior - 5" Partition (2-hr)** for Imperial (**Interior - 135mm Partition (2-hr)** for Metric) wall type in the preview area, as shown in Figure 3-24.

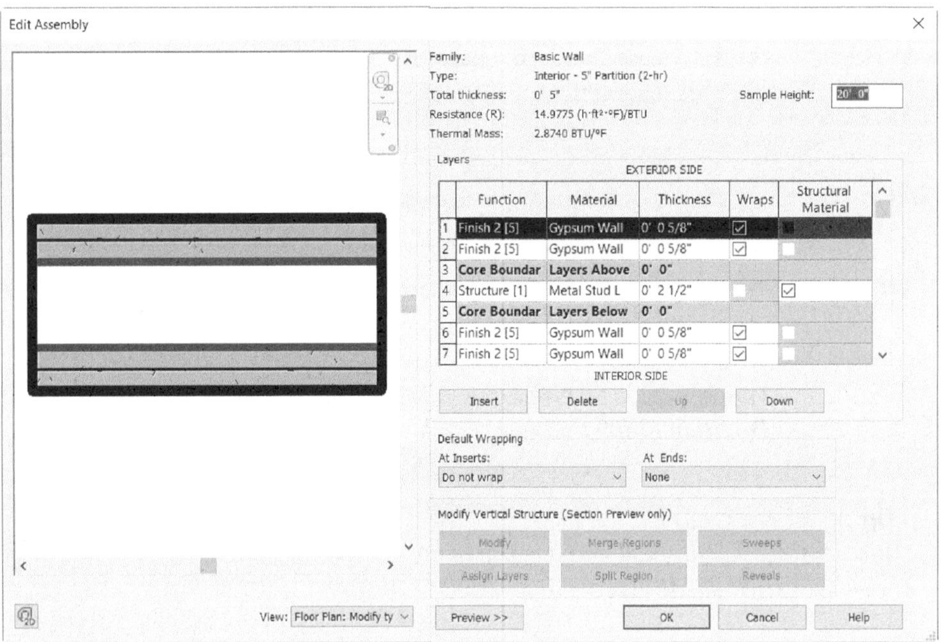

***Figure 3-24** The **Edit Assembly** dialog box for the **Interior - 5" Partition (2-hr)** wall type*

Tip

*In Autodesk Revit, you can add a structural wall to a project by choosing the **Wall: Structural** tool from **Architecture > Build > Wall** drop-down. The structural wall has analytical properties that can be used for structural analysis.*

ADDING WALL SWEEPS AND REVEALS

In an architectural project, wall sweep and wall reveal act as modifiers in a wall. Each type of wall sweep and wall reveal has predefined properties. You can select and use any type of wall sweep and wall reveal based on its usage in project. Wall sweep is used to add a baseboard, crown molding or other type of decorative horizontal or vertical projections to a wall. Wall reveal is used to add a decorative horizontal or vertical cutout to a wall. Wall sweep and wall reveal provide advancement to the building model by adding skirtings, projections and cutout to a building.

Note

Wall sweep and wall reveal can be added to a wall only in 3D view or in elevation view.

Wall Sweeps

Ribbon: Architecture > Build > Wall drop-down > Wall: Sweep

To add details to a wall, you can add a wall sweep by using the **Wall Sweep** tool. Wall Sweep can be selected either in an elevation view or in 3D view. Choose the **3D View** tool from the **Quick Access Toolbar**, the user interface will be displayed. Next, invoke the **Wall: Sweep** tool from the **Build** panel of the **Architecture** tab, as shown in Figure 3-25. On doing so, the **Modify | Place Wall Sweep** tab will be displayed. In the **Placement** panel of this contextual tab, the **Horizontal** tool is selected by default. As a result, the wall sweep will be added horizontally to the face of the wall. Select the required type of the wall sweep from the **Type Selector** drop-down list. Now, move the cursor over the face of the wall; a preview of the wall sweep along with the temporary dimensions will be displayed on the wall face. Click at the desired level of elevation; a wall sweep will be created, as shown in Figure 3-26. After adding the wall sweeps at desired faces of the wall, press ESC, or choose the **Modify** button from the **Select** panel to exit from the contextual tab. Similarly, you can add a vertical wall sweep at the face of the wall. To create a vertical wall sweep, choose the **Vertical** tool from the **Placement** panel.

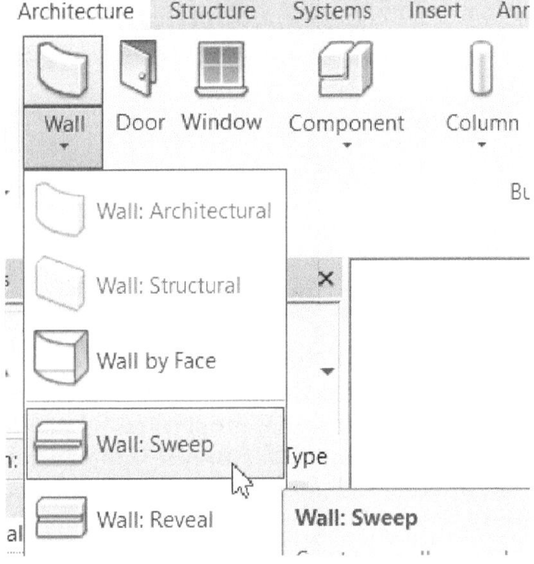

*Figure 3-25 Invoking the **Wall: Sweep** tool from the **Build** panel*

After adding the wall sweep to the wall, you can change the properties of the sweep such as its profile. To change the profile of the sweep, invoke the **Edit Type** button from the **Properties** palette; the **Type Properties** dialog box will be displayed. Now, choose the **Duplicate** button from the upper right corner of this dialog box; the **Name** dialog box will be displayed. In this dialog box, enter the desired name in the **Name** edit box and choose the **OK** button to return to the **Type Properties** dialog box. In **Type Properties** dialog box, you can select the desired wall sweep type from the **Profile** drop-down list by clicking on the value field of the corresponding parameter. You can edit the **Subcategory of Walls** by clicking on the corresponding value field of the **Type Parameter** area.

Tip

*You can add more options to the **Type-Selector** drop-down list by loading more families of profile into the drawings. To load more options, choose the **Load Family** tool from the **Load From Library** panel of the **Insert** tab; the **Load Family** dialog box will be displayed. In this dialog box, the predefined family profiles are available in **Profiles > Wall folder**.*

The methods to modify other **Type Properties** are discussed next

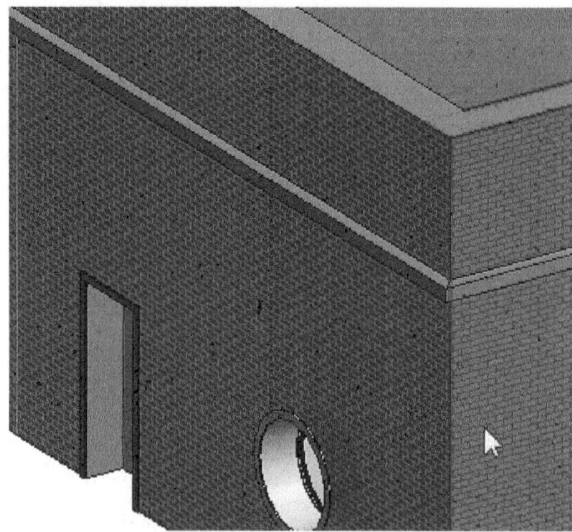

Figure 3-26 *Wall sweep added to the wall*

Modifying Type Properties

The **Type Properties** dialog box displays various type parameters of wall sweep such as **Constraints**, **Construction**, **Material and Finishes**, and **Identity Data**. To edit the parameters, click in the **Value** field corresponding to any of the parameters under these heads and then specify a desired value to it. To edit the material properties of the wall sweep click in the **Value** field corresponding to the **Material** parameter: a Browse button will be displayed. Choose the Browse button; the **Material Browser** dialog box will be displayed. You can use various options in this dialog box to specify the desired material for the wall sweep. Choose the **OK** button: the **Material Browser** dialog box will be closed and the specified material will be assigned to the wall sweep type.

Now, to create a copy of the original sweep type you can choose the **Duplicate** button from the top right corner in the **Type Properties** dialog box. On doing so, the **Name** dialog box will be displayed, and you will be prompted to assign a new name to the duplicate copy. Enter a name in this edit box and choose the **OK** button; a new sweep type is created which inherits the properties of the parent sweep type. Now, you can modify its parameters, as desired. The **Rename** button is also available on the top right corner. This button is used to give a new name to the selected sweep type without changing its properties.

Now, you will learn to modify the instance properties of the sweep type.

Modifying Instance Properties

You can modify various instance properties of the wall sweep by using the parameters in the **Properties** palette. The modification in these properties results in the change of the properties of only that particular instance in the project. The descriptions of various instance parameters are given next:

Instance Parameter	Description
Offset From Wall	Copies or moves a selected element to a specified distance from Wall face
Level	Level or reference plane of the base of a wall sweep and the properties shown only for Horizontal Sweep
Offset From Level	Specifies distance of sweep from level
Length	Indicates the length of a wall sweep
Image	Specifies the image file corresponding to a wall instance. This parameter can be used in the wall schedule to display the image of the wall instance.
Comments	Describes about the Wall Sweep
Mark	Add a mark or label to each sweep
Phase Created	Phase in which a wall sweep is created
Phase Demolished	Phase in which a wall sweep was demolished

Wall Reveals

Ribbon: Architecture > Build > Wall drop-down > Wall: Reveal

To complete the design of our wall, you need to add decorative cutout in the wall. To do so, you can use the wall reveal. To add a wall reveal, you need to be in an elevation view or in 3D view and then invoke the **Wall: Reveal** tool from the **Build** panel of the **Architecture** tab, refer to Figure 3-27; the **Modify | Place Reveal** tab will be displayed. In this contextual tab, select the desired orientation of the wall reveal by choosing either the **Horizontal** or **Vertical** tool from the **Placement** panel. Next, select the type of the wall reveal from the **Type Selector** drop-down list and then move the cursor over the face of the wall; a preview of the wall reveal with the temporary dimension will be displayed along the wall face. Click at desired level of elevation; a wall reveal will be added, as shown in Figure 3-28. You can add the wall reveal to other walls by clicking on their faces. After adding the wall reveal at desired faces of the wall, press **ESC** or choose the **Modify** button from the **Select** panel to exit the contextual tab. After adding the wall reveal to the wall, you can change the properties of the reveal such as its profile. To change the profile of the reveal, invoke the **Edit Type** button from the **Properties** palette; the **Type Properties** dialog box will be displayed. Choose the **Duplicate** button from the upper left corner of this dialog box; the **Name** dialog box will be displayed. In this dialog box, enter the desired name in the **Name** edit box and choose the **OK** button to return to the **Type properties** dialog box. In this dialog box, you can select the desired **Wall Reveal** type from the **Profile** drop-down list by clicking on the value field of this dialog box. You can edit the **Subcategory of Walls** by clicking on the corresponding value field in the **Type Parameter** area.

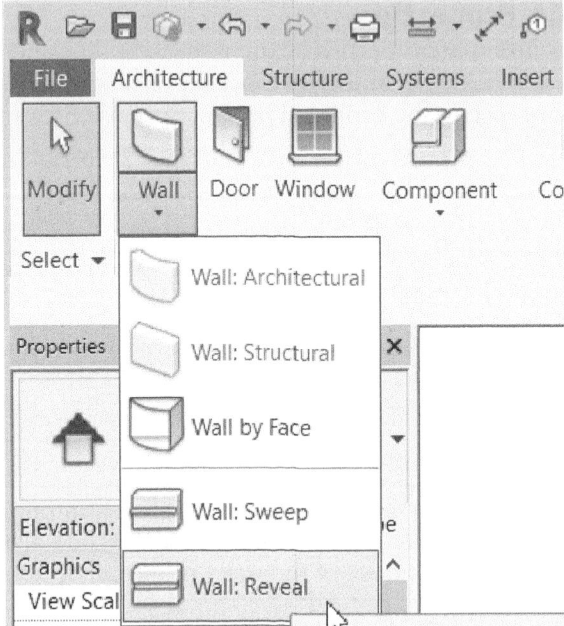

Figure 3-27 *Invoking the **Wall: Reveal** tool from the **Build** panel*

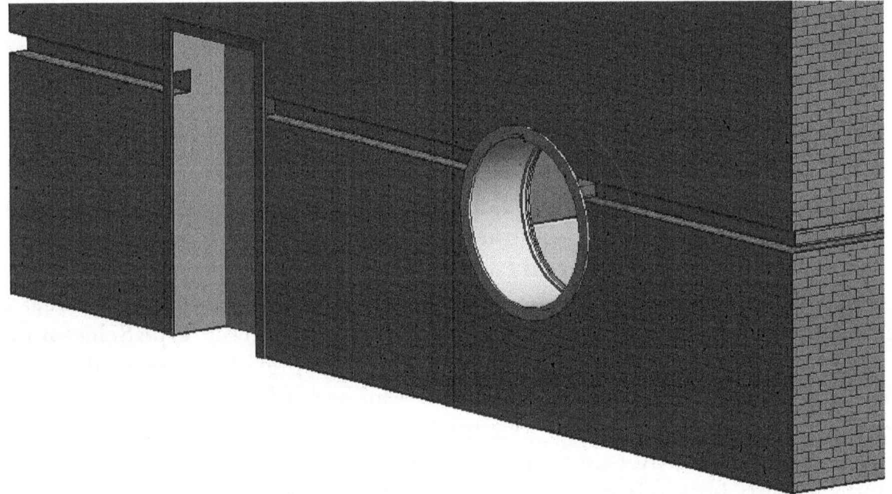

Figure 3-28 *Wall reveal added to the wall*

Now, you will learn to modify **Type Properties** and **Instance Properties** of the wall reveal.

Modifying Type Properties

To modify the type properties of the selected **Wall Reveal** type, choose the **Edit Type** button from the **Properties** palette; the **Type Properties** dialog box for the selected reveal type will be displayed.

The **Type Properties** dialog box displays the value of various parameters of **Wall Reveal**. The various type parameters are described in the following table:

Parameter	Description
Default Setback	By default, the default setback value in the edit box is 0'0". Wall reveal changes with the change in the value from positive to negative. The setback helps in making reveal type near windows and door trims.
Profile	Wall reveal is created by the profile family.

Modifying Instance Properties

To modify the instance properties of the selected **Wall Reveal** type, choose the reveal from the drawing window the **Properties** palette displays the **Instance Properties** of that reveal type. The various instance parameters are described next:

Instance Parameter	Description
Offset From Wall	Copies or moves a selected element to a specified distance from Wall face
Level	Level or reference plane of the base of a wall reveal and the properties shown only for Horizontal Sweep
Offset From Level	Specified distance of reveal from level
Length	Indicates the length of a wall reveal

Tip

*Wall sweep and wall reveal type can also be used directly by invoking the **Edit Type** button in the **Properties** palette of the wall. This dialog box is used only when sweep type or reveal is required throughout the building model along with the wall.*

TUTORIALS

The following tutorials are designed to familiarize you with the concepts of invoking the **Wall: Architectural** tool, selecting the wall type, modifying the wall properties, using the sketching tools, and sketching a wall with the given parameters.

All the files used in the tutorials can be downloaded from the CADCIM website. These files are compressed in zip file format and are required to be extracted before using them in the tutorials. The path of the files is as follows: *Textbooks > Civil/GIS > Revit Architecture > Exploring Autodesk Revit 2018 for Architecture*. For example, the tutorial file, *c02_Apartment_tut1.rvt* that is used in Tutorial 1 of Chapter 3 is compressed in the *c02_rvt_2018_tut.zip file*.

Tutorial 1 Apartment 1

In this tutorial, you will create the exterior walls of a two-room apartment based on the sketch plan shown in Figure 3-29. The dimensions have been given only for reference and are not to be used in this tutorial. The project file and the parameters to be used for creating the exterior walls are given next. **(Expected time: 30 min)**

1. Project file-
   For Imperial *c02_Apartment_tut1.rvt*
   For Metric *M_c02_Apartment_tut1.rvt*
2. Exterior wall type- **Basic Wall: Exterior - Brick on Mtl. Stud**.
3. Location line parameter- **Wall Centerline**; Top Constraint- **Up to Level 2.**

The following steps are required to complete this tutorial:

a. Open the *Apartment 1* project file created in Tutorial 1 of Chapter 2.
b. Invoke the **Wall**: **Architectural** tool from the ribbon.
c. Select the exterior wall type **Exterior - Brick on Mtl. Stud** from the **Properties** dialog box.
d. Modify **Top Constraint- Up to level: Level 2** and **Location Line - Wall Centerline** as wall properties using the **Properties** palette, refer to Figure 3-30.
e. Invoke the **Line** sketching tool and then sketch the exterior walls based on the given parameters, refer to Figures 3-31 through 3-38.
f. Save the project using the **Save As** tool.
   For Imperial *c03_Apartment1_tut1.rvt*
   For Metric *M_c03_Apartment1_tut1.rvt*
g. Close the project.

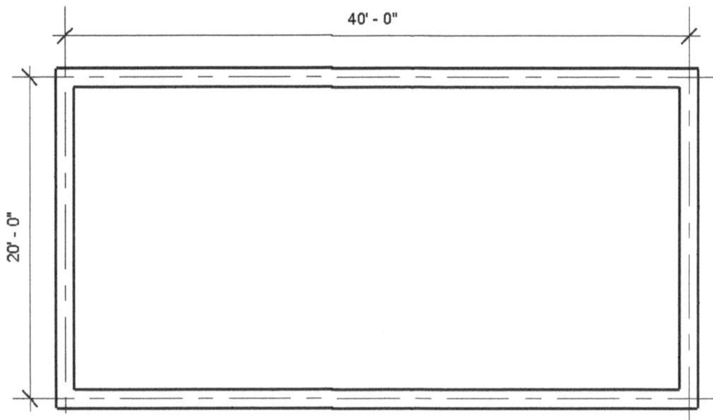

Figure 3-29 *Sketch plan for creating exterior walls for the Apartment 1 project*

Opening the Project File

Choose **Open > Project** from the **File** menu and open the *c02_Apartment1_tut1.rvt (M_c02_Apartment1_tut1.rvt for Metric)* project file. You can also download this file from *http://www.cadcim.com*. The path of the file is as follows: *Textbooks > Civil/GIS > Revit Architecture > Exploring Autodesk Revit 2018 for Architecture*.

Invoking the Wall: Architectural Tool and Selecting the Wall Type

To start sketching the wall, you must invoke the **Wall: Architectural** tool from the ribbon and select the wall type to be used **(Exterior - Brick on Mtl. Stud** in this case).

1. Invoke the **Wall: Architectural** tool from **Architecture > Build > Wall** drop-down; the **Modify | Place Wall** tab is displayed.

2. In the **Type Selector** drop-down list of the **Properties** palette, select the **Exterior - Brick on Mtl. Stud** wall type.

Modifying Properties of the Exterior Wall

After selecting the wall type, you need to modify the instance properties of the wall type using the **Properties** palette.

Note

*The default.rte or (DefaultMetric.rte for Metric) template file used for this project has two predefined levels: **Level 1** and **Level 2**.*

1. In the **Properties** palette, ensure that the **Location Line** parameter has **Wall Centerline** as the default value. Click on the column adjacent to the **Top Constraint** instance parameter; a drop-down list is displayed. Select **Up to level: Level 2** from this drop-down list, and choose the **Apply** button, as shown in Figure 3-30.

Tip

*If the **Properties** palette is not displayed in the User interface screen by default, select the **Properties** check box from **View > Windows > User-Interface** drop-down.*

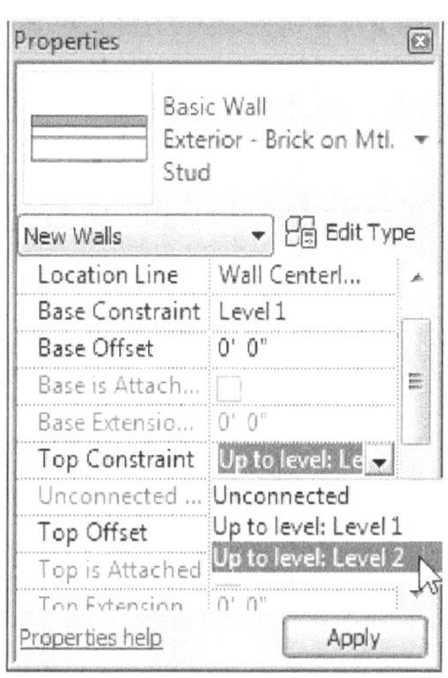

*Figure 3-30 Setting the **Top Constraint** parameter using the **Properties** palette*

Sketching the First Exterior Wall Segment

To sketch a wall, you need to choose an appropriate sketching tool from the **Draw** panel in the **Modify | Place Wall** tab. The exterior walls of the given sketch of the *Apartment 1* project can be created using the **Rectangle** tool. You will however use the **Line** tool to learn and understand the usage of this tool for sketching the straight walls.

1. Ensure that the **Line** tool is chosen in the **Draw** panel in the **Modify | Place Wall** tab and the **Chain** check box is cleared in the **Options Bar**.

2. Ensure that the **Allow** option is selected in the **Join Status** drop-down list.

3. Click between the four inward arrow keys to specify the start point of the first wall segment. Next, move the cursor toward the right hand side. On doing so, a wall segment starts from the specified point with temporary dimension appearing on it. The dimension changes dynamically as you move the cursor. This shows the length of the wall segment at any given location of the cursor.

4. Right-click in the drawing area; a shortcut menu is displayed. Choose the **Zoom In Region** option from the shortcut menu and zoom into the area to get a closer view of the sketched wall segment, as shown in Figure 3-31 (for zooming techniques, refer to Chapter 2- Starting an Architectural Project).

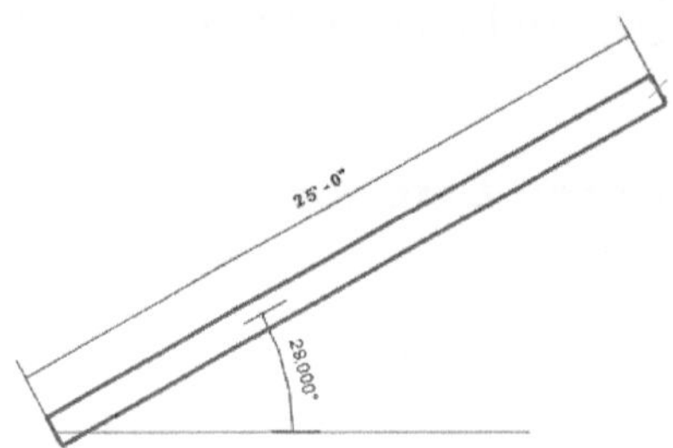

Figure 3-31 The temporary dimensions displayed on the wall

5. Move the cursor on the horizontal axis such that a dashed line appears at the central axis of the wall segment, as shown in Figure 3-32. Notice the two-sided arrow attached to the endpoint of the wall. This indicates that the wall segment being sketched is horizontal. A tooltip indicating the horizontal alignment is also displayed with two-sided arrow.

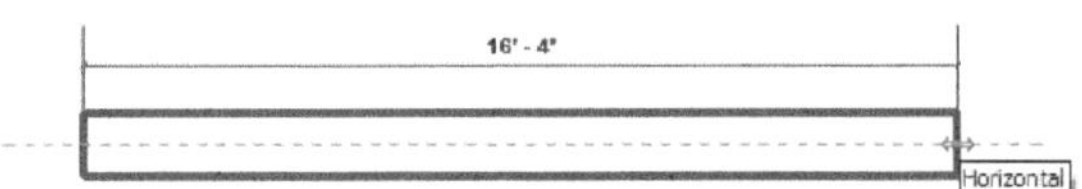

Figure 3-32 Sketching a horizontal wall segment

6. Move the cursor to the right until the temporary dimension shows a value more than 40'- 0"(12192 mm), as shown in Figure 3-33. Click at this location as the endpoint of the wall segment and press ESC twice; the wall is created. Note that, if the dimension is not displayed, you need to click on the created wall to display the dimension. Press ESC.

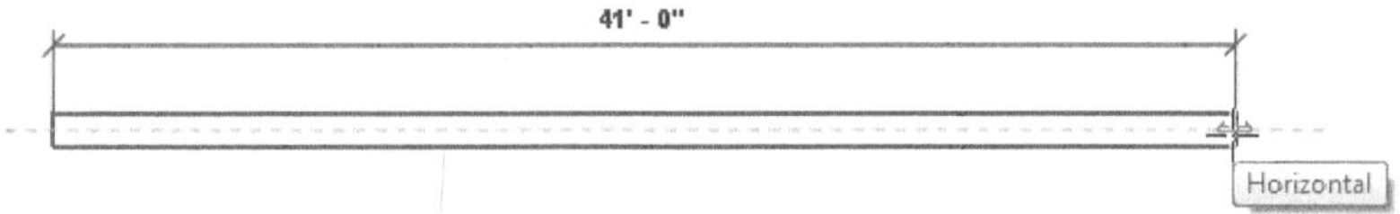

Figure 3-33 The sketched horizontal wall with its controls

Note

You can create a wall of exactly 40'0"(12192 mm) length using the dimension snaps set in the ***Snaps*** *dialog box. The only purpose of creating a wall of length more than the desired length is to explain how to modify the length of the sketched wall to the exact value.*

Modifying the Length of the Sketched Exterior Wall

You will now modify the length of the sketched wall to the actual dimension, as given in the *Apartment 1* sketch.

1. Select the created wall and click on its temporary dimension; an edit box appears showing the current dimension of the wall segment.

2. Enter **40' (12192 mm)** in the edit box, as shown in Figure 3-34 and then press ENTER; the length of the wall is modified to 40'0"(12192 mm). Press ESC to exit the **Modify | Walls** tab.

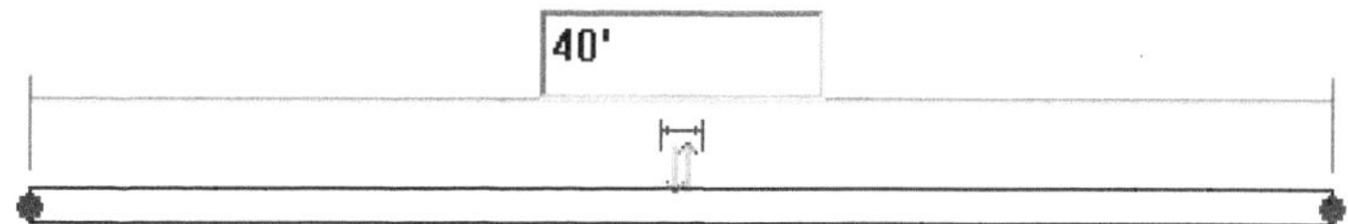

Figure 3-34 Modifying the length of a wall segment using temporary dimensions

Tip

*To exit the current tool, you can also right-click and choose **Cancel** from the shortcut menu displayed.*

Note

*By default, the exterior faces of the walls drawn from the left to right are on the upper face, and those drawn from top to bottom are on the right face. Similarly, the exterior faces of the walls drawn from right to left are on the lower face, and those drawn from the bottom to top are on the left side. Hence, you can minimize the use of the **flip** tool by sketching the walls in the appropriate direction.*

Sketching Other Exterior Wall Segments

In this section, you need to create other exterior wall segments using the **Endpoint** object snap tool.

1. Choose the **Wall: Architectural** tool from **Architecture > Build > Wall** drop-down. Now, bring the cursor close to the right endpoint of the first wall segment. When the cursor shows a square box at the endpoint (indicating the **Endpoint** object snap), as shown in Figure 3-35, click to specify the start point of the second wall segment.

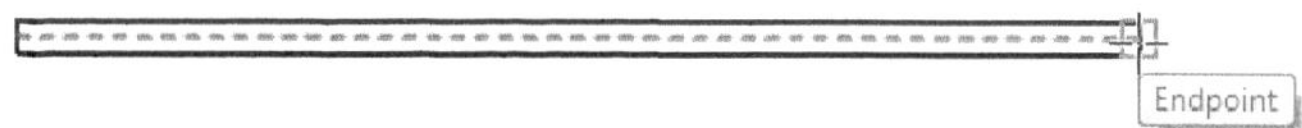

*Figure 3-35 Starting a second exterior wall segment using the **Endpoint** object snap option*

2. As you move the cursor, wall starts to get created dynamically, with one end attached to the specified point and the other end attached to the cursor. Move the cursor vertically downward. A dashed vertical line is visible inside the wall segment. Now, enter **20'0"(6096 mm)** as the value of the length; an edit box is displayed with the dimension that you have entered, as shown in Figure 3-36. Press ENTER; the second wall segment is sketched exactly to 20'0"(6096 mm) length.

   Notice that the intersection of the first and second wall segments has been intuitively filled or completed.

Figure 3-36 Creating the second exterior wall segment

3. To draw the third wall segment, select the **Chain** check box from the **Options Bar**.

4. Move the cursor close to the endpoint of the second wall segment and click when the endpoint object snap is displayed. On doing so, the third wall segment starts from this specified point. Move the cursor horizontally toward the left. Now, hold the SHIFT key while moving the cursor.

   Notice that the cursor can now move only in the orthogonal directions (in the horizontal and vertical direction). When the length of the wall segment is around 40'0"(12192 mm), a vertical dashed line originates from the start point of the first wall segment. The alignment line shows the point on the third wall segment that is in plumb with the first point. An intersection snap symbol indicated by an X appears at this point, as shown in Figure 3-37.

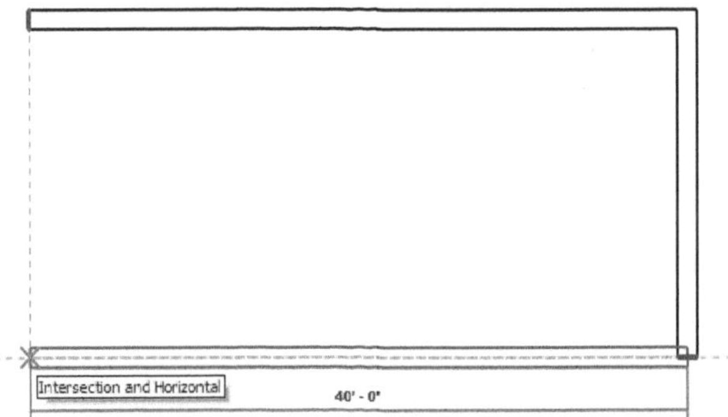

Figure 3-37 Creating the third wall segment

5. Click to specify the location of the endpoint of the third wall segment when the intersection snap symbol is displayed.

6. As you have enabled the **Chain** option, the next wall segment automatically starts from the last specified point. Move the cursor vertically upward and enter **25'(7620 mm)**, as shown in Figure 3-38, and then press ENTER. The fourth wall segment is created.

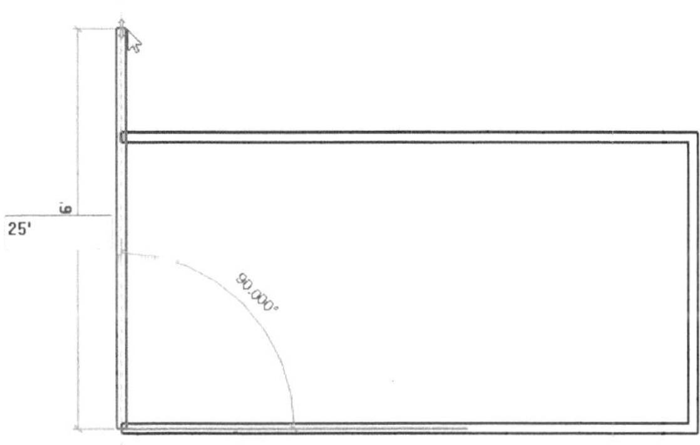

Figure 3-38 Sketching the fourth exterior wall segment

7. Press ESC twice to exit the **Wall: Architectural** tool.

Note

The purpose of creating a wall more than the desired length is only to explain how to stretch the wall to the exact length.

Stretching the Wall Segment

You will now stretch the wall segment to change its length to the desired dimension by using the drag controls.

1. Select the fourth wall segment to display its controls. The two blue dots at its two endpoints are the drag controls. Move the cursor near the upper dot; the color of the drag control symbol changes, as shown in Figure 3-39. Press and hold the left mouse button at this point and drag the cursor vertically downward and bring it close to the start point of the first wall segment. On doing so, the endpoint object snap is displayed at the intersection of two walls and the tooltip shows **Endpoint and Vertical**.

Figure 3-39 Using the drag control to modify the length of wall

2. Release the left mouse button at the intersection point and click; the first and fourth wall segments are joined at the corner with their ends completed.

Note that if these wall segments do not join at the corner on releasing the left mouse button, you need to click at their intersection.

3. Press ESC to remove the wall segment from the selection set. The external wall profile is completed for this tutorial, as shown in Figure 3-40.

Figure 3-40 *The completed exterior wall profile*

Saving the Project

In this section, you will save the project file using the **Save As** tool.

1. Choose **Save As > Project** from the **File** menu; the **Save As** dialog box is displayed. Create a folder with the name **c03_revit_2018_tut** and then save the file with the name **c03_Apartment1_tut1** (**M_c03_Apartment1_tut1**).

2. Choose the **Close** option from the **File** menu; the file is closed.

Tutorial 2 Club

Create the exterior walls of the club building and it's sketch plan is shown in Figure 3-41. The dimensions have been given only for reference and are not to be used in this tutorial. The parameters to be used for creating the exterior walls of the club building are given next.

(Expected time: 30 min)

1. Project file-
   For Imperial *c02_Club_tut2.rvt*
   For Metric *M_c02_Club_tut2.rvt*
2. Exterior wall type- **Exterior - Split Face and CMU on Mtl. Stud**.
3. Unconnected height of walls- **15'0" (4572 mm)**.
4. All inclined walls are at 45-degree to the horizontal axis.

The following steps are required to complete this tutorial:

a. Open the project file.
   For Imperial *c02_Club_tut2.rvt*
   For Metric *M_c02_Club_tut2.rvt*

b. Invoke the **Wall: Architectural** tool.
c. Select the exterior wall type:
   For Imperial **Exterior - Split Face and CMU on Mtl. Stud**
   For Metric **Exterior - Brick on Mtl. Stud**
d. Set the unconnected height to **15'0"** or **4572mm**.
e. Change the **Location Line** parameter to **Finish Face: Exterior**, refer to Figure 3-41.
f. Select the **Line** sketching option and sketch the inclined wall profile using the **Chain** option, refer to Figures 3-43 through 3-49.
g. Use the **Center-ends Arc** sketching option to create the curved wall, refer to Figures 3-46 and 3-47.
h. Save the project using the **Save As** tool.
   For Imperial *c03_Club_tut2.rvt*
   For Metric *M_c03_Club_tut2.rvt*
i. Close the project.

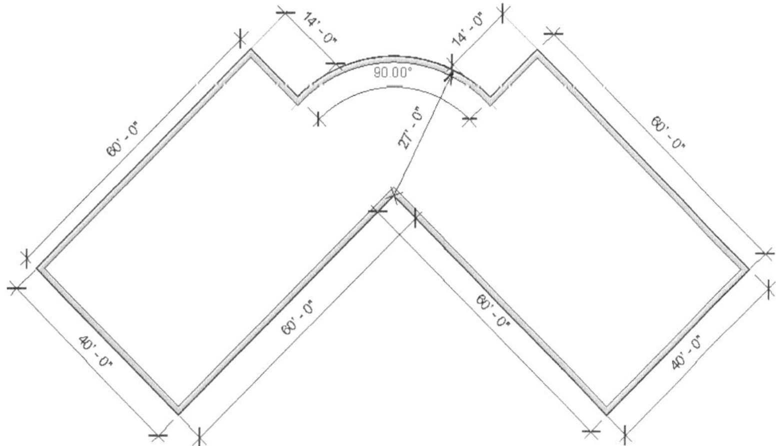

Figure 3-41 *Sketch plan for the Club project*

Opening an Existing Project

Choose **Open > Project** from **File** menu and open the *c02_Club_tut2.rvt (M_c02_Club_tut2.rvt* for Metric) project file created in Tutorial 2 of Chapter 2. You can also download this file from *http://www.cadcim.com*. The path of the file is as follows: *Textbooks > Civil/GIS > Revit Architecture> Exploring Autodesk Revit 2018 for Architecture*.

Invoking the Wall: Architectural Tool and Selecting the Wall Type

First, you will invoke the **Wall: Architectural** tool from the ribbon and then select the specified exterior wall type, as given in the project parameters.

1. Choose the **Wall: Architectural** tool from the **Architecture > Build > Wall** drop-down; the **Modify | Place Wall** tab is displayed.

2. In the **Properties** palette, select the required option from the **Type Selector** drop-down list.

For Imperial **Exterior - Split Face and CMU on Mtl. Stud**
For Metric **Exterior - Brick on Mtl. Stud**

Modifying Properties of the Exterior Wall

Next, you will use the **Properties** palette to modify the unconnected height to 15'0" or 4572mm. The dimensions given in the sketch are exterior wall face dimensions. Therefore, you need to set the **Location Line** parameter to **Finish Face: Exterior**.

1. In the **Properties** palette, click in the value field corresponding to the **Unconnected Height** parameter and replace the current value with **15'0"** (**4572mm**).

2. Click in the value field of the **LocationLine** parameter and select the **Finish Face: Exterior** option from the drop-down list displayed, as shown in Figure 3-42. Choose the **Apply** button to accept the specified values.

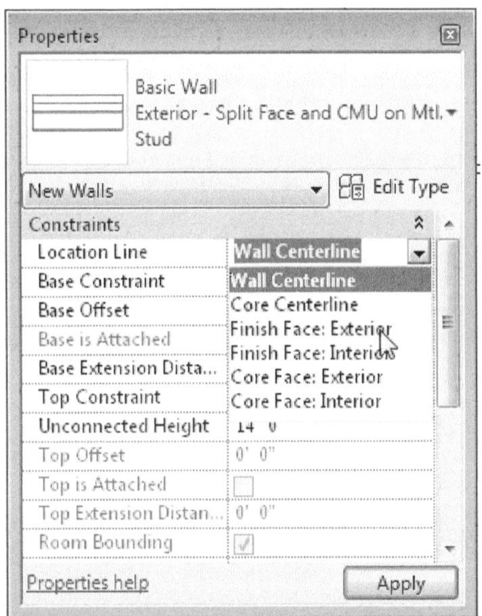

Figure 3-42 *Selecting the* ***Finish Face : Exterior*** *option for the* ***Location Line*** *parameter*

Sketching the Inclined Exterior Walls

Start creating the exterior wall profile by first sketching the inclined walls in a sequence such that the exterior face of the wall is on the external side. You need to select the **Chain** check box to sketch the continuous wall profile. Once you have created the first inclined wall, the other parallel and perpendicular walls can easily be created using the alignment lines and different object snaps options.

1. To create the straight wall, choose the **Line** tool in the **Draw** panel of the **Modify | Place Wall** tab, if it is not chosen by default.

2. In the **Options Bar**, select the **Chain** check box, if it is not selected. Also, select the **Allow** option from the **Join Status** drop-down list.

3. To start sketching the first inclined wall segment, click inside the four arrow keys in the drawing window and move the cursor upward toward the right and then move it to an inclination such that the angle subtended at the horizontal axis is 45 degrees.

4. Enter the value **14' (4267 mm)** to specify the length of the first wall segment; the value is displayed in the edit box, as shown in Figure 3-43. Press ENTER to create the first wall segment of the specified length.

5. As the **Chain** check box is selected in the **Options Bar**, the second wall segment will start from the last specified point. Now, move the cursor downward toward the right and right-click to invoke the shortcut menu. Next, choose **Snap Overrides > Perpendicular** from the shortcut menu displayed; the perpendicular snap symbol appears at the end of the wall. Enter **60'(18288 mm)**, see Figure 3-44; a wall is created perpendicular to the first inclined wall.

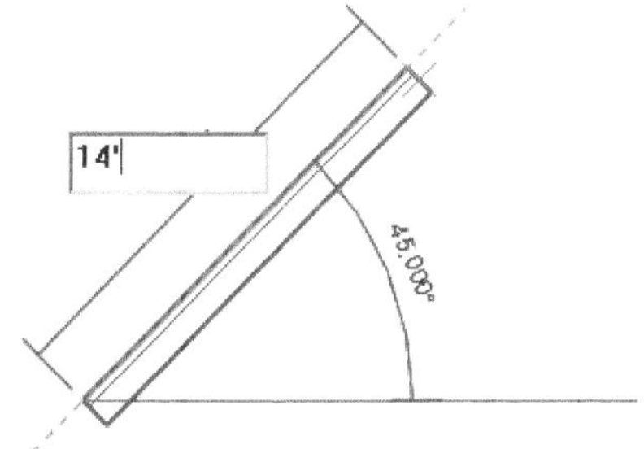

Figure 3-43 *Sketching the first inclined wall segment*

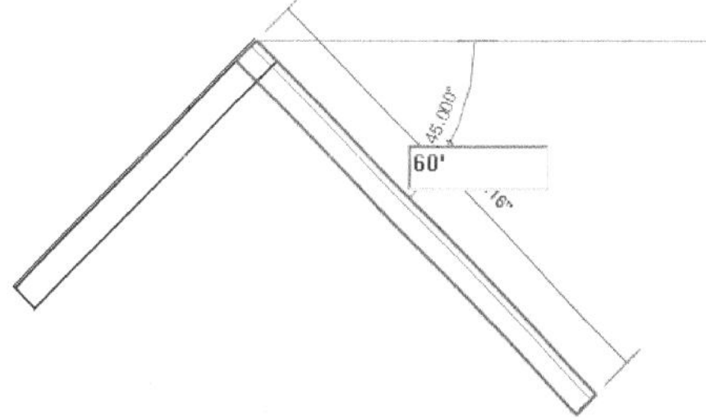

Figure 3-44 *Sketching the second inclined wall segment*

6. Similarly, for creating the next wall, move the cursor downward to the left and choose the perpendicular snap override as in step 5. Enter **40'(12192 mm)** as length, as shown in Figure 3-45. Now, press ENTER to create the third inclined wall.

7. To create the next wall, move the cursor upward toward the left and invoke the perpendicular snap override as in step 5. Enter **60' (18288 mm)** as the length of the wall segment and press ENTER to create the fourth inclined wall segment, as shown in Figure 3-46.

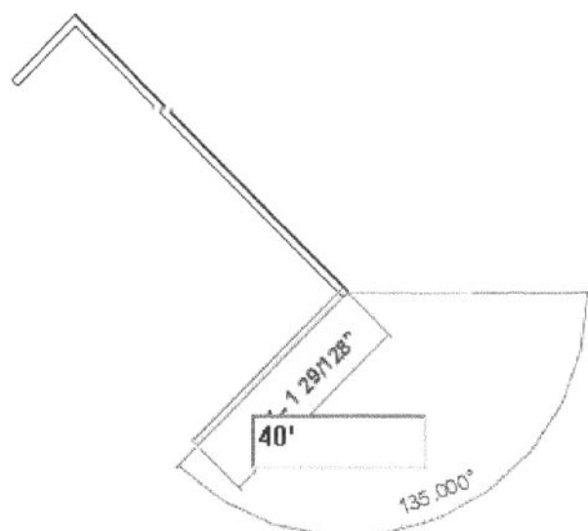

Figure 3-45 *Sketching the third inclined wall segment*

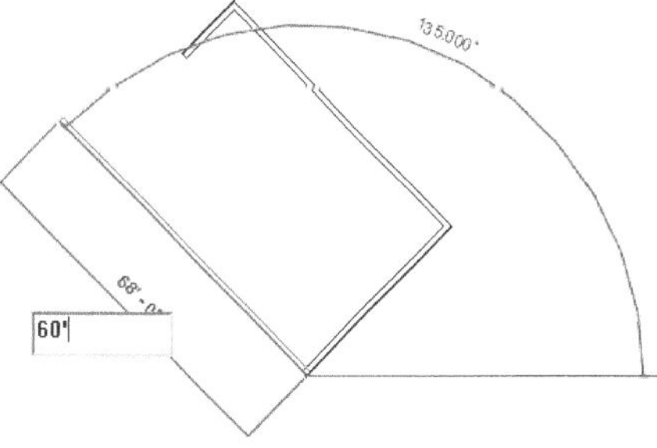

Figure 3-46 *Sketching the fourth inclined wall segment*

8. Similarly, create the fifth inclined wall segment of 60'(18288 mm) length, as shown in Figure 3-47.

9. Next, create the connected wall segment of 40'(12192 mm) length, as shown in Figure 3-48.

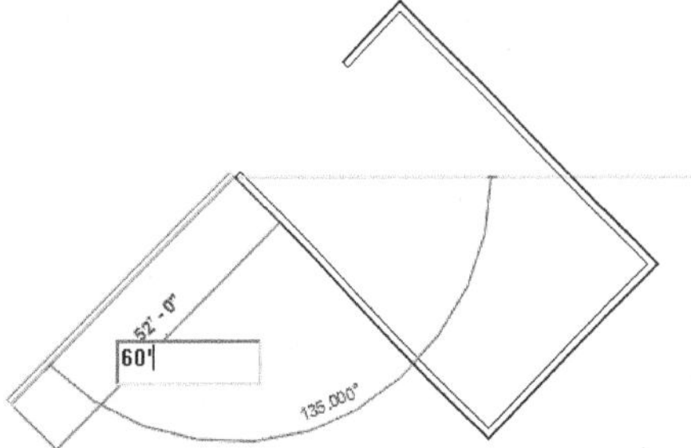

Figure 3-47 *Sketching the fifth inclined wall segment*

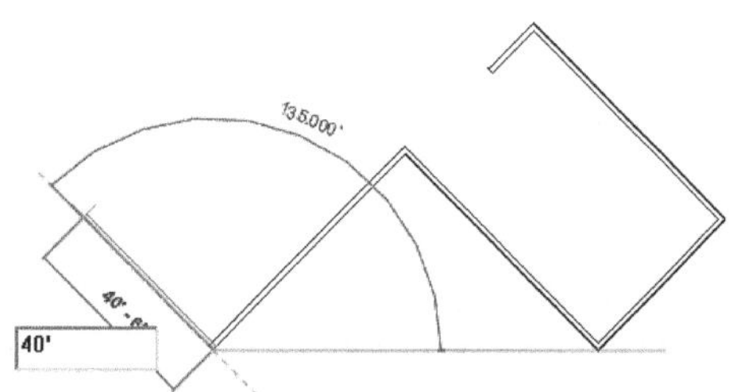

Figure 3-48 *Sketching the sixth inclined wall segment*

10. Now, create the next two wall segments of lengths 60'(18288 mm) and 14'(4267 mm) to complete the inclined wall exterior profile, as shown in Figure 3-49.

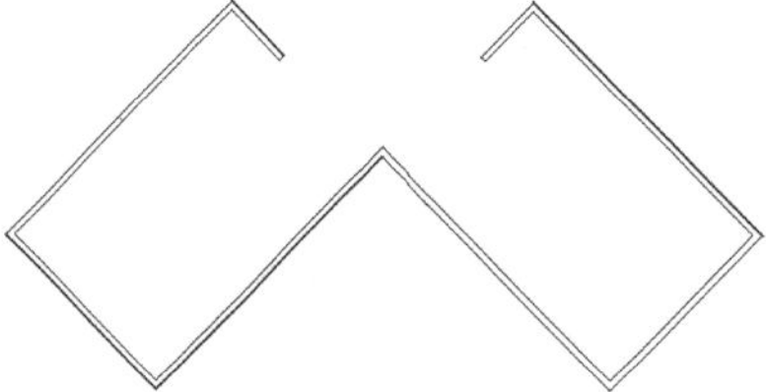

Figure 3-49 *The sketched inclined wall exterior profile*

11. Press the ESC key to discontinue the wall at this point and finish sketching the inclined walls.

Sketching the Curved Exterior Wall

Next, you will sketch the curved exterior wall profile based on the given parameters. You need to use the **Center-ends Arc** tool to create the curved wall segment.

1. Choose the **Center-ends Arc** tool in the **Draw** panel of the **Modify | Place Wall** tab. Move the cursor in the drawing window and click on the outer intersection of the inclined walls to specify the center of the curved wall, refer to Figure 3-50.

2. Move the cursor near the endpoint of the last sketched inclined wall segment. When 135-degree is displayed as the angular dimension, enter the value **27' (8100 mm)** as the radius of the curved wall and press ENTER, as shown in Figure 3-50. On doing so, the curved wall with the specified radius starts from the specified point.

Note

*While tracking the wall, if the perpendicular or other snapping symbol does not appear, you can right-click and choose **Snap Overrides**; a cascading menu will be displayed. Choose any snapping option from the cascading menu. On doing so, the desired snapping symbol will appear for the specified point or action.*

3. Move the cursor toward the right and click when the cursor snaps to the endpoint of the inclined wall, as shown in Figure 3-51. Now, press ESC twice to complete the exterior wall profile, as shown in Figure 3-52.

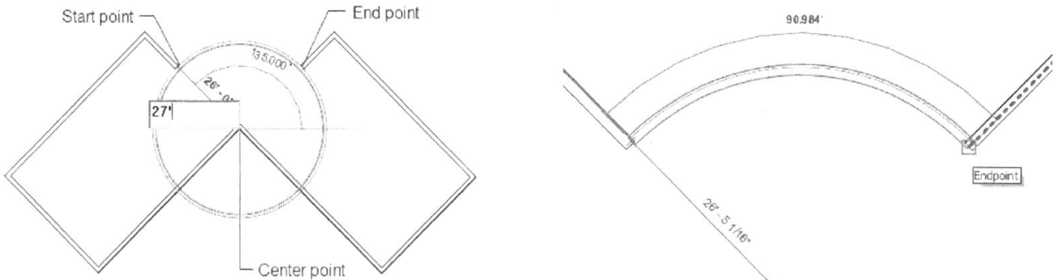

Figure 3-50 *Starting the curved wall segment*

Figure 3-51 *Completing the curved wall segment*

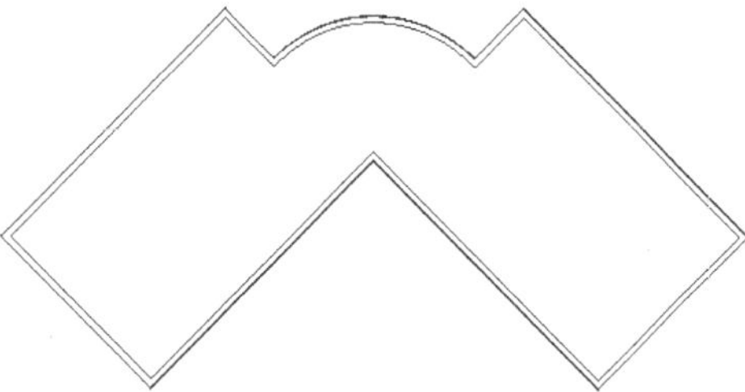

Figure 3-52 *Completed layout of the exterior walls for the Club project*

4. Choose the **Default 3D View** tool from **View > Create > 3D View** drop-down; a 3D view of the building model is displayed, as shown in Figure 3-53.

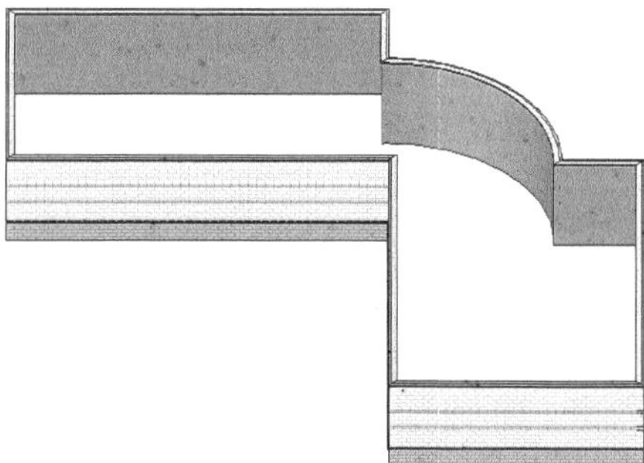

Figure 3-53 *3D view of the completed exterior wall profile*

5. From **View Control Bar**, choose the **Visual Style** button; a flyout is displayed. Choose the **Shaded** option from the flyout.

6. Under the **Floor Plans** head in the **Project Browser**, double-click on **Level 1** to return to the plan view.

Saving the Project

In this section, you will save the project file using the **Save As** tool.

1. Choose **Save As > Project** from **File** menu; the **Save As** dialog box is displayed. Now, browse to the folder **c03_revit_2018_tut** and enter **c03_Club_tut2** (**M_c03_Club_tut2** for Metric) and choose **Save**.

2. Choose the **Close** option from the **File** menu; the file is closed.

Tutorial 3 Apartment 1 - Interior Walls

In this tutorial, you will add interior walls to the apartment plan created in Tutorial 1 of this chapter. The interior walls to be created are the intermediate walls among various rooms, as shown in the plan sketch in Figure 3-54. The dimensions and text have been given for reference and are not to be created. The project file name and the parameters to be used for different elements are given next.

(Expected time: 30 min)

1. Project file-
   For Imperial *c03_Apartment1_tut1.rvt*
   For Metric *M_c03_Apartment1_tut1.rvt*
2. Interior wall type- **Interior - 5" Partition (2-hr)**.
3. Location line parameter- **Wall Centerline**.

The following steps are required to complete this tutorial:

a. Open the *Apartment 1* project file created earlier in this chapter.
b. Invoke the **Wall: Architectural** tool and select the required interior wall.
   For Imperial **Interior - 5" Partition (2-hr)**
   For Metric **Interior - 135mm Partition (2-hr)**
c. Set the location line parameter as **Location Line- Wall Centerline**.
d. Select the **Line** sketching tool to sketch the straight walls.
e. Sketch the interior walls based on the given parameters, refer to Figures 3-56 through Figure 3-62.
f. Edit the interior walls location to achieve clear internal distances, refer to Figures 3-63 and Figure 3-65.
g. Save the project using the **Save As** tool.
   For Imperial *c03_Apartment1_tut3.rvt*
   For Metric *M_c03_Apartment1_tut3.rvt*
h. Close the project.

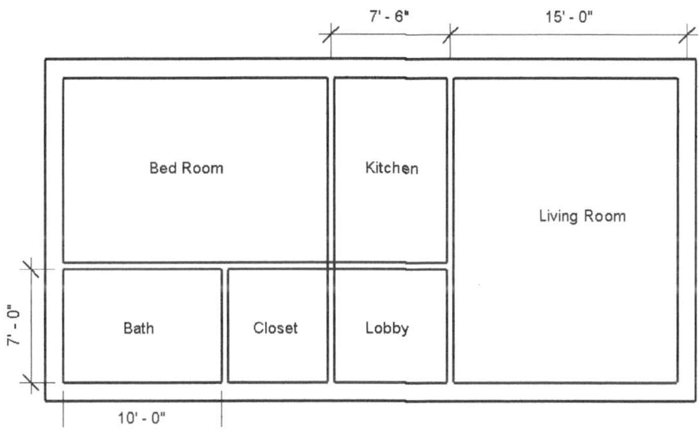

Figure 3-54 *Layout of internal walls for Apartment 1 project*

Opening the Project and Invoking the Wall: Architectural Tool

1. Choose **Open > Project** from the **File** menu and open the *c03_Apartment1_tut1.rvt (M_c03_Apartment1_tut1.rvt)* project created earlier in this chapter. You can also download this file from *http://www.cadcim.com*. The path of the file is as follows: *Textbooks > Civil/GIS > Revit Architecture > Exploring Autodesk Revit 2018 for Architecture*.

2. Invoke the **Wall: Architectural** tool from **Architecture> Build > Wall** drop-down.

Selecting the Interior Wall Type

1. On invoking the **Wall: Architectural** tool, the wall instance parameters are displayed in the **Properties** palette. In this palette, select the required option from the **Type Selector** drop-down list, as shown in Figure 3-55.

   For Imperial **Interior-5" Partition (2-hr)**
   For Metric **Interior - 135 mm Partition (2-hr)**

2. In the **Options Bar**, select the **Wall Centerline** option from the **Location Line** drop-down list, if it is not selected by default. Also, clear the **Chain** check box and select the **Allow** option from the **Join Status** drop-down list in the **Options Bar**.

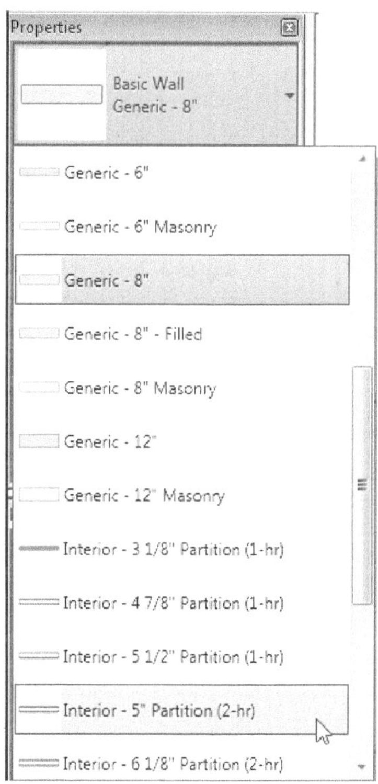

Figure 3-55 *Selecting the* ***Basic Wall: Interior - 5"Partition (2-hr)*** *wall type*

Sketching the First Interior Wall

After selecting the interior wall type, start sketching the interior walls. Notice that the **Line** tool is chosen as the default tool for sketching the walls.

1. Move the cursor near the top right endpoint of the wall structure and start moving the cursor toward left along the top horizontal wall. You will notice that a temporary

dimension appears which changes dynamically as you move the cursor away from it. This dimension shows the distance of the cursor from the nearest wall segment.

2. Type **15'(4572 mm)** from the keyboard, as shown in Figure 3-56. Now, press ENTER; the starting point of the first interior wall is specified.

3. Next, move the cursor vertically downward near the lower exterior wall segment. When the **Vertical and Nearest** symbol appears, as shown in Figure 3-57, click to specify the location of the endpoint of the wall segment; the first interior wall segment is sketched.

Sketching Other Interior Walls

Next, you will sketch the other horizontal and vertical interior walls by specifying their start point and endpoint using different object snap options.

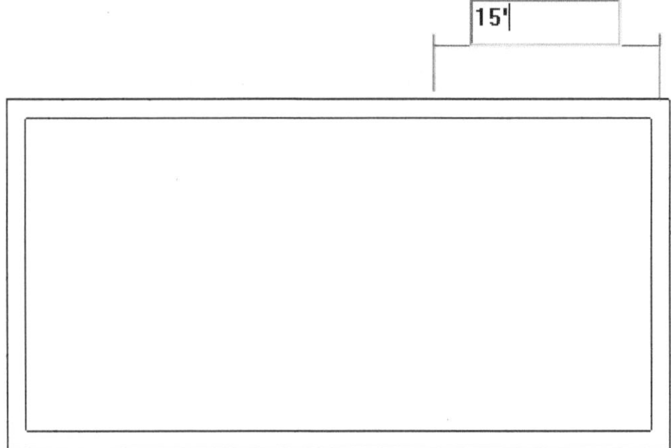

Figure 3-56 *Specifying the distance for starting the first interior wall segment*

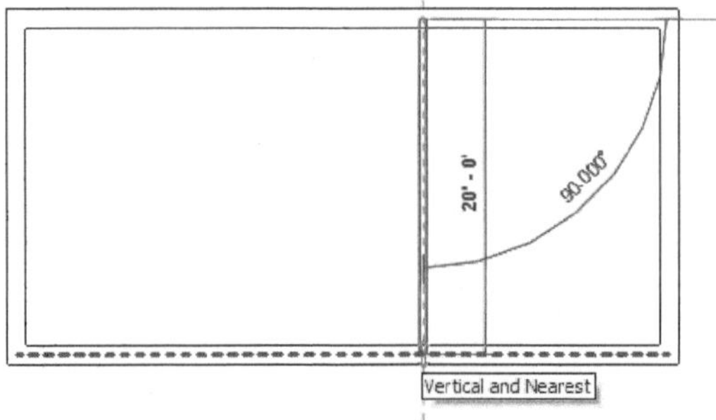

Figure 3-57 *Specifying the endpoint of the first interior wall segment*

1. To sketch the second interior wall, move the cursor to the upper endpoint of the interior wall you just created and then move the cursor horizontally toward the left. When the temporary dimension and the intersection object snap appears, enter **7'6"(2286 mm)**, as shown in Figure 3-58. Now, press ENTER; the start point of the second interior wall segment is specified on the upper horizontal exterior wall.

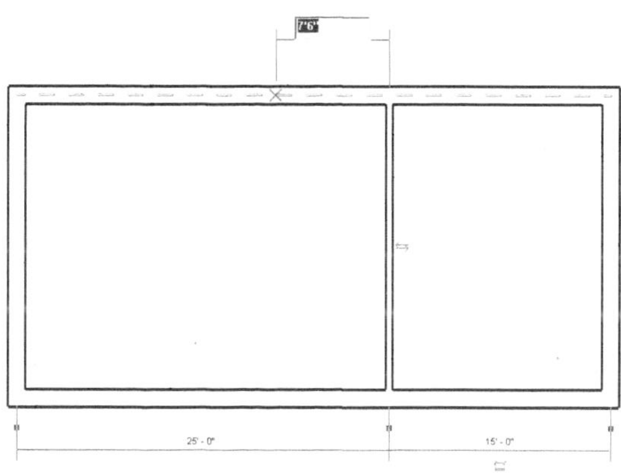

Figure 3-58 Specifying the starting point of the second interior wall

2. Press SHIFT and move the cursor downward. You will notice that the cursor moves parallel to the vertical axis while moving it downward. Click near the lower external wall when the **Vertical and Nearest** symbol appears, as shown in Figure 3-59.

   Next, you will sketch the interior walls of the bath. Since the internal dimensions have been provided for the interior walls, you will first sketch them using the wall center lines and later move them to get the exact clearance distance of the walls.

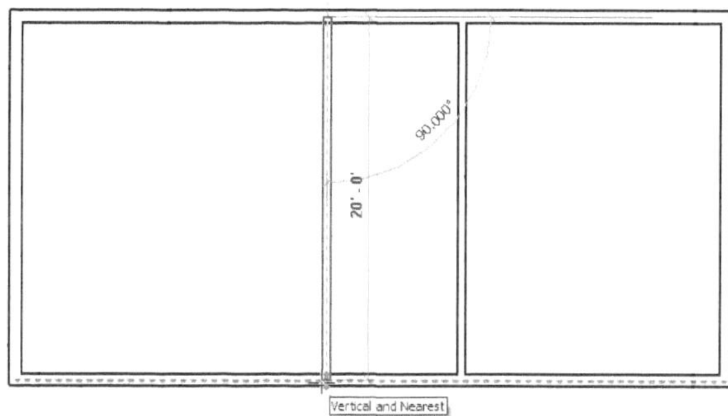

Figure 3-59 Sketching the second interior wall

3. Move the cursor to the lower left corner and then move it vertically upward. When the temporary dimension appears, enter **7'0"(2134 mm)** and then press ENTER to specify the starting point of the third interior wall, as shown in Figure 3-60.

Figure 3-60 Specifying the distance for sketching the third internal wall

4. Press SHIFT and move the cursor horizontally toward the right until it reaches the first vertical interior wall. When the **Horizontal and Nearest** object snap symbol appears, click to specify the location of the endpoint of the third interior wall, as shown in Figure 3-61, the wall segment is created.

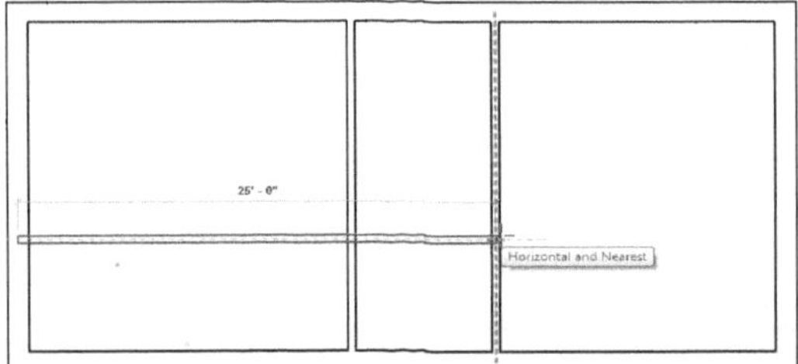

Figure 3-61 *Sketching the third interior wall segment*

5. Similarly, move the cursor near the lower left corner and then move it horizontally toward the right. When the temporary dimension and the intersection object snap appears, enter the value **10'0"**, as shown in Figure 3-62, and then press ENTER.

6. Press and hold the SHIFT key and move the cursor vertically upward until it reaches the horizontal interior wall. When the **Vertical and Nearest** symbol appears, click to specify the endpoint of the wall. Now, press ESC twice to finish the sketch of the wall.

Figure 3-62 *Sketching the interior walls of the bath*

Moving Walls Using Witness Lines

As the dimension of the bath walls will be measured from the centerline of the external walls, you need to move the interior walls such that the internal dimensions are 7'0"X10'0" as specified in the sketch. Use the witness lines and specify these dimensions.

1. Select the last created interior wall from the drawing; the selected interior wall shows the centerline distances and its controls.

2. Three blue dots define the extents of the dimensions. Click on the dot on the extreme left; the dot and the dimension witness line move to the interior face of the exterior wall, as shown in Figure 3-63.

3. Similarly, click twice on the next blue dot on the right to move it to the inner face of the third interior wall.

4. Now, click on the temporary dimension, enter the value **10'(3048 mm)**, and then press ENTER; the interior wall is moved to the desired distance 10'-0" from the interior face of the exterior wall, as shown in Figure 3-64.

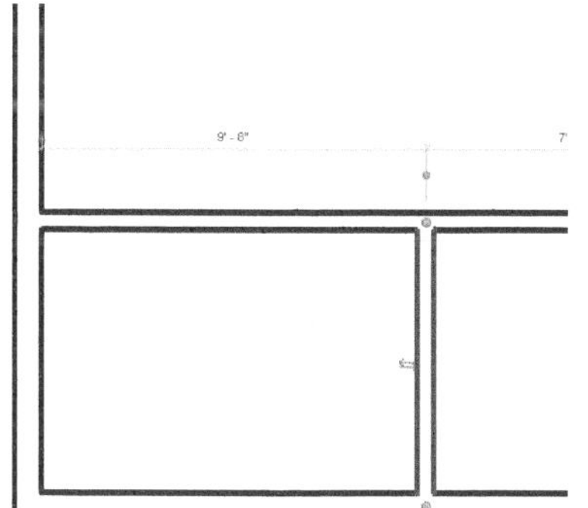

Figure 3-63 *The square dot moved*

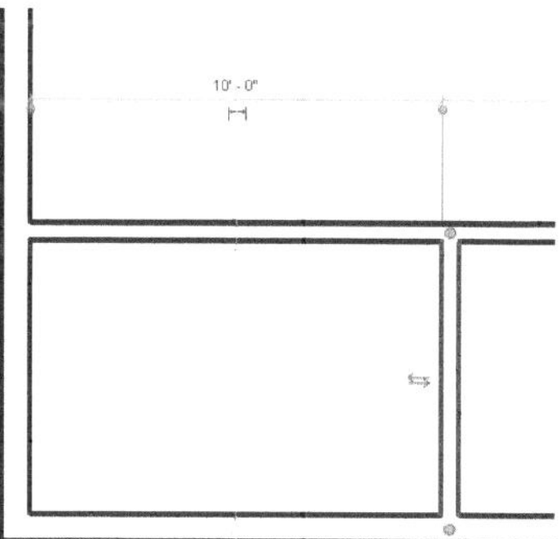

Figure 3-64 *The adjusted inner wall distance*

5. Similarly, to move the horizontal interior wall (common for the bath, kitchen and the closet), select it and move both the witness lines toward the inner face by clicking on the blue dots.

6. Now, click on the blue dots of temporary dimension from the lower external wall and the upper interior wall. Enter the value **7'(2134 mm)**, as shown in Figure 3-65, and press ENTER. On doing so, the interior wall is moved to the desired location. Now, press ESC to exit the **Modify | Walls** tab.

This completes the interior wall layout for the *Apartment 1* project, refer to Figure 3-65.

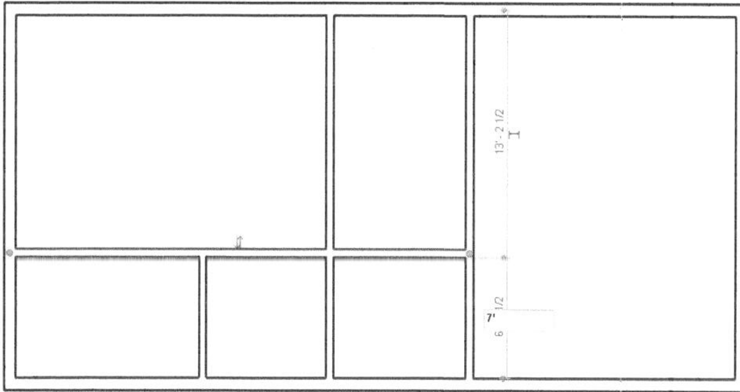

Figure 3-65 *Entering the value to adjust the dimension of the horizontal interior wall*

7. To view the building model in 3D, choose the **Default 3D View** tool from **View > Create > 3D View** drop-down. On doing so, the 3D view of the building model is displayed alongwith the **ViewCube** tool.

8. Now, choose the **Visual Style** button from the **View Control Bar**; a flyout is displayed. Choose the **Shaded** option from this flyout; the 3D view is displayed with the shading and edges visible, as shown in Figure 3-66.

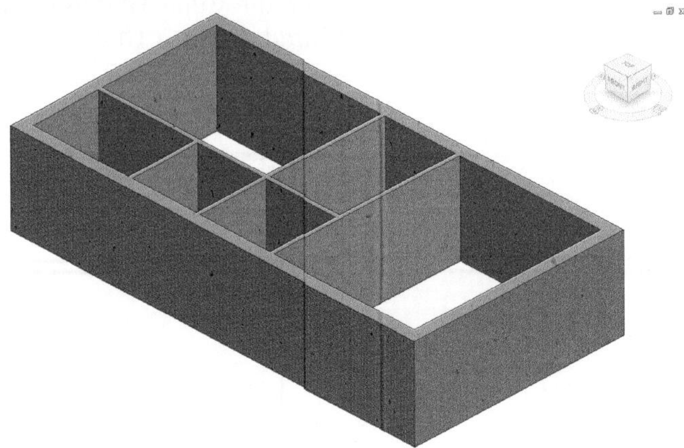

Figure 3-66 *3D view of the Apartment 1 building model*

Saving the Project

In this section, you will save the project file using the **Save As** tool.

1. Choose **Save As > Project** from **File** menu; the **Save As** dialog box is displayed. Now, browse to the folder **c03_revit_2018_tut** and enter **c03_Apartment1_tut3 (M_c03_Apartment1_tut3)** in the **File name** edit box and then choose **Save**.

2. Choose the **Close** option from the **File** menu; the file is closed.

Tutorial 4 Club - Interior Walls

Create the interior walls of the left portion of the club building whose exterior wall profile was created in Tutorial 2 earlier in this chapter. Create the walls based on the sketch plan shown in Figure 3-67. The dimensions are given for the centerlines of the walls and are displayed only for the purpose of drawing. You do not need to dimension or add text to the building. The project file name and the parameters to be used for different elements are given below.

(Expected time: 30 min)

1. Project file-
   For Imperial *c03_Club_tut2.rvt*
   For Metric *M_c03_Club_tut2.rvt*
2. Interior wall type -
   For Imperial **Interior - 6 1/8" Partition (2-hr)**.
   For Metric **Interior - 138mm Partition (1-hr)**.
3. Unconnected height of walls- **12'0"(3658 mm)**.

4. Location Line- **Wall Centerline**.
5. Inclined walls are parallel to the external walls and perpendicular to each other.

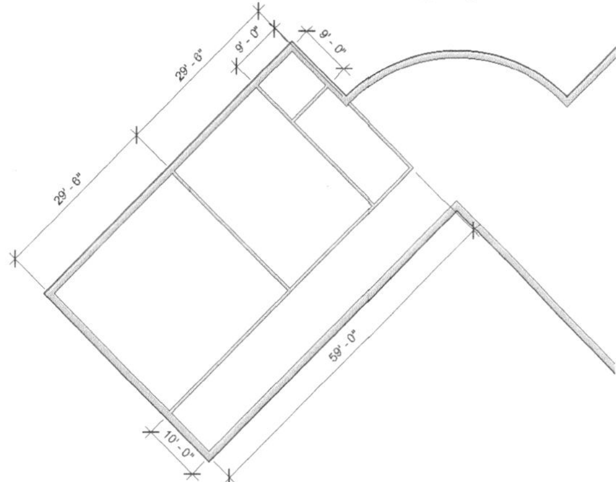

***Figure 3-67** Sketch plan for creating the interior wall of the left portion of the Club project*

The following steps are required to complete this tutorial:

a. Open the project file.
   For Imperial *c03_Club_tut2.rvt*
   For Metric *M_c03_Club_tut2.rvt*
b. Invoke the **Wall: Architectural** tool and select the required wall type, refer to Figure 3-68.
   For Imperial **Interior - 6 1/8" Partition (2-hr)**.
   For Metric **Interior - 138mm Partition (1-hr)**.
c. Set the unconnected height to **12'0"(3658 mm)**.
d. Ensure that the location line parameter is set to **Wall Centerline**.
e. Select the **Line** sketching option to create the straight walls.
f. Sketch the interior walls based on the given parameters, refer to Figures 3-69 through 3-75.
g. Save the project using the **Save As** tool.
   For Imperial *c03_Club_tut4.rvt*
   For Metric *M_c03_Club_tut4.rvt*
h. Close the project.

Opening the Existing Project and Invoking the Wall: Architectural tool

1. Open the *c03_Club_tut2.rvt (M_c03_Club_tut2.rvt)* project file by choosing **Open > Projects** from the **File** menu. You can also download this file from *http://www.cadcim.com*. The path of the file is as follows: *Textbooks > Civil/GIS > Revit Architecture > Exploring Autodesk Revit 2018 for Architecture*.

2. Click twice on **Level 1** under the **Floor Plans** head in the **Project Browser** and invoke the **Wall: Architectural** tool from **Architecture > Build > Wall** drop-down.

Selecting the Interior Wall Type

Before creating the interior walls, you need to select the wall type using the **Properties** palette.

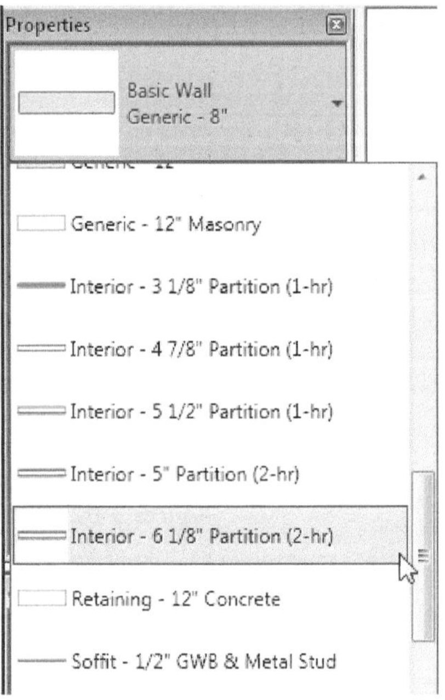

*Figure 3-68 Selecting the interior wall type from the **Properties** palette*

1. Select the required option from the **Type Selector** drop-down list in the **Properties** palette, as shown in Figure 3-68.
   For Imperial **Interior - 6 1/8" Partition (2-hr)**.
   For Metric **Interior - 138mm Partition (1-hr)**
2. Click in the value field corresponding to the **Top Constraint** parameter to display a drop-down list and ensure that the **Unconnected** option is selected in it.
3. Next, click on the value field corresponding to the **Unconnected Height** parameter, and replace the current value by entering the new value **12'0" (3658 mm)** in the cell.
4. Choose the **Apply** button to apply the changes made.

Sketching the Interior Walls

The interior walls to be created are straight in nature. Therefore you can use the **Line** tool from the **Draw** panel to create them.

1. Make sure that the **Wall Centerline** option is selected from the **Location Line** drop-down list in the **Options Bar**.
2. Clear the **Chain** check box in the **Options Bar**, if it is selected. Ensure that the **Allow** option is selected in the **Join Status** drop-down list.
3. Move the cursor close to the lower left corner, marked as 6, refer to Figure 3-69, and traverse upward along the centerline of extreme left wall of the building profile. When the temporary dimension appears, enter the value **10'(3048 mm)** and press ENTER to start the interior wall profile from the specified point, as shown in Figure 3-69.

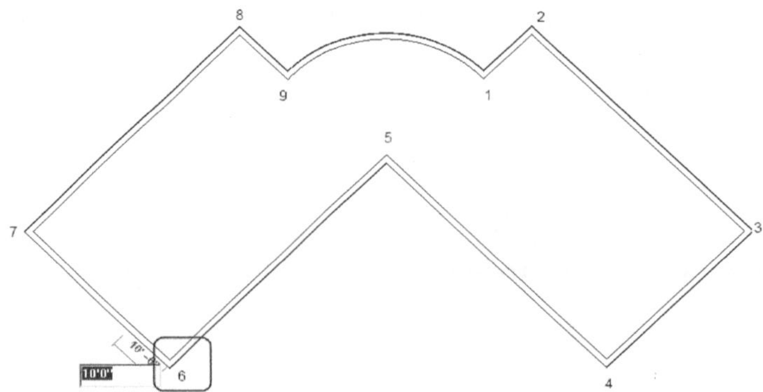

Figure 3-69 Specifying the start point of the first interior wall

4. Move the cursor 45 degrees upward to the right. When a dashed line appears, enter the value **59'(17983 mm)**, as shown in Figure 3-70 and then press ENTER.

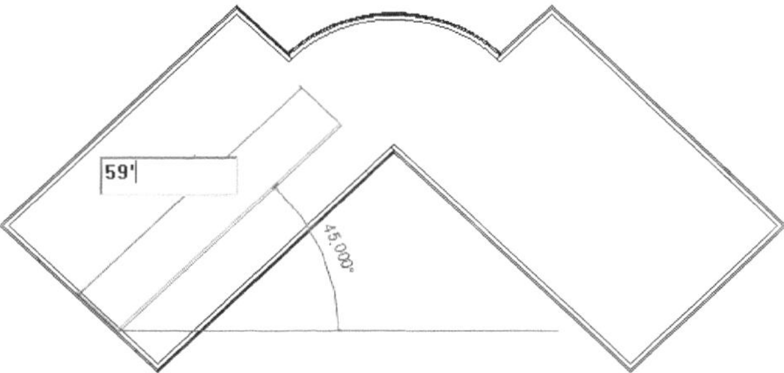

Figure 3-70 *Sketching the first interior wall of the Club project*

5. Start the next wall from the endpoint of the last created wall by clicking on its endpoint. Move the cursor upward toward the left such that it subtends an angle of 135 degrees with the horizontal and reaches the exterior wall displaying the **Nearest** object snap, as shown in Figure 3-71. Click to specify the endpoint of the wall.

6. Similarly, to start the next interior wall, bring the cursor close to the starting point of the last created wall (marked as 10), refer to Figure 3-71. Then, move the cursor away along the centerline of the wall until the temporary dimension appears. When the temporary dimension appears, enter the value **10'0"(3048 mm)** and press ENTER to specify the start point of the wall.

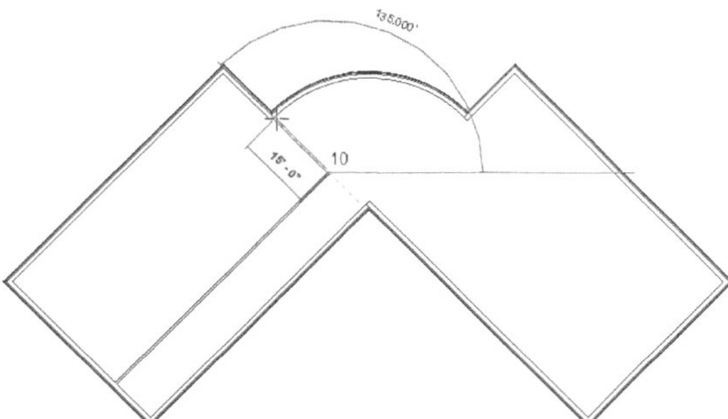

Figure 3-71 *Sketching the second interior wall*

7. Move the cursor upward toward the left such that it subtends an angle of 135 degrees with the horizontal until it reaches the exterior wall and the **Nearest** object snap is displayed, as shown in Figure 3-72. Click to specify the endpoint of the wall.

8. Create the next wall by moving the cursor away from the specified point. Next, move it downward toward the right. When the temporary dimension appears, enter the value **9'(2743 mm)** and press ENTER to start the wall, as shown in Figure 3-73.

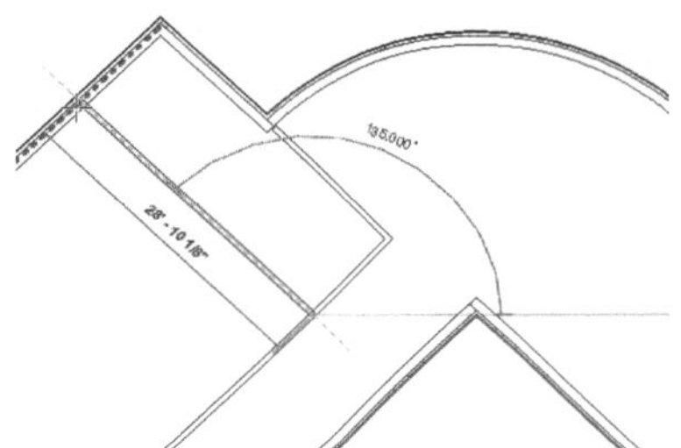

Figure 3-72 Sketching the third interior wall

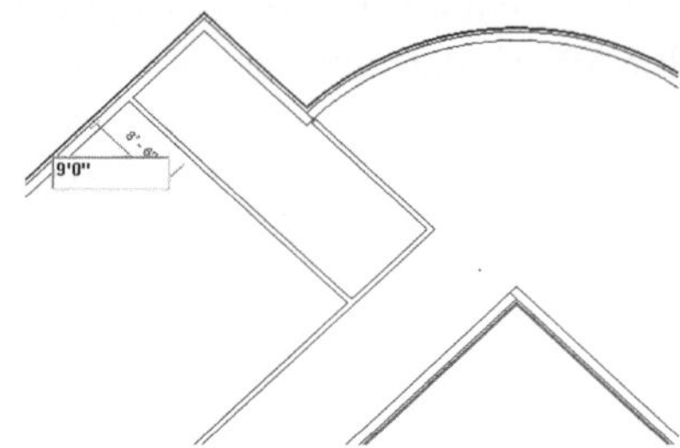

Figure 3-73 Specifying the distance of the fourth interior wall

9. Move the cursor upward toward the right. Click on the exterior wall to specify the endpoint of the interior wall when the **Nearest** object snap is displayed.

10. To create the next wall, bring the cursor close to the midpoint of the first interior wall until the **Midpoint** object snap appears, as shown in Figure 3-74. Click on the drawing to start the wall.

11. Move the cursor up toward the left upto the exterior wall such that it subtend an angle of 135 degrees with the horizontal and click when the **Nearest** object snap appears on the exterior wall, as shown in Figure 3-75. Click to specify the endpoint; the wall is created.

    This completes the interior wall layout for the left portion of the *Club* project.

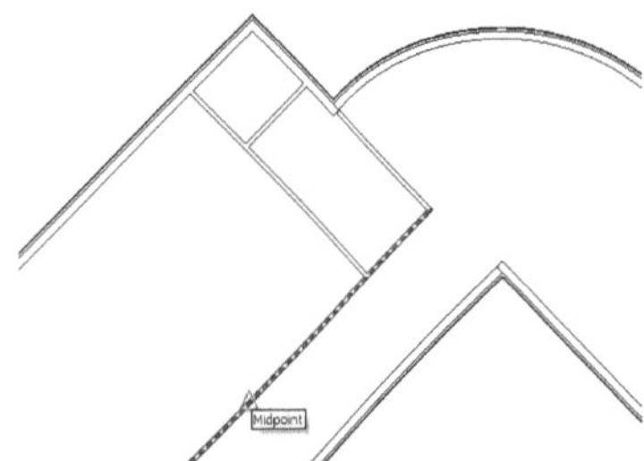

Figure 3-74 Starting the fifth interior wall from the midpoint of the first interior wall

Figure 3-75 Completing the interior walls

12. Choose the **Modify** button to exit the tool selection.

Saving the Project

In this section, you will save the project file using the **Save As** tool.

1. Choose **Save As > Project** from **File** menu; the **Save As** dialog box is displayed. Now, browse to the folder **c03_revit_2018_tut** and enter **c03_Club_tut4** (for Metric **M_c03_Club_tut4**) in the **File name** edit box and then choose **Save**.

2. Now, choose **Close** from **File** menu to close the file.

Tutorial 5 House-Stacked Wall

In this tutorial, you will create stacked walls and also add interior walls to the house plan. The interior walls to be created are the intermediate walls of the rooms, as shown in the plan sketch in Figure 3-76. The dimensions and text have been given for reference and are not to be created. The project file name and the parameters to be used for different elements are given next.

(Expected time: 45 min)

1. Project file-
   For Imperial *default.rte*
   For Metric *DefaultMetric.rte*
2. Interior wall type-
   For Imperial **Interior - 5 1/2" Partition (1-hr)**
   For Metric **Interior - 138 mm Partition (1-hr)**
3. Location line parameter- **Wall Centerline**.

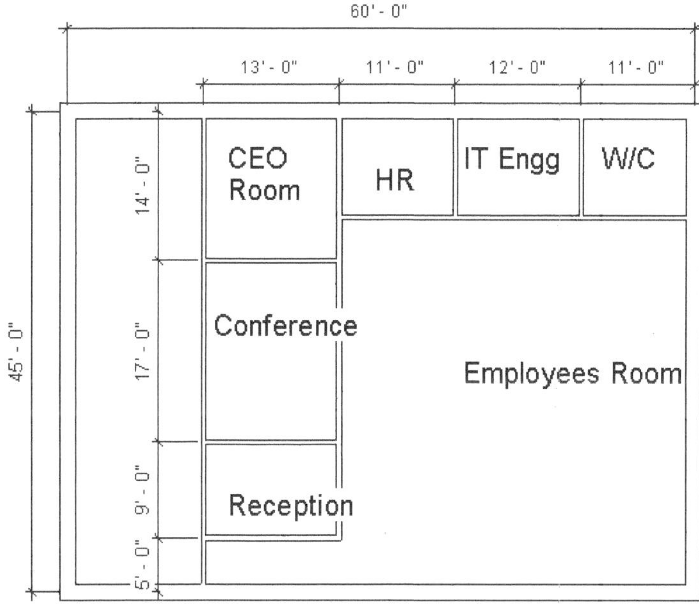

***Figure 3-76** Layout of internal walls for House project*

The following steps are required to complete this tutorial:

a. Open the project file.
   For Imperial *default.rte*
   For Metric *DefaultMetric.rte*
b. Invoke the **Wall: Architectural** tool and select the required wall type from the **Type Selector** drop-down list.
   For Imperial **Stacked Wall Exterior - Brick over CMU w Metal Stud**
   For Metric **Render on Brick on Block w Metal Stud**
c. Edit the wall type as **Stacked wall Exterior- EIFS over CMU w Metal Stud**.
d. Set the location line parameter as **Location Line- Wall Centerline**.
e. Select the **Rectangle** sketching tool to sketch the exterior walls.

f. Sketch the interior walls based on the given parameters.
g. Edit the interior walls location to achieve clear internal distances.
h. Save the project using the **Save As** tool.
   For Imperial *c03_Office_tut5.rvt*
   For Metric *M_c03_Office_tut5.rvt*
i. Close the project using the **Close** tool.

Opening a New Project

1. Choose **New > Project** from **File** menu; the **New Project** dialog box is displayed.

2. In this dialog box, choose the **Browse** button; the **Choose Template** dialog box is displayed.

3. In the **Choose Template** dialog box, select the required template file.
   For Imperial *default.rte*
   For Metric *DefaultMetric.rte*
   Then, choose the **Open** button; the selected template file is loaded in the **New Project** dialog box.

4. Now, choose the **OK** button; the selected template file is loaded.

Invoking the Wall: Architectural Tool and Selecting the Wall Type

In this section, you will create a stacked wall type.

1. Choose the **Wall: Architectural** tool from **Architecture > Build > Wall** drop-down; the **Modify | Place Wall** tab is displayed.

2. In the **Properties** palette, select the required option from the **Type Selector** drop-down list.
   For Imperial **Stacked Wall Exterior - Brick Over CMU w Metal Stud**
   For Metric **Stacked Wall Exterior - Brick Over Block w Metal Stud**

Modifying Exterior Wall Type

In this section, you will use the **Type Properties** dialog box to edit the wall type and the **Properties** palette to modify the unconnected height to 12'0"(3600 mm).

1. In the **Properties** palette, choose the **Edit Type** button; the **Type Properties** dialog box is displayed.

2. In this dialog box, choose the **Duplicate** button; the **Name** dialog box is displayed. Enter required name in the **Name** edit box.
   For Imperial **Exterior- EIFS Over CMU w Metal Stud**
   For Metric **Exterior- Render on Brick on Block w Metal Stud**
   Then, choose the **OK** button.

3. Choose the **Edit** button corresponding to the **Structure** parameter; the **Edit Assembly** dialog box is displayed.

4. In this dialog box, click on the first row under the value field of the **Name** column and select the required option from the drop-down list displayed.

For Imperial **Exterior- EIFS on Metal Stud**
For Metric **Exterior- Render on Brick on Block**

Ensure that **Variable** is selected under the **Height** column.

5. Similarly, click on the second row under the value field of the **Name** column and select the required option from the drop-down list displayed and enter the height as **5' (1524 mm)** under the **Height** column.
   For Imperial **Exterior- CMU on Metal Stud**
   For Metric **Exterior- Block on Metal Stud**

6. Choose the **Preview** button to view the wall type; a preview pane is displayed.

7. Now, choose the **OK** button from the **Edit Assembly** dialog box and the **Type Properties** dialog boxes to close them.

8. In the **Properties** palette, click in the value field corresponding to the **Unconnected Height** parameter and replace the current value with **12'0"(3600 mm)**.

9. Click in the value field of the **Location Line** parameter and select the **Finish Face: Exterior** option from the drop-down list displayed. Choose the **Apply** button to accept the specified values.

Sketching the Exterior Walls

In this section, you will learn to create the exterior walls.

1. To create the exterior wall, choose the **Rectangle** tool from the **Draw** panel of the **Modify | Place Wall** tab, if it is not chosen by default.

2. To start sketching the first inclined wall segment, click inside the four arrow keys in the drawing window and move the cursor downward toward the right and click again; a rectangle is created with temporary dimensions displayed along with it, as shown in Figure 3-77.

Figure 3-77 *Rectangle drawn with its temporary dimensions*

3. Press ESC twice to exit the currently selected tool.

4. Now, select the upper horizontal wall; the **Modify | Stacked Wall** tab is displayed.

5. In the **Options Bar**, choose the **Activate Dimensions** button; the dimensions are activated for vertical side.

6. Click on the vertical temporary dimension and enter **45'** (**13716 mm**) in the edit box displayed, as shown in Figure 3-78 and press ENTER.

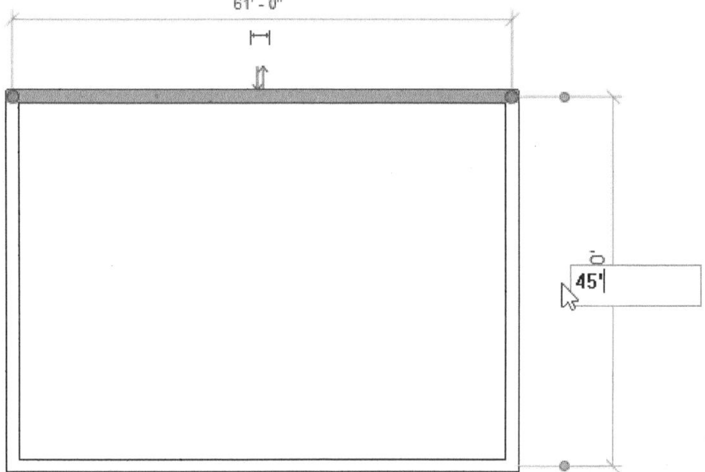

Figure 3-78 *Entering vertical dimension in the edit box*

7. Now, select the right wall and then activate the dimension using the **Activate Dimension** button from the **Options Bar**.

8. Click on the horizontal temporary dimension and enter **60'(18288 mm)** for the horizontal wall, as shown in Figure 3-79. Press ENTER.

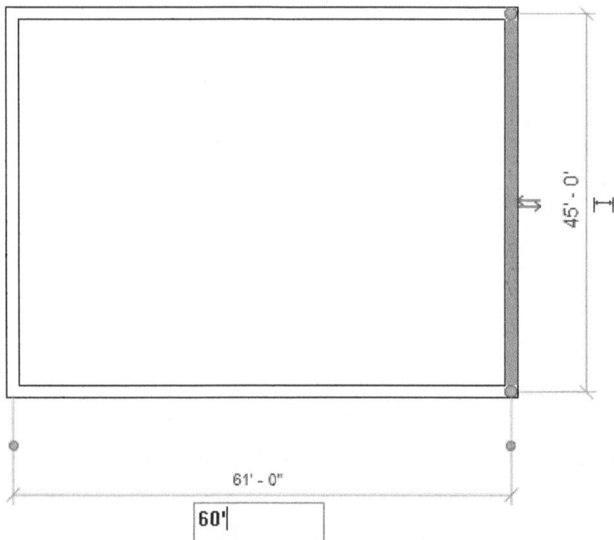

Figure 3-79 *Entering horizontal dimension in the edit box*

Selecting the Interior Wall Type

Before creating the interior walls, you need to select the wall type using the **Properties** palette.

1. Choose the **Wall: Architectural** tool from **Architecture > Build > Wall** drop-down.

2. Select the required option from the **Type Selector** drop-down list in the **Properties** palette, as shown in Figure 3-80.
   For Imperial **Interior - 5 1/2" Partition (1-hr)**
   For Metric **Interior- 138mm Partition (1-hr)**

3. Click in the value field corresponding to the **Top Constraint** parameter to display a drop-down list and ensure that the **Unconnected** option is selected in it.

4. Next, click on the value field corresponding to the **Unconnected Height** parameter, and replace the current value by entering the new value **12'(3658 mm)** in the cell.

5. Choose the **Apply** button to apply the changes made.

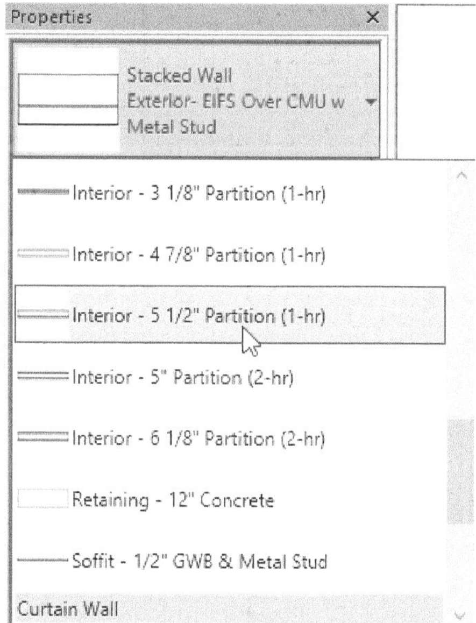

Figure 3-80 *Selecting the interior wall type from the* ***Properties*** *palette*

Sketching Interior Walls

In this section, you will sketch the horizontal and vertical interior walls by specifying their start point and endpoint using different object snap options.

1. To sketch the interior wall, move the cursor to the upper left corner of the exterior wall and then move the cursor horizontally toward the right. Enter **13'(3962 mm)** in the edit box as shown in Figure 3-81, when the temporary dimension and the intersection object snap appears. Now, press ENTER; the start point of the interior wall segment is specified on the upper horizontal exterior wall.

2. Press SHIFT and move the cursor downward. You will notice that the cursor moves parallel to the vertical axis while moving it downward. Click near the lower exterior wall, as shown in Figure 3-82 when the **Vertical and Nearest** symbol appears.

   Next, you will sketch the other interior walls.

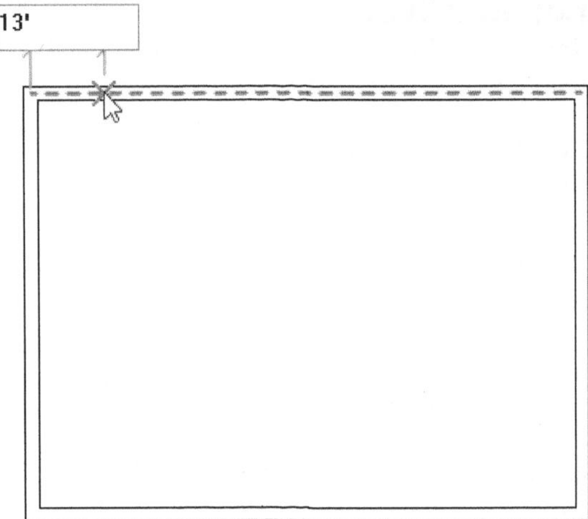

Figure 3-81 *Entering the value in the edit box*

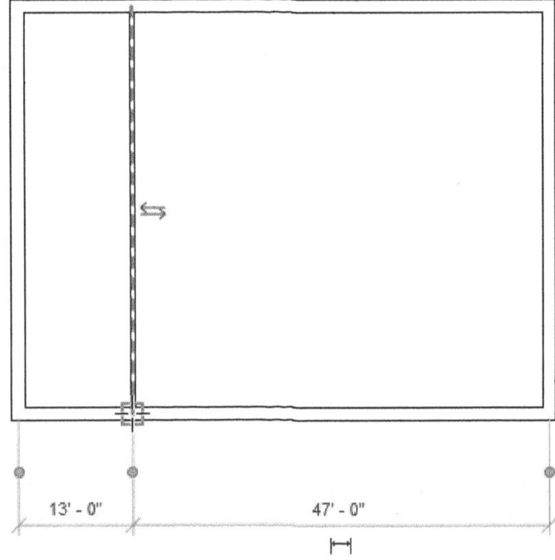

Figure 3-82 *Straight wall created till the lower exterior wall*

3. Move the cursor to the bottom of the wall just drawn and then move it vertically upward. When the temporary dimension appears, enter **5'0"(1524 mm)** and then press ENTER; the starting point of the third interior wall is specified, as shown in Figure 3-83.

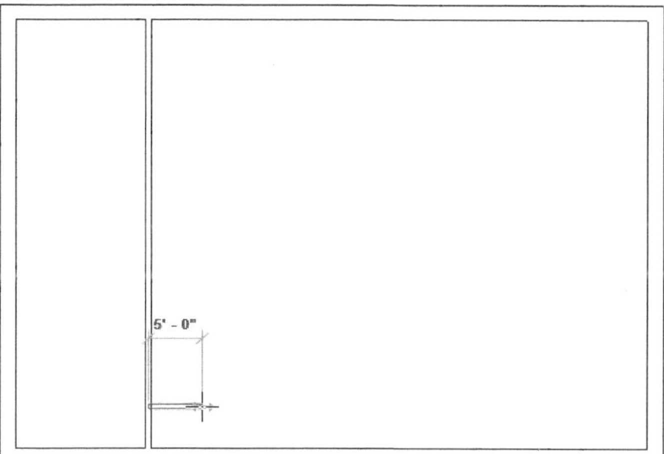

Figure 3-83 *Specifying the starting point of third interior wall*

4. Press SHIFT and move the cursor horizontally toward the right. When temporary dimension appears, enter **13'(3962 mm)** and then press ENTER; the wall segment is created.

5. Now, move the cursor vertically upward and click on the upper exterior wall, as shown in Figure 3-84.

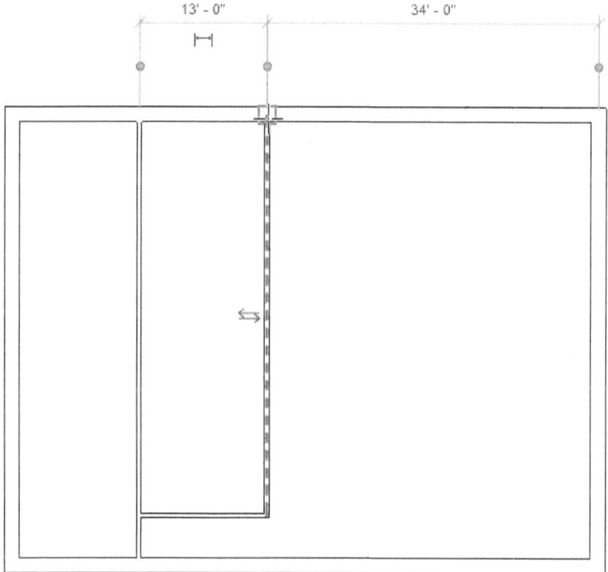

Figure 3-84 *The wall created extended upto the upper exterior wall*

6. Move the cursor near the upper right corner and then move it vertically downward. When the temporary dimension and the nearest object snap appear, enter the value **10'0"(3048 mm)** and then press ENTER.

7. Press and hold the SHIFT key and move the cursor horizontally toward left until it reaches the vertical interior wall. Next, click to specify the endpoint of the wall, as shown in Figure 3-85. Now, press ESC twice to finish the sketch of the wall.

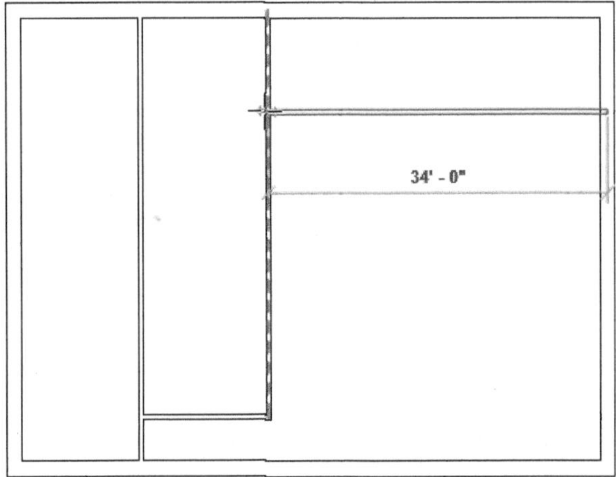

Figure 3-85 *Horizontal wall created at the distance of 10' from the outer exterior wall*

8. Similarly, sketch other walls, as shown in Figure 3-86.

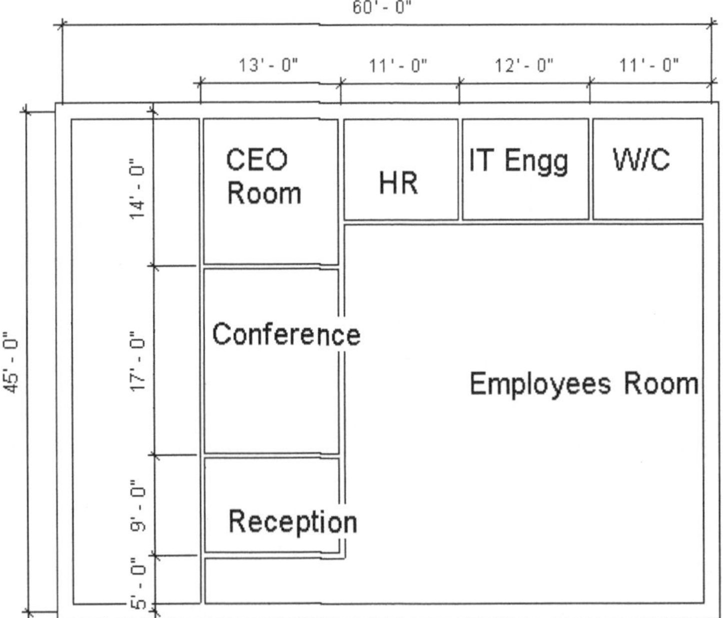

Figure 3-86 *Other interior walls for the project*

9. To view the building model in 3D, choose the **Default 3D View** tool from **View > Create > 3D View** drop-down. On doing so, the 3D view of the building model is displayed along with the **ViewCube** tool.

10. Now, choose the **Visual Style** button from the **View Control Bar**; a flyout is displayed. Choose the **Shaded** option from this flyout; the 3D view is displayed with shading and with edges visible, as shown in Figure 3-87.

Saving the Project

In this section, you will save the project file using the **Save As** tool.

1. Choose **Save As > Project** from **File** menu; the **Save As** dialog box is displayed. Enter **c03_office_tut5** in the **File name** edit box and then choose **Save**.

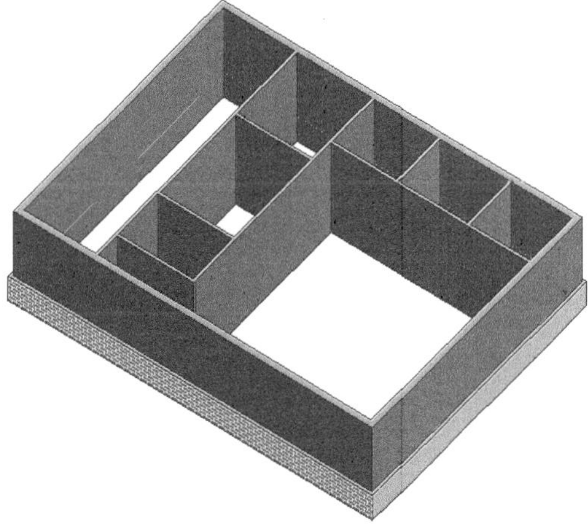

Figure 3-87 *3D view of a building with the shaded edges*

Self-Evaluation Test

Answer the following questions and then compare them to those given at the end of this chapter:

1. Which value of the Structural Usage parameter will turn a structural wall into an architectural wall?

   a) Bearing
   b) Non-bearing
   c) Structural combined
   d) Shear

2. A stacked wall is comprised of one or more _______ wall types.

   a) Generic
   b) Simple
   c) Basic
   d) Complex

3. You can use the ________ to view the instance parameters of an element.

   a) Properties palette
   b) Project Browser
   c) Filter
   d) Type Selector

4. The __________ option enables you to sketch continuous and end to end connected wall segments.

5. To create a wall starting at a specified distance from a point on an existing element, you can use the __________ option from the **Options Bar**.

6. You can select a wall type from the __________ drop-down list.

7. You can modify the instance properties of a wall type in the **Properties** palette. (T/F)

8. When you modify the instance properties of a wall, the instance properties of all the similar wall types used in the project are modified. (T/F)

9. You can create a wall type of your choice by combining various layers. (T/F)

10. By default, when you sketch a wall from left to right, the lower face becomes the external face. (T/F)

Review Questions

Answer the following questions:

1. Which of the following sketching tools can be used to create a straight wall?

   a) **Lines** b) **Circles**
   c) **Fillet Arc** d) **Center-ends Arc**

2. Which of the following keys can be used to constrain the cursor such that it moves along the orthogonal direction only?

   a) TAB b) SHIFT
   c) ALT d) F3

3. Which of the following sketching tools can be used to create a curved wall?

   a) **Polygon** b) **Line**
   c) **Fillet Arc** d) **Rectangle**

4. The __________ dimension appears after you specify the start point of a wall and move the cursor.

5. You can use the __________ option to create a curved wall by specifying the center and the endpoints.

6. The **Location Line** parameter is an instance property of a wall. (T/F)

7. The value of the **Function** parameter in the **Type Properties** dialog box for an exterior wall is **Exterior**. (T/F)

8. You can add or delete layers of a composite wall type to create a new wall type. (T/F)

9. Once a wall is sketched, its dimension and angle cannot be modified. (T/F)

10. The **Chain** option can be enabled or disabled without exiting the **Wall: Architectural** tool. (T/F)

11. The usage of the wall can be changed by modifying the value of the **Function** parameter. (T/F)

12. While using the **Wall: Architectural** tool, if you invoke any other tool, the **Wall: Architectural** tool will be exited. (T/F)

EXERCISES

Exercise 1 Apartment 2

Create the exterior and interior walls of the *Apartment 2*, based on Figure 3-88. The thick walls are the exterior walls and the thin walls are the interior walls. The dimensions and texts are not to be added. The project parameters for this exercise are given next.

(Expected time: 30 min)

1. Project file -
   For Imperial *c02_Apartment2_ex1.rvt.*
   For Metric *M_c02_Apartment2_ex1.rvt.*
2. Exterior wall type- **Exterior - Brick on Mtl. Stud.**
3. Interior wall type-
   For Imperial **Basic Wall: Interior - 5" Partition (2-hr).**
   For Metric **Basic Wall: Interior - 135mm Partition (2-hr).**
4. Height of the wall- **Top Constraint - Up to Level 2.**
5. Location line parameter for the exterior walls- **Wall Centerline.**
6. Name of the file to be saved-
   For Imperial **c03_Apartment2_ex1**
   For Metric **M_c03_Apartment2_ex1**

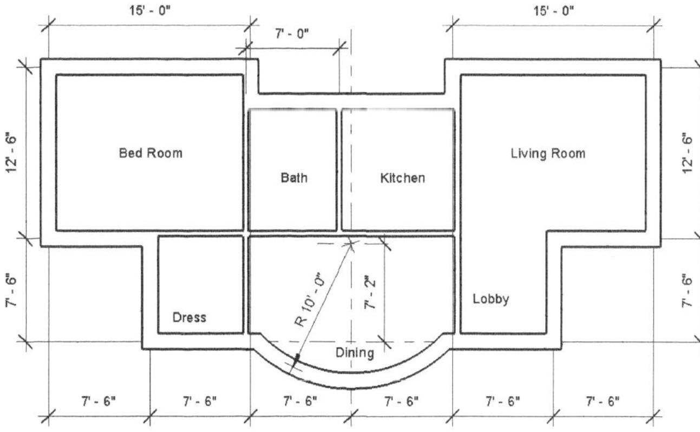

Figure 3-88 *The sketch plan for creating the exterior and interior walls for the Apartment 2 project*

Exercise 2 Elevator and Stair Lobby

Create the exterior walls of the *Elevator and Stair Lobby* project, based on Figure 3-89. Do not add dimensions or texts as they are given only for reference. The project parameters for this exercise are given next. **(Expected time: 30 min)**

1. Project file -
   For Imperial *c02_ElevatorandStairLobby_ex2.rvt*
   For Metric *M_c02_ElevatorandStairLobby_ex2.rvt*
2. Exterior wall type - **Basic Wall Exterior Brick on Mtl. Stud.**
3. Height of the wall - **Top Constraint- Up to Level 2.**
4. Location line parameter - **Wall Centerline.**
5. Name of the file to be saved -
   For Imperial **c03_ElevatorandStairLobby_ex2.**
   For Metric **M_c03_ElevatorandStairLobby_ex2.**

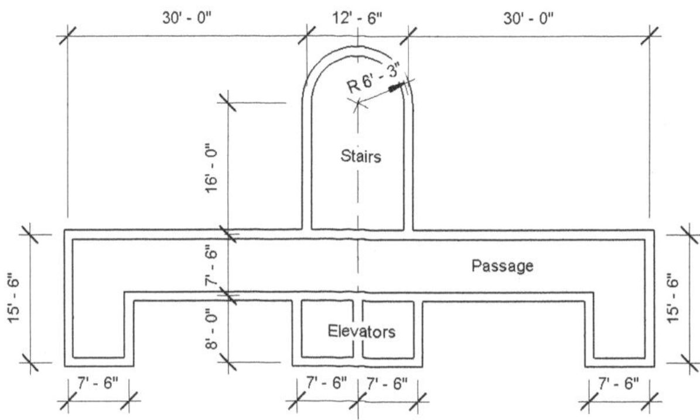

***Figure 3-89** Sketch plan for creating the exterior walls for the Elevator and Stair Lobby project*

Exercise 3 Club-Interior Walls

Create the interior walls of Hall 2 of the *Club* project based on Figure 3-90. Do not dimension the sketch as dimensions are given only for reference. The project parameters for this exercise are given next. **(Expected time: 30 min)**

1. Project file -
   For Imperial *c03_Club_tut4.rvt*
   For Metric *M_c03_Club_tut4.rvt*
2. Interior wall type-
   For Imperial **Basic Wall: Interior - 6 1/8" Partition (2-hr).**
   For Metric **Basic Wall: Interior - 138mm Partition (1-hr).**
3. Unconnected height of walls- **12'0"(3658 mm).**
4. Location Line- **Wall Centerline.**
5. Inclined walls are parallel to the external walls and perpendicular to each other.
6. Name for saving the file-

For Imperial **c03_Club_ex3**.
For Metric **M_c03_Club_ex3**.

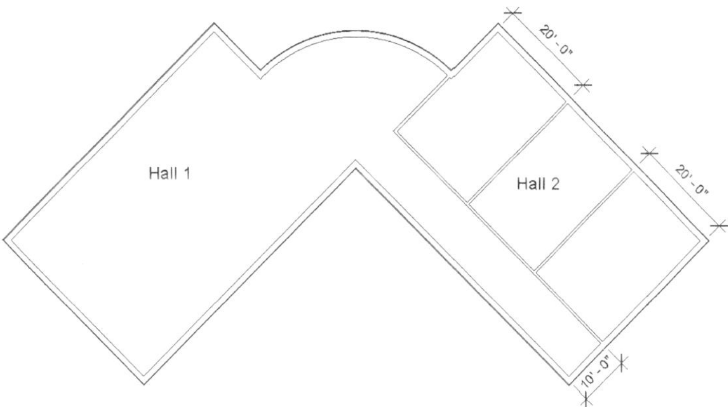

Figure 3-90 *Sketch plan for sketching the interior walls of right portion for the Club project*

Exercise 4 Residential Building- Walls

Create stacked wall type for exterior walls and also create the interior walls for *Residential Building-Walls* project, refer to Figure 3-91. Do not dimension the sketch as dimensions are given only for reference. The project parameters for this exercise are given next.

(Expected time: 30 min)

1. Project file -
   For Imperial *c02_residential_ex3.rvt*
   For Metric *M_c02_residential_ex3.rvt*
2. Exterior wall type-
   For Imperial **Stacked Wall: Exterior - Brick Over CMU w Metal Stud**
   For Metric **Stacked Wall: Exterior - Brick Over CMU w Metal Stud**
3. Exterior wall type-
   For Imperial **Generic- 5"**
   For Metric **Generic- 125mm**
4. Top Constraint- **Level 2**.
5. Location Line- **Wall Centerline**.
6. Inclined walls are parallel to the external walls and perpendicular to each other.
7. Name for saving the file-
   For Imperial **c03_residential_wall_ex4**.
   For Metric **M_c03_residential_wall_ex4**.

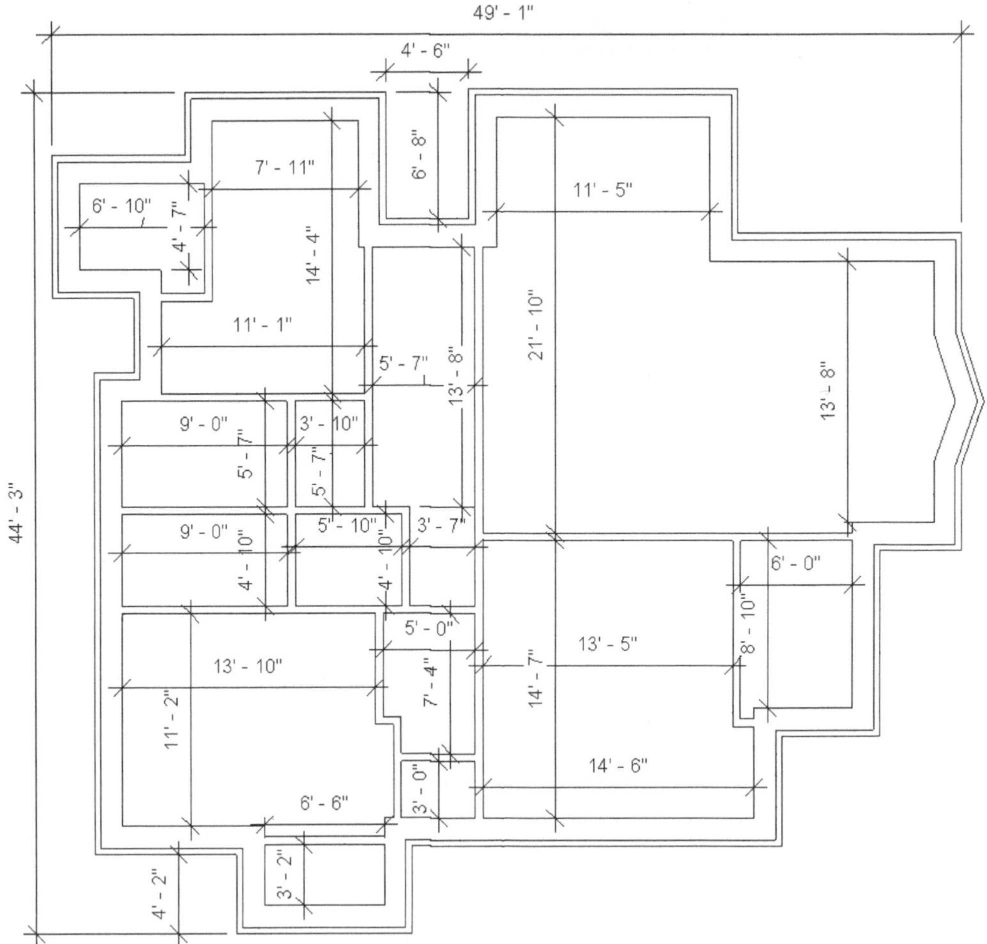

Figure 3-91 Sketch plan for sketching the interior walls of right portion for the Club project

Answers to Self-Evaluation Test

1. c, 2. c, 3. a, 4. **Chain**, 5. **Offset**, 6. **Type Selector**, 7. T, 8. F, 9. T, 10. F

Chapter 4

Using Basic Building Components-I

Learning Objectives

After completing this chapter, you will be able to:

- *Understand the concept of doors*
- *Understand various properties of doors*
- *Add doors to the exterior and interior walls*
- *Understand the concept of windows*
- *Understand various properties of windows*
- *Add windows to a building model*
- *Create door and window openings in walls*
- *Add openings to the walls*

INTRODUCTION

In the previous chapter, you learned to create different types of exterior and interior walls in a building profile. Similar to walls, the positioning of doors and windows also plays an important role in designing a building profile. In this chapter, you will learn the process of selecting and adding doors and windows to a building model. Autodesk Revit has several in-built families of doors and windows which help in adding different types of doors and windows in a building model. In Revit, doors and windows act as hosted components that can be added to any type of wall. In this chapter, you will also learn to use these components and modify their properties.

ADDING DOORS IN A BUILDING MODEL

A door is one of the most frequently used components in a building model. It helps in accessing various exterior and interior spaces in a project. Autodesk Revit provides a variety of predefined door types. You can access these door types by using the options from the **Type Selector** drop-down list of the **Properties** palette. You can also load other door types from the **US Imperial** or **US Metric** folder. A wall acts as a host element for doors. This means that a door can be placed only if there exists a wall. When you add a door to a wall, Autodesk Revit intuitively creates an opening in it. The procedure for adding doors to a building model is described next.

Adding Doors

You can add doors to a building model by using the **Door** tool. You can invoke this tool from the **Build** panel, as shown in Figure 4-1. Alternatively, you can type **DR** to invoke this tool.

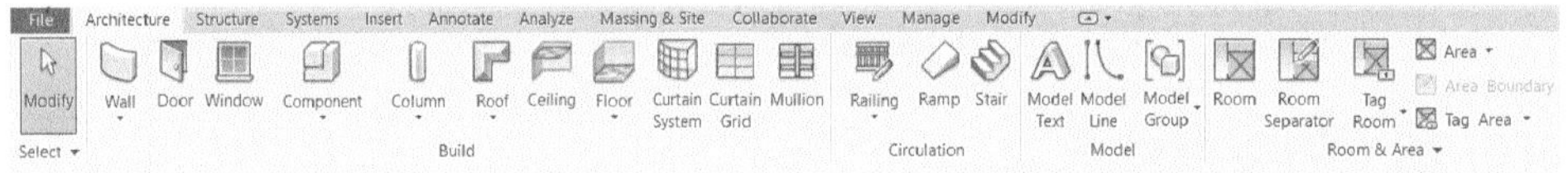

*Figure 4-1 Invoking the **Door** tool from the **Build** panel*

To add a door, invoke the **Door** tool; the **Modify | Place Door** tab will be displayed in the ribbon. Select the desired door type from the **Type Selector** drop-down list in the **Properties** palette and the instance properties of the door will be displayed, as shown in Figure 4-2. This drop-down list displays the in-built door types. Next, after selecting a door type, click on the desired location of a wall to add the door. After adding the door to the building model, you can view and modify its properties. To do so, select the door; the instance properties of the door will be displayed in the **Properties** palette, as shown in Figure 4-3. You will learn more about adding doors to a wall further in this chapter.

Now, to modify the type properties of the selected door type, choose the **Edit Type** button from the **Properties** palette; the **Type Properties** dialog box for the selected door type will be displayed, as shown in Figure 4-4. In this dialog box, change the parameters as per your requirement and then choose the **Preview** button to view the graphical image of the selected door type.

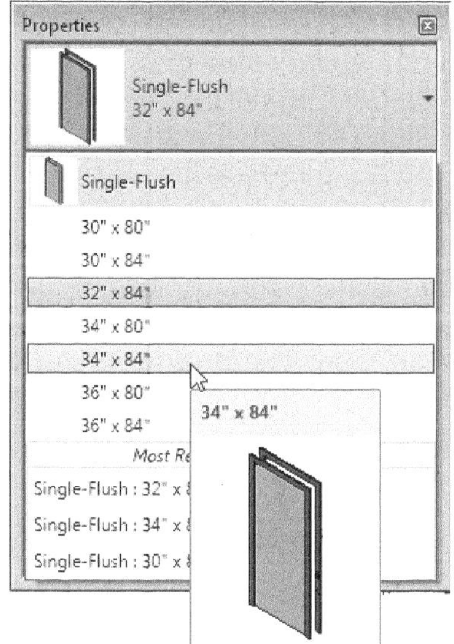

*Figure 4-2 Selecting the door type from the **Properties** palette*

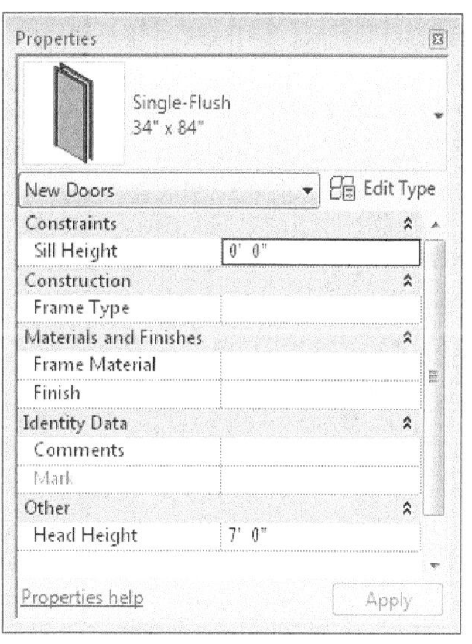

*Figure 4-3 The instance properties displayed for the **Single-Flush: 34" x 84"** door type*

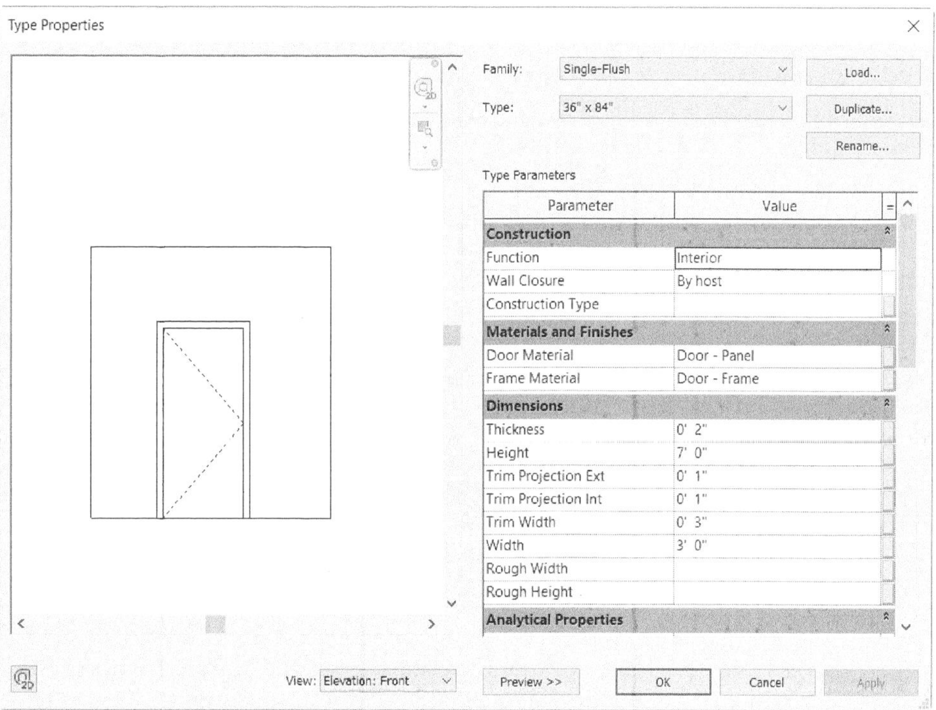

*Figure 4-4 The **Type Properties** dialog box*

Understanding Door Properties

The **Type Properties** dialog box displays the values of different parameters of a door. The type parameters are arranged under various heads based on their properties such as **Construction**, **Analytical Properties**, **Materials and Finishes**, **Dimensions**, **Identity Data**, and **IFC Parameters**. The parameters associated with each property are listed under each head. For example, the **Dimensions** head includes the dimensional type parameters associated with the door type such as **Height**, **Width**, **Trim Width**, and so on. You have the option of either using the default values for these parameters or modifying them to the desired values. However, before modifying the type properties of a predefined door type, it is recommended to create a copy of the original door type and modify the desired properties of the new door type. The **Duplicate** button available on the top right corner in this dialog box is used to create a copy of the door type. When you choose this button, the **Name** edit box will be displayed, prompting you to assign a name to the new door type. Enter a name in this edit box and choose the **OK** button; a new door type is created which inherits the properties of the parent door type. Now, its parameters can be modified as desired. Use the **Rename** button to give a new name to the selected door type. You can use the **Load** button provided on the top right corner of the dialog box to load a door type of the required family from the additional libraries.

Note

*Renaming a door type does not alter its properties. For example, if you rename **34"x 84"** to **36"x 84"**, its width will still remain 34", irrespective of its name.*

Door Type Properties

If you change the type properties of a door, the properties of all instances of that door type in the project will also change. The door type properties are described in the table given next:

Parameter Name	Description
Function	Specifies the function of door. You can set the door function value to Interior or Exterior. This value will be used at the time of scheduling
Wall Closure	Specifies the Wall Closure for the door type. In this case, you can set the layer wrapping for the door type
Construction Type	Specifies the type of construction for the door
Door Material	Specifies the finished material of the door panel. You can select the material of the door panel by clicking on the browse button in the value field. It displays **Material Browser - Door - Panel** dialog box. You can select the desired material from the **Name** list of the displayed dialog box
Frame Material	Specifies the finish material of the door frame and can be selected from the **Name** list of the **Material Browser-Door -Frame** dialog box displayed on clicking the browse button of the value field

Thickness	Specifies the thickness of the door
Height	Used to set the height of the door by editing in the value field
Trim Projection Ext	Specifies the thickness of the trim projection on the exterior side
Trim Projection Int	Specifies the thickness of the trim projection on the interior side
Trim Width	Specifies width of the trim at both sides of door
Width	Specifies width of the door and can be set to desired value
Rough Width	Specifies width of the door type used for scheduling or exporting
Rough Height	Specifies height of the door type used for scheduling or exporting
Assembly Code	Specifies the Assembly Code for the specified door type that can be selected from the hierarchical list
Keynote	This parameter is available for all model elements, detail components, and materials under identity data. You can add or edit the door keynote from the **Keynote** dialog box by clicking on the browse button in the value field of this parameter
Model	Specifies the name to be given to the model door type
Manufacturer	Specifies the name of the manufacturer of the door type
Type Comments	Specifies the comments entered for the door type. You can enter or select the additional information or comments to be added to the door type from the drop-down list, primarily for including in schedules
URL	Specifies the web link of the door type manufacturer
Description	Specifies the description of the door type
Fire Rating	Specifies the fire rating of the door type. You can edit the fire rating of the door type by clicking in the value field corresponding to the fire rating parameter
Cost	Specifies the cost of the door primarily used for costing purpose
Assembly Description	Specifies the description of the assembly of the door type
Type Mark	Specifies a unique value that may be generated in a sequence of creation of the door type

OmniClass	It is a classification system for the construction industry. It uses codes from OmniClass table to filter and identify shared content. A code consits of an OmniClass number and title
Analytical Properties	Specifies the Heat Transfer Coefficient, Thermal Resistance, Solar Heat Gain Coefficient, and Visual Light Transmittance. The values of these options are set by default for the materials available in the **Analytical Properties** drop-down list
Heat Transfer Coefficient	Helps in calculating heat transfer by convection or phase change between a solid or a liquid
Thermal Resistance	Measures temperature difference
Solar Heat Gain Coefficient	Specifies the Solar Heat Gain Coefficient for the door type. Solar radiations entering through a door directly absorbed and released inward
Visual Light Transmittance	Specifies the amount of visible light that passes through a glazing system
Analytical Construction	Specifies the desired construction

Some of the properties of the door are shown graphically in Figure 4-5.

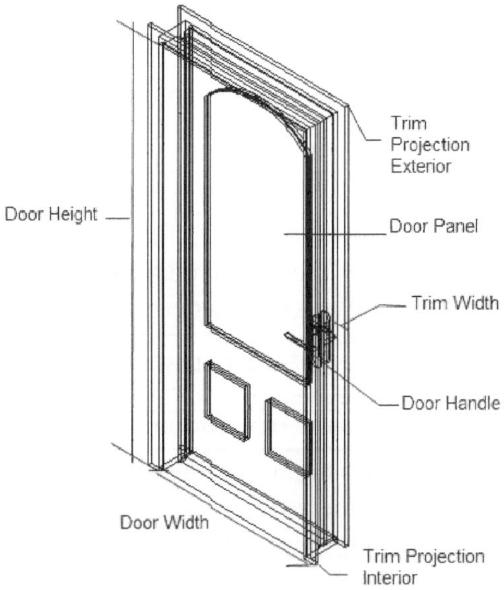

Figure 4-5 *The door properties*

Door Instance Properties

The door instance properties, available in the **Properties** palette, refer to the instance properties of a particular door. On changing these properties, the properties of only a particular instance in the project are changed. The description of various instance parameters is given in the table next:

Parameter Name	Description
Sill Height	Specifies the distance or height of the sill of the door from the specified level
Door Offset	Specifies the offset value of door from the wall instance
Frame Type	Specifies the type of frame used for the door instance
Show Grill	Specifies the presence of mullions in door
Threshold	Specifies to place the door threshold
Frame Material	Specifies the material used for the frame of the instance
Finish	Specifies the finish applied to the door and frame
Image	Specifies the image file corresponding to the door instance. This parameter can be used in the door schedule to display the image of the door instance
Comments	Specifies the comments for the door instance. It can be selected from the drop-down list
Mark	Specifies the mark of the selected door
Phase Created	Specifies the phase in which the door is to be created
Phase Demolished	Specifies whether the door is a part of the existing building or a new structure, or none
Threshold Offset	Specifies the value for the door threshold
Head Height	Specifies the height of the top of the door from the specified level

Adding a Door to a Wall

Doors can be added to a wall in the plan, section, elevation or a 3D view by clicking at the desired location on the wall. After invoking the **Door** tool and selecting the door type, move the cursor over the wall on which it is to be added. The '+' symbol over the cursor indicates that an element is being added. You will notice that the door symbol appears when the cursor is moved over the wall. When the cursor comes close to the upper or the lower face of the wall, the door symbol appears on it, as shown in Figure 4-6. Also, a temporary dimension appears depicting the distance of the center of the door opening from the adjacent walls or wall edges.

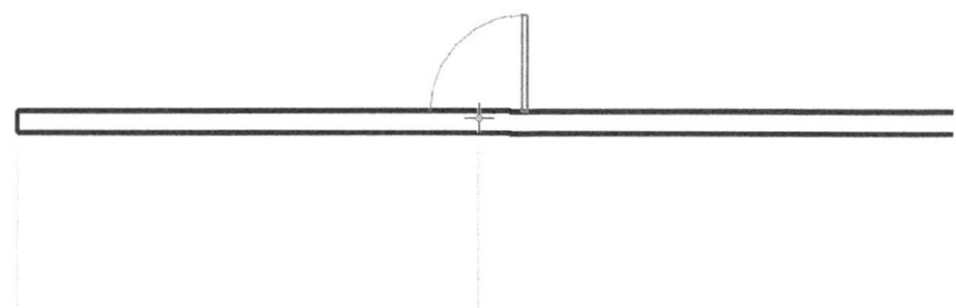

Figure 4-6 *Adding a door to a wall*

Using the temporary dimensions displayed, you can add the door at the desired location. Alternatively, you can first add the door at an approximate location on the wall and then modify its location to the exact dimension. When a door is added, an opening is automatically created in the wall and the edges are also completed, as shown in Figure 4-7. After selecting the door, you will notice that the horizontal and vertical twin arrow symbols appear in the door along with a tag number. To flip the swing-side of the door, click on the twin arrow key that appears parallel to the wall edge. To shift the door to the other side of the wall, click on the twin arrow key that appears perpendicular to the wall edge (vertical, in this case).

To move the added door to the exact dimension, click on the particular temporary dimension text and enter the exact value, as shown in Figure 4-8. The door shifts to the desired location.

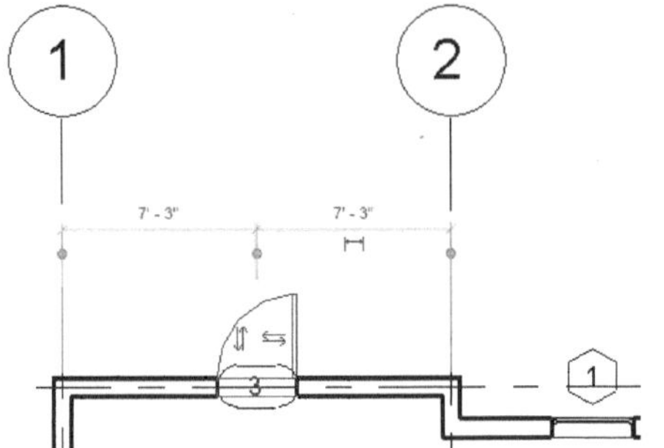

Figure 4-7 *A door added along with its controls*

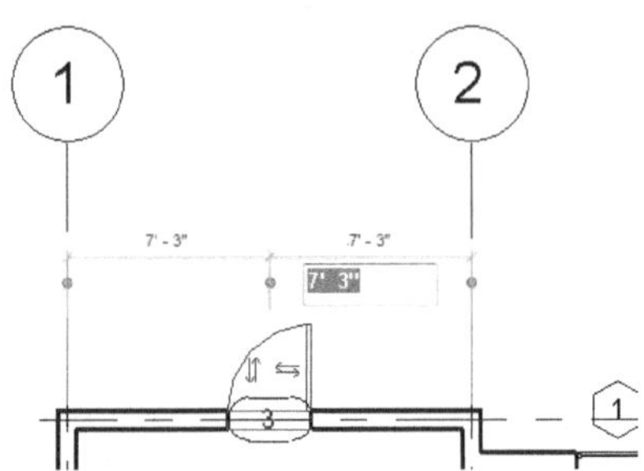

Figure 4-8 *Specifying the exact location of the door*

Tip

To flip the swing of the door, select the door and press the SPACEBAR. Each time you press the SPACEBAR, the door will cycle through all the four possibilities.

Note

A door can be placed in any type of wall regardless of the height of the door. Autodesk Revit 2018 displays alert messages if the door is not placed appropriately.

In Autodesk Revit, when doors are inserted, door tags are generated automatically. They assist in marking the doors and later arranging them in the form of a schedule. The door type tag number increases sequentially when you place a door by using the **Door** tool or when you copy and paste it into the building model. You can, however, give a specific mark or tag to doors individually. The visibility of door tags can be controlled by using the **Visibility/Graphics Overrides for Floor Plan** dialog box. This dialog box can be invoked by typing **VG**, or by selecting the desired door from the drawing and choosing the **Visibility/Graphics** tool in the **Graphics** panel in the **View** tab. Next, if you want to hide the door tags, choose the **Annotation Categories** tab from the **Visibility/Graphics Overrides for Floor Plan** dialog box and clear the **Door Tags** check box. When you invoke the **Door** tool, the option for adding a horizontal or vertical door tag becomes available in the **Options Bar**. You can set the orientation of the door tags to horizontal or vertical by selecting the **Horizontal** or **Vertical** option from the drop-down list displayed in the **Options Bar**.

To change a door type, select the particular instance; the properties and the type of the selected door will be displayed in the **Properties** palette. In the **Properties** palette, select a new door type from the **Type Selector** drop-down list; the selected door will be replaced with the new door type.

In Autodesk Revit, you can create a new door type by using various tools. To create a new door type, choose the **Model In-place** tool from the **Mode** panel of the **Modify | Place Door** tab; the **Name** dialog box will be displayed. In this dialog box, enter a name in the **Name** edit box and choose the **OK** button; the dialog box will be closed and the **Modify** tab will be displayed. Using the tools from this tab, you can create the doors that are specifically designed for that instance.

Note

*On invoking the **Model In-place** tool, the family editor mode will be activated. In this mode, you can use various massing tools from the **Architecture** tab to create an in-place door assembly.*

Apart from the door types available in the **Type Selector** drop-down list, you can use other door types from additional libraries. To access them, choose the **Load Family** tool in the **Mode** panel of the **Modify | Place Door**; the **Load Family** dialog box will be displayed. Additional door types are available in the **Doors** sub folder of the **US Imperial** folder. Select a door type to view its image in the **Preview** area, as shown in Figure 4-9. After selecting the door type, choose the **Open** button. The selected family of doors will be added to the **Type Selector** drop-down list in the **Properties** palette for that project.

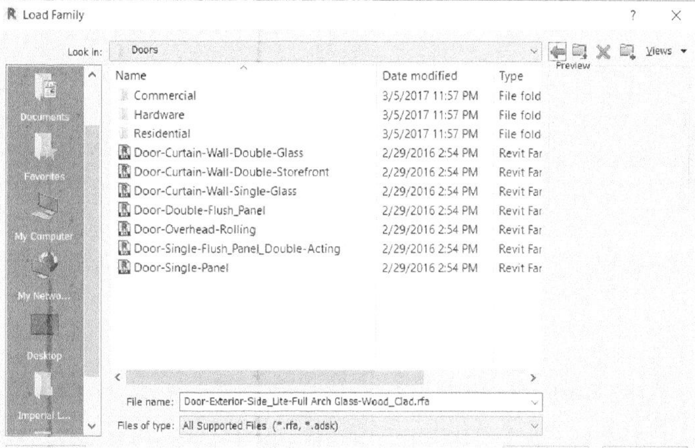

Figure 4-9 *Using the **Load Family** dialog box to load additional door types*

Tip

*Using the **Options Bar**, you can set certain parameters before placing the components. For example, before placing the door, you can set the horizontal or vertical position of door tags and select the leader as well.*

ADDING WINDOWS TO A BUILDING MODEL

Windows form an integral part of any building project. Autodesk Revit provides several in-built window types that can be easily used and added to a building model. Like doors, windows are also dependent on the walls that act as their host element.

Adding Windows

Ribbon: Architecture > Build > Window
Shortcut Key: WN

In Autodesk Revit, you can add windows to a building model by using the **Window** tool. To do so, invoke the **Window** tool from the **Build** panel of the **Architecture** tab, as shown in Figure 4-10; the **Modify|Place Window** tab will be displayed. In this tab, select the window type from the **Type Selector** drop-down list in the **Properties** palette, as shown in Figure 4-11. To add a building model, move the cursor over the wall and click to place it either in the upper face or in the lower face. After adding the window, you can view or change its instance parameters. To do so, select the window from the drawing; the **Properties** palette will be displayed, as shown in Figure 4-12. You can use this palette to view and modify various instance parameters of the selected window such as its Level, Head Height, Sill Height, and others. To modify and view the type parameters of the window, choose the **Edit Type** button in the **Properties** palette; the **Type Properties** dialog box will be displayed. In this dialog box, choose the **Preview** button to view the graphical image of the selected window type, as shown in Figure 4-13.

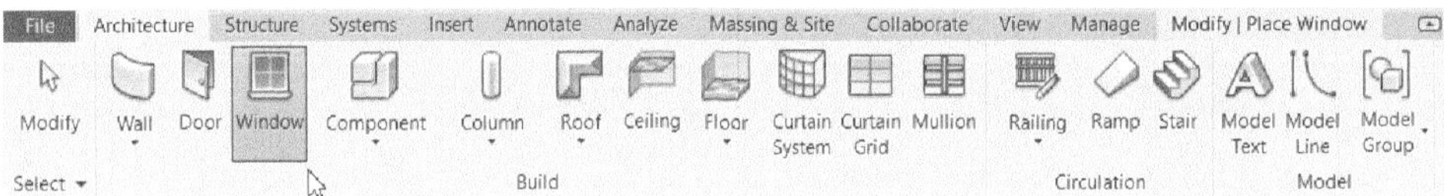

*Figure 4-10 Invoking the **Window** tool from the **Build** panel*

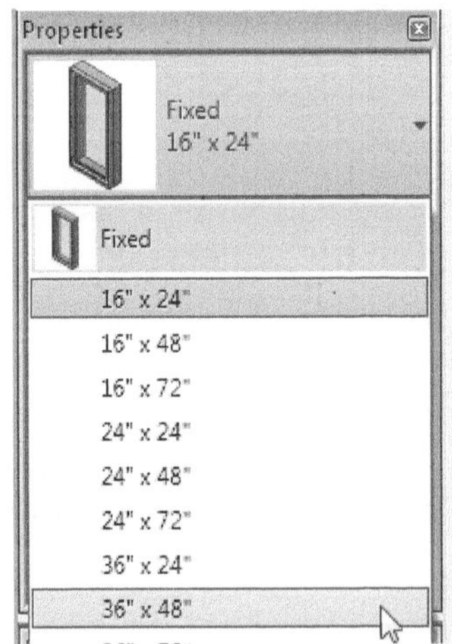

*Figure 4-11 Selecting the window type from the **Type Selector** drop-down list*

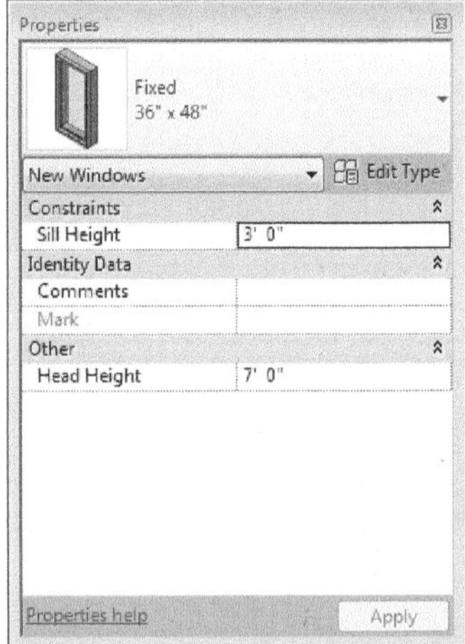

*Figure 4-12 The **Properties** palette for the **Fixed: 36" x 48"** window type*

Understanding Window Properties

The **Type Properties** dialog box displays the type parameters for different components of a window such as **Glass Pane Material**, **Sash Material**, **Default Sill Height**, **Width**, **Height**, and so on. You can click in the value column of each parameter and select from the available options or use the **Load** button provided on the top right corner of the dialog box to load a window family type from the additional libraries. The **Duplicate** button is used to create a copy of the window type with a different name. The new window inherits the properties of the parent window type and its parameters can be modified. By using the **Rename** button, you can give a new name to the selected window type. The window type properties are discussed next.

*Figure 4-13 The **Type Properties** dialog box for the **Fixed: 36" x 48"** window type with the **Preview** button chosen*

Window Type Properties

When you change the type properties of a window type, the properties of all instances of that window type in the project will also change. Various type parameters and their corresponding descriptions are given in the following table:

Parameter Name	**Description**
Wall Closure	Specifies layer wrapping for the window type
Construction Type	Specifies the construction type of the window
Glass Pane Material	Specifies the finish and material of the glass pane and can be selected from the **Material Browser-Glass** dialog box. This dialog box is displayed on clicking the browse button in the value field

Sash Material	Specifies the material assigned to the sash of the window
Height	Specifies the height of the window
Default Sill Height	Specifies the distance of the window from the bottom of the wall, its default value is 3'0". The default value of this parameter can be edited by clicking in the value field of the corresponding parameter
Width	Specifies the width of the window
Window Inset	Specifies the inset of the window from the wall face
Rough Width	Specifies the width used for scheduling or exporting
Rough Height	Specifies the height used for scheduling or exporting
Keynote	This parameter is available for all model elements, detail components, and materials under identity data
Model	Specifies the name to be given to the window type
Manufacturer	Specifies the name of the manufacturer of the window type
Type Comments	Additional information or comments to be added to the window type, primarily for creating schedules
URL	Specifies the weblink of the manufacturer
Description	Specifies the description of the window type
Assembly Description	Specifies the description of the assembly
Type Mark	Specifies the unique value assigned to each window
Cost	Specifies the cost of the window, primarily for costing purpose

Figure 4-14 shows the window properties such as height, width, and sill height.

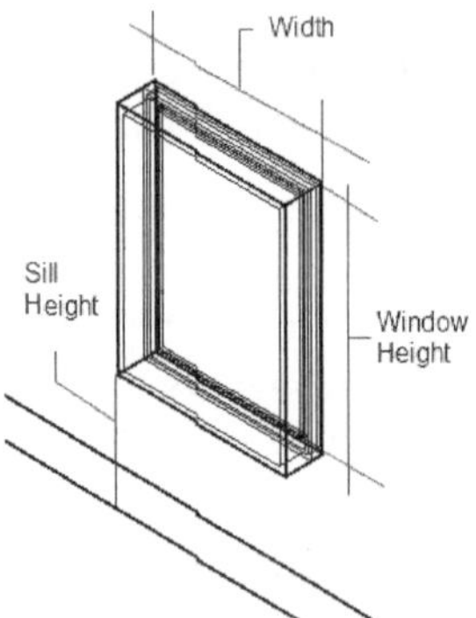

Figure 4-14 *Graphic showing the window properties*

Window Instance Properties

The parameters given in the **Properties** palette displays the window instance properties, and these prameter can be changed to change the instance properties of the selected window. The instance properties of a window are given in the table below.

Parameter Name	Description
Level	Shows the level to which the window belongs and can be used to move the window to a different level
Sill Height	Specifies the distance or height of the sill of the window from the specified level
Image	Specifies the image file corresponding to the window instance. This parameter can be used in the door schedule to display the image of the window instance
Comments	Specifies the window instance that is not covered in the type properties
Mark	Specifies or modifies the mark of the selected window
Phase Created	Specifies whether the window is part of a new construction or an existing construction
Phase Demolished	Specifies whether the window is a part of an existing building or new structure
Head Height	Specifies the height of the top of the window from the specified level

Adding a Window to a Wall

To add a window to a wall, invoke the **Window** tool from the **Architecture** tab of the ribbon and select the window type from the **Type Selector** drop-down list in the **Properties** palette. Next, move the cursor close to the wall on which it needs to be added. The window symbol appears when the cursor is moved over the wall. When the cursor comes close to the lower face of the wall, the window appears on that face. The window appears on the upper face when the cursor comes near to it, as shown in Figure 4-15. Also, notice a temporary dimension, which depicts the distance of the center of the window opening from the adjacent walls or wall edges.

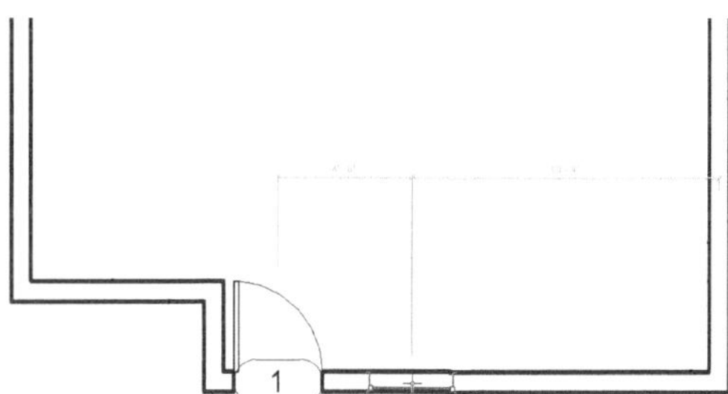

Figure 4-15 *Adding a window to an existing wall*

You can use the temporary dimensions to add the window by clicking at the appropriate location on the wall. Autodesk Revit automatically creates an opening in the wall and the edges also get completed, as shown in Figure 4-16.

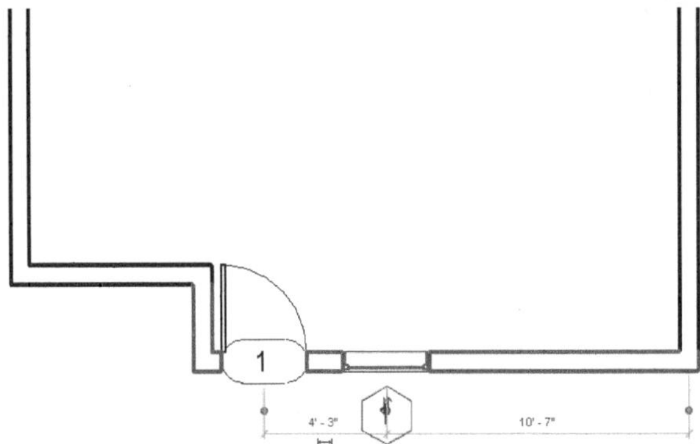

Figure 4-16 Window added to an existing wall

You will also notice a twin arrow symbol on the window, along with a tag number. Click on the symbol to flip the orientation of the window. The flip arrow symbol will appear on the side that is interpreted as the inner side of the window. You can specify the exact position of the window with respect to the adjacent walls or edges after placing it at the approximate location. To specify the dimensional location of a window, click on the particular temporary dimension text and type the exact dimension, as shown in Figure 4-17. The window will shift to the desired location.

Window tags are automatically generated in Autodesk Revit. Unlike doors, however, each window of the same type bears the same tag. Different window types have preassigned marks, which can be changed using the **Type Properties** dialog box. Window tags are used for creating the window schedule.

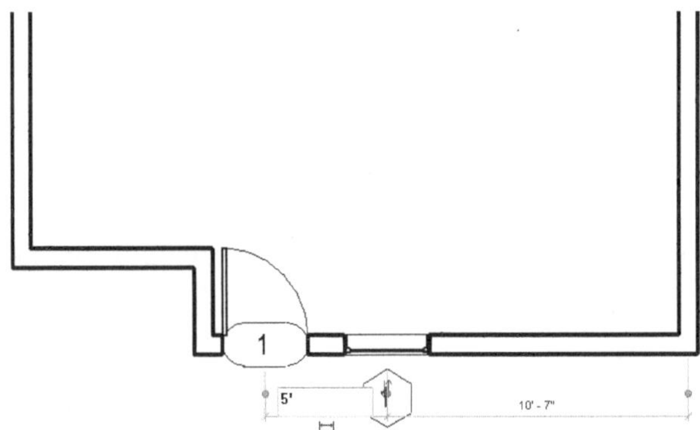

Figure 4-17 Changing the location of the added window

Tip

The depth of the window is automatically created based on the thickness of the host wall. If you change the type of the host wall of a window, the depth of the associated window will change accordingly.

Note

As you place windows in a project, the tag number assigned to them increase by one. You can also give them a specific tag number individually.

Similar to the door tags, the visibility of the window tags can also be controlled in the drawing. To hide the window tags, invoke the **Visibility/Graphics for Floor Plan** dialog box and choose the **Annotation Categories** tab from it. Next, clear the **Window Tags** check box.

Note

*On clearing the **Window Tags** check box in the **Annotation Categories** of the **Visibility/Graphics for Floor Plan** dialog box, the tags will get hidden, but will still remain a part of the project.*

In Autodesk Revit, you can create the windows that are specifically designed for a location or an instance. To do so, choose the **Model In-place** tool from the **Mode** panel of the **Modify |Place Window** tab; the **Name** dialog box will be displayed. In this dialog box, enter the name of the window type in the **Name** edit box and choose the **OK** button; the dialog box will be closed and the **Modify** tab will be displayed. Now, the family editor mode will be activated, and in this mode, you can use various tools to create the in-place window. Apart from the window types displayed in the **Type Selector** drop-down list, you can access other window types as well. To add other window types in the **Type Selector** drop-down list, choose the **Load Family** tool from the **Mode** panel of the **Modify | Place Window** tab; the **Load Family** dialog box will be displayed. In this dialog box, add additional window types from the **Library > US Imperial > Windows** folder. Alternatively, you can use the **Revit Web Content Library** to download more window types to your project.

DOORS AND WINDOWS AS WALL OPENINGS

Autodesk Revit also provides in-built opening types for door and windows. These types are available in the **Openings** subfolder of the **Libraries > US Imperial** folder for Metric (**Libraries > US Metric** folder for Metric) that can be accessed from the **Load Family** dialog box. To invoke this dialog box, choose the **Load Family** tool from the **Load from Library** panel of the **Insert** tab.

To add an opening for the door, invoke the **Load Family** dialog box and then from the **Openings** subfolder, select any of the following family types such as: For Imperial- **Opening with Trim**, **Opening**, **Opening-Door**, **Passage Opening-Cased**, **Opening-Window-Round, Passage Opening-Elliptical Arch, and Opening-Window-Square** or for Metric **M_Opening with Trim**, **M_Opening**, **M_Opening-Door**, **M_Passage Opening-Cased**, **M_Opening-Window-Round, M_Passage Opening-Elliptical Arch, and M_Opening-Window-Square**. After selecting any of the family type, choose the **Open** button in the **Load Family** dialog box; the selected family will be loaded in the project. Now, to place the selected opening type in the wall, choose the **Place a Component** tool from **Architecture > Build > Component** drop-down; the **Modify|Place Component** tab will be displayed. In the **Properties** palette, ensure that the desired opening type is selected in the **Type Selector** drop-down list. Next, click in a desired location in the wall to insert the door opening. In the **Properties** palette, you can also edit the width and height of the door opening.

Similar to adding a door opening, you can insert a window opening. To do so, invoke the **Load Family** dialog box and then select any of the two family types from the **Openings** sub folder:

Opening with Trim or **Opening**. To place the window opening in the wall you will follow the same method as used for inserting the door opening.

OPENINGS IN THE WALL

Ribbon:	Architecture > Opening > Wall

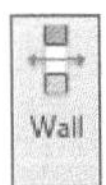

You can create rectangular openings in a curved or straight wall. To cut an opening in a wall, you can use a plan, elevation, or sectional view. Generally, the sectional or elevation view is preferred as locating and placing such views are easy. To cut a rectangular opening in a wall, open a preferred elevation or a section view in which the host wall of the opening is visible. (You will learn about creating the elevation and section views in Chapter 6 of this textbook). Next, choose the **Wall** tool from the **Opening** panel of the **Architecture** tab and then select the wall that will host the opening. Next, click in the desired area in the wall to mark the start point or the first corner point of the rectangular opening. As you move the cursor, a rectangle with its temporary dimensions appears. Click at the desired point in the wall to mark the other corner point of the rectangular opening. Now, you can use the temporary dimensions displayed on the opening to modify the placement of the opening. Next, choose the **Modify** button from the **Select** panel to exit the tool. After exiting the tool, you can select the created opening to modify its properties such as its height, top offset, base offset, and so on from the **Properties** palette.

Tip
Press the shortcut keys SM to snap the inserts to the midpoint of the wall. This is known as jump snap.

TUTORIALS

Tutorial 1 Apartment 1

In this tutorial, you will add doors and windows to the apartment project file created in Tutorial 3 of Chapter 3. Refer to Figure 4-18 for adding these elements. The dimensions and the text have been given for reference and are not to be added. The project file name and parameters to be used are given next. **(Expected time: 30 min)**

1. Project file-
   For Imperial *c03_Apartment1_tut3.rvt*
   For Metric *M_c03_Apartment1_tut3.rvt*

2. Door types to be used
   For Imperial
   1- **Single - Flush: 30"x 84"**
   2 and 3- **Door - Interior - Single - 4 - Panel - Wood - 36"x 84"**
   4- **Door-Exterior-Single-Two_lite - 48" x 96"**
   Door openings- **Passage Opening-Cased** resize to **7'0"**

   For Metric
   1- **M_Single - Flush: 0762 x 2134 mm**
   2 and 3- **M_Door -Interior-Single 4-Panel-Wood-0762 x 2134 mm**
   4- **M_Door-Exterior-Single-Two_lite - 1200 x 2400 mm**
   Door openings- **Passage Opening-Cased** resize to **2134 mm**

3. For Imperial — Window types to be used
   1- **Fixed: 24" x 48"**
   2- **Fixed: 48" x 48"** (with modified width)

   For Metric — Window types to be used
   1- **Fixed: 0610 x 1220 mm**
   2- **Fixed: 1220 x 1220 mm** (with modified width)

The following steps are required to complete this tutorial:

a. Open the file created in Chapter 3.
   For Imperial *c03_Apartment1_tut3.rvt*
   For Metric *c03_Apartment1_tut3.rvt*
   Invoke the **Door** tool.
b. Add doors at approximate locations, refer to Figures 4-19 through 4-24.
c. Load and add door openings, refer to Figure 4-25.
d. Place the door openings to the exact location based on the given parameters, refer to Figure 4-26 and Figure 4-27.
e. Invoke the **Window** tool. Select the window type by using the **Type Selector** drop-down list.
f. Place the windows at approximate locations.
g. Place the windows at the exact location as per the given dimensions, refer to Figures 4-28 through 4-34.
e. Save the project using the **Save As** tool.
   For Imperial *c04_Apartment1_tut1.rvt*
   For Metric **M_***c04_Apartment1_tut1.rvt*
f. Close the project.

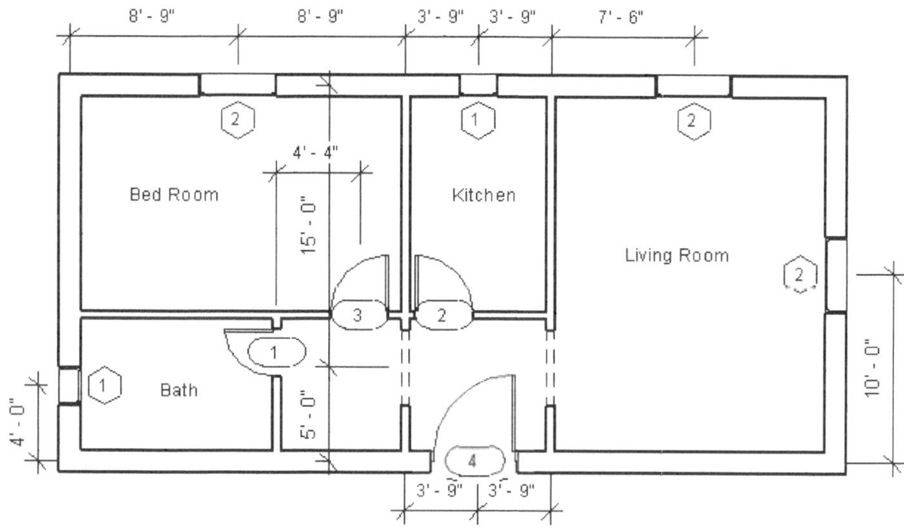

Figure 4-18 *Sketch for adding doors and windows to the Apartment 1 project*

Opening the Existing Project and Invoking the Door Tool

First, you need to open the specified project and invoke the **Door** tool from the **Architecture** tab.

1. Choose **Open > Project** from the **File** menu and open the *c03_Apartment1_tut3.rvt* for Imperial or *M_c03_Apartment1_tut3.rvt* for Metric project file created in Tutorial 3 of Chapter 3.

   You can also download this file from *http://www.cadcim.com*. The path of the file is as follows: *Textbooks > Civil/GIS > Revit Architecture > Exploring Autodesk Revit 2018 for Architecture*

2. Double-click on **Level 1** under the **Floor Plans** head in the **Project Browser**; the floor plan view is displayed.

3. Invoke the **Door** tool from the **Build** panel of the **Architecture** tab; the **Modify | Place Door** tab is displayed.

4. On invoking the **Door** tool, the properties of the door to be added are displayed in the **Properties** palette. In the palette, select the type of door from the **Type Selector** drop-down list.

   For Imperial **Single - Flush: 30" x 84"**
   For Metric **M_Single - Flush: 0762 x 2134 mm**

5. Ensure that the **Tag on Placement** tool is chosen from the **Tag** panel of the **Modify | Place Door** tab.

Adding Doors

In this section, you need to add doors at the approximate location and then modify its location by specifying the exact dimension. You will also use the **Load Family** tool to load the desired door type in the project.

1. Move the cursor close to the interior wall of the **Bath** area to display the door symbol, as shown in Figure 4-19. Notice that as you move the cursor, the side of the door is changed. Click on the interior wall; the door is created at the specified location.

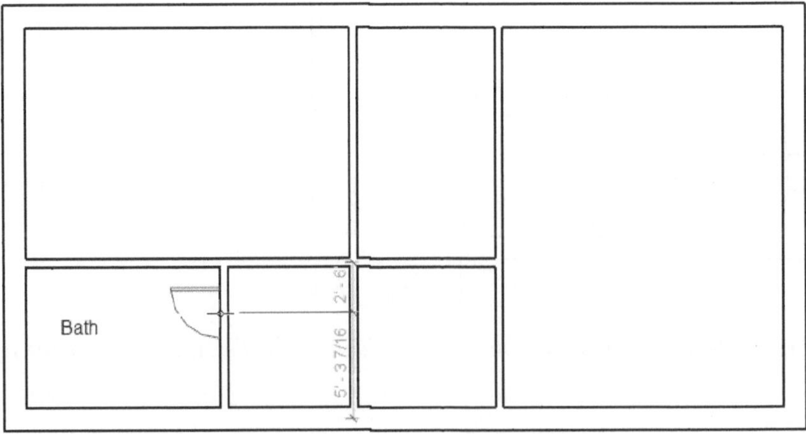

Figure 4-19 *Specifying the location of the bath door*

2. To move the door to the exact location, choose the **Modify** button in the **Select** panel of the **Modify | Doors** tab. Next, select the door added to the drawing; the selected door gets highlighted in blue with the controls and the related temporary dimensions displayed in it.

3. Since the location of the door is given with reference to the upper interior wall, click on the upper temporary dimension, and then enter **2'0"(610 mm)**, as shown in Figure 4-20. Next, press ENTER; the door moves to the specified location.

4. To place the door type 2, invoke the **Door** tool from the **Build** panel of the **Architecture** tab; the **Modify | Place Door** tab is displayed.

5. Choose the **Load Family** tool in the **Mode** panel of this tab; the **Load Family** dialog box is displayed.

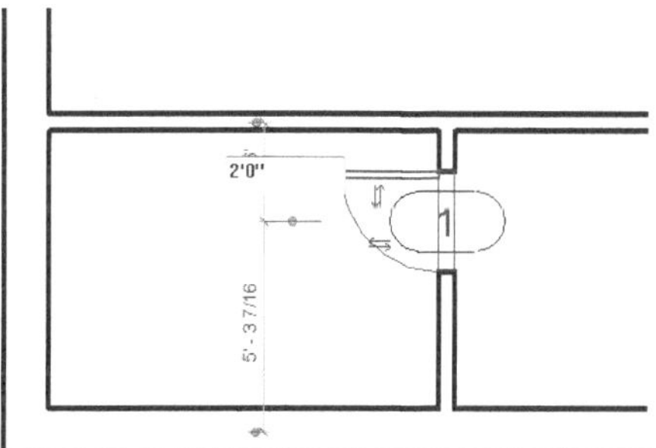

Figure 4-20 *Moving the door to the exact location*

6. In this dialog box, choose the **Doors > Residential** subfolder from the **US Imperial** folder. Next, select the required door family.
   For Imperial **Door - Interior - Single - 4 - Panel - Wood**
   For Metric **M_Door - Interior - Single - 4 - Panel - Wood**
   Next, choose the **Open** button; the **Specify Types** dialog box is displayed. In this dialog box, select the door type **36" x 84"(900 x 2100 mm)** from the **Types** area and choose the **OK** button.

7. Next, ensure that the following door type is selected in the **Type Selector** drop-down list.
   For Imperial **Door - Interior - Single - 4 - Panel - Wood - 36" x 84"**
   For Metric **M_Door - Interior - Single - 4 - Panel - Wood - 900 x 2100 mm**

8. Move the cursor near the interior wall common to the Lobby and the Kitchen areas, as shown in Figure 4-21, and click to add the kitchen door close to this location.

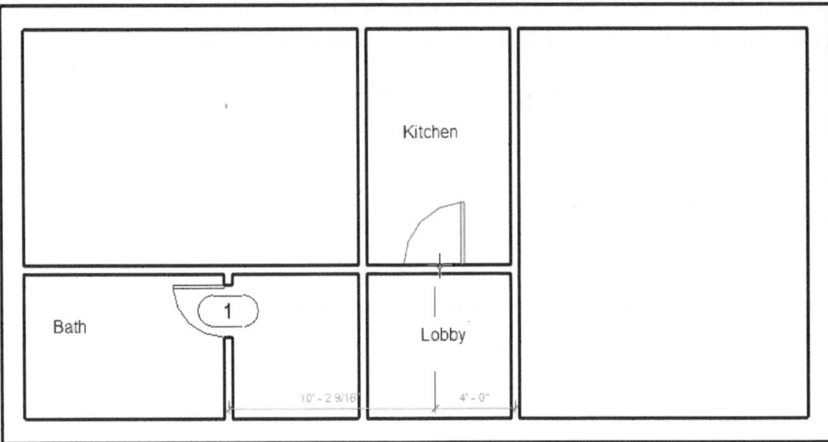

Figure 4-21 Adding the door to the kitchen area

9. Choose the **Modify** button from the **Select** panel. Next, select the door inserted in the drawing; the door gets highlighted and its controls are displayed.

   Notice that the door placed has the swing on the right side whereas the sketch shows a left side opening door, so you need to flip the swing side.

10. Click on the horizontal arrow key to flip the swing side. The swing side of the door is changed, as shown in Figure 4-22.

11. Click on the right side dimension to set it to **5'6" (1677 mm)**, as specified in the sketch plan.

12. Add the door of the same type in the bedroom area at a distance of **4'4" (1320 mm)** from the internal wall, as shown in Figure 4-23.

13. To create the entrance door of the apartment, choose the **Load Family** tool from the **Mode** panel of the **Modify | Place Door** tab; the **Load Family** dialog box is displayed. In this dialog box, add the **Door-Exterior-Single-Two-Lite** for Imperial (**M_ Door-Exterior-Single-Two-Lite** for Metric) family type from the **Doors > Commercial** subfolder in the **US Imperial** folder.

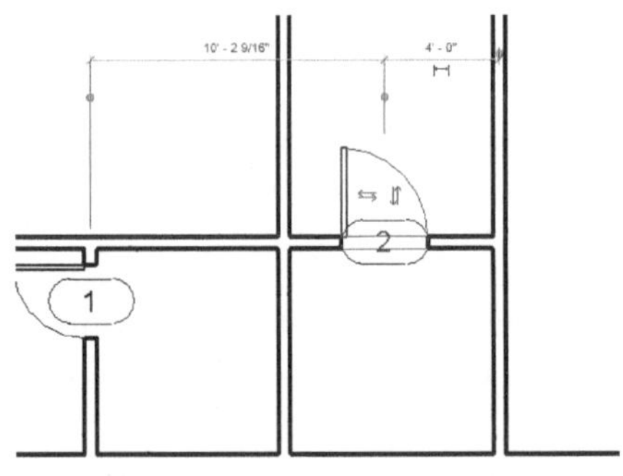

Figure 4-22 Using the flip control to change the swing side of the door

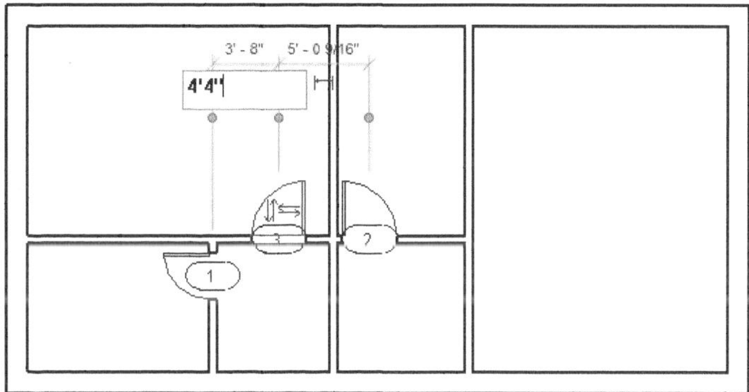

Figure 4-23 Specifying the location of the door in the bedroom area

14. Ensure that the **Door-Exterior-Single-Two_lite - 48" x 96"** option for Imperial or **M_Door-Exterior-Single-Two_lite - 1200 x 2400 mm** option for Metric is selected in the **Type Selector** drop-down list, and then add the door to the lobby area, as per the sketch plan, refer to Figure 4-24. While adding the door, you can use the spacebar to flip the door swing side.

15. After adding the door, choose the **Modify** button and select the recently created door; the temporary dimension is displayed. Click on the left of the temporary dimension and then enter the value **3'9"(1143 mm)**, as shown in Figure 4-24, to move the door to the exact location as given in the sketch plan. Now, press ESC to exit the **Modify | Doors** tab.

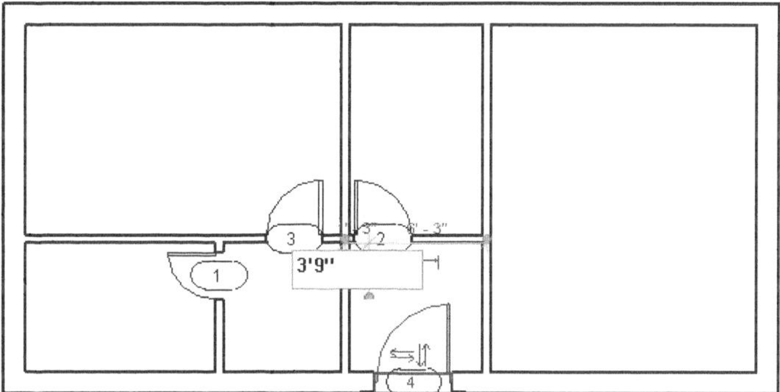

Figure 4-24 Specifying the location of the entrance door

Adding Door Openings

Next, you need to create two door openings in the lobby walls as given in the sketch plan. The openings can be loaded as door families but are added to the model as components.

1. Choose the **Insert** tab and then choose the **Load Family** tool from the **Load from Library** panel; the **Load Family** dialog box is displayed.

2. In the **Load Family** dialog box, select the **Passage Opening-Cased** family from the **Openings** sub-folder of the **US Imperial** folder or select the **M_Passage Opening-Cased** family from the **Openings** sub-folder of the **US Metric** folder. Next, choose the **Open** button to load this family; the **Passage Opening - Cased** family is added as a component type.

3. Invoke the **Place a Component** tool from **Architecture > Build > Component** drop-down; the **Modify | Place Component** tab is displayed.

4. Select the **Passage Opening - Cased 36" x 84"** option for Imperial or **M_Passage Opening - Cased 915 x 2134 mm** for Metric from the **Type Selector** drop-down list in the **Properties** palette, if it is not selected by default.

5. Move the cursor near the location shown in Figure 4-25 and then click to specify the location for the center of the opening. The opening is created.

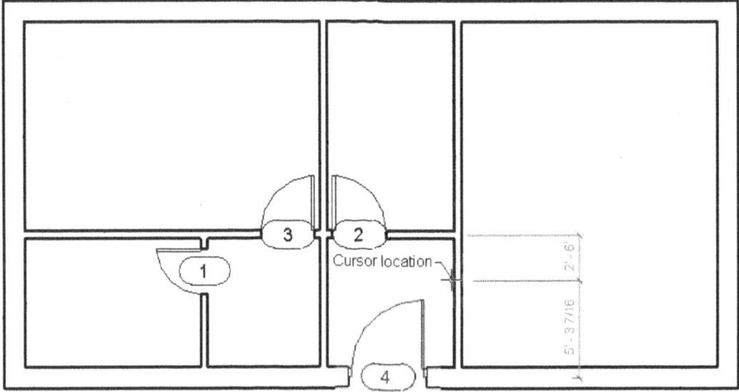

Figure 4-25 Adding openings

6. Now to modify the width of the opening, choose the **Modify** button from the **Select** panel. Select the recently created opening from the drawing; the **Modify | Generic Models** tab is displayed.

7. In this tab, choose the **Type Properties** tool from the **Properties** panel; the **Type Properties** dialog box is displayed.

8. Choose the **Duplicate** button; the **Name** dialog box is displayed. In this dialog box, enter **48" x 84"** for Imperial or **1220 x 2134 mm** for Metric in the **Name** edit box. Next, choose the **OK** button to close the **Name** dialog box.

9. Click in the **Value** field of the **Width** parameter and enter **4'0" (1220 mm)** as the new value.

10. Choose the **OK** button in the **Type Properties** dialog box to close it.

11. To move the opening to the exact location, click on lower temporary dimension, and enter **5'0"(1524 mm)**, as shown in Figure 4-26. Next, press ENTER and ESC to accept the value entered and exit the editing mode.

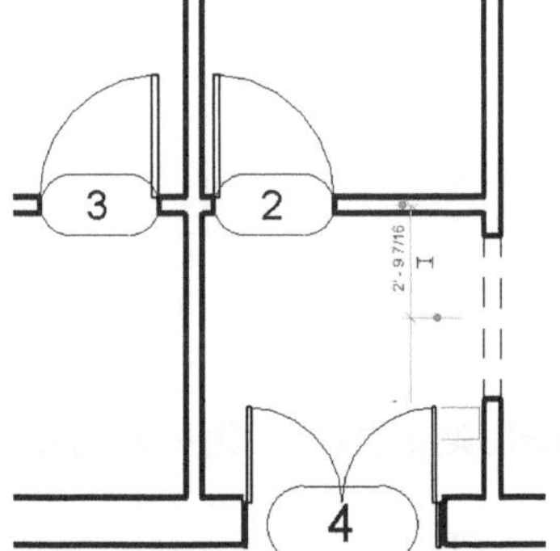

Figure 4-26 Specifying the exact location of the opening

12. Similarly, create the opening of the same size and at the same distance on the opposite wall to complete the creation of doors and opening for the *Apartment 1* project. After adding them, the layout plan of the project will look similar to the plan shown in Figure 4-27.

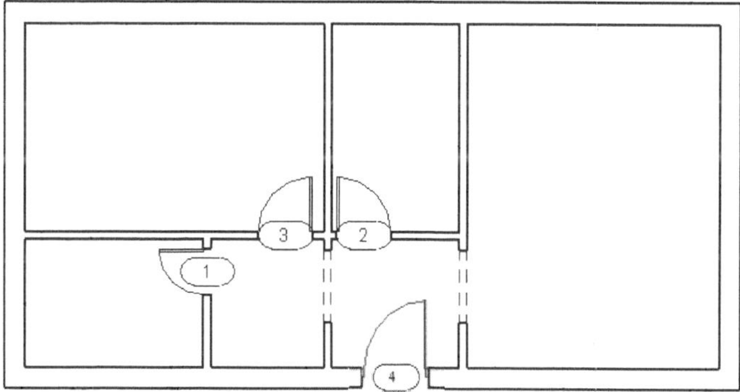

Figure 4-27 *Layout plan with all doors and openings added*

Tip
Doors and door openings can also be added to 3D view, sections, and elevations. You should, however, choose appropriate view to place the door. You can use the temporary dimensions to place the door at the exact location. In case you add a door incorrectly (for example, if the door is not entirely placed on the wall), Autodesk Revit displays a message, alerting you about the conflict and prompting you to take an appropriate action.

Adding Windows

The procedure of adding windows is quite similar to that of adding doors. Invoke the **Window** tool, select the window type, and add the window at an approximate location. You can then modify its location based on the sketch provided next in this tutorial.

1. Invoke the **Window** tool from the **Build** panel of the **Architecture** tab; the **Modify | Place Window** tab is displayed.

2. Ensure that the **Tag on Placement** tool is chosen from the **Tag** panel of the **Modify| Place Window** tab.

3. Click on the **Type Selector** drop-down list to view the in-built window types. To create the window number 1, select **Fixed 24" x 48"** for Imperial or **M_Fixed: 0610 x 1220 mm** for Metric from the drop-down list.

4. Move the cursor close to the exterior wall of the kitchen to display the window symbol, as shown in Figure 4-28. Add the window by clicking on the inner face of the exterior wall. The window is created at the specified location.

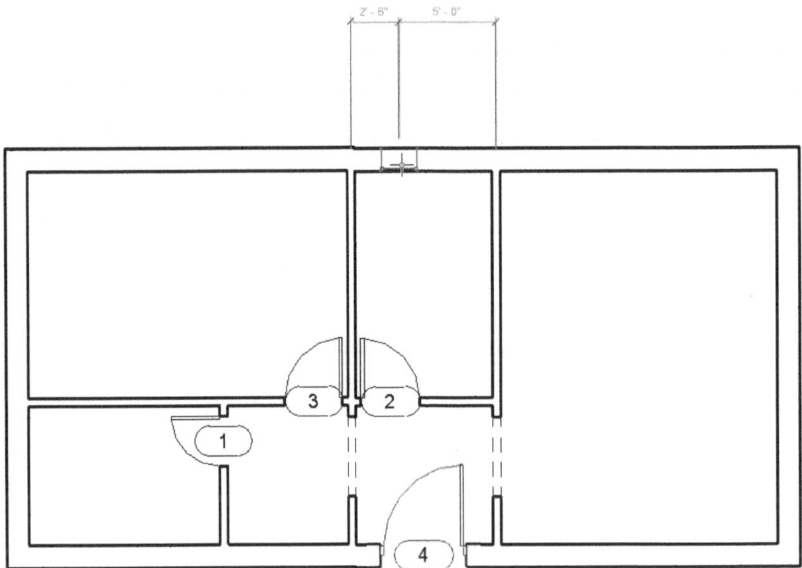

Figure 4-28 Adding the kitchen window to the exterior wall

5. To move the window to the exact location, choose the **Modify** button from the **Select** panel and then select the window from the drawing; it gets highlighted in blue and its controls are displayed.

6. Click on the left temporary dimension and enter **3'9"(1143 mm)**, as shown in Figure 4-29. Press ENTER; the window is moved to the specified location. Similarly, add another window of the same type near the external wall of the bath by invoking the **Window** tool from the **Build** panel, refer to Figure 4-18.

7. After adding the window in the external wall of the bath, you need to move it to the exact location. To do so, select the window; it is highlighted in blue. Click on the lower temporary dimension; an edit box is displayed. Enter **4'0"(1220 mm)** in the edit box, refer to Figure 4-30, and then press ENTER. The window is moved to the desired location. Press the ESC key and exit.

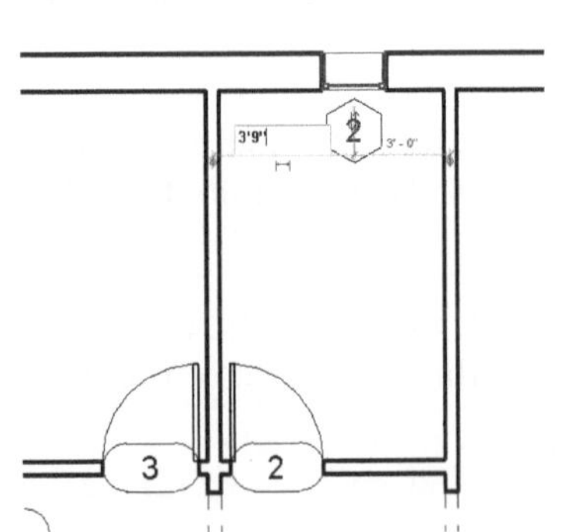

Figure 4-29 Specifying the exact location of the window

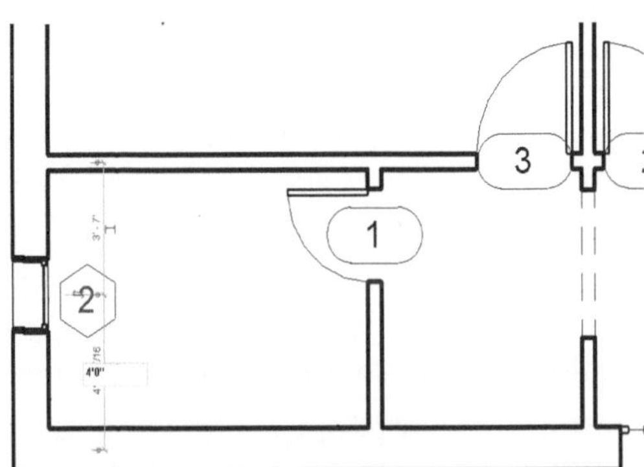

Figure 4-30 Specifying the location of the bath window

Now, you need to add the windows of type 2 to the drawing. These windows have a modified width of **4'0"(1220 mm)**. To add these windows, select the **Fixed: 24" x 48"** for Imperial or **M_Fixed: 0610 x 1220 mm** for Metric window type and create a window type duplicate. Modify window width to 4'0"(1220 mm) by using the **Type Properties** dialog box and add the window at the desired location.

8. Invoke the **Window** tool from the **Build** panel of the **Architecture** tab; the **Modify | Place Window** tab is displayed.

9. In the **Type Selector** drop-down list, select the **Fixed: 24" x 48"** (**M_Fixed: 610 x 1220 mm** for Metric) window type. Next, choose the **Edit Type** button in the **Properties** palette; the **Type Properties** dialog box is displayed.

10. In this dialog box, choose the **Duplicate** button; the **Name** dialog box is displayed. In the **Name** edit box, enter **48" x 48" (1220 x 1220 mm)** and then choose the **OK** button.

11. In the **Value** field for the **Width** type parameter, enter **4'0"(1220 mm)** and then choose the **Apply** and **OK** to close the **Type Properties** dialog box and return to the drawing window.

    Notice that the **Fixed: 48" x 48" (M_Fixed: 1220 x 1220 mm** for Metric) window type is added to the **Type Selector** drop-down list.

12. Move the cursor near the exterior wall of the bedroom and click to place the window. Press ESC twice to exit.

13. Now, select the added bedroom window; the window gets highlighted in blue color and its controls are displayed. Click on the temporary dimension displayed at the left and enter **8'9" (2667 mm)** to specify the location of the bedroom window, as shown in Figure 4-31. The window is moved to the desired location. Similarly, add the windows of the same type to the walls of the living room and specify their respective locations based on the sketch plan given, refer to Figures 4-32 and 4-33.

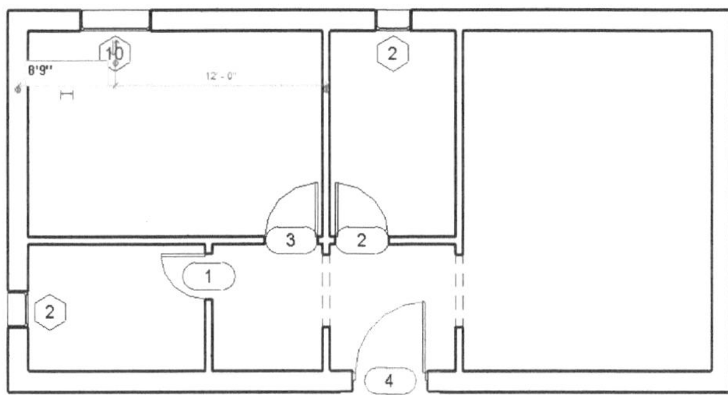

Figure 4-31 *Specifying the location of the bedroom window*

14. To change the window tag numbers, move the cursor over the number in any of the window tags marked 13 (tag number may vary) and double-click; an edit box is displayed. Enter **1** in the edit box and press ENTER; the **Revit** message box is displayed. Choose **Yes** in the message box; the window tag is renamed. Similarly, replace the other window tags marked 13 with the tag mark 1 and those marked 10 with the tag mark 2, refer to Figure 4-34. You will notice that the tag marks of other instances of the same window type are immediately modified.

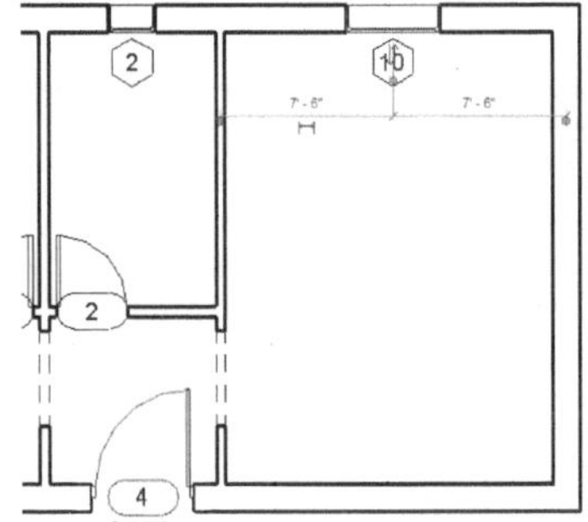

Figure 4-32 *Specifying the location of the first living room window*

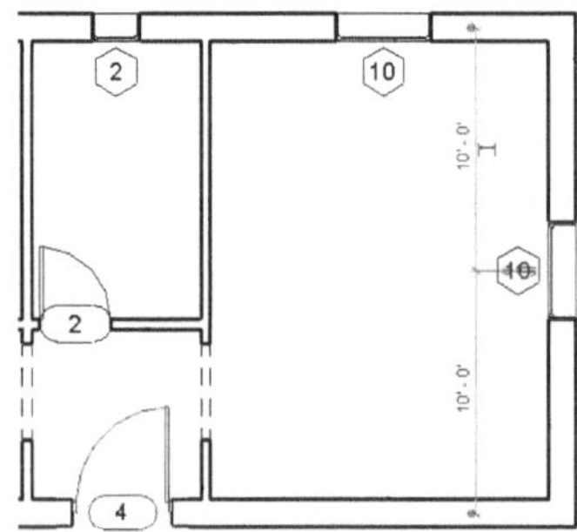

Figure 4-33 *Adding the second living room window using temporary dimensions*

The Level 1 plan should look similar to the plan shown in Figure 4-34.

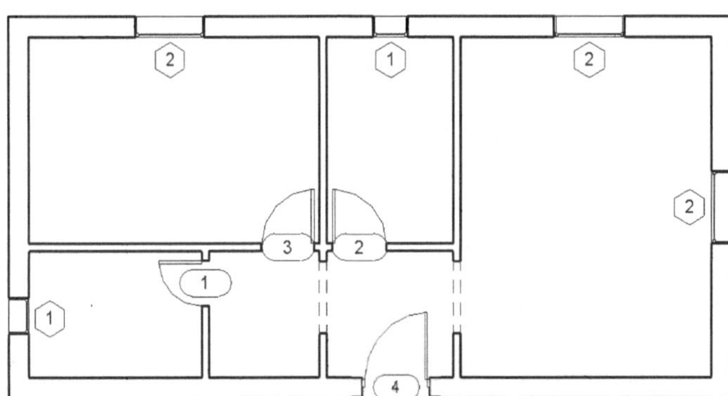

Figure 4-34 *Completed project plan with renamed window tags*

15. To view the plan in 3D, choose the **Default 3D View** tool from the **View > Create > 3D View** drop-down; the 3D view of the project is displayed, as shown in Figure 4-35.

Saving the Project

In this section, you will save the project file using the **Save As** tool.

1. Choose **Save As > Project** from **File** menu; the **Save As** dialog box is displayed. Create a folder with the name **c04_revit_2018_tut** and enter the desired name in the **File name** edit box.
   For Imperial **c04_Apartment1_tut1**
   For Metric **M_c04_Apartment1_tut1**
   Choose **Save**; the file is saved.

2. Choose **Close** from **File** menu to close the project file.

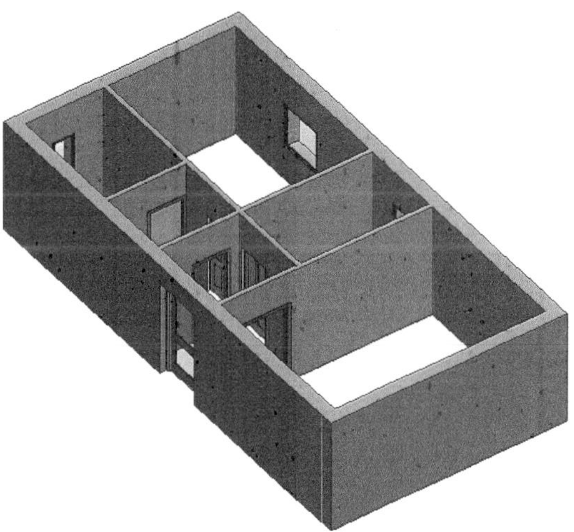

Figure 4-35 *3D view of the Apartment 1 project*

Tutorial 2 Club

In this tutorial, you will add doors and windows to Hall 1 and Lounge of the *Club* project created in Exercise 3 of Chapter 3. The centerline dimensions of the location of the doors and windows are given in Figure 4-36. You will create the doors and windows of Hall 2 in Exercise 2 later in this chapter. Use the following project file and parameters for this tutorial.

(Expected time: 30 min)

1. Project file-
   For Imperial *c03_Club_ex3.rvt*
   For Metric *M_c03_Club_ex3.rvt*

2. Door types to be used
   For Imperial 1, 2, and 3- **Door-Interior-Single-Full Glass Wood- 36" x 84"**
   4- **Door-Single-Panel: 36" x 84"**
   5- **Door- Double- Glass - 72"x 84"**
   For Metric 1, 2, and 3-
   M_Door-Interior-Single-Full Glass Wood- 900 x 2100 mm
   4- **M_Door- Single- Panel: 900 x 2100 mm**
   5- **M_Door- Double- Glass - 1830 x 2134 mm**

3. Window types to be used
   For Imperial 1- **Fixed: 36" x 48"**
   For Metric 1- **M_Fixed: 0915 x 1220 mm**

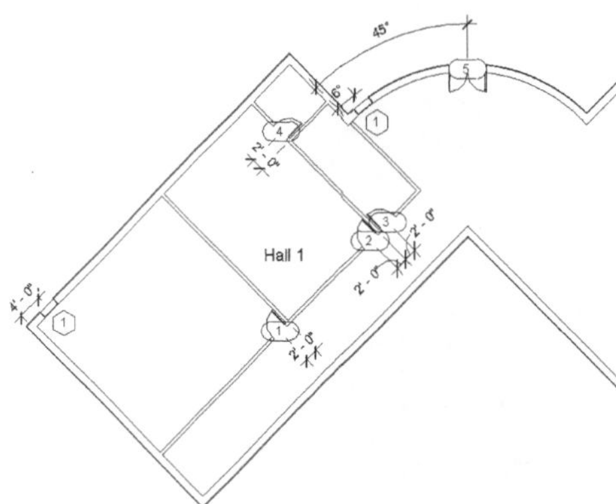

Figure 4-36 *Sketch plan for adding doors and windows to the Club project*

The following steps are required to complete this tutorial:

a. Open the file created in Chapter 3.
   For Imperial *c03_Club_ex3.rvt*
   For Metric *M_c03_Club_ex3.rvt*
   Invoke the **Door** tool.
b. Select the door type by using the **Type Selector** drop-down list.
c. Add the doors at approximate locations, refer to Figures 4-37 through 4-44.
d. Change the placement of the door to the desired location.
e. Invoke the **Window** tool and select the window type using the **Type Selector** drop-down list.
f. Add the windows at approximate locations, refer to Figures 4-45 through 4-47.
g. Modify the placement of windows to the exact location, based on the given sketch plan.
h. Save the project using the **Save As** tool.
   For Imperial *c04_Club_tut2.rvt*
   For Metric **M**_*c04_Club_tut2.rvt*
i. Close the project.

Opening the Existing Project and Invoking the Door Tool

First, you need to open the *Club* project and then invoke the **Door** tool.

1. Choose **Open > Project** from the **File** menu and open the *c03_Club_ex3.rvt* for Imperial *M_c03_Club_ex3.rvt* for Metric project file created in Exercise 3 of Chapter 3. You can also download this file from *http://www.cadcim.com*. The path of the file is as follows: *Textbooks > Civil/GIS > Revit Architecture > Exploring Autodesk Revit 2018 for Architecture*

2. Invoke the **Door** tool from the **Build** panel of the **Architecture** tab; the **Modify | Place Door** tab is displayed. Alternatively, type **DR**.

Selecting a Door Type

Select the door type 1 and add it to the project. The project parameters indicate that the door type is to be loaded from the **US Imperial** folder. To access the **US Imperial** folder, choose the **Load Family** tool from the **Mode** panel of the **Modify | Place Door** tab.

1. Choose the **Load Family** tool from the **Mode** panel in the **Modify | Place Door** tab; the **Load Family** dialog box is displayed.

2. In this dialog box, open the **Doors > Residential** folder and select the door type **Door-Interior-Single-Full Glass Wood**. Choose **Open** to load the family of this door type; the **Specify Types** dialog box is displayed. Select the **36" x 84"** from the **Types** area and choose the **OK** button.

3. Next, ensure that the **Door-Interior-Single-Full Glass Wood: 36" x 84"** option for Imperial or **M_Door-Interior-Single-Full Glass Wood- 900 x 2100 mm** option for Metric is selected by default in the **Type Selector** drop-down list.

Adding Doors

You can add a door at the desired location by clicking at an approximate point in its host wall and then modifying its location by specifying the exact dimension. First you need to add the door type 1 and then the other door types.

1. Move the cursor close to the interior wall face to display the door symbol, as shown in Figure 4-37. Notice that the side of the door changes as you move the cursor.

2. Place the door by clicking on the interior wall and then press ESC twice to exit. On doing so, the door is added to the exact location.

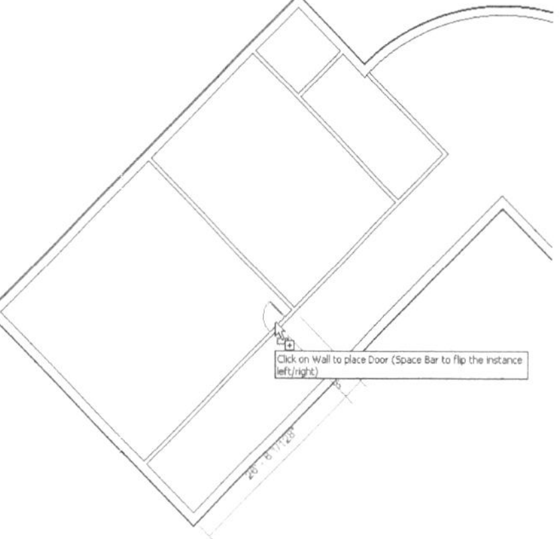

Figure 4-37 *Adding the door*

3. To move the door to the exact location, select the door; it gets highlighted in blue and its controls are displayed.

4. As the location of the door is given with reference to the interior wall, click on the right temporary dimension and enter **2'0"(610 mm)**, as shown in Figure 4-38. Press ESC to exit the setting of dimensions. The door moves to the desired location.

Note

Depending on the placement of the cursor, the door side and swing might not be same as desired. If required, click on the flip control arrows or the door swing arrows to achieve the desired orientation.

5. Add the next door using the same door type by clicking at the approximate location, as shown in Figure 4-39. Press ESC twice.

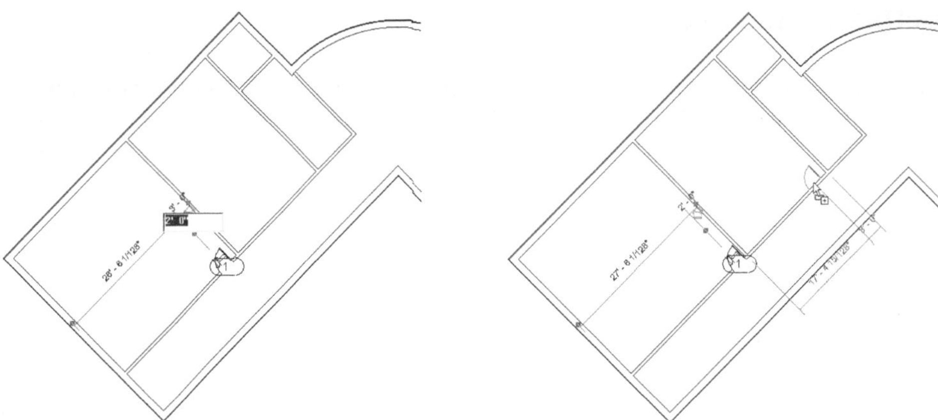

Figure 4-38 Editing the location of the door

Figure 4-39 Adding next door

6. Now, select the door and click on the temporary dimension between the door center and the interior wall and enter the value **3'0"(914.4 mm)** in the edit box, as shown in Figure 4-40. The door moves to the desired location.

7. Add another door at the location shown in Figure 4-41. You may need to use the flip arrows to orient the door swing in the desired direction.

8. To place the next door type, load the door and select **Door- Single- Panel - 36" x 84"** option for Imperial or **M_Door- Single- Panel - 900 x 2100 mm** option for Metric from the **Type Selector** drop-down list, as specified in the project parameters.

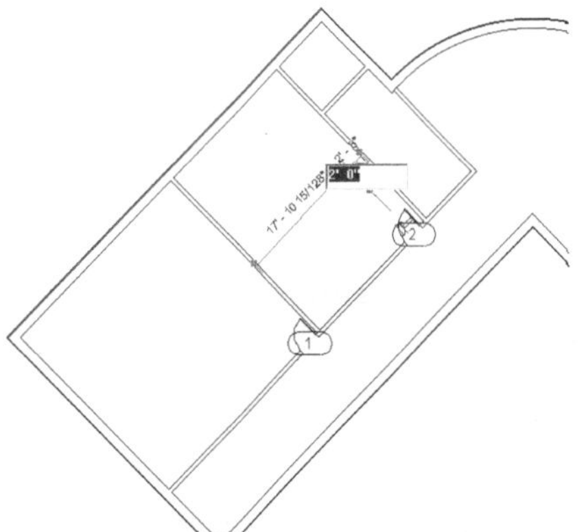

Figure 4-40 Editing the location of the next door

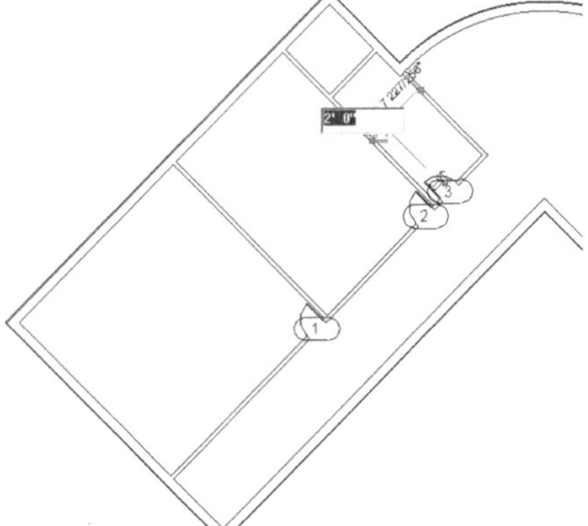

Figure 4-41 Specifying the location of the next door

9. Move the cursor near the interior wall and click to add the door close to the location, as shown in Figure 4-42. Press ESC to exit.

10. Select the door added last in the drawing; it gets highlighted in blue and its controls are displayed.

11. Click on the right side dimension and enter **3'0"(914.4 mm)**, as shown in Figure 4-42.

12. To create the entrance door, invoke the **Door** tool again and then choose the **Load Family** tool from the **Mode** panel; the **Load Family** dialog box is displayed. In the dialog box, load **Door- Double-Glass** from the **US Imperial > Doors** folder; the **Specify Types** dialog box is displayed. Select the **72" x 84"** in the **Types** area and choose the **OK** button.

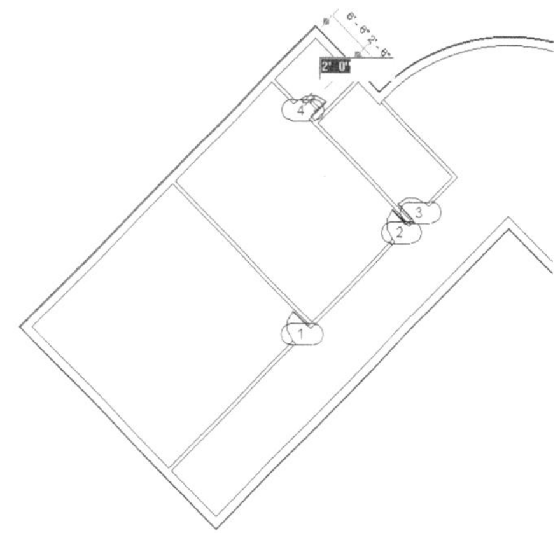

Figure 4-42 Adding a new door type

13. Ensure that the **Door- Double-Glass: 72" x 84"** door type is selected for Imperial or **M_Door- Double-Glass - 1830 x 2134 mm** for Metric from the **Type Selector** drop-down list in the **Properties** palette, if not selected by default.

14. Move the cursor near the main door location, as shown in Figure 4-43. Press SPACEBAR to flip the swing side of the door to the desired side, if required, and click to create the door.

15. Click on the temporary dimension and set the angle to 46 degrees, as shown in Figure 4-44. Press ENTER.

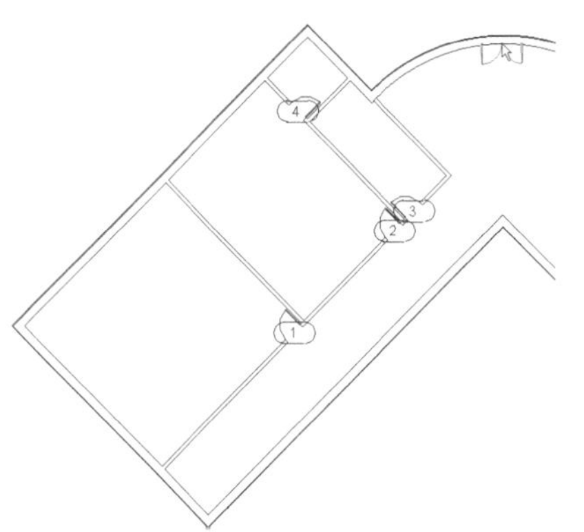

Figure 4-43 Adding the entrance door

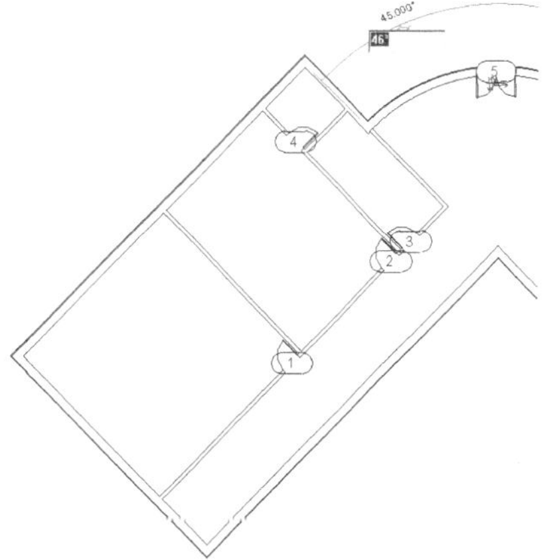

Figure 4-44 Specifying the angular dimension

16. Press ESC twice to exit the selection.

Adding Windows

The procedure for adding windows is similar to that for adding doors. After invoking the **Window** tool and selecting the required window type, click at the approximate location to add it. The location can then be modified to the exact dimension as specified in the sketch plan.

1. Choose **Window** from the **Build** panel of the **Architecture** tab; the **Modify | Place Window** tab is displayed.

2. Select the **Fixed 36" x 48"**option for Imperial **M_Fixed: 0915 x 1220 mm** for Metric from the **Type Selector** drop-down list in the **Properties** palette.

3. Move the cursor close to the exterior wall of Hall 1 to display the window symbol, as shown in Figure 4-45. Add the window by clicking on the exterior wall.

Tip
*If tags are displayed with doors and windows then choose the **Tag on Placement** tool from the **Tag** panel of the **Modify|Place Window** tab.*

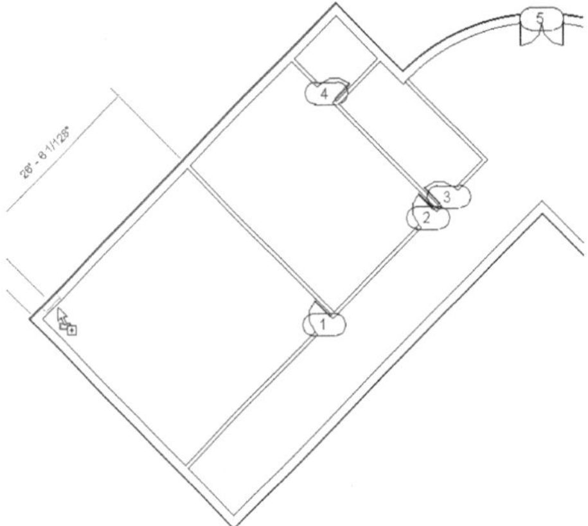

Figure 4-45 *Moving the cursor near the wall of Hall 1 to add window*

4. Next, to move the window to the exact location, choose the **Modify** button from the **Select** panel. Then, select the window, click on the lower temporary dimension, and enter **4'0"(1219 mm)**, as shown in Figure 4-46. The window moves to the desired location.

5. Repeat step 1 through step 3 to add another window by clicking near the left end of the curved wall, refer to Figure 4-47.

6. Select the window created and enter **6** as the angular dimension, as shown in Figure 4-47. The window moves to the desired location.

7. Next, select the window tag and click on the tag number; an edit box is displayed. Enter **1** in the edit box and press ENTER; the **Revit** message box is displayed. Choose **Yes**; the window tag is renamed.

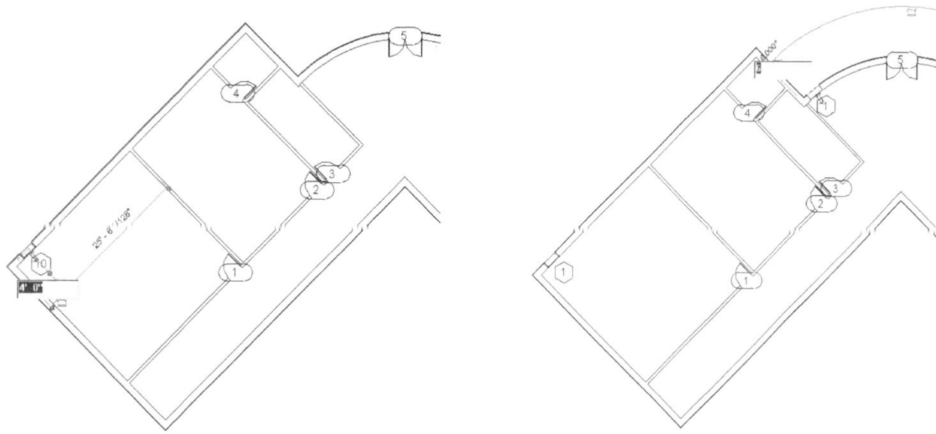

Figure 4-46 Editing the location of the window

Figure 4-47 Adding windows

Saving the Project

In this section, you will save the project file using the **Save As** tool.

1. Choose **Save As > Project** from the **File** menu and enter the required name in the **File name** edit box of the **Save As** dialog box.
   For Imperial **c04_Club_tut2**
   For Metric **M_c04_Club_tut2**
   Choose the save button. The project file is saved.

2. Choose **Close** from the **File** menu to close the project file.

Self-Evaluation Test

Answer the following questions and then compare them to those given at the end of this chapter:

1. Which of the following parameters of doors is an instance property?

   (a) **Frame Material** (b) **Thickness**
   (c) **Level** (d) **Fire Rating**

2. Which of the following shortcut keys is used for invoking the **Visibility/ Graphics Overrides** dialog box?

   (a) **VO** (b) **VD**
   (c) **VG** (d) **VB**

3. A loaded door type can be selected from the _________ drop-down list.

4. You can import and load additional door and window types by choosing the _________ button from the **Modify | Place Component** tab of the ribbon.

5. Using the _________ button in the **Type Properties** dialog box, a copy of an existing door type can be created.

6. The _________ type parameter indicates the height of a door.

7. You can add a door or a window to a project without creating a wall. (T/F)

8. The type parameters of a door can be modified in the **Properties** palette. (T/F)

9. You can change the swing side of a door after adding it to a wall. (T/F)

10. You can add windows to the plan view only. (T/F)

11. The door and window tags are automatically created in Autodesk Revit. (T/F)

12. In the **Type Properties** dialog box, the **Rename** button is used to change the name of a door or a window. (T/F)

Review Questions

Answer the following questions:

1. Which of the following parameters of the window cannot be modified in the **Properties** palette?

   (a) **Level** (b) **Assembly Code**
   (c) **Head Height** (d) **Mark**

2. Which of the following keys can be used to flip the swing side of a door before adding it to a wall?

   (a) TAB (b) SPACEBAR
   (c) ALT (d) ESC

3. Which of the following tab contains the Window **tool**?

   (a) **Design** (b) **Modify**
   (c) **Architecture** (d) **Insert**

4. Which of the following is a door instance parameter?

   (a) **Level** (b) **Thickness**
   (c) **Door** (d) **Material Height**

5. The door tag mark cannot be changed after the door is created. (T/F)

6. When you add a door or a window to a wall, Autodesk Revit automatically creates an opening in the host wall. (T/F)

7. Door tags increases automatically as you add doors to a project. (T/F)

8. You cannot control the visibility of the door and the window tags in the plan view. (T/F)

9. When you modify the width of a door type, its name is automatically modified. (T/F)

10. You can modify the width and height of a window in the **Properties** palette. (T/F)

11. While adding windows, you need to specify the thickness of the window with respect to the thickness of the wall. (T/F)

12. After placing a door at an approximate location on the wall, it can be modified to the exact location. (T/F)

EXERCISES

Exercise 1 Apartment 2

Add doors, windows, and openings to the *Apartment 2* project, created in Exercise 1 of Chapter 3, refer to Figure 4-48. The dimensions and text need not to be mentioned. Use the following project parameters: **(Expected time: 30 min)**

1. Project file-
   For Imperial *c03_Apartment2_ex1.rvt*
   For Metric *M_c03_Apartment2_ex1.rvt*

2. Door types to be used:
   For Imperial Bath and kitchen doors- **Door- Single - Panel: 36" x 84"**
   Bedroom and Lobby door- **Door-Interior-Double-Full Glass Wood - 36" x 84"**
   Door openings in dining (dashed lines)- **4'0" x 7'0"** using **Passage-Opening Cased : 36"x 84"**
   Distance of the door centerlines from wall centerlines- **2'0"**
   For Metric Bath and kitchen doors- **M_Door- Single- Panel: 0915 x 2134 mm**
   Bedroom door- **M_Door-Interior-Double-Full Glass Wood- 1500 x 2000 mm**
   Lobby door- **M_Double-Interior-Double-Full Glass Wood - 900 x 2100 mm**
   Door openings in dining (dashed lines)- **1220 x 2134 mm** using **M_Passage-Opening Cased : 0915 x 2134 mm**
   Distance of the door centerlines from wall centerlines- **610 mm**

3. Window types to be used
   For Imperial Bedroom and living room windows - **Fixed: 36" x 48"**
   Bath and kitchen windows- **Fixed: 24" X 48"**
   For Metric Bedroom and living room windows - **M_Fixed: 0915 x 1220 mm**
   Bath and kitchen windows- **M_Fixed: 0610 X 1220 mm**

4. File name to be saved-
   For Imperial **c04_Apartment2_ex1**
   For Metric **M_c04_Apartment2_ex1**

   For the distance of window centerlines from wall centerlines refer to Figure 4-48.

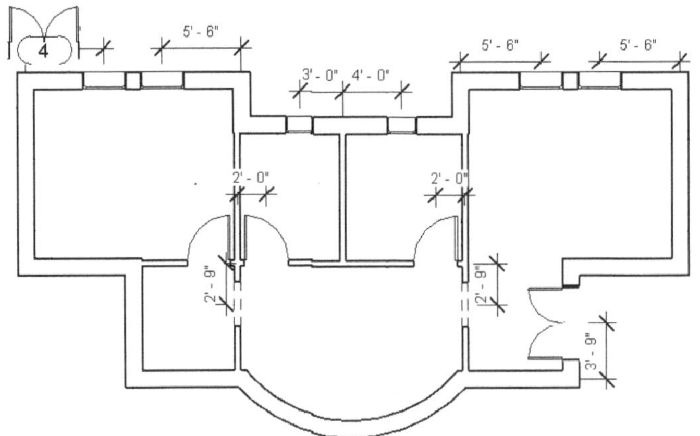

Figure 4-48 *Sketch plan for adding doors and windows to the Apartment 2 project*

Exercise 2 Elevator and Stair Lobby

Add doors, windows, and openings to the *Elevator and Stair Lobby* project created in Exercise 2 of Chapter 3, refer to Figure 4-49. Do not add text or dimensions as they are given for reference only. Use the following project parameters. **(Expected time: 30 min)**

1. Project File-
   For Imperial *c03_ElevatorandStairLobby_ex2.rvt*
   For Metric *M_c03_ElevatorandStairLobby_ex2.rvt*

2. Door types to be used-
   For Imperial **Single - Flush: 36" x 84",**
   Distance of door centerlines from wall centerlines- **2'6"**
   Door openings - **4'0" x 7'0"**
   Passage Opening-Cased- 36" x 84"
   For Metric **M_Single - Flush: 0915 x 2134 mm**
   Distance of door centerlines from wall centerlines- **762 mm**
   Door openings - **1220 x 2134 mm**
   Passage Opening-Cased- 0915 x 2134 mm

3. Window types to be used:
   For Imperial **Fixed: 36" x 48"**
   For Metric **M_Fixed: 0915 x 1220 mm**

4. File name to be saved-
   For Imperial **c04_ElevatorandStairLobby_ex2**
   For Metric **M_c04_ElevatorandStairLobby_ex2**

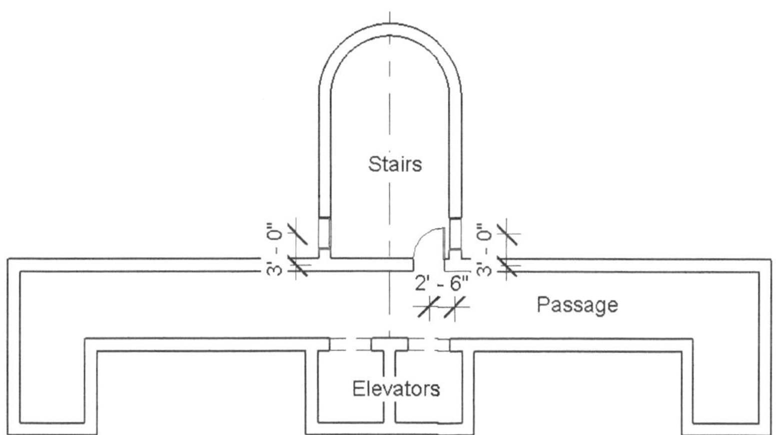

Figure 4-49 *Sketch plan for adding doors, windows, and openings to the Elevator and Stair Lobby project*

Exercise 3 Club - Hall 2

Add doors, windows and openings to Hall 2 of the *Club* project created in Tutorial 2 of this chapter, refer to Figure 4-50. The dimensions and text are given for reference and are not to be created. Use the following project parameters: **(Expected time: 30 min)**

1. Project-
   For Imperial *c04_Club_tut2.rvt*
   For Metric *M_c04_Club_tut2.rvt*

2. Door types to be used:
   For Imperial D1- **Door- Interior- Single- Full Glass Wood - 36" x 84"**
   For Metric D1- **M_Door- Interior- Single- Full Glass Wood - 0915 x 2134 mm**

3. Window types to be used:
   For Imperial W1- **Fixed: 36" x 48"**
   For Metric W1- **M_Fixed: 0915 x 1220 mm**

4. File name to be saved-
   For Imperial **c04_Club_ex3**
   For Metric **M_c04_Club_ex3**

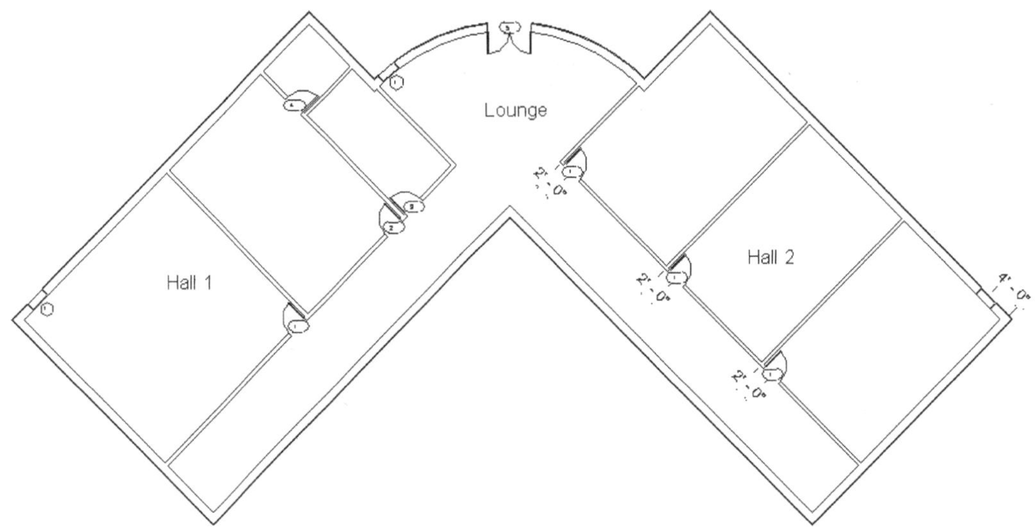

Figure 4-50 *Sketch plan for adding doors and windows to Hall 2 of the Club project*

Exercise 4 Residential Building- Doors and Windows

Add doors, windows, and openings to the *Residential Building* project created in Exercise 4 of Chapter 3, refer to Figure 4-51 and Figure 4-52. Do not add text or dimensions as they are given for reference only. Use the following project parameters. **(Expected time: 30 min)**

1. Project-
   For Imperial *c03_residential_wall_ex4.rvt*
   For Metric *M_c03_residential_wall_ex4.rvt*

2. Door types to be used:
   For Imperial D1- **Door- Exterior- Double- Full Glass Wood - 60" x 80"**
   D2- **Door- Interior- Single- Full Glass Wood - 36" x 84"**
   D3- **Door- Interior- Single- 1- Panel- Wood- 36" x 84"**
   D4- **Door- Interior- Single- 1- Panel- Wood- 30" x 80"**
   For Metric D1- **Door- Exterior- Double- Full Glass Wood - 1500 x 2000**
   D2- **Door- Interior- Single- Full Glass Wood - 0915 x 2134 mm**
   D3- **Door- Interior- Single- 1- Panel- Wood- 0915 x 2134 mm**
   D4- **Door- Interior- Single- 1- Panel- Wood- 0750 x 2000 mm**

3. Window types to be used:
   For Imperial W1- **Fixed: 24" x 24"**
   W2- **Fixed: 36" x 72"**
   For Metric W1- **M_Fixed: 0600 x 0600 mm**
   W2- **M_Fixed: 0900 x 1800 mm**

4. File name to be saved-
   For Imperial **c04_residential_door_window_ex4**
   For Metric **M_c04_residential_door_window_ex4**

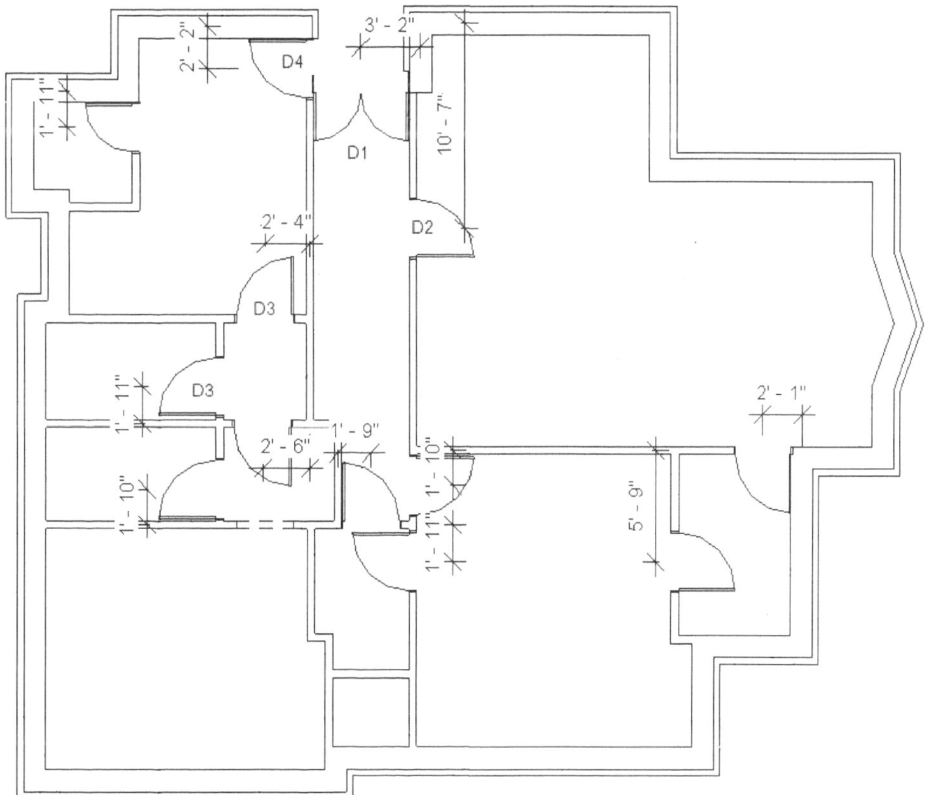

Figure 4-51 *Sketch plan for adding doors and openings to the residential building*

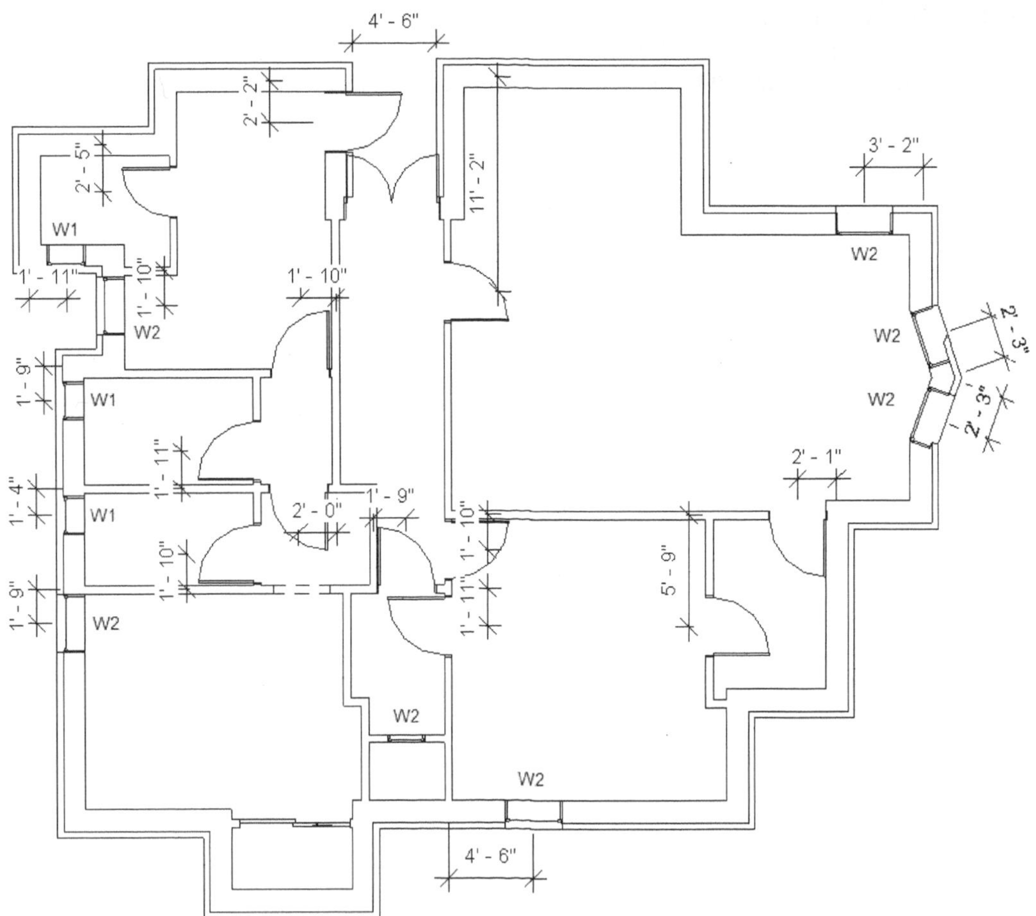

Figure 4-52 Sketch plan for adding windows to the residential building

Answers to Self-Evaluation Test

1. a, **2**. c, **3**. **Type Selector**, **4**. **Load Family**, **5**. **Duplicate**, **6**. **Height**, **7**. F, **8**. F, **9**. T, **10**. F, **11**. T, **12**. T

Chapter 5

Using the Editing Tools

Learning Objectives

After completing this chapter, you will be able to:

- *Create a selection set of elements*
- *Use the tools in the Status Bar*
- *Move and copy elements*
- *Use the Trim and Extend tools*
- *Use the Cut and Paste tools*
- *Use the Rotate, Mirror, and Offset tools*
- *Create an array of elements using the Array tool*
- *Use the Match, Align, Delete, Lock, and Group tools*
- *Split walls using the Split Elements and Split with Gap tools*

INTRODUCTION

In the previous chapter, you learned to create building elements such as walls, doors, and windows. In this chapter, you will learn to use various editing tools provided in Autodesk Revit. You can use these tools to add specific design requirements to the elements that you have created. Primarily, you will learn to select and edit elements using object controls and editing tools such as **Move**, **Copy**, **Trim**, **Extend**, **Cut**, **Delete**, **Rotate**, **Mirror**, **Array**, **Align**, **Match**, and so on. You will also learn to use different tools located in the **Status Bar**.

CREATING A SELECTION SET

In order to edit an element or a group of elements, you must first select them. To create a selection set, first you need to exit the currently invoked tool. To do so, choose the **Modify** button from the **Select** panel of the contextual tab or type **MD** to exit the current tool. After exiting the current tool, move the cursor near the element that you wish to select. On doing so, you will notice that it gets highlighted and its description is displayed in the **Status Bar**. For example, on highlighting a door, you might see **Doors: Single-Flush: 34"X84"** displayed in the **Status Bar**. In case, there are elements in proximity of the element to be selected, press the TAB key to cycle between them. Click to select the element when it is highlighted. By default a selected element will appear semi-transparent and blue in color. In the forthcoming sections, you will learn different methods of selecting multiple elements, restoring the selected elements, and removing elements from a selection.

Selecting Multiple Elements

The methods of selecting multiple elements are discussed next.

Using the CTRL Key

You can press and hold the CTRL key and click on the elements to add them to the current selection set. In case, you need to make multiple selections of the same type, release the CTRL key and when the elements are highlighted, press the TAB key.

Using the Selection Window

You can select elements by defining a selection window. To define a selection window, you need to click at a point in the drawing area which is close to the elements you desire to select. Next, drag the cursor to form a rectangle. You will notice that on dragging the cursor from left to right, the rectangle formed is of continuous lines and the elements that are completely inside it are selected, as shown in Figure 5-1. If you drag the cursor from right to left, a dashed rectangle appears and all items that are partially or fully inside it are selected, as shown in Figure 5-2.

Using the TAB Key (For Walls)

You can use the TAB key to select the walls that are joined together and form a continuous chain. To use this method, first highlight one of the walls and then press the TAB key. All the walls that are joined to the chosen wall are highlighted for selection.

Note

The usage of the TAB key for the selection of walls has certain limitations. It cannot be used if the walls are not properly joined together.

Tip

On defining a selection window, you will notice that the color of the selected elements has changed and the elements get highlighted in blue color, thereby making the selection easier.

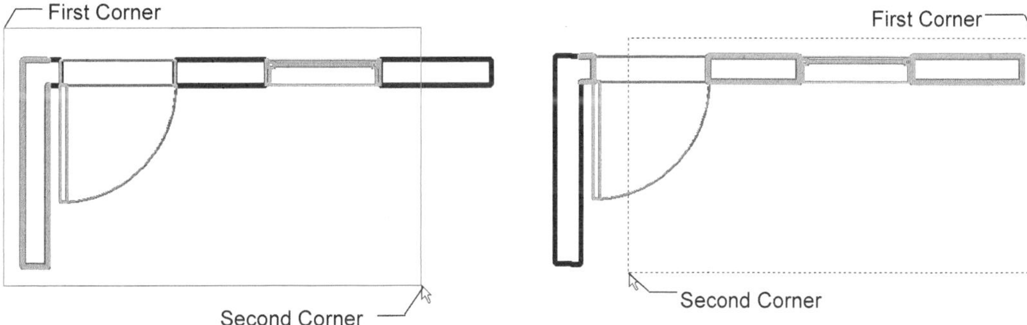

Figure 5-1 *Defining a selection window from left to right*

Figure 5-2 *Defining a selection window from right to left*

Using the Select All Instances Option

The **Select All Instances** option is used to select all the instances of an element type used in the project. To use this option, select a single instance and then right-click to display a shortcut menu. Now, choose the **Select All Instances** option in the shortcut menu; a flyout will be displayed. From the flyout, you can either choose the **Visible in View** option or the **In Entire Project** option. On choosing the **Visible in View** option from the flyout, the elements which have instances similar to that of the selected element in the current view will get selected. Alternatively, if you choose the **In Entire Project** option from the flyout, the elements which have instances similar to that of the selected element in the project will get selected. You can also select an element and type **SA** to select all its instances in the project.

Isolating Elements Using the Selection Box

The **Selection Box** tool is used to isolate elements in a 3D view. To isolate elements, first select the required element from the model and then choose the **Selection Box** tool from the **View** panel in the **Modify | <Elements>** contextual tab; the selected element will get isolated in the 3D view.

Selecting Elements Using the Advanced Tools

In Autodesk Revit, besides the basic selection tools discussed in the earlier chapters, you can use the advanced selection tools for selecting and modeling process. These advanced tools are available in the **Status Bar**, as shown in Figure 5-3. These tools are discussed next.

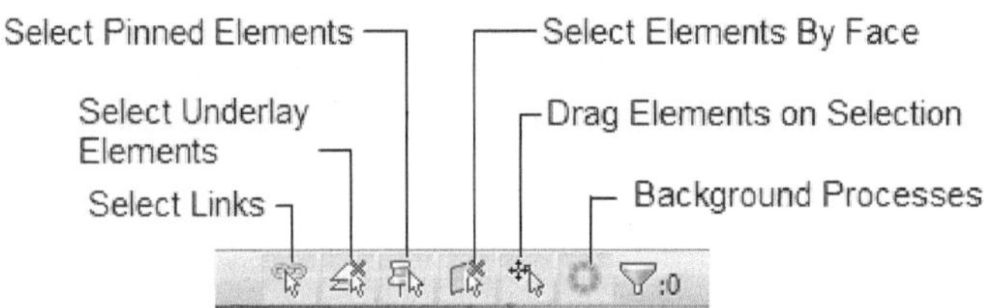

Figure 5-3 The tools in the ***Status Bar***

Select Links

In a project, you may require to select an entire linked model or an individual element inside the linked model. To do so, choose the **Select Links** tool from the **Status Bar** and then select the complete model or an individual part of the linked model.

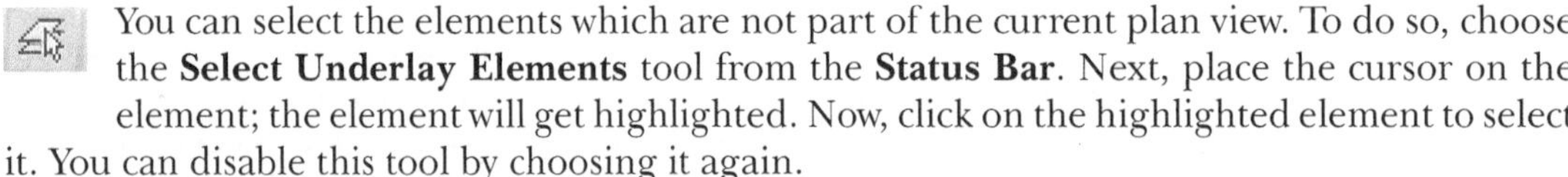

Tip

To select an individual element in a model, move and place the cursor on it and then press the TAB key; the element gets highlighted. Now, click on the highlighted element to select it.

Select Underlay Elements

You can select the elements which are not part of the current plan view. To do so, choose the **Select Underlay Elements** tool from the **Status Bar**. Next, place the cursor on the element; the element will get highlighted. Now, click on the highlighted element to select it. You can disable this tool by choosing it again.

Select Pinned Elements

You can select or deselect the pinned elements by using the **Select Pinned Elements** tool.

Select Elements by Face

This tool is used to select an element by enabling the selection of an element by face. To select an element using this tool, choose the **Select Elements by Face** tool from the **Status Bar**. Next, click at any point on the face of an architectural element such as a wall, floor and so on to select it. You can disable this tool by choosing it again.

Drag Elements on Secection

By using this tool, you can drag an element without selecting it first.

Background Processes

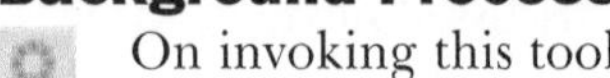

On invoking this tool from the **Status Bar**, a list of the processes, for example color fill, that will run in the background will be displayed.

Restoring the Selection

A selection cleared intentionally or unintentionally can easily be restored by using several methods. One method for restoring the previous selection is to choose the **Modify** button from the contextual tab and then right-click in the drawing area; a shortcut menu will be displayed.

From the shortcut menu, choose the **Select Previous** option; the previous selection will be restored. Alternatively, press CTRL+left arrow key to restore the previous selection.

Using the Filter Tool

You can use the **Filter** tool to filter the currently selected tools in your project. Select different types of elements to filter; the **Modify | Multi-Select** tab will be displayed. Now, choose the **Filter** tool from the **Selection** panel of the **Modify | Multi-Select** tab; the **Filter** dialog box will be displayed along with a list of categories of the currently selected elements, as shown in Figure 5-4. Alternatively, click on the filter icon displayed at the extreme right corner of the **Status Bar** to invoke the **Filter** dialog box.

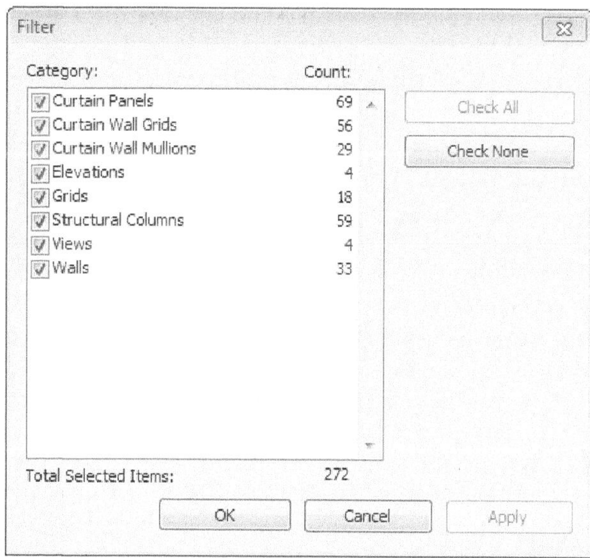

*Figure 5-4 The **Filter** dialog box displaying a list of categories*

In Revit, the **Filter** dialog box displays the count of the selected elements in each category, and the total number of elements currently selected at the bottom of the dialog box. You can clear the relevant check boxes to remove the elements corresponding to a specific family from the current selection. You can use the **Check All** button or the **Check None** button to select or clear all check boxes in the element categories displayed in the dialog box.

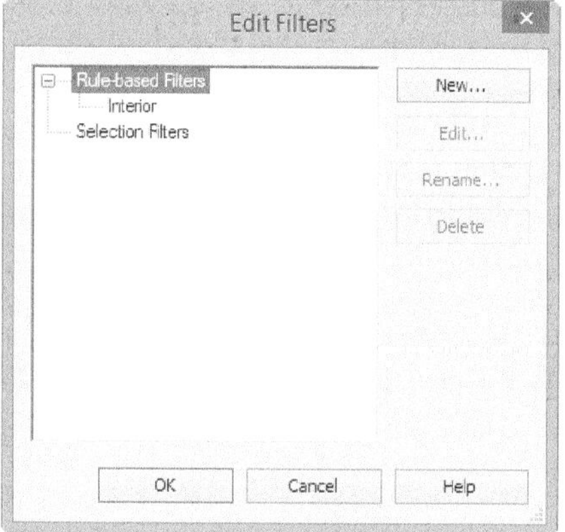

*Figure 5-5 The **Edit Filters** dialog box*

In Autodesk Revit, you can edit a selection set from a list by choosing the **Edit** tool from the **Selection** panel of the **Modify | Multi-Select** tab. On doing so, the **Edit Filters** dialog box will be displayed, as shown in Figure 5-5. In this dialog box, choose the **New** button; the **Filter Name** dialog box with three radio buttons will be displayed. In this dialog box, the **Define rules** radio button is selected by default. In the **Name** edit box of the dialog box, enter desired name for the entity to be selected and then choose the **OK** button. On doing so, the **Filters** dialog box will be displayed. In this dialog box, the name of the created filters will be displayed in the **Filters** area. Click on the desired filter name that you will edit. Next, in the **Categories** area, you can click on the **Filter list** drop-down list; a list of check boxes will be displayed. By default, all the check boxes are selected in the list. Clear all the check boxes except the **Architecture** check box. As a result, the categories that are relevant to the architectural properties will be displayed in the list box of the **Categories** area. If the filter rule for the selection requires the inclusion of the mechanical, electrical, structural, piping, or electrical properties, you can select the other check boxes such as

Structure, **Electrical**, **Mechanical**, or **Piping** from the list. The selection of multiple check boxes in the list will enable you to broaden the filter rule for selecting the elements in the drawings by the properties common to them. For example, if you are required to select walls, pipes, and columns of the same cost, in case then you need to select the **Architecture** and **Piping** check boxes from the list displayed on clicking the **Filter list** drop-down list.

On selecting the required check boxes, the categories common to the selected check boxes will be displayed in the list box below the **Filter list** drop-down list. From the list box, select the check boxes of the categories you require to add in the filter rules. After selecting the categories, you can use various options in the **Filter Rules** area to define the filter.

To define the filter rules, select the required parameter from the **Filter by** drop-down list in the **Filter Rules** area. If the desired parameter does not exist in the drop-down list you can create a parameter of your own. To do so, choose the button next to the **Filter by** drop-down list; the **Project Parameters** dialog box will be displayed. Choose the **Add** button; the **Parameter Properties** dialog box will be displayed. In this dialog box, select the **Project parameter** radio button and select the desired options from the **Discipline**, **Type of Parameter**, and **Group Parameter under** drop-down lists. When the **Shared Parameter** radio button is selected, the **Discipline** and **Type of Parameter** drop-down lists will get deactivated.

Note

*Project parameters in the **Parameter type** area can appear in schedules but not in tags whereas shared parameters can appear in schedules as well as in tags.*

In the **Parameter Data** area of the **Parameter Properties** dialog box, select the **Type** radio button to make the created parameter as a type parameter. You can select the **Instance** radio button to make the parameter as instance parameter in the project.

In the **Parameter Properties** dialog box, select the appropriate options from the **Categories** area to select the categories under which you want to display the created parameter and then choose the **OK** button; the **Parameter Value** dialog box will be displayed. In this dialog box, enter a desired value in the **Value** column corresponding to the created parameter and choose the **OK** button; the **Parameter Value** dialog box will be closed and the parameter defined will be added to the **Project Parameters** dialog box. Now, choose the **OK** button to close the **Project Parameter** dialog box and return to the **Filters** dialog box.

In the **Filters** dialog box, you can select the created parameter from the **Filter by** drop-down list and select the filter operators from various drop-down lists in the **Filter Rules** area to define the filter rules. After defining the filter rules in the **Filters** dialog box, choose the **OK** button; the **Filters** dialog box will be closed and you will return to the **Edit Filters** dialog box that contains the name of the filters created. In the **Edit Filters** dialog box, you can use the **Rename** button to change the name of the filter displayed in the list. You can delete any filter from the list by using the **Delete** button. You can use the **New** button to create a new filter definition. To close the **Edit Filters** dialog box, choose the **OK** button.

In the **Filter Name** dialog box, select the **Select** radio button and then choose the **OK** button. On doing so, the **Edit Selection Set** contextual tab will be displayed. In this environment, select the elements that you want to add or remove from the selection set. After making the selections, choose the **Finish Selections** button; you will exit from the **Edit Selection Set** contextual tab and the **Edit Filters** dialog box will be displayed.

If you want to retain the current selection then select the **Use current selection** radio button from the **Filter Name** dialog box. On doing so, the dialog box will be closed and the current selection will be used as the filter.

In the **Modify | Multi-Select** tab, you can choose the **Save** tool to save the current selection set. On choosing the **Save** tool, the **Save Selection** dialog box will be displayed. In this dialog box, enter the name of the selection set in the **Name** edit box and then choose the **OK** button; the current selection set will be saved. You can retrieve the saved selection by choosing the **Load** tool from the **Selection** panel of the **Modify | Multi-Select** tab.

Note

*In Autodesk Revit platform, the **Filter** icon is located at the lower right corner of the **Status Bar**. The number displayed next to the **Filter** icon indicates the number of currently selected elements.*

MOVING AND COPYING ELEMENTS

Moving and copying elements are frequent tasks that you need to perform while working in a project. In Revit platform, there are different options or methods by which you can perform these tasks. You can perform both copying and moving tasks at the same time. The methods used for moving and copying elements are described next.

Moving the Elements by Changing the Temporary Dimensions

When you create an element, its temporary dimension from a nearby object is also displayed. As explained in Chapters 3 and 4, you can move the element by changing this dimension. Click the temporary dimension and enter the new value to move the element to the desired location. For example, a door can be moved by specifying its new value from the adjacent wall or door (see Chapter 4).

Moving the Elements by Dragging

Dragging is a method used to move elements to the desired location. To drag an element, choose the **Modify** button from the **Select** panel and then select the element from the drawing. After making selection, move the cursor over the element, click and hold the left mouse button. Next, move the cursor toward the desired location. You will notice that the selected element moves along with the cursor, as shown in Figure 5-6. When the element reaches the desired location, release the left mouse button; the element is moved to the new location, as shown in Figure 5-7. Some elements such as walls can be moved only in a particular direction. The SHIFT key may be pressed to remove this constraint. Other elements can be moved in all directions. You can restrict the direction of movement of elements by pressing the SHIFT key.

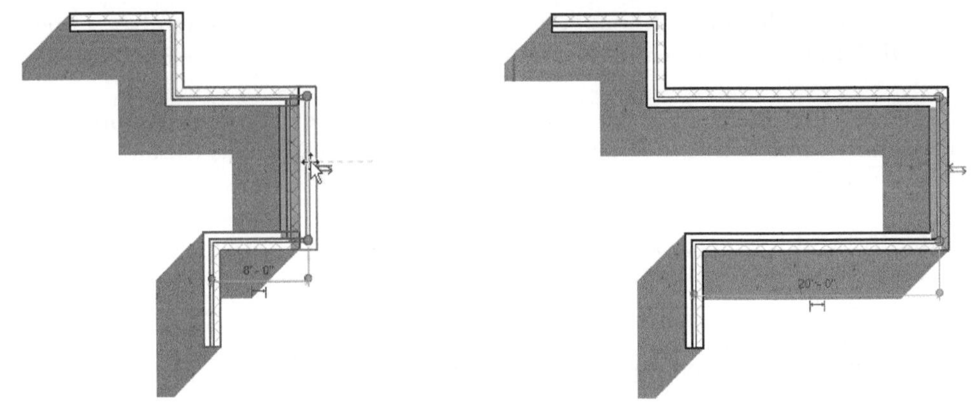

Figure 5-6 *Moving the walls by dragging*

Figure 5-7 *Moved wall with completed edges*

Note

In case of walls, the joined walls adjust and get completed automatically, refer to Figure 5-7.

Moving the Elements by Dragging the End-Joint Components

Using the drag control symbol, you can drag and move more than two components simultaneously provided they have a common joint. This feature is applicable for the line based components such as walls, beams, or braces. To drag the common joined elements, select one of the members of the common joint from the drawing and right-click; a shortcut menu will be displayed. Choose the **Select Joined Elements** option from the shortcut menu. All the members joined at the common end will be highlighted displaying the circular shaped drag controls, as shown in Figure 5-8. Bring the cursor at the common joint; the **Drag Wall End** tooltip will be displayed. Drag the common joint to a new location, as shown in Figure 5-9. You will notice that all the components joined to that common joint have been dragged. Doors and windows can be moved along their host walls only by picking and dragging them to a new location on the host wall. Autodesk Revit closes the old opening and automatically creates the opening at the new location.

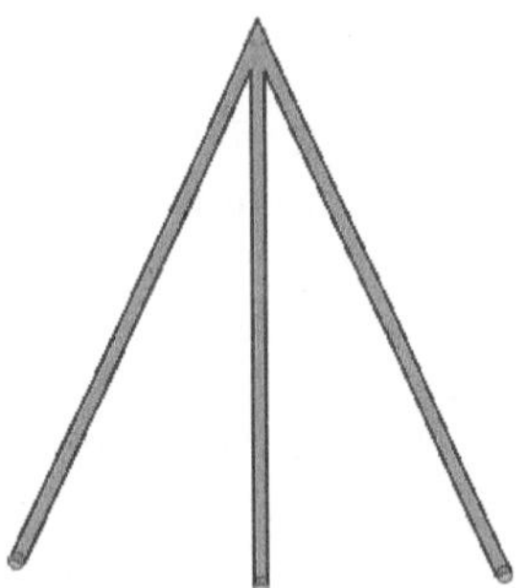

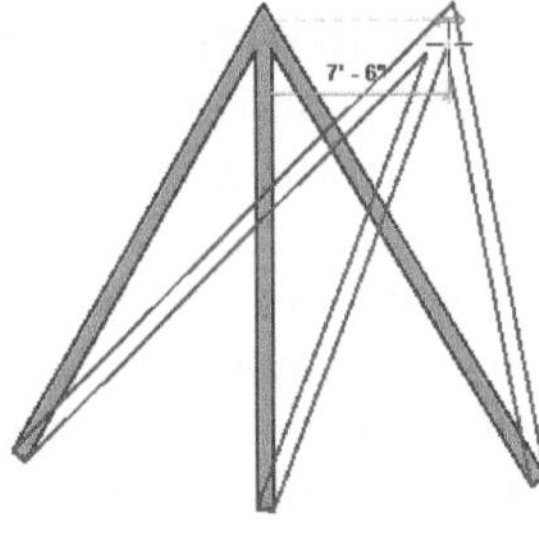

Figure 5-8 *Three walls joined at a common end*

Figure 5-9 *Dragging the end-joined walls simultaneously*

Moving the Elements by Selecting and Dragging

You can modify the location of an element by pressing and dragging the cursor over it. To do so, choose the **Drag Elements On Selection** tool and place the cursor on the desired element; the element gets highlighted. Now, press and drag the element and the element will get relocated.

Note

It is recommended to keep the ***Drag Elements On Selection*** *tool disabled to avoid accidental displacement of the elements.*

Using the Move Tool

Ribbon: Modify | (Elements / Components) > Modify > Move
Shortcut Key: MV

The function of the **Move** tool is similar to that of dragging with the only difference that the preview of the elements is not displayed. It is more useful for moving elements by a specific distance, thereby increasing the accuracy of the building model. To move elements, select them; a contextual tab will be displayed. Note that the name of the contextual tab will depend on the element type selected from the drawing. Invoke the **Move** tool from the **Modify** panel of the contextual tab, or type **MV**; the selected elements will be highlighted inside a dashed rectangle and the **Constrain**, **Disjoin**, and **Multiple** check boxes will be displayed in the **Options Bar**. These options have been discussed in the table given next.

Constrain	The selection of this check box, restricts the movement of the selected element along its collinear or perpendicular vectors.
Disjoin	By selecting this check box, you can break the association of an element with its associated elements and move it to a new location. For example, by selecting this check box from the **Options Bar**, you can move a wall without moving the joined wall. You can also move the elements from their current host element to another host element. For example, you can easily move a door or window from one wall to another. This option can be effectively used if the **Constrain** check box is cleared.
Multiple	The selection of this check box enables the creation of multiple copies of the elements by clicking at the desired location. It is enabled only when the **Copy** check box is selected.

Note

The ***Move*** *tool, like other editing tools such as* ***Copy***, ***Rotate***, ***Mirror***, ***Array***, *and* ***Scale***, *is only available after a selection is made. You can access these tools from the contextual tabs such as* ***Modify / Walls***, ***Modify / Windows***, *and others. The name of the contextual tab will depend upon the type of element or component you select.*

After invoking the **Move** tool, click in the drawing area to specify the start point for moving. Next, move the cursor to the desired location and click to specify the endpoint; the element will move to a new location. To move elements by a specific distance, enter the displacement value, after specifying the first point. An edit box is displayed with the specified value, as shown in Figure 5-10. Press ENTER to move the selected element by the specified value.

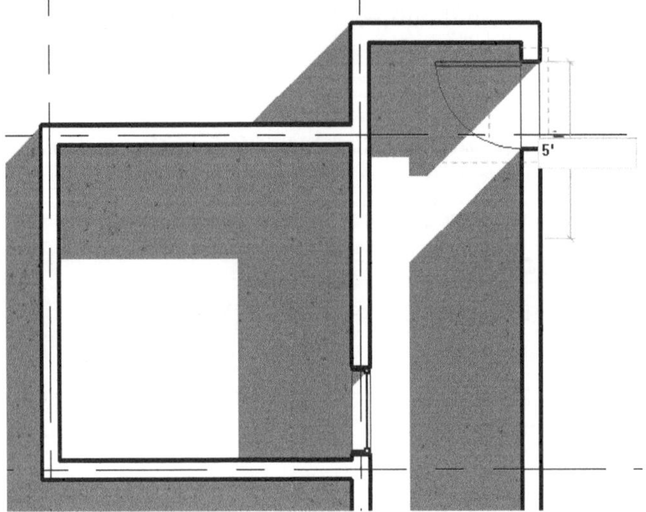

Figure 5-10 Moving elements through a specific distance

Using the Copy Tool

Ribbon: Modify | (Elements / Components) > Modify > Copy
Shortcut Key: CO

The usage of the **Copy** tool is similar to that of the **Move** tool. After invoking the **Copy** tool, click in the drawing window to specify the start point and then move the cursor to the desired distance. To specify the endpoint, click at the appropriate location. You can also specify the distance between the original and copied elements by entering the value.

Creating Multiple Copies of an Element

You can create several copies of the elements using the **Multiple** option from the **Options Bar** of the **Copy** tool. To do so, invoke the **Copy** tool and then select the **Multiple** check box in the **Options Bar**. To specify the start point, click in the drawing window. Move the cursor and click at the desired locations. Each successive click would result in a copy of the original element. Alternatively, you can enter the distance value in the edit box between the currently selected and next elements to create copies at a desired distance. The multiple copy option remains active until you choose some other tool or press the ESC key twice.

Tip

While copying elements, the specified distance should be in the direction of the new location. You can also use negative values to specify the distance in a direction opposite to that of the cursor movement.

TRIMMING AND EXTENDING ELEMENTS

You can trim or extend one or more elements to a boundary defined by the element of the same type. You can also extend or trim (if the elements intersect) the elements that are not-parallel to create a corner. You can trim or extend a reference line or a wall to another reference line or wall. In Autodesk Revit, you can trim and extend elements by using three tools namely: **Trim/ Extend to Corner**, **Trim/ Extend Single Element**, and **Trim/Extend Multiple Elements**. You can use these tools with walls, lines, beams, or braces. These tools are discussed next.

Using the Trim/Extend to Corner Tool

Ribbon:	Modify > Modify > Trim/Extend to Corner

This tool is used to extend a wall to another wall or to trim any extended portion of the building element at the apparent intersection to form a corner. For example, to extend a vertical wall to a horizontal wall, as shown in Figure 5-11, and to make a corner elbow, invoke the **Trim/Extend to Corner** tool from the **Modify** panel. Now, select the first element to be trimmed or extended, in this case, the horizontal wall. If you want to retain its left portion, then click anywhere on the wall on the left region of the apparent intersection, as shown in Figure 5-12. To select the next wall for trimming or extending, move the cursor near the vertical wall. As you move the cursor, you will notice that a dashed line appears showing the corner that will be formed, refer to Figure 5-13. When you click on the vertical wall, it is extended and the horizontal wall is trimmed to form the desired corner, refer to Figure 5-14.

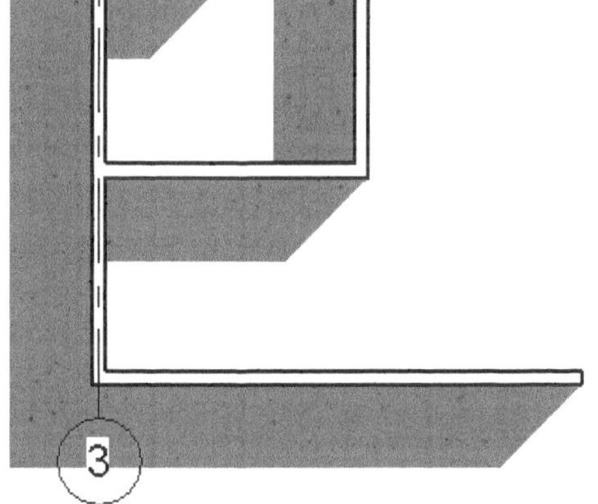

***Figure 5-11** Vertical wall extended to the horizontal wall*

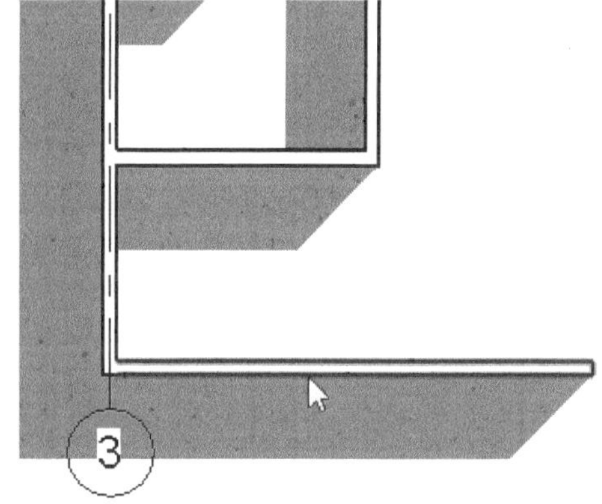

***Figure 5-12** Selecting the first wall to be trimmed/extended on the side to be retained*

Tip

*The **Trim/Extend to Corner** tool can be used with walls as well as with lines (for example, while creating 2D details for your project).*

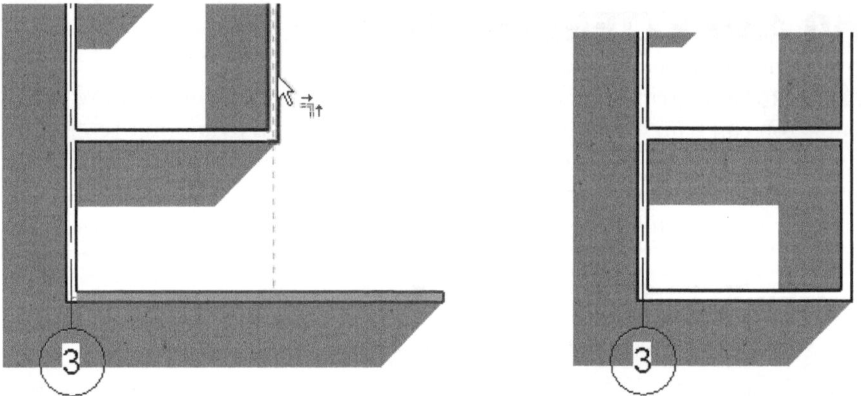

Figure 5-13 *Selecting the second wall to trim/extend* ***Figure 5-14*** *Trimmed and extended walls*

Using the Trim/Extend Single Element Tool

Ribbon: Modify > Modify > Trim/Extend Single Element

This tool enables you to extend or trim an element by defining a reference line or boundary. Using this tool, you can trim a wall or extend a wall to another wall without creating a corner at the intersection. You can also select the desired side of the wall to be retained. For example, use this option to trim the vertical wall at its intersection with the horizontal wall so that the lower portion of the vertical wall is retained. Invoke the **Trim /Extend Single Element** tool from the **Modify** panel and then select the horizontal wall as the cutting boundary. It is highlighted in red. To retain the lower portion of the inclined wall, move the cursor near it until a dashed line appears, refer to Figure 5-15. The profile that is created will be displayed as a dashed line. Click on the lower side of the vertical wall to retain the lower portion. The wall gets trimmed at the specified boundary, as shown in Figure 5-16. The **Trim /Extend Single Element** tool can also be used to extend an element to another element. For example, to extend a horizontal wall up to the vertical wall, invoke the tool and then select the latter as the defining boundary. On moving the cursor near the wall to be extended, you will notice that a dashed line appears, as shown in Figure 5-17. Now, click to extend the vertical wall up to the horizontal wall, as shown in Figure 5-18.

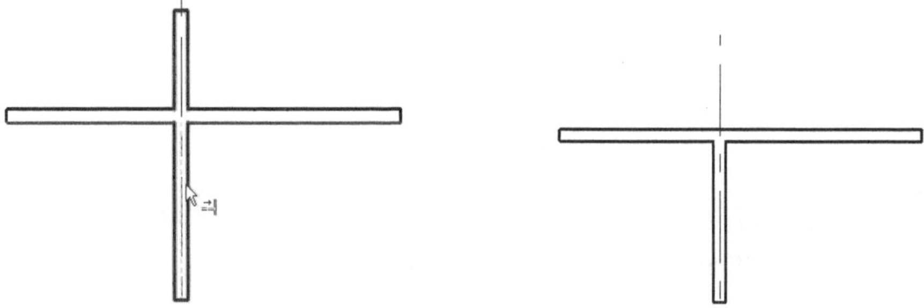

Figure 5-15 *Selecting the wall to be trimmed by clicking on the portion to be retained* ***Figure 5-16*** *Trimmed wall*

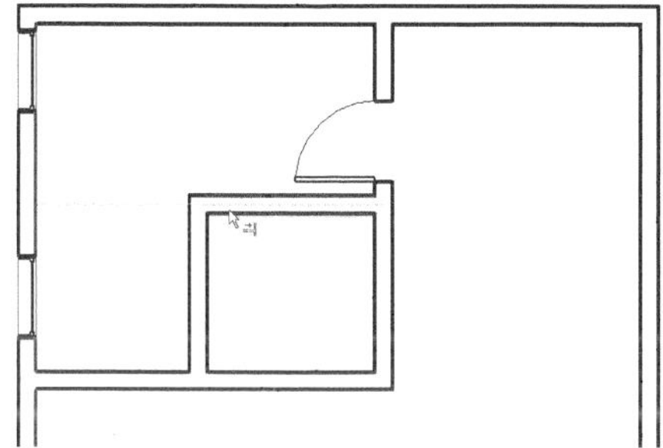

Figure 5-17 The dashed line on the wall to be extended

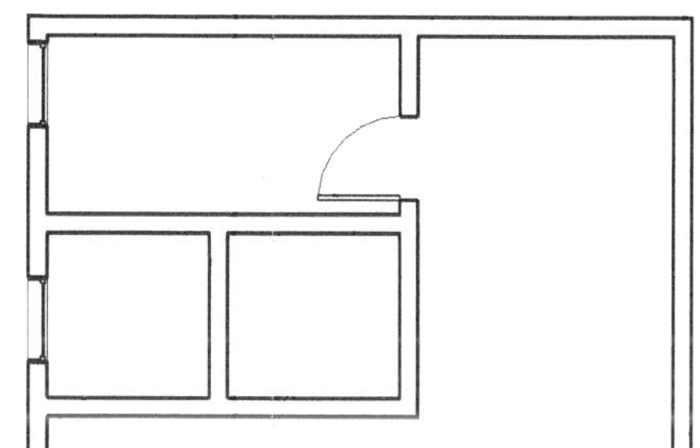

Figure 5-18 The extended wall

Using the Trim/Extend Multiple Elements Tool

Ribbon: Modify > Modify > Trim/Extend Multiple Elements

The **Trim/Extend Multiple Elements** tool enables you to extend or trim a number of elements using a common boundary or edge which can be defined by clicking on an element. After specifying the boundary, select the elements to be extended or trimmed. Autodesk Revit intuitively extends or trims them at the defined boundary. For example, you may need to extend and trim multiple vertical and inclined walls using the horizontal wall as the boundary such that the lower portions of the walls are retained. To do so, invoke the **Trim/ Extend Multiple Elements** tool from the **Modify** panel. On doing so, you will notice that a symbol of this tool appears along with the cursor. Then, click on the horizontal wall to define the cutting boundary and you will see it highlighted. To retain the lower portion of the wall, move the cursor near it until a dashed line appears, as shown in Figure 5-19. Now, click to trim the wall at the specified boundary. Similarly, you can click on the other inclined wall at the lower portion to trim it, refer to Figure 5-20. Without discontinuing the trim tool, move the cursor near the vertical wall which you want to extend, as shown in Figure 5-21, and then click on it. The wall is extended to the horizontal wall. To extend the next wall, move the cursor near it and click when the dashed line appears, as shown in Figure 5-22. Alternatively, you can use a selection box to select multiple elements to trim or to extend to a defined boundary.

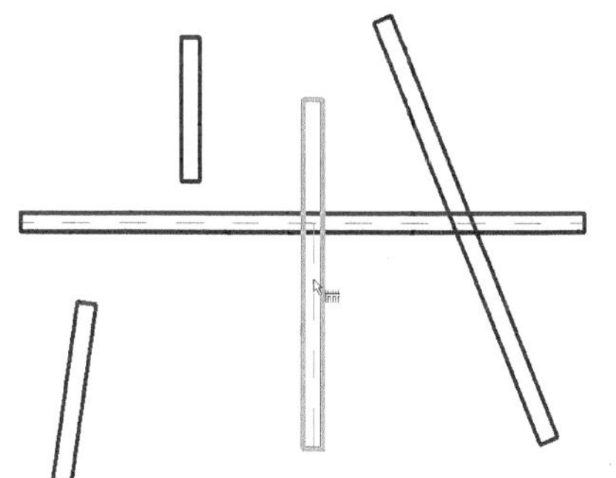

Figure 5-19 Selecting the wall to be trimmed

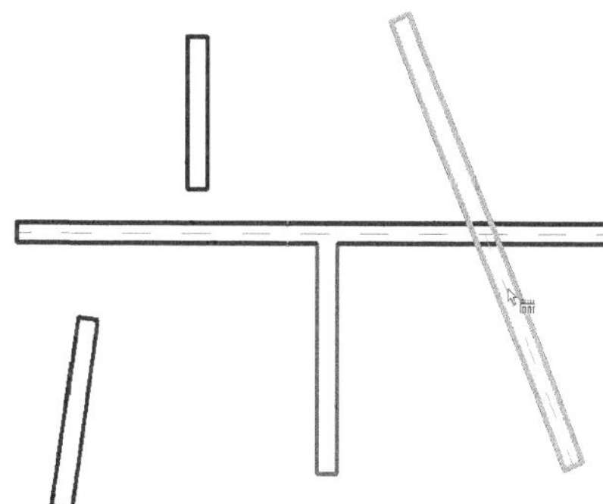

Figure 5-20 Selecting the inclined wall to be trimmed by clicking on the portion to be retained

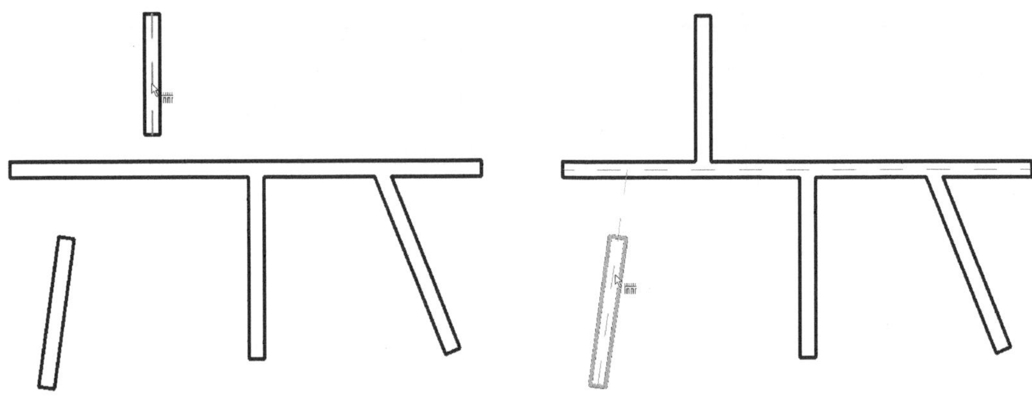

Figure 5-21 Selecting the wall to be extended

Figure 5-22 Selecting the next wall to be extended

Tip

While selecting walls or lines for trimming, ensure that the portion of the element to be retained is clicked. In trimming, the portion of the element on the other side of the intersection is removed.

CUTTING AND PASTING ELEMENTS

Using various cut and paste tools, you can cut some elements and then paste them at another location. You can use these tools efficiently to speed up your work and reduce the time taken in creating new elements. Various cutting and pasting tools are discussed next.

Cutting Elements

Ribbon: Modify | (Elements / Components) > Clipboard > Cut to Clipboard
Shortcut Keys: CTRL+X

The **Cut to Clipboard** tool is used to remove one or more elements from the project. The selected elements that are cut using this tool are copied on the clipboard where they stay until another selection is cut. When you cut an element and paste it to the clipboard, the existing selection is overwritten by the new one. These elements can then be pasted into the same or another project. The **Cut to Clipboard** tool becomes available only after a selection is made in the drawing. To create a selection set, you can use any selection tool described earlier in this chapter. Select the element(s) that you want to cut from the drawing area and choose the **Cut to Clipboard** tool from the **Clipboard** panel of the contextual tab. Alternatively, press the CTRL+X keys. On doing so, the selected elements will be removed from the project and pasted on the clipboard.

Copying Elements to the Clipboard

Ribbon: Modify | (Elements / Components) > Clipboard > Copy to Clipboard
Shortcut Keys: CTRL+C

This tool is used to create a copy of the selected elements on the clipboard and retain the original ones in the current project. Select the elements or components that you desire to copy from the drawing area and invoke the **Copy to Clipboard** tool from the **Clipboard** panel of the contextual tab. Alternatively, press the CTRL+C keys. A copy of the selected elements will be created on the clipboard.

Pasting Elements from the Clipboard

Ribbon: Modify | (Elements / Components) > Clipboard > Paste drop-down > Paste from Clipboard
Shortcut Key: CTRL+V

Paste from Clipboard

The **Paste from Clipboard** tool, which is used to add one or more elements from the clipboard to the project, becomes available only after the element(s) have been cut or copied to it earlier. The selection can be pasted on the current view or on a different view. To paste the elements from the clipboard to the drawing, invoke the **Paste from Clipboard** tool from the **Clipboard** panel. Alternatively, press the CTRL+V keys to paste the selected elements on the drawing view. You can then paste the element(s) at the desired location. To paste a single element, such as a door or a window on the clipboard, move the cursor to the desired location on the wall and click; the copied door or window will be placed in the host wall. If there are a number of elements in the pasted selection, they will appear in the preview box. If they are pasted into the same project, a temporary dimension will be displayed. This indicates the distance and direction of the cursor from the original selection. You can enter the value of the dimension and the angle to paste the elements. Alternatively, to paste the elements graphically, move the box to the desired location and click. Once these elements are pasted, they remain selected as a group in a dashed rectangular box and the **Modify | Model Groups** tab is displayed. Using this tab, you can use other editing tools such as **Move**, **Copy**, **Rotate**, **Align**, and so on to modify them. In the **Options Bar**, choose the **Activate Dimensions** button to view the dimensions of the pasted elements from the nearby element(s). After completing the pasting procedure, choose the **Finish** button from the **Edit Pasted** panel to return to the **Architecture** tab (default mode). To abort the pasting operation after the entities have been pasted and while the group of elements is selected, choose the **Cancel** button in the **Modify | Model Groups** tab. On doing so, the recently pasted group of elements will be removed from the project and you will exit from the **Paste from Clipboard** tool.

ROTATING ELEMENTS

Ribbon: Modify (Elements / Components) > Modify > Rotate
Shortcut Keys: RO

The **Rotate** tool is used to rotate elements about a specified axis or point. You can rotate an element about an axis perpendicular to its plan, elevation, and section views. In 3D view, elements rotate about an axis perpendicular to the current work plane. This tool is available only after the elements have been selected.

Note

*The **Rotate** tool has its limitations. For example, walls cannot be rotated in the elevation view. Dependent elements such as doors and windows cannot be rotated without their host elements.*

Select the element(s) or component(s) from the drawing that you need to rotate and invoke the **Rotate** tool from the **Modify** panel. Alternatively, you can type **RO** to invoke the **Rotate** tool. On invoking the **Rotate** tool, a rotation symbol is displayed at the center of the selected element(s). It represents the perpendicular axis or the center about which the elements will be rotated. You can snap to the symbol and drag it to the desired center of rotation.

Once the center of rotation has been specified, a ray is generated from this point, which moves along the direction of the cursor. Click at the desired start point of the rotation to display a line indicating its direction. You can use various object snap options to specify the start point of the rotation. Once the starting point has been specified, another line rotates with the cursor. A preview box, indicating the selected elements, also rotates with it. Now, move the cursor to the required angle and click in the drawing area to specify the second point of rotation. On doing so, the element will rotate toward a new direction. On rotating the entities, you will notice that a temporary angular dimension is displayed. You can enter the exact value of the angle of rotation, if required. This rotates the element to the specified angle. When you invoke the **Rotate** tool, five options are displayed in the **Options Bar**, as shown in Figure 5-23.

Figure 5-23 *Rotate options available in the **Options Bar***

Before rotating, you can select the **Disjoin** check box to break the association between the selected elements and the other associated elements. For example, you can independently rotate a wall that is joined to the other walls. The **Copy** option enables you to create a rotated copy of the selected element while retaining its original location. The **Angle** option can be used to rotate the elements by a specific angle. You can enter the value of the angle of rotation in the edit box. In the **Options Bar**, you can drag the rotation symbol or use the **Place** button to move the center of rotation to a different location. After you place the center of rotation you can choose the **Default** button to move the center of rotation to its default location. For example, to rotate a furniture element about its center by an angle of 90-degrees, click on the furniture element to select it. Next, invoke the **Rotate** tool from the **Modify** panel of the **Modify | Furniture** tab; the rotate symbol will be displayed at the center of the furniture element and a ray will be generated from it, as shown in Figure 5-24. You can now move the center of rotation, to a different location. To do so, choose the **Place** button and move the rotation symbol at the center of the bottom edge of the furniture element and click; the rotation symbol moves to the new location and the ray is now generated from this point, as shown in Figure 5-25. Next, move the cursor horizontally right and click when the generated ray will be parallel to the top and bottom edges of the furniture element, refer to Figure 5-26. To rotate the furniture element by 90-degrees angle, move the cursor counter-clockwise and click when the temporary dimension shows the desired angle value. As a result, the selected furniture element will rotate about the specified rotation point, as shown in Figure 5-27.

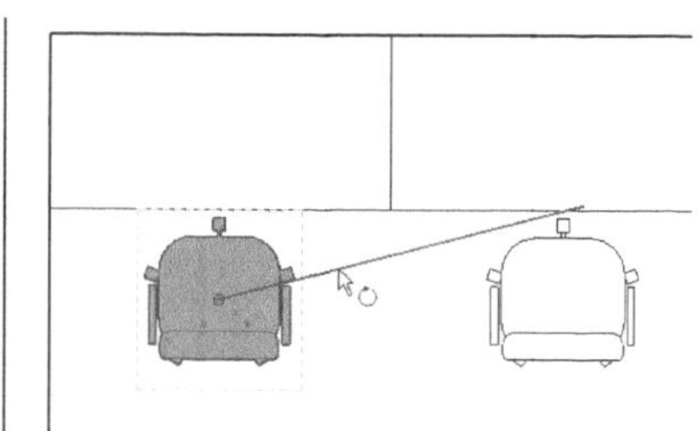

Figure 5-24 A ray generating from the center of the furniture element

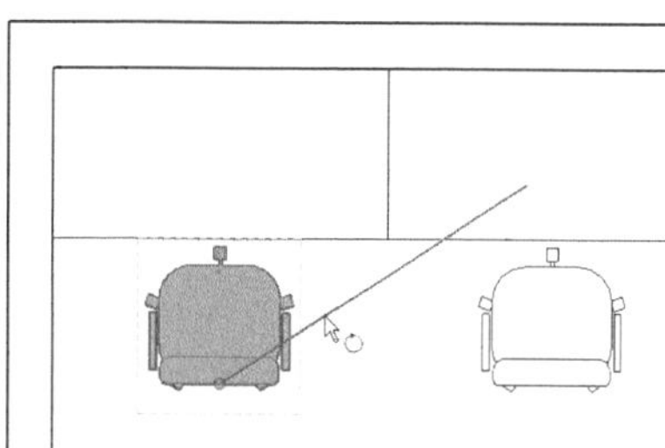

Figure 5-25 Dragging the center of rotation

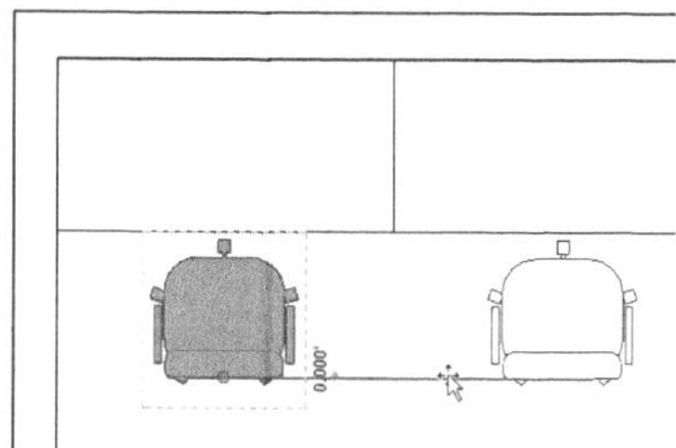

Figure 5-26 Snapping the rotation line using the object snap

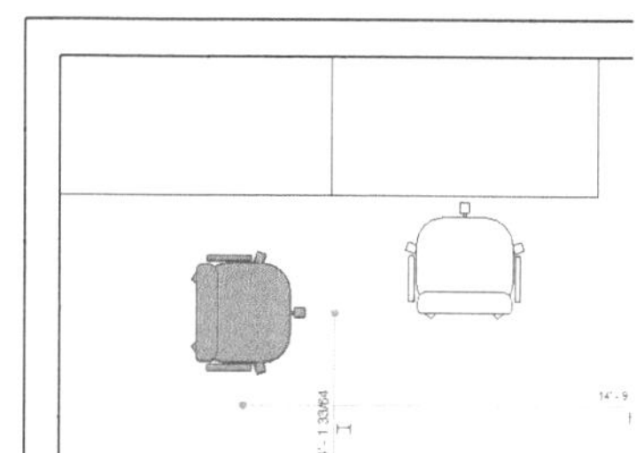

Figure 5-27 Using the temporary dimensions to rotate the element

MIRRORING ELEMENTS

In Autodesk Revit, you can create a mirror image of the elements selected from the drawing about an axis defined by an imaginary line passing through the two specified points. You can use various tools to mirror the selected elements. Using these tools, you can create a symmetrical profile and also create a copy of the elements which are equidistant from the specified axis. You can mirror elements using any of the two tools, **Mirror- Pick Axis** or **Mirror- Draw Axis**. These tools are available only after the elements to be mirrored have been selected. To mirror the element(s) in the drawing, select them and then choose **Mirror - Pick Axis** tool or **Mirror - Draw Axis** tool from the **Modify** panel of the contextual tab. Alternatively, you can type **MM** or **DM** to mirror elements. Note that when you type **MM**, the **Mirror - Pick Axis** tool is invoked and on typing **DM**, the **Mirror - Draw Axis** tool is invoked. On invoking these tools, you will be prompted to select the axis of reflection from the drawing area. Also, you will notice that the **Options Bar** displays the **Copy** option. By default, this option is selected, and therefore you will be able to create a mirrored copy of the elements. Clear the **Copy** check box if you do not require a copy. The two options to mirror the elements are discussed next.

Mirroring Elements Using the Mirror - Pick Axis Tool

Ribbon: Modify | (Elements / Components) > Modify > Mirror - Pick Axis
Shortcut Keys: MM

The **Mirror - Pick Axis** tool is represented symbolically by a cursor symbol and can be used to select an element defining the mirror axis. To use this tool, select the desired element(s) from the drawing and then choose the **Mirror - Pick Axis** tool from the

Modify panel; the mirror symbol will appear with the cursor in the drawing area. Next, move the cursor over the element that will define the mirror axis and click when the appropriate object snap appears. Figure 5-28 shows a floor plan with various elements selected for mirroring and the vertical gridline as the mirror axis. Figure 5-29 shows the elements created after mirroring.

Note

*Using the **Mirror - Pick Axis** tool, you can only select a line or a reference plane that the cursor can snap to. You cannot mirror elements about an imaginary axis created in the open space.*

Tip

*For mirroring elements about an inclined axis, you can create a line inclined at appropriate angle and then use the **Mirror - Pick Axis** tool to select it as the mirror axis.*

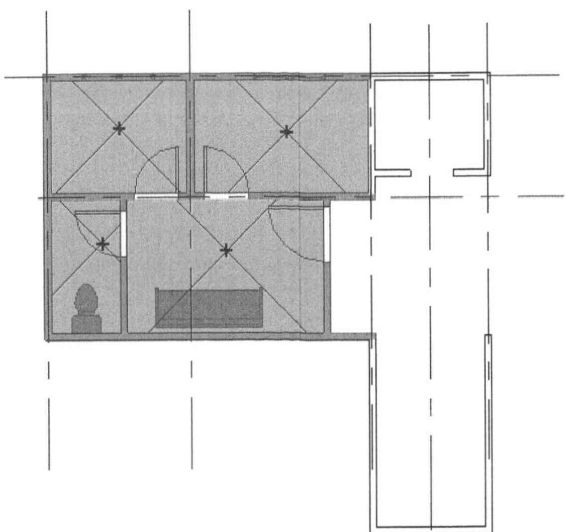

Figure 5-28 *Elements selected for mirroring*

Mirroring Elements Using the Mirror - Draw Axis Tool

Ribbon:	Modify (Elements / Components) > Modify > Mirror - Draw Axis

The **Mirror - Draw Axis** tool is represented by a pencil with mirror symbol. You can use this tool to mirror element(s) in the drawing about an axis that is defined by specifying two points in the drawing area. To use this tool, select the element(s) to be mirrored from the drawing and then choose the **Mirror - Draw Axis** tool from the **Modify** panel. Alternatively, type **DM**. Next, click in the drawing area to specify the start point of the mirror line; a ray will emerge from the specified point. Move the cursor to the desired location and click to specify the second point; the selected elements will be mirrored about the line which represents the mirror axis. Figure 5-30 shows the inclined mirror axis defined by two points. Figure 5-31 shows the mirrored elements about the specified inclined mirror axis.

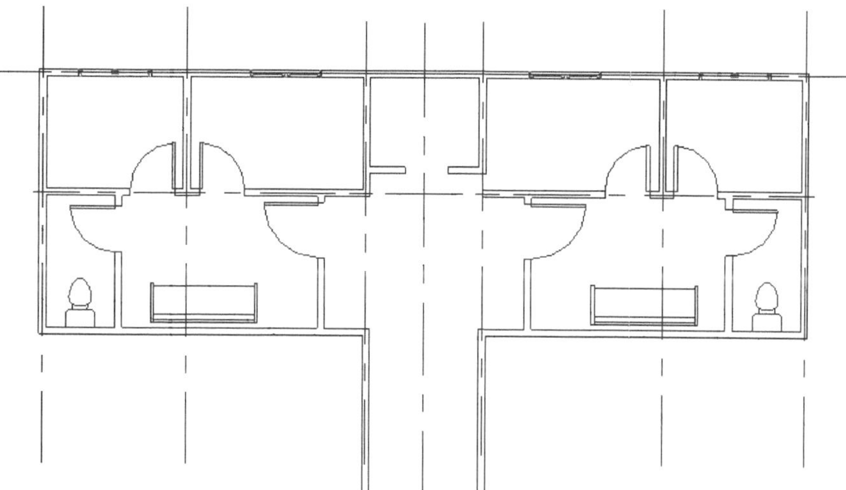

Figure 5-29 The floor plan after mirroring the elements

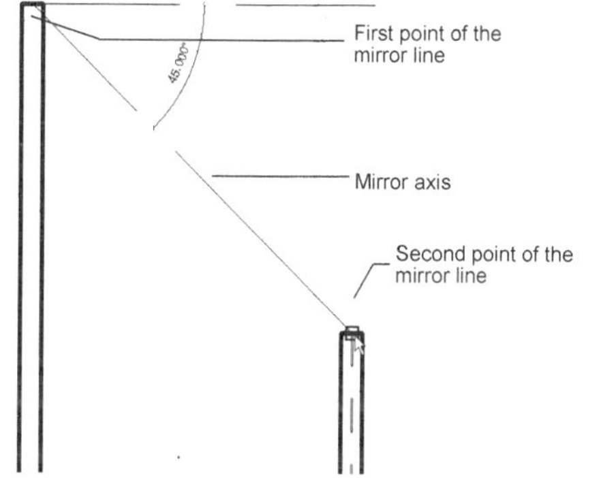

*Figure 5-30 Using the **Draw Mirror Axis** tool to define the mirror axis*

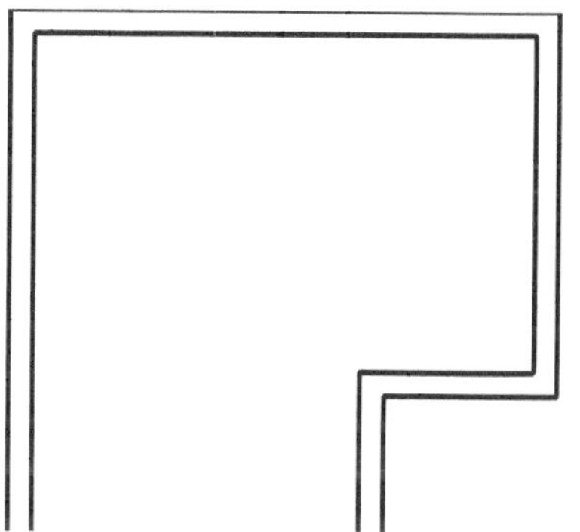

Figure 5-31 Sketched profile with the mirrored elements

CREATING AN OFFSET

Ribbon:	Modify > Modify > Offset
Shortcut Key:	OF

The **Offset** tool is used to create a copy of the selected element at a specified distance from the original element. You can select a single element or multiple elements. The selection can be made even after invoking this tool. By default, Autodesk Revit creates a copy of the selected element while creating an offset. To offset an element, invoke the **Offset** tool from the **Modify** panel of the **Modify** tab. Alternatively, you can type **OF** to invoke the **Offset** tool. On invoking the **Offset** tool, you will notice that the **Options Bar** displays the **Copy** check box. By default, this check box is selected. As a result, you will be able to create a copy of the element at the offset distance. Clear the **Copy** check box, if you do not require a copy. In this case, the object selected will be shifted to the offset distance and no copy will be created. The **Options Bar** also shows two radio buttons, **Graphical** and **Numerical**, which can be used to specify the mirror axis. The use of these options is discussed next.

Tip

*After creating the offset, the **Offset** text box in the **Options Bar** displays the distance through which the offset was created.*

The **Graphical** radio button is selected to specify the offset distance graphically in the drawing window. After selecting the elements and this option, click in the drawing area to specify the start point of the offset distance. A preview image of the selected element is displayed. Now, click again to specify the second point. The selected element is copied at a distance and in the direction defined by two specified points. As you move the cursor to specify the second point, the temporary dimension is displayed. To specify the exact offset distance, move the cursor in an appropriate direction and enter the offset value, as shown in Figure 5-32. Figure 5-33 shows the offset element created.

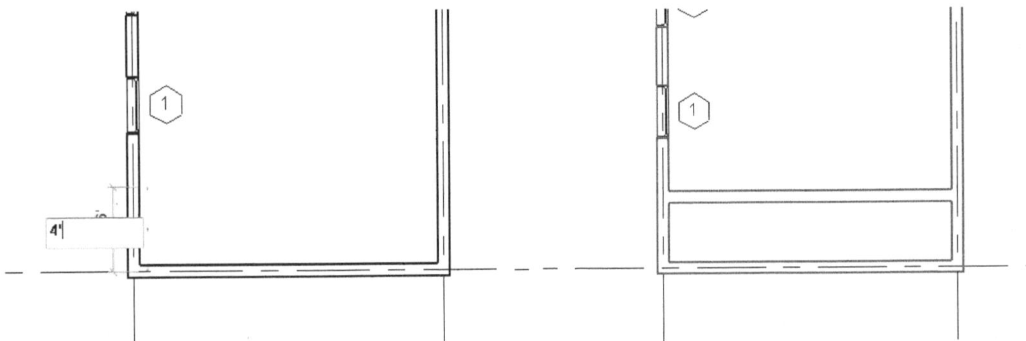

Figure 5-32 *Specifying the offset distance using the **Graphical** option*

Figure 5-33 *Offset wall created at the specified distance*

Tip

*To create a copy of the selected element to be offset, you can also press and hold the CTRL key if the **Copy** check box is not selected.*

The selection of the **Numerical** radio button from the **Options Bar** provides you the flexibility to create an offset by specifying the offset distance in the **Offset** edit box. This value must be a positive number. You can select the **Numerical** radio button to offset single element or a chain of elements. After specifying the offset distance, as you move the cursor near the element, a preview image profile of the selected element at the specified offset distance is displayed in the form of a dashed line. You have the option of changing the offset distance at this stage. You will notice that as you move the cursor over the element, the preview image flips sides. To select a chain of elements, press TAB when the preview image appears. All the connected elements are selected and the preview will change accordingly. Figure 5-34 shows the connected wall profile with its preview offset image. Click to offset the walls, when you see the preview image on the desired side. The offset is created at the specified distance entered in the **Offset** edit box. Figure 5-35 shows the offset wall profile created.

Note

You can offset elements only in the same work plane and not the elements created as in-place families.

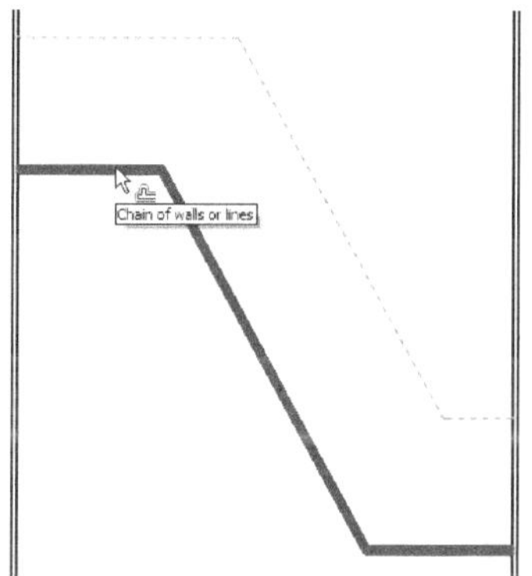

Created Offset Wall

Offset distance

Figure 5-34 *Previewing the offset and selecting a chain of walls using the TAB key*

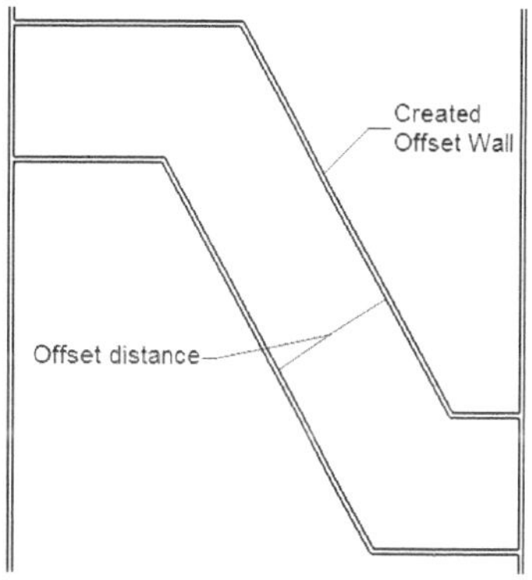

Figure 5-35 *An offset wall profile created at the specified distance*

In case, the wall selected for the offset has other dependent elements such as doors and windows, they are also copied and created in the offset. Figures 5-36 and 5-37 show a wall profile with the doors, windows, and its resultant offset.

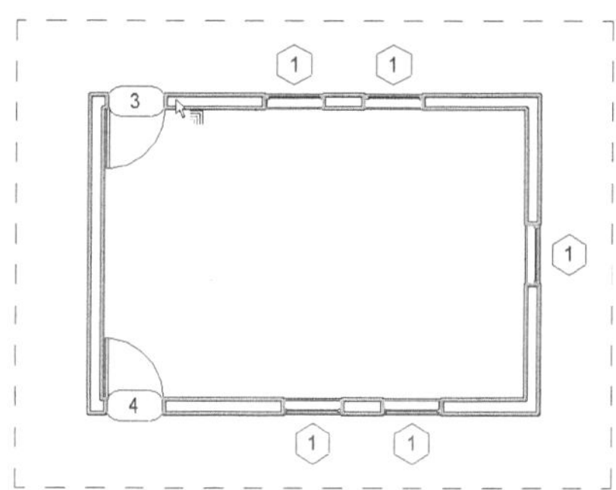

Figure 5-36 *Selecting the wall profile with the doors and windows inserted*

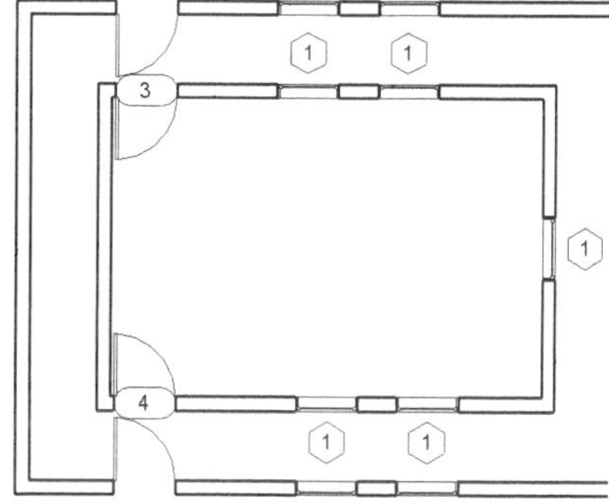

Figure 5-37 *Resulting offset with inserts copied at the specified offset distance*

CREATING AN ARRAY OF ELEMENTS

Ribbon: Modify | (Elements / Components) > Modify > Array

The **Array** tool creates copies of the selected element in a rectangular or radial pattern. It is available only after the elements are selected for an array. You can use any of the methods discussed earlier in this chapter to create a selection. Autodesk Revit provides you the option of arraying multiple elements that are associated as a group. Select the element(s) that you want to array from the drawing and then invoke the **Array** tool from the **Modify** panel. Alternatively, you can type **AR** to invoke the array tool. On invoking the **Array** tool, you will notice that the **Options Bar** displays certain array options. From the **Options Bar**, select the **Group and Associate** check box to create a group of the selected elements, which are then copied as a group rather than individual elements. Clear this check box, if you want to array elements individually. The two options available for creating an array are discussed next.

Linear

Linear, the default array option, can be used to create copies of the selected elements in a rectangular or linear pattern. In the **Options Bar**, additional options are available for creating an array. In the **Number** edit box, enter the number of copies you want to create. You can select the **2nd** radio button to specify the distance between items in the array. The **Last** option is used to specify the entire distance of the array. The items specified are then placed equidistantly between the first and the last specified points. You can use the **Activate Dimension** button to view various dimensions of the elements.

You can specify various options in the **Options Bar** either before or during the creation of an array. Using the **2nd** radio button, click at any point in the drawing window to specify the start point of the array distance. As you move the cursor in the desired direction, a temporary dimension is displayed. You have the option to either enter the value of the distance in that direction or simply move the cursor to the appropriate location and click. Autodesk Revit creates the array of the selected elements by calculating the distance and direction between the two specified points. After the second point is specified, you are prompted to enter the number of items for the array in an edit box. The number of items specified in the **Options Bar** appears as the default value. You have the option of overriding it and specifying a new number. An array of the selected items is created with the specified distance between each group of items. Figure 5-38 shows the selected elements and the distance between each element being specified. A preview of the array to be created is shown in Figure 5-39. You can use the **Constrain** check box in the **Options Bar** to restrict the movement of the cursor in orthogonal directions only. This helps in creating a horizontal or vertical linear array.

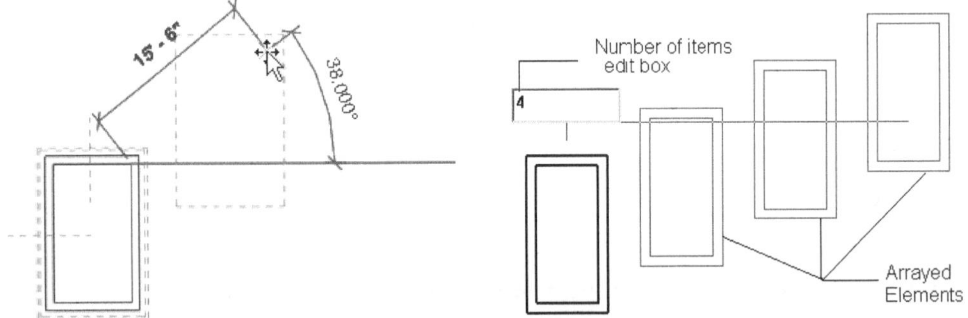

Figure 5-38 Specifying the distance and the angle for creating an array

Figure 5-39 A preview image of the arrayed items

You can select the **Last** radio button from the **Options Bar**, to create an array of elements between two points. Figure 5-40 shows the selection of the start point for specifying the array distance and the selected window to be arrayed. Move the cursor up to a distance that needs to be divided, as shown in Figure 5-41. As you click to specify the endpoint of the array distance, an edit box appears displaying the number of items in the array. You can specify the number in it, as shown in Figure 5-42, and press ENTER to complete the procedure. An array of the selected window is created on the wall, as shown in Figure 5-43.

Figure 5-40 Specifying the start point of the distance to array the selected window

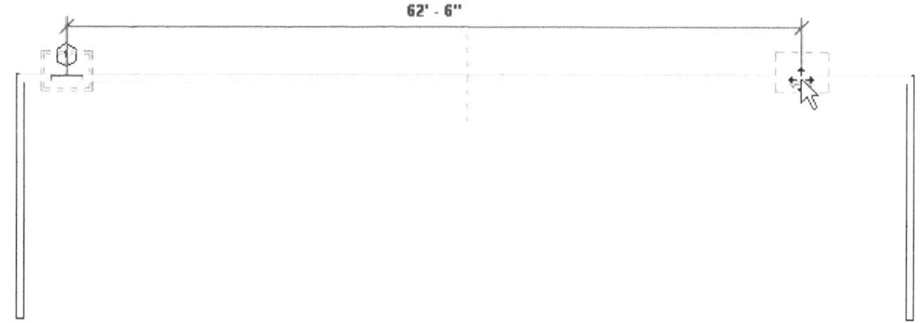

Figure 5-41 Specifying the endpoint of distance to array

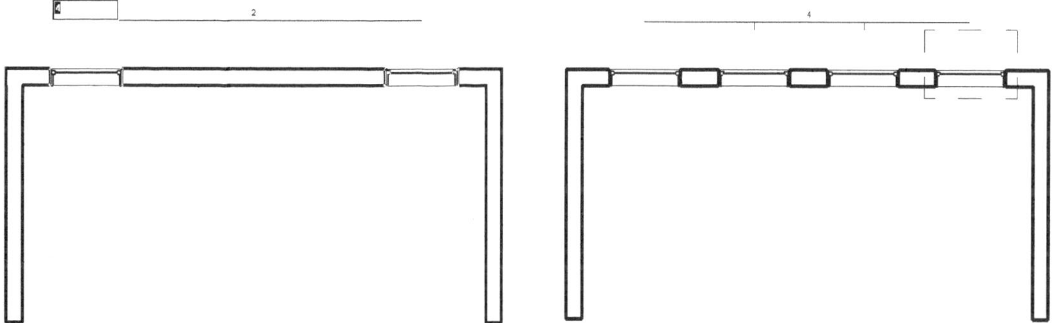

Figure 5-42 Specifying the number of items in an array

Figure 5-43 Array of windows created on the wall

Tip

Autodesk Revit displays error messages if the elements cannot be arrayed. For example, if the specified angle or the number of items do not fit into the length of the wall, or overlap each other, a suitable warning message is displayed to help you modify the settings accordingly.

Radial

You can create radial arrays using the **Radial** option available in the **Options Bar**. The other setting options available in the **Options Bar** such as **Group and Associate**, **Number**, **Move to: 2nd** and **Last** are the same as those given for the **Linear** option. The **Angle** edit box is provided to specify the angle about which the array is to be created. If the **Move To: 2nd** option is selected, the angle specified becomes the angle between each item, whereas if the **Move To: Last** option is selected, the number of items are created by equally dividing the specified angle. The procedure for creating a radial array is similar to that of using the **Rotate** tool, described earlier in this chapter. After selecting the element(s) of array and choosing the **Radial** option, you will notice that a rotational symbol is displayed at the center of the selection, which you can drag to the location to be used as the center of the array. Figure 5-44 shows a wall profile, in which the window is selected for an array with the center of the circular wall as its center. Next, click to specify the start point of the angle of the array. The example shows the creation of multiple windows within a specified angle. You can choose the **Move To: Last** option for this purpose. Move the cursor radially and click to specify the end point of the angle, as shown in Figure 5-45. An edit box is displayed prompting you to enter the number of items to be created between the specified angles, as shown in Figure 5-46. After specifying the number, press ENTER to complete the procedure. Figure 5-47 shows the resultant radial array of the windows. You will notice that the number of items are displayed in blue. You can click on it and enter a new value, if required. The two controls at the end of the arc can be used to resize it. The middle control can be used to modify the radius of the radial array, while the central control lets you drag it.

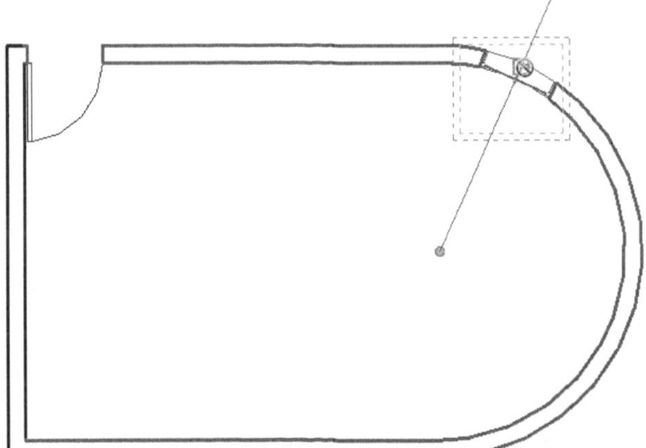

Figure 5-44 *Specifying the first point of the angle with the center of circular wall for the radial array of the selected window*

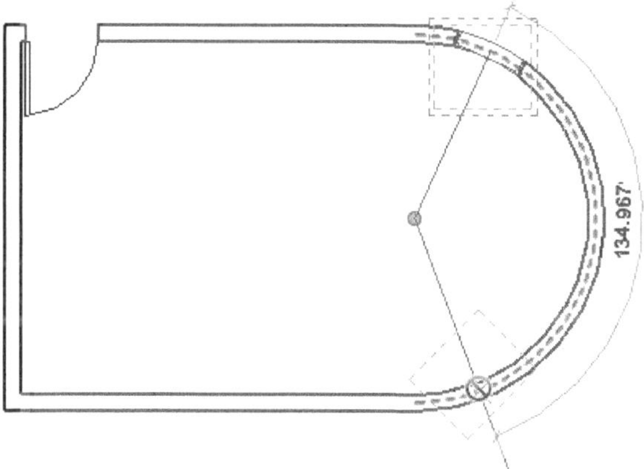

Figure 5-45 Specifying the second point of the angle for the radial array

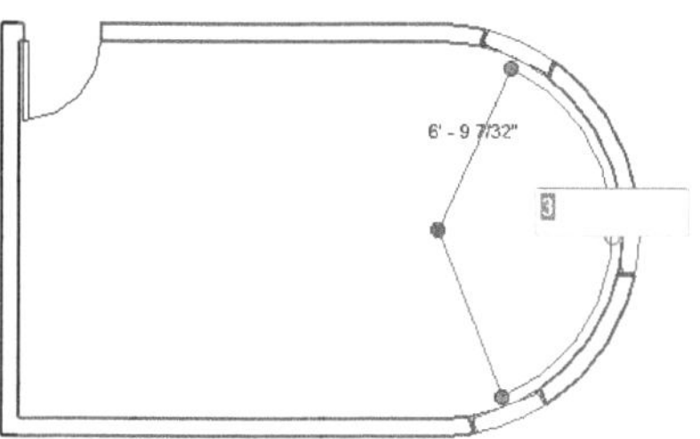

Figure 5-46 Specifying the number of items for the radial array

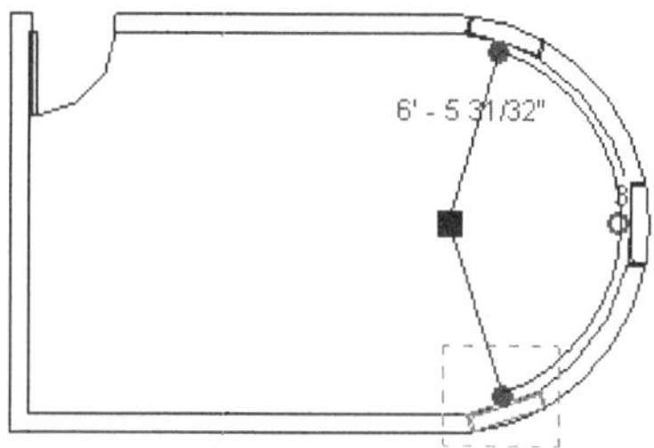

Figure 5-47 The resulting radial array with the last item highlighted

MATCHING ELEMENTS

Ribbon: Modify > Clipboard > Match Type Properties
Shortcut Keys: MA

In Autodesk Revit, you can use the **Match Type Properties** tool to copy the properties of a source element and transfer them to another element belonging to the same family. For example, you can select a wall and then another wall and match its properties with the first wall.

To match the property of a source element to another element of the same family, invoke the **Match Type Properties** tool from the **Clipboard** panel. After invoking this tool, you will notice that as you move the cursor in the drawing window, it changes to a paint brush. To select a type of element to match, move the paint brush near the element and click. The empty paint brush changes into a filled one indicating that the element type has been selected. To match another element of the same family type as the first selection, move the dropper over it and click. The dropper empties, indicating that the element type has been changed. In case of walls, the matching wall type does not change the instance parameters. Autodesk Revit has the improved feature of matching multiple family elements to a selected element of the same family.

ALIGNING ELEMENTS AND WORKING WITH CONSTRAINTS

Ribbon: Modify > Modify > Align
Shortcut Keys: AL

The **Align** tool is used to arrange elements in a collinear manner. You can choose an element that acts as a reference line or a plane along which the other elements can be aligned. When you align them, a padlock key will be displayed which represents the alignment constraint. Using this key, you can lock or unlock the alignment of the walls. Once you lock the alignment, the walls move together. The **Align** tool can be used only in plan or elevation views. In Autodesk Revit, you can use the **Align** tool to align multiple elements in your project at once. Invoke the **Align** tool from the **Modify** panel. In the **Options Bar**, the **Multiple Alignment** check box can be selected to align a number of elements to a common line. While aligning walls, you can choose to align the wall centerlines or wall faces by selecting the appropriate option from the **Prefer** drop-down list in the **Options Bar**. To select the reference line, click when the appropriate line is displayed. Figure 5-48 shows a wall profile and a wall centerline being selected as the reference line. To align another wall, you can move the cursor over it and click when the centerline snap is displayed. The second wall gets aligned to the first wall, as shown in Figure 5-49. You can click the padlock key to lock the alignment of these two walls. To align them to the third wall, select them as thc rcfcrcncc line, as shown in Figure 5 50. Since you have locked the alignment of the first two walls, both of them are aligned to the third wall centerline, as shown in Figure 5-51. You can click the padlock key to lock the alignment of all the three horizontal walls. You can also use the **Multiple Alignment** option and use one wall centerline as the reference line to align the other two walls.

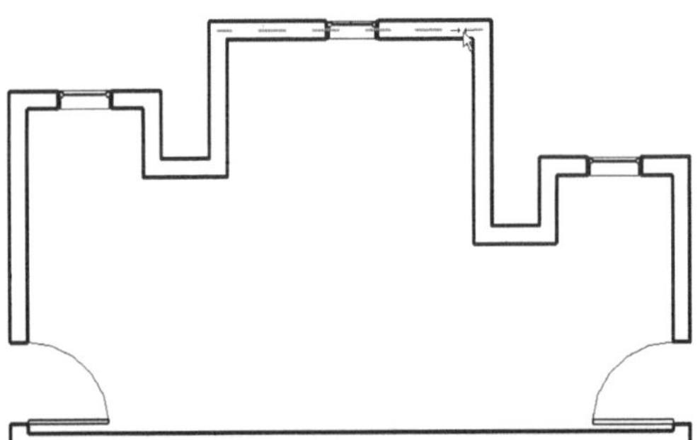

Figure 5-48 *Selecting the wall centerline as the alignment line*

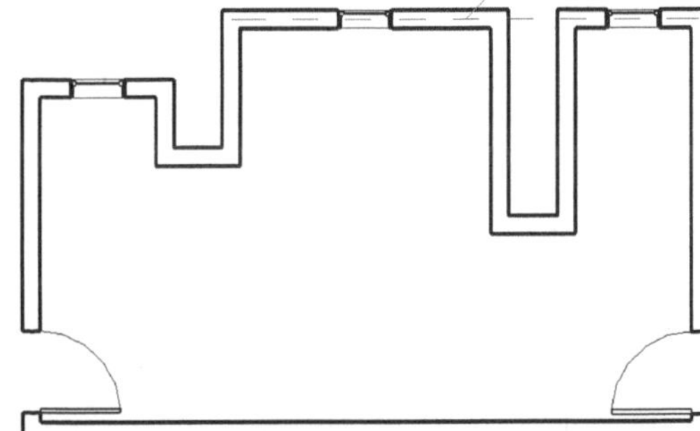

Figure 5-49 *The second wall aligned to the specified alignment line*

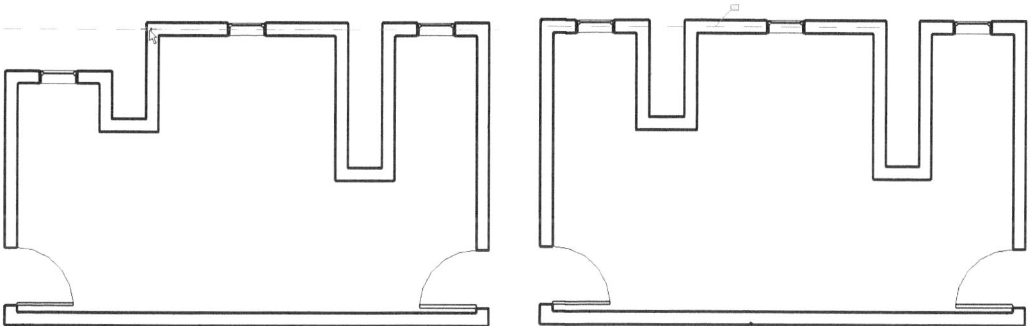

Figure 5-50 Specifying the reference line to align the walls

Figure 5-51 The resulting aligned walls

DELETING ELEMENTS

Using the **Delete** tool, you can remove the selected elements from the project. The deleted elements are permanently removed and are not pasted on the clipboard. The tool is available only after the elements have been selected. To invoke the **Delete** tool, select the element you want to delete, the contextual tab will be displayed. From the **Modify** panel of the contextual tab, choose the **Delete** tool; the selected elements will be deleted from the drawing. Alternatively, you can press the DELETE key or type **DE** to delete the selected elements.

SPLITTING ELEMENTS

Ribbon: Modify > Modify > Split Element
Shortcut Keys: SL

The **Split Element** tool is used to break a wall or a line into two parts at a specified point. Once a wall or a line is split, the parts can be edited independently. Invoke the **Split Element** tool from the **Modify** panel and select the element that you desire to split from the drawing. The **Options Bar** has the **Delete Inner Segment** check box, which you can select to delete the inner segment created between the two consecutive splits. On moving the cursor in the drawing window, you will notice that it changes to a cutting tool. Now, move the cursor over the wall or a line until the temporary dimension is displayed. You can move the cursor to the desired distance, as shown in Figure 5-52, and then click to specify the point of the split. A temporary dimension, indicating the location of the split, will be displayed. Click on it and enter the value of the distance, as shown in Figure 5-53. As a result, the split moves to the specified location. Similarly, you can click to specify the location of the second split, as shown in Figure 5-54. If the **Delete Inner Segment** check box is selected, the portion of the wall between these two split points is automatically removed, as shown in Figure 5-55; otherwise, the single wall is now split into three portions, each with a specified length. The walls can be split in the elevation or 3D view along a horizontal line. You can view the elevation by clicking the appropriate elevation name from the **Project Browser**. To split the wall, move the cursor and click to specify the location of the split. You can split the wall at the predefined levels by snapping to the reference lines or at any other level by clicking at the appropriate height.

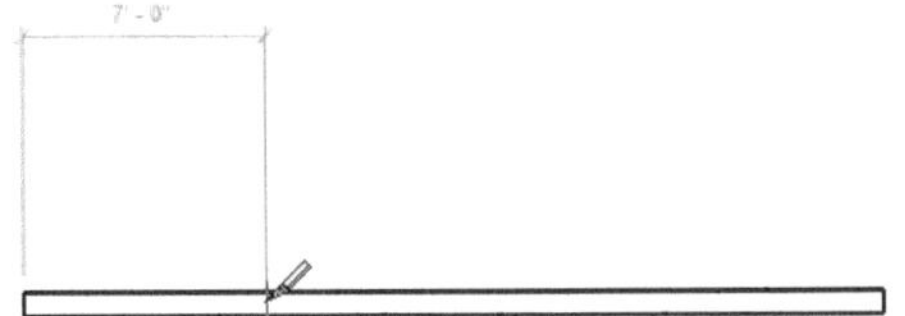

***Figure 5-52** Specifying the point of the split*

***Figure 5-53** Specifying the distance of the split by entering a value*

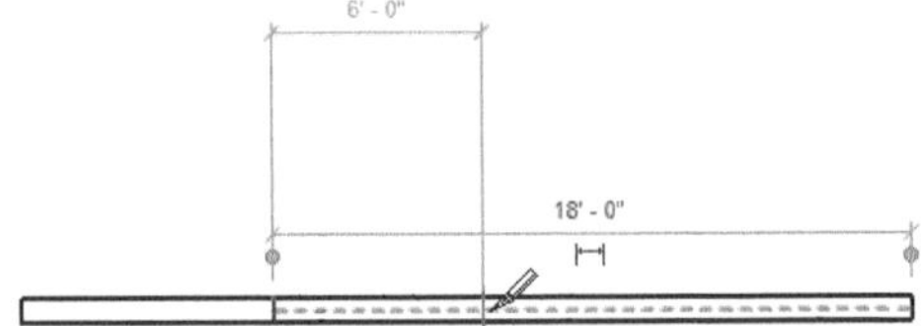

***Figure 5-54** Specifying the second point to split the wall segment*

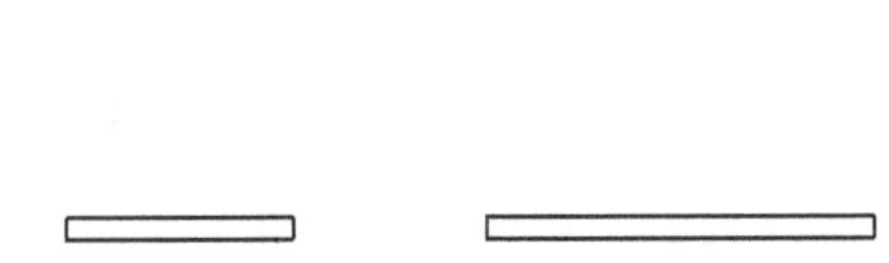

Figure 5-55** Single wall segment split at two points after selecting the **Delete Inner Segment** check box from the **Options Bar

To split a wall segment of a double story building at Level 2 in the elevation view, invoke the **Split Element** tool and move the cursor till it snaps to the Level 2 reference line. Click to split the wall into two portions. When a wall is split at the reference line, the base constraint for its upper portion is set to Level 2. And, the top constraint of its lower portion is set to Level 1. You can also split the wall at a location other than the reference line. For example, to split the middle portion of a wall in the elevation view, invoke the **Split Element** tool and click at the location shown in Figure 5-56; the wall will split horizontally into two. Now, click at another location to separate the middle segment. Next, click at a suitable place in the middle segment to split it vertically into two. You can now select and delete the lower portion of this middle wall to create an opening, as shown in Figure 5-57.

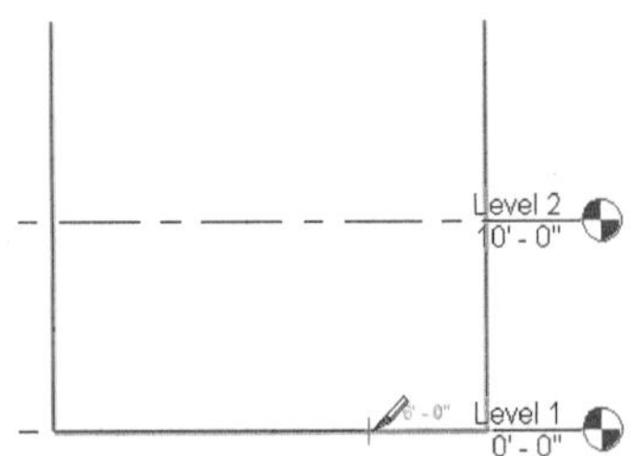

***Figure 5-56** Specifying the location of the split for the middle wall segment*

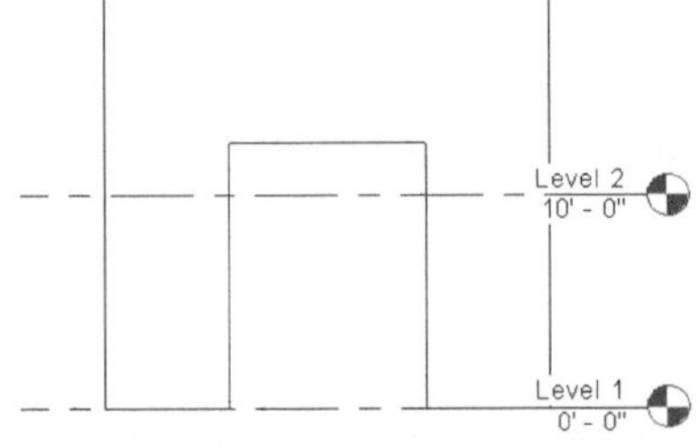

***Figure 5-57** The resulting wall after removing the lower portion of the split middle wall*

SPLITTING WITH GAP

Ribbon: Modify > Modify > Split with Gap

The **Split with Gap** tool is used to split a wall into two separate walls with a defined gap defined between them. To split a wall, invoke the **Split with Gap** tool from the **Modify** panel; the cursor will change to a cutting tool. In the **Options Bar**, enter a value in the **Joint Gap** edit box to set the spacing between two consecutive splits. Note that you can enter a value between 0 1/16" and 1' in the **Joint Gap** edit box. Next, move and place the cursor over the wall that you want to split. Click at the desired point in the wall; the wall will split into two separate walls with a gap value specified in the **Joint Gap** edit box.

SPLITTING FACES

Ribbon: Modify > Geometry > Split Face

The **Split Face** tool is used to split a face of a wall or a column into two separate regions. The splitting of the face of a wall or a column into different regions will help in applying different materials to each region. To split the face of a wall or column, invoke the **Split Face** tool from the **Geometry** panel; the cursor will change to a selection mode. Move the cursor toward the face of a wall or column and click when the face is highlighted. On doing so, the **Modify | Split Face > Create Boundary** tab will be displayed. From the **Draw** panel of this tab, choose a desired sketching tool and sketch the boundary line that will split the face. After sketching the boundary, choose the **Finish Edit Mode** button from the **Mode** panel; the face of the wall or column will be divided into two different regions and you can apply materials to them.

GROUPING ELEMENTS

Ribbon: Architecture > Model > Model Group drop-down > Create Group

Create Group

Grouping elements enables you to associate a single or a number of elements as a single entity or group. Once grouped, the elements act as a single entity. They can be selected as a single element so that you can move or copy a number of elements as a single unit. Each instance of the group acts as a single unit and any modifications made in the group are propagated in all its instances. For example, you may create a group with a cluster of walls, windows, and doors, and then create their multiple instances. When you modify the door type in one group, the change will reflect in all instances of the group. You can create three types of groups, model groups for the model elements, detail groups for the view-specific elements, and attached detail groups for view-specific elements associated with a specific model group. You can create groups either by selecting the elements first and then grouping them, or by creating groups first and then later adding the elements to the groups by selecting them from the project views. To create groups, invoke the **Create Group** tool from the **Model** panel of the **Architecture** tab; the **Create Group** dialog box will be displayed in which you can enter the name of the group.

Note

1. *If you invoke the **Create Group** tool after selecting the elements, the **Create Model Group** dialog box will be displayed.*

2. *You can invoke the Create Group tool from the Create panel of the Modify | (Elements/ Components) tab. Alternatively, type GP.*

Creating Groups by Selecting Elements in Project Views

You can create a group by selecting only the model elements from the project views or using the **Group Editor**. To create groups of elements, select the elements to be grouped and then choose the **Create Group** tool from the **Create** panel of the **Modify | Multi-Select** tab; the **Create Model Group** dialog box will be displayed, as shown in Figure 5-58. Alternatively, after selecting the elements to be grouped, choose the **Create Group** tool from **Architecture > Model > Model Group** drop-down; the **Create Model Group** dialog box will be displayed.

Note

*While creating a group, if you have selected one element type, the corresponding **Modify / (Elements / Components)** tab will be displayed instead of the **Multi-Select** tab.*

In the **Create Model Group** dialog box, specify the name of the group in the **Name** edit box and choose the **OK** button; the name of the created group will be automatically displayed under the **Group** heading in the **Project Browser**. The default name given to a model group is **Group 1** and the number in it increments as more groups are created. You can rename a group by selecting and right-clicking its name and choosing **Rename** from the shortcut menu.

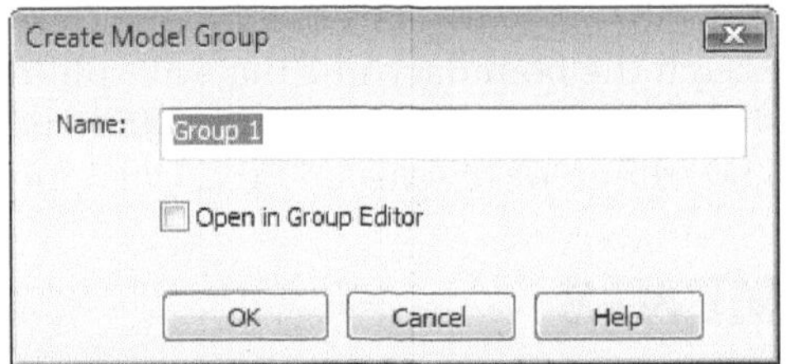

*Figure 5-58 The **Create Model Group** dialog box*

Creating Groups Using the Group Editor

The Group Editor allows you to create groups prior to the selection of the elements. You can create the **Model** group or the **Annotation** group based on the requirement and later on select the elements from the project views and add them to the groups. To do so, choose the **Create Group** tool from **Architecture > Model > Model Group** drop-down; the **Create Group** dialog box will be displayed, as shown in Figure 5-59. In this dialog box, specify the name of the group in the **Name** edit box. The **Group Type** area in this dialog box displays two radio buttons for creating group, **Model** and **Detail**. Specify the type of group by selecting the **Model** or **Detail** radio button and then choose the **OK** button; the screen will display edit mode with a yellow background and the **Edit Group** panel will be displayed in the **Architecture** tab. Figure 5-60 shows the options in the **Edit Group** panel. In the **Edit Group** panel, you can choose the **Add** button to add elements into a group. On choosing the **Add** button, the add (+) symbol will appear with the cursor. You can select the elements from the project view to group them. If there are no elements in the project view, you can create the elements using different tools from the **Build** panel in the **Architecture** tab. The elements will be automatically grouped. You can remove the elements from the existing group, attach details, and even view properties of the group using the respective buttons from the toolbar. Choose the **Finish** button after adding elements to the group.

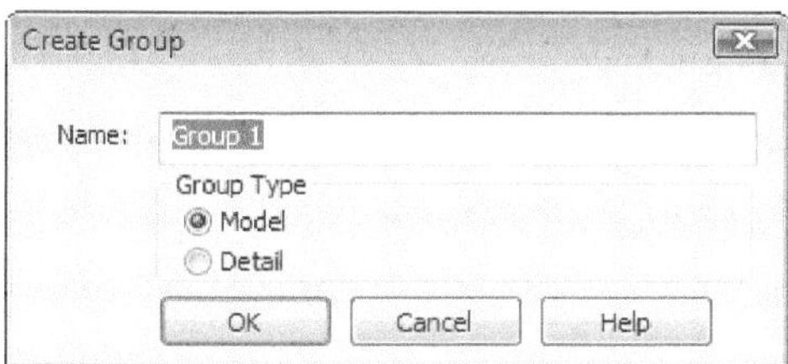

*Figure 5-59 The **Create Group** dialog box*

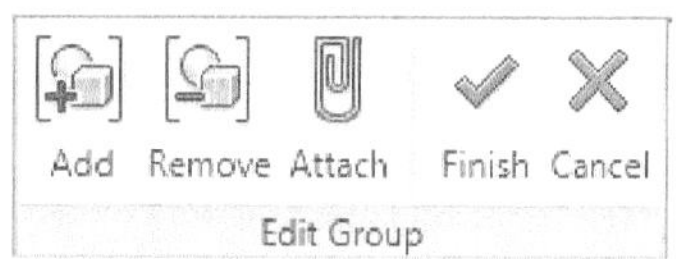

*Figure 5-60 The options in the **Edit Group** panel*

Creating a Detail Group

Revit allows you to group all the detail lines, fill regions, and the detail components separately. You will learn about them in Chapter 12 of this textbook. To group detail components, select them in the drawing and choose the **Create Group** tool from **Annotate > Detail > Detail Group** drop-down; the **Create Detail Group** dialog box will be displayed. Specify the name of the detail group in the **Name** edit box and choose the **OK** button; the name of the detail group will be displayed in the **Groups > Detail** head in the **Project Browser**.

Note

If you select incorrect components to add to a particular type of group, Revit will display a warning about the components that cannot be grouped together. For example, you cannot add tags, dimensions, and spot dimensions to a group of detail components.

Creating Model and Attached Detail Groups

Autodesk Revit allows you to group all the dimensions, tags, and the detail components as an attachment to the model group. This attached group consists of dimensions, tags, detail lines, or detail components that refer to the model group. To create an attached detail group, select the model elements and detail elements simultaneously using a crossing window; the **Modify | Multi-Select** tab will be displayed. Choose the **Create Group** tool from the **Create** panel; the **Create Model Group and Attached Detail Group** dialog box will be displayed, as shown in Figure 5-61. Enter the name of the model group in the **Name** edit box of the **Model Group** area. Next, enter a name of the detail group in the **Name** edit box of the **Attached Detail Group** area and choose the **OK** button; the attached detail group will be created consisting of the detail components, dimensions, and detail elements. The details will be attached automatically to the required model group and displayed in the **Project Browser** under the model group that it belongs to.

You can create a new group by duplicating an existing group. You can also modify the group without affecting the parent group. To create a duplicate group, select the group of which you want to create a duplicate in the **Project Browser** and right-click; a shortcut menu will be displayed. Choose **Duplicate** from the shortcut menu; a new group will be added to the **Project Browser** under the parent group. You can rename the group, if required.

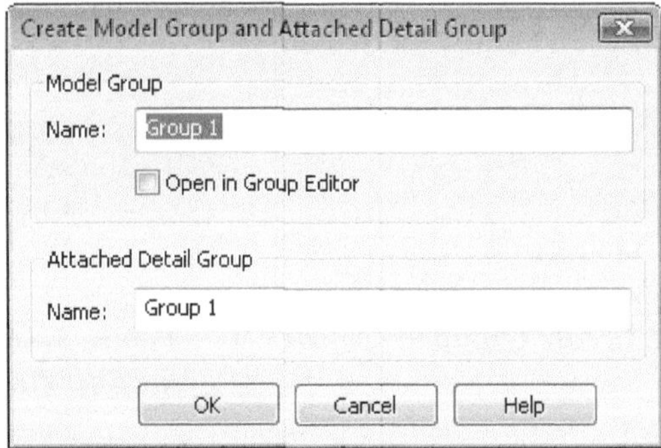

Figure 5-61 *The* ***Create Model Group and Attached Detail Group*** *dialog box*

Alternatively, to create a duplicate group, select the group of which you want to create a duplicate and then choose the **Type Properties** tool from the **Properties** panel of the **Modify | Multi-Select** tab; the **Type Properties** dialog box is displayed. Choose the **Duplicate** button and name the group in the **Name** dialog box displayed. Choose the **OK** button; the group will be added to the **Project Browser** with the new name.

Tip

You can group elements belonging to different families such as walls, doors, windows, furniture, into a single group. If dependent elements are grouped without their respective hosts, Autodesk Revit will display relevant error messages.

Note

In Revit, the detail group behaves as clipped element. On selecting the detail group, a clipped symbol will appear and the group will get selected even if the ***Select Pinned Element*** *option is disabled in the* ***Status Bar****. But on selecting the Model group and detail group together and making them a pinned element, the detail group will act as a pinned element and will not get selected on disabling the* ***Select Pinned Elements*** *option.*

Placing Groups

Once a group is created, you can easily place its instances in the project by dragging the group from the **Project Browser**. Select the required **Detail** or the **Model** group from the **Project Browser**, drag and drop it at the desired location in the drawing area, and then click to place it. Alternatively, to place a model group, choose the **Place Model Group** tool from **Architecture > Model > Model Group** drop-down; the **Modify | Place Group** tab will be displayed. Select the required group from the **Type Selector** drop-down list and click in the drawing area to place the model group.

Tip

The origin and rotation axis controls of a group are useful in saving time in positioning and swapping the group.

Alternatively, to place a detail group, choose the **Place Detail Group** tool from **Annotate > Detail > Detail Group** drop-down; the **Modify | Place Group** tab will be displayed. Now, select the desired detail group from the **Type Selector** drop-down list and click in the drawing area to place the detail group.

While placing a model group that has an attached detail group, you can control the display of the attached detail group. To do so, you need to place an instance of a model group that has a detail group attached with it in the drawing, and then select it; the **Modify | Model Groups** tab will be displayed. Now, choose the **Attached Detail Groups** tool from the **Group** panel; the **Attached Detail Group Placement** dialog box will be displayed. In the **Attached detail groups** area, a list of attached detail groups along with their corresponding check boxes will be displayed. You can select or clear the desired check box(es) to display or hide the detail group(s) along with the model group(s), when placed. Now, choose **OK**; the **Attached Detail Group Placement** dialog box will close and the selected model group will display or hide the attached detail group depending on whether the corresponding check box of the detail is selected or cleared in the **Attached Detail Group Placement** dialog box.

Once a group is placed in a drawing, you can position it at an appropriate location by moving or dragging it. Autodesk Revit provides the origin and rotation controls to set the position of the group. The origin control defines the base point of the grouped elements, whereas the rotation axis defines the rotation of the group. You can drag the two controls to the required location. By doing so, the orientation or position of the group will not change.

Swapping Groups

You can easily replace one group with another group. To do so, select a group from the drawing area; the **Modify | Model Groups** tab will be displayed. In the **Type Selector** drop-down list, the name of the available groups will be displayed. You can click on the **Model Group** drop-down list and select a different group to replace the selected group.

In case of swapping an attached detail group, Revit has the ability to update and replace the attached detail group of the old group with the attached detail group of the swapped group having the same name. Revit also displays a warning indicating the elements for which the reference could not be found out.

Modifying Groups

You can modify a group by ungrouping it. To modify a group, select it from the drawing; the **Modify | Model Groups** tab will be displayed. The **Group** panel of this tab displays the **Edit Group**, **Ungroup**, and **Link** buttons. On choosing the **Ungroup** button, the elements in the selected group will get disassociated and ungrouped. Using the **Edit Group** button, you can add or remove elements from the group and also attach details to it. When you choose this button, the screen will enter into the edit mode displaying the **Edit Group** panel, as shown earlier in Figure 5-60. The **Add** and **Remove** buttons can be chosen to add and remove elements from the group, respectively. After editing, choose the **Finish** button to complete the modifications. The **Cancel** button provides the option of discarding the modifications and returning to the **Modify | Model Groups** tab. You can use different editing tools on the grouped elements such as **Move**, **Copy**, **Mirror**, **Cut**, **Paste**, **Rotate**, and so on.

Excluding Elements from a Group

You can exclude elements from the group if some elements of a group overlap with the elements of the other group while placing them together. If the elements host some other elements such as doors and windows, Revit will automatically rehost the elements in the adjacent walls. To exclude an element from a group, place the cursor over the element that you want to exclude. Next, press TAB to highlight it, and click; a blue color icon will be displayed as shown by the cursor in Figure 5-62. When you place the cursor on the icon, a tooltip will be displayed prompting you to click on the icon to exclude the selected element. Click on the icon and press ESC; the element will be excluded from the group, and will not be displayed in the drawing. Alternatively, to exclude an element from the group, select the element in the drawing as explained above and right-click; a shortcut menu will be displayed. Choose **Exclude** from the shortcut menu; the element will disappear from the drawing and will be excluded from the group. The elements that are excluded will not be visible in the drawing and will not be included in the schedule. To restore the excluded elements in the group, select the group and right-click; a shortcut menu will be displayed. Choose **Restore All Excluded** from the shortcut menu; the elements will be restored in the group and will be displayed in the drawing.

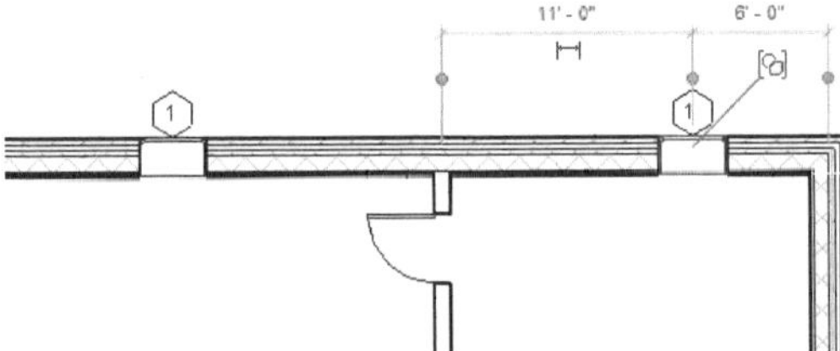

Figure 5-62 *Cursor showing an icon to exclude an element from the group*

Tip

You can use the shortcuts to exclude an element from a group. For example, select the element in the drawing and press EX, DELETE, or CTRL+X to exclude the selected element.

Saving and Loading Groups

In Revit, you can save the group as the Revit file with *.rvt* extension. You can edit the groups independent of the project in which they are loaded. To save groups, choose **Save As > Library > Group** from the **File** menu; the **Save Group** dialog box will be displayed, as shown in Figure 5-63. Select the group to be saved from the **Group To Save** drop-down list and then save it using either the same name as the group name or enter a new name in the **File name** edit box. The group(s) will be saved with the assigned name with *.rvt* extension in case of a project file, or *.rfa* extension in case of a family file. The saved groups can also be loaded into another Autodesk Revit project that is open in the current session by choosing the **Load as Group into Open Projects** tool from **Architecture > Model > Model Group** drop-down; the **Load into Projects** dialog box will be displayed. In this dialog box, the list box displays the name of the project files, along with their check boxes, that are opened in the current session. To load the group(s) to a specified file, you can select the check box that is displayed along with the file name, from the list box. In the **Include** area of the **Load into Projects** dialog box, you can select the **Attached Details**, **Levels**, or **Grids** check boxes, if you want to load the details, grids, and levels in the project with the group. The detail elements will be loaded in the project as attached detail groups. Now, choose

OK; the **Load into Projects** dialog box will close and the window of the selected project file(s) will be displayed. Notice that the group(s) that you have loaded is displayed under the **Groups** head in **Project Browser**.

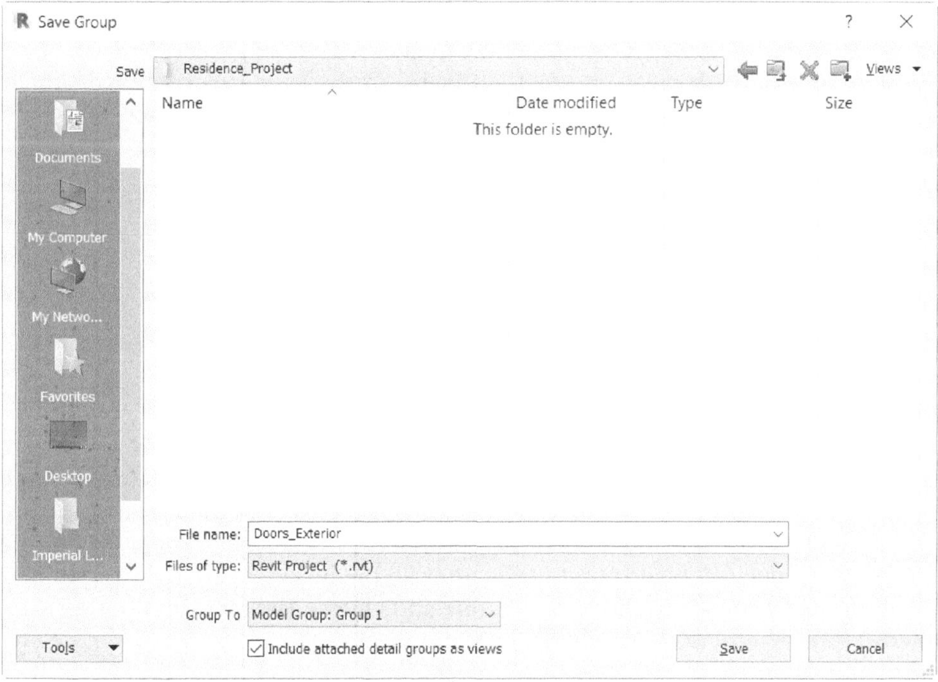

*Figure 5-63 The **Save Group** dialog box*

Converting Groups into Linked Models

To convert the groups into linked models, select the group to be converted into a linked model from the drawing; the **Modify | Model Groups** tab will be displayed. In this tab, choose the **Link** tool from the **Group** panel; the **Convert to Link** dialog box will be displayed, as shown in Figure 5-64.

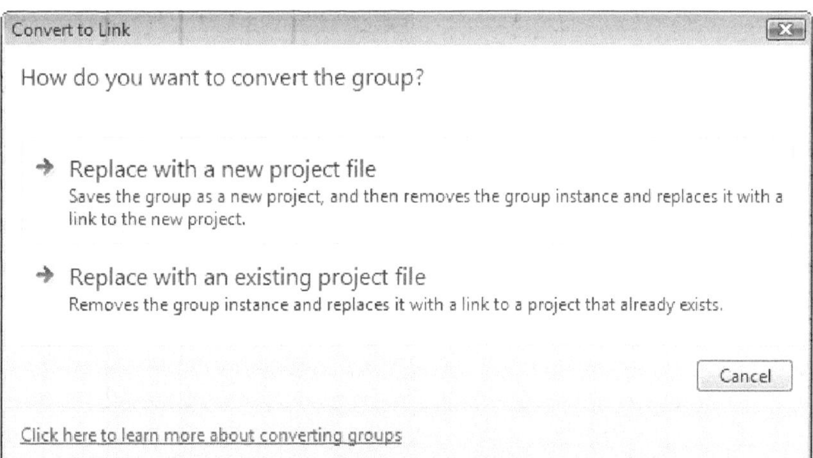

*Figure 5-64 The **Convert to Link** dialog box*

To create a new linked file, choose the **Replace with a new project file** button from the dialog box; the **Save Group** dialog box will be displayed. Specify the name in the **File name** edit box, browse to the required location, and choose the **Save** button to save the file. Choose the **Replace with an existing project file** button to replace the group with an already existing linked Revit model. On choosing this button, the **Open** dialog box will be displayed. Browse to the required location, select the existing file, and choose the **Open** button; the model group will be replaced by the existing linked file. You can choose the **Cancel** button to cancel the conversion.

If the name assigned to the linked group file already exists in the project then Revit will display a message box, as shown in Figure 5-65. Choose the **Yes** button to replace the group file. On choosing the **No** button, the **Save As** dialog box will be displayed. Enter a new name for the linked group file to save the file with a different file name.

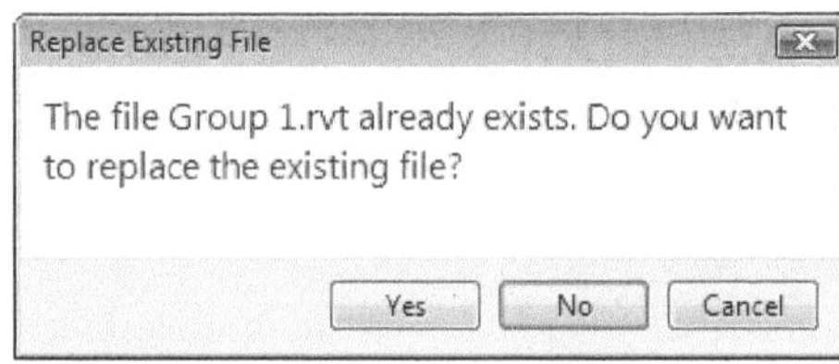

***Figure 5-65** The message box asking to replace the existing file*

Deleting Groups

The created groups can be deleted only after all the instances of the group are deleted from the project. To delete all the instances of a group, right-click on the group name in the **Project Browser** and choose **Select All Instances > In Entire Project** from the shortcut menu. Then, choose the **Delete** button from the **Modify** panel of the contextual tab or press the DELETE key. The name of the group will be displayed even after all the instances are deleted. To delete the group from **Project Browser**, right-click its name and choose **Delete** from the shortcut menu. The **Delete** option is available only when all the instances of the group have been deleted from the project.

Tip

*You can also create nested groups with sub-groups within groups. When you ungroup a group with sub-groups, the association between the sub-groups is terminated. The **Ungroup** button can be used again to edit individual elements in the sub-group. To delete or edit an element from an instance of a group, you need to ungroup it first and then modify the desired element. After the necessary changes are made, the elements can be regrouped.*

CREATING SIMILAR ELEMENTS

Ribbon: Modify (Elements / Components) > Create > Create Similar
Shortcut Key: CS

Autodesk Revit provides the **Create Similar** tool to create and place copies of an element or a group at specified points. This tool is available only after a selection has been made. To create an element similar to an existing element in the drawing, select it; the **Modify | (Elements / Components)** tab will be displayed. Now, choose the **Create Similar** tool from the **Create** panel; the creation tool which was used to create the selected element will be invoked. Now, create the element of similar instance parameter as that of the selected element in your drawing. For example, if you select a window from the drawing and then invoke the **Create Similar** tool, the **Modify | Place Window** tab will be displayed with the window type similar to that of the selected window, which is selected in the **Type Selector** drop-down list. Now, you can place windows with similar instance parameter as that of the selected window in the drawing. Alternatively, to invoke the **Create Similar** tool, select the element and then right-click; a shortcut menu will be displayed. Next, choose **Create Similar** from the shortcut menu; the **Create Similar** tool will be invoked.

PINNING AND UNPINNING ELEMENTS

Ribbon: Modify | (Elements / Components) > Modify > Pin / Unpin
Shortcut Key: PN, UP

Elements can be pinned to their position using the **Pin** tool. To do so, select an element from the drawing; the **Modify | (Elements / Components)** tab will be displayed. Invoke the **Pin** tool from the **Modify** panel. Alternatively, you can type **PN** to invoke the **Pin** tool. Once pinned, a graphical pushpin symbol appears with the element, as shown in Figure 5-66, indicating that it is pinned and cannot be moved from its position. You can also pin the position with respect to other elements and groups. Click on the pin symbol to pin or unpin an element. For example, you can pin the position of columns with the intersecting grid lines. Once pinned, the column and the grid lines cannot be moved without first unpinning their position. You can use the **Unpin** tool to unpin the position constraint for the pinned elements. Note that the **Unpin** tool will replace the **Pin** tool after an element is pinned.

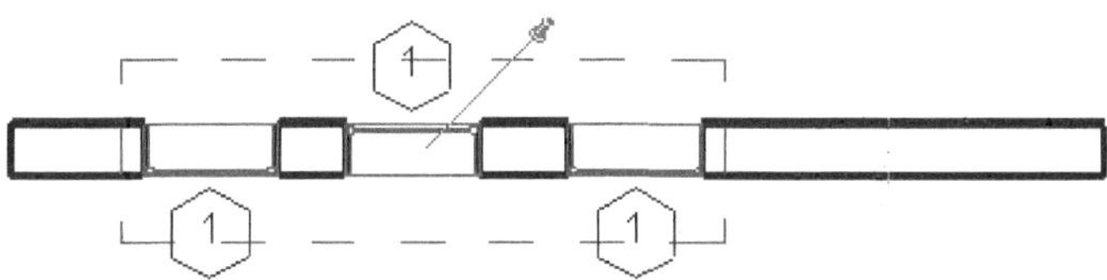

Figure 5-66 *Group of windows pinned at their position*

Note

The pin symbol is not visible after invoking other tools. The element or group must be selected to display the pin symbol. In Revit, you cannot delete the pinned elements. In case of multiple selection, if pinned elements get selected for deletion, then Revit will warn you that the elements are pinned and cannot be deleted. Also, it will instruct you to unpin the element.

SCALING ELEMENTS

Ribbon: Modify (Elements / Components) > Modify > Scale
Shortcut Key: RE

The **Scale** tool is used to modify the scale of a single or a selection of elements and is available only for walls, lines, images, *.dwg* and *.dxf* imports, reference planes and position of dimensions. After making a selection, invoke the **Scale** tool from the **Modify** panel. The **Options Bar** displays two radio buttons that can be selected for scaling, **Graphical** and **Numerical**.

You can select the **Graphical** radio button from the **Options Bar** to resize an element graphically. On selecting this radio button, you will be prompted to specify three points. First to specify the origin of scaling and the other two to define the scale vectors. Once the origin is specified, move the cursor and click to specify the length of the first vector. Move the cursor and click again to define the length of the second vector. Autodesk Revit calculates the proportion of the two vectors and resizes the selected element in the same proportion using the specified origin. The temporary dimensions displayed can also be used to resize the element to the desired scaling. For example, if the length of the first vector is 10' and the second vector is 15', the selected element is resized 1.5 times. Figure 5-67 shows a 10' long wall for which the left endpoint has been selected as the origin and the first vector whose length is 7'6". When you specify the length of the second vector as 15', as shown in Figure 5-68, Autodesk Revit calculates the proportion of the two vectors, 2 in this case, and scales the wall length to 20'.

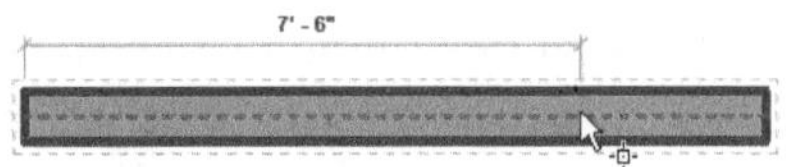

Figure 5-67 *Specifying the first vector for resizing the wall segment*

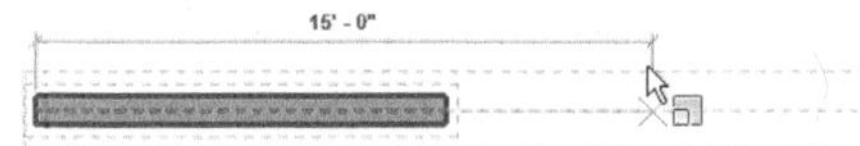

Figure 5-68 *Specifying the length of the second vector for resizing the wall segment*

You can select the **Numerical** radio button in the **Options Bar** and specify the numeric value of the scaling in the **Scale** edit box. You then need to specify the origin of the scaling by clicking it. Autodesk Revit instantly resizes the element by the specified scaling proportion. For example, when you resize a 10' long wall by a numerical factor of 2.5, its length is resized to 25'.

Tip

Scaling moves the position of the location line of the walls but does not change its height or thickness. You can use either the location line or the face of the wall for specifying the origin point.

USING DIAGNOSTIC TOOLS

Autodesk Revit provides tools to assist you in seeking information about the elements in the project. You can use these tools to measure distances and angles, get information of the element identification, and more.

Measuring Distance Between References and Along an Element

Ribbon: Modify > Measure > Measure drop-down > Measure Between Two References
Measure Along an Element

You can use the measure tools to quickly measure and temporarily display the length (and angle from the horizontal, if applicable) of individual walls or lines that you select in the project view (plan and elevation). The dimensions generated by this tool will remain on the screen until you exit from the current tool or start the next measurement.

In Revit, you have two measuring tools: **Measure Between Two References** and **Measure Along an Element**. You can invoke the **Measure Between Two References** tool to find out the exact distance between any two points and also the angle of the distance vector with the horizontal. Invoke this tool from the **Measure** panel; you will be prompted to select the start point. Now, move the cursor to the desired point and click; the start point of the line to be measured will be specified. Now, move the cursor towards the second point; a temporary dimension appears between the specified point and the current location of the cursor. Now, click to specify the location of the second point and the end of the line to be measured. A temporary dimension, along with the angular dimension, is created between the two specified points. Notice that in the **Options Bar**, the **Total Length** text box displays the running total for the length of the chain, if the **Chain** check box is selected.

For example, Figure 5-69 shows the temporary dimension created when two diagonal endpoints of a rectangular wall profile are selected. This temporary dimension or the tape measure value remains on the screen until another measurement or tool is invoked.

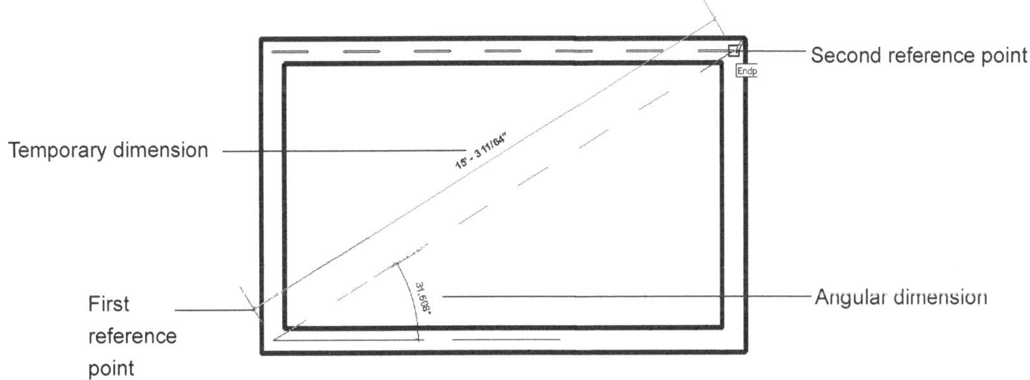

***Figure 5-69** The temporary dimension displayed using the **Measure Between Two References** tool*

You can invoke the **Measure Along an Element** tool to display the length and angle of an element along its axis line. Invoke this tool from the **Measure** panel and then select an element from the drawing; the temporary dimensions will be displayed along the axis of the element.

Tip

While using the measure tools, you can use the object snaps to measure the distance accurately. The location line snaps can also be used to get this information.

Selecting Elements Using the Element ID

In Autodesk Revit, each created element, group or annotation symbol is referred by a unique identification number. Error messages that are displayed refer to an element by its identification number. To display the identification of an element, select it from the drawing and then choose the **IDs of Selection** tool from the **Inquiry** panel of the **Manage** tab. On doing so, the **Element IDs of Selection** dialog box will be displayed, as shown in Figure 5-70. The **Id(s)** text box in this dialog box displays the identification number of the selected element.

You can invoke the **Select by ID** tool from the **Inquiry** panel of the **Manage** tab to identify and select an element by entering its identification number. On invoking this tool, the **Select Elements by ID** dialog box will be displayed, as shown in Figure 5-71. You can enter more than one Id using a ',' (comma) between them. Choose the **Show** button to preview the elements with the entered Ids in the drawing. Choose the **OK** button to create a selection of these elements.

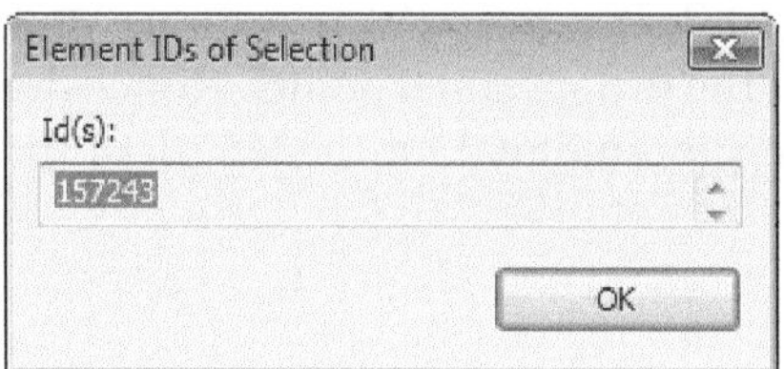

*Figure 5-70 The **Id(s)** text box showing the Id of the selected elements*

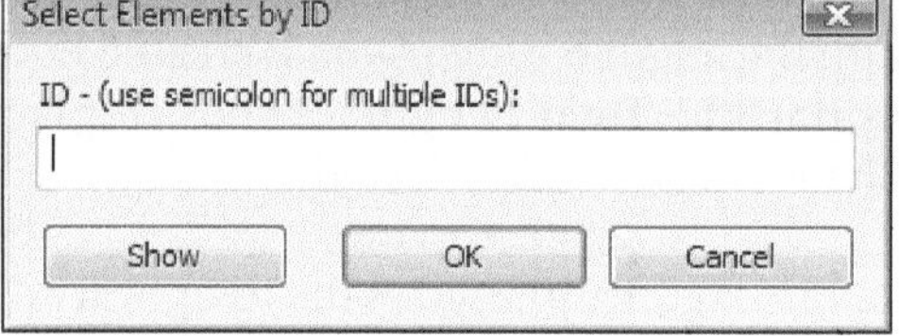

*Figure 5-71 The **Select Elements by ID** dialog box*

Note

When you select a chain of entities, the controls are displayed at joints and vertices. Select the control at the joint and drag it by pressing and holding the left mouse button. The joint remains intact.

ASSEMBLIES

In Revit, you can combine multiple elements to form a single entity called an assembly. The assembly include elements like model elements, annotations, detail items, groups, images, and so on. These assemblies help in identifying, classifying, and quantifying the unique element combinations in the model and are used for scheduling, tagging, and filtering.

The assemblies are listed as a type in the Project Browser. You can select the assembly type from the Project Browser and generate one or more types of isolated views of the assembly as well as parts lists, material takeoffs, and sheets. Assemblies can be placed in the project or assembly sheet views.

Creating Assemblies

To create an assembly, first select the elements that you want to include in the assembly; the **Modify | Multi- Select** tab will be displayed. Choose the **Create Assembly** tool from the **Create** panel of the **Modify | Multi-Select** tab; the **New Assembly** dialog box will be displayed. If the assembly includes elements of different categories like walls, doors and windows then the type name will depend on the option selected from the **Naming Category** drop-down list. If the assembly includes elements of same categories, the **Naming Category** drop-down list will be disabled and you can edit the type name in the **Type Name** edit box. Now, choose the **OK** button; the **New Assembly** dialog will be closed and the created assembly will be listed in the **Project Browser**.

Editing Assemblies

In Revit, you can add elements, remove elements, or can perform edits on the assembly. To edit an assembly, select it from the drawing area; the **Modify | Assemblies** dialog box will be displayed. In this tab, choose the **Edit Assembly** tool from the **Assembly** panel, you will enter into the editing mode and the floating **Edit Assembly** panel and origin with its planes in the drawing area will be displayed.

The origin determines the orientation of the assembly in relation to the project orientation. The planes of the origin helps in determining the orientation of assembly in the corresponding elevations while creating assembly views. On changing the type of an assembly instance, the origin of the new type is applied to that instance. When you select the assembly origin, the drag controls are displayed. You can use the drag controls to modify the origin.

This floating **Edit Assembly** panel will allow you to add or remove the elements from the drawing area. After adding or removing the desired elements from the assembly, choose the **Finish** button from the floating **Edit Assembly** panel, the created assembly will be modified.

You can remove the created assembly at any time from the project by choosing the **Disassemble** tool from the **Edit Assembly** panel of the **Modify | Assemblies** tab.

Creating Assembly Views and Sheets

You can create the assembly views and sheets for an assembly type. To create the assembly view, select the assembly; the **Modify | Assemblies** contextual tab will be displayed. Now, choose the **Create Views** tool from the **Assembly** panel of the **Modify | Assemblies** tab; the **Create Assembly Views** dialog box will be displayed. In this dialog box, you can set the view scale from the **Scale** drop-down list. You can also set your own scale value. To do so, choose the **Custom** option from the **Scale** drop-down list; the **Scale Value** edit box will be enabled. In the **Scale Value** edit box, you can set the scale value for the view. In the **Views to Create** area of the dialog box, all the check boxes are selected by default. As a result, all the views will be created for the assembly. For the assembly, you can create the schedules as well. To create a schedule, select the check box(es) from the **Schedule** drop-down list. You can include the sheets as well by selecting the required sheet from the **Sheet** drop-down list. You can also load the sheets, if required, by selecting the **Load** option from the **Sheet** drop-down list. Now, choose the **OK** button; the assembly views are created under the **Assembly** head in the **Project Browser**.

TUTORIALS

Tutorial 1 — Apartment 1

In this tutorial, you will modify the *c04_Apartment1_tut1.rvt* project file created in Tutorial 1 of Chapter 4. You will copy, move, and mirror the windows to create the project, refer to Figure 5-72. Do not add the dimensions and text as they are given only for reference. Use the following project parameters: **(Expected time: 30 min)**

The following steps are required to complete this tutorial:

a. Open the required file created in Chapter 4.
   For Imperial *c04_Apartment1_tut1.rvt*
   For Metric *M_c04_Apartment1_tut1.rvt*
b. Create the window type W5 using the **Window** tool, refer to Figure 5-73.
c. Use the **Copy** tool to create the windows at the desired locations, refer to Figures 5-74 and 5-75.
d. Use the **Group** tool to group the twin windows W3, refer to Figures 5-76 and 5-77.
e. Use the **Mirror** tool to mirror windows, refer to Figures 5-78 and 5-79.
f. Save the project using the **Save As** tool.
   For Imperial *c05_Apartment1_tut1.rvt*
   For Metric *M_c05_Apartment1_tut1.rvt*
g. Close the project.

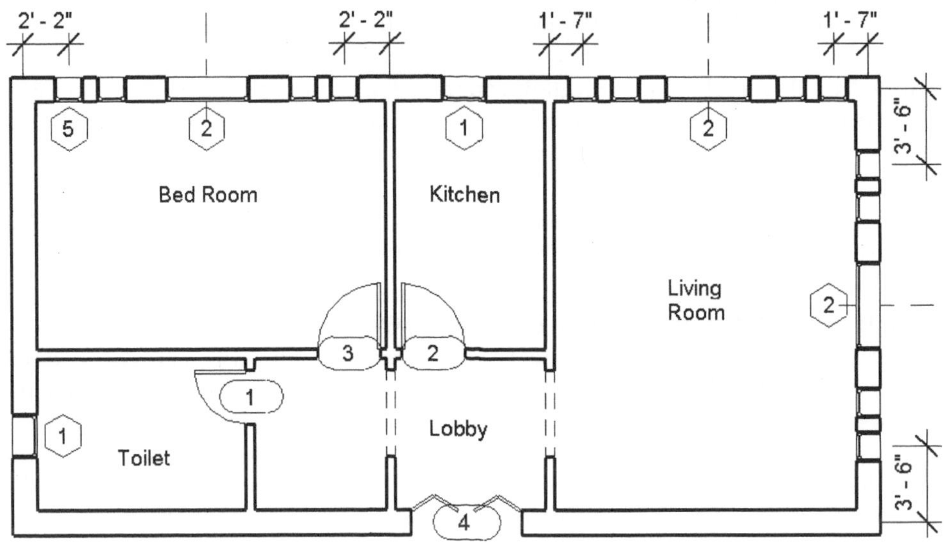

Figure 5-72 Sketch plan of the Apartment1 project

Opening the Project and Creating the Window

You need to open the specified project and add the left side bedroom window using the **Window** tool (see Adding Windows section in Chapter 4).

1. Choose **Open > Project** from the **File** menu and open the file created in Tutorial 1 of Chapter 4.

   For Imperial *c04_Apartment1_tut1.rvt*
   For Metric *M_c04_Apartment1_tut1.rvt*

   You can also download this file from *http://www.cadcim.com*. The path of the file is as follows: *Textbooks > Civil/GIS > Revit Architecture > Exploring Autodesk Revit 2018 for Architecture*

2. In the Project Browser, double-click on **Level 1** under the **Floor Plans** head.

3. Invoke the **Window** tool from the **Build** panel of the **Architecture** tab. Next, in the **Properties** palette, select the required option from the **Type Selector** drop-down list.

   For Imperial **Fixed 16"x48"**
   For Metric **Fixed 406 x 1220mm**

4. Click near the top exterior wall of the bed room to create a window and then modify the temporary dimensions, as shown in Figure 5-73. Press ESC twice to exit the **Window** tool.

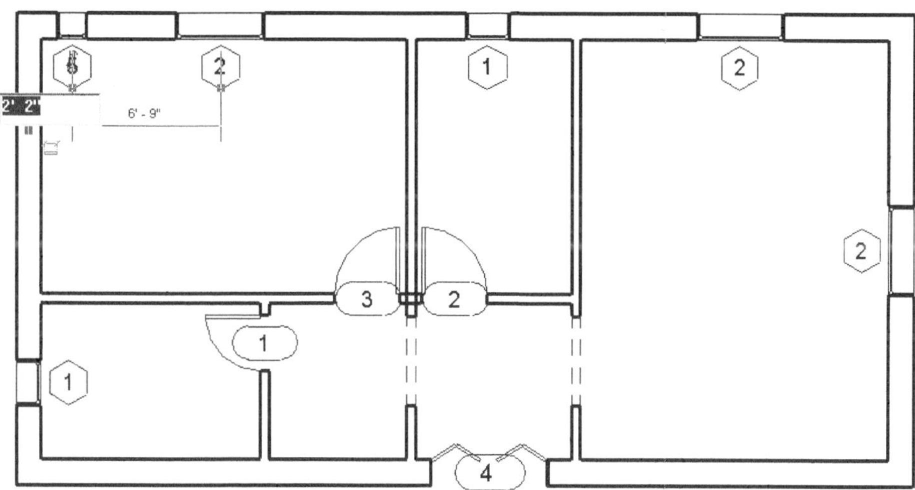

Figure 5-73 Modifying dimension to add window to the Apartment 1 project

Creating a Copy of the Window

Next, you need to copy the window type created in the previous section and then create another window at the specified distance.

1. Select the recently created window from the drawing area by clicking on it. On doing so, the **Modify | Windows** tab is displayed.

2. Invoke the **Copy** tool from the **Modify** panel; the window enclosed in the preview box is displayed indicating that it has been selected for copying. Ensure that the **Constrain** check box is selected in the **Options Bar**.

3. Move the cursor near the midpoint of the window you just created and click to specify the first point of the copy distance when the mid-point snap is displayed, as shown in Figure 5-74.

4. Move the cursor toward the right and type **2'0"(610 mm)** in the edit box displayed. Next, press ENTER; the window is copied at the specified distance, as shown in Figure 5-75. Now, press ESC to exit the **Modify | Windows** tab.

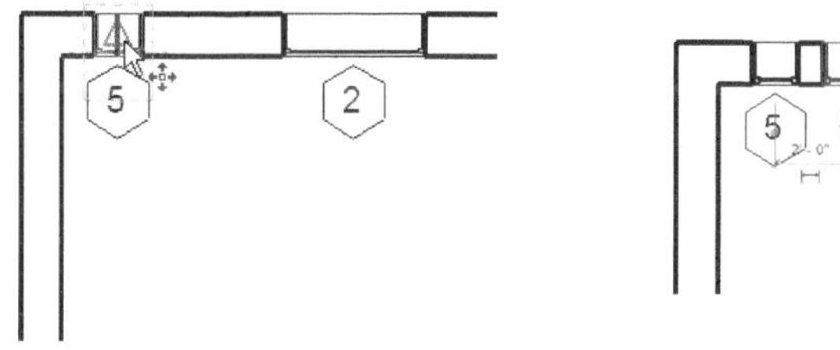

Figure 5-74 Specifying the first point of the copy distance

Figure 5-75 Specifying the distance at which the copy of the window will be placed

Grouping Windows

In this section, you will create a group using the **Create Group** tool. Since these windows appear at the same distance at all occurrences in the project, you can group them as a single entity and then create the copies. Use the pick box option for selecting the windows and then use the **Create Group** tool to group them.

1. Using the pick box selection method, select the two windows; the two windows are highlighted, refer to Figure 5-76.

2. Invoke the **Create Group** tool from the **Create** panel of the **Modify | Windows** tab; the **Create Model Group** dialog box is displayed.

3. Specify **2XW3** as the name of the group in the **Name** edit box and choose the **OK** button.

   The windows are grouped and a preview box is displayed. Also, the group origin controls are displayed, as shown in Figure 5-77.

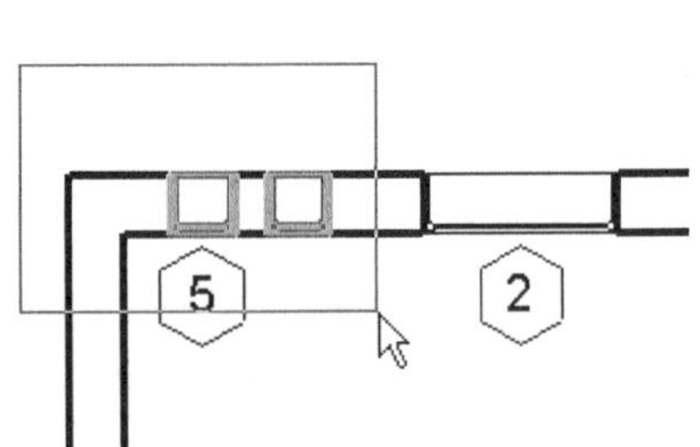

***Figure 5-76** Selecting the windows by using the pick box selection method*

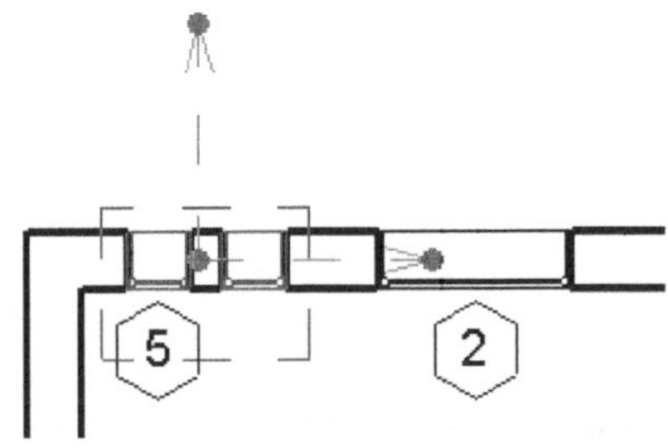

***Figure 5-77** Grouped windows with the group origin controls displayed*

Mirroring and Copying Windows

Now, the twin windows need to be mirrored and copied using the **Mirror - Pick Axis** tool. The sketch plan shows that the twin windows of the bedroom are equidistant from the center of the window tagged 2(W2). You will use this point to create a mirror axis to mirror the windows.

1. Invoke the **Mirror - Pick Axis** tool from the **Modify** panel in the **Modify | Model Groups** tab.
   The mirror tools are available because the created group is already selected and highlighted.

2. Move the cursor near the midpoint of the window tagged 2 (W2) until a vertical line is displayed, as shown in Figure 5-78. This line indicates the midpoint and the mirror axis. Click at this location; the windows are mirrored on the other side of the mirror axis, as shown in Figure 5-79.

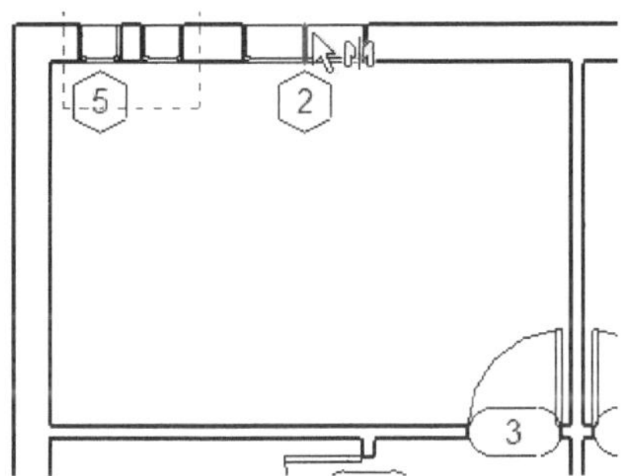

Figure 5-78 Specifying the mirror axis to mirror the twin windows

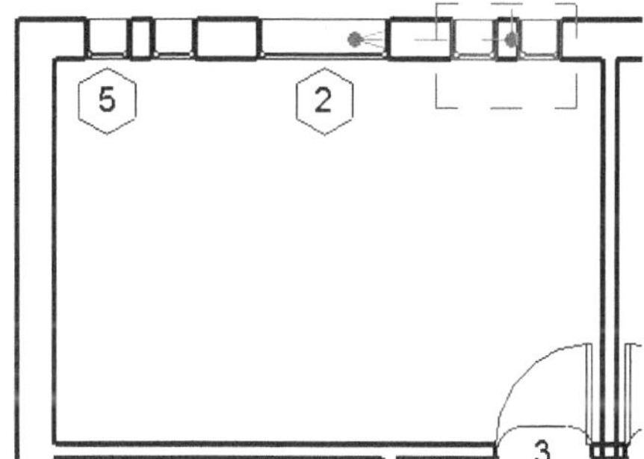

Figure 5-79 Windows created after mirroring

Placing Grouped Windows

Next, you need to place the grouped windows on the exterior wall of the living room by dragging and dropping the group in the drawing.

Activate Dimensions

1. In the **Project Browser**, click on the '+' sign in the **Groups** node of the **Project Browser** to display the created groups. Click on the '+' sign corresponding to the **Model** sub-node; it displays **2XW3** as the group in the project.

2. To place this group in the project, click on the group name in the **Project Browser** and drag and drop it on the exterior wall of the living room, as shown in Figure 5-80. Click to place the group.

3. Select the placed group, as shown in Figure 5-81, and choose the **Activate Dimensions** button from the **Options Bar**. Click on the left dimension and enter **1'7"(483 mm)**; the group moves to the desired location.

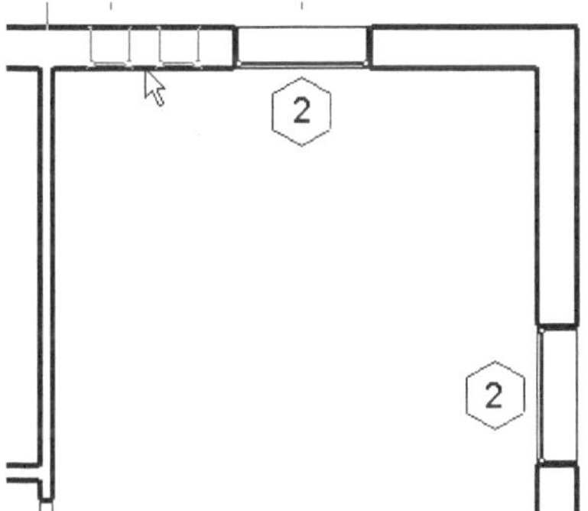

*Figure 5-80 Dragging and dropping a group from the **Project Browser***

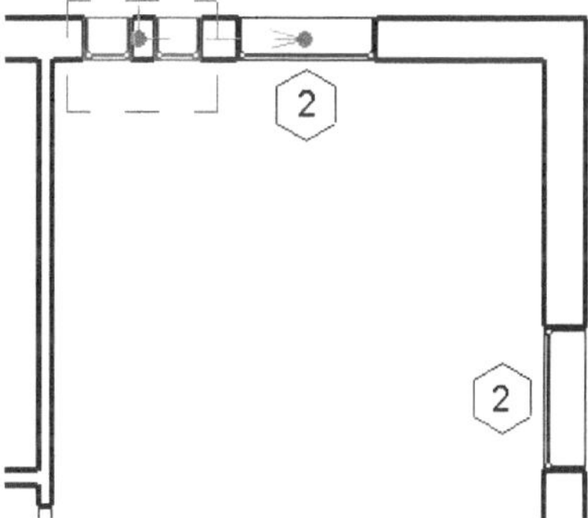

Figure 5-81 Selecting the group to move to the desired location

4. Create a mirror image of the twin windows using the midpoint of the central window as the mirror axis. The windows are mirrored, as shown in Figure 5-82.

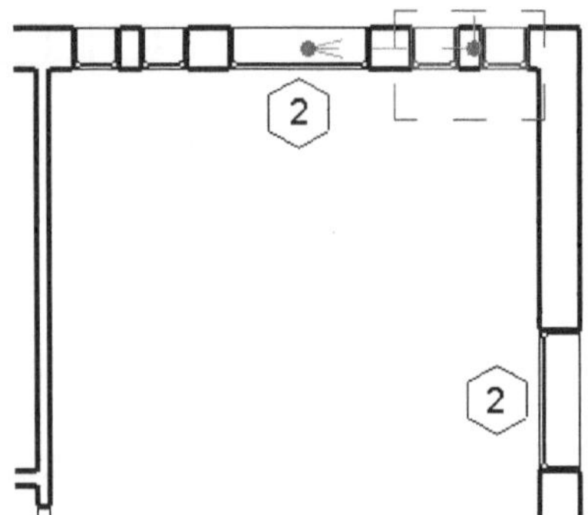

Figure 5-82 Mirrored windows

5. Repeat steps 1, 2, and 3 to place the window group on the upper side of the right exterior wall of the living room. Use the same distance parameter as specified in the sketch plan, refer to Figure 5-72. After placing the window group, create a mirror image of the group using the midpoint of the central window. Use the dimensions shown in Figure 5-72 to specify the exact location of the group. Press ESC to exit the **Modify | Model Groups** tab.

Saving the Project

In this section, you will save the project file using the **Save As** tool.

1. Choose **Save As > Project** from the **File** menu; the **Save As** dialog box is displayed.

   Enter the required file name in the **File name** edit box.

   For Imperial **c05_Apartment1_tut1**

   For Metric **M_c05_Apartment1_tut1**

   Choose the **Save** button; the file gets saved and the **Save As** dialog box is closed.

2. Choose **Close** from the **File** menu to close the project file.

   The completed project will look similar to the one shown in Figure 5-83.

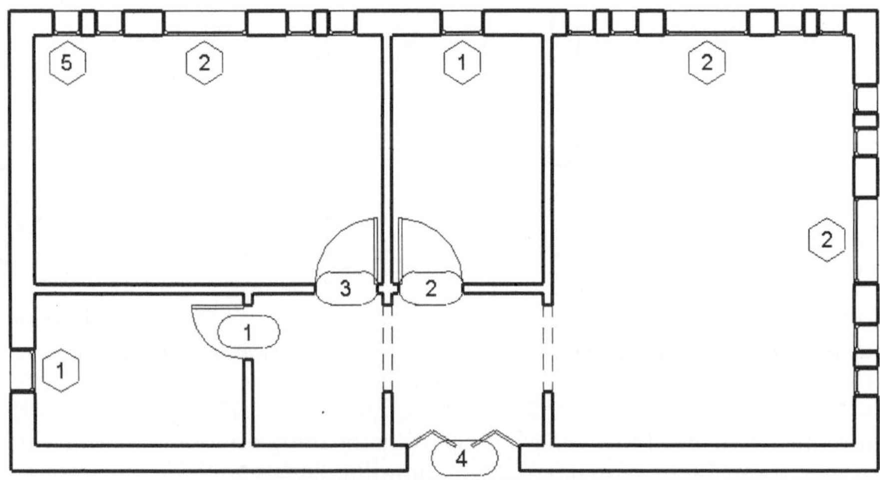

Figure 5-83 The completed Apartment 1 project

Tutorial 2 Club

In this tutorial, you will modify Hall 1 and Lounge of the *Club* project created in Tutorial 2 of Chapter 4. You will move and copy the windows to their desired locations and modify their size and type, refer to Figure 5-84. Do not create the dimensions and text as they are only for reference. Use the following project parameters: **(Expected time: 30 min)**

1. Project File-
   For Imperial *c04_Club_tut2.rvt*
   For Metric *M_c04_Club_tut2.rvt*

2. Window types to be used:
   For Imperial W1- **Fixed 36"x48"**
   For Metric W1- **Fixed 0915 x 1220 mm**

   The following steps are required to complete this tutorial:

a. Open the required file created in Chapter 4.
   For Imperial *c04_Club_tut2.rvt*
   For Metric *M_c04_Club_tut2.rvt*
b. Create an array of four windows of Hall 1 by selecting the **Linear** option of the **Array** tool, refer to Figures 5-85 and 5-86.
c. Create an array of windows of the Lounge by selecting the **Radial** option of the **Array** tool, refer to Figures 5-87 to 5-90.
d. Use the **Create Group** tool to group the four windows W1 as a single entity.
e. Use the **Mirror - Pick Axis** and **Mirror - Draw Axis** tools to mirror the grouped windows, refer to Figures 5-91 to 5-94.
f. Use the **Copy** tool to copy the grouped windows, refer to Figures 5-95 and 5-96.
g. Save the project using the **Save As** tool.
   For Imperial *c05_Club_tut2.rvt*
   For Metric *M_c05_Club_tut2.rvt*
h. Close the project.

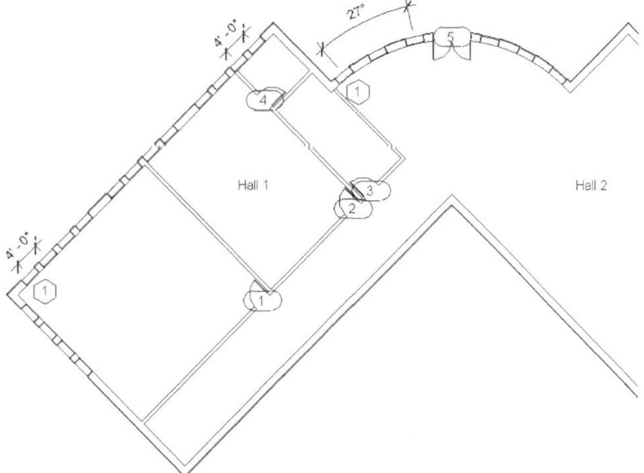

***Figure 5-84** Sketch plan for moving and copying the windows in the Club project*

Opening an Existing Project and Creating an Array of Windows

In Figure 5-84, notice that the windows of Hall 1 appear in three clusters of four windows each in the sketch plan. The four windows are equidistant, 4'0"(1220 mm) apart. You can create them using the **Linear** option of the **Array** tool. Similarly, to create the four windows of the Lounge, use the **Radial** option.

1. Choose **Open > Project** from the **File** menu and open the desired file.
   For Imperial *c04_Club_tut2.rvt*
   For Metric *M_c04_Club_tut2.rvt*

   You can also download this file from *http://www.cadcim.com*. The path of the file is as follows: *Textbooks > Civil/GIS > Revit Achitecture> Exploring Autodesk Revit 2018 for Architecture*

2. Move the cursor on the lower left window tagged 1(W1) of Hall 1 and click to select the window.

3. Invoke the **Array** tool from the **Modify** panel of the **Modify | Windows** tab; the window is enclosed in a dashed rectangular box indicating that it has been selected for creating an array. 

4. In the **Options Bar**, ensure that the **Linear** button is chosen and the **2nd** radio button is selected in the **Move To** area. Also, ensure that the **Constrain** check box is cleared.

5. In the **Number** edit box of the **Options Bar**, enter **4**.

6. Now, move the cursor near the midpoint of the selected window and click when the midpoint object snap is displayed, as shown in Figure 5-85; the start point of the linear array is specified. Ensure that the **Group and Associate** check box is selected.

7. Move the cursor upward along the wall incline and enter the value **4'0"(1220 mm)**, as shown in Figure 5-86; a text box with the number of array elements is displayed.

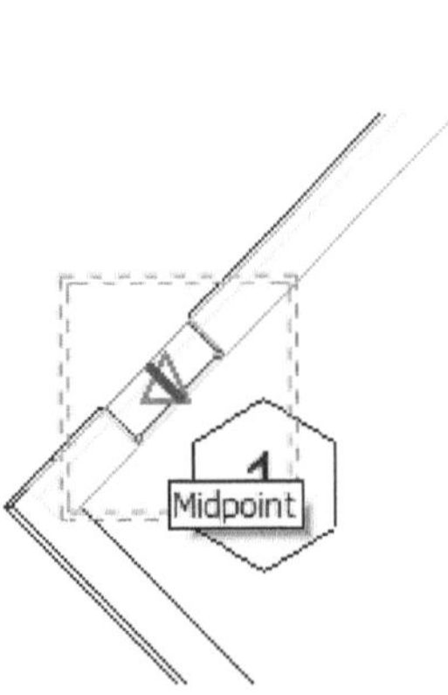

Figure 5-85 *Specifying the first point of the array distance*

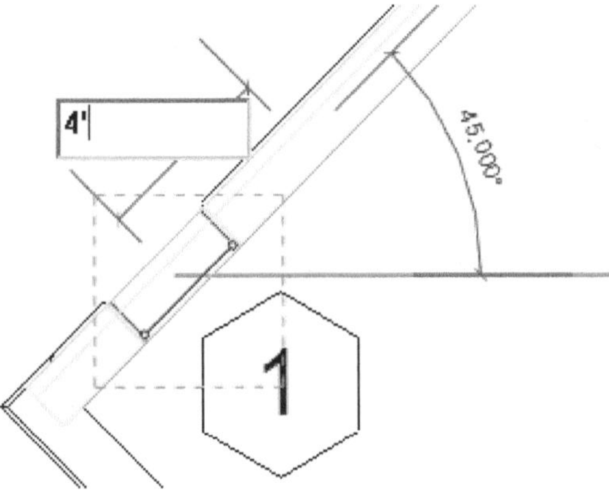

Figure 5-86 *Entering the value of the array distance*

8. Press ENTER to accept the value; an array is created. Notice that as you move the cursor, a preview box showing the location of the selected elements is displayed.

   Similarly, the windows of the Lounge can be created using the **Radial** option of the **Array**.

9. Move the cursor over the exterior window at the Lounge area tagged 1(W1), and click when it is highlighted; the window is selected.

10. Next, invoke the **Array** tool from the **Modify** panel of the **Modify | Windows** tab.

11. In the **Options Bar**, choose the **Radial** button. Also, ensure the **Group and Associate** check box is selected.

12. Select the **Last** radio button in the **Move To** area of the **Options Bar**. To create three windows, enter the value **3** in the **Number** edit box, if it is not entered by default.

    As the center of the required radial array is the center of the circular wall, you need to move the rotation point to it and then create the radial array.

13. In the **Options Bar**, choose the **Place** button and place the cursor at the center of the curved wall, as shown in Figure 5-87. Alternatively, you can move the cursor near the rotation key of the selected window and drag it to the center of the curved wall.

    Notice that the radial array line now originates from the new center point.

14. Move the cursor near the midpoint of the Lounge window and click when the **Midpoint** object snap is displayed, as shown in Figure 5-88; the start point of the radial array is specified.

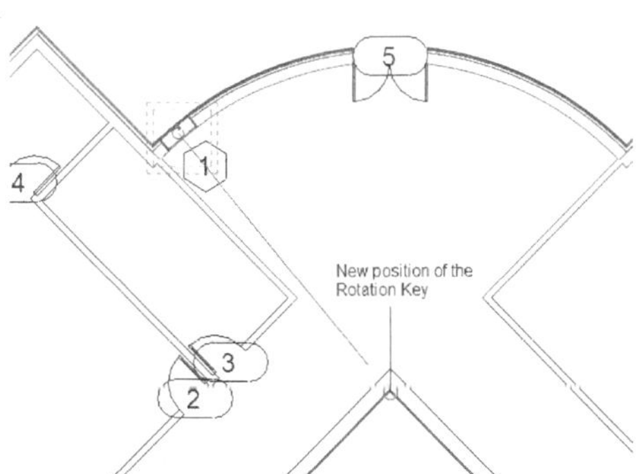

Figure 5-87 *Rotation key moved to the new rotation point*

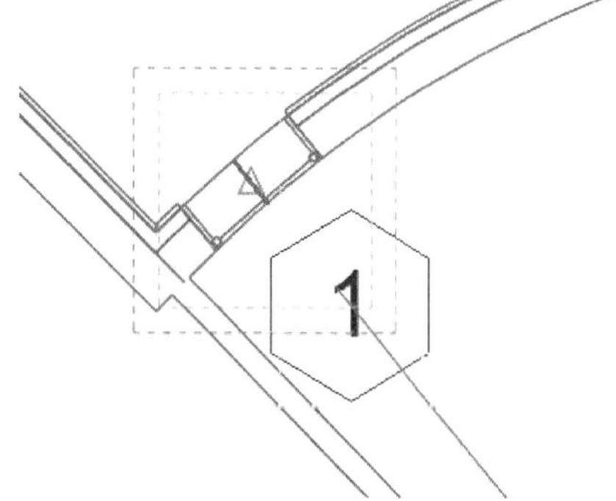

Figure 5-88 *Specifying the first point of the array*

15. Move the cursor clockwise along the curved wall and enter **27** as the temporary angular dimension, as given in the sketch plan and shown in Figure 5-89.

16. Next, press ENTER twice to accept the value specified for the angular dimension and the number of array elements; the radial array is created, as shown in Figure 5-90.

17. Choose the **Modify** button from the **Select** panel to exit the current selection.

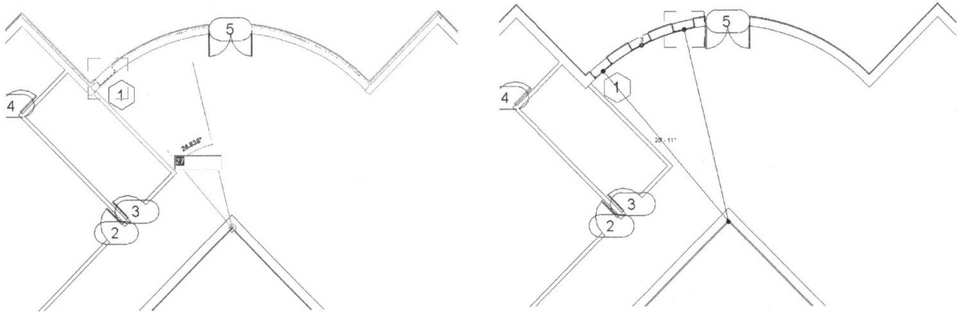

Figure 5-89 *Specifying the array angle* ***Figure 5-90*** *Radial array of the selected window*

Grouping the Cluster of Windows

The sketch plan shows the cluster of four Hall 1 windows appearing together. Group them for the ease of copying. You can use the **Create Group** tool to group the array of windows.

1. Move the cursor near the four windows of the Hall 1 and select them using the CTRL key.

2. Invoke the **Create Group** tool from the **Create** panel of the **Modify | Model Groups** tab; the **Create Model Group** dialog box is displayed. The default name of the group of windows in the dialog box is Group 1.

3. Specify **4XW1- Linear Windows** as the group name in the **Name** edit box.

4. Choose the **OK** button in the dialog box; the windows are grouped and the group name is displayed in the **Groups** node of the **Project Browser** in the **Model** subhead.

Mirroring the Grouped Windows

You need to mirror the grouped windows of Hall 1 and the radial windows of the Lounge using the **Mirror - Pick Axis** and **Mirror - Draw Axis** tools.

1. Move the cursor near the grouped windows of Hall 1 and click; the grouped windows are selected and highlighted, as shown in Figure 5-91.

2. Choose the **Mirror - Pick Axis** tool from the **Modify** panel of the **Modify | Model Groups** tab. Also, ensure that the **Copy** check box is selected in the **Options Bar**.

3. Move the cursor near the interior wall and click when the cursor snaps to the wall centerline; the wall centerline is selected as the mirror axis, as shown in Figure 5-92, and the grouped

windows are mirrored to the other end of the exterior wall. Ignore the error that is displayed due to the conflicts between the interior wall and the window. Now, choose the **Modify** button from the **Select** panel or press ESC to exit the current selection.

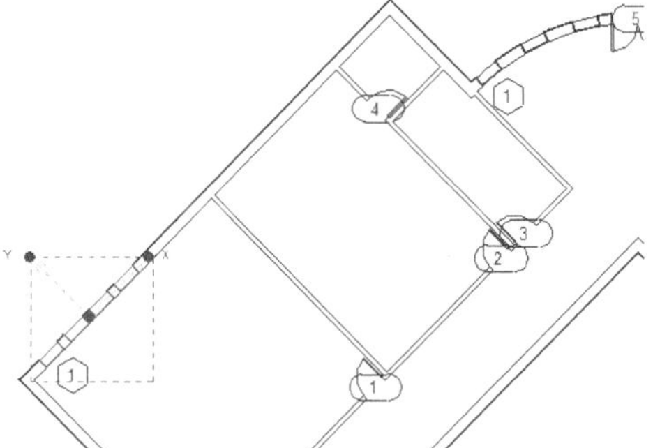

Figure 5-91 *Grouped windows selected and highlighted*

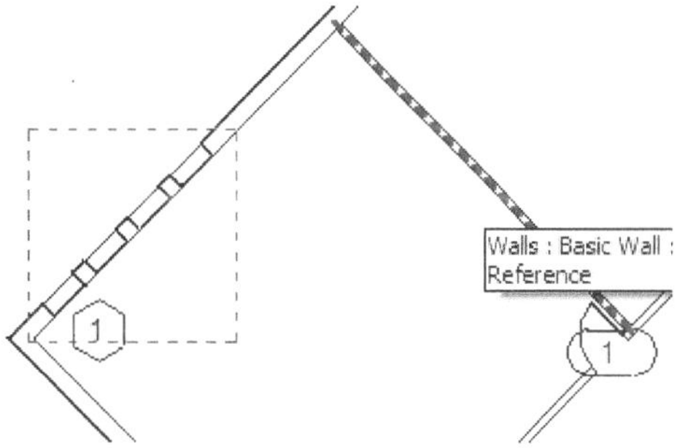

Figure 5-92 *Using the wall centerline as the mirror axis*

Notice that the same window type is also placed on the lower left perpendicular wall. You can use the **Mirror - Draw Axis** tool to mirror the grouped windows to the perpendicular wall.

4. Click on the original grouped windows to select them.

5. Invoke the **Mirror - Draw Axis** tool from the **Modify | Model Groups** tab.

6. In the **Options Bar**, ensure that the **Copy** check box is selected.

7. Move the cursor to the intersection of the two perpendicular walls and click when the endpoint object snap is displayed; the first point of the mirror line is specified.

8. Move the cursor horizontally and click when the dashed line is displayed, as shown in Figure 5-93; the second point of the mirror axis is specified. Now, choose the **Modify** button from the **Select** panel to exit from the current selection.

9. The grouped windows are mirrored to the perpendicular wall, as shown in Figure 5-94.

Similarly, mirror the three radial windows of the Lounge to the other side of the door using the **Mirror - Draw Axis** tool. Draw the vertical axis from the center of the curved wall as the mirror axis.

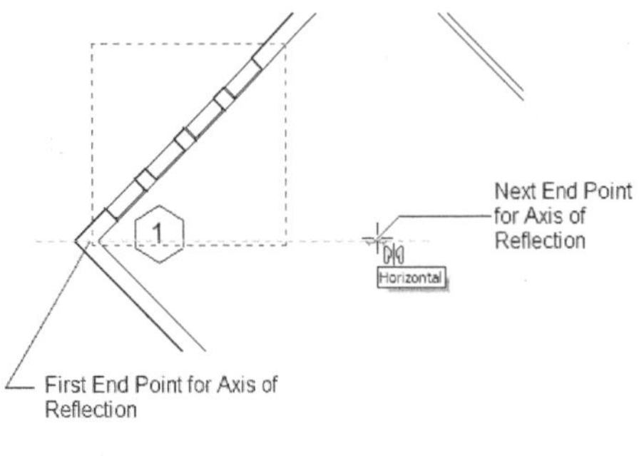

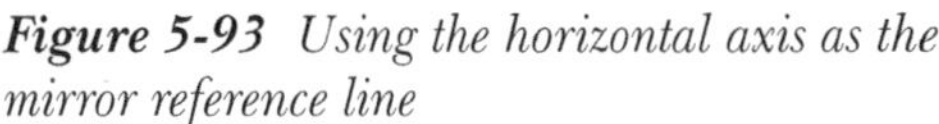
Figure 5-93 *Using the horizontal axis as the mirror reference line*

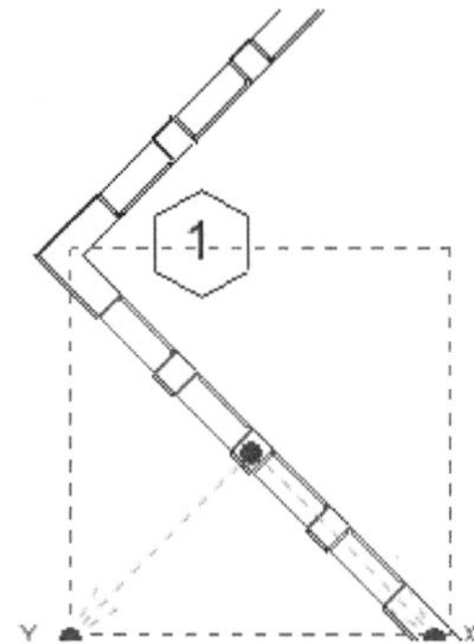

Figure 5-94 *Mirrored windows on the perpendicular wall*

Copying the Grouped Windows

You can use the **Copy** tool to copy the grouped windows of Hall 1.

1. Select the original grouped window of Hall 1.
2. Invoke the **Copy** tool from the **Modify | Model Groups** tab.
3. Select the group origin or the midpoint of the grouped windows as the start point of the copy distance.
4. Move the cursor upward along the external wall and choose the endpoint of the central internal wall as the second point of the copy distance, as shown in Figure 5-95. On doing so, the grouped window is copied at the desired location, as shown in Figure 5-96.

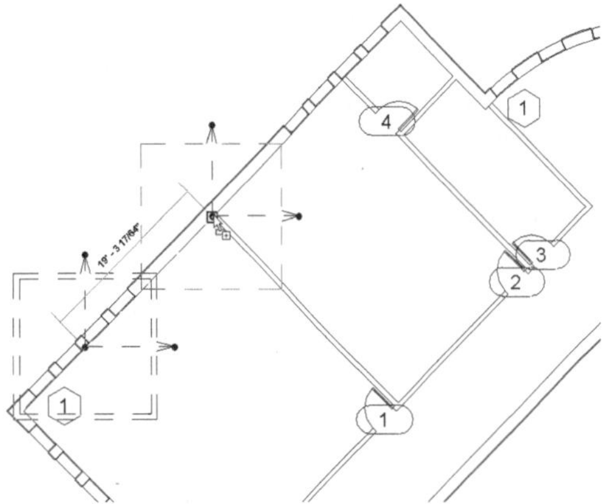

Figure 5-95 *Specifying the start and end points of the copy distance*

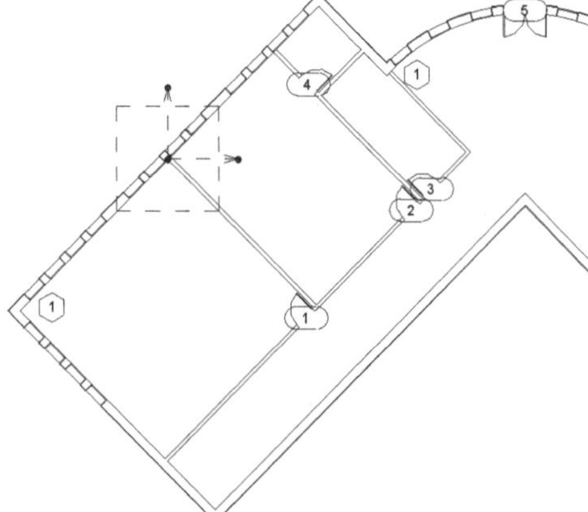

Figure 5-96 *Grouped windows copied*

Saving the Project

In this section, you will save the project file using the **Save As** tool.

1. Choose **Save As > Project** from the **File** menu; the **Save As** dialog box is displayed. Enter the required file in the **File name** edit box
   For Imperial **c05_Club_tut2**
   For Metric **M_c05_Club_tut2**
   Choose **Save**; the file is saved and the dialog box gets closed.

2. Choose **Close** from the **File** menu to close the project file.

Tutorial 3 Office-Assembly Views

In this tutorial, you will modify *Office* project. Refer to Figure 5-97. You will create, move, and copy the doors and windows to their desired locations and also create assembly of the stacked wall. Do not create the dimensions and text as they are only for reference. Use the following project parameters: **(Expected time: 30 min)**

1. Project File:
   For Imperial *c03_Office_tut5.rvt*
   For Metric *M_c03_Office_tut5.rvt*

2. Door types to be used:
   For Imperial **Door-Interior-Double-Sliding-2_Panel-Wood 72" x 84"**
   Door-Interior-Single-Full Glass-Wood 36" x 84"
   For Metric **M_Door-Interior-Double-Sliding-2_Panel-Wood 1800 x 2100 mm**
   M_Door-Interior-Single-Full Glass-Wood 0750/ x 2100 mm

3. Window types to be used:
   For Imperial W1- **Awning with Trim 36"x48"**
   For Metric W1- **Awning with Trim 0915 x 1220 mm**

The following steps are required to complete this tutorial:

a. Open the required file.
   For Imperial *c03_Office_tut5.rvt*
   For Metric *M_c03_Office_tut5.rvt*
b. Add doors and windows to the project.
c. Copy and mirror windows.
d. Create assembly using the **Create Assembly** tool.
e. Save the project using the **Save As** tool.
   For Imperial *c05_Office_tut3.rvt*
   For Metric *M_c05_Office_tut3.rvt*
f. Close the project.

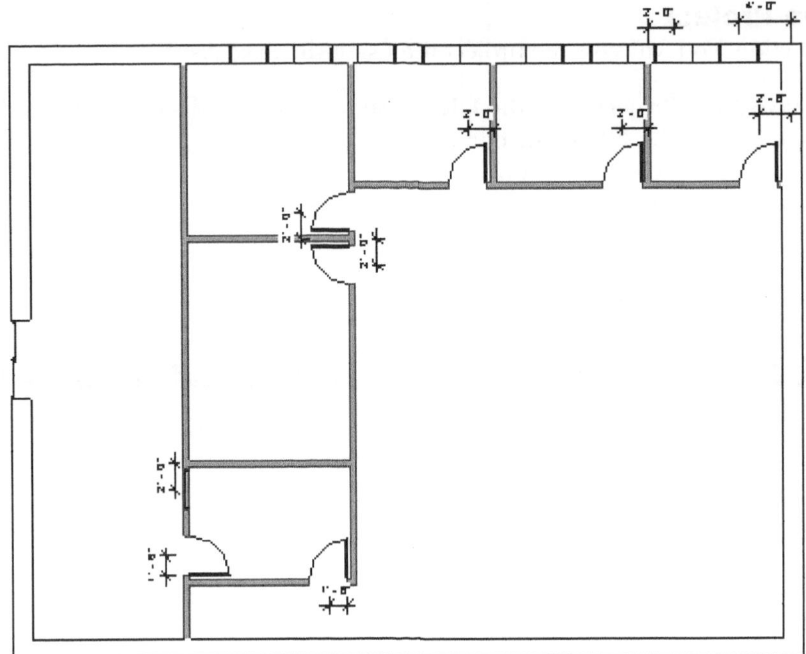

Figure 5-97 *Sketch plan for adding and copying the doors and windows in the Office project*

Opening the Project

In this section, you will open the existing project and also add doors and windows to the *Office* project.

1. Choose **Open > Project** from the **File** menu and open the desired file.
   For Imperial *c03_office_tut5.rvt*
   For Metric *M_c03_office_tut5.rvt*
   You can also download this file from *http://www.cadcim.com*. The path of the file is as follows: *Textbooks > Civil/GIS > Revit Architecture> Exploring Autodesk Revit 2018 for Architecture*

2. Double-click on **Level 1** under the **Floor Plans** head in the **Project Browser**; the floor plan view is displayed.

Adding Doors and Windows

In this section, you will add doors and copy and array the windows to the *Office* project.

1. Invoke the **Door** tool from the **Build** panel of the **Architecture** tab; the **Modify | Place Door** tab is displayed.

2. In this tab, choose the **Load Family** tool from the **Mode** panel; the **Load Family** dialog box is displayed.

3. Load the **Door-Double-Sliding** and **Door-Interior-Single-Full Glass-Wood** door types from the **US Imperial > Doors > Residential** folder (**US Metric > Doors > Residential** folder for Metric); the **Specific Types** dialog box is displayed. Load all the sizes of the type and then choose **Open** button; the loaded types are displayed in the **Type-Selector** drop-down list.

4. Select the required door type from the **Type-Selector** drop-down list.
   For Imperial **Door-Interior-Double-Sliding-2_Panel-Wood 72" x 82"**
   For Metric **M_Door-Interior-Double-Sliding-2_Panel-Wood 1800 x 2100 mm**

5. Now, place the door at the entrance, as shown in Figure 5-98.

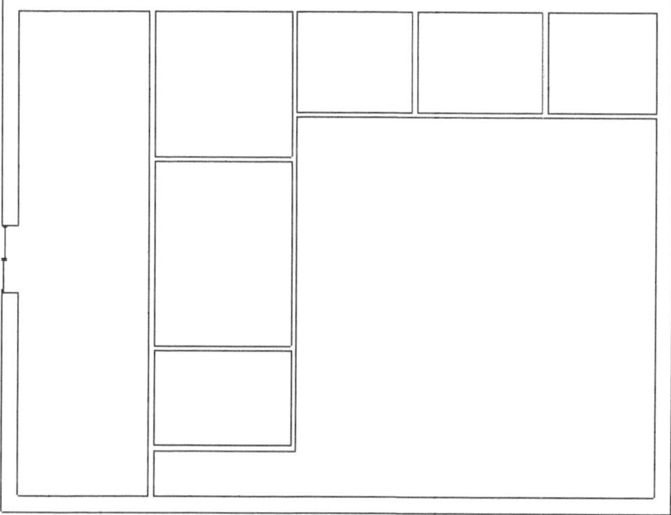

Figure 5-98 *Entrance door placed*

6. Select the desired door type from the **Type Selector** drop-down list.
   For Imperial **Door-Interior-Single-Full Glass-Wood 36" x 84"**
   For Metric **M_Door-Interior-Single-Full Glass-Wood 0750 x 2100 mm**
   Note that the **Tag on Placement** tool is not chosen in the **Modify|Place Door** tab.

7. Place the doors, as shown in Figure 5-99.

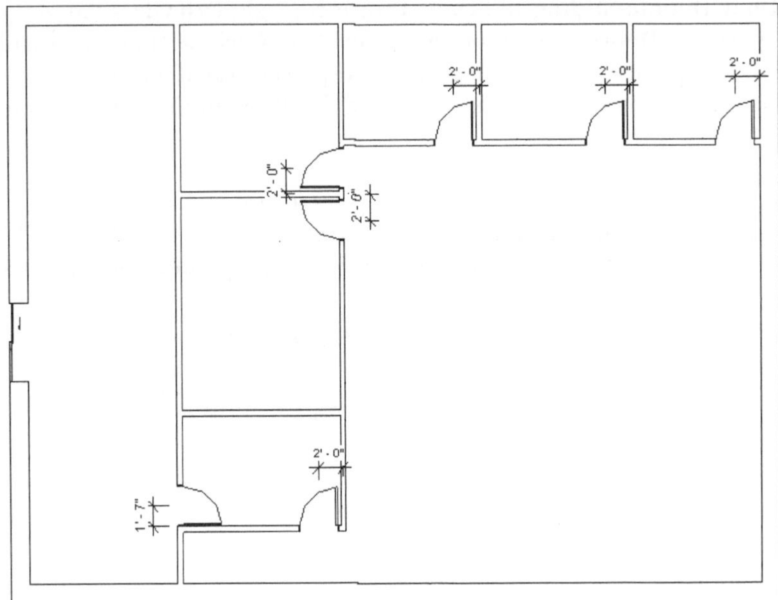

Figure 5-99 *Other doors in the building*

8. Invoke the **Window** tool from the **Build** panel of the **Architecture** tab; the **Modify| Place Windows** tab is displayed.

9. Repeat the procedure followed in steps 2 and 3 and load the **Awning with Trim** window type from **US Imperial > Windows** folder for Imperial (**US Metric > Windows** folder for Metric).

10. Select the window type **Awning with Trim: 36"x24"** from the **Type Selector** drop-down list.

11. Place the windows, as shown in Figure 5-100.

12. Press ESC twice to exit the current selection tool.

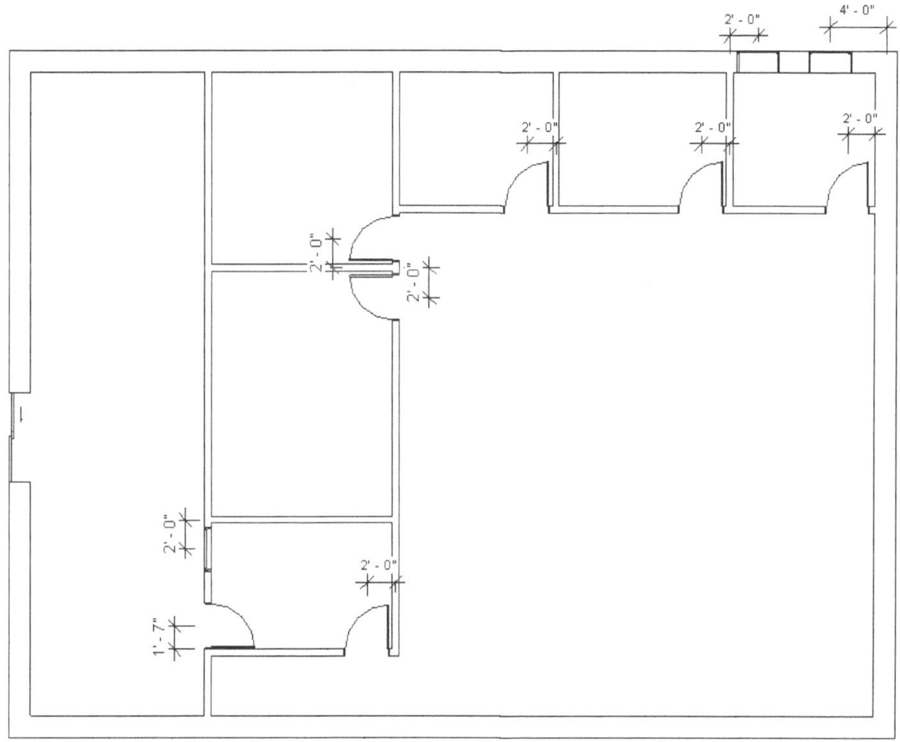

Figure 5-100 Windows placed at a specified distance

Copying and Mirroring Windows

Here, you will copy and mirror the windows.

1. Choose the windows that you want to copy; the **Modify|Windows** tab is displayed.

2. Invoke the **Copy** tool from the **Modify** panel of the **Modify | Windows** tab; the window is enclosed in a dashed rectangular box indicating that it has been selected for creating an array.

3. In the **Options Bar**, ensure that the **Multiple** check box is selected. Also, ensure that the **Constrain** check box is cleared.

4. Now, move the cursor near the midpoint of the selected window and click when the midpoint object snap is displayed; the start point of the copy is specified.

5. Move the cursor left along the wall and enter the value **5'** (for Metric **1927 mm**), as shown in Figure 5-101 and then press ENTER.

6. Press ENTER to accept the value; a copy of the window is created. Notice that as you move the cursor, a preview box showing the location of the selected elements is displayed.

7. Repeat the procedure followed in steps 5 and 6 to place other windows at a distance of **4'**, refer to Figure 5-102.

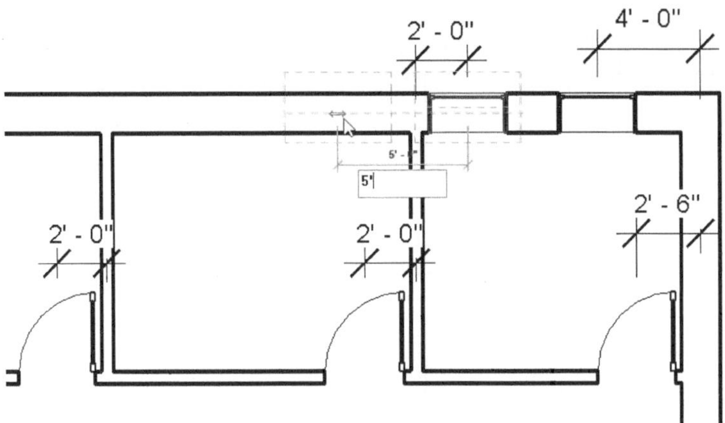

Figure 5-101 *Entering the value* ***5'*** *in the edit box*

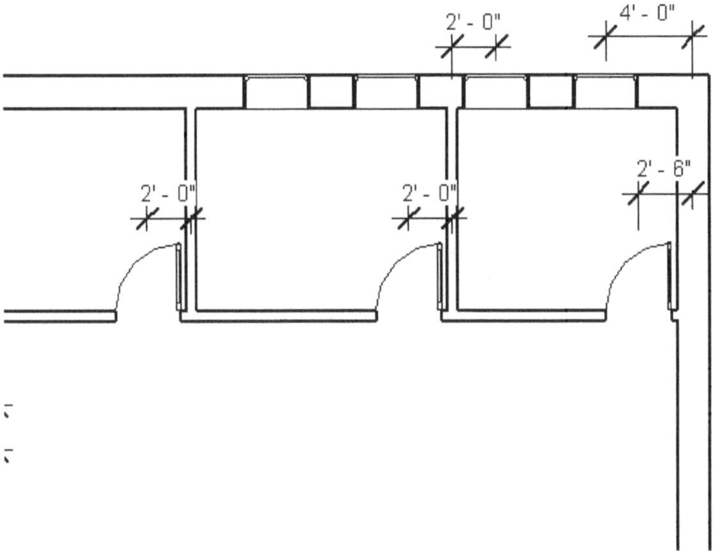

Figure 5-102 *Two other windows placed*

8. Select all the windows using the CTRL key; the windows get highlighted in blue and the **Modify| Windows** tab is displayed.
9. Now, choose the **Mirror-Pick Axis** tool from the **Modify** panel of the **Modify| Windows** tab.
10. Pick the axis when it gets highlighted in blue and click, refer to Figure 5-103; the windows are mirrored.

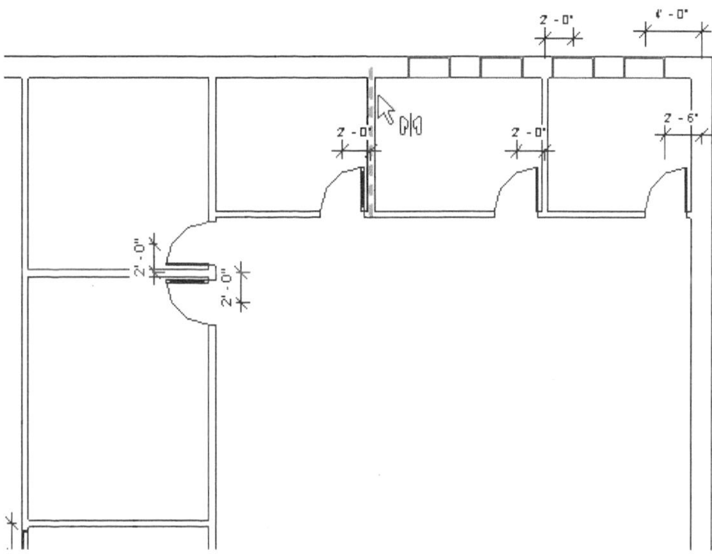

Figure 5-103 Picking the axis of wall to mirror windows

Creating Assemblies

Now, you will first create assemblies and then the views within that assembly.

1. Select the entire model which you have created; the **Modify | Multi-Select** tab is displayed.
2. In this tab, choose the **Filter** tool from the **Selection** panel; the **Filter** dialog box is displayed.
3. In this dialog box, choose the **Check None** button; all the check boxes are cleared.
4. Now, select the **Walls** check box and choose the **OK** button; the wall is highlighted in blue.
5. Choose the **Create Assembly** tool from the **Create** panel of the **Modify | Walls** tab; the **New Assembly** dialog box is displayed.
6. In this dialog box, enter **Wall Assembly** in the **Type Name** edit box and choose the **OK** button; the assembly is created with the name **Wall Assembly** under the **Assemblies** head in the **Project Browser**.
7. Now, select the assembly from the drawing area, as shown in Figure 5-104; the **Modify | Assemblies** tab is displayed.
8. Choose the **Create Views** tool from the **Assembly** panel of the **Modify | Assemblies** tab; the **Create Assembly Views** dialog box is displayed.
9. In this dialog box, ensure that all the check boxes are selected and then select the **Wall Schedule** check box under the **View type** list.

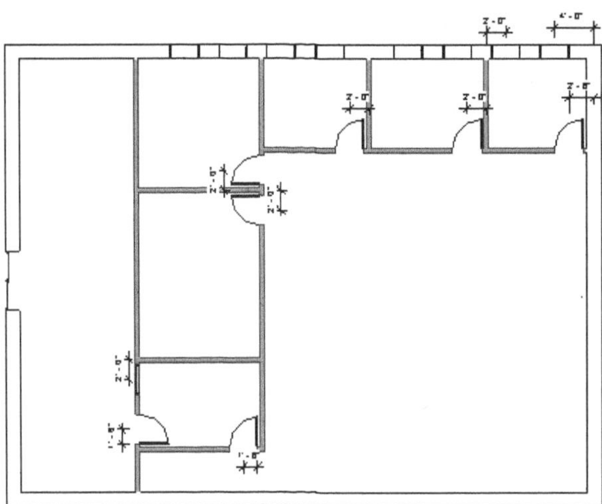

Figure 5-104 Selecting the assembly

10. Select the **Load** option from the **Sheet** drop-down list; the **Load Family** dialog box is displayed.

11. In this dialog box, select the required titleblock from the **US Imperial > Titleblocks** folder for Imperial (**US Metric > Titleblocks** folder for Metric).
    For Imperial **C 17 x 22 Horizontal**
    For Metric **A2 metric**

12. Choose the **Open** button; the sheet is loaded in the **Sheet** drop-down list.

13. Choose the **OK** button; the assembly views are displayed under the **Wall Assembly** head in the **Project Browser** and the view in the drawing area is changed.

14. Double-click on the **Detail View: Plan Detail** under the **Wall Assembly** head in the **Project Browser**; the plan detail view is displayed.

15. In the **Properties** palette, select the required option from the **View Scale** drop-down list.
    For Imperial **3/32" = 1'-0"**
    For Metric **1:100**

16. Double-click on **Sheet: A101 - Sheet** in the **Project Browser**; the sheet view is displayed.

17. Select **Detail View: Plan Detail** from the **Wall Assembly** head in the **Project Browser** and then drag it to the drawing area and place the view, as shown in Figure 5-105.

18. Repeat the procedure followed in step 17 and place the **Schedule: Material Takeoff**, **Schedule: Part List 1** and **Schedule: Wall Schedule** views in the sheet view, as shown in Figure 5-106.

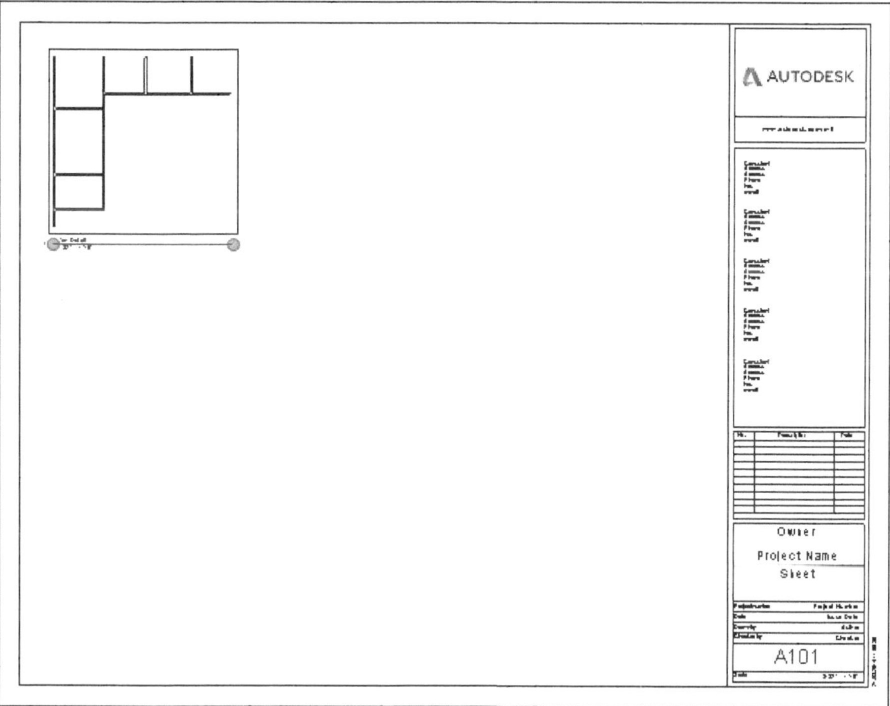

Figure 5-105 The Detail View: Plan Detail view placed on the sheet

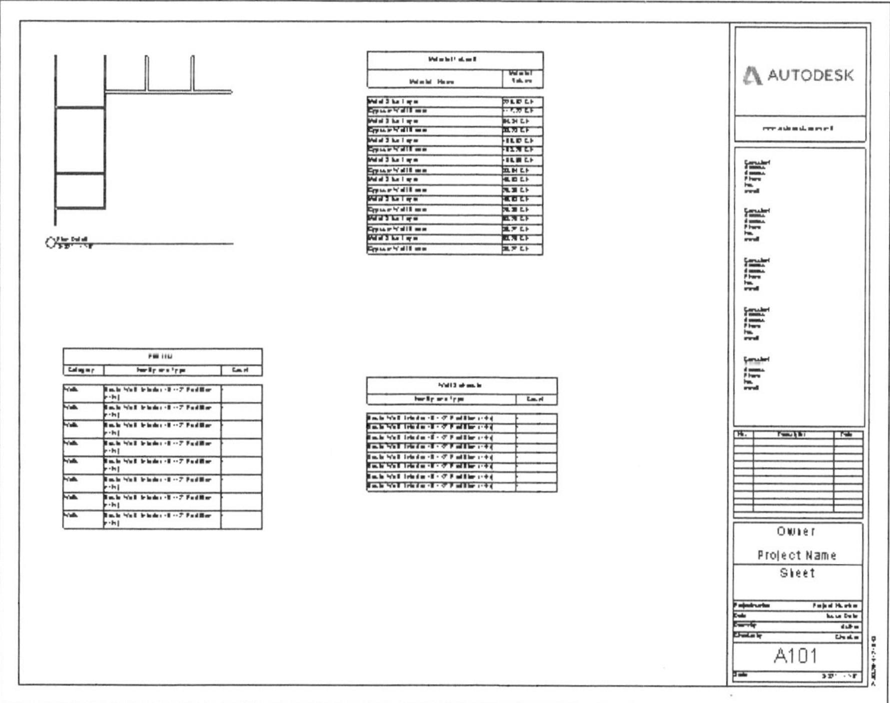

Figure 5-106 All assembly views arranged in sheet

After placing the schedule in the sheet, adjust the view by using the controls of schedule.

Saving the Project

In this section, you will save the project file using the **Save As** tool.

1. Choose **Save As > Project** from the **File** menu; the **Save As** dialog box is displayed. Specify the file name in the **File name** edit box:
   For Imperial **c05_office_tut3**
   For Metric **M_c05_office_tut3**
   Choose **Save**; the file is saved and the dialog box is closed.

2. Choose **Close** from the **File** menu to close the project file.

Self-Evaluation Test

Answer the following questions and then compare them to those given at the end of this chapter:

1. Which of the following panels contains the **Create Views** tool?

   (a) **Assembly** (b) **Modify**
   (c) **Create** (d) **Geometry**

2. While using the **Offset** tool, you can select the __________ radio button to create an offset at a specified distance.

3. You can break a wall into a number of segments using the __________ tool.

4. Using the ___________ tool, you can group a number of elements into a single entity.

5. You can use the ____________tool to measure the distance between any two points in a drawing window.

6. The____________ tool is used to copy the properties of a source element and transfer them to another element of the same family.

7. If a pick box is defined by dragging the cursor from left to right, the elements that are entirely enclosed in it are selected. (T/F)

8. After highlighting one element, you can press the CTRL key to select a chain of walls joined with each other. (T/F)

9. You can create multiple copies of an element by using the **Move** tool. (T/F)

10. You can rotate elements only in the plan view. (T/F)

11. When you mirror walls, the inserted elements such as doors and windows are also mirrored. (T/F)

Review Questions

Answer the following questions:

1. Which of the following tools is used to create copies of the selected elements?

   (a) **Match** (b) **Array**
   (c) **Lock** (d) **Group**

2. Which of the following keys should be kept pressed while adding elements to a selection?

   (a) TAB (b) SHIFT
   (c) CTRL (d) ESC

3. Which of the following tools can be used to restrict or lock the position of an element?

   (a) **Align** (b) **Place Similar**
   (c) **Copy** (d) **Pin Position**

4. In which of the following tabs the **Select by ID** tool is available?

   (a) **Insert** (b) **Modify**
   (c) **View** (d) **Manage**

5. You can save groups and use them in other Autodesk Revit projects. (T/F)

6. Once an element is locked, it is not possible to move it without removing the lock constraint. (T/F)

7. In Autodesk Revit, you cannot create nested groups. (T/F)

8. You cannot modify the number of items in a radial array after they have been created. (T/F)

9. While rotating an element, you can move the center of rotation by dragging it to the desired location. (T/F)

10. Using the **Trim/Extend Multiple Elements** tool, you can trim or extend multiple elements. (T/F)

11. The **Filter** tool is used to restore the selection of elements. (T/F)

EXERCISES

Exercise 1 Apartment 2

Add windows to the exterior wall of the dining area of the *Apartment 2* project created in Exercise 1 of Chapter 4 based on Figure 5-107. The dimensions and text are given only for reference and are not to be added. The parameters to be used for the project are given next.

(Expected time: 30 min)

1. Project-
   For Imperial *c04_Apartment2_ex1.rvt*
   For Metric *M_c04_Apartment2_ex1.rvt*
2. Window type to be added in the dining area-
   For Imperial **Fixed: 24"X48"**
   For Metric **Fixed: 0610 x 1220 mm**
3. Name of the file to be saved-
   For Imperial **c05_Apartment2_ex1**
   For Metric **M_c05_Apartment2_ex1**

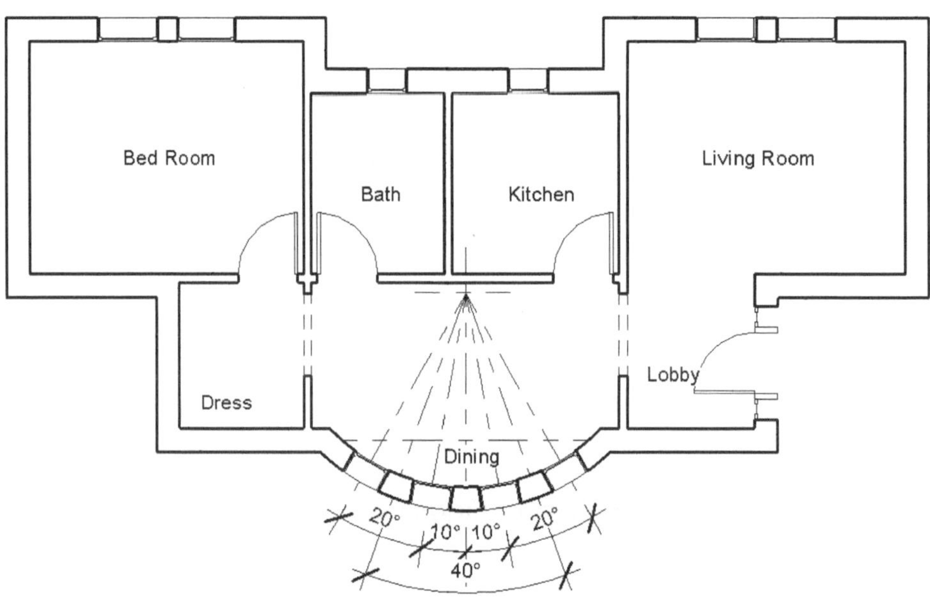

Figure 5-107 *Sketch plan for adding windows to the Apartment 2 project*

Exercise 2 Club

Add windows, as shown in Figure 5-108, to the Hall 2 of the *Club* project created in Tutorial 2 of this chapter. The dimensions and text have been given for reference and need not to be added.

(Expected time: 30 min)

1. Project File-
   For Imperial *c04_Club_ex3*
   For Metric *M_ c04_Club_ex3*

2. Window types to be used -
   For Imperial W1- **Fixed: 36" X 48"**
   For Metric W1- **Fixed: 0910 X 1220 mm**
3. Name of the file to be saved -
   For Imperial **c05_Club_ex2**
   For Metric **M_c05_Club_ex2**

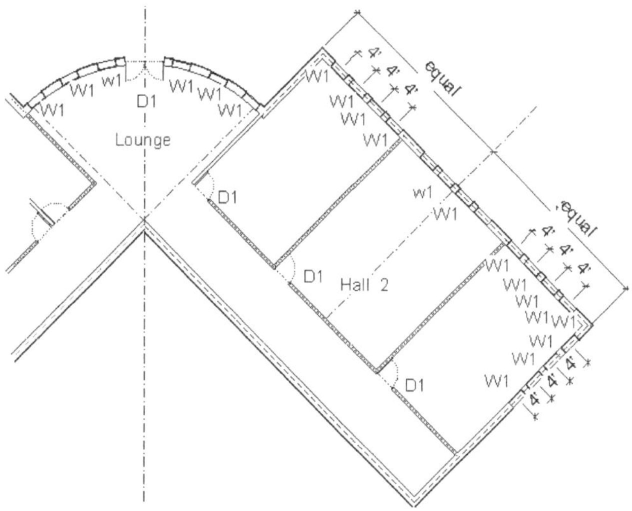

***Figure 5-108** Sketch plan for adding windows to Hall 2 of the Club project*

Exercise 3 Elevator and Stair Lobby

Add windows for the *Elevator and Stair Lobby* project created in Exercise 2 of Chapter 4, based on Figure 5-109. The dimensions and text have been given for reference and are not to be added. The parameters to be used for the elements are given next.

(Expected time: 15 min)

1. Project -
   For Imperial *c04_ElevatorandStairLobby_ex2.rvt*
   For Metric M_*c04_ElevatorandStairLobby_ex2.rvt*
2. Window type to be used:
   For Imperial W2- **Fixed 24" X 48"**
   For Metric W2- **Fixed 0610 X 1220 mm**
3. Name of the file to be saved-
   For Imperial **c05_ElevatorandStairLobby_ex3**
   For Metric **M_c05_ElevatorandStairLobby_ex3**

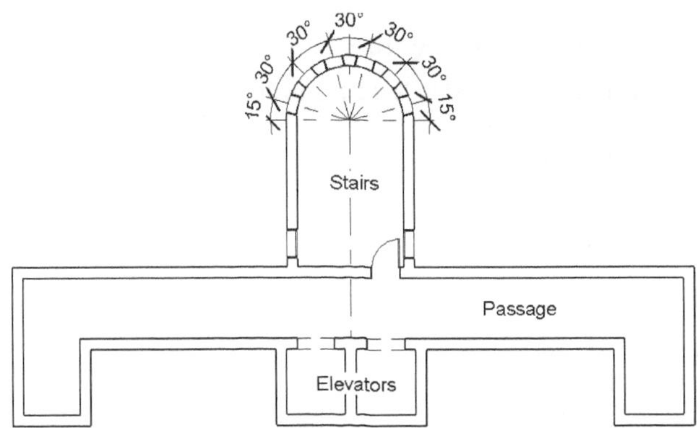

Figure 5-109 *Sketch plan for adding and creating windows for the Elevator and Stair Lobby project*

Exercise 4 — Office

Create the profile of an office building by using the tools learnt in this chapter. The exterior wall profile of the building is shown in Figure 5-110. The dimensions are given only for reference and need not to be added. The parameters to be used for various elements are given next.

(Expected time: 15 min)

1. Project Name to be given-
   For Imperial **c05_Office_ex4**
   For Metric **M_c05_Office_ex4**
2. Template file-
   For Imperial *Construction-Default*
   For Metric *Construction-DefaultMetric*
3. Exterior wall type-
   For Imperial **Basic Wall: Exterior - Brick on Mtl.Stud**
   For Metric **Basic Wall: Exterior - Brick on Mtl.Stud**
4. Unconnected height of walls-
   For Imperial **12'0"**
   For Metric **3600 mm**
5. All inclined walls are at an angle of 45-degree to the horizontal axis.

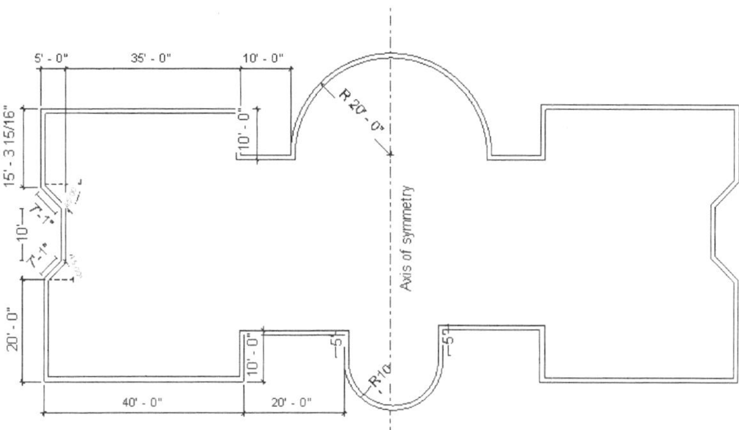

Figure 5-110 Sketch plan of the exterior wall profile of the office building

Exercise 5 Residential Building: Modify

In this exercise, copy the ground floor level to the first floor level and using the modification tools make changes in the plan created in Exercise 4 of Chapter 4.

(Expected time: 15 min)

1. Project-
   For Imperial *c04_residential_door_window_ex4*
   For Metric *M_ c04_residential_door_window_ex4*

2. Select the complete project using the crossing window and copy the model using the **Copy to Clipboard** tool. Then, paste it to the Level 2 using the **Aligned to Selected Levels** tool.

3. Delete the door displayed in the north view and the view will be as shown in Figure 5-111.

4. Name of the file to be saved-
   For Imperial **c05_residential_modify_ex5**
   For Metric **M_ c05_residential_modify_ex5**

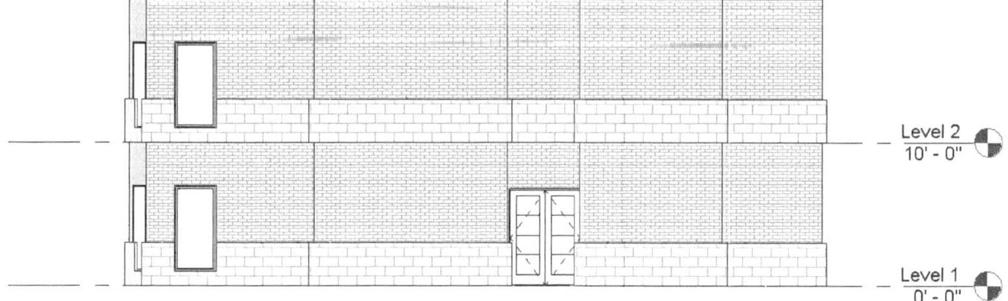

Figure 5-111 Sketch plan of the ***North*** *view of the Residential Building*

Answers to Self-Evaluation Test

1. c, 2. Numerical, 3. Split Element, 4. Create Group, 5. Measure Between Two References, 6. Match Type Properties, 7. T, 8. F, 9. F, 10. F, 11. T

Chapter 6

Working with Datum Plane and Creating Standard Views

Learning Objectives

After completing this chapter, you will be able to:

- *Understand the concept of levels*
- *Create multiple levels in a project*
- *Understand the concept of using grids in a project*
- *Create rectangular and circular grids in a project file*
- *Use the Work Plane and Reference Plane tools in a project*
- *Create a plan view in a project*
- *Create and understand the usage of elevation view*
- *Create section views and modify their properties*
- *Use the Scope Box tool*

INTRODUCTION

In the previous chapters, you learned to use editing tools to create groups and modify their properties in a project. In this chapter, you will learn to add datum elements and the procedure to create standard views in an architectural project. Datum elements and the non-physical elements form the basic framework in a project. These datum elements include levels, reference planes, and grids. Depending on the complexity of a project, you can use some or all of these components to systematize and provide a reference to a building model. These elements are also used for editing a project, creating schedules, and also creating other reference documentation for a project.

In Autodesk Revit, a standard view can be created and displayed with relative ease. Creating standard views in a project not only help in its presentation but also assist in creating and editing various building and stand-alone elements of a project.

WORKING WITH LEVELS

For a multistory building project, you need to specify floor levels within the building volume. Each floor level or story can contain a different set of building components. Levels, in a typical multistory building, may be understood as infinite horizontal planes that define each story. Revit uses levels as references for level-hosted elements such as floor, roof, and ceiling. The distance between levels can be used to define the story-height of a building model, as shown in Figure 6-1. Revit also provides flexibility to create a non-story level or a reference level such as sill level, parapet level, and so on. For example, a multistory office building may have different story heights for each floor. Building components such as exterior walls, windows, doors, and furniture may also differ on each floor. You can create levels based on the story height of a building. You can then create various building elements on each level such as an entrance door on the first floor level, bay windows on the second floor level, an elevator room on the roof level, and so on.

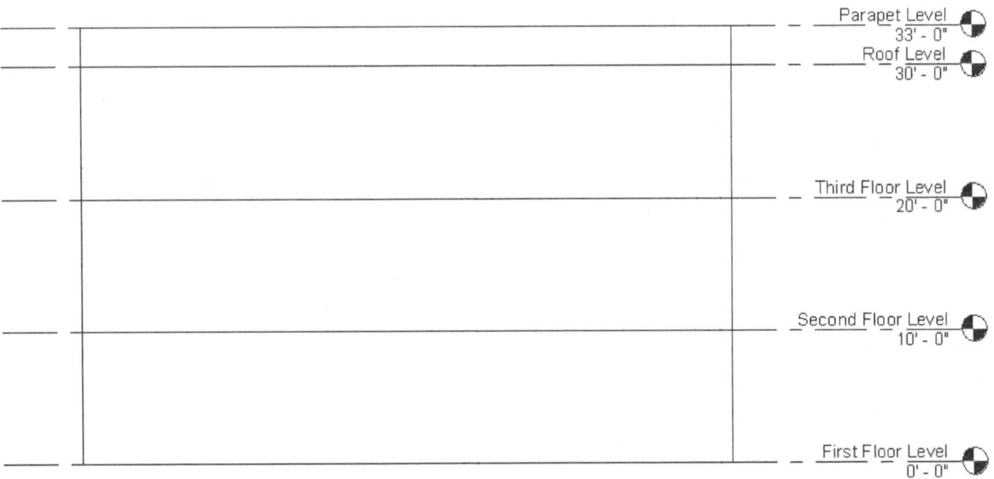

Figure 6-1 *Levels displayed in a multistory building project*

When you use the default template file for creating a new project file, it loads two predefined levels, **Level 1** and **Level 2**, which are displayed in the elevation view or section view. You can view any of the elevation or section views using the **Project Browser**. Levels can be added, renamed, and modified at any time during the project development.

Tip

In the conceptual design environment, the levels are displayed in 3D views. If you select a level in 3D view, the elevation and the name of the level will be displayed in the drawing area.

Understanding Level Properties

A typical level is represented by a level line, level bubble, level name, level elevation, and so on, refer to Figure 6-2. Using these parameters and controls, you can modify the appearance of a level. The level name is a modifiable parameter that is used to refer to each level. The level elevation is the distance of the level from the base level. The visibility of the level bubble on either side of the level line can be controlled by using the bubble display control. The length alignment control can be used to align levels lines. Autodesk Revit provides the 2D or 3D extents control for datums when they are selected. This enables you to change their extents in one or multiple views in which they are visible. When a datum is in the 3D mode, any modifications made in the 3D view will be propagated in all views of a building model. On the other hand, the 2D mode can be used to modify a datum in a specific view, thereby making it view-specific.

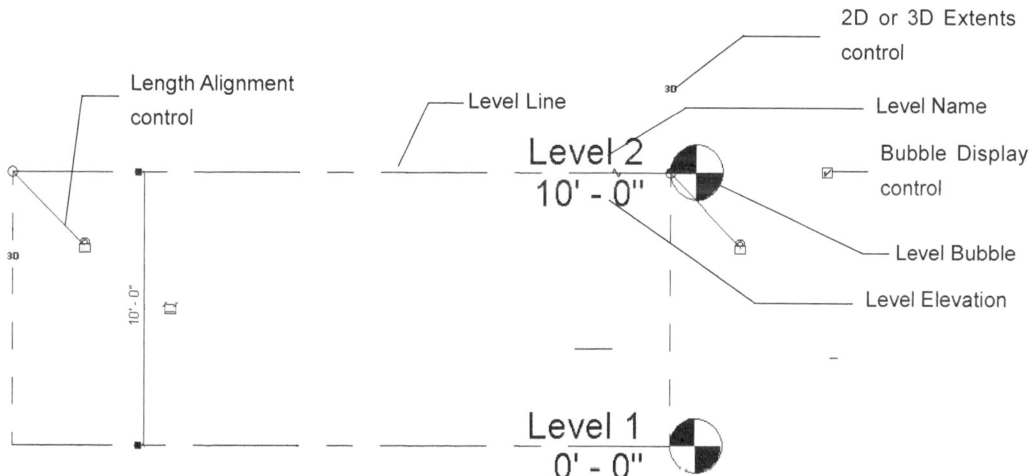

Figure 6-2 Various levels defined in the default template file

Note

The 3D extent of Revit helps in modifying the levels in all views whereas the 2D extent helps in modifying a level in the current view.

Like other building elements used in Revit project, levels also have associated types and instance properties. You can view and modify the instance properties of a level in the **Properties** palette, refer to Figure 6-3. You can also use the **Properties** palette to view and modify the type properties of the selected level. To do so, choose the **Edit Type** button in the **Properties** palette; the **Type Properties** dialog box will be displayed, as shown in Figure 6-4. You can use this dialog box to modify and view the type properties of the selected level from the drawing.

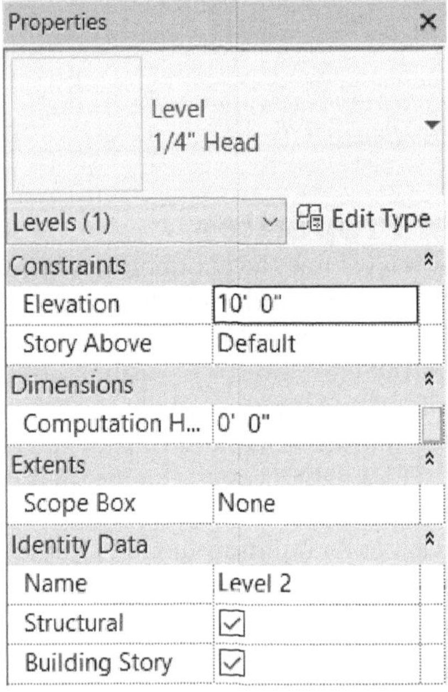

***Figure 6-3** The **Properties** palette for a level*

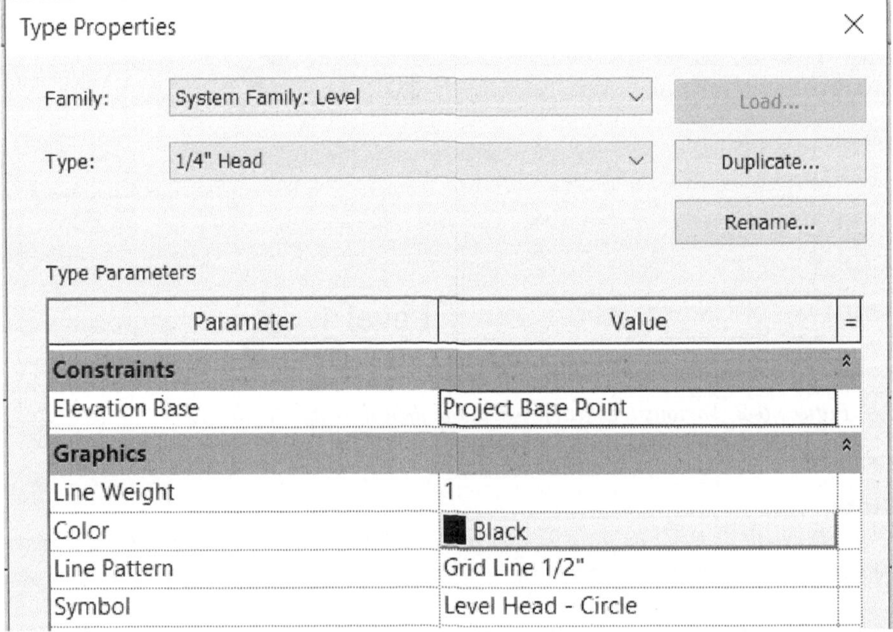

***Figure 6-4** Partial view of the **Type Properties** dialog box for a typical level*

Level Type Properties

The type properties of a level can be viewed and modified in the **Type Properties** dialog box of a level. When you change the type properties of a level, all its instances are also modified. In the **Type Properties** dialog box of a level, you can modify the value of a parameter by clicking in its corresponding **Value** field and selecting a new value from the drop-down list or entering a new value in the field. Different level type properties are described in the table given next.

Parameter Name	Value and Description
Elevation Base	Describes the elevation base value with respect to the project or the shared origin.
Line Weight	Specifies the weight of the line defining the level. It can be specified by clicking in its value field and selecting a desired option from the drop-down list displayed.
Color	Specifies to the color of the level line. The default color selected is black. You can select other colors from the displayed **Color** dialog box which appear on clicking in the value field corresponding to this parameter.
Line Pattern	Used to set the linetype of the level line.
Symbol	Specifies the symbol indicating the level and can be chosen from the drop-down list. The **None** option can be specified if the level head is not required.
Symbol at End 1 Default	Check box is selected if a bubble is required at the left end of the level line.
Symbol at End 2 Default	Check box is selected if a bubble is required at the right end of the level line.

Level Instance Properties

When you change the instance properties of a level, the properties of only the selected instance are changed. The different level instance properties are described in the following table:

Parameter Name	Value and Description
Elevation	Specifies the vertical height of the level from the elevation base.
Story Above	Specifies the next building story for the level.
Computation Height	Specifies the computation height for a level. This value is used to compute the area, perimeter, and volume of a room.
Name	Specifies the name assigned to the level. You can enter any name based on the project requirement.

Structural	By default, the check box corresponding to this parameter is cleared. You can select the check box to define the level as structural. For example, the level defined for the top of a foundation can be a structural level.
Building Story	By default, the check box corresponding to this parameter is selected. As a result, you can define a level as a functional story or a floor in the project.
Scope Box	Specifies the scope box assigned to the level that controls its visibility in different views.

Adding Levels

Ribbon: Architecture > Datum > Level
Shortcut Key: LL

In Revit, you can create multiple levels based on your project requirements. Note that the **Level** tool remains inactive in the **Datum** panel for all the plan views. The **Level** tool will only be active in an elevation or a section view. To create a level, invoke the **Level** tool from the **Datum** panel, as shown in Figure 6-5; the **Modify | Place Level** tab will be displayed. In this tab, choose any of the sketching options displayed in the **Draw** panel to create levels in your project. You can also invoke the **Level** tool by typing **LL**. In the **Modify | Place Level** tab, you can select a type of level from the **Type Selector** drop-down list to modify an existing level. This drop-down list has two types of levels, **Level: 1/4" Head** and **Level: No Head**. To make the level head visible, select the **Level: 1/4" Head** option. Else, select the **Level: No Head** option.

***Figure 6-5** Partial View of Choosing the **Level** tool from the **Datum** panel of the **Architecture** tab*

In the **Draw** panel of the **Modify | Place Level** tab, you can use the **Line** (default selection) or **Pick Lines** tool to sketch a level line. In the **Options Bar**, the **Make Plan View** check box is selected by default. As a result, when you will add a level in a project view, its associated plan view/s will be created. To specify the associated view/s to the level, choose the **Plan View Types** button displayed next to the **Make Plan View** check box; the **Plan View Types** dialog box will be displayed. In the **Select view types to create** area of this dialog box, three associated views will be displayed namely, **Ceiling Plan**, **Floor Plan** and **Structural Plan**. All three views are selected by default. You can select any one of them or all options from the **Select view types to create** area and then choose **OK** to close the dialog box; the selected view/s will be associated with the level. Alternatively, if you clear the **Make Plan View** check box, the associated views will not be created. The **Offset** edit box in the **Options Bar** can be used to add a level at a specified distance from the selected point or element.

To add a level, invoke the **Level** tool and move the cursor near the existing levels. On doing so, the temporary dimensions are displayed, indicating the perpendicular distance between the nearest level and the cursor. To add a level at the specified distance from the existing level, specify the perpendicular distance value, as shown in Figure 6-6.

Figure 6-6 *Specifying the distance of the new level from an existing level*

To sketch a level line, specify its start point and endpoint. The level elevation and the start point will be specified simultaneously. Click to specify the first point and move the cursor to the left or the right. You will notice that the level line, level name, and elevation appear and move with the cursor. On moving the cursor above the endpoint of the existing level line, a dashed alignment line will appear, indicating its alignment with the existing level, as shown in Figure 6-7. When the alignment line appears, click to specify the endpoint of the level line. You can also enter the elevation of the level by entering the value before specifying the start point.

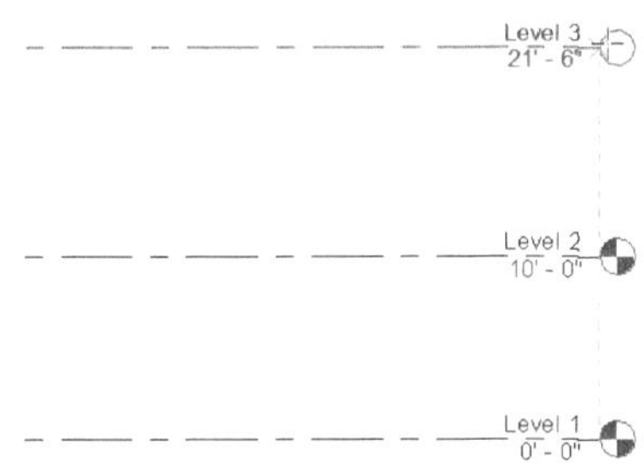

Figure 6-7 *Using the alignment line to specify the endpoint of the level line*

Note

Although you are required to specify the start point and the endpoint of the level lines, the levels corresponding to these lines are infinite horizontal planes. The placement of the level line can, however, be useful in the elevation and section views.

When you select a recently added level, it is highlighted and displays two square boxes, on the either side of the level, as shown in Figure 6-8. These boxes are used to control the visibility of the level bubble. They can be selected or cleared to make the bubble visible or invisible, respectively, at the desired side(s). The two small circles representing the drag controls for the level line can be used to increase or decrease its length by dragging. The padlocks act as the length alignment control for the alignment of all the level lines. When locked, the length of all the level lines is increased or decreased simultaneously. To modify the length of a single level line, unlock the control and then modify its length.

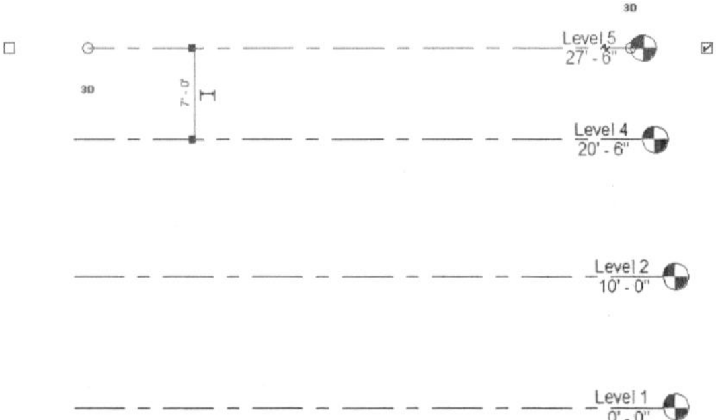

Figure 6-8 The highlighted level with its constraints and controls

Modifying Level Parameters

You can change a level type by selecting the level from the drawing and then selecting a different level type from the **Type Selector** drop-down list in the **Properties** palette. On doing so, the current level will be modified into the selected level. You can specify the properties of a level using the **Properties** palette before adding it. Some of the parameters of the level can also be modified by clicking on the level in the drawing window and entering the new value.

For example, after selecting a level, you can click on its name and assign a new name to it. As you start typing the new name, an edit box appears with the new value, as shown in Figure 6-9. Also, Autodesk Revit prompts you to specify whether you want to rename all the associated views such as the floor plan, ceiling plan, and so on. If you choose to rename the views, the name of the associated views will change in the **Project Browser**. Similarly, you can modify the elevation of a level by selecting it and entering the new temporary dimension value, as shown in Figure 6-10. When you enter the new value, the level automatically moves to the specified elevation.

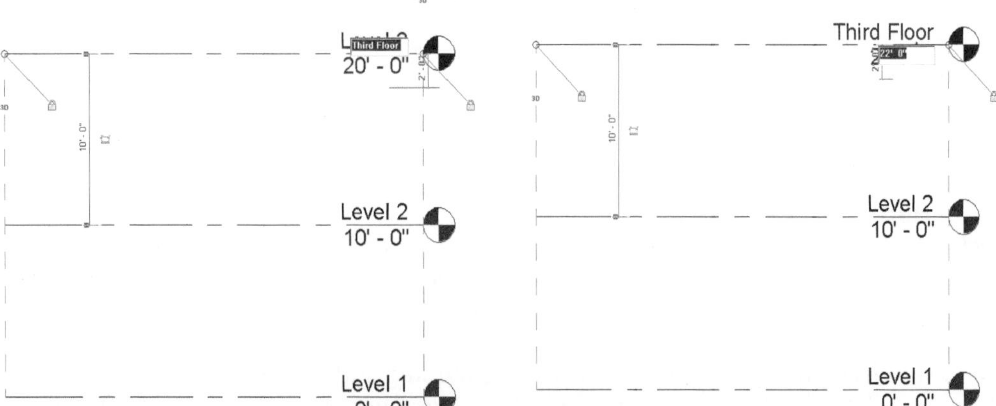

Figure 6-9 Editing the name of the level *Figure 6-10 Modifying the level elevation*

Tip

It is recommended that you name the levels based on the floor such as first floor, second floor, roof, and so on. This helps in referring to their corresponding plan views and also helps in editing level hosted elements. The names assigned to the levels are also reflected in the schedules created for the project.

You can also move levels by simply dragging them to the desired location. Click to select a level and drag the level(s) to the desired location. As you drag, the elevation level changes dynamically with respect to the cursor location. Hold the SHIFT key to move the level only in vertical direction. Next, release the mouse button at the appropriate location to complete the dragging process.

Tip

In addition to the level heads already loaded in Revit, you can load level heads from the ***US Imperial > Annotations*** *folder path.*

When you move the cursor near a level, it will be highlighted. Right-click on the highlighted level line; a shortcut menu will be displayed with various options. You can choose the **Go to Floor Plan** option from the shortcut menu to open the corresponding floor plan for the level. On choosing the **Find Referring Views** option from the shortcut menu, the **Go To View** dialog box will be displayed. In this dialog box, select the desired view from the list of views and then choose the **Open View** button; the view in which the selected level is visible will be displayed.

Tip

When you select a level, its distance from the adjacent levels is displayed. Click on the corresponding temporary dimension and enter the new value to move the level to the new location.

For certain levels, you may want to move the level bubble to a different location. When you select a level, you will notice that a break control appears below its name, next to the level bubble. This break control can be used to break the level line and move the level bubble away from it. On clicking this control, you will observe that the level name and the level bubble are also moved to the new location and an extension line is created, as shown in Figure 6-11. You can then use the blue dots to place the level bubble at the appropriate location.

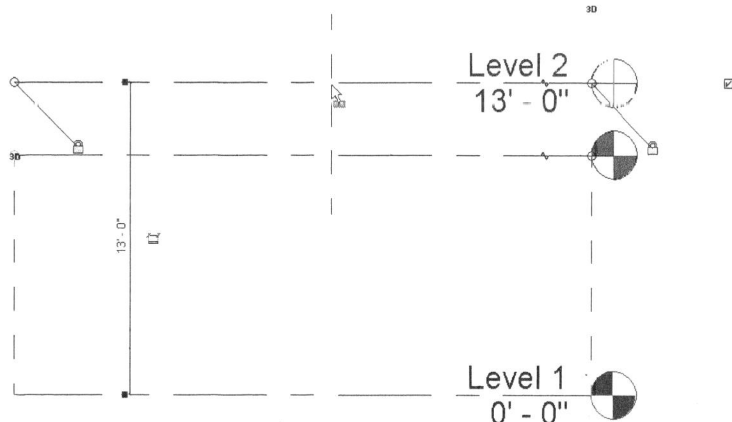

Figure 6-11 *Moving the level to a different location*

Tip

To view the floor plan of a level, you can move the cursor over the bubble and double-click. As a result, the corresponding floor plan view will be displayed in the viewing area.

HIDING ELEMENTS IN A VIEW

Revit allows you to hide elements and their categories, including annotations. You can also restore the visibility of hidden elements.

To hide an element in a view, select the view in which you want to hide a particular element or a category, select the element in the drawing, and then right-click to display a shortcut menu. In the shortcut menu, choose **Hide in View > Elements** / **Category** to hide an element or a category in the current view.

To restore the visibility of a hidden element or a category, choose the **Reveal Hidden Elements** button from the **View Control Bar**; the screen will enter the **Reveal Hidden Elements** mode with a magenta boundary and also a new panel **Reveal Hidden Elements** will be displayed in the ribbon. All hidden elements inside the magenta boundary will be displayed in magenta color. Select a hidden element and then choose the **Unhide Element** button from the **Reveal Hidden Elements** panel to restore the visibility of hidden element. Now, choose the **Toggle Reveal Hidden Elements Mode** button in the **Reveal Hidden Elements** panel to exit the **Reveal Hidden Elements** mode. Another method to restore the visibility of the hidden element(s) is to select the element(s) in the **Reveal Hidden Elements** mode and then right-click; a shortcut menu will be displayed. Choose **Unhide in View > Elements** / **Category** from the shortcut menu to restore the visibility of the hidden elements.

Tip

*After selecting the element(s) or a category in the **Reveal Hidden Elements** mode, you can type EU or VU to unhide the element(s) or the category in the current view.*

Controlling the Visibility of Levels

You can control the visibility of one level or all levels in any of the project views. When you select a level and right-click, a shortcut menu is displayed, as shown in Figure 6-12. Choose **Hide in View > Category** from the shortcut menu; the level category will be hidden in the current view. To hide a particular level, choose **Hide in View > Elements** from the shortcut menu; only the selected level will be hidden in the current view. The level will, however, be displayed in all other views.

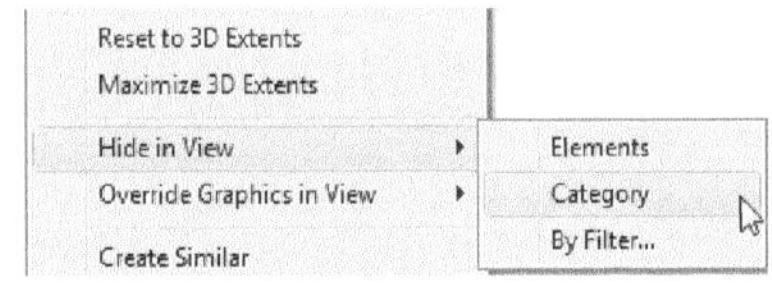

***Figure 6-12** Partial view of the shortcut menu displayed on selecting the level*

To hide all the levels in a project view, select any of the level in the project view. Next, choose the **Override by Category** tool from the **Modify | Levels > View > Override Graphics in View** drop-down; the **View-Specific Category Graphics** dialog box will be displayed. Clear the **Visible** check box in this dialog box and choose **OK**; all levels will be hidden from the current view. You can use the **Scope Boxes** feature to control the visibility of levels. You will learn about this feature later in this chapter.

Tip
After selecting the element, you can type EH or VH to hide an element or a category in the current view.

WORKING WITH GRIDS

Ribbon: Architecture > Datum > Grid
Shortcut Key: GR

Autodesk Revit provides you the option of creating rectangular or circular grids for your projects. Using these grids, you cannot only create building profiles easily but also place the structural elements at the specific locations and intersections.

Creating Grids

You can create the grid patterns based on the project requirements. Grid patterns can be rectangular or radial, depending on the project geometry. A rectangular grid pattern can be created using straight grid lines, whereas a radial grid pattern can be formed using arc grids. The created grids are visible in all plan, elevation, and section views.

To create a grid line, invoke the **Grid** tool from the **Datum** panel of the **Architecture** tab, as shown in Figure 6-13; the **Modify | Place Grid** tab and the **Properties** palette with the properties of grids will be displayed. The **Modify | Place Grid** tab, as shown in Figure 6-14, displays various options to draw and modify grids in a drawing. The **Draw** panel in this tab displays various tools to draw grids as lines and curves or to convert existing model lines into grids. In this **Properties** palette, you can modify the type and instance properties of the grid, before or after creating it. You can also change the type of grid by selecting a grid type from the **Type Selector** drop-down list.

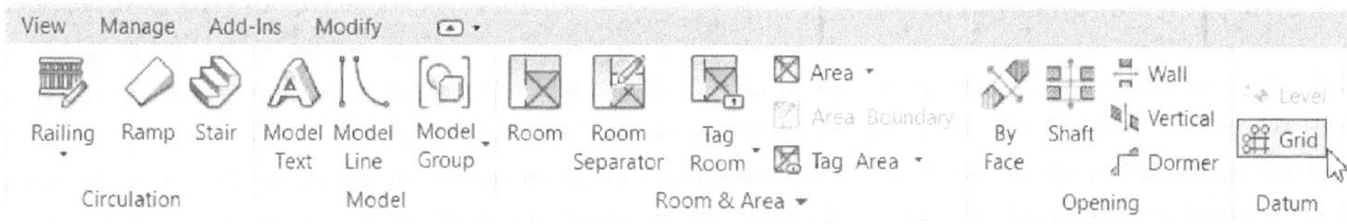

Figure 6-13 ***Partial view of*** *Invoking the* ***Grid*** *tool*

Figure 6-14 *Various options in the* ***Modify / Place Grid*** *tab*

Creating Grids Using the Draw Tools

To create a straight grid line, select any floor plan view from the **Project Browser** and then choose the **Grid** tool from the **Datum** panel in the **Architecture** tab; the **Modify | Place Grid** tab will be displayed. The **Line** tool in the **Draw** panel is chosen by default. As a result, you can start sketching the grid line by clicking at the appropriate location to specify the start point and then moving the cursor to the desired direction. As you move the cursor, you will notice that a grid line is created with one end fixed at the specified point and the other end attached to the cursor. A temporary angular dimension indicating the angle of the line with the horizontal axis is also displayed, refer to Figure 6-15. Click to specify the endpoint of the grid line when the appropriate angular dimension is displayed. You can also sketch an arbitrary inclined grid line and then click on the angular dimension to enter a new value of the angle. To draw orthogonal grids, hold the SHIFT key and restrain the movement of the cursor to the horizontal and vertical axes. When you click to specify the endpoint, a grid is created and its controls are highlighted, as shown in Figure 6-16. The recently added grid is highlighted and it displays one square box on either side. These boxes are used to control the visibility of the grid bubble. They can be checked or cleared to make the grid bubble visible or invisible at the desired side(s). The two circles, one on the either corner, can be dragged to extend or reduce the extents of the grid line.

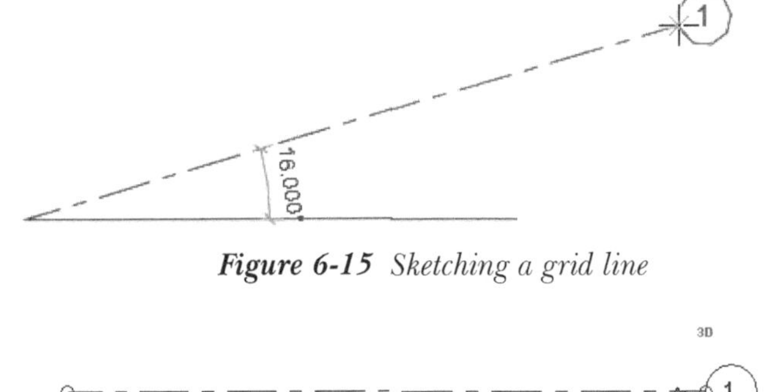

Figure 6-15 *Sketching a grid line*

Figure 6-16 *A horizontal grid line with its controls*

Similarly, when you sketch a new grid line near an existing one, a temporary dimension indicating the distance between the two grid lines is displayed. You can enter the value of distance in the displayed edit box, refer to Figure 6-17. Alternatively, you can move the cursor to the desired distance using the temporary dimensions. Once this is done, click to specify the start point of the second grid line. Move the cursor horizontally to the right and when the alignment line appears, click to specify the endpoint of the grid line; the second grid line is created. Notice that the name of this grid is 2. Autodesk Revit automatically numbers the grid lines as they are created.

Figure 6-17 *Specifying the distance of the second grid line*

Similarly, you can draw other parallel grid lines as well. These lines will be numbered automatically as you draw them, as shown in Figure 6-18. The **Offset** edit box in the **Options Bar** can be used to create a grid line that starts at a specified offset distance from a point defined on an existing element. The offset distance can be specified in the edit box in **Options Bar**. The shape of the resulting grid line depends on the selected sketching tool.

To create vertical grid lines, specify the start point above the first grid line. Now, move the cursor vertically downward and click below the last horizontal grid line to specify the endpoint. The procedure adopted for creating multiple horizontal grid lines can be used to create multiple vertical grid lines.

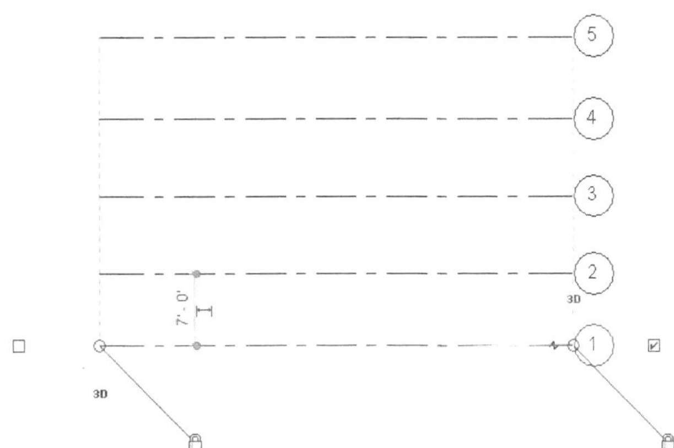

Figure 6-18 *Parallel grid lines automatically numbered*

In the same manner, you can create a rectangular grid pattern that is aligned at a given angle to the horizontal axis. You can also specify different angles for the grid lines and create the grid patterns based on the project requirement. Figure 6-19 shows some other examples of the rectangular grid patterns.

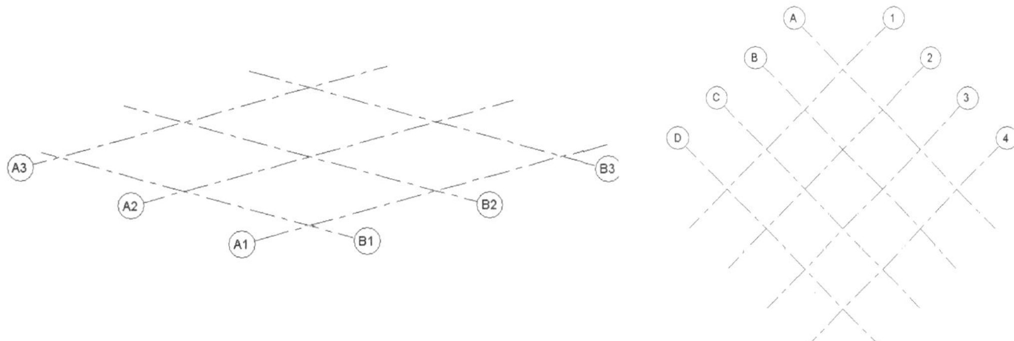

Figure 6-19 *Examples of the rectangular grid patterns*

In the **Draw** panel of the **Modify | Place Grid** tab, you can use the **Start-End-Radius Arc** and **Center-ends Arc** tools to create curved or radial grid patterns. The procedure of creating the curved grid lines using these options is similar to the sketching options for creating walls (see Chapter 3). You can create multiple curved grids using the tools in the **Draw** panel and specifying their radius in the **Radius** edit box in the **Options Bar**. You can specify a value in the **Radius** edit box in the **Options Bar** only if you select the check box located before it. Figure 6-20 shows an example of radial grid patterns created using the semicircular and straight grid lines.

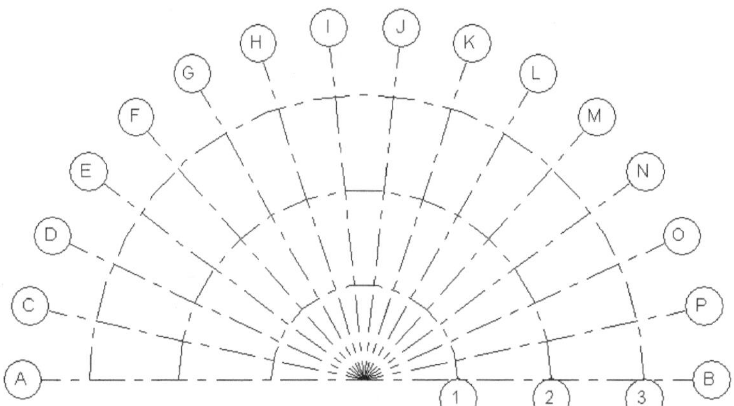

Figure 6-20 *An example of a radial grid pattern created using the semi-circular and straight grid lines*

Creating Grids Using the Multi-Segment Tool

You can use the **Multi-Segment** tool to sketch a multi-segmented grid in the project. To do so, choose the **Grid** tool from the **Datum** panel of the **Architecture** tab; the **Modify | Place Grid** tab will be displayed. In this tab, choose the **Multi-Segment** tool from the **Draw** panel; the **Modify | Edit Sketch** tab will be displayed. In the **Draw** panel of the tab, you can choose any of the sketching tools, displayed in the list box, to sketch the multi-segmented gridline. After choosing the desired sketching tool, you need to use various options in the **Options Bar** to control the creation of the gridline in the project. For example, select the **Chain** check box in the **Options Bar** to create grids in chain. In the **Offset** edit box, you can enter a value to specify the offset distance by which the grids will be offset from the clicked point in the drawing area. After setting the options in the **Options Bar**, click in the drawing area; a magenta colored gridline with a temporary dimension will emerge from the point at which you have clicked. Next, click in a desired point to create the first segment of the grid. Similarly, you can click on multiple points in the drawing area to create other segments. To finish the creation of the multi-segmented grids, choose the **Finish Edit Mode** button from the **Mode** panel of the **Modify | Edit Sketch** tab. Figure 6-21 shows a sketch with multi-segmented gridlines.

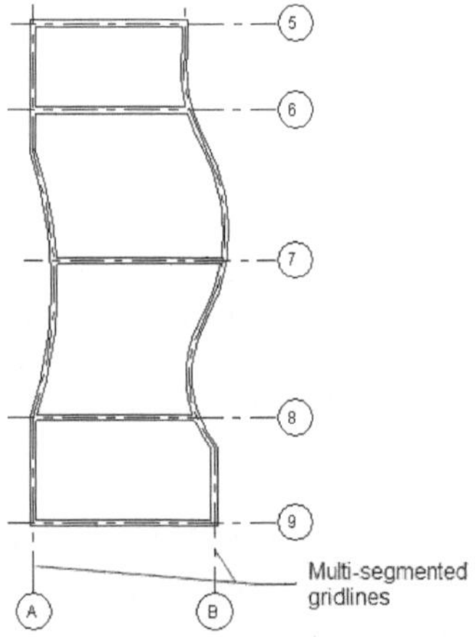

Figure 6-21 *An example of the multi-segmented grids in a floor plan*

Creating Grids Using the Pick Lines Tool

The **Pick Lines** tool is used to create grid lines that are aligned to the existing elements. When you select this tool from the **Draw** panel of the **Modify | Place Grid** tab and move the cursor near an existing element, the cursor snaps to certain object properties such as the interior face of the walls, centerlines of columns, and so on. Click when the desired property of the element is highlighted. Autodesk Revit automatically creates a grid line along the specified alignment of the element.

Tip

You can also use different editing tools such as ***Copy, Array, Mirror, Move,*** *and so on to create grid patterns. Revit numbers the grids intuitively. For example, if you array a grid named A, the new grids will sequentially be named as B, C, D, E, and so on.*

For example, to create grid lines for the interior wall profile, choose the **Pick Lines** tool from the **Draw** panel and move the cursor near the inclined exterior wall. As you move the cursor over the wall, it will snap to the interior and exterior faces. Click when the interior face is highlighted, as shown in Figure 6-22; a grid line aligned with the interior face of the wall will be created, as shown in Figure 6-23. Similarly, you can click on the other wall segments to create a grid pattern required for the building. Autodesk Revit also creates the curved grid lines, if a curved element is selected.

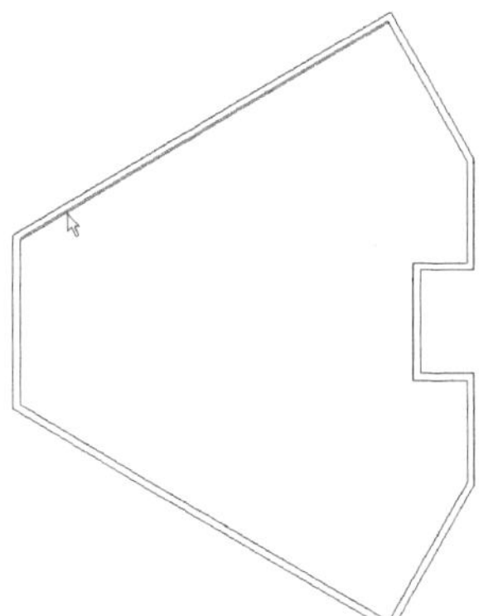

Figure 6-22 *Selecting the interior face to align the grid line*

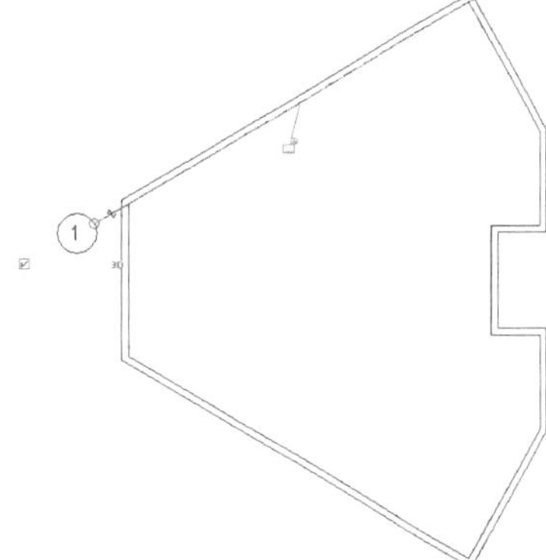

Figure 6-23 *Grid line created along the interior face of the selected wall using the* ***Pick Lines*** *tool*

If the cursor does not snap to the wall centerline, the grid lines along the centerlines of the walls will be created using the **Offset** edit box in the **Options Bar**. Specify the distance of the centerline from the interior face in the **Offset** edit box and then use the **Pick Lines** tool to select the interior face. The grid line aligned to the centerline of the wall is shown in Figure 6-24. Similarly, you can create other grid lines for the building project using the **Pick Lines** tool, as shown in Figure 6-25.

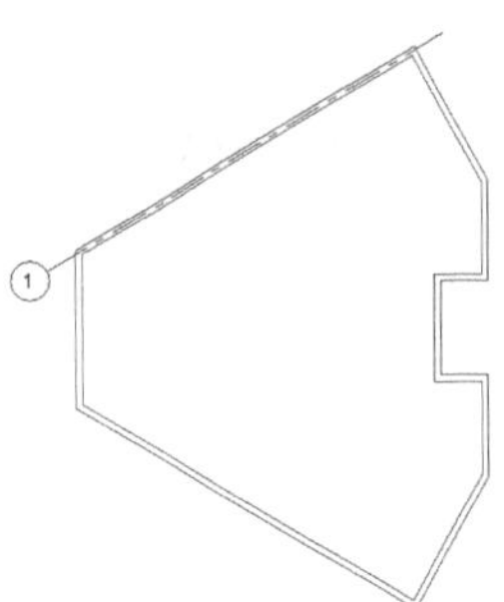

*Figure 6-24 Creating a grid line along the centerline of the wall using the **Offset** option*

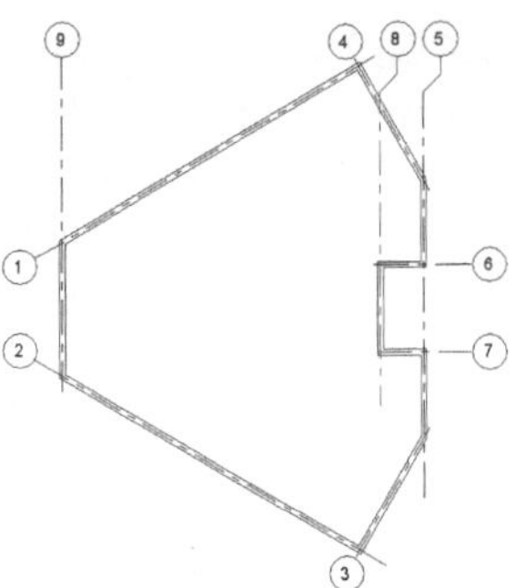

*Figure 6-25 Grid lines created using the **Pick Lines** tool*

Modifying Grids

As mentioned earlier, parameters of grids can be modified before or after grids are created. To modify a grid after it is created, you need to select the grid and modify its properties from the **Properties** palette.

For example, after selecting a grid, you can click on its name and assign it a new name. Similarly, you can modify the distance between grids by selecting the temporary dimension and entering a new value, as shown in Figure 6-26. When you enter a new value, the grid automatically moves to the specified distance.

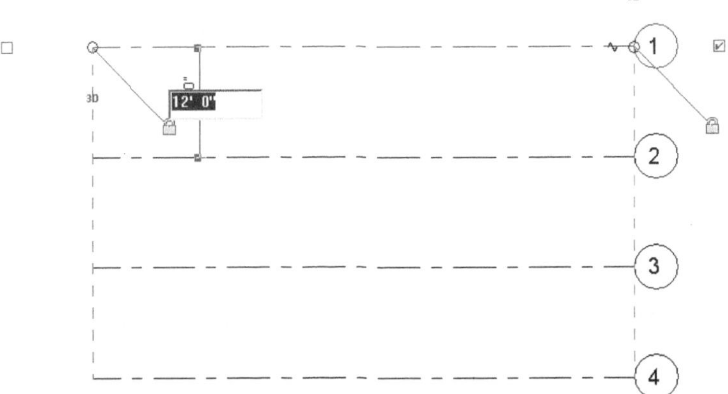

Figure 6-26 Modifying the distance between grids

You can also move the grids by simply dragging them to the desired location. Click to select a single grid. Hold the CTRL key while clicking to select multiple grids. You can now drag the grid(s) to the desired location. Hold the SHIFT key to restrain the movement of the cursor in the orthogonal direction.

When you move the cursor near a grid, it gets highlighted. Now, right-click; a shortcut menu will be displayed with various options. These options are **Select Previous**, **Select All Instances**, **Create Similar**, **Properties**, and so on.

For certain grids, you may need to move or offset the grid bubble to a different location. When you select a grid, a blue circle appears on each of its endpoints. The drag control, as mentioned earlier, controls the extents of the grid line. The grid line break control, which appears near the grid bubble, is used to create a grid bubble offset. You can click on this control and use the displayed drag controls to move the grid bubble to the desired location. The grid name also moves to the new location and an extension line is created. Figure 6-27 shows the newly created grid bubble offset.

Tip
The radial and rectangular array tools can be effectively used to create grid patterns suitable for the project.

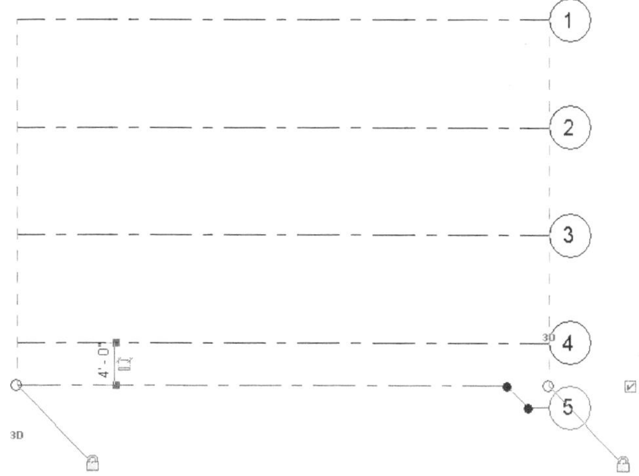

Figure 6-27 *A grid bubble offset created*

Grid Properties

Like levels, grids too have associated properties. A typical grid consists of a grid line, grid bubble, grid name, and other controls, as shown in Figure 6-28. The usage of the controls such as grid bubble visibility, 2D or 3D extents, and grid bubble break is similar to the usage described for levels.

To view and modify the properties of a grid, select it; the instance parameter of the selected grid will be displayed in the **Properties** palette. In this palette, choose the **Edit Type** button; the **Type Properties** dialog box will be displayed, as shown in Figure 6-29. You can use this dialog box to view and modify the type properties of the selected grid. The type properties of grids and their description are discussed next.

Tip
*It is recommended that you draw the grid lines with the endpoints aligned to each other. You can use the alignment line that is displayed when the cursor is moved to its proximity. The **Lock** constraints can be used to drag the extents of the single or multiple grid lines.*

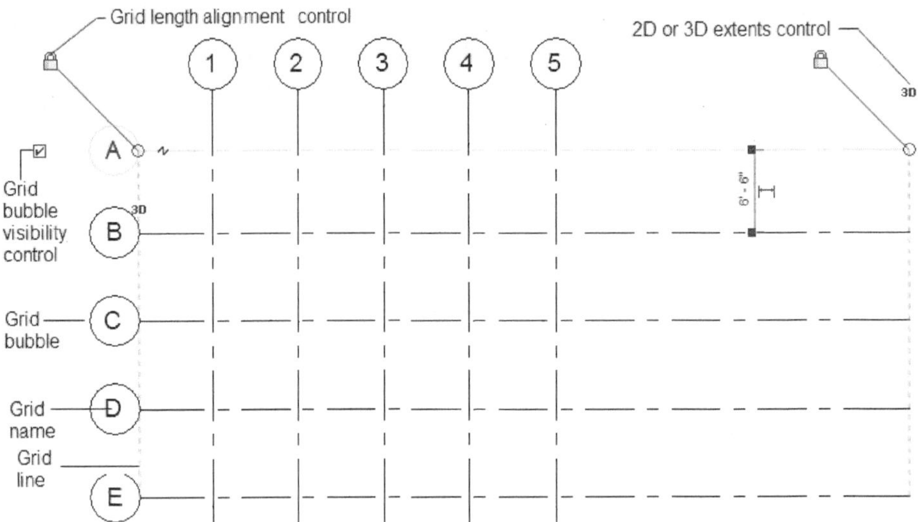

Figure 6-28 A typical grid line pattern with its controls

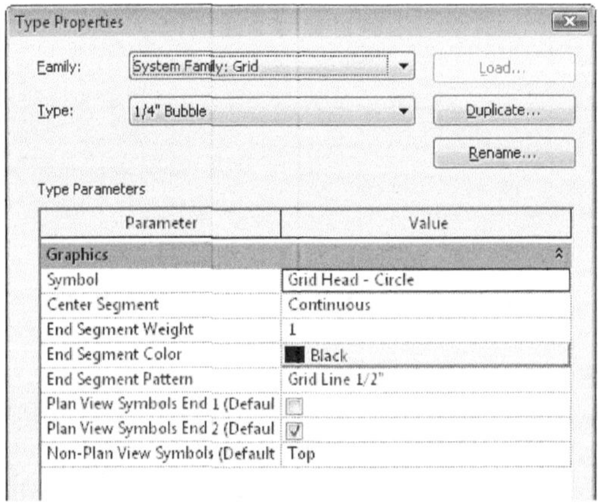
Type Properties

Family: System Family: Grid

Type: 1/4" Bubble

Load...

Duplicate...

Rename...

Type Parameters

Parameter	Value
Graphics	
Symbol	Grid Head - Circle
Center Segment	Continuous
End Segment Weight	1
End Segment Color	Black
End Segment Pattern	Grid Line 1/2"
Plan View Symbols End 1 (Defaul	☐
Plan View Symbols End 2 (Defaul	☑
Non-Plan View Symbols (Default	Top

Figure 6-29 Partial view of the ***Type Properties*** *dialog box of a grid*

Grid Type Properties

When the **Type Properties** of a grid is changed, the properties of all instance parameters related to it are also changed. You can click in the value field and select a new value from the drop-down list or enter a new value in that field. The properties of grid types are described next.

Parameter Name	Value and Description
Symbol	Specifies the display of the symbol at the end of the grid line. You can control the display of the symbol by selecting various options from the drop-down list

Center Segment	Specifies the display type of the center segment of the grid line. You can select **Continuous**, **None** or **Custom** from the drop-down list
Center Segment Weight	Specifies the line weight of the center segment, if the **Center Segment** parameter is set to **Custom**
Center Segment Color	You can assign a color to the center segment, if the **Center Segment** parameter is set to **Custom**
Center Segment Pattern	Specifies the line type of the segment at the center, if the **Center Segment** parameter is set to **Custom**. You can select various line patterns from the drop-down list
End Segment Weight	Specifies the line weight of the grid line, if the **Center Segment** parameter is set to **Continuous**. You can set the line weight of the end segments if the **Center Segment** parameter is set to **None** or **Custom**
End Segment Color	Specifies the color assigned to the grid line, if the **Center Segment** parameter is set to **Continuous**. You can set the color of the end segments if the **Center Segment** parameter is set to **None** or **Custom**
End Segment Pattern	Specifies the line type of the grid line if the **Center Segment** parameter is set to **Continuous**. You can set the line type of the end segments if the **Center Segment** parameter is set to **None** or **Custom**
End Segments Length	Specifies the length of each end segment as measured in the sheet if the **Center Segment** parameter is set to **None** or **Custom**
Plan View Symbols End 1(Default)	Specifies the default status for the visibility of the symbol at end 1 of the grid line in plan view. By default, the check box is cleared. If you select the check box, the visibility of the symbol at end 1 in the plan view will be turned on
Plan View Symbols End 2(Default)	Specifies the default status for the visibility of the symbol at end 2 of the grid line in the plan views. By default, the check box is selected. If you clear the check box, the visibility of the symbol at end 2 in the plan view is turned off

Non-Plan View Symbols (Default)	Specifies the default status for the visibility of the grid line in the sections and elevations, other than in the plan views. You can control the visibility of the symbol at the top and bottom of the grid line by selecting various options from the drop-down list

Note

*In the **Type Properties** dialog box, the **Center Segment Weight**, **Center Segment Color**, and **Center Segment Pattern** options will be available only when you choose the **Custom** option in the **Center Segment** drop-down list.*

Grid Instance Properties

When the instance properties of a grid are changed, only the properties of the selected instances are changed. The instance properties of grids are given next.

Parameter Name	Value and Description
Name	Specifies the name assigned to the grid. You can enter any name, based on the project requirement
Scope Box	Specifies the scope box assigned to the grid that controls its visibility in different views

Customizing the Grid Display

In Revit, you can customize the grid display according to your need. You can change the color, line weight, and line type of the entire grid line or part of the grid line such as center segment and end segment. At the same time, you can change the display of symbols at the end of the grid line.

Changing the Continuous Grid Line

A grid line is said to be continuous when the **Center Segment** parameter in the **Type Properties** dialog box is set to **Continuous**. You can change the line type, line weight, and color of the end segments using various options available in the **Type Properties** dialog box. Similarly, you can change the display of a symbol at the ends of the grid, using the other options available in the **Type Properties** dialog box.

Creating a Grid Line with Central Gap

In a grid line, you can create a gap between the two end segments. To do so, set the **Center Segment** parameter in the **Type Properties** dialog box to **None**. Simultaneously, you can change the display properties of the end segments, as discussed above. To create a grid, ensure that the **1/4" Bubble Custom Gap** option is selected in the **Type-Selector** drop-down list. On doing so, you will get grid pattern, as shown in Figure 6-30.

Figure 6-30 The grid line with a central gap

Creating a Grid Line with Center Segment

A grid line will appear with the center and end segments that have different display properties such as line color, line weight, and line pattern. To create a grid line with center segment, select **Grid : 1/4" Bubble** or the **Grid : 1/4" Bubble Custom Gap** option from the **Type Selector** drop-down list and choose the **Edit Type** button; the **Type Properties** dialog box will be displayed. In the **Type Properties** dialog box, select the **Custom** option corresponding to the **Center Segment** parameter. Now in the **Type Properties** dialog box, use various parameters to change the display properties such as color, lineweight, and line pattern for the end and center segments of a grid. Figure 6-31 shows a grid line with the center segment having a different line pattern as compared to its end segments.

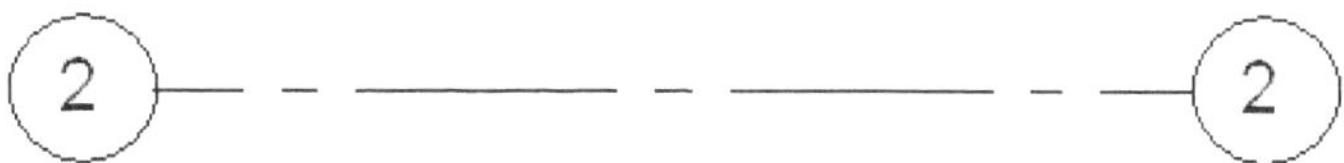

Figure 6-31 The grid line with a center segment

Controlling the Visibility of Grids

You can control the visibility of a grid or all grids in any of the project views. To control the visibility of a grid, select it and right-click, a shortcut menu will be displayed. Choose **Hide in View > Category** from the shortcut menu; the grid category will be hidden in the current view. Similarly, you can also hide one particular grid by choosing **Hide in View > Elements** from the shortcut menu. On doing so, the selected grid will be hidden in the current view. The grid will, however, be displayed in all other views.

Alternatively, you can control the visibility of grids by using the **Visibility/Graphic Overrides** dialog box. To invoke this dialog box, select a grid from the drawing; the **Modify | Grids** tab will be displayed. In the **View** panel of this tab, click on the **Override Graphics in View** drop-down and choose the **Override by Category** tool from the list displayed; the **View-Specific Category Graphics** dialog box will be displayed. In this dialog box, choose the **Open the Visibility Graphics dialog....** button; the **Visibility/Graphic Overrides for Floor Plan** dialog box will be displayed. In the **Annotation Categories** tab of this dialog box, clear the check box for the visibility of grids; the visibility of all grids will turn off in the current view. You can also control the visibility of grids using the Scope Box feature. You will learn more about this feature later in this chapter.

REFERENCE PLANES

Ribbon:	Architecture > Work Plane > Ref Plane
Shortcut Key:	RP

Reference planes are useful while sketching and adding building elements to a design. They can be used as datum planes to act as a guideline for creating elements. They can also be used effectively for creating new family elements. To create a reference plane, choose the **Ref Plane** tool from the **Work Plane** panel. On invoking the **Ref Plane** tool; the **Modify | Place Reference Plane** tab will be displayed. Select the tools from the **Draw** panel and start drawing the reference plane in the drawing. Alternatively, you can type **RP** to invoke the **Ref Plane** tool.

After invoking the tool, click at the desired location in the drawing window to start a line that defines the reference plane. Now, move the cursor to the new location and release the left button to specify the endpoint of the reference line; the reference plane will be created. To assign the reference plane a name, select it from the drawing. Next in the **Properties** palette, enter the name of the selected reference plane in the value field of the **Name** instance parameter.

WORK PLANES

As the name suggests, the work plane is a plane that can be used for sketching elements. In Autodesk Revit, you can create and edit only those elements that are in the current work plane. The work plane can be horizontal, vertical, or inclined at any specified angle. Each generated view has an associated work plane. This plane is automatically defined for some standard views such as floor plans. For others such as sections, elevations, and 3D views, you can set the work plane based on the location of the elements that are to be created or edited. The concept of work planes is especially useful for creating elements in elevations, sections, or inclined planes.

Setting a Work Plane

You can set a work plane based on your project requirement. To set a work plane, choose the **Set** tool from the **Work Plane** panel in the **Architecture** tab; the **Work Plane** dialog box will be displayed, as shown in Figure 6-32. It shows the current work plane and assists you in specifying the parameters to set a new work plane. The **Name** radio button has a drop-down list of available views. Select an available work plane from the drop-down list, which contains the names of levels, grids, and named reference planes. You can select the **Pick a plane** radio button in the **Work Plane** dialog box to set a work plane along an existing plane. On selecting this radio button and choosing the **OK** button in this dialog box, you will be prompted to select an existing plane in the drawing to which you want to align the work plane. The existing plane can be a face of a wall, floor, or roof. You can also select the **Pick a line and use the work plane it was sketched in** radio button from this dialog box to create a work plane that is coplanar with the plane on which the selected line was created.

Note

*In the project environment of Autodesk Revit, you can choose the **Viewer** tool from the **Work Plane** panel of the **Architecture** tab to display the **Workplane Viewer** window. In this window, you can modify the workplane dependent element easily.*

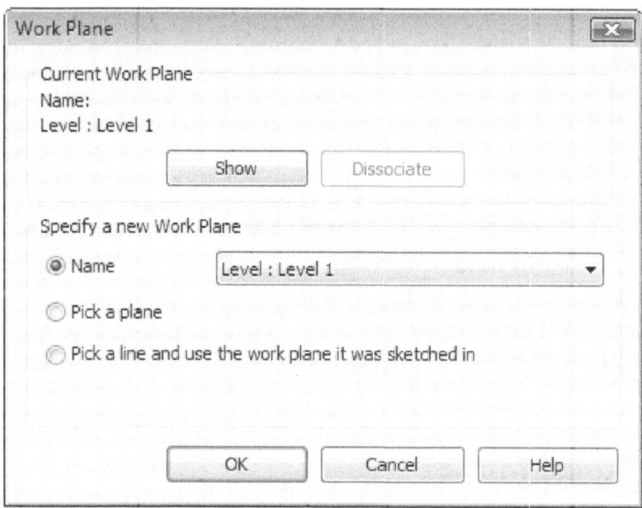

*Figure 6-32 The **Work Plane** dialog box*

Controlling the Visibility of Work Planes

You can control the visibility of the current work plane by choosing the **Show** button from the **Architecture** tab. As a result, the work plane appears as a grid in the current view, as shown in Figure 6-33. To hide it, choose the **Show** button again.

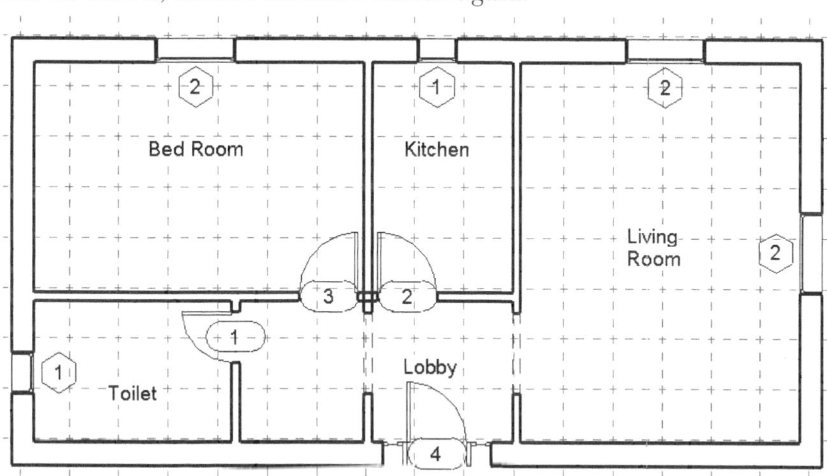

Figure 6-33 The display of the work plane as a grid

You can also set the grid spacing for a work plane by selecting it from the drawing. On doing so, the work plane gets highlighted. Specify the spacing by entering the new value in the **Spacing** edit box in **Options Bar**. You can snap to the work plane grid using the object snap tools. For example, these tools can be used to create wall profiles based on a square grid or a flooring pattern for an inclined ramp.

Tip

The drop-down list, next to the ***Name*** *radio button in the* ***Work Plane*** *dialog box shows all levels, grids, and reference planes that have been created in the project. If you select a plane that is perpendicular to the current view, the* ***Go to View*** *dialog box will be displayed and you can select the appropriate view from it.*

WORKING WITH PROJECT VIEWS

While working on the building model, you may need to view its different exterior and interior portions in order to add or edit the elements in the design. Revit provides various features and techniques that can be used to view the building model. In this section, you will recapitulate some concepts introduced earlier and also learn about the tools that will help you in working with the views.

Viewing a Building Model

The default template file has certain predefined standard project views, which are displayed in the **Views** head of the **Project Browser**, as shown in Figure 6-34. These include floor plans, ceiling plans, and elevations. To open any of these views, double-click on the name; the corresponding view will be displayed in the viewing area. You can control the visibility of the **Project browser** by selecting the **Project browser** check box from **View > Windows > User Interface** drop-down.

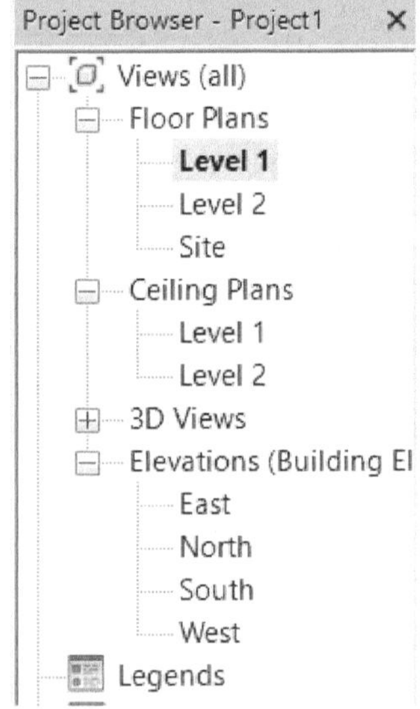

Figure 6-34 *The* ***Project Browser*** *showing the standard building views*

When you open a new project, the viewing area displays four inward arrow symbols in the floor plan view, which indicate the four side elevations: North, East, South, and West. You can use these symbols to view the appropriate building elevation by double-clicking on them.

Apart from these standard building views, you can use different viewing tools to view the building model from various angles. As described earlier (see Chapter 2), you can use the **Zoom** tool by choosing it from the navigation bar to zoom-in or zoom-out of the current view. You can also use the **Orient** tool to view the model using the preset standard viewpoints. The **SteeringWheels** and **ViewCube** tools assist you in navigating and viewing the model with various options. You can pan, zoom, walk, and change viewpoints using these tools.

To restrict the visibility of certain categories of elements, choose the **Visibility/Graphics** tool from the **Graphics** panel of the **View** tab; the **Visibility/Graphic Overrides** dialog box for the specific view will be displayed. The **Model Categories** tab of this dialog box contains a list of model elements such as walls, doors, windows, and so on, whereas the **Annotation Categories** tab contains annotations such as dimensions, door tags, and so on. You can clear the category of elements that you want to hide from the current view using this dialog box.

Visibility/Graphic Overrides of an Element

You can override the visibility and graphics of any element in a view. To do so, select an element and right-click; a shortcut menu will be displayed. Choose **Override Graphics in View > By Element** from the shortcut menu; the **View-Specific Element Graphics** dialog box will be displayed, as shown in Figure 6-35. The options in this dialog box are discussed next.

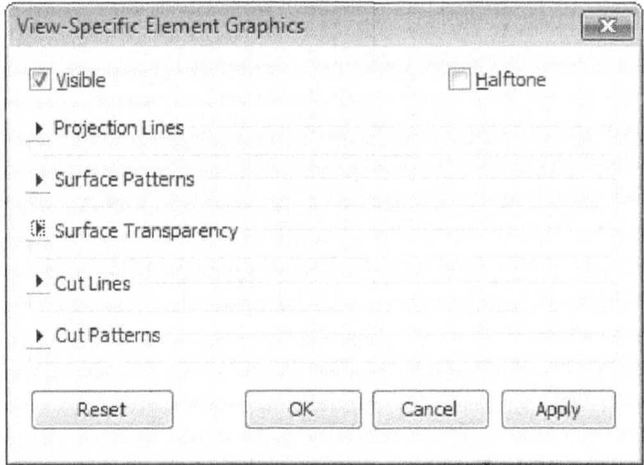

*Figure 6-35 The **View-Specific Element Graphics** dialog box*

Visible

The **Visible** check box controls the visibility of an element in a view. The check box is selected by default. Clear the check box to hide the selected element in the view.

Tip

*You can also use the keyboard shortcuts **VV** and **VG** to open the **Visibility/Graphics Overrides** dialog box.*

Halftone

Select the **Halftone** check box to adjust and blend the line color of an element with the background color.

Projection Lines

To view different options in the **Projection Lines** area, choose the arrow button located on the left of this area; the area will be expanded. In the expanded area, you can use any of the following options: **Weight**, **Color**, and **Pattern**. To set the line weight of the projection lines, you can select options from the **Weight** drop-down list. Similarly, to change the color of the projection lines, choose the button located on the right of the **Color** option; the **Color** dialog box will be displayed. Select the required color from the dialog box. Now, choose the **OK** button to close the dialog box. You can also change the pattern of projection lines. To do so, choose the button on the right of the **Pattern** option; the **Line Patterns** dialog box will be displayed. Select the required pattern of the projection lines from this dialog box. Next, choose the **OK** button to close the dialog box.

Surface Patterns

Choose the arrow button on the left of this option to expand the **Surface Patterns** area. You can change the visibility of the surface pattern by clearing the **Visible** check box. Select the color and pattern of the surface in the same way as explained earlier for the projection lines.

Surface Transparency

Choose the arrow button on the left of the **Surface Transparency** area to expand it. In this area, you can change the transparency of the selected element by moving the **Transparency** slider or by entering a suitable value in the edit box displayed next to the slider. Note that higher the value you enter in the edit box, more transparent will be the object.

Cut Lines

Choose the arrow button on the left of the **Cut Lines** area to expand it. In this area, you can change the weight, color, and pattern of the cut lines, as explained earlier for the **Projection Lines** area. Once you have edited the graphic settings of an element in the **View Specific Element Graphics** dialog box, choose the **Apply** and **OK** button to apply the settings and close the dialog box.

Cut Patterns

Expand the **Cut Pattern** area by choosing the arrow button on its left. In the expanded area, change the visibility, color, and pattern of the cut patterns. Once you have edited the visibility settings of an element in the **View Specific Element Graphics** dialog box, choose the **Apply** and then the **OK** button to apply the settings and close the dialog box.

Visibility/Graphic Overrides of an Element Category

To edit the visibility and graphics of an element category, open the required project view. Next, select an element of the required category and right-click; a shortcut menu will be displayed. Choose **Override Graphics in View > By Category** from the shortcut menu; the **View-Specific Category Graphics** dialog box for the loaded view will be displayed. In this dialog box, choose the **Open the Visibility Graphics dialog** button; the **Visibility/Graphic Overrides for Floor Plan** dialog box will be displayed, refer to Figure 6-36.

The dialog box contains the tabs to edit the visibility and graphic display of the models, annotations, and imported elements. Choose the required tab to edit the visibility and graphics of the selected category. In the **Visibility** column, clear or select the visibility check box available on the left of the category name to edit the visibility in the view. To specify overrides to a category, click on the name of the category in the **Visibility** column of the **Visibility/Graphics Overrides for Floor Plan** dialog box; the **Overrides** button will be displayed for the respective columns in the specified tab. To override patterns for the selected category, choose the **Override** button displayed in the **Patterns** column corresponding to the selected category; the **Fill Pattern Graphics** dialog box will be displayed. Set the visibility, color, and pattern for the **Visible**, **Color**, and **Pattern** options in the dialog box and choose the **OK** button. Similarly to override the transparency, of the selected object, choose the **Override** button displayed in the **Transparency** column; the **Surfaces** dialog box will be displayed. In this dialog box, you can use the **Transparency** slider to control the transparency of the selected element.

Similarly, click in the required columns in the **Visibility/Graphics Overrides for Floor Plan** dialog box to edit the graphic display of the category. Select the check boxes in the **Halftone** column if required. You can set the detail level of the selected category in the **Detail level** column. To do so, click in the **Detail Level** column and choose the down arrow displayed on the left. Select the detail level from the **Detail Level** drop-down list. Choose the **Apply** button to view the changes in the visibility and graphic display of the selected category. Choose the **OK** button to retain the changes and close the **Visibility/Graphics Overrides for Floor Plan** dialog box.

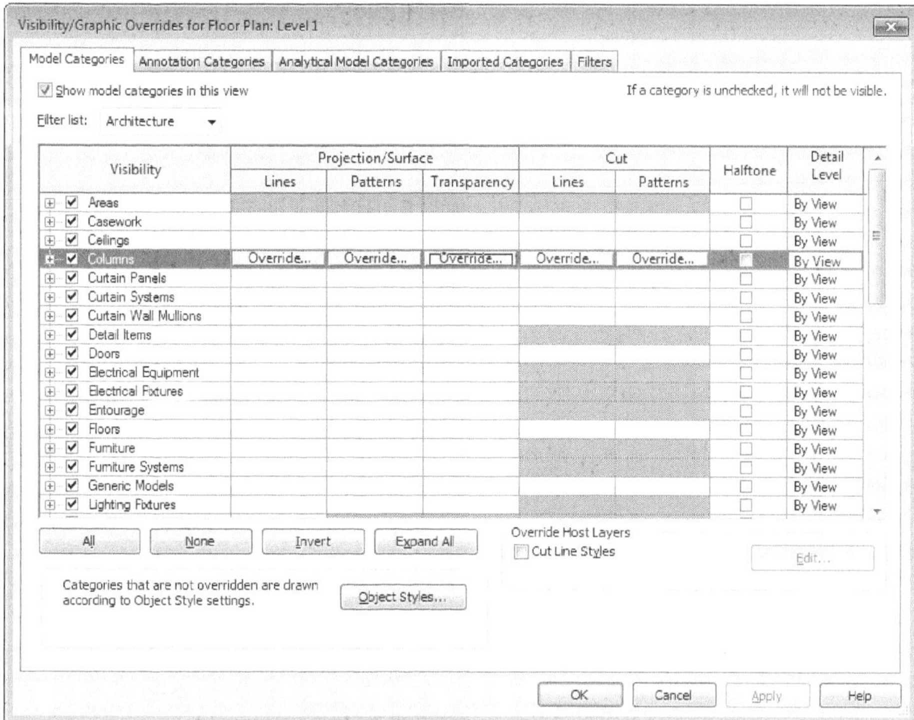

Figure 6-36 The ***Visibility/Graphic Overrides for Floor Plan*** *dialog box*

Making Elements Transparent

Revit provides you with a tool to make elements transparent so that you can see through an object. This tool can be used to view the interior of a building from the top, even after adding roofs or ceilings.

To make an element transparent, select the element and right-click; a shortcut menu will be displayed. Choose **Override Graphics in View > By Element** from the shortcut menu; the **View Specific Element Graphics** dialog box will be displayed. In this dialog box, choose the arrow on the left of the **Surface Transparency** area; the options in this area will be displayed. In this area, you can use the **Transparency** slider to control the transparency of the selected object. You can also increase the transparency by moving the slider toward right. Alternatively, you can enter a desired value in the edit box, next to the **Transparency** slider, to control the transparency of the selected element. After setting the transparency in the **Surface Transparency** area, choose the **OK** button; the selected element will become transparent and you will be able to see through it. Although the element becomes transparent, the edges and surface pattern of the element will still be visible. You can view the change before and after using the Transparency slider, refer to Figures 6-37 and 6-38.

Figure 6-37 Elements before selecting the ***Transparent*** *check box*

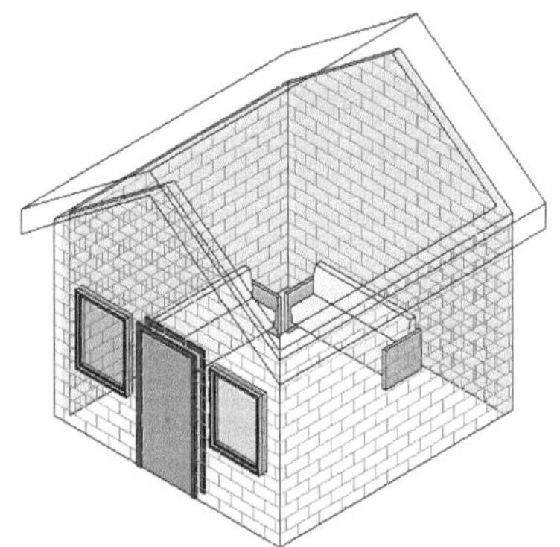

Figure 6-38 Elements after selecting the ***Transparent*** *check box*

Using the Temporary Hide/Isolate Tool

The **Temporary Hide/Isolate** tool can be used to hide or isolate elements temporarily from a project view. This tool will be available only after a selection has been made. Select the element or elements that you need to hide or isolate in the project view and then choose the **Temporary Hide/Isolate** tool from the **View Control Bar**; a cascading menu will be displayed. You can hide or isolate elements or their categories using the tools given in the cascading menu. The cascading menu contains six tools. On choosing any of the tools from it, a cyan color border will be displayed in the drawing area, indicating that the elements in the drawing are in the **Temporary Hide/Isolate** mode. You can choose the **Hide Element** tool from the cascading menu, as shown in Figure 6-39, to hide the selected element in a view. On choosing the **Isolate Element** tool, only the selected elements will be displayed while the rest will be hidden in the view. The **Hide Category** tool is used to hide all the elements of the category of the selected element. The **Isolate Category** is used to display only the elements belonging to the category of the selected element in the view.

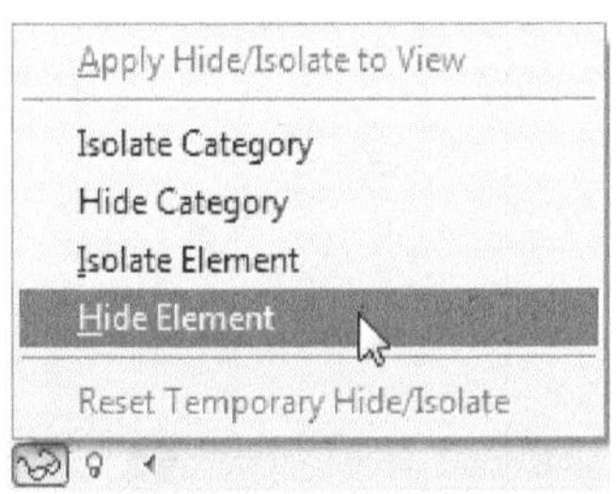

Figure 6-39 Choosing the ***Hide Element*** *tool*

The **Reset Temporary Hide/Isolate** tool is used to revert to the original view without saving the temporary hide or isolate changes in the view. The **Apply Hide/Isolate to view** option is used to hide or isolate the temporary hidden or isolated elements permanently in the view. After you choose this tool, the blue boundary becomes invisible and the temporarily hidden or isolated elements and categories are permanently hidden or isolated. On hiding or isolating an element or category, the sunglasses symbol of the **Temporary Hide/Isolate** tool in the **View Control Bar** is highlighted in the same color as that of the boundary, indicating that certain elements have been hidden temporarily. When you choose the **Reset Temporary Hide/Isolate** option, the sunglasses symbol is no longer highlighted.

Revealing and Unhiding Elements

To reveal and unhide the hidden elements in the view, choose the bulb icon from the **View Control** bar to invoke the **Reveal Hidden Elements** tool. On doing so, a magenta color border will be displayed and the hidden elements will be highlighted in the same color. Select the required elements and choose the **Unhide Element** or the **Unhide Category** button from the **Reveal Hidden Elements** panel in the **Architecture** tab. Now, again you need to click the bulb icon to exit the **Reveal Hidden Elements** mode. You can also exit by choosing the **Toggle Reveal Hidden Elements Mode** button from the **Reveal Hidden Elements** panel of the **Architecture** tab. You will notice that all the hidden elements and categories will be displayed in the view.

Plan Views

In Autodesk Revit, you can use the floor and ceiling views to view the building model plan. By default, Autodesk Revit opens the floor plan view when you create a new project. The default template file contains two floor plans and two corresponding ceiling plans. These views are enlisted under the **Floor Plans** and **Ceiling Plans** heads in the **Project Browser**.

Adding a Plan View

As described earlier, when you add levels in the project view, Autodesk Revit automatically adds their corresponding floor and ceiling plan views in the **Project Browser**. To create new plan views for the added levels that do not contain associated plans in the **Project Browser**, choose the **Floor Plan** tool from **View > Create > Plan Views** drop-down; the **New Floor Plan** dialog box will be displayed, as shown in Figure 6-40.

Figure 6-40 *The **New Floor Plan** dialog box*

In the **New Floor Plan** dialog box, the **Floor Plan** option is selected by default in the **Type** drop-down list, refer to Figure 6-40. You can edit the existing type or create a new type by choosing the **Edit Type** button. On choosing the **Edit Type** button; the **Type Properties** dialog box will be displayed. In this dialog box, you can edit various type parameters for the existing view type or choose the **Duplicate** button and create a new type. Choose the **OK** button to return to the **New Floor Plan** dialog box. In this dialog box, you can select the appropriate level to create the plan view in the list box displayed. You can also select multiple levels by holding the SHIFT key. The **Do not duplicate existing views** check box can be cleared to create a plan view for a level that has an already existing plan view. The duplicate view is created and added in the **Project Browser** with the suffix (1). The number in the brackets increments as more copies of the plan view are added. The appropriate scale for the new view can be selected from the **Scale** drop-down list.

Note

*While creating a level, if you have cleared the **Make Plan View** check box in the **Options Bar**, then its corresponding plan view will not be created.*

Modifying the Plan View Properties

To modify the view properties of a plan view or any other project view, select the project view from the **Project Browser**; the properties of the selected view will be displayed in the **Properties** palette. Using this palette, you can modify the parameters related to the current view such as **View Scale**, **Display Model**, **Detail Level**, **View Name**, and so on. The **View Range** parameter in the **Extents** category controls the visibility and appearance of the elements in the view by defining the extent of horizontal plane of the view. The crop region parameter defines the boundary of a view and can be turned on or off using the **Crop Region Visible** check box. You can also access the tools related to the visibility settings of the view using the **View Control Bar** available near the bottom left corner of the drawing window.

Elevation Views

An elevation view refers to the view of the building model from four sides, North, East, South, and West. The four side elevation views are automatically created by Autodesk Revit when the default template file is used. Using the elevation view, you cannot only visualize the building from its exterior but also create the views of the interior walls of various internal spaces.

For example, for a residential building, you can easily view the four side elevations and also create the elevation views of the walls of the interior spaces such as kitchen and bathroom. In the plan view, the elevation is represented by the elevation symbol pointing in the direction of the elevation view side.

Creating an Elevation View

To create an elevation view, invoke the **Elevation** tool from **View > Create > Elevation** drop-down; the **Properties** palette for the elevation will be displayed. In this palette, select the type of elevation from the **Type Selector** drop-down list. From this drop-down list, you can select any of the two options: **Building Elevation** or **Interior Elevation**. To create an exterior elevation, select the **Building Elevation** option and move the cursor in the viewing area in the drawing. On doing so, the elevation symbol will appear. On moving the cursor near the exterior walls, you will notice that the arrow head of the elevation symbol has changed its alignment perpendicular to the wall, as shown in Figure 6-41. Now, click when the elevation arrow head symbol points toward the desired direction; the new elevation view will be created and added to the list of elevations in the **Project Browser**. Revit automatically numbers the elevation names. When you select the elevation symbol created, its controls are displayed, as shown in Figure 6-42.

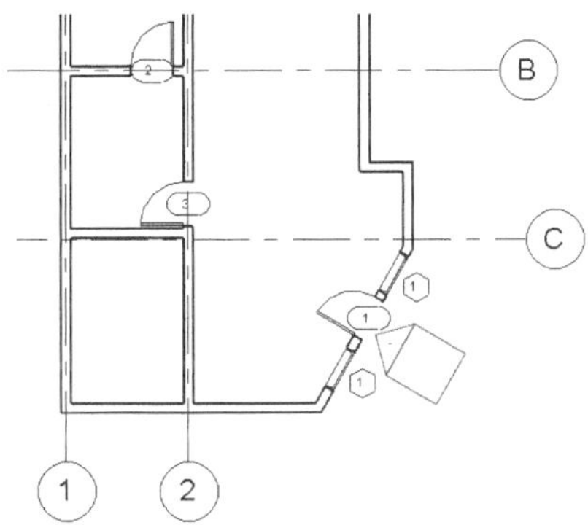

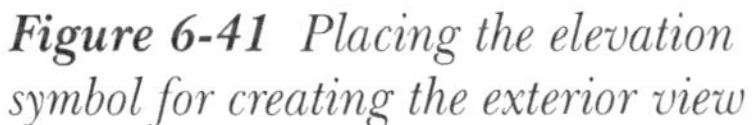
Figure 6-41 *Placing the elevation symbol for creating the exterior view*

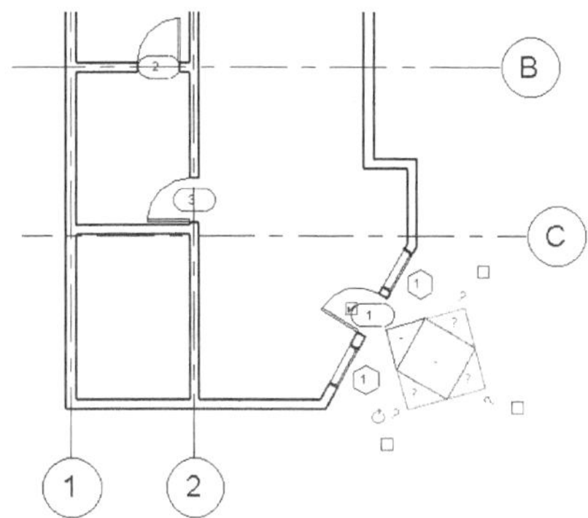

Figure 6-42 *Controls of the elevation symbol*

Similarly, to create an elevation view of the interior walls of an interior space of a building model, invoke the **Elevation** tool and select the **Interior Elevation** option from the **Type Selector** drop-down list. Next, move the cursor near the interior wall in the interior space; the elevation symbol will appear. Place this symbol inside the space, as shown in Figure 6-43. When you select the elevation symbol, its controls are displayed. Using the check box(es) in these controls, you can create the elevation of the desired walls, as shown in Figure 6-44. The rotate symbol can be used to rotate the elevation symbol in the desired direction.

You can also set the width of the elevation view using the clip plane control. When you click the arrow head of the elevation symbol, the clip plane is displayed as a blue line with the drag control dots on its two ends, as shown in Figure 6-45. You can drag them to resize the width of the elevation view. For the interior elevation views, Autodesk Revit automatically extends the clip plane to the extents of the room. You can drag the blue dots to increase or decrease the extents of the elevation view, as shown in Figure 6-46.

Note

*In Revit, elevations are added in **Project Browser** under two different headings, **Elevations (Building Elevation)** and **Elevations (Interior Elevation)**. All the exterior elevations are added under the **Elevations (Building Elevation)** heading and all the interior elevations are added under the **Elevations (Interior Elevation)** heading.*

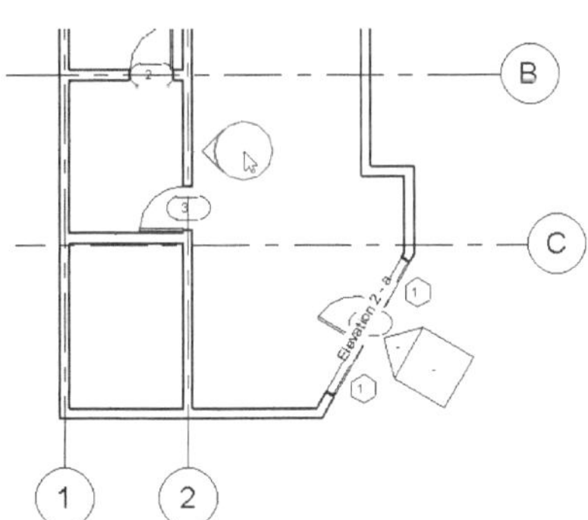

Figure 6-43 *Placing the elevation symbol for creating the interior elevation view*

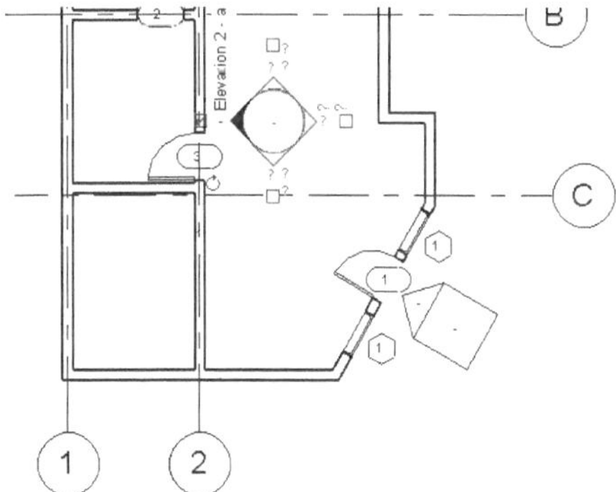

Figure 6-44 *Adding the interior view by using the elevation controls*

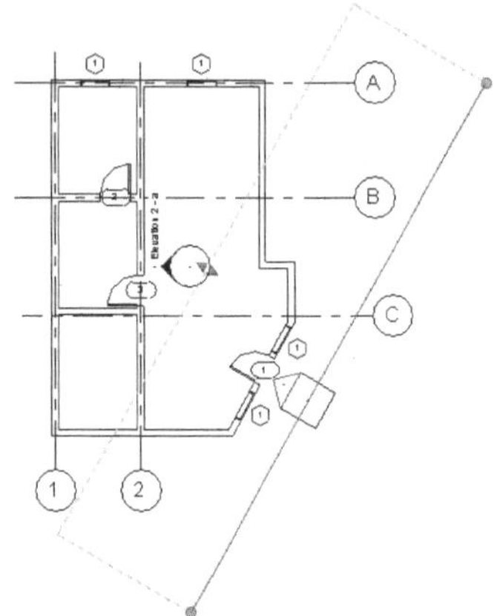

Figure 6-45 The clip plane drag controls

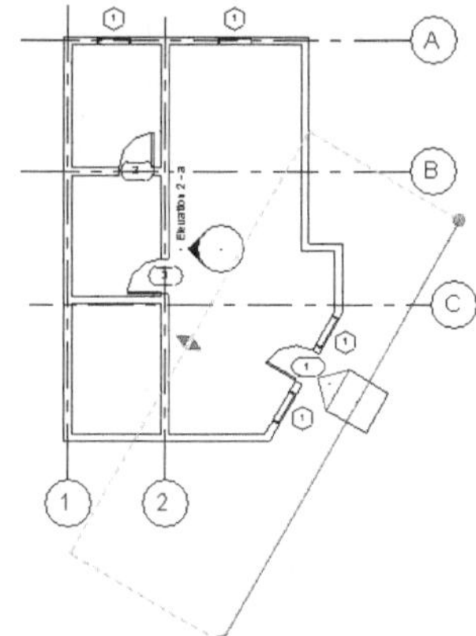

Figure 6-46 Dragged clip plane controls

To rename the elevation view created, right-click on the view name in the **Project Browser**; a shortcut menu will be displayed. Choose the **Rename** option from the shortcut menu; the **Rename View** dialog box will be displayed. In this dialog box, enter a name in the **Name** edit box and choose the **OK** button; the elevation view will be renamed.

There are various methods to display an elevation view. The first method is by double-clicking on the name of the elevation in the **Project Browser**. When you do so, the corresponding elevation view will be displayed in the drawing window. Second method to display the elevation view is to double-click on the arrow head of the elevation symbol to display its corresponding elevation view. The third method is to right-click on the elevation symbol to display a shortcut menu. Choose **Find Referring Views** from the shortcut menu; the **Go To View** dialog box is displayed, as shown in Figure 6-47. Next, select the view to be displayed from this dialog box and then choose the **Open View** button or double-click on the name of the view. The other method to display the elevation view is to select the arrow head of the elevation symbol and then right-click to display a shortcut menu. Next, choose the **Go to Elevation View** option from the shortcut menu displayed; the corresponding elevation will be displayed in the drawing area.

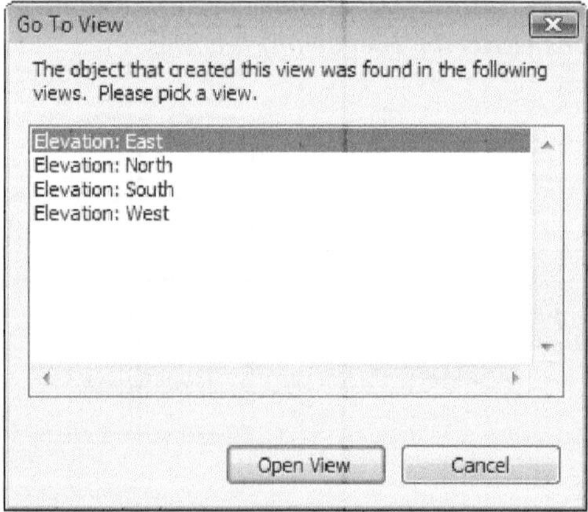

Figure 6-47 The ***Go To View*** *dialog box*

You can modify the properties associated with elevation views by using the **Properties** palette. This palette is displayed with instance parameters when you select the required view or when the required view is displayed in the drawing area.

Note
While working on the floor plan, if the created building model extends beyond the clip planes of the four side elevation views, the corresponding elevations no longer show the complete exterior views. Instead an elevation view that is cut through the building model will be displayed. You can drag the clip plane controls symbol beyond the extent of the building profile to retain the view as a complete exterior elevation view.

Tip
*You can also change the elevation view symbol by selecting it and then choosing the **Edit Type** button from the **Properties** palette to display the **Type Properties** dialog box. You can then select and modify different parameters to create the desired elevation view symbol.*

Section Views

Section views are generated by cutting sections through the building model. These views are created to display various wall elevations, floor heights, and special vertical features of the project. They are also useful in creating and editing elements added to the interior spaces of the building model.

For example, in an office building, to emphasize the salient features of the central atrium, you may need to show a section through the central atrium. Autodesk Revit enables you to create it with relative ease. You can also modify the sectional view to create a section that displays the interior spaces.

Creating a Section View

To create a section view, invoke the **Section** tool from the **Create** panel of the **View** tab. On doing so, the **Modify | Section** tab will be displayed. The options in the **Modify | Section** tab are used to specify the section type to be created and to specify the instance and its type properties. The section can be created in the plan, elevation, and section views. You can create different types of section views such as the building section, wall section, and detail section. You can choose the section view type to be created from the **Type Selector** drop-down list in the **Properties** palette. In the **Options Bar** you can use the **Reference other view** check box to create a reference section that acts as a reference for another view. Notice that the reference sections are not added as an additional section in the list of section views in the **Project Browser**.

To create a building section, invoke the **Section** tool from the **Create** panel and move the cursor to the viewing area; the cursor will change into a cross symbol, and you will be prompted to draw the section line in the current view. Click at the appropriate location to specify the start point. To create a section through the entire building, click near the exterior face of the building profile. As you move the cursor, a section line will appear with one end fixed at the specified point and the other end attached to the cursor. You can even create a section line at any angle. To create a horizontal or vertical section view, move the cursor horizontally or vertically across the building profile, as shown in Figure 6-48 and click to specify the endpoint. The section line along with its controls is shown in Figure 6-49. It is represented by a section head and a line. The section head indicates the direction toward which the section will be created.

Note that, the methods used for displaying the section views are similar to the ones described for the elevation view.

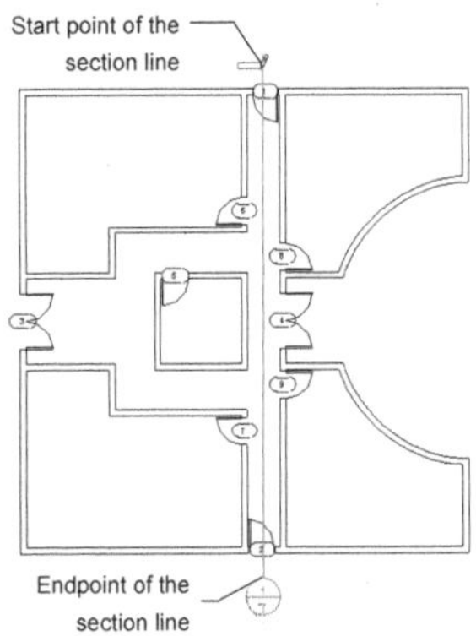

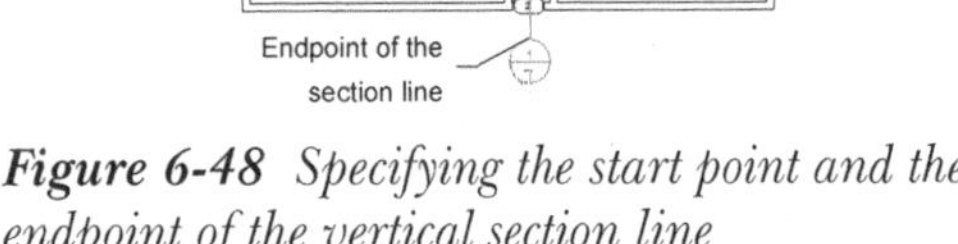

Figure 6-48 Specifying the start point and the endpoint of the vertical section line

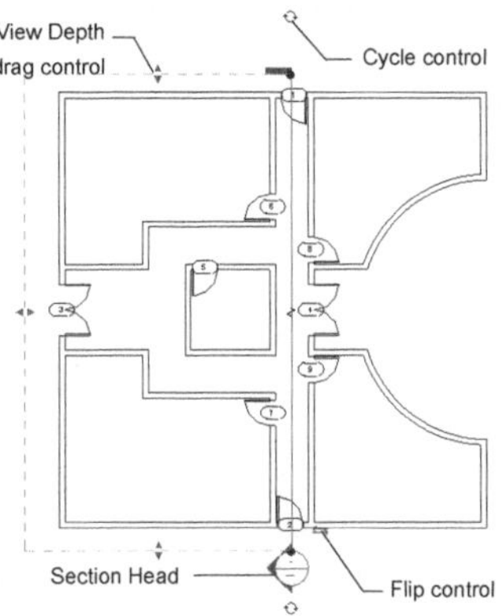

Figure 6-49 The vertical section line and its controls

Modifying a Section View

After creating a section view, you can modify the location of the section line of the section view by dragging it, as shown in Figure 6-50. When you drag a section line, the corresponding section view is updated immediately, refer to Figure 6-51.

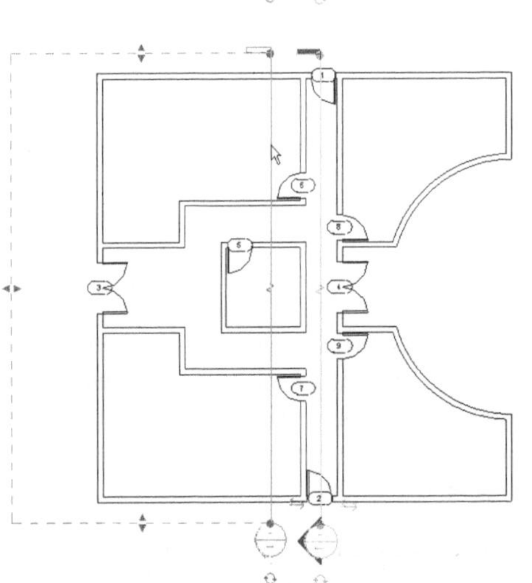

Figure 6-50 Dragging the section line

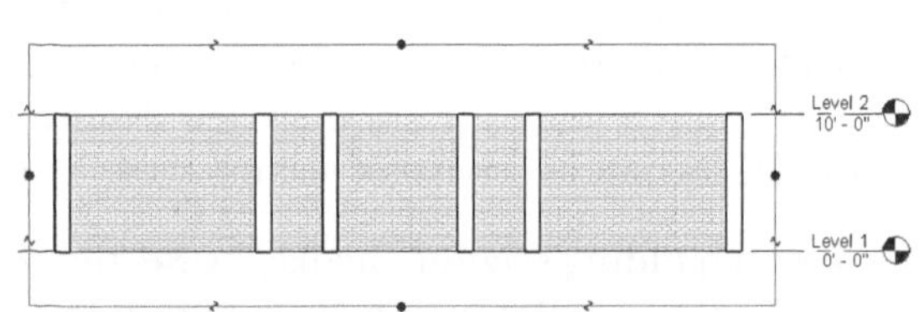

Figure 6-51 The updated section view

You can modify the parameters of the section view by using the controls available on the section view line. When selected, the created section line shows its controls. The twin arrow symbol represents the flip tool that can be used to flip the viewing side of the section view. By default, the section head appears on one side. The cyclic control on both the ends of the section line can be used to change the visibility of the section head and tail at the respective end. You can click on the symbol to hide or display them. Click on the break line symbol, which appears in the middle of the section line, to break it. You can then resize the two section lines to the required extent of the view. To rejoin the section line, click on the break line control again.

When you create a section view, Autodesk Revit intuitively creates its view depth, which is the extent of the view in the current view. It is represented by a dashed line the blue arrows as drag controls. To modify the view depth, drag the arrows to the desired location. The section view shows only those elements that are within the view depth. For example, Figure 6-52 shows the modified view depth with its corresponding updated section view. Notice that the west wall is not visible in the section view because it is not within the view depth.

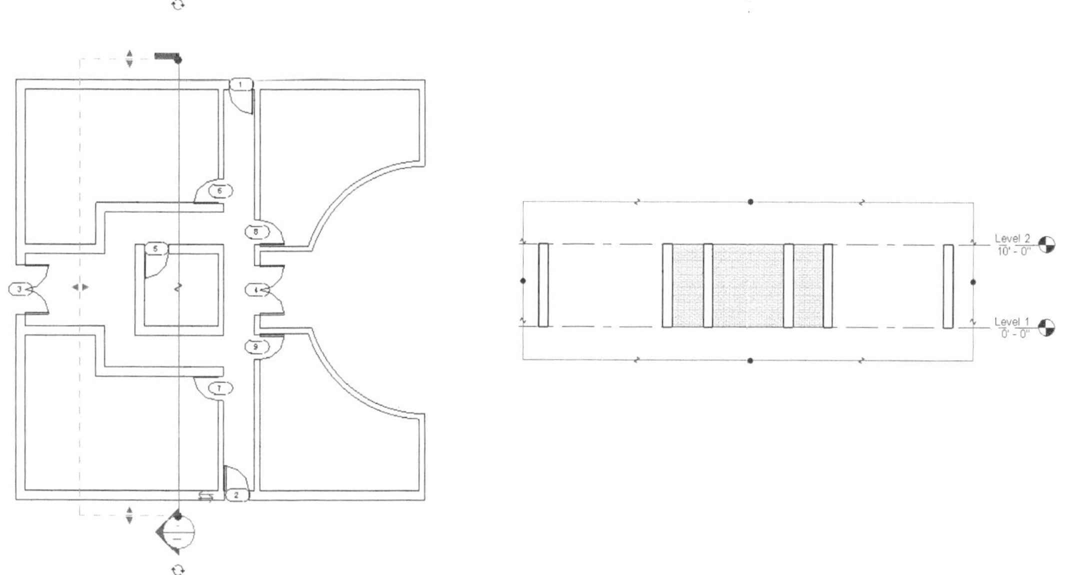

Figure 6-52 *The modified view depth with its corresponding updated section view*

To modify the properties of a section view, select its section line, the **Properties** palette will be displayed with the instance parameters of the section view, as shown in Figure 6-53. Using this palette, you can modify various instance properties such as **View Name**, **View Scale**, **Crop Region Visible**, and so on by clicking in the corresponding **Value** column and selecting a new value from the drop-down list if available, or by entering a new value in that field.

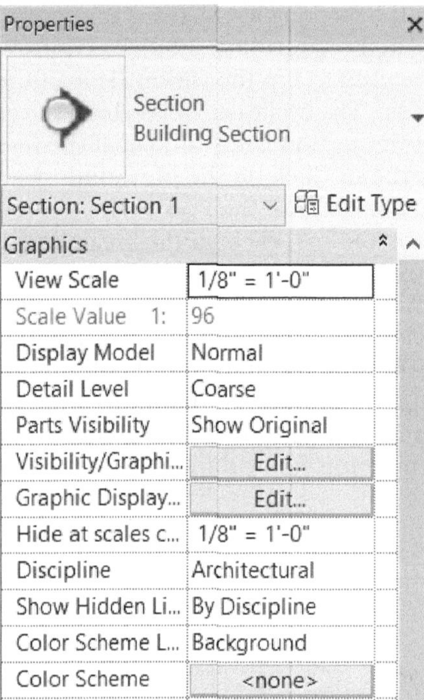

***Figure 6-53** The **Properties** palette for a section view*

You can choose the **Edit Type** button to display the **Type Properties** dialog box and modify the type properties of the section view such as **Callout Tag**, **Section Tag**, and **Reference Label**.

Tip

By default, when you create a section line horizontally from left to right, the section view faces upward, whereas if you create it from right to left, it faces downward. Similarly, when you create it vertically from bottom to top, the section view faces toward the left, whereas if you create it from top to bottom, it faces toward the right.

Creating a Segmented Section

Autodesk Revit enables you to split the section into segments that are orthogonal to the direction of the section view. This enables you to show different parts of the building model in the same section view.

To create a segmented section, create a straight section line in the drawing and then choose the **Split Segment** tool from the **Section** panel of the **Modify | Views** tab. On doing so, a split symbol will be attached to the cursor. Move it over the section line and click at the point from where you want to split it. Move the cursor perpendicular to the section line; it will break from the specified point and you can move the cursor in the desired direction to split the section line along the head or tail side. Click again to specify the location of the split. The segmented section will be created and the section view will be modified immediately, as shown in Figure 6-54.

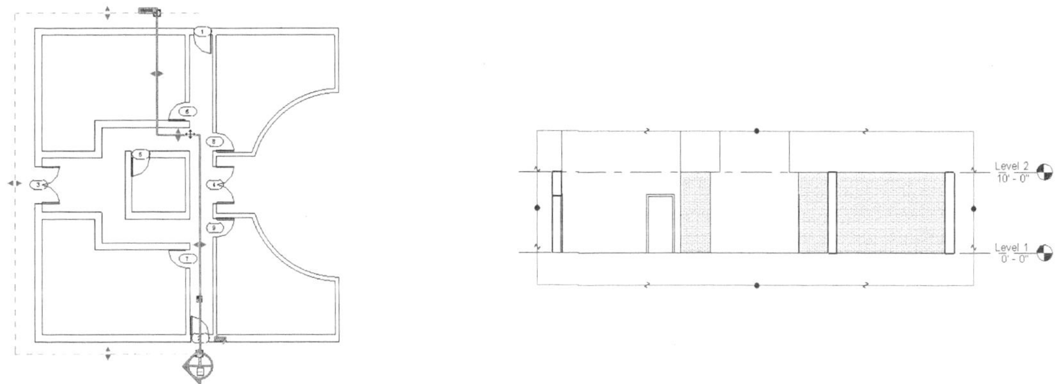

Figure 6-54 The segmented section line with the modified section view

Controlling the Visibility of a Section Line

The section line is visible in plan, section, and elevation view, if the view range of the created views intersects the crop region of the current view. The section line created in one view is visible and created simultaneously in all the other views.

You can also control the visibility of the section line in the views. Select the section line, right-click, and choose **Hide in View > Element** from the shortcut menu. It becomes hidden in the current view.

Note

The section of elements is displayed when a section is cut through them. Sections through in-place elements are not available; therefore they are not displayed in the section view.

Creating a Detail and a Wall Section View

In Autodesk Revit, you can create different types of section views. The types of section views will depend upon the type you will select from the **Type Selector** drop-down list in the **Properties** palette. From the **Type Selector** drop-down list you can select any of the three different types of section views such as detail, building, or wall section view.

To create a detail section view from the building model, select the **Detail View : Detail** option from the **Type Selector** drop-down list of the **Properties** palette. Similarly, to create a building section or a wall section of the building model, select the **Section : Building Section** or the **Section : Wall Section** option from the **Type Selector** drop-down list. After clearing a wall section using the **Section : Wall Section** type, you will notice that its section view has been added to the list of sections under the subhead **Sections (Wall Sections)** in the **Project Browser** and you can display it by double-clicking on the section name. Similarly, a section view created as a building section or a detail section will be displayed in the subhead **Sections (Building Sections)** or **Detail Views (Detail)**, respectively. You will learn more about these views in the later chapters.

Using the Scope Box Tool

With the **Scope Box** tool, Autodesk Revit provides you the option of controlling the visibility of the datum elements in the project views. As described earlier in this chapter, the datum planes have an infinite scope and extend throughout the project. Using the **Scope Box** tool, you can limit the boundary for the visibility of the datum planes. You can also specify the views in which these datum planes become visible.

Note

The ***Scope Box*** *tool is activated only in the plan view and it is view specific.*

Creating a Scope Box

The Scope box can be created in the plan view by invoking the **Scope Box** tool. You can invoke this tool from the **Create** panel of the **View** tab. Once this tool has been invoked, the **Options Bar** displays the **Name** and **Height** edit boxes. You can enter the name and height of the scope box using these edit boxes.

To create the Scope Box, move the cursor in the viewing area. It changes into a cross symbol, prompting you to draw the scope box in the plan view. To define the scope box, click on its upper left corner, move the cursor to the lower right corner, and then click to specify the diagonally opposite ends. The rectangle should be drawn in such a way that the elements that need to be visible are enclosed in it. The scope box with the assigned name is created. When it is selected, the drag controls are visible on it, as shown in Figure 6-55. These drag controls can be used to resize the scope box.

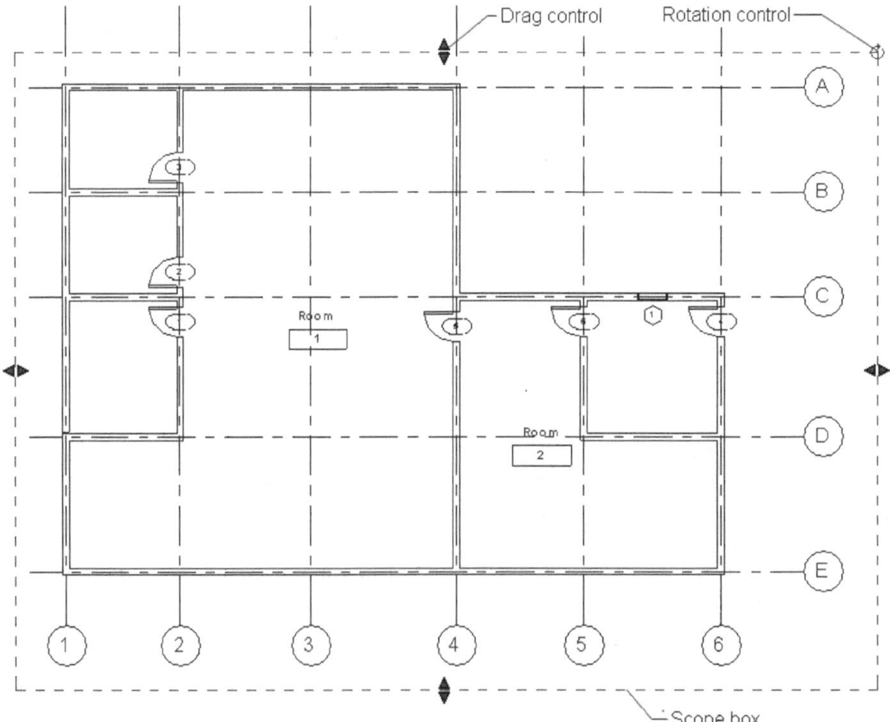

Figure 6-55 *Drag controls displayed on selecting the scope box*

Applying the Scope Box

The visibility of datum planes can be controlled by associating them with the scope box. You can select a datum such as a grid, a level, or a reference plane, and then in the **Properties** palette, click on the value column for the **Scope Box** parameter and select the name of the scope box from the drop-down list displayed. Now, choose the **Apply** button to apply the property to the selected datum. The datum now appears only in those views whose cutting planes intersect the scope box.

Controlling the Visibility of the Scope Box

The scope box can be resized to limit its visibility for certain views. Its visibility can also be controlled for each view. To control the visibility of the scope box, select it; the instance properties of the selected scope box will be displayed in the **Properties** palette. In the **Parameters** area of the palette, choose the **Edit** button displayed in the value field for the **Views Visible** parameter; the **Scope Box Views Visible** dialog box will be displayed. This dialog box lists all views types and view names available in the project. In the **Scope Box Views Visible** dialog box, the **Automatic visibility** column shows the current visibility of scope boxes for corresponding views. You can click in the value field in the **Override** column for a specific view. On doing so, a drop-down list will be displayed, as shown in Figure 6-56. The drop-down list has three options: **None**, **Visible**, and **Invisible**. You can select any of the options from the drop-down list displayed to override the automatic visibility setting.

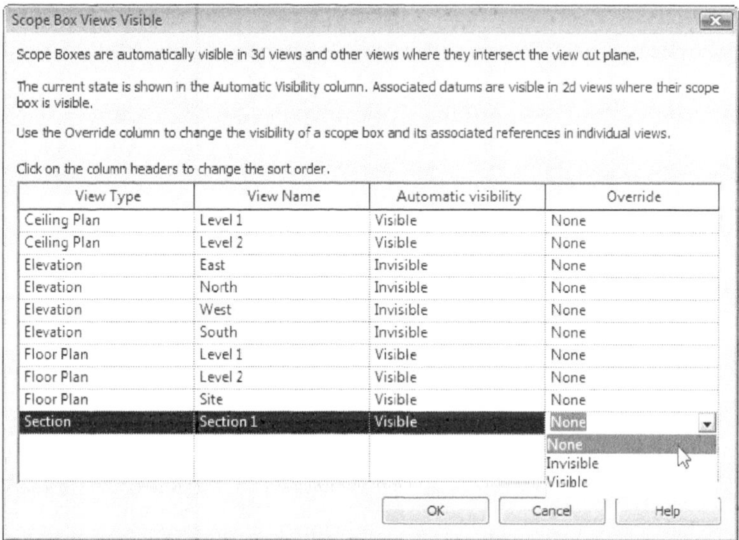

Figure 6-56 Controlling the visibility of the scope boxes using the ***Scope Box Views Visible*** *dialog box*

TUTORIALS

Tutorial 1 Apartment 1

In this tutorial, you will add levels and grids to the *c05_Apartment1_tut1.rvt (M_c05_Apartment1_tut1.rvt* for Metric) project. Also, you will create wall elevation for the kitchen walls and sections using the Figure 6-57 as reference. Do not create the dimensions and text as they have been given only for your reference. Use the following project parameters:

(Expected time: 30 min)

1. Rename Level 1 as **First Floor** and Level 2 as **Second Floor**

2. Levels to be added:
   For Imperial **Third Floor- Elevation 20'0"**
   Fourth Floor- Elevation 30'0"
   Roof Floor- Elevation 40'0"
   For Metric **Third Floor- Elevation 6000 mm**
   Fourth Floor- Elevation 9000 mm
   Roof Floor- Elevation 12000 mm

   Note that in the metric template level 2 is at 4000 mm. Change that level to 3000 mm and then add further levels.

3. Grids and sections to be created using Figure 6-57 as reference. The horizontal section to be renamed as **Section X** and the vertical section as **Section Y**.

The following steps are required to complete this tutorial:

a. Open the file created in Chapter 5.
   For Imperial *c05_Apartment1_tut1.rvt*
   For Metric *M_c05_Apartment1_tut1.rvt*
b. Add levels using the **Level** tool, refer to Figures 6-58 through 6-61.
c. Add grids using the **Grid** tool, refer to Figures 6-62 through 6-64.
d. Create section views using the **Section** tool, refer to Figures 6-64 and 6-66.
e. Create and view the four interior wall elevations of the kitchen walls, refer to Figures 6-67 and 6-68.
f. Save the project using the **Save As** tool.
   For Imperial *c06_Apartment1_tut1.rvt*
   For Metric *M_c06_Apartment1_tut1.rvt*
g. Close the project.

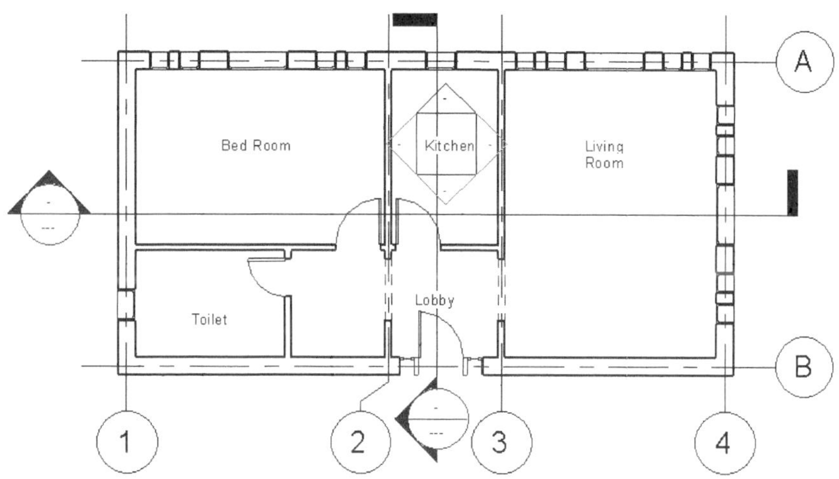

Figure 6-57 Sketch plan for adding grids, sections, and elevations to the Apartment 1 project

Opening an Existing Project and Hiding Tags

Before starting this tutorial, you need to open the specified project, and then you need to hide the door and window tags to simplify the project view using the **Visibility/Graphics** tool.

1. To open the specified project, choose **Open > Project** from the **File** menu and then open the *c05_Apartment1_tut1.rvt* file (for Metric *M_c05_Apartment1_tut1.rvt*), created in Tutorial 1 of Chapter 5. You can also download this file from *http://www.cadcim.com*. The path of the file is as follows: *Textbooks > Civil/GIS > Revit Architecture > Exploring Autodesk Revit 2018 for Architecture*

2. Ensure that the **Floor Plans** view for Level 1 is opened. Next, to hide the doors and windows tags, choose the **Visibility/Graphics** tool from the **Graphics** panel of the **View** tab; the **Visibility/Graphic Overrides for Floor Plan** dialog box is displayed.

3. Choose the **Annotation Categories** tab from the dialog box and clear the check boxes for **Door Tags** and **Window Tags**.

4. Choose the **Apply** button to apply the changes and then the **OK** button to close the dialog box and return to the drawing window.

Adding Levels

In this section, you will learn to create levels in the elevation view.

1. Move the cursor to the **Project Browser** and double-click on **North** under the **Elevations (Building Elevation)** head. The north elevation with the existing levels is displayed in the drawing window. Make sure that the **Hidden Line** option is selected in the **Visual Style** menu of the **View Control Bar**. Select the levels and drag the endpoints of the level lines near the building profile; the view is adjusted, as shown in Figure 6-58.

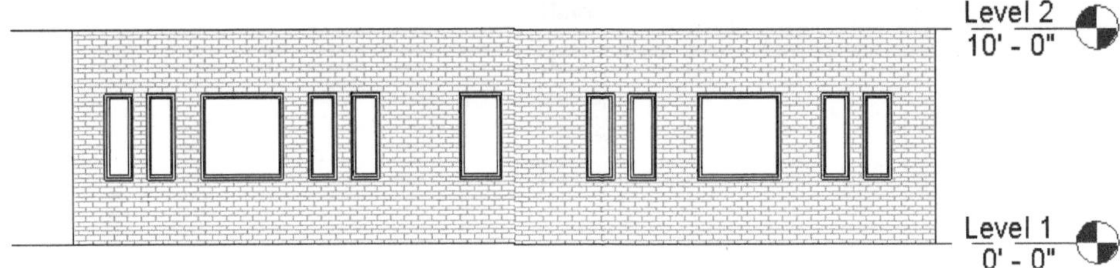

Figure 6-58 The north elevation view of the Apartment 1 project

2. Invoke the **Level** tool from the **Datum** panel of the **Architecture** tab.

Note

*In the metric unit system, by default, the Level 2 is at 4000 mm. Shift the Level 2 to 3000 mm by clicking on the value and entering the value as **3000**.*

3. Next, move the cursor near the left endpoint of the level line of Level 2 and then move it upward and when the alignment line appears, enter **10'0"(3000 mm)** as the distance of the new level from the Level 2, as shown in Figure 6-59.

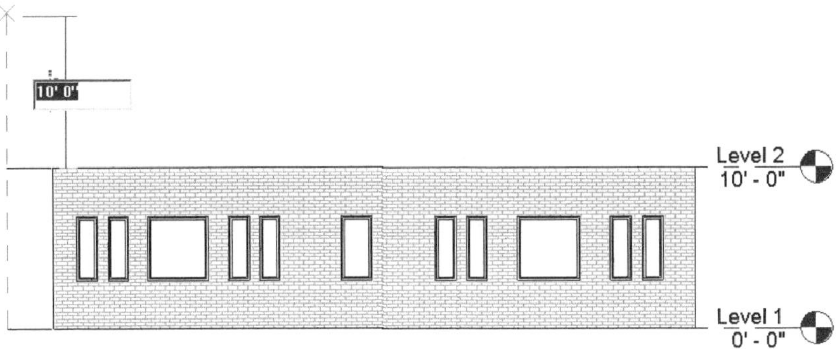

Figure 6-59 Specifying the distance of the new level

4. Move the cursor toward right until the alignment line is displayed above the Level 2 bubble, as shown in Figure 6-60, and click to complete the level line. The new level line is created showing the level name as **Level 3**, and the elevation as **20'0"(6000 mm)**. Press ESC to exit.

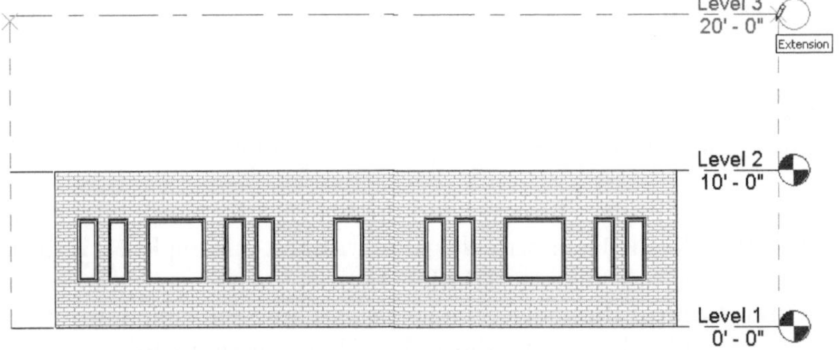

Figure 6-60 Creating the new level line using the alignment line

5. Repeat the procedure followed in steps 3 and 4 to create two more levels, Level 4 and Level 5 above Level 3 at a distance of **10'0"(3000 mm**) each. Press ESC twice to exit the **Level** tool.

   Notice that the **Project Browser** now shows the floor and ceiling plans for Level 3, Level 4, and Level 5.

6. To rename the levels, move the cursor over Level 1 under the **Floor Plans** head in the **Project Browser** and then right-click to display a shortcut menu.
7. Choose the **Rename** option from the shortcut menu; the **Rename View** dialog box is displayed.
8. In the **Rename View** dialog box, enter **First Floor** in the **Name** edit box and choose the **OK** button. Autodesk Revit prompts you to verify whether you want to rename the corresponding levels and views.
9. Choose the **Yes** button to rename the levels and views. Level 1 is renamed to **First Floor** in the elevation view.

10. Repeat the procedure followed in steps 6 through 9 to rename Level 2 as **Second Floor**, Level 3 as **Third Floor**, Level 4 as **Fourth Floor**, and Level 5 as **Roof**. Figure 6-61 shows all levels renamed in the north elevation.

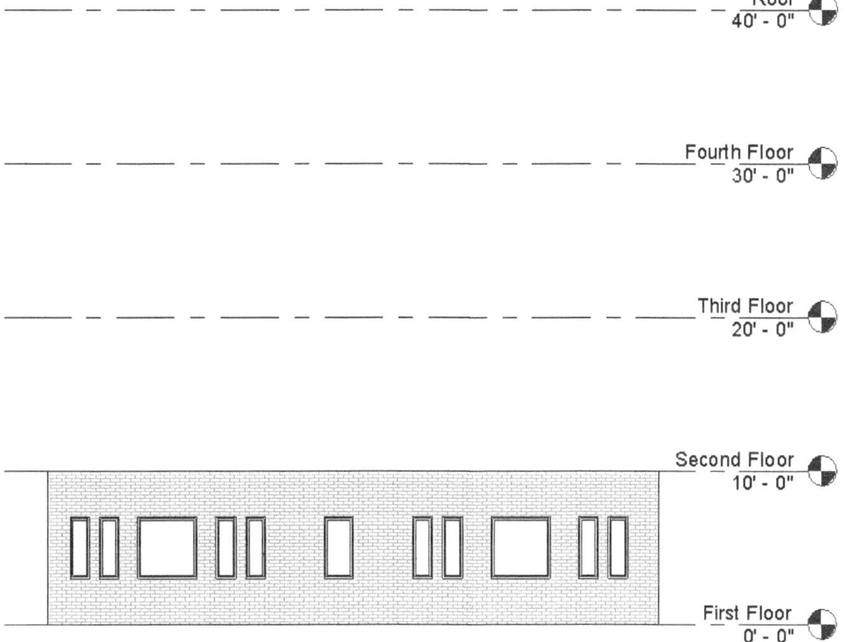

Figure 6-61 *North elevation showing the renamed levels*

Adding Grid Lines

You can use the plan view to add grids to the project using the **Grid** tool. Grids are automatically numbered as they are created. You will create grids in the sequence, as shown in the sketch plan.

1. Double-click on **First Floor** from the **Floor Plans** head in the **Project Browser** to display the ground floor plan in the drawing window.

2. Next, choose the **Grid** tool from the **Datum** panel of the **Architecture** tab; the **Modify | Place Grid** tab is displayed.

   Notice that the sketch plan shows the grid lines as the centerlines of walls. You can use the **Line** tool (default) from the **Draw** panel to create them.

3. Now, ensure that the **Line** tool is chosen in the **Draw** panel.

4. Move the cursor near the top left corner of the exterior wall profile and move the cursor up till a vertical extension line is displayed. Click to specify the start point of the grid line when the temporary dimension of 3'0"(900 mm) is displayed from the centerline of the exterior wall, as shown in Figure 6-62.

5. Move the cursor vertically downward and click outside the south wall to specify the endpoint of the grid line, as shown in Figure 6-63.

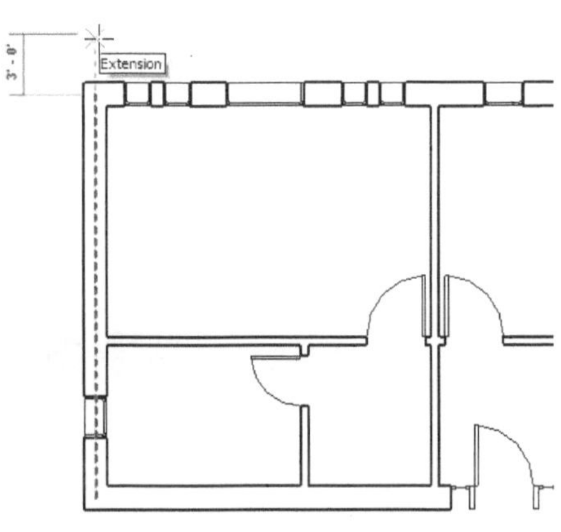

Figure 6-62 *Specifying the start point of the grid line*

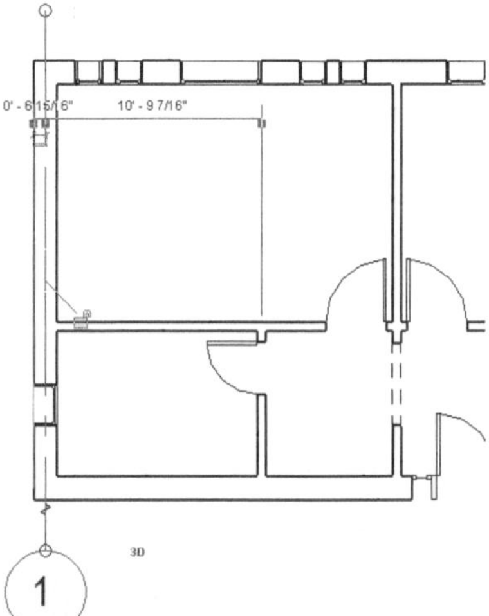

Figure 6-63 *Specifying the end point of the first vertical grid line*

Note

*If grid lines are not visible in the drawing, choose the **Visibility/Graphics** tool from the **Graphics** panel of the **View** tab to display the **Visibility/Graphic Overrides for Floor Plan** dialog box. In the **Annotation Categories** tab of this dialog box, select the **Grids** check box.*

The same procedure can be followed to draw grid lines for the interior walls. As the thickness of the interior wall is 5"(127 mm), you can specify 2 1/2"(64 mm) as the offset distance to draw grid lines for the interior walls.

6. Repeat the procedure followed in steps 3, 4, and 5 to create other vertical and horizontal grid lines in the sequence of their numbers using the alignment line feature. After adding grid lines, press ESC twice to exit. Figure 6-64 shows the floor plan after adding grid lines.

7. To rename the grid 5, select it and then click on its name. The edit box with the current number is displayed.

8. Enter the value **A** in the edit box and press ENTER to rename the grid.

9. Repeat steps 7 and 8 to rename the grid 6 as **B**.

Note

You can rename a grid by selecting it from the drawing and then entering a value corresponding to the value column for the **Name** *parameter in the* **Properties** *palette. The entered value will be the new name of the grid.*

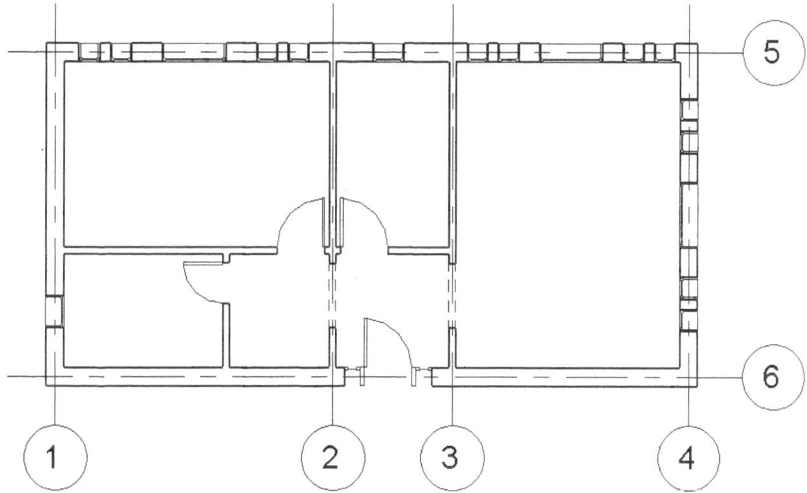

Figure 6-64 The horizontal and vertical grids created for the wall centerlines

Creating Section Views

The Section views can be created by using the **Section** tool.

1. Choose the **Section** tool from the **Create** panel of the **View** tab.

2. Move the cursor near the midpoint of the west wall. Click to specify the start point of the section line, refer to Figure 6-65.

3. Move the cursor horizontally across the building plan until you cross the exterior face of the east wall, as shown in Figure 6-65. Click to specify the endpoint of the section line.

The section view is created and the name **Section 1** is displayed in the **Sections (Building Section)** head in the **Project Browser**.

4. Repeat the procedure followed in steps 2 and 3 to create a transverse section through the apartment building, as shown in Figure 6-66. Choose a point outside the main entrance as the start point and move the cursor vertically upward beyond the exterior wall of the kitchen to specify the endpoint of the section line. As the bubble of the grid line 2 touches the section line, you can move the grid bubble using the **Modify the grid by dragging its model end** tool.

5. Select the grid line 2 and click on the **Add elbow** symbol displayed near the grid bubble.

6. Drag the two blue dots to a location outside the exterior wall, refer to Figure 6-66. Press ESC to exit.

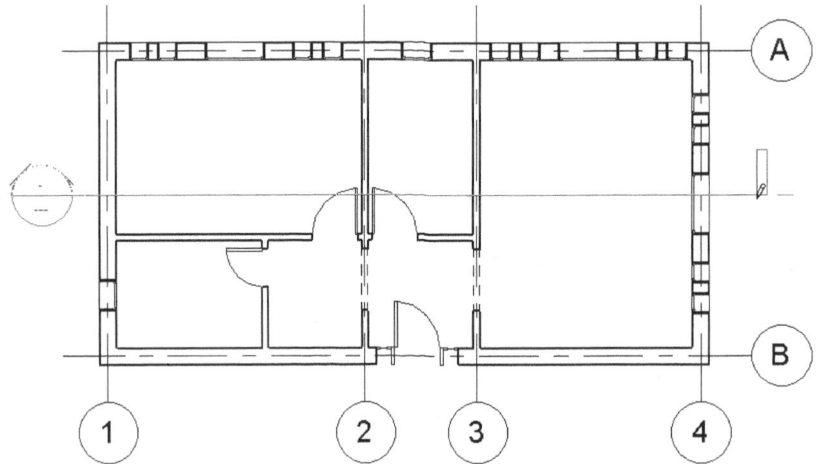

Figure 6-65 *Creating a section line for the section view*

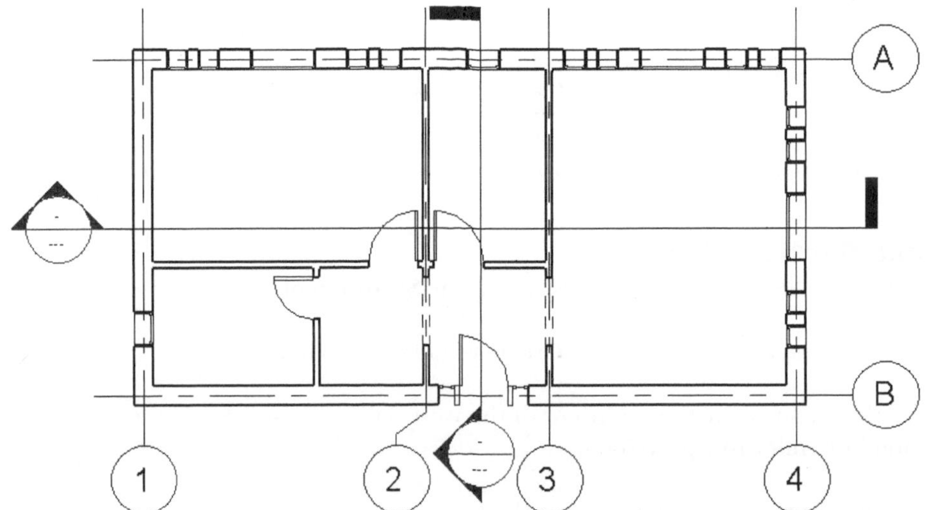

Figure 6-66 *The section lines created for the section views*

7. Click on the '+' symbol on the left of the **Sections (Building Section)** head in the **Project Browser** to display the section name created. Right-click on **Section 1** and then choose **Rename** from the shortcut menu; the **Rename View** dialog box is displayed.

8. Enter **Section X** in the **Name** edit box of the **Rename View** dialog box and then choose **OK**; the section view is renamed.

9. Similarly, rename **Section 2** as **Section Y**.

10. Double-click on **Section X** to display the corresponding section in the drawing window, as shown in Figure 6-67.

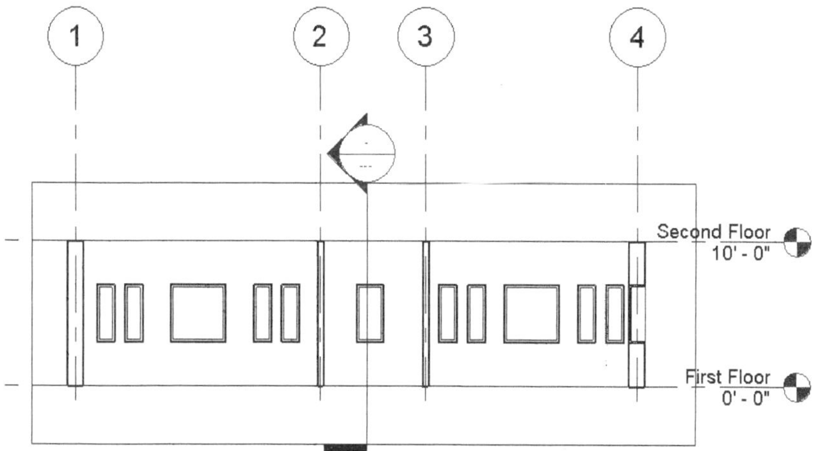

Figure 6-67 *Section view of* ***Section X***

Creating Elevation Views

To create the interior wall elevation of the kitchen walls, use the **Elevation** tool. You can use the first floor plan view to create new elevations.

1. Double-click on the name **First Floor** in the **Floor Plans** head of the **Project Browser** to display the first floor plan in the drawing window.

2. Choose the **Elevation** tool from **View > Create > Elevation** drop-down.

3. Move the cursor and place on a wall near the door in the kitchen area until the arrowhead points upward, toward the kitchen window and click to create the elevation.

4. Press the ESC key twice to exit the **Elevation** tool.

5. Select the elevation symbol to display its controls.

6. Click to select all the three cleared check boxes to create interior elevations. The new elevations are added under the **Elevations (Building Elevation)** head in the **Project Browser**.

7. Rename the elevation A, B, C, and D as **Kitchen-North Wall**, **Kitchen-East Wall**, **Kitchen-South Wall**, and **Kitchen-West Wall**, respectively, using the shortcut menu displayed on right-clicking the elevation views.

8. Double-click on the **Kitchen-North Wall** option in the **Project Browser** to display the corresponding elevation view. The crop-region can be picked by selecting the box. On selecting the box, drag controls appear. Drag the view crop region using the drag controls and grids of the kitchen area, as shown in Figure 6-68. Similarly, create the **Kitchen- South Wall** elevation, as shown in Figure 6-69.

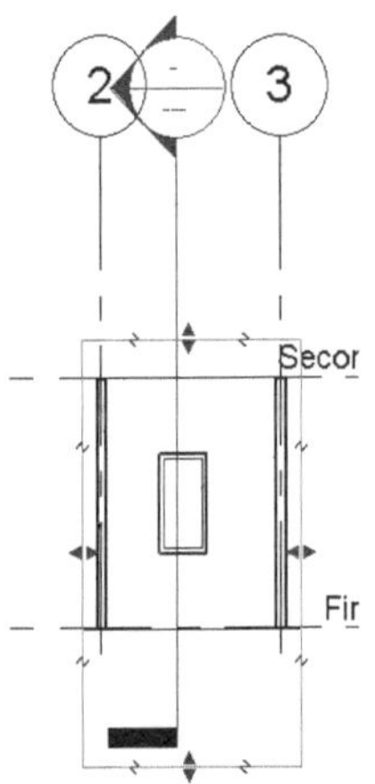

Figure 6-68 *The Kitchen-North Wall elevation*

Figure 6-69 *The Kitchen-South Wall elevation*

Note

*If the crop-region boundary is not visible in the drawing, then choose the **Show Crop Region** button from the **View Control Bar**.*

9. Double-click on **First Floor** under the **Floor Plans** head in the **Project Browser** to return to the floor plan view.

Saving the Project

In this section, you will save the project file using the **Save As** tool.

1. Choose **Save As > Project** from the **File** menu; the **Save As** dialog box is displayed. Enter **c06_Apartment1_tut1** in the **File name** edit box and then choose **Save** to save the project.

2. Choose the **Close** option from the **File** menu.

Tutorial 2 Club

In this tutorial, you will add levels and grids to the *c05_Club_ex2.rvt (M_c05_Club_ex2.rvt)* project created in Exercise 2 of Chapter 5. Also, you will create sections in the sketch plan shown in Figure 6-70. Do not create dimensions and texts as they have been given only for reference. Use the following project parameter. **(Expected time: 30 min)**

1. Rename Level 1 as the **First Floor** and move the Roof level to **15'0"(4572 mm)** elevation. Rename the Level 2 as **Roof** in Metric unit system.

2. Grids and sections to be created in the sketch plan are shown in Figure 6-70.

The following steps are required to complete this tutorial:

a. Open the file.
   For Imperial *c05_Club_ex2.rvt*
   For Metric *M_c05_Club_ex2.rvt*
b. Modify levels by dragging, refer to Figures 6-71 and 6-72.
c. Add grids using the **Grid** tool, refer to Figures 6-73 and 6-74.
d. Create section views using the **Section** tool, refer to Figure 6-75 through Figure 6-77.
e. Save the project using the **Save As** tool.
   For Imperial *c06_Club_tut2.rvt*
   For Metric *M_c06_Club_tut2.rvt*
f. Close the project.

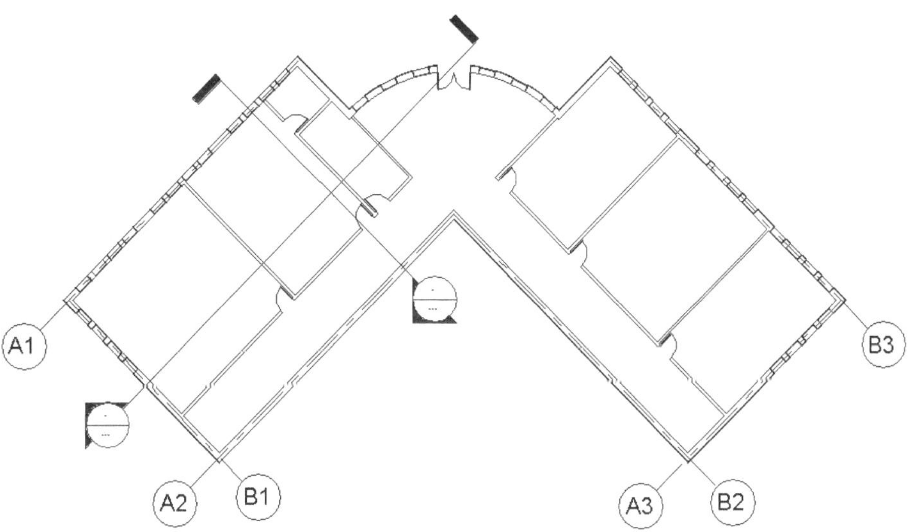

Figure 6-70 *Sketch plan for adding grids and creating section views for the Club project*

Opening the Existing Project and Hiding Tags

To start with the tutorial, you need to open the Club project file and hide the door and window tags using the **Visibility/Graphics** tool.

1. Choose **Open > Project** from the **File** menu and open the required file.
   For Imperial *c05_Club_ex2.rvt*
   For Metric *M_c05_Club_ex2.rvt*
   You can also download this file from *http://www.cadcim.com*. The path of the file is as follows: *Textbooks > Civil/GIS > Revit Architecture > Exploring Autodesk Revit 2018 for Architecture*

2. Choose the **Visibility/Graphics** tool from the **Graphics** panel of the **View** tab; the **Visibility/Graphics Overrides for Floor Plan** dialog box for the plan view is displayed.

3. Choose the **Annotations Categories** tab and clear the check boxes for **Door Tags** and **Window Tags**.

4. In the **Visibility/Graphics Overrides for Floor plan** dialog box, choose the **Apply** and **OK** buttons to apply the changes and close it.

Modifying Levels

You can use the **Elevation** tool to display any exterior elevation of the project. You will open the north elevation and then drag the level to the specified distance.

1. Move the cursor to the **Project Browser** and double-click on **North** under the **Elevations (Building Elevation)** head. The north elevation is displayed within the existing levels in the drawing window.

2. Choose the **Zoom In Region** tool from the **Navigation Bar** to enlarge the right portion of the elevation showing the levels, as shown in Figure 6-71. Ensure that the **Hidden Line** option is chosen in the **View Control Bar** for Visual Style.

   Notice that the wall extends beyond the roof level line. This is because you have used the explicit parameter for the wall height. You can now move the level to the wall top.

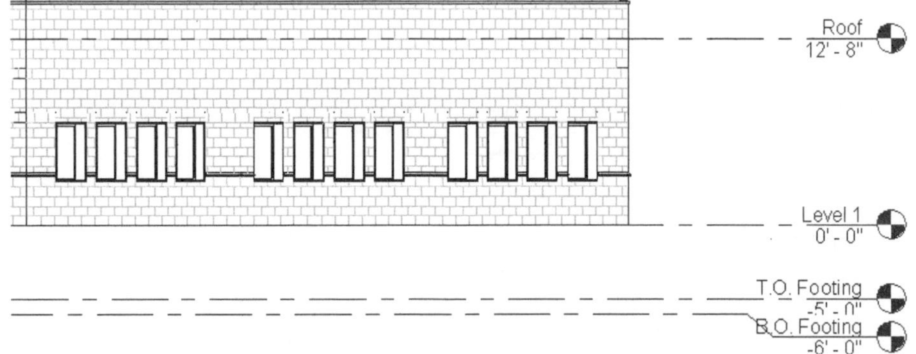

Figure 6-71 *Existing levels for the Club project*

3. Move the cursor near the roof level line and click when it gets highlighted. Drag it to the top of the wall. The elevation in the level bubble now shows **15' - 0" (4572 mm** for Metric) as its elevation from the base.

4. To rename the levels, move the cursor over **Level 1** in the **Project Browser** and right-click; a shortcut menu is displayed.

5. Choose the **Rename** option from the shortcut menu; the **Rename View** dialog box is displayed.

6. In this dialog box, enter **First Floor** in the **Name** edit box. Next, choose the **OK** button. You are prompted to verify whether you want to rename the corresponding levels and views.

7. Choose the **Yes** button to rename the levels and views. The level is immediately renamed in the elevation view, as shown in Figure 6-72.

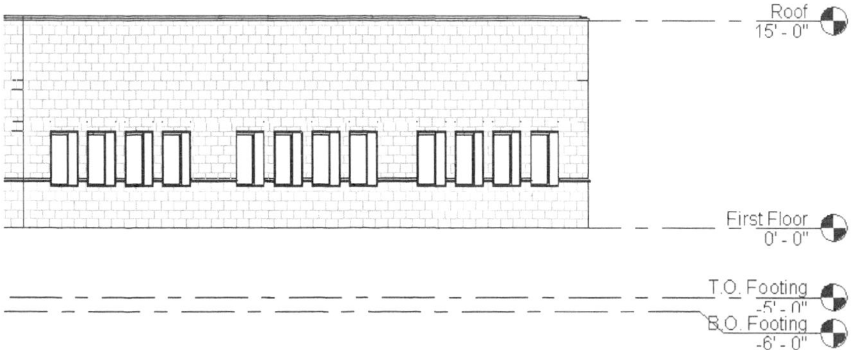

***Figure 6-72** Renamed levels and views for the Club project*

Similarly, rename the level 2 as **Roof** in the Metric unit system.

Creating Grid Lines

You will use the plan view to add grids to the project using the **Grid** tool. The grids are automatically numbered as they are created. You will, however, rename them based on the names given in the sketch plan.

1. Double-click on **First Floor** from the **Floor Plans** head of the **Project Browser** to display the first floor plan in the drawing window.

2. Choose the **Grid** tool from the **Datum** panel of the **Architecture** tab.

   Notice that the sketch plan shows the grid lines as the centerlines of the walls. Use the **Line** tool to create grid lines at the centerline of the walls. You may need to zoom into the area for Revit to snap to the wall centerlines.

3. Choose the **Line** tool, if it is not chosen by default in the **Draw** panel of the **Modify | Place Grid** tab.

4. Zoom into the west corner of Hall 1 and move the cursor near the exterior wall intersection, marked 1, refer to Figure 6-73. Use the TAB key to toggle between the object snaps at the intersection and click when a dashed line appears in the center of the wall on which the grid 1 is to be created, refer to Figure 6-74.

5. Move the cursor along the exterior wall and click when the cursor crosses the lower exterior wall intersection, as shown in Figure 6-73. The first grid line is created.

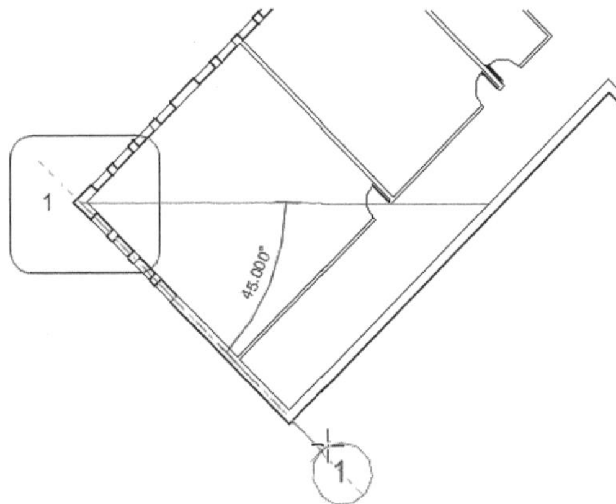

Figure 6-73 *Grid line created using the **Line** tool in the **Draw** panel*

6. Repeat the procedure followed in steps 4 and 5 to create other grid lines for the external walls, as shown in the Figure 6-74. Press ESC twice to exit.

   The completed plan with grids will be similar to the one shown in Figure 6-74.

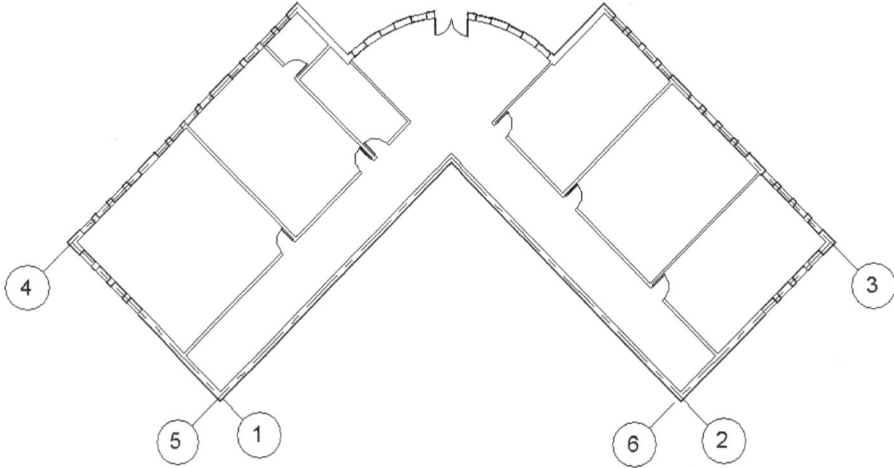

Figure 6-74 *Grids created for the Club project*

7. To rename the grid number 4, double-click on it; an edit box with the current grid number is displayed.

8. Enter the new value **A1** in the edit box to rename the grid.

9. Repeat the procedure followed in steps 7 and 8 to rename all other grid numbers based on the sketch plan, refer to Figure 6-70.

Creating Section Views

The Section views can be created by using the **Section** tool.

1. Choose the **Section** tool from the **Create** panel of the **View** tab.

2. Move the cursor over the wall of the grid A1, refer to Figure 6-70 and drag it downward. When the temporary dimension appears, enter **20'**(**6000 mm**) in the edit box displayed; the start point of the section line is specified. Now, drag it straight to draw the section across the building, refer to Figure 6-75.

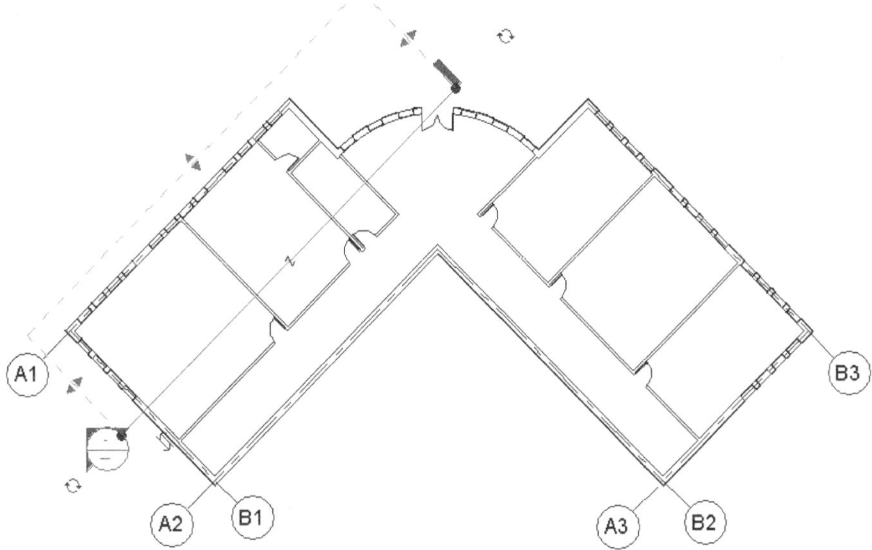

Figure 6-75 *The section line created*

3. Move the cursor diagonally upward across the building plan until you cross the exterior face of the lobby wall. Click to specify the endpoint of the section line, as shown in Figure 6-75. The name, **Section 1** is displayed in the **Sections (Building Sections)** head in the **Project Browser**.

4. Repeat the procedure followed in steps 2 and 3 to create a transverse section through Hall 1 of the club building, as shown in Figure 6-76.

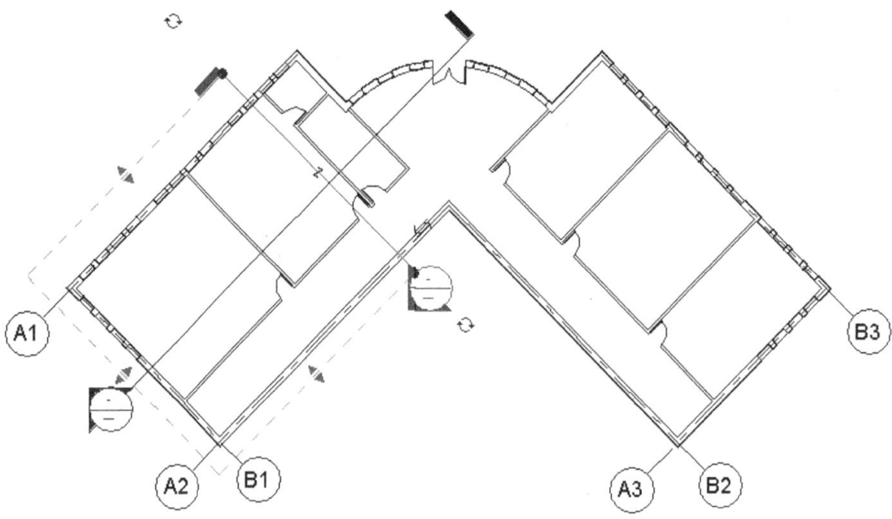

Figure 6-76 Creating the second section line

5. Right-click on the name **Section 1** under the **Section (Building Section)** in the **Project Browser**, and then choose the **Rename** option from the shortcut menu displayed; the **Rename View** dialog box is displayed.

6. In the **Rename View** dialog box, enter **Section X** in the **Name** edit box and choose the **OK** button.

7. Repeat the procedure followed in steps 5 and 6 to rename **Section 2** as **Section Y**, as specified in the sketch plan.

8. Double-click on **Section X** in the **Project Browser** to display the corresponding section in the drawing window, as shown in Figure 6-77.

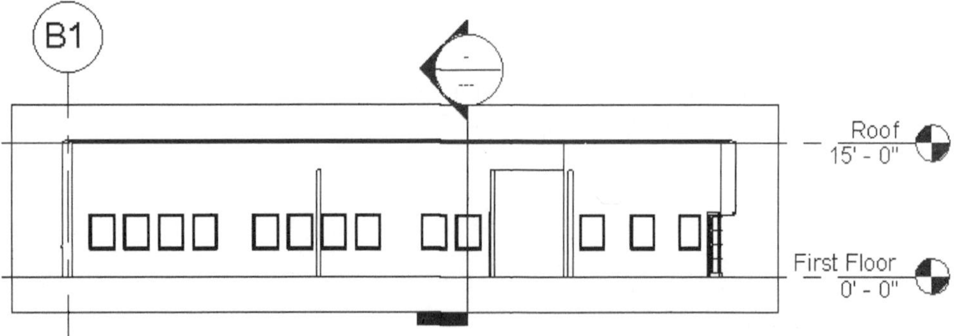

Figure 6-77 Displaying the section view for the Club project

9. Double-click on **First Floor** under the **Floor Plans** head in the **Project Browser** to display the floor plan of the first floor.

Saving the Project

In this section, you will save the project file using the **Save As** tool.

1. Choose **Save As > Project** from the **File** menu and enter the required name **c06 _Club_tut2** (for Metric **M_c06 _Club_tut2**) in the **File name** edit box of the **Save As** dialog box. Next, choose the **Save** button.

2. Choose **Close** from the **File** menu to close the file.

Tutorial 3 Office

In this tutorial, you will add levels to the *c05_office_tut3.rvt (M_c05_office_tut3.rvt)* project created in tutorial 3 of Chapter 5. Also, you will add floor levels to the above project. Use the following project parameter. **(Expected time: 30 min)**

1. Rename Level 1 as the **Ground Floor**.
   Rename Level 2 as **First Floor** and change its height to **12'**.

2. Add other two levels at a height of **12'** and rename added levels as **Second Floor** and **Roof**, respectively.

The following steps are required to complete this tutorial:

a. Open the file.
   For Imperial *c05_office_tut3.rvt*
   For Metric *M_c05_office_tut3.rvt*
b. Add two levels above the existing levels.
c. Copy the existing floors to above levels.
d. Save the project using the **Save As** tool.
   For Imperial *c06_Office_tut3.rvt*
   For Metric *M_c06_Office_tut3.rvt*
e. Close the project.

Opening the Existing Project

To start with the tutorial, you need to open the Office project file and hide the door and window tags using the **Visibility/Graphics** tool.

1. Choose **Open > Project** from the **File** menu and open the required file.
   For Imperial *c05_office_tut3.rvt*
   For Metric *M_c05_office_tut3.rvt*
   You can also download this file from *http://www.cadcim.com*. The path of the file is as follows: *Textbooks > Civil/GIS > Revit Architecture > Exploring Autodesk Revit 2018 for Architecture*

2. Choose the **Visibility/Graphics** tool from the **Graphics** panel of the **View** tab; the **Visibility/Graphics Overrides for Floor Plan** dialog box for the plan view is displayed.

3. Choose the **Annotations Categories** tab and clear the check boxes for **Door Tags** and **Window Tags**.

4. In the **Visibility/Graphics Overrides for Floor plan** dialog box, choose the **Apply** and **OK** buttons to apply the changes and close it.

Adding Levels

In this section, you will learn to create levels in the elevation view.

1. Move the cursor to the **Project Browser** and double-click on **North** under the **Elevations (Building Elevation)** head. The north elevation with the existing levels is displayed in the drawing window. Make sure that the **Hidden Line** option is selected in the **Visual Style** menu of the **View Control Bar**. Select the levels and drag the endpoints of the level lines near the building profile.

2. Change the height of level 2 to **12'0"(3600 mm)**.

3. Invoke the **Level** tool from the **Datum** panel of the **Architecture** tab.

Note

*In the metric unit system, by default, the Level 2 is at 4000 mm. Shift the Level 2 to 3600 mm by clicking on the value and entering the value as **3600**.*

4. Next, move the cursor near the left endpoint of the level line of Level 2 and then move it upward and when the alignment line appears, enter **12'0"(3600 mm)** as the distance of the new level from the Level 2.

5. Move the cursor toward right until the alignment line is displayed above the Level 2 bubble and click to complete the level line. The new level line is created showing the level name as **Level 3**, and the elevation as **24'0"(7300 mm)**, as shown in Figure 6-78. Press ESC to exit.

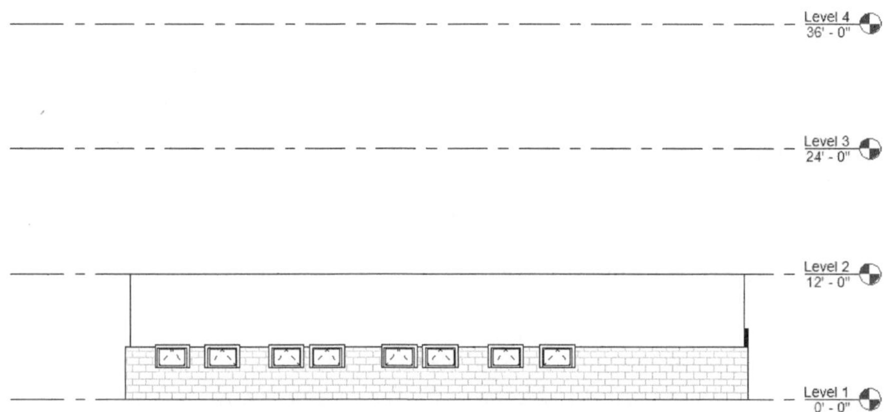

Figure 6-78 *Adding levels using the alignment line*

6. Repeat the procedure followed in steps 4 and 5 to create one more level, Level 4 above Level 3 at a distance of **12'0"(3600 mm**) each. Press ESC twice to exit the **Level** tool.

   Note that the **Project Browser** now shows the floor and ceiling plans for Level 3 and Level 4.

7. To rename the levels, move the cursor over Level 1 under the **Floor Plans** head in the **Project Browser** and then right-click to display a shortcut menu.
8. Choose the **Rename** option from the shortcut menu; the **Rename View** dialog box is displayed.
9. In the **Rename View** dialog box, enter **Ground Floor** in the **Name** edit box and choose the **OK** button. Autodesk Revit prompts you to verify whether you want to rename the corresponding levels and views.
10. Choose the **Yes** button to rename the levels and views. Level 1 is renamed to **Ground Floor** in the elevation view.
11. Repeat the procedure followed in steps 7 through 10 to rename Level 2 as **First Floor**, Level 3 as **Second Floor** and Level 4 as **Roof**. Figure 6-79 shows all levels renamed in the north elevation.

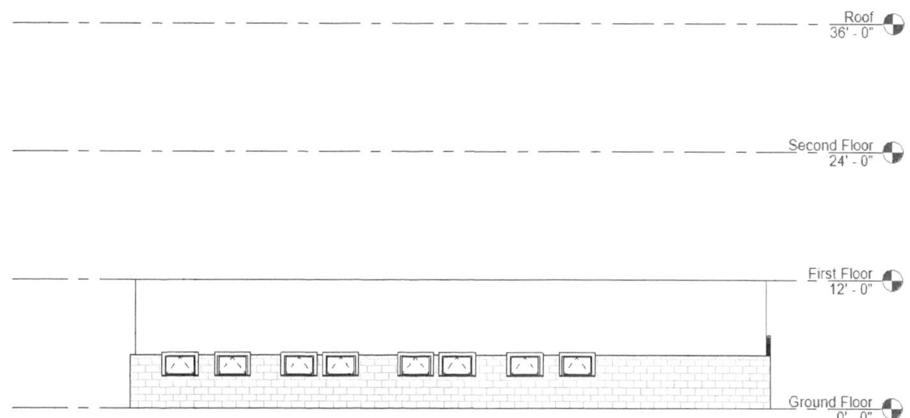

Figure 6-79 *North elevation showing the renamed levels*

Extending Walls to the Topmost Level

As described earlier, it is better to extend the exterior walls to the top story, instead of stacking them one above the other. To extend the exterior wall height, you need to set the **Top Constraint** parameter to the topmost level and then use the 3D view to view the changes.

1. To change the current view to a 3D view, double-click on **3D** under the **3D Views** head in the **Project Browser**.
2. Now, move the cursor near the exterior wall and press the TAB key; the chain of exterior walls is highlighted.
3. Click to select the exterior walls; the **Modify | Walls** tab is displayed.
4. In the **Properties** palette for the **Top Constraint** instance parameter, select the **Up to level: Roof** option.
5. Replace the current value of the **Top Offset** parameter with **3'0" (900 mm)** as specified in the project parameters.
6. Choose the **Apply** button in the **Properties** palette. The exterior walls are extended to 3'0" (900 mm) above the roof level, as shown in Figure 6-80. Press ESC to exit the tool.

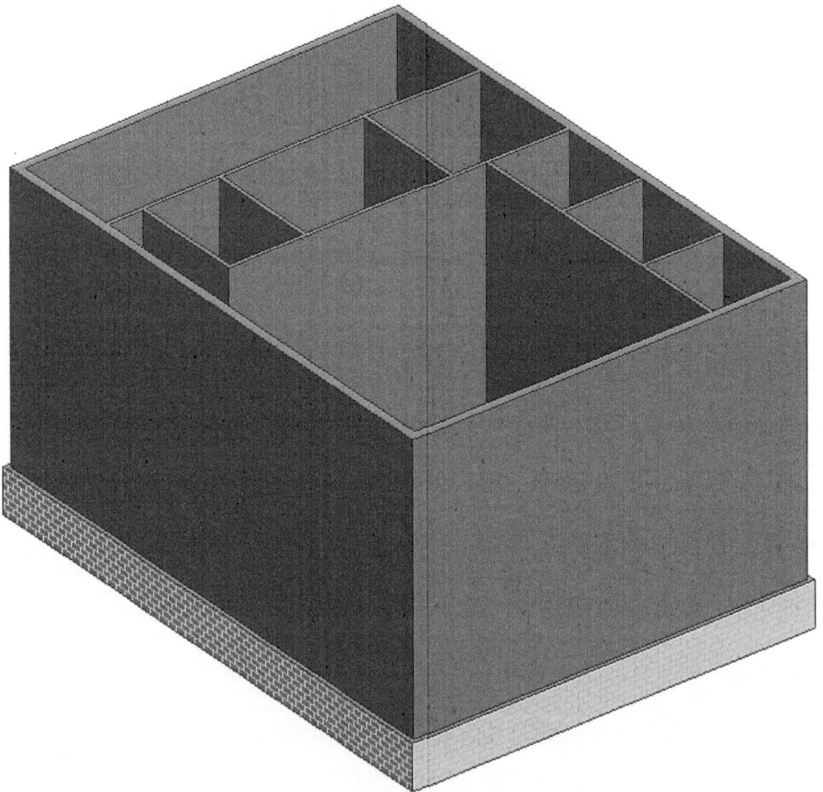

Figure 6-80 *Extending the exterior walls to the topmost level*

Copying Elements to Upper Levels

You can now select all elements except the exterior walls and use the **Aligned to Selected Levels** tool to copy them to the upper levels. The following steps describe the general procedure for copying elements to different levels by using the **Aligned to Selected Levels** tool.

1. In the 3D view, select all elements except the exterior walls by creating a selection window from the left to right. All elements, including the interior walls, doors, windows, and components need to be selected.

Note

To exclude the exterior walls, select all elements first and then press the SHIFT key and select the exterior walls.

2. Choose the **Copy to Clipboard** tool from the **Clipboard** panel of the **Modify | Multi-Select** tab.

3. Now, choose the **Aligned to Selected Levels** tool from the **Modify | Multi-Select > Clipboard > Paste** drop-down; the **Select Levels** dialog box is displayed.

4. In this dialog box, select the **First Floor** and **Second Floor** levels by pressing and holding the **CTRL** button, as shown in Figure 6-81.

5. Choose the **OK** button to close the **Select Levels** dialog box. The selected elements and components are pasted on the three upper levels as shown in figure 6-82.

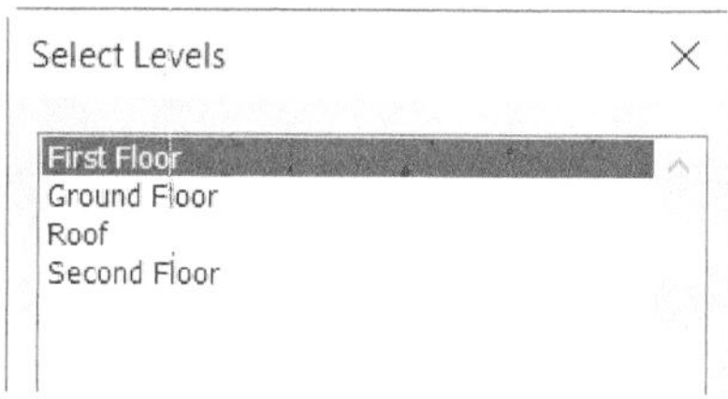

Figure 6-81 *Specifying levels to paste the selected elements*

Saving the Project

In this section, you will save the project file using the **Save As** tool.

1. Choose **Save As > Project** from the **File menu** and enter the required name **c06 _Club_tut2** (for Metric **M_c06 _Club_tut2**) in the **File name** edit box of the **Save As** dialog box. Next, choose the **Save** button.

2. Choose **Close** from the **File menu** to close the file.

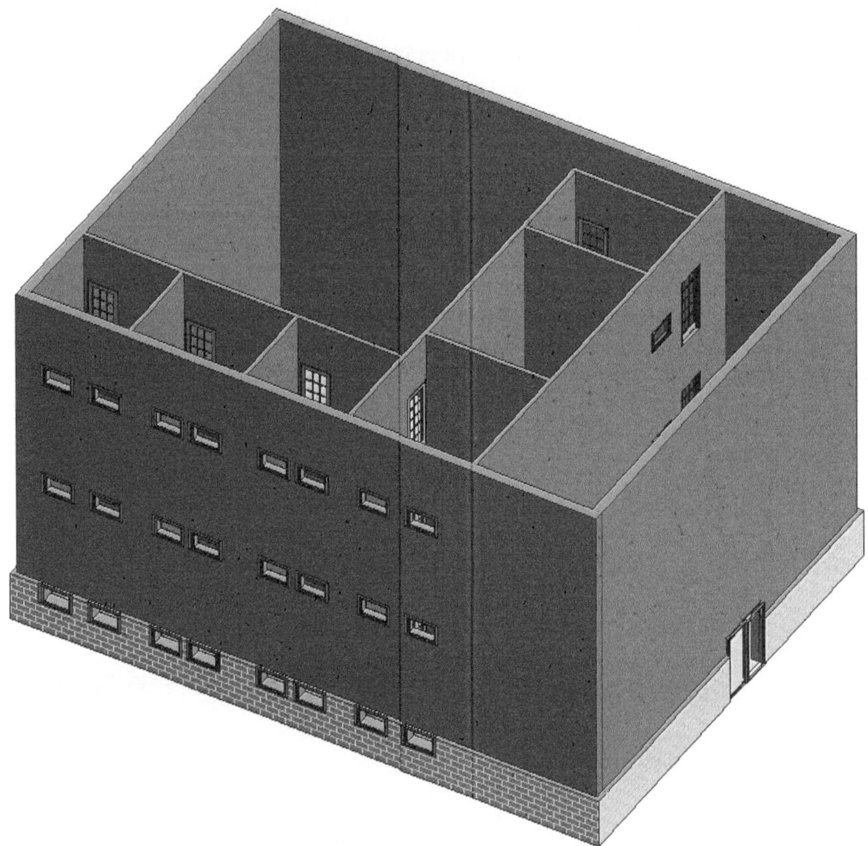

Figure 6-82 *Components pasted on the upper levels*

Self-Evaluation Test

Answer the following questions and then compare them to those given at the end of this chapter:

1. Which of the following grid properties can you modify?

   (a) **Name** (b) **Type**
   (c) **Position** (d) **Elevation**

2. The **Project Browser** shows a logical organization of all views, schedules, sheets, groups, linked Revit models, and other parts of the ____________.

   (a) Current project (c) User interface
   (b) Properties palette (d) View control bar

3. Using the _________ tool, you can create grids by picking elements.

4. You can change the viewing side of a section by clicking on the _________ symbol.

5. You can select the _________ type of section from the **Type Selector** drop-down list to create a detail section view.

6. To assign a new name to a section view, right-click on the name of the view in the **Project Browser** and then choose the _________ option from the shortcut menu.

7. The _________ tool can be used to limit the visibility of a datum in a portion of a view.

8. Levels, once created, cannot be modified. (T/F)

9. You can control the visibility of a level head. (T/F)

10. When you move a level, its elevation is modified automatically. (T/F)

11. In Revit, grids are numbered automatically. (T/F)

12. You cannot copy or array grids. (T/F)

Review Questions

Answer the following questions:

1. Which of the following tools is used to hide the elements belonging to the same category?

   (a) **Delete** (b) **Hide/Isolate**
   (c) **Hidden Lines** (d) **Zoom**

2. Which of the following keys needs to be held to add elements to a selection?

   (a) TAB (b) SHIFT
   (c) CTRL (d) ESC

3. Which of the following tools can be used to limit the visibility of a datum to a certain portion of a view?

   (a) **Hide/Isolate** (b) **Hidden lines**
   (c) **Scope Box** (d) **Dynamic View**

4. You must place an elevation tag to generate an elevation_______.

   (a) View (b) Parameter
   (c) Element (d) Sheet

5. Which of the following tools is used to turn off the visibility of any element in a view.

   (a) **Visual styles** (b) **Visibility/graphic overrides**
   (c) **Object styles** (d) **Display styles**

6. You can control the visibility of grids in each view. (T/F)

7. A work plane cannot be rotated or moved. (T/F)

8. You can align the elevation view based on the orientation of walls. (T/F)

9. Modifications made in any one view are propagated immediately to all other views. (T/F)

10. You can also create detail section views using the **Section** tool. (T/F)

11. Using the **Grid** tool, you can create radial grid patterns. (T/F)

12. The **Scope Box** tool can be used to limit the visibility of grids in a portion of a view. (T/F)

EXERCISES

Exercise 1 Apartment 2

Add levels and grids to the *c05_Apartment2_ex1.rvt (M_c05_Apartment2_ex1.rvt* for Metric*)* project created in Exercise 1 of Chapter 5. Create the wall elevation for the dining room walls and also sections in the sketch plan shown in Figure 6-83. Do not create dimensions and texts as they are given only for your reference. Use the parameters given below.

(Expected time: 30 min)

1. Rename Level 1 as the **First Floor** and Level 2 as the **Second Floor**.
   In Metric unit system, shift the Level 2 to **3000** mm.
2. Levels to be added:
   For Imperial **Third Floor- Elevation 20'0"**
   Fourth Floor- Elevation 30'0"
   Roof- Elevation 40'0"
   For Metric **Third Floor- Elevation 6000 mm**
   Fourth Floor- Elevation 9000 mm
   Roof- Elevation 12000 mm
3. Grids and Sections to be created in the sketch plan shown in Figure 6-83. Name the horizontal section as **Section X1** and the vertical section as **Section Y1.**
4. Name of the file to be save-
   For Imperial **c06_Apartment2_ex1**
   For Metric **M_c06_Apartment2_ex1**

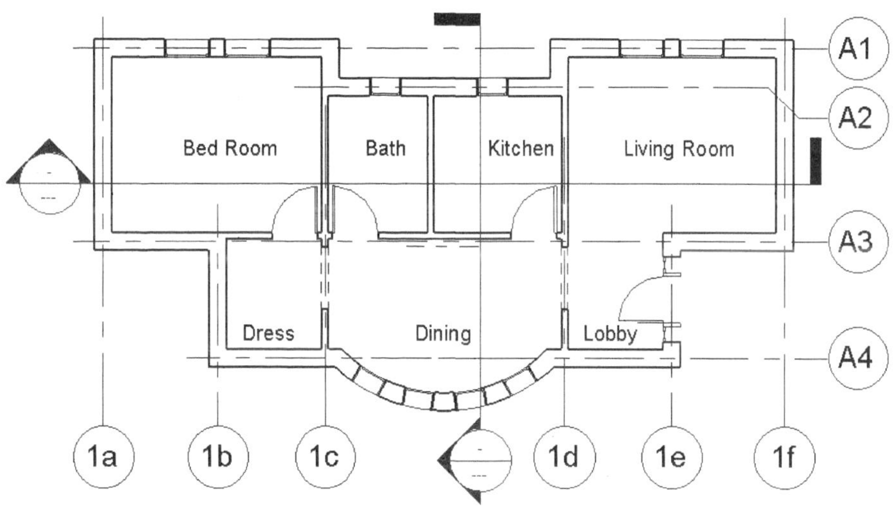

Figure 6-83 Sketch for adding grids and sections to the Apartment 2 project

Exercise 2 Elevator and Stair Lobby

Add levels and grids to the *Elevator and Stair Lobby* project created in Exercise 3 of Chapter 5. Do not create the dimensions and texts as they are given only for reference. Use the following project parameters:

(Expected time: 30 min)

1. Rename Level 1 as **First Floor** and Level 2 as **Second Floor**
2. Levels to be added:

   For Imperial **Third Floor- Elevation 20'0"**
   Fourth Floor- Elevation 30'0"
   Roof Floor- Elevation 40'0"

   For Metric **Third Floor- Elevation 6000 mm**
   Fourth Floor- Elevation 9000 mm
   Roof- Elevation 12000 mm
3. Grids and Sections are to be created in the sketch plan shown in Figure 6-84. Name the horizontal section as **Section H** and the vertical section as **Section V**.
4. Name of the file to be saved-

   For Imperial **c06_ElevatorandStairLobby_ex2**
   For Metric **M_c06_ElevatorandStairLobby_ex2**

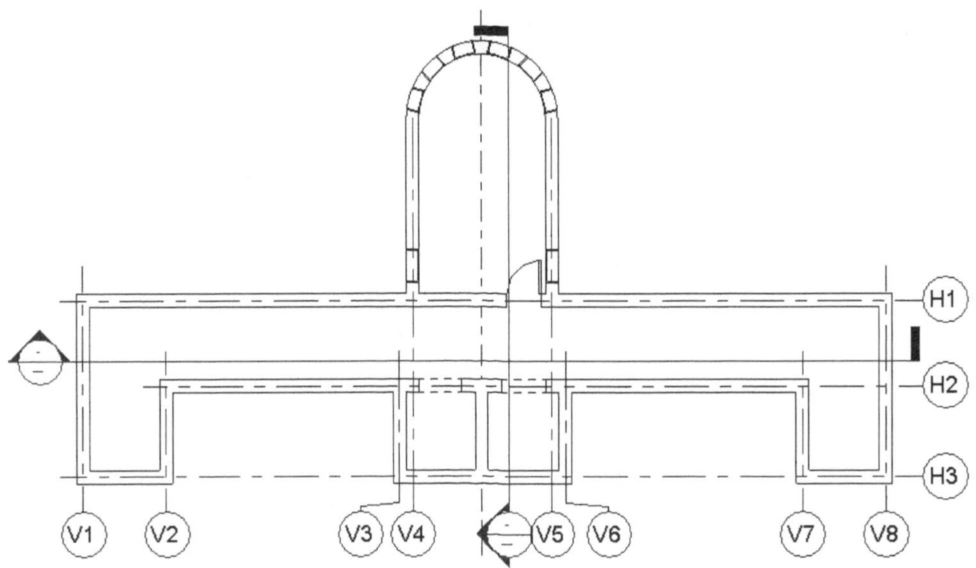

Figure 6-84 *Sketch plan for creating grids and sections for the Elevator and Stair Lobby project*

Exercise 3 — Residential Building- Levels

Add levels and grids to the *Residential Building* project created in Exercise 4 of Chapter 4. Do not create the dimensions and texts as they are given only for reference. Use the following project parameters: **(Expected time: 30 min)**

1. Rename Level 1 as **Ground Floor** and Level 2 as **First Floor**
2. Levels to be added:
   For Imperial **Roof- Elevation 20'0"**
   For Metric **Roof- Elevation 6000 mm**
3. Sections are to be created in the sketch plan shown in Figure 6-85. Name the horizontal section as **Section X** and the vertical section as **Section Y**.
4. Name of the file to be saved-
   For Imperial **c06_residential_level_ex3**
   For Metric **M_c06_residential_level_ex3**

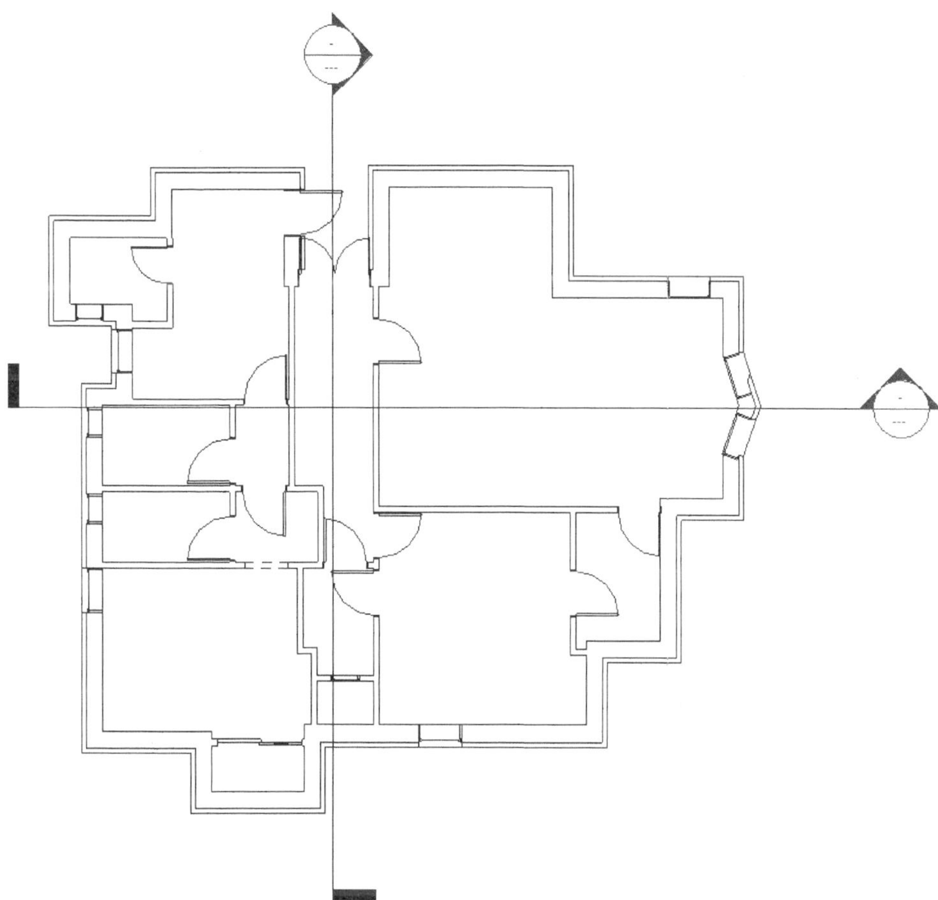

Figure 6-85 *Sketch plan for creating sections for the Residential Building project*

Answers to Self-Evaluation Test

1. d, 2. a, 3. Pick Line, 4. Flip Section, 5. Detail View: Detail, 6. Rename, 7. Scope Box, 8. F, 9. T, 10. T, 11. T, 12. F

Chapter 7

Using Basic Building Components-II

Learning Objectives

After completing this chapter, you will be able to:
- *Understand the concept of floor*
- *Create floors using the Floor tool*
- *Create roofs using the Roof tool*
- *Use the shape editing tools for floor, roof, and slabs*
- *Create ceilings using the Ceiling tool*
- *Create openings in the floor, roof, and ceiling*
- *Create rooms using the Room tool*
- *Join walls with the other walls and roofs*

INTRODUCTION

In the earlier chapters, you learned to use levels, grids, and datums in a project. Also, you have learned that elements such as walls, doors, windows, and so on can be added from the library of in-built elements provided in Autodesk Revit. This chapter describes creation of sketched elements such as floors, roofs, and ceilings in a project. For creating these sketched elements, you need to draw sketch.

CREATING ARCHITECTURAL FLOORS

Ribbon: Architecture > Build > Floor drop-down > Floor: Architectural

You can add a floor to the current level of a building model using the **Floor: Architectural** tool. You can invoke this tool from the **Build** panel of the **Architecture** tab. On invoking this tool, the **Modify | Create Floor Boundary** contextual tab will be displayed, as shown in Figure 7-1.

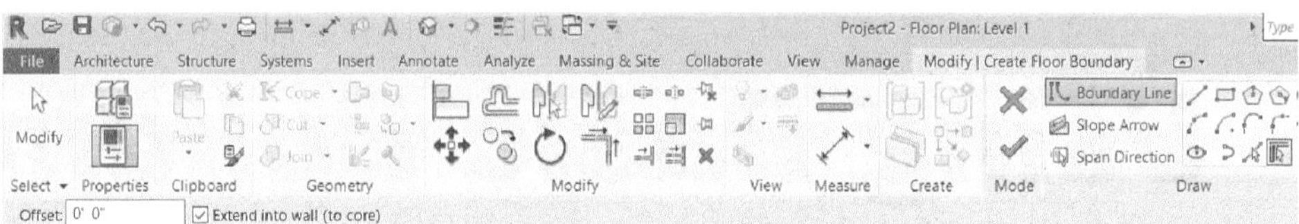

*Figure 7-1 The **Modify / Create Floor Boundary** tab*

You can use this tab to draw, annotate, and edit a floor boundary for your building model as well as to assign properties to it. The **Draw** panel of the **Modify | Create Floor Boundary** tab consists of various tools that are used to draw the floor sketches. These sketches define the boundary of the floor. To define the boundary of the floor, you can either pick the existing walls or sketch the boundary in the plan view by using lines or sketch the boundary in the 3D view, provided that the work plane is set to the plan view.

Similar to the other model components, the floor too has associated type and instance properties. Once you sketch the floor, the **Properties** palette will display the instance parameters of the floor, as shown in Figure 7-2. The **Type Selector** drop-down list in this palette displays the floors available in Autodesk Revit's library, refer to Figure 7-2. This palette can be used to modify the instance properties of the floor such as the level at which the floor is to be created, the height offset of the floor from the specified level, and so on. To modify the type properties of a floor, choose the **Edit Type** button from the **Properties** palette; the **Type Properties** dialog box will be displayed, as shown in Figure 7-3. You can set the type parameters for the floor in it. You can also create a new floor type by using the **Duplicate** button. To edit the structural elements of the floor, choose the **Edit** button in the **Value** column for the **Structure** type parameter; the **Edit Assembly** dialog box will be displayed, showing the structure of the floor type with its different layers. In the **Edit Assembly** dialog box, the **Insert** or **Delete** button can be used to customize the new floor type based on the specific project requirement.

Note

The type and instance properties vary depending upon the floor type selected. Autodesk Revit Help provides a detailed explanation of all the properties associated with the floor types.

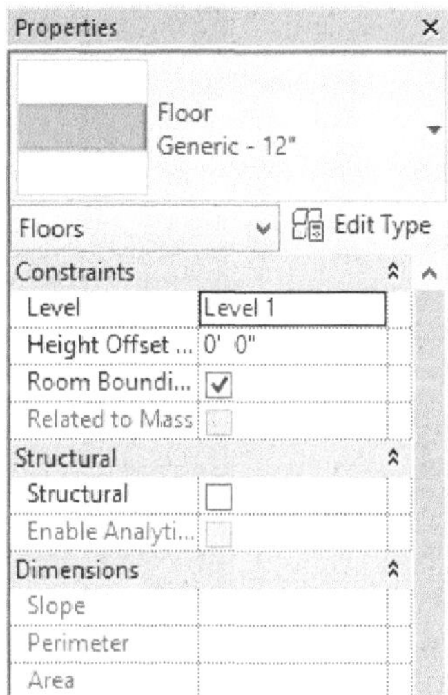

*Figure 7-2 Partial View of The **Properties** palette displaying the instance parameters*

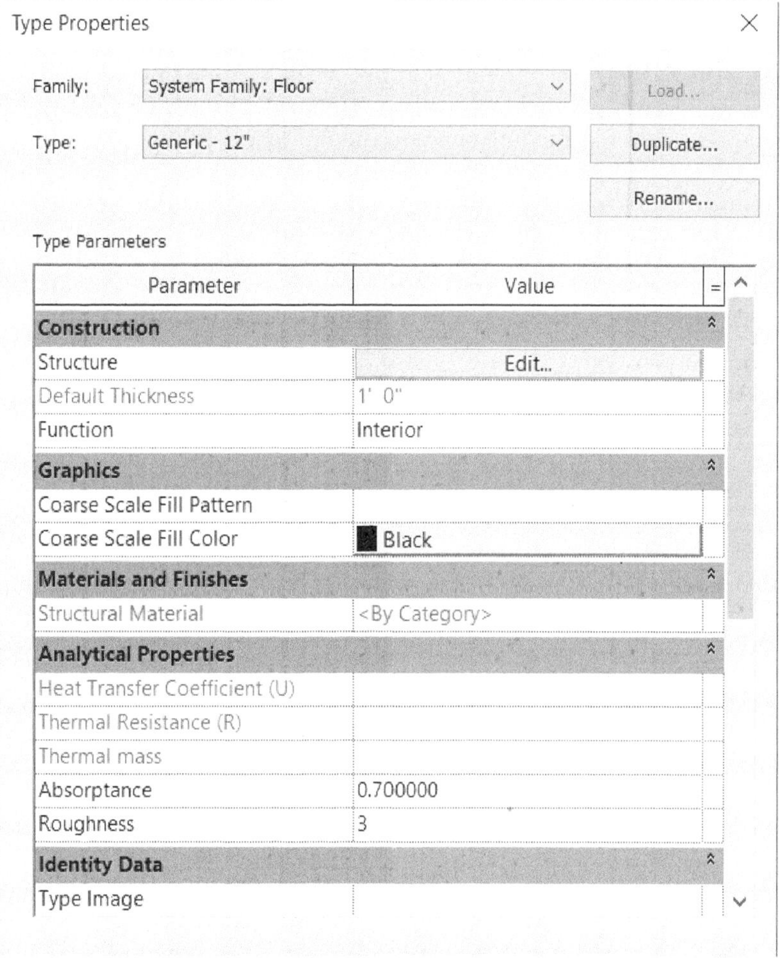

*Figure 7-3 The **Type Properties** dialog box*

Tip

*The **Preview** button in the **Type Properties** dialog box can be used to display a graphical image of the floor type which changes when you add or remove a layer to the floor structure.*

Sketching the Floor Boundary

To create a floor, you need to sketch its boundary. There are two methods to sketch a boundary. The first method is to pick the already created walls using the **Pick Walls** tool to define the floor boundary. The other method to define the floor boundary is to draw the floor profile using the draw tools such as line, rectangle, polygon, arc, and others from the **Draw** panel of the **Modify | Create Floor Boundary** tab.

By default, the **Pick Walls** tool is chosen in the **Draw** panel of the **Modify | Create Floor Boundary** tab. This tool can be used to sketch the floor for the spaces bound by the connected walls. The **Option Bar** displays the **Offset** edit box; which can be used to specify the offset distance of the floor sketch line from an existing wall. The **Extend into wall (to core)** check box is used to extend the floor to the wall core and assists in creating a joint between the floor and the wall core. If the **Pick Walls** tool is not chosen by default, then invoke this tool and move the cursor near the wall. You will notice that as the cursor is brought near the face of the wall, a dashed line appears along its inner or outer face. You can choose either of the faces of the wall to sketch the floor. Click when the dashed line appears at appropriate location; a magenta line with flip and drag controls as well as two parallel lines will be displayed on the wall, refer to Figure 7-4. The flip control can be used to flip the line between the two faces of the wall.

Similarly, you can select other walls to define the floor boundary. The sketched boundary must form a closed profile with all edges connected to each other.

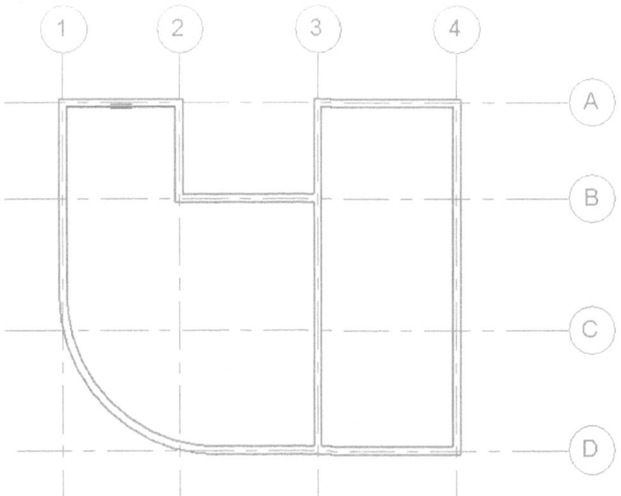

Figure 7-4 *A boundary line created from one of the wall faces while sketching the floor boundary*

Tip
You can also use the TAB key to select a chain of wall segments to create the floor boundary.

After completing the floor boundary, you can edit it by using the drag controls and various tools in the **Modify** panel of the **Modify | Create Floor Boundary** tab. For example, you can drag the sketched line of the floor boundary to a new location by using the drag controls, as shown in Figure 7-5. After the floor profile has been sketched, choose the **Finish Edit Mode** button from the **Mode** panel; the floor will be created and highlighted in blue. As the floor created will not be visible in the plan view, you can use the **Default 3D View** tool from the **Quick Access Toolbar** to view it.

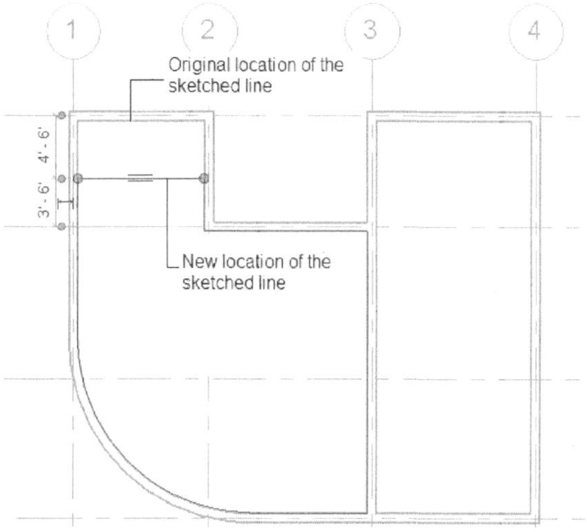

***Figure 7-5** Dragging the sketched floor boundary*

Tip
In case the sketched profile does not form a closed loop, Revit displays an error message informing that the lines are not connected. Also, you are asked whether you want to quit sketching or continue editing the sketch. To rectify the error, you can choose the ***Continue*** *option, make the correction, and then proceed.*

The other option to sketch the floor profile is to draw it using the sketching tools from the **Draw** panel. You can choose the appropriate sketching tool to sketch the floor boundary based on its shape. The functions of the sketching tools are the same as those used for creating a wall. When you use the **Line** tool, the **Chain** check box in the **Options Bar** can be selected to sketch the lines that are connected end-to-end. The **Offset** edit box in the **Options Bar** can be used to sketch lines at a specified offset distance from a point on an existing element. Using the editing tools in the **Modify** panel of the **Modify | Create Floor Boundary** tab, you can edit the sketched profile.

In the sketched floor boundary, you can provide slope. To do so, invoke the **Slope Arrow** tool from the **Draw** panel; a list box containing tools to draw the slope arrow will be displayed. The list box contains two tools: **Line** and **Pick Lines**. The **Line** tool is chosen by default in the display panel. You need to specify the start point and endpoint of the arrow in the drawing. After specifying the start point and endpoint, you can modify its instance properties in the **Properties** palette.

Using this palette, you can modify the associated properties such as specification method to define the slope arrow, the level at which the tail of the slope arrow will rest, height offset at the tail of the arrow, and more. You can attain the desired slope in the floor using the instance properties in the **Properties** palette.

After you complete the profile and add specifications for the floor, choose the **Finish Edit Mode** button from the **Mode** panel; the floor will be created and the **Modify | Floors** tab will be displayed. In this tab, you can use various modification tools to modify the floor created. This tab consists of ten panels: **Properties**, **Clipboard**, **Geometry**, **View**, **Modify**, **Measure**, **Create**, **Mode**, **Draw** and **Work Plane**.

Tip

*You can also create floor from a mass floor using the **Floor by Face** tool from **Architectural > Build > Floor** drop-down. The method of creating a mass floor from a massing object is explained in Chapter 10.*

In Autodesk Revit, you can also create a structural floor in a building model. The structural floor is capable of carrying loads and transferring it to other active structural members. It actively participates in the structural analysis of the building. This makes it different from the floor that you will add using the **Floor: Architectural** tool. To add a structural floor, you can invoke the **Floor: Structural** tool from **Architecture > Build > Floor** drop-down.

In an architectural floor, you can create a slab edge under the existing floor. To do so, invoke the **Floor: Slab Edge** tool from the **Floor** drop-down in the **Build** Panel of the **Architecture** tab. On invoking this tool, the **Modify | Place Slab Edge** tab will be displayed. Now, place the cursor at the desired edge of the floor; the edge will get highlighted. Click at the highlighted edge; slab under the floor will be created as shown in Figure 7-6. After clicking on the edge, two flip arrows will be displayed at the selected edge. You can flip the direction of the slab using these arrows. After doing so, you can change the properties in the **Properties** palette by modifying the type and instance properties of the slab created. To modify the type properties, choose the **Edit Type** button from the **Properties** palette; the **Type Properties** dialog box will be displayed. In this dialog box, you can specify the desired values in the **Value** fields of the parameters either by entering a new value or selecting an option from the drop-down list in the **Type Properties** dialog box. Similarly, you can modify the instance properties of a slab by entering a new value or by selecting an option from the drop-down list displayed in the value field of the corresponding parameter.

Note

If you place a slab segment at the adjacent side of the existing slab edge, both the existing and the new segment will mitter and form one continuous slab.

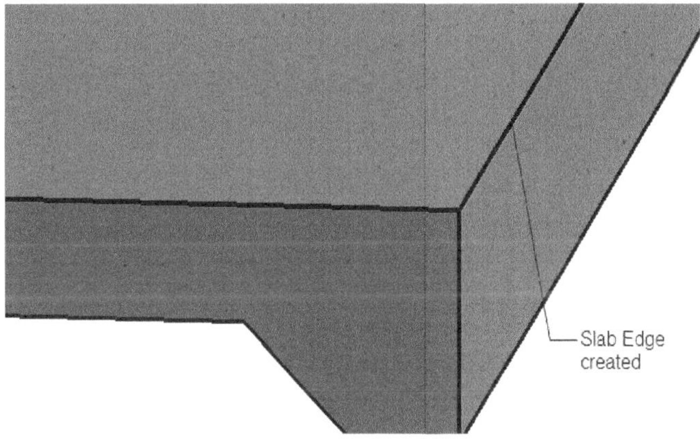

Figure 7-6 Slab edge displayed at one face

CREATING ROOFS

A roof is a structure that covers the uppermost part of a building. The primary function of a roof is to protect the building and its contents from rain. The other functions of a roof depend upon the nature of the structure that it is protecting. For dwellings, a roof can protect against heat, cold, sunlight, and wind.

In Autodesk Revit, you can create a roof structure using various tools displayed in the **Roof** drop-down in the **Build** panel of the **Architecture** tab, as shown in Figure 7-7. You can use the extrusions or mass instances present in the drawing to create a roof.

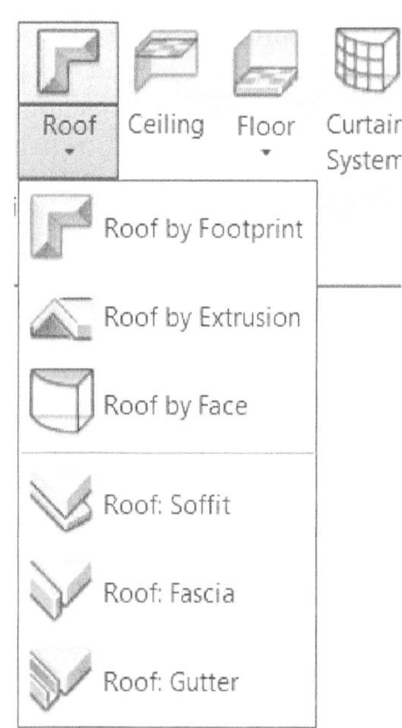

***Figure 7-7** Various tools displayed in the **Roof** drop-down*

Creating Roofs by Footprint

Ribbon: Architecture > Build > Roof drop-down > Roof by Footprint

Roof by Footprint The roof footprint is a two dimensional sketch of the perimeter of a roof. In Autodesk Revit, you can create a roof footprint by drawing lines or picking walls that will define the perimeter of the roof to be created.

The sketch of the footprint which is to be created, will be placed at the same level of the plan view where it was sketched. The sketch of the footprint should be a closed loop geometry that may also contain other closed loops, which will define the opening in the roof.

In Autodesk Revit, you can invoke the **Roof by Footprint** tool from **Architecture > Build > Roof** drop-down. On invoking this tool, the **Lowest Level Notice** dialog box will be displayed. This dialog box contains a drop-down list. From this drop-down list, you can select the required level to sketch the roofprint in which it will be created. By default, **Level 2** is selected in the drop-down list, as shown in Figure 7-8. Therefore, by default, Autodesk Revit sketches the footprint in **Level 2**. However, you can specify different levels in the drop-down list of the **Lowest Level Notice** dialog box and then choose the **Yes** button; the dialog box will be closed and the **Modify|Create Roof Footprint** tab will be displayed. The **Modify|Create Roof Footprint** tab contains tools to draw, annotate, edit, and change the properties of the roof to be created. To draw a footprint, choose the required drawing tools from the **Draw** panel of the **Modify|Create Roof Footprint** tab. In the **Draw** panel, the **Pick Walls** tool is chosen by default. You can use this tool to draw the footprint of the roof by selecting walls. Alternatively, you can use sketching tools such as line, rectangle, circle, or ellipse to draw the footprint from the **Draw** panel. While drawing the roof footprint, you can set the overhang distance of the roof by entering a value in the **Overhang** edit box in the **Options Bar**. You can also change the slope definition of the line that constitutes the footprint. To do so, select the **Defines slope** check box in the **Options Bar**. As such, when you draw the footprint, you can define the slope value of the line by clicking on it and changing the existing slope value in the edit box that will be displayed. You can also extend the roof to the wall core by selecting the **Extend to wall core** check box from the **Options Bar**. Figure 7-9 shows the completed roof footprint for a rectangular wall profile with a specified offset distance and a defined slope. After completing the sketch of the footprint, choose the **Finish Edit Mode** button in the **Mode** panel of the **Modify | Create Roof Footprint** tab; the **Modify|Roofs** tab will be displayed.

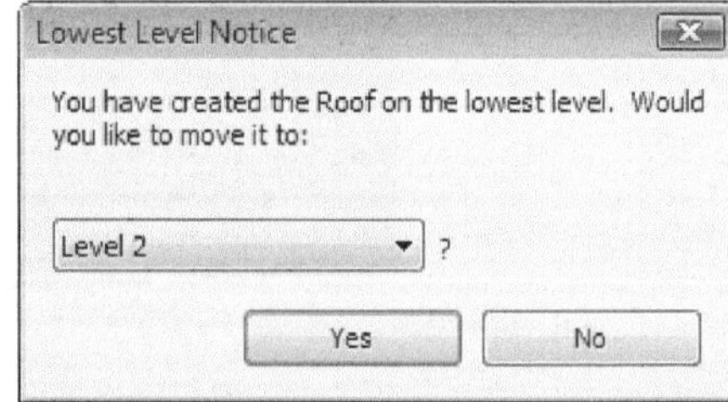

***Figure 7-8** Specifying the level to sketch the roof footprint*

Note

*While drawing the roof for the first time in a project or while drawing it at Level 1, the **Lowest Level Notice** dialog box will be displayed.*

In the **Modify | Roofs** tab, you can use various tools for modifying the created roof such as modifying the instance and type properties, editing the footprint, and other modification tools. After modifying the roof, press ESC to exit from the roof creation tool. Now, you can choose the **{3D}** option from the **Project Browser** to view the created roof, as shown in Figure 7-10. You can create a gable roof from the roof footprint by setting the two parallel lines of the roof footprint as sloping. To do so, select the roof that you want to create as a gable roof from the drawing; the **Modify | Roofs** tab will be displayed. In this tab, choose the **Edit Footprint** tool from the **Mode** panel; the **Modify | Roofs > Edit Footprint** tab will be displayed. Also, the footprints of the roof will be displayed in the drawing area.

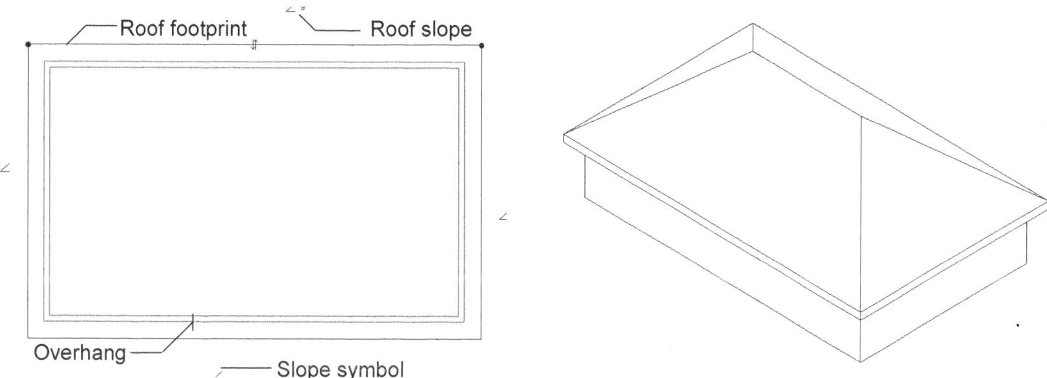

Figure 7-9 Roof footprint of a rectangular wall profile

Figure 7-10 Hip roof created

Now, select a footprint line from the drawing and clear the **Defines Slope** check box in the **Options Bar** to remove the slope parameter. Similarly, select the footprint line parallel to the previously selected line and remove the slope. Alternatively, to modify the slope of a footprint line, select it; the **Properties** palette will be displayed. In this palette, select or clear the **Defines Roof Slope** check box in the value column of the **Defines Roof Slope** parameter. Selecting the **Defines Roof Slope** check box helps you create a sloping edge of the roof footprint, whereas clearing the check box enables you to remove the slope. For example, for a given rectangular profile, you can select the longer edges of the roof footprint as sloping, as shown in Figure 7-11. Next, after setting the slopes for the footprint, choose the **Finish Edit Mode** button from the **Mode** tab to complete the sketch. The resulting roof shape resembles the illustration shown in Figure 7-12.

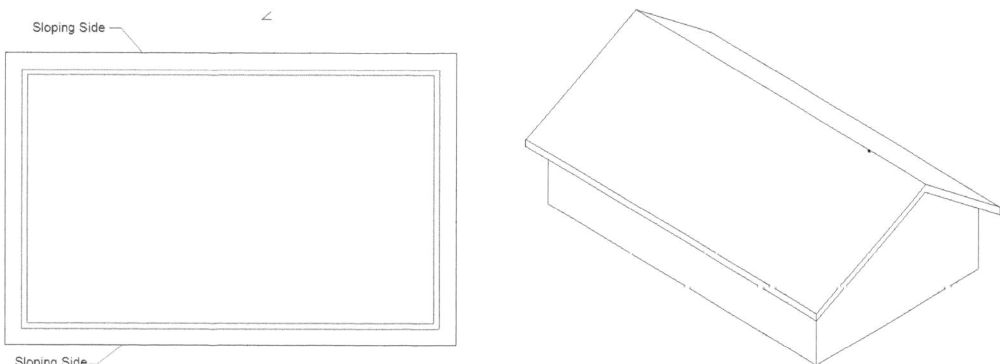

Figure 7-11 Sketching the roof footprint by longer edges

Figure 7-12 Resulting gable roof

A shed roof can be created by selecting only one edge of the roof footprint as the sloping side. Figure 7-13 shows the selected sloping side for the rectangular wall profile. The resulting roof is shown in Figure 7-14.

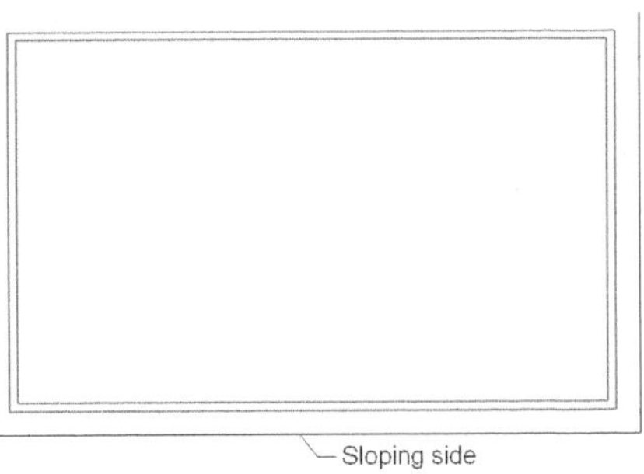

Figure 7-13 Specifying the sloping side

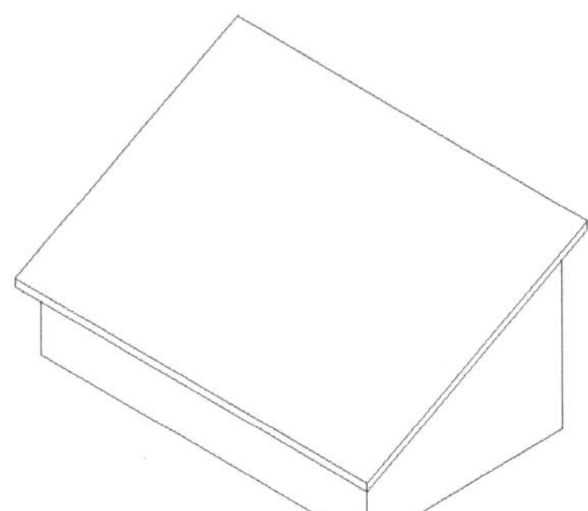

Figure 7-14 Resulting shed roof

A flat roof is created if no sloping parameter is assigned to a line. To create a flat roof, clear the **Defines Slope** check box before sketching the roof footprint. Alternatively, enter the value **0** for the roof slope control while sketching the roof profile.

Note

*To select roof, open the view in which it has been created because it might not be visible in the lowest plane. The sloping roof may appear to be cut off at a level because of the intersection of the roof and the work plane of the level. Double-click on **Site** in the **Floor Plans** head of the **Project Browser** to view the entire roof profile.*

Creating Roofs By Extrusion

Ribbon: Architecture > Build > Roof drop-down > Roof by Extrusion

The second method of creating a roof is by using the **Roof by Extrusion** tool. You can sketch the roof profile and then extrude it to create the roof by using this tool. The profile can be created in the elevation view by using a specific work plane. Also, the profile created must have a series of connected lines that do not form a closed boundary.

To create a roof by extrusion, invoke the **Roof by Extrusion** tool from the **Build** panel; the **Work Plane** dialog box will be displayed, as shown in Figure 7-15. In this dialog box, select the work plane for sketching the roof profile.

You can choose an existing work plane by selecting the **Name** radio button and then selecting its name from the corresponding drop-down list. By default, the **Pick a plane** option is selected. You can also select an existing plane by using this option. When you select this option, Autodesk Revit prompts you to select a work plane or an element defining a plane to sketch the roof profile. The **Pick a line and use the work plane it was sketched in** radio button is used to select a line and to use the work plane, in which it was sketched for sketching the roof profile. You can also create a work plane that is coplanar to the work plane of the file.

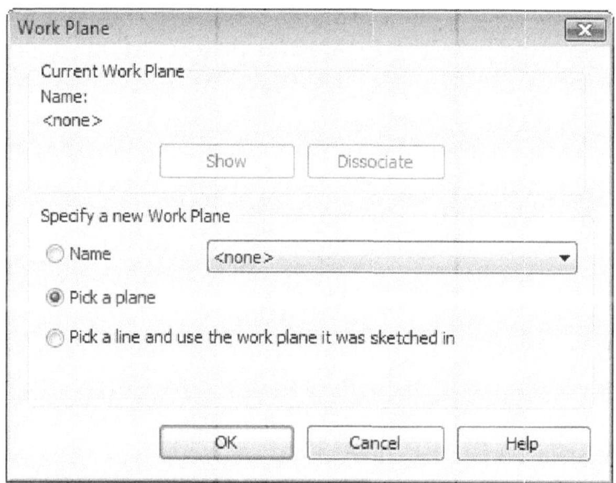

***Figure 7-15** Specifying the work plane for sketching the roof profile in the **Work Plane** dialog box*

If the selected plane is perpendicular to the existing view, the **Go to View** dialog box will be displayed. In this dialog box, you can select a view from the different views available to set the work plane. For example, you can select the **East** or **West** elevation view option to make the sketch parallel to the screen or you can select the **3D View** option to place the roof sketch at an angle to the screen. On selecting a work plane, the **Roof Reference Level and Offset** dialog box will be displayed, as shown in Figure 7-16.

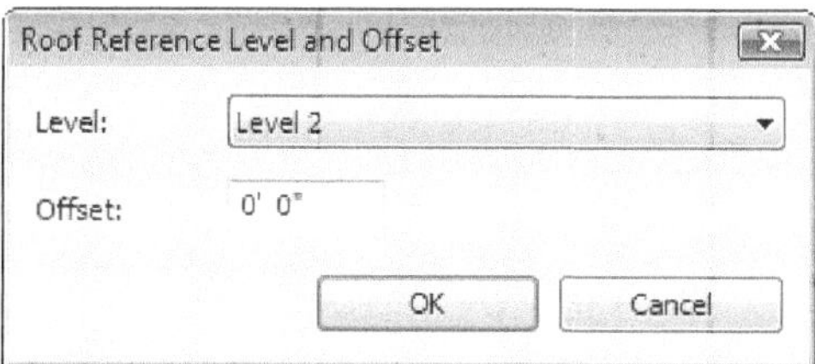

***Figure 7-16** The **Roof Reference Level and Offset** dialog box*

You can specify the base level of the roof by selecting the required option from the **Level** drop-down list. The default level in the drop-down list is the highest level in the project. The **Offset** edit box can be used to specify the offset distance of the roof from the base level. Specify a positive value to create the roof above the specified base level and a negative value to create the roof below the specified base level. Then, choose the **OK** button in the **Roof Reference Level and Offset** dialog box; a reference plane will be generated automatically at the offset distance from the specified level and the **Modify | Create Extrusion Roof Profile** tab will be displayed. From this tab, you can use various tools to draw, annotate, and modify a roof. To draw a profile, you can use the sketching tools available in the **Draw** panel. While or after sketching the roof profile, you can dimension it using various dimension tools that will be displayed in the **Dimension** panel. While sketching the roof profile, you can also use various editing tools such as **Trim**, **Extend**, **Align**, **Split**, and **Offset**. You can also modify the sketched profile by using various tools such as **Move**, **Copy**, **Mirror**, **Array**, **Scale**, and **Delete** in the **Modify** panel of the **Modify | Create Roof Extrusion Profile** tab.

After you sketch the roof profile, you can change the instance and type properties of the roof for which the profile will be created from the **Properties** palette. In this dialog box, you can change the family and the type of the roof to be created. To do so, select the desired family and then select its type from the **Type Selector** drop-down list. After selecting the desired family and its type for the roof, you can change various instance parameters like start and end values of the extrusion, the reference level, the offset of the level, and other parameters of the roof. To change values of these parameters, click on their respective value fields in the **Properties** palette, and change the existing value by entering a new value or by selecting a new option from the drop-down list. In the **Properties** palette, choose the **Edit Type** button; the **Type Properties** dialog box will be displayed. You can use this dialog box to change the type parameters of the roof such as structural, coarse scale fill and color, and the parameters that reveal the identity of the roof. After changing the type parameters in the **Type Properties** dialog box, choose the **OK** button to exit the dialog box and return to the drawing and editing mode of the roof with the **Modify | Create Extrusion Roof Profile** tab displayed.

Note

*For sketching roof profile, you can draw reference planes at the specified work plane before you invoke the **Roof by Extrusion** tool. To draw reference planes, align your view with the desired elevation view and then choose the **Reference Plane** tool from the **Work Plane** panel in the **Architecture** tab; you will enter the sketching mode. Sketch the desired reference planes, as shown in Figure 7-17, and then invoke the **Roof by Extrusion** tool. Now, you can sketch the roof profile using these reference planes, as shown in Figure 7-18.*

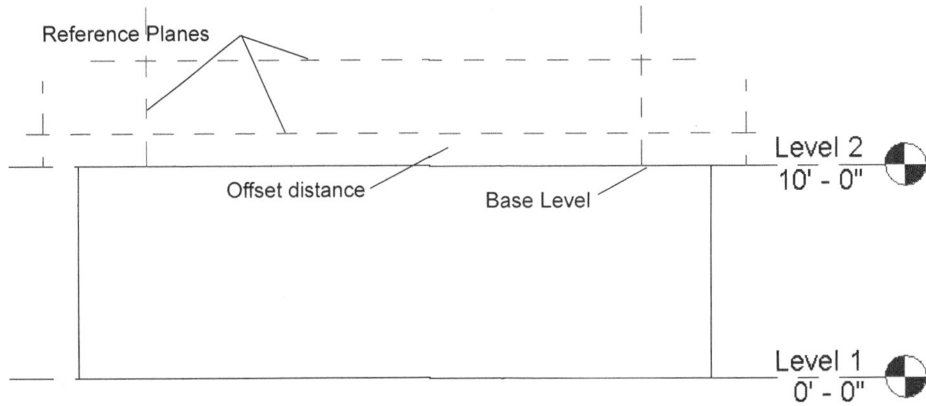

Figure 7-17 *Sketching reference planes to sketch the roof profile*

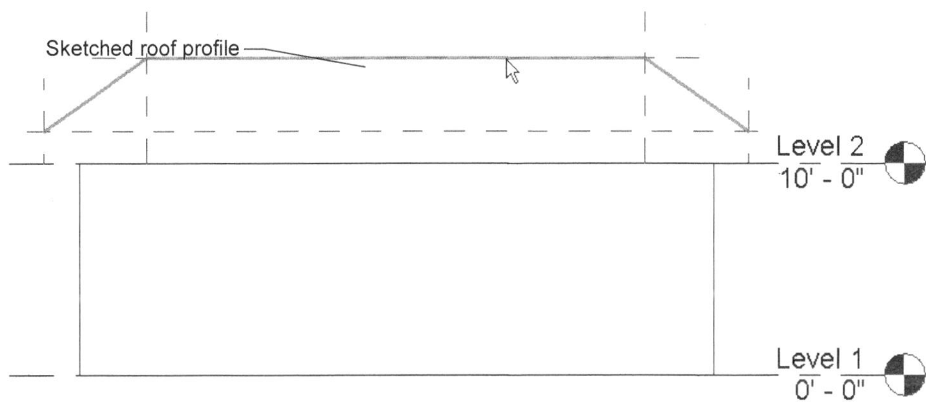

Figure 7-18 *Sketching the roof profile by using the reference planes*

Now, you can finish the sketch of the extrusion profile and the creation of the roof by choosing the **Finish Edit Mode** button from the **Mode** panel of the **Modify | Create Extrusion Roof Profile** tab. After you finish the sketching of the roof profile and create the roof view, you can use the **ViewCube** navigation tool to change the view to display the other views of the roof for better visualization.

Note

For a sketch to be valid, the sketched profile should have lines and/or curves that are connected end-to-end. Also, it should not form a closed loop if it is to be extruded.

After creating the roof, you will notice that the walls do not go up to the roof soffit, as shown in Figure 7-19. To extend the unconnected walls to the roof soffit, select the walls; the **Modify | Walls** tab will be displayed. In this tab, choose the **Attach Top/Base** tool from the **Modify Wall** panel; the **Options Bar** for the attaching options will be displayed. The **Options Bar** displays two radio buttons: **Top** and **Base**. To attach the wall top to the roof, select the **Top** radio button. Similarly, to attach the selected wall base to the roof, select the **Base** radio button. After selecting the desired radio button, select the roof; the selected walls will be extended and attached to the roof soffit, as shown in Figure 7-20.

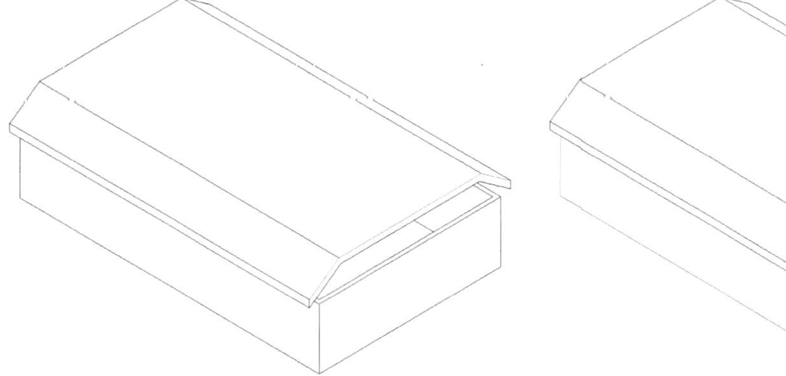

Figure 7-19 *Walls unattached to the roof soffit*

Figure 7-20 *Extending and attaching the walls to the roof*

In Autodesk Revit, you can create and add soffit, fascia, or gutter to the created roof. You can invoke the tools to create these structures by choosing the **Roof Soffit/Fascia/Gutter** tool from the **Roof** drop-down in the **Build** panel of the **Architecture** tab.

Note

The examples given in this chapter are elementary in nature and their purpose is to explain the basic methods of creating roofs. Using the described techniques, you can experiment with roof shapes and forms to create roofs that are suitable for your project. Autodesk Revit empowers you to create a variety of dynamic roof forms using a combination of these tools.

Modifying Roof Properties and Editing Shapes

In Autodesk Revit, you can modify the properties and edit the shape of the roof that you have created for the building model. The properties of a roof can be classified into the following three categories:

a) **Roof Boundary Line Properties** - properties of the lines used in sketching the roof footprint such as length, slope angle, offset from the base, and so on.

b) **Roof Instance Properties** - instance properties of the selected roof such as maximum ridge height, base offset from level, and so on.

c) **Roof Type Properties** - properties of the roof, composition, and cost such as structure, thickness, material, and so on.

Tip

You can combine different roof shapes and join or unjoin them by selecting the corresponding roof and then choosing the ***Join Geometry /Unjoin Geometry*** *tool from the* ***Join*** *drop-down in the* ***Geometry*** *panel of the* ***Modify*** *tab.*

You can modify the roof instance and type properties by using the **Properties** palette. To modify these properties from the palette, select the desired roof; the properties related to it will be displayed in the **Properties** palette. You can select a roof type from the **Type Selector** drop-down list in this palette, as shown in Figure 7-21.

The **Properties** palette, as shown in Figure 7-22, lists various instance parameters under the following five main headings: **Constraints**, **Construction**, **Dimensions**, **Identity Data**, and **Phasing**.

Note

The number of headings and parameters can increase depending upon the options selected from the ***Type Selector*** *drop-down list in the* ***Properties*** *palette.*

The parameters under the **Constraints** head are used to specify the boundary and level constraints for the selected roof. The **Base Level** parameter is used to set the level for the footprint of the selected roof. To change this parameter, click in the corresponding **Value** field and select the desired level from the drop-down list displayed. By default, the top most level is selected. The **Room Bounding** parameter displays a check box in its corresponding value field. This check box is selected by default, which indicates that the selected roof is part of the room boundary. If this check box is cleared, it means the roof is not a part of the room boundary. The **Related to Mass** parameter contains a check box in its value field. If the check box is selected, it indicates that the selected roof is generated from an existing mass element in the drawing. The selection of the check box for the **Related to Mass** parameter is a read-only parameter and it depends upon the method by which the selected roof will be created. The **Base Offset From Level** parameter is used to specify the distance of the selected roof above or below the level where it is being sketched. To modify the existing value in the value field, click on it and enter a suitable value.

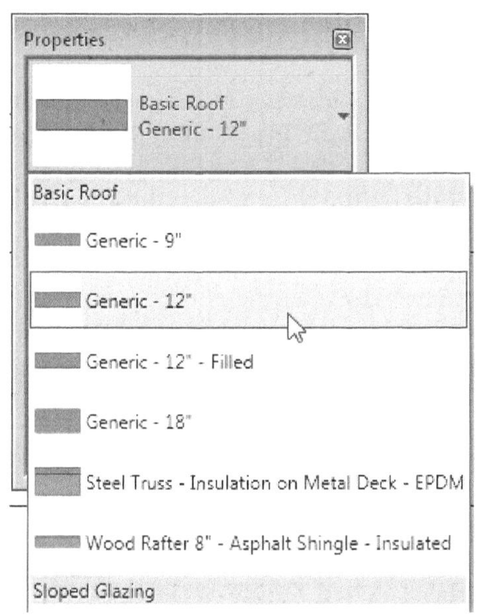

Figure 7-21 Selecting an option from the ***Type Selector*** *drop-down list*

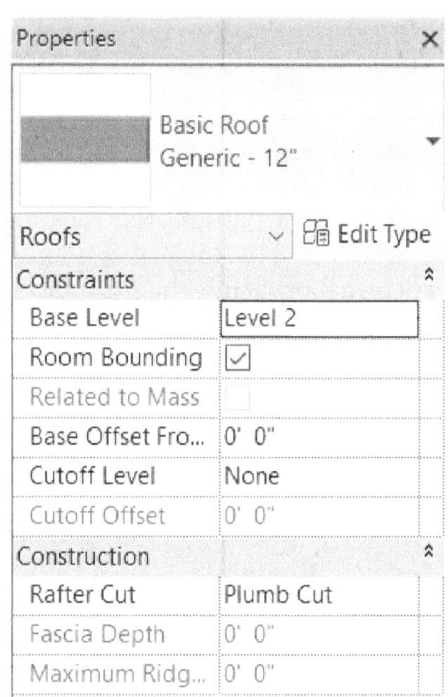

Figure 7-22 *The* ***Properties*** *palette displaying various instance properties of a roof*

The parameters under the **Construction** head of the **Properties** palette are used to specify various values related to the construction of the roof. The parameters that can be used to specify values under this head are: **Rafter Cut**, **Fascia Depth**, **Rafter or Truss**, and **Maximum ridge height**. The **Rafter Cut** parameter specifies the rafter cut on the eave of the roof. For this parameter, you can specify any of the three values such as **Plumb Cut**, **Two-Cut Plumb**, and **Two-Cut Square**, by clicking on the corresponding field in the **Value** column and selecting the desired option from the drop-down list that will be displayed. The **Fascia Depth** parameter displays the length of the lines that will define the fascia on the selected roof. The **Maximum ridge height** parameter displays the maximum height of the top of the roof above the base level of the building model. The value displayed for this parameter is a read-only value.

The parameters under the **Dimensions** heading in the **Properties** palette are used to specify the dimensional properties of the selected roof such as **Slope**, **Thickness**, **Volume**, and **Area**. The **Slope** parameter is used to specify the slope of the selected roof. This parameter initially displays a value if there is a slope-defining line. If there is no slope-defining line, the parameter is blank and disabled. You can change its value by clicking in its value field and then entering a desired value. The **Thickness** parameter displays the thickness of the roof. Similarly, the **Volume** and

Area parameters display the volume and area of the selected roof in their corresponding value fields. The values displayed in the **Value** field of the **Volume** and **Area** parameters are read-only and so you cannot change them.

The **Identity Data** and **Phasing** headings in the **Properties** palette of the selected roof contain the parameters that specify the values related to the identification and phasing information.

Tip
You can add a glazed roof to your model. To do so, select the ***Sloped Glazing : Sloped Glazing*** *option from the* ***Type Selector*** *drop-down list in the* ***Properties*** *palette while adding or modifying a roof in a model.*

After specifying the instance parameters in the **Properties** palette, you can view and specify the type properties of the selected roof. To do so, choose the **Edit Type** button displayed in the **Properties** palette of the selected roof; the **Type Properties** dialog box will be displayed, as shown in Figure 7-23. In this dialog box, choose the **Edit** button displayed in the **Value** column of the **Structure** parameter; the **Edit Assembly** dialog box will be displayed. In this dialog box, you can modify various type parameters such as layer composition, material, thickness, and so on. Use the **Insert** and **Delete** buttons to add or remove layers in the existing assembly. The total thickness of the roof is calculated by adding the individual thickness of all the layers. After specifying the type parameters, choose the **OK** button; the **Edit Assembly** dialog box will be closed. Now, choose the **OK** button again to return to the settings of the **Modify|Roofs** tab in your drawing.

In the **Modify | Roofs** tab, you can use various editing tools such as **Copy**, **Rotate**, **Move**, and **Mirror** to edit or copy the roof created. You can also edit the geometry of the footprints of the selected roof. To do so, choose the **Edit Footprint** tool from the **Mode** panel; the **Modify | Roofs > Edit Footprints** tab along with the sketched profile of the selected roof in the sketched mode will be displayed. Now, you can modify the sketch profile by using the drag controls and other editing tools that are displayed in the **Modify | Roofs > Edit Footprints** tab.

For a roof generated using the **Roof by Footprint** tool, each line segment of the sketched footprint can be assigned a slope parameter individually to create sides with the desired slope. You can also specify the pitch for each sloping side of the roof. To define the slope, select the line; the **Properties** palette will be displayed. Next, enter the value of the instance parameters such as overhang, rise, and so on. You can enter the value of the rise per 12" of the horizontal length in the value column of the **Slope** parameter. After editing the profile of the selected roof, choose the **Finish Edit Mode** button from the **Mode** panel of the **Modify | Roofs > Edit Footprints** tab; Revit will exit from the footprint editing mode and the **Modify|Roofs** tab will be displayed. Press ESC to exit the displayed tab.

Note
The instance parameters displayed in the instance parameters table depend upon the roof type selected. You can experiment with these parameters to modify the roof to a desired shape.

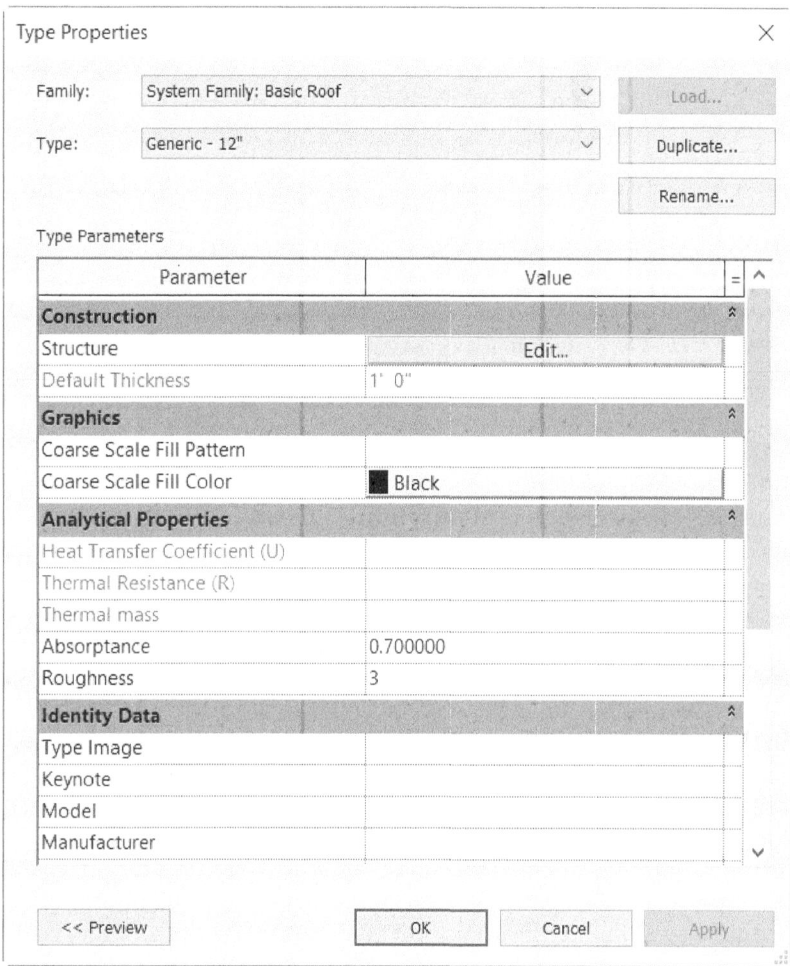

*Figure 7-23 The **Type Properties** dialog box for the selected roof*

SHAPE EDITING TOOLS FOR FLOORS

Autodesk Revit provides you with a set of shape editing tools. Using these tools, you can modify the horizontal surface of floors, roofs (without slope), and structural floors by adding slopes to the surfaces for draining. You can add slopes to the horizontal surfaces without defining the sloping edges. To do so, you need to add low or high elevation points to the horizontal surface of the selected floor, roof, or structural floor, thereby splitting the surface into subregions, which in turn slope into different directions. These tools basically belong to the Revit Structure program, but you can also access these tools in Revit Architecture.

To access the shape editing tools, select the floor, roof, or structural floor created in the drawing; the shape editing tools will be displayed in the **Shape Editing** panel of the **Modify | Floors** tab of the ribbon, as shown in Figure 7-24. The shape editing tools are **Modify Sub Elements**, **Add Point**, **Add Split Line**, **Pick Supports**, and **Reset Shape**. These tools are discussed next.

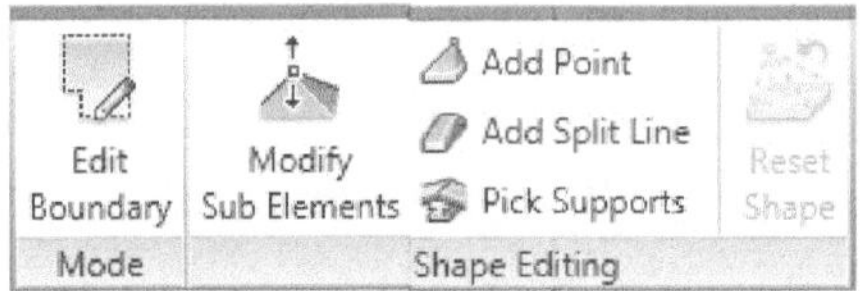

***Figure 7-24** The shape editing tools displayed in the **Shape Editing** panel*

Tip

Autodesk Revit generates roofs based on the sketch profile and values of the instance and type parameters. In case the roof profile is not continuous or the inputs given are invalid, an error message is displayed. Based on the error description, you can take necessary corrective actions.

Modify Sub Elements

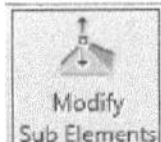

This tool helps you select and modify the points or edges on a selected slab, floor, or roof surface. On invoking the **Modify Sub Elements** tool from the **Shape Editing** panel, a green colored boundary line and green colored corner grips will be displayed at the corners, as shown in Figure 7-25.

On selecting an edge, the edge will be highlighted in blue color and a drag control symbol consisting of two arrows and a square will be displayed. Drag the arrows to move the selected point or edge vertically to different elevations. Drag the square control to move the selected point or edge in the horizontal direction. Figure 7-26 shows the drag control symbol displayed after selecting the left corner point and Figure 7-27 shows the floor after dragging the corner point vertically upward. Instead of dragging the selected point or the edge by using the drag controls, you can type the elevation value in the **Elevation** edit box in the **Options Bar**. On doing so, the selected point or the edge will move to the specified elevation value. If you select an edge, the drag control symbol will be displayed at the center of the edge. The edge can be modified by dragging the center point control to different elevations but the other two points of an edge will remain at the same elevation.

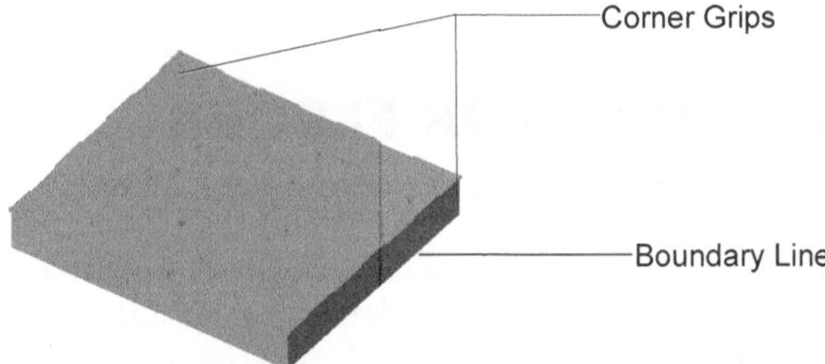

***Figure 7-25** The boundary line and the corner grips displayed after selecting the floor*

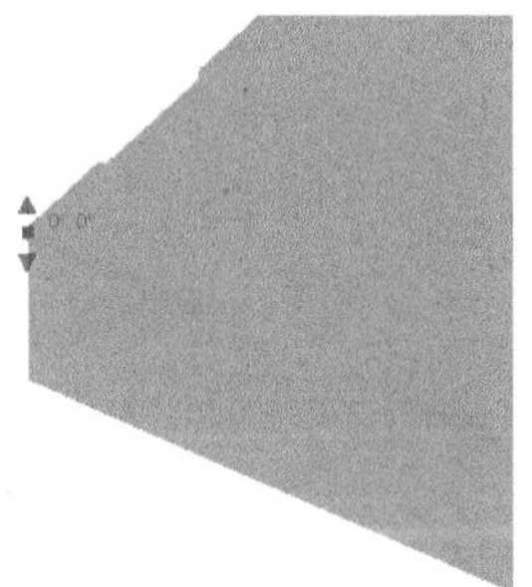

Figure 7-26 Drag control symbol displayed after selecting the left corner point

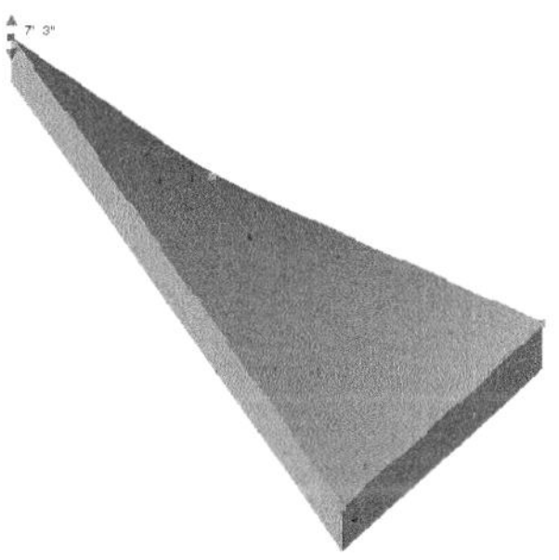

Figure 7-27 The floor after dragging the left corner point vertically upward

Note

The shape editing tools are available only after selecting the existing space floor, roof (without slope), or slab.

Add Point

This tool is used to assign a spot elevation by adding single or multiple points to the surface. These points are then used to modify the geometry of the selected slab, floor or roof. On invoking this tool, the **Elevation** edit box and the **Relative** check box will be displayed in the **Options Bar**. The **Relative** check box is selected by default, which means that the point will be added at a specified elevation relative to the surface to which it is added. You can specify the elevation value in the **Elevation** edit box. By default, the elevation value is **0'0"** which means that the points will be added on the surface on which they are created. On clearing the **Relative** check box, the points will be added on the surface at the elevation value displayed in the **Elevation** edit box. This value represents the project elevation. Figure 7-28 shows the floor after adding a point at the center and dragging the point vertically downward.

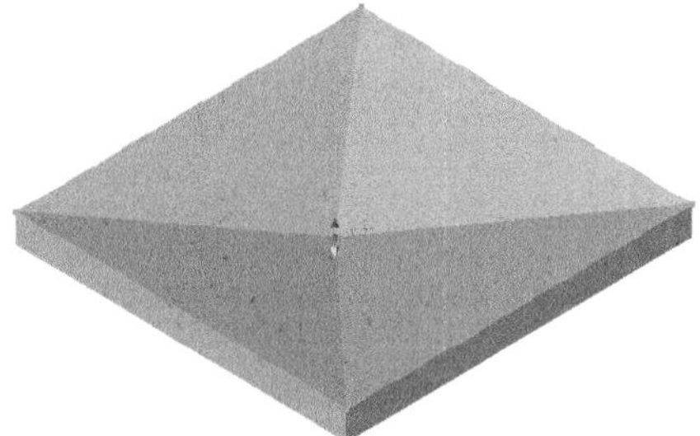

Figure 7-28 Adding a point at the center of the surface and then dragging the point

Add Split Line

Add Split Line

This tool is used to split or divide the slab, floor, or roof surface into different sub regions by adding the split lines to the surface. These split lines act as edges and split the surface into different regions. You can then drag these split edges to different elevations, thereby providing slopes to these subregions. Each subregion created will slope independently in different directions. To add split lines, invoke this tool and select a vertex, edge, point, or face of the surface to start the split line. Select another vertex, point, or edge to complete the split line between the points, vertices, or edges. Figure 7-29 shows the floor shape after adding three split edges, one joining the two corners and the other two joining the centers of two edges.

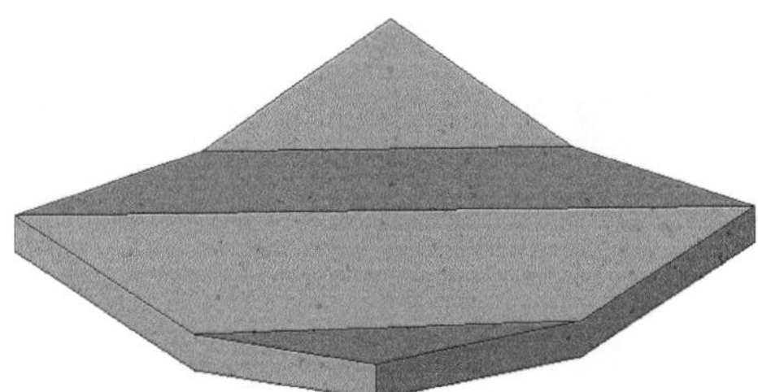

Figure 7-29 The floor after adding three split lines and dragging them to different elevations

Pick Supports

This tool is used to select the beams to define the split lines. Invoke this tool and select the beams from the drawing for reference; a new split edge will be created using the elevations of the endpoints of the picked reference. The elevations will shift from the bottom face to the top face of the selected slab or roof according to the slab or roof thickness.

Reset Shape

This tool allows you to reset the geometry and shape of the slab, floor, or roof. After invoking this tool, the selected floor, roof, or slab reverts to the original shape.

CREATING CEILINGS

Ribbon: Architecture > Build > Ceiling

You can add a ceiling to a building model by using the **Ceiling** tool. To do so, invoke this tool from the **Build** panel; the **Modify | Place Ceiling** tab with various tools for creating the ceiling will be displayed. Since the ceilings are not visible in the floor plan, they are created in the ceiling plan. You can add a ceiling to a project using three different methods: by automatic ceiling, by sketching the ceiling, and by using the pick walls method.

Creating an Automatic Ceiling

The first method to add a ceiling to a project is by creating an automatic ceiling. To do so, choose the **Ceiling** tool from the **Build** panel; the **Modify | Place Ceiling** tab will be displayed. In this tab, the **Automatic Ceiling** tool is selected by default in the **Ceiling** panel. In the **Properties** palette, select the ceiling type from the **Type Selector** drop-down list. You can select different types of built-in ceiling that can be used from this list. Now, to add the ceiling to the entire room, open the ceiling plan, move the cursor inside the room, and click when the ceiling boundary is displayed. Autodesk Revit will automatically create ceiling from the center of the room. For example, when you move the cursor inside the room for creating an automatic ceiling, its boundary is highlighted in red, as shown in Figure 7-30. Click to create the ceiling automatically. If you have created the ceiling in a floor plan, Autodesk Revit will display a warning indicating that the ceiling created will not be visible in it. You can then open the ceiling plan of the corresponding level to view the created ceiling, as shown in Figure 7-31. You can also open the section view through the room to view the cross-section of the ceiling.

Figure 7-30 Selecting the room to create an automatic ceiling

Figure 7-31 Automatic ceiling created

Sketching a Ceiling

You can sketch a ceiling boundary and create a ceiling. To do so, choose the **Ceiling** tool from the **Build** panel; the **Modify | Place Ceiling** tab will be displayed. In this tab, choose the **Sketch Ceiling** tool from the **Ceiling** panel; the **Modify | Create Ceiling Boundary** tab will be displayed. This tab contains various tools for sketching and modifying the ceiling boundary. To start the sketch of a ceiling boundary, choose the **Boundary Line** tool from the **Draw** panel; a list box containing various drawing tools will be displayed on the right in this panel, as shown in Figure 7-32. The **Line** tool is chosen by default in the **Draw** panel. You can use this tool and other drawing and modification tools displayed in the **Modify | Create Ceiling Boundary** tab to complete the sketch. Figure 7-33 shows a ceiling boundary that is sketched using various tools displayed in the **Modify| Create Ceiling Boundary** tab. After completing the sketch, choose the **Finish Edit Mode** button from the **Mode** panel of the **Modify | Create Ceiling Boundary** tab; the ceiling will be created within the sketched profile, as shown in Figure 7-34. Display the section view to view the ceiling in it. The ceiling will appear at a certain height from the floor level, as shown in Figure 7-35.

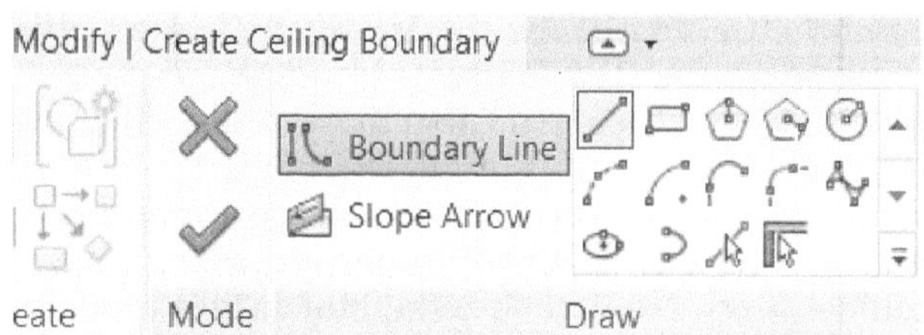

Figure 7-32 The list box containing the tools to sketch the boundary line

Figure 7-33 *Sketching the ceiling boundary*

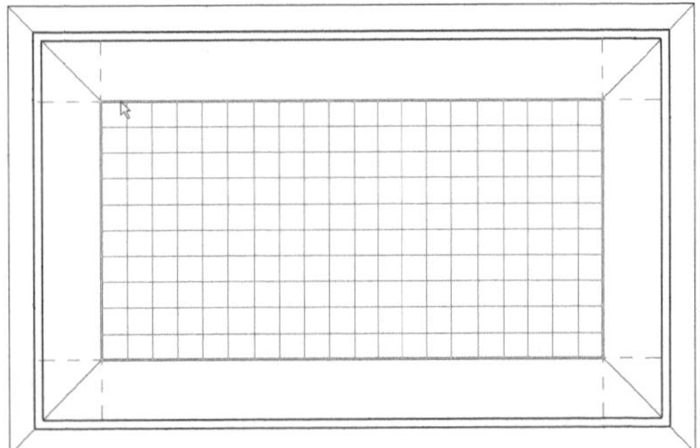

Figure 7-34 *Ceiling created within the sketched boundary*

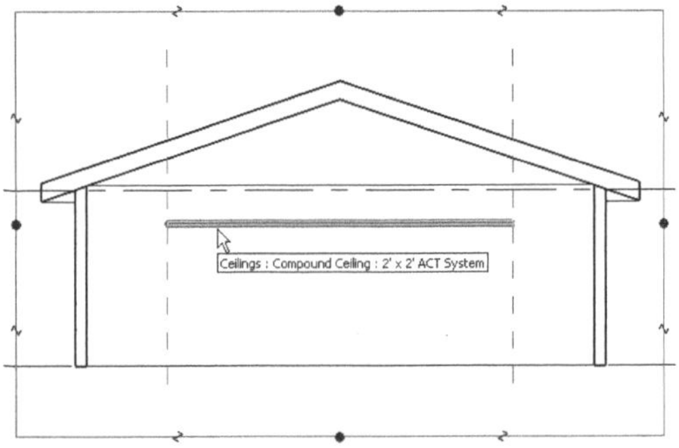

Figure 7-35 *Ceiling displayed in the section view*

Using the Pick Walls Method

The third method to create the ceiling is by picking the wall faces. This is a common method for creating ceilings. To create a ceiling by picking the wall faces, choose the **Ceiling** tool from the **Architecture** tab; the **Modify | Place Ceiling** tab will be displayed. In this tab, choose the **Sketch Ceiling** tool from the **Ceiling** panel; the **Modify | Create Ceiling Boundary** tab will be displayed. In this tab, choose the **Pick Walls** tool from the list box of the **Draw** panel; you will be prompted to pick the walls to define the boundary of the ceiling. Specify the offset value for the ceiling in the **Offset** edit box in the **Options Bar**. Select the **Extend into Wall (to core)** check box, if you want the offset to be measured from the core layer of the walls. Next, pick the walls to create the sketch for the ceiling. In the **Properties** palette, select the ceiling type from the **Type Selector** drop-down list. Next, choose the **Finish Edit Mode** button from the **Mode** panel of the **Modify | Create Ceiling Boundary** tab; the ceiling will be created.

Modifying a Ceiling

You can modify a ceiling after it has been created. To modify the ceiling, select it; the **Modify|Ceiling** tab will be displayed. From this tab, you can use various modification and editing tools to make changes on the selected ceiling. For editing the selected ceiling, you can use the editing tools such as **Copy**, **Rotate**, **Move**, and **Mirror**. You can also modify the properties of the selected ceiling based on its sketch. To do so, choose the **Edit Boundary** tool from the **Mode** panel; the **Modify | Ceiling > Edit Boundary** tab will be displayed and the sketch mode will be activated for the selected ceiling in the drawing. Now, you can modify the sketch profile by using the drag controls and other editing tools. Select the edge(s) of the ceiling boundary; the instance properties for the selected edges(s) of the ceiling profile will be displayed in the **Properties** palette. In this palette, you can enter the required values of various instance parameters for the selected edge(s) of the ceiling boundary.

You can view and edit the instance properties of a ceiling. To do so, select the ceiling from the drawing; the instance properties of the ceiling will be displayed in the **Properties** palette. This palette displays the instance parameters of the selected ceiling such as the level, height offset from level, and so on, as shown in Figure 7-36.

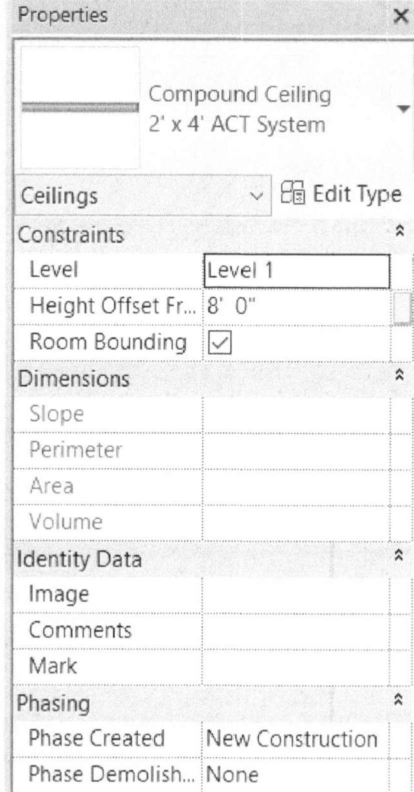

Figure 7-36 *Partial view of the **Properties** palette with various instance properties*

Being a level-based element, ceilings are created at a specified distance from the base level. This distance is specified in the **Height Offset From Level** instance parameter in the **Properties** palette. For example, to create a ceiling at 10' height from Level 2, you can select it as the value for the **Level** instance parameter and enter the value **10'** in the **Height Offset From Level** instance parameter.

The **Edit Type** button in the **Properties** palette is used to invoke the **Type Properties** dialog box. Choose the **Edit Type** button; the **Type Properties** dialog box for the selected ceiling type will be displayed, as shown in Figure 7-37. In the **Type Properties** dialog box, you can create a duplicate type as the new ceiling type. To do so, choose the **Duplicate** button; the **Name** dialog box will be displayed. In this dialog box, enter a name for the new ceiling type in the **Name** edit box and choose **OK**; the **Name** dialog box will close and a new type of ceiling will be created. In the **Type Properties** dialog box, choose the **Edit** button in the **Value** column for the **Structure** type parameter to display the **Edit Assembly** dialog box. This dialog box displays the structure of the ceiling type with its various layers. The **Insert** or **Delete** button can be used to customize the new ceiling type based on the specific project requirement.

Note

*When you select the created ceiling in the section view and choose **Edit**, Autodesk Revit displays the **Go To View** dialog box. You can select the view that you want to open for editing the ceiling boundary sketch.*

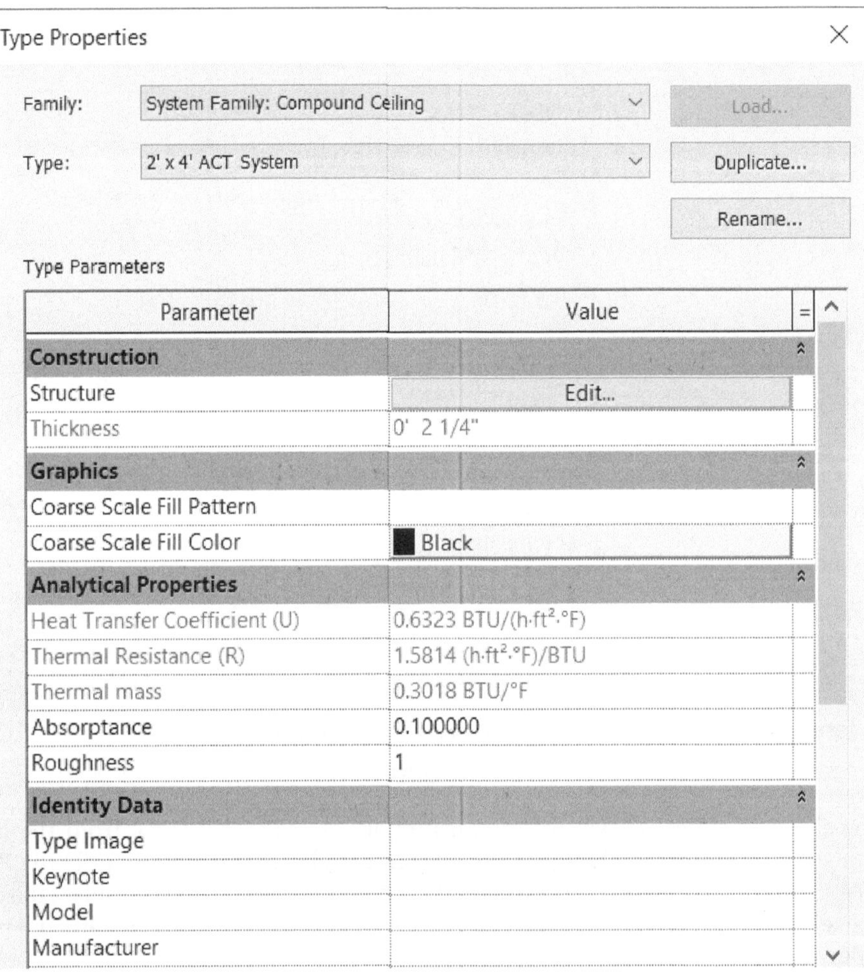

***Figure 7-37** The partial view of the **Type Properties** dialog box for the selected ceiling type*

ROOMS

Room is a part of Autodesk Revit building elements. Autodesk Revit provides you the flexibility of creating rooms independent of room tags. Rooms can be created only in the plan view. You can also add rooms from the room schedules. Rooms and areas have the same graphical representation.

Adding Rooms

Ribbon: Architecture > Room & Area > Room

You can add rooms to the plan view by using the **Room** tool. To do so, invoke this tool from the **Room & Area** panel, as shown in Figure 7-38; the **Modify|Place Room** tab will be displayed. Now, as you move the cursor inside a closed boundary that you need to define as a room in the drawing, a symbol with a cross hair graphics attached to the cursor will appear. Notice that the size of this cross hair graphics will change according to the area of the room space of the closed boundary. Before you insert the room, you can select the type of room from the **Type Selector** drop-down list in the **Properties** palette. You can select any of the three options namely, **Room Tag**, **Room Tag With Area**, and **Room Tag With Volume** from the **Type-Selector** drop-down list. You can select the **Room Tag** option to display the inserted room with the tag only. Similarly, you can select the **Room Tag With Area** or **Room Tag With Volume** option from the **Type Selector** drop-down list to attach the room tag to the room to display the information regarding the area or volume of the room. After selecting the required option from the **Type Selector** drop-down list, choose the **Highlight Boundaries** tool from the **Room** panel of the **Modify | Place Room** tab; the **Autodesk Revit 2018** message box will be displayed, informing that the room bounding elements are highlighted in the drawing. Choose the **Close** button to close the message box.

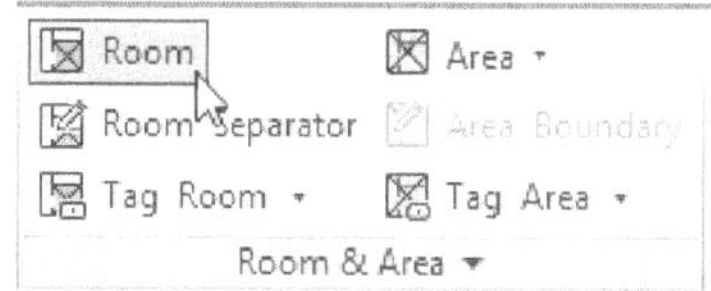

Figure 7-38 *Invoking the* ***Room*** *tool*

Rooms can also be automatically placed in closed and bounded areas greater than 0.25 square feet. Rooms will be created according to the parameters specified in the **Options Bar**. To automatically place the rooms, choose the **Place Rooms Automatically** tool from the **Room** panel of the **Modify | Place Room** contextual tab; a dialog box will be displayed showing the number of rooms created.

To add a room with a room tag, choose the **Tag on Placement** tool from the **Tag** panel. You can specify a level up to which the boundary of a room will extend vertically or upward. To do so, select an option from the **Upper Limit** drop-down list in the **Options Bar**. For example, if you have added a room to the floor plan of **Level 1** and you desire to extend the room to **Level 2**, select the **Level 2** option from the **Upper Limit** drop-down list. You can extend the room boundary above the level specified in the **Upper Limit** drop-down list. To do so, click in the **Offset** edit box in the **Options Bar**. The default value displayed in this edit box is **10'**. You can enter a positive value to extend the room boundary above the level that you have selected from the **Upper Limit** drop-down list. Similarly, you can enter a negative value to extend the room boundary below the selected level. You can orient the room tag horizontally or vertically in reference to the current view, or align it with the walls and boundary lines present in the building model. To specify the orientation of the room tag, select an option from the drop-down list displayed next to the **Offset** edit box in the **Options Bar**. You can select the **Leader** check box to place the room tag with a leader.

To add a room, click in an area enclosed by the room-bounding elements such as walls, as shown in Figure 7-39. The room will be added and the area of the room will be equal to the area enclosed by the walls.

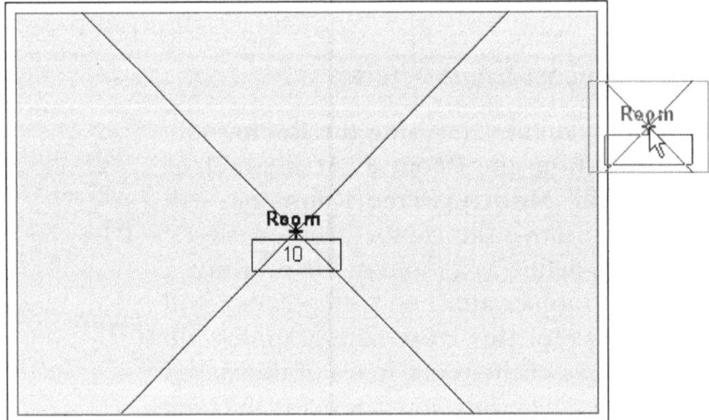

Figure 7-39 *The graphical representation of the room*

You can also add a room in a free space or in an area that is not enclosed completely, and then add walls or other room bounding elements to the room. In such an instance, the room will be created and the area of the room will be equal to the area enclosed by the walls added later. Figure 7-40 shows a room added to the area that is not enclosed and Figure 7-41 shows the room after enclosing the area by adding a wall segment. On placing a room in a free space or in an area that is not enclosed, Autodesk Revit will display a warning message that the room is not in a properly enclosed region.

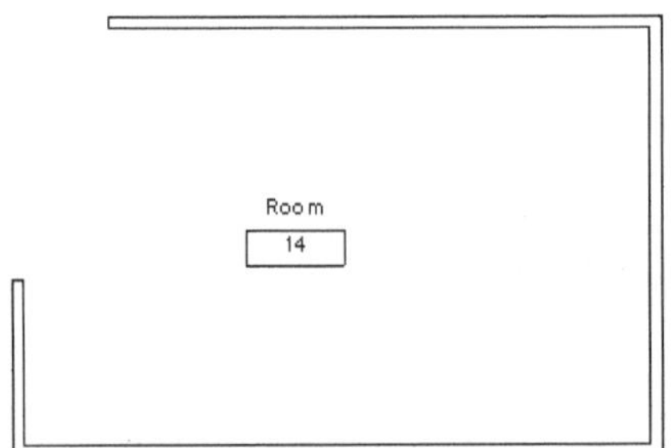

Figure 7-40 *Room added in an open boundary*

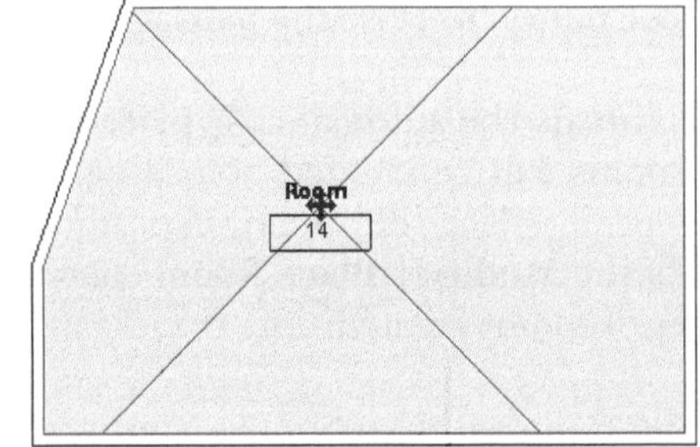

Figure 7-41 *Room created after adding the wall segment*

Creating Rooms from Room Schedules

Revit provides you with the flexibility to add rooms from the room schedules. You can add a new room in a room schedule and place the same room in the plan view. To do so, invoke the **Room** tool and select the room type from the **Room** drop-down list in the **Options Bar**. Next, select the room tag from the **Type Selector** drop-down list. The room types will be available in the **Room** drop-down list only when you have added rooms to a room schedule. After selecting the room type from the drop-down list, click in the drawing to place the room; a room with a room tag will be added in the drawing.

Note

If you do not select the room type from the ***Room*** *drop-down list in the* ***Options Bar****, a new room will be created and will be numbered after the last number of the room in the schedule.*

Room Bounding Elements

You can use different elements as room bounding elements. hese elements define the boundary of the room and help in calculating the area and volume of the room. Walls, roofs, ceilings, curtain systems, floors, columns, and room separation lines can be used as room bounding elements. Autodesk Revit calculates the areas based on the area enclosed by room bounding elements and the room height.

Modifying Room Properties

You can modify the room properties by changing the values of the room parameters in the **Properties** palette. To do so, select the room and click when the crosshair graphics is displayed; the **Properties** palette will be displayed, as shown in Figure 7-42.

Understanding Room Instance Parameters

The different instance parameters of the room are described in the table given next.

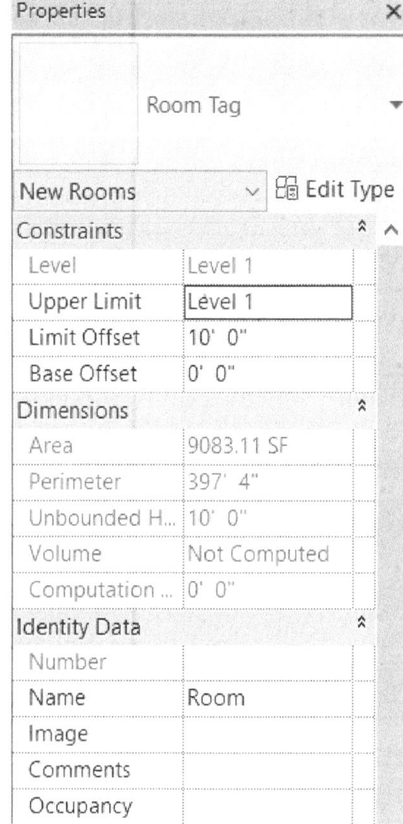

Figure 7-42 The ***Properties*** *palette displaying the properties of a room*

Instance Parameter	Value and Description
Level	Specifies the base level of the room. Level 1 is the default value
Upper Limit	Specifies the upper boundary of the room. The specified level and the value defines the upper limit of the room. The level can be selected from the **Level** drop-down list by clicking on value column of corresponding parameter

Instance Parameter	Value and Description
Limit Offset	Specifies the value specified to be added in the level to set the total height of the room. This parameter can have negative value. The default value set is 10'. A new value can be entered by clicking in the value field of this parameter
Base Offset	Specifies the value specified to be added in the level to set the total height from the base of the room
Area	Specifies the total area calculated using the room bounding elements
Perimeter	Defines the perimeter of the room
Unbounded Height	Total height defined by the sum of the room base level, upperlimit and limit offset
Volume	Specifies the total volume of the room. The volume is computed only when you select the **Areas and Volumes** radio button in the **Area and Volume Computations** dialog box
Computation Height	Specifies the height from where the total height of the room is calculated
Number	Specifies the room number assigned according to the number of rooms added
Name	Specifies the room name. The default name is **Room**. Any name can be assigned to the room
Comments	Some specific comments or description about the room can be entered in this section
Occupancy	Specifies the type of occupancy for structure that can be specified as per the requirement. This parameter can be defined by any name.
Department	Specifies the department of the room based on the functionality of the room
Base/Ceiling Finish	A user-defined parameter, defines any type of finish for the base and the ceiling such as GWB
Wall/Floor Finish	Specifies the finish for the walls of the room such as metal paints and coatings of the walls and tiles for the floor
Occupant	Specifies the name of a person, group, or any organization of the occupant
Phase	Specifies the name of the phase in which the room is created

Calculating Room Volumes

To enable the volume computations and calculate room volumes, choose the **Area and Volume Computations** tool from the **Room & Area** panel; the **Area and Volume Computations** dialog box will be displayed. In the **Volume Computations** area of the **Computations** tab, select the **Areas and Volumes** radio button. By default, the **Areas only** radio button is selected in the **Volume Computations** area. Next, choose the **OK** button; the volume computation of room will be enabled and displayed in its instance properties. To view the calculated volume of a room, select it from the drawing; the **Properties** palette will be displayed. In the **Properties** palette, the value in the value column of the **Volume** parameter shows the computed volume of the room.

Note

In Revit, the volume calculations of room are done considering the finish face of the room-bounding element. When you select a room, the outline and the color fill display the exact periphery and the enclosed area used for calculating the volume of the room.

While computing the room volume, the room volume calculation engine of Autodesk Revit looks up and down from the measurement height to access the vertical limit of the room-bounding element. You can set the lower and upper limits of the room-bounding elements using the **Properties** palette. The **Base Offset** parameter in the value column in this palette defines the limit of the lower boundary that is used to limit the extent of the room with no floors or prevent floors to leak from floor openings while computing the volume of the room.

The volume is also displayed in the drawing view if the rooms are added in the drawing view with the **Room Tag With Volume** option selected from the **Type Selector** drop-down list.

Cutting Openings in a Wall, Floor, Roof, and Ceiling

In Autodesk Revit, you can create an opening in the wall, floor, roof, structural floor, ceiling, and structural elements such as beams and braces using any of the tools available in it. To create an opening, invoke any of these tools from the **Opening** panel of the **Architecture** tab, as shown in Figure 7-43. From this panel, you can choose any of these five options, **By Face**, **Wall**, **Vertical**, **Shaft**, or **Dormer** to create an opening.

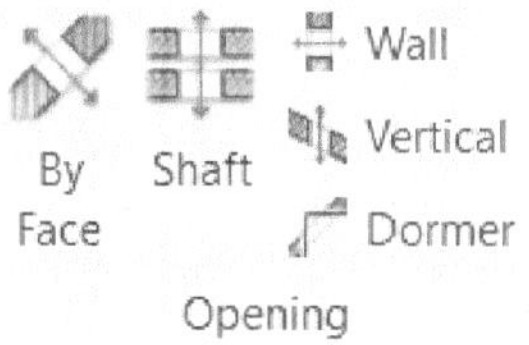

Figure 7-43 *Various opening tools in the* ***Opening*** *panel*

You can use the **By Face** tool to cut openings on the faces of roofs, floors, or ceilings in the building model. This tool is useful in a project when you need to cut an opening in a floor for stairway or skylight opening. You can also use this tool for creating any cut-out in the roof for a chimney. To do so, invoke this tool from the **Opening** panel; you will be prompted to select a planar face of a roof, floor, ceiling, beam, or column. Select the face on which you want to create an opening, as shown in Figure 7-44. Once you select the face, the **Modify | Create Opening Boundary** tab will be displayed. In this tab, you can use various tools to sketch the opening in any view. Now, open the required view and sketch the opening using the reference planes, as shown in Figure 7-45. After sketching the opening boundary on the selected face, choose the **Finish Edit Mode** button from the **Mode** panel to finish the sketch of the opening and then exit the **Modify | Create Opening Boundary** tab. Figure 7-46 shows the resulting opening perpendicular to the selected face.

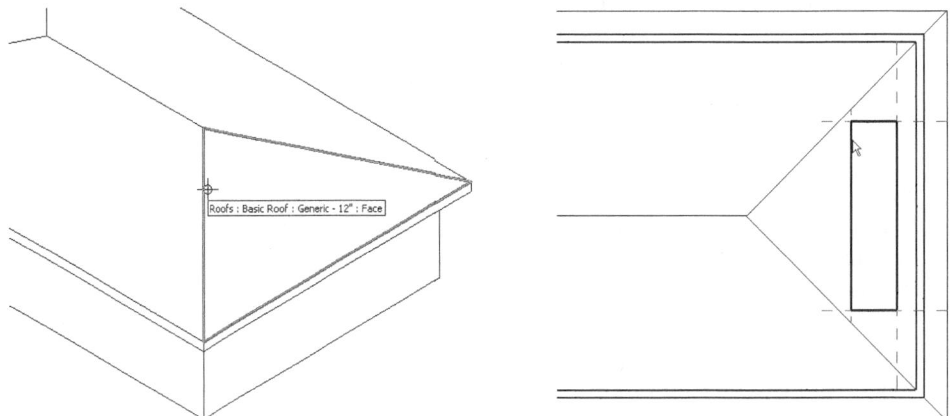

Figure 7-44 *Selecting the face to be cut of the roof*

Figure 7-45 *Sketching the opening in the ceiling plan using the reference planes*

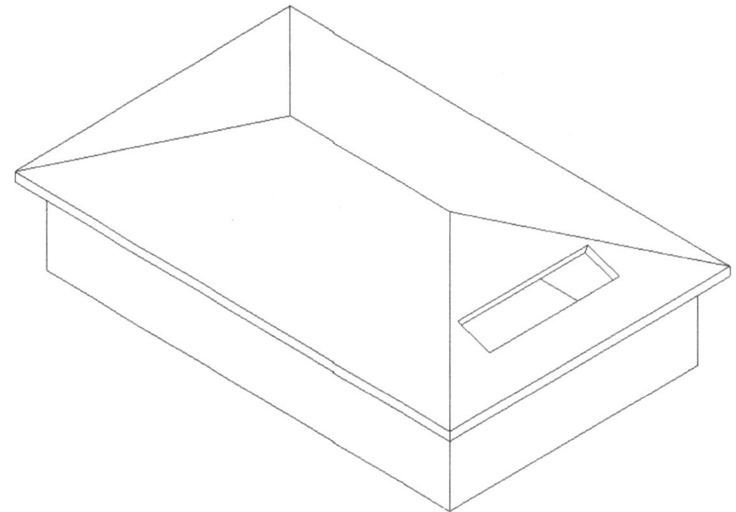

Figure 7-46 *Resulting opening perpendicular to the selected face*

To cut a vertical opening, choose the **Vertical** tool from the **Opening** panel and select the required ceiling, roof, or floor; the **Modify | Create Opening Boundary** tab will be displayed. You can use various tools from this tab to sketch the boundary of the opening. Sketch the opening in the appropriate view using the sketching tools. After sketching the opening boundary, choose the **Finish Edit Mode** button from the **Mode** panel; a vertical opening will be created in the selected element. You can use the sketching tools to draw a sketch of appropriate size, as shown in Figure 7-47. The opening can also be viewed in the 3D view, as shown in Figure 7-48.

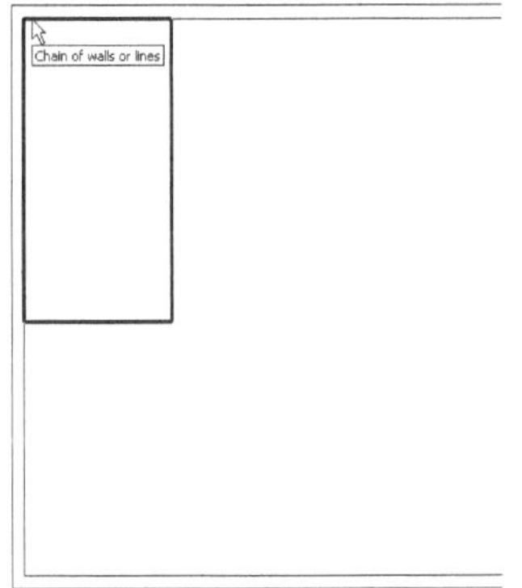

Figure 7-47 *Sketching the roof opening in the ceiling plan view*

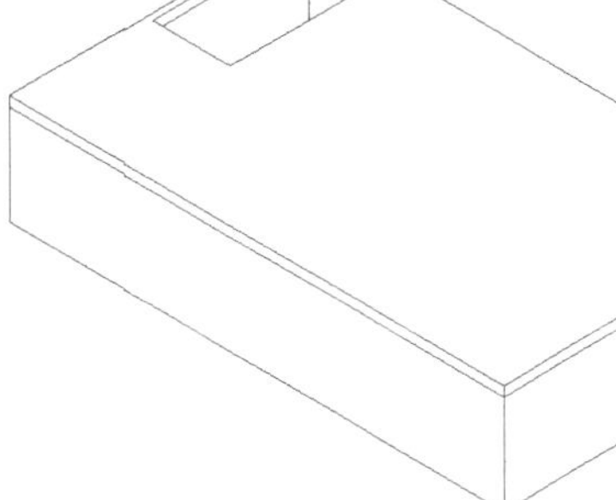

Figure 7-48 *Roof opening in the 3D view*

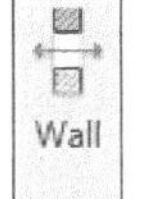

To create a rectangular opening in a wall, choose the **Wall** tool from the **Opening** panel in the **Architecture** tab; you will be prompted to select a wall. Select the wall in which you want to cut an opening and then sketch a rectangular opening of the required size by clicking and dragging the cursor.

To create a dormer opening in the dormer roof, choose the **Dormer** tool from the **Opening** panel; you will be prompted to select the roof in which you want to create a dormer opening. Select the roof; the screen will enter the sketch mode. Choose the **Pick Roof/ Wall Edges** tool from the **Pick** panel of the **Modify | Edit Sketch** tab and pick the boundary of the dormer to create the dormer opening. Next, choose the **Finish Edit Mode** button from the **Mode** panel; a dormer opening will be created.

Note

The boundary that you will pick for the dormer opening in a roof should be an edge of the selected roof, wall, or both, and should form a closed loop.

To cut an opening up to the entire height of a building, choose the **Shaft** tool from the **Opening** panel; the **Modify | Create Shaft Opening Sketch** tab will be displayed. Choose a suitable sketching tool from this tab to create an opening of the required shape. Next, choose the **Finish Edit Mode** button from the **Mode** panel; the opening will be created passing through the entire height of the building. Make sure that before sketching the opening, you select the required work plane and the view to sketch the opening.

You can also specify the levels that will be cut by the opening. It will help you to restrict the opening to a particular level. To specify the levels, select the opening; the **Modify | Shaft Openings** tab will be displayed. Select a level for the **Base Constraint** parameter in the **Properties** palette to start the opening. Next, select a level for the **Top Constraint** parameter to end the opening. The opening will be cut through the selected levels.

JOINING WALLS WITH OTHER ELEMENTS

In Autodesk Revit, walls are not attached to a floor and roof automatically. If needed, they can be attached using the **Attach Top/Base** tool. For example, using the **Attach Top/Base** tool, you can attach the structural layer of a wall to a floor without attaching its finish layer. Similarly, if you need to detach a wall, you can use the **Detach Top/Base** tool.

Using the Attach Top/Base and Detach Top/Base Tools

To attach walls to other elements, first select the walls to be attached; the **Modify | Walls** tab will be displayed. Next, choose the **Attach Top/Base** tool from the **Modify Wall** panel; the **Options Bar** will prompt you to choose whether you want to attach the element to the top or to the bottom of the wall. To attach the floor to the wall, select the **Base** radio button and to attach a roof or a ceiling, select the **Top** radio button. After selecting the required radio button, select the element(s) to be attached to the wall(s); they will be attached to the top/base of the selected wall(s) and the **Options Bar** will return to the previous options allowing you to attach or detach more elements to the already selected walls.

The wall attachment status can be checked from its instance properties. To do so, select the desired wall; the instance parameters of the selected wall will be displayed in the **Properties** palette. In this palette, the **Top is Attached** and **Base is Attached** instance parameters show the status of attachments for the selected walls, as shown in Figure 7-49. The selection of the check box corresponding to the **Top is Attached** parameter in the value column indicates that the selected wall is attached to an element at its top. Similarly, the selection of the check box displayed in **Value** column of the **Base is Attached** parameter indicates that the selected wall is attached to an element at its base. After you attach walls to other elements, you can detach them. To do so, invoke the **Detach Top/Base** tool from the **Modify** panel of the **Modify | Walls** tab. The usage of this tool is similar to the **Attach Top/Base** tool that has already been discussed.

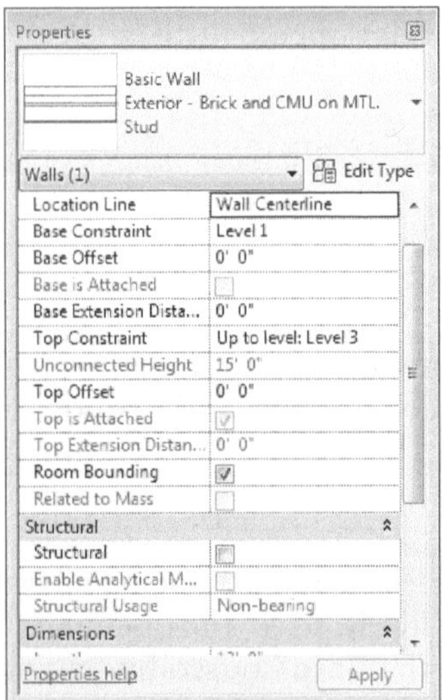

Figure 7-49 *Checking the status of attachments to walls in the* ***Properties*** *palette*

TUTORIALS

Tutorial 1 Apartment 1

In this tutorial, you will add a floor and a ceiling to the *c06_Apartment1_tut1.rvt* project created in Tutorial 1 of Chapter 6. Also, you will attach walls to the floor. To complete this tutorial, you need to use the following project parameters: **(Expected time: 30 min)**

1. Floor type -
   For Imperial **Floor: LW Concrete on Metal Deck**.
   For Metric **160mm Concrete With 50mm Metal Deck**
2. Ceiling type-
   For Imperial **Compound Ceiling: GWB on Mtl. Stud**,
   For Metric **Compound Ceiling: Plain**
   Level- 8'6" from the floor level.

   The following steps are required to complete this tutorial:

a. Open the required file.
b. Hide the annotation tags such as the section line, grids, and the elevation tag.
c. Create the floor using the **Floor** tool, refer to Figures 7-50 through 7-52.
d. Create the ceiling using the **Ceiling** tool, refer to Figures 7-53 and 7-54.
e. Attach walls to the floor.
f. Save the project using the **Save As** tool.
   For Imperial *c07_Apartment1_tut1.rvt*
   For Metric *M_c07_Apartment1_tut1.rvt*
g. Close the project.

Opening the Project File and Hiding Annotation Tags

To start with this tutorial, open the specified project file and then hide the annotation symbols and tags such as section line, grids, and elevation tags using the **Visibility/Graphics** tool.

1. Choose **Open > Project** from the **File** menu and then open the *c06_Apartment1_tut1.rvt* (*M_c06_Apartment1_tut1.rvt* for Metric) file created in Tutorial 1 of Chapter 6. You can also download this file from *http://www.cadcim.com*. The path of the file is as follows: *Textbooks > Civil/GIS > Revit Architecture> Exploring Autodesk Revit 2018 for Architecture*

2. Choose the **Visibility/Graphics** tool from the **Graphics** panel of the **View** tab; the **Visibility/ Graphics Overrides for Floor Plan: First Floor** dialog box is displayed.

3. Choose the **Annotation Categories** tab and clear the check boxes under the **Visibility** parameter for **Elevations**, **Grids**, and **Sections**.

4. Now, choose the **Apply** button and then the **OK** button; the specified settings are applied to the plan view and you return to the drawing window.

Creating the Floor

In the following set of steps, you will add floor to the apartment plan using the **Floor** tool.

1. Choose the **Floor: Architectural** tool from **Architecture > Build > Floor** drop-down; the **Modify | Create Floor Boundary** tab is displayed along with the **Options Bar**. Notice that the drawing area fades when you invoke the **Floor** tool, which indicates that you are in the sketch mode.

2. In the **Options Bar**, select the **Extend into wall (to core)** check box, if it is not selected. Also notice that the **Pick Walls** tool is chosen by default in the **Draw** panel.

3. Move the cursor near the center of the north wall of the apartment plan, and press the TAB key when the wall is highlighted.

4. When the chain of walls is highlighted, click to sketch the floor boundary; the boundary is sketched and appears as a magenta rectangle, as shown in Figure 7-50.

5. Choose the **Finish Edit Mode** button from the **Mode** panel to complete the sketching of the floor.

6. Next, you need to assign the type to the floor.
   Select the option from the **Type Selector** drop-down list in the **Properties** palette, as shown in Figure 7-51.

   For Imperial **Floor : LW Concrete on Metal Deck**
   For Metric **160mm Concrete With 50mm Metal Deck**

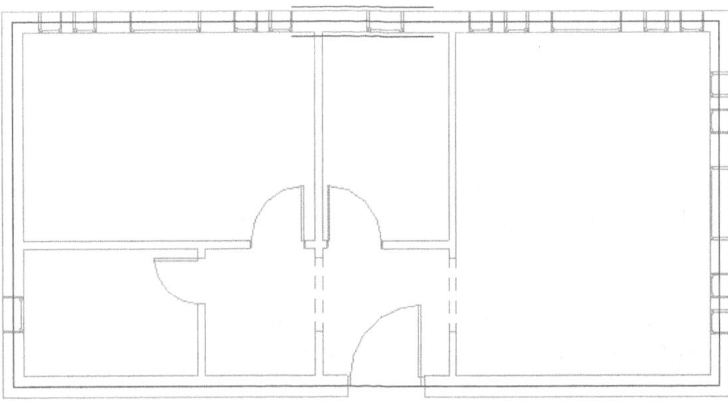

Figure 7-50 *The floor boundary sketched using the* ***Pick Walls*** *tool*

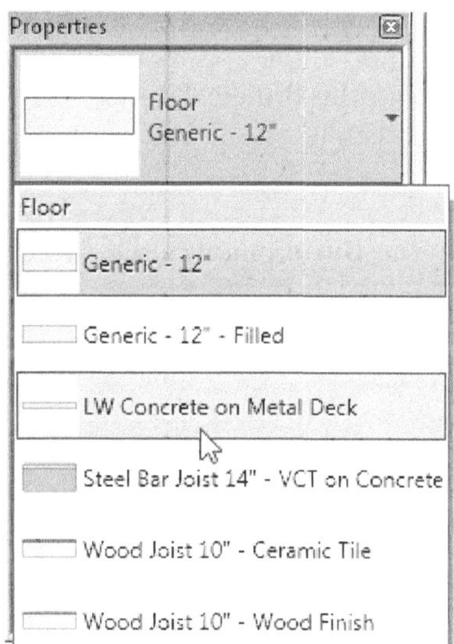

Figure 7-51 *Selecting the* ***LW Concrete on Metal Deck*** *floor type*

7. Choose the **Modify** button from the **Select** panel of the **Modify | Floor** tab to exit the **Floor: Architectural** tool. The floor is created for the *Apartment 1* project, as shown in Figure 7-52.

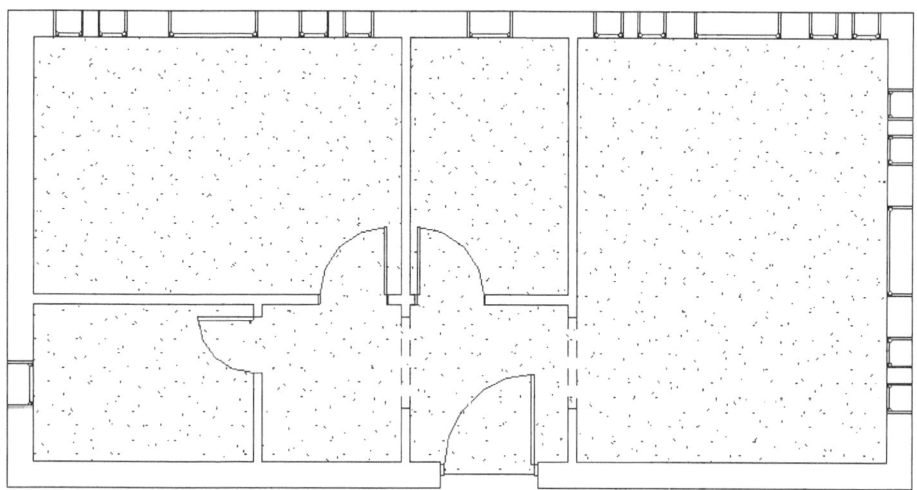

Figure 7-52 *The* ***LW Concrete on Metal Deck*** *type of the floor created*

Creating the Ceiling

After creating the floor for the apartment, you need to add a ceiling to it. For this you need to transform the current view to the ceiling plan view.

1. Double-click on **First Floor** from the **Ceiling Plans** head in the **Project Browser**.

As you open this view, you will notice the appearance of the annotation tags. Repeat steps 2, 3, and 4 given in the **Opening the Project File and Hiding Annotation Tags** section in this tutorial to hide various grids, elevation, window, and section tags from the first floor ceiling plan view.

2. Invoke the **Ceiling** tool from the **Build** panel of the **Architecture** tab; the **Modify | Place Ceiling** tab is displayed.

3. Click on the **Type Selector** drop-down list in the **Properties** palette and then select the desired option from it.

For Imperial	**Compound Ceiling : GWB on Mtl. Stud**
For Metric	**Compound Ceiling : Plain**

Next, you need to define the clear height of the ceiling.

4. In the **Properties** palette, click on the value field of the **Height Offset From Level** instance parameter and enter **8'6"(2590 mm)**. Then, choose the **Apply** button; the new height is assigned to the ceiling.

5. Move the cursor inside any room; the room boundary is highlighted. Now, click inside the highlighted boundary area; the ceiling is created. Notice that the created ceiling is not distinctly visible in the ceiling plan because the ceiling type selected has a plain GWB board finish.

6. Repeat step 5 to create individual ceilings for every room in the *Apartment 1* project. After creating all the ceilings, press ESC twice to view them in the 3D view of the project.

7. Click on the + symbol for the **3D Views** head in the **Project Browser** and double-click on **{3D}**; the 3D view of the apartment project with the created ceiling is displayed. You can move the cursor over the ceiling of any room to highlight it and display the ceiling type, as shown in Figure 7-53.

Attaching Walls to the Floor

In this section, you will use the **Attach** tool to attach walls to the floor so that you get a clear intersection between the floor and the wall. You need to use the section view to attach the floor.

1. Double-click on **Section X** in the **Project Browser**.

2. Now, move the cursor near the external wall that is cut in the section, and when it is highlighted, press TAB to highlight all the exterior walls.

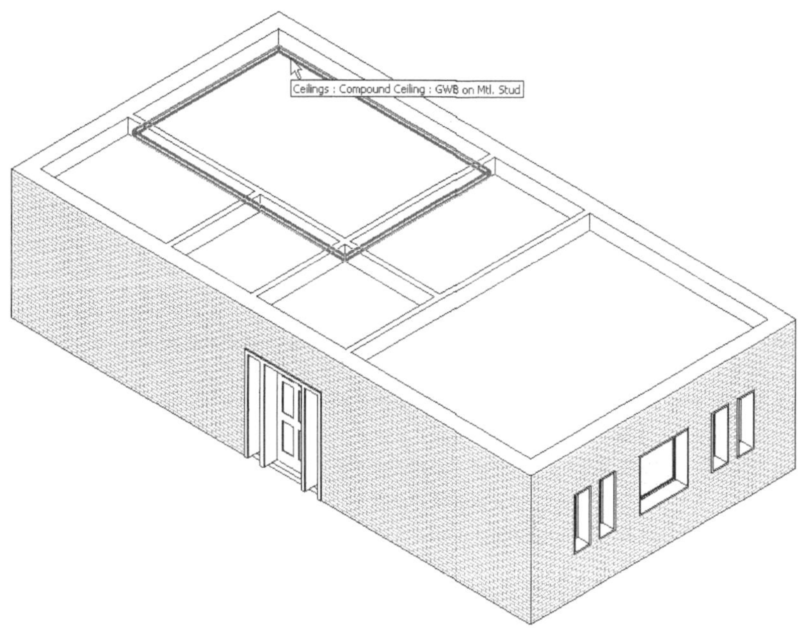

Figure 7-53 *Highlighting and displaying the ceiling type for bedroom*

3. Click to select the chain of exterior walls in the section view and then choose the **Attach Top/Base** tool from the **Modify Wall** panel of the **Modify | Walls** tab; the **Options Bar** is displayed.

4. From the **Options Bar**, select the **Base** radio button.

5. Move the cursor near the floor and click when it is highlighted; the floor is attached to walls, as shown in Figure 7-54.

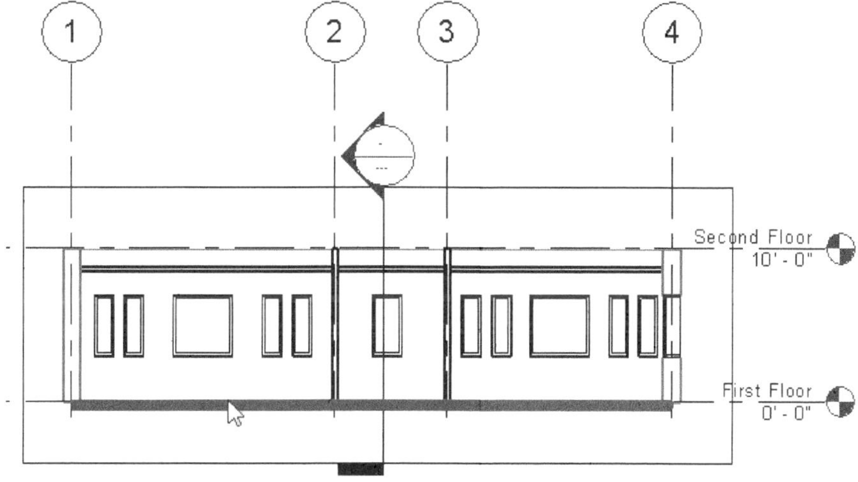

Figure 7-54 *Selecting the floor to attach it with the exterior walls*

6. Double-click on **First Floor** in the **Floor Plans** head in the **Project Browser**; the corresponding floor plan in the drawing window is displayed.

Note

In this section of the tutorial, as you attach walls with the floor, you may not find any difference in the wall and the floor intersections as compared to when they were not attached. To see the difference, attach the wall with the floor and then enter a positive value in the value column corresponding to the ***Height Offset From Level*** *instance parameter in the* ***Properties*** *palette.*

Saving the Project

In this section, you will save the project file using the **Save As** tool.

1. Choose **Save As > Project** from the **File** menu; the **Save As** dialog box is displayed. Enter required name in the **File name** edit box
   For Imperial **c07_Apartment1_tut1**
   For Metric **M_c07_Apartment1_tut1**
   Choose **Save**; the project file is saved.

2. Now, choose **Close** from the **File** menu to close the file.

Tutorial 2 Club

In this tutorial, you will add a floor, ceiling, and a roof to the *Club* project created in Tutorial 2 of Chapter 6. In this tutorial, you will also attach floor and ceilings to walls. Figure 7-55 shows a 3D View of the *Club* project after adding roofs and other elements. Use the following project parameters to complete this tutorial: **(Expected time: 30 min)**

1. Floor type -
   For Imperial **LW Concrete on Metal Deck.**
   For Metric **160mm Concrete With 50mm Metal Deck**
2. Ceiling type-
   For Imperial **Compound Ceiling: 2'x 2' ACT System**
   For Metric **Compound Ceiling: 600 x 600 mm Grid**
   Level- 11'0" from floor level.
3. Roof type for Hall 1 and Hall 2- Hip roof-
   For Imperial **Basic Roof: Insulation on Metal Deck-EPDM**
   For Metric **Basic Roof: Steel Bar Joist Steel Deck- EPDM Membrane**
   Roof shape for Hall 1 and Hall 2- Hip roof with Slope as 4"/12" (8.46 mm)
   Roof level for Hall 1 and Hall 2- Roof
   Roof type for Lounge-
   For Imperial **Basic Roof: Insulation on Metal Deck - EPDM**
   For Metric **Basic Roof: Steel Deck-EPDM Membrane**

   Roof shape for Lounge- Flat
   Roof level for Lounge- **Roof**; Base Offset from level **-1'4"(406 mm)**
   Overhang for all roofs- 4'0" (1220 mm) from the outer face of the exterior walls

The following steps are required to complete this tutorial:

a. Open the required project file.
   For Imperial *c06_Club_tut2.rvt*
   For Metric *M_c06_Club_tut2.rvt*
b. Hide the annotation tags such as section line, grids, and elevation tag.
c. Create the floor using the **Floor** tool, refer to Figure 7-56.
d. Create the ceiling using the **Ceiling** tool.
e. Create the roof using the **Roof by Footprint** tool, refer to Figures 7-57 through 7-63.
f. Attach all walls to the floor.
g. Save the project using the **Save As** tool.
   For Imperial *c07_Club_tut2.rvt*
   For Metric *M_c07_Club_tut2.rvt*
h. Close the project.

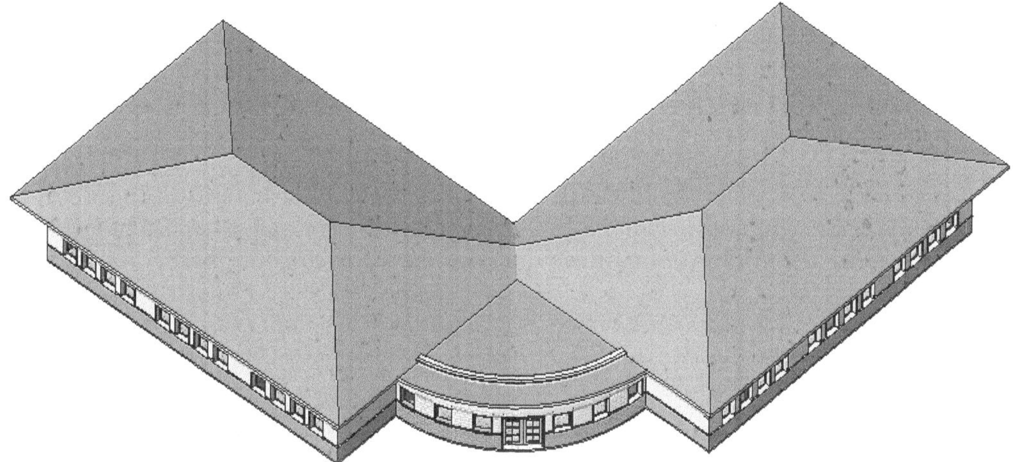

Figure 7-55 *Sketch view for adding roof to the Club project*

Opening the Project File and Hiding Annotation Tags

In this section, you will open the *Club* project that was created in Tutorial 2 of Chapter 6 and then hide annotation symbols and tags before you start creating floor, ceiling, and roof in the next section.

1. Choose **Open > Project** from the **File** menu and then open the *c06_Club_tut2.rvt* (*M_c06_Club_tut2.rvt* for Metric) file created in Tutorial 2 of Chapter 6. You can also download this file from *http://www.cadcim.com*. The path of the file is as follows: *Textbooks > Civil/GIS > Revit Architecture> Exploring Autodesk Revit 2018 for Architecture*

2. After the specified file is opened, ensure that the **First Floor** for the **Floor Plans** is the current view selected and then choose the **Visibility/Graphics** tool from the **Graphics** panel of the **View** tab; the **Visibility/Graphics Overrides for Floor Plan: First Floor** dialog box is displayed.

3. Select the **Annotation Categories** tab to open annotation categories.

4. Clear the check boxes under the **Visibility** parameter for **Elevations**, **Grids**, and **Sections** in the dialog box.

5. Choose **Apply** and then **OK** to apply the settings to the plan view and close the dialog box to return to the drawing window.

Creating the Floor

In the following steps, you will add a floor to the club plan using the **Floor** tool.

1. Invoke the **Floor: Architectural** tool from **Architecture > Build > Floor** drop-down; the **Modify | Create Floor Boundary** tab is displayed.

2. Ensure that the **Pick Walls** tool is chosen in the **Draw** panel. Clear the **Extend into wall (to core)** check box in the **Options Bar**.

3. Move the cursor near any exterior wall of the club building plan until it gets highlighted. When the exterior wall is highlighted, press the TAB key; all the exterior walls get highlighted and dashed lines appear in the walls indicating the extents of the floor.

4. When the chain of walls is highlighted, click to sketch the floor boundary. Ensure that the floor boundary line is sketched on the outer face of the exterior wall, as shown in Figure 7-56. If required, use the flip control to move the floor profile to the outer face

Note

While sketching the floor boundary, make sure it is in a closed loop. Else, a warning message will be displayed and the floor will not be created.

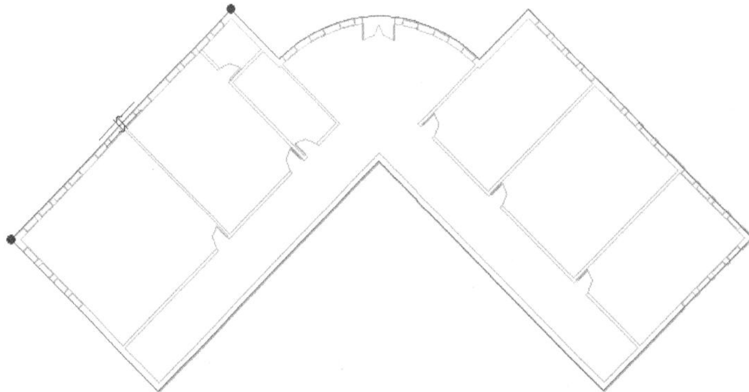

Figure 7-56 *The sketched floor boundary*

5. Now, finish the sketch of the floor by choosing the **Finish Edit Mode** button from the **Mode** panel.

6. Next, you need to assign a type to the floor.

In the **Properties** palette, select the desired option from the **Type Selector** drop-down list.

For Imperial **LW Concrete on Metal Deck**
For Metric **160mm Concrete With 50mm Metal Deck**

To exit from the **Floor: Architectural** tool, choose the **Modify** button from the **Select** panel.

Creating the Ceiling

In this section, you will add ceiling to the *Club* project in the ceiling plan using the **Ceiling** tool.

1. To change the project view to the ceiling plan.
   Double-click on the **First Floor** from the **Ceiling Plans** head of the **Project Browser**; the first floor ceiling plan is displayed in the drawing.

2. Now, assign a type to the ceiling.
   Invoke the **Ceiling** tool from the **Build** panel of the **Architecture** tab; the properties for the proposed ceiling are displayed in the **Properties** palette.

3. In the **Properties** palette, click on the **Type Selector** drop-down list and select the required option from it.
   For Imperial **Compound Ceiling: 2' x 2' ACT System**
   For Metric **Compound Ceiling: 600 x 600mm Grid**

4. Now, you need to assign height to the ceiling.
   In the **Properties** palette, click in the value field of the **Height Offset From Level** instance parameter and enter **11'0"(3353 mm)**. Then, choose the **Apply** button.

5. Now, move the cursor inside the building profile and notice that each space boundary is highlighted, when you move it inside the boundary.

6. Click inside each room to create the ceiling at the specified height. It appears as a square grid in the first floor ceiling plan.

Note
Sketch the ceiling for uneven room.

7. Press ESC to exit from the **Ceiling** tool.

Creating the Roof

In this section, first you will create the hip roof for Hall 1 using the **Roof by Footprint** tool and then similarly create roofs for the Lounge and the Hall 2 areas.

1. First, change the project view to the floor plan of the first floor.
   Double-click on **First Floor** from the **Floor Plans** head of the **Project Browser**; the floor plan of the first floor is displayed.

2. Invoke the **Roof by Footprint** tool from **Architecture > Build > Roof** drop-down.

3. In the **Options Bar**, select the **Defines slope** check box and enter **4'0"** (**1220 mm**) in the **Overhang** edit box.

4. Choose the **Pick Walls** tool, if not chosen, from the **Draw** panel of the **Modify | Create Roof Footprint** tab.

5. Move the cursor near the exterior wall of Hall 1, facing northwest, and click when the dashed line appears on the outer side, as shown in Figure 7-57. The roof boundary line is sketched.

6. Similarly, create boundary lines by using the other three exterior walls of Hall 1 at the same offset distance. The boundary lines are sketched, as shown in Figure 7-58.

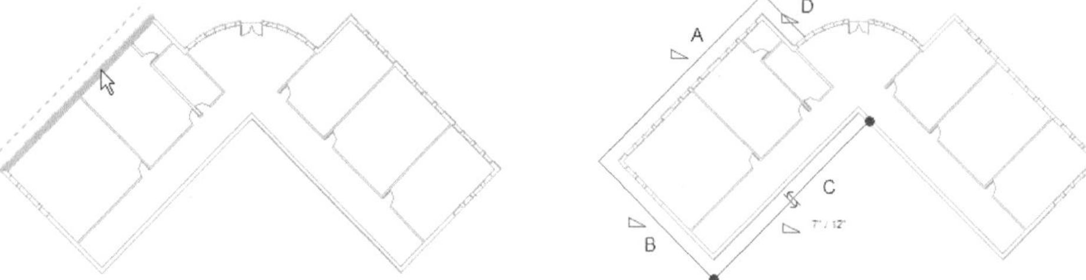

Figure 7-57 Sketching the roof profile *Figure 7-58 Completing the roof profile of Hall1*

7. Next, you need to join the boundary lines marked as C and D, refer to Figure 7-58. To do so, choose the **Trim/Extend to Corner** tool from the **Modify** panel of the **Modify | Create Roof Footprint** tab and select the two lines marked as C and D to complete the closed rectangular profile of the roof of Hall 1. After completing the profile, press the ESC key to exit the **Trim/Extend to Corner** tool.

8. In the **Properties** palette, click on the value column for the **Base Level** instance parameter and select **Roof** as the base level.

9. Next, click on the value column for the **Base Offset From Level** instance parameter and ensure that **0' 0"(0 mm)** is entered as the base level offset value. Then, choose the **Apply** button.

   To set appropriate slope for the hip roof, you must select the sketch boundary and then set its slope properties.

10. First select one of the four boundary lines, and then select the rest by using the CTRL key; the instance properties for the selected boundary lines are displayed in the **Properties** palette.

11. In the **Properties** palette, replace the current value present in the value column of the **Slope** instance parameter by entering **4" / 12"(18.46°)** as the new value of the pitch, as specified in the project parameters, and then choose the **Apply** button.

12. Next, choose the **Finish Edit Mode** button from the **Mode** panel of the **Modify | Create Roof Footprint** tab; the **Revit** message box is displayed.

13. In the message box, choose the **Yes** button to attach the highlighted walls to the roof.

14. Next, to assign a type to the created roof, select the desired option from the **Type Selector** drop-down list in the **Properties** palette.

    For Imperial **Basic Roof : Insulation on Metal Deck-EPDM**
    For Metric **Basic Roof : Steel Bar Joist Steel Deck-EPDM Membrane**

15. Double-click on **North** from the **Elevations (Building Elevation)** head in the **Project Browser** to view the roof, refer to Figure 7-59. Make sure the **Shaded** option is chosen in the **View Control Bar**.

Figure 7-59 *North elevation of the Club project with the created roof*

In the following steps, you will create a flat roof for the **Lounge** area of the Club building.

16. Double-click on **Roof** in the **Floor Plans** head of the **Project Browser**.

17. Invoke the **Roof by Footprint** tool from **Architecture > Build > Roof** drop-down.

18. In the **Options Bar**, clear the **Defines slope** check box.

19. Ensure that the **Overhang** edit box shows **4'0"(1220 mm)** as the overhang value.

20. Choose the **Wireframe** option from the **Visual Style** menu of the **View Control Bar**.

21. Now, move the cursor near the curved wall of the Lounge area. Click when the dashed line appears on the outer face of the wall to sketch the roof boundary curve, as shown in Figure 7-60.

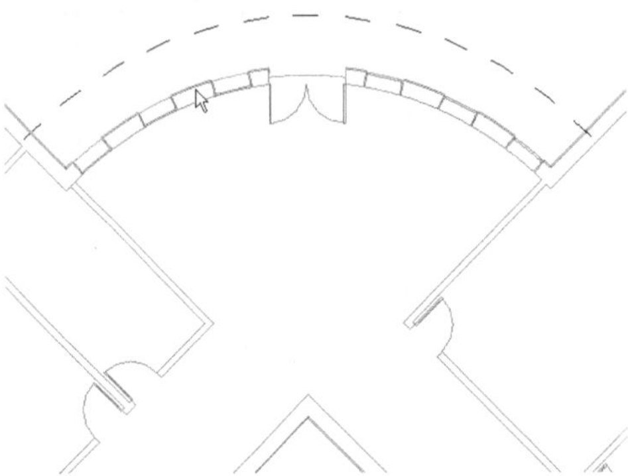

Figure 7-60 Sketching the curved roof profile

To sketch the other two lines for the Lounge roof, you need to use the **Line** tool from the **Draw** panel of the **Modify | Create Roof Footprint** tab.

22. Ensure that the **Boundary Line** tool is chosen in the **Draw** panel, and then choose the **Line** tool from the list box.

23. Clear the **Chain** check box in the **Options Bar**.

24. Ensure that the **Defines slope** check box in the **Options Bar** is cleared. Sketch the two lines to complete the boundary of the Lounge roof, as shown in Figure 7-61.

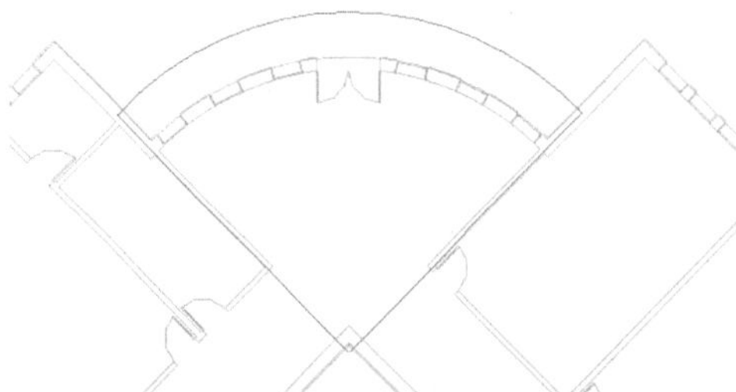

Figure 7-61 The completed roof profile of the Lounge

25. In the **Properties** palette, click on the value column for the **Base Level** instance parameter and ensure that the **Roof** option is selected from the drop-down list displayed.

26. Enter the value **-1'4" (-407 mm)** in the value column for the **Base Offset From Level** parameter as specified in the project parameter.

27. Choose the **Apply** button to apply the specified properties to the roof.

28. Next, choose the **Finish Edit Mode** button from the **Mode** panel of the **Modify | Create Roof Footprint** tab.

On choosing the **Finish Edit Mode** button; the **Revit** message box displays asking whether you would like to attach highlighted walls to the roof. Choose the **OK** button; the walls will be attached to the roof.

29. Next, to assign a type to the flat roof.
 Select the **Basic Roof : Insulation on Metal Deck-EPDM** option **Basic Roof : Steel Bar Joist Steel Deck-EPDM Membrane** from the **Type Selector** drop-down list in the **Properties** palette. Press **ESC** to exit from the **Floor: Architectural** tool.

 Now, you need to create roof for Hall 2. Since the roof of Hall 2 is identical to the roof of Hall 1, you can use the **Mirror-Draw Axis** tool to mirror the roof of Hall 1 to create the roof of Hall 2.

30. Double-click on **Roof** in the **Floor Plans** head in the **Project Browser** to display the roof plan of the club building.

31. Before you use the **Mirror-Draw Axis** tool, you need to display the grids in the drawing. Choose the **Visibility/Graphics** tool from the **Graphics** panel; the **Visibility/Graphic Overrides for Floor Plan : Roof Framing** dialog box is displayed.

32. Choose the **Annotation Categories** tab, select the **Grids** check box if it is not selected in the **Visibility** column, and then choose **OK**; the **Visibility/Graphic Overrides for Floor Plan : Roof Framing** dialog box is closed.

33. Now, select the roof of Hall 1; the **Modify | Roofs** tab is displayed.

34. Choose the **Mirror - Draw Axis** tool from the **Modify** panel; you are prompted to pick the start point for the axis of reflection.

35. Click at the point of intersection of the grids A2 and B2 to specify the start point for the axis.

36. Next, click at any point vertically up, as shown in Figure 7-62. Press ESC to exit the modification mode.

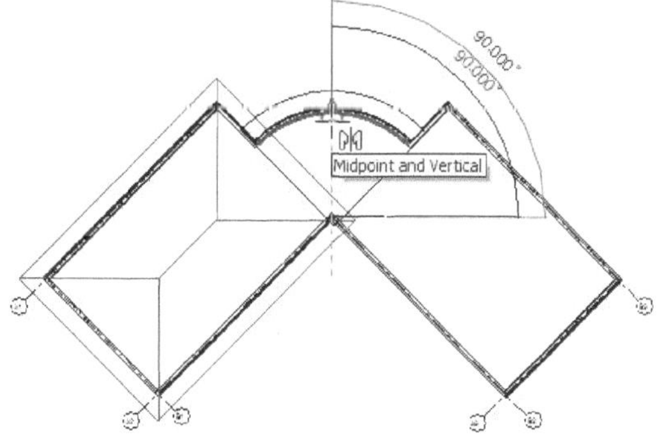

Figure 7-62 *Mirroring the roof of Hall 1*

37. Double-click on **North** in the **Elevations** node of the **Project Browser** to view the north elevation of the club building, as shown in Figure 7-63.

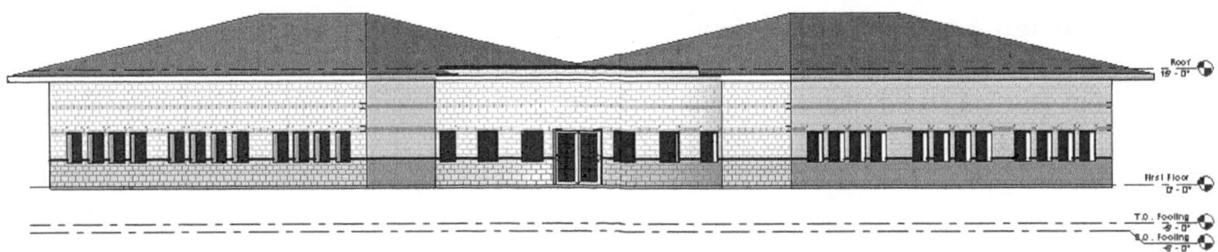

Figure 7-63 *North elevation of the Club project with the completed roof profile*

Attaching Walls to the Floor

While creating the roof, you have already attached the walls to its bottom. Now, you need to attach the walls to the floor using the **Attach** tool.

1. Double-click on **Section X** under the **Sections (Building Section)** head in this **Project Browser** to display the corresponding section view in the drawing window.

2. Move the cursor near the exterior wall, and when it is highlighted, press the TAB key; all the exterior walls get highlighted. Now, click to select the chain of exterior walls in the section view.

3. In the **Modify | Walls** tab, choose the **Attach Top/Base** tool from the **Modify Wall** panel; the options for attachment are displayed in the **Options Bar**.

4. Select the **Base** radio button in the **Options Bar**.

5. Next, move the cursor near the floor and click when it is highlighted; the walls get attached to the floor. Now, choose the **Modify** button from the **Select** panel to exit the modification tool.

   This completes the tutorial of creating floor, ceiling, and roof for the *Club* project.

6. Double-click on **First Floor** in the **Floor Plans** head of the **Project Browser** to display the first floor plan in the drawing window.

Saving the Project

In this section, you will save the project file using the **Save As** tool.

1. Choose **Save As > Project** from **the File** menu; the **Save As** dialog box is displayed. Enter required name in the **File name** edit box

   For Imperial **c07_Club_tut2**
   For Metric **M_c07_Club_tut2**

   Choose **Save**; the project file is saved.

2. Choose **Close** from the **File** menu to close the file.

Tutorial 3 Office

In this tutorial, you will add a floor and a ceiling to the *c06_Office_tut3.rvt* project created in Tutorial 3 of Chapter 6. To complete this tutorial, you need to use the following project parameters: **(Expected time: 30 min)**

1. Floor type -
   For Imperial **Floor: LW Concrete on Metal Deck.**
   For Metric **160mm Concrete With 50mm Metal Deck**
2. Ceiling type-
   For Imperial **Compound Ceiling: GWB on Mtl. Stud,**
   For Metric **Compound Ceiling: Plain**
   Level- 9' from the floor level.

   The following steps are required to complete this tutorial:

a. Open the required file.
b. Create the floor using the **Floor** tool, refer to Figures 7-64 and 7-66.
c. Create the ceiling using the **Ceiling** tool, refer to Figures 7-67.
d. Save the project using the **Save As** tool.
   For Imperial *c07_Office_tut3.rvt*
   For Metric *M_c07_Office_tut3.rvt*
e. Close the project.

Opening the Project File

To start with this tutorial, open the specified project file .

1. Choose **Open > Project** from the **File** menu and then open the *c06_Office_tut3.rvt* (*M_c06_Office_tut3.rvt* for Metric) file created in Tutorial 3 of Chapter 6. You can also download this file from *http://www.cadcim.com*. The path of the file is as follows: *Textbooks > Civil/GIS > Revit Architecture> Exploring Autodesk Revit 2018 for Architecture.*

Creating the Floor

In the following set of steps, you will add floor to the apartment plan using the **Floor** tool.

1 Choose the **Floor: Architectural** tool from **Architecture > Build > Floor** drop-down; the **Modify | Create Floor Boundary** tab is displayed along with the **Options Bar**. Notice that the drawing area fades when you invoke the **Floor** tool, which indicates that you are in the sketch mode.

2. In the **Options Bar**, select the **Extend into wall (to core)** check box, if it is not selected. Also notice that the **Pick Walls** tool is chosen by default in the **Draw** panel.

3. Select the rectangle tool from the **Draw** panel of the **Modify|Create Floor** Boundary Tab**.**

4. Create rectangle from the external face of the wall, as shown in Figure 7-64.

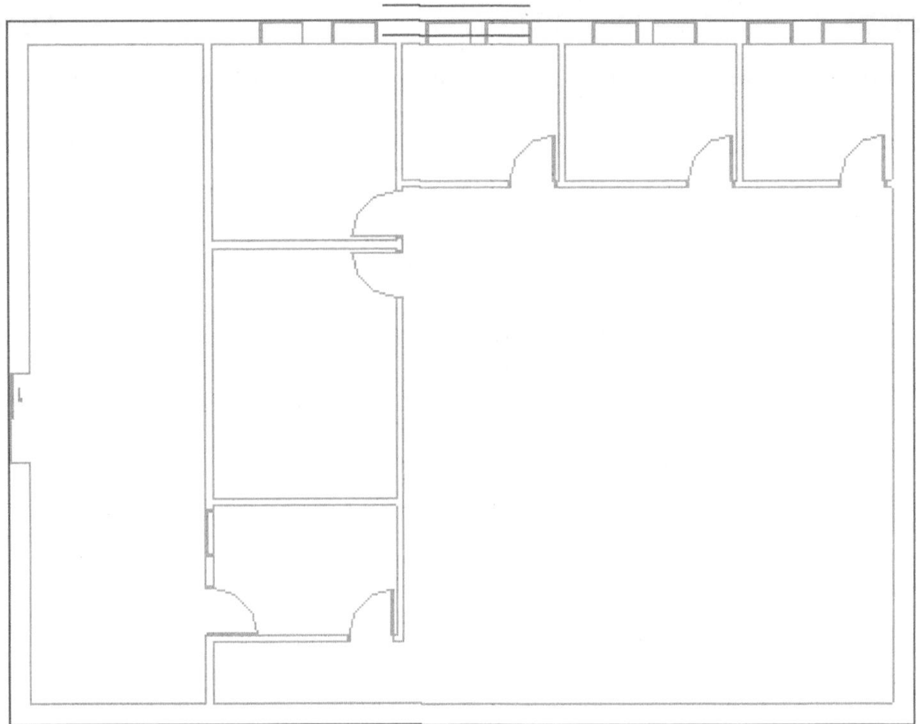

*Figure 7-64 The floor boundary sketched using the **Pick Walls** tool*

5. Choose the **Finish Edit Mode** button from the **Mode** panel to complete the sketching of the floor.

6. Next, you need to assign the type to the floor.

   Select an option from the **Type Selector** drop-down list in the **Properties** palette, as shown in Figure 7-65.

   For Imperial **Floor : LW Concrete on Metal Deck**
   For Metric **160mm Concrete With 50mm Metal Deck**

7. Choose the **Modify** button from the **Select** panel of the **Modify | Floor** tab to exit the **Floor: Architectural** tool. The floor is created for the *Office* project, as shown in Figure 7-66.

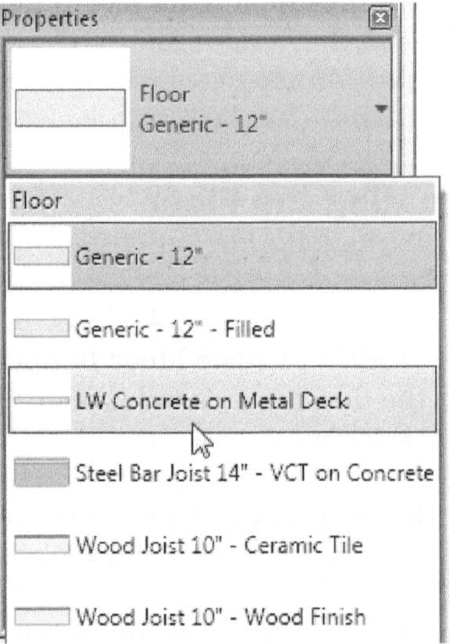

*Figure 7-65 Selecting the **LW Concrete on Metal Deck** floor type*

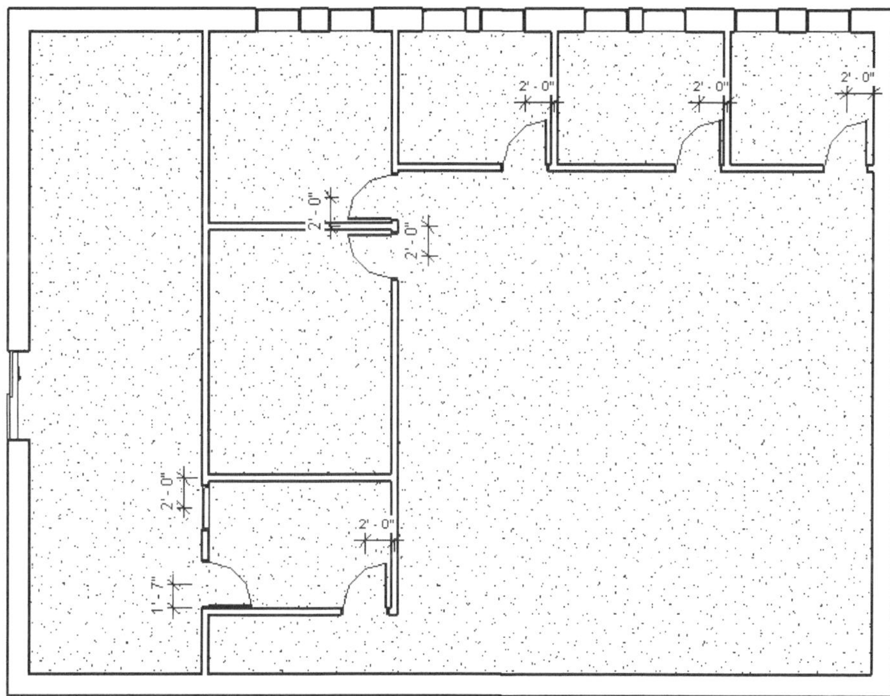

*Figure 7-66 The **LW Concrete on Metal Deck** type of the floor created*

Copying Floor to Upper Levels

You can now select floor and use the **Aligned to Selected Levels** tool to copy them to the upper levels. The following steps describe the general procedure for copying floor to different levels by using the **Aligned to Selected Levels** tool.

1. Double-click on the **North** elevation view and select the floor made at Ground Level.
2. Choose the **Copy to Clipboard** tool from the **Clipboard** panel of the **Modify | Multi-Select** tab.
3. Now, choose the **Aligned to Picked Level** tool from the **Modify | Floors > Clipboard > Paste** drop-down; the level symbol gets attached with the cursor.
4. Now, in the drawing area select the First Floor level; the floor is created at that level.
5. Similarly follow the step 2 and step 3 to copy the floor to the other levels.

Creating the Ceiling

After creating the floor for the apartment, you need to add a ceiling to it. You will use the **Ceiling** tool to create the ceiling for the apartment in the ceiling plan.

1. To start creating the ceiling, the first thing you need to do is to transform the current level view to the ceiling plan view of the ground floor.

Double-click on the **Ground Floor** from the **Ceiling Plans** head in the **Project Browser**.

2. Invoke the **Ceiling** tool from the **Build** panel of the **Architecture** tab; the **Modify | Place Ceiling** tab is displayed.
   For Imperial **Compound Ceiling : GWB on Mtl. Stud**
   For Metric **Compound Ceiling : Plain**
   Next, you need to define the clear height of the ceiling.

3. In the **Properties** palette, click on the value field of the **Height Offset From Level** instance parameter and enter **9' (2800 mm)**. Then, choose the **Apply** button; the new height is assigned to the ceiling.

4. Move the cursor inside any room; the room boundary is highlighted. Now, click inside the highlighted boundary area; the ceiling is created. Notice that the created ceiling is not distinctly visible in the ceiling plan because the ceiling type selected has a plain GWB board finish.

5. Repeat step 5 to create individual ceilings for every floor and for every room in the *Office* project. After creating all the ceilings, press ESC twice to view them in the 3D view of the project.

6. Click on the + symbol for the **3D Views** head in the **Project Browser** and double-click on **{3D}**; a 3D view of the office project with the created ceiling is displayed. You can move the cursor over the ceiling of any room to highlight it and display the ceiling type. The section view of ceiling is shown in Figure 7-67.

Saving the Project

In this section, you will save the project file using the **Save As** tool.

1. Choose **Save As > Project** from the **File** menu; the **Save As** dialog box is displayed. Enter required name in the **File name** edit box
   For Imperial **c07_Office_tut3**
   For Metric **M_c07_Office_tut3**
   Choose **Save**; the project file is saved.

2. Now, choose **Close** from the **File** menu to close the file.

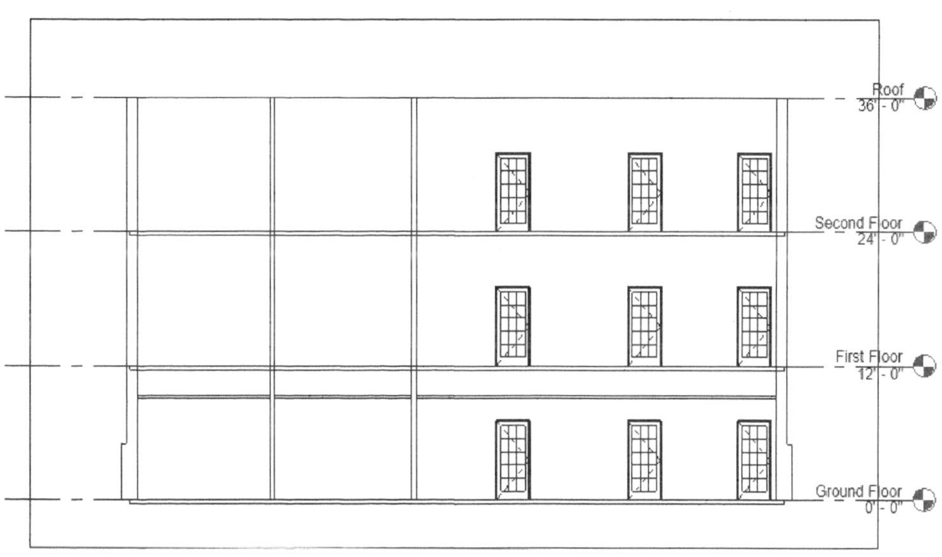

Figure 7-67 Sectional View of the ceiling created

Self-Evaluation Test

Answer the following questions and then compare them to those given at the end of this chapter:

1. When you model a roof, it gets automatically associated with a ________.

   (a) Level (b) Wall
   (c) View (d) Material

2. To define the extents of a room, you must use room bounding elements or room separation________.

   (a) Families (b) Parameters
   (c) Lines (d) Tags

3. Using the ________ drop-down list, you can select a ceiling type to be created.

4. The slope of a boundary line can be specified in the value column of the ________instance parameter.

5. You can use the ________ tool to create a roof profile by sketching its boundaries in a closed loop.

6. You can create an opening in a roof by using the ________ tool.

7. The ________ tool can be used to attach walls to a floor.

8. Floors once created cannot be modified. (T/F)

9. You can sketch a floor in the section view. (T/F)

10. You can use the shape editing tools to modify the horizontal surface of a floor. (T/F)

11. You can use the **Chain** tool to sketch the roof footprint. (T/F)

12. A floor is created even if the sketched profile is not closed. (T/F)

Review Questions

Answer the following questions:

1. Which of the following options can be used to convert a sloping roof to a flat roof?

   (a) **Opening** (b) **Slope**
   (c) **Join/Unjoin** (d) **Define Slope**

2. Which of the following options can be used to create a roof overhang?

   (a) **Define Slope** (b) **Offset**
   (c) **Overhang** (d) **Extend to wall core**

3. Which of the following tools can be used to limit the visibility of a datum in a view?

   (a) **Visibility/Graphics** (b) **Hidden lines**
   (c) **Scope Box** (d) **Steering Wheels**

4. When modeling a floor, the floor ________ must be a closed loop.

   (a) Type (b) Boundary
   (c) Slope (d) Function.

5. Which TWO statements about roof sketching methods are true?
   (a) A roof footprint is a 3D sketch of the perimeter of a roof.
   (b) You set the start and end points of a roof to determine the depth of the extrusion.
   (c) You can draw a footprint by sketching the profile of the top of the roof in an elevation or section view.
   (d) A roof footprint sketch must be a closed loop.

6. A reference plane can be used to provide guides for sketching a roof profile. (T/F)

7. You can modify the slope of a roof after it has been created. (T/F)

8. An automatic ceiling is generated with the center of the room as its center. (T/F)

9. You can create an opening in the ceiling using the **Cut** tool. (T/F)

10. You can select only the sloping side to create an opening perpendicular to its face. (T/F)

11. Walls can be attached to the floors using the **Join Geometry** tool. (T/F)

12. You cannot copy a floor, roof, or ceiling from one project to another. (T/F)

EXERCISES

Exercise 1 Apartment 2

Create a floor and a ceiling on the First Floor level of the *c06_Apartment2_ex1.rvt* (*M_c06_Apartment2_ex1.rvt* for Metric) project created in Exercise 1 of Chapter 6. Attach the walls to the floor. Use the following project parameters: **(Expected time: 30 min)**

1. Floor type -
   For Imperial **Floor: LW Concrete on Metal Deck**
   For Metric **160mm Concrete With 50mm Metal Deck**
   Extents to wall core.

2. Ceiling type-
   For Imperial **Compound Ceiling: GWB on Mtl Stud**
   For Metric **Compound Ceiling: Plain**
   Level- 8'6" (2591 mm) from the First Floor level.

3. Name of the file to be saved-
   For Imperial **c07_Apartment2_ex1**
   For Metric **M_c07_Apartment2_ex1**

Exercise 2 Elevator and Stair Lobby

Create a floor and ceiling on the First Floor level of the *c06_ElevatorandStairLobby_ex2.rvt (M_c06_ElevatorandStairLobby_ex2.rvt* for Metric*)* project created in Exercise 2 of Chapter 6. Attach the walls to the floor. Also, create openings in the floor and ceiling based on Figure 7-68. Use the following project parameters. Hide the grids and sections of the building and do not create the floor and ceiling in the elevator shafts. **(Expected time: 30 min)**

1. Floor type -
   For Imperial **LW Concrete on Metal Deck**
   For Metric **160mm Concrete With 50mm Metal Deck**
   Extents to wall core.

2. Ceiling type-
   For Imperial **GWB on Mtl Stud**
   For Metric **Plain**
   Level- 8'6" (2591 mm) from the floor level.
3. Name of the file to be saved-
   For Imperial **c07_ElevatorandStairLobby_ex2**
   For Metric **M_c07_ElevatorandStairLobby_ex2**

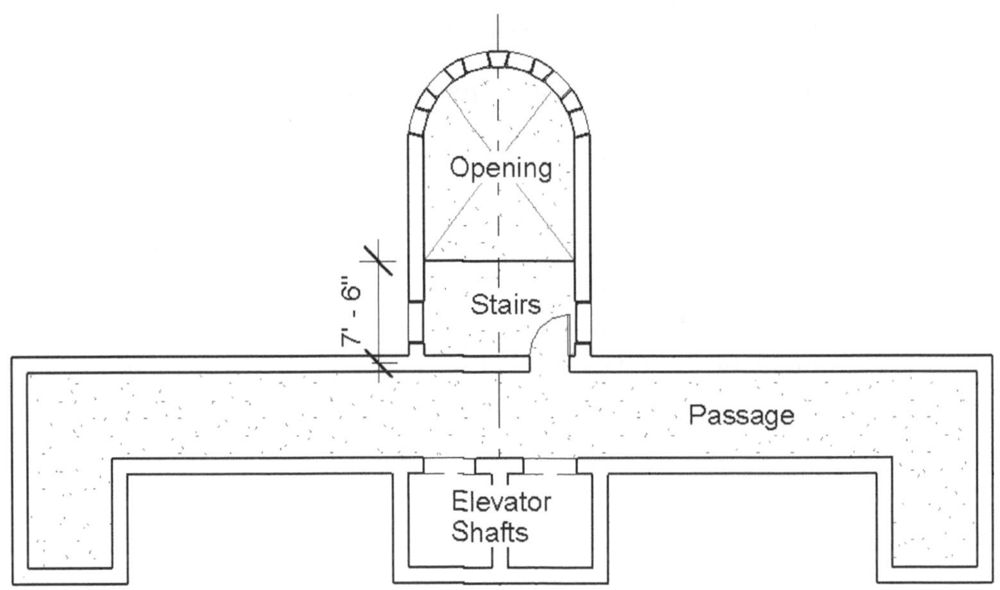

Figure 7-68 Sketch plan for creating an opening for the Elevator and Stair Lobby project

Exercise 3 Residential Building: Floor

Create a floor and ceiling on the Ground Floor level and then copy it to the First Floor level of the project created in Exercise 3 of Chapter 6. Attach the walls to the floor. Use the following project parameters. Hide the sections of the building. **(Expected time: 30 min)**

1. Floor type -
   For Imperial **Generic- 6" (Customized)**
   For Metric **Generic- 150mm**

2. Ceiling type-
   For Imperial **Generic**
   For Metric **Plain**
   Level- 8' (2400 mm) from the floor level.
3. Name of the file to be saved-
   For Imperial **c07_residential_floor_ex3**
   For Metric **M_c07_residential_floor_ex3**

Answers to Self-Evaluation Test

1. a, **2.** c, **3. Type Selector**, **4. Slope**, **5. Roof by Extrusion**, **6. Opening**, **7. Attach Top/Base**, **8.** F, **9.** F, **10.** T, **11.** T, **12.** F

Chapter 8

Using Basic Building Components-III

Learning Objectives

After completing this chapter, you will be able to:

- *Add components to a building model*
- *Create stairs using the Stairs tool*
- *Add railings to various locations in a project using the Railing tool*
- *Understand the procedure of adding ramps to a building model*
- *Add curtain walls with doors and mullions*
- *Copy elements from one level to another*

INTRODUCTION

This chapter describes the usage of building elements such as freestanding components, stairs, railings, ramps, and curtain walls. In addition, the chapter discusses how to copy elements to different levels.

USING COMPONENTS IN A PROJECT

Autodesk Revit provides various freestanding components that can be placed in a project. These include furniture items, plumbing fixtures, electrical fittings, trees, and many other family elements. Unlike other dependent elements, these freestanding components do not have any predefined associativity with other elements. However, it enables you to assign certain restrictions to their placement.

Adding Components

Ribbon:	Architecture > Build > Component drop-down > Place a Component
Shortcut Key:	CM

You can add components to a building model using the **Place a Component** tool. This tool can be invoked from the **Build** panel. On invoking this tool, the **Modify | Place Component** tab will be displayed. You can use the options in this tab to select the component type and specify the properties of the component to be inserted, load components from the predefined library, or create a new component in the drawing. Alternatively, type **CM** to invoke the **Place a Component** tool.

Revit provides different in-built component types. You can select them from the **Type Selector** drop-down list in the **Properties** palette, as shown in Figure 8-1. You can also load additional component types from the **US Imperial** folder. To do so, choose the **Load Family** tool from the **Mode** panel of the **Modify | Place Component** tab; the **Load Family** dialog box will be displayed. In this dialog box, browse to the **US Imperial** folder and select the required component from the specific sub-folder. After you select the required component and close the **Load Family** dialog box, the selected component will be added in the **Type Selector** drop-down list.

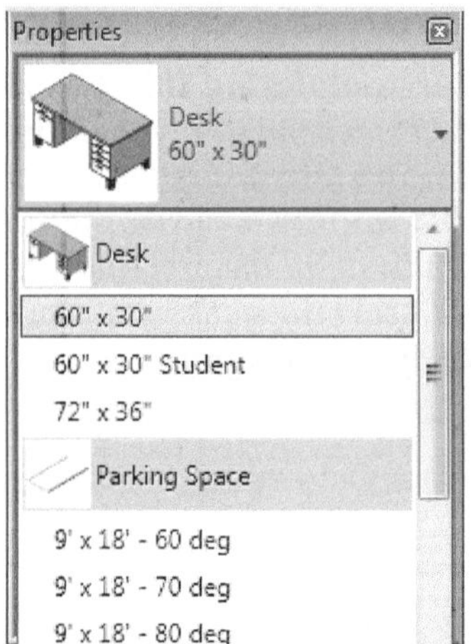

***Figure 8-1** The **Type Selector** drop-down list displaying different component types*

After selecting the component from the **Type Selector** drop-down list, select the **Rotate after placement** check box in the **Options Bar**, so that you can rotate the component after placing it. Now, move the cursor to the area where you want to add it. You will notice a component symbol attached to the cursor. Moreover, the temporary dimensions will display the distance of the component from the nearby elements. To place the component, click at the desired location; the temporary dimensions will be highlighted. Click on the appropriate dimension to enter a new value; the component will move to a new distance. As you have selected the **Rotate after placement** check box, the **Rotate** tool will be invoked when you add a component in the project. You can then rotate it graphically. To understand the concept of adding components, consider an example.

If you need to add a kitchen sink to a kitchen layout plan, choose the **Place a Component** tool from **Architecture > Build > Component** drop-down; the **Modify | Place Component** tab will be displayed. In this tab, choose the **Load Family** tool from the **Mode** panel; the **Load Family** dialog box will be displayed. In this dialog box, the **US Imperial** folder with a list of sub-folders will be opened. Select the **Plumbing** sub-folder and choose the **Open** button; the files of different family types of plumbing fixtures will be displayed in the selected sub-folders. Select the desired file and choose the **Open** button; the **Load Family** dialog box will close and the selected family type will be added to the **Type Selector** drop-down list. As you add the component to the **Type Selector** drop-down list, it gets selected automatically. Now, when you move the cursor to the floor plan of the kitchen, an image of the sink will be attached to it and the temporary dimension will appear, as shown in Figure 8-2. Click to add the sink at the appropriate location, as shown in Figure 8-3. Invoke the **Modify** tool from the **Select** panel to exit this tool.

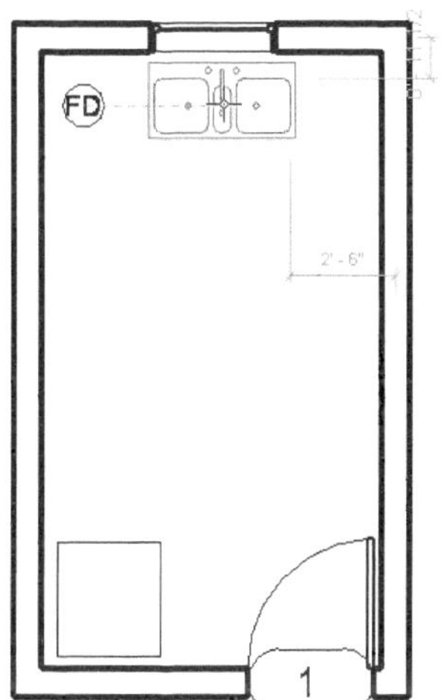

Figure 8-2 *Adding a component using the temporary dimension*

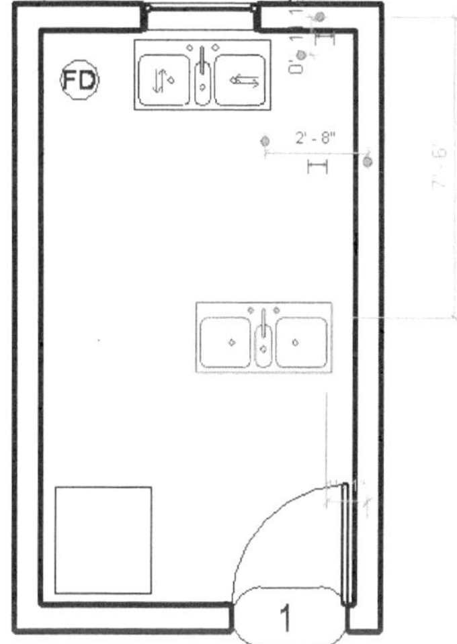

Figure 8-3 *The added component with its controls and temporary dimensions*

After you have inserted the desired component in the drawing, you can lock its position with certain elements such as walls. To do so, select the component inserted; the **Options Bar** will be displayed. In **Options Bar**, you can select the **Moves With Nearby Elements** check box to lock the position of the selected component to the nearest element displayed around it. For example, the sink can be locked to its supporting wall by selecting it and then selecting the **Moves With Nearby Elements** check box in the **Options Bar**. The component is locked to the nearby wall. Now, the kitchen sink will move with the wall, as shown in Figure 8-4. Figure 8-5 shows the new location of the sink. The component can, however, be moved freely in its plane of insertion.

You can create components that are specific to a project requirement. For example, while designing the interior of an office space, you may require different shapes and type of workstations to be inserted in your drawing. Therefore, to create and add different types of workstation cubicles, you can use the **Model In-Place** tool. Invoke this tool from **Architecture > Build > Component** drop-down; the **Family Category and Parameters** dialog box will be displayed. Select the desired family category from the list available in the **Family Category** area and then choose the **OK** button. On doing so, the **Name** dialog box will be displayed. In this dialog box, enter a name in the **Name** edit box and then choose **OK**; the dialog box will be closed and the **Family Editor** interface will be opened. You can use various tools from the ribbon in this interface to create in-place models and then specify their datum and in-place properties. After you create the in-place model, choose the **Finish Model** button from the **In-Place Editor** panel in the **Create** tab.

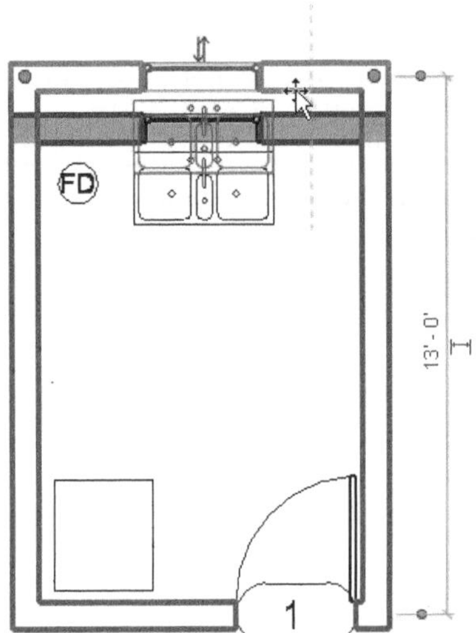

Figure 8-4 Moving the wall with the locked sink

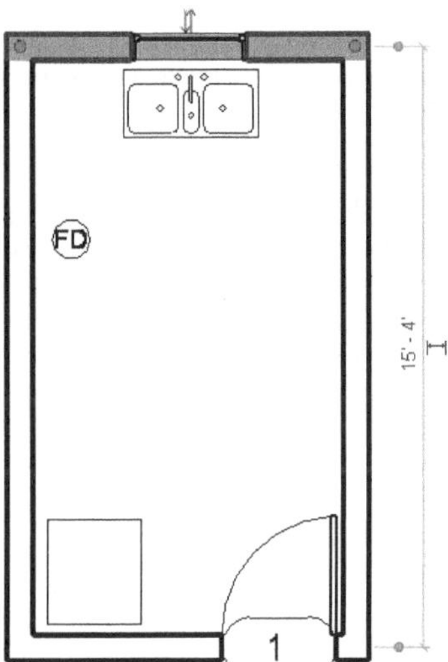

Figure 8-5 Resulting wall and the moved sink

After you place a component in the drawing, you can modify its instance and type properties. To do so, select a component from the drawing; the **Modify <Family Category>** tab will be displayed and the instance properties for the selected component of a specific family category will be displayed in the **Properties** palette. In this palette, various instance parameters such as level, information about the host, phases created and demolished and so on are displayed with their current values, as shown in Figure 8-6. In this palette, you can modify the current values of various parameters to the desired values. The value of the **Level** parameter indicates the current level on which the component is placed. To change the current value of this parameter, click on its corresponding value field and select the new level from the drop-down list to move the selected component to the new level. Other parameters in the instance parameters table depend on the component selected. Various instance parameters of the components can be modified using this table. In the **Properties** palette, you can also view and modify the type properties of the selected component.

Choose the **Edit Type** button in this palette; the **Type Properties** dialog box will be displayed, as shown in Figure 8-7. In the **Type Parameters** area of this dialog box, you can view the parameters and then modify them. Alternatively, you can display the **Type Properties** dialog box by choosing the **Type Properties** tool from the **Properties** panel of the **Modify < Family Category>** tab.

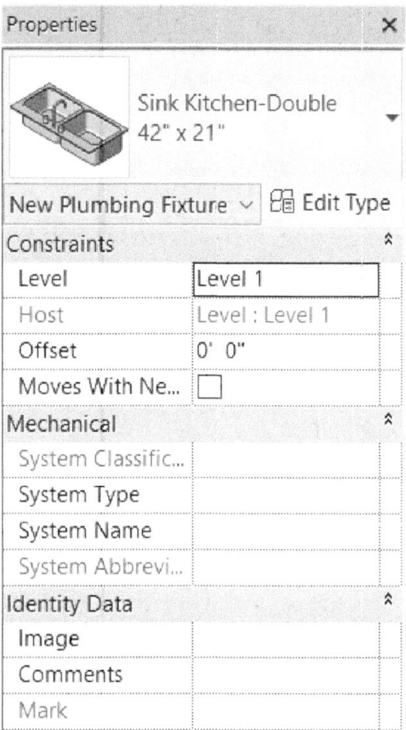

Figure 8-6 Instance parameters in the ***Properties*** *palette for the component* ***Sink Kitchen-Double 42" x 21"***

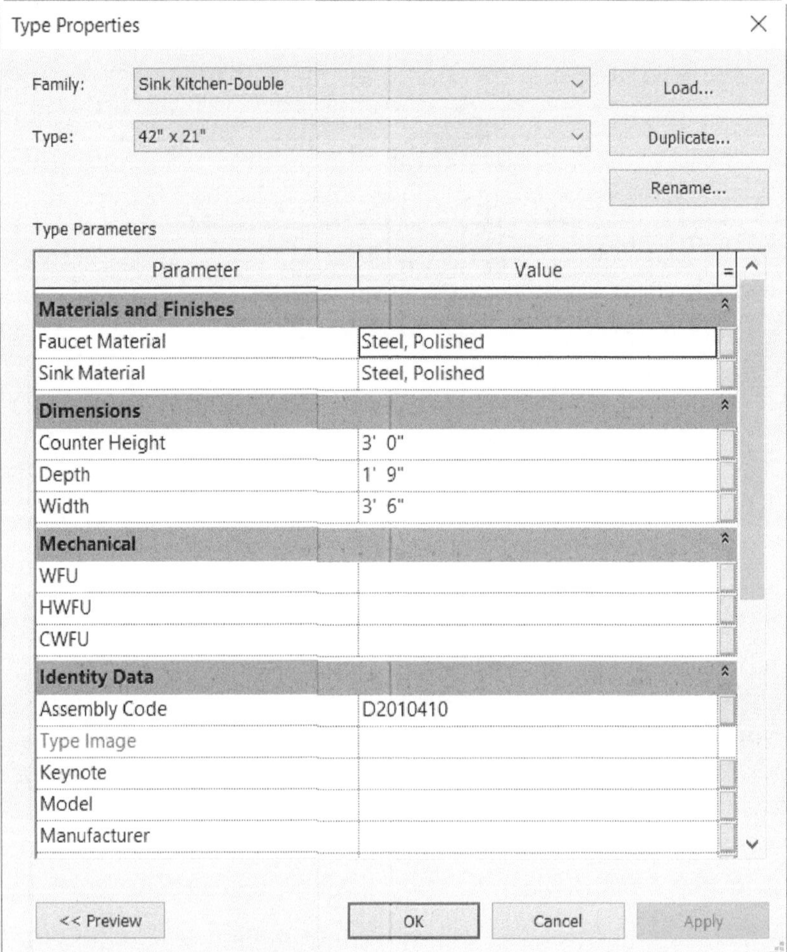

Figure 8-7** The **Type Properties** dialog box for the component **Sink Kitchen-Double 42" x 21"

ADDING STAIRS

Ribbon:	Architecture > Circulation > Stair

In Autodesk Revit, you can create a variety of stair shapes such as straight, curved, and spiral stairs with ease. In Revit, stairs are parametric elements; therefore, you can create them by specifying the rules for risers, treads, and stringers. You can create stairs in your building design both in the plan and 3D views.

In Autodesk Revit, stairs can be added in individual components, such as Run, Landing, and Supports. To do so, invoke the **Stair** tool from the **Circulation** panel; the **Modify | Create Stair** tab will be displayed. In the **Component** panel of this tab, you can choose the **Run**, **Landing**, or **Support** tool based on the requirement. Some of these tools are discussed next.

Run Tool

You can use the **Run** tool to create a run of a stair. To create the run of stair, invoke the **Stair by Component** tool from the **Circulation** panel; the **Modify | Create Stair** tab will be displayed. In the **Components** panel of this tab, ensure that the **Run** tool is chosen. As a result, a list of tools to create the stair run is displayed in the list box displayed in the **Components** panel. The list box contains the **Straight**, **Full-Step Spiral**, **Center-Ends Spiral**, **L-Shape Winder**, **U-Shape Winder**, and **Create Sketch** tool. Some of these tools are discussed next.

Straight Tool

This tool is used to create a stair run with a straight flight. This tool can be invoked from the **Component** panel of the **Modify | Create Stair** tab. As you invoke the **Straight** tool, various options related to the creation of a straight run are displayed in the **Options Bar**. The **Location Line** drop-down list in the **Options Bar** is used to specify the reference line for creating the stairs. You can select the following options from the drop-down list: **Exterior Support: Left**, **Run: Center**, **Run: Left**, **Run: Right**, and **Exterior Support: Right**. The **Run: Center** option is selected by default. To offset the stair run from the specified reference line, you can specify the offset value in the **Offset** edit box. In the **Options Bar**, enter a value in the **Actual Run Width** edit box to specify the run width for stairs. The **Automatic Landing** check box in the **Options Bar** is selected by default. As a result, the landing will be created at the turn between the flight. If you clear this check box, the landing will not be created. You need to specify the instance parameters of the stair run in the **Properties** palette. Select an option from the **Type Selector** drop-down list to specify the type of the stair. Click in the **Value** field corresponding to the **Base Level** parameter and select an option from the displayed drop-down list to assign the level to the base of the stair. You can specify an offset distance by which the base of the stair will be offset from the selected level. To specify the offset value, click in the **Value** field corresponding to the **Base Offset** parameter and enter a value. Similarly, you can set the level and offset distance for the top of the stair by selecting a desired option for the **Top Level** parameter and by specifying a desired value to the **Top Offset** parameter. In the **Properties** palette, the other parameters that you can specify for the stair are **Multistory Top Level**, **Desired Number of Risers**, **Actual Tread Depth**, **Tread/Riser Start Number**, and so on. After specifying the desired parameters, you can start creating the stair in the drawing view. To do so, click in the drawing window to specify the start point of the run. On doing so, a stair run will start from the desired point and the preview of the stair run will be displayed along with the cursor, as shown in Figure 8-8. Next, click again at a desired point to specify the endpoint of the stair run. On specifying the endpoint, the stair run will be created, as shown in Figure 8-9. To finish the stair creation, choose the **Finish Edit Mode** button from the **Mode** panel of the **Modify | Create Stairs** tab. Now, you can view the three-dimensional view of the created stair, refer to Figure 8-10, by choosing the **Default 3D View** tool from the **Create** panel of the **View** tab.

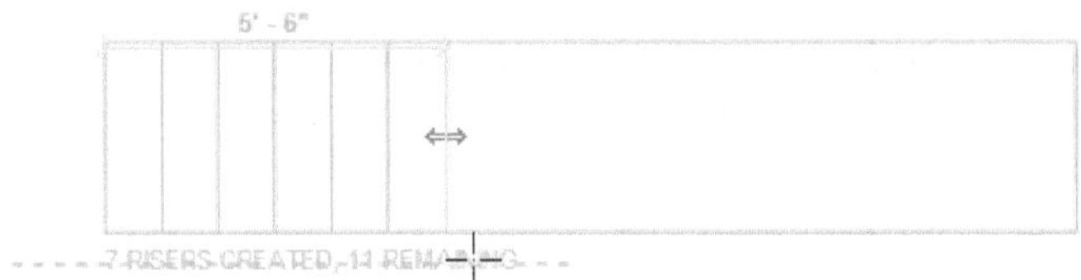

Figure 8-8 *Preview of the stair run on specifying the start point*

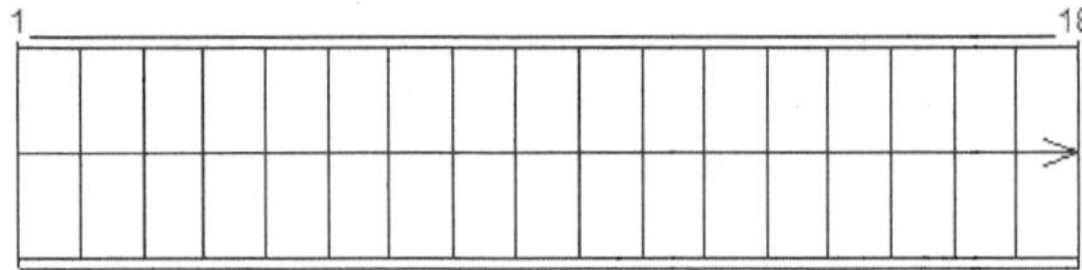

Figure 8-9 *The straight stair run created on specifying the endpoint*

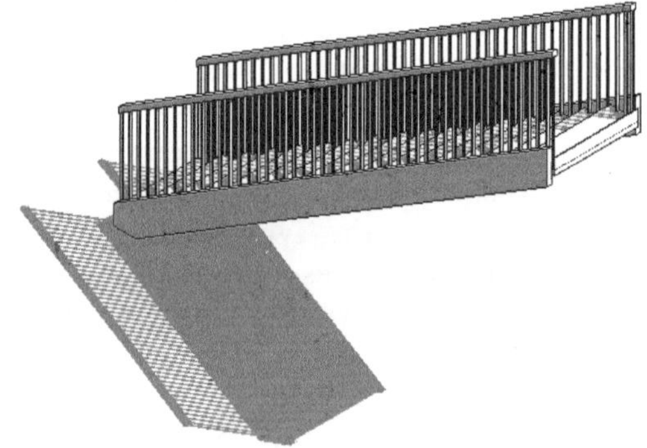

Figure 8-10 *The three-dimensional view of the straight stairs*

Full-Step Spiral Tool

You can use this tool to create a spiral run by specifying its start point and the center. To create a spiral run, choose this tool from the **Components** panel of the **Modify | Create Stair** tab; you will be prompted to specify the center of the stair. Click at the desired location in the drawing area to specify the center of the spiral stair. On doing so, the preview of the spiral stair will appear with cursor. You can move the cursor away from the specified center of the spiral stair and click at desired point to specify the radius of the stair. On doing so, the spiral stair will be created at the specified center, as shown in Figure 8-11. Choose the **Finish Edit Mode** button from the **Mode** panel of the **Modify | Create Stair** tab to complete the creation of the spiral stair.

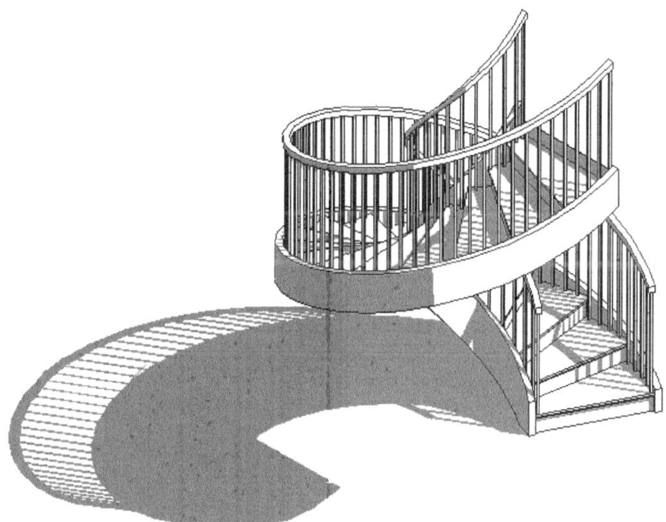

Figure 8-11 The three-dimensional view of the spiral stairs

Center-Ends Spiral Tool

This tool helps to create a spiral run that is less than 360 degrees by specifying the center point, start point, endpoint, and the direction of the turn. To create a spiral run by using this tool, choose the **Stair by Component** tool from the **Stair** drop-down in the **Circulation** panel; the **Modify | Create Stair** tab will be displayed. Next, choose the **Center-Ends Spiral** tool from this tab; you will be prompted to specify the center of the stair. Click in the drawing area to specify the center; a preview of the stair will be displayed. Next, click to specify the start point of the stair; you will be prompted to specify the end point. Click in the desired location to complete the stair creation. Note that the turn of the stair can be changed and the end point can be specified on the side where the turn of the stair is be placed. The process of creating a spiral stair by using the **Center-Ends Spiral** tool has been illustrated in Figure 8-12 through 8-15.

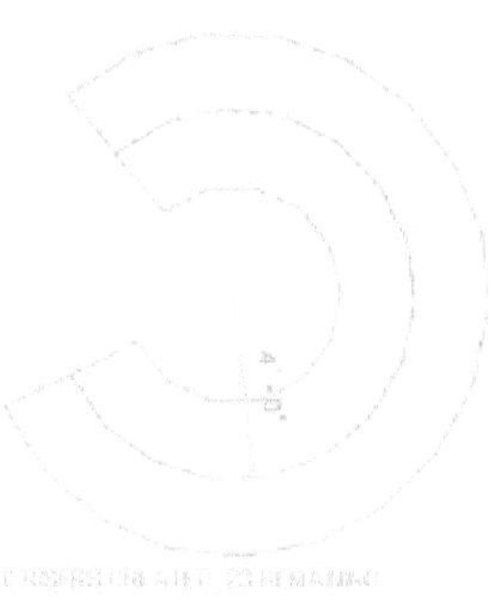

Figure 8-12 Specifying the center of the spiral stairs

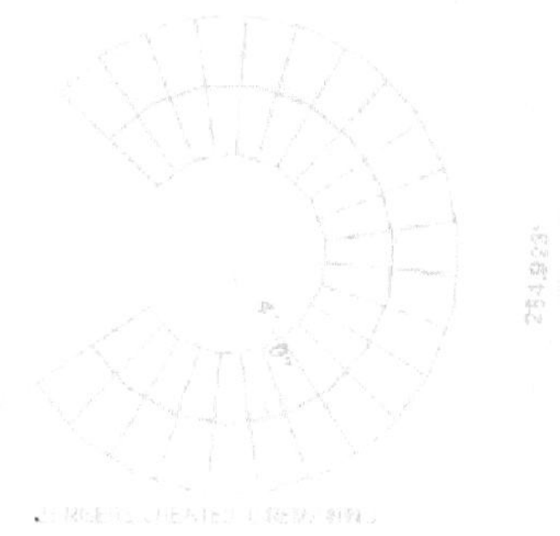

Figure 8-13 Specifying the start point of the spiral stairs

L-Shape Winder Tool

This tool in the **Component** panel of the **Modify|Create Stair** tab helps you to create a L-shape stair with a winder. The winder in a stair consists of steps at the turn that are narrower on one side. These steps are placed to change the direction of landing. The L-shape winder can be created by specifying the start point of the run at the lower end. You can also change the direction of the run by pressing SPACEBAR.

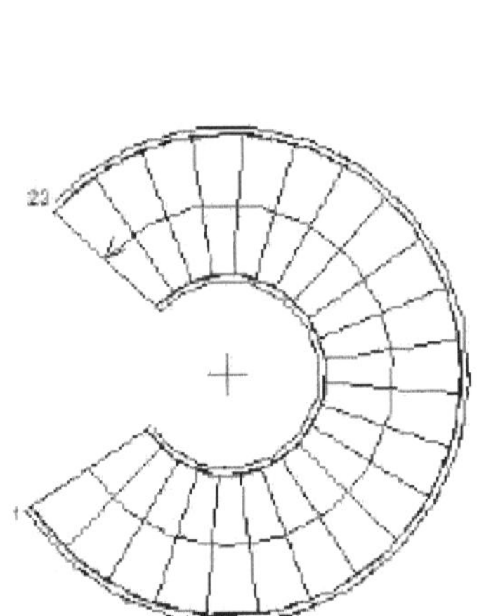

Figure 8-14 *Specifying the turn of the spiral stairs*

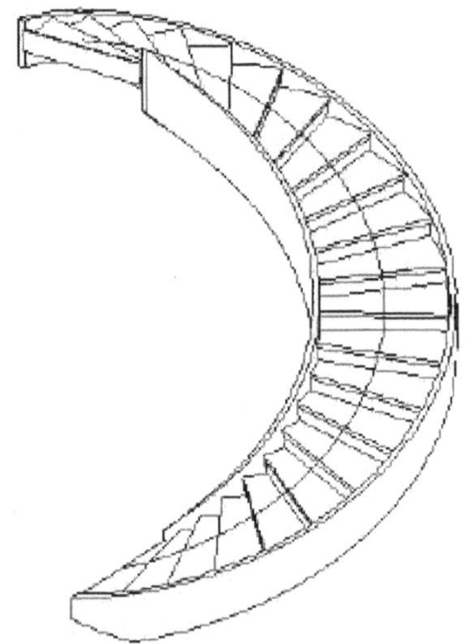

Figure 8-15 *Three dimensional view of the spiral stairs using the* ***Center-Ends Spiral*** *tool*

U-Shape Winder Tool

You can use this tool to create a U-shape stair with winders at turn. To create such stairs, invoke this tool from the **Components** panel of the **Modify | Create Stair** tab, a preview of the U-shape stairs will be displayed in the drawing area. Also, various options and properties of the stairs will be displayed in the **Options Bar** and the **Properties** palette, respectively. In the **Options Bar**, you can select an option from the **Location Line** drop-down list to specify the reference line for the stair. In the **Relative Base Height** edit box, enter a value to specify the height of the base of the stair run relative to its base level. In the **Options Bar**, you can select the **Mirror Preview** check box to flip the start and end of the stair run to be added to the drawing. Figure 8-16 and Figure 8-17 show plans of a U-shape stair created with the **Mirror Preview** check box cleared and selected, respectively.

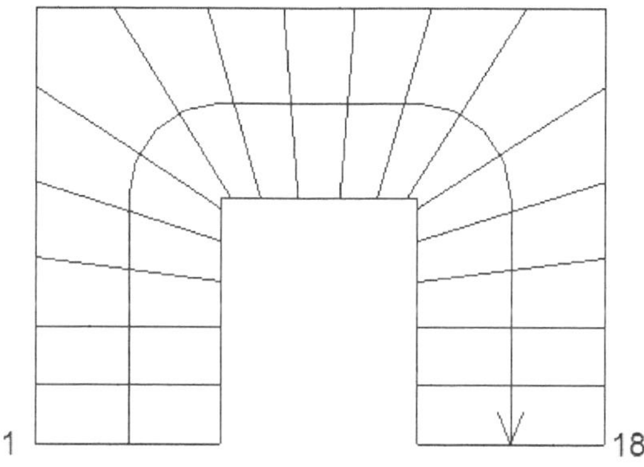

Figure 8-16 *The U shaped winder stair run created with the* ***Mirror Preview*** *check box cleared*

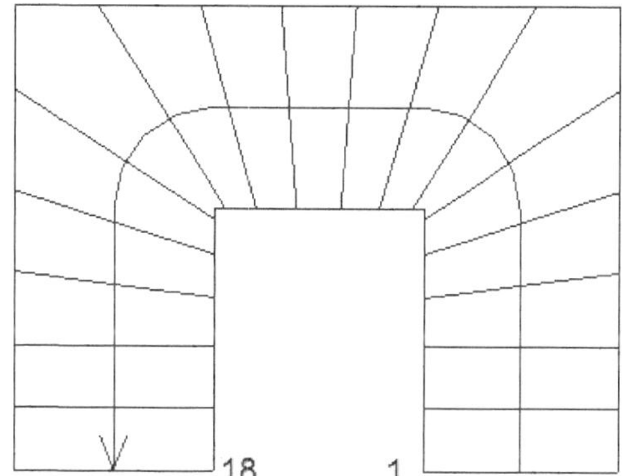

Figure 8-17 *The U shaped winder stair run created with the* ***Mirror Preview*** *check box selected*

In the **Properties** palette, you can select a stair type from the **Type Selector** drop-down list. You can also specify the parameters for setting the base level, actual depth of the tread, desired number of risers, start number for tread or riser, and so on. Now, click in the desired point in the drawing area, the U-shape stair with winder will be added in the project view. In the **Mode** panel of the **Modify | Create Stair** tab, choose the **Finish Edit Mode** button to finish the creation of stair run.

Landing Tool

This tool is used to create a landing between two runs. To create landing, choose the **Stair by Component** tool from **Architecture > Circulation > Stair** drop-down; the **Modify| Create Stair** tab will be displayed. From the **Components** panel of this tab, choose the **Landing** tool; the **Pick Two Runs** and **Create Sketch** tools are displayed in the list box next to it. You can use the **Pick Two Runs** tool to create a landing by selecting two runs of a stair. On invoking this tool, you will be prompted to select the first run. Click on the first run of the stair; the stair run will be selected and highlighted, as shown in Figure 8-18. Also, you will be prompted to select the second stair run. Click on the second stair run; a landing will be created between the first and second stair runs, as shown in Figure 8-19.

Alternatively, you can use the **Create Sketch** tool in the **Components** panel to create a custom based landing by sketching it in the project view. When sketching a landing using this tool, you need to define the boundary and the stair path. The stair path defines the walk line or the direction of the landing in the stair. Invoke the **Create Sketch** tool from the list box in the **Components** panel; the **Modify | Create Stair > Sketch Landing** tab will be displayed. In the **Draw** panel of this tab, you can use the **Boundary** and **Stairs Path** tools to define the boundary of the landing and path of the stair, respectively. To create the boundary of the landing, choose the **Boundary** tool from the **Draw** panel, if it is not chosen by default. On doing so, various tools to sketch the boundary of the landing will be displayed next to the **Boundary** tool. You can choose a tool or a combination of the tools as per requirement of the project. As you sketch the boundary of the landing, you need to specify options related to the sketching tool you have chosen in the **Options Bar**. Also, you need to specify various properties of the landing in the **Properties** palette. You can specify the height at which the landing will be created. To do so, enter a desired value in the value field of the **Relative Height** parameter. The value entered for this parameter will be measured in reference to the base of the stair. Now, create the boundary of the landing using the desired sketching tools. Next, choose the **Stairs Path** tool from the **Draw** panel to define the path of the stair run. Figure 8-20 shows a sketched boundary and the stair path of the landing. Now, choose the **Finish Edit Mode** button from the **Mode** panel to finish the sketching of the landing and the stair path; the landing between the runs will be created and the **Modify | Create Stair** tab will be displayed. In this tab, you can choose the **Edit Sketch** tool from the **Tools** panel to modify the sketch of the landing. Now, choose the **Finish Edit Mode** button from the **Mode** panel to exit the stair creation mode. Figure 8-21 displays a three-dimensional view of a stair run with a custom sketched landing.

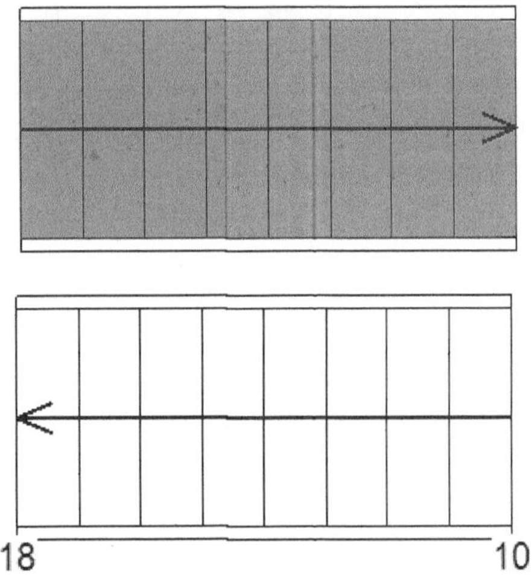

***Figure 8-18** The first stair run highlighted*

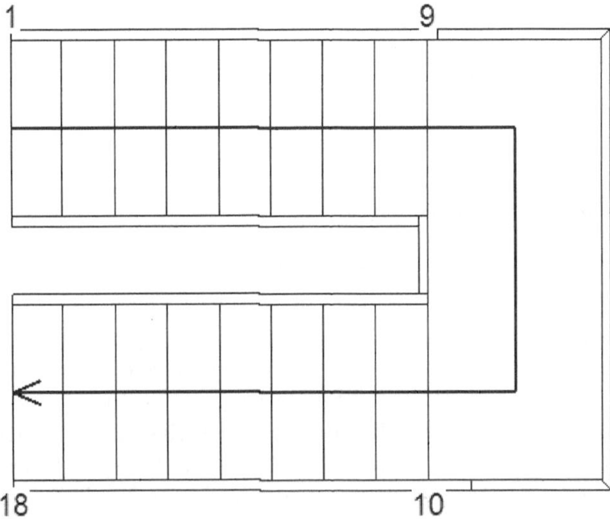

***Figure 8-19** Landing created between the first and second stair run*

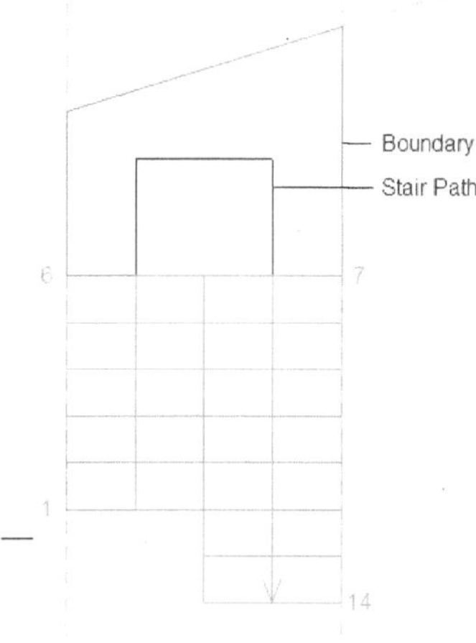

Figure 8-20 *Sketched boundary and the stair path of a landing*

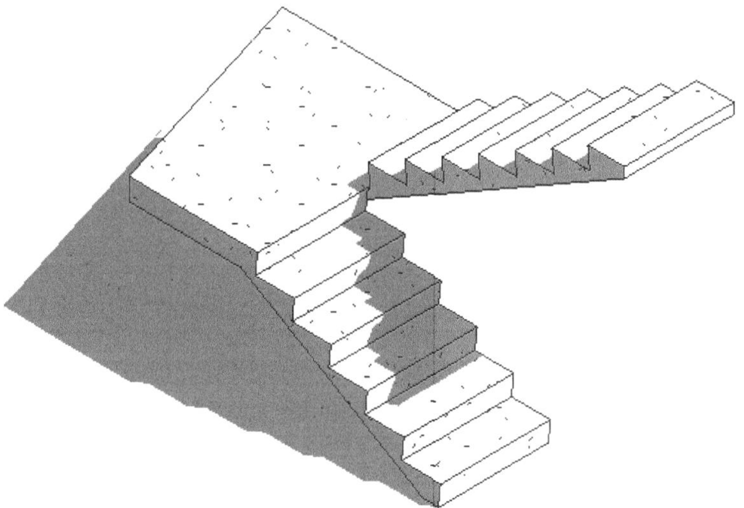

Figure 8-21 *Three-dimensional stair runs with custom based landing*

Support Tool

You can use this tool to add a stringer or a carriage by selecting an individual path on a run or landing. Invoke this tool from the **Components** panel of the **Modify | Create Stair** tab; you will be prompted to pick the edge of a stair run or landing to place the support. Choose the **Finish Edit Mode** button from the **Mode** panel; the support will be added to the stairs run, as shown in Figure 8-22.

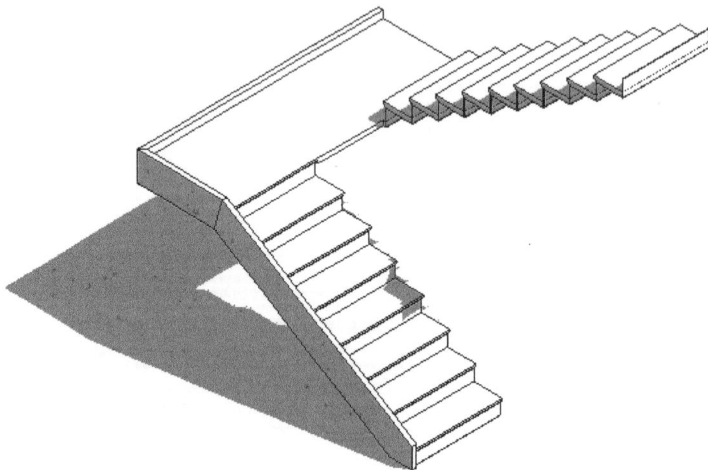

Figure 8-22 Support added to the stair runs

Connect Levels Tool

You can use the **Connect Levels** tool to create stairs that continue from the base level to the upper level of a multistory building. After creating a staircase at one level, invoke this tool from the **Multistory Stairs** panel of the **Modify/Create Stair** tab; the **Go To View** dialog box will be displayed, as shown in Figure 8-23. In this dialog box, you can choose the required view and then choose the **Open View** button; the selected view will be displayed. In the elevation view, select the levels upto which you want to create the staircase. Next, choose the **Finish Edit Mode** button from the **Mode** panel; the staircase is created upto the desired level. Figure 8-24 shows an example of staircase created upto 5th level.

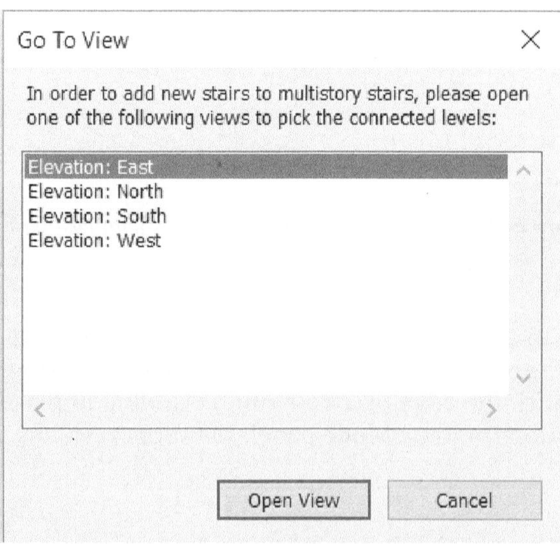

Figure 8-23 The ***Go To View*** *dialog box*

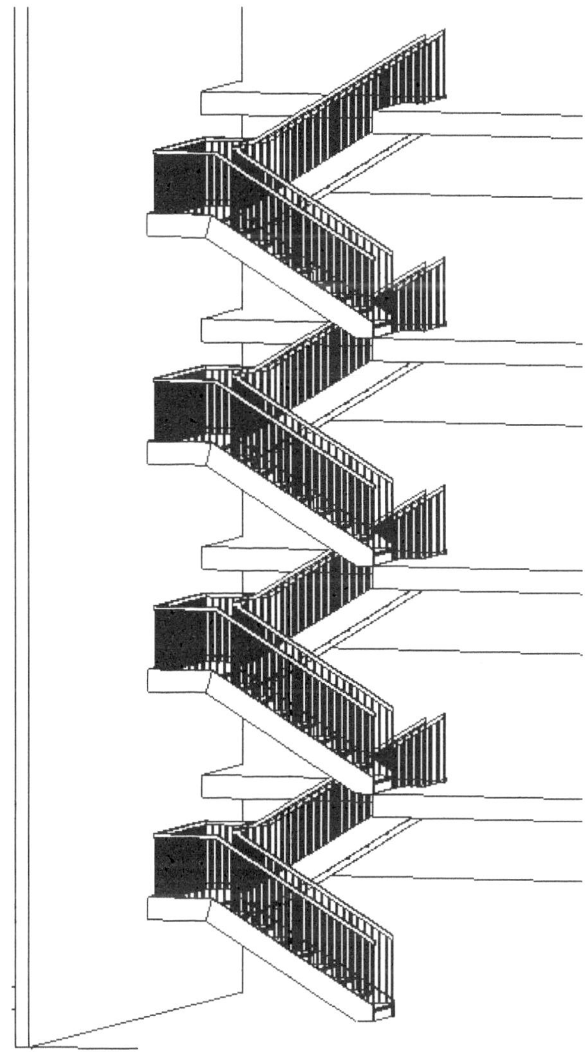

Figure 8-24 The 3D view of the staircase

Modifying Stairs Properties

You can specify the properties of stairs before creating them and then you can modify its properties. To modify the stairs after you create them, select the stairs; the properties of the stairs will be displayed in the **Properties** palette, as shown in Figure 8-25. In the **Properties** palette, the **Base Level** parameter indicates the level from which the stairs will start, and the **Top Level** parameter indicates the level at which they will end. By default, the current level is set as the base level, and the next story level is set as the top level.

The parameters under the **Dimensions** section are used to specify different dimensional parameters for the stairs. You can determine the number of risers in the stairs by specifying a value in the **Value** column of the **Desired Number of Risers** parameter. In the **Value** column for the **Actual Tread Depth** parameter, you can specify a value for the depth of the treads in a stair. Other instance parameters can also be modified in the **Properties** palette.

You can choose the **Edit Type** button from the **Properties** palette for viewing and modifying the type properties. On choosing this button, the **Type Properties** dialog box will be displayed, as shown in Figure 8-26. In the **Type Properties** dialog box, you can choose the **Edit** button for specifying the calculation rules. When you choose this button, the **Stair Calculator** dialog box will be displayed. This dialog box can be used to set new rules to calculate the slope of the stairs. In the **Type Properties** dialog box, you can enter the **Minimum Tread Depth**, **Minimum Run Width** and the **Maximum Riser Height** in their corresponding value columns. Other type parameters that can also be specified in the **Type Properties** dialog box include **Tread Thickness**, **Riser Thickness**, **Nosing Length**, and so on. The **Monolithic Stairs** check box can be selected to create the stairs made up of only a single material.

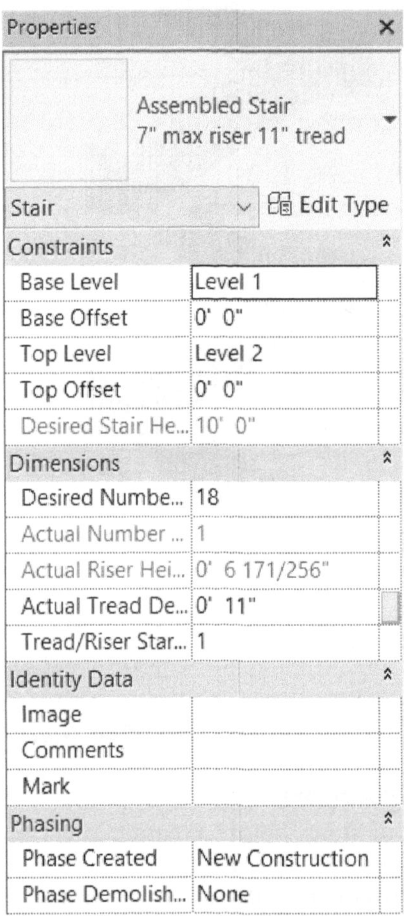

Figure 8-25 *The* ***Properties*** *palette displaying various instance properties of the selected stairs*

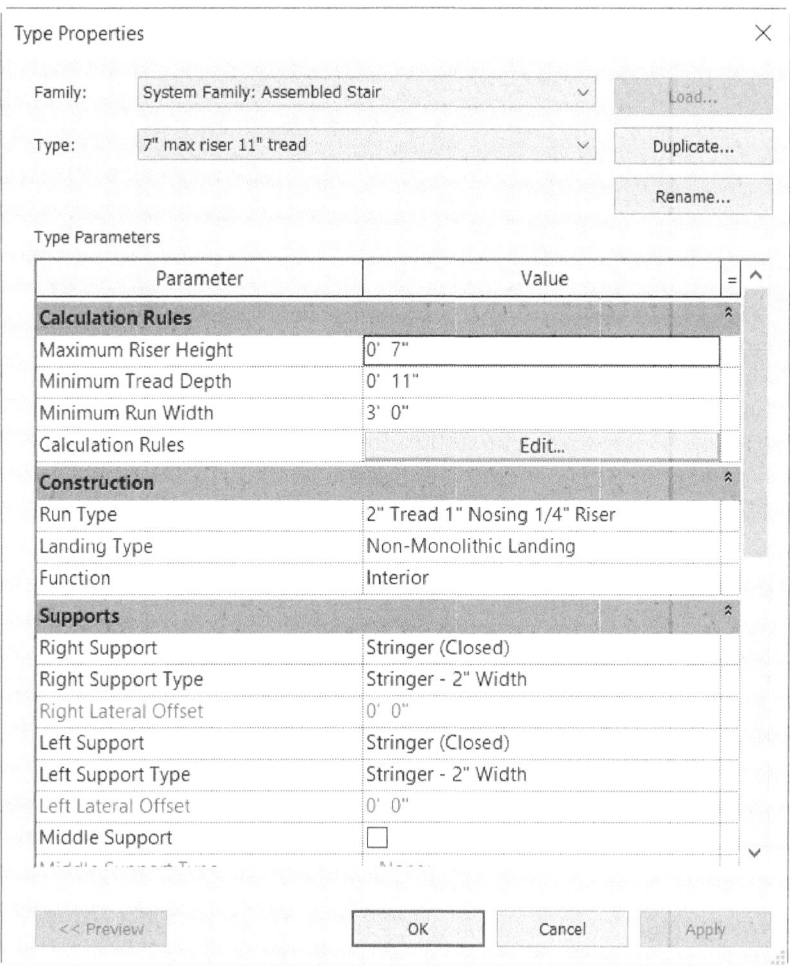

*Figure 8-26 The **Type Properties** dialog box for stairs*

Tip

You can experiment with different types and instance properties to create the required stairs.

Note

*While creating stairs, you can specify the type of railings that will be attached to it. To do so, choose the **Railings Type** tool from the **Tools** panel of the **Modify / Create Stairs Sketch** tab; the **Railings Type** dialog box will be displayed. Select the railings type from the drop-down list and choose the **OK** button to confirm the selection.*

Tip

1. *The instance and type parameters depend on the selected component type. Revit empowers you to modify these parameter(s) as per requirement.*

2. *The rules and calculations set in the **Stair Calculator** dialog box are only applicable if they are set before the creation of the stairs. You cannot modify the rules of the created stairs using this dialog box.*

ADDING RAILINGS

Enhanced

Railings are automatically generated with the stairs but they can also be created by specifying their profile. You can also create them for other locations in the building project such as terraces, passages, and so on. You can select and modify their properties to achieve the desired railing configuration. In Revit, you can add railing by sketching its path or by placing it in a stair or a ramp in the project. The methods of adding a railing by sketching a path and placing it on a host such as stair and ramp are discussed next.

Adding Railings by Sketching the Path

Ribbon: Architecture > Circulation > Railing

You can add railing in a project by sketching its path. To do so, you can use the **Sketch Path** tool. Invoke this tool from **Architecture > Circulation > Railing** drop-down; the **Modify | Create Railing Path** tab will be displayed. This tab displays various sketching tools to sketch the railing path. You can sketch the railing path with or without a host as per the requirement of the project. The host to the railing can be a floor stairs, ramps and so on. To select a host, choose the **Pick New Host** tool from the **Tools** panel of the **Modify | Create Railing Path** tab; you will be prompted to select an element in the drawing on which the railing is to be created. Select the host if required. In the **Properties** palette, you can select the type of the railing. To assign a type to the railing, select an option from the **Type Selector** drop-down list. In the **Properties** palette, you can also assign various instance parameters such as **Base Level**, **Base Offset**, **Tread / Stringer Offset**, and so on to the railing. Now, to sketch the railing path, choose any of the drawing tools from the list box that will be displayed in the **Draw** panel of the **Modify | Create Railing Path** tab to sketch. For example, you can use the **Line** tool to define a specific railing path, as shown in Figure 8-27. You can use the **Ref Plane** tool to assist you in sketching the railing boundary, if required. After completing the sketch of the railing path, choose the **Finish Edit Mode** button from the **Mode** panel; the railing will be created, as shown in Figure 8-28.

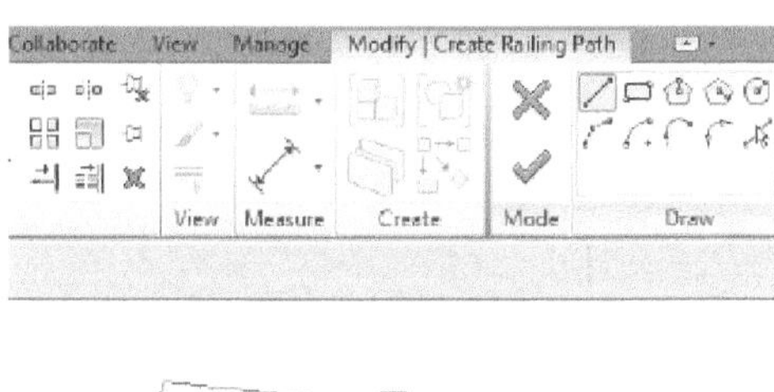

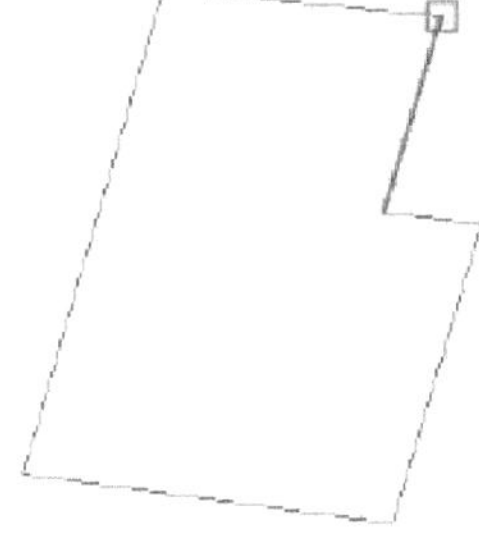

Figure 8-27 *Using the* ***Line*** *tool to create the boundary for a railing*

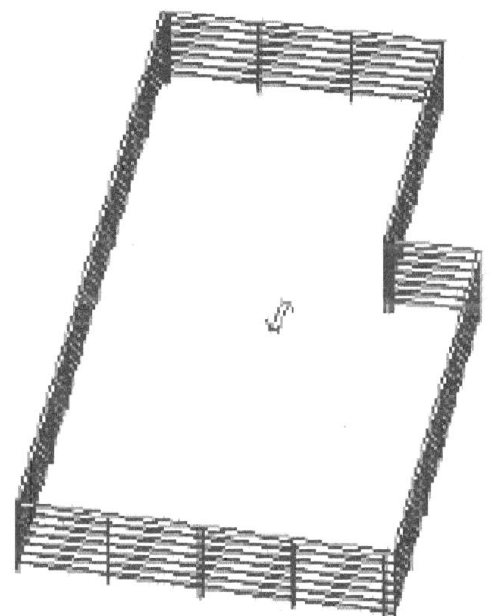

Figure 8-28 *3D view of the railing created*

Note

You can now sketch railings onto the top faces of floors, slabs, slab edges, walls, or roofs. Balusters and railings adjust to the slope of irregular surfaces

Adding Railings by Placing On Stair/Ramp

Ribbon: Architecture > Circulation > Railing

The **Railing** tool allows you to add railings to the entire stair tower or an individual staircase. Such railings can be edit from one instance to all in a group. In Revit 2018, you can attach railing to building staircase and the toposurface for model fencing, road barriers, or outdoor handrails. The example of railing added to building staircases and toposurface is shown in Figure 8-29.

Modifying Railing Properties

You can modify the properties and parameters of a railing before or after creating it. To specify the properties and parameters of a railing, you can use various instance properties displayed in the **Properties** palette. To specify the type properties of the proposed railing, choose the **Edit Type** button in the **Properties** palette; the **Type Properties** dialog box will be displayed. In this dialog box, the **Edit** buttons in the value column for the **Rail Structure** and **Baluster Placement** type parameters can be chosen to view and modify the parameters of the railing such as rail type, baluster type, baluster spacing, and so on. The **Baluster Offset** parameter indicates the offset distance of the baluster from the sketched rail boundary.

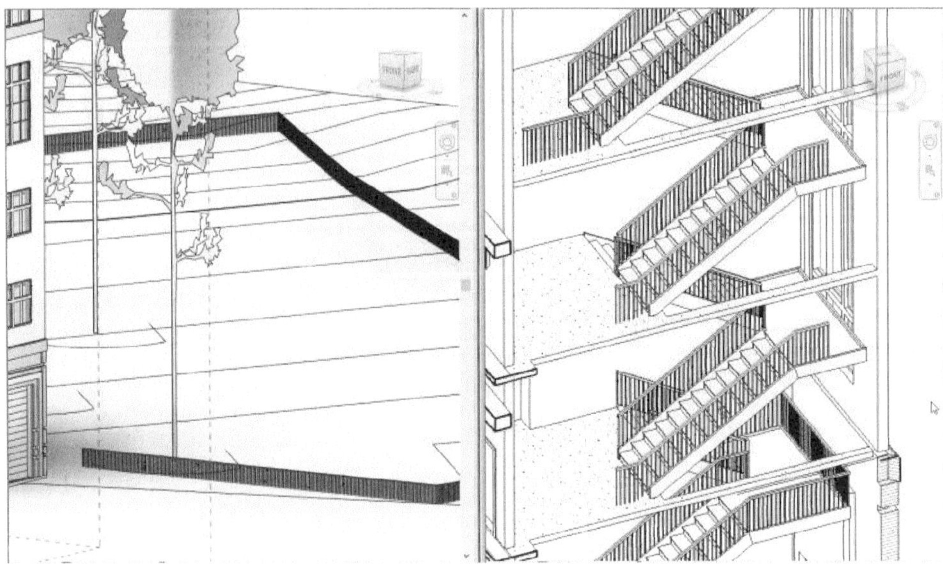

Figure 8-29 Railing added to building staircase and toposurface

Apart from the preloaded baluster types, you can load additional ones by choosing the **Load Family** tool from the **Load from Library** panel in the **Insert** tab. On choosing the **Load Family** tool, the **Load Family** dialog box will be displayed. In this dialog box, open the **US Imperial >Railings > Balusters** and select the desired file(s) for adding baluster type(s) in the project. After selecting the desired file(s), choose the **Open** button in the **Load Family** dialog box; the dialog box will close and the selected baluster type(s) will be loaded into the project.

Note

Railings are associated with their hosts and get modified with the changes in the host element. For example, if the stairs are deleted, the railing will also be deleted. You can, however, delete the railing independent of its hosts.

Modifying Railing Joints

You can modify the joint type of a joint in a railing. To do so, open the plan or the 3D view in which the railing you wish to edit is visible. Next, select the railing; the **Modify | Railings** tab is displayed. Choose the **Edit Path** tool from the **Mode** panel; the **Modify | Railings > Sketch Path** tab will be displayed and the railing path will be displayed in the sketch mode. In the **Modify | Railings > Sketch Path** tab, choose the **Edit Joins** tool from the **Tools** panel and then move the cursor along the path of the railing. As you move the cursor along the path, you will notice a snap is displayed at the intersection of the railing path or at the point where the two paths join. Click, when the snap is displayed, and then from the **Rail Join** drop-down list in the **Options Bar**, select an option to specify the type of join. Similarly, you can click on other joins in the railing path and change their type as per the project requirement. After you finish assigning the type to the joins, choose the **Finish Edit Mod**e button from the **Mode** panel of the **Modify Railings > Edit Path** tab to finish editing of the railing joins.

ADDING RAMPS

Ribbon: Architecture > Circulation > Ramp

You can create ramps in Autodesk Revit in a manner similar to creating stairs. The **Ramp** tool is used to create ramps and can be invoked from the **Circulation** panel. On invoking this tool, the **Modify | Create Ramp Sketch** tab will be displayed. Also, the properties used for creating the ramp will be displayed in the **Properties** palette. You can use various tools and options in this tab to create the sketch of the ramp. In the **Properties** palette, you can assign properties and type to the ramp.

The **Draw** panel of the **Modify | Create Ramp Sketch** tab contains various sketching tools that can be used to create the sketch of the ramp boundary. These tools and their applications are similar to those present in the **Draw** panel of the **Modify | Create Ramp Sketch** tab.

After sketching the ramp boundary for the proposed ramp, you need to view and assign properties to it. To do so, you can use various properties displayed in the **Properties** palette of the ramp. The instance properties of the ramp can be specified in this palette. In the **Properties** palette, the **Width** parameter indicates the width of the ramp, whereas the **Base Level** parameter indicates the level from where the ramp will start, and the **Top Level** parameter indicates the level at which the ramp will end. The slope and width of the ramp can be specified even before it is created. Next, to view and modify the type properties of the proposed ramp, choose the **Edit Type** button in the **Properties** palette; the **Type Properties** dialog box will be displayed. In this dialog box, the value of the **Maximum Incline Length** parameter indicates the maximum length of the ramp before a landing is required. Specify the maximum slope of the ramp in the **Ramp Max Slope (1/x)** parameter value. The **Shape** parameter is used to create a ramp with a solid base or a slab. Figure 8-30 shows an example of sketching a ramp by specifying the start point and the endpoint.

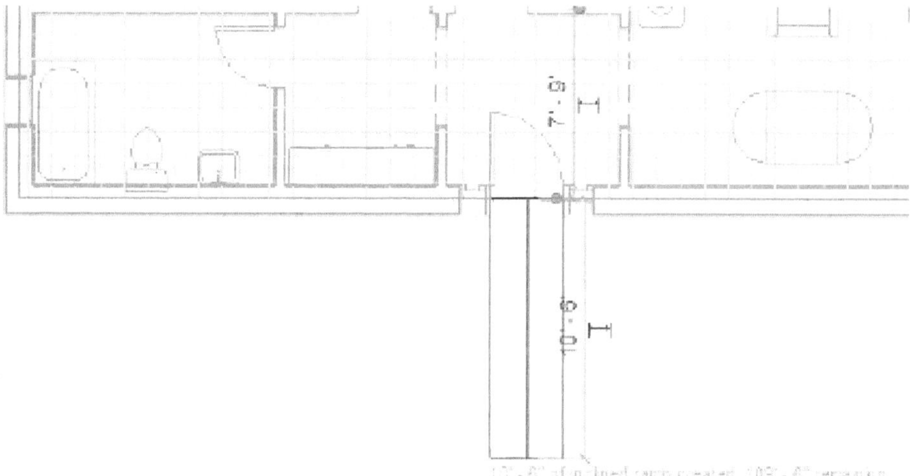

Figure 8-30 *Sketching the ramp run*

After specifying the instance and type properties of the ramp, you can specify the type of railing to be used for it. To do so, choose the **Railing** tool from the **Tools** panel of the **Modify | Create Ramp Sketch** tab; the **Railings** dialog box will be displayed. In this dialog box, select the railing type from the available drop-down list and choose the **OK** button; the **Railings** dialog box will close and the selected railing type will be assigned to the ramp.

Next, click in the drawing area to specify the start point of the ramp. On doing so, a rectangle shaped geometry will be displayed. This geometry will show the total size required for creating the ramp. The ramp size can be calculated based on the current ramp property settings. The required length of the ramp is also displayed on specifying the first point of the ramp run. Next, specify the endpoint of the ramp and choose the **Finish Edit Mode** button from the **Mode** panel of the **Modify | Create Ramp Sketch** tab. This creates the ramp with the given parameters, as shown in Figure 8-31. If the specified length of the ramp is less or more than the required length, Autodesk Revit will display a warning message box showing the error and its cause, as shown in Figure 8-32. You can ignore the error, if possible, or rectify the sketch or the properties to create the desired ramp using curtain systems in a project.

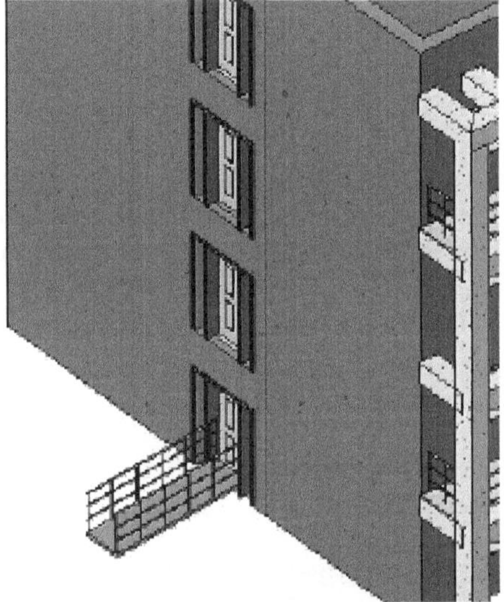

Figure 8-31 *3D view of resultant ramp*

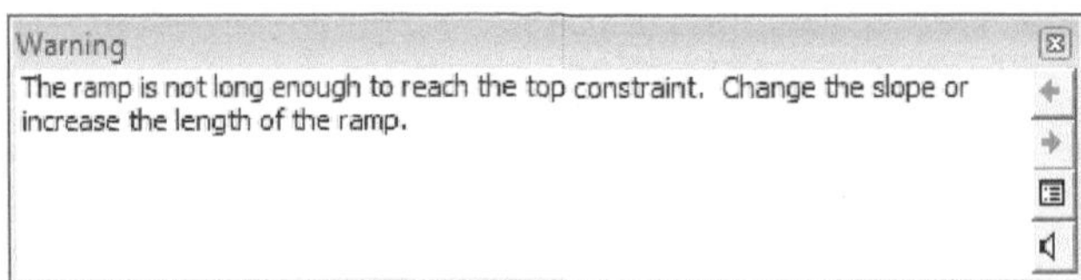

Figure 8-32 *The* ***Warning*** *message box showing the error type*

USING CURTAIN SYSTEMS IN A PROJECT

In Autodesk Revit, a typical curtain system comprises the panels, curtain grid, curtain wall, and mullions, as shown in Figure 8-33. Each of these elements can be modified individually. A curtain system can be added by using the **Wall: Architectural** tool or by using the specific curtain system tools. You can also generate the curtain systems of different shapes and configurations. A curtain system created using the **Wall: Architectural** tool is also referred to as a curtain wall. You can create curved, sloping, and store front curtain systems.

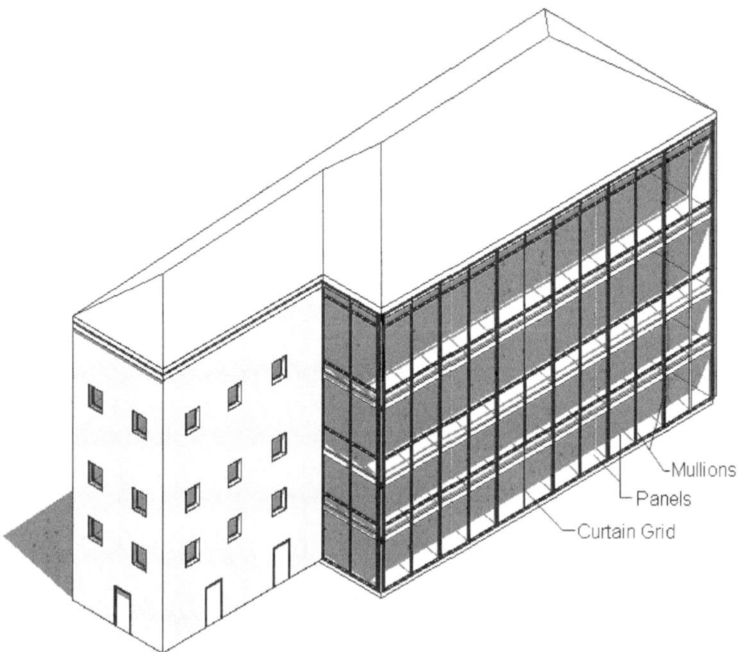

Figure 8-33 *Typical curtain system elements*

Creating a Curtain Wall Using the Wall: Architectural Tool

A curtain wall can be created by using the **Wall** tool. To create a curtain wall, invoke the **Wall** tool and select the required type from the **Type Selector** drop-down list in the **Properties** palette, as shown in Figure 8-34. Note that the **Type Selector** drop-down list displays three different types of curtain wall options such as **Curtain Wall 1**, **Exterior Glazing**, and **Storefront** under the **Curtain Wall** head. After selecting the desired curtain wall type from the **Type Selector** drop-down list, you can start sketching the proposed curtain wall by using the sketching tools available in the **Properties** palette.

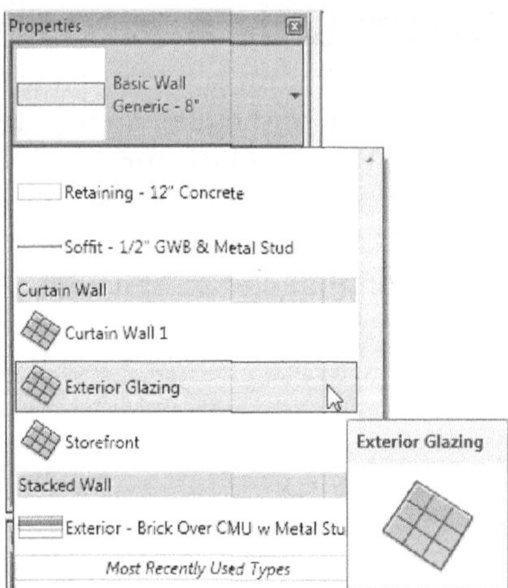

***Figure 8-34** Selecting the curtain wall type from the **Type Selector** drop-down list in the **Properties** palette*

Alternatively, select any wall and replace it with the predefined curtain wall using the **Type Selector** drop-down list. If you select the **Curtain Wall** option as a wall type from the **Type Selector** drop-down list, a curtain wall will be created with a single panel. Even a curved curtain wall is first created as a straight curtain wall. You can then use the **Curtain Grid** tool in the **Build** panel of the **Architecture** tab to add curtain grids at a specific distance to give the desired shape, refer to Figure 8-35. The other two curtain wall types available in the **Type Selector** drop-down list have predefined curtain grids. They can, however, be modified to the desired spacing.

Tip

Autodesk Revit enables you to create elements with minimum faults by warning you about the errors in their creation. The parametric building elements associate with each other and help in creating designs that have the least discrepancies.

Creating a Curtain Wall by Picking Lines

You can create a curtain wall from existing lines in a drawing. The existing lines can be model lines or edges of elements, such as roofs, curtain panels, and other walls. To create a curtain wall by using the existing lines, choose the **Pick Lines** tool from the **Draw** panel of the **Modify | Place Wall** tab; you will be prompted to select an edge or a line from the drawing. Select the desired edge or line from the drawing; the curtain wall will be created.

For example, you can select the edge of a floor slab or any line in a different level to create the curtain wall. Figure 8-35 shows a flat and a curved curtain system created by using the **Pick Lines** tool. Note that the curved curtain system appears flat when it is created and acquires the actual curved form when the curtain grids are added.

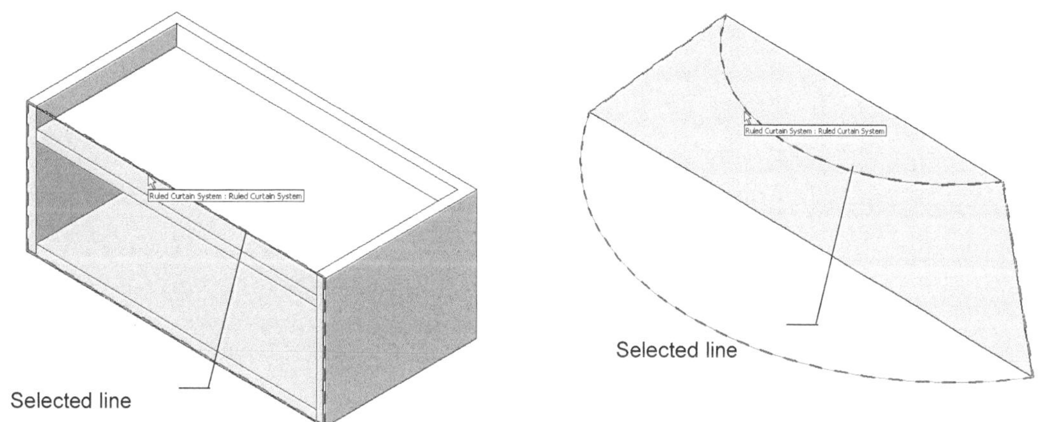

*Figure 8-35 A flat and a curved curtain system created using the **Pick Lines** tool*

Creating a Curtain System on a Face

Ribbon: Architecture > Build > Curtain System

Curtain System

You can create a curtain system on a face by using the **Curtain System** tool. This tool is effective for creating a curtain system on the solids and faces created by using the massing tools (the use of massing tools is described in Chapter 10). After creating a massing geometry, invoke this tool from the **Curtain Build** panel; the **Modify | Place Curtain System by Face** tab will be displayed and you will be prompted to select a face that will be used to create the curtain system. The selected face can be flat or with a single or double curved faces. After selecting the face, choose the **Create System** tool from the **Multiple Selection** panel in the **Modify | Place Curtain System by Face** tab; a curtain system will be created based on the face selected. The type of the curtain system will be based on the default value selected in the **Type Selector** drop-down list in the **Properties** palette.

You can change the existing type and properties of the curtain system from the **Properties** palette. You can change the existing values in this palette and create a new type.

To create a new type of a curtain system, choose the **Edit Type** button from the **Properties** palette; the **Type Properties** dialog box will be displayed. In this dialog box, choose the **Duplicate** button; the **Name** dialog box will be displayed. Type a name in the **Name** edit box and choose the **OK** button; the **Name** dialog box will close. Now, you can change the values of different parameters of the newly created type in the **Type Properties** dialog box.

In the **Type Properties** dialog box, the parameters in the **Grid 1** Pattern and **Grid 2** Pattern heads specify how the grid lines in the curtain system will be generated. The parameters displayed under the **Grid 1 Pattern** and **Grid 2 Pattern** heads specify the settings for generating vertical grid lines and the horizontal grid lines, respectively.

After changing the values for the new type in the **Type Properties** dialog box, choose **Apply** and then choose **OK**; the changed properties will be applied to the created curtain system and the dialog box will close. Figure 8-36 shows an example of a curtain system created using the **Curtain System** tool.

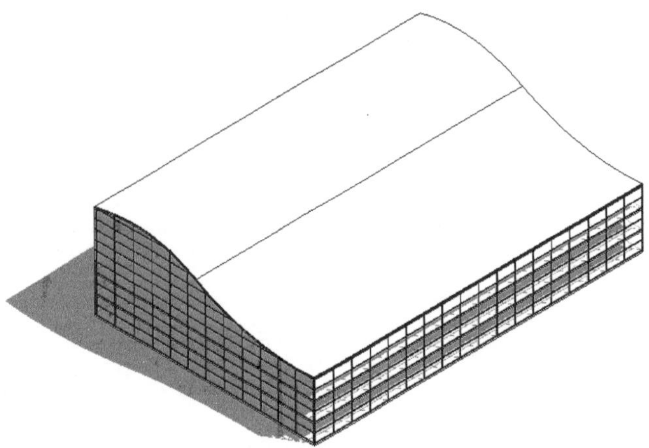

***Figure 8-36** Example of curtain systems created using the **Curtain System** tool*

Adding Curtain Grids

Ribbon: Architecture > Build > Curtain Grid

Curtain Grid

Curtain grids are added to a curtain system to define its geometry and form a grid for adding mullions. Invoke the **Curtain Grid** tool from the **Build** panel; a preview image of the grid will be displayed on the panels. Also, the **Modify | Place Curtain Grid** tab will be displayed. The **Placement** panel of this tab displays three tools: **All Segments**, **One Segment**, and **All Except Picked**. The **All Segments** tool is invoked by default and lets you place grid segments on all panels where the preview appears. The **One Segment** tool, if invoked, will create a grid segment only in the panel where the preview appears. Similarly, on invoking the **All Except Picked** tool, you can place grid segments on all panels except those you select to exclude.

After you select any tool from the **Placement** panel, move the cursor to a curtain wall or a curtain system where you wish to add the curtain grids. On doing so, a dashed line will appear, indicating the position to place the curtain grid. A horizontal dashed line appears when the cursor is near a vertical edge, and a vertical dashed line will appear when the cursor is close to a horizontal edge. Click at the desired locations to add the curtain grids. The object snap options displayed can also be used for this purpose. Figure 8-37 shows two examples of a curtain grid added to a curtain system by using the **All Segments** and **One Segment** tools.

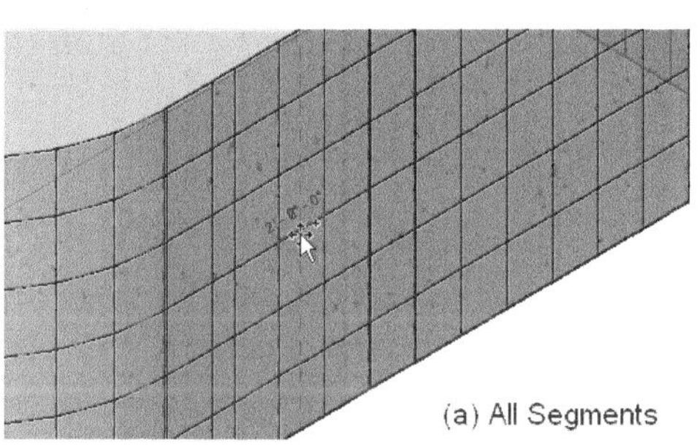

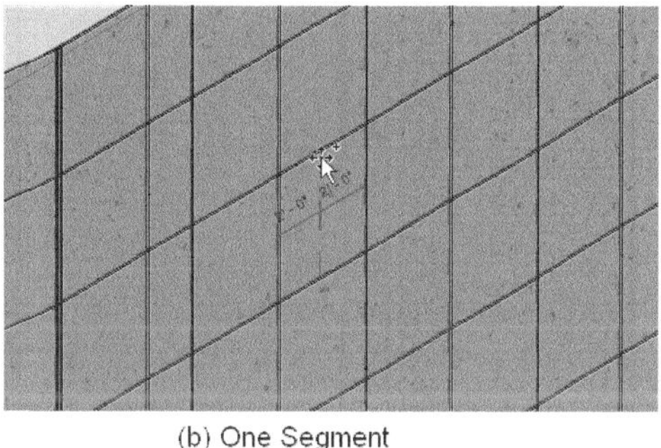

Figure 8-37 *Adding curtain grids to a curtain system by using the* ***All Segments*** *and* ***One Segment*** *tools*

Tip

When you create curtain grids individually using the ***Curtain Grids*** *tool, you can delete or drag each curtain grid to achieve the appropriate curtain grid pattern.*

Modifying Curtain System Panels

On creating a curtain grid, the curtain system is divided into curtain system panels. Each portion between the curtain grids is treated as a single curtain system panel. By default, each panel is treated as a glazed system panel. However, Autodesk Revit enables you to modify the properties of each panel. You can create a solid panel or an empty panel. To modify a system panel, select it using the crossing selection method and the **Filter** tool (if required); the **Properties** palette will display the type and properties of the system panel. In the **Properties** palette, the **System Panel : Glazed** option is selected by default in the **Type Selector** drop-down list. In this drop-down list, you can select the **Empty System Panel : Empty** or **System Panel : Solid** option to replace the selected panel(s) with an empty or solid panel, respectively. In this manner, you can create a combination of solid and glazed panels for a curtain system. Figure 8-38 shows the curtain panels of three different types added to a curtain system.

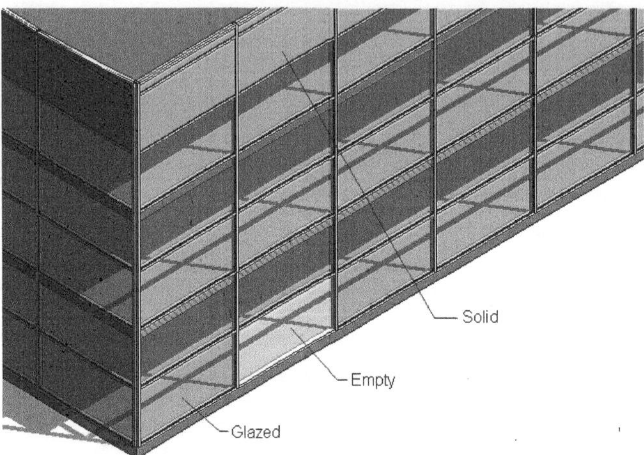

Figure 8-38 Example of different curtain panels added in the curtain system

Adding Doors and Awnings to a Curtain System

The doors and curtain wall awnings can be added to a curtain system by replacing the curtain system panel with them. To add doors and the awning to the curtain wall panel, first you need to load their family types. To do so, choose the **Insert** tab and then choose the **Load Family** tool from the **Load from Library** panel; the **Load Family** dialog box will be displayed. In this dialog box, browse the **US Imperial** folder and load the curtain wall double glass and single glass doors, and awnings from the **Doors** and **Windows** sub-folders, respectively. However, before adding doors, ensure that the curtain panel to be replaced is of the desired door size. This may require you to remove certain curtain grid segments. To remove a grid segment from a grid system, select the grid and choose the **Add/Remove Segments** button in the **Curtain Grid** panel of the **Modify | Curtain Wall Grids** tab. Now, click on the segment to be removed and click anywhere outside the curtain system; the grid segment will be removed. Similarly, you can also add the removed curtain grid segment in a curtain grid system. To do so, select the grid from which a segment has been removed; the removed segment will be highlighted with a dashed line. Now, choose the **Add/Remove Segments** button from the **Curtain Grid** panel of the **Modify | Curtain Wall Grids** and click on the highlighted dashed line; the removed grid will be added. Once the panel of the desired size has been created in the curtain system, select it from the drawing; the **Modify | Curtain Panels** tab will be displayed. From the **Type Selector** drop-down list select any loaded curtain wall doors and awnings. The selected curtain wall doors or awnings will be added to the selected panel.

Adding Mullions

Ribbon: Architecture > Build > Mullion

Once you have created the curtain grid, you can use the **Mullion** tool to add mullions to the segments of curtain grid segments. To use the **Mullion** tool, invoke it from the **Build** panel; the **Modify | Place Mullion** tab will be displayed. Also, the properties of the mullion will be displayed in the **Properties** palette. In this palette, you can select the mullion type from the **Type Selector** drop-down list. Autodesk Revit provides you with six main types of mullions: **Circular Mullion**, **L Corner Mullion**, **Quad Corner Mullion**, **Rectangular Mullion**, **Trapezoid Corner Mullion**, and **V Corner Mullion**. By default, the **Rectangular Mullion** type is selected in the **Type Selector** drop-down list. After selecting a type from the **Type Selector** drop-down list, you can change the type properties of the mullion you want to place. To do so, choose the **Edit Type** button from the **Properties** palette; the **Type Properties** dialog box will be displayed. In this dialog box, change the type parameters, where required, in their corresponding value field and then choose **OK**; the desired change will be applied and the **Type Properties** dialog box will close. Now, you can use the tools from the **Placement** panel in the **Modify | Place Mullion** tab to place the mullions using the curtain grids. The tools available in the **Placement** panel for placing mullions are **Grid Line**, **Grid Line Segment**, and **All Grid Lines**. You can use the **Grid Lines** tool to place a mullion across the entire grid line. Similarly, you can use the **Grid Line Segment** or **All Grid Lines** tool to place a mullion on the individual segment of the grid line or on all grid lines. After you invoke the desired tool, move the cursor near the curtain grid and click when it is highlighted; the mullion will be created on it. This step can be repeated to create mullions for the desired curtain grids, as shown in Figure 8-39. The length of the mullion created for the curtain grid will be equal to the length of the curtain grid. After the mullions are added on a curtain grid, you can control mullion joins. To do so, select the mullion; the **Modify | Curtain Wall Mullions** tab will be displayed. In the **Mullion** panel of this tab, you can choose the **Make Continuous** or **Break at Join** tool to control the mullion joins. You can choose the **Make Continuous** tool to extend the ends of mullions at a join so that they appear as one continuous mullion Alternatively, you can choose the **Break at Join** tool to trim the ends of mullions at a join so that they appear as separate mullions.

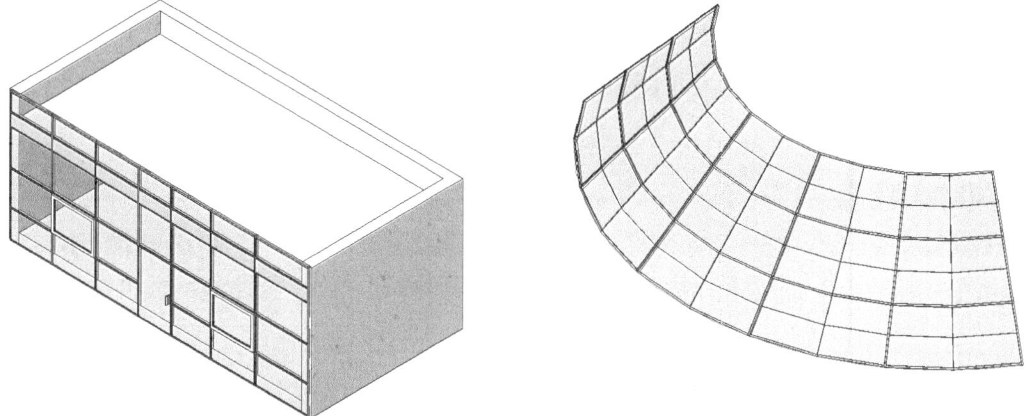

Figure 8-39 *Adding mullions to a curtain system using the* ***Mullion*** *tool*

COPYING ELEMENTS FROM ONE LEVEL TO ANOTHER

As described earlier, you can copy elements in the same work plane using the **Copy to Clipboard**, **Cut to Clipboard**, and **Paste** tools. For multistory building projects, you need to use the **Paste** tool to copy the elements such as doors, windows, furniture elements, and so on from one level to another level, exactly above or below their original location.

Select the elements to be copied to the other level. The **Filter** tool can be useful in selecting the elements of the same family. After you select the elements, invoke the **Copy to Clipboard** tool from the **Clipboard** panel of the **Modify | (Elements / Components)** tab; the selected elements will be copied to the clipboard.

Using the Pasting Tools

After copying the elements to the clipboard, choose the **Paste** drop-down from the **Clipboard** panel; a list of pasting tools will be displayed. Based on the required result, you need to choose the appropriate tool from the list. These tools are discussed next.

The **Paste from Clipboard** tool is used to paste elements from the clipboard into the current view.

The **Aligned to Current View** tool is used to paste elements into the current view which is different from the view in which the elements were copied. For example, you can copy elements from a plan view to a callout view.

The **Aligned to Same Place** tool is used to copy elements to the same place from they were copied from. This option is useful for developing different design options for the same location.

The **Aligned to Picked Level** tool is used to paste elements into levels by selecting their corresponding level line. You need to be in the elevation view for selecting the level line to paste the elements.

The **Aligned to Selected Levels** tool, the most frequently used tool, enables you to choose the level(s) for pasting the elements. You can choose the desired level(s) from the list of existing levels in the **Select Levels** dialog box.

The **Aligned to Selected Views** tool is useful for copying view specific elements such as dimensions from one level to another.

TUTORIALS

Tutorial 1 — Apartment 1

In this tutorial, you will add furniture and sanitary elements to the first floor level of the *c07_Apartment1_tut1.rvt* project created in Tutorial 1 of Chapter 7. The approximate location of components is shown in Figure 8-40. The text has been given for reference and is not to be created. Extend the exterior walls to 3'0" above the top floor level and copy all interior walls, doors, windows, and other elements at the same location on all three upper floors. Also, create a flat roof for the top floor. Use the following parameters for different components to be added: **(Expected time: 30 min)**

Alphabets in Figure 8-40 represent the furniture and plumbing components to be used, as given below.

1. Furniture Components

   For Imperial: Furniture components from the **Furniture** folder of the **US Imperial**:

   A- **Bed-Shaker: Double 56" x 78"**
   B- **Entertainment Center-72" x 72" x 24"**
   C- **Dresser-72" x 60" x 18"**
   D- **Sofa-72"**
   E- **Table-Dining Oval-36" x 72"**
   F- **Table-Coffee-36" x 72"**

G- **Chair-Corbu**
H- **Table-End:24" x 24"** (modify height to 15")

For Metric: Furniture components from the **Furniture** folder of the **US Metric**:
A- **Bed-Shaker: Double 1422 x 1981 mm**
B- **Entertainment Center- 1830 x 1830 x 610 mm**
C- **Dresser- 1220 x 1525 x 0610 mm**
D- **Sofa- 1830 mm**
E- **Table-Dining Oval- 0915 x 1830 mm**
F- **Table-Coffee- 0915 x 1830 x 0457 mm**
G- **Chair-Corbu**
H- **Table-End- 0610 x 0610 mm** (modify height to 381 mm)

2. Plumbing Components
For Imperial: Plumbing components from **Speciality Equipment > Domestic** and **Plumbing** folders of **US Imperial**
J- **Kitchenette-Medium**: 8'6" (modified width)
K- **Toilet-Domestic-3D**
L- **Tub-Rectangular-3D**
M- **Sink Vanity-Square**: **20" x 18"**

For Metric: Plumbing components from **Speciality Equipment > Domestic** and **Plumbing** folders of **US Metric**
J- **Kitchenette-Medium**: 2591 mm (modified width)
K- **Toilet-Domestic-3D**
L- **Tub-Rectangular-3D**
M- **Sink Vanity-Square**: **500 x 440 mm**

3. Top floor roof type-
For Imperial **Basic Roof : Generic 9"** - Flat
For Metric **Basic Roof : Generic 400 mm** - Flat

The following steps are required to complete this tutorial:

a. Open the project file, invoke the **Place a Component** tool, and load the components from the additional libraries using the **Load Family** tool.
b. Add and position the components at their desired location in the building model using the **Rotate** and **Move** tools, refer to Figures 8-41 and 8-42.
c. Extend the exterior walls to **3'0"(914 mm)** above the top most level, refer to Figure 8-43.
d. Select the doors, windows, floor, ceiling, and components, and copy them to all upper floors using the **Aligned to Selected Levels** tool, refer to Figure 8-44
e. Create the roof of the topmost floor using the **Roof** tool, refer to Figure 8-45.
f. Save the project using the **Save As** tool.
For Imperial *c08_Apartment1_tut1.rvt*
For Metric *M_c08_Apartment1_tut1.rvt*
g. Close the project.

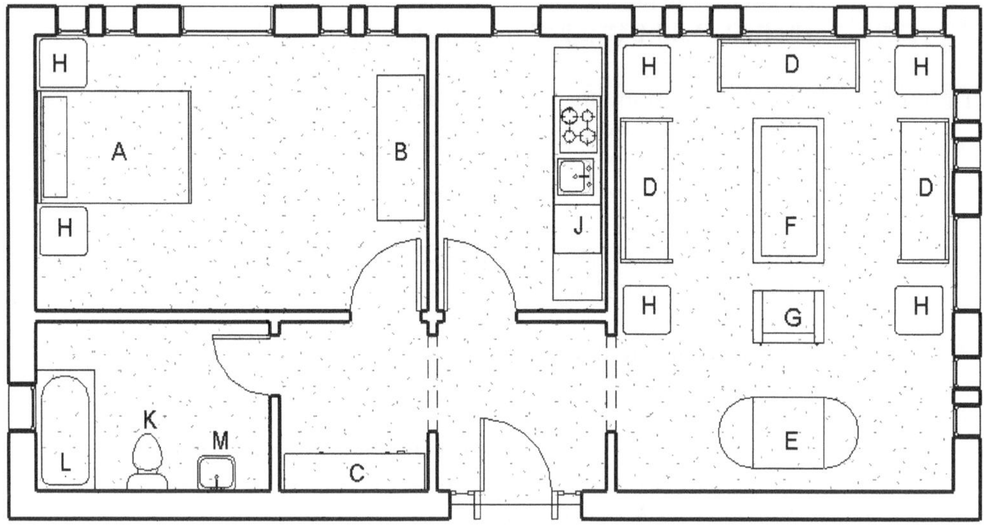

Figure 8-40 Sketch plan for adding furniture and plumbing components to the Apartment 1 project

Opening the Project File and Loading Components from Additional Libraries

In this section of the tutorial, you will first open the specified project file and add the components to the first floor plan view by using the **Component** tool. You will use the **Load Family** tool to load the components from the specified additional libraries.

1. Choose **Open > Project** from the **File** menu and open the *c07_Apartment1_tut1.rvt* file created in Tutorial 1 of Chapter 7 and make sure that the first floor plan is displayed. You can also download this file from *http://www.cadcim.com*. The path of the file is as follows: *Textbooks > Civil/GIS > Revit Architecture > Exploring Autodesk Revit 2018 for Architecture*.

2. Next, you need to place the components as specified in the project parameters. To do so, invoke the **Place a Component** tool from **Architecture > Build > Component** drop-down; the **Modify | Place Component** tab is displayed.

3. Next, you need to load additional components to the drawing. To do so, choose the **Load Family** tool from the **Mode** panel; the **Load Family** dialog box is displayed.

4. In the **Load Family** dialog box, select the desired folder to open it.
   For Imperial **US Imperial > Furniture**
   For Metric **US Metric > Furniture**

5. In this folder, select the following furniture types from their corresponding folders and load them one by one.
   For Imperial: **Bed-Shaker** (Folder: Beds), **Chair-Corbu** (Folder: Seating), **Dresser** (Folder: Storage), **Entertainment Center** (Folder: Storage), **Sofa** (Folder: Seating), **Table-Dining Oval** (Folder: Tables), **Table-Coffee** (Folder: Tables), and **Table-End** (Folder: Tables).

For Metric: **M_Bed-Shaker** (Folder: Beds), **M_Chair-Corbu** (Folder: Seating), **M_Dresser** (Folder: Storage), **M_Entertainment Center** (Folder: Storage), **M_Sofa** (Folder: Seating), **M_Table-Dining Oval** (Folder: Tables), **M_Table-Coffee** (Folder: Tables), and **M_Table-End** (Folder: Tables).

6. After selecting the required families, choose the **Open** button; the **Load Family** dialog box is closed and the selected type becomes available in the **Type Selector** drop-down list in the **Properties** palette. At this stage, it is recommended that you do not click in the drawing area or press ESC.

7. Invoke the **Load Family** dialog box. In this dialog box, choose the **Fixtures** folder from **US Imperial > Plumbing > Architectural** folder (For Metric, **US Metric > Plumbing > Architectural** folder). In the **Fixture** folder, load the following fixture types from their corresponding folders:

   For Imperial: **Sink Vanity- Square** (Folder: Sinks), **Toilet-Domestic-3D** (Folder: Water Closets), and **Tub-Rectangular-3D** (Folder: Bathtubs).

   For Metric: **M_Sink Vanity- Square** (Folder: Sinks), **M_Toilet-Domestic-3D** (Folder: Water Closets), and **M_Tub-Rectangular-3D** (Folder: Bathtubs).

8. Repeat step 3 to invoke the **Load Family** dialog box. In this dialog box, access the **Domestic** folder from **US Imperial > Speciality Equipment** (for Metric: **US Metric > Speciality Equipment**) and load folder from **US Imperial > Speciality Equipment** and load **Kitchenette-Medium** (for Metric **M_Kitchenette-Medium**) into the project file.

Adding and Positioning Components in the Building Model

You can now select the component type from the **Type Selector** drop-down list and add it to the building model. Different editing tools like **Rotate**, **Copy**, and **Move** can be used to position the components at their desired location and in the required direction. The steps below describe the procedure for a single component, **Bed-Shaker**. The following steps can then be used to add and position other furniture and plumbing components. As mentioned earlier, the exact location of the components is not important for this tutorial.

1. In the **Type Selector** drop-down list of the **Properties** palette, select the **Bed-Shaker : Double 56" x 78"**option, as specified in the parameters for the project.

2. Select the **Rotate after placement** check box in the **Options Bar**.

3. Move the cursor near the west wall of the bedroom and click at the desired location, as shown in Figure 8-41; the component is temporarily placed and the **Rotate** tool is invoked, as shown in Figure 8-42.

4. Move the cursor vertically upward and click when the dashed rectangle (indicating the direction of the bed) is horizontally positioned, as shown in Figure 8-43; the bed is added. Now, press ESC. Depending on the point selected for the placement, you may need to use the **Move** tool to move the component to the desired position.

5. Repeat steps 1 to 4 for adding and positioning the components in the building model at locations based on the given sketch plan, refer to Figure 8-40. The components are listed next according to their placements in sketch plan.
   For Imperial: **Entertainment Center : 72"x 72" x 24"**
   Dresser : 72" x 60" x 18"
   Sofa : 72"
   Table-Dining Oval : 36" x 72"
   Table-Coffee : 36" x 72" x 18"
   Chair-Corbu
   Table- End : 24" x 24"
   Kitchenette - Medium : Kitchenette - Medium
   Toilet-Domestic-3D
   Tub-Rectangular-3D
   Sink Vanity-Square : 20" x 18"

   For Metric: **Entertainment Center : 1830 x 1830 x 610 mm**
   Dresser : 1220 x 1525 x 0610 mm
   Sofa : 1830 mm
   Table-Dining Oval : 0915 x 1830 mm
   Table-Coffee : 0915 x 1830 x 0457 mm
   Chair-Corbu
   Table- End : 0610 x 0610 mm
   Kitchenette - Medium : Kitchenette - Medium
   Toilet-Domestic-3D
   Tub-Rectangular-3D
   Sink Vanity-Square : 0500 x 0440 mm

6. After adding all components, press ESC twice.

Tip
On the basis of dimensions, you can place the components from the neighboring elements. To do so, select the component to display its temporary dimensions. Select the appropriate temporary dimension and enter the new value. The component is moved to the exact location.

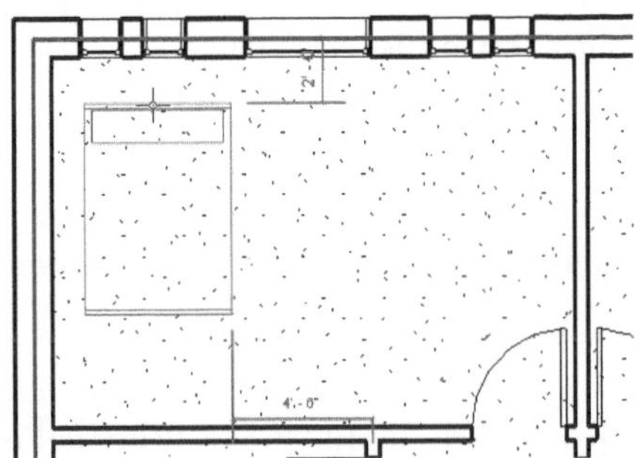

Figure 8-41 *Placing a component temporarily*

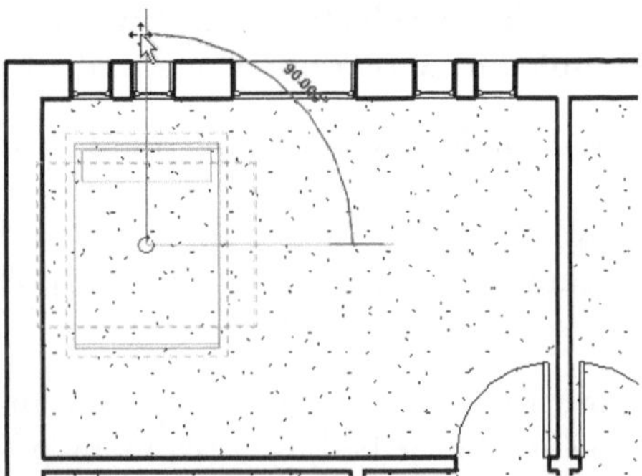

Figure 8-42 *Rotating the component*

Modifying the Added Components

The width of the **Kitchenette - Medium** and the height of the **Table- End : 24" x 24"** components can be modified by using the **Type Properties** dialog box.

1. Select the **Kitchenette-Medium : Kitchenette - Medium** component placed in the building model; the **Modify | Specialty Equipment** tab is displayed.

2. Choose the **Edit Type** button from the **Properties** palette; the **Type Properties** dialog box is displayed.

Note

Create a new type for the ***Kitchenette-Medium : Kitchenette - Medium*** *component if it already does not exist.*

3. In the **Type Properties** dialog box, choose the **Duplicate** button; the **Name** dialog box is displayed.

4. Enter **8'6" (2591 mm)** in the **Name** edit box and choose the **OK** button to close it.

5. In the **Type Properties** dialog box, enter **8'6" (2591 mm)** as the value for the **Cabinet Width** type parameter.

6. Choose the **OK** button to close this dialog box. The **Kitchenette - Medium** component is modified to the new size. You may need to use the **Move** tool to reposition the component at the desired location.

7. Similarly, select the **Table-End : 24" x 24"** (for Metric **Table- End : 0610 x 0610 mm**) component, access the **Type Properties** dialog box, and then modify the value of the **Height** parameter to **1'3" (381 mm)**. This modifies the height of all instances of the component.

8. Choose the **OK** button; the **Type Properties** dialog box is closed.

   The first floor plan after adding and positioning the components should appear similar to the sketch plan given for this tutorial.

Extending Walls to the Topmost Level

As described earlier, it is better to extend the exterior walls to the top story, instead of stacking them one above the other. To extend the exterior wall height, you need to set the **Top Constraint** parameter to the topmost level and then use the 3D view to view the changes.

1. To change the current view to a 3D view, double-click on **3D** under the **3D Views** head in the **Project Browser**.

2. Now, move the cursor near the exterior wall and press the TAB key; the chain of exterior walls is highlighted.

3. Click to select the exterior walls; the **Modify | Walls** tab is displayed.

4. In the **Properties** palette for the **Top Constraint** instance parameter, select the **Up to level: Roof** option.

5. Replace the current value of the **Top Offset** parameter with **3'0" (915 mm)** as specified in the project parameters.

6. Choose the **Apply** button in the **Properties** palette. The exterior walls are extended to 3'0" (915mm) above the roof level, as shown in Figure 8-43. Press ESC to exit the tool.

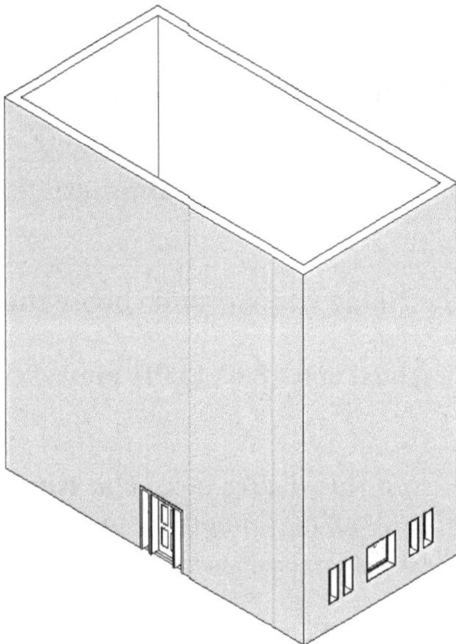

Figure 8-43 *Extending the exterior walls to the topmost level*

Copying Elements to Upper Levels

You can now select all elements except the exterior walls and use the **Aligned to Selected Levels** tool to copy them to the upper levels. The following steps describe the general procedure for copying elements to different levels by using the **Aligned to Selected Levels** tool.

1. In the 3D view, select all elements except the exterior walls by creating a selection window from the left to right. All elements, including the interior walls, floor, ceiling, doors, windows, and components need to be selected.

Note

To exclude the exterior walls, select all elements first and then press the SHIFT key and select the exterior walls.

2. Choose the **Copy to Clipboard** tool from the **Clipboard** panel of the **Modify | Multi-Select** tab.

3. Now, choose the **Aligned to Selected Levels** tool from the **Modify | Multi-Select > Clipboard > Paste** drop-down; the **Select Levels** dialog box is displayed.

4. In this dialog box, select the **Second Floor**, **Third Floor**, and **Fourth Floor** levels by pressing and holding the CTRL button, as shown in Figure 8-44.

5. Choose the **OK** button to close the **Select Levels** dialog box. The selected elements and components are pasted on the three upper levels.

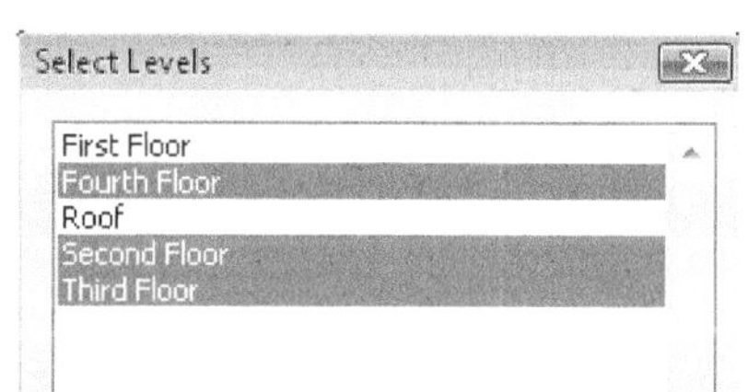

Figure 8-44 *Specifying levels to paste the selected elements*

Adding Roof to the Top Floor

The top floor is still without a roof. Therefore, you need to use the **Roof** tool to create a flat roof. It is recommended that you create the roof in its corresponding floor plan.

1. Double-click on **Roof** from the **Floor Plans** head in the **Project Browser** to display the roof plan.

2. Choose the **Roof by Footprint** tool from **Architecture > Build > Roof** drop-down; the **Modify | Create Roof Footprint** tab is displayed.

3. Choose the **Pick Walls** tool from the **Draw** panel, if not chosen by default, and then clear the **Defines slope** check box in the **Options Bar**, if selected.

4. Move the cursor near the exterior wall of the plan, and when it is highlighted, press the TAB key to highlight the chain of exterior walls. Click to select them. The roof boundary is displayed. Ensure that it is displayed on the inner face. If it is not displayed on the inner face, click on the flip arrow to flip the selection.

5. Choose the **Finish Edit Mode** button from the **Mode** panel to create the roof boundary at the roof plan level.

6. Next, select the **Basic Roof : Generic - 9"** option (for Metric **Basic Roof : Generic - 400 mm**) from the **Type Selector** drop-down list in the **Properties** palette, as specified in the project parameters.

7. Double-click on **3D** under the **3D Views** head in the **Project Browser** to display the 3D view of the multistory apartment. You can use the **ViewCube** tool from the drawing window to view the other sides of the building model, as shown in Figure 8-45.

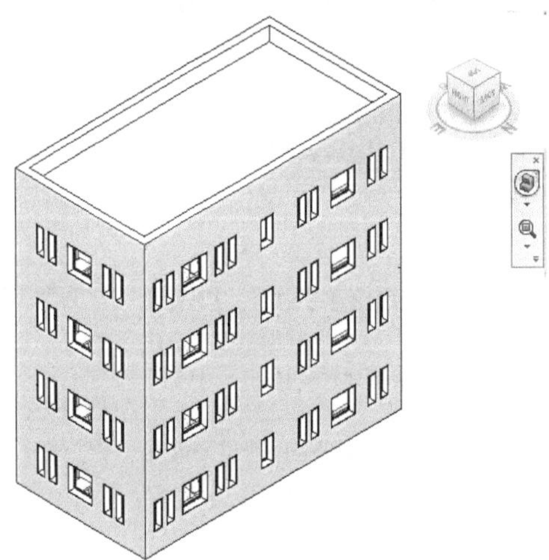

Figure 8-45 Completed multistory apartment

8. Double-click on **First Floor** from the **Floor Plans** head in the **Project Browser** to return to the first floor plan.

Saving the Project

In this section, you will save the project file using the **Save As** tool.

1. Choose **Save As > Project** from **the File** menu and enter the desired name in the **File name** edit box of the **Save As** dialog box.

   For Imperial **c08_Apartment1_tut1**
   For Metric **M_c08_Apartment1_tut1**

   Next, choose **Save**; the project file is saved.

2. Choose **Close** from the **File** menu to close the project file.

Tutorial 2 Club

In this tutorial, you will modify the two walls of the *Club* project created in Tutorial 2 of Chapter 7 into curtain walls and add mullions to all curtain grids. Figure 8-46 shows the walls that are to be modified. Use the parameters given next for the different components to be added.

(Expected time: 30 min)

1. Curtain wall type - **Curtain Wall: Exterior Glazing**
   Curtain grid spacing:
   For Imperial Horizontal- **5'0"**, Vertical- **5'0"**
   For Metric Horizontal- **1524 mm**, Vertical- **1524 mm**

2. Mullion type
   For Imperial **Rectangular Mullion: 1.5" x 2.5" Rectangular,**

For Metric **Rectangular Mullion: x 2.5" Rectangular**,

The following steps are required to complete this tutorial:

a. Open the *c07_Club_tut2.rvt* project file created in Tutorial 2 of Chapter 7.
b. Select the walls and modify them into curtain walls using the **Type Selector** drop-down list.
c. Modify the vertical and horizontal spacing for curtain grids.
d. Add mullions using the **Mullion** tool, refer to Figures 8-47 and 8-48.
e. Save the project using the **Save As** tool.
   For Imperial *c08_Club_tut2.rvt*
   For Metric *M_c08_Club_tut2.rvt*
f. Close the project.

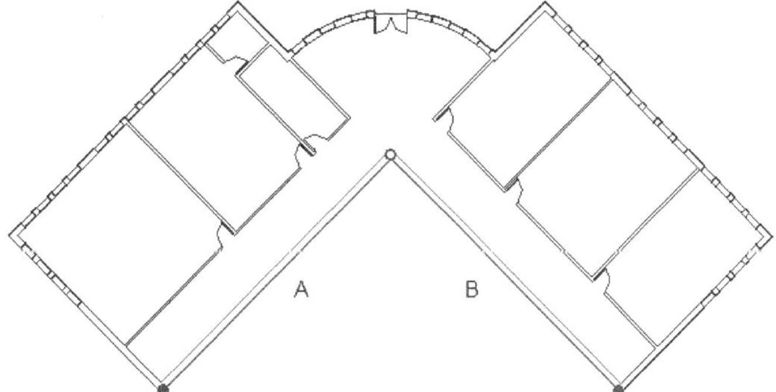

Figure 8-46 *Sketch plan for modifying the existing walls into curtain walls for the Club project*

Opening the Project File and Modifying the Wall Type

To modify the walls into curtain walls, first you need to open the *c07_Club_tut2.rvt* project file and then make sure that the **First Floor** plan is the current view.

1. Choose **Open > Project** from the **File** menu and open the *c07_Club_tut2.rvt* file, created in Tutorial 2 of Chapter 7. Also, open the first floor plan using the **Project Browser**. You can also download this file from *http://www.cadcim.com*. The path of the file is as follows: *Textbooks > Civil/GIS > Revit Architecture> Exploring Autodesk Revit 2018 for Architecture*.

2. Select the two walls marked A and B using the CTRL key, refer to the sketch plan; the **Modify | Walls** tab is displayed.

3. In the **Properties** palette, select the **Curtain Wall: Exterior Glazing** option from the **Type Selector** drop-down list. Autodesk Revit displays an error message indicating that the curtain wall cannot be joined to the exterior wall. Choose the **Unjoin Elements** button to proceed. The walls are replaced by the selected curtain wall type.

Modifying the Curtain Wall Parameters

Next, you will modify the vertical and horizontal spacing of the curtain grid using the **Type Properties** dialog box based on the given project parameters.

1. Ensure that the curtain walls are still selected. Next, choose the **Edit Type** button from the **Properties** palette; the **Type Properties** dialog box is displayed.

2. In the **Value** columns of the **Spacing** type parameter in the **Vertical Grid** pattern and **Horizontal Grid** pattern heads, enter the value **5'0"(1524 mm)**.

3. Choose the **Apply** and then **OK** button to return to the drawing window. The curtain wall grid is modified to the new spacing.

Modifying Curtain System Panels

Now, you need to replace the top row of the curtain wall panel with solid panels to hide the ceiling.

1. Open the **South** elevation using the **Project Browser**.

2. Select the top row of curtain panels using the crossing window; the **Modify | Curtain Panels** tab or the **Modify | Multi-Select** tab is displayed.

3. If the **Modify | Multi-Select** tab is displayed, choose the **Filter** tool from the **Selection** panel; the **Filter** dialog box is displayed.

4. In the **Filter** dialog box, clear all check boxes except the **Curtain Panels** check box and then choose the **OK** button to close the dialog box; the **Modify | Curtain Panels** tab is displayed.

5. In the **Properties** palette, select **System Panel : Solid** from the **Type Selector** drop-down list to replace the selected panels. Press ESC to exit.

Adding Mullions

Mullions can be added using the **Mullion** tool. You need to choose the **All Grid Lines** option to add mullions to all curtain grids.

1. Choose the **Mullion** tool from the **Build** panel of the **Architecture** tab; the **Modify | Place Mullion** tab is displayed.

2. In the **Properties** palette, select the desired mullion type from the **Type Selector** drop-down list.

   For Imperial **Rectangular Mullion: 1.5" x 2.5"**
   For Metric **Rectangular Mullion: 50 x 150 mm**

3. Choose the **All Grid Lines** tool from the **Placement** panel.

4. Move the cursor in the left curtain grid area and click when the curtain wall of Hall 1 is highlighted, as shown in Figure 8-47; the mullions are automatically added to all the curtain grids. Similarly, add mullions to the Hall 2 curtain walls.

5. Choose the **Visual Style** button from the **View Control Bar** and choose the **Shaded** option from the flyout displayed to view the shaded South elevation, as shown in Figure 8-48.

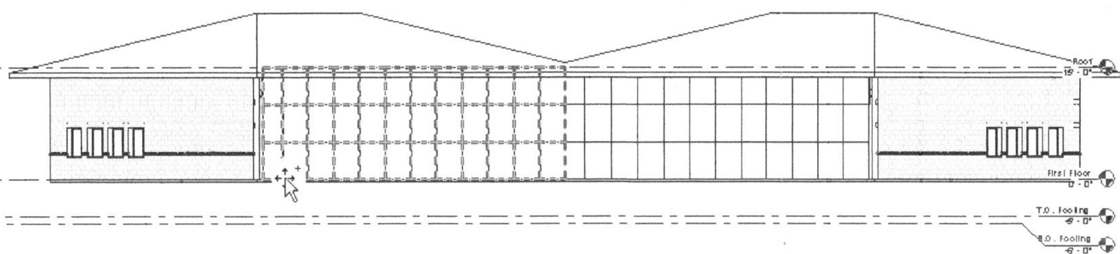

Figure 8-47 Selecting a curtain wall to add mullions

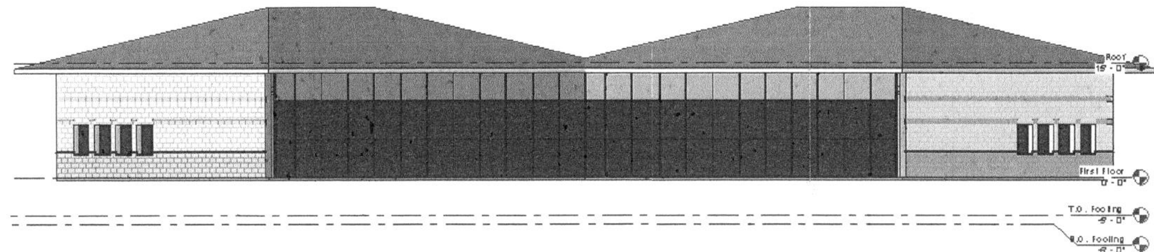

Figure 8-48 South elevation of the club project showing the curtain wall created with mullions

6. Double-click on the **First Floor** in the **Floor Plans** head in the **Project Browser** to return to the first floor plan view.

Saving the Project

In this section, you will save the project file using the **Save As** tool.

1. Choose **Save As > Project** from the **File** menu and enter the required name in the **File name** edit box of the **Save As** dialog box.

   For Imperial **c08_Club_tut2**
   For Metric **M_c08_Club_tut2**

   Next, choose **Save**; the project file is saved.

2. Choose **Close** from the **File** menu to close the file.

Tutorial 3 Elevator and Stair Lobby

In this tutorial, you will open the *Elevator and Stair Lobby* project created in Exercise 2 of Chapter 7 and extend the walls to 3'0"(915 mm) above the roof level. You can also download this file from the *www.cadcim.com*. Copy all doors, windows, and components at the same location on all upper floors. Also, create a flat roof for the stairs portion at the roof level. Add stairs to the project based on the project parameters, as shown in Figure 8-49. The texts and dimensions have been given for reference and are not to be created. Use the project parameters given next. **(Expected time: 45 min)**

1. Stairs: **Width- 5'0"(1524 mm), Minimum Tread Depth- 11"(279 mm), Maximum Riser Height- 7"(178 mm)**

2. Roof type-
   For Imperial **Basic Roof : Generic 9 " - Flat**
   For Metric **Basic Roof : Generic 400mm - Flat**

The following steps are required to complete this tutorial:

a. Open the project file and extend the walls using the **Top Constraint** parameter.
b. Copy the elements such as door, windows, floor, ceiling, and openings to the upper floors using the **Paste** tool.
c. Create the flat roof at the top most floor using the **Roof** tool, refer to Figure 8-50.
d. Add stairs to the project using the **Stairs** tool, refer to Figures 8-51 through 8-55.
e. Create railings for the stairs at the fourth floor, refer to Figures 8-56 and 8-57.
f. Save the project using the **Save As** tool.
   For Imperial *c08_ElevatorandStairLobby_tut3*
   For Metric *M_c08_ElevatorandStairLobby_tut3.rvt*
g. Close the project.

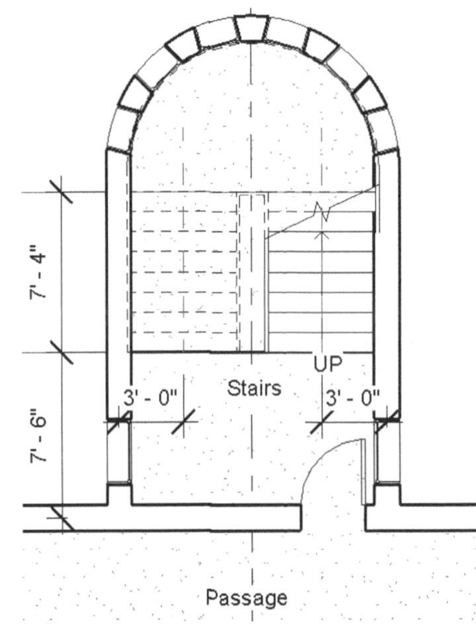

Figure 8-49 *Sketch plan for adding stairs to the Elevator and Stair Lobby project*

Opening the Project File and Extending the Walls

First, open the *c07_ElevatorandStairLobby_ex2.rvt* project. The walls can be extended by setting the **Top Constraint** parameter to the roof level.

1. Choose **Open > Project** from the **File** menu and open the **c07_ElevatorandStairLobby_ex2.rvt** (for Metric **M_c07_ElevatorandStairLobby_ex2.rvt**) file created in Exercise 2 of Chapter 7 and ensure that the first floor plan is opened.

You can also download this file from *www.cadcim.com*. The path of the file is as follows: *Textbooks > Civil/GIS > Revit Architecture> Exploring Autodesk Revit 2018 for Architecture*.

2. Select all elements using the crossing method and then choose the **Filter** tool from the **Selection** panel in the **Modify | Multi-Select** tab; the **Filter** dialog box is displayed.

3. In the **Filter** dialog box, clear all check boxes except the **Walls** check box and choose **OK**; all walls in the project are selected.

4. In the **Properties** palette, click in the **Value** field corresponding to the **Top Constraint** instance parameter and select the **Up to level: Roof** option from the drop-down list displayed.

5. Enter **3'0"(915 mm)** in the **Value** field for the **Top Offset** parameter and then choose the **Apply** button. Now, press ESC to exit the selection.

Copying Elements to Upper Floors

In this section, you will select elements and components using the **Filter** tool and use the **Paste** tool to copy them to the upper levels.

1. Select all elements using the crossing method and then choose the **Filter** tool from the **Selection** panel of the **Modify | Multi-Select** tab; the **Filter** dialog box is displayed.

2. Clear the check box corresponding to **Walls** in the **Filter** dialog box and then choose the **OK** button; the dialog box is closed.

3. Next, choose the **Copy to Clipboard** tool from the **Clipboard** panel of the **Modify | Multi-Select** tab is displayed.

4. Choose the **Aligned to Selected Levels** tool from **Modify | Multi-Select > Clipboard > Paste** drop-down; the **Select Levels** dialog box is displayed.

5. While holding the CTRL key, select the **Second Floor**, **Third Floor**, and **Fourth Floor** levels and then choose **OK**; the **Select Levels** dialog box closes. The selected elements and the components are pasted at the specified levels. Press ESC to exit the selection.

6. To view the multistory building model and exit from the current selection, choose **3D** from the **Project Browser**.

Adding Roof to the Roof Floor

You need to use the **Roof** tool to create a flat roof at the top floor level.

1. Double-click on **Roof** from the **Floor Plans** head in the **Project Browser** to display the roof floor plan.

2. Choose the **Roof by Footprint** tool from **Architecture > Build > Roof** drop-down; the **Modify | Create Roof Footprint** tab is displayed.

3. Ensure that the **Defines slope** check box is cleared in the **Options Bar**. Also, ensure that the **Pick Walls** tool is chosen by default in the **Draw** panel of the **Modify | Create Roof Footprint** tab.

4. Sketch the roof using the **Pick Walls** tool. Ensure that the roof boundary is created on the inner face and is connected end-to-end.

Note

You can also create the roof separately for elevator, lobby, and stairs area.

5. Choose the **Finish Edit Mode** button from the **Mode** panel to create the roof at the roof level.

6. In the **Properties** palette, click in the **Type Selector** drop-down list and select the required option from it.

   For Imperial **Basic Roof : Generic -9"**
   For Metric **Basic Roof : Generic -400 mm**

7. Double-click on **3D** under the **3D Views** head in the **Project Browser** to display the 3D view of the multistory apartment.

8. Right-click on the **ViewCube** tool; a shortcut menu is displayed. Choose **Orient to a Direction > Northwest Isometric** from the shortcut menu.

   The northwest view of the building model is displayed in the drawing window, as shown in Figure 8-50.

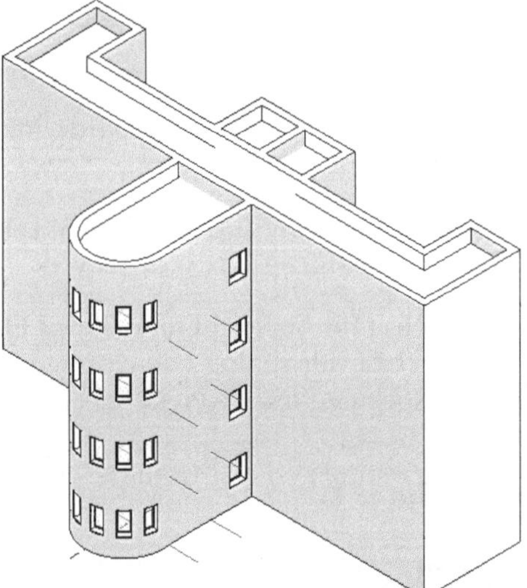

Figure 8-50 *The Northwest view of the Elevator and Stair Lobby project*

Adding Stairs

To add stairs to the project, you should first open the appropriate view. For most of the locations, you will find it easier to sketch the stairs in the plan view. Since the stairs start from the first floor, you can open the corresponding floor plan. Use the **Run** tool to sketch the stair run and the **Boundary** tool to create the semicircular landing. Before sketching the stairs, draw reference planes to assist you in sketching the run.

1. Double-click on the **First Floor** from the **Floor Plans** head of the **Project Browser**.
2. Choose the **Stair by Sketch** tool from the **Architecture > Circulation > Stair** drop-down; the **Modify | Create Stairs Sketch** tab is displayed.
3. In the **Properties** palette, click in the value field corresponding to the **Width** instance parameter and type **5'0"(1524 mm)** and select the default stair type from the **Type Selector** drop-down list.
4. After setting the stairs properties, you can draw the reference planes. To do so, invoke the **Ref Plane** tool from the **Work Plane** panel; the **Place Reference Plane** tab is displayed.
5. Draw the reference planes, as shown in Figure 8-51 (Dimensions have been given only for reference).

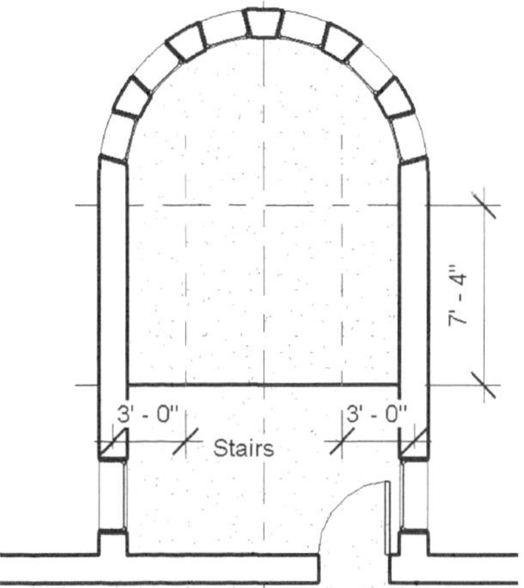

Figure 8-51 *Drawing reference planes to locate the start point and the endpoints of the stair run*

6. After drawing the reference planes, press ESC. Next, choose the **Modify | Create Stairs Sketch** tab and then choose the **Run** tool from the **Draw** panel.
7. Move the cursor near the start point of the first run and click when the **Endpoint** object snap appears, refer to Figure 8-52.
8. Move the cursor vertically up until the **Intersection** object snap appears and click to sketch the first end of the run of stairs, as shown in Figure 8-53.

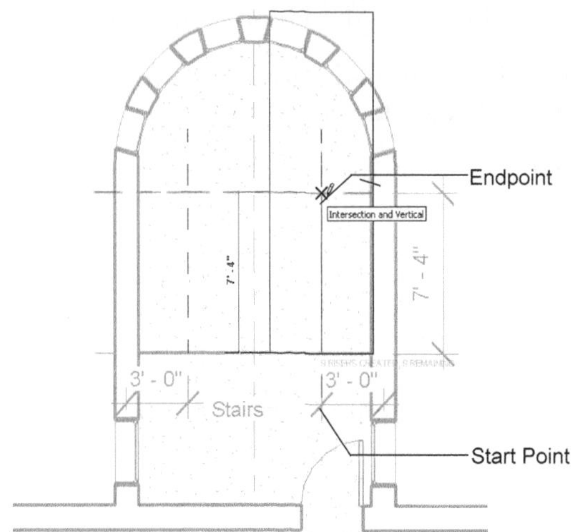

Figure 8-52 Specifying the start point and the endpoint of the first run of stairs

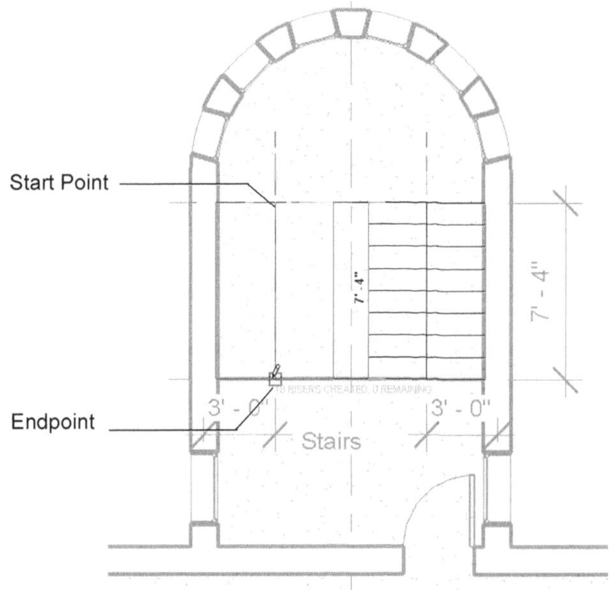

Figure 8-53 Specifying the start point and the endpoint of the second run of stairs

9. Similarly, click to specify the start point of the next run of stairs, as shown in Figure 8-54.

10. Move the cursor vertically downward and click when the intersection object snap appears, refer to Figure 8-55. On doing so, the stairs are sketched with the rectangular mid-landing, as shown in Figure 8-56. You can now edit their boundary and sketch the profile of the landing using the **Boundary** tool.

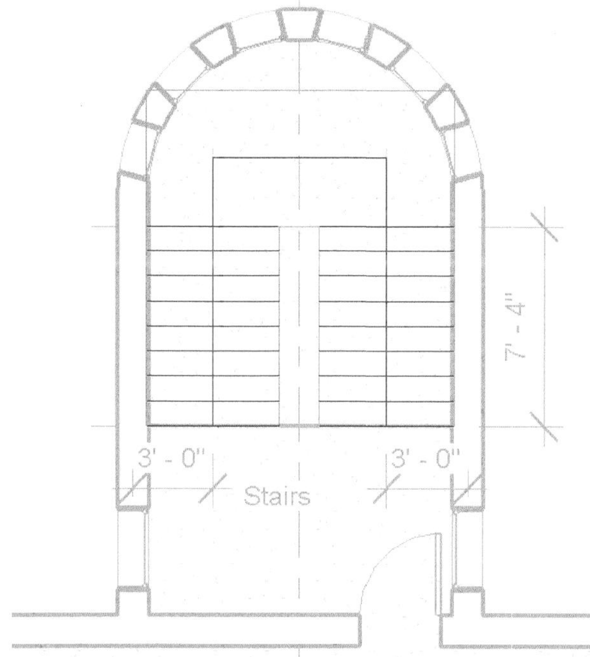

Figure 8-54 *Sketch of the stairs with two runs*

11. Choose the **Modify** button from the **Select** panel.

12. Now, select the three boundary lines of the mid-landing and press the DELETE key.

13. Invoke the **Boundary** tool from the **Draw** panel and use the **Pick Lines** tool and other modification tools to draw the semicircular boundary of the landing, as shown in Figure 8-55.

Note

While sketching the semicircular boundary for the landing of the stairs, make sure that its endpoints join with the endpoints of the boundary of the stairs.

14. Now, invoke the **Connect Levels** tool from the **Multistory Stairs** panel of the **Modify/Create Stair** tab; the **Go To View** dialog box is displayed. Choose the required view and then select the **Fourth Floor** level. Next, choose the **Finish Edit Mode** button from the **Mode** panel; the staircase is added upto the fourth floor level. By default, railings are created on both sides of the stairs. You can delete it from the drawing by selecting it and then pressing DELETE.

Creating Railings

The next step is to complete the railing of the stairs at the fourth floor level.

1. Double-click on the **Fourth Floor** from the **Floor Plans** head in the **Project Browser** to display the corresponding floor plan. Next, choose **Visual Style > Wireframe** from the **View Control Bar** to display the view in wireframe.

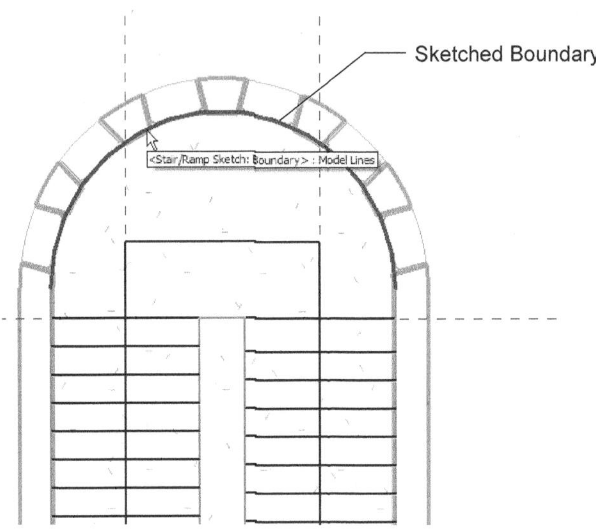

Figure 8-55 Sketching a new boundary for the mid-landing

2. Now, choose the **Sketch Path** tool from the **Architecture > Circulation >Railing** drop-down; the **Modify | Create Railing Path** tab is displayed. Also, Autodesk Revit enters the sketch mode with the **Line** tool invoked from the **Draw** panel of the **Modify | Create Railing Path** tab.

3. Sketch the line defining the railing, as shown in Figure 8-56.

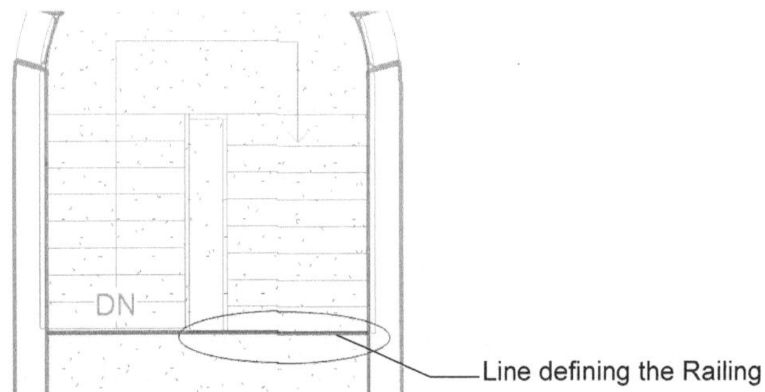

Figure 8-56 Sketching the railing at the roof level

4. Choose the **Finish Edit Mode** button from the **Mode** panel to create the railing.

5. Double-click on **Section V** from the **Sections (Building Section)** head in the **Project Browser** to view the section through the stairs. Increase the size of the section boundary box to display the complete building section. It appears similar to the illustration shown in Figure 8-57.

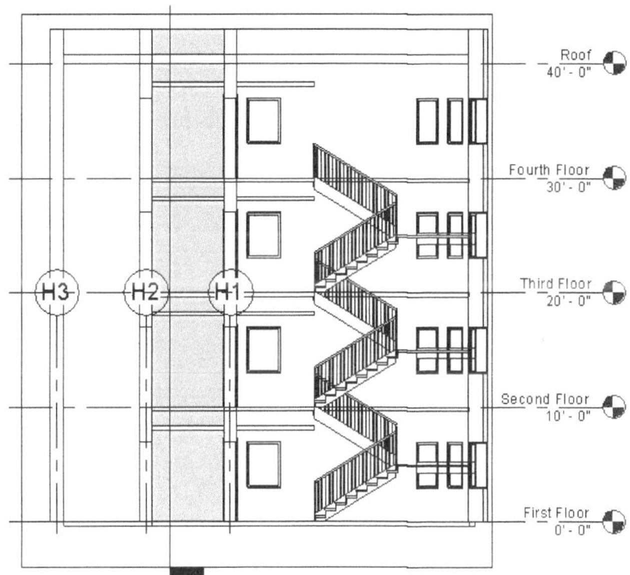

Figure 8-57 Section through the stairs

6. Return to the first floor plan view using the **Project Browser**.

Saving the Project

In this section, you will save the project file using the **Save As** tool.

1. Choose **Save As > Project** from the **File** menu and enter **c08_ElevatorandStairLobby_tut3** in the **File name** edit box of the **Save As** dialog box. Next, choose **Save** to save the project file.

2. Choose **Close** from the **File** menu to close the project file.

Tutorial 4 Office

In this tutorial, you will open the *Office* project created in Tutorial 3 of Chapter 7. You can also download this file from the *www.cadcim.com (Textbooks > Civil/GIS > Revit Architecture> Exploring Autodesk Revit 2018 for Architecture)*. Create a flat roof for the stairs portion at the roof level. Also create an opening for the stairs. Add stairs to the project based on the project parameters shown in Figure 8-58. The texts and dimensions have been given for reference and are not to be created. Use the project parameters given next. **(Expected time: 45 min)**

1. Stairs
   Width: 5'0"(1500 mm), Minimum Tread Depth: 11"(275 mm), Maximum Riser Height: 7"(175 mm)

2. Roof type:
   For Imperial **Basic Roof : Generic 9 " - Flat**
   For Metric **Basic Roof : Generic 400mm - Flat**

The following steps are required to complete this tutorial:

a. Create the flat roof at the topmost floor using the Roof tool, refer to Figure 8-59.
b. Add stairs to the project using the Stairs tool, refer to Figure 8-60.
c. Create railings for the stairs, as shown in Figure 8-61.
d. Create opening in the floor.
e. Save the project using the Save As tool.
   For Imperial *c08_Office_tut4*
   For Metric *M_c08_Office_tut4.rvt*
f. Close the project.

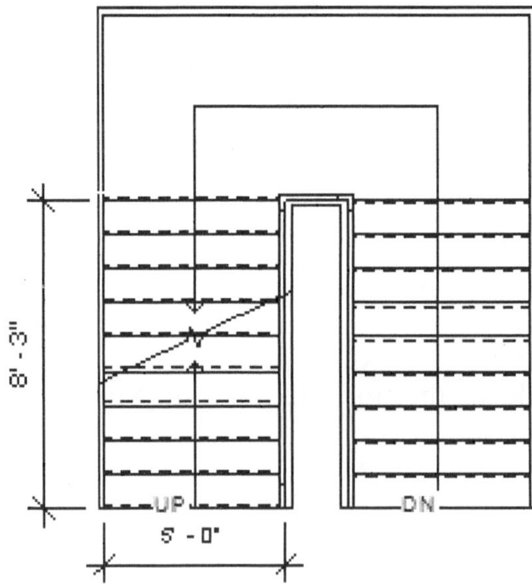

Figure 8-58 *Sketch plan for adding stairs to the Office project*

Adding Roof to the Roof Floor

In this section, you will use the **Roof** tool to create a flat roof at the top floor level.

1. Double-click on **Roof** from the **Floor Plans** head in the **Project Browser** to display the roof floor plan.

2. Choose the **Roof by Footprint** tool from **Architecture > Build > Roof** drop-down; the **Modify | Create Roof Footprint** tab is displayed.

3. Ensure that the **Defines slope** check box is cleared in the **Options Bar**. Choose the **Rectangle** tool and enter **18"(450 mm)** in the **Offset** edit box as the overhang value.

4. Sketch the roof using the **Rectangle** tool. Ensure that the roof boundary is created and is connected end-to-end.

5. In the **Properties** palette, select the required option from the **Type Selector** drop-down list.
   For Imperial **Basic Roof : Generic -9"**
   For Metric **Basic Roof : Generic -400 mm**

6. Double-click on **3D** under the **3D Views** head in the **Project Browser** to display the 3D view of the multistory apartment.

7. Right-click on the **ViewCube** tool; a shortcut menu is displayed. Choose **Orient to a Direction > Northwest Isometric** from the shortcut menu; the northwest view of the building model is displayed in the drawing window, as shown in Figure 8-59.

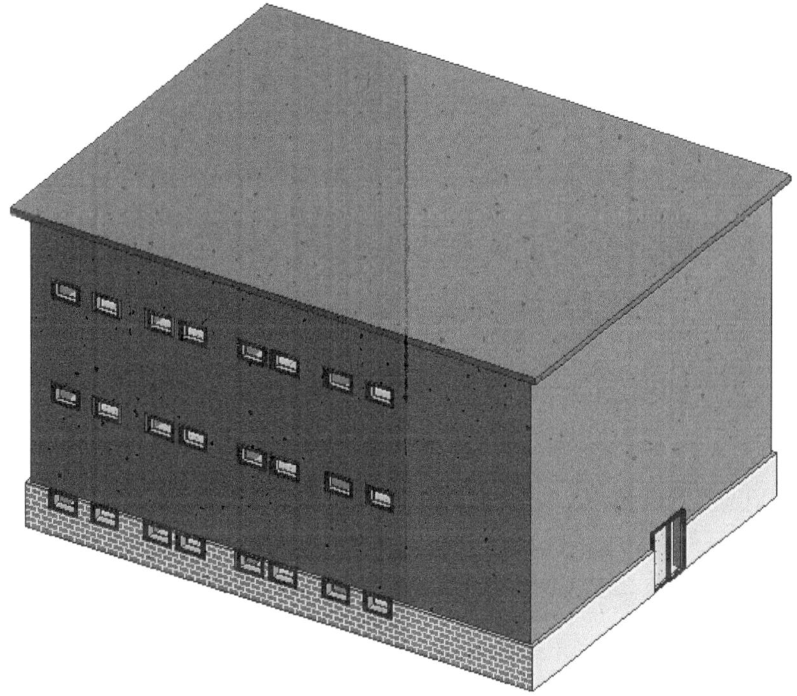

Figure 8-59 *The Northwest view of the building model*

Adding Stairs

To add stairs to the project, you should first open the appropriate view. For most of the locations, you will find it easier to sketch the stairs in the plan view. Since the stairs start from the first floor, you can open the corresponding floor plan. Use the **Run** tool to sketch the stair run and the **Boundary** tool to create the semicircular landing. Before sketching the stairs, draw reference planes to assist you in sketching the run.

1. Double-click on the **Ground Floor** from the **Floor Plans** head of the **Project Browser.**

2. Choose the **Stair** tool from the **Circulation** panel of the **Architecture** tab; the **Modify | Create Stair** tab is displayed.

3. In the **Options bar**, click in the value field corresponding to the **Actual Run Width** edit box and type **5'0"(1500 mm)** and select the **Monolithic** stair type from the **Type Selector** drop-down list.

Note

For metric tutorial, you are required to set the number of risers 20 next to the ***Desired Number of Risers*** *parameter in the* ***Properties*** *palette.*

4. After setting the stairs properties, move the cursor to the left area of the building and create stair.

5. Click to specify the start point of the next run of stairs.

6. Move the cursor to left and click when the intersection object snap appears, as shown in Figure 8-60. Select the **Run:Left** option in the **Location Line** drop-down list and then create the stairs, as shown in Figure 8-61.

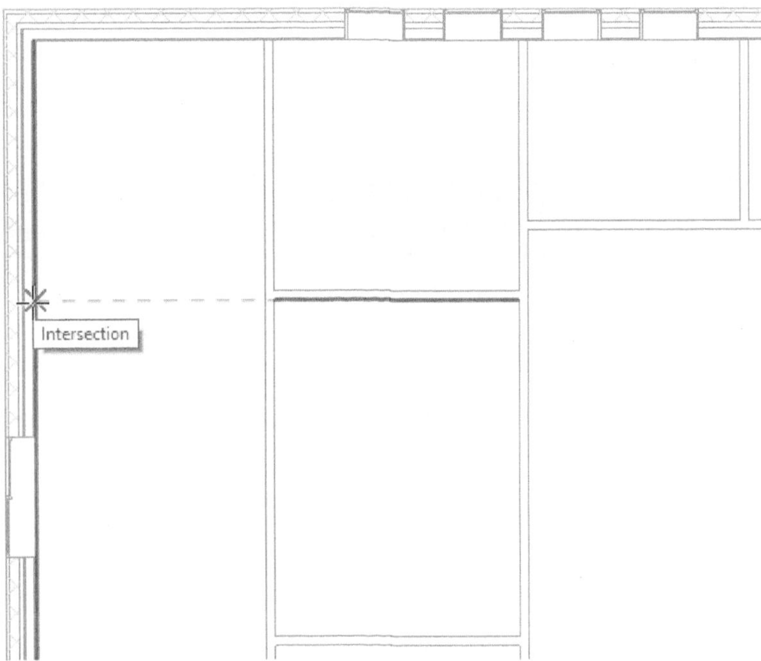

Figure 8-60 *Object Snap for the staircase*

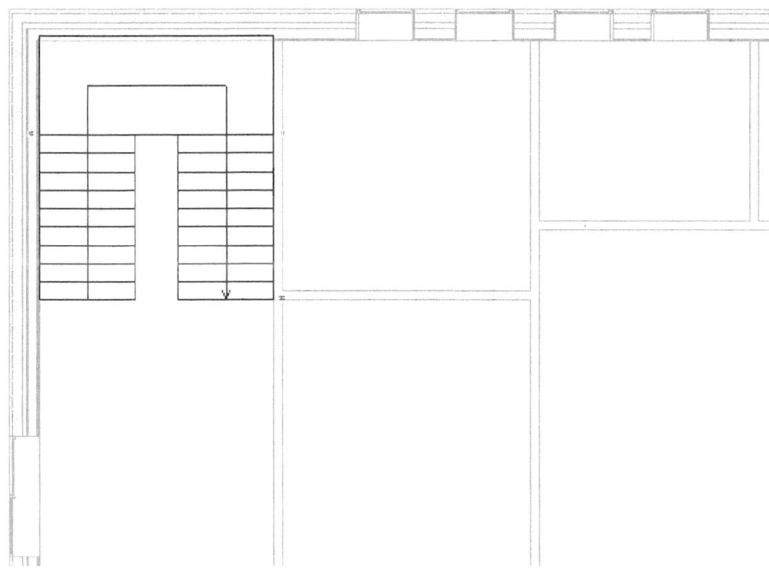

Figure 8-61 *Sketch of the stairs with two runs*

7. Now, invoke the **Connect Levels** tool from the **Multistory Stairs** panel of the **Modify/Create Stair** tab; the **Go To View** dialog box is displayed. Choose the **Elevation:North** view and then choose the **Open View** button; the north elevation view is displayed.

8. Now, select the **Select Floor** level from the elevation view and then choose the **Finish Edit Mode** button; the staircase is created at the second floor level, as shown in Figure 8-62. By default, railings are created on both sides of the stairs. You can delete the wall side railing from the drawing by selecting it and then pressing DELETE.

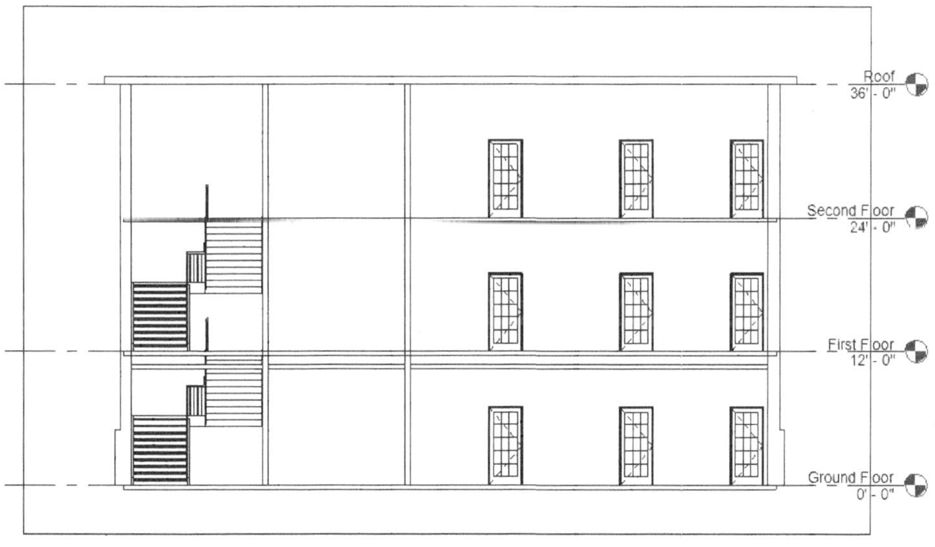

Figure 8-62 *Section through the stairs*

Creating Opening in The Floor

1. Double-click on the Ground Floor under the **Floor Plans** in the **Project Browser**; the ground floor plan is displayed.

2. Select the **By Face** tool from the **Opening** panel of the **Architecture** tab; the cursor is changed into cross hair.

3. Select the face of the ceiling; the **Modify|Create Opening Boundary** contextual tab is displayed.

4. In this tab, choose the **Rectangle** tool from the **Draw** panel and create the rectangle around the stairs area, as shown in Figure 8-63.

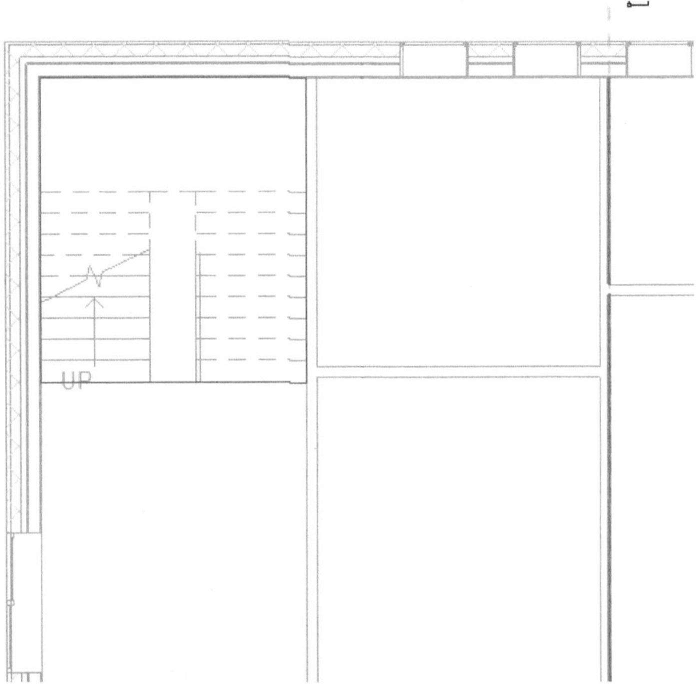

Figure 8-63 *Rectangle created for the Opening*

5. Choose the **Finish Edit Mode** button; the opening is created.

6. Double-click on the **First Floor** under the **Floor Plan** head in the **Project Browser** and select the created opening and then choose the **Copy to Clipboard** tool from the **Clipboard** panel.

7. Now, select the **Aligned to Select Levels** option from the **Paste** drop-down list; the **Select Levels** dialog box is displayed.

8. In this dialog box, select the **First Floor**, **Second Floor**, and **Roof** options and then, choose the **OK** button; the opening is created to all levels.

Note

*Check whether the openings are created in all faces of ceiling or floor, or not. If not, then create the opening using the **By Face** tool.*

Saving the Project

In this section, you will save the project file using the **Save As** tool.

1. Choose **Save As > Project** from the **File** menu and enter **c08_Office_tut4** in the **File name** edit box of the **Save As** dialog box. Next, choose **Save** to save the project file.

2. Choose **Close** from the **File** menu to close the project file.

Self-Evaluation Test

Answer the following questions and then compare them to those given at the end of this chapter:

1. You can lock components with other elements by using the _________ option.

2. After selecting the stairs, you can choose the _________ button from the **Modify | Create Stairs Sketch** tab of the ribbon to modify the sketch and the properties of the selected stairs.

3. You can use the _________ tool to break the boundary line at landings.

4. The _________ tool is used to add mullions to a curtain grid.

5. For curtain grids, you can enter a value for the _________ parameter to set the spacing between the vertical curtain grids.

6. Components can be moved from one level to another level by dragging. (T/F)

7. You cannot modify the properties of in-built components. (T/F)

8. You can add mullions to curtain walls by selecting curtain grids individually. (T/F)

9. You can change the direction of stairs after it has been created. (T/F)

10. The **Paste** tool can be used to copy elements from one level to multiple levels. (T/F)

Review Questions

Answer the following questions:

1. Which of the following parameters can be used to create stairs from the lowest to the top level in a multilevel building model?

   (a) **Top Level** (b) **Base Level**
   (c) **Multistory Top Level** (d) **Stair Rules**

2. Which of the following tools can be used to draw guidelines to sketch the stairs?

   (a) **Ref Plane** (b) **Work Plane**
   (c) **Lines** (d) **Grid**

3. Which of the following options can be used to add mullions partially along curtain grids?

   (a) **All Empty Segments** (b) **Entire Grid Line**
   (c) **Curtain Grid** (d) **Grid Line Segment**

4. By modifying the **Level** instance parameter, you can move component from one level to another. (T/F)

5. The rules set in the **Stair Calculator** cannot be modified. (T/F)

6. While sketching stairs, Autodesk Revit displays the number of created and remaining treads. (T/F)

7. You can use the **Cut** tool to break a boundary line at mid-landings. (T/F)

8. For curtain walls, doors can be added by replacing the panels with the curtain wall door. (T/F)

9. You can modify the slope of the ramp after creating it. (T/F)

10. You can use combination of the **Run** and **Boundary** tools to create stairs. (T/F)

EXERCISES

Exercise 1 Apartment 2

Add furniture and sanitary components to the *c07_Apartment2_ex1.rvt* project created in Exercise 1 of Chapter 7. The approximate location of the components is given in Figure 8-64. The text has been given only for reference and is not to be created. Extend the exterior walls to 3'0" above the roof level and copy all interior walls, interior doors, windows, and components at the same location on all the three upper floors. Also, create a flat roof at the roof level. Use the following parameters for various components to be added. The Northeast 3D view of the completed project should appear similar to the illustration shown in Figure 8-65.

(Expected time: 30 min)

Alphabets in Figure 8-62 represent the furniture and plumbing components to be used, as given below.

1. Furniture Components
   For Imperial: Furniture components from the **Furniture** folder of the **US Imperial**:
   A- **Bed Shaker: Double 56" x 78"**
   B- **Entertainment Center: 72" x 72" x 24"**
   C- **Dresser- 72" x 60" x 18"**
   D- **Sofa: 72"**
   E- **Table-Ellipse : 72" x 36"**

F- **Table-Coffee : 36" x 72" x 18"**
G- **Table-End: 24" x 24"**

For Metric: Furniture components from the **Furniture** folder of the **US Metric**:
A- **Bed Shaker: Double 1422 x 1981 mm**
B- **Entertainment Center: 1830 x 1830 x 0610 mm**
C- **Dresser- 1220 x 1525 x 0610 mm**
D- **Sofa: 1830 mm**
E- **Table-Ellipse : 1800 x 0900 mm**
F- **Table-Coffee : 0915 x 1830 x 457 mm**
G- **Table-End: 0610 x 0610 mm**

2. Plumbing Components
For Imperial: Plumbing components from the **Plumbing Fixtures** folder of the **US Imperial**:
J- **Kitchenette-Medium**: **8'6"** (modified size)
K- **Toilet-Domestic-3D**
L- **Tub-Rectangular-3D**
M- **Sink Vanity- Square: 24" x 19"**

For Metric: Plumbing components from the **Plumbing Fixtures** folder of the **US Metric**:
J- **Kitchenette-Medium**: **2591 mm** (modified size)
K- **Toilet-Domestic-3D**
L- **Tub-Rectangular-3D**
M- **Sink Vanity- Square 0610 x 0483 mm**

3. Roof type- **Basic Roof: Generic 400mm** - Flat.

4. Name of the file to be saved-
For Imperial **c08_Apartment2_ex1**
For Metric **M_c08_Apartment2_ex1**

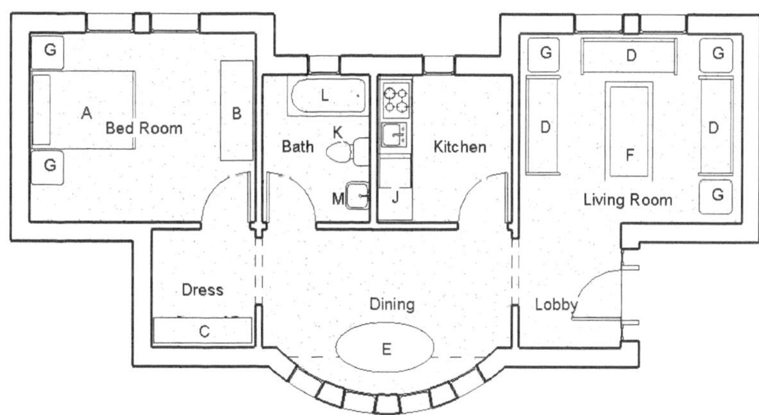

Figure 8-64 *Sketch plan for adding components to the Apartment 2 project*

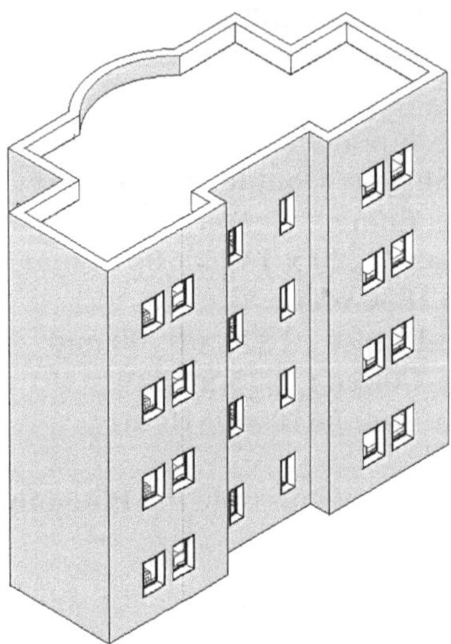

Figure 8-65 The Northeast 3D view of the Apartment 2 project

Exercise 2 Residential Building: Components

Add furniture and sanitary components to the project created in Exercise 3 of Chapter 7. The approximate location of the components is given in Figure 8-66. The text has been given only for reference and is not to be created. Extend the exterior walls to 3'0" above the roof level and copy all interior doors, windows, and components at the same location on all upper floors. Also, create a flat roof at the roof level. Use the following parameters for various components to be added. **(Expected time: 30 min)**

Alphabets in Figure 8-64 represent the furniture and plumbing components to be used, as given below.

1. Furniture Components

For Imperial: Furniture components from the **Furniture** folder of the **US Imperial**:

A- **Bed Shaker: Double 56" x 78"**
B- **Bed Standard: King 78" x 80"**
C- **Cabinet- File 2 Drawer 18" x 29"**
D- **Entertainment Center: 58" x 58" x 24" (Customized)**
E- **Dresser- 72" x 60" x 18"**
F- **Dresser- 48" x 72" x 24"**
G- **Sofa Pensi: 84"**
H- **Table-Coffee : 36" x 72" x 18"**
I- **Table- Dining Round w Chairs 60" Diameter**
J- **Table-End: 24" x 24"**
K- **TV-Flat Screen: 42"**
L- **TV-Flat Screen: 56"**

For Metric: Furniture components from the **Furniture** folder of the **US Metric**:

A- **Bed Shaker: Double 1422 x 1981 mm**
B- **Bed Standard: King 1981 x 2032 mm**
C- **Cabinet- File 2 Drawer 457 x 734 mm**

D- **Entertainment Center: 1450 x 1450 x 0610 mm (Customized)**
E- **Dresser- 1830 x 1525 x 0457 mm**
F- **Dresser- 1220 x 1830 x 0610 mm**
G- **Sofa Pensi: 2134 mm**
H- **Table-Coffee : 0915 x 1830 x 18"**
I- **Table- Dining Round w Chairs 1525mm Diameter**
J- **Table-End: 0610 x 0610 mm**
K- **TV-Flat Screen: 1070mm**
L- **TV-Flat Screen: 1270mm**

2. Plumbing Components
   For Imperial: Plumbing components from the **Plumbing Fixtures** folder of the **US Imperial**:
   M- **Tub- Rectangular 3D (4'10" Customized)**
   N- **Toilet- Domestic-3D**
   O- **Sink Vanity- Round: 19" x 19"**

   For Metric: Plumbing components from the **Plumbing Fixtures** folder of the **US Metric**:
   M- **Tub- Rectangular 3D (115mm Customized)**
   N- **Toilet- Domestic-3D**
   O- **Sink Vanity- Round: 480 x 480 mm**

3. Domestic Components
   For Imperial: Domestic components from the **Domestic** sub folder of the **Speciality Equipments** folder of the **US Imperial**:
   P- **Kitchenette-Small**: **54"**
   Q- **Refrigerator 30" x 32" RH**
   R- **Microwave 32" x 18" x 20"**
   For Metric: Domestic components from the **Domestic** sub folder of the **Speciality Equipments** folder of the **US Metric**:
   P- **Kitchenette-Small**: **1372mm**
   Q- **Refrigerator 660 x 760 mm**
   R- **Microwave 815 x 450 x 500 mm**

4. Flat Roof
   For Imperial: **Generic-6"**
   For Metric: **Generic- 150mm**

5. Name of the file to be saved:
   For Imperial **c08_residential_component_ex2**
   For Metric **M_c08_residential_component_ex2**

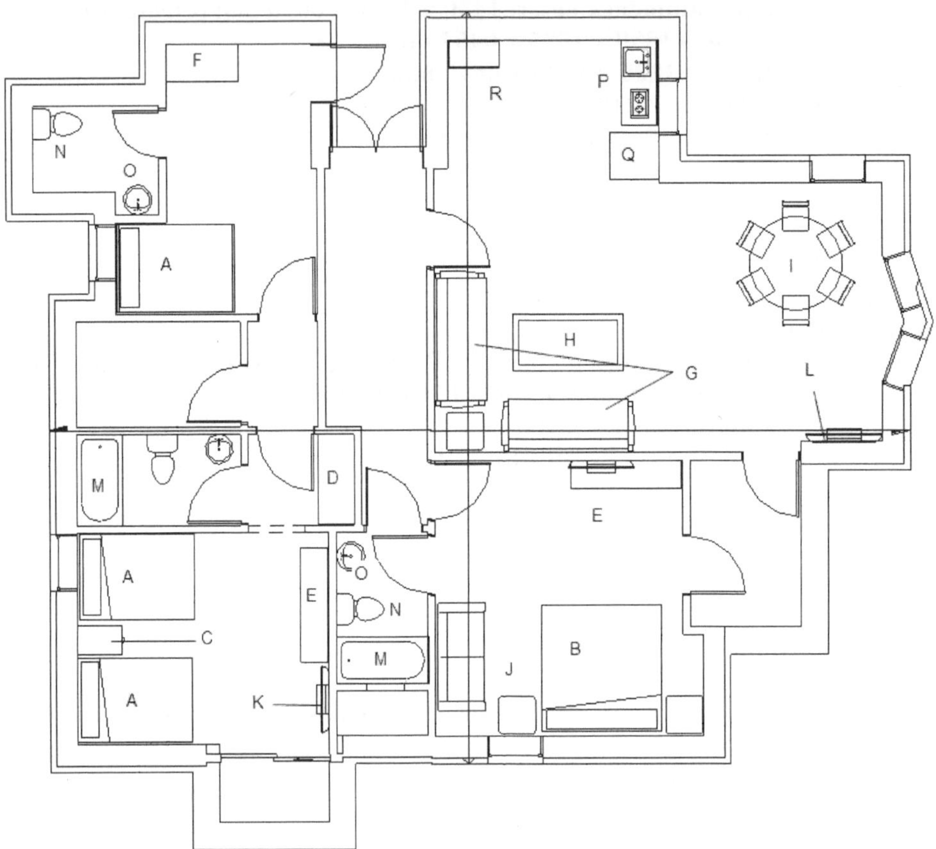

Figure 8-66 *Sketch plan for adding components to the residential project*

Answers to Self-Evaluation Test

1. Move with Nearby Elements, **2.** Modify Sketch, **3.** Split, **4.** Mullion, **5.** Spacing, **6.** F, **7.** F, **8.** T, **9.** T, **10.** T

Chapter 9

Adding Site Features

Learning Objectives

After completing this chapter, you will be able to:
- *Create contoured sites using the Toposurface tool*
- *Modify the site parameters*
- *Add property lines to the site plan using the Property Line tool*
- *Add building pads in the site plan using the Building Pad tool*
- *Add parking components to the site plan*
- *Add site components and plantations to the site plan*

INTRODUCTION

In the previous chapters, you learned the usage of different building elements such as walls, doors, windows, stairs, ramps, curtain wall, and so on. Now, in this chapter, you will learn to create contoured sites and modify the site parameters. Moreover, you will also learn to add property line, building pad, parking components, and so on to the site plan with the help of various tools available in Revit.

WORKING WITH SITE FEATURES

Autodesk Revit provides you with various tools to create site features. These tools can be accessed from the **Model Site** and **Modify Site** panels in the **Massing & Site** tab, refer to Figure 9-1.

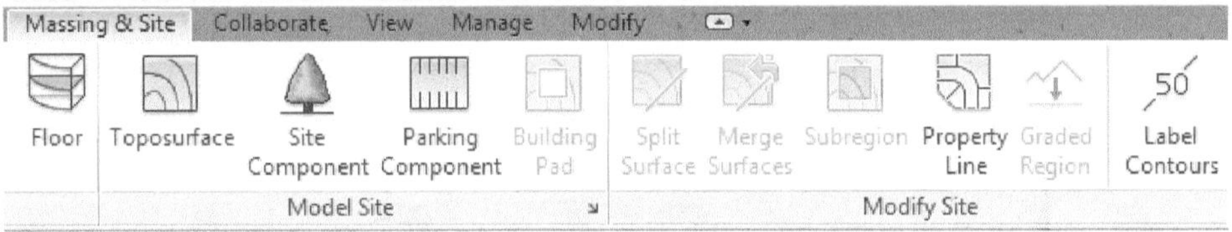

*Figure 9-1 Tools in the **Massing & Site** tab*

Note

*In the **Massing & Site** tab, the tools in the **Conceptual Mass** and **Model by Face** panels are used for creating building massing and are not useful for creating site features.*

The **Model Site** panel in the **Massing & Site** tab consists of various tools that are used for creating site features. These tools are **Toposurface**, **Site Component**, **Parking Component**, and **Building Pad**. In the **Model Site** panel, there is an inclined arrow placed at the lower right corner. On clicking the arrow, the **Site Settings** dialog box will be displayed. You can use this dialog box to change different settings related to the entire site. The options in this dialog box will be discussed later in this chapter. In the **Model Site** panel of the **Massing & Site** tab, the **Building Pad** tool will be inactive by default. To activate this tool, open a 3D view or a site plan view and create a toposurface in the drawing. A toposurface is a contoured site that can be generated using the **Toposurface** tool in the **Model Site** panel. The **Building Pad** tool is used to create a pad for placing a building block. Similarly, you can use the **Site Component** and **Parking Component** tools to insert components like trees, bollards, building signs, planters, parking space, and so on.

The tools in the **Modify Site** panel in the **Massing & Site** tab can be used to modify the site features in your drawing. The tools available in this panel are **Split Surface**, **Merge Surface**, **Subregion, Property Line**, and **Graded Region**. You can modify the created surfaces using the **Split Surface** and **Merge Surface** tools. The **Subregion** tool enables you to create smaller regions on a toposurface. The **Property Line** tool demarcates the extent of the site.

The **Graded Region** tool can be used to create a graded region. This graded region is created from an existing toposurface in the current phase. In the graded region, you can add or delete points, change the elevations of points, and also simplify the surface within it.

Tip

You can also generate a toposurface by picking points at different elevations. To do so, first pick points at one elevation, change the elevation, and then pick points at the new elevation.

Creating a Toposurface

Ribbon: Massing & Site > Model Site > Toposurface

A toposurface, also called topographical surface, is a graphical representation of the terrain of the site of a building project. The topograhical surfaces comprises of contour lines to represent elevation of the terrain. To create a toposurface for a building project, invoke the **Site** floor plan view or a **{3D}** view from the **Project Browser** and then invoke the **Toposurface** tool from the **Model Site** panel. On doing so, the **Modify | Edit Surface** tab will be displayed. The tools displayed in this tab are shown in Figure 9-2. They can be used to sketch and create topographical surfaces which are defined by picking the elevation points.

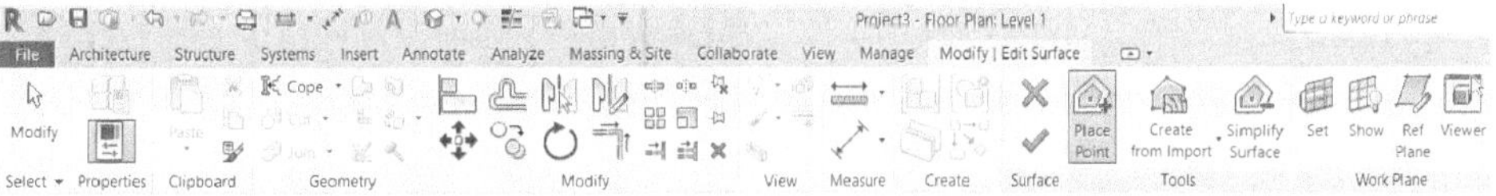

Figure 9-2 *Tools displayed in the **Modify / Edit Surface** tab*

In the **Modify | Edit Surface** tab, the **Place Point** tool in the **Tools** panel is chosen by default. This tool can be used to pick elevation points to define the profile of the surface. When this tool is invoked, the **Elevation** edit box and a drop-down list become available in the **Options Bar**. The **Elevation** edit box is used to specify the elevation of the points. You can select the **Absolute Elevation** option from the drop-down list, if it is not selected by default, to pick points at the specified distance (elevation) from the base level. However, if you create the second or the subsequent surfaces, or edit an existing surface by placing more points at the specified elevation, the **Relative to Surface** option will become available in the drop-down list. You can select this option to pick points at the specified distance, above or below a selected surface. After specifying the distance (elevation), move the cursor and pick the points in the site plan view. On picking three points, Revit will generate a triangle, as shown in Figure 9-3.

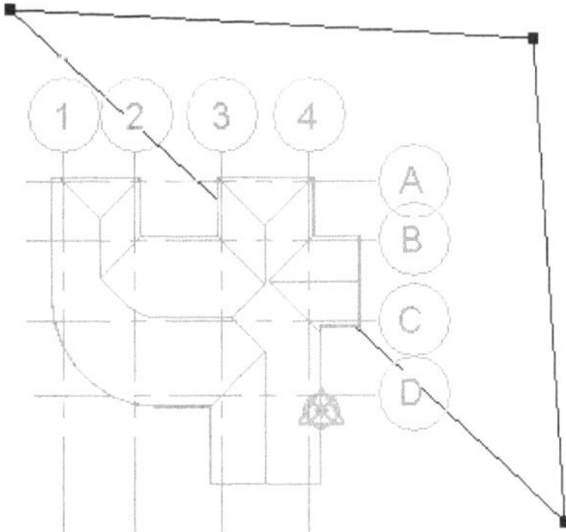

Figure 9-3 *A triangular surface generated by picking three points*

On picking additional points, you will notice that the elevation points join to form a continuous loop, as shown in Figure 9-4.

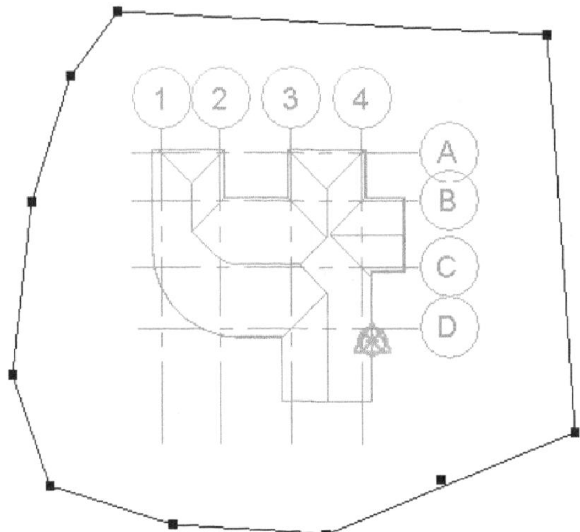

Figure 9-4 *Picking elevation points to sketch the toposurface*

In Autodesk Revit, you can generate a toposurface automatically from a 3D contour data that can be imported to your drawing. The file format of the imported data can be DWG, DXF, or DGN. Similarly, you can generate a toposurface automatically from a point file that can be in CSV or TXT format. Note that the points in a point file can be generated by a Civil Engineering software application. In Revit, you can generate a toposurface from a 3D contour data by choosing the tools from the **Create from Import** drop-down in the **Tools** panel of the **Modify | Edit Surface** tab. On doing so, a drop-down menu will be displayed. In this drop-down menu, you can choose any of the following two tools: **Select Import Instance** or **Specify Points File**. Choose the **Select Import Instance** tool to create a toposurface using the 3D contour data that has been imported to your drawing. Similarly, you can choose the **Specify Points File** tool to create a toposurface from a point file. As mentioned above, this point file will have points that are generated by a Civil Engineering application software and it will provide contour data that is created using a regularized grid of elevation points. Revit will import these points from the specified point file and then generate a toposurface.

Note

*The 3D contour data must be imported to your drawing before you create a toposurface from the contour data. To import the data, you can use the **Import CAD** tool from the **Import** panel of the **Insert** tab of the Ribbon. You will learn more about this tool in Chapter 16(free download).*

Before you create a toposurface, you can make specific settings to clean the unwanted spot elevations in a surface for a specified accuracy level. To do so, choose the **Simplify Surface** button from the **Tools** panel in the **Modify | Edit Surface** tab; the **Simplify Surface** dialog box will be displayed. In this dialog box, enter a suitable value in the **Accuracy** edit box and choose the **OK** button; the dialog box will close and the surface accuracy value will be assigned to the proposed surface. Now, you can pick points at different elevations to define the contours of the site. In this way, you can sketch different closed curves with different elevation points defining various levels in the toposurface. Complete the contour and choose the **Finish Surface** button from the **Surface** panel of the **Modify | Edit Surface** tab; the surface will be created. Figure 9-5 shows the sketched concentric contour lines in a toposurface. You can view the newly created toposurfaces in the elevation view, as shown in Figure 9-6. You can also set different properties of toposurfaces before or after creating them. To modify a toposurface, select it from the drawing; the **Modify | Topography** tab will be displayed. You can modify the locations of points in the surface by choosing various tools such as **Move**, **Copy**, **Mirror-Pick Axis**, **Mirror-Draw Axis**, and **Rotate** from the **Modify** panel of the **Modify | Topography** tab.

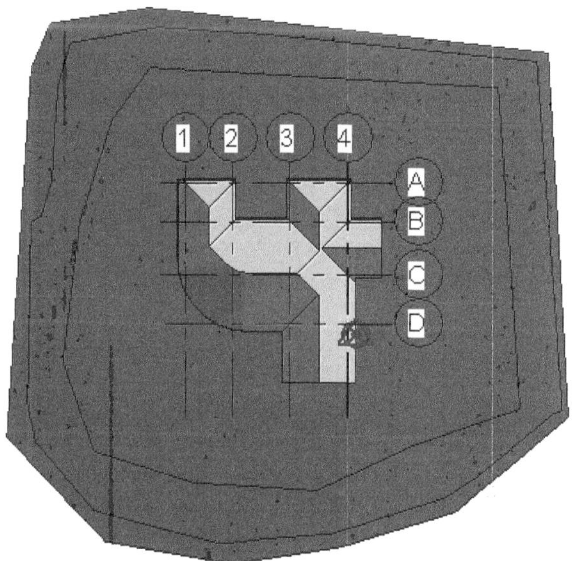

Figure 9-5 *Sketched concentric contour lines*

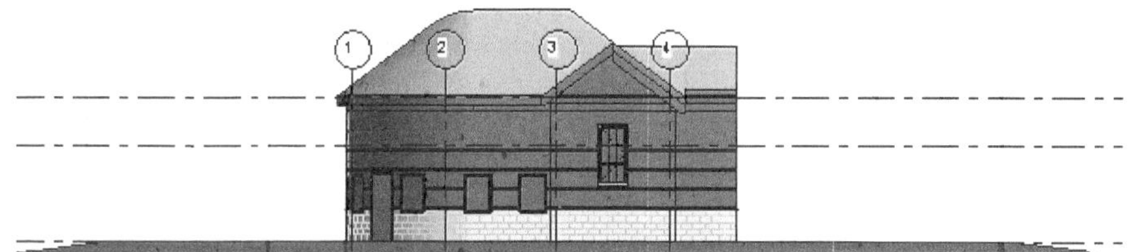

Figure 9-6 *Toposurfaces in the elevation view*

Creating Topographical Subregions

Ribbon: Massing & Site > Modify Site > Subregion

The **Subregion** tool is used to create a region on a toposurface. This tool is available only after a toposurface has been created. In a project, you can use the region created by the **Subregion** tool to represent various site features such as parking lots, pedestrian pavements, and so on. You can also assign different materials to each subregion. This tool can be effectively used to create conceptual site plans. Autodesk Revit also calculates the area of each subregion for scheduling purposes.

To create a region on a toposurface, choose the **Subregion** tool from the **Modify Site** panel in the **Massing & Site** tab; the **Modify | Create Subregion Boundary** tab will be displayed. From the **Draw** panel of the **Modify | Create Subregion Boundary** tab, you can invoke the **Line** tool and different sketching tools to sketch the subregion profile. After you have sketched the profile, choose the **Finish Edit Mode** button from the **Mode** panel to create the subregion. Once the subregion has been created, you can modify it. To do so, select the required subregion in the toposurface from the drawing; the **Modify | Topography** tab will be displayed. From this tab, choose the **Edit Boundary** button from the **Subregion** panel; the **Modify | Edit Boundary** tab will be displayed. You can use various tools from this tab to modify the sketch of the selected subregion.

Splitting a Topography

Ribbon: Massing & Site > Modify Site > Split Surface

The **Split Surface** tool is used to split a toposurface into two surfaces and then different materials can be assigned to them. In the project, you can use this tool to depict water bodies, special site features, and so on. To split a surface, invoke this tool from the **Modify Site** panel; you will be prompted to select the surface that you want to split from the drawing. On selecting the surface, the **Modify | Split Surface** tab will be displayed and Autodesk Revit will enter the sketch mode. In the **Modify | Split Surface** tab, you can use various sketching tools to draw lines, circles, polygons, and so on to split a selected surface. These tools are displayed in the list box available in the **Draw** panel. In the list box in the **Draw** panel, the **Line** tool is chosen by default. You can choose other tools like **Circle**, **Rectangle**, **Ellipse**, and **Pick Lines** to draw the profile of the boundary that will split the selected surface into two parts.

A split surface can be sketched by using two methods. In the first method, you need to create a closed loop that does not touch the boundaries of a surface, as shown in Figure 9-7.

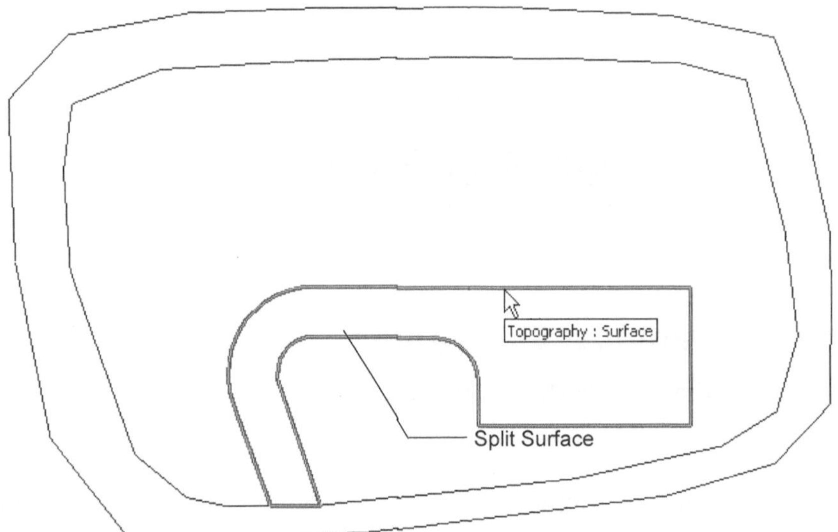

Figure 9-7 *Splitting a topographical surface using the* ***Split Surface*** *tool*

In the second method, you need to create an open line with both ends lying on the boundary. You can assign the new split surface a new material. To do so, select the split surface from the drawing; the instance properties of the surface will be displayed in the **Properties** palette. In this palette, click on the value column for the **Material** instance parameter and choose the new material; the new material will be assigned to the new split surface. Now, you can view the assigned material in the split surface in 3D view with the **Shaded** option enabled. The view will appear similar to the illustration shown in Figure 9-8.

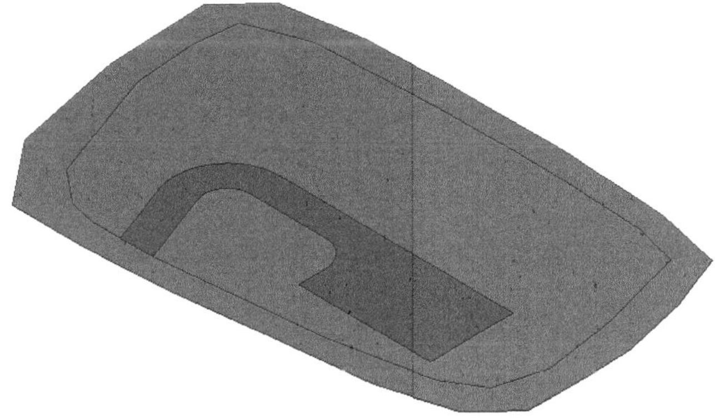

Figure 9-8 *3D view of the split toposurface with assigned materials*

Merging Toposurfaces

Ribbon: Massing & Site > Modify Site > Merge Surfaces

You can merge or rejoin the split surfaces when they overlap or share a common edge. To do so, invoke the **Merge Surfaces** tool from the **Modify Site** panel. Next, select the primary surface. The primary surface is the one whose properties are acquired by the resulting merged surface. Now, select the secondary surface, as shown in Figure 9-9; the two selected surfaces will merge, as shown in Figure 9-10.

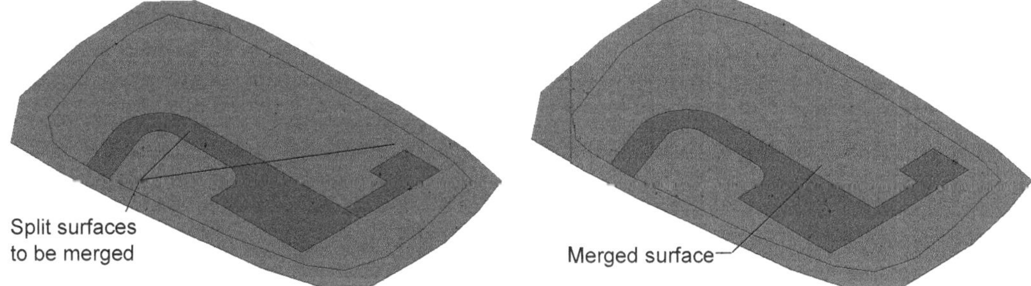

Figure 9-9 *Selecting the two split surfaces to be merged*

Figure 9-10 *The resulting merged surface*

Tip

To develop a site, you can create pavement patterns, road linkages, or special features for various building blocks and then merge them using the ***Merge Surfaces*** *tool.*

Grading Toposurfaces

Ribbon: Massing & Site > Modify Site > Graded Region

Grading is configuring the toposurface of the land by adding or removing earthen material to shape it for the project. Autodesk Revit provides you with the option of modifying the toposurface that indicates the shape change in the surface during construction. This can be done by using the **Graded Region** tool. This tool works only with the existing toposurface and is used to grade the topographical surface. To grade the plain topographical surface, choose the **Graded Region** tool from the **Modify Site** panel of the **Massing & Site** tab; the **Edit Graded Region** dialog box will be displayed, as shown in Figure 9-11. This dialog box provides you with two options to edit the existing toposurface.

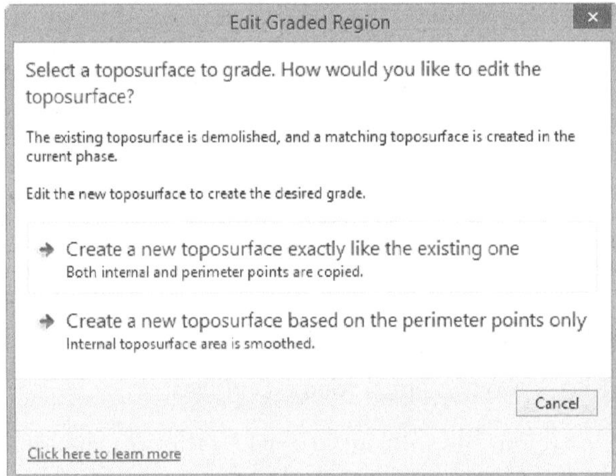

Figure 9-11 The ***Edit Graded Region*** *dialog box*

Select the **Create a new toposurface exactly like the existing one** option to create the new toposurface similar to the existing one but with the graded region. On selecting this option, you will be prompted to select the existing toposurface from the drawing area to create another toposurface as the existing one. Select the toposurface; the **Modify | Edit Surface** contextural tab with the existing points of the surface will be displayed and the new surface will be generated using those points. Now, you can add more points in this toposurface by using the **Place Point** tool and also by adding the elevation value to it.

Select the **Create a new toposurface based on the perimeter points only** option to edit the existing toposurface. On selectng the option, you will be prompted to select the toposurface for which you want to edit the points. Select the toposurface; you will be prompted to add other points, if any, or edit the elevation of existing points.

After editing the toposurface, choose the **Finish Surface** button; the new toposurface will be created and displayed with the graded region in the drawing area.

Tip

The ***Graded Region*** *tool is used to modify the toposurface. You can modify the toposurface phase assignment, define new elevation points on the contoured toposurface, and demolish the old toposurface by using this tool.*

Creating a Topography Using Imported Data

Autodesk Revit provides you with the option of importing data and using it to create a toposurface. Based on the type of the data imported, Revit automatically creates a toposurface. The data imported can be 3D data consisting of contours in the DWG, DXF, or DGN format, or the point files consisting of points.

Creating a Surface Using the Point File Data

As has been discussed already in the previous sections, you can import a point file into the current project and create a toposurface. To do so, choose the **Toposurface** tool from the **Model Site** panel in the **Massing & Site** tab; the **Modify | Edit Surface** tab will be displayed. In this tab, choose the **Specify Points File** tool from **Tools > Create from Import** drop-down; the **Select File** dialog box will be displayed. In the **Files of type** drop-down list, select the required file format to import the data. You can select the **CSV Files** option to import the file in the CSV format or select the **Comma delimited Text** to import the file in the text form. Navigate to the required location using the **Look in** drop-down list and select the required file. Next, choose the **Open** button from the **Select File** dialog box; the **Format** dialog box will be displayed. In this dialog box, select an option from the **One unit in the file equals one** drop-down list to assign the drawing units to the imported points. After assigning the units, choose the **OK** button to close the **Format** dialog box. On doing so, the point data will be imported and the toposurface will automatically be created based on the coordinates of points in the imported point file. Next, choose the **Finish Surface** button from the **Surface** panel in the **Modify | Edit Surface** tab; the toposurface will be created.

Another method to create a toposurface is by using the 3D contour data. To do so, you need to import the 3D contour data by using the DWG, DXF or DGN format. You can import the required 3D contour data by choosing the **Import CAD** tool from the **Import** panel of the **Insert** tab. After you have imported the required data, choose the **Select Import Instance** tool from **Modify |Edit Surface > Tools > Create from Import** drop-down and select the imported 3D data from the drawing view; the **Add Points from Selected Layers** dialog box will be displayed. Select the layers to which you want to apply the elevation points and choose the **OK** button; a toposurface based on the elevations points will be placed along the contour lines.

Note

The data imported in the point file must contain the numeric x, y, and z coordinate values in the CSV or the TXT format. The other numeric information about the points should be given after the x, y, and z values in the file.

SETTING THE SITE PROPERTIES

You can change the settings of the toposurface related to the entire site. To do so, choose the **Massing & Site** tab and then choose the **Site Settings** button displayed as an inclined arrow at the lower right corner of the **Model Site** panel; the **Site Settings** dialog box will be displayed, as shown in Figure 9-12. The parameters in the **Contour Line Display** area of the dialog box are used to control the display of contours in the views. The **At Intervals of** edit box is used to specify the intervals at which the contour lines will appear. The **Passing Through Elevation** is the base level at which the contours start. For example, if you set the contour intervals at 10 and pass through elevation value of 5 in the **Passing Through Elevation** edit box, then 5 will be the base level of contour. So, each line will appear at an interval of 10, and the contour will appear as -5, 5,15, 25, 35 and so on.

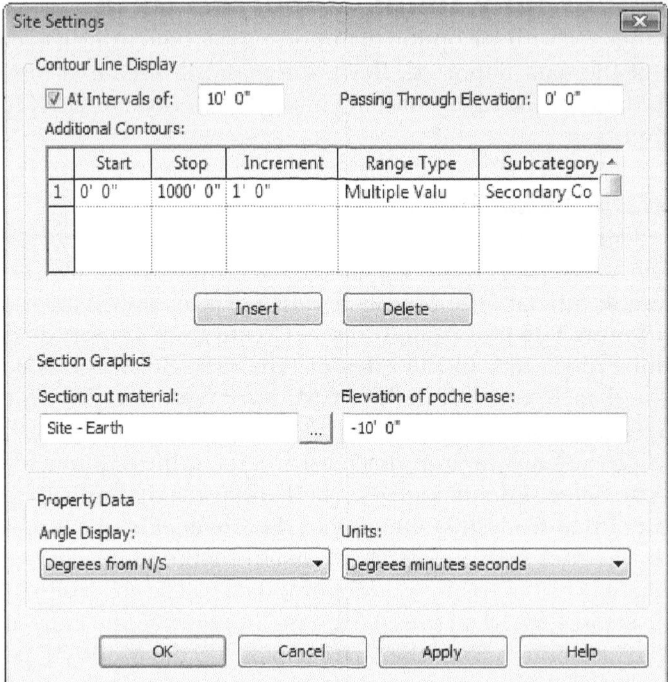

***Figure 9-12** The **Site Settings** dialog box*

Additional contours can also be generated between the sketches by specifying the parameters in the **Additional Contours** table in the **Site Settings** dialog box. Choose the **Insert** button to add the additional contours. In the **Additional Contours** area, the **Start** column displays the elevation at which the contour lines become visible, and the **Stop** column displays the level at which they are no longer displayed. The **Increment** column value is used to set the interval for each additional contour. The **Range Type** column can be used to insert single or multiple additional contours. On selecting the **Single Value** option, the **Stop** and **Increment** edit boxes will be disabled. The **Subcategory** column is used to assign the subcategory under which the contours will be added. You can assign a material to the site when it is cut in section view. To do so, choose the button on the right of the **Section cut material** edit box in the **Section Graphics** area; the **Materials Browser** dialog box will be displayed. Select the material from the **Materials Browser** dialog box, such as **Grass**, **Earth**, **Water**, and so on. The **Elevation of poche base** edit box is used to set the depth of the cross-section of the topographical elements such as earth. Choose the **OK** button to close the **Site Settings** dialog box.

ADDING PROPERTY LINES

Ribbon: Massing & Site > Modify Site > Property Line

The **Property Line** tool is used to demarcate and define the extents of the property of a building project based on the survey data. Property lines can be sketched only in the plan views; therefore, these lines can be created only when a plan view, preferably a site plan view, is selected. Property lines can be added by two methods. The first method is by entering distances and bearings and the second method is by sketching. On invoking the **Property Line** tool from the **Massing & Site** tab, the **Create Property Line** window will be displayed, as shown in Figure 9-13. This window displays two options: **Create by entering distances and bearings** and **Create by sketching**. If you select the first option, you will be able to use a table having details of distances and bearings to create a property line. Alternatively, you can choose the second option to create property lines by sketching.

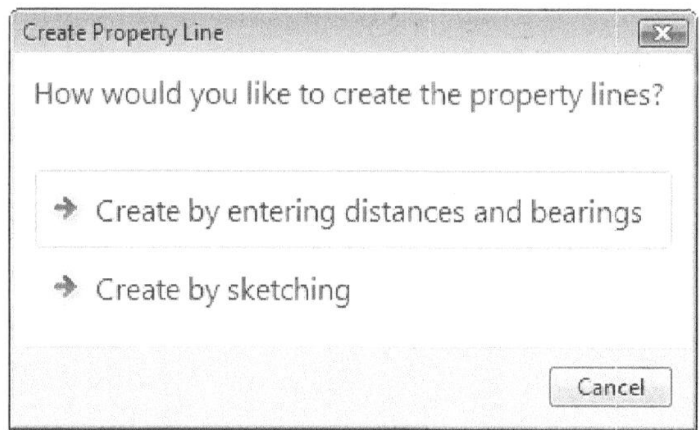

Figure 9-13 *The* ***Create Property Line*** *window showing the methods for creating the property line*

Sketching Property Lines

When you choose the **Create by sketching** option from the **Create Property Line** dialog box, the **Modify | Create Property Line Sketch** tab will be displayed. The **Draw** panel of this tab displays various sketching tools that can be used to draw the geometry of a property line. Choose the appropriate sketching tools and then the **Finish Edit Mode** button from the **Mode** panel to exit the sketching option and create the property line. The property line appears as a dashed line in the site plan view. Figure 9-14 shows an example of a property line created for a contoured site (highlighted for illustration).

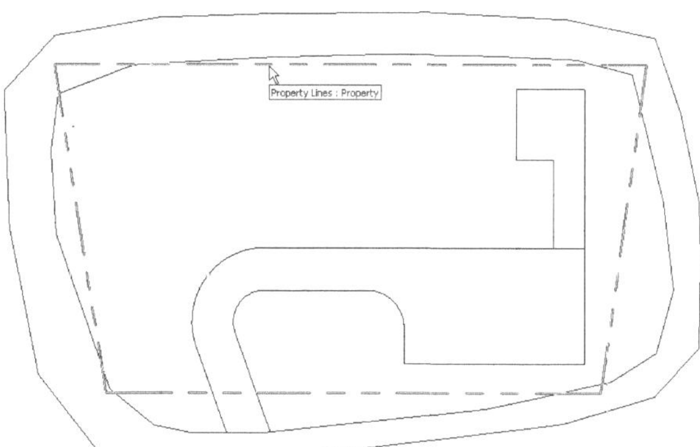

Figure 9-14 *Sketched property lines (highlighted)*

Creating Property Lines Using Distances and Bearings

You can also create property lines by entering survey data into the project. To do so, choose the **Create by entering distances and bearings** option from the **Create Property Line** window; the **Property Lines** dialog box will be displayed, as shown in Figure 9-15.

In the **Deed Data** area of this dialog box, you can view and enter the bearings and distances of the line segments that constitute the property line. The **Deed Data** area contains seven columns, namely **Distance, N/S, Bearing, E/W, Type, Radius**, and **L/R**. You can view and edit the bearing distance of the line segment in the **Distance** column. The **N/S** and **E/W** columns specify the North/South and East/West directions, respectively. Click on the field of the **N/S** column; a drop-down list will be displayed. Select the **N** or the **S** option from the drop-down list to specify the direction reference. Similarly, you can select the **E** or **W** option from the drop-down list in the **E/W** column. The **Bearing** column in the **Deed Data** area of the **Property Lines** dialog box displays the angle that the line segment of the property line subtends with the directions. To specify angle value of a line segment, click on the corresponding field of the **Bearing** column and enter a value in the edit box displayed. The value displayed in the **Type** column will specify whether a specified line segment will be an arc or a line. Click on the corresponding field of the **Type** column; a drop-down list containing two options, **Line** and **Arc** will be displayed.

To assign a type to the property line segment, select any of these options. Notice that on selecting the **Arc** option from the drop-down list, the fields corresponding to the **Radius** and **L/R** columns will be activated. Click on the field corresponding to the **Radius** column and enter a value in the edit box displayed. Similarly, click on the field of the **L/R** column; a drop-down list will be displayed. From this drop-down list, you can select any of the two options: **L** or **R**. You can select **L**, if you want the arc to appear on the left of the line segment and **R**, if you want the arc to appear on the right of the line segment.

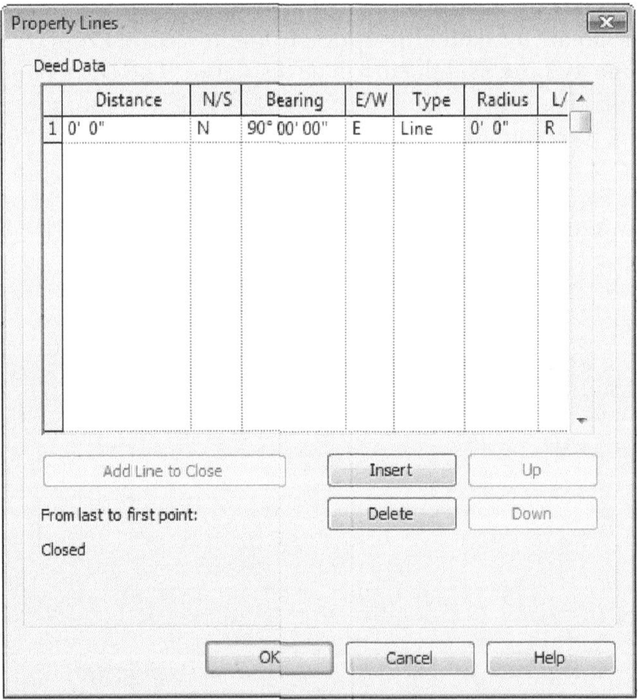

*Figure 9-15 The **Property Lines** dialog box showing the distance and bearing of various property line segments*

You can choose the **Add Line to Close** button in the **Deed Data** area of the **Property Lines** dialog box to add a line segment such that the line connects the first and the previous line segment to close the geometry. This button will remain inactive in its default state, unless a positive value is entered for the first line segment in the **Distance** column.

You can choose the **Insert**, **Delete**, **Up**, or **Down** button in the **Deed Data** area to add, delete or reorder a line segment of the property line. After you specify the line segments of the property line, choose the **OK** button, the **Property Lines** dialog box will close. Now, click in the drawing area; a property line will be created.

In Autodesk Revit, you can convert a sketched property line to a table-based property line. To do so, select a property line from the drawing and choose the **Edit Table** tool from the **Property Lines** panel in the **Modify | Property Lines** tab. On doing so, Autodesk Revit displays a warning that the sketched property lines once converted into the table-based property lines cannot be converted back. It also warns that the constraints applied while sketching will be lost during the conversion process. You can choose the **Yes** button to proceed. The sketched property lines are converted into the table-based property lines.

The **Deed Data** table shows the distance and bearing of various line segments constituting the selected property line. These bearings are given with respect to the true north setting for the project. To set the true north for the project, ensure that you are in the **Site** view and then click in the value field corresponding to the **Orientation** parameter in the **Properties** palette and select the **True North** option from the drop-down list displayed. Next, choose the **Rotate True North** tool from **Manage > Project Location > Position** drop-down and rotate the site by clicking and specifying the angle in the drawing area.

Creating Building Pads

Ribbon: Massing & Site > Model Site > Building Pad

In a project, you can develop a level area for your building model in the site. This level area, which provides a minimal slope for a building drainage, is called a building pad. The creation of a building pad provides you more flexibility in the design as you will not be dictated by grade elevations, floor transitions, building shapes or other consideration. In Revit, you can create a building pad by using the **Building Pad** tool. To do so, invoke this tool from the **Model Site** panel of the **Massing & Site** tab; the **Modify | Create Pad Boundary** tab will be displayed.

Note

The building pad is a toposurface hosted element and can be added only to an existing topographical surface. This ***Building Pad*** *tool will be activated in the* ***Model Site*** *panel only if there is an existing toposurface in the drawing.*

On displaying the **Modify | Create Pad Boundary** tab, Revit enters the sketch mode. Before creating the building pad geometry, make sure that the **Boundary Line** button in the **Draw** panel is chosen by default. Now, if the building block has already been placed, choose the **Pick Walls** tool (default) from the **Draw** panel in the **Modify | Create Pad Boundary** tab. Select the desired walls and choose the **Finish Edit Mode** button from the **Mode** panel; the building pad will be created along the periphery of the desired walls that you have picked. Alternatively, you can create the building pad boundary by invoking other sketching tools such as **Line**, **Circle**, **Ellipse**, and so on from the list box in the **Draw** panel of the **Modify | Create Pad Boundary** tab.

You can assign the desired properties to the building pad to be created. To do so, you can use the properties available in the **Properties** palette, as shown in Figure 9-16. The **Level** parameter in this palette can be used to specify the level of the building pad. You can specify the height of the pad from the specified level in the value column of the **Height Offset From Level** instance parameter. You can choose the **Edit Type** button to display the **Type Properties** dialog box, as shown in Figure 9-17. You can modify the structural parameters and also create a new building pad using this dialog box.

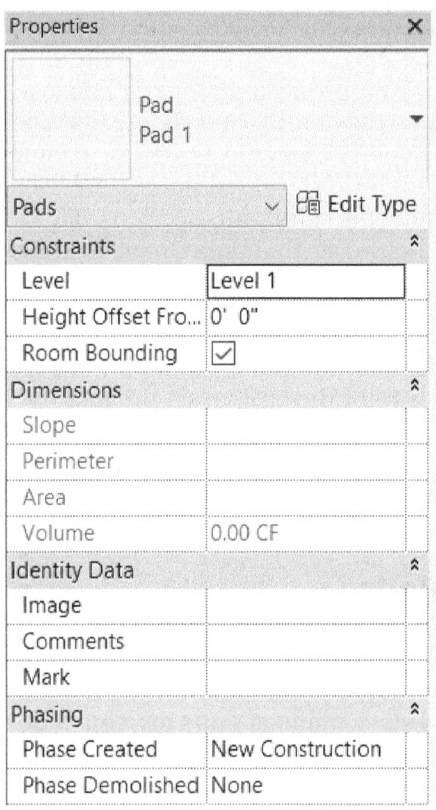

***Figure 9-16** The **Properties** palette for a building pad*

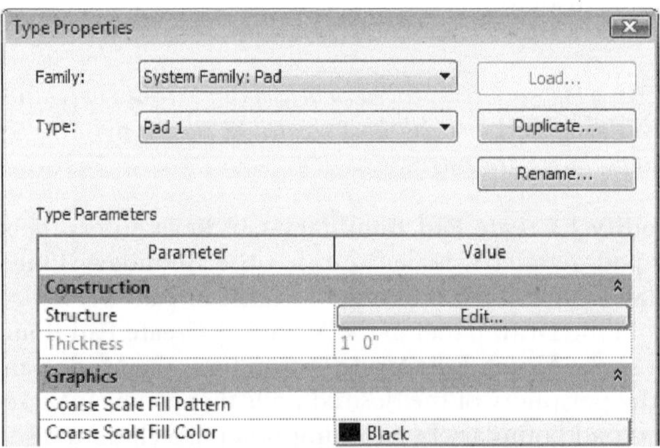

***Figure 9-17** The partial view of the **Type Properties** dialog box for a building pad*

Based on the level specified in the pad properties, the building pad may not be visible in the site plan view. To view it, you need to generate a section view through the site. Figure 9-18 shows an example of the building pad (highlighted) created on a contoured site.

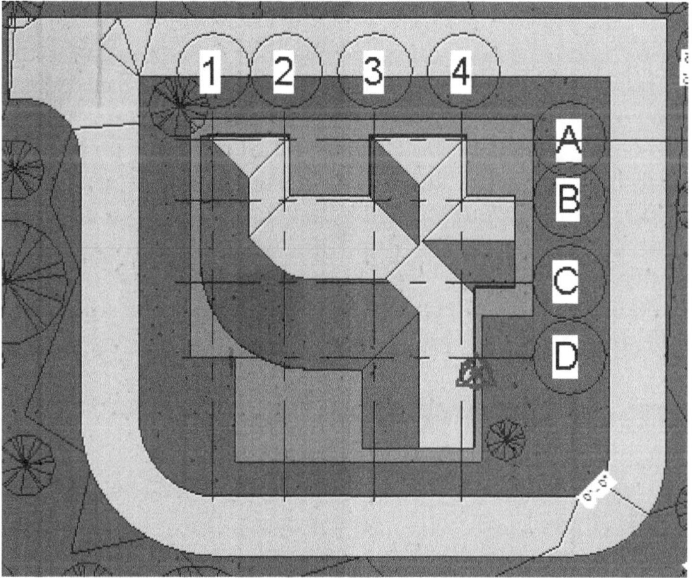

Figure 9-18 *Building pad created on a contoured site*

Autodesk Revit automatically creates a puncture of the required depth at the location of the building pad. When you generate a transverse section view through the building pad, it appears similar to the illustration shown in Figure 9-19.

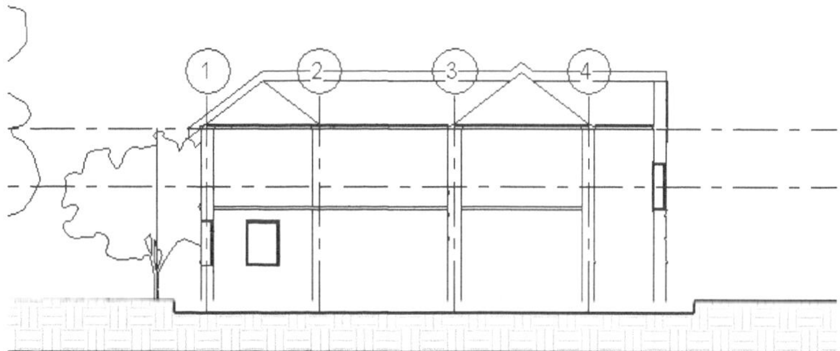

Figure 9-19 *Section view of the resulting building pad*

Adding Slope to Building Pads

While creating a building pad, sometimes it is necessary to provide a slope for drainage facilities. Revit allows you to add slopes to the building pads while creating the project. To create a slope in the building pad, sketch the boundary of the building pad and then choose the **Slope Arrow** tool from the **Draw** panel in the **Modify | Create Pad Boundary** tab; the list box next to the **Slope Arrow** tool will display two tools: **Line** and **Pick Lines**. In the list box, the **Line** tool is invoked by default. Now, click on the pad to specify the first point of the slope arrow and then drag the cursor in the required direction; a blue colored dotted line with a pink colored arrow head will follow the cursor. Next, click to specify the endpoint of the slope arrow; the controls of the arrow head and a temporary dimension indicating the length of the slope arrow will be displayed.

Now, in the **Properties** palette, click in the value column corresponding to the **Specify** instance parameter; a drop-down list will be displayed. In this drop-down list, you can select either the **Height at Tail** option or the **Slope** option. In the slope line, the start point is called as tail and the endpoint is called as head. Select the **Height at Tail** option from the drop-down list to set values for various parameters such as **Level at Tail**, **Height Offset at Tail**, **Level at Head**, and **Height Offset at Head**. These parameters will help you create a slope in the building pad based on your requirement. Similarly, select the **Slope** option from the drop-down list for the **Specify** parameter and specify the slope of the building pad in the **Slope** instance parameter. After specifying the desired values in the **Properties** palette, choose the **Apply** button to accept the specified values and close the dialog box.

ADDING SITE COMPONENTS

Ribbon: Massing & Site > Model Site > Site Component

You can add different site components such as trees, bollards, building signs, planters, and so on to a site using the **Site Component** tool. The procedure for adding site components is similar to that of adding building components (for more information, refer to the Adding Components section in Chapter 8).

Invoke the **Site Component** tool from the **Model Site** panel in the **Massing & Site** tab; the **Modify | Site Component** tab will be displayed. In the **Properties** palette, select the component to be added from the **Type Selector** drop-down list and insert it into the drawing. You can add other components in your drawing apart from those available in the **Type Selector** drop-down list. To do so, choose the **Load Family** button in the **Mode** panel of the **Modify | Site Component** tab; the **Load Family** dialog box will be displayed. You can use this dialog box to load site components from the libraries available in the **US Imperial > Site** folder location. This folder contains four subfolders: **Accessories**, **Logistics**, **Parking**, and **Utilities**. Each subfolder contains elements related to its title. For example, the **Utilities** subfolder contains elements such as **Fire Hydrant**, **Manhole**, and so on.

After choosing the desired components from the **Load Family** dialog box, choose the **OK** button; the components chosen will be added to the **Type Selector** drop-down list in the **Properties** palette. Now, you can choose the appropriate component type to add it to the site.

To add planting components to the site, load the plantation elements from the **Planting** subfolder in the **US Imperial** folder using the **Load Family** dialog box. Next, select the tree type from the **Type Selector** drop-down list and add it to the site in the site plan view, as shown in Figure 9-20.

After you add trees to the site, they automatically get attached to the topographical level at the specified point of placement. The added components can be viewed in the section or 3D view of the site. The trees appear as simple lines unless the view is rendered. Figure 9-21 shows a rendered view of the contoured site with trees.

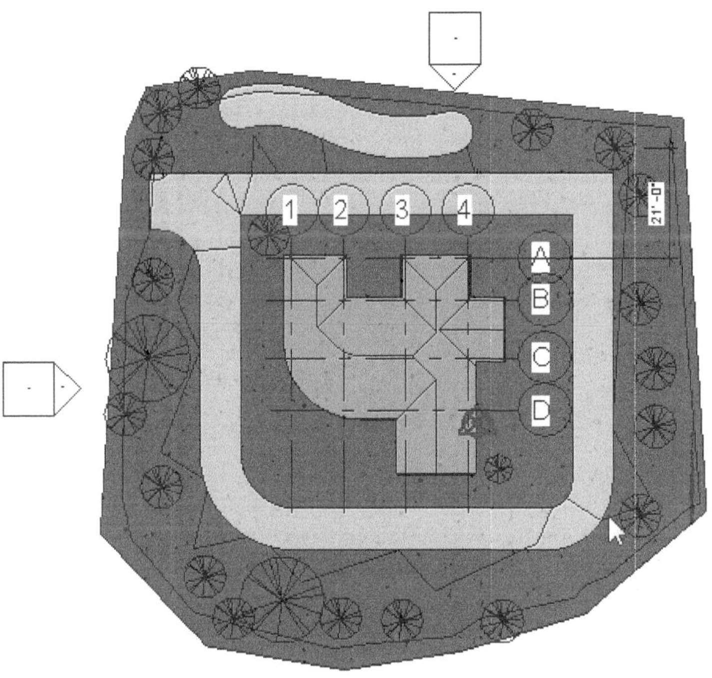

Figure 9-20 *Adding planting components to a contoured site*

Figure 9-21 *Rendered view of the contoured sites with trees*

ADDING PARKING COMPONENTS

Ribbon: Massing & Site > Model Site > Parking Component

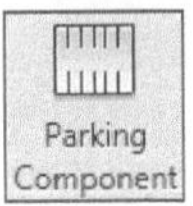

You can add parking components by using the **Parking Component** tool. To add parking components, invoke this tool from the **Model Site** panel; the **Modify | Parking Component** tab will be displayed and the type and properties for the proposed parking components will be displayed in the **Properties** palette. In this palette, select the appropriate type of parking space from the **Type Selector** drop-down list and add it to the site plan. Similar to a building pad, parking components are toposurface hosted components. You can add as many parking spaces as required. The **Rotate after placement** check box can be selected from the **Options Bar** to invoke the **Rotate** tool and rotate the parking component after you have placed it.

ADDING LABELS TO CONTOURS

Ribbon: Massing & Site > Modify Site > Label Contours

The **Label Contours** tool is used to label the elevation levels of toposurfaces or contours. To invoke this tool and add labels to the contours or toposurfaces displayed in the drawing, choose the **Label Contours** tool from the **Modify Site** panel; the **Modify | Label Contours** tab will be displayed. In this tab, choose the **Edit Type** button from the **Properties** panel; the **Type Properties** dialog box will be displayed. In this dialog box, specify the font and size of the text. Next, choose the **OK** button to accept the specified values and close the dialog box.

To add labels, sketch a line that intersects the contour to be labeled. To create labels for multiple contours, sketch a line that intersects all of them. Autodesk Revit automatically adds labels to each contour based on their respective elevations. Figure 9-22 shows the example of labels added to alternate contours.

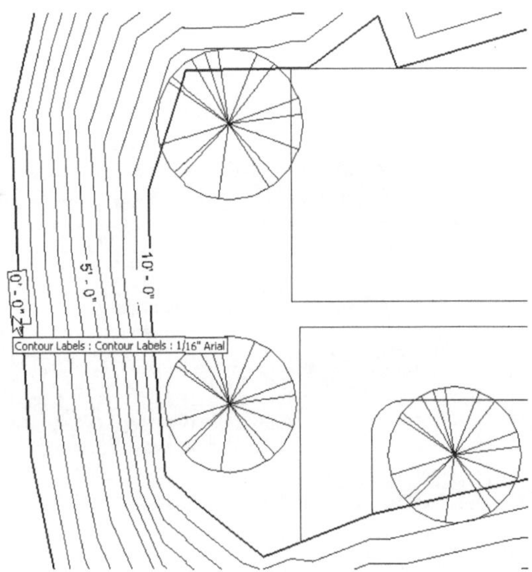

Figure 9-22 *Labels added to the contours*

TUTORIAL

Tutorial 1 Site Plan

In this tutorial, you will create a contoured site plan for an apartment complex on the basis of Figure 9-23. The approximate locations and sizes of roads, parking components, building pads and site components are also given. You can assume the missing dimensions. The texts and dimensions have been given only for reference and are not to be created. Given below are the parameters for various components to be added.

(Expected time: 2hr 15 min)

1. Project file parameters:
   Template file-
   For Imperial ***default.rte***
   For Metric ***DefaultMetric.rte***

   File name to be assigned-
   For Imperial *c09_SitePlan_tut1.rvt*
   For Metric *M_c09_SitePlan_tut1.rvt*

2. Property size:
   For Imperial **600'0" X 500'0"** (Extents of property line)
   For Metric 180000 X 15000 mm

3. Site settings:
   Contours at **1'0"(300 mm)** intervals
   Site material- **Grass**, Road material- **Asphalt**
   Elevation of Poche base-
   For Imperial **5'0"**
   For Metric **1500 mm**

4. Building pads:
   Apartment blocks-3 Nos. building pads- size **106'0" X 151'0" (31800 X 45300 mm)** - placed symmetrically about the center of the design scheme
   Club 1 and Club 2-symmetrical building pads as per the dimensions given in sketch plan
   Building pad level-Level 2

5. Width of the straight pedestrian walkway- **8'(2400 mm)**, circular- **12'(3600 mm)**.

6. Parking Component:
   For Imperial **Parking Space: 9' X 18': 90 deg**
   For Metric **Parking Space: 4800 X 2400 mm- 90 deg**

7. Site Component:
   For Imperial **Tree - Deciduous: Red Ash - 25'** placed on Level 2.
   For Metric

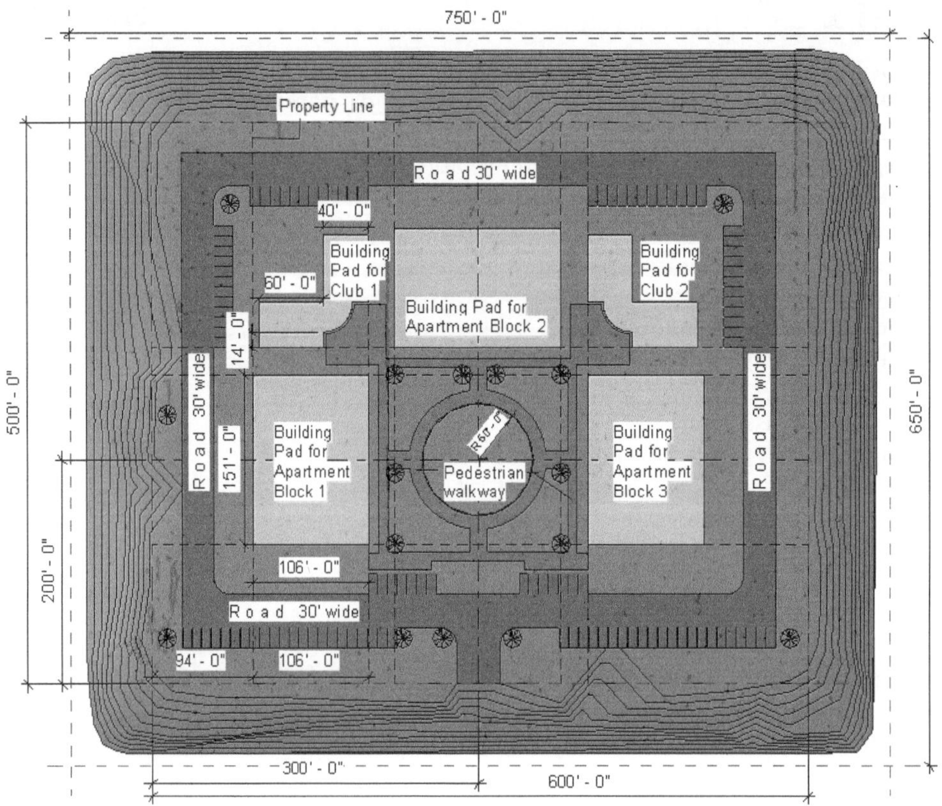

Figure 9-23 Sketch plan for creating the site plan with contours, site components, and building pads

The following steps are required to complete this tutorial:

a. Open a new project file using the default template file and open the **Site Plan** view.
b. Create reference planes to assist in sketching contours.
c. Modify the site setting to create additional contours at **1'0"** interval.
d. Use the **Topographies** tool to sketch the contours, refer to Figures 9-24 through 9-26.
e. Create property line using reference planes and the **Property Line** tool, refer to Figure 9-27.
f. Add building pads using the **Building Pad** tool, refer to Figures 9-28 through 9-30.
g. Use the **Subregion** tool to create roads, refer to Figures 9-31 and 9-32.
h. Add parking components using the **Parking Component** tool, refer to Figures 9-33 through 9-35.
i. Add site components using the **Site Component** tool, refer to Figures 9-36 through 9-39.
j. Save the project using the **Save As** tool.
   For Imperial *c09_SitePlan_tut1.rvt*
   For Metric *M_c09_SitePlan_tut1.rvt*
k. Close the project.

Opening a New Project File and the Site Plan View

In this section, you will open a new project file using the **New** tool. As mentioned earlier, the site contours should be created in the **Site** view. Therefore, you will open the **Site** view using the **Project Browser**. You can also hide the elevation tags using the **Visibility/Graphics** tool.

1. Choose the **New** option under the **Projects** head from the interface screen; the **New Project** dialog box is displayed.

2. Choose the **Browse** button; the **Choose Template** dialog box is displayed.

3. In the **Choose Template** dialog box, select the *default* template file from the **US Imperial** folder (For Metric select the *DefaultMetric* template file from the **US Metric** folder) and choose **Open**; the **New Project** dialog box is displayed. Next, choose the **OK** button; the dialog box closes and a new project file opens in the drawing window.

4. In the **Project Browser**, double-click on **Site** under the head **Floor Plans** to display the site plan view.

5. Select the elevation symbol in the drawing window and right-click; a shortcut menu is displayed.

6. Choose **Hide in View > Category** from the shortcut menu; the elevation symbol get hidden in the site plan view. Similarly, select the project base point and the survey point symbols in the drawing window and then hide them.

Creating Reference Planes

Before creating contours, you need to draw reference planes to provide guidelines for sketching the site periphery and contour profile. In this section, you will draw the reference planes for the contour profile.

1. Invoke the **Ref Plane** tool from the **Work Plane** panel in the **Architecture** tab.

2. Move the cursor to the drawing window and click on the upper left corner of the screen to start creating the first reference plane.

3. Now, move the cursor horizontally to the upper right corner of the screen and click to end the reference plane.

4. Next, to create the second reference plane, move the cursor to the lower left corner of the drawing window in alignment with the first reference plane and then click at an appropriate location; the creation of the second reference plane starts.

5. Now, move the cursor to the lower right corner and click to end the second reference plane. Notice that a temporary dimension appears between the two reference planes.

6. Now, click on the value of the temporary dimension; an edit box is displayed. Enter **650'0"(198120 mm)** in the edit box and press ENTER.

7. Similarly, create two vertical reference planes at a distance of **750'0"** (**228600**).

8. Now, right-click on the open area of the drawing window; a shortcut menu is displayed. Choose the **Zoom To Fit** option from the shortcut menu; the screen view fits to the extent of the sketched reference plane, offering more clarity to the view displayed.

9. Press ESC twice to exit the **Ref Plane** tool.

10. Now, use the dragging method to extend the four reference planes, horizontally and vertically, such that they intersect each other, as shown in the sketch plan in Figure 9-23.

Modifying the Site Settings

Before creating the contours, you need to modify the site settings to achieve the desired contour layout. In this section, you will use the **Site Settings** dialog box to set parameters for creating additional contours. Then, you will create three topographical surfaces to generate all site contours, as shown in the sketch plan.

1. Choose the **Massing & Site** tab and then choose the inclined arrow button placed on the right of the **Model Site** panel; the **Site Settings** dialog box is displayed.

2. Make sure that the check box that is placed before the **At Intervals of** edit box is selected and then enter **1'0" (304.8 mm)** in the **At Intervals of** edit box. Also, ensure that in the **Passing Through Elevation** edit box 0' 0" (0) is entered.

3. Now, in the **Site Settings** dialog box, choose the **Insert** button to insert additional contours.

4. In the **Increment** column of the **Additional Contours** table, ensure that for Imperial **1' 0"** and for Metric **1000** is set as the default value.

5. In the **Section Graphics** area, choose the browse button under the **Section cut material** edit box; the **Material Browser** dialog box is displayed. In this dialog box, enter **Grass** as the material in the **Searches for Material** edit box and press ENTER; the Grass material is displayed in the Autodesk Material Library.

Note

If the Autodesk Library panel is not displayed, then choose the ***Shows/Hides library panel*** *button from the right side of the* ***Project Materials: All*** *pane.*

6. Double-click on Grass in **Autodesk Material Library**, it is added under the **Project Materials: All** area.

7. Select the material under the **Project Materials: All** area and choose **OK** to accept the other specified values and to close the **Material Browser** dialog box.

8. In the **Section Graphics** area of the **Site Settings** dialog box, enter **-5'0" (-1525 mm)** in the **Elevation of poche base** edit box.

9. Now, choose **OK**; the specified setting is applied and the **Site Settings** dialog box is closed.

Creating Site Contours

In this section, you will use the **Topographies** tool and the **Point** tool and also pick points to generate the desired profile of contours. The contours should be created from the lowest to the highest level to be fully visible. You can first create a topographical surface at the base level and then create two more surfaces at **5'0"(1525 mm)** and **10'0"(3048 mm)** levels, respectively. On doing so, the Autodesk Revit automatically generates the intermediate contours at **1'0"** (304.8 mm) level.

1. Choose the **Toposurface** tool from the **Model Site** panel in the **Massing & Site** tab; the **Modify | Edit Surface** contextual tab is displayed. Ensure that the **Place Point** tool in the **Tools** panel is invoked, the **Elevation** edit box in the **Options Bar** shows **0'0"** as the elevation, and the **Absolute Elevation** option is selected (default option) in the drop-down list.

2. Move the cursor to the upper left corner and click to start the topographical surface. Ensure that the toposurface is drawn within the sketched reference plane.

   Click on multiple points to form a closed loop, as shown in Figure 9-24. The exact shape of the toposurface profile is not important for this tutorial.

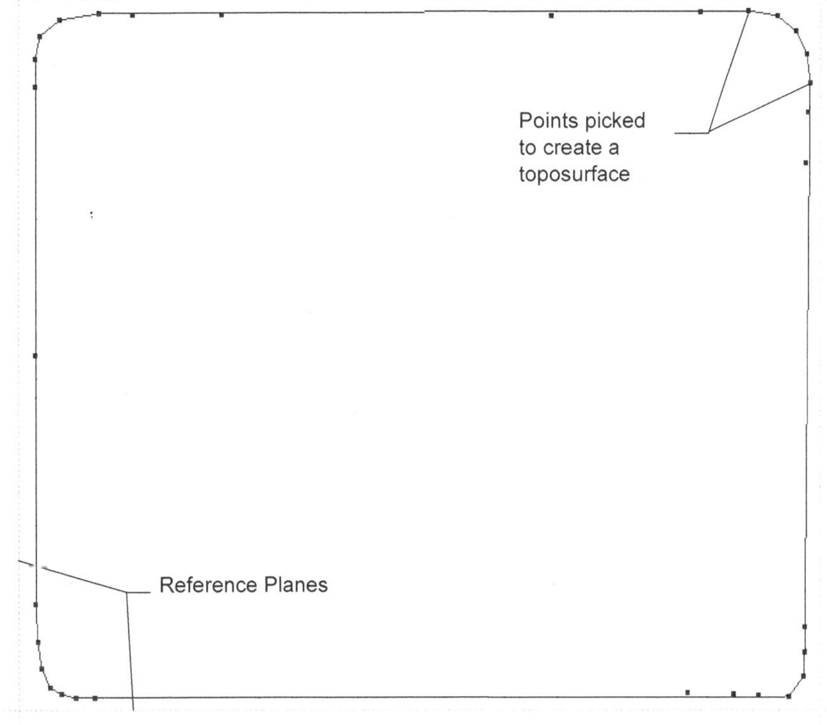

Figure 9-24 *Picking points to sketch the lowest topographical surface of the site plan*

3. Choose the **Finish Surface** button from the **Surface** panel in the **Modify | Edit Surface** tab to complete the lowest topographical surface.

4. Select the toposurface created; the **Modify | Topography** tab is displayed. In this tab, choose the **Edit Surface** tool from the **Surface** panel; the **Modify | Edit Surface** tab is displayed.

5. Choose the **Place Point** tool from the **Tools** panel.

6. In the **Options Bar**, enter **5'0" (1525 mm)** in the **Elevation** edit box and press ENTER.

7. Next, move the cursor to the upper left corner of the toposurface created and click inside it to start the second topographical surface.

8. Click on multiple points along the inner surface of the first profile to create the second topographical surface, as shown in Figure 9-25. You will notice that as you pick the points, Autodesk Revit automatically generates the intermediate contours at **5'0"** level.

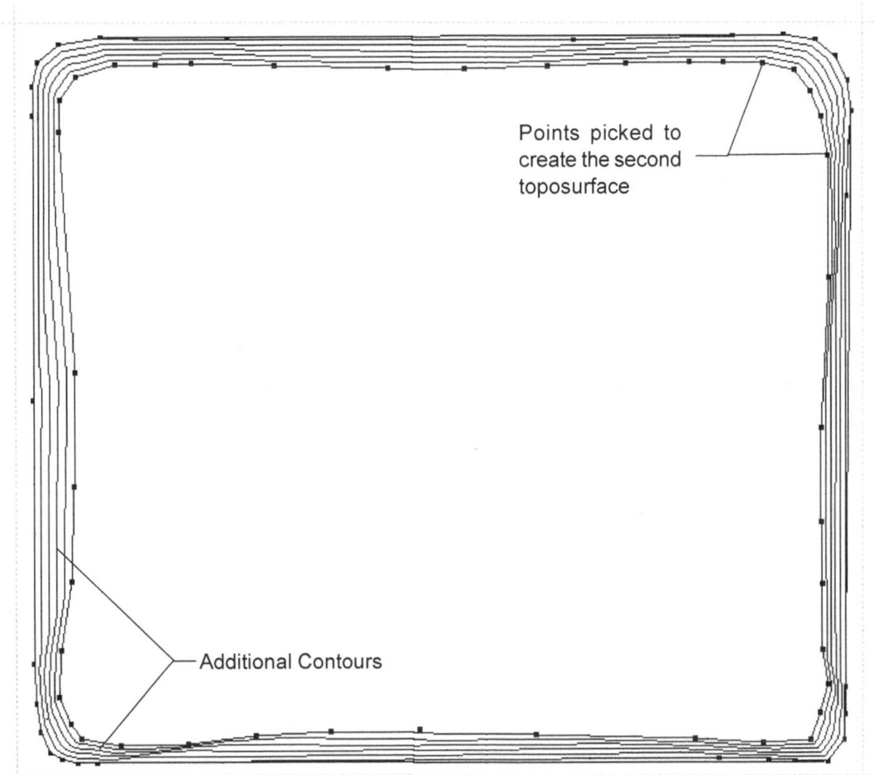

Figure 9-25 *Picking points to sketch the topographical surface at **5'0"** level*

9. Choose the **Finish Surface** button from the **Modify | Edit Surface** tab to create the second topographical surface.

10. Similarly, using the **Edit Surface** tool create the third topographical surface at **10'0"** (3048mm) level from the second toposurface, as shown in Figure 9-26.

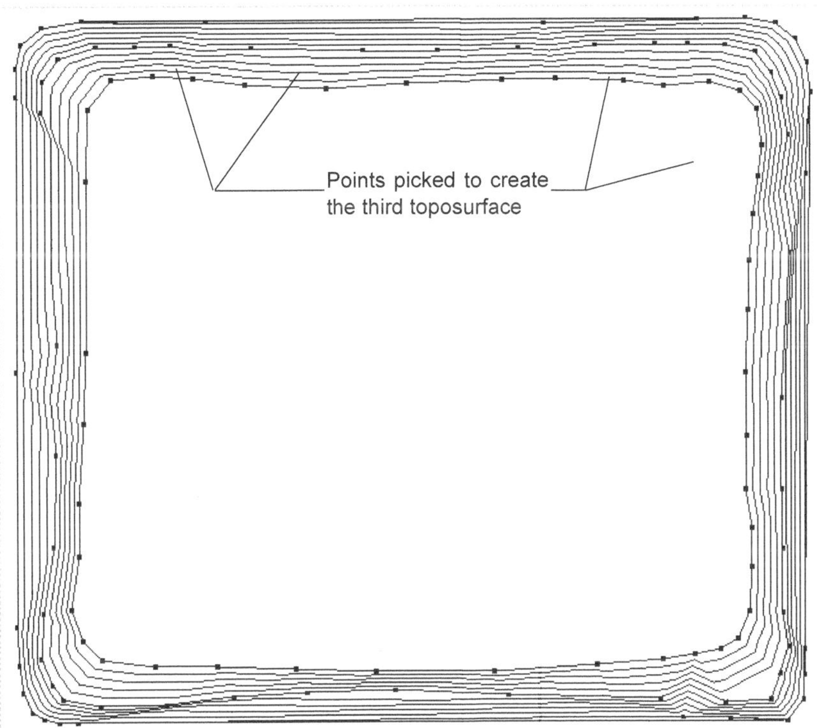

Figure 9-26 *Picking points to sketch the third topographical surface at **10'0"** level*

11. After creating the toposurface, choose the **Finish Surface** tool from the **Surface** panel of the **Modify|Edit Surface** tab.

Adding the Property Line

In this section, you will create a property line of an appropriate length using the **Property Line** tool. You will create reference planes to locate the corner of the property line.

1. Choose the **Architecture** tab, and then invoke the **Ref Plane** tool from the **Work Plane** panel. Now, you can start creating the desired reference planes.

2. Create two horizontal reference planes at a distance of **500' (152400 mm)** and two vertical reference planes at a distance of **600' (182880 mm)**, intersecting at the four corners of the property line, as specified in the sketch plan.

3. Choose the **Massing & Site** tab and then choose the **Property Line** tool from the **Modify Site** panel; the **Create Property Line** window is displayed.

4. In this window, choose the **Create by sketching** option; the **Modify | Create Property Line Sketch** tab is displayed.

5. From the **Draw** panel in the **Modify | Create Property Line Sketch** tab, choose the **Rectangle** tool.

6. Now, sketch the rectangular property line by selecting the two diagonal intersections of the reference planes created in step 2. The temporary dimensions displayed can be used to verify the size of the sketched rectangle.

7. Choose the **Finish Edit Mode** button to finish sketching the property line. Figure 9-27 shows the property line created (highlighted for illustration purpose).

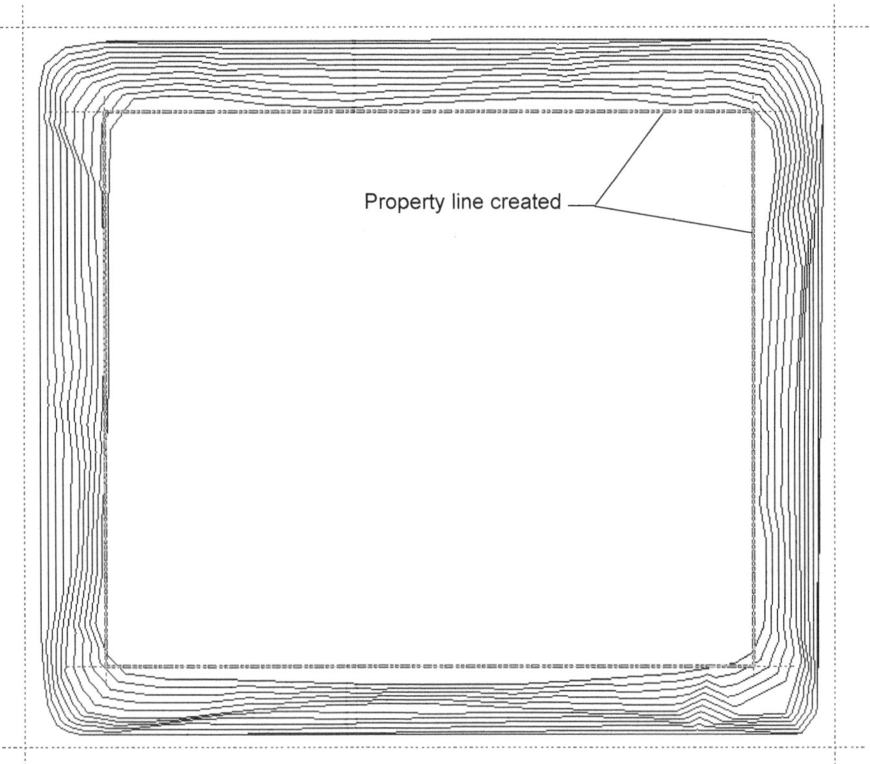

Figure 9-27 *Property line created for the site plan*

Adding the Building Pads

The next step is to add building pads to the site plan. They are placed symmetrically around the central point of the layout. You will first create a single apartment block building pad and then use the **Radial Array** tool to create multiple copies of the building pad. The club-building pad can be added using the sketching tools. But, first you must locate the center of the design scheme using the reference planes.

1. Choose the **Architecture** tab and then choose the **Ref Plane** tool from the **Work Plane** panel.

2. Create a horizontal reference plane at a distance of **200'** (**60960 mm**) from the lower horizontal property line. Now, create a vertical reference plane between the midpoint of the two horizontal property lines, as given in the sketch plan. Their point of intersection is the center of the design scheme. Similarly, create additional reference planes to locate building pads, which are shown as reference lines in the sketch plan.

3. Choose the **Massing & Site** tab and then choose the **Building Pad** tool from the **Model Site** panel; the **Modify | Create Pad Boundary** tab is displayed.

4. In the **Properties** palette, select the **Level 2** option from the drop-down list displayed in the value field of the **Level** instance parameter.

5. Ensure that the **Boundary Line** button is chosen in the **Draw** panel, and then invoke the **Rectangle** tool from the list box.

6. Sketch the Apartment Block 1 building pad with the dimension **106' X 151' (32308 x 46024 mm)** by clicking on the two diagonal intersection points on the reference planes, refer to Figure 9-28.

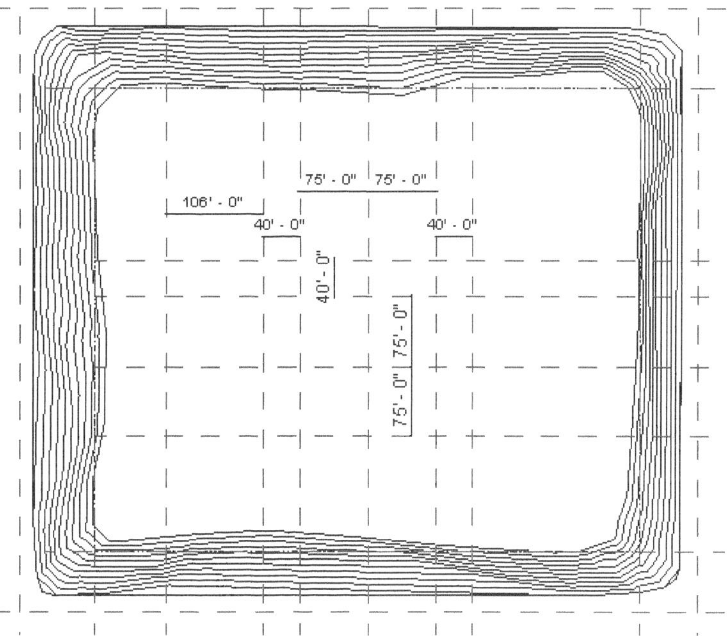

Figure 9-28 *Reference Plane dimensions*

7. Choose the **Finish Edit Mode** button from the **Mode** panel in the **Modify |Create Pad Boundary** tab to add the building pad, as shown in Figure 9-29; the **Modify|Pads** tab is displayed.

8. Select the created building pad, if not selected, to create its radial array and then choose the **Array** tool from the **Modify** panel in the **Modify | Pads** tab.

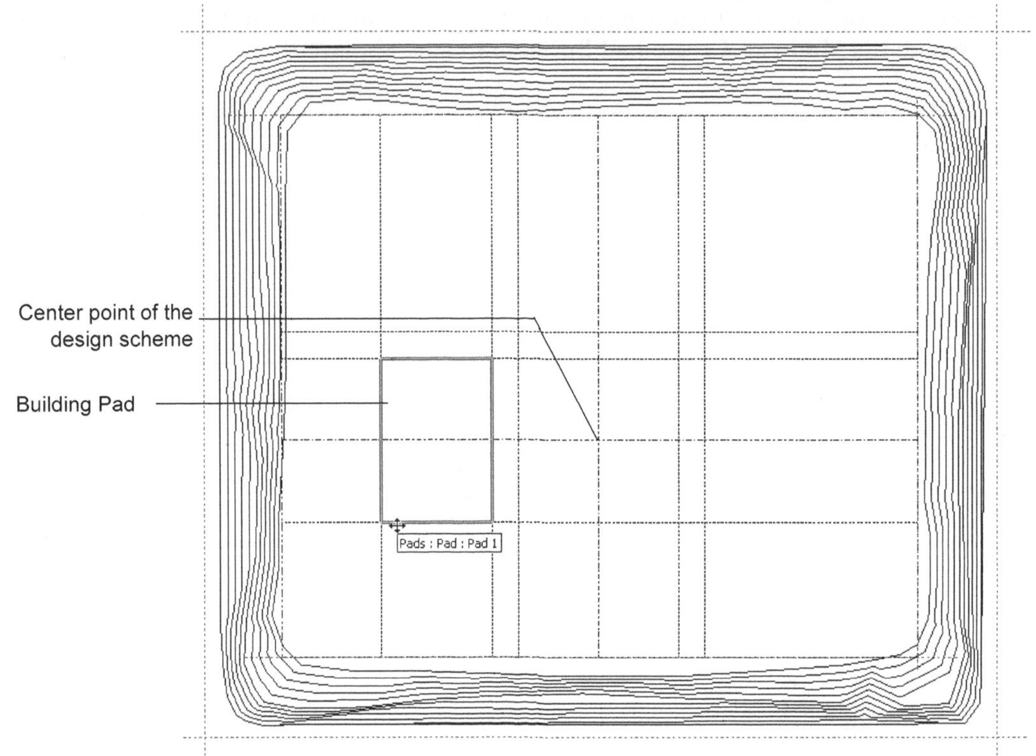

Figure 9-29 *Creating reference planes and adding the building pad (highlighted)*

9. Choose the **Radial** button from the **Options Bar** and then create the two additional building pads by moving the center of the radial array to the center of the design scheme, as shown in Figure 9-30.

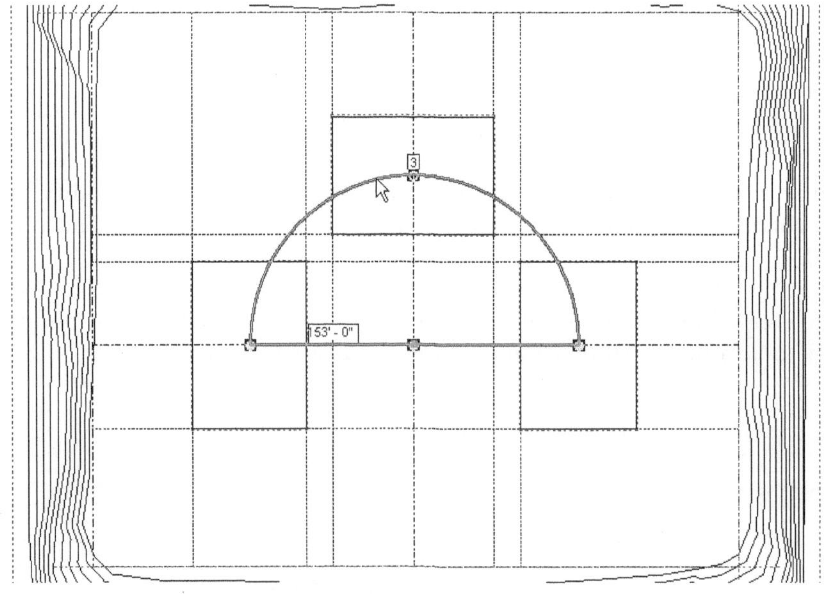

Figure 9-30 *Creating a radial array of the building pad*

10. Similarly, sketch the building pad for the club building based on the dimensions and location, refer to Figure 9-31. Use the **Mirror - Pick Axis** tool or the **Mirror-Draw Axis** tool to create a copy of this pad, as shown in Figure 9-31.

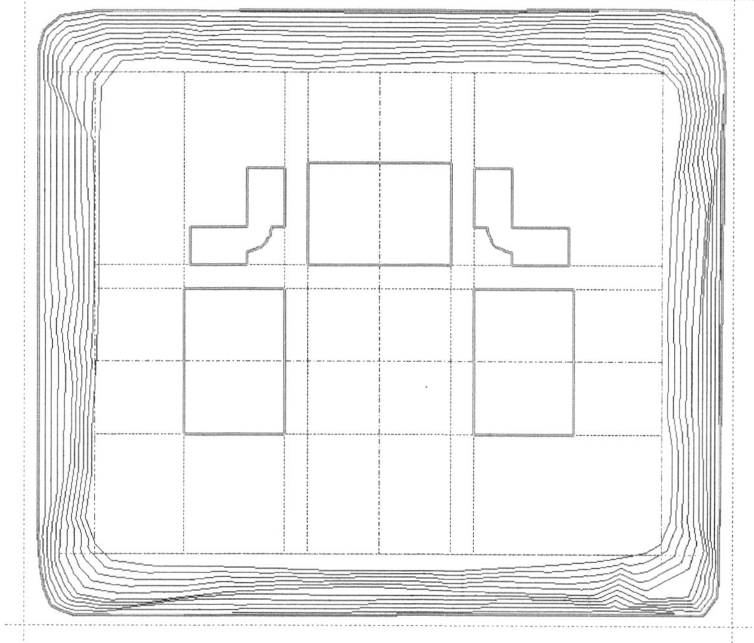

Figure 9-31 *Creating the building pads for the club buildings*

Creating Roads Using the Subregion Tool

Now, create roads for the site plan using the **Subregion** tool. You can create a subregion on the topographical surface in such a manner that a separate surface is created for the road. It can then be assigned a different material. You can use the sketching tools to sketch the road profile.

1. Before you create subregions for the road and the pedestrian walkway, the first thing you need to do is sketch the reference planes for them according to the dimensions and locations given in the sketch plan, refer to Figure 9-23. To do so, choose the **Architecture** tab and invoke the **Ref Plane** tool from the **Work Plane** panel to create reference planes to locate all corners of the outer profile of the road and the references for the pedestrian walkway.

2. Now, create a subregion for the road. To do so, choose the **Massing & Site** tab and then choose the **Subregion** tool from the **Modify Site** panel; the **Modify | Create Subregion Boundary** tab is displayed.

3. Next, use the sketching tools in the **Draw** panel to sketch the road profile according to the sketch plan.

4. After you sketch the road profile, choose the **Finish Edit Mode** button from the **Mode** panel; the topographical subregion is created and displayed as shown in Figure 9-32 (highlighted for illustration purpose).

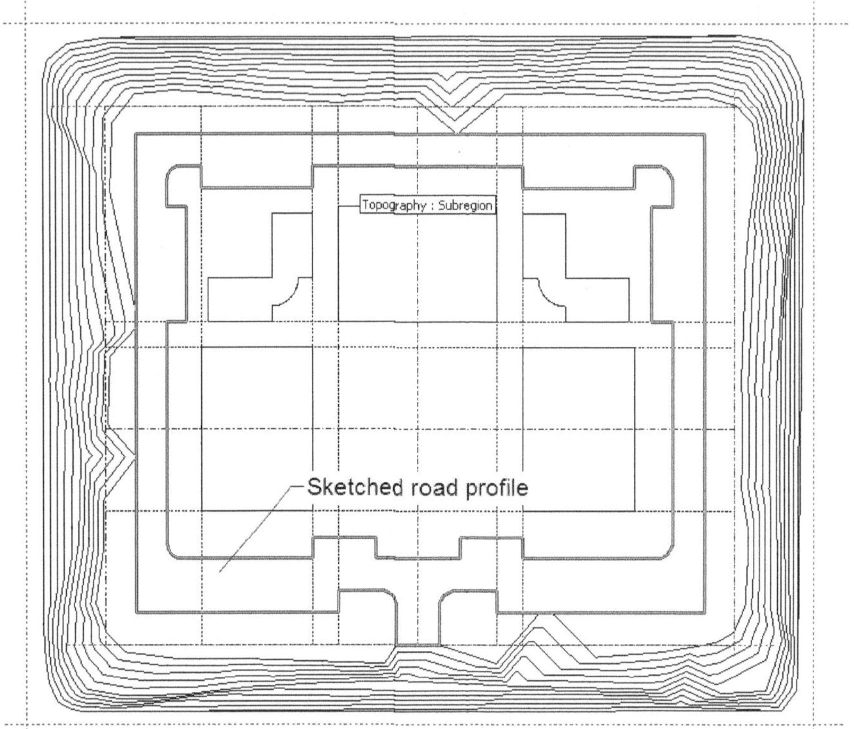

***Figure 9-32** Creating the road profile (highlighted) using the **Subregion** tool*

5. Similarly, create another subregion for the pedestrian walkway to enter each apartment block, as shown in Figure 9-33, by using the available sketching and editing tools.

   After creating contours, building pads, and subregions, you need to assign the appropriate material to their surface. This tutorial introduces you to the concept of applying materials to various elements. You will learn more about using materials in Chapter 15.

6. To apply a material to the road subregion, select it; the instance properties of the selected subregion are displayed in the **Properties** palette.

7. In this palette, click on the value field for the **Material** instance parameter and then choose the **Browse** button on the right of the edit box to display the **Material Browser** dialog box.

8. From the list of names, select **Asphalt Shingle** and then choose the **OK** button; the **Material Browser** dialog box is closed.

9. Similarly, select the site contours toposurface and apply the material **Grass** to it.

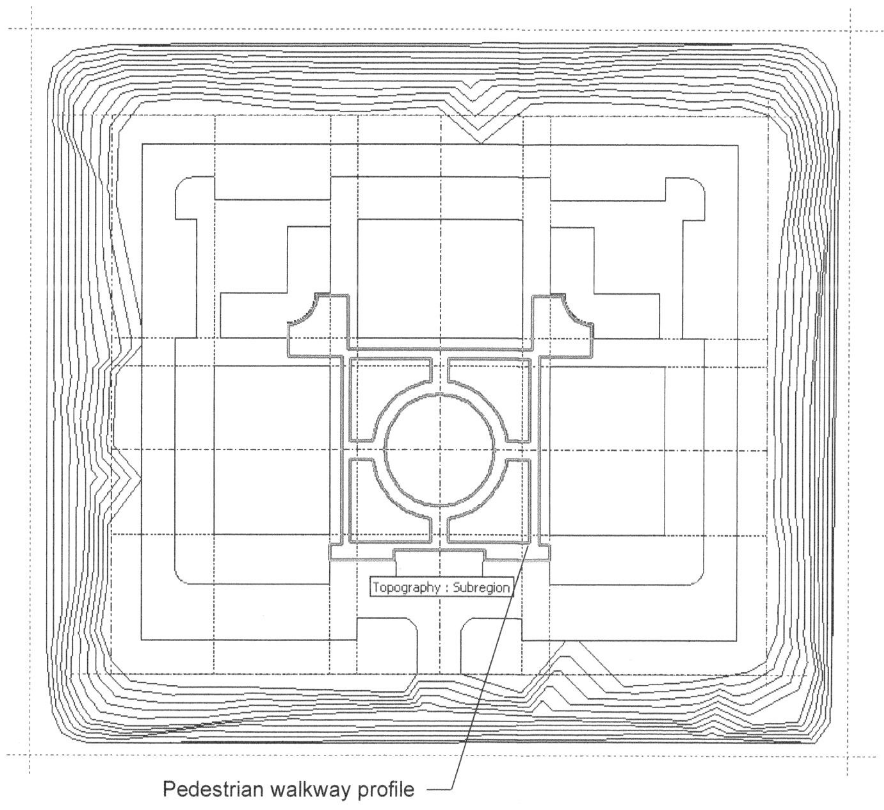

Figure 9-33 Pedestrian walkway profile created

Adding Parking Components

In this section, you will add the parking components to the site plan using the **Parking Component** tool.

1. Choose the **Massing & Site** tab and then choose the **Parking Component** tool from the **Model Site** panel; the **Modify |Parking Component** tab is displayed.

2. In the **Properties** palette, select the **Parking Space: 9' X 18'-90 deg (4800 X 2400 mm- 90 deg)** option from the **Type Selector** drop-down list, as specified in the component parameters for the project.

3. Move the cursor near the entrance of the lower left corner of the site and click near the location shown in Figure 9-34. (You may need to use the **Zoom In Region** tool to enlarge the portion of the site). The selected parking component is added to the site plan. Depending upon the point selected for placement, you may need to use the **Move** or **Flip** tool to orient the component to the desired position.

4. Create multiple copies of the added parking component using the **Array** tool. Choose the **Linear** button from the **Options Bar** and create an array of 7 components placed consecutively, as shown in Figure 9-35.

5. Repeat steps 1 to 4 and add the same parking component to the other seven places in the project. The site plan appears similar to the illustration shown in Figure 9-36.

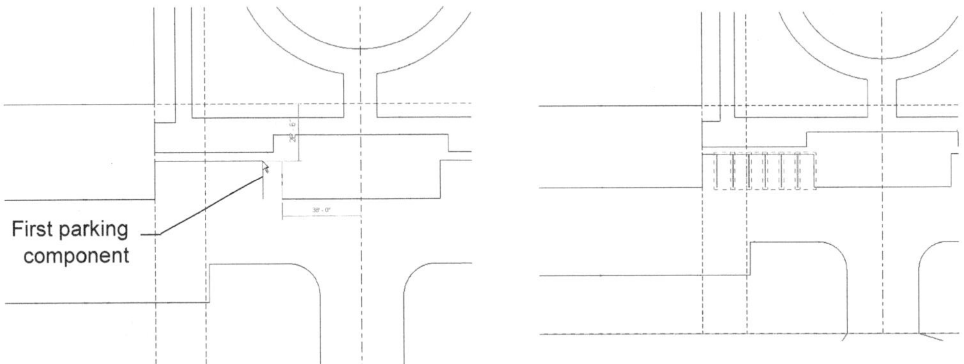

Figure 9-34 *Adding the parking component*

Figure 9-35 *Creating an array of the parking components*

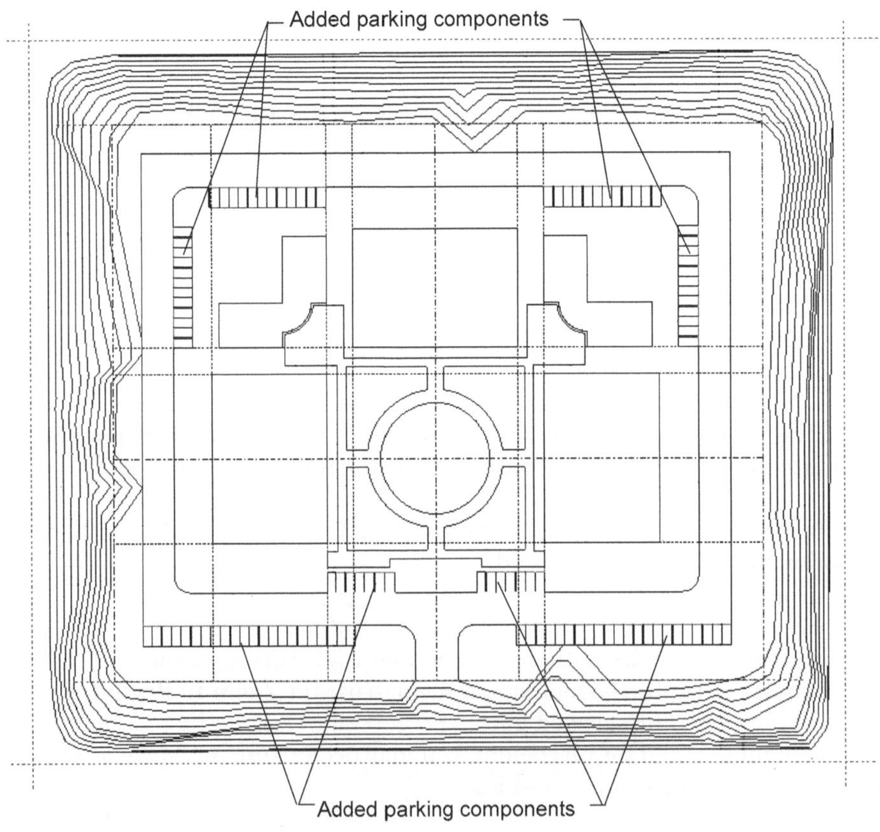

Figure 9-36 *Parking components added*

Adding Site Components

In this section, you will add site components from the in-built library of Autodesk Revit. The procedure is the same as that of adding parking components.

1. Choose the **Site Component** tool from the **Model Site** panel in the **Massing & Site** tab.

2. Next, you need to load the desired site component from the library. To do so, choose the **Load Family** tool from the **Mode** panel; the **Load Family** dialog box is displayed.

3. Now, browse to **US Imperial > Planting** and select **RPC Tree - Deciduous** and then choose **Open**.

4. Next, in the **Properties** palette, select the required option from the **Type Selector** drop-down list, as specified in the site component parameters for the project.
   For Imperial **RPC Tree - Deciduous : Red Ash-25'**
   For Metric **RPC Tree - Deciduous : Red Ash- 7.6 Metres**

5. Move the cursor to the site plan and click to add the planting component. Add multiple trees by clicking points on the site plan.

   The trees can be placed at an approximate location, as given in the sketch plan.

6. Next, select all trees from the site plan; the instance properties of the selected trees are displayed in the **Properties** palette.

7. Now, select **Level 2** from the drop-down list corresponding to the **Level** parameter.

   The complete site plan with site components appears similar to the illustration given in Figure 9-37.

Creating Sections through the Site

You can use the **Section** tool to create section lines horizontally and vertically through the site.

1. Choose the **View** tab and then invoke the **Section** tool from the **Create** panel.

2. Create horizontal section line from the left to the right across the center of the design scheme.

3. Similarly, create a vertical section line from the bottom to the top across the center. The two section lines are created and their corresponding views are added under the **Sections (Building Section)** head in the **Project Browser**.

4. Using the **Project Browser**, rename the horizontal section **Section1** as **Longitudinal Section** and the vertical section **Section 2** as **Transverse Section**.

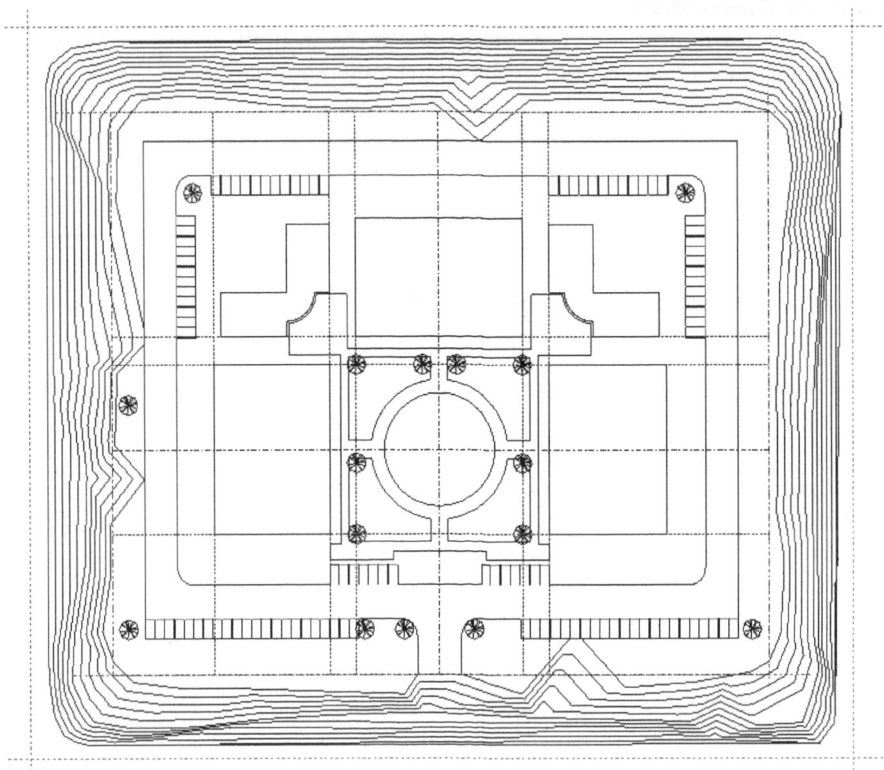

Figure 9-37 *Complete site plan with site components*

5. Double-click on **Longitudinal Section** under the **Sections (Building Section)** head in the **Project Browser** to view the longitudinal section.

6. Double-click on **Transverse Section** under the **Sections (Building Section)** head in the **Project Browser** to view the transverse section.

   You may need to increase the view range box by dragging the section box from the top or the bottom. Also, drag the levels to the sides of the section view. Ensure that the scale of the view shown in the **View Control Bar** is 1"=20'0" (1: 100).

7. Choose **Visual Styles > Shaded** from the **View Control Bar** to display the shaded view of the Longitudinal and Transverse sections, as shown in Figure 9-38 and Figure 9-39.

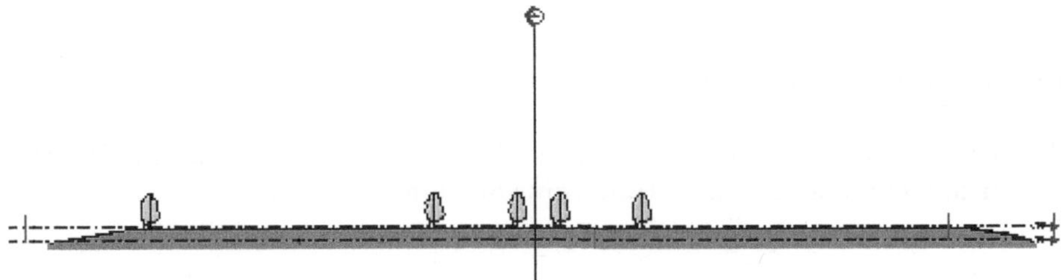

Figure 9-38 *Longitudinal section through the site*

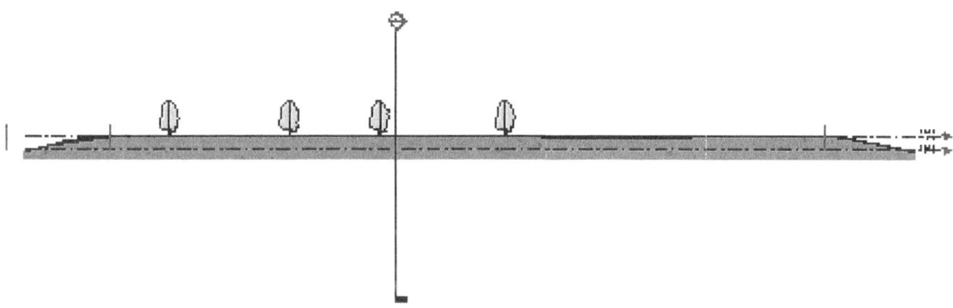

Figure 9-39 *Transverse section through the site*

8. Similarly, open the site plan and choose **Visual Styles > Shaded** from the **View Control Bar** to display the shaded view of the site plan, as shown in Figure 9-40.

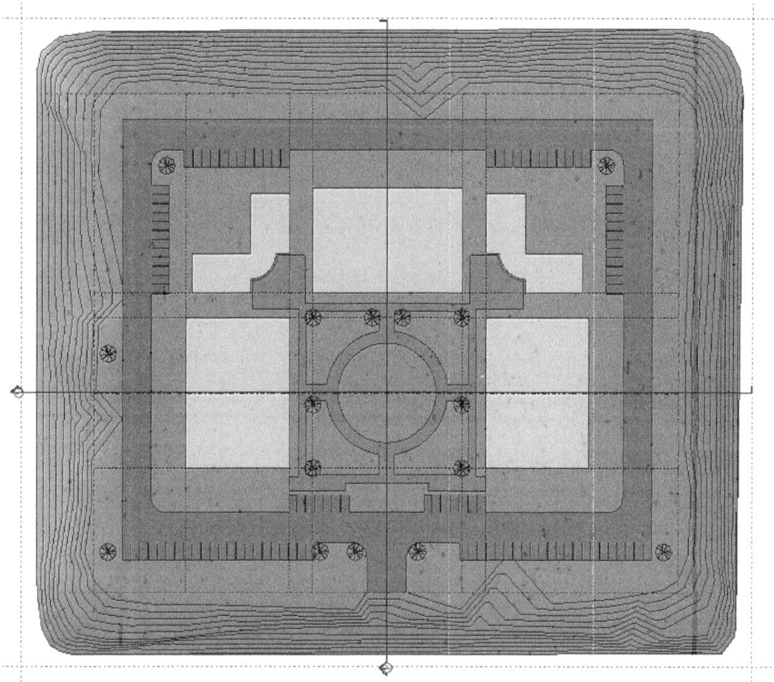

Figure 9-40 *Complete site plan*

Saving the Project

In this section, you will save the project file using the **Save As** tool.

9. Choose **Save As > Project** from the **File** menu to save the project. Specify the file name in the **File name** edit box and choose **Save**.
   For Imperial **c09_SitePlan_tut1**
   For Metric **M_c09_SitePlan_tut1**
   The project file is saved.

10. Choose **Close** from the **File** menu to close the project file.

Tip

*The modified material properties are not visible in the hidden lines view type. You can choose the **Visual Style** button in the **View Control Bar** and then choose **Shaded** option from the menu to graphically view the modified materials.*

Self-Evaluation Test

Answer the following questions and then compare them to those given at the end of this chapter:

1. Which of the following tools helps to insert the entourages in the project?

   (a) **Parking Component** (b) **Topographies**
   (c) **Site Component** (d) **Split Surface**

2. Which of the following tools helps to define the extents of the project?

   (a) **Property Line** (b) **Graded Region**
   (c) **Subregion** (d) **Building Pad**

3. The __________ tool is used to join two topographical surfaces that overlap or have a common edge.

4. The depth of the cross-section of the topographical surface can be specified in the ________ edit box of the **Site Settings** dialog box.

5. The __________ tool is used to add a building pad to a topographical surface.

6. The __________ option can be chosen to invoke the **Rotate** tool immediately after placing a parking component.

7. After creating a topographical surface, you can choose the __________ button from the **Modify |Topography** tab to edit it.

8. You can pick points at different elevation levels while creating a toposurface. (T/F)

9. When you pick points to create a toposurface, they automatically join to form a loop. (T/F)

10. A toposurface can be split along a straight line only. (T/F)

11. The specified depth and height offset is automatically cut in the toposurface. (T/F)

12. When you add site components, they get attached at the elevation level of the point picked on the toposurface. (T/F)

Review Questions

Answer the following questions:

1. Which of the following parameters can be used to specify the distance of a building pad from the base level?

   (a) **Level** (b) **Structure**
   (c) **Height Offset from level** (d) **Thickness**

2. Which of the following tools is used to create a region on a toposurface?

   (a) **Topographies** (b) **Pad**
   (c) **Subregion** (d) **Parking component**

3. Which of the following site setting parameters can be used to create additional contours?

   (a) **At Intervals of** (b) **Additional Contours**
   (c) **Passing Through Elevation** (d) **Elevation of poche base**

4. While creating a topographical surface, the **Relative to Surface** option is used to pick points relative to the base level. (T/F)

5. The properties of a toposurface cannot be modified after its creation. (T/F)

6. The **Split Surface** tool is used to break the created toposurface into two separate surfaces. (T/F)

7. On merging two toposurfaces, the merged toposurface acquires the properties of the toposurface that was selected first. (T/F)

8. The **Work Plane** tool is used to draw multiple guidelines for locating points before creating a property line. (T/F)

9. The thickness of a building pad cannot be specified. (T/F)

10. A property line, once added, cannot be edited. (T/F)

EXERCISES

Exercise 1 Site Plan

Create the peripheral pedestrian walkway for the *Site Plan* project created in Tutorial 1 of this chapter, as shown in Figure 9-41. The sketch plan shows the pathway in white. You can assume the width of the walkway at various locations. Assign the material **Site - Sand** to the created pathway surface. Save the file as *c09_SitePlan_ex1.rvt (M_c09_SitePlan_ex1.rvt).*

(Expected time: 30 min)

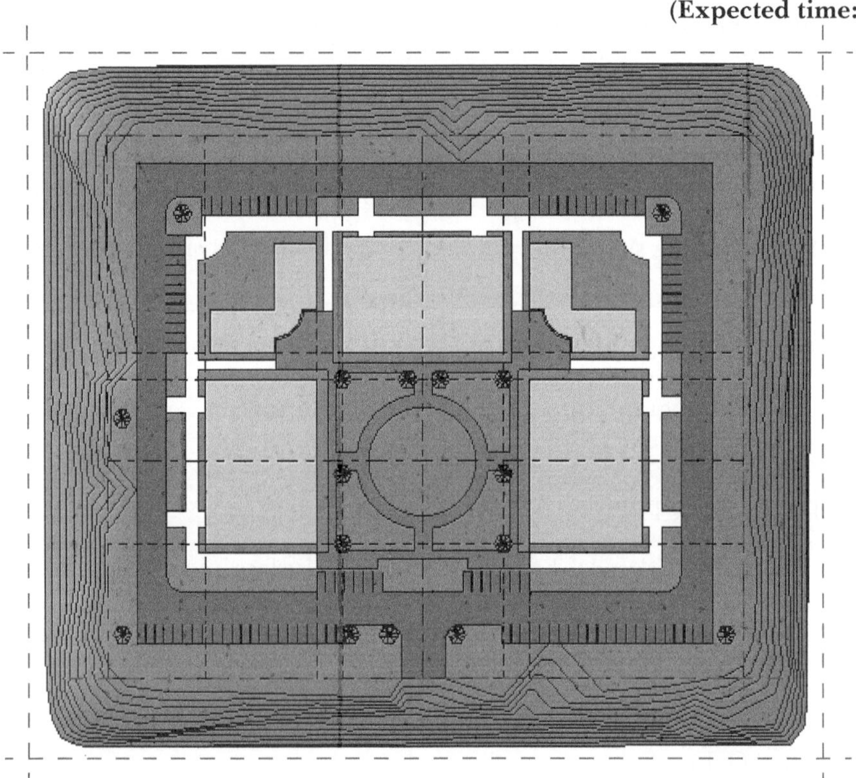

Figure 9-41 *Sketch plan for adding the peripheral pedestrian walkway to the Site Plan project*

Exercise 2 Museum Site Plan

Create the site plan for a new project, a museum, by adding a site toposurface, road subregion, pedestrian walkway subregion, parking components, and trees, based on the illustration given in Figure 9-42. The dimensions and texts have been given only for reference and are not to be added. The site plan is symmetrical along the diagonal axis and you can assume the missing dimensions. **(Expected time: 30 min)**

1. Project file parameters:
   For Imperial Template File- *default.rte*
   For Metric Template File- *DefaultMetric.rte*

   File name to be assigned:
   For Imperial *c09_MuseumSitePlan_ex2.rvt*
   For Metric *M_c09_MuseumSitePlan_ex2.rvt*

2. Property size:
   For Imperial **150'0" X 150'0"** (Extents of property line)
   For Metric **45720 X 45720 mm**

3. Site settings:
   Contours at 1'0" (304.8 mm) intervals, top of site level- **5'0" (1525 mm)**
   Site material- **Site - Grass**, Road material- **Asphalt**, Walkway material- **Sand**
   Elevation of poche base- **-5'0" (-1525 mm)**

4. Building Pad: Level - **5'0" (1525 mm)**
   As per the dimensions given in the sketch plan - placed symmetrically along the diagonal axis.
   Building pad base level- **Level 2**

5. Parking Component-
   For Imperial **Parking Space: 9' X 18'-90 deg**
   For Metric **Parking Space: 4800 X 2400- 90 deg**

6. Site Component-
   For Imperial **RPC Tree - Deciduous: Red Ash-25'**
   For Metric **RPC Tree - Deciduous: Red Ash-7.6 Metres**

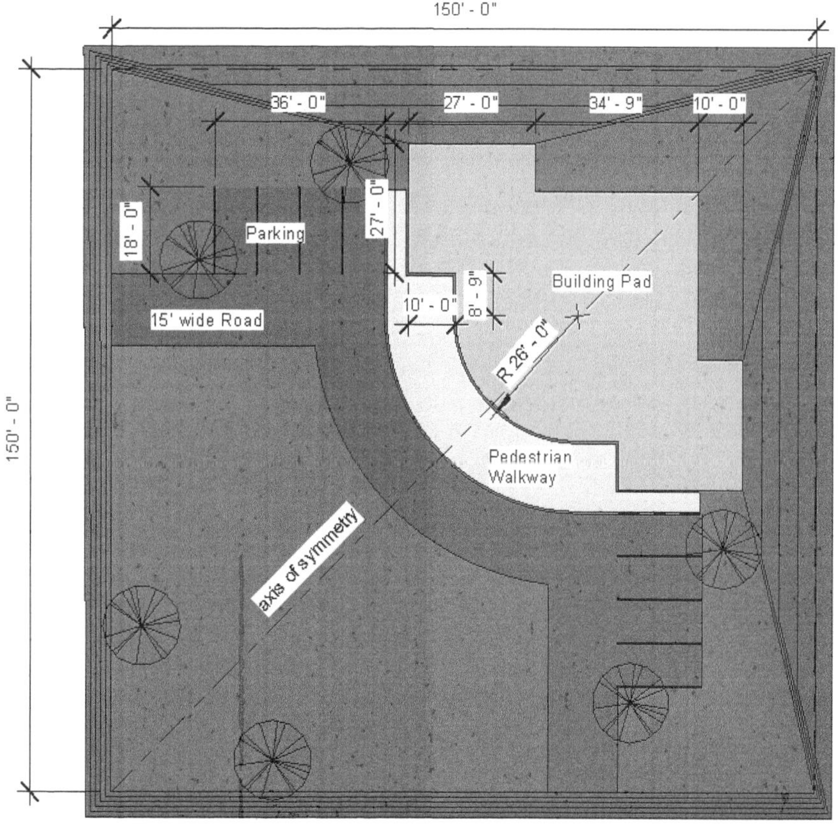

Figure 9-42 *Sketch plan for creating the site plan for the Museum project*

Answers to Self-Evaluation Test

1. c, 2. a, 3. Merge Surface, 4. Elevation of poche base, 5. Building Pad, 6. Rotate after placement, 7. Edit Surface, 8. T, 9. T, 10. T, 11. T, 12. T

Chapter 10

Using Massing Tools

Learning Objectives

After completing this chapter, you will be able to:

- *Understand the concept of massing in Revit*
- *Create massing geometries using the Massing tool*
- *Cut massing geometries using the Void Form tools*
- *Convert a massing geometry into building elements*
- *Add other building elements to a converted geometry*
- *Create conceptual massing in conceptual design environment*
- *Create a family and its types*

INTRODUCTION

In the earlier chapters, you learned to use different building elements and components to create a building model. These building elements are parametrically associated and enable you to generate a building model based on specific design requirements such as wall types, door width, window height, and so on. Each of the elements must be assigned specific properties to achieve the desired element parameters, thereby making a building model accurate. Needless to say, this is a fairly time-consuming procedure. Autodesk Revit provides you with an alternative and much easier method to create a building model, known as massing.

UNDERSTANDING MASSING CONCEPTS

At the conceptualization stage of a project, you may want to study it in terms of its building volumes and shapes. You may also want to convey the basic idea of the structure of a building in a three-dimensional form without putting in a lot of detailing. This can be achieved by using various tools for creating massing geometries.

The tools for creating massing geometry not only enable you to conceive and create a variety of building shapes and volumes with relative ease but also convey the potential design in terms of building masses and geometric shapes. You can create and edit geometric shapes and amalgamate them to form a building structure. This process can be compared to the creation of building a model using foam blocks. You have the freedom of choice to add or cut geometric shapes and join different blocks or masses to form an assembly. Figure 10-1 shows a group of volumes that can be created to represent the building volume and mass.

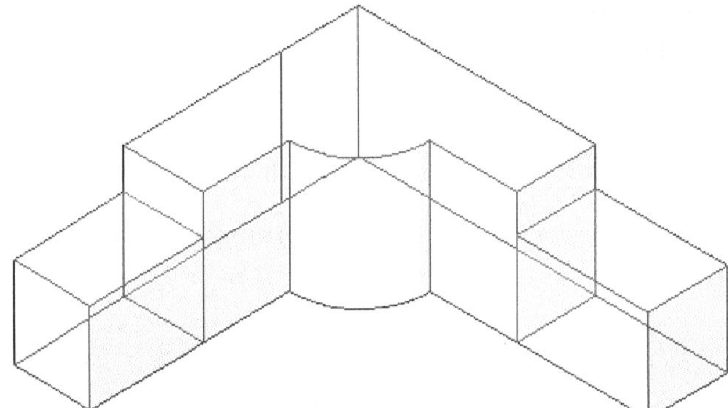

Figure 10-1 *Building blocks created using the massing geometry*

Revit also enables you to convert a building mass into building elements. Building blocks can be transformed into an assembly of individual building elements such as walls, roof, and floor. The transformation carried out by using the tools provided for replacing massing faces with predefined wall, roof, and floor types, allows you to convert the same building mass into a building model. You can then develop it into a detailed building model by incorporating individual building elements with specified parameters.

Revit provides a much-needed continuity in the design development of a building project by using the same building model from its conceptualization to completion. It also enables you to control the visibility of geometry between the building volumes (massing) and building elements (shell) during the initial stages of project development. Other project information such as its total area can also be extracted from the building massing.

It is, however, important to understand the limitations of the massing tool. This tool is only meant for conceptual design development using simple geometric shapes. You can place the predefined massing family elements provided in additional libraries. Autodesk Revit attempts to translate the massing geometry into building elements or shell. So, it is not recommended to be used for the development of a detailed geometry such as columns, cavity walls, footing, and so on.

CREATING THE MASSING GEOMETRY

In Autodesk Revit, you can create the massing geometry in any of these three environments: Family Editor, Conceptual Design, and Project.

To create the massing geometry in the Family Editor environment, choose **New > Family** from the **File** menu; the **New Family - Select Template File** dialog box will be displayed. In this dialog box, choose the *Generic Model.rft* file (commonly used) from the **English_I** folder [for Metric the *Metric Generic Model.rft* file (commonly used) from the **English** folder] and then choose the **Open** button; a new file will open in the Family Editor environment. In the new file, create the massing geometry using various tools available in the ribbon.

The Conceptual Design environment is a new environment in Revit. This environment is a type of Family Editor that provides the advanced modeling tools and techniques for creating massing families. To start creating a mass in this environment, choose **New > Conceptual Mass** from the **File** menu; the **New Conceptual Mass - Select Template File** dialog box will be displayed. In this dialog box, select the **Mass** template file from the **Conceptual Mass** folder and then choose **Open**; a new file will be displayed in the Conceptual Design environment. In the new file, you can create the massing geometry using the tools available in the **Create** tab of the ribbon, as shown in Figure 10-2.

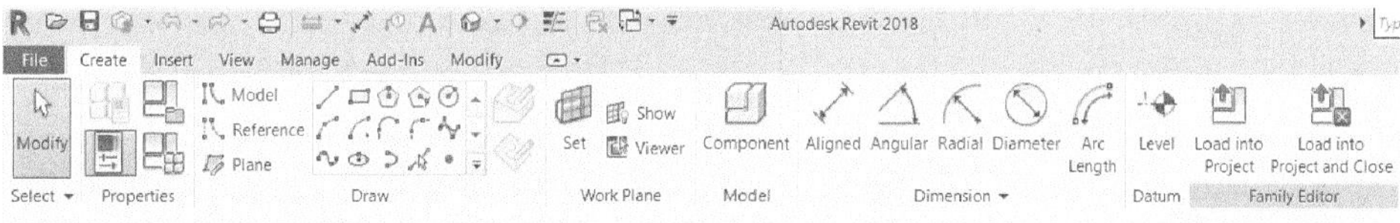

Figure 10-2 *Various tools in the* ***Create*** *tab of the ribbon*

The Project environment is the most common environment used in a project design. To start creating a mass in this environment, open a new file or an existing file by choosing **New > Project** or **Open > Project** from the **File** menu. After opening a new file or an existing file, choose the **Massing & Site** tab. In this tab, the massing tools can be accessed from the **Conceptual Mass** panel. The **Conceptual Mass** panel contains the following tools for massing: **In-Place Mass**, **Show Mass by View Settings**, and **Place Mass**.

The options in the **Model by Face** panel are used to convert the conceptual mass created into real building elements like walls, floors, roofs, and curtain systems. As such, these tools are also called the Building Maker tools.

When you create shapes in massing, Autodesk Revit creates its corresponding building elements. It is, therefore, imperative to consider the associativity of the massing and shell elements. The massing elements may need to be transformed into individual building elements simultaneously. Therefore, the massing geometry must be created accordingly.

For example, when you create a complex geometric massing shape and convert faces into building elements, you may find that some planes do not acquire the desired building element characteristics. The inclined planes and the curved surfaces are converted into in-place roofs.

Creating a Massing Geometry in the Family Editor

As discussed earlier, the Family Editor environment provides tools to create massing geometry. To create a new mass, choose **New > Family** from the **File** menu; the **New Family - Select Template File** dialog box will be displayed. In this dialog box, select the *Generic Model.rft* file (commonly used) from the **English_I** folder [for Metric the *Metric Generic Model.rft* file (commonly used) from the **English** folder] and choose **Open**; a new file will open using the selected template file.

In the Family Editor environment, the **Create** tab contains tools to create massing geometry. These tools can be used to create massing geometries in solid or in void form.

To create a solid form, invoke the **Extrusion** / **Blend** / **Revolve** / **Sweep** / **Swept Blend** tool from the **Forms** panel of the **Create** tab. These tools are used to create different solid forms. Similarly, to create a void form, choose the **Extrusion** / **Blend** / **Revolve** / **Sweep** / **Swept Blend** tool from the **Void Forms** drop-down in the **Forms** panel. You can create a massing geometry using any of these massing tools or a combination of the **Solid** and **Void** tools. The usage of these tools for creating simple massing geometries is described next. However, a designer can select the appropriate tool judiciously depending on the massing geometry to be created. Various tools used to create a solid or a void geometry are explained in the next sections.

Creating an Extrusion

Ribbon: Create > Forms > Extrusion

The **Extrusion** tool is used to create a massing geometry by adding height to a sketched profile. You can invoke this tool from the **Forms** panel in the **Create** tab of the ribbon in the Family Editor. On doing so, the **Modify | Create Extrusion** tab will be displayed. In this tab, you can specify different options to sketch an extrusion profile and create a massing geometry. Figure 10-3 shows different options in the **Modify | Create Extrusion** tab.

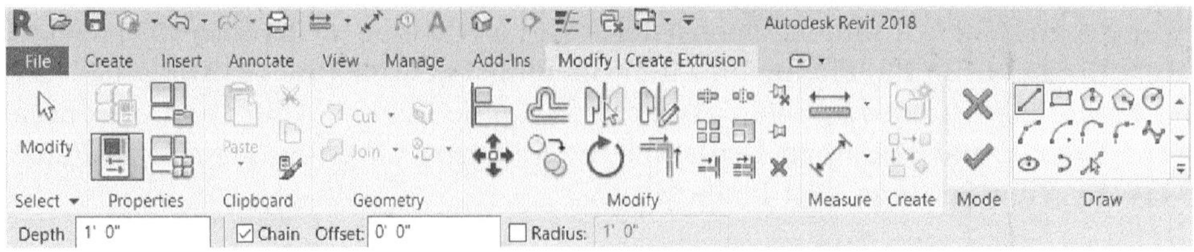

*Figure 10-3 Different options in the **Modify / Create Extrusion** tab*

To create an extrusion, first you need to define the work plane to sketch a profile. To do so, you can invoke the **Set** tool available in the **Work Plane** panel of the **Modify | Create Extrusion** tab. After specifying the work plane, you can invoke the **Reference Plane** tool in the **Datum** panel of the **Create** tab to draw reference planes for locating exact points to sketch a profile. To sketch the 2D profile to be extruded, you can invoke any of the sketching tools available in the **Draw** panel of the **Modify | Create Extrusion** tab. You can invoke the appropriate tool (s) depending on the shape of the profile that must form a closed loop. In the **Properties** panel, choose the **Properties** tool to display the **Properties** palette, if it is not displayed by default. In this palette, you can specify the start and end levels of extrusion and other properties. The **Extrusion Start** instance parameter in the **Properties** palette indicates the start level of extrusion from the base level. The **Extrusion End** parameter indicates the top level of extrusion. The difference between these two parameters is calculated as the depth of the extrusion. You can also enter its value in the **Depth** edit box of the **Options Bar**. Autodesk Revit assumes the depth of extrusion from the base level. After sketching the profile, choose the **Finish Edit Mode** button from the **Mode** panel to finish the sketch of the profile for extrusion.

For example, to create a high-rise building, invoke the **Extrusion** tool from the **Forms** panel. In the **Options Bar**, you can specify the height of extrusion in the **Depth** edit box and also if required, select the **Chain** check box if it is not selected by default. Next, in the **Draw** panel of this tab, the **Line** tool (invoked by default) can be used to sketch the extrusion profile. You can also use other sketching tools available in the **Draw** panel to sketch the profile. Sketch the base of the specified dimension using temporary dimensions, as shown in Figure 10-4. After the profile is completed, choose the **Finish Edit Mode** button to extrude the sketched profile to the specified depth. The building mass created can be seen in the 3D view, as shown in Figure 10-5.

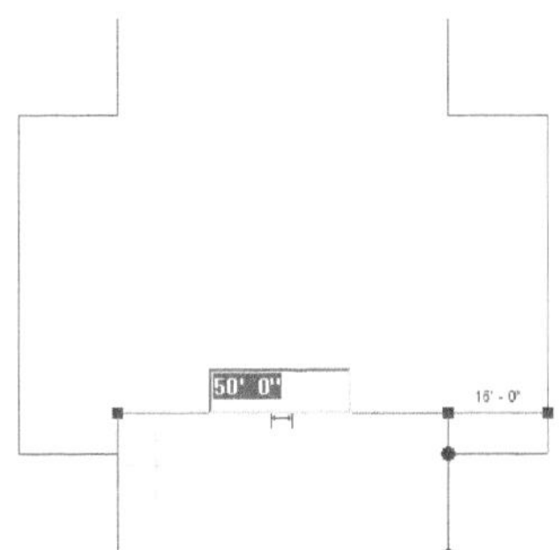

Figure 10-4 *Sketch of a building profile to be extruded*

Figure 10-5 *Massing geometry created by using the **Extrusion** tool*

Creating a Revolved Geometry

Ribbon: Create > Forms > Revolve

The **Revolve** tool is used to create a solid geometry by revolving a profile about an axis. This tool can also be used to create shapes such as domes, donuts, cylinders, and so on. To create a revolved geometry, invoke this tool from the **Forms** panel; Autodesk Revit enters the sketch mode and the **Modify | Create Revolve** tab will be displayed, as shown in Figure 10-6.

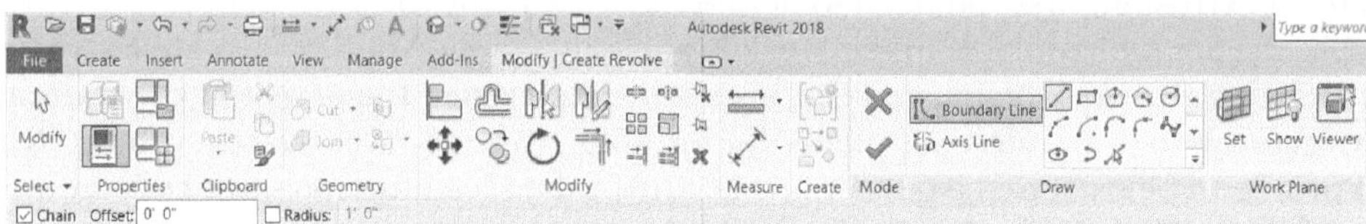

*Figure 10-6 Options in the **Modify / Create Revolve** tab*

In the **Draw** panel, the **Boundary Line** tool is chosen by default. As a result, various sketching tools used to sketch the profile of the revolved geometry are displayed in a list box of this panel. Before invoking any of the sketching tools, you need to set the work plane. To do so, choose the **Create** tab, and then choose the **Set** tool from the **Work Plane** panel; the **Work Plane** dialog box will be displayed. In this dialog box, you can use various options to specify the required work plane for sketching the profile of the revolved geometry. After selecting the required plane, you can sketch the profile of the revolved geometry.

To sketch this profile, choose the **Modify | Create Revolve** tab. Next, you can use various sketching tools from the list box in the **Draw** panel. The sketched profile must be a single closed loop or multiple closed loops that do not intersect. After defining the profile, you need to define the axis about which the profile will revolve. To do so, invoke the **Axis Line** tool from the **Draw** panel; two tools, **Line** and **Pick Line**, will be displayed in the list. The **Line** tool is used to draw a line that can be used as an axis and the **Pick Line** tool is used to pick a line or an edge to define the axis of revolution. After completing the sketch and defining the axis of revolution, choose the **Finish Edit Mode** button from the **Modify | Create Revolve** tab; the **Modify | Revolve** tab will be displayed and the revolved geometry will be created.

In the **Modify | Revolve** tab, you can change the instance property of a revolved geometry in the **Properties** palette. In this palette, you can set the start and end angles of revolution. The default values for these two parameters are 0-degree and 360-degree, respectively.

For example, to create a dome, you can sketch the profile and define the axis for it, as shown in Figure 10-7. Before you start the sketch, you need to set the work plane that is perpendicular to the horizontal plane. The resultant revolved massing geometry with the axis and its profile is shown in Figure 10-8. Figure 10-9 shows an example of the revolved geometry in which the **End Angle** and **Start Angle** parameters in the **Properties** palette have been assigned the values 180.000° and 0.000°, respectively.

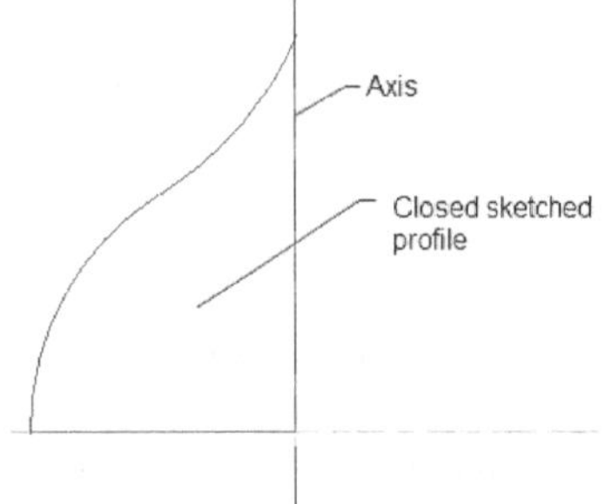

Figure 10-7 Sketching a closed profile for a revolved geometry

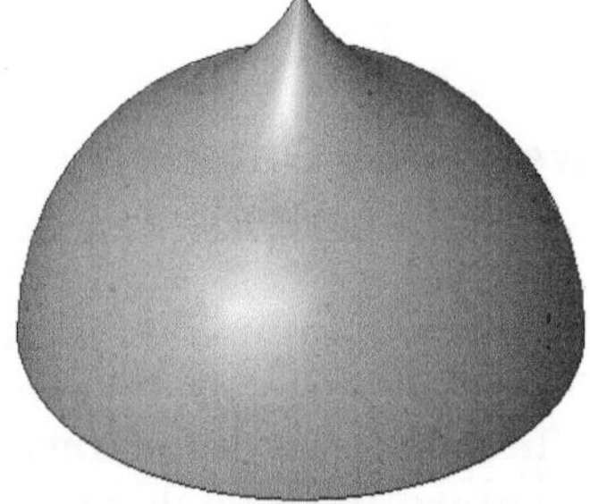

*Figure 10-8 Massing geometry created by using the **Revolve** tool*

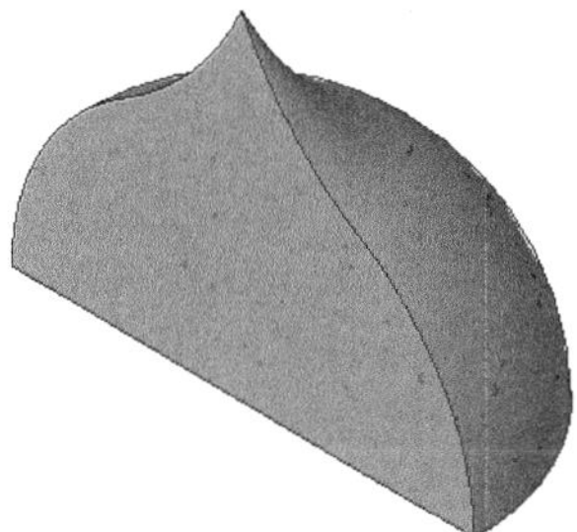

Figure 10-9 *Revolved geometry created by revolving the profile at an angle of 180 degrees*

Tip

In Autodesk Revit, you can quickly edit the revolve angle of a revolved geometry by selecting the geometry from the drawing and then changing the temporary angular dimension displayed in the geometry.

Creating a Sweep

Ribbon: Create > Forms > Sweep

The **Sweep** tool is used to create a massing feature by selecting a profile along a sketched path. To create a massing feature by sweeping a profile, invoke the **Sweep** tool from the **Forms** panel; the sketch mode will be invoked and the **Modify | Sweep** tab will be displayed, as shown in Figure 10-10. The **Sketch Path** tool in the **Sweep** panel of the **Modify | Sweep** tab is used to sketch the path to be used for extrusion. On invoking this tool, the **Modify | Sweep** tab will be replaced by the **Modify | Sweep > Sketch Path** tab, which contains tools to draw path.

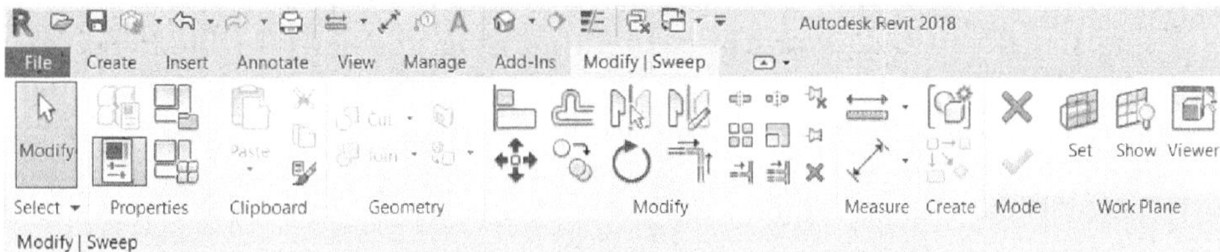

Figure 10-10 *Options in the **Modify / Sweep** tab with its tools*

Using the tools from the **Draw** panel, you can sketch the desired shape of the path, which can be an open or closed profile. After sketching the path, choose the **Finish Edit Mode** button from the **Mode** panel; the **Modify | Sweep** tab will be displayed. In this tab, you can sketch a profile or load a profile for the sweep geometry. To sketch a profile, choose the **Edit Profile** tool from the **Sweep** panel in the **Modify | Sweep** tab; the **Go To View** dialog box will be displayed. In this dialog box, select an appropriate view and sketch the profile using different sketching tools. After sketching the profile, choose the **Finish Edit Mode** button from the **Mode** panel; the **Modify | Sweep > Edit Profile** tab will be displayed. In this tab, choose the **Finish Edit Mode** button from the **Mode** panel; a sweep geometry will be created. Figure 10-11 shows the example of a 2D path with a sketched profile and Figure 10-12 shows the resulting massing shape.

Autodesk Revit also provides in-built profiles that can be used in projects. These profiles are available in the **Profile** drop-down list in the **Sweep** panel of the **Modify | Sweep** tab. You can also choose the **Load Profile** button from the **Sweep** panel and access additional profiles in the **Profiles** subfolder in the **US Imperial** folder (for Metric **US Metric** folder). You can modify the properties of the sweep profile such as its **Structural**, **Mechanical**, and **Others**. To do so, select the massing created by the **Sweep** tool; the **Modify | Sweep** tab will be displayed. In this tab choose the **Edit Sweep** tool from the **Mode** panel; the properties of the sweep model will be displayed in the **Properties** palette. In this palette, click on the value field corresponding to the **Part Type** parameter under the **Mechanical** head; a drop-down list will be displayed. You can select an option from the displayed drop-down list to specify a part type to the sweep model. In the **Properties** palette, select the check box corresponding to the **Can host rebar** parameter to allow the sweep mass to host rebar for structural detailing.

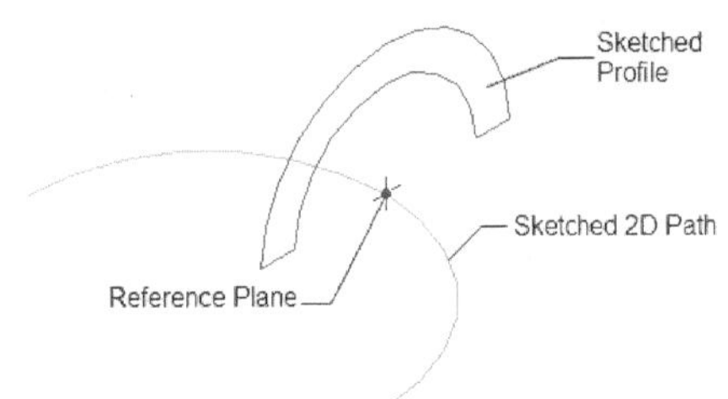

Figure 10-11 *Sketching the profile and the 2D path for creating a sweep*

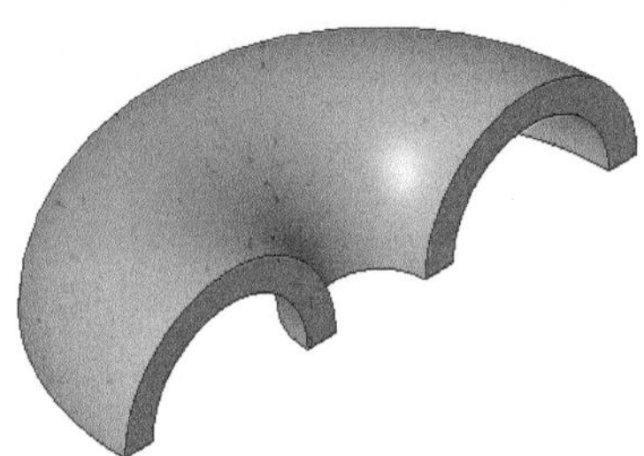

Figure 10-12 *Massing geometry created by using the* ***Sweep*** *tool*

Creating a Blend

Ribbon:	Create > Forms > Blend

Using the **Blend** tool, you can create a massing geometry by blending or linking two profiles. To create a massing geometry using this tool, invoke it from the **Forms** panel; the **Modify | Create Blend Base Boundary** tab will be displayed. The tools in this tab are used to create and edit a blend. Figure 10-13 shows various tools in the **Modify | Create Blend Base Boundary** tab.

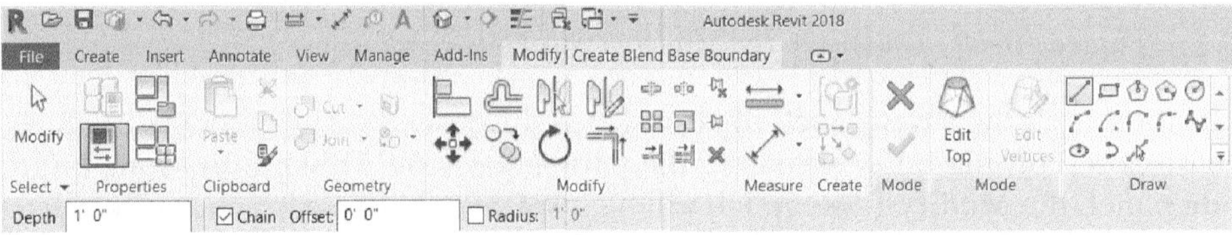

Figure 10-13 *Different tools in the* ***Modify / Create Blend Base Boundary*** *tab*

After setting the work plane, you can sketch the base profile using different sketching tools available in the **Draw** panel. In the **Properties** palette, you can specify values in the value fields of the **First End** and **Second End** instance parameters to set the height of the blend geometry. After completing the base profile, you can choose the **Edit Top** option from the **Mode** panel in the **Modify | Create Blend Base Boundary** tab to display the **Modify | Create Blend Top Boundary** tab. In this tab, you can sketch the profile of the top of the blend geometry in any work plane. The depth of the blend geometry can be specified in the **Depth** edit box available in the **Options Bar**.

The **Edit Vertices** tool in the **Mode** panel of the **Modify | Create Blend Top Boundary** tab will be available only after both the base and top profiles are sketched. This tool enables you to specify the connectivity between the vertices of their profiles. After sketching both the profiles, choose the **Finish Edit Mode** button from the **Mode** panel to create the blend geometry. Figure 10-14 shows two circular profiles being sketched as the base and top profiles. The resulting geometry is shown in Figure 10-15.

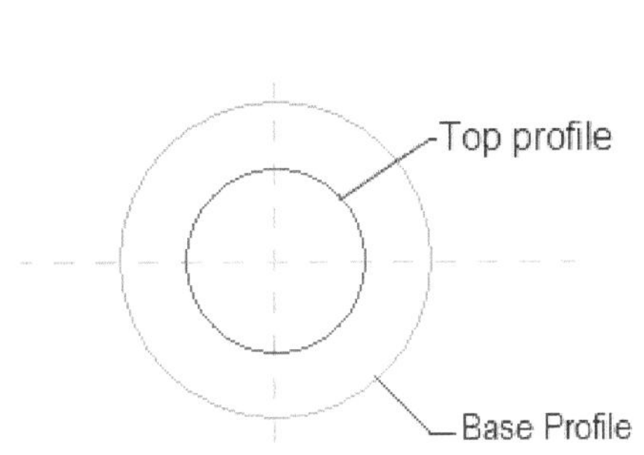

***Figure 10-14** Sketching the base and top profiles to create a blend geometry*

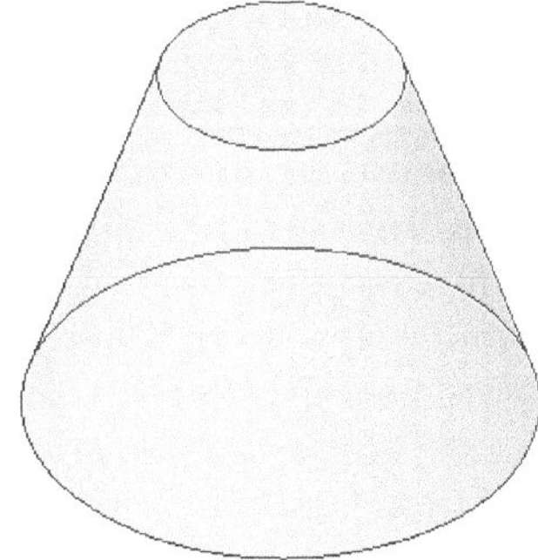

***Figure 10-15** Resulting shape after blending the base and top profiles*

Creating a Swept Blend

Ribbon: Create > Forms > Swept Blend

The solid swept blend geometries are created by using the **Swept Blend** tool. This tool has combined features of the **Sweep** and **Blend** tools. A geometry created using the **Swept Blend** tool consists of a path and two different profiles drawn at the either end of the path.

To create a swept blend geometry, choose the **Swept Blend** tool from the **Forms** panel; the screen will enter into the sketch mode and the **Modify | Swept Blend** tab will be displayed, as shown in Figure 10-16.

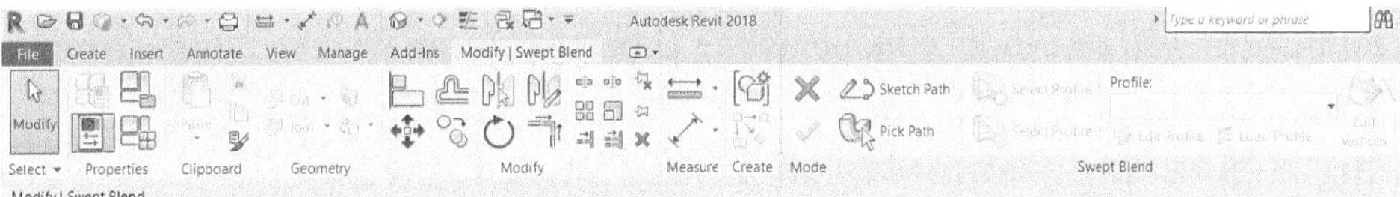

***Figure 10-16** Different options in the **Modify / Swept Blend** tab*

The **Modify | Swept Blend** tab contains various tools to sketch and edit the path and profiles of a solid swept blend geometry. Figure 10-17 shows the graphical representation of the solid swept blend geometry.

To create the geometry, first you need to sketch the 2D path. To do so, choose the **Sketch Path** tool from the **Swept Blend** panel; the sketch mode will be invoked. You can use various sketching tools in the **Draw** panel to sketch the 2D path. Next, choose the **Finish Edit Mode** button from the **Mode** panel of the **Modify | Swept Blend > Sketch Path** tab. Alternatively, you can define the 2D path for the solid swept blend geometry by choosing the **Pick Path** tool from the **Swept**

Blend panel and then selecting an existing open curve or the edges of elements. The desired 2D path is always an open geometry consisting of single segment. Once you have sketched or picked the 2D path, you need to define a profile at either end. Choose the **Select Profile 1** tool from the **Swept Blend** panel and then choose the **Edit Profile** tool from the **Edit** panel; the **Go To View** dialog box will be displayed. Choose the required option from this dialog box and then choose the **Open View** button; the view will change based on the option chosen and the **Modify | Swept Blend > Edit Profile** tab will be displayed. Sketch the first profile at the end of the 2D path where you can see the reference plane with a red dot prominently displayed by using the appropriate sketching tools from the **Draw** panel. Next, to finish the sketching of the first profile, choose the **Finish Edit Mode** button from the **Mode** panel of the **Modify | Swept Blend > Edit Profile** tab. Similarly, you can define the second profile. To do so, choose the **Select Profile 2** option from the **Swept Blend** panel and then choose the **Edit Profile** option from the **Mode** panel in the **Modify | Swept Blend** tab; the **Modify | Swept Blend > Edit Profile** tab will be displayed. Sketch the second profile and then choose the **Finish Edit Mode** button from the **Mode** panel; the **Modify | Swept Blend** tab will be displayed. Now, choose the **Finish Edit Mode** button from the **Mode** panel; the solid swept blend geometry will be created, as shown in Figure 10-18.

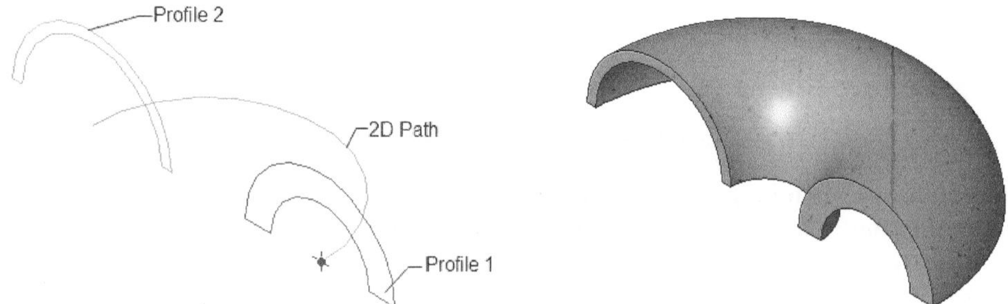

Figure 10-17 *The profiles and the 2D path for creating a swept blend geometry*

Figure 10-18 *Massing geometry created by using the **Swept Blend** tool*

Editing a Massing Geometry in the Family Editor

In Autodesk Revit, you can easily edit a massing geometry. It can be edited using drag controls or by editing massing parameters.

Resizing a Massing Geometry by Using Drag Controls

On selecting a massing geometry, a number of drag controls will be displayed as arrows. You can use the drag control to drag the desired face. The entire massing geometry is automatically updated based on the dragged face. For example, Figure 10-19 shows a cuboid with drag controls displayed on all its faces. When you drag a plane of the cuboid using drag controls, Autodesk Revit immediately updates the geometry, as shown in Figure 10-20.

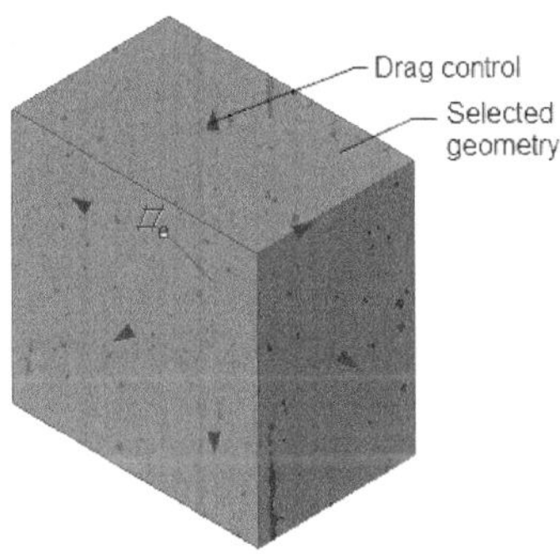

Figure 10-19 *The geometry with the drag controls*

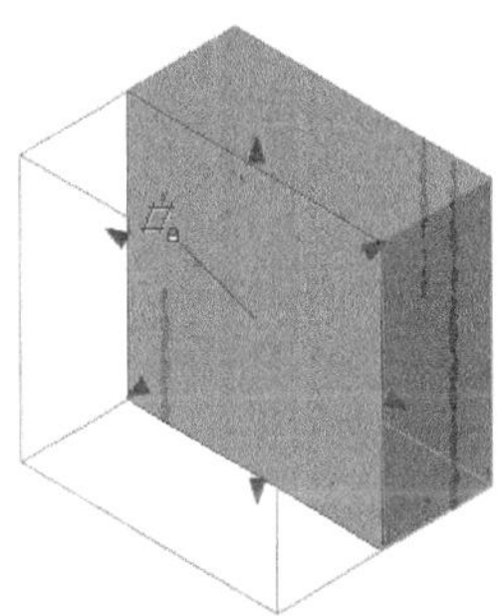

Figure 10-20 *The massing geometry resized using the drag controls*

Editing a Massing Geometry

The parameters of a massing geometry can be modified in the Family Editor. For example, select a massing geometry created by using the **Extrusion** tool; the **Modify | Extrusion** tab will be displayed. In this tab, choose the **Edit Extrusion** tool from the **Mode** panel; the **Modify | Extrusion > Edit Extrusion** tab will be displayed. From the **Draw** panel of this tab, you can use various sketching tools to alter the sketch of the extrusion profile. You can also change the properties of extrusion like height, material, and visibility from the **Properties** palette. In this palette, you can change the height of extrusion by changing the values of the **Extrusion End** and **Extrusion Start** parameters. Similarly, you can change other parameters. Next, in the **Modify | Extrusion > Edit Extrusion** tab, choose the **Finish Edit Mode** button from the **Mode** panel; the editing of the selected extruded mass will be finished.

As discussed earlier, you can also edit other massing geometries such as Sweep, Swept Blend, Revolve, and Blend.

To a certain extent, massing features can also be modified like other building elements. You can use the editing tools such as Mirror, Copy, Group, Array, and so on along with the massing tools.

Creating Cuts in a Massing Geometry by Using the Family Editor

You can cut a massing geometry by creating a void form in it. This void form is cut or subtracted from the massing geometry it intersects. You can create void forms by using the tools displayed in the **Void Forms** drop-down in the **Forms** panel of the **Create** tab. The **Void Forms** drop-down displays five tools: **Void Extrusion**, **Void Blend**, **Void Revolve**, **Void Swept Blend**, and **Void Sweep**. You can choose an appropriate tool to generate the shape and volume of the void form. The method of creating a void form using these tools is similar to that of creating a solid form.

When any of the tools from the **Void Forms** drop-down is invoked, a contextual tab is displayed. For example, if you invoke the **Void Extrusion** tool, the **Modify | Create Void Extrusion** tab will be displayed. You can use the options in this tab to sketch the profile for the extruded void geometry. After sketching the profile of the extruded void geometry, choose the **Finish Edit Mode** button from the **Mode** panel of the **Modify | Create Void Extrusion** tab; the **Modify | Void Extrusion** tab will be displayed. From this tab, you can use various editing options to modify the extruded void geometry. Next, click in the drawing area or press ESC; the void form will automatically cut its shape and volume from the intersecting massing geometry.

For example, Figure 10-21 shows the profile of an arcade sketched using the **Void Extrusion** tool. Now, when you choose the **Finish Edit Mode** button from the **Modify | Create Void Extrusion** tab, the cutting geometry, an arcade in this case, is generated and automatically cut from the larger massing geometry. Figure 10-22 shows the resulting massing geometry.

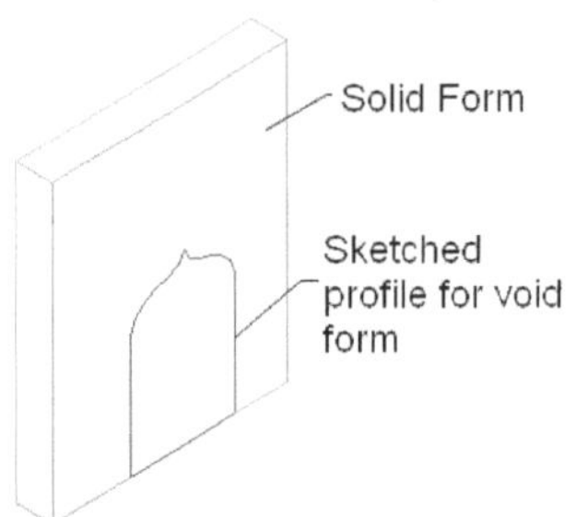

*Figure 10-21 The profile for creating a void form using the **Void Extrusion** tool*

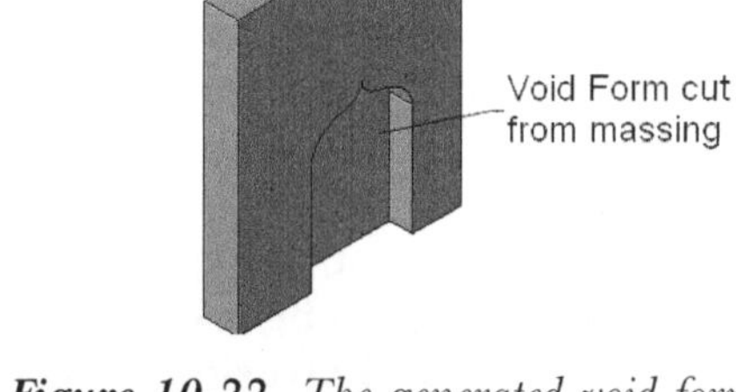

Figure 10-22 The generated void form and the resulting massing geometry

Similarly, you can also use the **Void Revolve**, **Void Sweep**, **Void Blend**, and **Void Swept Blend** tools from the **Void Forms** drop-down to create the void form. For example, to create a tunnel through a building block, you can use the **Void Sweep** tool to sketch a semicircular profile and specify its path, as shown in Figure 10-23. The resulting void form will be cut from the cuboid to create an arched opening through the building block, as shown in Figure 10-24.

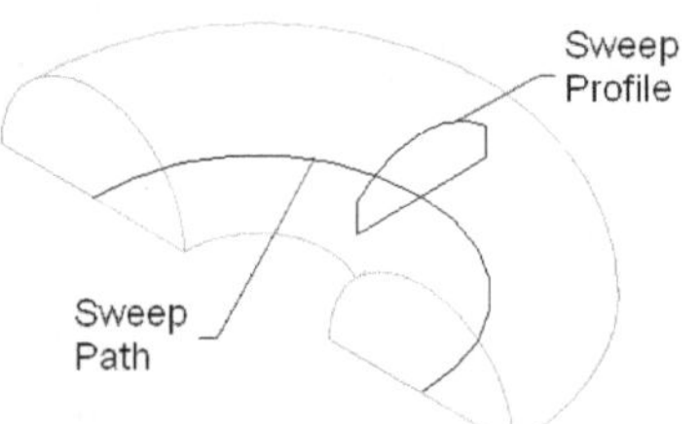

Figure 10-23 Sketching the profile for creating a void form

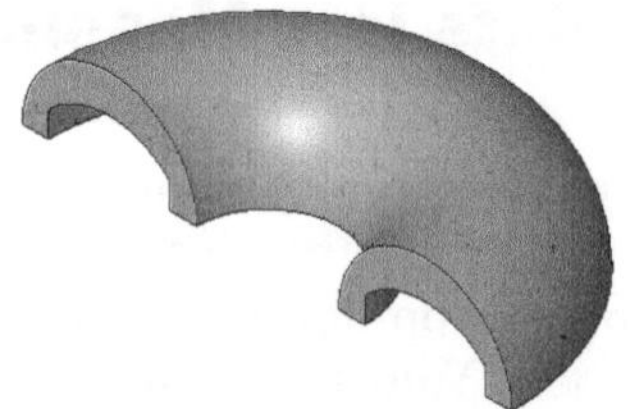

Figure 10-24 The generated void form and the resulting massing geometry

You can also use various editing tools such as **Copy**, **Mirror**, **Array**, and so on to create multiple copies of the void form profile for a single massing geometry. For example, a commercial building block has a semicircular vertical cut as the void form on one of its sides, you can select the 2D profile of the void form and use the **Copy** tool to create its duplicate.

Loading Massing Geometry into the Project

After creating massing geometries in the Family Editor, you can load them into the Project environment. To do so, choose the **Load into Project** tool from the **Family Editor** panel of the **Modify** tab; the current project file will appear if one project file is opened on the screen. Note that if more than one project file is opened in the current session, the **Load into Projects** dialog box will be displayed, as shown in Figure 10-25. In this dialog box, you can select the check box(es) to select the project(s) in which the created mass will be loaded. After selecting the required check box(es), choose **OK**; the mass will be loaded into the selected project file(s) corresponding to the check boxes selected. In this project file, the **Modify | Place Component** tab is chosen and you will notice that the mass created in the Family Editor appears in the drawing area along with the cursor.

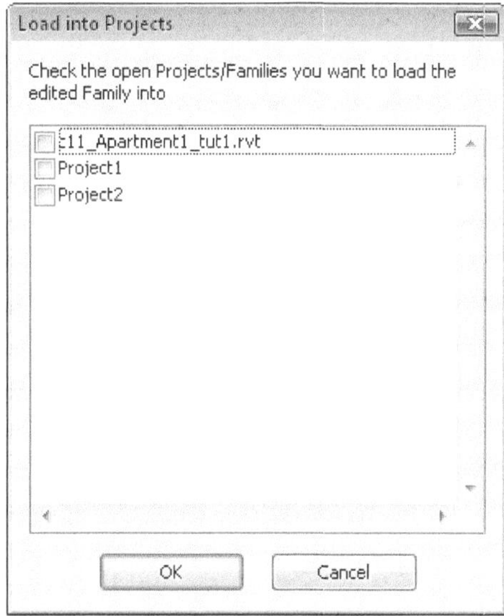

*Figure 10-25 The **Load into Projects** dialog box*

Placing the Massing Geometry in a Project

In the Project environment of Autodesk Revit, you have the option to add a predefined massing geometry to the project using the **Place Mass** tool. To add a predefined geometry, invoke this tool from the **Conceptual Mass** panel of the **Massing & Site** tab; the **Massing - Show Mass Enabled** window will be displayed. Choose the **Close** button from the window; the **Revit** message box will be displayed. Choose the **Yes** button from this message box; the **Load Family** dialog box will be displayed. In this dialog box, browse to the **Mass** subfolder in the **US Imperial** folder and then select a massing family. After selecting the massing family, choose the **Open** button; the **Load Family** dialog box will be closed. Also, the **Modify | Place Mass** tab will be displayed and the selected family will be loaded into the project. Now, click in the drawing area to place the loaded massing geometry.

In Revit, you can either align a mass geometry with the selected faces of the components created or place it on the defined work plane based on your requirement. To place a mass geometry on a selected face, choose the **Place on Face** tool from the **Placement** panel of the

Modify | Place Mass tab and then place the cursor on the face of the component with which you want to align the massing geometry. You will notice that the mass geometry is aligned with the face on which the cursor is placed. Now, you can click to place the mass on the plane. Similarly, while placing a mass in a drawing, you can place it at a desired level. To do so, choose the **Place on Work Plane** tool from the **Placement** panel of the **Modify | Place Mass** tab; the options for placing the mass will be displayed in the **Options Bar**. In the **Options Bar**, select the required level from the **Placement Plane** drop-down list and click in the drawing area; a mass will be created in the selected level. Before aligning the mass geometry to a desired face or in a work plane, you can also rotate it about an axis. To do so, select the **Rotate after placement** check box from the **Options Bar**. After placing the mass geometry in the drawing, you can edit its geometrical properties such as height, width, radius, and so on, depending upon the type of geometry created. To do so, modify the instance parameters displayed in the **Properties** palette. In the **Dimensions** category of the **Properties** palette, you can select the desired dimension instance parameter and change its value in its respective value field.

Creating the In-Place Mass in a Project

In the Project environment, you have the option to create an in-place massing geometry by using the **In-Place Mass** tool. Invoke this tool from the **Conceptual Mass** panel of the **Massing & Site** tab; the **Name** dialog box will be displayed. In this dialog box, enter the name of the mass in the **Name** edit box and choose **OK**; the **Create** tab will be displayed. You can use the options in this tab to sketch the massing profile and convert it into a solid or void form. To sketch the profile for the mass, choose the **Model** tool from the **Draw** panel; the **Modify | Place Lines** tab will be displayed. You can use various sketching tools available in the **Draw** panel of this tab. While sketching, you can also use the **Reference Plane** tool from the **Draw** panel to draw references for the sketch. After sketching the profile, you can use any of the tools displayed in the **Create Form** drop-down in the **Form** panel. The **Create Form** drop-down displays two tools: **Solid Form** and **Void Form**. You can use the **Solid Form** tool to create a solid form and the **Void Form** tool to create a void form. To use any of the tools from the **Create Form** drop-down, you need to select the sketched profile from the drawing and then invoke the **Solid Form** or **Void Form** tool. After invoking any of these tools; the **Modify | Form** tab will be displayed. In this tab, you specify the settings to change the instance property of the mass created, divide the surfaces of the mass, and modify geometrical elements of the mass.

You can change the instance properties of the massing geometry like material and visibility from the **Properties** palette. After changing the instance properties of the selected massing geometry, you can change the geometrical property of the surface by adding edges and profiles. The tools for changing the geometrical properties are: **X-Ray**, **Add Edge**, and **Add Profile**. You can invoke these tools from the **From Element** panel of the **Modify | Form** (solid form) tab.

The **X-Ray** tool in the **Element** panel of the **Modify | Form** tab is used to display the geometry skeleton like vertices and edges of the mass. The **Add Edge** tool can be used to add edges to the form of the mass and the **Add Profile** tool is used to add profile to the surface of the mass. Figure 10-26 shows the added edge and profile in the **X-Ray** mode.

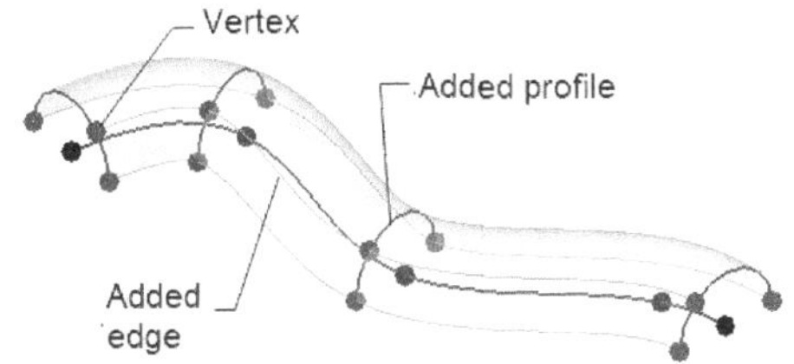

Figure 10-26 *Massing geometry with added edge and profile in the **X-Ray** mode*

Dividing Edges or Paths

You can divide a line or edge of a form to define the nodes on which the components can be placed. On dividing a line or edge, nodes are applied to the division points that denote the position of the points of placement for components. You can divide a line or an edge of a form by using any of the following methods: Specifying number of divisions, Specifying distance between divisions, or by using the point of intersection between the line or edge with the levels, reference planes, or divided paths. To divide a path on an edge, select a form from the project view; the **Modify | Mass** tab will be displayed. In this tab, choose the **Edit In-Place** tab; the form will be displayed in the editable mode. Select an edge of the form; the **Modify | Form** tab will be displayed. In this tab, choose the **Divide Path** tool from the **Divide** panel; the properties of the path division will be displayed in the **Properties** palette. Also the selected edges will display 6 nodes in equal division along its edge. You will also notice the number **6** displayed above the edge. You can click on the number and enter a different numerical value in the edit box displayed to increase the number of nodal divisions along the edge.

MASSING IN CONCEPTUAL DESIGN ENVIRONMENT

Conceptual design is the very first phase of a design process. The primary objective of a conceptual design is to create a representation of the idea generated for creating the building mass of a project. For creating a building project, conceptual design is very important for architects, engineers, and designers as it helps in finding out the final representation of the design intent. It thus enables them to create more specific sets of plans.

In Revit, you can create conceptual designs in any of the following environments: Conceptual Design Environment and Revit Project Environment. The Conceptual Design Environment is used to create massing families as conceptual designs that reside outside the Project Environment. These families can be loaded in the Revit Project Environment that forms the basis to create detail design by applying walls, roofs, floors, and curtain systems to them. In the Revit Project Environment, you can create conceptual designs by using the **In-Place Mass** or **Place Mass** tool from the **Conceptual Mass** panel in the **Massing & Site** tab. In this environment, you cannot create 3D reference planes and view 3D levels.

Interface of the Conceptual Design Environment

To open the interface of the Conceptual Design Environment, choose **New > Conceptual Mass** from the **File** menu. On doing so, the **New Conceptual Mass-Select Template File** dialog box will be displayed. In this dialog box, select the **Mass.rft** file from the **Conceptual Mass** folder in the **English_I** folder (for Metric the **Metric Mass.rft** file from the **Conceptual Mass** folder in the **English** folder) and then choose the **Open** button; the interface of the Conceptual Design Environment along with the settings of the selected template file will be displayed, as shown in Figure 10-27. From the interface of the **Conceptual Massing Environment**, you can use various tools in the ribbon to create the conceptual mass.

Figure 10-27 The Conceptual Design Environment interface

Creating Masses in Conceptual Design Environment

In the Conceptual Design Environment, you can create the conceptual mass by using various tools from the ribbon. The ribbon of the Conceptual Design Environment, as shown in Figure 10-28, consists of the following tabs: **Create**, **Insert**, **Views**, **Manage**, and **Modify**. The **Create** tab is chosen by default. From the **Create** tab, you can access the tools required to create the Conceptual Mass. From the **Workplane** panel of the **Create** tab, you can choose any of the tools such as **Set**, **Show**, and **Viewer** that can be used for setting, showing, and viewing workplane to be used to create the conceptual mass. You can choose the **Level** tool in the **Datum** panel to add levels that will assist in the creation of its conceptual mass. You can add levels in 3D and elevation views in the Conceptual Design Environment. The **Draw** panel of the **Create** tab contains tools that can be used to sketch conceptual mass. In this panel, you can use the **Model**, **Reference**, and **Plane** tool to sketch the model lines, reference lines and reference planes to create the conceptual mass. When you choose the **Model** or **Reference** tool from the **Draw** panel, the **Draw on Face** and the **Draw on Work Plane** will be activated. You can use any of these tools to specify the plane in which conceptual mass will be created. Also, on choosing the **Model** or **Reference** tool from the **Draw** panel, a contextual tab will be displayed along with various options in the **Options Bar**. This tab contains options that help in sketching the model or reference line. In the **Family Editor** panel of the **Create** tab, you can choose the **Load into Project** tool to load the conceptual mass into the project file. From the **Dimension** panel of the **Create** tab, you can choose various tools to dimension the sketch of the conceptual mass. In the ribbon of the Conceptual Design Environment, the tools in the other tabs such as **Insert**, **View**, **Manage**, and **Modify** are same as those in the Project Environment. In the next sections, the method and the tools involved in the process of drawing and creating the conceptual mass are discussed.

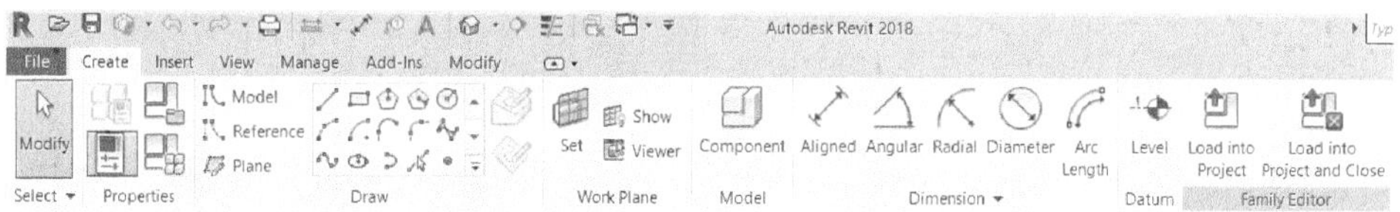

Figure 10-28 The Ribbon of the Conceptual Design Environment

Sketching the Conceptual Design Environment

To sketch a profile of the conceptual mass in the Conceptual Design Environment, you can use the floor plan views or the 3D views depending upon the project requirement. You can draw a profile of the conceptual mass with or without using references. You can use the references to create constraints and reference for the conceptual mass. To draw references for the profile conceptual mass, you can invoke the **Reference** tool from the **Draw** panel of the **Create** tab. After invoking the **Reference** tool, you can draw the reference by using various sketching tools such as **Line**, **Rectangle**, **Circle**, **Pick Lines**, and **Point Elements** from the list box displayed next to it.

After sketching the reference, you will sketch the model lines for the profile of the conceptual mass. To do so, choose the **Model** tool from the **Draw** panel; the **Modify | Place Lines** tab will be displayed. In the **Draw** panel of this tab, you can use the sketching tools such as **Line**, **Rectangle**, and others to sketch the conceptual mass. When you invoke a sketching tool, its corresponding options are displayed in the **Options Bar**. These options assist in sketching the profile. After you sketch the conceptual mass, you can also use various editing tools such as **Offset**, **Move**, **Copy**, and others from the **Modify** panel of the **Modify | Place Lines** tab to edit the sketch. Figure 10-29 displays a sketched profile of a conceptual mass. After sketching the conceptual mass, select it; the **Modify | Line** tab will be displayed. In the **Form** panel of this tab, you can click on the **Create Form** drop-down and choose the **Solid Form** or the **Void Form** tool from the drop-down menu. You can choose the **Solid Form** tool to create a solid from the sketched lines. Alternatively, choose the **Void Form** tool to create a void or cavity in an existing solid. On choosing the **Solid Form** tool from the **Create Form** drop-down, the **Modify | Form** tab will be displayed. Also, the selected sketch line will extrude to a certain height and will appear along with its temporary dimensions. Figure 10-30 displays a solid created by extruding sketched lines.

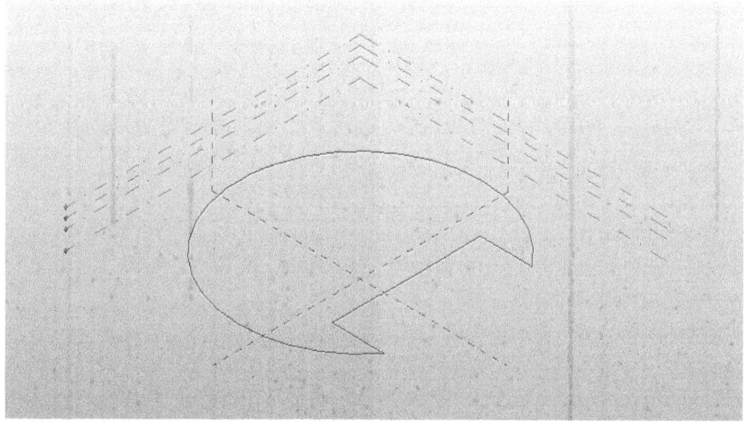

Figure 10-29 Sketched profile of a conceptual mass

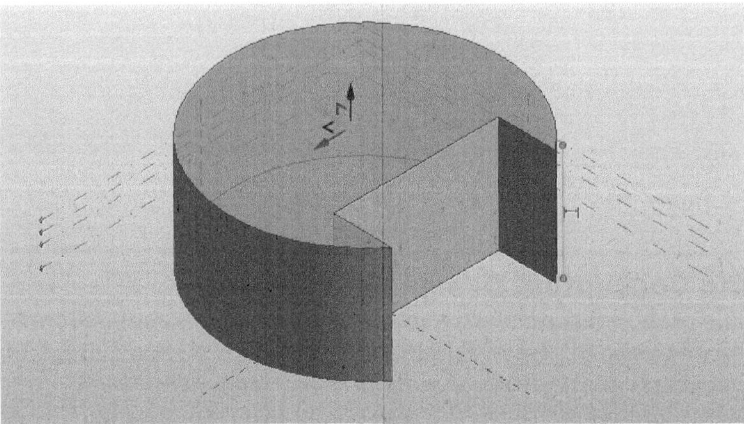

Figure 10-30 *Solid created by extruding the sketched lines*

After creating a solid, you can edit its profile. To do so, select the extruded face of the solid profile and then choose the **Edit Profile** tool from the **Mode** panel of the **Modify | Form** tab. On doing so, the profile of the selected face will enter the sketch mode, as shown in Figure 10-31. You can edit the sketch using various tools in the **Modify Form > Edit Profile** tab. After editing the sketched profile, choose the **Finish Edit Mode** button from the **Mode** panel to return to the **Modify | Form** tab.

Figure 10-31 *Profile of the selected face in the editing mode*

You can divide the surfaces of a conceptual mass, add profile and edge to its form, display the geometric skeleton of its form, and dissolve the surfaces of its form. The various tools that you can use to perform these functions are **Divide Surface**, **X-Ray**, **Add Profile**, **Add Edge**, and **Dissolve**. These tools are discussed next.

Using X-Ray

The **X-Ray** tool can be used to display the underlying geometric skeleton of a selected form. The mode in which the geometric skeleton of the selected form will be displayed is called the X-Ray mode. In this mode, as the surfaces become transparent this allows you to directly interact with the individual elements. It is to be noted that at a time only one form in all the model will be visible in the X-Ray mode. To switch the display of a form to the X-Ray mode, select it and then choose the **X-Ray** tool from the **Form Element** panel of the **Modify | Form** tab. Once you switch the form to the X-Ray mode, you can select the element again and choose the **X- Ray** tool to restore its visibility to its previous mode.

Adding Profiles

Add Profile

After you create a conceptual mass, you can add cross-section profiles to it. An edge is a profile that may be a single line, chain of connected lines, or a closed loop, depending upon the geometry of the form. The added profile can be used to generate a form or edit the geometry of the existing form. To add a profile to a form, select it and then choose the **Add Profile** tool from the **Form Element** panel of the **Modify | Form** tab. On doing so, the cursor changes to a cross mark and at the **Status Bar**, you will be prompted to insert a new profile at the cross-section of the form element. Move the cursor on the surface of the form, the surface of the form will be highlighted in a blue border and a probable profile will be displayed at the position of the cursor. Click at a desired point on the surface of the form to add the profile. Note that the added profile in the form will only be visible in the X-Ray mode. Figure 10-32 displays a form with added profiles.

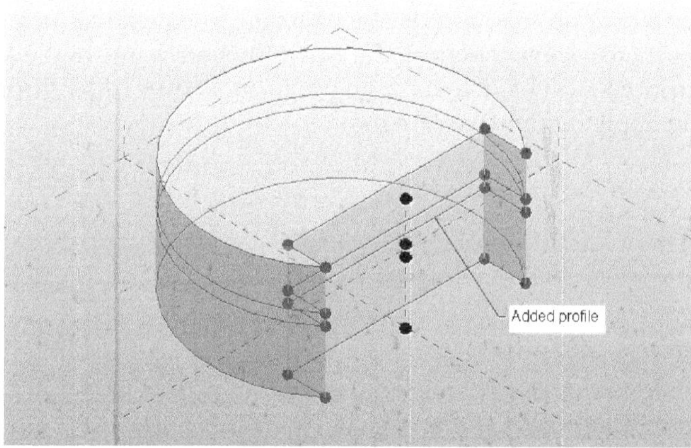

Figure 10-32 *Profiles added in the form*

Adding Edges

Add Edge

After you create a conceptual mass, you can add edges to it. To add an edge select the form and then choose the **Add Edge** tool from the **Form Element** panel of the **Modify | Form** tab. On doing so, the cursor will change into a cross mark. Place the cursor on the surface of the form; an edge will appear at the point of the cursor. Click at the desired point on the surface of the form and add the edge to it, as shown in Figure 10-33.

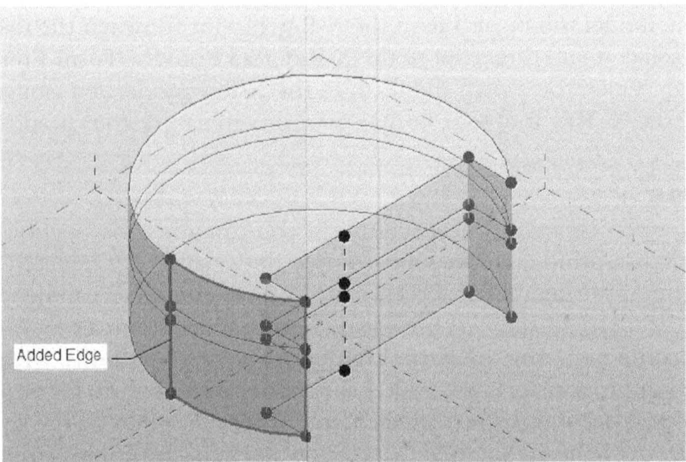

Figure 10-33 Edge added to the form

Dissolve

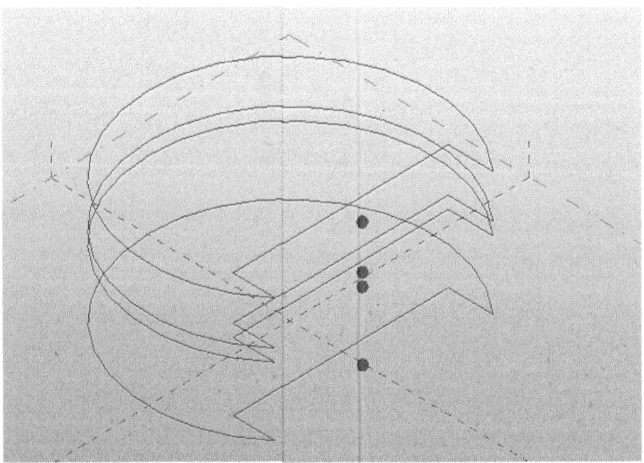

You can delete the surface of the form and retain its profile. You can also edit the retained profiles and recreate a form. To delete the surface of a form, select the form and choose the **Dissolve** tool from the **Form Element** panel of the **Modify | Form** tab. On doing so, the surface(s) will be deleted from the form. Figure 10-34 displays a form with its surfaces removed on applying the **Dissolve** tool.

Figure 10-34 Surfaces removed from the form

Tip

You can divide the surface of the form. To do so, select the surface of the form and then choose the ***Divide Surface*** *tool from the* ***Form Element*** *panel of the* ***Modify / Form*** *tab. On doing so, the* ***Modify / Divided Surface*** *tab will be displayed. You can use various tools from the displayed tab and options from the* ***Options Bar*** *to divide the selected surface.*

CREATING BUILDING ELEMENTS FROM THE MASSING GEOMETRY USING BUILDING MAKER TOOLS

After generating the shape and volume of massing forms, you can convert them into building elements such as walls, floors, roofs, and curtain systems. You can select the faces of the generated massing geometry and replace them with the desired building element. To convert faces into building elements, you can use various tools from the **Model by Face** panel of the **Massing & Site** tab in the ribbon.

Creating Walls by Selecting Faces

Ribbon: Massing & Site > Model by Face > Curtain System

You can convert the faces of the placed mass into walls. To do so, choose the **Wall** tool from the **Model by Face** panel of the **Massing & Site** tab; the **Modify | Place Wall** tab will be displayed. In this tab, select the wall type to be used for conversion from the **Type Selector** drop-down list. In the **Draw** panel of this tab, make sure that the **Pick Faces** option is chosen. In **Options Bar**, select the appropriate values of the **Level**, **Height**, and **Location Line** from their respective drop-down lists.

Now, to convert the faces into walls, move the cursor over the massing geometry. You will notice that the faces that can be converted are highlighted. Next, click on the desired face to make the conversion. You can use the TAB key to select all the faces of the massing geometry that can be converted into walls. Figure 10-35 shows the selected faces of the massing geometry and Figure 10-36 shows the walls created.

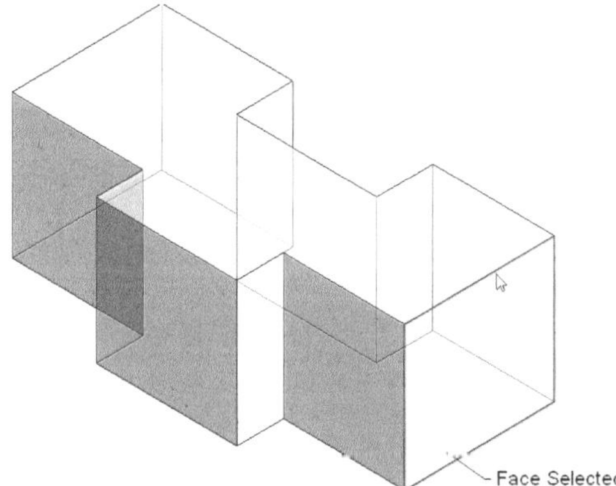

Figure 10-35 *Selected wall face*

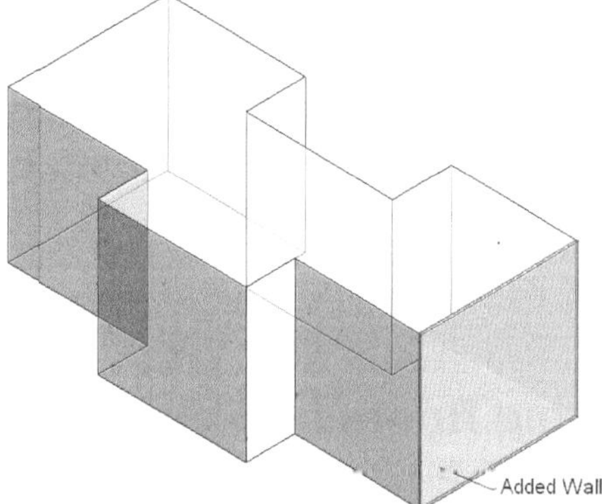

Figure 10-36 *Wall face converted into walls*

Creating Floors by Selecting Faces

Ribbon: Massing & Site > Model by Face > Floor

To create a floor in a massing geometry, first you need to define the floor area faces by selecting the massing geometry and then choosing the **Mass Floors** tool from the **Model** panel of the **Modify | Mass** tab. On doing so, the **Mass Floors** dialog box will be displayed. Select the levels at which the floor area faces are required and choose the **OK** button. Autodesk Revit will automatically generate the floor area faces based on the massing geometry and the defined levels.

Next, to add the floor to the floor area faces, you need to invoke the **Floor by Face** tool from the **Conceptual Mass** panel; the **Modify | Place Floor by Face** tab will be displayed. You can select a floor type from the **Type Selector** drop-down list. Next, move the cursor over the massing geometry; the floor area faces will be highlighted. Now, you can choose the **Select Multiple** tool from the **Multiple Selection** panel and use the crossing options to create a selection of multiple floor area faces. Next, choose the **Create Floors** button in the **Multiple Selection** panel of the **Modify | Place Floor by Face** tab to create floors. Autodesk Revit will convert all the selected floor area faces into the selected floor type. Figure 10-37 shows the floor area faces generated for a multistory building. The floors created are shown in Figure 10-38.

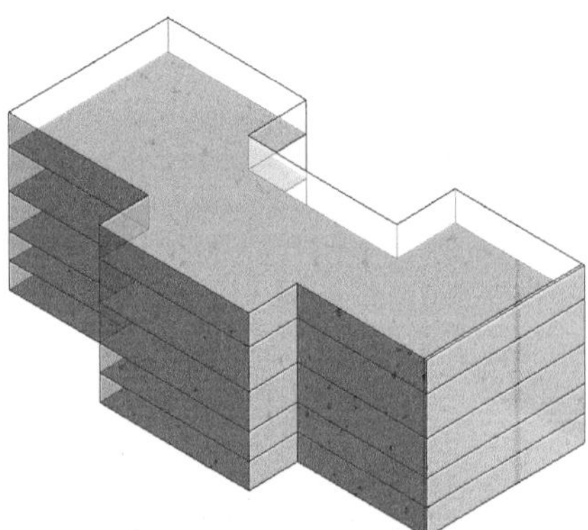

Figure 10-37 *Generated floor area faces*

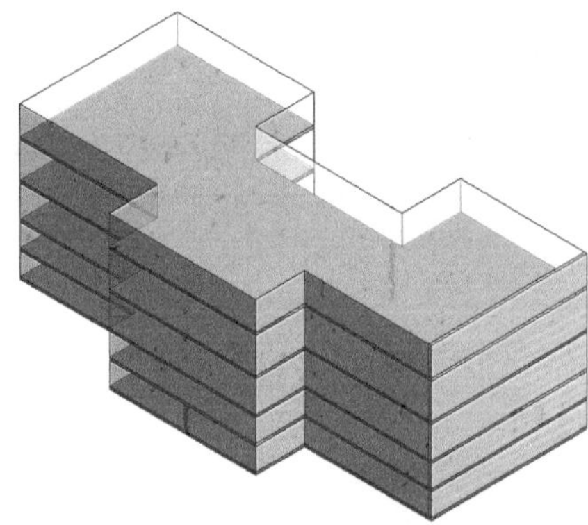

Figure 10-38 *Floor area faces converted into floors*

Creating Roofs by Selecting Faces

Ribbon: Massing & Site > Model by Face > Roof

You can use the **Roof** tool in the **Massing & Site** tab to convert the massing faces into roofs. Faces can be horizontal planes of any shape or those created by using the **Extrusion**, **Revolve**, **Blend**, **Sweep**, or **Swept Blend** tool.

Invoke the **Roof** tool from the **Model by Face** panel; the **Modify | Place Roof by Face** tab will be displayed. From this tab, select the roof type to be used from the **Type Selector** drop-down list. Next, move the cursor over the massing geometry and click to select the highlighted face. Next, choose the **Create Roof** button in the **Multiple Selection** panel to convert it into a roof. Figures 10-39 and 10-40 show the top face of a multistory building converted into a roof.

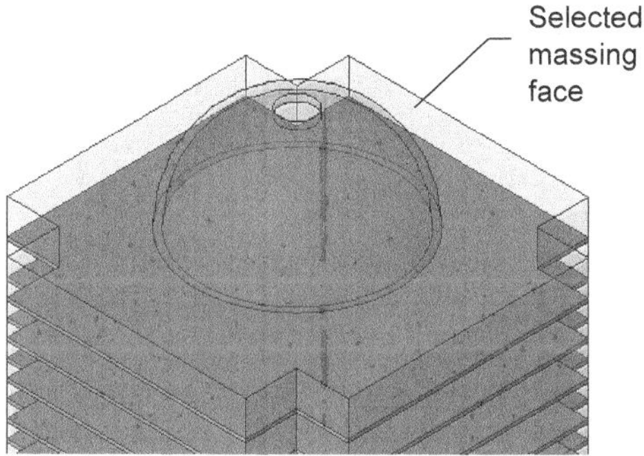

Figure 10-39 *The top face selected for conversion into a roof*

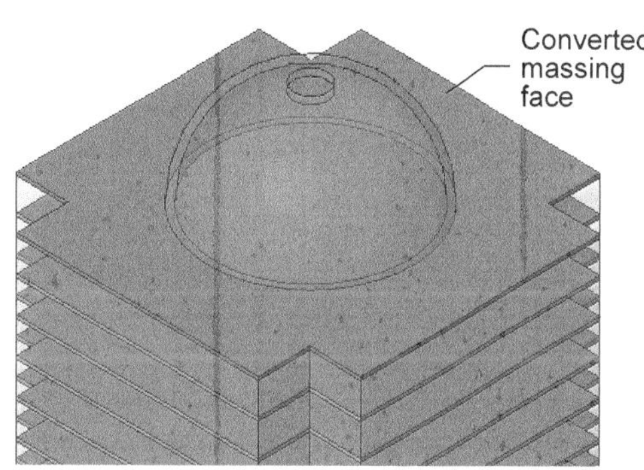

Figure 10-40 *The top face of the massing geometry converted into a roof*

Creating Curtain Systems by Selecting Faces

Autodesk Revit provides you with the **Curtain System** tool to convert the planar and non-planar faces into curtain systems. Invoke this tool from the **Model by Face** panel; the **Modify | Place Curtain System by Face** tab will be displayed. In this tab, select the curtain system type from the **Type Selector** drop-down list. In the **Properties** palette, you can modify the instance and type properties of the curtain system before creating it. Next, move the cursor over the face that needs to be converted into the curtain system and click to select it. Choose the **Create System** tool from the **Multiple Selection** panel to create the curtain system. Figure 10-41 shows the example of a curtain system of a dome. You can then add mullions to the curtain system using the **Mullions** tool, as shown in Figure 10-42. Figure 10-43 shows another example of using the **Curtain System** tool to convert non-planar massing faces into curtain systems.

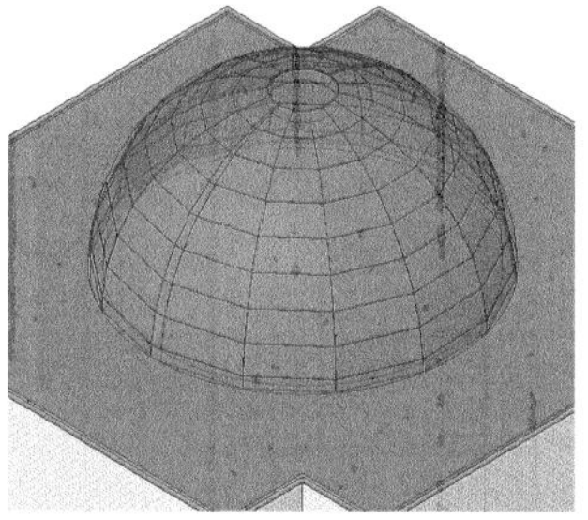

Figure 10-41 *Creating a curtain system using the **Curtain System** tool*

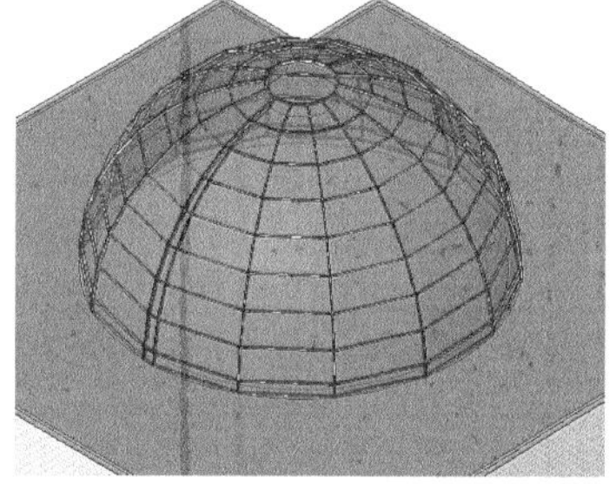

Figure 10-42 *Mullions added to the curtain system using the **Mullions** tool*

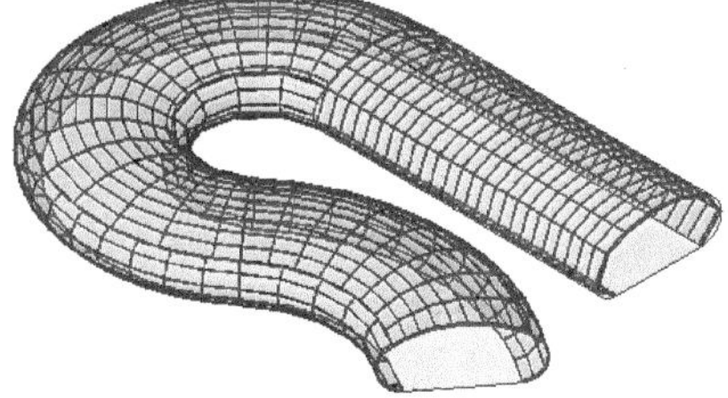

Figure 10-43 *Converting non-planar massing faces into curtain systems with mullions*

Controlling the Visibility of a Massing Geometry

To hide or display a massing geometry, choose the **Show Mass by View Settings** tool from **Massing & Site > Conceptual Mass > Show Mass by View Settings** drop-down. However, the use of this tool has a temporary effect on the visibility of the massing forms. When a project file is closed, the show mass settings are not saved in it. Therefore, next time when you will open the project file, the massing forms will not be visible.

To display massing form permanently in a project file, invoke the **Visibility/Graphics** tool from the **Visibility/Graphics** panel of the **View** tab; the **Visibility/Graphics Overrides** dialog box for the current view will be displayed. In this dialog box, select the check box for the **Visibility** parameter of the **Mass** model category.

Adding other Building Elements

After converting the massing geometry into basic building elements, you can add other building elements such as doors, windows, roofs, and so on to the basic building elements. You can also use various editing tools to copy, edit, and delete the converted building elements.

Figure 10-44 shows the example of a building model in the plan view with modified wall type and added windows. You can use the editing tools such as **Mirror**, **Array**, and **Paste Aligned** to copy elements and create a building model of desired shape with specified parameters, as shown in Figure 10-45.

Like other building models, you can also create the standard building views of the converted massing model. Autodesk Revit also provides the facility to extract the areas and other statistical figures of the created massing geometry.

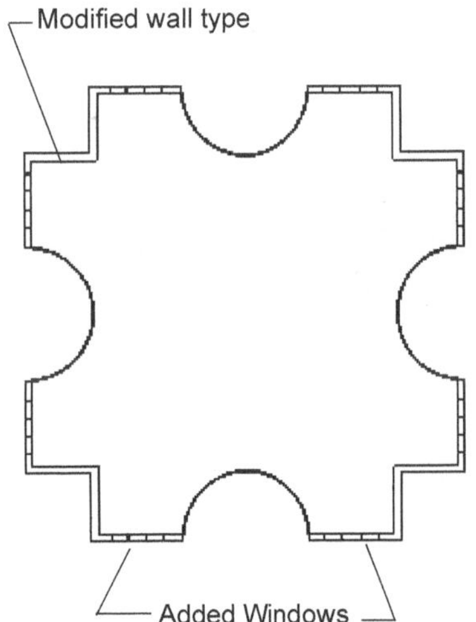

Figure 10-44 *Plan view showing the modified wall type and added windows*

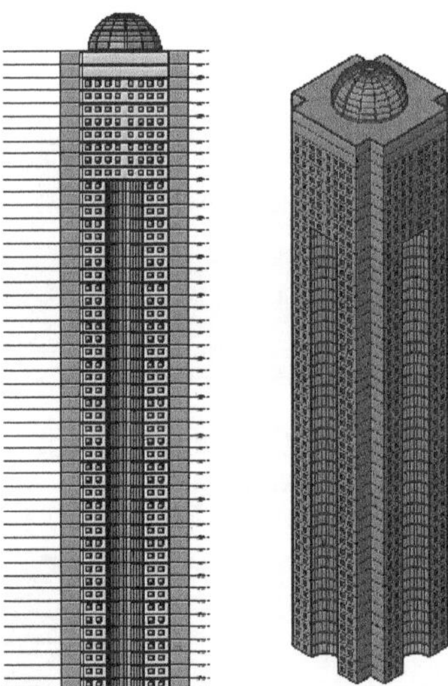

Figure 10-45 *A multistory building with building components*

Tip

*With the **Massing** tool, Autodesk Revit enables you to create a variety of shapes and volumes. Based on the desired geometry, you can use a combination of tools. The massing geometry can also be used to generate the rendered views of conceptual building volumes. This can prove to be an effective tool for communicating the design intent to the entire project team before starting the detailed project plans.*

CREATING FAMILIES

Revit family is defined as a collection of parametric components or elements having similar graphical representation, utility, and common parameters. By nature, all the elements used in Revit are family-based. A Revit family has a wide range of collections starting from a wall to a window and extended up to two-dimensional annotations or symbols required for your project. In Autodesk Revit, each family inherits the character of some specific type. Each type is a member of Revit family that consists of certain parameters known as **Type Parameters**. These parameters are constant for identical types. For example, a **Single-Flush** door family can have different types such as **Single-Flush : 36" x 84"** in Imperial (**Single-Flush : 0915 x 2134 mm** in Metric), **Single-Flush : 30" x 84"** (**Single-Flush : 0915 x 2032 mm** in Metric), and others. You can access these types from the **Type Selector** drop-down list.

In Autodesk Revit, families are useful tools as they are driven by the Revit parametric change engine. This engine helps to reflect the changes made in a family throughout the project. You can edit the parameters of a family after you have created it in a project using the **Revit Family Editor**. The **Revit Family Editor** is an interface that allows you to create or make changes in a family. At the same time, it helps you add or modify specific parameters of your model while defining it as a family type.

While creating a project, you may need to define a family inside another family. This type of family is called nested family. For example, if you are creating a window family, you can create another family inside it for hardware items such as knobs, bolts, and so on. The use of nested family adds details to the family you have created.

In Autodesk Revit, there are three types of families: System families, In-place families, and Standard component families. These families are differentiated on the basis of their creations and utilities in a project.

The System families include the most common building components that are frequently used in a project such as walls, floors, roofs, and ceilings. You cannot create a new system family of your own, but you can create duplicate families and modify their properties as per your need. The In-place families are project-specific, therefore, you can use them when you need to create a unique component for a specific project. For example, you may need to design a unique table, featuring curved edges and material finishes, specific to the flooring of a dining area. In such a case, you can use the In-place families for creating the table. Also, you can save this table for further use. In Revit, the Standard component families are the basic components that are commonly used in a building design. These families are not project-specific. Whenever a need arises, you can download these families from common libraries. You can place the Standard component families in a project template so that they can be used whenever you start a new project. Revit allows you to load the required family of door, window, and so on from the in-built Revit library. To do so, choose the **Load Family** tool from the **Load from Library** panel in the

Insert tab; the **Load Family** dialog box will be displayed. Select the required file for the family from the appropriate folder and then choose **Open**; the family will be loaded into the project.

In Autodesk Revit, you can save a selected family or all the families loaded in the current project or template to a location on your system or to a network location. To save a family loaded in the current project choose **Save As > Library > Family** from the **File** menu; the **Save Family** dialog box will be displayed. In this dialog box, browse to a folder location to save the family file. Next, in the **File name** edit box, enter the name of the file and then select an option from the **Family to save** drop-down list to specify a family or all families loaded in the project. Next, choose the **Save** button; the selected family will be saved at the specified location. Note that in-place families and system families, such as walls, and patterns cannot be saved. Revit also enables you to create your own customized families and then use them in a project. There are two methods that you can use to create a family. These methods are discussed next.

Creating In-Place Families

This method is used to create custom families such as the furniture for reception and workstations in a building model. You can create a family while working on a project. The family created is saved within the project and gets updated according to the changes made in the project.

To create an In-Place family, choose the **Model In-Place** tool from **Architecture > Build > Component** drop-down; the **Family Category and Parameters** dialog box will be displayed. In the **Family Category** area, select an option from the **Filter list** drop-down list to filter the list of categories that will be displayed in the list box displayed below it. Double-click on the required category from the list box; the **Name** dialog box will be displayed. In this dialog box, enter a name for the family in the **Name** edit box and then choose the **OK** button; the sketch mode will be invoked and the options in the **Create** tab will be displayed. Sketch the reference planes and set the work plane to help you sketch the geometry for the family using the required sketching tools from the **Model** panel and the **Forms** panel. After creating the massing geometry, choose the **Finish Model** button from the **In-Place Editor** panel; a family will be created. After creating the geometry of a family, you can assign materials to the family and create family types with different dimensions.

Creating Families Using Standard Family Templates

In this method, you can create a new family by using certain standard in-built family templates as platform. These templates provide you with some parameters, reference planes, and dimensions in different views that are already saved in templates. You have to create the geometry for a family in the required view. To do so, you need to sketch reference planes, dimension reference planes, label dimensions, and then sketch the profile for the family using the required sketching tools. Once you have created the profile, apply materials to it and create family types by assigning different dimensions to the geometry. At the end, give a name to the template, save it, and load the family into the project to use it in your drawing.

The steps to create a family are explained next with an example of an arch-shaped panel window, as shown in Figure 10-46. The window is created using a standard template.

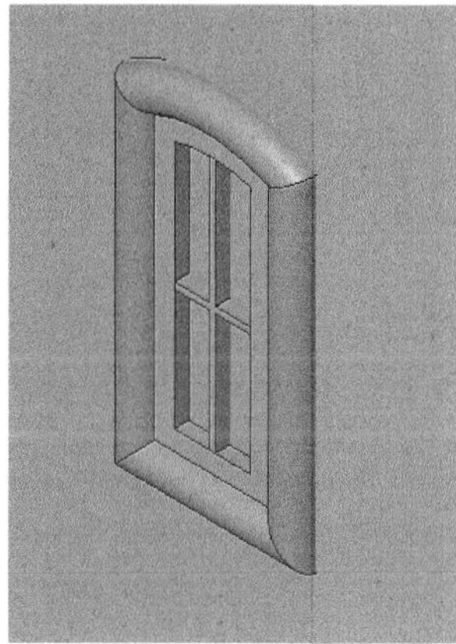

Figure 10-46 An arch-shaped window with panels

Selecting a Template

The first step to create a family using standard template is to select a suitable template to be used as a platform. To do so, choose **New > Family** from the **File** menu; the **New Family - Select Template File** dialog box will be displayed. In this dialog box, select the required template for Imperial from the **Family Templates > English_I** folder, select the **Generic Model.rft** file (for Metric from the **Family Templates > English** folder and then select the **Metric Generic Model.rft** file). For creating an arch-shaped window with panels, select the **Generic Model wall based** template and choose the **Open** button; the template with a geometry and a reference plane will be displayed in the drawing area. Choose the **Tile Windows** tool from the **Windows** panel of the **View** tab to display all the views saved in the template, as shown in Figure 10-47.

Figure 10-47 Different views saved in the template

Adding Reference Planes

Once you have selected the template, the next step is to add reference planes to the required view. You can do so by using the **Reference Plane** tool. To add reference planes, open the

Elevations : Placement Side view and then invoke the **Reference Plane** tool from the **Datum** panel of the **Create** tab; the **Modify | Place Reference Plane** tab will be displayed. Invoke the **Line** tool from the **Draw** panel of this tab and sketch reference planes based on the dimensions of the geometry. Sketching the reference planes helps you sketch the geometry of the plane easily. Figure 10-48 shows the reference planes sketched for the arch-shaped window.

Dimensioning

To use the tools for dimensioning, choose the **Annotate** tab and then choose any of the dimensioning tools from the **Dimension** panel, and dimension the reference planes. Dimensioning the sketched reference planes helps you control the parametric geometry, refer to Figure 10-48.

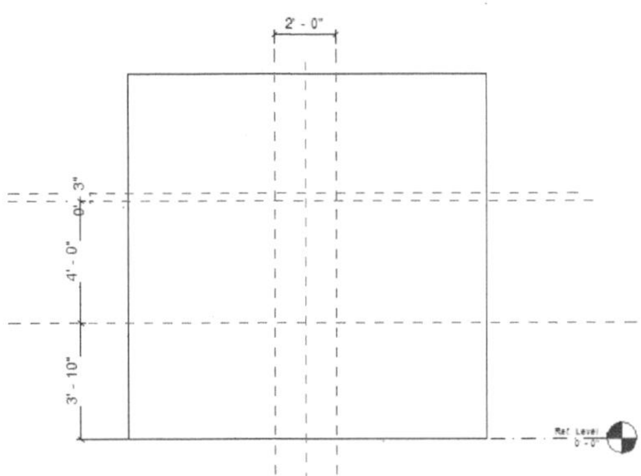

Figure 10-48 Dimensioning the sketched reference planes

Labeling the Dimensions

After dimensioning the reference planes, you need to label dimensions. The dimensions that are labeled become the type and instance parameters for a family. To label dimensions, select the dimension and right-click; a shortcut menu will be displayed. Choose **Label** from the shortcut menu; a drop-down list will be displayed. Select **Add Parameter** from the drop-down list, as shown in Figure 10-49; the **Parameter Properties** dialog box will be displayed. In this dialog box, enter labels for sill height, height, width, and rise, as shown in Figure 10-50.

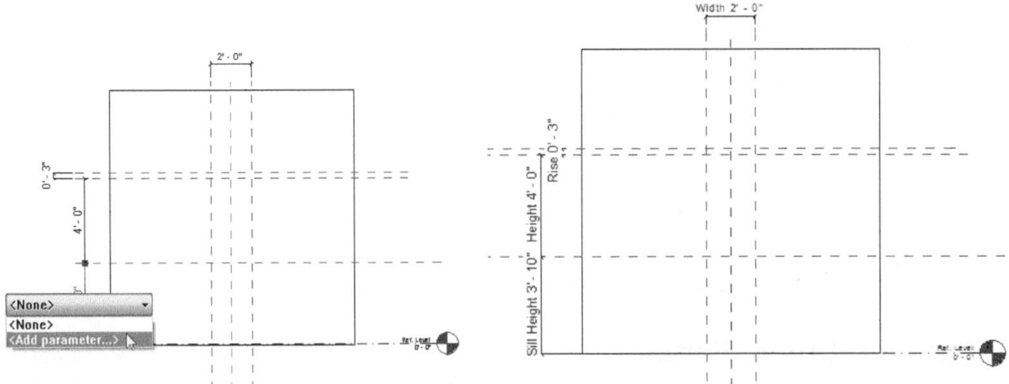

*Figure 10-49 The drop-down list displayed after choosing the **Label** option from the shortcut menu*

Figure 10-50 The reference planes after being labeled

Creating an Opening

After dimensioning and labeling the dimensions, the next step is to create an opening in the window. The shape of the opening depends upon the shape of the window. To create an opening, invoke the **Opening** tool from the **Model** panel of the **Create** tab; the sketch mode will be invoked. Next, use the required sketching tools and sketch the opening for the window. You can sketch the opening of any shape based on the shape of the window. Next, choose the **Finish Edit Mode** button from the **Mode** panel of the **Modify | Create Opening Boundary** tab to finish the sketch of the opening. Figure 10-51 shows an arch-shaped opening created using the **Line** and **Start-End-Radius Arc** tools. Now, you can see the opening in a 3D view.

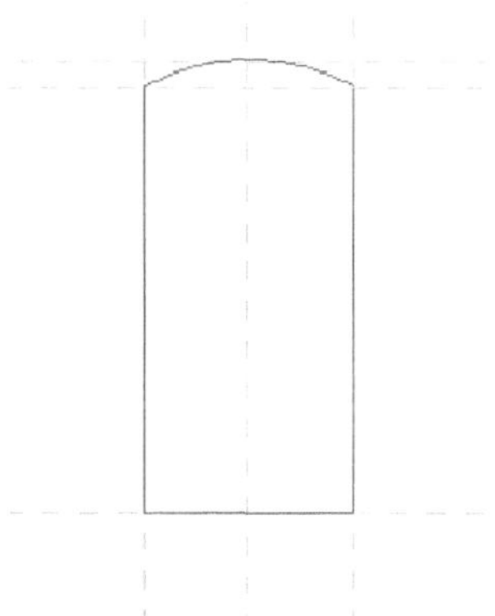

Figure 10-51 *Sketching the arch-shaped opening for the window*

Adding Reference Planes for Sash and Glass

You need to add reference planes to place the window frame, sash, and glass. These planes can be added on the right or left elevation view. Figure 10-52 shows three planes added to the right elevation view at a distance of 0' 1"(25 mm) and 0' 1.5"(38 mm) from the center reference plane and at the exterior edge of the wall. You can also give names to the reference planes. To do so, select the required plane and in the **Properties** palette, enter a name in the value column for the **Name** parameter. The reference planes can be named as Sash, Glazing, and Exterior.

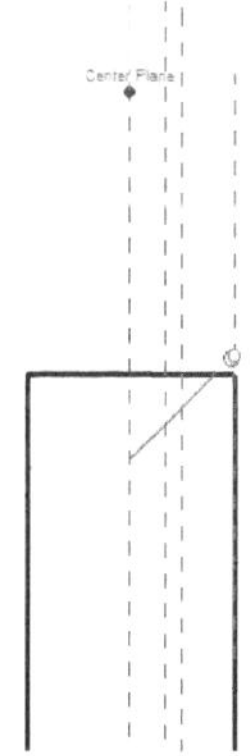

Figure 10-52 *The right elevation view with three reference planes*

Creating a Solid Sweep

The next step is to create a solid sweep for the window frame using the **Sweep** tool in the required view. To use this tool, you need a profile and a path. To sketch a path, change the current view to the **Placement Side** view and then choose the **Sweep** tool from the **Forms** panel of the **Create** tab; the screen will enter into the sketch mode. Invoke the **Sketch Path** tool from the **Sweep** panel of the **Modify | Sweep** tab, and sketch the path similar to the shape of the opening. Make sure that the path and the opening overlap each other. After sketching the 2D path, choose the **Finish Edit Mode** button from the **Mode** panel of the **Modify | Sweep > Sketch Path** tab; the path will be sketched and the **Modify| Sweep** tab will be displayed.

Next, you need to sketch the profile for creating the solid sweep feature. To do so, choose the **Select Profile** tool and then the **Edit Profile** tool from the **Sweep** panel of the **Modify | Sweep** tab; the **Go To View** dialog box will be displayed. Select the required view from the dialog box and choose the **Open View** button; the corresponding view will open with a wall and a red circular symbol. This symbol represents the point of intersection of the path and the profile. Sketch the profile using the sketching tool from the **Draw** panel of the **Modify | Sweep > Edit Profile** tab and then choose the **Finish Edit Mode** button from the **Mode** panel. Next, choose the **Finish Edit Mode** button from the **Mode** panel of the **Modify | Sweep** tab to create the sweep geometry. Figure 10-53 shows a circular profile sketched on the right elevation view with the red symbol at the center. Open the 3D view and choose **Visual Style > Shaded** from **View Control Bar**. Figure 10-54 shows the 3D view of the sweep. This completes the geometry of the window frame.

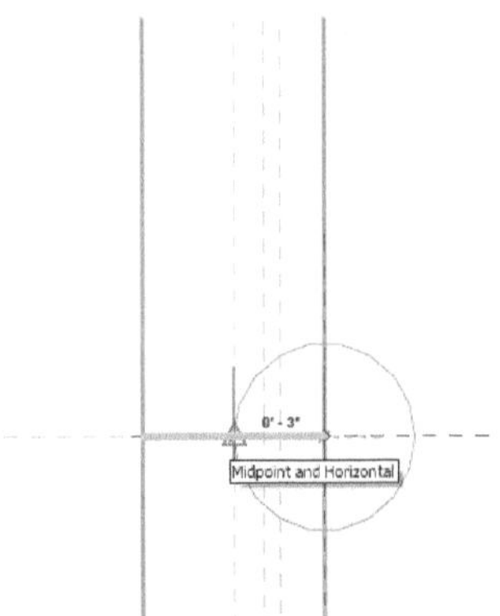

Figure 10-53 *A circular profile sketched in the right elevation view*

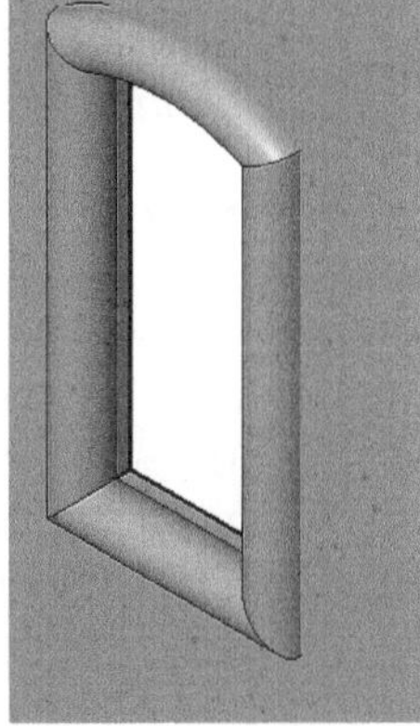

Figure 10-54 *The 3D view of the sweep created*

Adding the Sash to the Window

After creating the geometry for the window, you need to add sash or frame to the window using the **Extrusion** tool. Before you invoke the **Extrusion** tool, you need to change the current view to the **Placement Side** view and then set the work plane. To do so, first double- click on **Placement Side** under the **Elevations** head in the **Project Browser** and then invoke the **Set** tool from the **Work Plane** panel of the **Create** tab; the **Work Plane** dialog box will be displayed. In this dialog box, ensure that the **Name** radio button is selected, and then select **Reference Plane : Sash** from the drop-down list displayed next to the **Name** radio button. Now, choose **OK**; the current work plane will be set. Now, invoke the **Extrusion** tool from the **Forms** panel of the **Create** tab; the **Modify | Create Extrusion** tab will be displayed. In the **Options Bar**, enter values for the depth and the offset for extrusion in the **Depth** and **Offset** edit boxes. Next, invoke the **Pick Lines** tool from the **Draw** panel and click to pick the inner lines and arc by using the TAB key. Again, pick the lines and arc that you just added to create an offset. Next, to create an extrusion geometry, choose the **Finish Edit Mode** button from the **Mode** panel. Figure 10-55 shows the offset created for sash in the **Placement Side** view after selecting it. The depth and offset values of extrusion are set to **0'3"(76 mm)**.

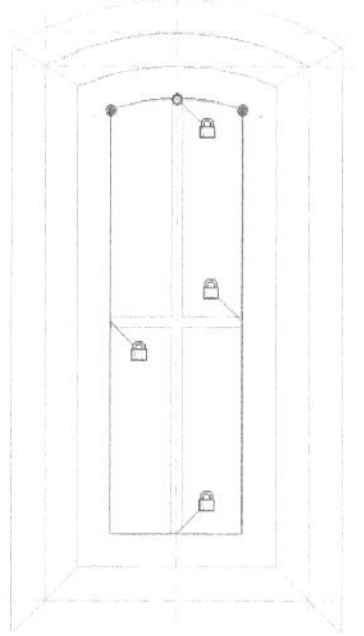

Figure 10-55 *Offset created for the solid extrusion of the sash in the* ***Placement Side*** *view*

Creating Panels

After adding sash, you need to add wooden panels using the **Extrusion** tool. To do so, choose the **Extrusion** tool from the **Forms** panel. Next, sketch the panel in any pattern using the appropriate sketching tool and then extrude the sketch. Figure 10-56 shows a vertical panel and a horizontal panel created using the **Rectangle** sketch tool. Next, to create an extrusion geometry, choose the **Finish Edit Mode** button from the **Mode** panel. Figure 10-57 shows the 3D view of the window with sash and panels.

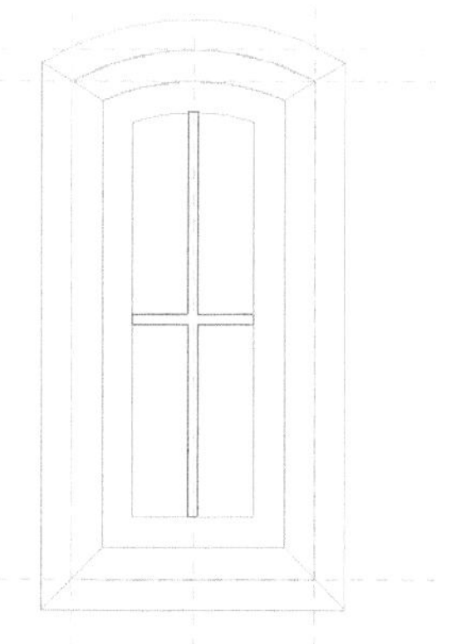

Figure 10-56 *The vertical and horizontal panels created using the* ***Rectangle*** *sketch tool*

Figure 10-57 *3D view of the window with sash and panels*

Adding the Glass

The next step after creating panels is to add glass to the window using the **Extrusion** tool. To add the glass, invoke the **Set** tool from the **Work Plane** panel; the **Work Plane** dialog box will be displayed. From the **Name** drop-down list, select the reference plane sketched earlier to place the glass. Open the required view and invoke the **Extrusion** tool. Enter the required values for depth and offset in the **Depth** and **Offset** edit boxes in **Options Bar**. Using the **Pick Lines** tool from the **Draw** panel, pick the inner sides of sash and lock them. Locking the sides will enable them to change according to the geometry. Figure 10-58 shows the locked lines for creating the glass. Choose the **Finish Edit Mode** button to complete the sketch.

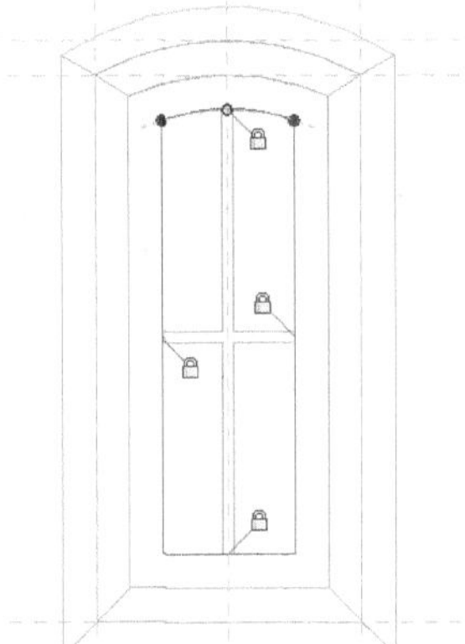

Figure 10-58 *Lines picked and locked to add the glass*

Assigning Materials

Once you have created the arch-shaped window with frame and panels, the next step is to assign materials to different components of the arch-shaped window. To do so, choose the **Materials** tool from the **Settings** panel of the **Manage** tab; the **Material Browser** dialog box will be displayed. In this dialog box, double-click on the name of the desired material in the **Autodesk Materials** area; the material will be displayed in the **Project Materials: All** area. Next, select the **Duplicate Selected Material** option from the **Creates and duplicates a material** drop-down list located at the lower left corner of the **Material Browser** dialog box; the material will be duplicated and displayed in the **Project Materials: All** area. Select the duplicated material, if it is not selected, and right-click; a shortcut menu will be displayed. Choose the **Rename** option from this menu and rename the material.

Now to apply this material, you need to select the required category and then apply the material to that category. To do so, invoke the **Family Category and Parameters** tool from the **Properties** panel of the **Create** tab; the **Family Category and Parameters** dialog box will be displayed. Ensure that the **Architecture** check box is selected in the **Filter list** drop-down list. Select the **Windows** category from the **Family Category** area and choose the **OK** button. Now, you need to assign this material to the required components of the window such as solid sweep and sash.

To assign the materials, select the sweep geometry in the **Placement Side** view or the 3D view and in the **Properties** palette, set the value for the **Subcategory** parameter to **Frame / Mullion**. In the **Material** parameter, click in the value column; a browse button will be displayed on the right. Choose the Browse button; the **Materials Browser** dialog box will be displayed. In the **Project**

Materials: All area of this dialog box, select the material that you have duplicated or renamed and choose the **OK** button to apply it. You can also edit the visibility/graphics overrides by choosing the **Edit** button in the **Value** column for the **Visibility/Graphics Overrides** parameter. Choose the **Apply** button in the **Properties** palette. Open the 3D view and choose **Visual Style > Shaded** from **View Control Bar** to view the assigned material in the shade mode. Similarly, select the solid extrusion created for the sash and panels and assign the material as explained above. You can assign the same material or select any other material from the **Material Browser** dialog box. To apply a glass material to the solid extrusion of glass, select the extrusion and then set the value for the **Subcategory** and **Material** parameters to **Glass** in the **Properties** palette. Next, choose the **Apply** button. Open the 3D view and then view the family in the shade mode. Figure 10-59 shows 3D view of an arch-shaped window with panels after assigning the Wood/Oak, Red, Stained, and Dark Polished material to the frame. The procedure for assigning materials is discussed in detail in Chapter 15.

Figure 10-59 *The final 3D view of the arch-shaped window with panels*

Creating Family Types

After creating family, you need to create family types by assigning different dimensions to geometry. To create family types, invoke the **Family Types** tool from the **Properties** panel in the **Create** tab; the **Family Types** dialog box will be displayed, as shown in Figure 10-60. Choose the **New** button from the **Family Types** area; the **Name** dialog box will be displayed. Enter a name in the **Name** dialog box and choose the **OK** button to save the settings by this name. Change the value of the **Height** and **Width** parameters and choose the **OK** button. You have finished creating one of the family types of the window. Similarly, assign different values to the **Height** and **Width** parameters and name the types accordingly. Figure 10-61 shows the family types created for the arch-shaped window family in the **Name** drop-down list. Select the window and then select the types from the **Name** drop-down list to check whether the window changes according to the type selected.

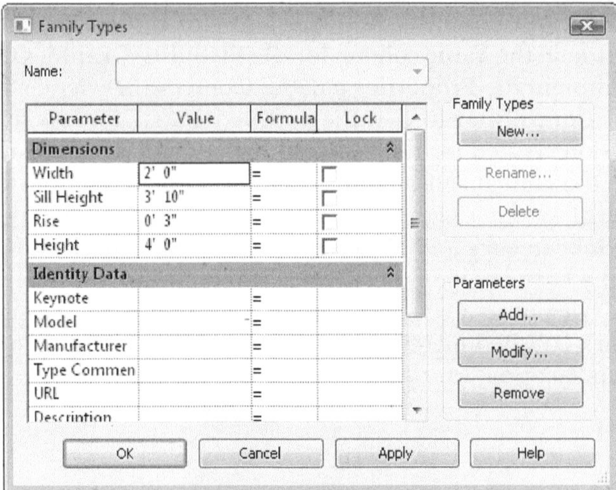

*Figure 10-60 The **Family Types** dialog box*

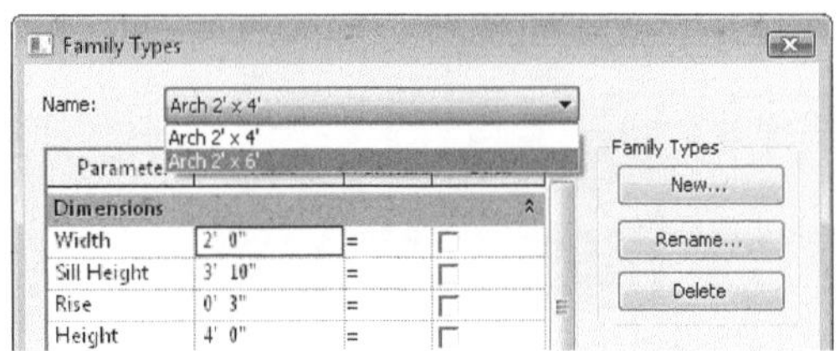

*Figure 10-61 The **Name** drop-down list displaying different family types for Arch-Shaped window*

Loading the Family

Once you have created the family, you need to save it and then load it into the required project. Save the family at the required location and choose the **Load into Project** option from the **Family Editor** panel in the **Modify** tab, to load it into the current project. Once you have loaded the family, you will notice that the family types will be added to the **Type Selector** drop-down list after invoking the **Place Component** tool. Figure 10-62 shows the family types of the arch-shaped window added to the **Type Selector** drop-down list. Select the window loaded and verify if the window changes based on the types selected from the **Type Selector** drop-down list. If the family types are not responding, select and edit that particular type. This happens mostly when the elements are not locked.

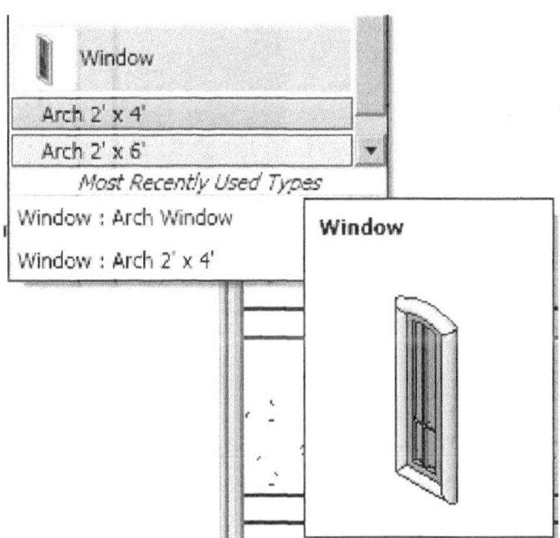

*Figure 10-62 The **Type Selector** drop-down list*

TUTORIALS

Tutorial 1 Office Building 2

In this tutorial, you will create massing geometry for a five-story office building based on the shape shown in Figure 10-63. It consists of a 50'0" X 50'0" (15240 X 15240 mm) central hall that is 60'0"(18288 mm) high. It has a 30'0"(9144 mm) diameter cylindrical atrium with a hemispherical dome at the top level. The central hall is flanked by the right and left wings that are 40'0"(12192 mm) high. The entrance area is 30'0"(9144 mm) high. Use the dimensions of the building given in the floor plan shown in Figure 10-64 and the dimensions of the elevation shown in Figure 10-65. The dimensions and the text have been given for reference and are not to be created. After creating the massing geometry, convert it into building elements with the parameters given next. **(Expected time: 1 hr 15 min)**

1. Project parameters:

   For Imperial — Template File- *default.rte*,
   File name to be assigned- *c10_Office-2_tut1.rvt*
   Floor to floor height of the building - **10'0"**

   For Metric — Template File- *DefaultMetric.rte*,
   File name to be assigned- *M_c10_Office-2_tut1.rvt*
   Floor to floor height of the building - **3048 mm**

2. Building Element types for the converted shell elements:

   For Imperial — Floor: **Floor : LW Concrete on Metal Deck**
   Walls: Central Hall- **Basic Wall: Exterior - Brick on CMU**
   Left and Right Wing, and Entrance- **Curtain Wall: Exterior Glazing**
   (Spacing 5'0" horizontal, 10'0" vertical)
   Flat Roof: **Roof : Generic 9"**

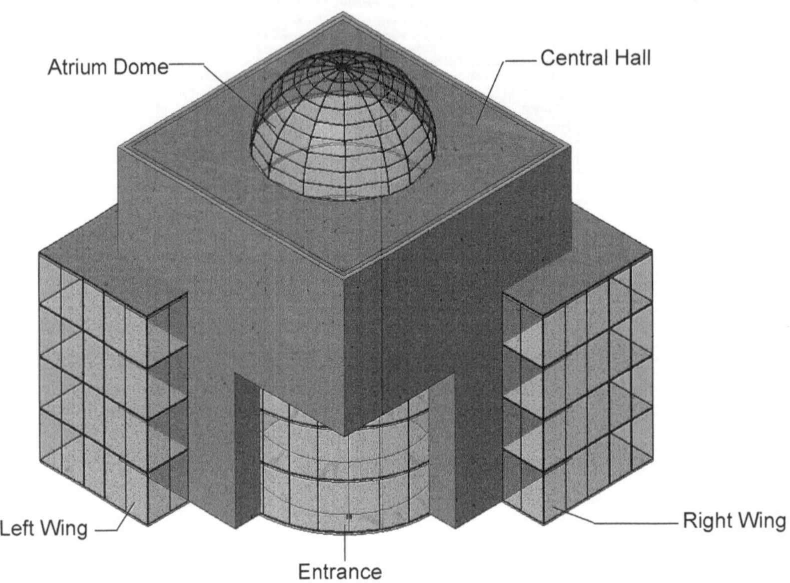

Figure 10-63 *3D sketch view of the office building*

Curtain system for dome: Spacing **3'6"** horizontal, **7'0"** vertical; Mullion type

For Metric Floor: **Floor : LW Concrete on Metal Deck**
Walls: Central Hall- **Basic Wall: Exterior - Brick on CMU**
Left and Right Wing, and Entrance- **Curtain Wall: Exterior Glazing**
(Spacing 1524 mm horizontal, 3048 mm vertical)
Flat Roof: **Roof : Generic 400 mm**
Curtain system for dome: Spacing **1067 mm** horizontal, **2134 mm** vertical; Mullion type

The following steps are required to complete this tutorial:

a. Open a new project file by using the default template file and adding levels.
b. Create a massing geometry using the **Form** tool, refer to Figures 10-66 through 10-69.
c. Cut the geometry based on the sketch plan to create the atrium and the entrance using the **Void Form** tool, refer to Figures 10-70 through 10-73.
d. Use the **Solid Form** tool to generate the atrium dome, refer to Figures 10-74 through 10-76.
e. Convert the massing geometry into the specified building elements, refer to Figures 10-77 through 10-81.
f. Save the project using the **Save As** tool.
For Imperial *c10_Office-2_tut1.rvt*
For Metric *M_c10_Office-2_tut1.rvt*
g. Close the project.

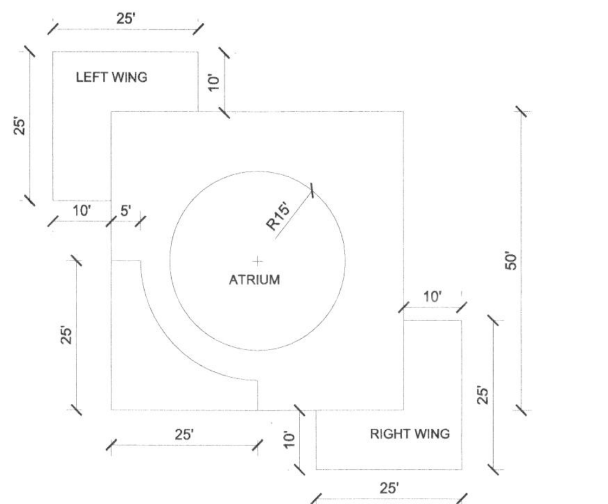

Figure 10-64 Sketch plan for the office building

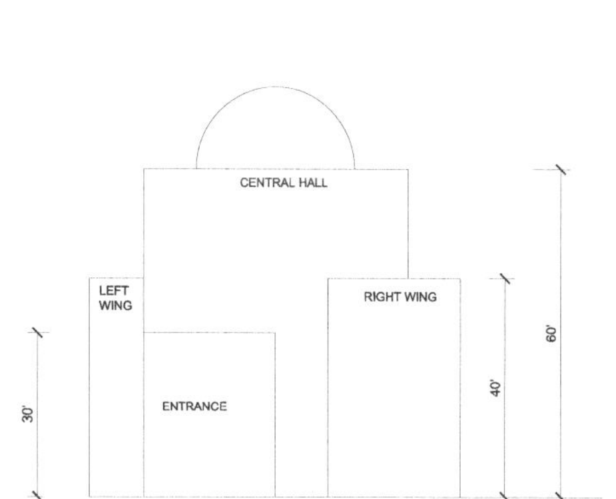

Figure 10-65 Elevation for the office building

Opening the Project File and Adding Levels

You need to first open a new project file using the **New** tool. As the building is five-story high, you need to create four additional levels and rename them according to the floor levels.

1. Choose **New > Project** from the **File** menu; the **New Project** dialog box is displayed.
2. Select the **Architectural Template** option from the drop-down list in the **Template file** area, if it is not selected by default.
3. Choose the **OK** button to close the **New Project** dialog box; the new project file is opened in the drawing window.
4. In the **Project Browser**, double-click on **South** in the **Elevations (Building Elevation)** head to display the corresponding view.
5. Choose the **Level** tool from the **Datum** panel in the **Architecture** tab.
6. Add four levels above level 2 at an elevation of **10'0" (3048 mm)** each. (For more information on adding levels, refer to Adding Levels section in Chapter 6)
7. Rename the levels as follows:
   Level 1- First Floor
   Level 2- Second Floor
   Level 3- Third Floor
   Level 4- Fourth Floor
   Level 5- Fifth Floor
   Level 6- Roof

   Choose the **Yes** button in the **Revit** conformation box to rename the corresponding views.

Creating the Massing Geometry

Now, you can start creating the massing geometry using the tools for massing. The central hall and the two wings can be generated using the **Form** tool.

Note

The massing geometry can be created using different methods and tools. The steps given below describe a general procedure to create massing geometry. The steps and methods may vary depending on the design intent.

1. Double-click on the **First Floor** under the **Floor Plans** head in the **Project Browser** to display the corresponding plan.

2. Choose the **In-Place Mass** tool from the **Conceptual Mass** panel of the **Massing & Site** tab; the **Massing - Show Mass Enabled** message box is displayed.

3. Choose **Close** from this message box; the **Name** dialog box is displayed.

4. In the **Name** edit box of the **Name** dialog box, enter the name **Central Hall** and then choose the **OK** button.

5. Invoke the **Rectangle** sketching tool from the **Draw** panel of the **Create** tab.

6. Move the cursor in the area lying in the mid of the four elevation tags and sketch a square with **50'0"(15240 mm)** side. After sketching the square, choose the **Modify** button.

7. Now, select the created square and choose the **Solid Form** tool from **Modify|Lines > Form > Create Form** drop-down; the **Modify |Form** tab is displayed.

8. Next, choose the **Default 3D** tool from the **Create** panel of the **View** tab; the 3D view of the mass created is displayed.

9. Now, move the cursor over the top face of the box created, refer to Figure 10-66, and click when the edges of the faces are highlighted. On doing so, two temporary dimensions are highlighted.

10. Click on the value of the lower dimension (dimension that specifies the height of the box) and enter **60' (18288 mm)** in the edit box. Now, press ENTER; the box is resized to the height 60' (18288 mm).

11. Choose the **Modify** button and then right-click in the drawing area; a shortcut menu is displayed. Choose **Zoom To Fit** from the shortcut menu; the box created can now be viewed completely.

12. Now, choose the **Finish Mass** button from the **In-Place Editor** panel of the **Modify** tab; the Central Hall massing is created.

    Similarly, you need to create the left and right wings of the building using the **Form** tool. You will sketch the profile in the first floor plan view and extrude it to a height of **40'0" (12192 mm)**, as specified in the sketch plan.

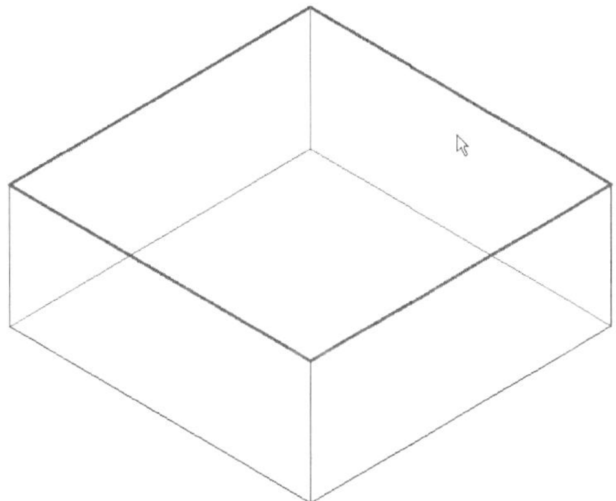

Figure 10-66 *Selecting the top face of the central hall*

13. Create the mass for left and right wings of the building. Double-click on **First Floor** under the **Floor Plans** head in the **Project Browser** to display the corresponding plan.

14. Now, choose the **In-Place Mass** tool from the **Conceptual Mass** panel of the **Massing & Site** tab; the **Name** dialog box is displayed.

15. In the **Name** dialog box, enter the name **Wings** and choose the **OK** button.

16. Invoke the **Line** tool from the **Draw** panel of the **Create** tab and ensure that the **Chain** check box is selected in the **Options Bar**.

17. Move the cursor near the lower right corner of the square and sketch the profile based on the dimensions given in the sketch plan, refer to Figure 10-64. The profile for the right wing is sketched, as shown in Figure 10-67.

    Note that the sketch for the wings should be a closed sketch.

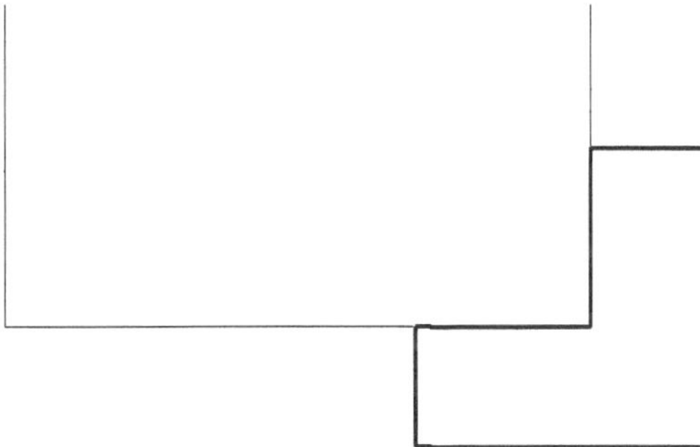

Figure 10-67 *Sketched profile for the right wing*

18. Choose the **Modify** button from the **Select** panel to clear the current selection.

19. Now, select the sketched profile for the right wing and choose the **Mirror - Draw Axis** tool from the **Modify** panel of the **Modify | Lines** tab.

20. Draw a line from the top right corner to the bottom left corner of the central square to define the mirror axis line. The profile is mirrored at the diagonally opposite corners of the square, as shown in Figure 10-68.

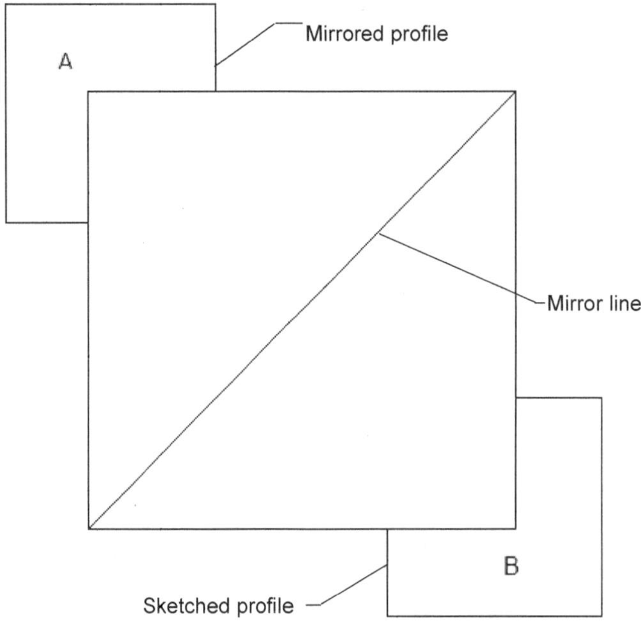

Figure 10-68 *Creating a mirror copy of the sketched profile*

21. Now, ensure that the mirrored profile is selected and the **Modify | Lines** tab is chosen.

22. Choose the **Solid Form** tool from the **Modify | Lines > Form > Create Form** drop-down.

23. Next, select the other profile at the lower right corner and repeat step 22.

24. Choose the **Modify** button from the **Select** panel and then choose the **Default 3D** tool from the **Create** panel of the **View** tab; the 3D view of the mass created is displayed.

25. Now move the cursor over the top face of the created mass marked as A (refer to Figure 10-68) and then click on the face when it is highlighted. On doing so, two temporary dimensions are displayed.

26. Click on the value of the lower displayed dimension and enter **40'** (**12192mm**) in the edit box.

27. After entering the value in the edit box, press ENTER; the selected face of the mass will be extended to a height of 40' from the First Floor level and the mass corresponding to it is resized.

28. Next, select the top face of the other mass marked B and repeat steps 25 to 27.

29. Now, after you create the masses for the wings, choose the **Modify** button in the **Select** panel; the current selection is cleared.

30. Now, choose the **Finish Mass** button from the **In-Place Editor** panel of the **Modify** tab; the masses for the wings are created.

31. Now, move the cursor over the **ViewCube** tool and right-click; a shortcut menu is displayed. Choose **Orient to a Direction > Northeast Isometric** from the shortcut menu; the 3D view of the created mass geometry is displayed, as shown in Figure 10-69.

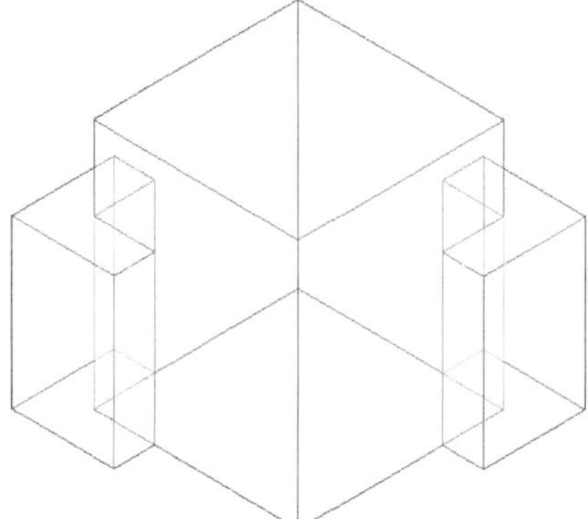

Figure 10-69 *The* ***Northeast Isometric*** *view of the central hall and the two wings*

Cutting the Massing Geometry

After creating the desired building blocks, you can now cut them to create the atrium and the entrance. The **Void Form** tool can be used to create the desired void geometry.

1. Double-click on **First Floor** under the **Floor Plans** head in the **Project Browser** to display the first floor plan view.

2. Choose the **Central Square** hall; the **Modify | Mass** tab is displayed.

3. Choose the **Edit In-Place** tool from the **Model** panel of the **Modify | Mass** tab; the **Modify** tab is displayed.

4. Next, choose **Visual Style > Wireframe** from **View Control Bar**.

5. Draw reference planes diagonally to locate the center of the square by using the **Plane** tool from the **Draw** panel of the **Modify** tab. After creating the reference planes, choose the **Modify** button from the **Select** panel to clear the current selection.

6. Now, invoke the **Circle** tool from the **Draw** panel of the **Modify** tab.

7. Move the cursor at the center of the square. Use the reference planes to locate the center and click to specify it.

8. Move the cursor to the right and enter the value **15'0" (4572mm)**. Next, press ENTER; the circle of **30'0"** diameter is created. Now, press ESC twice to exit and then select the circle created.

9. Choose the **Void Form** tool from the **Modify | Lines > Form > Create Form** drop-down; two circular images are displayed.

10. Choose the left image and then choose the **View** tab. Next, choose the **Default 3D** tool from the **Create** panel; the 3D view of the mass created is displayed.

11. Now, select the two segments of the circle profile of the void created by using the CTRL key, as shown in Figure 10-70. On selecting the segments, the corresponding pivot points are displayed. Hold and drag the blue segments till they cross the upper face of the central hall. Choose the **Modify** button.

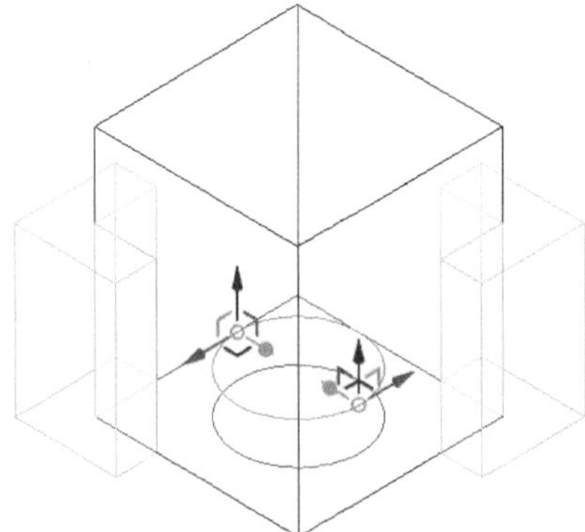

Figure 10-70 *The segments selected for the circular void*

12. Now, double-click on **First Floor** under the **Floor Plans** head in the **Project Browser** to display the corresponding plan.

13. Next, choose the **Modify| Form** tab and invoke the **Center-ends Arc** tool from the **Draw** panel.

14. Move the cursor to the center of the atrium circle and then click. Next, move the cursor horizontally toward the left and enter the value **20'0"** (**6096mm**) to specify the radius. Now, press ENTER.

15. Move the cursor counterclockwise and click to create a quarter arc, as shown in Figure 10-71.

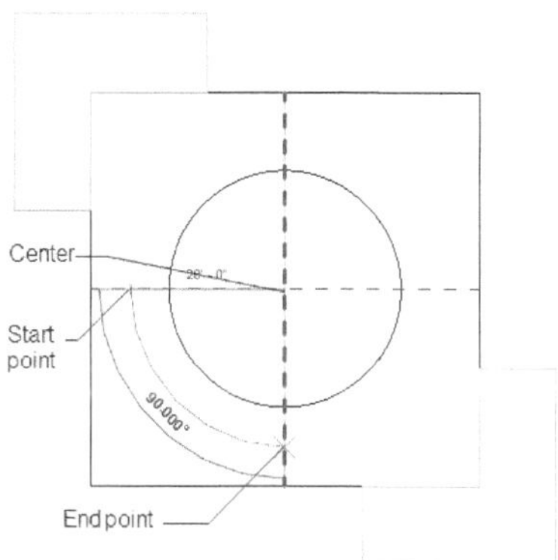

Figure 10-71 Sketching an arc to create a cutting geometry

16. Choose the **Line** sketching tool and ensure that the **Chain** check box is selected.
17. Sketch the profile of the cutting geometry, as shown in Figure 10-72.

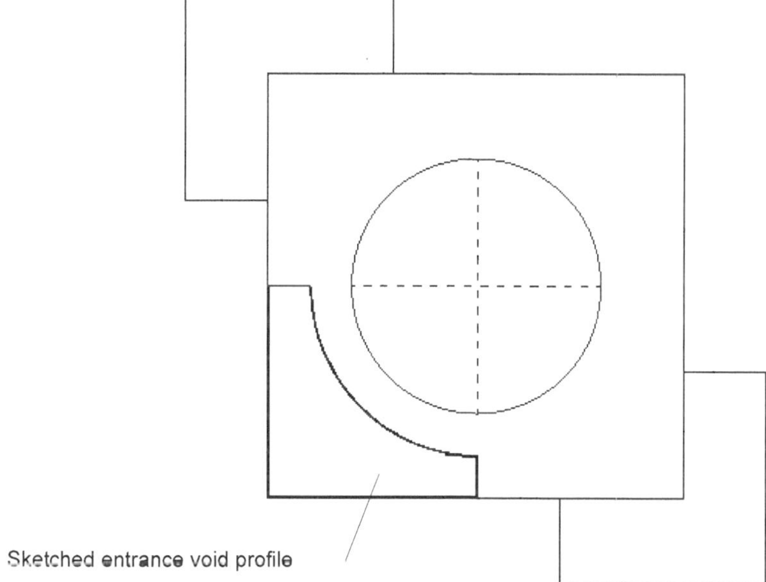

Figure 10-72 Profile of the cutting geometry

18. Choose the **Modify** button from the **Select** panel and then select the profile that was created recently; the **Modify | Lines** tab is displayed.
19. Choose the **Void Form** tool from the **Modify | Lines > Form > Create Form** drop-down; the void mass is created.
20. Next, choose the **View** tab and then choose the **Default 3D** tool from the **Create** panel; the 3D view of the created mass is displayed.

21. Now, move and place the cursor over the **ViewCube** tool and right-click; a shortcut menu is displayed.

22. Choose **Orient to a Direction > Front Left Isometric** from the shortcut menu.

23. Next, select the top face of the void geometry created, as shown in Figure 10-73.

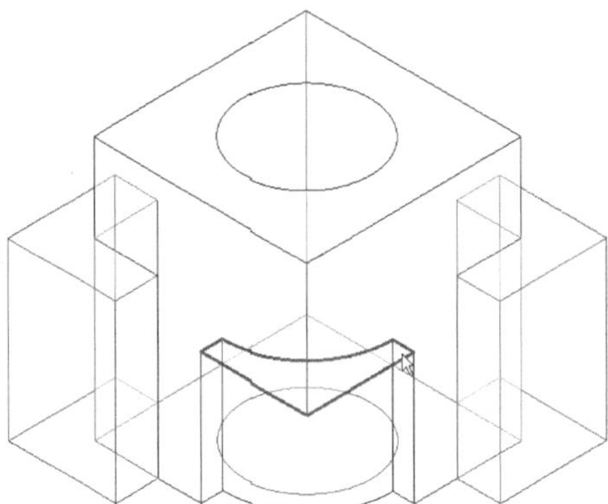

Figure 10-73 Selecting the face of the void geometry to edit the height

24. After selecting the top face, click on the dimension value of the temporary dimension that is displayed at the bottom. Enter **30'** in the displayed edit box and press ENTER.

25. Now, choose the **Modify** button from the **Select** panel and then choose the **Finish Mass** button from the **In-Place Editor** panel of the **Modify** tab.

26. Next, right-click on the drawing area and choose **Zoom To Fit** from the shortcut menu.

Creating the Atrium Dome

The atrium dome can be added using the **Form** tool. It is a hemispherical dome having a radius of **20'0"(6096 mm)** which is same as the radius of the atrium.

1. Choose the **In-Place Mass** tool from the **Conceptual Mass** panel of the **Massing & Site** tab; the **Name** dialog box is displayed.

2. In this dialog box, enter **Dome** in the **Name** edit box and choose the **OK** button.

3. Choose the **Set** tool from the **Work Plane** panel of the **Create** tab; you are prompted to pick a plane.

4. Select the right side entrance wall as the work plane, as shown in Figure 10-74. Note that to confirm that the selected face has been assigned the current work plane, choose the **Show** button from the **Work Plane** panel of the **Create** tab; the selected plane is highlighted.

5. Now, choose the **Reference** tool from the **Draw** panel of the **Create** tab and invoke the **Line** tool.

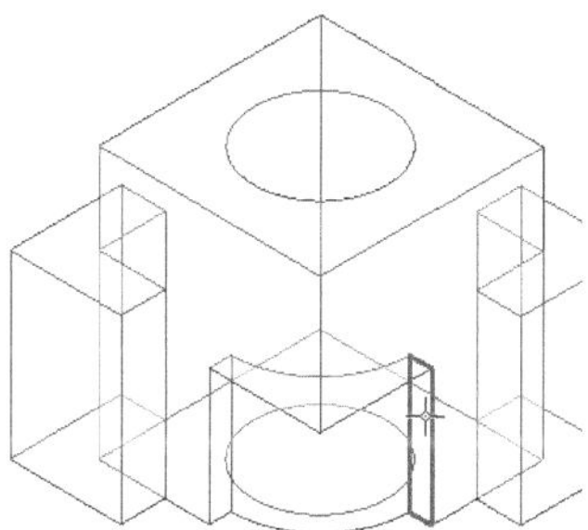

Figure 10-74 Selecting the right side entrance wall as the work plane

6. Sketch the reference lines for the dome, as shown in Figure 10-75.

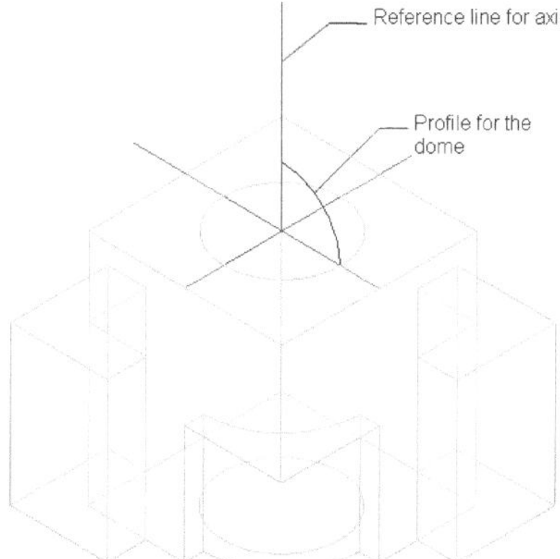

Figure 10-75 The reference line and the profile for the dome

7. Now, choose the **Model** tool from the **Draw** panel of the **Modify** tab and then invoke the **Center-ends Arc** sketching tool from the **Draw** panel.

8. Using the center of the atrium roof as the center of the curve, sketch a quarter arc, refer to Figure 10-75. Next, choose the **Modify** button to clear the current selection.

9. Select the reference line that defines the vertical axis and then select the arc using the CTRL key, refer to Figure 10-75.

10. Now, choose the **Solid Form** tool from the **Form** panel; the dome is created, as shown in Figure 10-76.

11. Choose the **Finish Mass** button from the **In-Place Editor** panel of the **Modify** tab to finish the creation of the dome geometry. Ignore the warning message displayed, if any. Now, choose the **Modify** button from the **Select** panel.

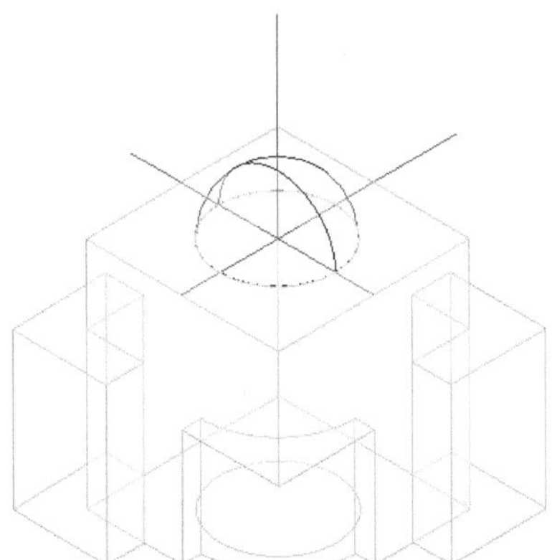

Figure 10-76 The dome created for the Atrium

Converting Massing Geometry into Building Elements

You can now convert the massing geometry into building elements using the **Floor**, **Wall**, and **Roof** tools. In order to create floors, you must first create different floor area faces.

1. Select the **Central Hall** and **Wings** massing geometries by holding the CTRL key; the **Modify | Mass** tab is displayed.

2. Choose the **Mass Floors** tool from the **Model** panel; the **Mass Floors** dialog box is displayed.

3. In the **Mass Floors** dialog box, select the check boxes for all the floors and choose the **OK** button; the floor area faces are created for the selected floors. Now, choose the **Modify** button.

4. Next, choose the **Floor** tool from the **Model by Face** panel of the **Massing & Site** tab; the **Modify | Place Floor by Face** tab is displayed.

5. In the **Properties** palette, select **Floor: LW Concrete on Metal Deck** (for Metric **160mm Concrete with 50mm Metal Deck**) from the **Type Selector** drop-down list.

6. Using the crossing window, select all the floor faces and then choose the **Create Floor** tool from the **Multiple Selection** panel; Autodesk Revit creates floors at the floor area faces. Now, choose **Visual Style > Shaded** from the **View Control Bar**. The shaded view of the model is shown in Figure 10-77.

7. Now, choose the **Wall** tool from the **Model by Face** panel of the **Massing & Site** tab; the **Modify | Place Wall** tab is displayed.

8. In the **Properties** palette, select the **Basic Wall : Exterior - Brick on CMU** wall type from the **Type Selector** drop-down list.

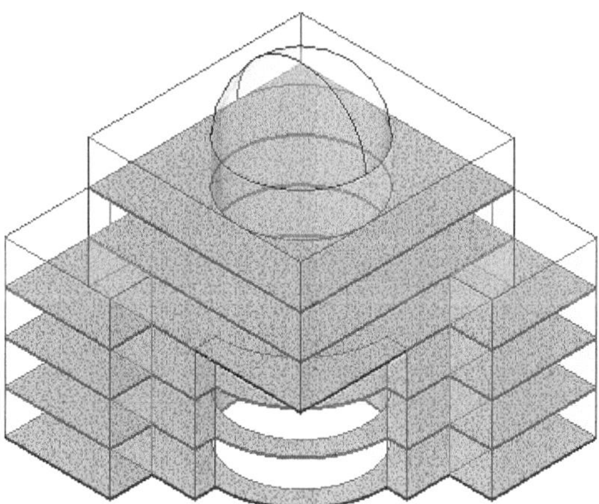

Figure 10-77 *Floor areas of the massing converted into floors*

9. Now, move the cursor over the central hall massing geometry and when an exterior wall is highlighted, click to convert the wall face into the selected wall type.

10. Similarly, click on the other exterior walls of the central hall including the two side walls of the entrance. The resultant 3D view is shown in Figure 10-78.

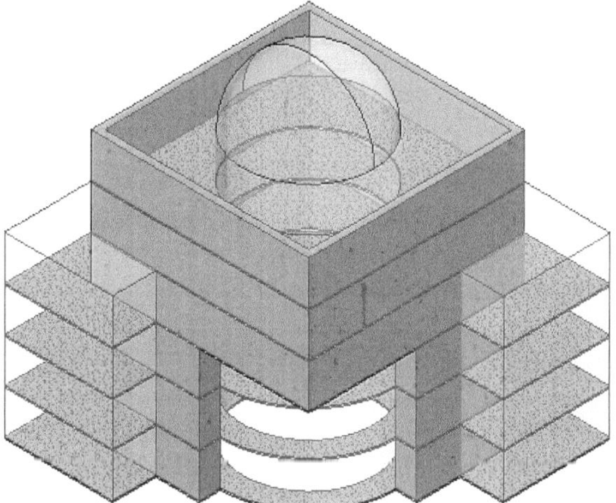

Figure 10-78 *Converting the massing into walls*

11. Next, in the **Properties** palette, select the **Curtain Wall : Exterior Glazing** wall type from the **Type Selector** drop-down list.

12. Choose the **Edit Type** button in the **Properties** palette; the **Type Properties** dialog box is displayed.

13. In the **Type Properties** dialog box, enter **5'0"(1524 mm)** in the **Value** field of the **Spacing** parameter in the **Vertical Grid** category and **10'0"(3048 mm)** for the **Spacing** parameter in the **Horizontal Grid** category.

14. Now, choose **Apply** and **OK**; the **Type Properties** dialog box is closed and the specified parameters are applied to the selected type.

15. Next, highlight and click on the exterior walls of the right and left wings to convert them into the selected exterior glazing walls.

16. Similarly, convert the curved entrance wall into the exterior glazing wall type. The 3D view now appears similar to the illustration shown in Figure 10-79. Now, choose the **Modify** button.

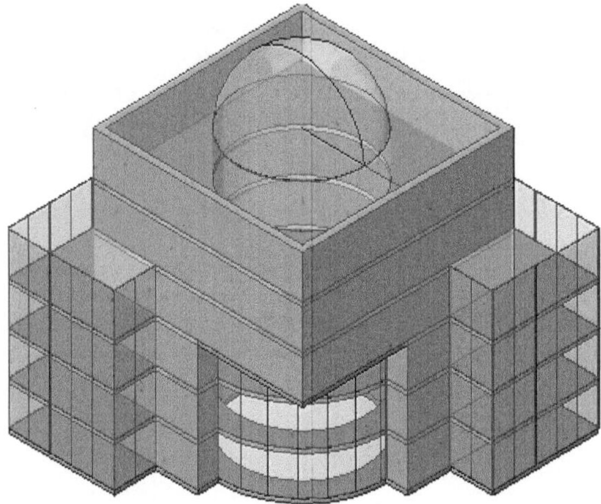

Figure 10-79 *Converting the entrance wall massing into walls*

17. Next, choose the **Roof** tool from the **Model by Face** panel of the **Massing & Site** tab; the **Modify | Place Roof by Face** tab is displayed.

18. In the **Type Selector** drop-down list, select the specified roof type.
    For Imperial **Basic Roof : Generic - 9"**
    For Metric **Basic Roof : Generic - 300 mm**

19. Highlight the roof face of the central hall and click.

20. Now, choose the **Create Roof** tool from the **Multiple Selection** panel of the **Modify | Place Roof by Face** tab; the roof is created on the selected face.

21. Similarly, create the roof of the same type for the two wings. After creating the roofs, the 3D view appears similar to the one shown in Figure 10-80. Next, you will create the curtain wall system for the dome.

22. To create a curtain system for the dome, choose the **Curtain System** tool from the **Model by face** panel of the **Massing & Site** tab; the **Modify | Place Curtain System by Face** tab is displayed.

23. Choose the **Type Properties** tool from the **Properties** panel; the **Type Properties** dialog box is displayed.

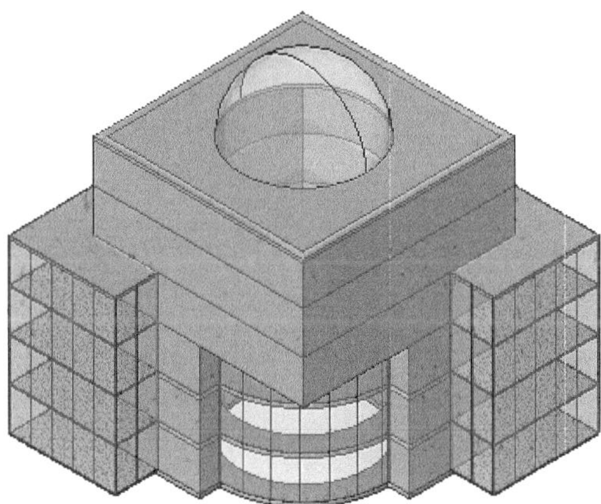

Figure 10-80 *Converting the massing into roof*

24. Choose the **Duplicate** button; the **Name** dialog box is displayed. Enter **3'6" X 7'0" (1067 x 2134 mm)** in the edit box and then choose the **OK** button.

25. Enter the values **7'0"** (**2134 mm**) and **3'6"(1067 mm)** in the **Value** fields of the **Spacing** parameters under the **Grid 1 Pattern** and **Grid 2 Pattern** categories, respectively.

26. Choose the **OK** button; the **Type Properties** dialog box is closed.

27. Now, select both the curved faces of the dome and then choose the **Create System** tool from the **Multiple Selection** panel of the **Modify | Place Curtain System by Face** tab. The curved surfaces of the dome are converted into curtain systems. Now, choose the **Modify** button.

28. Next, you need to add a door to the entrance. To start with, choose the **Insert** tab and then choose the **Load Family** tool from the **Load from Library** panel; the **Load Family** dialog box is displayed.

29. In this dialog box, browse to the **US Imperial > Doors** folder and then choose the **Door-Curtain-Wall-Double-Glass** (for Metric M_ **Door-Curtain-Wall-Double-Glass**) family file. After choosing the file, choose **Open**; the selected file is loaded in the drawing.

30. Choose the **Modify** button and then select the two curtain panels of the exterior glazing by the window selection process.

31. Invoke the **Filter** tool from the right end of the Status Bar; the **Filter** dialog box is displayed.

32. In the **Filter** dialog box, clear all the check boxes except the **Curtain Panel** check box and then choose the **OK** button; the **Filter** dialog box is closed and selection is done, as shown in Figure 10-81.

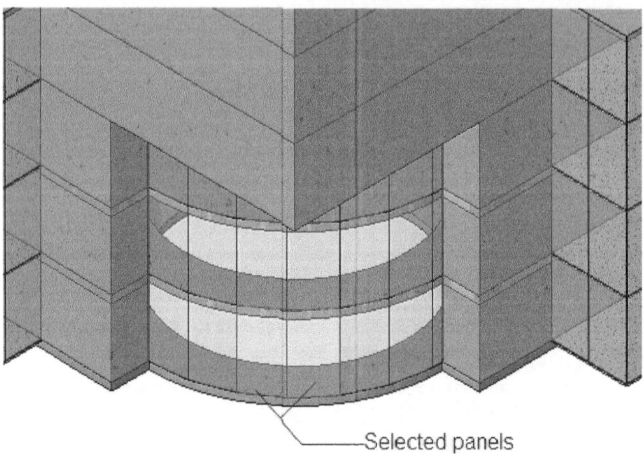

***Figure 10-81** Selecting panels from the glazing*

33. From the **Type Selector** drop-down list, select the **Curtain Wall Dbl Glass** option. Next, choose the **Modify** button.

34. To add mullions to the exterior glazing, choose the **Mullion** tool from the **Build** panel of the **Architecture** tab; the **Modify | Place Mullion** tab is displayed.

35. In the **Type Selector** drop-down list, select the desired mullion type.
    For Imperial **Rectangular Mullion : 1" Square**
    For Metric **Rectangular Mullion : 30 mm Square**.

36. Next, choose the **All Grid Lines** tool from the **Placement** panel and move the cursor over the exterior glazings. Click on each face of the glazing when it is highlighted. Add all the curtain systems to the project, including the exterior wing walls, the curved entrance wall, and the dome. Use the **Grid Line Segment** tool from the **Placement** panel to add grids, if required.

    The completed 3D view of the project appears similar to the one shown in Figure 10-63.

Saving the Project

In this section, you will save the project file using the **Save As** tool.

1. Choose **Save As > Project** from the **File** menu; the **Save As** dialog box is displayed.
2. Enter **c10_Office-2_tut1** in the **File name** edit box and choose **Save**; the file is saved.
3. Now, choose **Close** from the **File** menu to close the Autodesk Revit session.

Tutorial 2 Architectural Column

In this tutorial, you will create an architectural column, as shown in Figure 10-82. Some of the dimensions are given and some are to be assumed. After creating the massing geometry, load it into the project to apply in a building model, refer to Figure 10-83.

(Expected Time: 50 min)

1. Project parameters:

   For Imperial — Template File- *Generic Model.rfa*,
   File name to be assigned- *c10_archicolumn_tut2.rvt*
   Floor to floor height of the column - **10'0"**

   For Metric — Template File- *Metric Generic Model.rfa*,
   File name to be assigned- *M_c10_archicolumn_tut2.rvt*
   Floor to floor height of the column - **3048 mm**

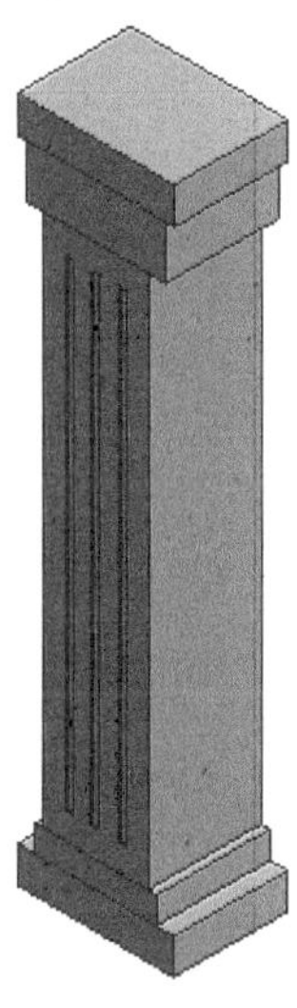

Figure 10-82 *An architectural column*

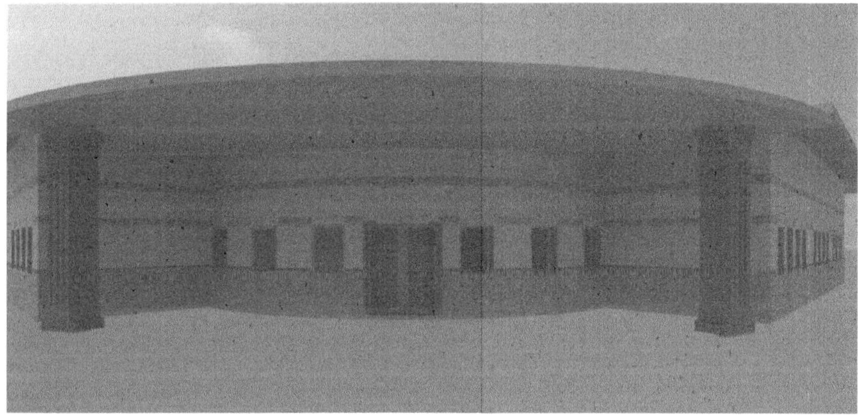

Figure 10-83 *An architectural column in a building model*

The following steps are required to complete this tutorial:

a. Open a new family using the default template file.
b. Create reference planes using the **Reference Planes** tool, refer to Figures 10-84 through 10-90.

c. Create the architectural column using the **Forms** tool, refer to Figures 10-91 through 10-98.
d. Cut the geometry based on the sketch plan using the **Void Form** tool, refer to Figures 10-100 through 10-104.
e. Modify the column by assigning material.
f. Download and open the project file.
g. Use the Family and load it into the project, refer to Figures 10-107 through 10-109.
h. Save the project using the **Save As** tool.
   For Imperial *c10_clubarchicolumn_tut2.rvt*
   For Metric *M_c10_clubarchicolumn_tut2.rvt*
i. Close the project.

Opening the Family and Creating Reference Planes

In this section, you will create reference planes to form the architectural column.

1. Choose **New > Family** from the **File** menu; the **New Family - Select Template File** dialog box is displayed.

2. In this dialog box, browse to the *English_I* folder (*English* folder for Metric) and select the **Generic Model.rft** (**Metric Generic Model.rft**) template file. Now, choose the **Open** button; the selected template file is opened.

3. In the **Project Browser**, double-click on **Back** under the **Elevations (Elevation 1)** head; the corresponding view is displayed.

4. Choose the **Reference Plane** tool from the **Datum** panel in the **Create** tab; the **Modify | Place Reference Plane** contextual tab is displayed.

5. Choose the **Line** tool from the **Draw** panel, if it is not selected by default.

   Now, you will create reference planes.

6. Move the cursor to the left end of the **Reference level** and then move the cursor upward till the alignment line appears.

7. Enter **8"** (**203.2mm**) in the edit box displayed, as shown in Figure 10-84 and press ENTER; the cursor snap appears. Now, draw the reference plane by dragging the cursor in the horizontal direction, as shown in Figure 10-85.

***Figure 10-84** Entering value 8" on the appearance of alignment line*

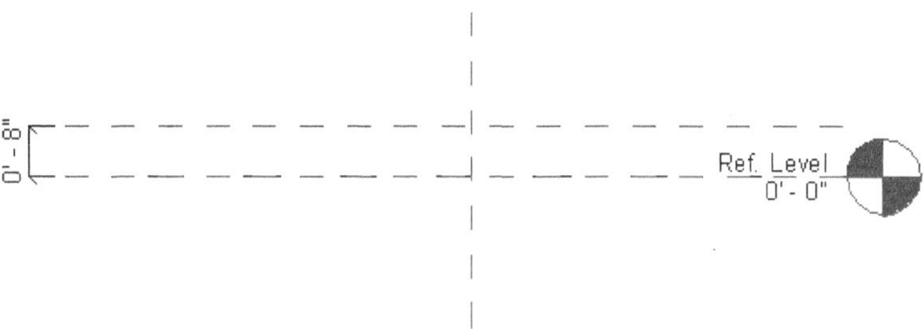

Figure 10-85 *Reference plane drawn at a height of 8"*

8. Similarly, sketch other reference planes at heights **6"(152 mm)**, **6"(152 mm)**, **9'(2743 mm)**, **6"(152 mm)**, **1'(305 mm)**, and **8"(203 mm)**, as shown in Figure 10-86. Choose the **Modify** tool from the **Select** panel to clear the selection.

9. Select the **Center(Left/Right)** reference plane; a pinned symbol is displayed. Click on this symbol to unpin it. Next, drag the vertical reference line so that it crosses the topmost reference line, as shown in Figure 10-87.

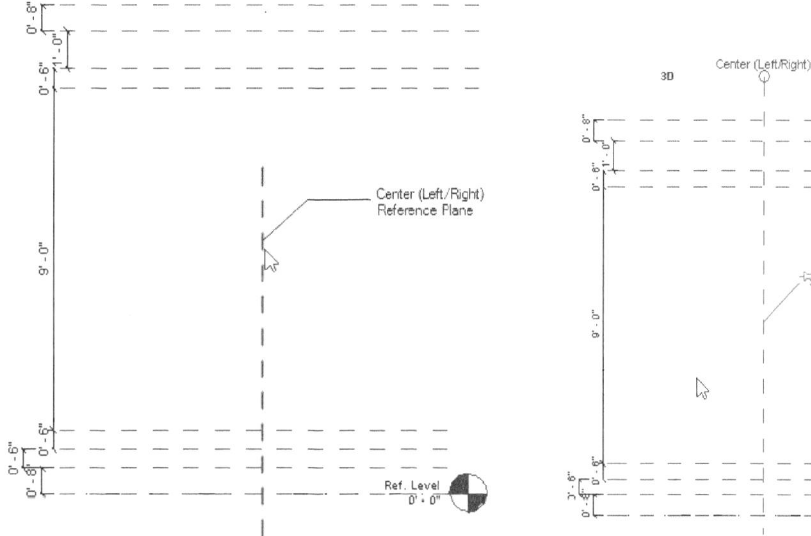

Figure 10-86 *Reference planes drawn at specified heights*

Figure 10-87 *The* ***Center(Left/Right)*** *reference plane stretched to the top*

10. Click anywhere in the drawing area; the selection is cleared.

    Next, you will sketch the vertical reference plane.

11. Invoke the **Reference Plane** tool from the **Datum** panel of the **Create** tab; the **Modify | Place Reference Plane** contextual tab is displayed.

12. In this tab, the **Line** tool is chosen by default. Now, place the cursor at the bottom of the **Center(Left/Right)** reference plane and then move the cursor toward left; an alignment line appears. Enter **6"**(**152 mm**) in the edit box displayed, as shown in Figure 10-88 and press ENTER. Move the cursor in vertical direction and draw a line parallel to the **Center(Left/Right)** reference plane, as shown in Figure 10-89.

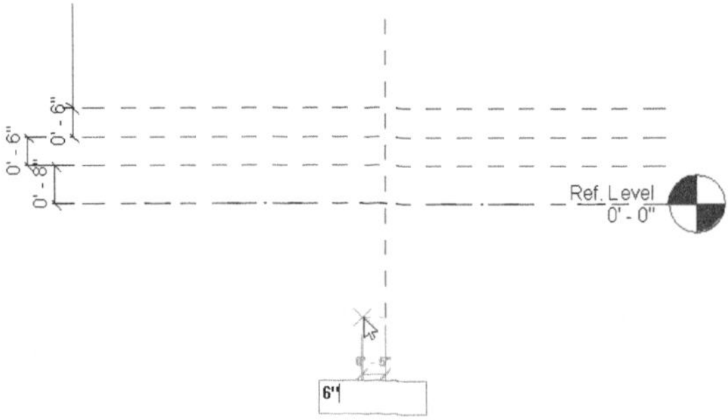

Figure 10-88 Drawing a 6" reference plane to the left of the ***Center(Left/Right)*** *reference plane*

13. Similarly, sketch other reference planes each at a distance of **6"**(**152 mm**), **2"**(**51 mm**), and **4"**(**102 mm**) from the respective reference planes, as shown in Figure 10-90.

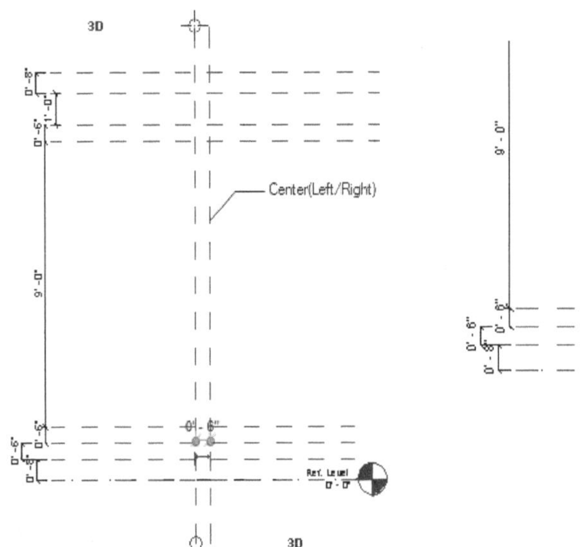

Figure 10-89 Vertical reference plane drawn to the left of the ***Center(Left/Right)*** *reference plane*

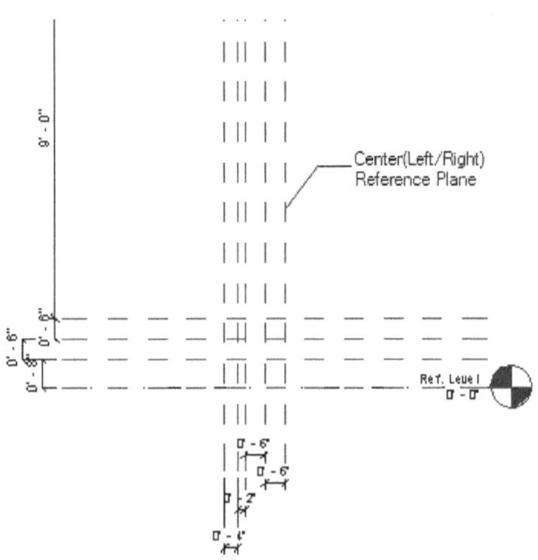

Figure 10-90 Vertical reference planes drawn to the left of the ***Center(Left/Right)*** *reference plane at specified distances*

14. Repeat the procedure followed in steps 11 through 13 to sketch the vertical reference planes at the other side of the **Center(Left/Right)** reference plane.

15. Press the ESC button twice to clear the selection.

Creating the Architectural column

Now, you will create an architectural column using the **Extrusion** and **Void Extrusion** tools.

1. In the **Project Browser**, double-click on **Front** in the **Elevation (Elevation 1)** head; the front view is displayed in the drawing.

2. Right-click on the drawing area; a shortcut menu is displayed. Choose the **Zoom to Fit** tool to fit into the drawing.

3. Choose the **Extrusion** tool from the **Forms** panel of the **Create** tab; the **Modify|Create Extrusion** contextual tab is displayed.

4. Invoke the **Rectangle** sketching tool in the **Draw** panel of the **Modify|Create Extrusion** tab.

5. Move the cursor in the drawing and draw a rectangle of **10' x 2'** (**3048 x 610 mm**) starting at a point where the third reference plane from the top intersects the second reference plane at the left of the **Center(Left/Right)** reference plane. The rectangle ends at the point where sixth reference plane from the top intersects the second reference plane to the right of the **Center(Left/ Right)** reference plane, refer to Figures 10-91 and 10-92.

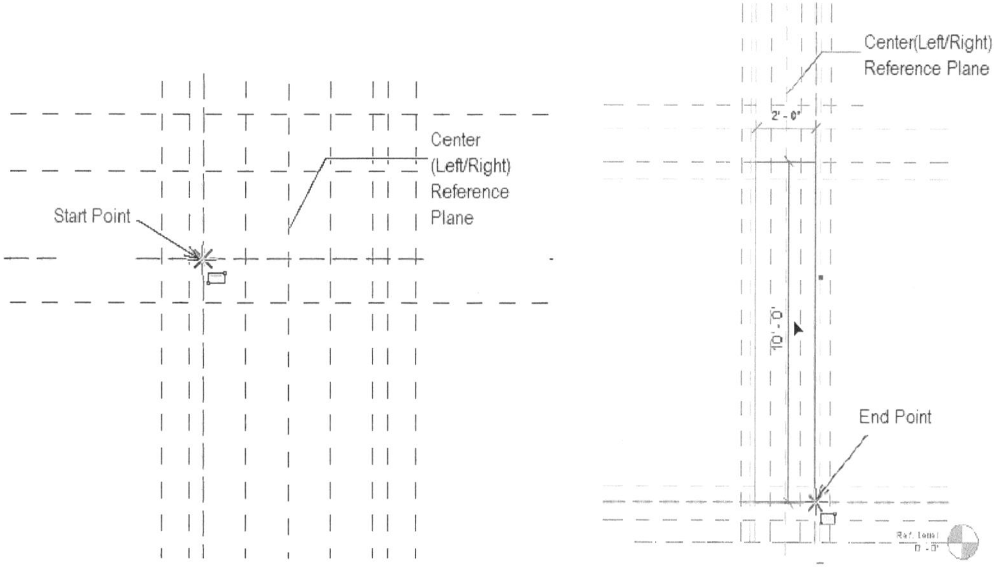

Figure 10-91 Starting point to draw a rectangle

Figure 10-92 End point of a rectangle

6. Choose the **Finish Edit Mode** button from the **Mode** panel of the **Modify|Create Extrusion** contextual tab; the **Modify | Extrusion** contextual tab is displayed.

7. In the **Properties** palette, enter **7'10" (2388 mm)** in the **Extrusion Start** value field. Similarly, enter **10' (3048 mm)** in the **Extrusion End** value field. Choose the **Apply** button to apply the changes and then press ESC; the selection is cleared.

Now, you will create the base of the column.

8. Choose the **Extrusion** tool from the **Forms** panel of the **Create** tab; the **Modify | Create Extrusion** tab is displayed.

9. Invoke the **Rectangle** tool from the **Draw** panel of this tab.

10. Place the cursor at the intersection of the reference planes, which is next to the left corner of the column at the base. Now, click to draw a rectangle starting from point P1, and ending at point P2, as shown in Figures 10-93 and 10-94.

11. In the **Properties** palette, enter **7'10"(2388 mm)** in the **Extrusion Start** parameter value field and enter **10'(3048 mm)** in the **Extrusion End** value field. Choose the **Apply** button to apply the changes.

12. Choose the **Finish Edit Mode** button and then press ESC.

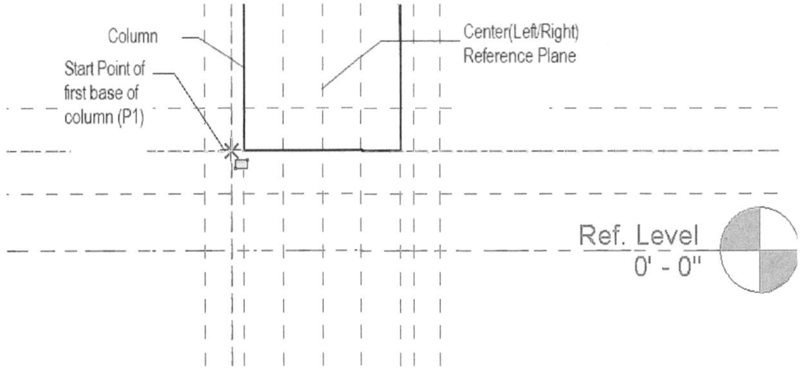

***Figure 10-93** Starting point of rectangle drawn at the base*

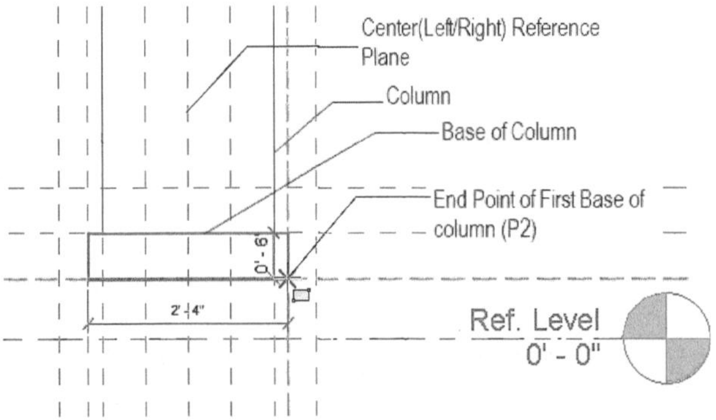

***Figure 10-94** Ending point of rectangle drawn at the base*

13. Similarly, draw another rectangular base exactly below the drawn rectangle using the **Extrusion** tool, starting from the point P3 and ending at point P4, as shown in Figure 10-95. Next, enter values for the **Extrusion End** and **Extrusion Start** parameters as stated earlier.

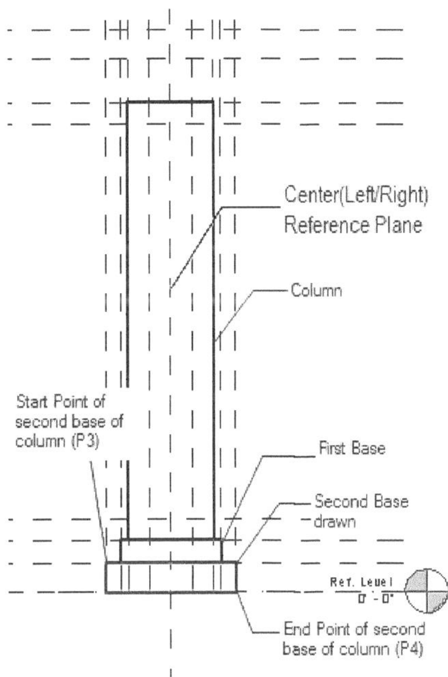

***Figure 10-95** Rectangle drawn below to form the base of an architectural column*

14. Choose the **Finish Edit Mode** button to complete the rectangle and press ESC twice.

    Now, you will create the crown of the column.

15. Choose the **Extrusion** tool from the **Forms** panel of the **Create** tab; the **Modify | Create Extrusion** tab is displayed.

16. Invoke the **Rectangle** tool from the **Draw** panel of the contextual tab.

17. Now place the cursor at the intersection of the reference planes lying next to the left corner of the column at the top. Now, click on the point which is specified as point P5 and draw a rectangle from point P5 ending at point P6, as shown in Figure 10-96.

18. Choose the **Finish Edit Mode** button from the **Mode** panel of this contextual tab.

19. In the **Properties** palette, enter **7'10" (2388 mm)** in the **Extrusion Start** parameter value field and enter **10'(3048 mm)** in the **Extrusion End** parameter, if the values are not entered. Now, choose the **Apply** button to apply the changes.

20. Now, to create the main crown of an architectural column, follow steps 14 and 16. Start drawing the rectangle at point P7 ending at point P8, as shown in Figure 10-97. In the **Properties** palette, enter values for the **Extrusion Start** and **Extrusion End** parameters as stated earlier.

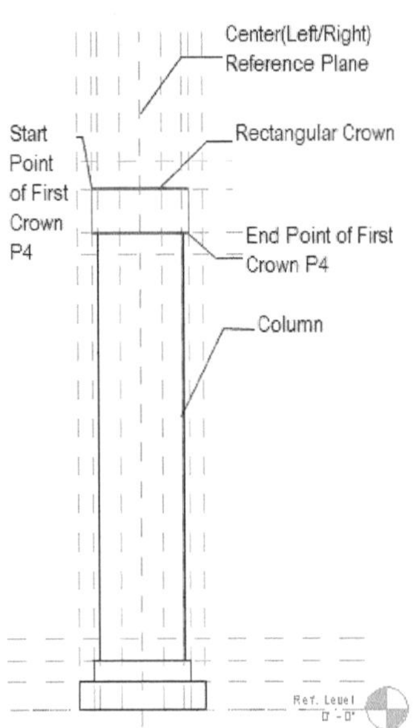

Figure 10-96 Rectangular crown of an architectural column

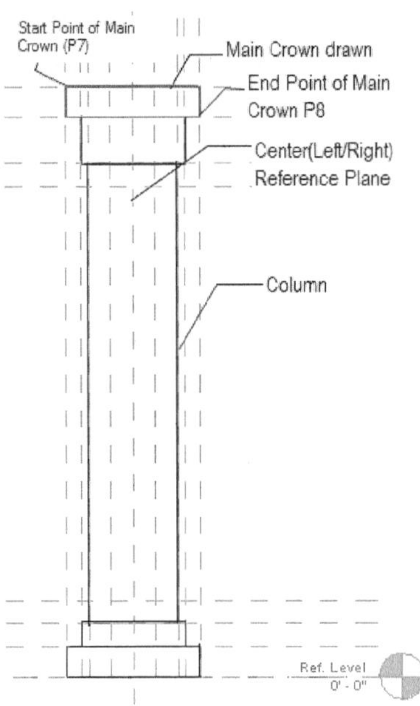

Figure 10-97 Main rectangular crown of an architectural column

21. Choose the **Finish Edit Mode** button from the **Mode** panel of the contextual tab. Figure 10-98 shows the crowns created in an architectural column.

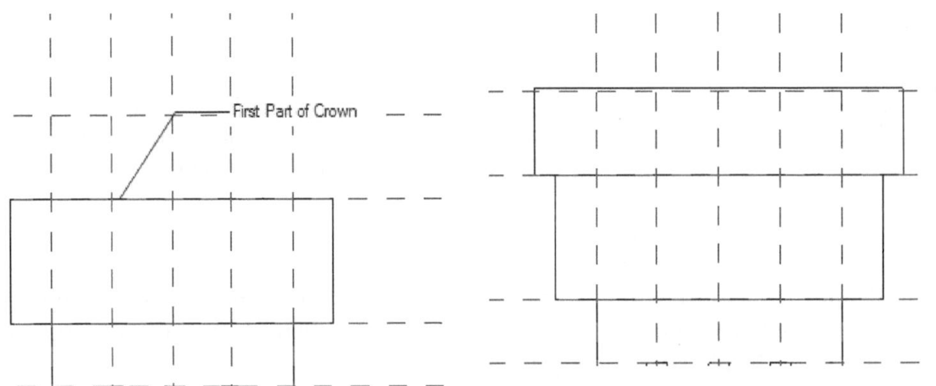

Figure 10-98 Crown created in an architectural column

Cutting the Geometry

After creating the desired column mass in a family, you can cut the geometry using the **Void Forms** tool.

1. To create void in geometry, choose the **Void Extrusion** tool from **Create > Forms >Void Forms** drop-down, as shown in Figure 10-99; the **Modify | Create Void Extrusion** contextual tab is displayed.

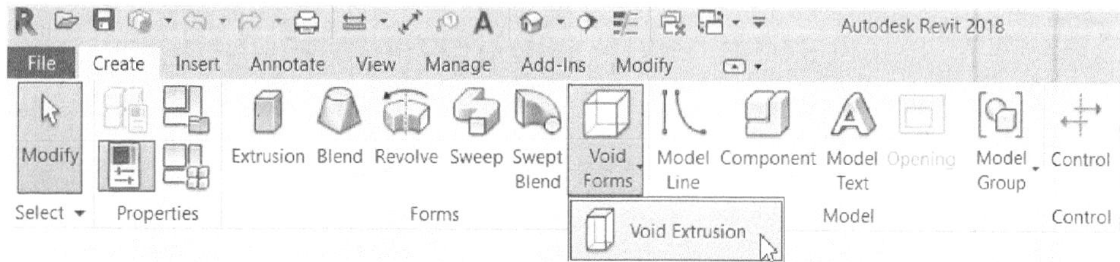

*Figure 10-99 Invoking the **Void Extrusion** tool from the **Void Forms** drop-down*

2. Invoke the **Line** tool from the **Draw** panel of the tab displayed and ensure that the **Chain** check box is selected. Draw void extrusion in the column at three reference planes inside the flange.

3. Now, move the cursor over the base of the column at the reference plane R1 inside the flange of the column and then draw a horizontal line moving in the left direction. Enter **1"** (**25.4mm**) in the edit box displayed and press ENTER, as shown in Figure 10-100.

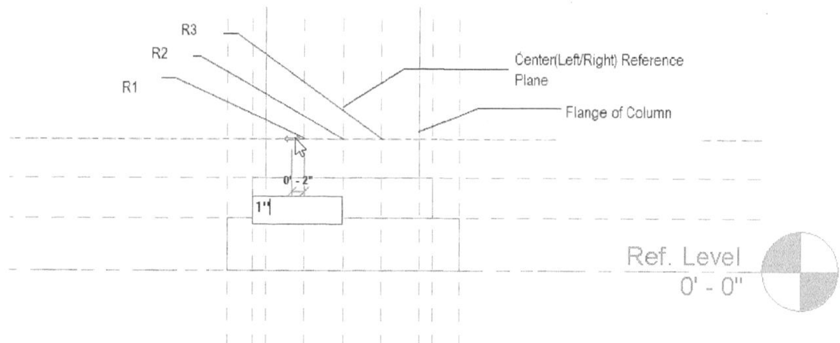

Figure 10-100 Line of 1" drawn on the reference line inside the flange of column

4. Move the cursor upward and enter **9'** (**2743 mm**) in the edit box displayed. Press ENTER and then move the cursor in the horizontal direction toward right. Enter **2"(51 mm)** in the edit box and press ENTER. Now, move the cursor downward, enter **9'** in the edit box and press ENTER. Next, move the cursor inward to complete a rectangle, as shown in Figure 10-101 through Figure 10-103. Choose the **Finish Edit Mode** button to form extrusion.

5. In the **Properties** palette, enter **9'6" (2896 mm)** in the **Extrusion Start** parameter and enter **10'(3048 mm)** in the **Extrusion End** parameter. Choose the **Apply** button to apply the changes.

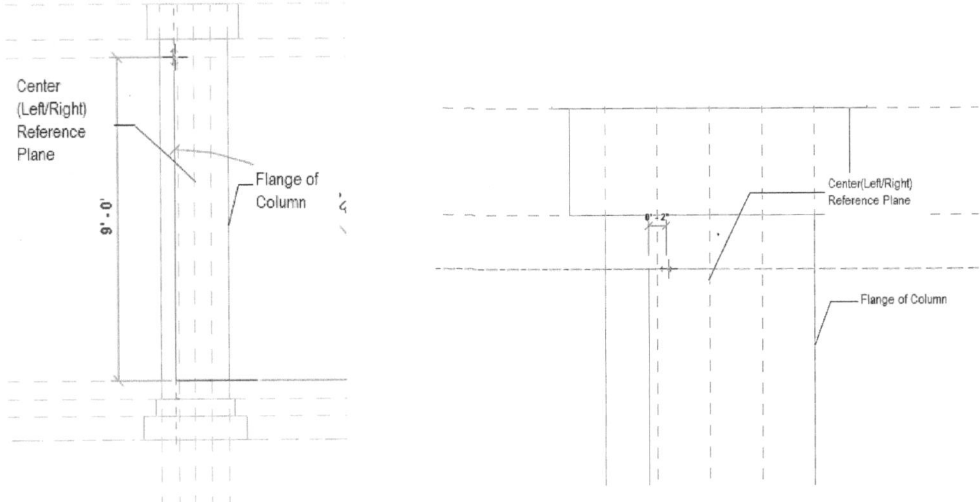

Figure 10-101 *Vertical line of 9' is drawn*

Figure 10-102 *Horizontal line of 2" drawn moving toward east*

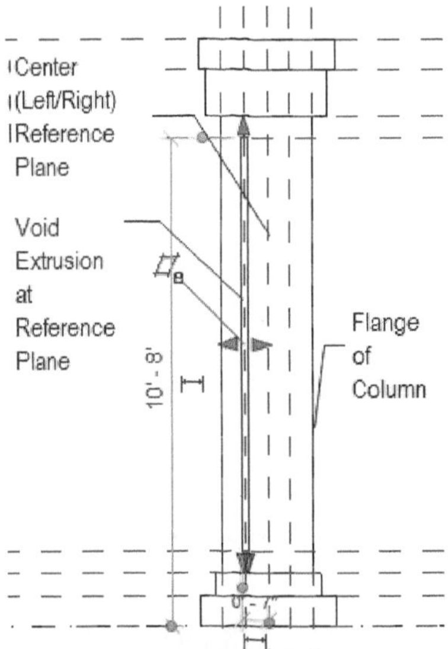

Figure 10-103 *Resultant void extrusion*

6. Similarly, draw two more void extrusions at reference planes R2, and R3, as shown in Figure 10-104 and enter values as specified for the first void extrusion in the **Properties** palette.

7. Choose the **Finish Edit Mode** button from the **Mode** panel of the **Modify|Create Void Extrusion** tab.

8. Now, select the **Default 3D** tool from the **Create** panel of the **View** tab to view the column in three dimensions. Choose the **Visual Style > Shaded** from the **View Control Bar**; the shaded view in three dimensions is displayed, as shown in Figure 10-105.

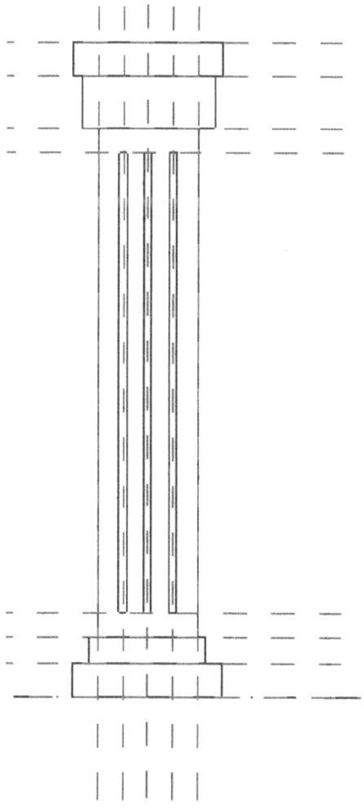

Figure 10-104 *Void extrusion formed at the three reference planes*

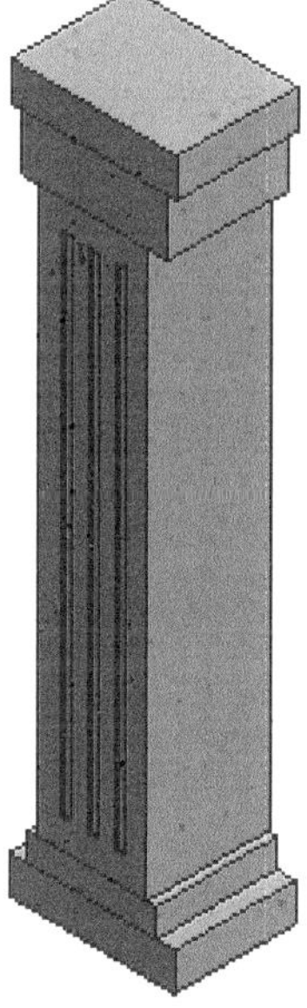

Figure 10-105 *Three dimensional View of an architectural column with the* ***Shaded*** *style*

Assigning Material to Column

In this section, you will assign material and then apply that material over the column.

1. Select the complete element by using the CTRL key; the **Modify|Extrusion** contextual tab is displayed.

2. In the **Properties** palette, click on the value field corresponding to the **Material** parameter under the **Material and Finishes** head; a browse button is displayed. Choose the browse button; the **Material Browser** dialog box with the **Material Editor** pane is displayed.

3. In the **Material Browser** dialog box, click on **Default** in the **Project Materials: All** area; the **Material Editor** pane displays the properties of this material.

4. In this dialog box, select the **Duplicate Selected Material** option from the **Creates or Duplicate Material** drop-down list; the material is duplicated and is displayed in the **Project Materials: All** area.

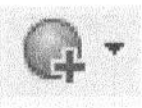

5. Select the duplicate material and right-click on it; a shortcut menu is displayed. Choose the **Rename** option from the shortcut menu and rename the material as **Concrete**.

6. Choose the **Appearance** tab in the **Material Editor** pane; the **Material Editor** pane will display the appearance properties of the selected material. Choose the **Replaces this asset** button in this tab; the **Asset Browser** dialog box is displayed.

7. In this dialog box, click on the **Appearance Library** arrow; a list of material is displayed. Select the **Concrete>Cast-In-Place** option from the list.

8. Next, select the **Flat - Broom Gray** material from the material list in the right pane in the **Asset Browser** dialog box and click on the double-arrow button; the material is assigned to the column.

9. Choose the **Close** button from the **Asset Browser** dialog box; the dialog box is closed and you can see the updated preview in the **Material Editor** pane.

10. In the **Appearance** tab, select the **Transparency** check box and set the value of the **Amount** spinner to **0** and then choose the **Apply** button to apply the changes.

11. Next, choose the **Graphics** tab in the **Material Editor** pane and select the **Use Render Appearance** check box. Choose the **Apply** button to apply the changes and then choose the **OK** button; the **Material Browser** dialog box is closed.

12. Choose **Save As > Family** from the **File** menu; the **Save As** dialog box is displayed. Enter **architecture_column** in the **File name** edit box, as shown in Figure 10-106. Choose the **Save** button from this dialog box; the family is saved.

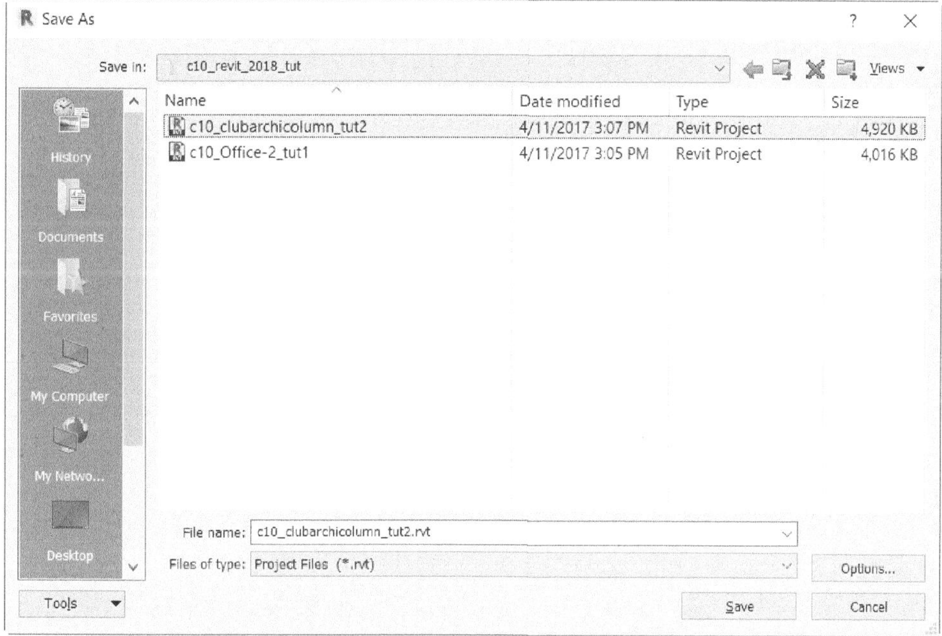

*Figure 10-106 The **Save As** dialog box*

Downloading and Opening the File

Before loading the family, you need to download the tutorial data to your computer.

1. Log on to *www.cadcim.com* and browse to *Textbooks > Civil/GIS > Revit Architecture > Exploring Autodesk Revit 2018 for Architecture*. Next, select *c14_rvt_2018_tut.zip* file from the **Tutorial Files** drop-down list and then choose the corresponding **Download** button to download the data file.

2. Extract the contents of the zip folder to the following location:
   C:\RevitArchi_2018

   Notice that the *c14_rvt_2018_tut* folder is created within the *RevitArchi_2018* folder.

3. Choose **Open > Project** from the **File** menu; the **Open** dialog box is displayed. Now, browse to *C:\RevitArchi_2018\ c14_rvt_2018_tut\ c14_club_tut2.rvt* and choose the **Open** button.

Loading an Architectural Column in Project

In this section, you will load the architectural column in the project.

1. In the Club project, double-click on **Site** in the **Floor Plans** head in the **Project Browser**; the plan will be opened in the drawing window.

2. Now, select **architectural column-3D View{3D}** from the **Switch Windows** drop-down list in the **Windows** panel of the **View** tab; the family is displayed.

3. Choose the **Load into Project** tool from the **Family Editor** panel in the **Modify** tab; you will be prompted to place that column.

Note

*If more than one project is opened in Revit, then on choosing the **Load into Project** tool; the **Load into Projects** dialog box is displayed. Select the check box corresponding to the project in which you want to load the family.*

4. Now, using the **Rotate** and **Move** tools, place the column at corners C1 and C2, as shown in Figure 10-107.

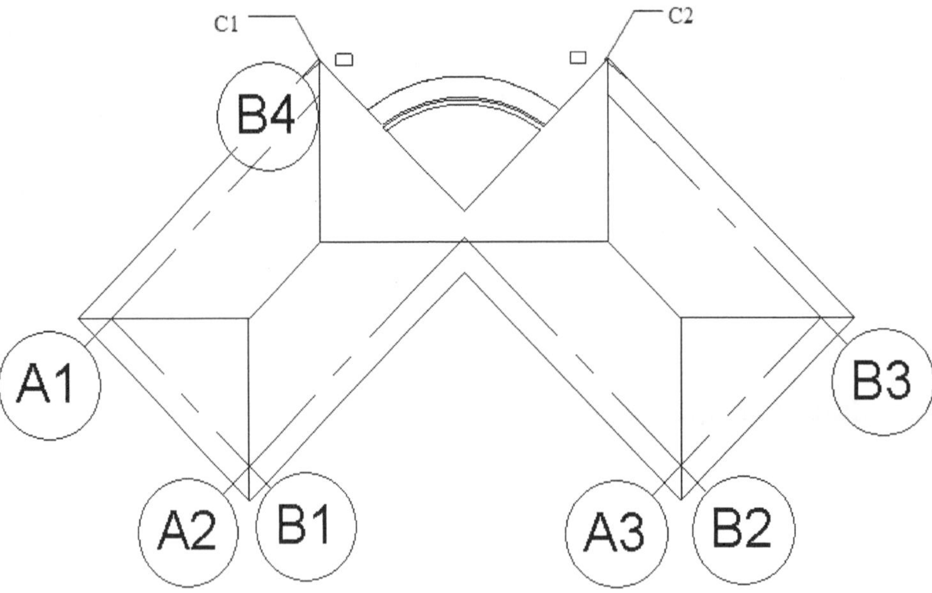

Figure 10-107 *Placing the column at the corner using the **Rotate** and **Move** tools*

5. After placing the column, invoke the **Roof by Footprint** tool from the **Architecture > Build > Roof** drop-down; the **Modify | Create Roof Footprint** tab is displayed.

6. Sketch the roof in the arc form using the **Line** and **Start-End-Radius Arc** tools from this tab, as shown in Figure 10-108. Now, choose the **Finish Edit Mode** button from the **Mode** panel.

7. In the **Properties** palette, click on the value field corresponding to the **Base Level** parameter and select the **Roof** option from the drop-down list displayed. Similarly, click in the value field of the **Base Offset From Level** edit box and enter **-2'2"(660 mm)**. Choose the **Apply** button; the desired changes are applied to the drawing.

8. Choose the **Modify** button from the **Select** panel to clear the selection; the architectural column is loaded to the project, as shown in Figure 10-109.

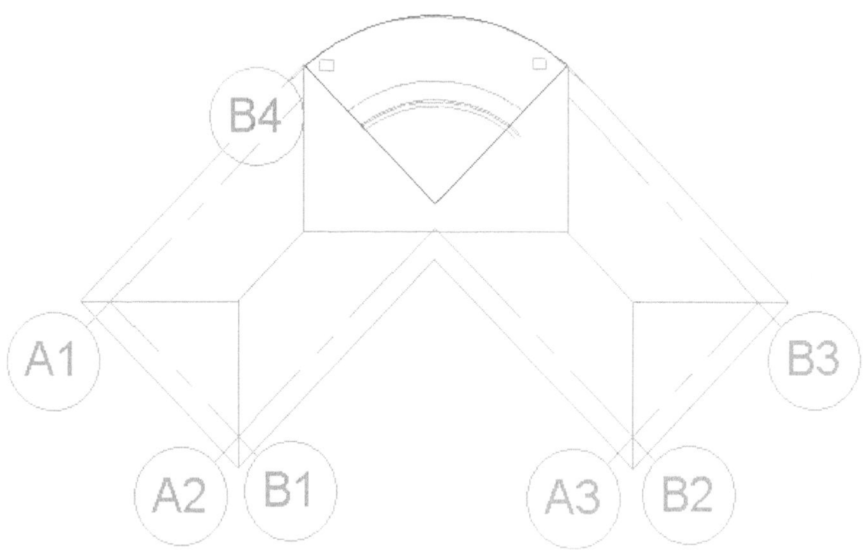

Figure 10-108 *Roof sketched using the* ***Line*** *and* ***Start-end-radius arc*** *tool*

Figure 10-109 *The architectural column loaded in the project*

9. Choose **Save As > Project** from the **File** menu; the **Save As** dialog box is displayed. Enter the required name in the **File name** edit box and choose **Save**; the project file is saved.
   For Imperial **c10_clubarchicolumn_tut2**
   For Metric **M_c10_clubarchicolumn_tut2**

10. Now, choose **Close** from the **File** menu; the file is closed.

Self-Evaluation Test

Answer the following questions and then compare them to those given at the end of this chapter:

1. Which of the following dialog boxes is displayed on choosing the **Model-In Place** tool from the **Component** drop-down.

   (a) **Family Category and Parameters** (b) **Load Family**
   (c) **Massing- Show Mass Enabled** (d) **Revit**

2. Which of the following tools in the **Element** panel of the **Modify | Form** tab is used to display the geometry skeleton like vertices and edges of the mass.

   (a) **Add Edge** (b) **Add Profile**
   (c) **X-Ray** (d) **Divide Edges**

3. The _________ tool is used to add massing by sketching a profile and defining an axis.

4. The ________ tool is used to specify the connection of vertices while using the **Blend** tool.

5. Using the _________ tool, you can display or hide a massing geometry.

6. The start point and endpoint of a solid extrusion can be specified in the _________ dialog box.

7. To modify a massing geometry, select it and then choose the ________ button from the **Options Bar** to modify its profile and properties.

8. The **Extrusion** tool is used to create the massing perpendicular to the sketched profile. (T/F)

9. Using the **Blend** tool, you can link two profiles at different levels. (T/F)

10. You cannot specify a negative value in the **Depth** edit box. (T/F)

11. A massing geometry once created cannot be resized. (T/F)

12. The **Void form** option is used to create a cut in a massing geometry. (T/F)

Review Questions

Answer the following questions:

1. Which of the following parameters in the **Properties** palette can be used to specify the extrusion from the base level?

   (a) **Level** (b) **Extrusion End**
   (c) **Depth** (d) **Extrusion Start**

2. Which of the following tools is used to create a curved tube?

   (a) **Blend** (b) **Revolve**
   (c) **Extrude** (d) **Sweep**

3. Which of the following tools can be used to create a sphere?

   (a) **Sweep** (b) **Revolve**
   (c) **Extrude** (d) **Blend**

4. From which of the following panels, the **Curtain System** tool is invoked?

   (a) **Circulation** (b) **Model by Face**
   (c) **Model Site** (d) **Conceptual Mass**

5. The drag controls can be used to resize a massing geometry. (T/F)

6. You can use the editing tools such as **Move**, **Mirror**, **Copy**, and so on while sketching a massing geometry. (T/F)

7. The **Blend** tool extrudes a profile along a defined path. (T/F)

8. You can extrude multiple closed profiles using the **Extrude** tool. (T/F)

9. The **Work Plane** tool can be used to define a plane in which the profile is to be sketched. (T/F)

10. You can load additional profiles while using the **Sweep** tool. (T/F)

11. Once a massing geometry has been converted into building elements, it cannot be viewed as a massing geometry. (T/F)

12. Mullions are added to a curtain wall without the presence of grids. (T/F)

EXERCISES

Exercise 1 Office

Create a massing geometry for an office building that consists of two identical 400'0" high towers with a connecting passage at 200'0" height. Each tower has a 50'0" X 50'0" base with an offset of 5'0" at 200'0" and 300'0" levels. There are two masts on each tower with a base radius of 2'6" and the top radius of 0'6" The connecting passage is 150'0" long and has a width and height of 25'0" with a vault roof. The plan view of the building is shown in Figure 10-110. The 3D, elevation, and shaded views of the building are shown in Figures 10-111, 10-112, and 10-113, respectively. The dimensions and text have been given for reference and are not to be created. Assume the missing dimensions proportionate to the building design. After creating the massing, convert it into the building elements with the parameters given next.

(Expected time: 45 min)

1. Project file parameters:
   Template File- **Architectural Template**,
   File Name to be assigned- *c10_OfficeTowers_ex1.rvt*

2. Building element types for the converted shell elements:
   Floor: **Floor : LW Concrete on Metal Deck**
   Walls: Towers- **Curtain Wall: Exterior Glazing**
   (horizontal and vertical spacing- 10'0")
   Connecting Passage- **Curtain Wall: Curtain Wall 1**
   Roof: **Basic Roof : Generic 9"**

After completion, the building model will appear similar to the illustration given in Figure 10-113.

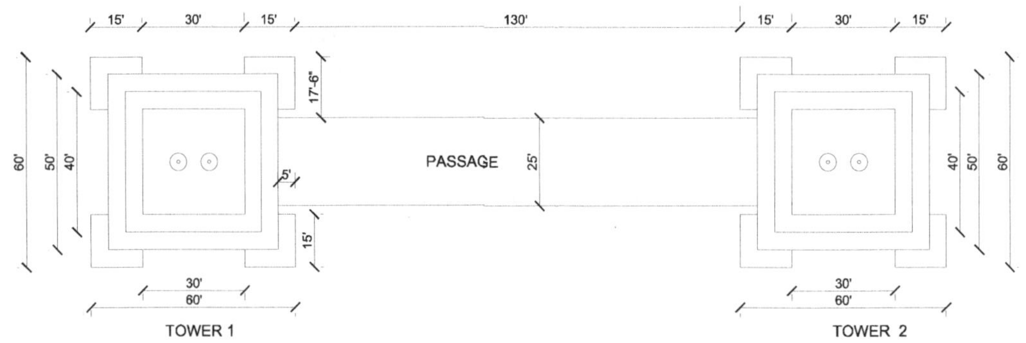

Figure 10-110 Sketch plan for a multistory office building

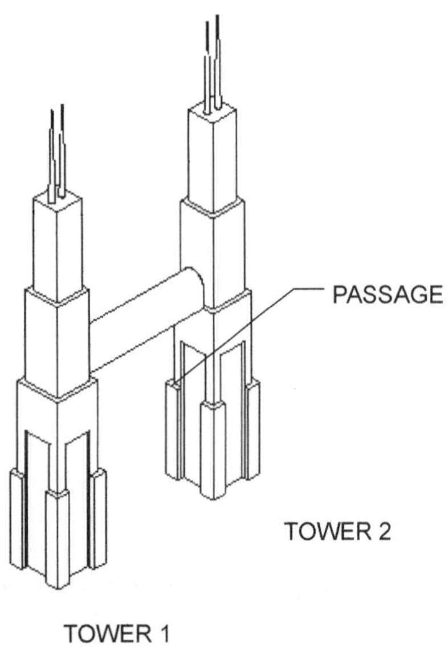

Figure 10-111 3D view of the building

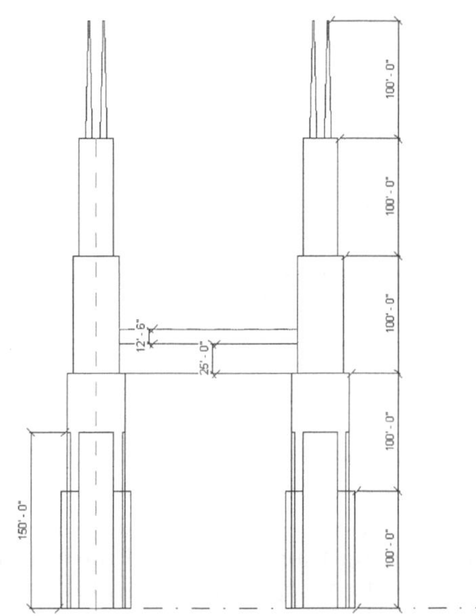

Figure 10-112 Elevation view of the building

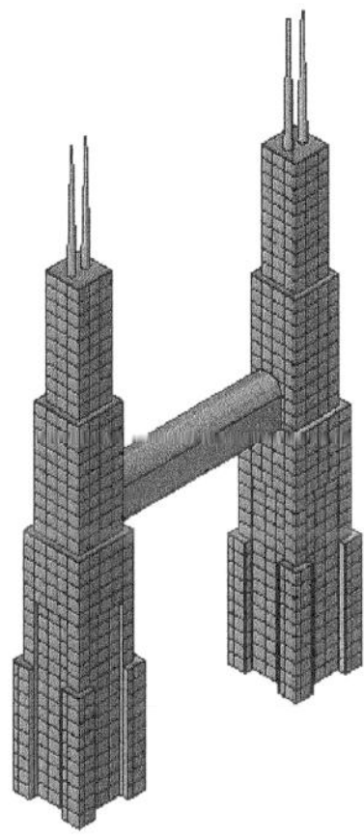

Figure 10-113 Shaded 3D view of the building

Exercise 2 Stadium

Create a massing geometry for a Stadium. Its plan view is shown in Figure 10-114. It consists of the field area and stands. In the stands, the tread of the lower tier is 3'0" and the riser is 1'0". Similarly, the tread of the lower-tier is 3'0"and the riser is 1'6". The cross-section view of stands is shown in Figure 10-115. Assume the missing dimensions proportionate to the sketch plan. Use the following building parameters.

(Expected time: 30 min)

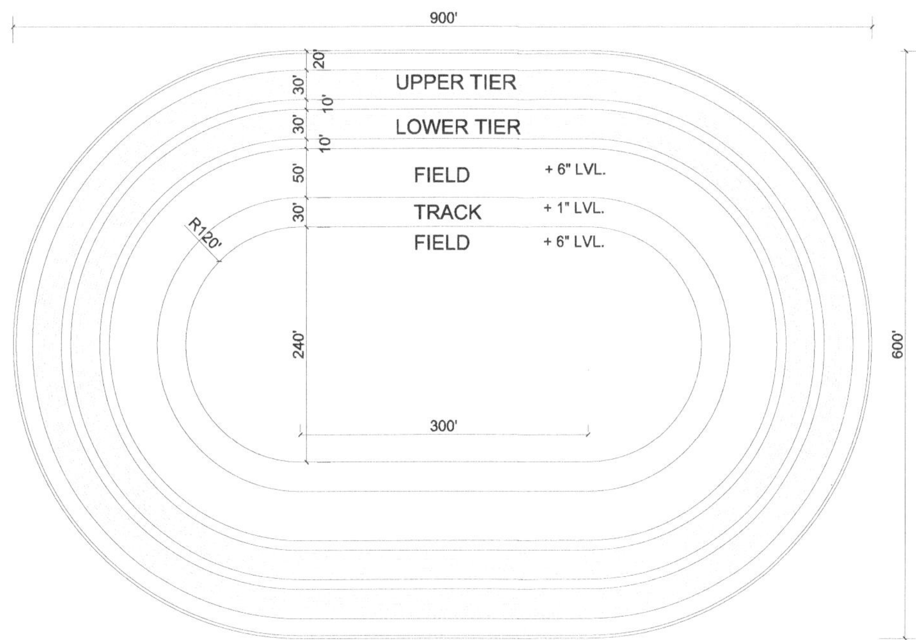

Figure 10-114 Sketch plan of the Stadium

1. Project file Parameters:
   Template file- **Architectural Template**,
   File name to be assigned- *c10_Stadium_ex2.rvt*

   After completion, the building model will appear similar to the illustration given in Figure 10-116.

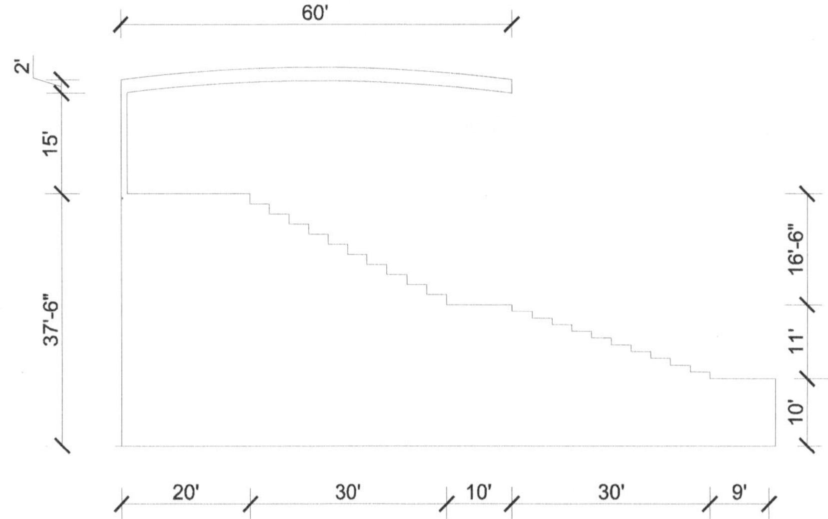

Figure 10-115 *Cross-section view of the stands*

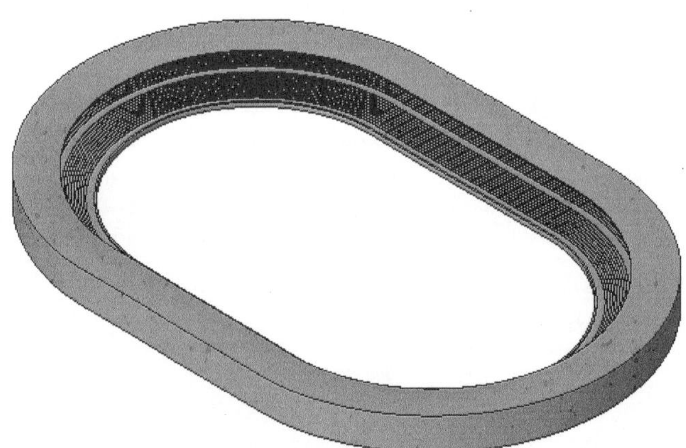

Figure 10-116 *3D view of the stadium*

Answers to Self-Evaluation Test

1. Massing- Show Mass Enabled, 2. X-Ray, 3. Revolve, 4. Edit Vertices, 5. Show Mass, 6. Properties, 7. Edit, 8. T, **9.** T, **10.** F, **11.** F, **12.** T

Chapter 11

Adding Annotations and Dimensions

Learning Objectives

After completing this chapter, you will be able to:

- *Add tags to building elements using the Tag tool*
- *Add room tags to the interior spaces using the Room Tag tool*
- *Add symbols to project view using the Symbol tool*
- *Create dimensions using various dimensioning tools*
- *Modify dimensions based on the given parameters*
- *Add spot elevation to a building model using the Spot Elevation tool*

INTRODUCTION

In the previous chapters, you learned to create and add different building elements to a project. This will help you to convey the design intent of the project, graphically. However, in order to execute a building or an interior project from drawings into reality, you need to add documentation to the drawing. In this chapter, you will learn to add tags to elements and spaces, create dimensions, use annotations, create schedules and details, and add dimensions to the elements. In later chapters of this book, you will learn about the tools that are used to document an Autodesk Revit project and add content to it. You will also learn to compose and plot sheets in the later chapters.

ADDING TAGS

You can easily tag various elements in a building model. A tag is a useful annotation that assists in identifying the tagged building element. When you design complex building models using Autodesk Revit, tags play an important role in arranging various elements in schedules. You can then add necessary description for each tagged element in tabulated form. Figure 11-1 shows the usage of various tags in an interior layout.

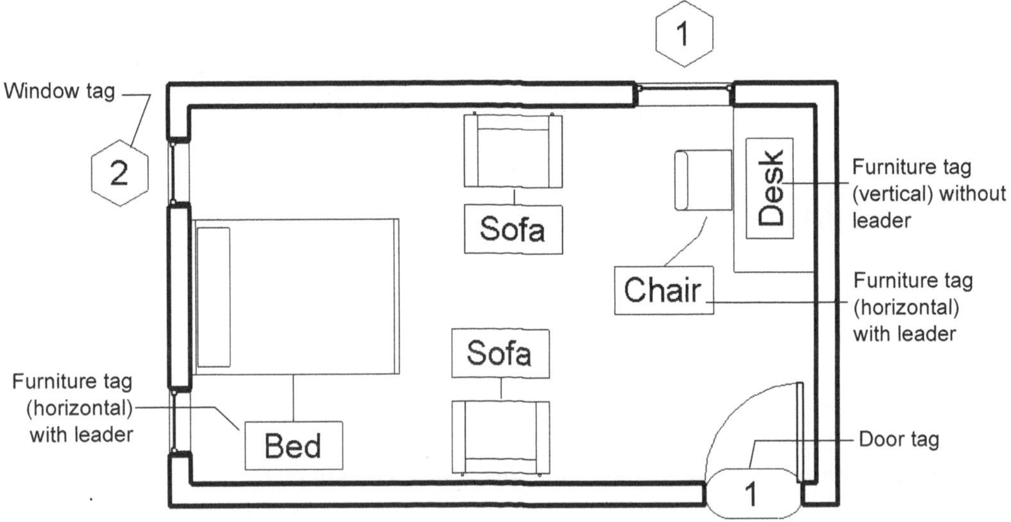

***Figure 11-1** Various tags in an interior layout*

Autodesk Revit provides various tools that are used to add and edit tags. When you open the default template file, tags of a certain category of elements are preloaded. Therefore, when you add the elements such as doors and windows, Autodesk Revit automatically tags them. For the other elements, you need to load their respective tags from the Autodesk Revit library. Like other annotations, tags are also view-specific and they appear only in the view they have been created in. You can control the visibility of tags by choosing the **Visibility/Graphics** tool from the **Graphics** panel of the **View** tab. On doing so, the **Visibility/Graphic Overrides for <current view >** dialog box will be displayed. The **Annotation Categories** tab of this dialog box contains the list of tag categories such as **Door Tags**, **Window Tags**, **Furniture Tags**, **Electrical Fixture Tags**, and so on. You can select the appropriate check boxes to control the visibility of each category of tags. The methods used for tagging the elements are described next.

Tagging Elements by Category

Ribbon: Annotate > Tag > Tag by Category

To attach a tag to an element based on the element category, choose the **Tag by Category** tool from the **Tag** panel of the **Annotate** tab, as shown in Figure 11-2. On doing so, the **Modify |Tag** contextual tab will be displayed and the parameters related to placing and orienting will be displayed in the **Options Bar**. In the **Options Bar**, you can select the **Horizontal** or **Vertical** option from the drop-down list displayed on the left, based on the desired direction of the text in the tag, refer to Figure 11-1. The **Leader** check box is selected by default in the **Options Bar**. As a result, a leader will be displayed with the tag. You can clear this check box, if you do not require a leader to be displayed with the tag. As the **Leader** check box is selected, the options in the drop-down list displayed on the right of it will be enabled. From this drop-down list, you can select two options: **Attached End** and **Free End**. On selecting the **Attached End** option from the drop-down list, you will not be able to move the end of the leader with the tag away from the element category it is attached to. As you select the **Attached End** option from the drop-down list, the edit box on its right gets enabled. In this edit box, you can specify the length of the leader or the distance of the tag from the attached element. Alternatively, if you select the **Free End** option from the drop-down list, the end of the leader can be moved away from the element it is attached to.

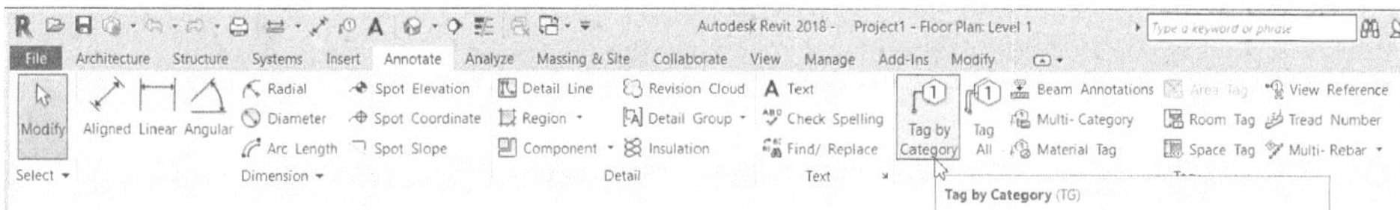

*Figure 11-2 Choosing the **Tag by Category** tool from the **Annotate** tab*

Loading Tags and Symbols

By default, Autodesk Revit loads tags and symbols for certain categories of elements such as areas, drawing sheets, walls, and so on. To insert tags in the drawing area, you can choose the **Loaded Tags And Symbols** tool from the **Tag** drop-down of the **Annotate** tab; the **Loaded Tags And Symbols** dialog box will be displayed. This dialog box displays the category-wise list of the loaded tags with their loaded symbols, as shown in Figure 11-3. In this dialog box, you can control the display of the categories in the categories list by clicking on the **Filter list** drop-down list and selecting the check box(es) of the catagory(ies) that you want to display in the list.

In case, the category of elements to be tagged does not have its corresponding tag or symbols already loaded, choose the **Load Family** button from the **Loaded Tags And Symbols** dialog box; the **Load Family** dialog box will be displayed, as shown in Figure 11-4.

You can select various categories of tags from the **Library > US Imperial > Annotations** folder path as required. The **Preview** area of the **Load Family** dialog box displays a preview image of the selected tag, refer to Figure 11-4. You can select the appropriate tag from the list and choose the **Open** button to load it into the project. On doing so, the desired tag will be added to the list of loaded tags for the corresponding element category in the **Loaded Tags And Symbols** dialog box.

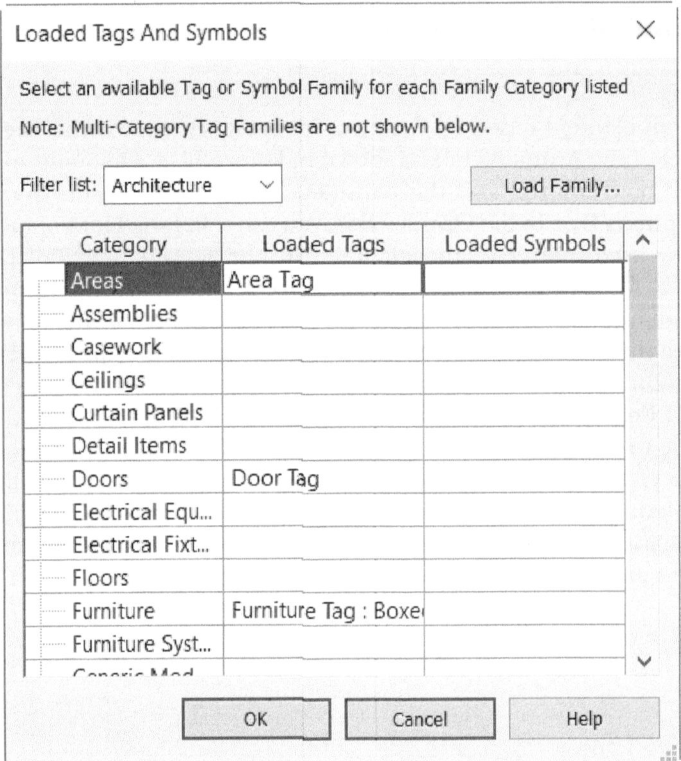

Figure 11-3 *The **Loaded Tags and Symbols** dialog box displaying the list of loaded tags*

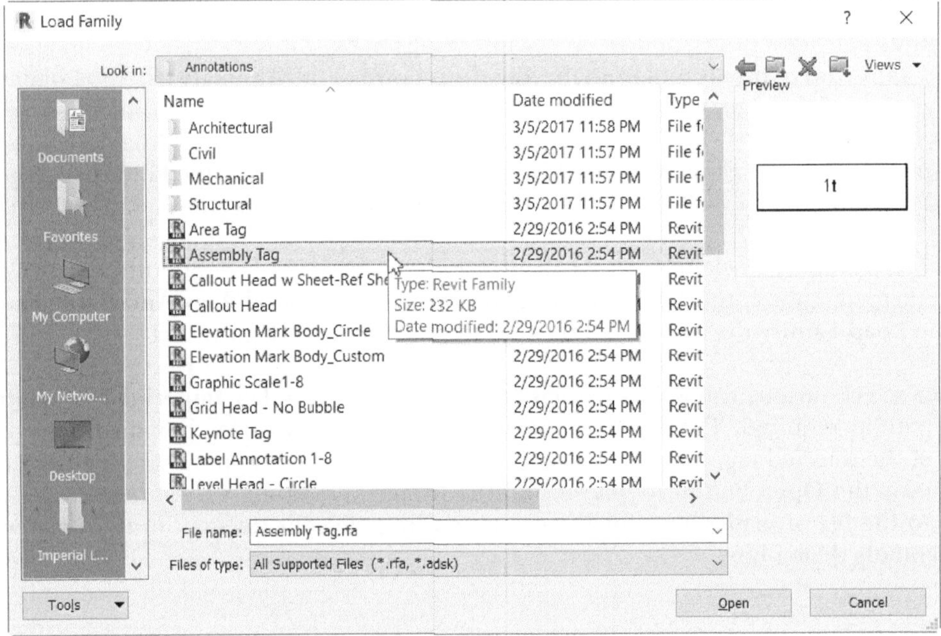

Figure 11-4 *The **Load Family** dialog box*

Another method of loading the tags is to invoke the **Tag by Category** tool and select the element to be tagged. In case, you select an element that does not have a corresponding tag already loaded, the **No Tag Loaded** message box will be displayed, as shown in Figure 11-5. This message box will inform that you have not loaded a tag for the selected object type. Choose the **Yes** button; the **Load Family** dialog box will be displayed. From this dialog box, select the desired file and choose the **Open** button; the tag will be loaded. After loading, when you move the cursor near the element, a preview image of the tag will be displayed along with it. Move the cursor to the desired position and click when the tag appears to place it. Next, select different elements of the same category and tag them individually. The added tag appears similar to the illustration shown in Figure 11-6. When you select a tag, its controls will be displayed, as shown in Figure 11-7.

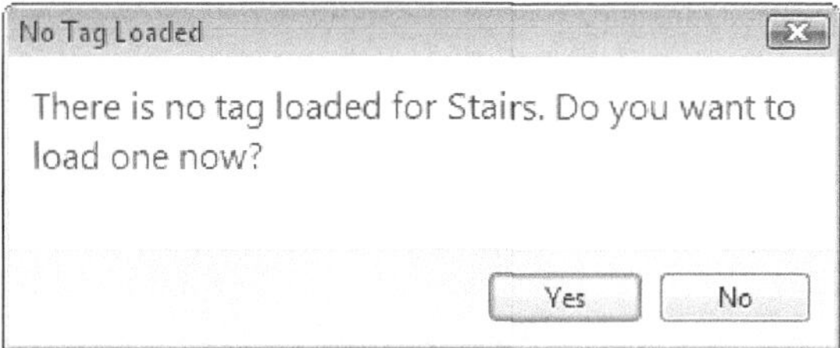

*Figure 11-5 The **No Tag Loaded** message box for loading tags*

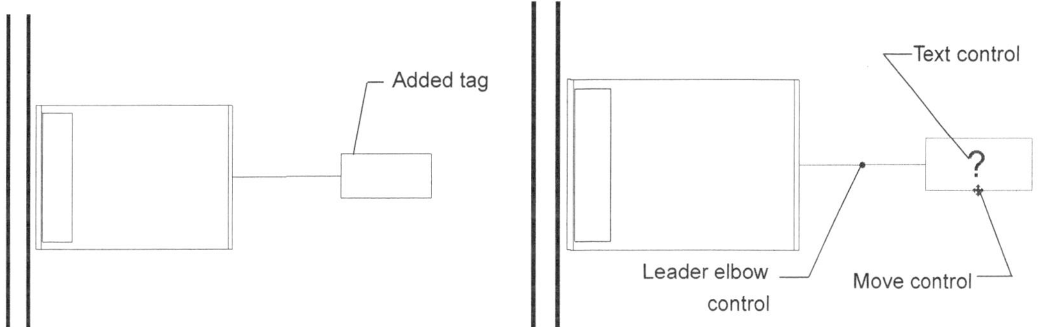

Figure 11-6 An example showing the element and the added furniture tag

Figure 11-7 The selected tag with its controls

The move control displayed with the tag can be used to move the tag to the desired location. The leader elbow control can be used to adjust the leader. The ? control can be used to enter text for the label of the tag. When you add a label, Autodesk Revit displays the message box informing you that you are changing a type parameter of the tag and that it could affect many elements. Choose **Yes** to continue; the entered value appears as the label in the tag.

Editing Tags

You can also edit an added tag easily. You can edit not only the tag label but also the tag type. To edit a tag, select the added tag and then select the desired tag type from the **Type Selector** drop-down list in the **Properties** palette to replace it with the existing tag type. The options available in the **Options Bar** can be used to convert a horizontal tag into a vertical one and vice versa. You can also add or remove the leader for an added tag using the **Leader** check box. You can modify the instance properties of the selected tag in the **Properties** palette. In this palette, you can modify the visibility of the leader using the check box for the **Leader Line** parameter. The direction of the tag label can also be modified using the **Orientation** parameter.

To modify the type parameter of the selected tag, choose the **Edit Type** button from the **Properties** palette; the **Type Properties** dialog box will be displayed. In this dialog box, you can select the arrowhead type for the leader from the drop-down list in the **Value** column of the **Leader Arrowhead** type parameter. Alternatively, you can invoke the **Type Properties** dialog box of the selected tag by choosing the **Type Properties** tool from the **Properties** panel of the contextual tab to modify the type properties.

Tip
It is easier to first add tags to all elements and then add the labels, or edit them individually. Autodesk Revit displays the alignment line to facilitate the placement of multiple tags at desired locations.

Note
*The contextual tab contains a set of tools that relate only to the context of that tool or element. For example, for a selected door tag, the name of the contextual tab will be **Modify / Door Tags**.*

Tagging All Elements in a View

Ribbon: Annotate > Tag > Tag All

The **Tag All** tool is used to tag all elements that are visible in the current view. On choosing this tool, the **Tag All Not Tagged** dialog box will be displayed, as shown in Figure 11-8. In this dialog box, there are two radio buttons: **All objects in current view** and **Only selected objects in current view**. By default, the **All objects in current view** radio button will be selected. The **Only selected objects in current view** radio button will be active and ready for selection only when objects to be tagged are selected prior to invoking the **Tag All Not Tagged** dialog box. The selection of the **All objects in current view** radio button ensures that all objects present in the current view will be tagged, provided their categories are selected from the **Category** column of the **Tag All Not Tagged** dialog box. The table below the radio buttons displays the list of category tags of all elements present in the current view and their corresponding loaded tags.

Note
*If the category of element you wish to tag does not appear in this list, you need to load the corresponding tag family and then use the **Tag All** tool.*

You can select only one category at a time. Select the category of elements to be tagged and the tag type to be used from the **Tag All Not Tagged** dialog box, as shown in Figure 11-8. You can select the **Leader** check box to add a leader to the elements. You can also modify the length and orientation of the leader in the dialog box by entering a value in the **Leader Length** edit box and selecting an option from the **Tag Orientation** drop-down list, respectively. Next, choose the **Apply** button to apply the settings to the current view. For example, you can tag all furniture elements in a layout plan view by using the **Tag All** tool, as shown in Figure 11-9.

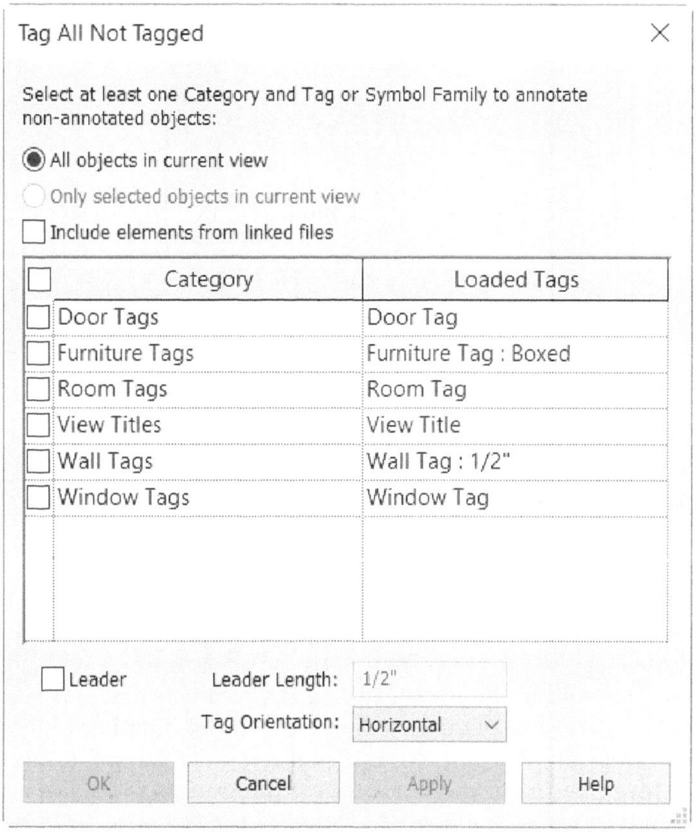

Tag All Not Tagged

Select at least one Category and Tag or Symbol Family to annotate non-annotated objects:

All objects in current view

Only selected objects in current view

Include elements from linked files

Category	Loaded Tags
Door Tags	Door Tag
Furniture Tags	Furniture Tag : Boxed
Room Tags	Room Tag
View Titles	View Title
Wall Tags	Wall Tag : 1/2"
Window Tags	Window Tag

Leader Leader Length: 1/2"

Tag Orientation: Horizontal

OK Cancel Apply Help

Figure 11-8 *Selecting the category of elements to be tagged from the* ***Tag All Not Tagged*** *dialog box*

In Revit, you can use the **Tag All** tool to tag rooms or areas. If you tag the elements whose visibility has been turned off, the **Tag Visibility Enabled** message box will be displayed. This message box displays a message informing that the visibility of all elements, whose visibility is turned off, will be turned on while adding tags. Choose **Yes** to continue; the tags will be added to all elements belonging to the selected category. You can then edit them individually. This process needs to be repeated for tagging elements category-wise.

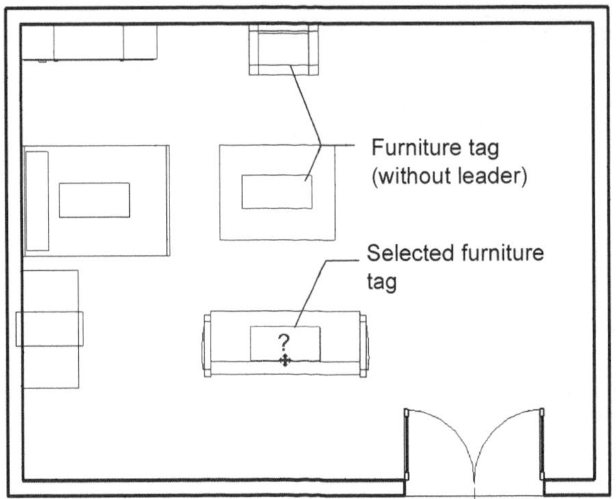

Figure 11-9 *The furniture elements tagged using the **Tag All** tool*

Tagging Treads or Risers

In a project view, you can display the numbering of treads or risers for a run in a component based stair. The numbering for the run can be displayed in a plan, elevation, or in a section view. Like any other annotation, the numbering in the treads or risers is view-specific. To add the numbers of tread or risers in a plan view, choose the **Tread Number** tool from the **Tag** panel of the **Annotate** tab; you will be prompted to pick a reference line of a stair to place the Stair or Tread number. Move the cursor and place it over the stair at a location where you desire to place the numbers. You can place the numbers in any of the following locations of the stair run: Left, Right, Center, Left Quarter, and Right Quarter. Click on the desired reference line on the stair run; the riser or tread will be numbered along the stair path, as shown in Figure 11-10.

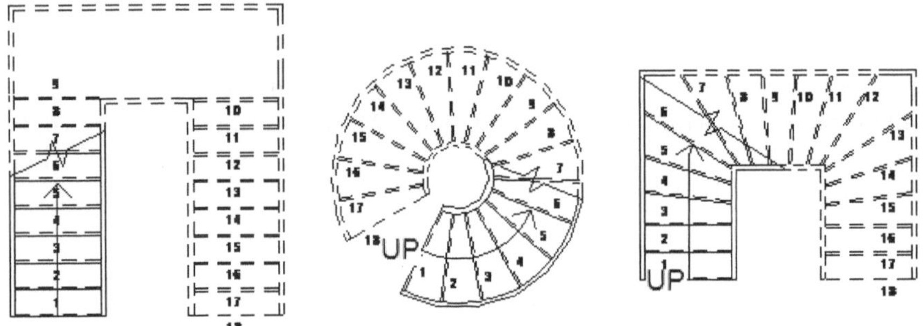

Figure 11-10 *Stairs with tread numbers*

Note

You cannot annotate the treads or risers in the sketch mode.

ROOM TAGS

Room tags are useful annotation tools for your drawing and they help you set information about the type of occupancy and define the enclosed area and volume. Autodesk Revit enables you to define and add a nomenclature to various interior and exterior spaces in a building project. This is important not only for identifying each space, but also for creating a room-wise project schedule. In Autodesk Revit, a room is also treated as an element of the project similar to the other elements such as a wall, door, or window.

In a building model, rooms and their tags are interrelated to each other. You can add a room with a tag. To do so, choose the **Room** tool from the **Room & Area** panel of the **Architecture** tab; the **Modify | Place Room** tab will be displayed. In the **Tag** panel of this tab, the **Tag on Placement** option is selected by default. As a result, the room added will have a tag. If you want to add a room without a tag, invoke the **Room** tool, deselect the **Tag on Placement** option from the **Tag** panel, and click at the desired place. You can add the room tag later by using the **Room Tag** tool from the **Tag** panel of the **Annotate** tab.

Autodesk Revit provides you with the option to keep the tag either in its original position or inside the room that has been moved. When you move a room that has a tag attached to it, an alert message will be displayed in the **Autodesk Revit 2018** dialog box, informing that the room tag is outside of its room. To enable the room tag such that it adjusts itself within the room at the new position, choose the **Move to Room** button from the displayed dialog box; the room tag will automatically move inside the room. Next, choose the **OK** button; a leader will be added to the room tag and the room tag will be placed outside the room that has been moved.

Room Separation

Ribbon: Architecture > Room & Area > Room Separator

Rooms are the defined spaces in a building and are used for specific utilities in a building project. They are divided into different parts to define the purpose of their utilization. They can be separated by a wall or without a wall depending upon the need of the project and the nature of the space. Revit defines a room by assessing the interior edges of the walls bounding the space. While working on large projects, you may need to define rooms by specifying the room boundary by using the **Room Separator** tool. This tool helps you add room-bounding lines to separate and adjust the room boundaries and create separate boundary enclosures without the intervention of a wall.

Invoke the **Room Separator** tool from the **Room & Area** panel; the **Modify | Place Room Separation** tab will be displayed. In this tab, the **Draw** panel displays various sketching tools that can be used to sketch the lines defining the separation boundary of the room. You can also use the **Pick Lines** tool from the **Draw** panel to pick the elements that define the room separation lines. To control the visibility of the separation lines, choose the **Visibility/Graphics** tool from the **Graphics** panel of the **View** tab; the **Visibility/Graphics Overrides for <contextual view>** dialog box will be displayed. From this dialog box, choose the **Model Categories** tab and expand the **Lines** group by clicking on the **(+)** sign in the **Visibility** column of the **Model Categories** tab. Now, if you select the check box beside the **Room Separation** option, the separation lines will be visible in the plan view and can be printed. If you clear the check box, the separation lines will be hidden in the plan view but the room boundaries will be retained. There may be instances when you do not want to use a particular wall as a room-defining wall. In this case, set the property of that wall as non-room bounding by clearing the check box for the **Room Bounding** instance parameter. On doing so, the selected wall will not be considered while defining the room.

For example, Figure 11-11 shows a 3D view of a room that has an intermediate wall with an arched opening. Assume that you want to ignore it while defining the entire room. To do so, clear the check box corresponding to the **Room Bounding** instance parameter in the **Properties** palette. Autodesk Revit will ignore the intermediate wall and the room boundaries will be extended to the exteriors walls, refer to Figure 11-12. In this manner, you can add identification to each space and later create a schedule of areas. You will learn more about creating schedules in Chapter 12 of this textbook.

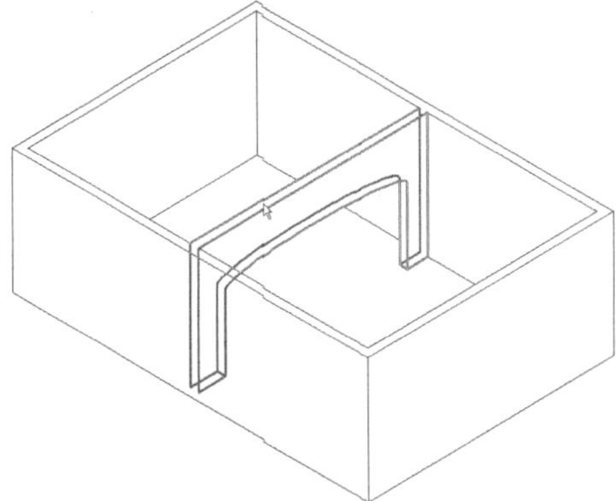

Figure 11-11 *An intermediate room with a wall having an arched opening*

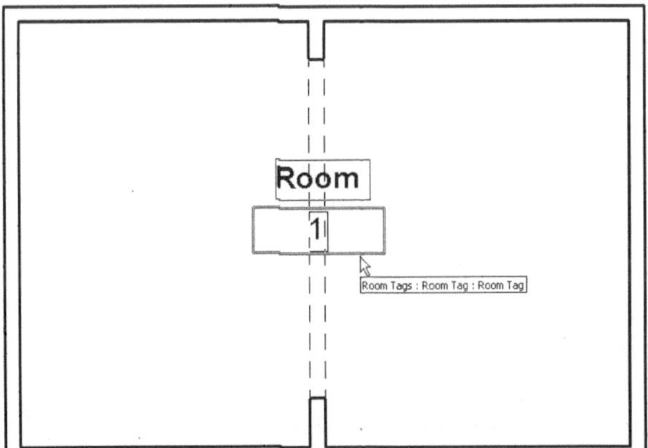

Figure 11-12 *Defining a room by changing the* ***Room Bounding*** *parameter of the intermediate wall*

Tagging Rooms

Ribbon: Architecture > Room & Area > Tag Room drop-down > Tag Room
Shortcut Key: RT

To add room tags, choose the **Tag Room** tool from the **Room & Area** panel; the **Modify | Place Room Tag** tab will be displayed. From the **Type Selector** drop-down list of the **Properties** palette, you can select any of these three options, **Room Tag**, **Room Tag With Area**, and **Room Tag With Volume**. To display the room tag along with its area, select the **Room Tag With Area** option in the **Type Selector** drop-down list. Similarly, you can display the volume of the room along with its tag by selecting the **Room Tag With Volume** option from the **Type Selector** drop-down list. By default, the **Room Tag** option is selected from the **Type Selector** drop-down list. As a result, the room tag is displayed without its area and volume. Now, after you select a specific type for the Room tag to be inserted, you can specify its instance and type properties from the **Properties** palette.

In **Options Bar** of the **Modify | Place Room Tag** tab, various options are displayed. These options work similar to the options described for the tags earlier in this chapter. When you move the cursor inside the room to be tagged, its boundaries will be highlighted. This indicates that the room is enclosed.

Note

If the room is not enclosed by bounding walls, the room tag will still be displayed. This means the room tags can also be added to the spaces that are not enclosed. However, the parameters such as area, perimeter, and so on will not be generated for these spaces in the schedule.

When you select any room tag, controls will be displayed on it. You can click on the text control to add a label to the room tag. Figure 11-13 shows an example of an interior layout plan with various room tags.

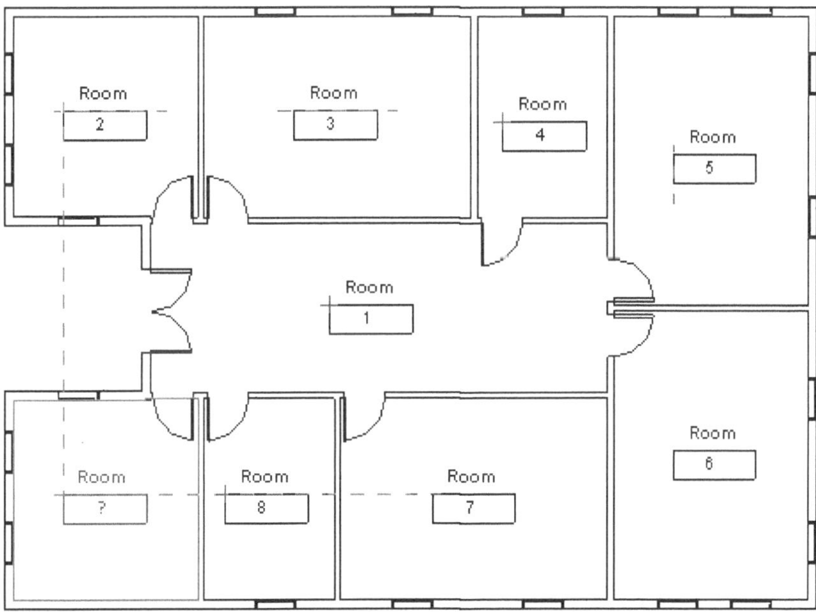

Figure 11-13 *An interior layout plan with various room tags*

Tip

By default, the room tags are visible in the floor plan in which they are created. Autodesk Revit automatically numbers them sequentially.

KEYNOTES

Keynote is a type of tag family. It is available for all model elements, detail components, and materials. Although you can add annotations to detail views using the **Text** tool, when it comes to labeling the components in detail, it is preferable to use keynotes. In keynoting, pre-defined list of notes is used. The notes are organized in a keyed list defined in a separate text file.

The keynoting data provided in Revit is based on a separate text file containing the list of different keynotes. In Autodesk Revit, keynoting can be done by following any of the two systems, the 1995 CSI (Construction Specifications Institute) Master Format system, and the revised version of the 1995 CSI Master Format system, which was introduced in the year 2004.

The 1995 CSI (Construction Specifications Institute) Master Format system is widely used in the United States. This format system follows 16 divisions to organize construction processes and materials and uses a tab-delimited series of keys matching the descriptive labels. In this system, you do not need to actually utilize the keys in order to use the keynoting functionality to label your drawings. Revit can add either the keys or the descriptive labels.

The revised version of the 1995 CSI Master Format system, introduced in the year 2004, has not yet seen widespread acceptability amongst the AEC professionals. This revised version is based upon 50 divisions to organize construction processes and materials.

Revit's keynote files (*RevitKeynotes_Imperial.txt*, *RevitKeynotes_Imperial2004.txt*, and *RevitKeynotes_Metric.txt*) are stored as an ASCII text file format in the **US Imperial** folder. These files can be opened in a notepad and can be modified according to the company's keynoting system.

Loading Keynote File

Before you can use keynoting in a project, you must first load a keynote file. To do so, choose the **Keynoting Settings** tool from the **Annotate > Tag > Keynote** drop-down; the **Keynoting Settings** dialog box will be displayed, as shown in Figure 11-14. The **File locations** edit box in the **Keynote Table** area of this dialog box displays the path of the keynote file. To change the file path or to select a different keynote file, choose the **Browse** button next to the **File Location** edit box; the **Browse for Keynote File** dialog box will be displayed. Choose the desired keynote file from this dialog box and choose the **Open** button; the **Reload Successful** message box will be displayed showing that the keynote table reloaded successfully. Choose the **OK** button; the desired file will now replace the previous file and its path will be displayed in the **File Location** edit box.

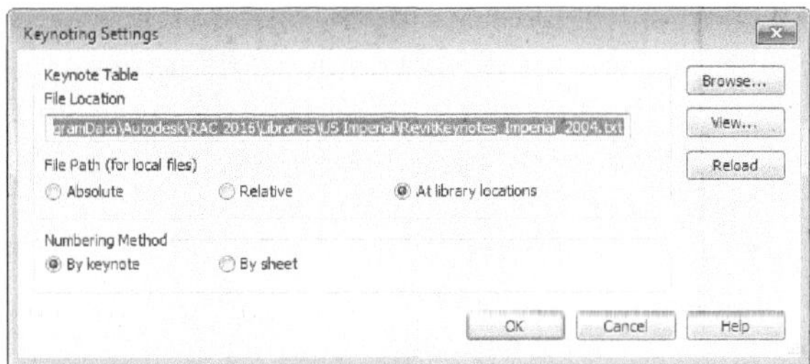

***Figure 11-14** The **Keynoting Settings** dialog box*

After you specify the desired file, choose the **View** button next to the **Keynote Table** area to display the **Keynotes** dialog box. This dialog box displays the keynotes but does not allow you to edit them. Next, choose the **OK** button to close it. Again in the **Keynoting Settings** dialog box, use other options and choose the **OK** button; the dialog box will close and the specified standards in the file will now be assigned to all the keynotes to be placed after the new settings.

Placing Keynotes

In Autodesk Revit, there are three types of keynotes that you can use to detail your drawing. The three types of keynotes are: Element, Material, and User.

The Element keynote annotates building elements. The tag reads the keynote assigned to the element in the model such as the keynote assigned to a wall or door, not to the individual layers or components of the wall or door. To add the Element keynotes in the detail view of your drawing, choose the **Element Keynote** tool from **Annotate > Tag > Keynote** drop-down; the **Modify | Place Element Keynote** tab will be displayed. Now, in the **Properties** palette, click on the **Type Selector** drop-down list and select the desired type from the list displayed. From the **Type Selector** drop-down list, you can select any of these four options of Keynote Tags: for Imperial **Keynote Tag Keynote Number**, **Keynote Tag Keynote Number-Boxed-Large**, **Keynote Tag Keynote Number-Boxed-Small**, or **Keynote Tag Keynote Text** (for Metric **M_Keynote Tag Keynote Number**, **M_Keynote Tag Keynote Number-Boxed-Large**, **M_Keynote Tag Keynote Number-Boxed-Small**, or **M_Keynote Tag Keynote Text**). If you select the **Keynote Number** option from the drop-down list, the added keynote will only display the keynote number in your drawing.

However, if you select the **Keynote Number-Boxed-Large** or **Keynote Number-Boxed-Small** option, keynote will be displayed with a number inside a large or a small box, respectively. If you select the **Keynote Text** option from the **Type Selector** drop-down list, the keynote will be displayed only with the keynote text in the drawing.

After you select a type from the **Type Selector** drop-down list, you can use the options in the **Options Bar** of the **Modify | Place Element Keynote** tab to select the keynote tag orientation (horizontal or vertical) from the drop-down list, and select or clear the **Leader** check box to show or hide the keynote tag leader.

After using the options from the **Options Bar**, move the cursor in the drawing area and click over the relevant element that you want to tag; an arrowhead will appear at this location. Next, click for the second point of the first segment for the leader. Now, click again to specify the final point for the end of the second segment of the leader and the location of the keynote tag. If the element already has a value assigned for the keynote, it will automatically appear in the tag. If the keynote is not yet assigned, the **Keynotes - <path of the keynote file>** dialog box will be displayed, as shown in Figure 11-15. Select any of the keynote values from the hierarchies in the **Key Value** column. Next, choose the **OK** button; the **Keynotes** dialog box will be closed and a keynote value will be assigned to the desired element and will display in the drawing.

The Material keynote annotates building materials. The text in the tag reads the keynote assigned to the material, such as the layers of a wall or the components of a door. The User keynote annotates the user-defined components. This type of keynote, will always display the **Keynotes** dialog box on clicking the relevant element. On doing so, you can select the keynote that you want to assign, thus overriding any predefined keynote. Since it is an override, it will not update if you later modify the type or material of the selected element. To add the Material or User keynote to your drawing, choose the **Material Keynote** or **User Keynote** tool from **Annotate > Tag > Keynote** drop-down. The method of placing any of these two keynotes is the same as that of placing the Element keynote.

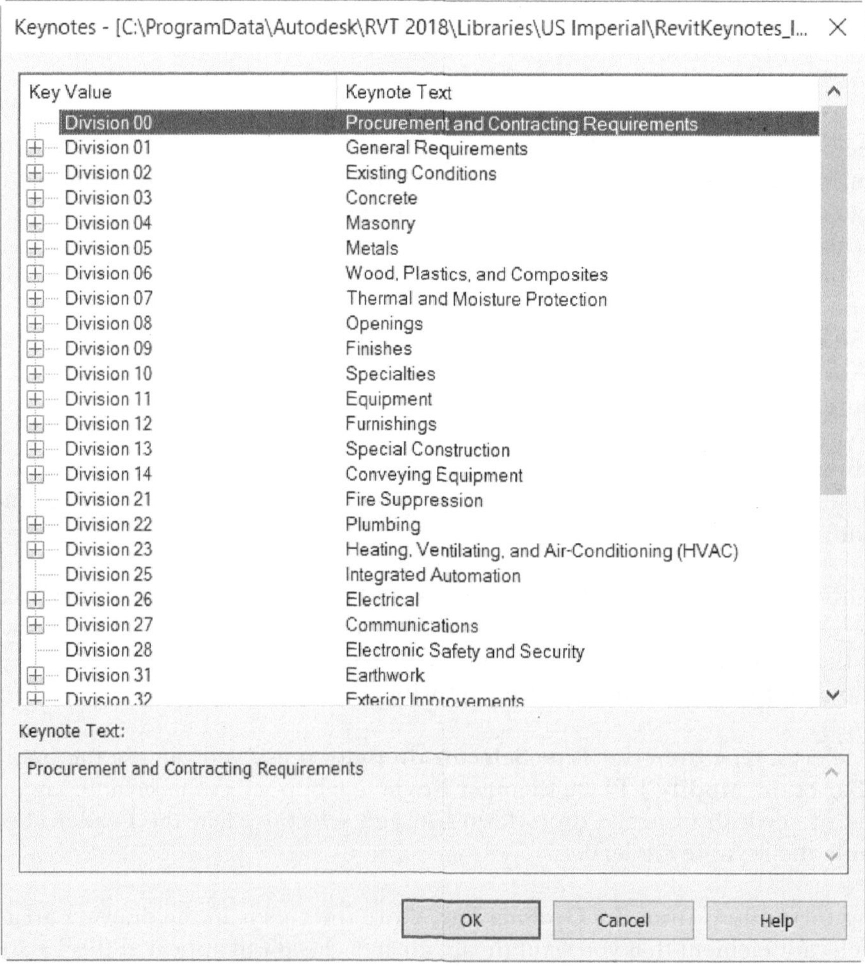

*Figure 11-15 The **Keynotes** dialog box*

The **Type Properties** and **Material Browser** dialog box can be used to assign the keynote values to different elements. To assign a keynote value in the **Type Properties** dialog box, select the desired element from the drawing and then choose the **Edit Type** button in the **Properties** palette; the **Type Properties** dialog box will be displayed. Click in the value column of the **Keynote** parameter; a **Browse** button will be displayed on the right. Choose this button; the **Keynotes** dialog box will be displayed. Choose the required keynote division and then choose the **OK** button; the **Keynotes** dialog box will be closed and the keynote number will be displayed in the **Value** column of the **Type Properties** dialog box. Again, choose the **OK** button to close the **Type Properties** dialog box; the selected elements and the other elements of the same type, and the element particular to the materials will automatically take the assigned keynote values.

Similarly, to assign a keynote value in the **Material Browser** dialog box, first invoke the **Type Properties** dialog box and then choose the **Edit** button in the **Value** column corresponding to the **Structure** parameter. On doing so, the **Edit Assembly** dialog box will be displayed. In this dialog box, click on the field under the **Material** column corresponding to the **Structure** function; a browse button will be displayed on the right. Choose this button; the **Material Browser** dialog box will be displayed. In this dialog box, choose the **Identity** tab; the information about the material will be displayed. In the **Revit Annotation Information** area, enter the desired keynote value in the **Keynote** edit box. Alternatively, you can choose the browse button next to the **Keynote** edit box; the **Keynotes** dialog box will be displayed. Choose the required keynote division and then choose the **OK** button; the keynote number will be displayed in the **Keynote** edit box. Now, choose the **OK** button; the **Keynotes** dialog box and the **Material Browser** dialog box will be closed.

Note

*The **Edit Assembly** dialog box will be displayed only for the **Wall** types.*

Adding Keynote Legends

Ribbon: View > Create > Legends drop-down > Keynote Legend

A keynote legend defines the keynote along with its property and functional description in tabulated format.

To create a new keynote legend, choose the **Keynote Legend** tool from the **Create** panel; the **New Keynote Legend** dialog box will be displayed. Specify a legend name in the **Name** edit box of the dialog box and choose the **OK** button; the **Keynote Legend Properties** dialog box will be displayed. To assign properties and parameters to the keynote legend, you can choose various tabs such as **Fields**, **Filter**, **Sorting/Grouping**, **Formatting**, and **Appearance** from the **Keynote Legend Properties** dialog box. Next, choose the **OK** button to exit the **Keynote Legend Properties** dialog box; a keynote legend will be added in the drawing. A keynote legend has two columns: **Key Value** and **Keynote Text**. **Key Value** in the legend lists all keynotes of the elements in the project that are tagged with a keynote and the **Keynote Text** column lists the description of the associated **Key Value** in the **Keynote Legend**.

A keynote legend gives information only about the elements that are tagged with a keynote. To view the keynote legend created by you, expand the **Legends** group in the **Project Browser**; the **Keynote Legend** will be displayed under the **Legends** node.

ADDING SYMBOLS

Ribbon:	Annotate > Symbol > Symbol

The **Symbol** tool is used to add 2D annotation drawing symbols to a project view to make it more informative. For example, you can use the **Symbol** tool to insert a north symbol, graphical scale, centerline symbol, and so on into a specific project view. Like other annotations, symbols are also view-specific in character.

When you choose the **Symbol** tool from the **Symbol** panel, the **Modify | Place Symbol** tab will be displayed. Now, from the **Type Selector** drop-down list which shows the loaded symbols in the project, select the required symbol. The instance and type properties depend on the selected symbol. You can modify the instance and type properties of a symbol from the **Properties** palette. The **Number of Leaders** spinner available in the **Options Bar** enables you to add multiple leaders to a single symbol. If the **Rotate after placement** check box is selected, the **Rotate** tool will be invoked as soon as you place the symbol. As a result, you can reorient the symbol after placing it.

The selected symbol can be added to the project view by clicking at the desired location. Figure 11-16 shows an example of the centerline symbol added to a plan view. Multiple instances of the symbol can then be placed by clicking on the locations of other instances.

Figure 11-16 *Adding the centerline symbol to the plan view*

ADDING DIMENSIONS

Dimensions play a crucial role in the presentation of a project. Although the building model conveys the graphical image of the design, yet to materialize it at the site, the building view must provide information and statistics regarding each element. Since the design drawing is used for the actual construction of a project, it is essential to describe the building parts in terms of actual measurement parameters such as length, width, height, angle, radius, diameter, and so on. All these information can be added into the project using dimensions. The information conveyed through dimensions is, in most cases, as important as the project view itself. It ensures that the project drawings are read and interpreted in appropriate way. Adding dimensions also ensures that there are no discrepancies between various elements used in the generation of the building drawings.

In an Autodesk Revit project, you can add dimensions based on the actual dimensions of the created elements. In other words, they are as truthful as the project elements themselves. The units play an important role in describing the detailing with which the project is required to be constructed. For example, the use of fractional inches indicates the amount of detailing that has been considered while generating the design. It also reflects the extent of detailing and the precision required for the accomplishment of the project. Therefore, the dimensions are used, not only to specify the sizes of elements, but also as the instructions to the persons involved in the project such as cost estimators, project managers, site engineers, contractors, supervisors, and so on.

You can dimension straight lines and arcs as well. There are two types of dimensions that can be created for an element: temporary dimensions and permanent dimensions. The temporary dimensions appear while creating or selecting the element, but they are not displayed in project views. On the other hand, the permanent dimensions appear in the views in which they are created and describe a particular size or distance.

In Revit, you can create linear dimensions, referencing circle, ellipse, or arc centers as well as dimensions from the intersection of lines, walls and references. The size of dimensions is based on the selected scale for the project. However, you can modify various parameters of the dimension. Autodesk Revit automatically calculates the dimensions of the selected element from the nearby elements.

You can also format the dimension texts as you do for the normal texts and can also adjust the width factor of the dimension text. You can set the dimension text as underlined, italicized, and bold by using the **Type Properties** dialog box.

The dimensioning options provided in Autodesk Revit enable you to dimension elements in a variety of ways. You can choose the option that is most suitable for the dimensioning of a particular element type. Remember that the dimensioning conventions and standards followed in the industry should also be considered while dimensioning a project.

Types of Dimensions

In Autodesk Revit, you can use two types of dimensions: temporary and permanent. By default, the temporary and permanent dimensions use the units settings specified in the initial start-up of the project. The temporary dimensions are not view-specific, whereas the permanent dimensions are view-specific. It means that if you change the view, the permanent dimensions will not be visible. These two types of dimensions are discussed in detail in the next section.

Temporary Dimensions

Autodesk Revit displays a dimension when you draw an element or place a component in a view. The dimension that appears dynamically to assist you in drawing and placing elements for your project is called temporary dimension. This type of dimension is not view-specific and can be seen in any view when you draw or select an element. The temporary dimensions help you in positioning the elements at the desired location and references. While sketching the lines instantly of a desired length and angle, the temporary dimensions can also help you speed up your drafting work.

Temporary dimension appears only in three instances. First, when you draw any element; second, when you select any element; and third, when you place any component in your project. In Autodesk Revit, temporary dimensions are displayed in blue color.

When you place a component in your project, the temporary dimension becomes a useful tool to guide the exact placing of the component with respect to a fixed element or a component. While placing a component, the temporary dimensions are created to the nearest perpendicular element or component with a predefined snap increment settings to assist in the proper placement of the component, as shown in Figure 11-17.

While using the temporary dimension, you can set the point of reference of the element you are placing or considering for reference. To change settings of the temporary dimension, choose the **Temporary Dimensions** tool from **Manage > Settings > Additional Settings** drop-down; the **Temporary Dimension Properties** dialog box will be displayed, as shown in Figure 11-18. This dialog box contains two areas: **Walls** and **Doors and Windows**. You can change the measurement reference of the temporary dimension for walls by selecting any one of the four radio buttons namely, **Centerlines**, **Center of Core**, **Faces**, and **Faces of Core** in the **Walls** area of the **Temporary Dimension Properties** dialog box. To change the point of references for placing and referring doors and windows, you can select any of the two options namely: **Centerlines** and **Openings** from the **Doors and Windows** area of the **Temporary Dimension Properties** dialog box.

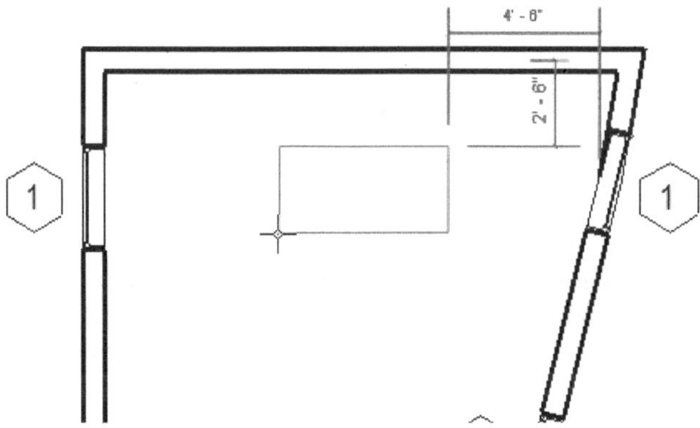

Figure 11-17 *Temporary dimensions displayed while placing a component*

These settings will help you set the references of walls, doors, and windows for temporary dimensions while creating or placing the elements or components in your model.

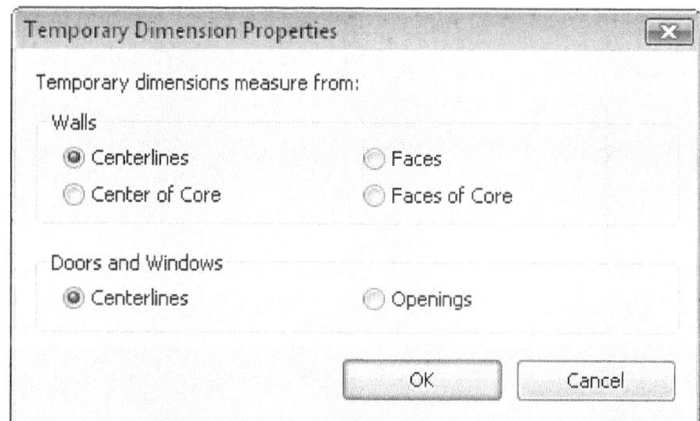

*Figure 11-18 The **Temporary Dimension Properties** dialog box*

Permanent Dimensions

Permanent dimensions are the dimensions that are placed during the documentation of the drawing. These dimensions occur in two states, modifiable and non-modifiable. After you have placed the permanent dimension using the appropriate dimension tools, you can adjust it according to your requirement. To do so, select the reference object of the required dimension; the state of the permanent dimension will change from non-modifiable to modifiable. A permanent dimension in its modifiable state allows you to change the current dimension provided that the dimension is not locked. The non-modifiable state of permanent dimensions refers to a state in which the size of the text and other related components appear in its true size.

Dimensioning Terminology

Before using the dimensioning tools, it is important to understand the dimensioning terms that are used in Autodesk Revit. Figure 11-19 shows common dimensioning terminologies that are discussed next.

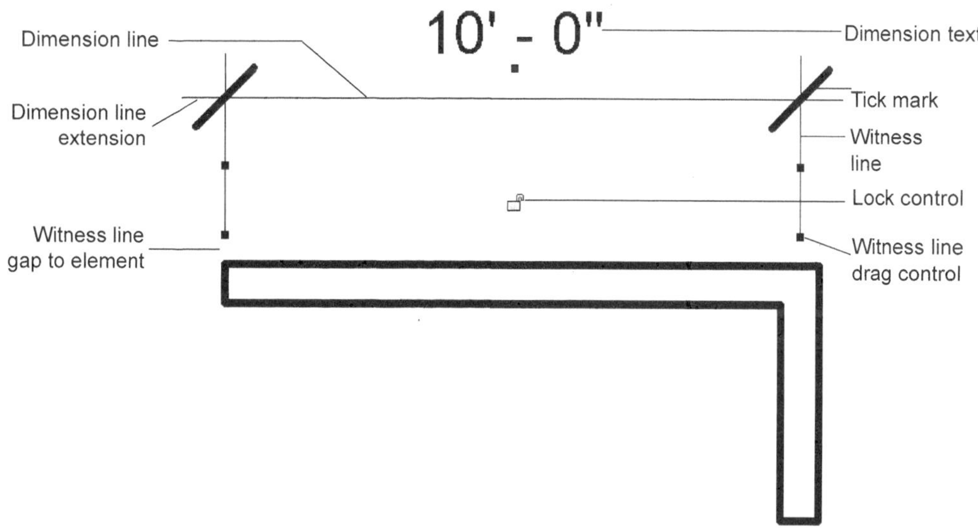

Figure 11-19 Various dimensioning terms

Dimension Line

The dimension line indicates the distance or angle that is being measured. By default, this line has tick marks at both the ends and the dimension text is placed along the dimension line. For angular or radial dimensions, this line is an arc.

Dimension Text

The dimension text represents the actual measurement (dimension value) between the selected points, as calculated by Autodesk Revit. This value cannot be modified manually, but you can add prefixes or suffixes to it. Note that the dimension text value is automatically updated when the size of the element is modified.

Tick Marks

Tick marks are added at the intersection of the dimension line with the witness line. As the drafting standards differ from company to company, Autodesk Revit allows you to select the tick marks from a range of in-built symbols. You can also modify its parameters.

Witness Lines

Witness lines are generated from the selected element and extend toward the dimension line. Generally, they are generated perpendicular to the dimension line. You can use the witness line drag controls to move them to the desired location. Another method of moving them is to select them and then choose the **Edit Witness Lines** button from the ribbon, or right-click and then choose the **Edit Witness Lines** option from the shortcut menu displayed. The dimension value automatically changes to the new distance between the witness lines. You can also control the parameters of the witness lines such as the gap to the element, extension beyond the dimension line, type, and so on.

Adding Permanent Dimensions

Permanent dimensions are added specifically for a particular measurement. In Autodesk Revit, you can access various dimensioning tools from the **Dimension** panel in the **Annotate** tab, as shown in Figure 11-20. You can choose the appropriate dimension type and the dimension tool to add dimensions to the element. The usage of these dimensioning tools is described next.

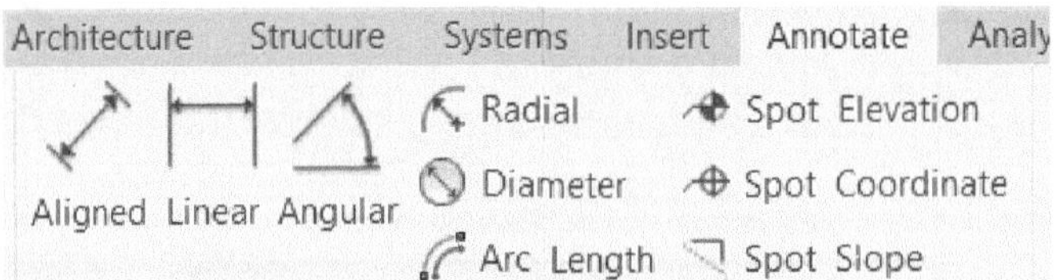

***Figure 11-20** Dimensioning tools in the **Dimension** panel of the **Annotate** tab*

Aligned Dimensions

Ribbon:	Annotate > Dimension > Aligned

The **Aligned** tool is used to dimension two orthogonal references or points such as the wall ends. To dimension two orthogonal references, invoke the **Aligned** tool from the **Dimension** panel; the **Modify | Place Dimensions** tab will be displayed. To change the type for the aligned dimension, select an option from the **Type Selector** drop-down list in the **Properties** palette. Next, to set the snap point for the cursor, select an option from the first drop-down list in the **Options Bar**. For example, if you select the **Wall centerlines** option from the drop-down list, the cursor will snap to the centerline of the wall when placed above the wall. Next, select **Individual References** from the **Pick** drop-down list. Now, place the cursor at a reference point on an element; the reference point will be highlighted when the system allows you to place the dimension. Now, left-click to specify the reference and then place the cursor at the location you want to place the next reference point and click. As you move the cursor upward, a dimension line will appear. Move the cursor away from the component and left-click again; a permanent aligned dimension will appear, as shown in Figure 11-21. This tool can also be used to dimension between the center of the arc wall and other walls or lines.

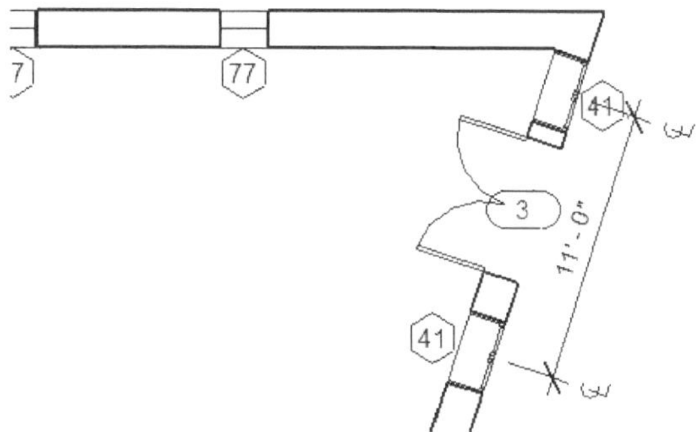

Figure 11-21 *Dimension created using the* ***Aligned*** *dimension tool*

If you select **Entire Walls** from the drop-down list in the **Options Bar**, the **Options** button will be activated. Choose the **Options** button; the **Auto Dimension Options** dialog box will be displayed. Select the check boxes in the dialog box. You can now dimension the openings, doors, windows, and the intersecting walls simultaneously. You can also define the references for dimensioning by selecting the **Centers** or **Widths** radio button in the **Select references** area. After selecting various options in the **Auto Dimension Options** dialog box, choose the **OK** button; the dialog box will close. Now, click on the wall that you want to dimension and then move the cursor away from the wall. Click again in the drawing. You will see that the walls, doors, and openings are dimensioned separately according to the references defined in the **Auto Dimension Options** dialog box.

Linear Dimensions

Ribbon: Annotate > Dimension > Linear

The **Linear** tool is used to dimension straight elements and distances. It measures the shortest distance between the two specified points. To dimension straight elements, invoke this tool from the **Dimension** panel; the **Modify | Place Dimensions** tab will be displayed. From the **Type Selector** drop-down list in the **Properties** palette, select an option to assign a type to the linear dimension that you want to create. After selecting this option, select the first point by clicking at the appropriate location. After selecting the first point, select the second point of reference for the dimension; the dimension line appears. You can now move the cursor to the desired location and click to place the dimension. The created dimension displays various parameter controls. You can invoke any other tool or press ESC to exit the **Linear** tool. The linear dimension will be created, as shown in Figure 11-22.

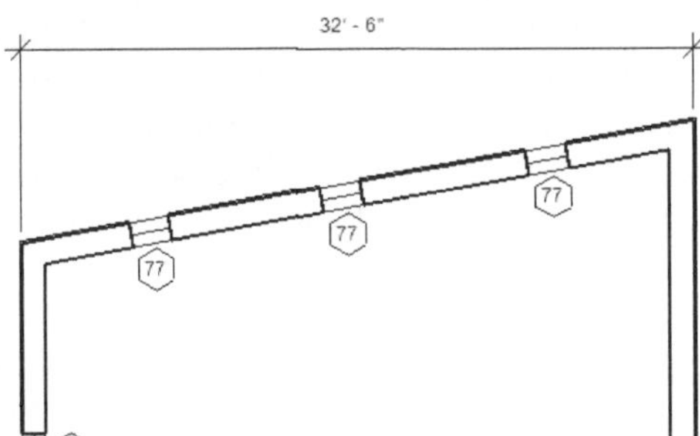

*Figure 11-22 Dimension created using the **Linear** dimension tool*

Angular Dimensions

Ribbon: Annotate > Dimension > Angular

The **Angular** tool is used to dimension an angle. This tool creates a dimension arc (dimension line in the shape of an arc with tick marks at both ends) to indicate the angle between two non-parallel elements, as shown in Figure 11-23. To dimension or measure an angle, invoke the **Angular** tool from the **Dimension** panel; the **Modify | Place Dimension** tab will be displayed. From the **Type Selector** drop-down list in the **Properties** palette, select an option from the list of types displayed. After selecting an option from the drop-down list, move the cursor and then click to place the dimension. This option can also be used to dimension when the angular dimension appears on the desired angle, as shown in Figure 11-24.

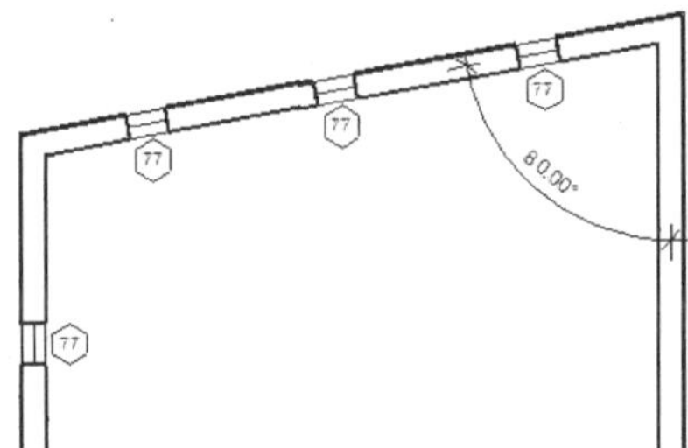

*Figure 11-23 Dimension created between two walls using the **Angular** tool*

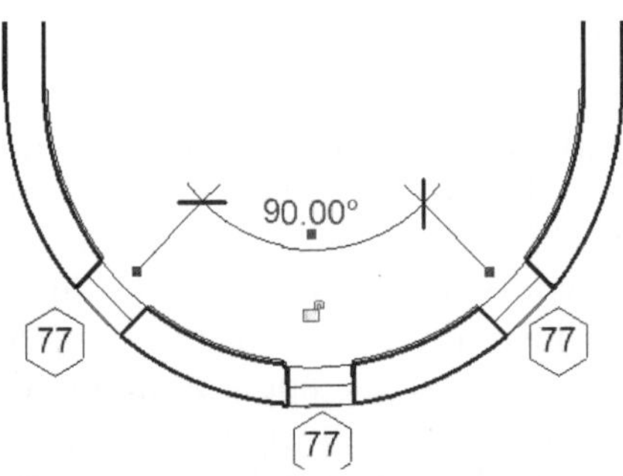

*Figure 11-24 Angular dimension created for an arc wall using the **Angular** tool*

Radial Dimensions

Ribbon: Annotate > Dimension > Radial

The **Radial** tool is used to dimension the radius of a circular or an arc profile, as shown in Figure11-25. The dimension text generated by Autodesk Revit has a prefix **R**, which indicates a radial dimension. To create a radial dimension, invoke this tool from the **Dimension** panel; the **Modify | Place Dimensions** tab will be displayed.

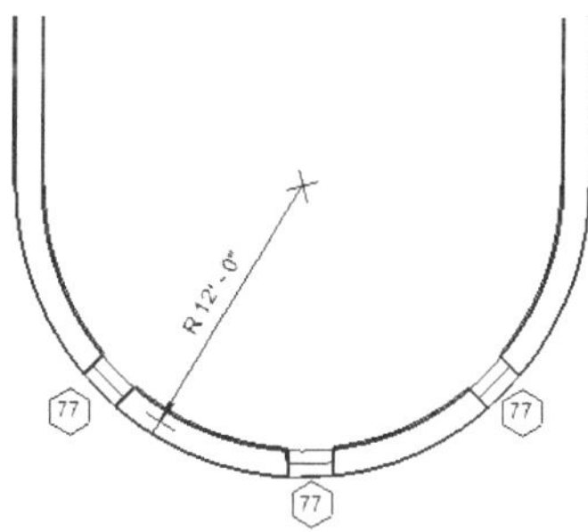

Figure 11-25 *Radial dimension created for an arc wall using the* ***Radial*** *tool*

From the **Type Selector** drop-down list, select an option from the list of types displayed. After selecting this option, move the cursor near the profile and click when the appropriate snap option appears; a center mark for the radial dimension will automatically be generated. Move the cursor and place the dimension.

Diametric Dimensions

Ribbon: Annotate > Dimension > Diameter

The **Diameter** tool is used to dimension the diameter of a circular or an arc profile. The dimension text generated by Autodesk Revit has a prefix **ø**, which indicates a diametric dimension. To create a diametric dimension, invoke this tool from the **Dimension** panel; the **Modify | Place Dimensions** tab will be displayed. Place the cursor on the curve of a circle or arc, and then click; a temporary dimension displaying the diameter of the curve will be displayed. Move the cursor along the dimension line, and click to place the diametric dimension.

Tip

You can press the TAB key to switch the reference point for the dimension between a wall face and a wall centerline.

Arc Length Dimensions

Ribbon: Annotate > Dimension > Arc Length

The **Arc Length** tool can be used to dimension an arc wall, based on its overall length. Invoke this tool from the **Dimension** panel; the **Modify | Place Dimensions** tab will be displayed. Now, select the dimension type from the **Type Selector** drop-down list.

Now, move the cursor near the arc wall and click to specify the radial point. Select the start and end references that will define the points between which the arc length is to be measured. Move the cursor away from the arc wall and click to place the arc length dimension; the arc length dimension will be created, as shown in Figure 11-26.

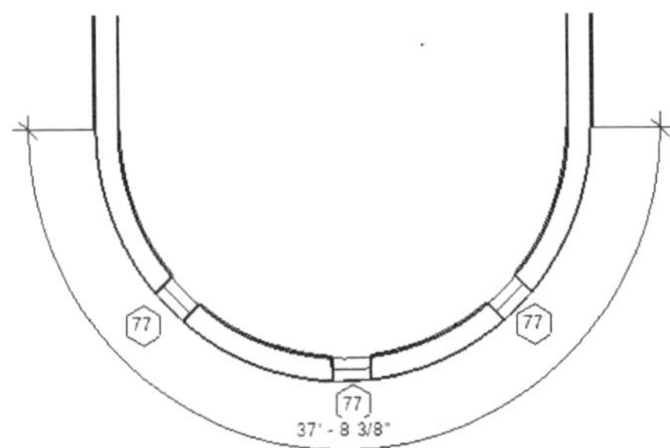

Figure 11-26 *Dimension created for an arc wall using the* ***Arc Length*** *tool*

Adding Alternate Dimension Units

In a project, besides the main dimensions, you can also display alternate dimensions in your model. These alternate dimensions can be both permanent and spot dimension types. The alternate dimension units display both imperial and metric units simultaneously in drawings. To add an alternate dimension to the main dimension in a project, select any of the dimension tool from the **Dimension** panel of the **Annotate** tab; the **Modify | Place Dimension** contextual tab and various related instance properties in the **Properties** palette will be displayed. Now, in the **Properties** palette, choose the **Edit Type** button; the **Type Properties** dialog box will be displayed. In this dialog box, choose the **Duplicate** button; the **Name** dialog box will be displayed. Enter the name **Alternate Units** in the **Name** edit box and choose the **OK** button to return to the **Type Properties** dialog box. Now, in the **Type Properties** dialog box, click on the **Value** field corresponding to the **Alternate Units** parameter; a drop-down list with the **None**, **Right**, and **Below** options will be displayed. You can select an option as per your requirement. On selecting the **Right** option, the alternate units will be displayed in-line to the primary units, and on selecting the **Below** option, the alternate units will be displayed below the primary units. Now, click on the **Value** field corresponding to the **Alternate Units Format** parameter; the **Format** dialog box will be displayed. In this dialog box, select the **Meters** option from the **Units** drop-down list, select the '**m**' option from the **Units Symbol** drop-down list and then choose the **OK** button; the **Format** dialog box will be closed. You can also assign square brackets '[]' to the **Alternate Prefix** and **Alternate Suffix** value fields. Now, choose the **OK** button; the **Type Properties** dialog box will be closed and the drawing window will be displayed.

To assign alternate units to a building model in the drawing, select the **Linear Dimension Style Alternate Units** option from the **Type Selector** drop-down list. Now, the cursor will change and the witness line of the selected dimension is subjected to change, as shown in Figure 11-27. You can select one of the options such as **Wall Centerline**, **Wall Faces**, **Center of core**, **Faces of core** from the drop-down list available in the **Options Bar** of the **Modify | Place Dimension** tab. Next, place the cursor at the face of the wall; primary units along with alternate dimension units will be displayed, as shown in Figure 11-28.

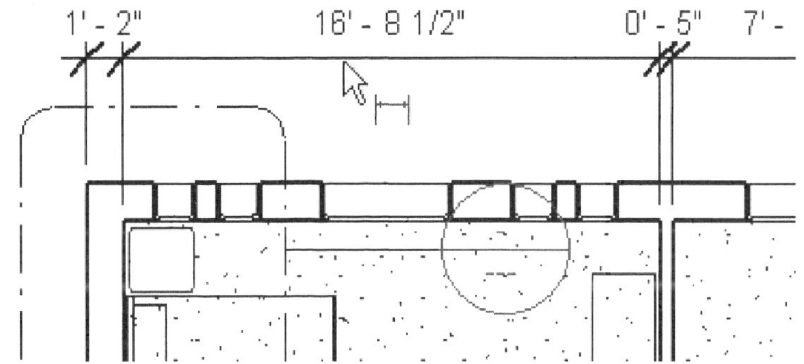

Figure 11-27 The witness line is subjected to change

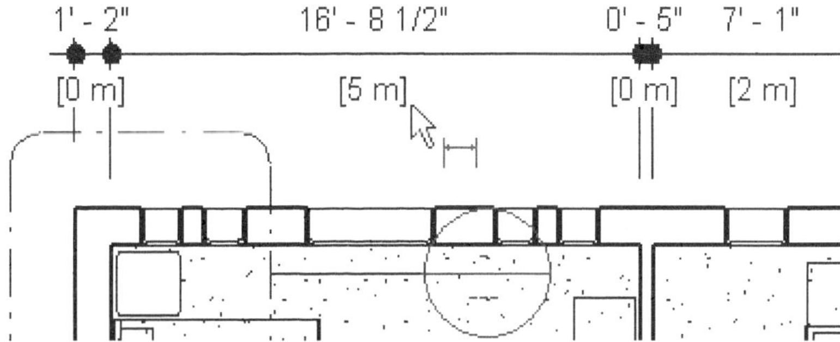

Figure 11-28 The primary units along with alternate units

Baseline and Ordinate Dimensions

You can dimension a series of elements and components simultaneously. This can be done by using the baseline and ordinate dimensioning techniques.

A baseline dimension is a stacked dimension that originates from a common baseline. It creates a referenced dimension from the first witness line which acts as a base for adding dimension, as shown in Figure 11-29. An ordinate dimension is generated to show the level of a particular point measured from a fixed point, called datum, as shown in Figure 11-30. The ordinate dimension of a point shows the measurement of its perpendicular distance from the datum or the origin point. Note that you can use the baseline and ordinate dimensioning techniques only for linear and aligned dimensions.

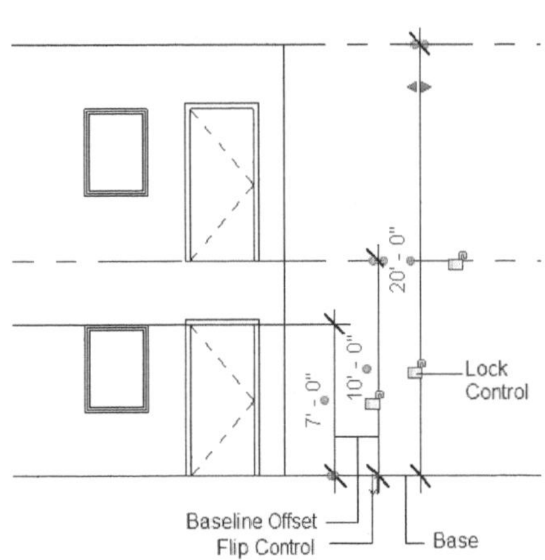

Figure 11-29 The selected baseline dimension and its components

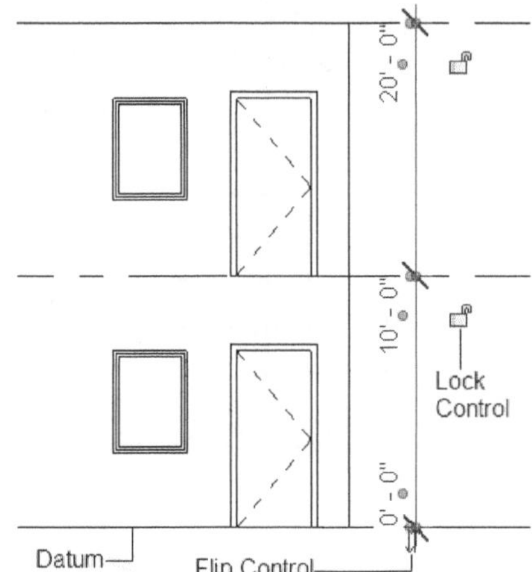

Figure 11-30 The selected ordinate dimensions and their components

Methods of Creating and Placing Baseline and Ordinate Dimensions

To create a baseline dimension or an ordinate dimension, choose the **Aligned** or **Linear** dimension tool from the **Dimension** panel in the **Annotate** tab; the **Modify | Place Dimensions** tab will be displayed. To create a new dimension style by using the baseline or ordinate dimension technique, choose the **Type Properties** tool from the **Properties** panel; the **Type Properties** dialog box will be invoked. Choose the **Duplicate** button from this dialog box and name the new dimension style in the **Name** dialog box as per the standard nomenclature system followed for the baseline or ordinate dimension.

To create a baseline dimension, in the **Type Properties** dialog box, click on the **Value** field corresponding to the **Dimension String Type** parameter and select the **Baseline** for creating a baseline dimension. Similarly, you can also set the value of the **Dimension String Type** parameter to **Ordinate** for creating an ordinate dimension. You can also invoke the **Type Properties** dialog box for the linear or aligned dimension type by choosing the **Linear Dimension Types** tool from the **Dimension** panel in the **Annotate** tab.

After creating the style for the baseline or ordinate dimension, you can use it in your project. To start dimensioning, use the same method as discussed earlier. After invoking any of the dimension tools (**Linear** or **Aligned**), select the desired type from the **Type Selector** drop-down list. To create a baseline dimension, select the first point for the dimension in the drawing area. This is the origin of the baseline dimension. Next, continue to select the necessary reference points and when you have reached the last reference point, move the cursor away from the last element, and click; the baseline dimension will be displayed.

You can control the distance between the consecutive baseline dimension lines before or after placing the dimensions in the drawing. To do so, enter the **Baseline Offset** value in the **Options Bar** to adjust the distance between the dimension lines. Similarly, to create an ordinate dimension, select the desired dimension style. Next, select a fixed point called datum (00) and then select other points in a series to get the perpendicular distance of these points with respect to the datum.

Editing Dimensions

You can edit various properties of a dimension before or after creating it. To modify any dimension in the drawing, select it; the **Modify | Dimensions** tab will be displayed. From this tab, you can use various options to modify and edit the dimension selected. The **Type Selector** drop-down list displays various in-built dimension types available in Autodesk Revit. You can select the appropriate dimension type from the drop-down list to assign it to the selected dimension.

Modifying Dimension Parameters

You can modify various parameters of a dimension, such as the dimension text font, gap of the witness line from the element, and so on, to achieve the desired dimension style. To do so, select the dimension created and then you can use various parameters in the **Properties** palette. You can add a leader to the dimension by selecting the check box corresponding to the **Leader** instance parameter. To access and modify the type parameters, choose the **Edit Type** button in the **Properties** palette; the **Type Properties** dialog box will be displayed, as shown in Figure 11-31. You can create a new dimension style with the parameters most suitable to the project by using the **Duplicate** button. Various type parameters and their usage are described next.

Tip

*You can invoke the **Type Properties** dialog box for individual type directly by choosing the corresponding tool from the **Dimension** panel.*

Using the **Leader** parameter, you can specify the type of line to draw for the leader. You can select the **Arc** or **Line** option from the drop-down list corresponding to its **Value** column. You can specify the type of tick mark for the leader by selecting an option from the **Value** column corresponding to the **Leader Tick Mark** parameter. You can specify the condition for the display of the leader. To do so, select an option from the drop-down list in the **Value** column corresponding to the **Show Leader When Text Moves** parameter. For the **Tick Mark** parameter, you can select the mark type to be used as the tick mark. Select the desired mark from the drop-down list in the **Value** column. The **Line Weight** parameter sets the line weight or thickness for the dimension line. You can select the value ranging from 1 to 16, depending on the desired thickness. The **Tick Mark Line Weight** parameter sets the thickness of the tick mark line. The **Dimension Line Extension** parameter sets the distance of the extension of the dimension line beyond its intersection with the witness line.

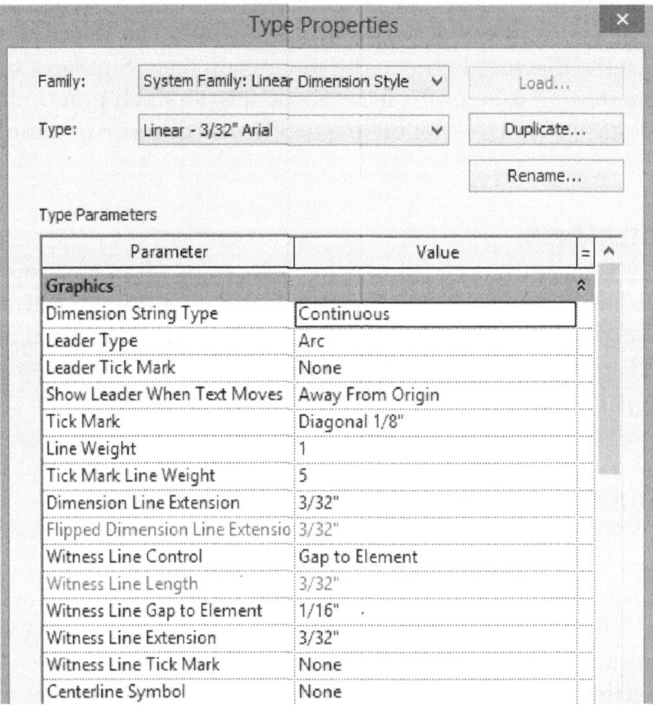

***Figure 11-31** The partial view of the **Type Properties** dialog box for dimensions*

In an equality dimension you can change the default label from **EQ** to a different text description for the dimension type. To do so, you can use the **Equality Text** parameter under the **Other** head. Also, you can assign an equality formula that is used to display equality dimension labels. An equality formula can be used for aligned, linear, or arc dimension types. This formula will allow you to display a single label for equality dimensions applied for more than two segments. For example, if an equality dimension includes three consecutive segments of length 5' (1524 mm), and you desire to display a single label displaying 3' x 5' (914 x 1524 mm) text, then you can use the equality formula.

To define the equality formula, choose the button displayed in the **Value** field corresponding to the **Equality Formula** parameter; the **Dimension Equality Formula** dialog box will be displayed. You can use this dialog box to define the way the single label will be displayed in the dimension. In the **Type Properties** dialog box, apart from various dimension settings, you can also set various parameters for the dimension texts such as **Text Size**, **Text Offset**, and so on. After modifying the parameter(s), choose the **Apply** button to apply the changes.

Controlling the Display of Tick Marks and Dimension Arrows

Revit provides you the flexibility to control the display of tick marks and dimension arrows while dimensioning small segments. When the dimensioning segments are too small to accommodate the dimension arrow, Revit flips the dimension arrows on the exterior side and displays diagonal tick marks, as shown in Figures 11-32 through 11-34.

To control the display of the tick marks and the arrow of a dimension, you need to select the dimension and invoke the **Type Properties** dialog box by choosing the **Type Properties** tool from the **Properties** panel. In the **Type Properties** dialog box of the dimension, there are two parameters: **Flipped Dimension Line Extension** and **Interior Tick Mark**. These parameters are enabled only when the **Tick Mark** parameter is set to **Arrow** type. The **Flipped Dimension Line Extension** parameter controls the length of the dimension line beyond the arrows, after the arrows are flipped. The **Interior Tick Mark** parameter displays the type of tick marks to be displayed in case the small multiple segments need to be dimensioned. You can lock the permanent dimensions once you have finished adding them to the project and add linear dimensions automatically to linear walls.

Figure 11-32 *Dimension arrows replaced by the tick marks*

Figure 11-33 *Dimension arrows on the interior side of the witness lines*

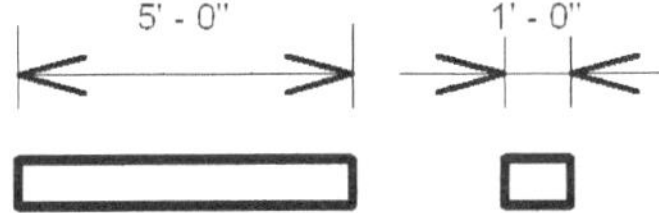

Figure 11-34 *The flipping of arrows on the exterior side in case of small segments*

Locking Dimensions

On adding a permanent dimension, a lock control symbol is displayed. It also appears when you select a permanent dimension. This symbol can be used to lock or unlock the dimension for the element. When the symbol is unlocked, you can modify the element that the dimension refers to. In such cases, the dimension is also modified with the element. When you lock a dimension, the element that it refers to is also locked with it. This means that you cannot modify the element or the distance between the points to which it refers to. You can, however, move the element along with the dimension. Once the dimension is locked, you must unlock it to change its value.

Creating Linear Wall Dimensions Automatically

Autodesk Revit provides the option to create dimensions automatically for linear walls. To do so, invoke the **Aligned** tool from the **Dimension** panel of the **Modify | Place Dimensions** tab and then select the **Entire Walls** option from the **Pick** drop-down list in **Options Bar**. This option enables you to pick a linear wall and create the dimensions associated with it. Next, choose the **Options** button from the **Options Bar**; the **Auto Dimension Options** dialog box will be displayed. In this dialog box, you can select the required references to create the dimensions. You can add dimensions to openings or to the walls intersecting with the selected wall. You can also specify whether to use the center of openings or their widths for giving reference. After selecting the appropriate option, select the linear wall to add the dimensions. When the **Openings** option is selected from the **Auto Dimension Options** dialog box, Autodesk Revit will create the dimensions that refer to the center or widths of openings. When you select the **Intersecting Walls** option, the automatic dimensions refer to all perpendicular walls intersecting the selected wall.

ADDING SPOT DIMENSIONS

Besides adding spot elevations, Revit also allows you to add coordinates. The spot dimensions are the dimensions that display the elevation level and the coordinates of a point with respect to the base level. They can be placed in the plan, elevation, or 3D views. You can add spot dimensions on non-horizontal and non-planar surfaces. You can use the spot elevation to specify the elevation level of points on a ramp, road, topographical surface, stairs, and other features. The properties of the spot elevation are similar to the properties of dimensions.

Placing a Spot Dimension

To place a spot dimension, choose the **Spot Elevation**, **Spot Coordinate** or **Spot Slope** tool from the **Dimension** panel of the **Annotate** tab; the **Modify | Place Dimensions** tab will be displayed. From this tab, select the type of spot dimension symbol to be used from the **Type Selector** drop-down list. Move the cursor near the edge of the element and click to select the point of reference when the edge of the element is highlighted. If you have selected the spot dimension without a leader, it will be placed at the selected point. If the type of spot dimension selected is with a leader, an arrow will start from the specified point. Move the cursor and click to locate the elbow of the leader. Now, move the cursor to the desired location and click again to place the spot dimension; the spot dimension will be created. Figure 11-35 show the spot elevations added to the plan view and Figure 11-36 shows the spot elevations and spot coordinates added to a 3D view.

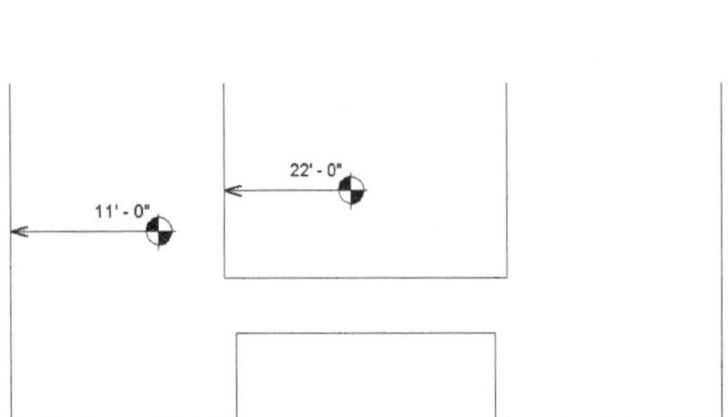

Figure 11-35 *Placing the spot elevation in the plan view*

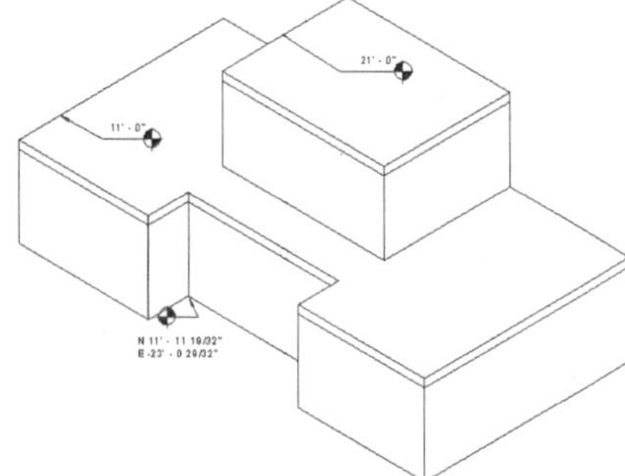

Figure 11-36 *Placing the spot elevation in the 3D view*

You can dimension the elevation of the top and bottom edges of elements or masses with thickness using the **Spot Elevation** dimensioning tool. When you place a spot elevation in your drawing, you can place it with a leader or without a leader. You can also add supplementary text along with the spot elevation and spot coordinates. You can maintain the relative location of the spot elevation and spot coordinates with respect to the referenced element when the elements are rotated. To do so, select the **Rotate with Component** check box in the **Type Properties** dialog box for the spot elevation and spot coordinates. You can display both the spot elevation and the spot coordinates in your project by using the **Spot Coordinate** tool.

Note

On choosing the spot elevation/coordinate, you will notice that similar to a temporary dimension, Autodesk Revit displays the temporary spot elevation/coordinates on moving the cursor to the required points.

Modifying Spot Dimension Properties

Similar to other dimensions, you can also modify various properties of spot dimensions before or after creating them. To modify the instance parameters of a spot dimension, select it; the instance properties of the selected spot dimension will be displayed in the **Properties** palette. In this palette, you can select the check box in the value field corresponding to the **Leader** parameter to display the leader with the spot dimension. In the **Properties** palette, you can specify other instance parameters to specify the settings of the text and the leader. You can modify the type properties of the spot dimension. To do so, select a spot dimension and choose the **Type Properties** tool from the **Properties** panel; the **Type Properties** dialog box will be displayed, as shown in Figure 11-37. An important property of the spot dimension is the elevation origin. By default, Autodesk Revit assumes the project origin as the base level. It then calculates the distance or the elevation of the spot level from this origin. You can use the default settings or specify a different elevation origin to calculate the spot elevations. This can be done by setting the value of the **Elevation Origin** type parameter to **Relative**. You can also select a placed spot level and modify its relative base level.

The **Type Properties** dialog box is used to modify the properties that affect the appearance of the spot level dimensions. The **Symbol** type parameter in this dialog box is used to specify the symbol for representing the spot dimension. Click in the corresponding **Value** column and select the symbol from the drop-down list. If you need the dimensions with a leader line, select the **Leader** check box in the **Options Bar**. The line weight and arrow type of the leader line is specified in the **Leader Line Weight** and **Leader Arrowhead** parameters, respectively.

The parameters such as **Text Size, Text Offset from Leader**, **Text Location**, **Text Font**, and so on can be set for the text used for representing the spot elevation. If required, you can also add suffix or prefix to the spot elevation using the **Suffix** and **Prefix** instance parameters.

Converting Temporary Dimensions to Permanent Dimensions

As described in the earlier chapters, temporary dimensions appear while you create various elements such as walls, doors, windows, and so on. They can be used to specify the size and location of the elements in the building model, refer to Chapter 3, Creating Walls. You can move or resize an element by clicking on the temporary dimension and entering a new value. When you create an element, a conversion control symbol will also be displayed along with the temporary dimension, as shown in Figure 11-38. When you click on this symbol, the temporary dimension will be converted into a permanent dimension, as shown in Figure 11-39.

Type Properties

Family: System Family: Spot Elevations — Load...

Type: Target w Leader — Duplicate...

Rename...

Type Parameters

Parameter	Value
Constraints	
Rotate with Component	☐
Graphics	
Leader Arrowhead	Arrow 30 Degree
Leader Line Weight	1
Leader Arrowhead Line Weig	5
Color	Black
Symbol	Spot Elevation - Target Filled
Text	
Width Factor	1.000000
Underline	☐
Italic	☐
Bold	☐
Suppress Spaces	☐
Text Size	3/32"
Text Offset from Leader	1/16"
Text Font	Arial
Text Background	Opaque
Units Format	1' - 5 1/2" (Default)
Alternate Units	None

<< Preview | OK | Cancel | Apply

Figure 11-37 *The* ***Type Properties*** *dialog box for spot dimension*

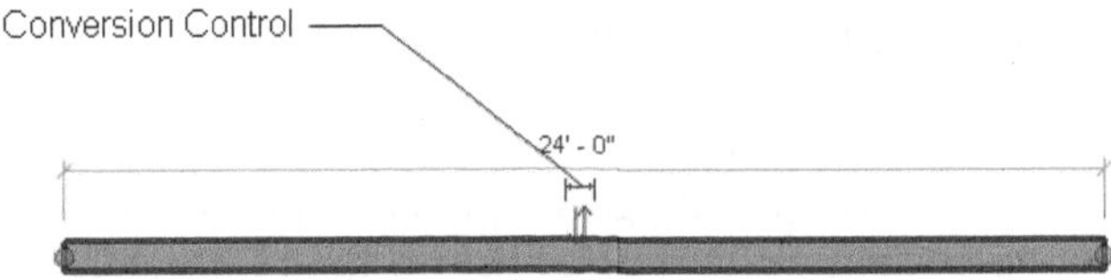

Figure 11-38 *A temporary dimension with the conversion control*

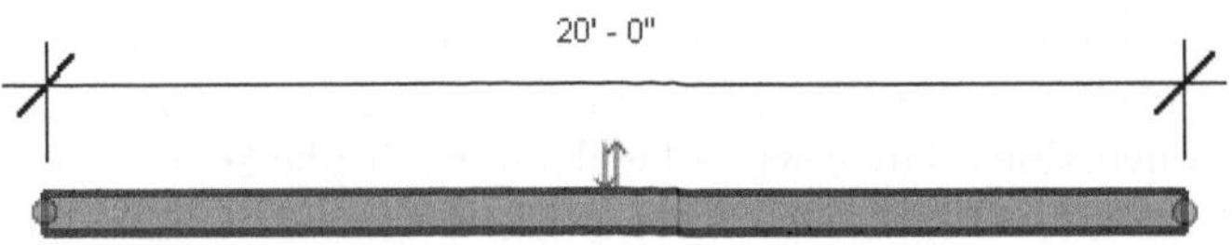

Figure 11-39 *Permanent dimension*

Tip

As described earlier, the temporary dimensions can be used to move or copy the elements to the desired locations. For example, when you modify the temporary dimension of a selected wall segment, it is modified as per the value of the length. Thus, in Autodesk Revit, building elements and their dimensions are parametrically associated with each other.

TUTORIAL

Tutorial 1 Apartment 1

In this tutorial, you will first add rooms to the enclosed spaces of the *Apartment 1* project created in Tutorial 1 of Chapter 8, and then name the rooms by using the **Room Tag** tool. You will also tag the furniture and then dimension the ground floor plan view based on the sketch plan shown in Figure 11-40. The dimensions shown on the top and right sides of the plan are referenced to the wall centerlines, whereas the dimensions on the bottom and left side are referenced to the wall faces. The exact location of the tags and dimensions is not important in this tutorial. Use the parameters given below for creating the dimensions.

(Expected time: 45 min)

1. Room tag- **Room Tag: Boxed**
2. Furniture tag- **Furniture Tag: Standard** with leader arrowhead- **Arrow 30 Degree**
3. Dimension Parameters:
   Dimension type to be based on the following options:
   For Imperial **Linear w Center - 3/32" Arial** and **Linear - 3/32" Arial**
   For Metric **Diagonal Center - 2.5 mm Arial** and **Linear - 3/32" Arial**

   New dimension type names- **Linear Dimension - CL** and **Linear Dimension - Faces**
   Tick Mark- For Imperial **Dot Filled 1/16"**
   For Metric **Filled Dot 3mm**
   Witness Line Gap to Element- For Imperial **1/4"**
   For Metric **6.35mm**

   The following steps are required to complete this tutorial:

a. Open the specified project file and the first floor plan view.
b. Use the **Room** and **Room Tag** tools and add rooms and room tags, refer to Figures 11-41 through 11-45.
c. Invoke the **Tag** tool and then load and add the furniture tags, refer to Figures 11-46 through 11-49.
d. Invoke the **Dimension** tool and set the type parameters.
e. Add dimensions to the project plan view using the wall centerlines as the reference, refer to Figures 11-50 through 11-52.
f. Add dimensions using automatic dimensioning with wall faces as the reference, refer to Figure 11-54.
g. Save the project using the **Save As** tool.
   For Imperial *c11_Apartment1_tut1.rvt*
   For Metric *M_c11_Apartment1_tut1.rvt*
h. Close the project.

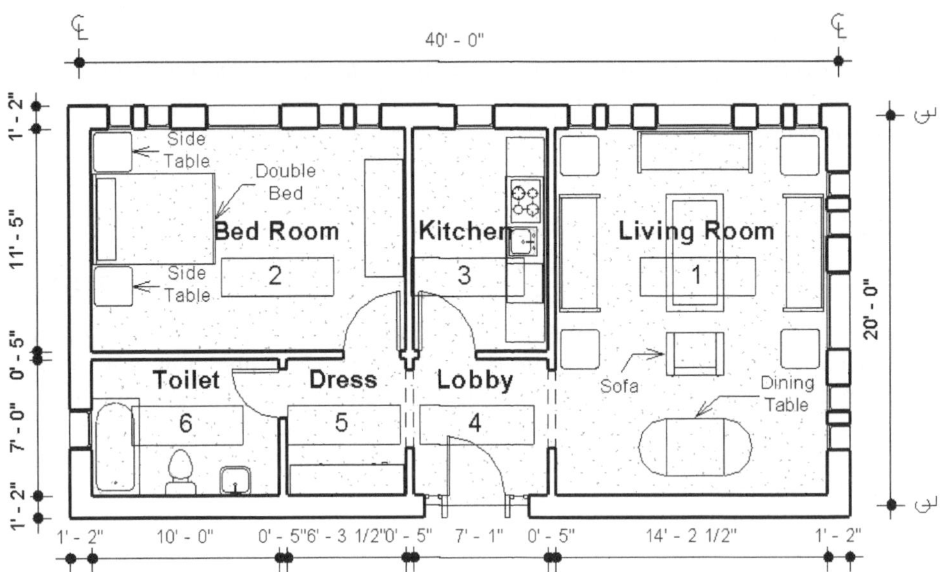

Figure 11-40 Sketch plan for adding room tags, furniture tags, and dimensions to the Apartment 1 project

Opening the Project File

1. To begin this tutorial, open the file that you have created in Tutorial 1 of Chapter 8 for the *Apartment 1* project.
   Choose **Open > Project** from the **File** menu and open *c08_Apartment1_tut1.rvt*. You can also download this file from *http://www.cadcim.com*. The path of the file is as follows: *Textbooks > Civil/GIS > Revit Architecture > Exploring Autodesk Revit 2018 for Architecture*.
2. After you open the file, double-click on **First Floor** in the **Floor Plans** head from the **Project Browser**; the first floor plan is displayed.

Adding Room and Room Tags

In this section of the tutorial, you will first add rooms (without a tag) to the enclosed space. To add room tags to the interior spaces, you need to invoke the **Room Tag** tool. The room tag is preloaded in the default template file. As this template will be used in this tutorial, you do not need to load it. Next, you need to move the cursor inside the enclosed space and click to add the room tag. You can then click on the tag and rename it. Autodesk Revit sequentially numbers the room tags. Therefore, you need to add them based on the sequence given in the sketch plan.

Note

In a building project, you can add rooms with tags attached to them and then rename the tags according to the space functionality. In this section of the tutorial, the rooms are added without tags and then the tags are added to make you understand the use of the ***Room*** *tool and the* ***Room Tag*** *tool separately.*

1. Invoke the **Room** tool from the **Room & Area** panel in the **Architecture** tab; the **Modify | Place Room** tab is displayed. Now, as you move the cursor in the drawing area, you will

notice a blue rectangle along with the default text **Room** attached to it. Next, you need to ensure that while adding rooms, the tags should not appear.

Note that the **Tag on Placement** button is not chosen in the **Tag** panel.

2. Move the cursor inside the living room (for location refer to Figure 11-40), and click in the enclosed space. Notice that when you click inside the enclosed space, it is shaded with blue color and the shading becomes transparent. Also, notice that the room is marked by two diagonal lines and a rectangle showing the extent of the enclosed space.

3. Without exiting the **Room** tool, repeat step 2 to add room to the kitchen, toilet, bed room, dress, and lobby, refer to Figure 11-40. Note that after adding the last room, you need to add press ESC to exit.

4. After adding the rooms to the spaces, you need to tag them.
Choose the **Room Tag** tool from the **Tag** panel of the **Annotate** tab; the **Modify | Place Room Tag** tab is displayed. Notice that when you invoke the **Room Tag** tool, all rooms in the drawing are displayed in a blue transparent shade with the diagonal lines showing their extents.

5. Move the cursor inside the living room; a Room tag attached to the cursor is displayed, as shown in Figure 11-41. Click to add the tag, as shown in Figure 11-42. Now, press ESC to exit from the **Room Tag** tool.

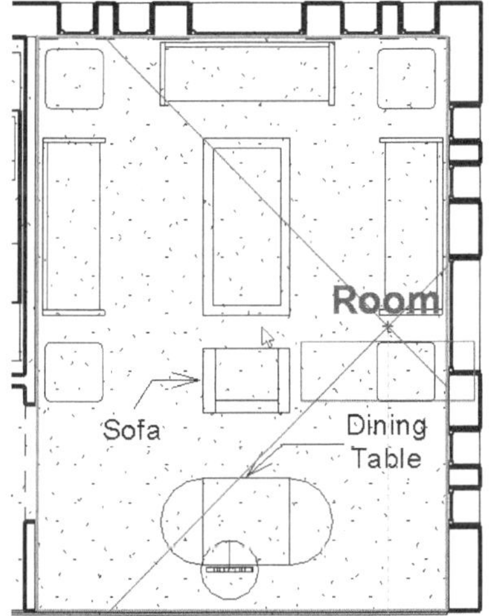

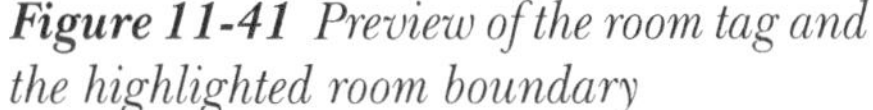

Figure 11-41 *Preview of the room tag and the highlighted room boundary*

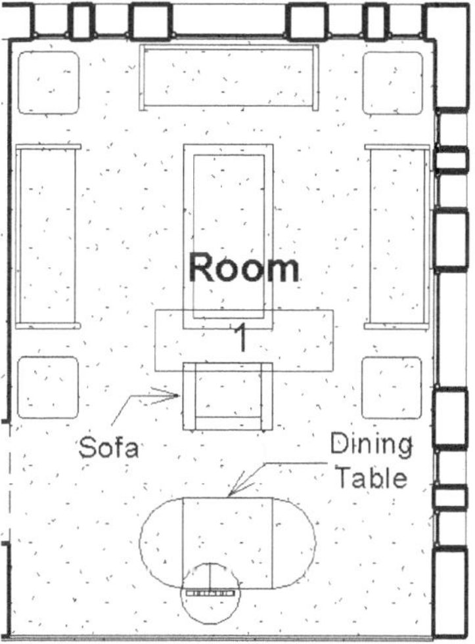

Figure 11-42 *The room tag added*

6. Select the room tag marked **1**(in the living room) and click on the text **Room**; an edit box is displayed.

7. Type **Living Room** in the edit box, as shown in Figure 11-43. Now, press ENTER and then ESC. The room tag is renamed, as shown in Figure 11-44.

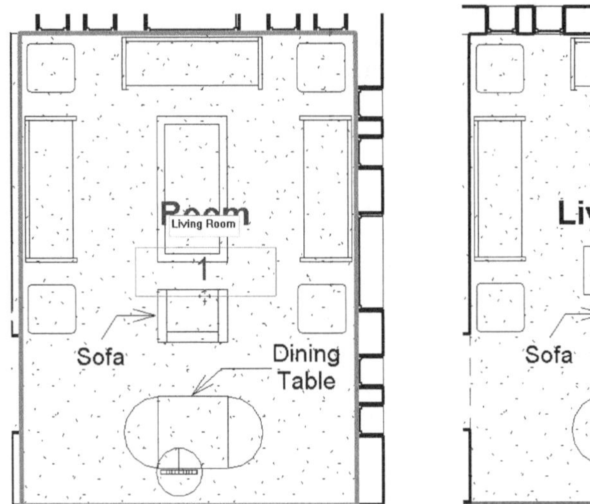

Figure 11-43 Renaming the room tag

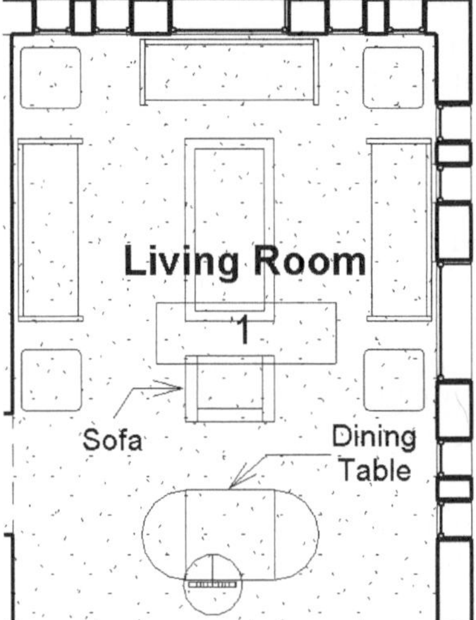

Figure 11-44 The renamed room tag

8. Repeat steps 5 to 7 to add and rename the room tags of the other rooms in the first floor plan in the sequence of the room tag numbers shown in the sketch plan. Also, refer to the sketch, as shown in Figure 11-40, to name the respective rooms.

Note

Depending on the view scale, the text height and other parameters of the room tag are automatically calculated by Autodesk Revit.

9. Click on each room tag and rename it based on the given sketch plan. Rename the tags for the bed room, kitchen, toilet, lobby, and dress. The completed room tags on the first floor level are shown in Figure 11-45.

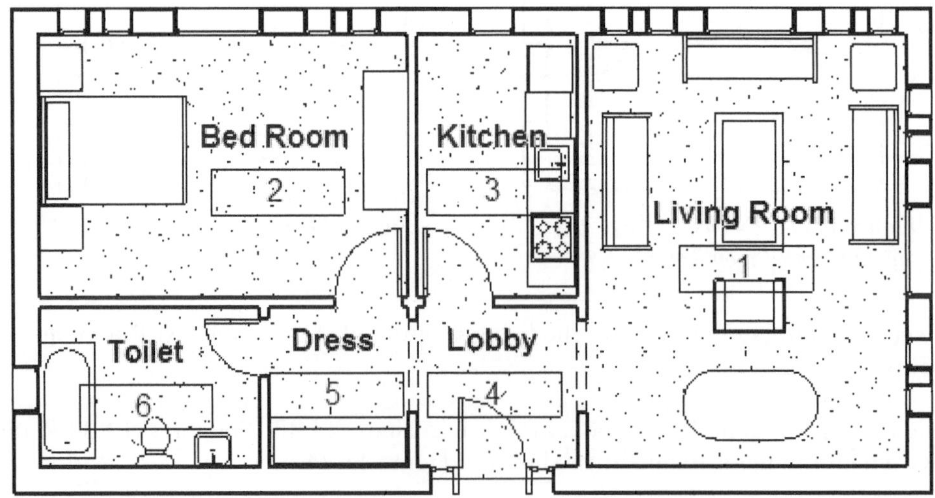

Figure 11-45 The room tags added to all rooms in the first floor plan view

Adding Furniture Tags

In this section of the tutorial, you will use the **Tag** tool to add tags to the furniture items. The furniture tags were not loaded into this project file initially. Therefore, when you select a furniture item, Autodesk Revit prompts you to load the furniture tag from its library. You can load the furniture tag and then add tags to the items. You can also set the properties of the leader as specified in the project parameters. The added tags can then be suitably renamed.

1. Choose the **Annotate** tab and then choose the **Tag by Category** tool from the **Tag** panel.

2. Move the cursor over the bed in the bedroom and click when it is highlighted.

   On doing so, Autodesk Revit displays a message box informing that no tag is loaded for the element type selected and prompts you to load the tag.

3. In the message box, choose the **Yes** button; the **Open** dialog box is displayed.

4. Browse to the **Annotations > Architectural** folder and select **Furniture Tag** from the list of family files.

5. Choose the **Open** button to load the furniture tag.

6. Move the cursor over the bed and click when the furniture tag is displayed at an appropriate location; the furniture tag is added without a name and a "?" symbol, as shown in Figure 11-46.

7. Press ESC and select the furniture tag added in the previous step. On doing so, the **Modify | Furniture Tags** tab is displayed.

8. From the **Type Selector** drop-down list, select **Furniture Tag: Standard** to replace the boxed tag with a standard furniture tag without a box, as given in the project parameters.

9. Next, click on the tag name marked **?** to display the edit box and enter the name **Double Bed** in it, as specified in the sketch plan shown in Figure 11-47. Next, press ENTER; Autodesk Revit displays a message box informing that you are changing a type parameter and it could affect many elements.

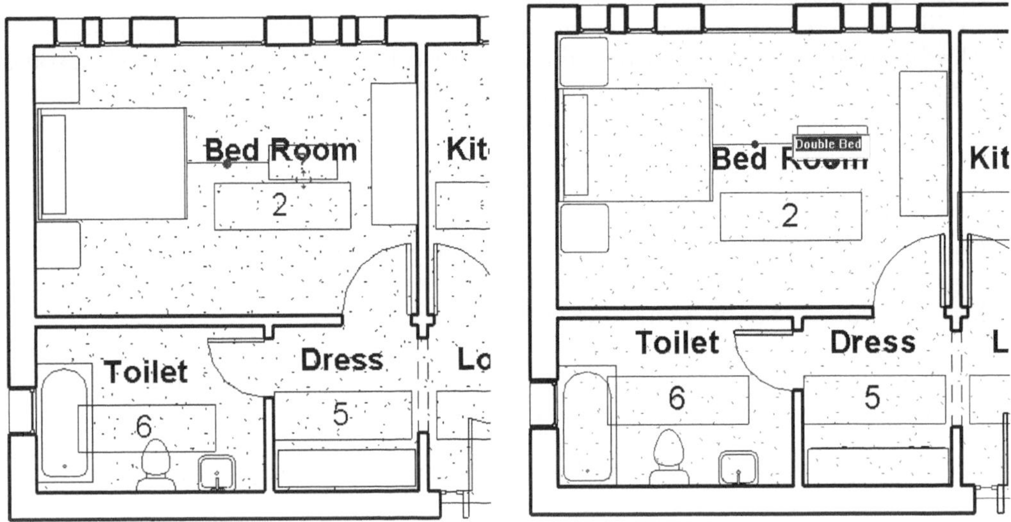

*Figure 11-46 Using the **Tag** tool to add a furniture tag*

Figure 11-47 Renaming the furniture tag

10. Choose **Yes** in the message box; the furniture tag is renamed.

    Next, you need to add an arrowhead to the furniture tag leader as per the parameters given.

11. Choose the **Edit Type** button from the **Properties** palette; the **Type Properties** dialog box is displayed.

12. Click in the **Value** column for the **Leader Arrowhead** parameter and select **Arrow 30 Degree** from the drop-down list.

13. Choose **Apply** and then **OK**; the **Type Properties** dialog box closes and the arrowhead is added to the furniture tag leader.

14. Drag the furniture tag upward to the new location using the move control, as shown in Figure 11-48.

15. Drag the leader elbow control represented by the blue dot upward in such a way that the leader appears similar to that shown in Figure 11-49.

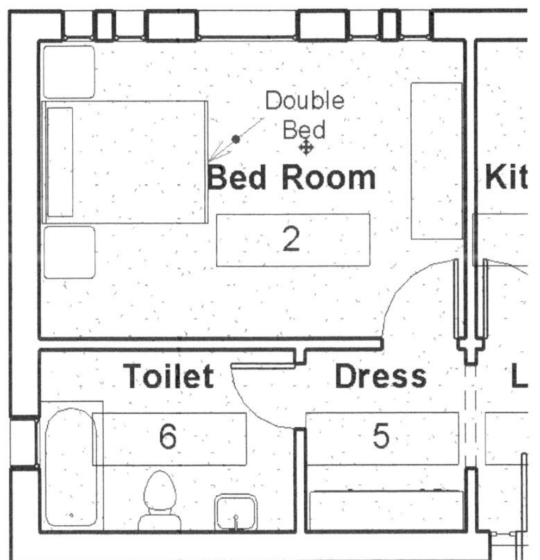

Figure 11-48 Dragging the furniture tag to a new location

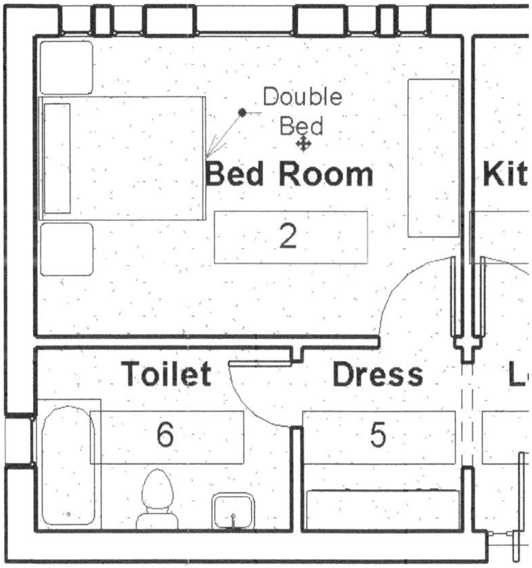

Figure 11-49 Adjusting the tag leader at the new tag location

16. Similarly, add other furniture tags to various furniture items in the **First Floor** plan view based on the given sketch plan.

Invoking the Dimension Tool and Setting the Dimension Parameters

In this section of the tutorial, you will add dimensions to the project view. Note that the sketch plan shows two types of linear dimensions, centerline and wall faces. You will select appropriate dimension type from the **Type Selector** drop-down list. Further, you will use the **Type Properties** dialog box to create a new dimension style and set the parameters for the new dimension type as specified in the project parameters.

1. To start dimensioning the project view.

   Invoke the **Aligned** tool from the **Dimension** panel of the **Annotate** tab; the **Modify | Place Dimensions** tab is displayed.

2. Select the required dimension style from the **Type Selector** drop-down list.
   For Imperial **Linear Dimension Style: Linear w Center - 3/32" Arial**
   For Metric **Linear Dimension Style: Diagonal Center - 2.5mm Arial**

3. Choose the **Edit Type** button from the **Properties** palette; the **Type Properties** dialog box is displayed.

4. Choose the **Duplicate** button to display the **Name** dialog box.

5. Enter **Linear Dimension - CL** in the **Name** edit box and choose the **OK** button.

6. Click in the **Value** column corresponding to the **Tick Mark** type parameter and select **Dot Filled 1/16" (Filled Dot 3mm)** from the drop-down list as specified in the project parameters.

7. Click in the **Value** column corresponding to the **Witness Line Gap to Element** type parameter and enter the value **1/4"(6 mm)**.

8. Choose the **Apply** button and then the **OK** button to close the **Type Properties** dialog box.

9. Repeat steps 2 to 5 to create another dimension style using the **Linear Dimension Style: Linear - 3/32" Arial** (**Linear Dimension Style: Diagonal - 2.5mm Arial** for Metric) and rename it to **Linear Dimension - Wall Faces**. Modify the **Tick Mark** and **Witness Line Gap to Element** parameters to the values used for the **Linear Dimension - CL** dimension style.

Adding Dimensions to the Project View

Now, add dimensions to the project plan. As all the dimensions to be added are linear dimensions, use the **Linear** option to create them. In the following steps, you will add dimensions to the project plan using different methods. First, you will create centerline dimensions on the right and topsides of the plan view using the **Wall centerline** and **Individual References** options. Next, you will use the **Wall faces** and **Entire Walls** options to create interior dimensions of various rooms placed on the left and bottom of the plan view.

1. Select **Linear Dimension - CL** from the **Type Selector** drop-down list.

2. Ensure that the **Wall centerlines** option is selected from the drop-down list displayed in the **Options Bar**, and **Individual References** is selected in the **Pick** drop-down list.

3. Move the cursor over the south wall near the right corner of the plan view until the object snap for the wall centerline is highlighted, as shown in Figure 11-50. Click to start the dimension.

4. Move the cursor vertically upward until the object snap for the centerline of the north wall is displayed. Now, click to specify the endpoint of the dimension distance; the dimension line is displayed and the dimension moves with the cursor, as shown in Figure 11-51.

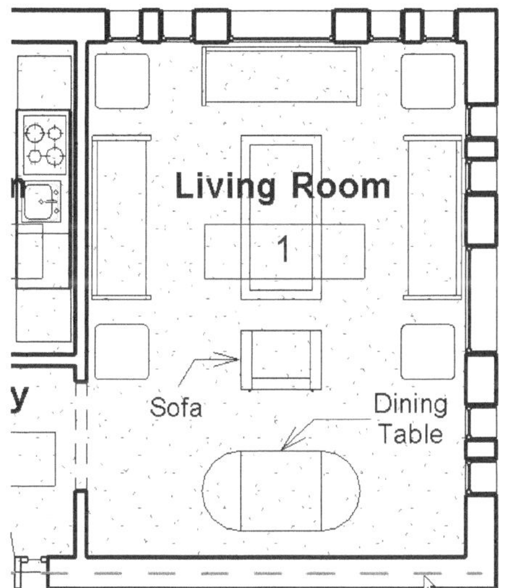

Figure 11-50 Selecting the wall centerline reference to start a dimension

Figure 11-51 Selecting the second wall centerline reference

5. Move the cursor toward the right until it crosses the exterior wall and click to specify the location of the dimension. The dimension is created and its controls are highlighted, as shown in Figure 11-52.

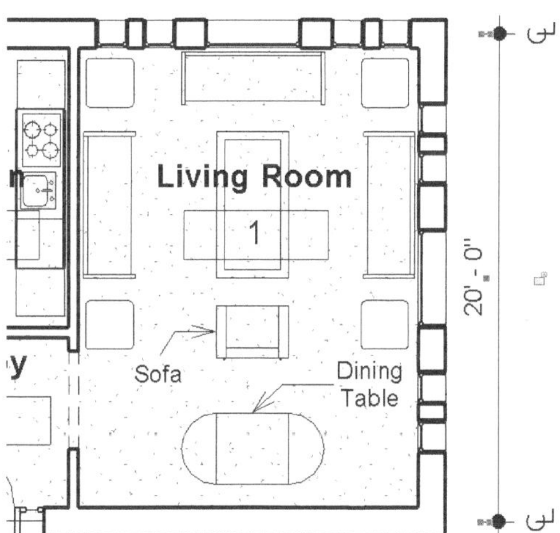

Figure 11-52 The dimension with its controls

6. To add dimensions to the north wall.

   Choose the **Entire Walls** option from the **Pick** drop-down list in the **Options Bar**.

7. Move the cursor over the north wall and click when it is highlighted.

Autodesk Revit automatically selects the centerlines of the end walls and displays the dimension.

8. Move the cursor such that the dimension appears above the north wall, as shown in Figure 11-53, and click to place the dimension.

***Figure 11-53** Adding dimensions to the north wall*

9. Select the **Wall faces** option from the drop-down list on the left of the **Options Bar**.

10. Choose the **Options** button in the **Options Bar** to display the **Auto Dimension Options** dialog box.

11. Select the **Intersecting Walls** check box and choose the **OK** button.

12. Move the cursor over the west wall and click when it is highlighted; the dimensions are displayed.

13. Move the cursor such that the dimensions appear on the left side of the west wall and click to add them, as shown in Figure 11-54.

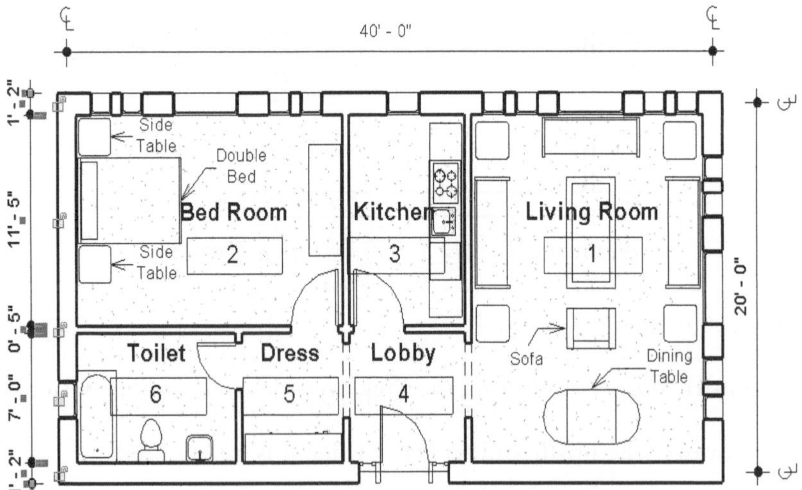

***Figure 11-54** Dimensions added to the west wall*

14. Using the above settings, add dimensions to the south wall.

Saving the Project

In this section, you will save the project file using the **Save As** tool.

1. Choose **Save As > Project** from the **File** menu; the **Save As** dialog box is displayed. Enter **c11_Apartment1_tut1 (M_c11_Apartment1_tut1)** in the **File name** edit box and then choose **Save**.

2. Choose **Close** from the **File** menu to close the project file.

The completed *Apartment 1* plan view appears similar to the sketch plan given for this tutorial.

Self-Evaluation Test

Answer the following questions and then compare them to those given at the end of this chapter:

1. The **Tag** tool is available in the __________ tab.

2. The __________ tool is used to tag all elements in the view that are not tagged.

3. Using the __________ tool, you can sketch the room separation boundary while adding a room tag.

4. The distance of the witness line from the selected element can be set in the **Value** column for the __________ type parameter.

5. The __________ tool is used to create a radius dimension.
6. When you drag a room tag, the leader is set automatically. (T/F)

7. You cannot control the visibility of tags in a project view. (T/F)

8. You can edit the tags added to a project view after adding them. (T/F)

9. Autodesk Revit automatically detects the boundary of a room while adding a room tag. (T/F)

10. Radial dimensions are used to dimension the angle between two inclined walls. (T/F)

Review Questions

Answer the following questions:

1. Which of the following parameters can be modified to convert a room-bounding wall into a non-room bounding wall?

   (a) **Unconnected Height** (b) **Base Constraint**
   (c) **Room Bounding** (d) **Top Constraint**

2. Which of the following options of the **Dimension** tool is used to create a dimension at an angle between the two points on an arc?

   (a) **Linear** (b) **Radial**
   (c) **Angular** (d) **Arc Length**

3. Which of the following type parameters is used to modify the distance between the dimension text and the dimension line?

   (a) **Witness Line Length** (b) **Witness Line Extension**
   (c) **Text Offset** (d) **Witness Line Gap to Element**

4. If an element whose tag is not loaded is selected for tagging, Autodesk Revit will prompt you to load the corresponding tag. (T/F)

5. You can add a leader to a room tag even after the tag is added. (T/F)

6. A permanent dimension can be converted into a temporary dimension. (T/F)

7. Temporary dimensions can be used to resize walls. (T/F)

8. When you select more than one element, the temporary dimensions can be made visible using the **Activate Dimensions** button. (T/F)

9. You cannot change the room tag type after adding it. (T/F)

10. The **Load from Library** tool can be used to load tags. (T/F)

EXERCISES

Exercise 1 Club

Add rooms (without tags), room tags, and dimensions (linear, radial, and angular) to the first floor plan view of the *Club* project created in Tutorial 2 of Chapter 8, based on the sketch plan shown in Figure 11-55. Use the **Room Separator** tool to demarcate and tag the entrance lounge and passages. Note that dimensions for the east side hall are referenced to the wall centerlines, while those for the west hall are referenced to the wall faces. You can provide suitable names to the modified dimension styles. Ensure that the scale for the first floor plan view is set to 1/16"=1'0" (1: 200). The exact location of the room tags and dimensions is not important for this exercise. Use the following parameters for creating room tags and dimensions.

(Expected time: 30 min)

1. Room Tags:
   Room Tag with Area

2. Dimension Parameters:
   For Imperial Tick Mark- **Arrow Filled 30 Degree**
   Witness Line Gap to Element- **1/8"**

Text Size- **1/8"**
Text Offset- **1/16"**

For Metric Tick Mark- **Arrow Filled 30 Degree**
Witness Line Gap to Element- **3mm**
Text Size- **3mm**
Text Offset- **6mm**

3. Name of the file to be saved-
   For Imperial **c11_Club_ex1**
   For Metric **M_c11_Club_ex1**

Note

Dimensions and area values may deviate slightly from that shown in the sketch plan.

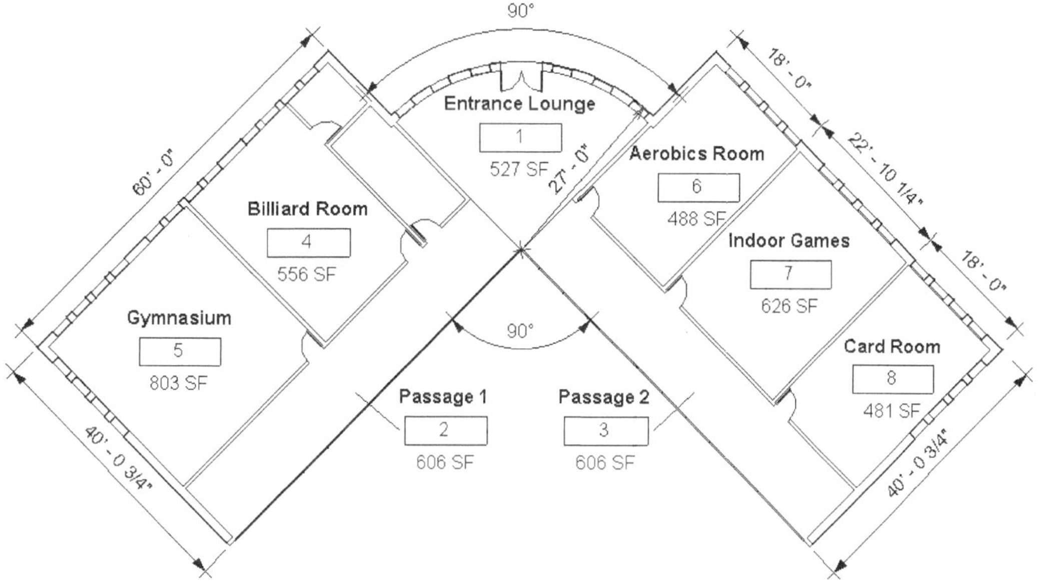

Figure 11-55 *Sketch plan for adding room tags and dimensions to the Club project*

Exercise 2 Elevator and Stair Lobby

Add text and dimensions to the first floor plan view of the *Elevator and Stairs Lobby* project created in Tutorial 3 of Chapter 8. Figure 11-56 shows partial first floor sketch plan of the project. The dimensions are to be added symmetrically on both sides of the vertical axis. Ensure that the view plan scale is set to 1/8"=1'0" (1: 400). All dimensions have wall centerlines as the reference. The exact location of the tags and dimensions is not important for this exercise. Use the following parameters for creating the dimensions. **(Expected time: 30 min)**

1. Dimension Parameters:

   For Imperial
   - Dimension type to be based on: **Linear w Center 3/32" Arial**
   - New dimension type name- **Linear 3/32" Arial-Stairs**
   - Tick Mark- **Diagonal 1/8"**
   - Witness Line Gap to Element- **1/8"**

   For Metric
   - Dimension type to be based on: **Diagonal Center 2.5 mm Arial**
   - New dimension type name- **Linear 2.5 mm Arial-Stairs**
   - Tick Mark- **Diagonal 3mm**
   - Witness Line Gap to Element- **3mm**

2. Name of the file to be saved-

   For Imperial **c11_ElevatorandStairLobby_ex2**

   For Metric **M_c11_ElevatorandStairLobby_ex2**

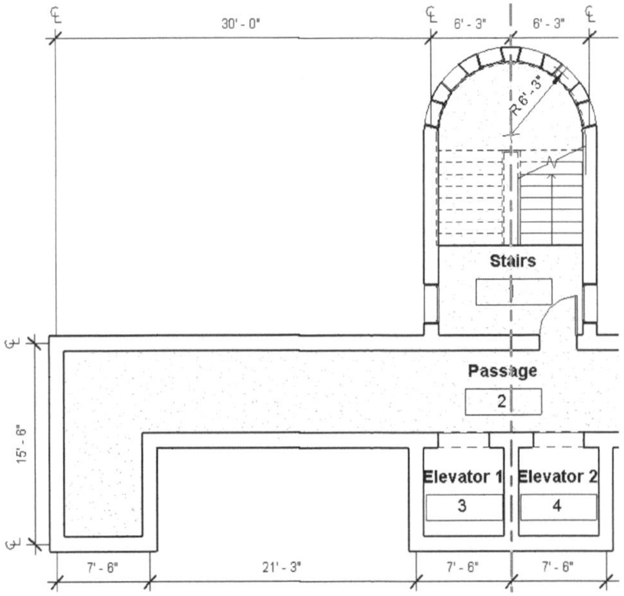

Figure 11-56 Partial sketch plan for adding text and dimensions to the Elevator and Stair Lobby project

Exercise 3 Building 1

Create the wall profile shown in Figure 11-57 using the wall centerline dimensions given in the plan. Also, create the dimensions for the profile. You can assume various dimension parameters for this exercise. Save the project file as *c11_Building1_ex3.rvt(M_c11_Building1_ex3.rvt).*

(Expected time: 15 min)

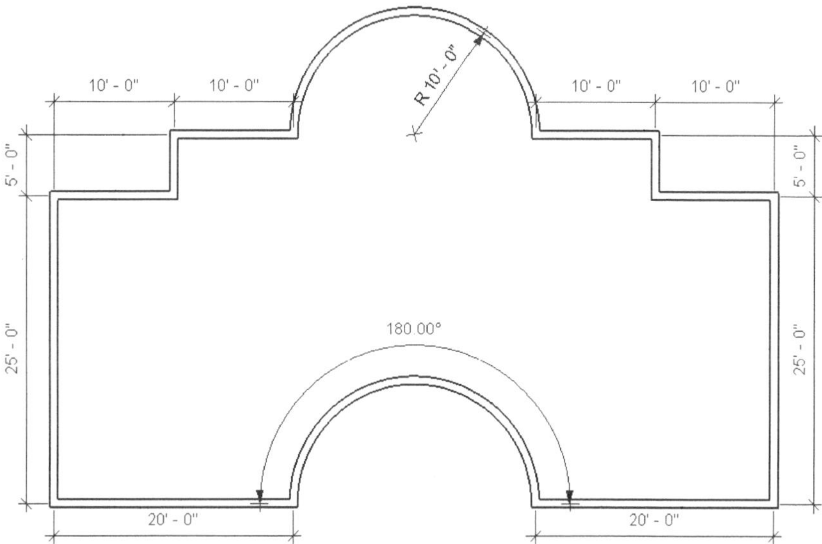

Figure 11-57 *Sketch plan for creating the wall profile and dimensions*

Exercise 4 Annotations

Add text and dimensions to the floor plan view of the residential project created in Exercise 2 of Chapter 8. Figure 11-58 shows the first floor sketch plan of the project. The dimensions are to be added symmetrically on both sides of the vertical axis. Ensure that the view plan scale is set to 1/8"=1'0" (1: 100). All dimensions have wall centerlines as the reference. The exact location of the tags and dimensions is not important for this exercise. Use the following parameters for creating the dimensions. **(Expected time: 30 min)**

1. Dimension Parameters:

   For Imperial Dimension type to be based on: **Linear 3/32" Arial**
   Witness Line Gap to Element- **1/16"**

   For Metric Dimension type to be based on: **Linear 2.5 mm Arial**
   Witness Line Gap to Element- **3mm**

2. Name of the file to be saved-

   For Imperial **c11_residential_annonations_ex4**
   For Metric **M_c11_residential_annotations_ex4**

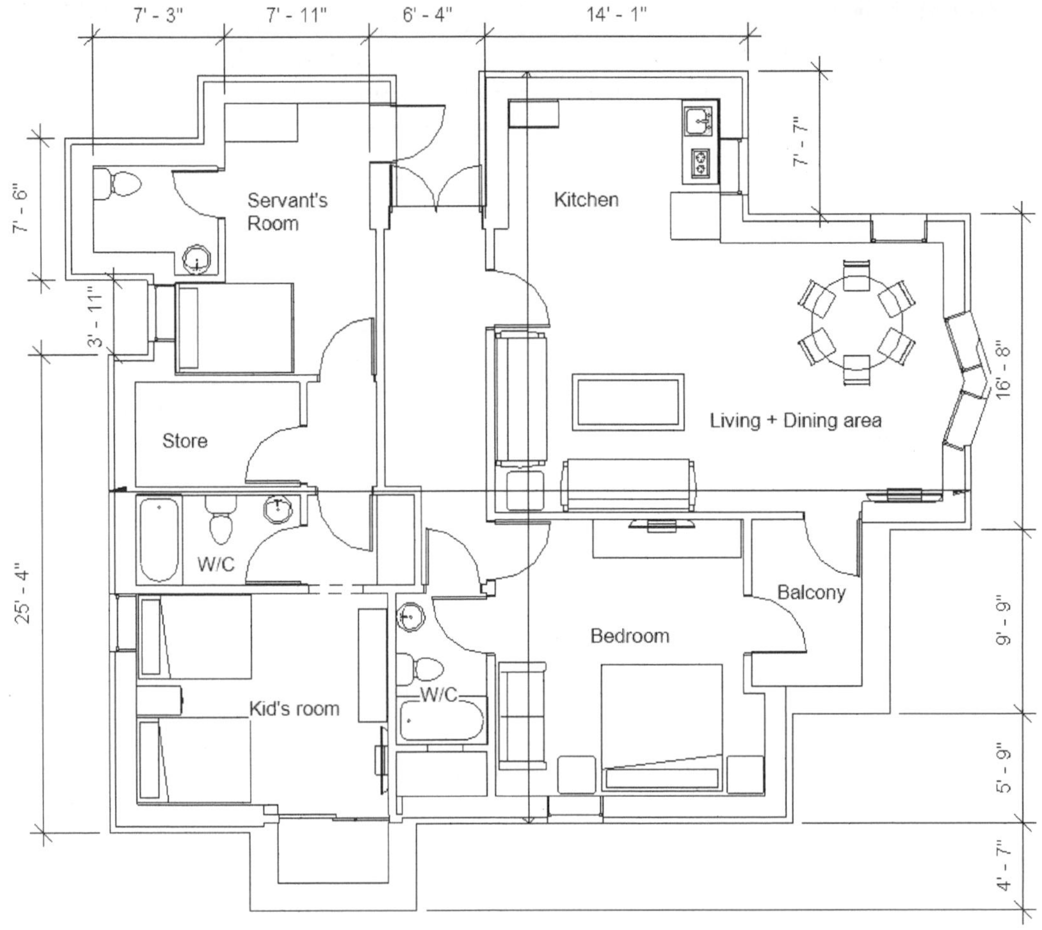

Figure 11-58 Sketch plan for adding text and dimensions to the Residential project

Answers to Self-Evaluation Test

1. **Annotate**, **2.** **Tag All**, **3.** **Room Separator**, **4.** **Witness Line Gap to Element**, **5.** **Radial**, **6.** T, **7.** F, **8.** T, **9.** T, **10.** F

Chapter 12

Creating Project Details and Schedules

Learning Objectives

After completing this chapter, you will be able to:

- *Create a callout view*
- *Create project details*
- *Add crop region to the model*
- *Create a drafting detail*
- *Add text notes to the project detail*
- *Add model text to a building model*
- *Add revision cloud and revision tag to the project detail*
- *Create project schedules*

PROJECT DETAILING IN Autodesk Revit

For a building or an interior project, details are as important as the building design. Apart from enabling architects and building industry professionals to convey their ideas about materializing a project on site, details describe the materials to be used for construction and their usage. The interconnection of various materials used in a project can be explained graphically using the enlarged views of specific locations. The extent of detailing provided for a project also describes the precision desired while using materials. It can also be used to describe the procedure to be followed for achieving the design intent. For example, you may want to describe the procedure for fabricating a furniture item or explain the interconnection of various materials on the floor or roof joint. The information provided through details helps the fabricator, builder, or contractor understand the architect's concept of achieving the desired design intent. The executing agency can then construct the project based on these details.

Autodesk Revit empowers architects and other building industry professionals to create details with relative ease. This chapter describes the general procedure of adding details to a Revit project. There are two basic methods of creating details:

1. **Using the project view**: This method is used to create details based on project views. This means you can enlarge the desired portion of a project view using the callout view, and then sketch the detail over it.

2. **Creating a drafted detail**: The second method is to sketch the details that do not use a project view. This can be done by using drafting view. The drafting details are not parametrically associated with a building model.

Based on the detailing required, you can select the method that is more suitable to the project requirement.

CREATING DETAILS IN A PROJECT

This method uses an enlarged portion of a building model view to create the project detailing. You can create a callout view by using plan, section, elevation, or detail view as its parent view. A new view is added to the **Project Browser** and is displayed under the same head as the parent view. The callout view is dependent on its parent view and is deleted if the parent view is deleted.

You can then sketch detail lines over the callout view to create the detail. Autodesk Revit provides various in-built detail components that can also be added to the detail view. In addition to this, while detailing you can crop views, sketch boundaries, and fill the sketched boundary with required filling material. Also, you can add break lines, dimensions, and annotations to the detailed views. The various tools and methods to create detailed views are discussed next.

Callout View

A callout view is used to display an enlarged view of a part of a building model. This view is important for detailing. Creating a callout view is a common practice amongst engineers as it helps them to view the project more precisely and with a higher detail. In an architectural project, callout is used to show details of the basic building elements in a model. You can create callout in plan view or in elevation view. Note that, the callout tag added to these views will be linked to the callout view.

A callout tag consists of the following parts: callout bubble, callout head, and leader line, as shown in Figure 12-1. The callout bubble is the line drawn around that part of the model that you want to enlarge. The callout head is the symbol that represents the callout displaying detail number and sheet number of a model. The line connecting the callout bubble to the callout head is called the leader line.

You can create callout views either by sketching or by creating a rectangle. The methods of creating and displaying callout view, modifying callout view properties, and adding detail lines to a callout view are discussed in the next section.

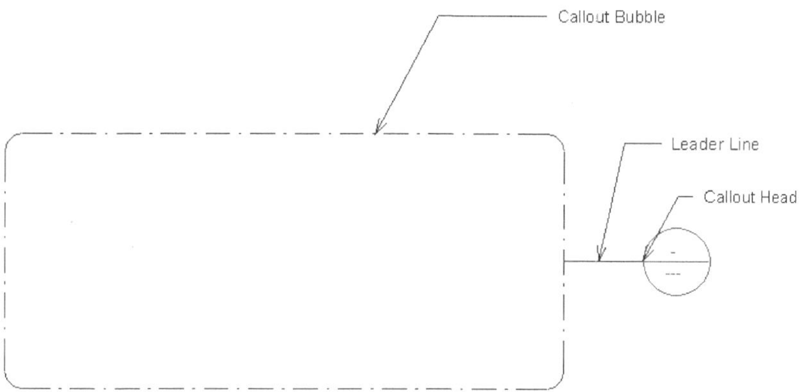

Figure 12-1 *A callout tag*

Creating a Callout View Using the Rectangle Tool

Ribbon: View > Create > Callout drop-down > Rectangle

As mentioned above, a callout view is used to give a detailed description about some specific section of a model around which it is drawn. To create a callout view, invoke the **Rectangle** tool from the **Callout** drop-down in the **Create** panel; the **Modify | Callout** tab will be displayed. In the **Properties** palette, the **Type Selector** drop-down list displays the type of callout view to be generated. There are two options in this drop-down list: **Detail View : Detail** and **Floor Plan : Floor Plan** (for current view). You can select the **Detail View : Detail** option for providing the detailed information about a specific part in a building model. Similarly, you can select the **Floor Plan : Floor Plan** (for current view) option to provide more information about a part of the current view. The **Scale** drop-down list in the **Options Bar** can be used to set the view scale. The check box on the right of the **Scale** drop-down list is cleared by default. You can select this check box to create a reference callout. When you select the check box, the **Reference other view** drop-down list will be activated. From this drop-down list, you can select an option to specify the existing view that the callout will refer to. After selecting the desired type and option, move the cursor to the top left corner of the area that you want to enlarge and then drag it toward the lower right corner of the area to create a callout bubble, as shown in Figure 12-2. Release the left mouse button when the required area is enclosed in it.

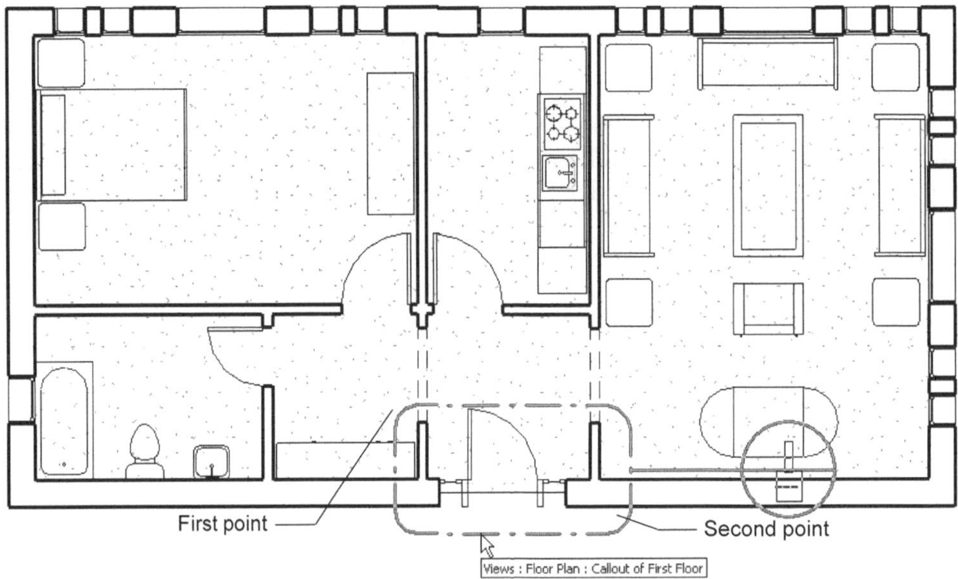

Figure 12-2 A callout bubble showing the first and second points

Creating a Callout View Using the Sketch Path Tool

Ribbon: View > Create > Callout drop-down > Sketch Path

In Autodesk Revit, you can create a customized callout view by using the draw tools. To do so, invoke the **Sketch Path** tool from the **Create** panel of the **View** tab; the **Modify | Edit Profile** tab will be displayed. In the **Draw** panel of this tab, the **Line** tool is selected by default. You can also select other sketching tools to create a callout of desired type. Next, choose the **Finish Edit Mode** button to exit the **Modify | Edit Profile** tab. In the **Properties** palette, the **Type Selector** drop-down list displays the type of callout view to be generated. There are two options in this drop-down list: **Detail View : Detail** and **Floor Plan : Floor Plan** (for current view). You can select the **Detail View : Detail** option for providing detailed information of a specific part in a building model. Similarly, you can select the **Floor Plan : Floor Plan** (for current view) option to provide more information about a part of the current view.

Displaying a Callout View

After you create a callout in the existing view, a new callout view is added to the **Project Browser** under the parent category. The parent category is the category in which the callout view is created. Therefore, if you create a callout view in the section view, the callout view will be added under the **Sections** heading in the **Project Browser**. Double-click on its name in the **Project Browser** under the **Sections** heading to display the corresponding callout view in the drawing window. Figure 12-3 shows an example of a callout view.

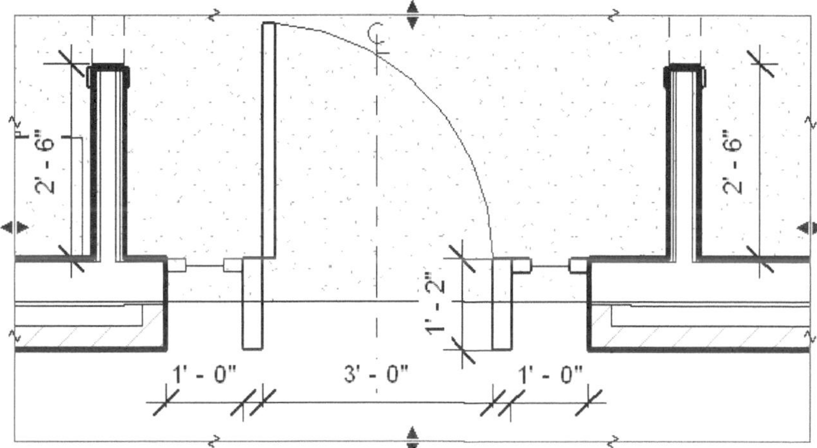

Figure 12-3 A callout view displayed

Alternatively, highlight the callout bubble and right-click to display the shortcut menu. Choose **Go To View** from the shortcut menu to display the callout view.

Modifying Callout View Properties

You can modify the appearance of a callout bubble in the parent view by using the bubble controls. These controls are displayed when the callout view is selected. The drag controls can be used to modify the extent of a callout view. The rotation control is used to rotate a callout bubble along with its leader and tag. The leader elbow control can be dragged to some desired location.

The instance properties of the callout view are different for different types of callouts. To modify the instance properties of a callout view, select it from the drawing; the instance properties of the selected callout view will be displayed in the **Properties** palette. In the **Properties** palette shown in Figure 12-4, the **View Name** instance parameter under the **Identity Data** head is used to specify a name for a callout view. The title for the sheet can be entered in the **Title on Sheet** parameter. The **Display Model** parameter under the **Graphics** head is used to set the display type for the view of a building model. By default, this parameter is set to **Normal**. You can set the value of the **Display Model** parameter to **Halftone** from its corresponding drop-down list to display the model element in the current view as a faded image. You can select the **Do not display** option from the drop-down list corresponding to the **Display Model** parameter to hide the model element in the current view. The **Range: Base Level** parameter under the **Underlay** head can be used to set the display of model elements that are displayed in other levels and are not visible in the current view. By default, the **Range: Base Level** parameter is set to **None**. You can select a level under this head to make the elements of the selected level visible in the current view. The elements that are displayed as underlay appear dimmed. The **View Template** parameter under the **Identity** head can be used to assign a view template to each view in a project. By default, the **None** option is selected in this parameter. To assign an existing view template or to create a new template and assign it to the current view, choose the **<None>** button displayed corresponding to the **View Template** parameter; the **Apply View Template** dialog box will be displayed, as shown in Figure 12-5. In the **View Templates** area of this dialog box, you can select the desired options from the **Discipline filter** and **View type** drop-down lists to limit the view templates that will be displayed in the **Names** list box. In the **Names** list box, you can select the desired template to be assigned to the view. On selecting a template from the **Names** list box, its corresponding parameters will be displayed in the **View Properties** area. You can modify the parameter as per the requirement of the project. In the **View Templates** area, you can select an existing view template and choose the **Rename** button; the **Rename** dialog box will be displayed. In the **New** edit box, enter the desired name and choose the **OK** button; the selected template is renamed and will be displayed in the **Names** list box. In the **View templates** area, you can choose the **Delete** and **Duplicate** buttons to delete an existing view template and create a copy of an existing view template, respectively. To apply a view template to the current view, select the view template from the **Names** list box and choose the **Apply** button. To close the **Apply View Template** dialog box, choose the **OK** button.

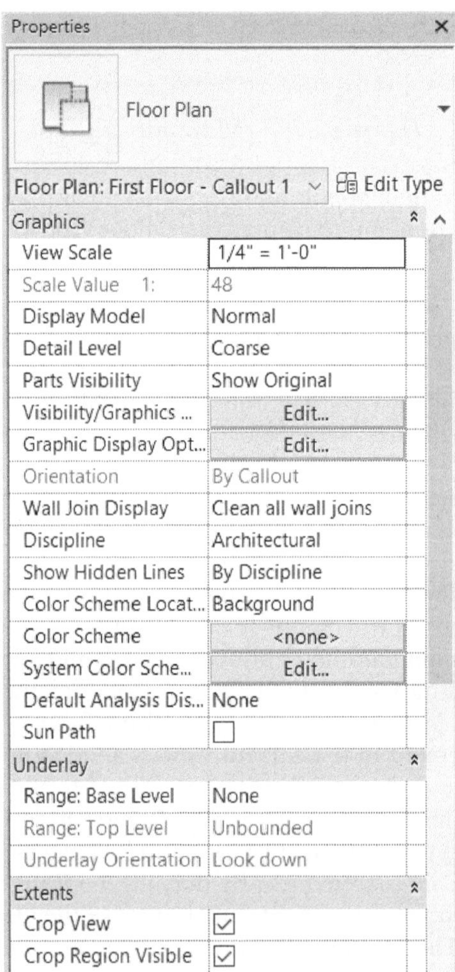

***Figure 12-4** The partial view of the **Properties** palette displaying the instance properties of a callout view*

The amount of details to be displayed in the callout view can be controlled by using the **Detail Level** parameter under the **Graphics** head. From the drop-down list corresponding to this parameter, you can select any of the three options: **Coarse**, **Medium**, and **Fine**. The **Coarse** option is selected by default in the drop-down list. As a result, model elements are displayed with less details in the current view. You can select the **Fine** option from this drop-down list to display the layers of various materials used in a building model. On selecting the **Fine** option, additional lines are displayed in the callout view. These lines describe composite materials. The **Edit** button in the **Value** column for the **Visibility /Graphics Overrides** parameter can be used to control the visibility of different models and annotation elements in the callout view. The **View Scale** instance parameter is used to set the scale for the callout view. You can use the drop-down list in the **Value** column to select a scale for the callout view.

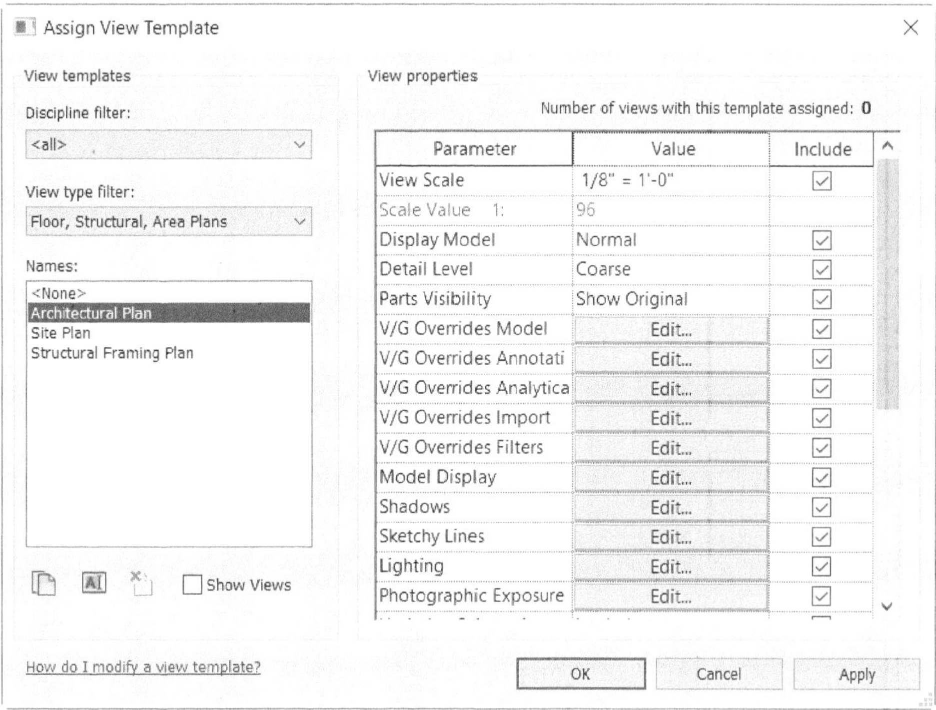

*Figure 12-5 The **Apply View Template** dialog box*

Adding Details to the Callout View

Autodesk Revit provides various tools to add details to a callout view. In the callout view, you can sketch lines using the **Detail Line** tool and add the detail components provided in the Autodesk Revit's library.

Adding Detail Lines

Ribbon: Annotate > Detail > Detail Line
Shortcut Key: DL

The **Detail Line** tool is used to create lines for a detail view. Detail lines are view-specific and appear only in the view in which they are created. You can use the callout view of a building model and trace detail lines over the image using their varying thicknesses. You can invoke the **Detail Line** tool from the **Detail** panel of the **Annotate** tab. On doing so, the **Modify | Place Detail Lines** tab will be displayed. In the **Line Style** panel of this tab, you can select the type of detail line from the **Line Style** drop-down list. You can select appropriate detail line based on its usage. Alternatively, you can select a type by clicking in the **Value** field corresponding to the **Line Style** parameter in the **Properties** palette and then selecting an option from the drop-down list displayed. For example, wide lines can be used to show masonry elements whereas thin lines can be selected to represent lighter materials such as glass and aluminum. The **Draw** panel of the **Modify | Place Detail Lines** tab displays the sketching tools to draw these lines. To add detail lines, you can trace over the underlay elements. On doing so, you will notice that the cursor snaps at various elements on the underlay lines. The entire detail can be sketched using a variety of line thicknesses to achieve the desired graphical representation. You can also add dimensions and symbols to details. Figure 12-6 shows an example of a detail view created over a callout view (shown as underlay) using lines, dimensions, and symbol. However, after completing a detail, you can hide the underlay callout view using the **Display Model** parameter.

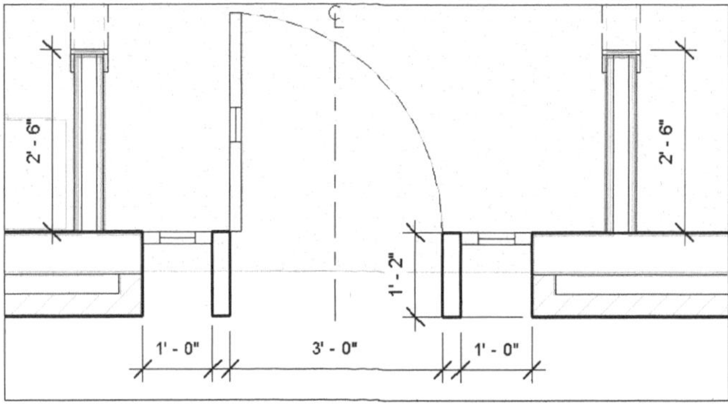

Figure 12-6 *Adding detail lines in the callout view*

Tip

You can use the TAB key to cycle between various reference snap options such as the wall centerline, wall faces, wall cores, and so on. Left-click when an appropriate snap option is highlighted.

CROP REGIONS

Crop regions help to crop views to exclude the unwanted content thereby reducing the view size. Revit has two types of crop regions that allow you to crop views for the model and annotation categories. You can control the visibility of the crop region from **View Control Bar**. The two types of crop regions are discussed next.

Model Crop Region

You can use the model crop region to crop all model elements such as doors, windows, walls, and so on.

Annotation Crop Region

The annotation crop region crops all the annotation elements such as tags, dimensions, keynotes, and so on. All the elements that are touched partially by the annotation crop region boundary are cropped fully to avoid the partial display of annotations. Figure 12-7 shows both the annotation and model crop regions with drag controls.

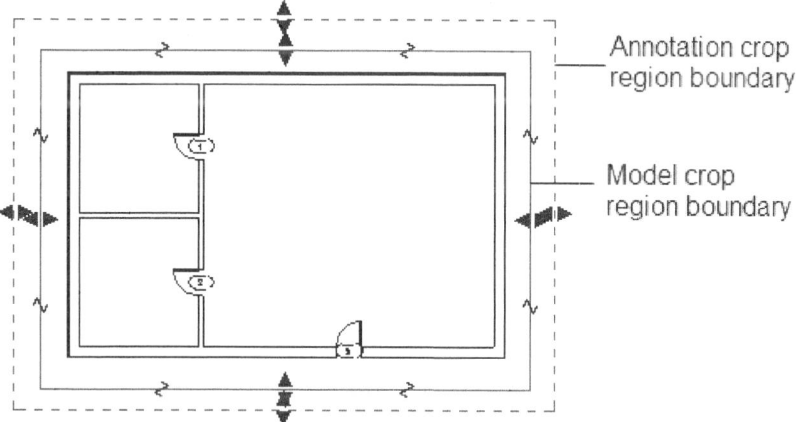

***Figure 12-7** The model crop and annotation crop regions with drag controls*

Note

By default, the annotation crop region is displayed in the callout and duplicate dependent views, but this region is not visible in the primary view. Annotations such as door and window tags will not be visible in the annotation crop region if they are a part of the hidden elements or the model crop region.

To view the crop region boundary, choose the **Show Crop Region** button from the **View Control Bar**; the crop region boundary will be displayed with drag controls. You can resize the crop region using the drag controls. Next, choose the **Crop View** button from the **View Control Bar**; the resized crop region boundary will be displayed.

To hide or show the crop regions, choose the **Show Crop Region** or **Hide Crop Region** button from the **View Control Bar**. To show or hide the annotation crop region in the drawing, you can use various options in the **Properties** palette. In this palette, you can select or clear the check box displayed in the value field corresponding to the **Annotation Crop** parameter. Next, hover the cursor over the drawing and place the cursor over the crop boundary; a colored annotation boundary will be displayed. Click in the drawing to display the annotation crop region boundary along with the drag controls.

Creating the Filled Region

Ribbon: Annotate > Detail > Region drop-down > Filled Region

Filled Region

The **Filled Region** tool is used to create a two-dimensional, view-specific fill pattern within a closed boundary. You can invoke the **Filled Region** tool from the **Detail** panel. On doing so, the **Modify | Create Filled Region Boundary** tab will be displayed and the sketch mode will be activated. In this tab, you can select an option from the **Line Style** drop-down list in the **Line Style** panel to select the desired line type. The sketching tools in the **Draw** panel can be used to sketch the boundary of various shapes and sizes. You can change the region properties of the fill pattern within the closed boundary. To do so, choose the **Edit Type** button from the **Properties** palette to display the **Type Properties** dialog box. Next, click in the **Value** field for the **Fill Pattern** parameter type; a button on the right of the field will be displayed. Choose the button; the **Fill Patterns** dialog box will be displayed, as shown in Figure 12-8.

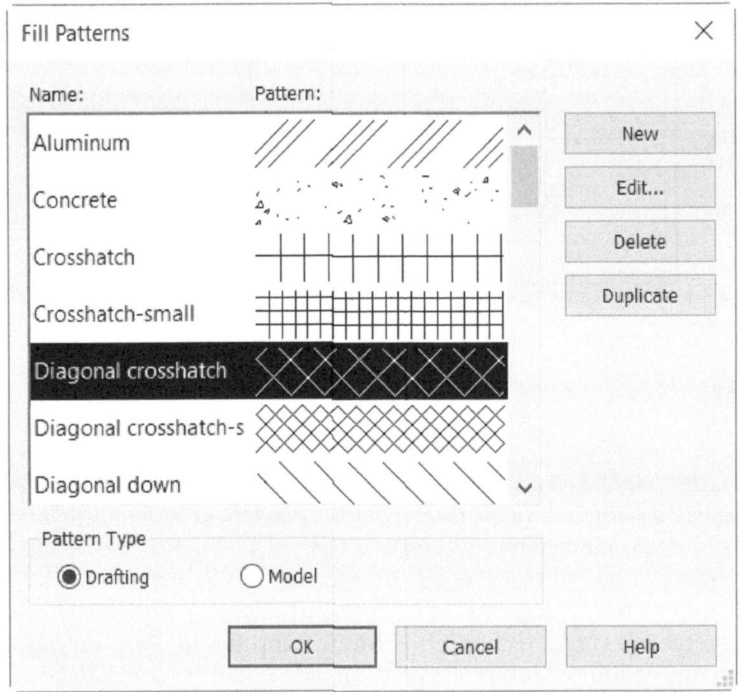

***Figure 12-8** The **Fill Patterns** dialog box displaying fill patterns*

You can create two types of patterns: Model and Drafting. The Model patterns represent model elements such as brick, sand, carpet, and so on. They are fixed with respect to the model element and are scaled with it. On the other hand, the Drafting patterns are surface patterns that represent materials in a symbolic form. For example, a masonry-concrete block is represented by a diagonal cross-hatch pattern. The density of the drafting patterns is fixed with respect to the drawing sheet.

Tip

*To create a custom pattern, choose the **New** button from the **Fill Patterns** dialog box; the **New Pattern** dialog box will be displayed. From this dialog box, you can use various options to create a custom pattern for the filled region.*

To create the Model or Drafting pattern, select the **Model** or the **Drafting** radio button in the **Pattern Type** area of the **Fill Patterns** dialog box.

Note

You can use both the model and drafting patterns for the elements in your project. However, on the cut element surfaces in the plan or section view, you can only create drafting patterns.

After selecting the type of pattern from the **Pattern Type** area, select the fill pattern from the display box. Next, choose the **OK** button from the **Fill Patterns** dialog box; this dialog box will close and the selected pattern will be assigned to the **Fill Pattern** parameter in the **Type Properties** dialog box. Choose the **OK** button to close the **Type Properties** dialog box. Next, from the **Draw** panel of the **Modify | Create Filled Region Boundary** tab, you can use various sketching tools to sketch the boundary for the filled region. Next, choose the **Finish Edit Mode** button from the **Mode** panel; the filled pattern will be created within the sketched boundary.

In this way, you can use the **Region** tool to create a pattern by sketching an enclosed boundary. In the detailed view, you can use various patterns to represent different materials with respect to their usage.

Viewing the Area of Filled Region

Revit allows you to view the surface area of the filled region. To do so, select the filled region; the instance properties will be displayed in the **Properties** palette. In this palette, the value of the **Area** parameter in the value column displays the area of the filled region. The area is defined by project units like square meters or square feet.

Adding Detail Components

Ribbon: Annotate > Detail > Component > Detail Component

Autodesk Revit provides various in-built components that can be added to the detail using the **Detail Component** tool. To add components, invoke this tool from the **Detail** panel; the **Modify | Place Detail Component** tab will be displayed. In the **Properties** palette, you can select different types of detail components from the **Type Selector** drop-down list. To select additional types of detail components, choose the **Load Family** tool from the **Mode** panel; the **Load Family** dialog box will be displayed. In this dialog box, choose **US Imperial > Detail Items (Detail Components)**; the **Detail Items** folder will open. This folder contains several subfolders containing various element family files that can be loaded into a project. For example, you can load typical details for a window jamb in metal or wood and use them in the callout detail. The **Structural** folder contains subfolders with a variety of detail components in concrete and wood. After selecting the detail component, move the cursor in the drawing area and click to place it. Thus, you can create details by adding different detail components such as wooden members, steel elements, and so on. Figure 12-9 shows the cross-section of a typical steel column encasement detail. This detail has been created using metal studs and GW board that have been loaded from Autodesk Revit's library of detail components.

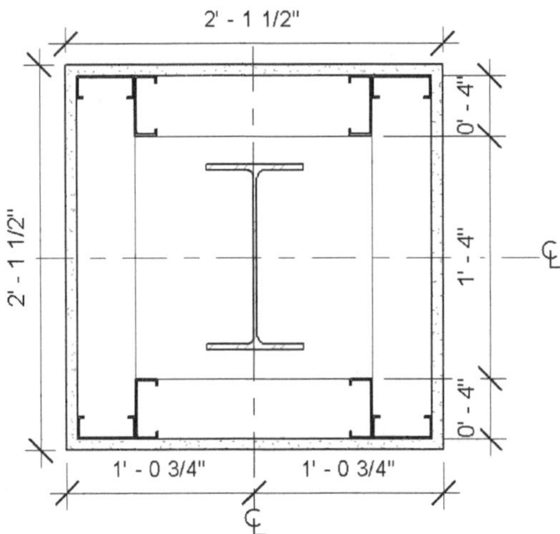

Figure 12-9 Creating a detail view using detail components

Adding an Insulation Barrier

Ribbon: Annotate > Detail > Insulation

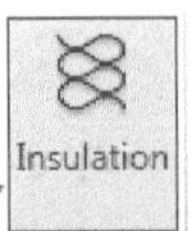

The **Insulation** tool is used to add insulation barrier to a detail view. To add a barrier, invoke this tool from the **Detail** panel; the **Modify | Place Insulation** tab will be displayed. In the **Draw** panel of this tab, you can select any of the two tools: **Lines** and **Pick Lines** to draw the insulation barrier in a detail view. The **Width** edit box in the **Options Bar** is used to enter the value of thickness of insulation barrier. The selection of the **Chain** check box enables you to create a continuous graphical representation. You can enter a value in the **Offset** edit box to create the insulation barrier at an offset distance from a reference. The drop-down list next to the **Offset** edit box shows three options : **to center**, **to near side**, and **to far side**. These options can be used to select an option to specify the reference of the offset or location for the insulation barrier. After specifying the options in the **Options Bar**, click in the drawing area to start insulation and move the cursor in the desired direction. As you move the cursor, the preview image of insulation graphics will be displayed. Click to specify the endpoint of the insulation barrier. After creating the insulation barrier, you can modify its properties. To do so, select the created insulation barrier from the drawing; the instance properties will be displayed in the **Properties** palette. In this palette, the **Insulation Bulge to Width Ratio (1/x)** instance parameter can be used to change the bulge of the insulation graphic. Figure 12-10 shows an example of an insulation barrier added to the detail view.

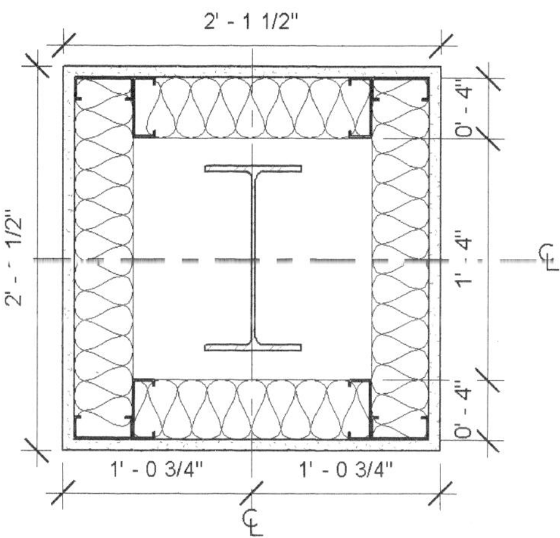

Figure 12-10 *An insulation barrier added to the detail view*

Adding a Break Line

A break line is added to a detail view as a detail component. To add a break line to a detail view, invoke the **Detail Component** tool from the **Annotate > Detail > Component** drop-down; the **Modify | Place Detail Component** tab will be displayed. If the required break line is not loaded in the drawing, choose the **Load Family** tool from the **Mode** panel and load the *Break Line.rfa* family file by browsing **US Imperial > Detail Items (Detail Components)** and choosing the **Div 01-General** folder in the **Load Family** dialog box. After you have selected the file, choose the **Open** button; the **Load Family** dialog box will close and the selected family type will be added to the **Type Selector** drop-down list. Click in the **Type Selector** drop-down list, select the **Break Line : Break Line** option from it, and then move the cursor to the required location and click to add the break line. After placing the break line, you can choose the **Rotate** tool from the **Modify** panel, if required, to orient the break line perpendicular to the element to be discontinued. On doing so, Autodesk Revit will automatically break the element at the specified location. In this manner, you can add as many break lines as you want to the detail, as shown in Figure 12-11. The two ends of the break line must intersect the edges of the component(s), in order to discontinue their visibility. You can also use the grips to extend the limit of the break line. The grips will be displayed on selecting the break line.

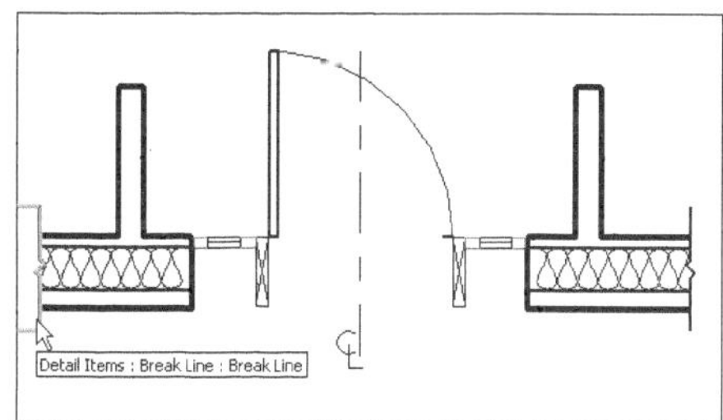

Figure 12-11 *Break lines added to the detail view*

Adding Text Notes

Text notes can be added to a detail view by using the **Text** tool. To do so, invoke this tool from the **Text** panel of the **Annotate** tab; the **Modify | Place Text** tab will be displayed. Now, from the **Type Selector** drop-down list in the **Properties** palette, select the desired text type. You can also create a new text type or change the existing instance and type properties. To create a new text type or modify the existing type, choose the **Type Properties** tool from the **Properties** panel of the **Modify | Place Text** tab; the **Type Properties** dialog box will be displayed. In this dialog box, you can specify various type parameters such as color, line weight, text font, text size, width factor, and so on. These parameters can be specified in their respective value columns. After specifying the type parameters, choose **Apply** and then the **OK** button to close the **Type Properties** dialog box. In the **Paragraph** panel of the **Modify | Place Text** tab, you can choose the **Align Left**, **Align Center**, or **Align Right** button to set the horizontal alignment of the text to be inserted.

In Autodesk Revit, you can insert a text with or without a leader. To do so, choose any of the four buttons namely, **No Leader**, **One Segment**, **Two Segments**, and **Curved** from the **Leader** panel of the **Modify | Place Text** tab. By default, the **No Leader** button is chosen. As a result, the text will be inserted without a leader. To attach a leader to the text, choose the **One Segment**, **Two Segments**, or **Curved** button from the **Leader** panel to display the text with a single segment, double segments, or a curved segment leader. After selecting the required option from the **Modify |Place Text** tab, click in the drawing area. Depending upon the option selected from the **Leader** panel, you need to click once or twice in the drawing area. On doing so, a text box will be displayed. Enter the text note in the text box and click in the drawing area again to finish the writing of the text. Figure 12-12 shows the added text and the leader in the detail view. The detailed description of adding text to a project view is described later in this chapter.

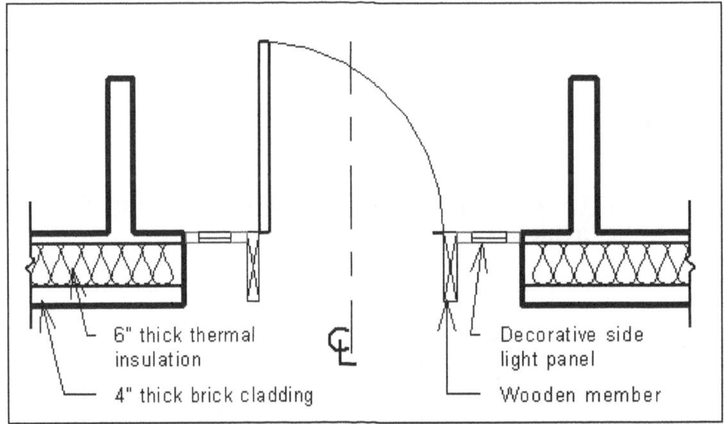

Figure 12-12 *Text notes added to the detail view*

CREATING DRAFTED DETAILS

Drafted details are created for the details that are not referenced to the existing project views. These details are not linked to a building model, therefore, they do not get updated with it. To create a drafted detail, first create a drafting view and then use the drafting tools provided in

Autodesk Revit to sketch the detail. You can also import in-built details from Autodesk Revit's detail library and use them. The created drafted detail can then be used as a reference detail.

Creating a Drafting View

To create a drafting view, invoke the **Drafting View** tool from the **Create** panel of the **View** tab; the **New Drafting View** dialog box will be displayed, as shown in Figure 12-13. This dialog box is used to set the name and scale for the drafting view.

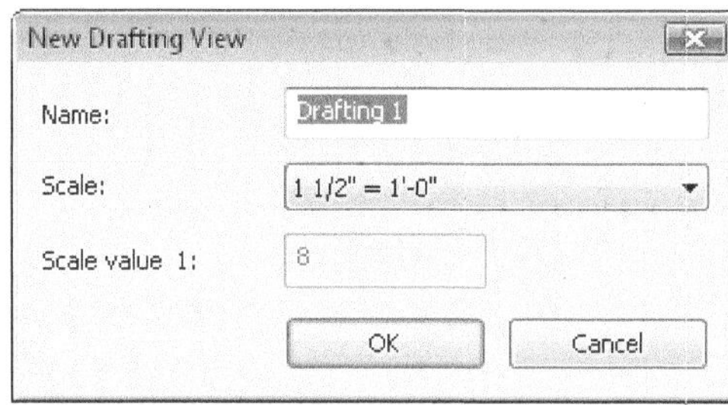

***Figure 12-13** The **New Drafting View** dialog box*

Enter a name for the drafting view in the **Name** edit box. Select the scale for the detailing from the **Scale** drop-down list. If the required scale is not available in the drop-down list, the **Custom** option can be selected to specify the scale of the drafting view. The created drafting view is added under the **Drafting Views** subhead in the **Project Browser**.

Note

The drafting views do not use project views. As a result, when you create drafting views, project views are not displayed in the drawing window.

Drafting a Detail

The method of drafting a detail in the drafting view is similar to the one used in the callout view. In a callout view, lines are traced over the enlarged project view whereas in a drafting view, the project view is not available and a new detail is drafted as if you were drafting on a blank sheet.

To draft a detail, you can use the tools in the **Annotate** tab of the ribbon. The usage of the tools of the **Annotate** tab is similar to their usage in a callout view. The **Detail Lines** tool enables you to draw lines with varying thickness. The **Place a Component** tool is used to add in-built detail components from Autodesk Revit's detail library. The **Insulation** tool enables you to add a graphical insulation symbol to the drafted detail. You can create graphical patterns to represent various building materials using the **Region** tool. You can also add dimensions, text notes, and break lines to complete the drafted detail.

Line Style Settings

Ribbon:	Manage > Settings > Additional Settings drop-down > Line Styles

Line Styles

Autodesk Revit provides a variety of line styles that can be used not only in detail views but also in a building model. To view these line styles, choose the **Line Styles** tool from the **Settings** panel; the **Line Styles** dialog box will be displayed. This dialog box displays the list of predefined line styles, as shown in Figure 12-14.

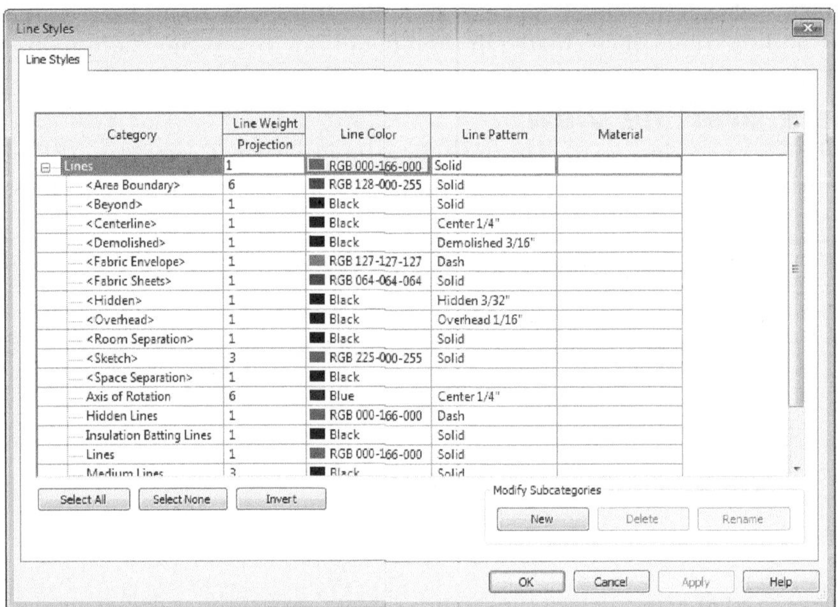

*Figure 12-14 The **Line Styles** dialog box displaying the list of in-built lines styles*

Each line style is listed with its parameters such as weight, color, pattern and material. You have the option to change any or all of these parameters. The column for the **Line Weight** parameter displays a drop-down list of the available line weights. Click twice in the **Line Color** column to display the **Color** dialog box and then select the color to be assigned to the corresponding line style from the dialog box. The **Line Pattern** column displays a drop-down list showing the available line patterns.

Creating a New Line Style

Apart from using these predefined line styles, you can also create a new line style. To do so, choose the **New** button from the **Modify Subcategories** area in the **Line Styles** dialog box; the **New Subcategory** dialog box will be displayed, as shown in Figure 12-15. In this dialog box, specify a new line style name in the **Name** edit box, select an option from the **Subcategory of** drop-down list, and then choose the **OK** button; the new line style will be added to the list of existing line styles. Now, you can set its parameters such as **Line Weight**, **Line Color**, **Line Pattern**, and **Material** to create a new line style. The new line style will be stored only in the project in which it is created.

The **Delete** and **Rename** buttons in the **Line Styles** dialog box can be used to delete or rename the new line styles. Other buttons such as **Select All**, **Select None**, and **Invert** can be used to create a selection of the listed line styles. Note that by default some of these buttons will be inactive.

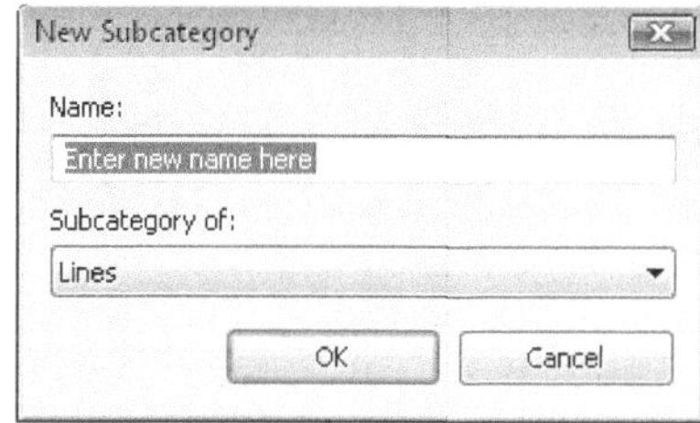

***Figure 12-15** The **New Subcategory** dialog box*

Using Line Weights

Ribbon: Manage > Settings > Additional Settings > Line Weights

The **Line Weights** tool is used to control the display of line widths in various scales of a project view. To do so, invoke this tool from the **Settings** panel of the **Manage** tab; the **Line Weights** dialog box will be displayed. This dialog box has three tabs: **Model Line Weights**, **Perspective Line Weights**, and **Annotation Line Weights**, as shown in Figure 12-16.

The **Model Line Weights** tab displays line weights for modeling elements such as walls, doors, windows, and so on. Line weights depend on view scale. This means when elements are displayed at an enlarged scale, model lines are displayed with a greater thickness or weight. The table in the **Line Weights** dialog box shows the width of each defined line weight for the corresponding scale. In this dialog box, sixteen different line weights have been defined for six different view scales. To modify a line weight, click in the appropriate cell of the table and enter a new value. The **Add** button is used to add a new scale. On choosing this button, the **Add Scale** dialog box will be displayed. The new scale can be set by selecting it from the drop-down list in the **Add Scale** dialog box. After setting the scale of the line style, choose the **Line Weights** dialog box. The **Delete** button can be used to delete an added or a predefined view scale.
The **Perspective Line Weights** tab controls line widths for various elements in the perspective view. It contains a list of sixteen model line weights. You can enter a new model line weight in the corresponding cell.

The **Annotation Line Weights** tab controls line weights for various annotations such as dimension lines, section lines, and so on. The line weights for annotation symbols are independent of the scale at which they are viewed. This means a dimension line is displayed at the same thickness value irrespective of the view scale. There are sixteen predefined annotation line weights that can be selected from different tabs in the **Line Weights** dialog box. You can click and change their values.

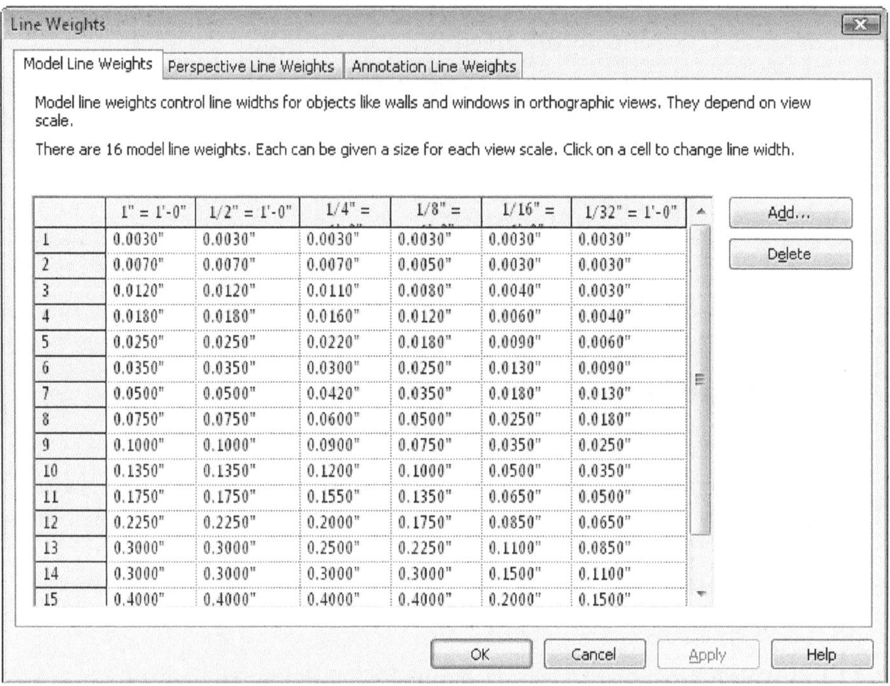

*Figure 12-16 The **Line Weights** dialog box*

Using Line Patterns

Ribbon: Manage > Settings > Additional Settings > Line Patterns

Line Patterns

The **Line Patterns** tool is used to control line patterns. Invoke this tool from the **Settings** panel; the **Line Patterns** dialog box will be displayed, as shown in Figure 12-17. This dialog box displays the names of the predefined lines along with their corresponding patterns. Line patterns are a series of dashes, dots, and spaces. You can modify the properties of the predefined line patterns. To do so, select a line pattern and choose the **Edit** button; the **Line Pattern Properties** dialog box will be displayed, refer to Figure 12-18.

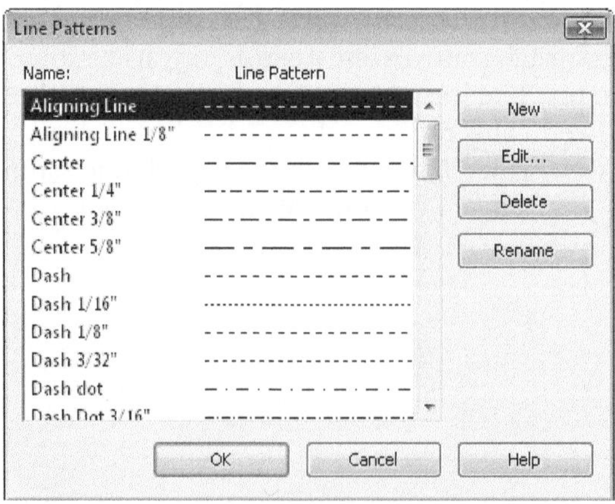

*Figure 12-17 The **Line Patterns** dialog box*

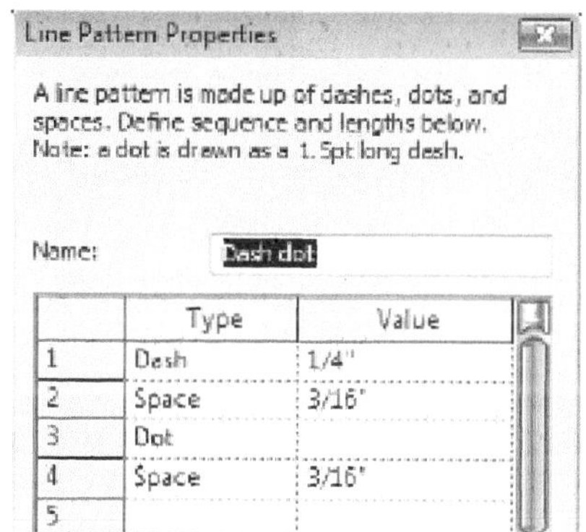

***Figure 12-18** The partial view of the **Line Pattern Properties** dialog box for the **Dash dot** line pattern*

To create a new line pattern, choose the **New** button from the **Line Pattern** dialog box; the **Line Pattern Properties** dialog box will be displayed. In this dialog box, enter a name for the line pattern in the **Name** edit box. In the **Type** column of this dialog box, you can specify the type of the line pattern and in the **Value** column, you can specify a value for the specified line pattern.

ADDING TEXT NOTES

Text notes form an important part of a project detail. They not only help in adding the specification for various building elements but also help in conveying the specific design intent. Autodesk Revit provides a variety of options to add text notes to a building model detail view by using the **Text** tool.

Creating Text Notes

Ribbon: Annotate > Text > Text
Shortcut Key: TX

Invoke the **Text** tool from the **Text** panel; the **Modify | Place Text** tab will be displayed, as shown in Figure 12-19. The buttons in the **Leader** panel of this tab are used to align text. You can align text to the left, center, or right of the text box. Autodesk Revit enables you to create text notes with or without a leader. A leader is a line that connects the text note to the referred portion of a project view. To attach a leader to a text note, you can use any of these four tools, **No Leader**, **One Segment**, **Two Segments**, and **Curved** available in the **Leader** panel. The **No Leader** tool is chosen by default in this panel and is used to create a text without a leader line. The **One Segment**, **Two Segments**, or **Curved** tool can be used to create a textnote with a single segment, two segments, or a curved leader, respectively, as shown in Figure 12-20. To use the **One Segment** tool, click at the location of the start point of the leader or the arrow. As you move the cursor, the leader extends with it. Next, click at the required location to place the text note and then type its content. If you choose the **Two Segments** tool, you need to specify one more point for the elbow of the leader. If you choose the **Curved** tool, you need to specify two points: one for the start point and the other for the endpoint of the arc leader.

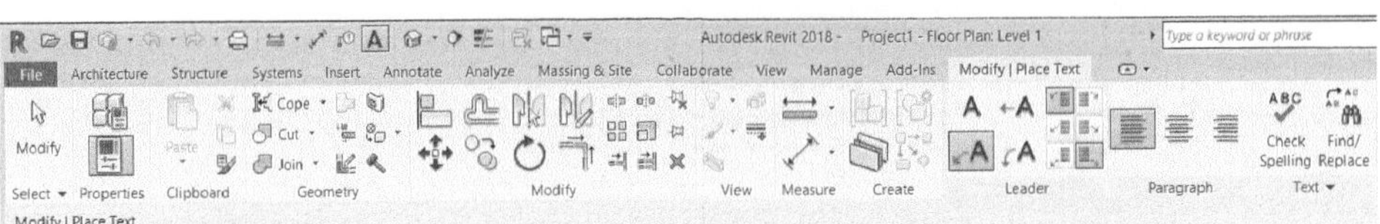

*Figure 12-19 Text options available in the **Modify / Place Text** tab*

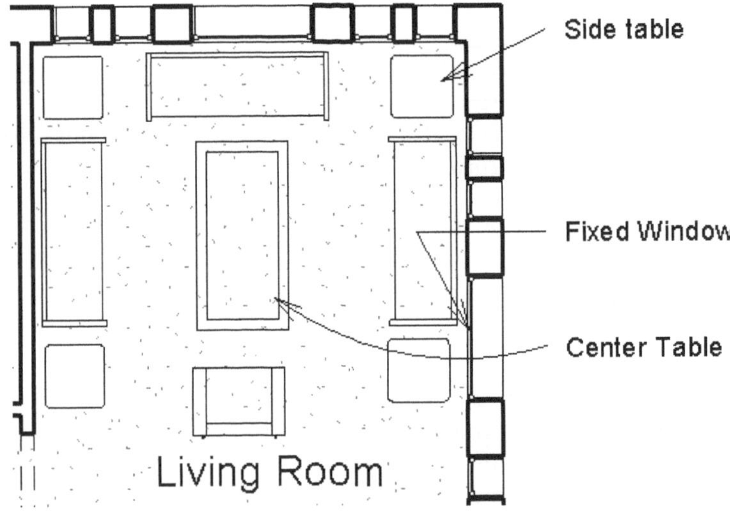

*Figure 12-20 Leaders created using the **One Segment, Two Segments**, and **Curved** options*

After setting the options for the placement of leader, you can set the alignment of the text. To do so, you can choose any of the three tools, **Align Left**, **Align Center**, or **Align Right** from the **Paragraph** panel. The **Align Left** tool is chosen by default in this panel. As a result, the text will be aligned on the left margin in the text box. You can choose the **Align Center** tool to align the text evenly between the left margin and the right margin of the text box. You can choose the **Align Right** tool to align the text to the right margin of the text box.

After setting the desired options for placing the leader line and the text alignment, move the cursor near the desired location and click to add the text note. To add a text note, invoke the **Text** tool and choose the appropriate alignment and leader options from the **Modify | Place Text** tab. As you move the cursor in the drawing window, the cursor will change into a text note symbol. If the **No Leader** tool is chosen, click near the desired location to add the text note; a text box and the **Edit Text** tab with various tools to edit the text will be displayed. In this text box, you can enter the text using the tools present in the **Edit Text** tab.

In the **Font** panel of the the **Edit Text** contextual tab, you can use the **Bold**, **Italics**,**Underline** tool, or their combinations to format the text as required. In the **Font** panel, you can also use the **Subscript**, **Superscript**, **All Caps** tool, or their combination to format the text. In the **Paragraph** panel, you can use various tools to edit the paragraph of the text that you will insert. For instance, you can use the **List** tools in the **Paragraph** panel to list bullets, numbers, or alphabets in the text. You can also use the **Decrease Indent** or **Increase Indent** tool to move the paragraph to the left or right within the text note. After writing text in the text box, choose the **Close** button in the **Edit Text** panel to exit the **Edit Text** tab. Now, choose the **Modify** button in the **Select** panel of the **Modify | Place Text** tab to exit the **Text** tool.

Editing Text Notes

You can either set the text note properties before creating the text note or can edit its properties afterwards. When you select a text note after it is created, its controls are displayed, as shown in Figure 12-21. You can use them to edit the parameters of a text note. In the selected text note, one blue dot on each side represents the stretch controls that can be used to modify its size. The rotation control placed at the top right corner of the text note is used to rotate it. The location of the leader arrow head remains in its original position and only the text note is rotated. The leader tail automatically adjusts to the rotated text note. You can also drag the location of the leader elbow and the leader head by using the drag control dots. The drag control is used to change the location of the text note.

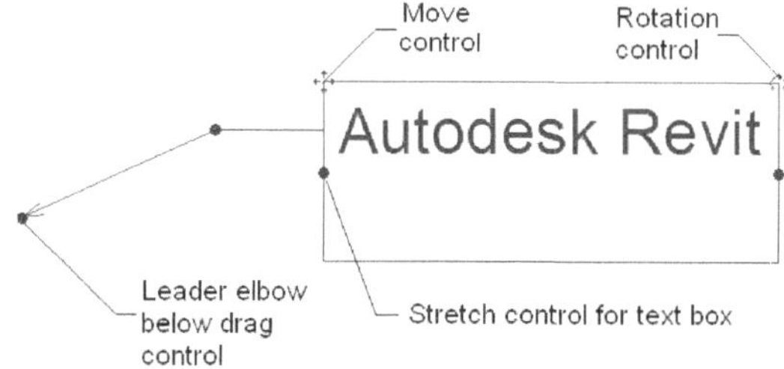

***Figure 12-21** Editing the text note using its controls*

As you select the created text note, the **Modify | Text Notes** tab will be chosen. In this tab, you can use various editing tools such as **Copy**, **Mirror**, **Rotate**, **Array**, and so on to edit and arrange the text note. Figure 12-22 shows various options in the **Modify | Text Notes** tab for editing and modifying the selected text.

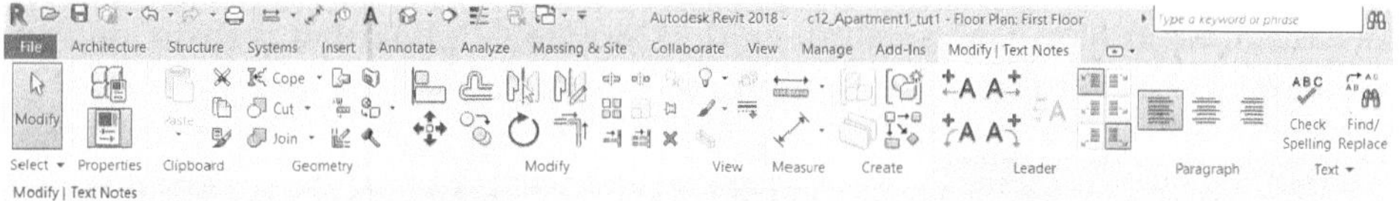

***Figure 12-22** Text note editing options in the **Modify / Text Notes** tab*

The alignment of the text note can be modified by choosing the appropriate alignment option from the **Leader** panel. You can use the appropriate add leader options such as **Add Right Side Straight Leader**, **Add Left Side Straight Leader**, **Add Left Side Arc Leader**, and **Add Right Side Arc Leader** from the **Leader** panel to add a leader to a text note created without a leader. You can also use any of these options to add multiple leaders. The **Remove Last Leader** button in the **Leader** panel is used to remove the most recently added leader to a text note. To modify a text note, select the text inside the text box displayed with it, click inside the text box, and then enter the new note. You can also modify the instance properties of the text note such as font style and text size in the **Properties** palette. In this palette, the value assigned to the **Horizontal Align** parameter specifies the horizontal text alignment of the selected text. To change this value, click on the value column and select the desired alignment option from the drop-down list displayed. The **Arc Leaders** instance parameter specifies whether or not an arc leader will be attached to a text. The value column of this parameter displays a check box. By default, this check box is cleared. You can select this check box to attach an arc leader to the text note.

You can also edit the type properties of a text using the **Properties** palette. To do so, choose the **Edit Type** button from the **Properties** palette; the **Type Properties** dialog box will be displayed, as shown in Figure 12-23.

Using this dialog box, you can edit the font of a text by clicking in the **Value** column corresponding to the **Text Font** parameter and then selecting the required text font from the drop-down list displayed. The **Text Size** parameter is used to specify the size of the text note. The **Tab Size** parameter is used to set the tab spacing used in text notes. The tab spacing can be inserted by pressing the TAB key. You can also select the check boxes for the **Bold**, **Italic**, and **Underline** parameters to set the format of the text note. Choose the **OK** button to close the **Type Properties** dialog box. The **Type Selector** drop-down list in the **Properties** palette of the selected text note displays the available text types. You can select the appropriate type from the available text types before creating text notes. Alternatively, you can select a text note that was created earlier and then select the new text type from the **Type Selector** drop-down list to replace the old text type. You can also use the **Copy to Clipboard** and **Paste from Clipboard** tools from the **Modify| Text Notes** tab to copy the text notes from one level to multiple levels. You can also edit the font in the text or list the text by bulleting, numbering, or adding alphabets to it. To insert the number, bullet, or alphabet before a text, click in the desired place. On doing so, the **Edit Text** contextual tab will be displayed. In this tab, you can use various options in the **Paragraph** panel to insert the list. To exit the **Edit Text** contextual tab, choose the **Close** button from the **Edit Text** panel.

The **Type Selector** drop-down list in the **Properties** palette displays the available text types. You have the option to select the appropriate type before creating a text. Alternatively, you can select a created text note and then select a new text type from the **Type Selector** drop-down list to replace the old text type. You can also use the **Copy to Clipboard** and **Paste** tools from the **Modify | Text Notes** tab to copy text notes from one level to multiple levels.

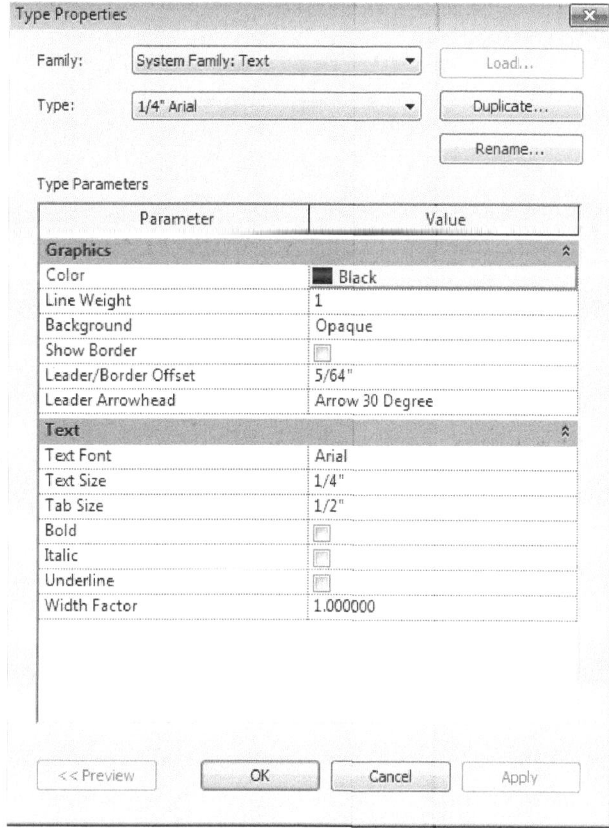

***Figure 12-23** The **Type Properties** dialog box for text notes*

Creating a Model Text

Ribbon:	Architecture > Model > Model Text

The **Model Text** tool enables you to create a text that acts as a 3D building element. The added texts are visible in all related views. They are rendered as a part of a building model and not as annotation symbols. The model text can be added to a selected level or a plane.

To add the model text to a building model, invoke the **Model Text** tool from the **Model** panel. On doing so, the **Edit Text** dialog box will be displayed and you will be prompted to enter the model text notes. After entering the text notes, choose the **OK** button to close the dialog box. The preview image of the text note entered will be displayed in the drawing window attached to the cursor. Click to place the model text at the desired location. Now, you can select the model text and modify its properties. Figure 12-24 shows an example of a model text added to the facade of a building.

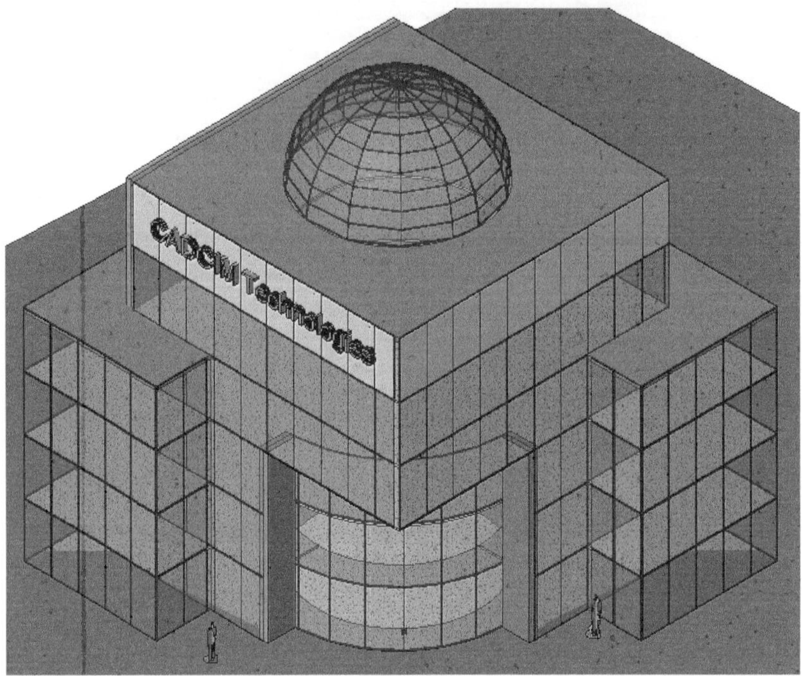

Figure 12-24 *Model text added to a building model*

Tip

You should set the work plane before invoking the ***Model Text*** *tool because model text can be placed only in the current work plane.*

Modifying Model Text Properties

You can modify the properties of the model text before or after creating it. To edit the model text, select it from the drawing; the **Modify | Generic Models** tab will be displayed. You can use options in this tab to modify the content of the text, properties (instance and type) of the text, existing work plane of the text, and so on. In the **Modify | Generic Models** tab for the selected text, modification options are available in specific panels. To edit contents in the selected text, choose the **Edit Text** tool from the **Text** panel of the **Modify | Generic Models** tab; the **Edit Text** dialog box will be displayed. Enter suitable content in the dialog box and choose **OK**; the dialog box will be closed and the modified content will be displayed in the model text.

To change the instance and type properties of the selected text, you can use various parameters in the **Properties** palette. In this palette, choose the **Edit** button in the **Value** column of the **Text** instance parameter to enter new text. The **Horizontal Align** parameter can be used to set the alignment or justification of the text to left, center, or right. The **Depth** instance parameter can be used to set the depth or extrusion height of the text characters. You can also select and assign materials to the model text using the **Material** parameter. You can access the type parameters of the model text. To do so, choose the **Edit Type** button from the **Properties** palette; the **Type Properties** dialog box will be displayed. This dialog box displays the type parameters for the model text. The function of parameters such as **Text Font**, **Text Size**, **Bold**, **Italic**, and so on is similar to those described for text notes. Figure 12-25 shows another example of model text added to a building model.

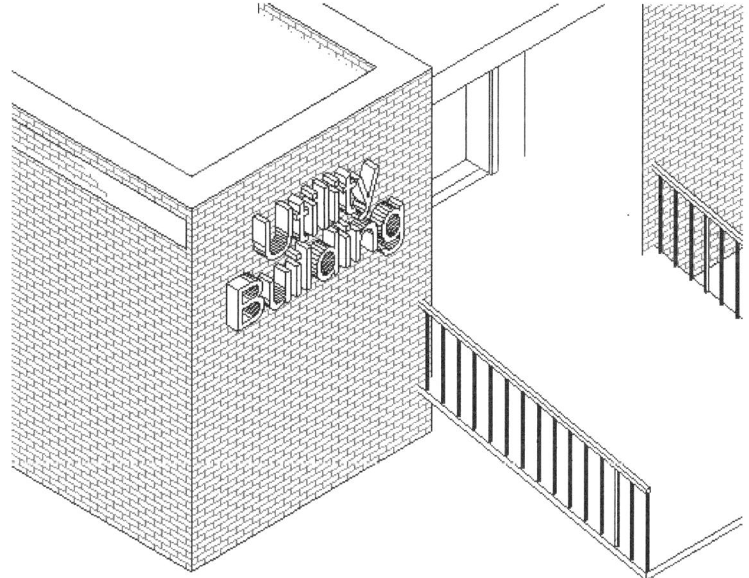

Figure 12-25 An example showing the model text added to a building model

Note

If a project view intersects the model text, it will be shown as a cut. You can however set the view range parameter to make it appear complete

Tip

*You can also use the editing tools such as **Copy, Move, Rotate, Array, Mirror** and so on for editing the model text.*

REVISION CLOUDS

While creating project plans, you may need to revise a portion of a project view and issue the revised drawings to the concerned authorities. The revision cloud is added to refer and to indicate the revised portion. Except 3D views, you can add the revision cloud to any project view such as floor plans, elevations, sections, and so on. Autodesk Revit enables you to create the revision clouds of the desired shape and size. You can also add a revision tag to the revision cloud for referring to the revisions made to a specified area.

Creating the Revision Cloud

Ribbon: Annotate > Detail > Revision Cloud

To create a revision cloud, invoke the **Revision Cloud** tool from the **Detail** panel; the **Modify | Create Revision Cloud Sketch** tab will be displayed. You can use various sketching tools in the tab to sketch, edit a sketch, and assign properties to the revision cloud. To sketch the revision cloud, choose any of the drawing tools from the **Draw** panel, move the cursor near the revised area, and click at the desired location to start creating the revision cloud. On moving the cursor, you will notice that a curved bubble-shaped line is displayed. Click to specify the next point of the cloud outline. In this way, you can click at multiple points to sketch the revision cloud of desired size and shape enclosing the portion of the view that needs to be referred for revision. You can choose other standard tools to create revision cloud such as line, rectangle, and so on. You can use SPACEBAR to flip the direction of the cloud. Next, choose the **Finish Edit Mode** button from the **Mode** panel of the **Modify | Create Revision Cloud Sketch** tab to create the revision cloud, as shown in Figure 12-26.

Revit allows you to hide revision clouds in a view. To hide a revision cloud, select the required revision cloud and right-click; a shortcut menu will be displayed. Then, choose **Hide in view > Category** from the shortcut menu. Hiding clouds in a view does not have any effect on revision tables and schedules.

Note
If you have tagged the revision cloud, hiding the revision cloud will also hide the tag associated with it.

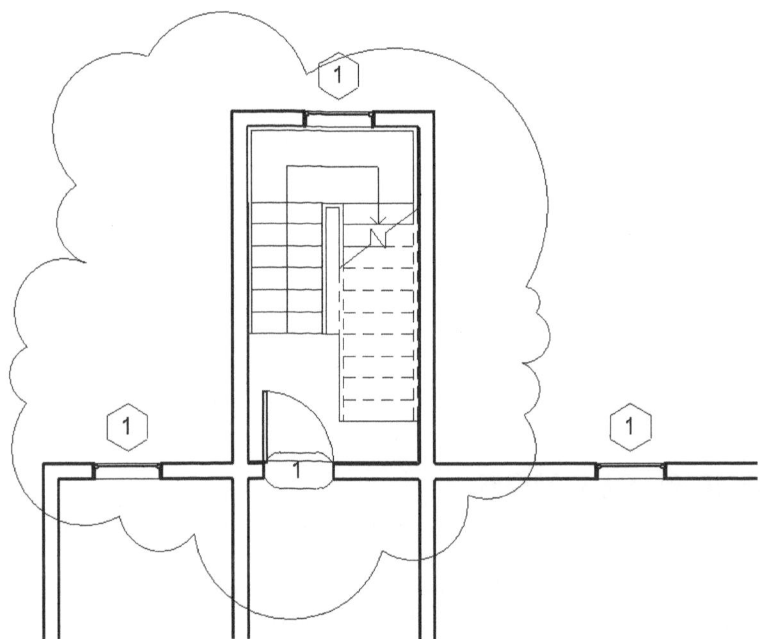

Figure 12-26 *The revision cloud created around the portion to be referred for revision*

Adding a Revision Tag

While working on projects, you may need to use multiple revision clouds in a project view. To identify and mark each revision cloud, you can add revision tags to it.

A revision tag can be added using the **Tag by Category** tool. To add a revision tag, invoke the **Tag by Category** tool from the **Tag** panel of the **Annotate** tab and then move the cursor near the revision cloud. Click in the drawing area when the cloud is highlighted; the revision tag will be placed. In case it is not loaded in the project file, Autodesk Revit will prompt you to load it. You can load the *Revision Tag.rfa* family file from the **US Imperial > Annotations** folder. Now, you can move the cursor over the revision cloud and click to place the revision tag. A leader will automatically be added to the revision tag because the **Leader** check box in the **Options Bar** is selected by default. You can then use the drag controls to direct the leader toward the revision cloud, as shown in Figure 12-27. However, you can remove the leader from the revision tag by selecting it and then clearing the **Leader** check box in **Options Bar**. Once you have added the revision tags, Autodesk Revit will enable you to create revision schedules to be placed on the drawing sheet. You will learn more about creating schedules in the next section.

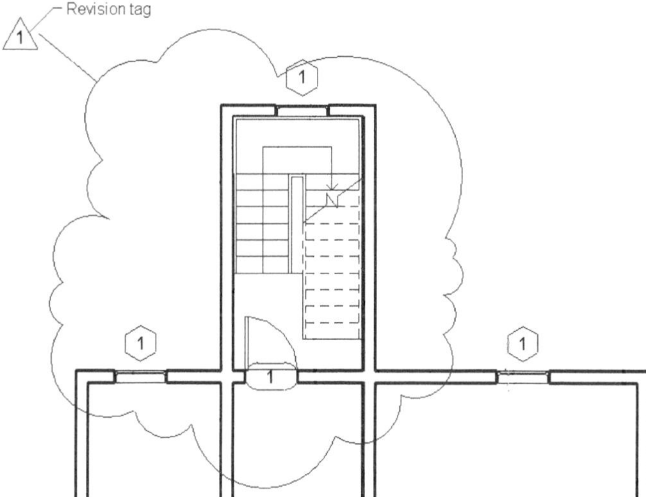

Figure 12-27 *A revision tag added to the revision cloud*

Controlling the Visibility of the Revision Tag

Revit allows you to control the visibility of revision tags before adding revision clouds to a drawing. To specify the visibility settings, choose the **Sheet Issues/Revisions** tool from **Manage > Settings > Additional Settings** drop-down; the **Sheet Issues/Revisions** dialog box will be displayed. In the **Show** column of the dialog box, the **Cloud and Tag** option is selected by default. Click in the **Show** column cell and select any of the following visibility options:

None

This option will turn off the display of both the revision cloud and the tag in the drawing.

Tag

This option will display the tag, but not the revision cloud. You can hover the cursor in the drawing and select the revision cloud when it gets highlighted.

Cloud and Tag

This is the default option and displays both the revision cloud and the tag, if loaded in the drawing.

USING SCHEDULES IN A PROJECT

Schedule is another format for providing project information. In a building project, there may be different items that can be used a number of times at different locations. Schedules are primarily used to provide information regarding these items in a tabulated form. For each item, the schedule tables provide information regarding its size, material, cost, finish, level, and so on. These schedules can then be used by associated agencies for various purposes. They can assist the fabricating agency to manufacture all such items. The quantity surveyors and estimators can calculate the quantity and cost of the grouped items.

For example, in a building model, a particular window type may be used a number of times in the same layout plan on different floors. Using schedules, you can group these windows in different ways based on their parameters such as location in a project, floor, size of the window, material of construction, and so on.

Schedules are created by extracting information from a building model. In Revit, all elements are parametric. This means that they have several properties associated with them. When you use these elements, the associated information is automatically added to the building model. This information can be then extracted for the creation of schedules.

The power of Autodesk Revit's parametric change engine enables you to modify elements in a building model at any stage of the project development. The changes are reflected immediately in all project views. As elements are bidirectionally associated, the entire project information is updated immediately and the necessary changes in schedules are reflected automatically. Conversely, when you modify an element in a schedule, all its instances are immediately updated in all project views. Autodesk Revit also enables you to create schedules based on common group properties of different categories of items. For example, you can create a schedule of all rooms in a project that have the same floor, ceiling, and wall finish. These are termed as Key Schedules.

Note

Some of the parameters of wall such as Base Constraint, Base Offset, Top Constraint, Top Offset, and Unconnected Height are included in the Wall Schedule and Material Takeoff.

Generating a Schedule

Ribbon:	View > Create > Schedules drop-down > Schedule/Quantities

In Autodesk Revit, you can create a schedule by using the **Schedule/Quantities** tool. You can invoke this tool from the **Create** panel. On doing so, the **New Schedule** dialog box will be displayed, as shown in Figure 12-28.

In the **New Schedule** dialog box, various categories of building elements are listed in the **Category** list. By default, all the check boxes are selected in the **Filter List** drop-down. You can select one or more disciplines from the **Filter List** drop-down list. Then, you can select the required category from the **Category** list to create a schedule. For example, to generate a door schedule, you can select **Doors** from the **Category** list. The **Wall Sweeps** category in the **Category** list is used to create a schedule for wall sweeps. The category selected for creating a schedule is displayed in the **Name** edit box. The **Schedule building components** radio button is used to create a schedule of building elements. The **Filter List** drop-down list is used to display all the

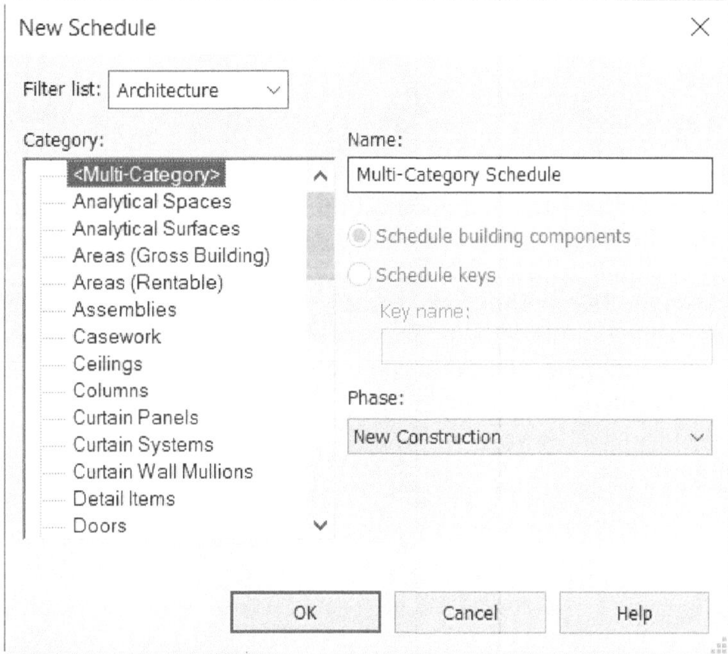

Figure 12-28 *The* ***New Schedule*** *dialog box*

discipline categories. In this drop-down list, you can select the check box of the discipline you want to display. When you choose the **OK** button, the **Schedule Properties** dialog box will be displayed, as shown in Figure 12-29.

The **Schedule Properties** dialog box has the options to set the properties of the elements, formatting, and appearance in a schedule. It contains five tabs: **Fields**, **Filter**, **Sorting/Grouping**, **Formatting**, and **Appearance**. The options in the **Fields** tab can be used to select the headings of a schedule. Select the required headings from the **Available fields** list and then choose the **Add** button to add fields to the **Scheduled fields** area. Choose the **Remove** button to remove the selected scheduled fields. You can use the **Move parameter up** and **Move parameter down** buttons to move and arrange the fields in the desired order. By choosing the **New Parameter** button, you can add your own custom field. You can choose the **Add Calculated Parameter** button to create a field that is a percentage of another field. You can choose the **Combined Parameters** button to combine the parameters for the schedule. The **Include elements in links** check box can be selected to include elements from the linked Revit files into the schedules as well as drawing files of model elements such as doors, walls, rooms, and so on.

The options in the **Filter** tab enable you to restrict the display of elements based on certain rules. Based on their parameters and values, you can use maximum four filters for a schedule. For example, to display doors on Level1, you can use the **Level** parameter as one filter and the number **1** as the other filter. The options in the **Sorting/Grouping** tab can be used to sort and group rows in a schedule. The parameter for sorting a schedule can be selected from the **Sort by** drop-down list. You can sort it in the ascending or descending order by selecting appropriate radio button. For example, to arrange doors types in the ascending order of their width, choose **Width** as the **Sort by** parameter and the **Ascending** button. The **Grand totals** check box can be selected to display the sum total of all the elements. On selecting the **Grand Totals** checkbox the **Custom grand total title** edit box will be enabled. In this edit box, you can enter the title for the **Grand Total** in the schedule.

The **Formatting** tab enables you to set the parameters related to the appearance of headings. You can select a heading from the **Fields** list and enter a new heading name in the **Heading** edit box. The orientation and the alignment of the heading can be specified by selecting the desired options from the **Heading orientation** and **Alignment** drop-down lists, respectively. The **Field Format** button is used to format the appearance of fields with numerical values. Select the required option from the **Show conditional format on sheets** drop-down list to display the sum total of the values entered in these fields. You can select the **Hidden field** check box to hide a field in a schedule. On doing so, you can sort out or filter a schedule by using the selected field without actually displaying it in the schedule.

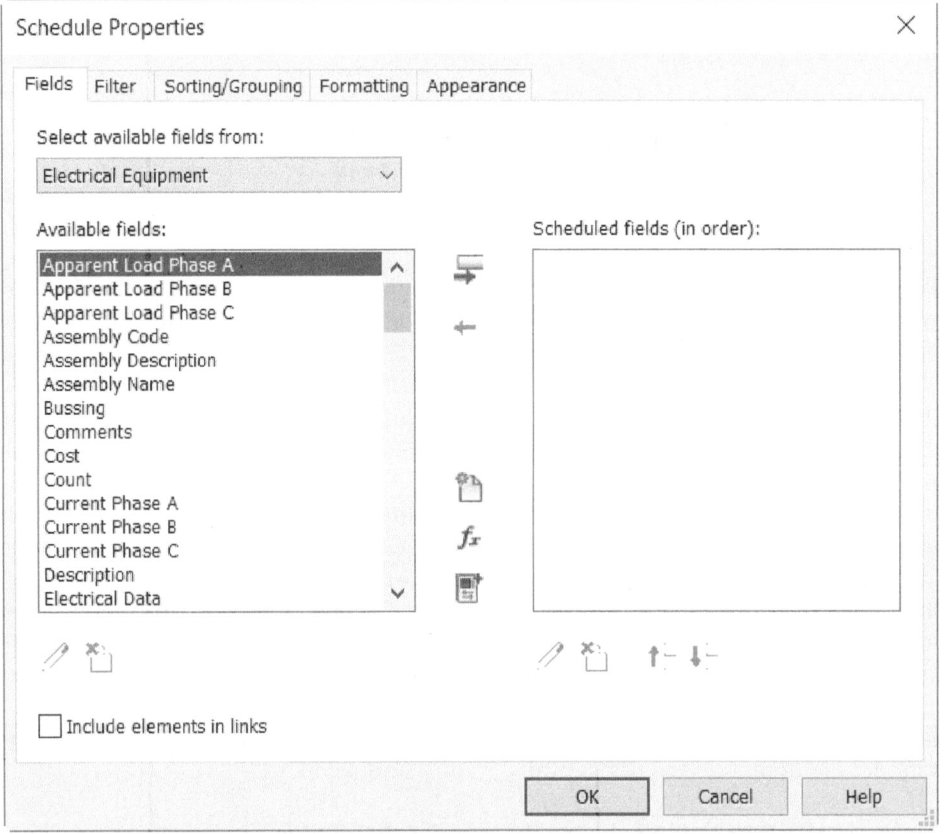

Figure 12-29 *The* ***Schedule Properties*** *dialog box*

The options in the **Appearance** tab can be used to change the appearance of the schedule view. You can use various parameters such as **Header text**, **Body text**, and so on to modify the appearance of a schedule.

When you choose the **OK** button from the **Schedule Properties** dialog box it will be closed and the schedule will be created. Autodesk Revit scans the building model for the category of elements and displays the schedule based on the parameters specified. Figure 12-30 shows an example of a window schedule with the scheduled fields.

Window Schedule					
Type Mark	Width	Height	Level	Count	Comments
1	3' - 0"	4' - 0"	Ground Floor	1	
1	3' - 0"	4' - 0"	Ground Floor	1	
2	4' - 0"	4' - 0"	Ground Floor	1	
2	4' - 0"	4' - 0"	Ground Floor	1	
2	4' - 0"	4' - 0"	Ground Floor	1	
3	1' - 4"	4' - 0"	Ground Floor	1	
3	1' - 4"	4' - 0"	Ground Floor	1	
3	1' - 4"	4' - 0"	Ground Floor	1	
3	1' - 4"	4' - 0"	Ground Floor	1	
3	1' - 4"	4' - 0"	Ground Floor	1	
3	1' - 4"	4' - 0"	Ground Floor	1	
3	1' - 4"	4' - 0"	Ground Floor	1	
3	1' - 4"	4' - 0"	Ground Floor	1	
3	1' - 4"	4' - 0"	Ground Floor	1	
3	1' - 4"	4' - 0"	Ground Floor	1	
3	1' - 4"	4' - 0"	Ground Floor	1	
3	1' - 4"	4' - 0"	Ground Floor	1	
1	3' - 0"	4' - 0"	First Floor	1	
1	3' - 0"	4' - 0"	First Floor	1	
2	4' - 0"	4' - 0"	First Floor	1	

Figure 12-30 *A window schedule*

You can modify the properties of a schedule even after creating it. To do so, click on the schedule name in the **Project Browser** and from the **Properties** palette, choose the **Edit** button in the **Value** column for the **Fields**, **Filter**, **Sorting/Grouping**, **Formatting**, and **Appearance** instance parameters to access their respective tabs in the **Schedule Properties** dialog box.

For example, the schedule shown in Figure 12-30 can be edited to create a simplified schedule in which the doors with a particular type mark are grouped together. You can access the options in the **Sorting/Grouping** tab, select the **Grand totals** check box and clear the **Itemize every instance** check box to summarize the schedule. On doing so, the modified schedule will be displayed, as shown in Figure 12-31.

Window Schedule					
Type Mark	Width	Height	Level	Count	Comments
1	3' - 0"	4' - 0"		8	
2	4' - 0"	4' - 0"		12	
3	1' - 4"	4' - 0"		48	

Figure 12-31 *The modified window schedule*

Tip

You can modify the appearance of a schedule by dragging the columns to the desired width.

After calculating the required material quantity, you can use the cost per unit to calculate the total estimated cost for that item. For example, to calculate the total cost of walls for a project, first create a wall schedule showing the area of each wall type. Next, enter the value of the cost per square feet for each wall type directly in the created schedule. Autodesk Revit automatically assigns the cost to all instances of the same wall type. In the **Fields** tab of the **Schedule Properties** dialog box, you can then use the **Add Parameter** button in the **Schedule Properties** dialog box to add a new column for **Total Cost** for each type of wall. Use the **Calculate Value** button and assign the formula **Cost*Area/1'^2** to calculate the total cost of each type of wall (the factor 1'^2 is used to suppress the units). In the **Formatting** tab, select the **Calculate total** check box for the **Total Cost** column and generate the total cost of the walls in the building project. This procedure can be adopted for each category of elements such as windows, doors, floor, roof, furniture, and so on. The gross total cost of all building elements can then be calculated.

Tip

*The **Schedule/Quantities** tool can be used to create schedules of the elements related to a building model. For example, you can create wall schedules showing values of wall parameters such as length, height, volume, area, and so on. The values of these parameters can then be used to calculate the required quantity of materials such as brick, plaster, paint, and so on. Similarly, you can create furniture schedule, room schedule, structural schedule, and so on to create an inventory of the dependent and stand-alone elements used in a project. These schedules help you arrange the elements in a tabular form.*

Exporting Schedule to Excel Sheet

In Autodesk Revit, you can export a schedule to MS Office Excel to generate a spreadsheet. To do so, from the **File** menu, choose **Export > Reports > Schedule**; the **Export Schedule** dialog box will be displayed, as shown in Figure 12-32. Enter the name of file in the **File Name** edit box and select the **Delimited text (*.txt)** from the **File of type** drop-down list. Next, choose the **Save** button; the modified **Export Schedule** dialog box will be displayed, refer to Figure 12-33.

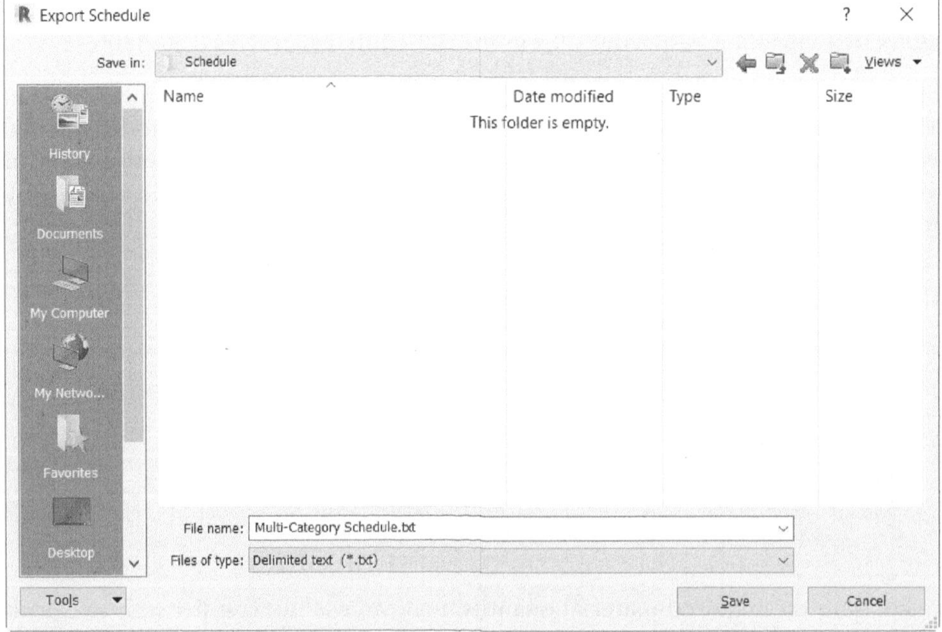

Figure 12-32 *The **Export Schedule** dialog box*

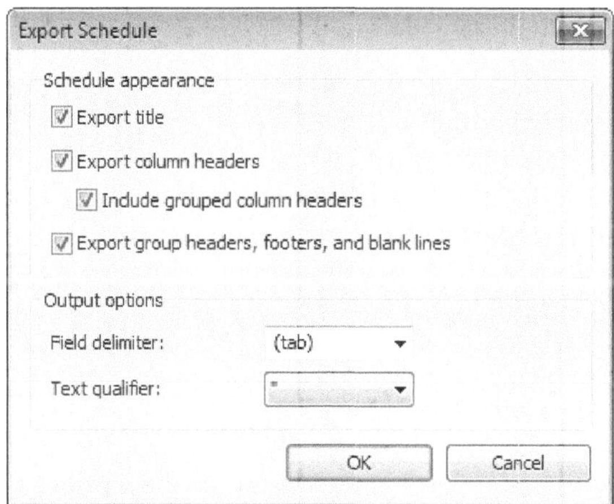

*Figure 12-33 The **Export Schedule** dialog box with schedule appearance and output parameters*

The **Export Schedule** dialog box consists of the **Schedule Appearance** and **Output options** areas.

In the **Schedule Appearance** area, the **Export title** check box is selected by default. As a result, the title of the schedule will be exported to the spreadsheet. On clearing this check box, the title of the schedule will not be exported to the spreadsheet. The **Export column header** check box is also selected by default in the **Schedule Appearance** area. As a result, the **Include grouped column header** check box will be activated and selected. Therefore, the columns and the grouped columns will be exported to the spreadsheet. On clearing these check boxes, the column and the grouped columns will not be exported to the spreadsheet.

The **Export group headers, footers, and blank lines** check box is selected by default. As a result, the header and footer of the schedule will be exported to the spreadsheet. On clearing this check box, the header and footer will not be exported.

The **Output options** area specifies how you want to display the data in the output file. The fields in the output file can be separated by tabs, spaces, commas, or semi-colons. You can select one of these option from the **Field delimiter** drop-down list to separate the text in the field. Select the desired options from the **Text qualifier** drop-down list to specify the text in each field of the file. Next, choose the **OK** button to close the dialog box; the schedule file will be saved at the desired location. To open the saved schedule file in an excel sheet, you need to choose **Start > All Programs > MS Office > Excel 2013**. On doing so, the program will be loaded and the user interface screen will be displayed. Now, choose the **File** button; the **File** menu will be displayed. From the **File** menu, choose **Open** and select the desired file; the file will be displayed in an excel sheet. If required, you can edit Schedule/Quantities in this sheet.

Creating a Legend View

Ribbon:	View > Create > Legends drop-down > Legend

Legend

Legends are created to list the symbols and annotations used in project views.

You can create them for various elements used in a project such as wall types, tag type, symbols, and so on. A legend is created as a view.

To create a legend, choose the **Legend** tool from the **Create** panel; the **New Legend View** dialog box will be displayed, as shown in Figure 12-34. Enter a name for the legend in the **Name** edit box. You can set the scale for the legend by selecting the scale from the **Scale** drop-down list. To set a scale other than the options available in the drop-down list, select the **Custom** option and specify the scale in the **Scale value 1:** edit box. Once you choose the **OK** button in the **New Legend View** dialog box, a new view will open in the drawing window and will be added under the **Legends** head in the **Project Browser**. You can then use various tools to create the desired legend type. Next, you will add legend components to the opened legend view. To do so, choose the **Legend Component** tool from **Annotate > Detail > Component** drop-down; the **Options Bar** will display the associated tools and options. The **Family** drop-down list displays family elements. The required view for the legend can be selected from the **View** drop-down list. The **Host Length** edit box can be used to specify the length of the legend symbol for the selected family type. You can select the desired family element and create a legend. You can use the **Text** tool in the **Text** panel of the **Annotate** tab to add text notes to the legend view. The **Detail Lines** tool can be used to create a tabulated legend with lines.

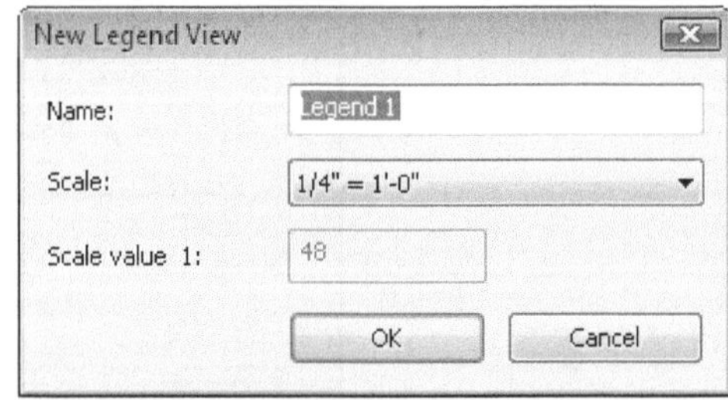

***Figure 12-34** The **New Legend View** dialog box*

Similarly, the **Symbol** tool can be used to create a legend of the symbols used in a project. For example, you can create a legend for all the tags used in the project documentation using the **Symbol** tool, as shown in Figure 12-35.

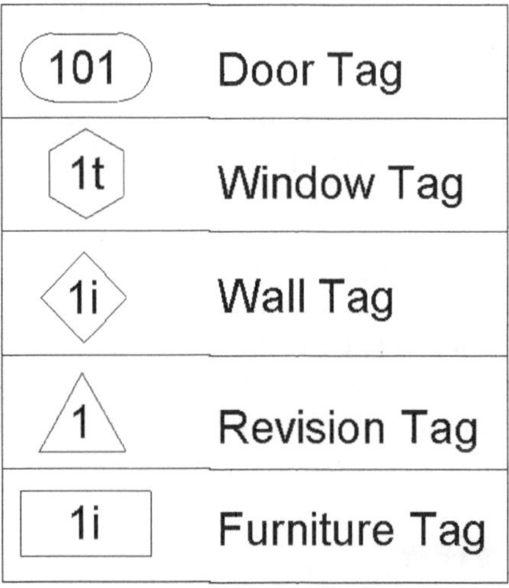

***Figure 12-35** A tag legend*

TUTORIALS

Tutorial 1 Apartment 1 - Callout View

In this tutorial, you will create a callout view of the kitchen door jamb in the *Apartment 1* project represented by a highlighted rectangle with a cursor, as shown in Figure 12-36. You will use the *c11_Apartment1_tut1.rvt* file created in Tutorial 1 of Chapter 11. You need to add the detail lines, detail components, text notes, and break lines to complete the door jamb detail, as shown in Figure 12-37. Use the parameters given in the figure and those given below to create it.

(Expected time: 1hr)

1. Callout view parameters:
   Callout view name to be assigned- **Door Jamb Detail**
   View Scale- **1 1/2" = 1'-0"** View Scale- **1:10**
   Detail Level- **Fine**

2. Detail component to be loaded from the **US Imperial > Detail Items (Detail Components) > Div 06-Wood and Plastic > 061100-Wood Framing** and **US Imperial > Detail Items (Detail Components) >Div 08-Openings > 081400-Wood Doors** folder locations.

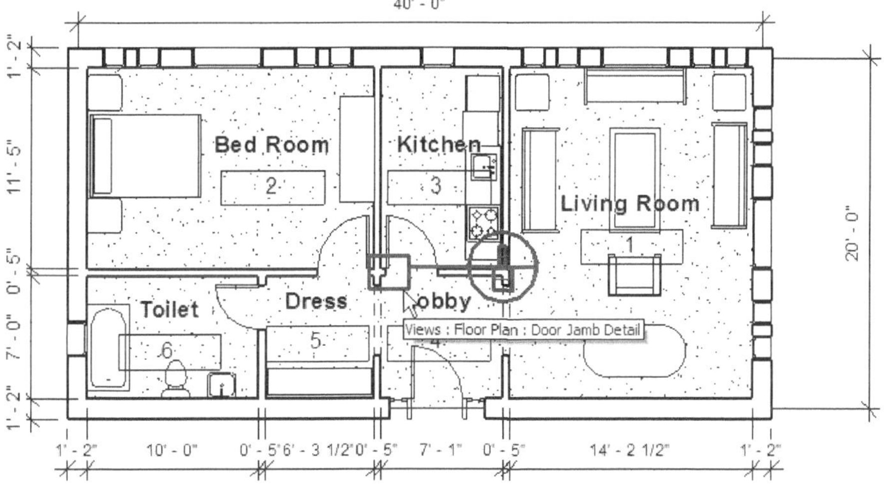

Figure 12-36 Sketch plan for adding a callout view to the Apartment 1 project plan

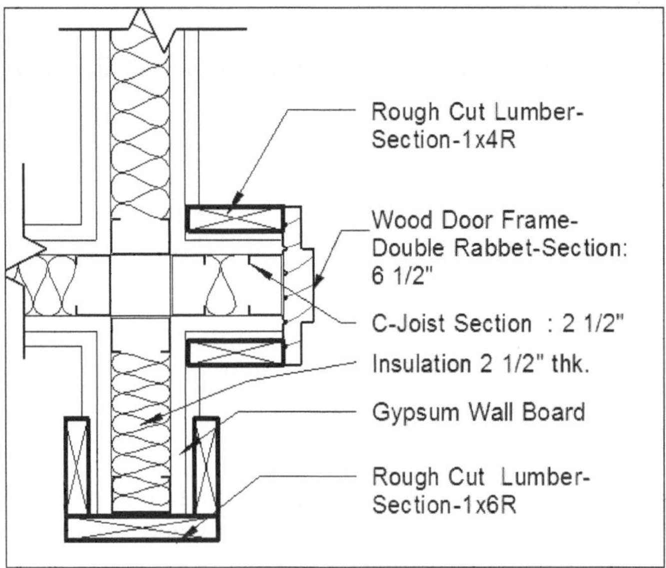

Figure 12-37 *The callout view of the Apartment 1 project*

3. Insulation instance parameters:
   Insulation Width: **2 1/2" (64 mm)**
   Insulation Bulge to Width Ratio: **3**

4. Text note parameters:
   Text Size: **3/32" (2.4 mm)**
   Leader Arrowhead: **Arrow Filled 15 - Degree**
5. Load the break line from **US Imperial > Detail Items (Detail Components)** folder (For Metric **US Metric > Detail Items (Detail Components)** folder) with the following modified parameters:
   Values for the **Right** and **Left** instance parameter: **0' 4" (102 mm)**
   Values for the **Jag Depth**, **Jag Width**, and **Masking depth** parameters: **0' 2" (51 mm)**

   The following steps are required to complete this tutorial:

a. Open the specified project file and then create the callout view using the **Callout** tool, refer to Figure 12-37.
b. Display the view and set its parameters, refer to Figure 12-38.
c. Use the callout view as an underlay and add detail components using the **Detail Component** tool, refer to Figures 12-39 through 12-41.
d. Add detail lines to the callout view using the **Detail Lines** tool, refer to Figures 12-42 through 12-43.
e. Use the **Insulation** tool to add insulation to the detail, refer to Figures 12-45 and 12-46.
f. Invoke the **Text** tool and add the text notes after setting the parameters, refer to Figures 12-47 through 12-49.
g. Add break lines to complete the detail callout view.

h. Save the project using the **Save As** tool.
   For Imperial *c12_Apartment1_tut1.rvt*
   For Metric *M_c12_Apartment1_tut1.rvt*

i. Close the project.

Opening the Project File and Creating the Callout View

1. To start a project, choose **Open > Project** from the **File** menu and open the *c11_Apartment_tut1.rvt* file created in Tutorial 1 of Chapter 11. The first floor plan is displayed. You can also download this file from *http://www.cadcim.com*. The path of the file is as follows: *Textbooks > Civil/GIS > Revit Architecture > Exploring Autodesk Revit 2018 for Architecture*

2. Choose the **Zoom in Region** tool from the **Navigation Bar** and zoom near the area inside the rectangle, refer to Figure 12-36.

3. Next, choose the **Rectangle** tool from the **View > Create > Callout** drop-down; the **Modify | Callout** tab is displayed.

4. Click at two points to define the callout view rectangle, as shown in Figure 12-38.

   The callout view created is displayed as **First Floor- Callout 1** under the **Floor Plans** head in the **Project Browser**.

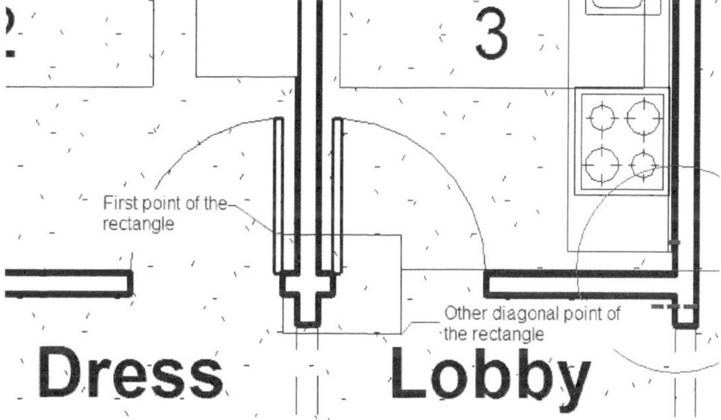

Figure 12-38 *Defining the rectangle to create a callout view*

Displaying the Callout View and Setting View Parameters

1. To display the callout view, double-click on the callout view name **First Floor- Callout 1** under the **Floor Plans** head in the **Project Browser**.

   Now, select the door element in the callout view and right-click; a shortcut menu is displayed. Choose **Hide in view > Category** from the shortcut menu; the doors in this view are now hidden, as shown in Figure 12-39.

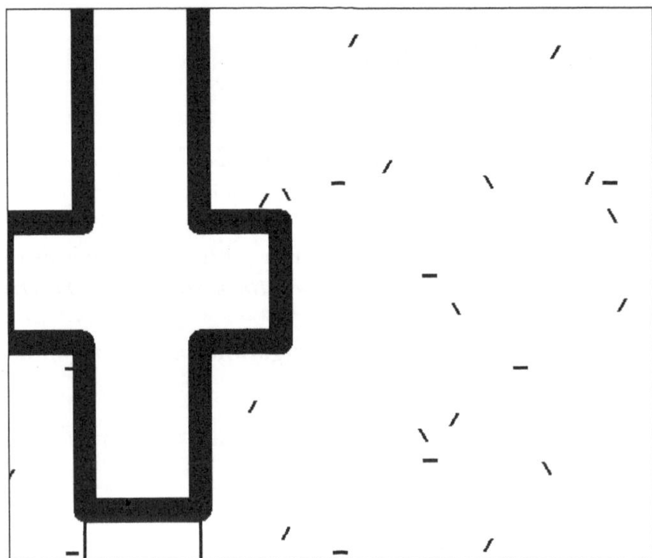

Figure 12-39 Callout view displayed in the viewing area

2. In the **Properties** palette, click in the **Value** field for the **View Name** instance parameter and enter **Door Jamb Detail**.

3. For the **View Scale** parameter, click in its value field and select the desired option from the corresponding drop-down list.
   For Imperial **1 1/2" = 1'- 0"**
   For Metric **1 : 10**

4. Similarly, click in the value fields for the **Display Model** and **Detail Level** parameters and then select **Halftone** and **Fine** from the corresponding drop-down lists.

Adding Detail Components

In this section of the tutorial, you will add detail components by using the callout view as an underlay. Further, you will load the desired components, place them at the required location, and then modify their sizes.

1. Choose the **Annotate** tab and then choose the **Detail Component** tool from the **Component** drop-down of the **Detail** panel; the **Modify | Place Detail Component** tab is displayed.

   Next, you need to load the components according to the project parameters.

2. Choose the **Load Family** tool from the **Mode** panel; the **Load Family** dialog box is displayed.

3. Navigate to **US Imperial > Detail Items > Div 08-Openings > 081400-Wood Doors** and select the **Wood Door Frame-Double Rabbet-Section** file (**US Metric > Detail Items**

>Div 08- Doors and Windows > 08200-Wood and Plastic Doors > 08210- Wood Doors and select the **M_Wood Door Frame-Double Rabbet-Section** file). Now, choose **Open**; the selected file is loaded and it will be available in the **Type Selector** drop-down list.

4. Choose the **Type Properties** tool from the **Properties** panel; the **Type Properties** dialog box is displayed.

5. Choose **Duplicate**; the **Name** dialog box is displayed. Enter **6 1/2" (165 mm)** in the **Name** edit box and choose **OK**. Now, in the **Value** fields for the **Width** and **Stop** parameters, enter **0' 6 1/2" (165 mm)** and **0' 3" (76 mm)**, respectively.

6. Now, choose **OK**; the **Type Properties** dialog box will close.

7. Choose the **Load Family** tool from the **Mode** panel; the **Load Family** dialog box is displayed. In this dialog box, navigate to **US Imperial > Detail Items > Div 06-Wood and Plastic > 061100-Wood Framing** and select the **Rough Cut Lumber-Section** file (for Metric **US Metric > Detail Items > Div 06-Wood and Plastic > 06100- Rugh Carpentry > 06110- Wood Framing** and select the **M_Rough Cut Lumber-Section** file). Next, choose **Open**; the **Specify Types** dialog box is displayed.

8. Choose **1x4R** and **1x6R** in the **Type** column using the CTRL key and then choose **OK**; the **Specify Types** dialog box will close and the selected types will now be available in the **Type Selector** drop-down list in the **Properties** palette.

9. From the **Type Selector** drop-down list, select **Wood Door Frame-Double Rabbet-Section: 6 1/2" (165 mm)**.

10. Select the **Rotate after placement** check box available in the **Options Bar**.
11. Move the cursor to the viewing area and click near the door jamb location to place the door frame. Rotate it 90 degrees in counterclockwise direction to achieve the correct orientation and then click again. Next, choose the **Modify** button from the **Select** panel. Then, select the placed door frame and use the **Move** tool and the **Midpoint** snap option to move the door frame to the location shown in Figure 12-40. Choose the **Modify** button from the **Select** panel.

12. Similarly, using the **Detail Component** tool and the editing tools, place the **Rough Cut Lumber-Section : 1x4R** component at the locations shown in Figure 12-41.

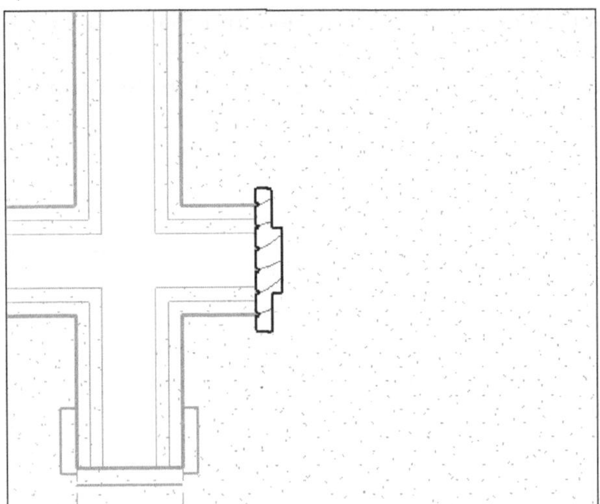

Figure 12-40 *Adding the door frame as a detail component*

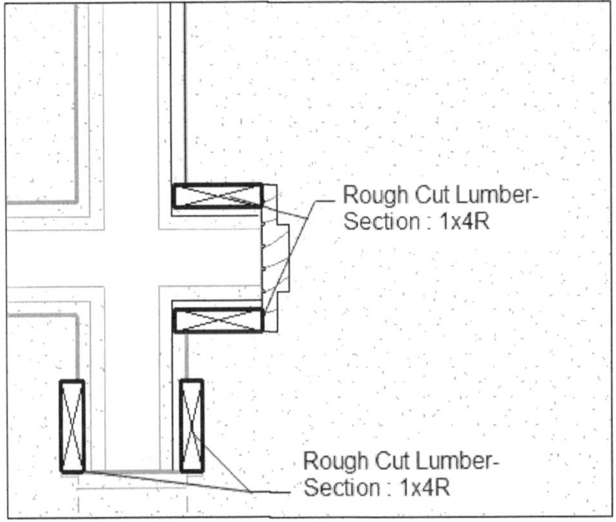

Figure 12-41 *Adding the wood board as a detail component*

You need to place another wood board of **6 1/2"** (165 mm) length. You can select and modify the properties of a similar component to create a new one.

13. Next, invoke the **Detail Component** tool and select the **Rough Cut Lumber-Section : 1x6R** option from the **Type Selector** drop-down list.

14. Choose the **Edit Type** button from the **Properties** palette; the **Type Properties** dialog box is displayed.

15. Choose the **Duplicate** button; the **Name** dialog box is displayed. Enter **1x 6.5R** in the **Name** edit box.

16. In the **Type Properties** dialog box, enter the value **0' 6 1/2" (165 mm)** in the **Value** column for the **Depth** dimension parameter.

17. Choose **OK**; the **Type Properties** dialog box is closed.

18. Ensure that the detail component **Rough Cut Lumber-Section : 1x6.5R** is selected in the **Type Selector** drop-down list and place it at the location, as shown in Figure 12-42.

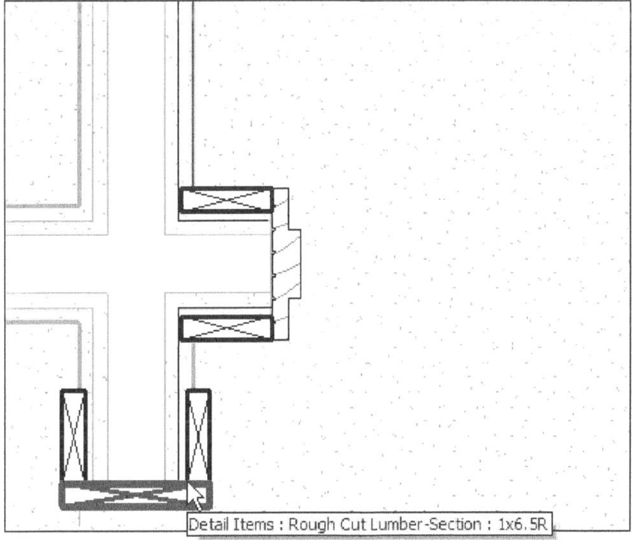

Figure 12-42 *The modified wood board added as a detail component*

Adding Detail Lines to the Project Detail

1. Choose the **Detail Line** tool from the **Detail** panel of the **Annotate** tab; the **Modify | Place Detail Lines** tab is displayed.

2. Ensure that the **Thin Lines** option is selected in the **Line Style** drop-down list in the **Line Style** panel. Now, use the snap options to sketch thin lines at 5/8" distance, depicting the double layer gypsum wall board in the callout view. You can also use the **Mirror**, **Offset**, and **Copy** tools to create detail lines. After adding the thin lines, the detail view will appear similar to the graphic shown in Figure 12-43.

3. After you create the details lines, you will add metal studs to support the gypsum boards. To do so, choose the **Detail Component** tool from **Annotate > Detail > Component** drop-down; the **Modify | Place Detail Component** tab is displayed.

4. Choose the **Load Family** tool from the **Mode** panel; the **Load Family** dialog box is displayed. Now, browse to the **US Imperial > Detail Items > Div 05-Metals > 054200-Cold-Formed Metal Joist Framing** folder and select the **C Joist-Section** file (for Metric **US Metric > Detail Items > Div 05-Metals > 05400-Cold-Formed Metal Framing > 05420-Cold-Formed Metal Joists** folder and select the **M_C Joist-Section** file). Now, choose **Open**; the selected file will now be loaded and can be selected from the **Type Selector** drop-down list.

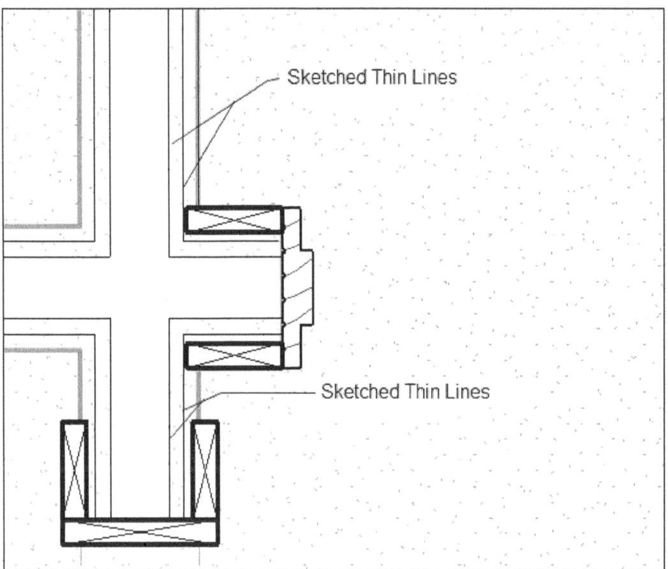

Figure 12-43 The detail lines added to the callout view

5 Ensure that the **C Joist-Section : 5 1/2" (140mm)**is selected in the **Type Selector** drop-down list and then choose the **Edit Type** button from the **Properties** palette; the **Type Properties** dialog box is displayed.

6. Choose **Duplicate**; the **Name** dialog box is displayed. Enter **2 1/2" (64 mm)** in the **Name** edit box and then choose **OK** to close the **Name** dialog box.

7. Now, in the **Type Properties** dialog box, click in the **Value** fields of the **Width** and **Depth** parameters and enter **2 1/2" (64 mm)** and **1 1/2" (38 mm)**, respectively.

8. Choose **OK**; the **Type Properties** dialog box closes and the new type of joist section is selected in the **Type Selector** drop-down list.

9. Move the cursor in the drawing area and then use the editing tools to add the selected type of joist to the detail view, as shown in Figure 12-44.

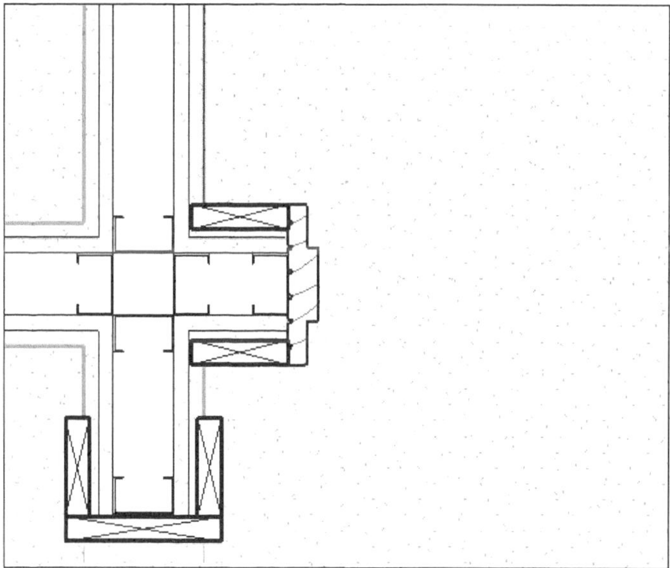

Figure 12-44 The medium detail lines added to the detail view

Adding an Insulation to the Detail

After you have added detail components and detail lines, you will add insulation between the metal joist framing members by using the **Insulation** tool.

1. To add insulation, choose the **Insulation** tool from the **Detail** panel of the **Annotate** tab; the **Modify | Place Insulation** tab is displayed.

2. Ensure that the **Line** tool is chosen in the **Draw** panel. Next, enter **0' 2 1/2" (64 mm)** in the **Width** edit box in the **Options Bar**.

3. Move the cursor to the drawing window and click to specify the location of the start point and end point of the insulation, as shown in Figure 12-45. Now, press ESC twice; the insulation is created.

4. Next, select the insulation that you have recently created; the **Modify | Insulation Batting Lines** tab is displayed.

5. In the **Properties** palette, click in the value column of the **Insulation Bulge to Width Ratio (1/x)** parameter and enter **3**. Now, choose **Apply**; the type property of the selected component gets modified.

6. Similarly, to add other insulations, repeat steps 1 to 3 of this section. Refer to Figure 12-46 for location.

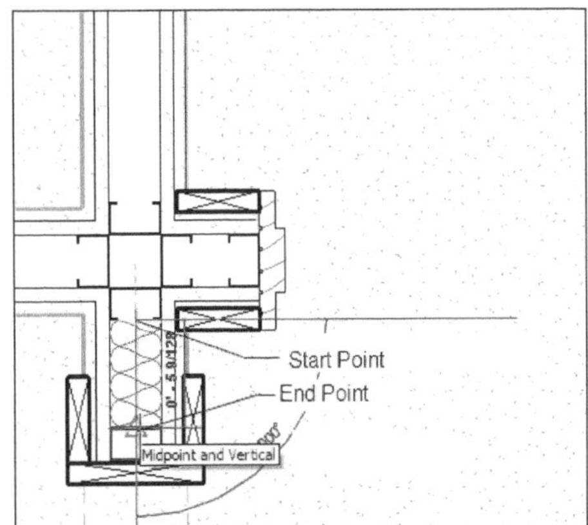

Figure 12-45 Sketching the insulation

Figure 12-46 The insulations added to the detail view

Adding Text Notes to the Detail

You need to add text notes to the detail. Use an existing text note style as a template and create a new text type by modifying its parameters, as given in the project parameters.

1. Choose the **Text** tool from the **Text** panel of the **Annotate** tab; the **Modify | Place Text** tab is displayed.
2. From the **Type Selector** drop-down list, select **Text: 3/32" Arial (2.5mm Arial)**.
3. In the **Properties** palette, choose the **Edit Type** button; the **Type Properties** dialog box is displayed.
4. Choose **Duplicate** from the dialog box; the **Name** edit box is displayed.
5. Enter the name **Text Notes** in the **Name** edit box and choose **OK**.
6. In the **Type Properties** dialog box, ensure that the value for the **Text Size** type parameter is **3/32" (2.5 mm)**.
7. For the **Leader Arrowhead** parameter, select **Arrow Filled 15 Degree** from the drop-down list.
8. Choose **Apply** and **OK**; the settings are applied to the text notes and the **Type Properties** dialog box closes.
9. To add the text note with two segment leaders, choose the **Two Segments** tool from the **Leader** panel of the **Modify | Place Text** tab. If you want to create a text note with two segment leaders, you need to specify three points. The first point specifies the location of the leader head, the second point specifies the leader elbow, and the third point specifies the start point of the text.
10. Click on the door panel, refer to Figure 12-47, to specify the first point and move the cursor upward in the right direction and then click to specify the elbow point. Next, move the cursor horizontally toward right and click to specify the endpoint of the leader (start point of the text), as shown in Figure 12-47.

11. Enter the text **Wood Door Frame - Double Rabbet-Section**: **6 1/2** " (for Metric **Wood Door Frame - Double Rabbet-Section**: **165 mm**) in the edit box, as shown in Figure 12-48. Click outside the text box to complete the text note.

12. Similarly, add other text notes at appropriate locations, as shown in Figure 12-49, and press ESC when you have completed entering the text.

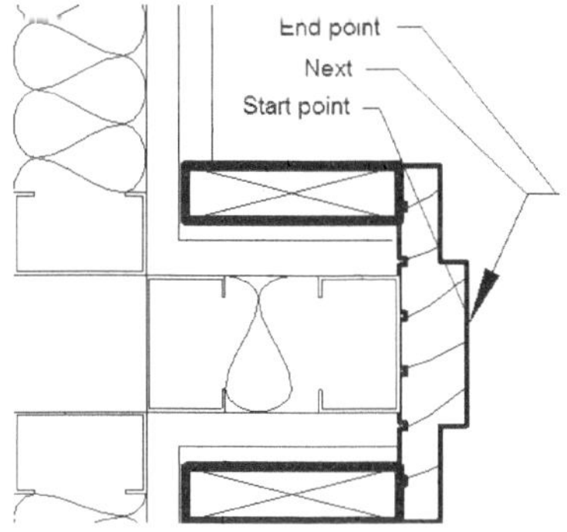

Figure 12-47 Specifying three points for creating the text note with two segment leaders

Figure 12-48 Writing the text for the text note

Adding Break Lines

In this section of the tutorial, you will add break line symbols to the continuing walls at the left and right by using the **Detail Component** tool.

1. Choose the **Detail Component** tool from **Annotate >Detail > Component** drop-down; the **Modify | Place Detail Component** tab is displayed.

2. Choose the **Load Family** tool from the **Mode** panel; the **Load Family** dialog box is displayed. Now, browse to **US Imperial > Detail Items (Detail Components) > Div 01 - General** folder and select the **Break Line** file. Choose **Open**; the **Load Family** dialog box closes, and the **Break Line** option gets selected in the **Type Selector** drop-down list.

3. Move the cursor in the drawing view and add the first break line horizontally at the top of the callout view, refer to Figure 12-37.

4. After you add the first break line, choose the **Modify** button from the **Select** panel and then select the break line you have recently added; the **Modify | Detail Items** tab is displayed.

5. In the **Properties** palette, click in the value fields of the **right** and **left** instance parameters and enter **0' 4" (102 mm)**.

6. Similarly, click in the value fields of the **Jag Depth**, **Jag Width**, and **Masking depth** parameters and enter **0' 2" (51 mm)**. Now, choose **Apply** so that the specified instance parameters are assigned to the selected break line.

   Next, you need to add a vertically aligned break line on the left of the callout view, refer to Figure 12-37.

7. Copy the first break line, place it at the specified location, and then rotate it. Use the **Copy** and **Rotate** tools to add this line.

8. In the **Project Browser**, click on the **Door Jamb Detail** sub-head under the **Floor Plans** head; the instance properties of the callout view are displayed in the **Properties** palette.

9. In the **Properties** palette, click in the value field of the **Display Model** instance parameter and select the **Do not display** option from the drop-down list to restrict the display of the building model. Next, choose the **Apply** button.

   The completed tutorial resembles the detail sketch plan, as shown in Figure 12-49.

Saving the Project

In this section, you will save the project file using the **Save As** tool.

1. Now, choose **Save As > Project** from the **File** menu; the **Save As** dialog box is displayed. Enter **c12_Apartment1_tut1** (for Metric **M_c12_Apartment1_tut1**) and choose **Save**; the project file is now saved.

2. Now, close the project file by choosing **Close** from the **File** menu.

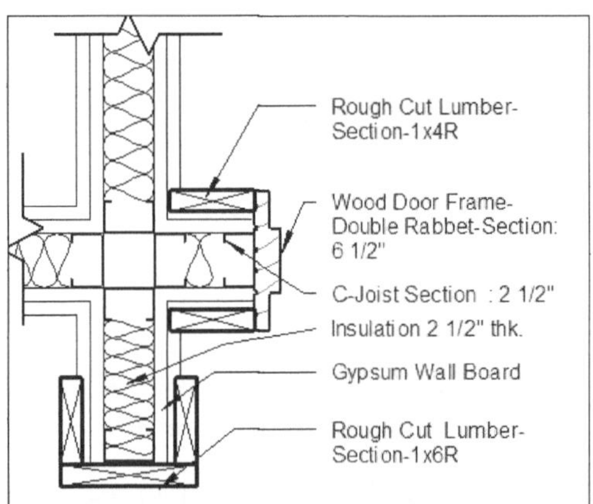

Figure 12-49 *Text added to the callout detail*

Tutorial 2 Apartment 1 - Schedules

In this tutorial, you will create the door, room, and wall schedule for the *Apartment 1* project, based on the schedule given in Figures 12-50, 12-51, and 12-52. **(Expected time: 30 min)**

The following steps are required to complete this tutorial:

a. Open the project file and then invoke the **Schedule/Quantities** tool.
b. Set the schedule properties for creating a door schedule using the **Schedule Properties** dialog box, based on the schedules given.
c. Create the door schedule.
d. Set the schedule properties for creating the room schedule using the **Schedule Properties** dialog box based on the schedules given.

e. Create the room schedule.
f. Create the wall schedule.
g. Save the project using the **Save As** tool.
    For Imperial *c12_Apartment1_tut2.rvt*
    For Metric *M_c12_Apartment1_tut2.rvt*
h. Close the project.

Opening the Project File and Invoking the Schedule/Quantities Tool

1. Choose **Open > Project** from the **File** menu to open the *Apartment 1* project created in the previous tutorial. You can also download this file from *http://www.cadcim.com*. The path of the file is as follows: *Textbooks > Civil/GIS > Revit Architecture > Exploring Autodesk Revit 2018 for Architecture.*

2. Double-click on the **First Floor** under the **Floor Plans** head in the **Project Browser** to open the first floor plan.

3. Invoke the **Schedule/Quantities** tool from **View > Create > Schedules** drop-down; the **New Schedule** dialog box is displayed.

Setting the Parameters for the Door Schedule

1. In the **New Schedule** dialog box, choose **Doors** from the **Category** list and ensure that the **Schedule building components** radio button is selected. Choose the **OK** button; the **Schedule Properties** dialog box is displayed. You can now set the desired parameters based on the door schedule given in Figure 12-50.

Door Schedule				
Type Mark	Level	Width	Height	Count
4	First Floor	2' - 6"	7' - 0"	1
4	Fourth Floor	2' - 6"	7' - 0"	1
4	Second Floor	2' - 6"	7' - 0"	1
4	Third Floor	2' - 6"	7' - 0"	1
8	First Floor	3' - 0"	7' - 0"	1
8	First Floor	3' - 0"	7' - 0"	1
8	Fourth Floor	3' - 0"	7' - 0"	1
8	Fourth Floor	3' - 0"	7' - 0"	1
8	Second Floor	3' - 0"	7' - 0"	1
8	Second Floor	3' - 0"	7' - 0"	1
8	Third Floor	3' - 0"	7' - 0"	1
8	Third Floor	3' - 0"	7' - 0"	1
15	First Floor	3' - 0"	7' - 0"	1
15	Fourth Floor	3' - 0"	7' - 0"	1
15	Second Floor	3' - 0"	7' - 0"	1
15	Third Floor	3' - 0"	7' - 0"	1
Grand total: 16				

Figure 12-50 *Door schedule for the Apartment 1 project*

2. In the **Fields** tab, use the CTRL key and select **Count**, **Height**, **Level**, **Type Mark**, and **Width** from the **Available fields** list.

3. Choose the **Add parameter(s)** button to add these fields to the **Scheduled fields** list. The fields in the **Scheduled fields** list need to be arranged in the same order as they appear in the schedule. To do so, use the **Move parameter up** and **Move parameter down** buttons.

4. Select the **Type Mark** option in the **Scheduled fields** list and choose the **Move parameter up** button thrice to move this field to the top of the list.

5. Similarly, using the **Move parameter up** and **Move parameter down** buttons, arrange the other fields in the following order: **Level**, **Width**, **Height**, and **Count** after the **Type Mark** field.

   Notice that the door schedule to be created is arranged according to the type marks. For this reason, you need to use the **Sorting/Grouping** tab to create this sorting.

6. In the **Schedule Properties** dialog box, choose the **Sorting/Grouping** tab to display its contents.

7. Select the **Type Mark** option from the **Sort by** drop-down list.

8. Select the **Grand totals** check box to generate the total count.

9. Choose the **OK** button to close the **Schedule Properties** dialog box.

   Autodesk Revit displays the created schedule in the drawing window, refer to Figure 12-50. The Door Schedule is added under the **Schedules/Quantities** head in the **Project Browser**.

Setting the Parameters for the Room Schedule

1. Choose the **View** tab and then invoke the **Schedule/Quantities** tool from the **Schedules** drop-down in the **Create** panel; the **New Schedule** dialog box is displayed.

2. Choose **Rooms** from the **Category** list and choose the **OK** button; the **Schedule Properties** dialog box is displayed. You will use this dialog box to set the desired room schedule parameters.

3. Hold the CTRL key and select **Area**, **Level**, **Name**, **Number**, and **Perimeter** from the **Available fields** list in the **Fields** tab.

4. Choose the **Add** button to add these fields to the **Scheduled fields** list.

5. Using the **Move parameter up** and **Move parameter down** buttons, arrange the fields in the following order: **Name**, **Number**, **Level**, **Area**, and **Perimeter**.

6. Choose the **Sorting/Grouping** tab to display its contents.

7. Select the **Number** option from the **Sort by** drop-down list and select the **Grand totals** check box.

Note

*The total area of the room is shown in Figure 12-51. Now, use the **Formatting** tab to calculate the total area.*

8. Choose the **Formatting** tab to display its contents.

9. Select **Area** from the **Fields** list and then select the **Calculate totals** from the drop-down list displayed and ensure that the **Show conditional format on sheets** check box is selected.

10. Choose the **OK** button to close the **Schedule Properties** dialog box.

Autodesk Revit displays the Room Schedule in the drawing window, refer to Figure 12-51. Its name is added under the **Schedules/Quantities** head in the **Project Browser**.

Room Schedule				
Name	Number	Level	Area	Perimeter
Living Room	1	First Floor	268 SF	66' - 1 1/2"
Bed Room	2	First Floor	191 SF	56' - 3 1/2"
Kitchen	3	First Floor	81 SF	37' - 0 1/2"
Lobby	4	First Floor	50 SF	28' - 2"
Dress	5	First Floor	44 SF	26' - 7"
Toilet	6	First Floor	70 SF	34' - 0"
Grand total: 6			703 SF	

***Figure 12-51** Room schedule for the Apartment 1 project*

Setting the Parameters for the Wall Schedule

1. Choose the **View** tab and then invoke the **Schedule/Quantities** tool from the **Schedules** drop-down in the **Create** panel; the **New Schedule** dialog box is displayed.

2. Now, choose **Walls** from the **Category** list and choose the **OK** button; the **Schedule Properties** dialog box is displayed.

3. In the **Fields** tab, press and hold the CTRL key and select **Area**, **Family**, **Length**, **Type**, and **Volume** from the **Available fields** list.

4. Choose the **Add parameter(s)** button to add these fields to the **Scheduled fields** list.

5. Arrange the other fields in the following order: **Family**, **Type**, **Length**, **Volume**, and **Area** using the **Move parameter up** and **Move parameter down** buttons.

6. In the **Sorting/Grouping** tab, select the **Type** option from the **Sort by** drop-down list and then select the **Grand totals** check box. Clear the **Itemize every instance** check box.

7. Choose the **Formatting** tab to display its contents.

8. Select **Area** from the **Fields** list and select the **Calculate totals** option from the drop-down list displayed.

9. Similarly, select the **Calculate totals** check box for the **Length** and **Volume** fields.

10. Choose the **OK** button to close the **Schedule Properties** dialog box.

    Autodesk Revit displays the wall schedule in the drawing window and its name is added under the **Schedules/Quantities** head in the **Project Browser**.

11. You can adjust the column width of the schedule to accommodate the text in the **Type** column using the dragging tool. The created wall schedule appears similar to the schedule given in Figure 12-52.

Wall Schedule				
Family	Type	Length	Volume	Area
Basic Wall	Exterior - Brick on Mtl. Stud	120' - 0"	5196.19 CF	4494 SF
Basic Wall	Interior - 5" Partition (2-hr)	291' - 2"	948.91 CF	2277 SF
Grand total: 24		411' - 2"	6145.09 CF	6771 SF

Figure 12-52 *Wall schedule for the Apartment 1 project*

This completes the tutorial for creating the schedules for the *Apartment 1* project.

12. Double-click on **First Floor** under the **Floor Plans** head in the **Project Browser**.

Saving the Project

In this section, you will save the project file using the **Save As** tool.

1. Choose **Save As > Project** from the **File** menu; the **Save As** dialog box is displayed. Enter **c12_Apartment1_tut2** (for Metric **M_c12_Apartment1_tut2**) in the **File name** edit box and choose **Save**; the project file is saved.

2. Choose **Close** from the **File** menu to close the project file.

Tutorial 3 Road Section Detail

In this tutorial, you will create a new drafting detail of road section, as shown in Figure 12-53. Also, you will use the **Filled Region** tool to sketch the detail elements and the fill region. Use the parameters given below to create the section. **(Expected time: 30 min)**

1. Drafting view parameters:
   Drafting view name to be assigned- **Road Section Detail**
   View Scale- **1" = 1'-0"**
   Detail Level- **Fine**

2. Dimension parameters:
   Dimension style: **Linear Dimension Style: Linear 3/32" Arial**

3. Filled Region parameters:
   Hidden for the earth fill and **Medium** for the other lines
   Fill patterns to be used- **Concrete** and **Earth**

4. Text note parameters:
   Text type- **Text: 3/32" Arial**
   Leader Arrowhead: **Arrow Filled 30 Degree**

5. Break line to be loaded from the **US Imperial > Detail Items (Detail Components)** folder and the parameters to be adjusted as per the given sketch.

   The following steps are required to complete this tutorial:

a. Open a new project file and create a drafting view using the **Drafting View** tool.
b. Set the drafting view parameters.
c. Use the **Filled Region** tool to create elements with fill patterns.
d. Add text notes.
e. Add break lines to complete the detail.
f. Save the project using the **Save As** tool.
   For Imperial *c12_RoadSectionDetail_tut3.rvt*
   For Metric *M_c12_RoadSectionDetail_tut3.rvt*
g. Close the project.

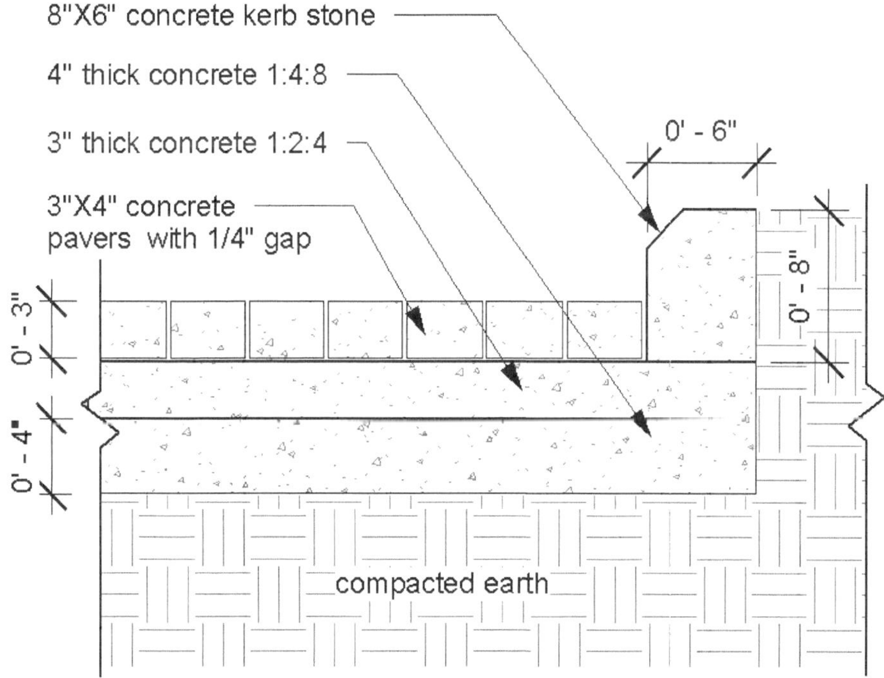

Figure 12-53 *Sketch for creating the drafting detail of a road section*

Opening a New Project File and Creating the Drafting View

1. Choose **New > Project** from the **File** menu and open a new project using the default template file.

2. Choose the **View** tab and choose the **Drafting View** tool from the **Create** panel; the **New Drafting View** dialog box is displayed.

3. In the **New Drafting View** dialog box, enter the name **Road Section Detail** in the **Name** edit box.

4. Select **1"=1'-0"** (**1:50**) from the **Scale** drop-down list and choose the **OK** button to return to the drawing window. The drafting view created is displayed under the **Drafting Views (Detail)** head in the **Project Browser**.

Creating Detail Elements Using the Fill Patterns

1. Choose the **Annotate** tab and then invoke the **Filled Region** tool from the **Region** drop-down in the **Detail** panel; the **Modify | Create Filled Region Boundary** tab is displayed.

2. Now, from the **Line Style** drop-down list in the **Line Style** panel, select **Medium Lines**.

3. In the **Draw** panel, choose the **Rectangle** tool.

4. Sketch a rectangle which is **3'0"** in length and **0'4"** in height.

5. Use the **Zoom in Region** tool to zoom in the rectangle created.

6. Choose the **Edit Type** button from the **Properties** palette; the **Type Properties** dialog box is displayed.

7. Choose **Duplicate**; the **Name** dialog box is displayed. Enter **Concrete** in the **Name** edit box and choose **OK**. Notice that the **Concrete** option is selected from the **Type** drop-down list in the **Type Properties** dialog box.

8. Click in the **Value** column of the **Fill Pattern** parameter and then click on the **Browse** button to display the **Fill Patterns** dialog box.

9. Choose **Concrete** from the list of patterns and choose the **OK** button to return to the **Type Properties** dialog box.

10. Choose the **OK** button to close the **Type Properties** dialog box.

11. Choose the **Finish Edit Mode** button from the **Mode** panel in the **Modify | Create Filled Region Boundary** tab; the sketched rectangle is filled with the selected fill pattern, as shown in Figure 12-54. Press ESC to exit.

***Figure 12-54** Sketched rectangle with the fill pattern*

12. Similarly, use the **Filled Region** tool to sketch another rectangle measuring **3'0"** in length and **0'3"** in height above the filled region that has already been created, refer to Figure 12-53.

13. Sketch the profile of the kerb stone at the top right corner of the upper rectangle, refer to Figure 12-53, by using the **Filled Region** tool and then the **Line** tool from the **Draw** panel of the **Modify | Create Filled Region Boundary** tab. The kerb stone is created along with the concrete fill pattern.

Tip
While sketching the kerb stone or paver block, ensure that the lines drawn in the sketch should be continuous without overlapping each other.

14. Use the **Filled Region** tool to sketch one paver block measuring **4"** in length and **3"** in height at a distance of **1/4"** from the kerb stone. Use the **Offset** tool for placing the block at the specified distance. Use the **Thin Lines** option as the linetype and the **Concrete** option as the fill pattern.

15. Use the **Array** tool to create 7 copies at a distance of **4 1/4"**(center to center), as shown in Figure 12-55.

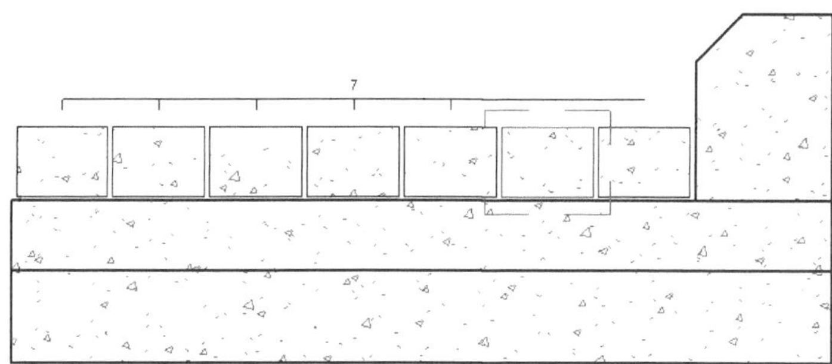

Figure 12-55 *Sketched road section with pavers*

16. Invoke the **Filled Region** tool again and select **<Invisible lines>**from the **Line Style** drop-down list.

17. Sketch the outer profile of the earth, as given in the sketch detail.

18. Choose the **Edit Type** button from the **Properties** palette; the **Type Properties** dialog box is displayed.

19. Choose **Duplicate**; the **Name** dialog box is displayed. Enter **Earth** in the **Name** edit box and choose **OK**.

20. In the **Type Properties** dialog box, click in the **Value** field of the **Fill Pattern** instance parameter and choose the **Browse** button; the **Fill Patterns** dialog box is displayed. Choose the **Earth** pattern name and then choose **OK**; the **Fill Patterns** dialog box closes. Next, choose **OK** to close the **Type Properties** dialog box.

21. Choose the **Finish Edit Mode** button from the **Mode** panel; the earth fill pattern is displayed in the drawing, as shown in Figure 12-56.

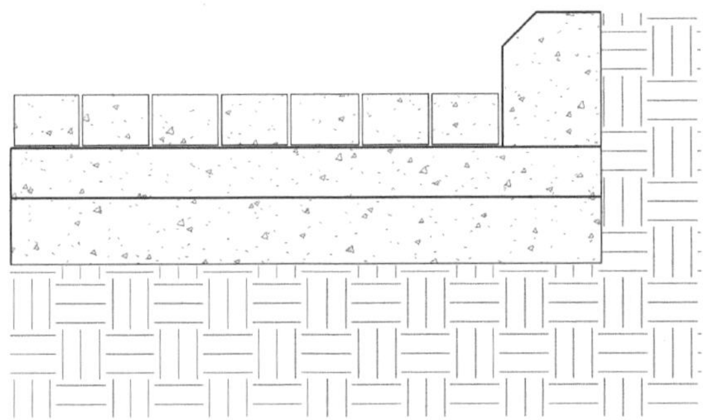

Figure 12-56 Sketched earth with the fill pattern

Adding Dimensions to the Detail View

1. Choose the **Aligned** tool from the **Dimension** panel of the **Annotate** tab; the **Modify | Place Dimensions** tab is displayed.

2. In the **Properties** palette, ensure that the **Linear Dimension Style: Linear 3/32" Arial** option (for Metric **Linear Dimension Style: Linear 3mm Arial**) is selected from the **Type Selector** drop-down list.

3. Now, move the cursor near the top left corner of the sketch and create a vertical dimension of **0' 3" (76.2 mm)** representing the thickness of the paver.

4. Similarly, add other dimensions to the detail view, as shown in Figure 12-57. Press ESC to exit.

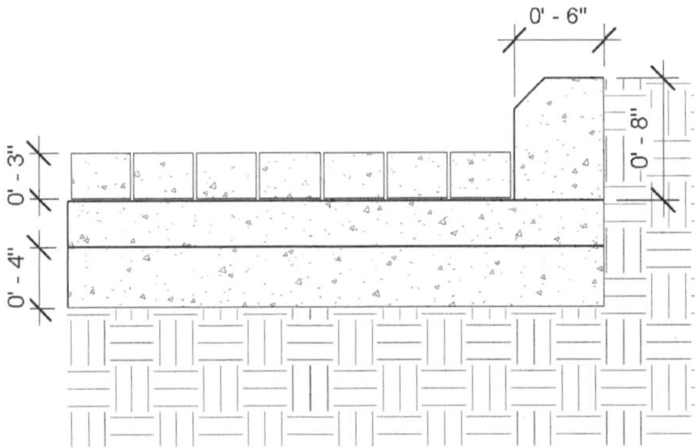

Figure 12-57 Dimensions added to the detail view

Adding Text Notes

1. Choose the **Text** tool from the **Text** panel of the **Annotate** tab; the **Modify | Place Text** tab is displayed.

2. Choose the **Two Segments** tool from the **Format** panel.

3. From the **Type Selector** drop-down list, select **Text : 3/32" Arial**.

4. Now, choose the **Type Properties** tool from the **Properties** panel; the **Type Properties** dialog box is displayed.

5. Click on the **Value** field of the **Leader Arrowhead** type parameter and select the **Arrow Filled 30 Degree** option. Then, choose **OK** to exit the dialog box.

6. Click at the top of the paver to specify the first point and subsequently specify two more points to indicate the location of the elbow and text note. Add the text note **8"X6" concrete kerb stone**, as shown in Figure 12-58.

7. Add text notes based on the given sketch section. Press ESC twice.

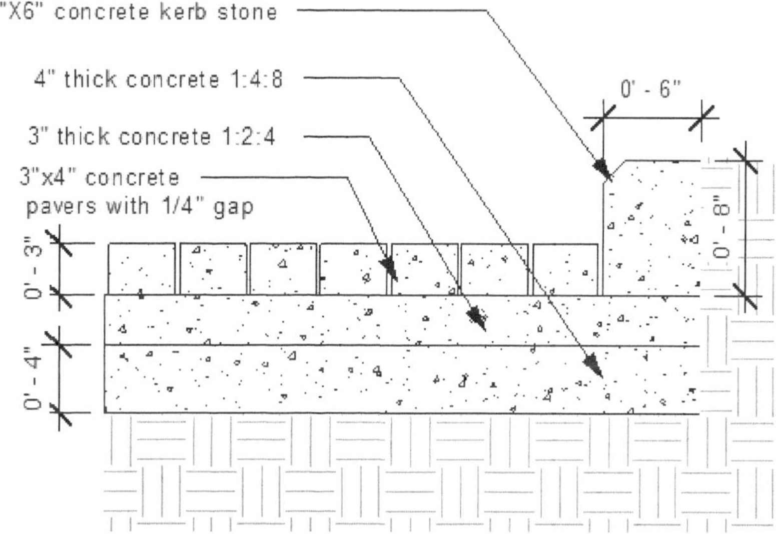

Figure 12-58 *Text notes added to the detail view*

Adding Break Lines

In this section of the tutorial, you will add break lines at the left and right sides in the drafting detail view using the **Detail Component** tool.

1. Choose the **Detail Component** tool from **Annotate > Detail > Component** drop-down; the **Modify | Place Detail Component** tab is displayed.

2. Now, choose the **Load Family** tool from the **Mode** panel; the **Load Family** dialog box is displayed.

3. Now, browse to **US Imperial > Detail Items > Div 01-General** folder and then select the **Break Line** file (for Metric **M_Break Line**).

4. Now, choose **Open**; the selected break line type is displayed in the **Type Selector** drop-down list.

5. Select the **Rotate after placement** check box from the **Options Bar**.

6. Now, add two instances of the break line, refer to Figure 12-53.

7. Use the drag controls to modify the size of the break line based on the given sketch.

   The detail view is now complete.

Saving the Project

In this section, you will save the project file using the **Save As** tool.

1. Choose **Save As > Project** from the **File** menu; the **Save As** dialog box is displayed. Enter **c12_RoadSectionDetail_tut3** (for Metric **M_c12_RoadSectionDetail_tut3**) in the **File name** edit box and choose **Save**; the project file is saved.

2. Now, choose **Close** from the **File** menu; the *c12_RoadSectionDetail_tut3.rvt* (for Metric *M_c12_RoadSectionDetail_tut3.rvt*) file closes.

Self-Evaluation Test

Answer the following questions and then compare them to those given at the end of this chapter:

1. Which of the following is a type of keynote?

   (a) Element (b) Structure
   (c) Material User (d) Keynoting

2. Which of the following schedule types helps you show the details regarding the assembly of a component?

   (a) Note block (b) Drawing list
   (c) View list (d) Material takeoff

3. The __________ tag can be added to indicate the revisions made to some portion of a project view.

4. The __________ tool is used to create schedules in a project.

5. The __________ parameter is used to set the display of a project view as an underlay.

6. The __________ tool is used to add a graphical representation of an insulation barrier to a detail view.

7. The __________ type of detail view does not use an existing project view.

8. You can create a text note without a leader. (T/F)

9. A text note cannot be moved without moving a leader. (T/F)

10. A drafted detail uses an enlarged portion of a project view as an underlay. (T/F)

11. The **Add Right Side Arc Leader** tool can be used to add a curved leader to the right side of the text note. (T/F)

12. Detail items can be loaded from Autodesk Revit's library. (T/F)

Review Questions

Answer the following questions:

1. Which of the following tools can be used to add a 3D text to a building model?

   (a) **Text** (b) **Detail Component**
   (c) **Level** (d) **Model Text**

2. Which of the following parameters can be modified to control the extent of details shown in a project view?

   (a) **View Scale** (b) **Display Model**
   (c) **Detail Level** (d) **Referencing Detail**

3. Which of the following instance parameters is used to set the alignment of text notes?

   (a) **Horizontal Align** (b) **Text Size**
   (c) **Tab Size** (d) **Background**

4. Which of the following options is used to change the fill pattern display for wall cuts in plan?

   (a) Projection/surface pattern (b) Cut pattern
   (c) Line styles (d) Cut line styles

5. Drag controls can be used to resize a text note. (T/F)

6. A model text is visible only in the view in which it is created. (T/F)

7. You can use various editing tools such as **Move**, **Copy**, **Rotate**, and so on to edit a model text created. (T/F)

8. You can resize the extents of a callout view by using drag controls. (T/F)

9. A text note can be assigned multiple leaders. (T/F)

10. When a text note is dragged to a new location, the leader adjusts automatically. (T/F)

11. The **Region** tool is used to create detail elements by defining a boundary and assigning a fill pattern. (T/F)

EXERCISES

Exercise 1 Club - Drafted Detail

In the *Club* project created in Exercise 1 of Chapter 11, create a drafted detail based on the sketch given in Figure 12-59. Load the required detail items (detail components). Use wide and thin lines to sketch the detail lines. Assume the parameters for adding text notes, dimensions, and break lines. The exact placement of the elements is not important for this exercise. Save the project file as *c12_Club_ex1.rvt (for Metric M_c12_Club_ex1.rvt).*

(Expected time: 30 min)

To add the Window jamb detail component in the Project, you need to download the *Window Jamb - Metal Fixed Flush.rfa* file from the website: *www.cadcim.com*

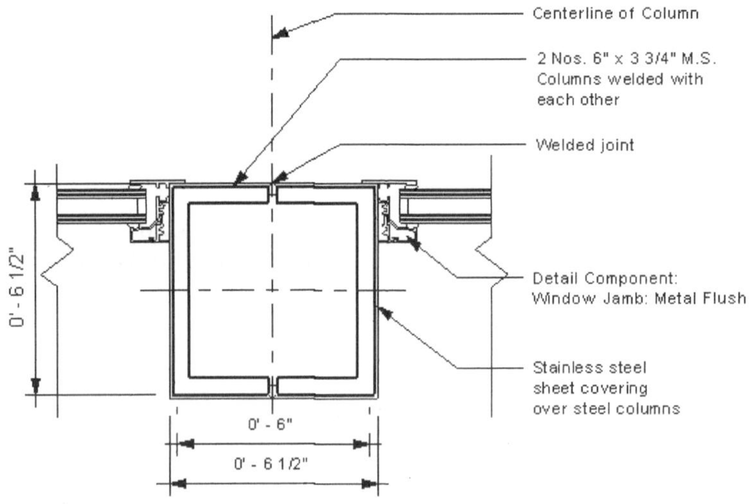

***Figure 12-59** Sketch plan for creating a drafted detail for the Club project*

Exercise 2 General- Sketch Detail

Create the drafted detail based on the sketch detail shown in Figure 12-60. Use the **Fill Region** tool to create elements and fill patterns. Assume the parameters for adding text notes and dimensions. The exact placement of the elements is not important for this exercise. Save the project file as *c12_sketchdetail_ex2.rvt* (for Metric *M_c12_sketchdetail_ex2.rvt)*

(Expected time: 30 min)

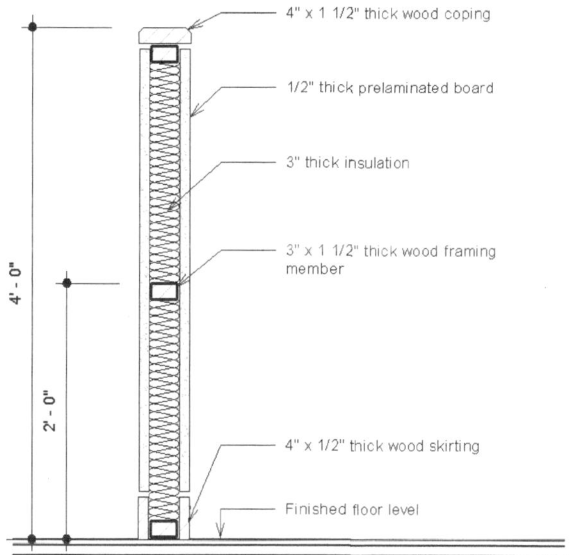

Figure 12-60 *Sketch detail for creating a drafted detail*

Exercise 3 Club - Schedules

Create the room and wall schedules for the *Club* project created in Exercise 1 of Chapter 11, based on the schedules shown in Figures 12-61 and 12-62. Use the predefined room schedule available in the **Project Browser** and edit it as per the given fields. Save the project file as *c12_clubschedule_ex3.rvt* (for Metric *M_c12_clubschedule_ex3.rvt*)

(Expected time: 30 min)

Room Schedule				
Name	Number	Level	Area	Perimeter
Entrance	1	First Floor	527 SF	93' - 2 1/4"
Passage 1	2	First Floor	606 SF	138' - 1 1/4"
Passage 2	3	First Floor	606 SF	138' - 0"
Billiard Ro	4	First Floor	556 SF	95' - 8 1/4"
Gymnasiu	5	First Floor	803 SF	113' - 4 1/4"
Aerobics	6	First Floor	488 SF	90' - 10"
Indoor Ga	7	First Floor	626 SF	100' - 8 1/4"
Card Roo	8	First Floor	481 SF	90' - 4 1/4"
Grand total: 8			4692 SF	860' - 2 1/2"

Figure 12-61 *Room schedule for the Club project*

Wall Schedule				
Family	Type	Length	Area	Volume
Basic Wall	Exterior - Split F	13' - 1 1/2"	200 SF	236 CF
Basic Wall	Exterior - Split F	58' - 10 1/4"	709 SF	836 CF
Basic Wall	Exterior - Split F	38' - 10 1/4"	501 SF	593 CF
Basic Wall	Exterior - Split F	38' - 10 1/4"	521 SF	614 CF
Basic Wall	Exterior - Split F	58' - 10 1/4"	713 SF	837 CF
Basic Wall	Exterior - Split F	13' - 1 1/2"	189 SF	222 CF
Basic Wall	Exterior - Split F	42' - 5 1/4"	480 SF	567 CF
Basic Wall	Interior - 6 1/8"	59' - 0"	635 SF	324 CF
Basic Wall	Interior - 6 1/8"	28' - 10 1/4"	315 SF	161 CF
Basic Wall	Interior - 6 1/8"	15' - 8 3/4"	185 SF	94 CF
Basic Wall	Interior - 6 1/8"	9' - 0"	98 SF	50 CF
Basic Wall	Interior - 6 1/8"	28' - 10 1/4"	336 SF	172 CF
Basic Wall	Interior - 6 1/8"	59' - 0"	635 SF	324 CF
Basic Wall	Interior - 6 1/8"	15' - 8 3/4"	185 SF	94 CF
Basic Wall	Interior - 6 1/8"	28' - 10 1/4"	336 SF	172 CF
Basic Wall	Interior - 6 1/8"	28' - 10 1/4"	336 SF	172 CF
Curtain Wall	Exterior Glazing	58' - 10 1/4"	880 SF	
Curtain Wall	Exterior Glazing	58' - 10 1/4"	883 SF	

Figure 12-62 *Wall schedule for the Club project*

Answers to Self-Evaluation Test

1. a, **2.** a, **3.** Revision, **4.** Schedule/Quantities, **5.** Display Model, **6.** Insulation, **7.** Drafting view, **8.** T, **9.** F, **10.** F, **11.** T, **12.** T

Chapter 13

Creating and Plotting Drawing Sheets

Learning Objectives

After completing this chapter, you will be able to:

- *Add drawing sheets to a project*
- *Add views to a drawing sheet*
- *Modify view properties of a drawing sheet*
- *Pan the viewport*
- *Add schedules to a drawing sheet*
- *Modify a building model in a drawing sheet*
- *Create dependent views*
- *Add matchline to dependent views*
- *Add views to sheet*
- *Add view reference*
- *Print drawing sheets and project view*
- *Select and modify the printer settings*

INTRODUCTION

In the previous chapters, you learned to create views of a building model. You also learned to add information to the views and create additional detail views. The views should be organized in proper format and sequence, and should also be stored on paper. The organized drawing sheets can be issued to the concerned agencies during progressive stages of the project. The printed drawing sheets enable a better understanding of the project and also results in smooth coordination between the associated agencies. They also form a printed reference for the modifications and detailing that are carried out during the project development and execution.

Using Autodesk Revit, you can easily compose the building views on a drawing sheet. You can first choose the appropriate title block for the drawing sheet and then add the desired views to it. You can control the visibility of various categories and set the scale for the printing of each view. You can also modify the building model and create new views. Having composed the drawing sheets, you can print them on the desired print media using various settings. This chapter explains the general procedure for creating, composing, and printing drawing sheets.

CREATING DRAWING SHEETS

In Autodesk Revit, drawing sheets are treated like views in a project. They are defined by a border and a title block. Therefore, to create a drawing sheet, you first need to add a sheet view to the project.

Adding a Drawing Sheet to a Project

Ribbon: View > Sheet Composition > Sheet

Sheet

To add a drawing sheet to a project, choose the **Sheet** tool from the **Sheet Composition** panel; the **New Sheet** dialog box will be displayed. This dialog box has two areas: **Select titleblocks** and **Select placeholder sheets**. Select the required title block for the drawing sheet from the list of title blocks. To load drawing sheets other than the ones in the list of title blocks in the **Select titleblocks** area, choose the **Load** button from the **New Sheet** dialog box; the **Load Family** dialog box will be displayed. Next, choose **US Imperial > Titleblocks** (for Metric **US Metric > Titleblocks**); the list of titleblocks family files will be displayed, as shown in Figure 13-1. Select the desired family file from the list to load it into your project and choose the **Open** button; the title block corresponding to the selected family file will be added to the list of title blocks in the **Select titleblocks** area. Select a titleblock from the list and choose the **OK** button; a titleblock of the selected family will be displayed in the drawing window, as shown in Figure 13-2.

A titleblock is used to convey the project information and the drawing sheet title. The project information includes client, project name, project title, project number, date of issue of drawing, drawing sheet number, scale, and so on.

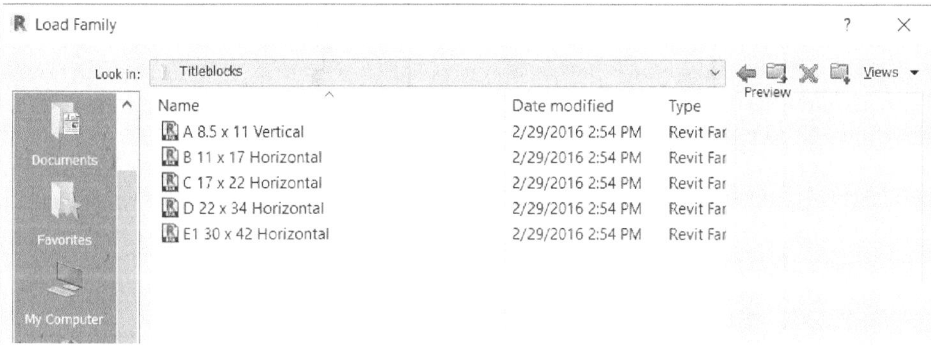

Figure 13-1 *Partial view of the* **Load Family** *dialog box displaying the list of titleblocks family*

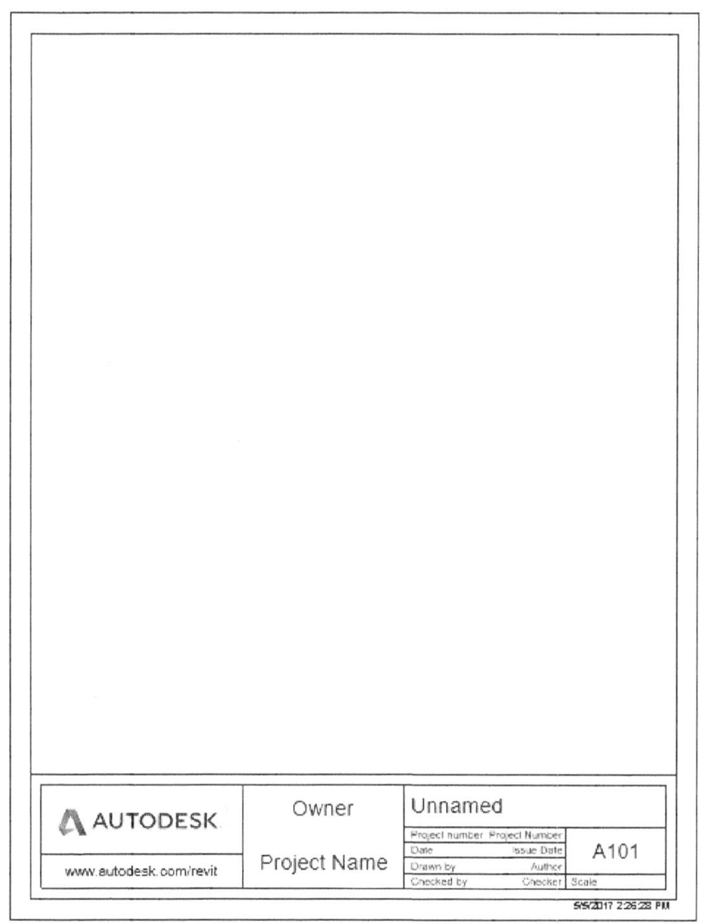

Figure 13-2 *Sheet view with the selected title block*

The project information can be added to a project using the **Project Information** tool. Invoke this tool from the **Settings** panel of the **Manage** tab; the **Project Information** dialog box will be displayed. In this dialog box, you can add the project information such as the **Author**, **Project Issue Date**, **Project Status**, and **Client Name** in the **Value** field of their respective parameters. Figure 13-3 shows the partial view of the **Project Information** dialog box displaying the instance parameters. Other project related information such as the name of the client or the owner, the address of the project, its name and number can also be entered in the corresponding **Value** fields. The information entered in this dialog box is automatically entered in the title block. The other information provided in the sheet such as sheet name, sheet number, drawn by, scale, and so on may vary from sheet to sheet, and these are treated as instance parameters for the title block. To enter these information, select the title block; the instance parameters will be displayed in the **Properties** palette. Add relevant information to the palette and choose **Apply**; the added information will be updated in the selected title block.

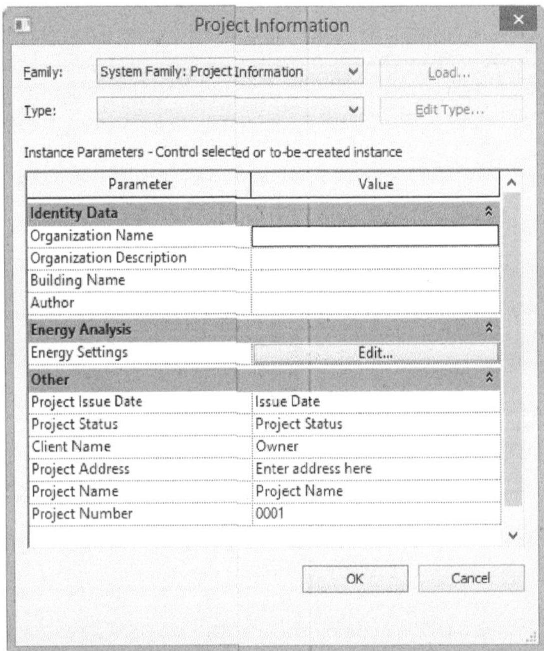

***Figure 13-3** The **Project Information** dialog box with the project related information*

You can enter the project related information directly by selecting the title block, clicking on the appropriate parameter, and then entering a value in the displayed edit box. The entered values are saved as project information for the other sheet views. As you add sheets to a project, their names and numbers are displayed in the **Sheets(all)** head of the **Project Browser**.

Note

*In the new drawing sheets, only the information which will be entered in the **Project Properties** dialog box will be displayed. Also, as you add a new sheet, the sheet number will increment automatically in a sequence.*

Tip

In a project, there can be many drawing sheets. The information provided in the title block plays an important role in identifying the drawing sheets.

Adding Views to a Drawing Sheet

Ribbon: View > Sheet Composition > Place View

To add views to a drawing sheet, choose the **Place View** tool from the **Sheet Composition** panel; the **Views** dialog box will be displayed with a list of views to be added to the drawing sheet, as shown in Figure 13-4. Select the required view and choose the **Add View to Sheet** button. On doing so, the selected view will appear as a viewport represented by a rectangle attached to the cursor. Move this cursor to the drawing area in the sheet and click in the preferred location to add the selected view. Next, in the **Properties** palette, change the **View Scale** parameter by selecting a suitable scale from the drop-down list in its **Value** field and choose **Apply**. The added view will adjust to the specified scale and appear in the sheet, as shown in Figure 13-5.

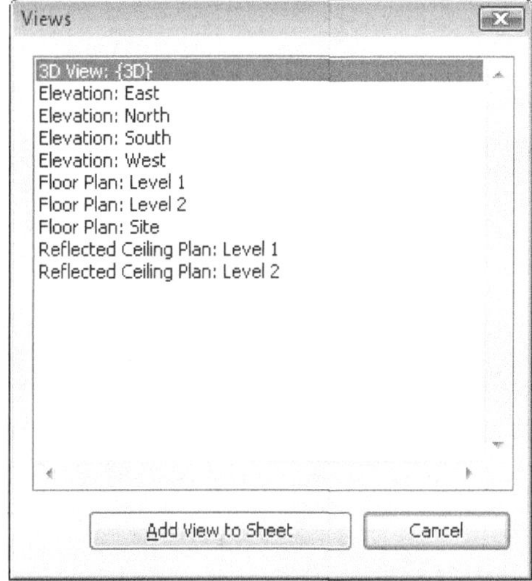

***Figure 13-4** The **Views** dialog box with the list of views to be added to the drawing sheet*

The viewport of the inserted view displays a label line at the bottom left corner. The label line shows the view name, view scale, and view number, as shown in Figure 13-6. In this manner, you can add a number of views to the same drawing sheet and create a complete set of drawing sheets for a project. You can modify various properties associated with the viewport in the **Properties** palette.

Tip

*To quickly open a sheet on which a view is placed, right-click on a view in the **Project Browser**; a shortcut menu will be displayed. Choose the **Open Sheet** option from the menu.*

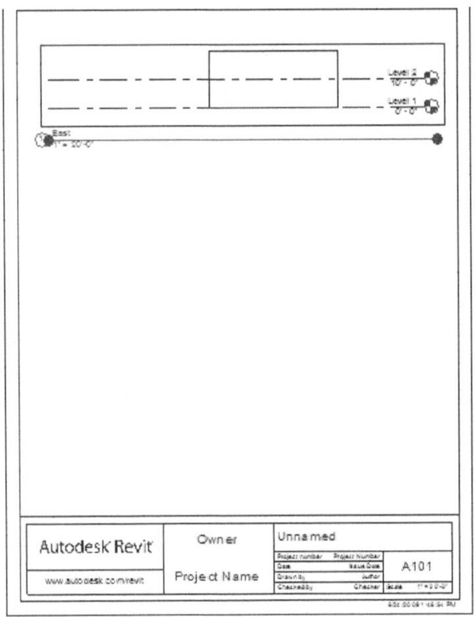

Figure 13-5 The added view in the title block

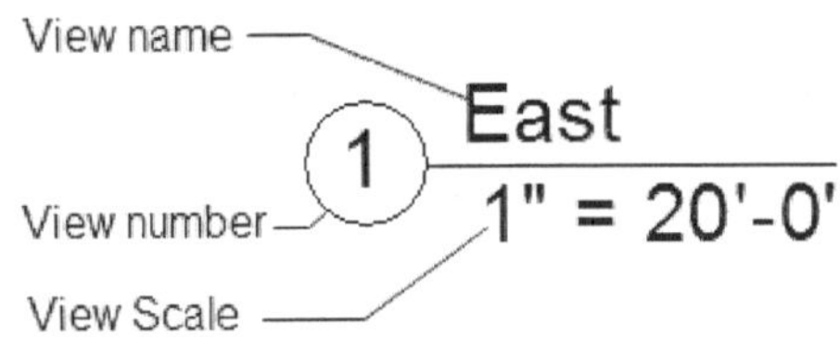

Figure 13-6 Parameters in the label line of the viewport

Modifying View Properties

To modify the properties associated with a view in a sheet, select the viewport corresponding to it; the **Properties** palette and the **Options Bar** will be displayed. The **Properties** palette for the viewport displays various instance parameters associated with the viewport, as shown in Figure 13-7. Based on the requirement, you can modify these values. In the **Properties** palette, click on the value column corresponding to the **View Scale** parameter and select an option from the drop-down list displayed to modify the scale of the view. In the palette, you can select the **Coarse**, **Medium**, or **Fine** option from the drop-down list corresponding to the value column of the **Detail Level** instance parameter to define the level of details to be displayed in a view. To control the visibility of different categories of elements in each viewport, choose the **Edit** button for the **Visibility/Graphics Overrides** parameter; the **Visibility/Graphics Overrides for Elevation (current view)** dialog box will be displayed for the corresponding view. In this dialog box, you can control the visibility of various model and annotation elements. In the **Properties** palette, you can rename the corresponding view of the selected viewport by entering a name in the value column corresponding to the **View Name** parameter. In the **Properties** palette, you can click on the value column corresponding to the **Rotation on Sheet** instance parameter to rotate the view clockwise or counterclockwise. Alternatively, you can rotate the view by selecting an option from the **Rotation on Sheet** drop-down list in the **Options Bar**. You can edit the type properties of the selected view in the sheet.

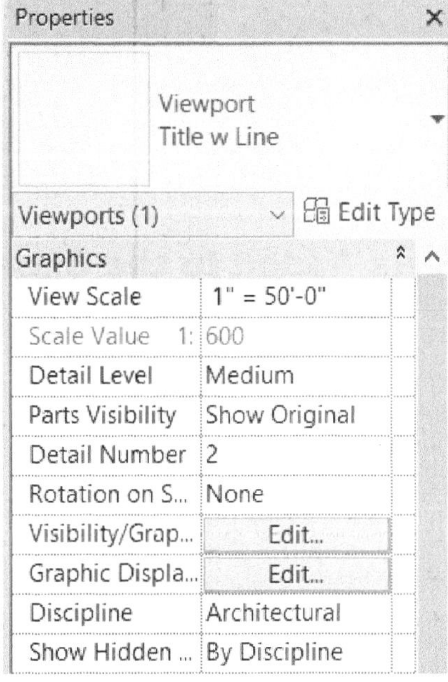

*Figure 13-7 The **Properties** palette for the viewport*

Tip
*A view can also be added by simply dragging its name from the **Project Browser** into the sheet view.*

To do so, choose the **Edit Type** button in the **Properties** palette; the **Type Properties** dialog box will be displayed, refer to Figure 13-8. In this dialog box, you can use various parameters to control the visibility of the title and extension lines associated with the view in the sheet. In the **Type Properties** dialog box, you can also modify the line weight color, and line pattern of the label line associated with the view.

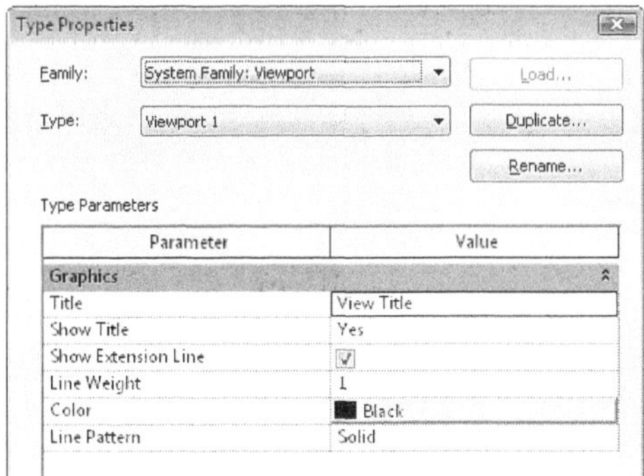

*Figure 13-8 The partial view of the **Type Properties** dialog box for the viewport*

In the **Properties** palette, you can click in the value column corresponding to the **Detail Level** parameter and select any of the options, **Coarse**, **Medium**, and **Fine** from the drop-down list to specify the level of details in the view.

Tip

The modifications made to the visibility of the elements in the viewport are also reflected in the actual view. To retain the visibility settings for the original view, make its copy and then add it to the drawing sheet. One project view cannot be added to more than one drawing sheet. However, its copy can be created and added to different drawing sheets.

Panning the Viewports Added to the Sheet

In Revit, you can accurately place the views added to the sheet by panning or moving them. To pan the view, select a viewport, right-click, and choose **Activate View** from the shortcut menu. You will notice that only the view, which is selected in the drawing is activated (You will learn more about it in the next section). Now, right-click again to display a shortcut menu. Choose the **Pan Active View** option from the displayed shortcut menu; the cursor will convert into a symbol with four arrows. Press and hold the left mouse button and drag the mouse to move the entities in the viewport. Once you have panned and placed the entities at the appropriate location in the sheet, choose **Deactivate View** from the shortcut menu to revert to the sheet.

Tip

*The **Visibility/Graphics Overrides** tool is used effectively in the project drawings. Using the same building model, you can create multiple viewports in the drawing sheet and display or hide different categories of elements in each viewport. For example, you can create multiple viewports for a residence plan and selectively display certain elements such as flooring pattern, false ceiling layout, furniture arrangement, and so on in each viewport.*

Adding Schedules to a Drawing Sheet

You can easily add the schedules created in a project to a drawing sheet. To do so, drag the schedules created (required schedules) from the **Project Browser** and drop them into the drawing sheet; the preview image of the schedule will be attached to the cursor. Move the cursor and click at the desired location in the drawing to place the schedule. The selected schedule will appear with blue triangles for each column and a break line on the right side, as shown in Figure 13-9.

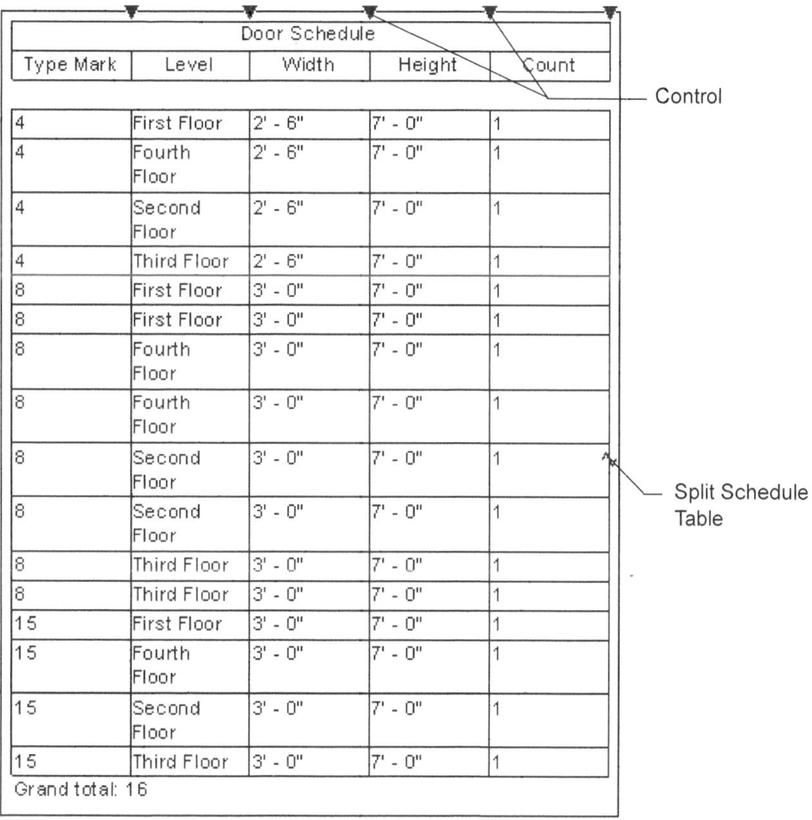

Door Schedule				
Type Mark	Level	Width	Height	Count
4	First Floor	2' - 6"	7' - 0"	1
4	Fourth Floor	2' - 6"	7' - 0"	1
4	Second Floor	2' - 6"	7' - 0"	1
4	Third Floor	2' - 6"	7' - 0"	1
8	First Floor	3' - 0"	7' - 0"	1
8	First Floor	3' - 0"	7' - 0"	1
8	Fourth Floor	3' - 0"	7' - 0"	1
8	Fourth Floor	3' - 0"	7' - 0"	1
8	Second Floor	3' - 0"	7' - 0"	1
8	Second Floor	3' - 0"	7' - 0"	1
8	Third Floor	3' - 0"	7' - 0"	1
8	Third Floor	3' - 0"	7' - 0"	1
15	First Floor	3' - 0"	7' - 0"	1
15	Fourth Floor	3' - 0"	7' - 0"	1
15	Second Floor	3' - 0"	7' - 0"	1
15	Third Floor	3' - 0"	7' - 0"	1

Grand total: 16

Figure 13-9 *Schedule with controls added to a drawing sheet*

You can modify the appearance and properties of a schedule. The blue triangles representing the controls for the column width can be dragged to modify the width of each column in the schedule. The break line in the right border represents the split control. It can be used to split the schedule table into multiple sections. When the split control is used, the schedule is split into two sections, as shown in Figure 13-10. These sections are placed adjacent to each other. In this manner, the schedule can be split into a number of sections that fit into the drawing sheet.

Door Schedule				
Type Mark	Level	Width	Height	Count
4	First Floor	2' - 6"	7' - 0"	1
4	Fourth Floor	2' - 6"	7' - 0"	1
4	Second Floor	2' - 6"	7' - 0"	1
4	Third Floor	2' - 6"	7' - 0"	1
8	First Floor	3' - 0"	7' - 0"	1
8	First Floor	3' - 0"	7' - 0"	1
8	Fourth Floor	3' - 0"	7' - 0"	1
8	Fourth Floor	3' - 0"	7' - 0"	1
8	Second Floor	3' - 0"	7' - 0"	1

Door Schedule				
Type Mark	Level	Width	Height	Count
8	Second Floor	3' - 0"	7' - 0"	1
8	Third Floor	3' - 0"	7' - 0"	1
8	Third Floor	3' - 0"	7' - 0"	1
15	First Floor	3' - 0"	7' - 0"	1
15	Fourth Floor	3' - 0"	7' - 0"	1
15	Second Floor	3' - 0"	7' - 0"	1
15	Third Floor	3' - 0"	7' - 0"	1

Grand total: 16

Figure 13-10 *The schedule table split into two sections*

The sections of a schedule can be moved using the move control available in the center of the schedule section. Moreover, the sections of a schedule can be resized by dragging the blue dot at its end. When the schedule section is resized, the additional or reduced rows are automatically adjusted between the sections. However, the last section cannot be resized as it contains the remaining rows.

Note

The schedule sections can neither be deleted individually nor moved from one drawing sheet to another. For these operations, the entire schedule is treated as a single entity.

The split sections of a schedule can be rejoined again. As they are sequential, therefore a section can be joined only to its previous or next section. To join a split section, drag a section using the move control over the previous or the next section; the two schedule sections will be merged together into a single schedule section.

As already mentioned, you can adjust the width of the columns in a schedule by dragging the blue triangle control for the respective columns. When a column width is modified, the column width of all schedule sections will be modified automatically.

If a building model is modified after making the schedule, then the schedule will be updated automatically. To edit it, right-click on the schedule in the drawing sheet and then choose the **Edit Schedule** option from the shortcut menu.

Modifying a Building Model in a Drawing Sheet

You can modify a building model directly from the views added to a drawing sheet. To do so, you need to activate a view and make the desired modifications in it. To activate a view from a drawing sheet, select the viewport; the **Modify | Viewports** tab will be displayed. In this tab, choose the **Activate View** button from the **Viewport** panel; the view in the selected viewport will be activated. In the activated view, you can work on the building model as in any other project view. The desired elements can be edited using the editing tools. New elements can also be added to the model. When the building model is edited, the parametric change engine of Autodesk Revit modifies other project views immediately. As a result, all the project views are updated automatically. For example, the modifications made to the location of a furniture item in an activated viewport of the drawing sheet are also made in the corresponding floor plan, sections, and other associated views.

Tip

Another method to activate or deactivate a viewport is to move the cursor over the project view and right-click; a shortcut menu will be displayed. From the shortcut menu, you can choose the ***Activate View*** *or* ***Deactivate View*** *option to activate or deactivate the specified viewport.*

After making the necessary modifications, choose the **Deactivate View** tool from **View > Sheet Composition > Viewports** drop-down to return to the drawing sheet view.

New views can also be added to the project when the viewport is activated. You can create a new plan, elevation, section, callout, detail view, and so on, while working in the activated view. The activated view can then be deactivated. Also, the newly created views can be added to the drawing sheet.

CREATING GUIDE GRIDS

Figure 13-11 *The* ***Assign Guide Grid*** *dialog box*

Guide Grid is a customizable grid available in Revit sheets. It is used to place the drawing view in place in the sheet. To create a Guide Grid, choose the **Guide Grid** tool from the **Sheet Composition** panel of the **View** tab; the **Assign Guide Grid** dialog box will be displayed, as shown in Figure 13-11. In this dialog box, the **Create new** radio button is selected by default. You can enter a name for the Guide Grid in the **Name** edit box and choose the **OK** button; the Guide Grid will be displayed over the sheet in the drawing area, as shown in Figure 13-12. On creating a Guide Grid, it gets added as an instance property under the **Other** head in the **Properties** palette. Now, select the Guide Grid from the drawing area; the drag controls will be displayed. You can use the drag controls to resize the Guide Grids in the drawing area. The **Properties** palette displays the instance properties of the selected Guide Grid. In the **Properties** palette, you can specify guide spacing in the **Guide Spacing** edit box to increase or decrease the spacing of the grids. You can also rename the guide name under the identity data in the **Name** edit box in the **Properties** palette.

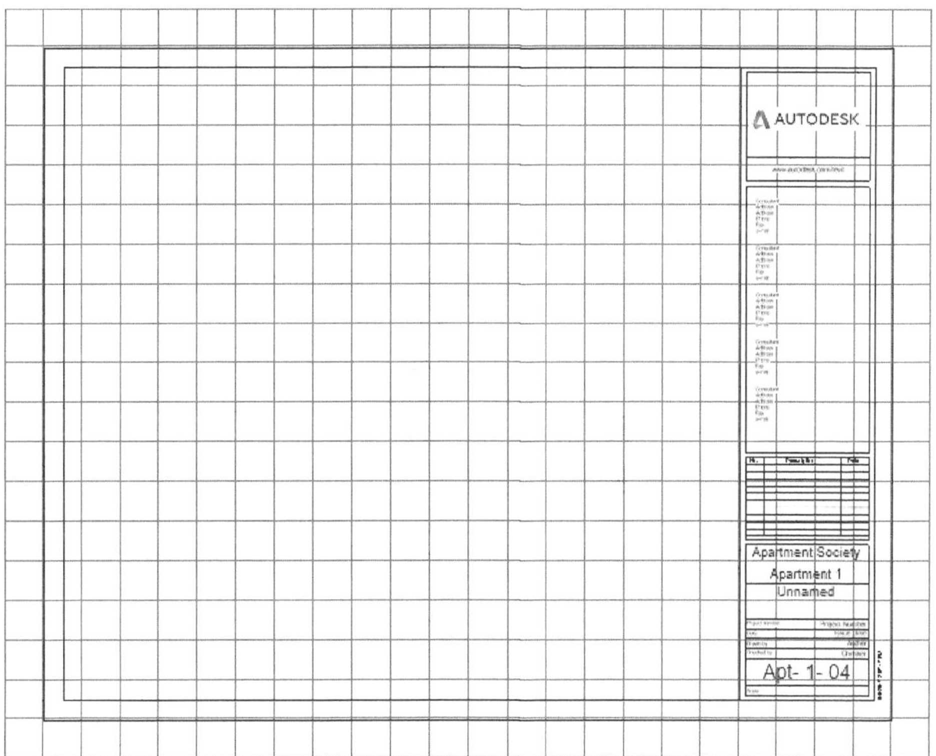

Figure 13-12 *The Guide Grid displayed over the sheet*

Note

In the current project, you can place the existing Guide Grid in a new sheet. To place an existing Guide Grid, open the new sheet and select an option from the ***Guide Grid*** *drop-down list in the* ***Properties*** *palette.*

DUPLICATING DEPENDENT VIEWS

You can create multiple copies of the project views in Revit. These multiple views are called duplicate views. All the duplicate views are dependent on the original view from which they are created. Therefore, these dependent views are automatically updated if any changes are made in the original view. Dependent views are useful when you want to use or place the same view on more than one sheet. It is also useful in case of huge projects when the overall project view is too large to fit in a single sheet. In such cases, you can crop the parent view into small segments using the crop regions, create dependent views from them, and then place the cropped dependent views on the sheet.

Creating Dependent Views

You can create a dependent view from a plan, elevation, section, and callout view. To create a dependent view, open the view from which you want to create duplicate view and choose the **Duplicate as Dependent** tool from **View > Create > Duplicate View** drop-down. Alternatively, select the required view name in the **Project Browser** and right-click; a shortcut menu will be displayed. Choose **Duplicate View > Duplicate as Dependent** from the shortcut menu; the primary view will display a crop region boundary which will be added to the **Project Browser** as a dependent view under the primary view. Select the crop region boundary to display the drag controls. Now, using the drag controls, resize and crop the primary view to include only the required portion of the view in the dependent view. Next, select the name of the dependent view in the **Project Browser** and right-click; a shortcut menu will be displayed. Choose the **Rename** option from the shortcut menu; the **Rename View** dialog box will be displayed. Enter a name for the dependent view in the dialog box and choose the **OK** button; the duplicate view will be renamed. Again, open the primary view and choose the **Show Crop Region** button from **View Control Bar** to display the crop region boundary. Similarly, create another dependent view. In this way, you can crop the primary view and create multiple dependent views. Figure 13-13 shows primary view and Figures 13-14 and 13-15 show two dependent views with the crop boundaries.

Tip

The views added to the drawing sheet are displayed in the ***Project Browser*** *below the sheet name under the* ***Sheets(all)*** *subhead. You can delete a selected view from the sheet view. To do so, highlight the view name and right-click. Next, choose the* ***Remove From Sheet*** *option from the shortcut menu and delete the selected view.*

Note

When you duplicate a view, the view will open in the drawing area and the default name for the duplicate view will be <view name>-Duplicate 1.

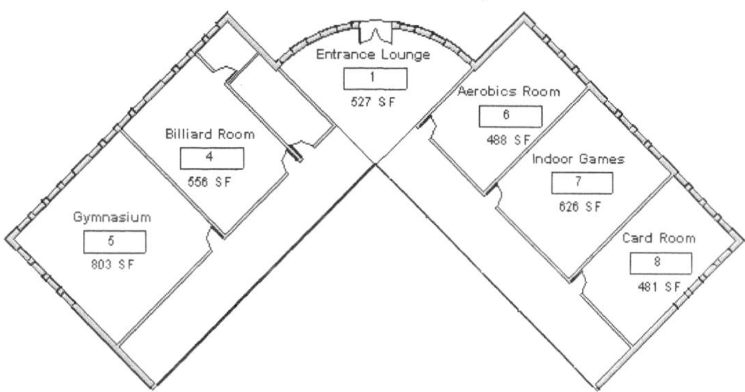

Figure 13-13 A primary view

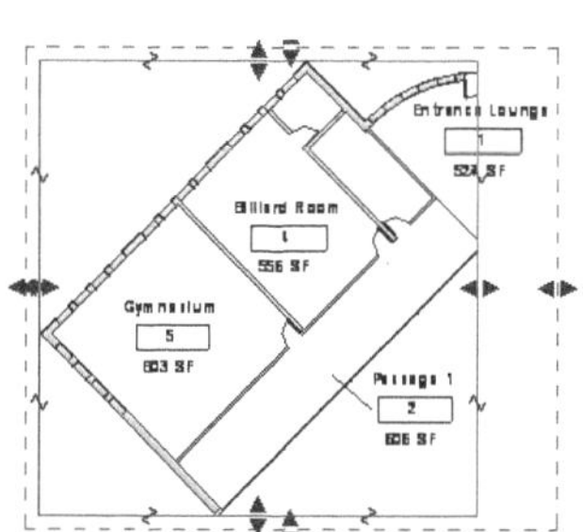

Figure 13-14 The left dependent view showing the left portion of the drawing with crop regions

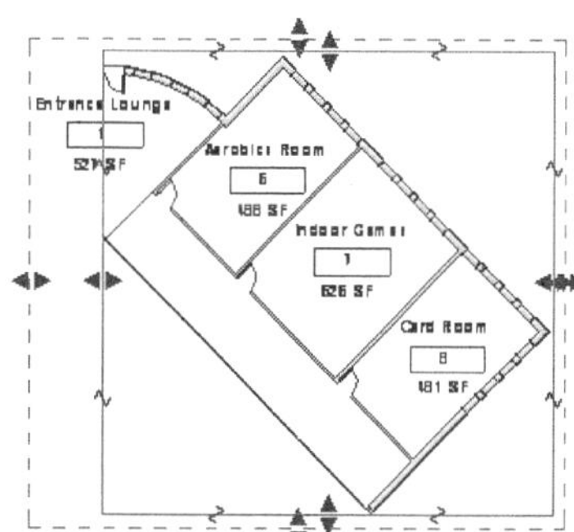

Figure 13-15 The right dependent view showing the right portion of the drawing with crop regions

To navigate to the primary view from the dependent view, select the crop region boundary of the dependent view and right-click; a shortcut menu will be displayed. Choose the **Go to Primary View** option from the shortcut menu; the primary view will be displayed on the screen. You can also navigate to the dependent views from the primary view. To do so, choose the **Show Crop Region** button from the **View Control Bar**, if the crop regions are not displayed in the primary view. On doing so, the crop regions for all dependent views will be displayed. Select the crop region of the required dependent view and right-click; a shortcut menu will be displayed. Choose **Go to View** from the shortcut menu; the respective dependent view will open. You can display the primary or the dependent views by double-clicking on their respective view names in the **Project Browser**.

Adding Matchline to Dependent Views

Matchlines are the graphical representation of a split in views. These are the sketch lines that indicate the area where a view is split. To add a matchline, open the primary view from which the dependent views are created. Next, choose the **Show Crop Region** button from the **View Control Bar**; the crop regions of both the primary and dependent views will be displayed. Choose the **Matchline** tool from the **Sheet Composition** panel in the **View** tab; the **Modify | Create Matchline Sketch** tab will be displayed and the screen will enter the sketch mode. Sketch a matchline using the sketching tools in the **Draw** panel of the **Modify | Create Matchline Sketch** tab to show the split. After sketching the matchline, choose the **Finish Edit Mode** button from the **Mode** panel of the **Modify | Create Matchline Sketch** tab; the matchline will be displayed, as shown in Figure 13-16. You can also edit the length and shape of the matchline. To do so, select the matchline; the **Modify | Matchline** tab will be displayed. In this tab, choose the **Edit Sketch** button from the **Mode** panel; the **Modify | Matchline > Edit Sketch** tab will be displayed. On invoking this tab, the screen will enter the sketch mode. Modify the sketch of the matchline as required and then choose the **Finish Edit Mode** button from the **Mode** panel in the **Modify | Matchline > Edit Sketch** tab.

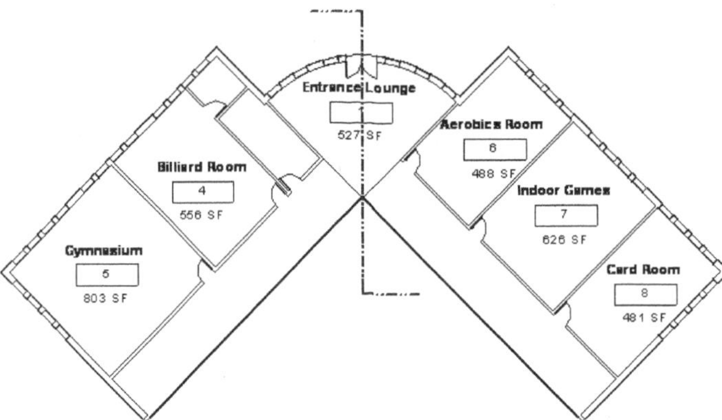

Figure 13-16 *Matchline showing the area where you want to split the drawing*

To modify the display of the matchline, select the matchline and right-click in the drawing; a shortcut menu will be displayed. Choose **Override Graphics in View > By Element** from the shortcut menu; the **View-Specific Element Graphics** dialog box will be displayed. You can modify the display properties of the matchlines, such as **Weight**, **Pattern**, and **Color**, in the dialog box and choose the **OK** button.

In Revit, you can configure the settings of the matchline upto a certain level. For example, there may be a building with 35 floors and you want the same settings of the floor upto level 30. To do so, select the matchline. Then, in the **Properties** palette, click in the **Value** column for the **Top Constraint** parameter and select the **Level 30** option from the drop-down list. On doing so, you will notice that the matchline is displayed only upto level 30. From level 31 onward, you can again configure different settings for the building model.

Adding View Reference

You can add a view reference in the primary view after you have placed the cropped dependent views on the sheet. A view reference is a symbol that is used to refer the dependent view available in the same or different sheet.

To add a view reference, select the primary view on the sheet and right-click; a shortcut menu will be displayed. Now, choose the **Activate View** option from the shortcut menu; the selected view will be highlighted. Next, invoke the **View Reference** tool from the **Tag** panel of the

Annotate tab. Now, select the dependent view to be referred to from the **Target View** drop-down list available in the **Options Bar** and then click in the selected drawing view to add the view reference. After adding the required view references, right-click, and then choose **Deactivate View** from the shortcut menu to deactivate the selected view. Now, if you double-click on the view reference tag, the respective referred view will open.

Note

If a plan view is split into two duplicate views, left and right, then to add a view reference to a right side view, when you select the left duplicate view, the view reference tag will be visible in the view except the left view (referred view).

PRINTING IN Autodesk Revit

The created building model and project views can be stored in the computer's hard disk or on a temporary media. It also becomes imperative to print these views as a hard copy at various stages of the project. During the initial stages of the project development, you may need to print certain project views and discuss them with the others in your organization or with the clients. As the project progresses, other professional agencies such as structural, electrical, plumbing, HVAC, landscape, and so on become involved with the project. The printed drawings assist in a proper coordination between these agencies. The project may also require approval from statutory bodies and other departments. Printed drawings and project views explain the project and can be submitted as a complete set to obtain their approval.

Another important use of the printed drawings is during the construction process. The printed views such as plans, section, elevations, details, and 3D views convey the architect's or interior designer's concept of the project to all the executing agencies involved. These views provide the information and necessary details to materialize the project on the site. They can also explain the procedure for executing the job and the level of detailing/finishing that is desired by the designers.

Using Autodesk Revit, you can easily print the created project views or composed drawing sheets at any time during the project development. This section explains the general procedure for printing. You can print the current window, visible portion of the current window, or the selected view/sheet using the **Print** tool. The printing process involves selecting the correct output device (printer or plotter), specifying the area to be plotted, specifying the paper size, and other settings.

Printing Drawing Sheets and Project Views

The **Print** tool is used to print project views and drawing sheets. You can invoke this tool from the **File** menu. On invoking the **Print** tool, the **Print** dialog box will be displayed, as shown in Figure 13-17.

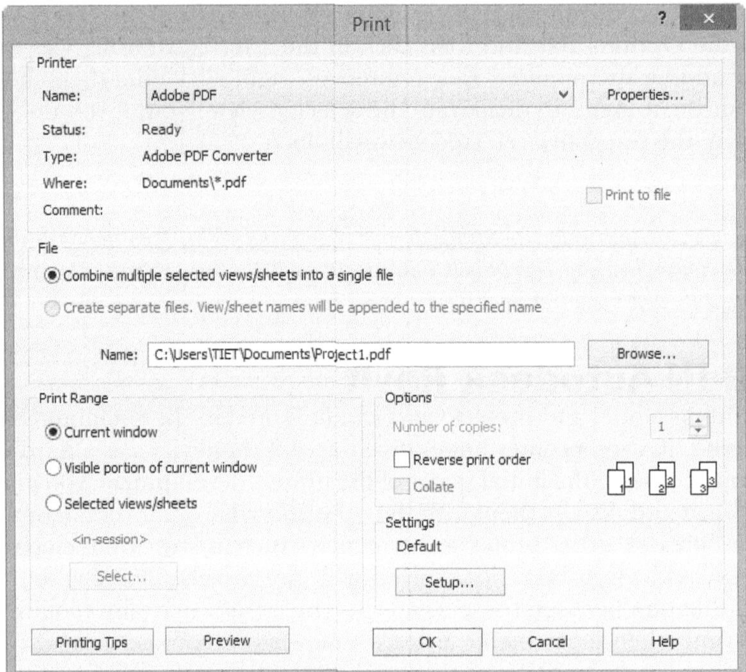

*Figure 13-17 The **Print** dialog box*

You have the option of using the default values in this dialog box. In case, the values conform to your requirements, you can choose the **OK** button and start printing directly. Otherwise, you can alter the print specifications using the options provided in the **Print** dialog box. The print options available in this dialog box are explained next.

Selecting and Modifying the Printer Settings

You can select a printing device from the **Name** drop-down list in the **Print** dialog box. This dialog box displays the information regarding the selected printer in the **Status**, **Type**, **Where**, and **Comment** fields below the printer name. The **Properties** button is used to set various printer properties. If you choose this button, a dialog box with a set of printer properties corresponding to the selected printer will be displayed, refer to Figure 13-18.

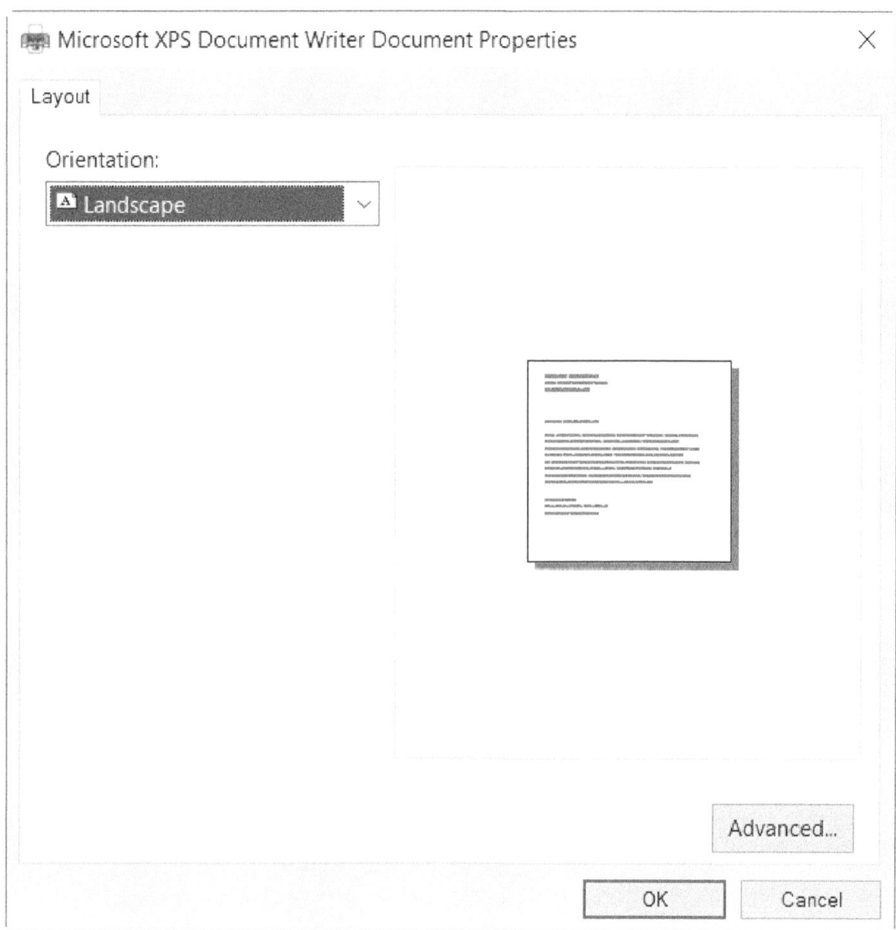

***Figure 13-18** The **Microsoft XPS Document Writer Document Properties** dialog box*

The printer properties depend on the type of printer selected from the **Name** drop-down list in the **Print** dialog box. In Figure 13-19, the **Layout** tab, displays the options related to the **Orientation** of the paper.

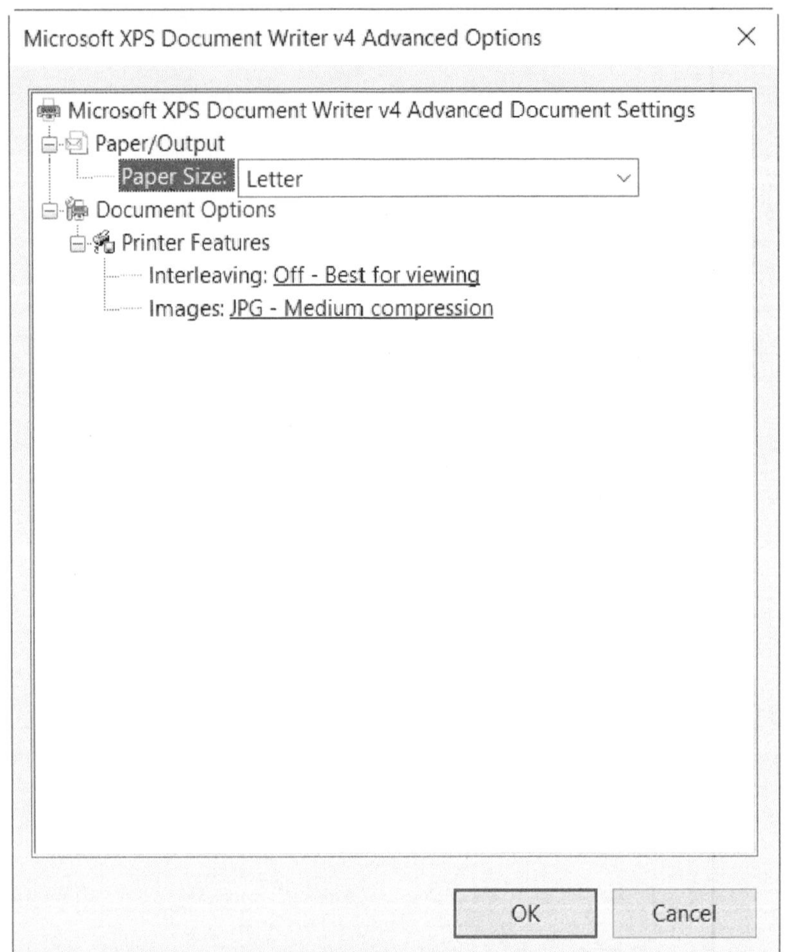

Figure 13-19 *The **Microsoft XPS Document Writer v4 Advanced Options** dialog box displayed for the selected printer*

Choose the **Advanced** button in this tab; the **Microsoft XPS Document Writer Advanced Options** dialog box will be displayed. You can modify and set printing preferences such as **Paper Size**, refer to Figure 13-20. Some of the major options used for printing are discussed next.

Note

*The appearance and options available in the **Print** dialog box depend on the type of printer selected and the operating system used.*

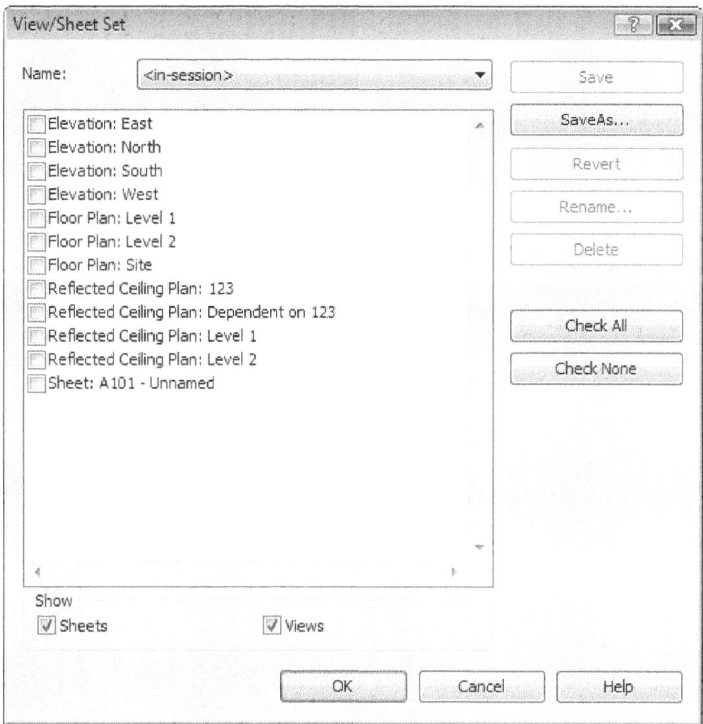

***Figure 13-20** The **View/Sheet Set** dialog box displaying the created views and sheets*

Setting the Print Range

The **Print Range** area in the **Print** dialog box has three radio buttons: **Current window**, **Visible portion of current window**, and **Selected views/sheets**. You can select any of these radio buttons to specify the parameters of the view to be printed. The **Current window** radio button can be selected to print the project view that is currently displayed in the drawing window while the **Visible portion of current window** radio button is used to print only the portion of the view that is currently displayed in the drawing window.

You can select the **Selected views/sheets** radio button to select project views or drawing sheets for printing. On selecting this radio button, the **Select** button that is located below it will be activated. Choose this button; the **View/Sheet Set** dialog box will be displayed, as shown in Figure 13-20. It contains a list of views that have been created and also the drawing sheets in the project. This dialog box can be used to select project views and create drawing sets. You can select views by selecting their corresponding check boxes. Now, to save the settings, choose the **Save As** button; the **New** dialog box will be displayed. In this dialog box, enter the name of the setting and choose **OK**; the **Name** dialog box will close. The name of the new selection set can be selected from the **Name** drop-down list in the **View/Sheet Set** dialog box. You can choose the **Rename** button to rename a set. You can delete a set by choosing the **Delete** button. Similarly, you can choose the **Check All** and **Check None** buttons to select and deselect all the listed views and sheets. You can also control the display of views and sheets by using their respective check boxes in the **Show** area placed at the bottom of the **View/Sheet Set** dialog box.

Using the Print Setup Dialog Box

File menu: Print > Print Setup

In Revit, you can specify various options for printing a drawing sheet. To do so, invoke the **Print Setup** dialog box by choosing **Print > Print Setup** from the **File** menu or choose the **Setup** button in the **Settings** area of the **Print** dialog box; the **Print Setup** dialog box will be displayed, as shown in Figure 13-21.

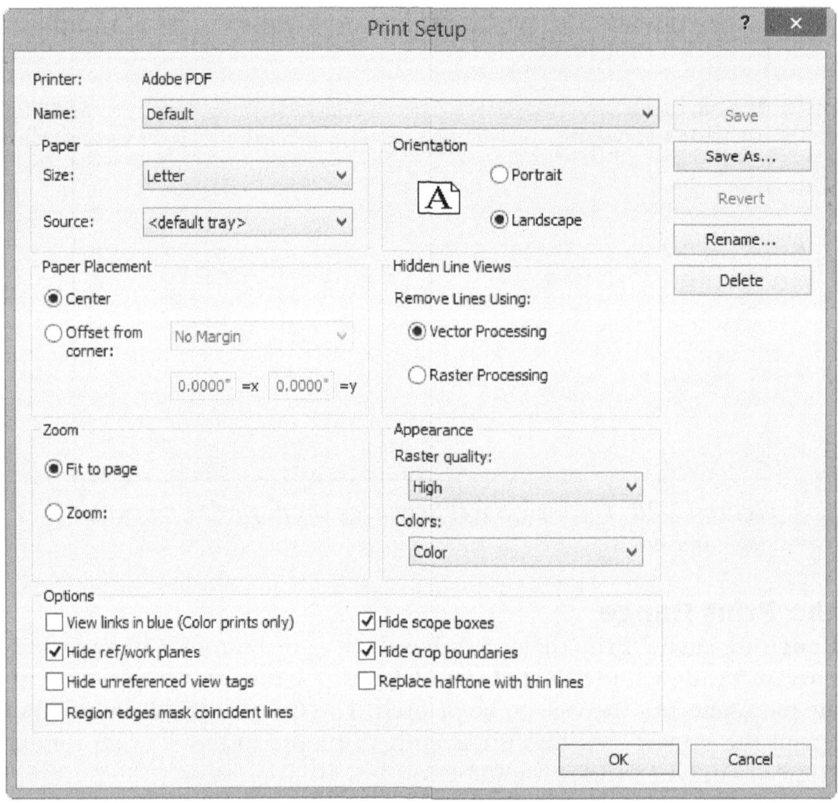

Figure 13-21 *The* ***Print Setup*** *dialog box*

This dialog box displays various setup options related to the printing procedure. The selected printer name is displayed at the top in the **Print Setup** dialog box. The **Name** drop-down list displays the name of the print settings that have been saved in the project. The **Size** drop-down list in the **Paper** area displays a list of paper sizes available for the selected printer. From this drop-down list, you can select the required size of paper to print the project view such as A5, A4, A3, and so on. From the **Source** drop-down list, you can select an option to specify the source of the paper. The **Portrait** or **Landscape** radio button can be selected to specify the orientation of the paper.

The **Paper Placement** area specifies the placement or the location of the view on the paper. The **Center** radio button can be selected for printing the view at the center of the paper. Selecting the **Offset from corner** radio button enables you to specify the offset distance of the view from the corner. You can select any of the three options, **No Margin**, **Printer limit**, or **User defined** to specify the offset distance. When the **User defined** option is selected, the **x** and **y** edit boxes get enabled where you can enter the X and Y offset distances. In the **Hidden Line Views** area, you can choose an option to increase the print performance for printing hidden lines in various views such as elevations, sections, 3D, and so on. When the **Vector Processing** radio button is selected in this area, the time taken to hide the lines will depend on the number and complexity of the views processed. This option produces smaller print files and decreases the print time. On the other hand, if the **Raster Processing** radio button is selected, the actual dimension of the print will be considered. As a result, larger print files will be produced, which will take more processing time.

Tip

*You can also invoke the **Print Setup** dialog box by choosing the **Setup** button from the **Print** dialog box.*

Note

*In a view, the elements that are hidden using the **Temporary Hide/Isolate** tool will be shown in print.*

The **Fit to page** radio button in the **Zoom** area can be selected to fit the view to the selected paper size. The **Zoom** radio button can be used to enlarge or reduce the view to a specified percentage. The **Appearance** area of the **Print Setup** dialog box displays the options for specifying the print quality and color. The **Raster quality** drop-down list in the **Appearance** area displays the **Low**, **Medium**, **High**, and **Presentation** options that enable you to select the required quality of print. Note that a higher quality of print will take more time to print. The **Colors** drop-down list in this area is used to specify whether the view is to be printed as **Black Lines**, **Grayscale**, or **Color**. When you select the **Black Lines** option, all text, lines, pattern lines, and edges will be printed in black. However, all raster images and solid patterns will be printed in grayscale. To print all the elements in grayscale, select the **Grayscale** option. The **Color** option can be used to print the project views in color. The printer, however, must support colored printing.

The **Options** area provides other print setting options. By default, the view links are printed in black. The **View links in blue** check box can be used to print the view links in blue. The options for hiding various annotations and elements such as scope boxes, reference/work planes, and crop boundaries are also provided in this section of the **Print Setup** dialog box.

Previewing the Print Setup

Before printing a project view or a drawing sheet, you can preview it using the **Print Preview** tool. This tool can be invoked by choosing the **Preview** button in the **Print** dialog box. When you invoke this tool, Autodesk Revit displays a draft version of the drawing sheet in the preview window, as shown in Figure 13-22. The displayed image acts as a preview of the hard copy that will be printed and is based on the set print parameters. If the displayed image does not conform to the desired result, you can use the **Close** button to close the preview and make the necessary modifications in the print setup till the desired result is achieved. While in the preview window, you can use the **Zoom In** and **Zoom Out** buttons to enlarge or reduce the view. On achieving the desired preview image, proceed to print the drawing using the **Print** tool.

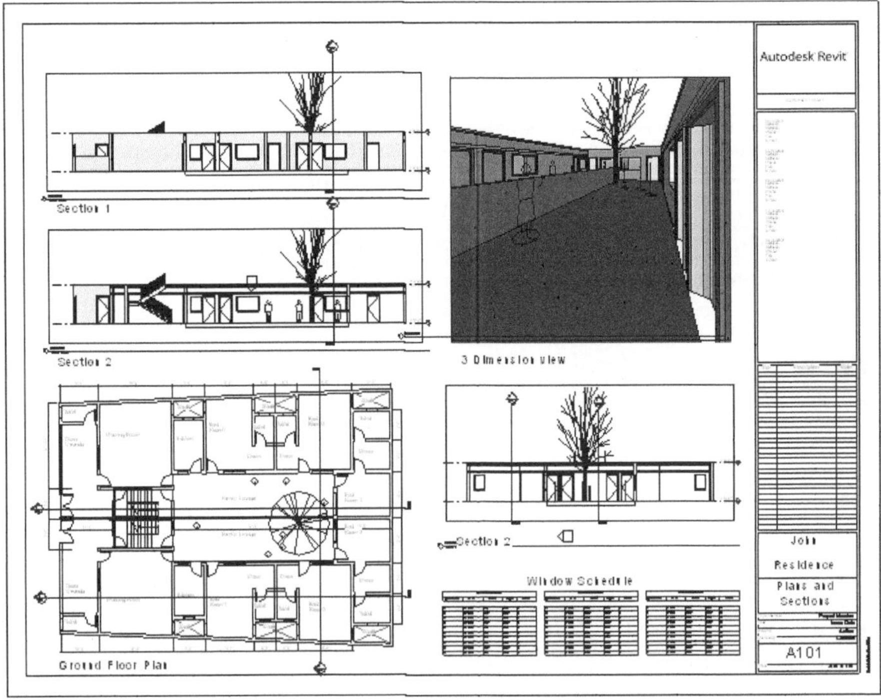

Figure 13-22 *Previewing the print settings displayed using the* ***Print Preview*** *tool*

TUTORIAL

Tutorial 1 Apartment 1

In this tutorial, you will create a drawing sheet for the *Apartment 1* project created in Tutorial 2 of Chapter 12, and then add the first floor plan, north elevation, longitudinal section, room schedule, and door schedule to the sheet, as shown in Figure 13-23. You will also add the following project and sheet information in the sheet title block:

(Expected time: 30 min)

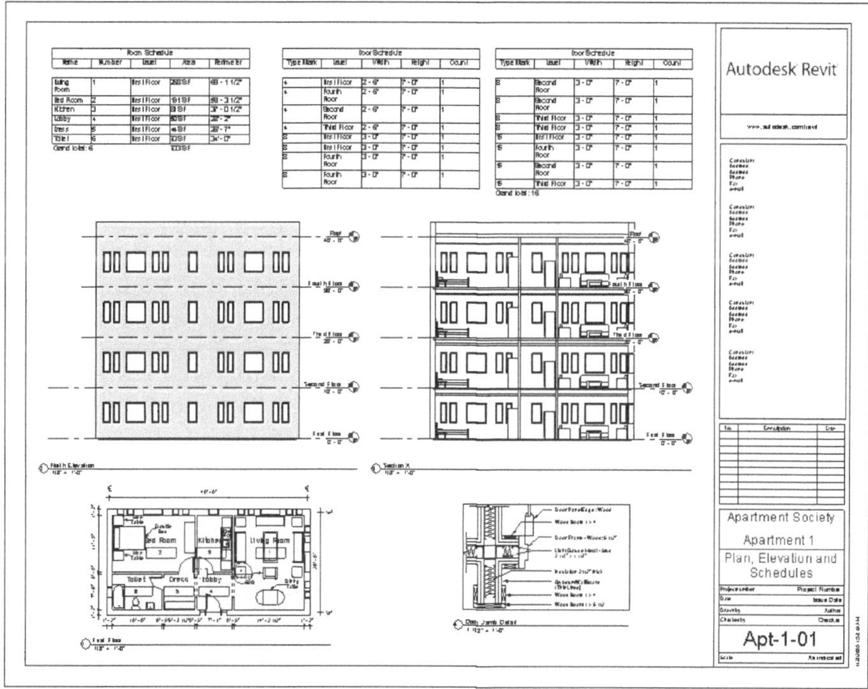

Figure 13-23 Sheet layout for creating a drawing sheet for the Apartment 1 project

1. Drawing sheet parameters:
   Titleblock to be used-
   For Imperial **C17 x 22 Horizontal** from the **US Imperial > Titleblocks** folder.
   For Metric **A2 metric** from the **US Metric > Titleblocks** folder.

2. Project information:
   Owner name: **Apartment Society**
   Sheet title: **Apartment 1**
   Sheet name: **Plan, Elevation and Schedules**
   Sheet number: **Apt-1-01**

   The following steps are required to complete this tutorial:

a. Add a sheet by using the **New Sheet** tool and by loading the specified titleblock.
b. Add the project information to the sheet titleblock.
c. Add views to the sheet view and compose the drawing sheet.
d. Modify the visibility settings of the added views using the **Activate View** tool.
e. Add schedules to the sheet.
f. Edit schedules to compose them on the sheet.
g. Save the project using the **Save As** tool.
   For Imperial *c13_Apartment1_tut1.rvt*
   For Metric *M_c13_Apartment1_tut1.rvt*
h. Close the project.

Adding a Sheet to the Project

First, you need to open the project file and create a new sheet view. You can load the titleblock from the specified folder.

1. Choose **Open > Project** from the **File** menu and open the *c12_Apartment1_tut2.rvt* (for Metric *M_c12_Apartment1_tut2.rvt*) file created in Tutorial 2 of Chapter 12. You can also download this file from *http://www.cadcim.com*. The path of the file is as follows: *Textbooks > Civil/GIS > Revit Architecture > Exploring Autodesk Revit 2018 for Architecture*

2. Choose the **Sheet** tool from the **Sheet Composition** panel in the **View** tab; the **New Sheet** dialog box is displayed.

3. Choose the **Load** button; the **Load Family** dialog box is displayed. In this dialog box, choose the titleblock **C 17 x 22 Horizontal** from **US Imperial > Titleblocks** folder (for Metric **A2 metric** from the **US Metric > Titleblocks** folder). On doing so, the specified titleblock is added to the list in the **Select titleblocks** area in the **New Sheet** dialog box.

4. Choose the **OK** button to close the **New Sheet** dialog box and create the sheet view by using the loaded titleblock.

Adding the Project Information to the Sheet Titleblock

In this section, you need to add the project information to the titleblock using the **Properties** palette. Further, you need to directly enter other project parameters in the title block.

1. Select the titleblock from the drawing window. Then, in the **Properties** palette, click in the value fields for the **Sheet Name** and **Sheet Number** parameters and enter **Plan, Elevation and Schedules** and **Apt-1-01**, respectively.

2. Choose **Apply**. You will notice that the values entered in the **Properties** palette are displayed in the sheet.

3. Next in the titleblock, click in the **Owner** field and enter **Apartment Society** in the edit box. Now, press ENTER to view the new value in the sheet.

4. Similarly, you need to click on the **Project Name** field in the titleblock in the drawing area and enter **Apartment 1** in the edit box and then press ENTER. Now, the project details appear in the titleblock, as shown in Figure 13-24.

Figure 13-24 *Project information in the titleblock of the sheet view*

Adding Project Views to the Drawing Sheet

In this section, you need to add the specified project views by dragging their name from the **Project Browser** in the sheet. Further, you need to place the project views at their designated place in the sheet based on the sheet layout.

1. Drag **First Floor** from the **Floor Plans** head in the **Project Browser** into the drawing sheet. The view appears in the form of a rectangle in the sheet view.

2. Next, move the cursor to the lower left area of the titleblock such that the corner of the rectangle is close to the lower left corner of the drawing sheet. Next, click to place the view. The first floor plan view is added to the sheet and appears enclosed in a rectangle.

3. In the **Project Browser**, click on the **North** elevation node under the **Elevations(Building Elevation)** head and then right-click to display the shortcut menu. From the shortcut menu, choose the **Rename** option; the **Rename View** dialog box is displayed. In the **Name** edit box of this dialog box, enter **North Elevation** and then choose the **OK** button; the **Rename View** dialog box is closed and the view is renamed.

4. Drag **North Elevation** and **Section X** from the **Project Browser** and add them to the specified locations in the sheet, refer to Figure 13-25. The three views are added to the sheet, as shown in Figure 13-25.

5. Next, drag the **Door Jamb Detail** view from the **Project Browser** and add it to the desired location in the sheet, refer to Figure 13-23.

Note

You may need to hide the annotations that are not needed to be viewed in the sheet.

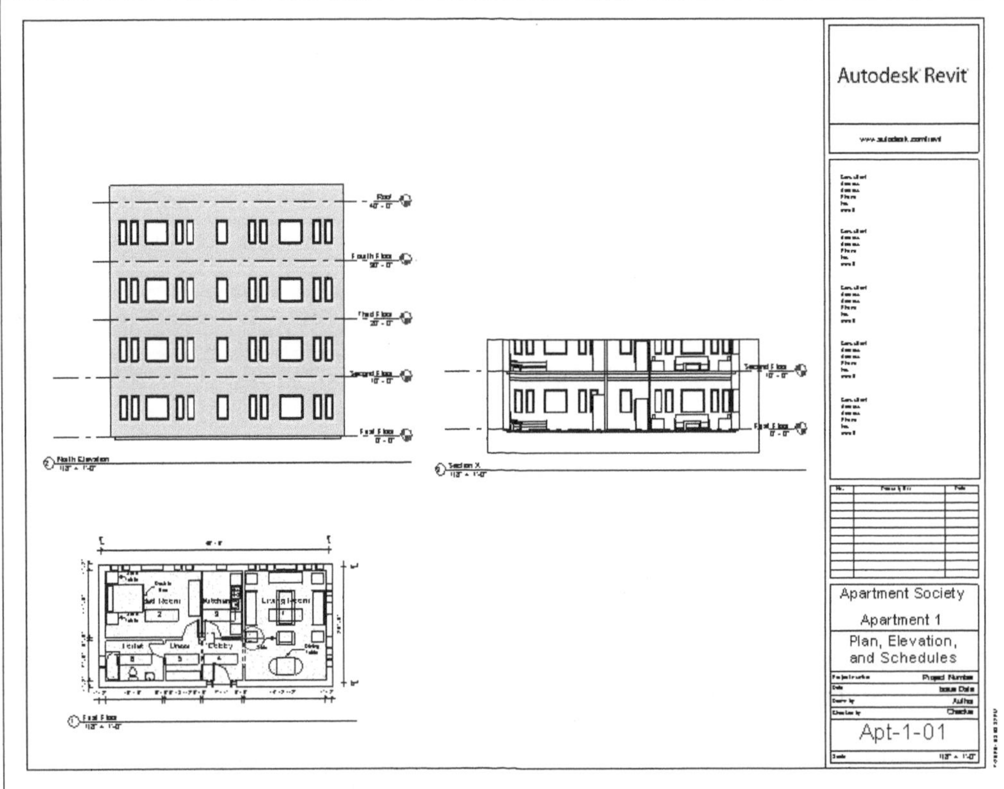

Figure 13-25 Project views added to the drawing sheet view

Modifying the Visibility of the Added Project Views

Notice that the project views in the drawing sheet given for this tutorial do not show the grids and section lines but show the complete section view. You can access each project view directly from the drawing sheet using the **Activate View** tool. Then, you can modify their visibility settings.

1. Select the **North Elevation** view from the drawing or highlight the view and then right-click to display the shortcut menu. Choose the **Activate View** option from the shortcut menu. On doing so, all the views except the selected one become grey. You can now use the editing tools to modify the building model and the visibility settings of the activated view.
2. Choose the **Visibility/Graphics** tool from the **Graphics** panel in the **View** tab; the **Visibility/Graphics Overrides for Elevation: North Elevation** dialog box is displayed.
3. In the **Annotation Categories** tab, clear the check boxes for **Grids** and **Sections** in the **Visibility** column. Choose **OK** to close the dialog box and return to the drawing window.
4. Right-click in the drawing window, and then choose the **Deactivate View** option from the shortcut menu.

5. Repeat step 1 for activating the **Section X** view from the sheet. Next, repeat steps 2 to 4 to turn off the display of grids and sections in the activated view.

6. In the **Properties** palette for the **Section X** view, ensure that the check box corresponding to the **Crop Region Visible** parameter is selected. Next, in the sheet, select the boundary of the section view to display the view range controls.

7. Increase the size of the view range and display the entire section view by using the drag control located on the top as shown in the drawing sheet for this tutorial. You may use the **Zoom** tool to zoom in the section view. Next, right-click and choose **Deactivate View** from the shortcut menu.

Adding Schedules to the Drawing Sheet

Next, you need to add schedules to the drawing sheet in the same manner as you did in the case of the project view. Autodesk Revit, however, gives you the flexibility to divide larger schedules into smaller panels to accommodate them in the drawing sheet.

1. Drag **Room Schedule** from the **Schedules/Quantities** head in the **Project Browser**.

2. Move the cursor to the top left corner of the titleblock. The schedule is displayed and moves along with the cursor. Click to drop and add the room schedule at the location shown in the drawing sheet.

3. Similarly, drag and drop **Door Schedule** from the **Project Browser** to the drawing sheet. The door schedule is long and therefore you can use the **Split Schedule Table** tool to split it into two parts.

4. Click on the **Split Schedule Table** control available in the middle of the right edge of the door schedule, as shown in Figure 13-26. The schedule is divided into two parts and the second part is placed on the right of the first part, refer to Figure 13-23.

*Figure 13-26 Using the **Split Schedule Table** tool to split the table into two parts*

Saving the Project

In this section, you will save the project file using the **Save As** tool.

1. Choose **Save As > Project** from the **File** menu; the **Save As** dialog box is displayed. Enter **c13_Apartment1_tut1 (M_c13_Apartment1_tut1** for Metric) in the **File name** edit box and then choose **Save**.
2. Next, choose **Close** from the **File** menu to close the project file.

Self-Evaluation Test

Answer the following questions and then compare them to those given at the end of this chapter:

1. The __________ tool is used to activate a view added to a sheet.
2. The __________ control is used to split a schedule table into multiple parts.
3. You can access the **Type Properties** dialog box for a sheet by choosing the __________ button from the **Properties** palette.
4. The __________ option in the **Print** dialog box enables you to create a print file.
5. The __________ radio button in the **Print Setup** dialog box needs to be selected to fit the view to the selected paper size.
6. You can load additional titleblocks from the Autodesk Revit's Library. (T/F)
7. You can enter the project information directly in the titleblock. (T/F)
8. A view can be added to a sheet by using the dragging method. (T/F)
9. Once a view is added to a sheet, its parameters and properties cannot be modified. (T/F)
10. You can preview a print document before printing it. (T/F)

Review Questions

Answer the following questions:

1. Which of the following parameters cannot be used to specify the print range of a project view for printing?

(a) **Selected views/sheets** (b) **Visible portion of current window**
(c) **Size** (d) **Current window**

2. Which of the following tools can be used to add a project view to a sheet?

   (a) **Callout** (b) **Sheet**
   (c) **Drafting View** (d) **Add View**

3. Which of the following tools can be used to adjust the location of an added schedule in a sheet view?

   (a) **Move** (b) **Offset**
   (c) **Align** (d) **Array**

4. Which of the following steps is required to place a schedule on a sheet?

   (a) Click on the schedule in the project browser and drag it onto the sheet.
   (b) Right-click on the schedules in the **Project Browser** and click Send to Sheet.
   (c) Define the schedule as a hosted view in the sheets properties palette.
   (d) Define the schedules sheet location in its view properties.

5. Which of the following options is displayed in the Section Tag after placing a section view?

   (a) The view scale (b) The view name
   (c) The sheet number (d) All sheets referenced.

6. The elements edited in a project view are automatically updated in a sheet view. (T/F)

7. The schedules added to a sheet can be moved to another sheet. (T/F)

8. When you edit a building parameter, the schedules added to a sheet are automatically updated. (T/F)

9. You can modify the **View Scale** parameter of a project view after adding it to a sheet. (T/F)

10. The visibility settings of a view are modified after adding it to a sheet. (T/F)

11. You can create your own titleblock by modifying the titleblock available in Autodesk Revit's library. (T/F)

12. Apart from printing sheet views, you can also directly print project views. (T/F)

EXERCISES

Exercise 1 Club

Create a drawing sheet for the *Club* project created in Exercise 3 of Chapter 12. Add the first floor and roof plan, north elevation, sections, and room schedule to the sheet, as shown in Figure 13-27. Use the following project and sheet information parameters:

(Expected time: 30 min)

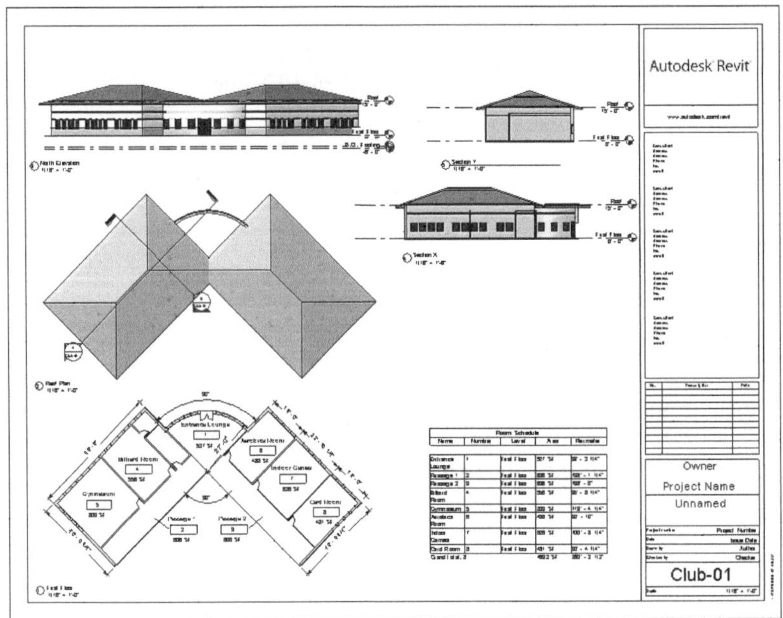

Figure 13-27 *Sheet view for creating a drawing sheet for the Club project*

1. Drawing sheet parameters:
   Title block to be used:
   For Imperial **C 17 x 22 Horizontal** from **US Imperial > Titleblocks** folder.
   For Metric **A2 metric** from **US Metric > Titleblocks** folder.

2. Project information:
   Owner name: **Club House**
   Sheet title: **Club Building**
   Sheet name: **Project Drawings**
   Sheet number: **Club-01**

3. Name of the file to be saved-
   For Imperial **c13_Club_ex1**
   For Metric **M_c13_Club_ex1**

Note
The Club project has been created using the Commercial-Default.rte template and therefore it already contains various sheet views. Some of the views have already been placed in them. You need to create a copy of the views and then add them to the new sheet that you create. You may also need to modify the view scale.

Exercise 2 Urban House

Create a drawing sheet for the *i_Urban_House.rvt* project. You can download the *i_Urban_House.rvt* file from *http://www.cadcim.com*. The path of the file is as follows:

Textbooks > Civil/GIS > Revit Architecture > Exploring Autodesk Revit 2018 for Architecture. In the drawing sheet, add the ground floor plan, first floor plan, second floor plan, south elevation, east elevation, and the 3D View 1, as shown in Figure 13-28. Use the titleblock **E1: 30 X 42 Horizontal** (for Metric **A0 metric** titleblock) for this exercise. All the views, except the 3D view, should be 1/8"=1'0"(for metric 1:100) view scale.

(Expected time: 30 min)

Save the file as:

For Imperial *c13_UrbanHouse_ex2.rvt*

For Metric *M_c13_UrbanHouse_ex2.rvt*

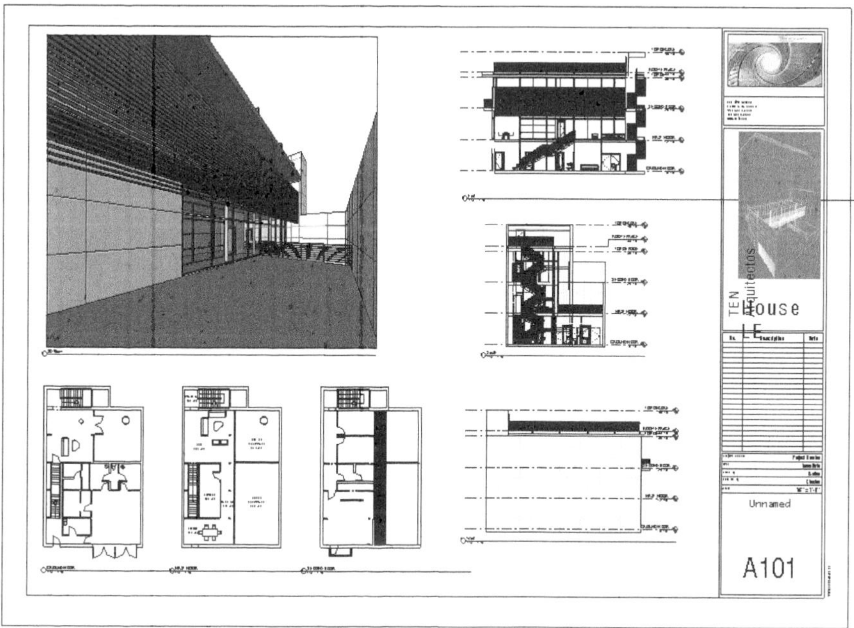

Figure 13-28 *Sheet view for creating a drawing sheet for the Urban House project*

Answers to Self-Evaluation Test

1. Activate View, 2. Split Schedule Table, 3. Edit Type, 4. Print to File, 5. Fit to Page 6. T, 7. T, 8. T, 9. F, 10. T

Chapter 14

Creating 3D Views

Learning Objectives

After completing this chapter, you will be able to:

- *Generate orthographic view of a building model*
- *Use the Navigation tools to view a building model*
- *Generate perspective view using the Camera tool*
- *Modify the properties of perspective view*
- *Lock and unlock 3D view*
- *Use the section view*

INTRODUCTION

A three-dimensional view is a powerful medium of developing and presenting architectural and interior design concepts. Viewing a building model in all the three dimensions helps the architects and interior designers to visualize various building forms and shapes. It also conveys their vision of project to the clients, who, in most cases, are unable to understand the architectural drawings. The exterior 3D views of a building not only depict its overall scale, shape, and volume but can also represent the proposed exterior finishes as envisaged by the architects. The interior 3D views can be used to represent various interior elements such as interior partitions, furniture, plants, and interior finishes.

The use of computer graphics in the preparation of three-dimensional exterior and interior views gives numerous advantages to designers. The inevitable alterations in a building model during the design development can easily be studied with respect to their implications on the three-dimensional aspect of design. Software also enables the designers to develop design alternatives with different exterior and interior materials.

As described in the previous chapters, a building model of a project created using Autodesk Revit is an amalgamation of various three-dimensional elements such as walls, doors, windows, floor, roof, stairs, furniture, and so on. Each of these elements is a three-dimensional parametric entity. Autodesk Revit's powerful parametric technology enables the designers to create and edit these elements, and study them in all the three dimensions simultaneously. Autodesk Revit provides various tools to view these elements in 3D.

This chapter deals with the tools used for generating 3D views of a structure. It describes the procedure for generating new orthographic and perspective views for a building model. The ease of generating 3D views in Autodesk Revit gives a major advantage to all the users. They can also easily modify the view properties to achieve the desired effect in the exterior or interior 3D views.

THREE-DIMENSIONAL (3D) VIEWS

In Autodesk Revit, you can display a variety of three-dimensional (3D) views. There are two basic types of 3D views that can be created and viewed.

Orthographic View: An orthographic view is a 3D view of a building model in which all the elements are displayed in their actual sizes, irrespective of their distance from the source. This view is displayed automatically as a default 3D view. Once this view has been displayed, you can then use various tools to modify its properties.

Perspective View: A perspective view is displayed by placing a camera and specifying its eye elevation and target position.

Generating Orthographic View

Ribbon: View > Create > 3D View drop-down > Default 3D View

In Autodesk Revit, the default 3D view is an orthographic view. To view a building model in orthographic projection, invoke the **Default 3D View** tool from the **Create** panel; the current view will change into the default 3D view.

Note

*In Revit, there is no default {3D} view in the **Project Browser**. However, when you invoke the **Default 3D View** tool from the **Create** panel, the default {3D} view is added to the **Project Browser**.*

When you create an orthographic 3D view for the first time in a project, a camera is automatically placed at the default position (southeast corner) and the corresponding view is displayed in the drawing window. The default view is named as **{3D}** and is added under the **3D Views** head of the **Project Browser**. Figure 14-1 shows an example of the 3D view of a building model displayed using the **Default 3D View** tool.

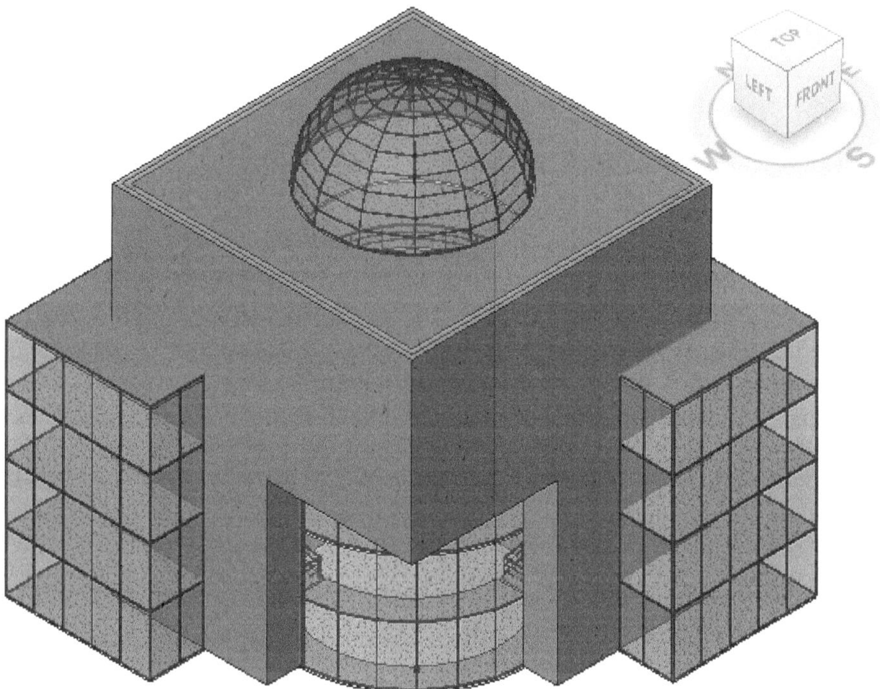

Figure 14-1 *3D view of a building model displayed using the **Default 3D View** tool*

Tip

*You can rename the default 3D view in the Project Browser. After renaming it, when the **Default 3D View** tool is invoked from the **View** tab, Autodesk Revit will create another default view under the **{3D}** head in the Project Browser.*

Dynamically Viewing Models Using Navigation Tools

The 3D environment of Revit has two important tools for navigation: SteeringWheels and ViewCube. You can use these tools to navigate through 3D views easily. These tools have already been discussed in brief in Chapter 2.

The SteeringWheels, as shown in Figure 14-2, is a tracking menu that enables you to navigate easily within the exterior and interior faces of a model. The ViewCube helps you simplify the switching of views from one point to another, as shown in Figure 14-3.

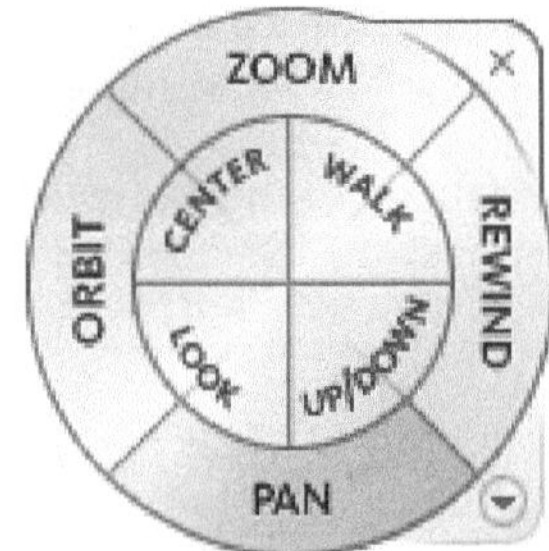

Figure 14-2 *The tools in the SteeringWheels*

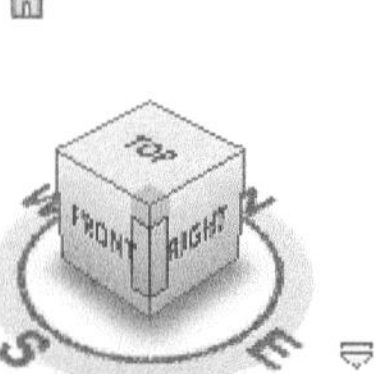

Figure 14-3 *The tools in the ViewCube*

Note

*If the SteeringWheels is not displayed by default, press F8 or invoke it from the **Navigation Bar**. You can also display or hide the SteeringWheels navigation by pressing Shift+W keys.*

Using the Navigation Tools in SteeringWheels

In Autodesk Revit, you can invoke nine navigation tools from the SteeringWheels. These tools are **CENTER, FORWARD, LOOK, ORBIT, PAN, REWIND, UP/DOWN, WALK,** and **ZOOM**. The availability of these tools depends upon the type of wheels being used. Different types of SteeringWheels have been discussed in Chapter 2. Various tools in the SteeringWheels are discussed next.

CENTER Tool

The **CENTER** tool is used to specify a point on a model as the center of the current view. While using this tool, you can adjust the location of the center of the current view by clicking and dragging the cursor to the defined point. As you drag the cursor, the cursor takes the shape of a sphere, as shown in Figure 14-4. Next, click at the desired place to specify the center of the view. When you release the mouse button, the model pans until the sphere is centered in the view and you return to the SteeringWheels.

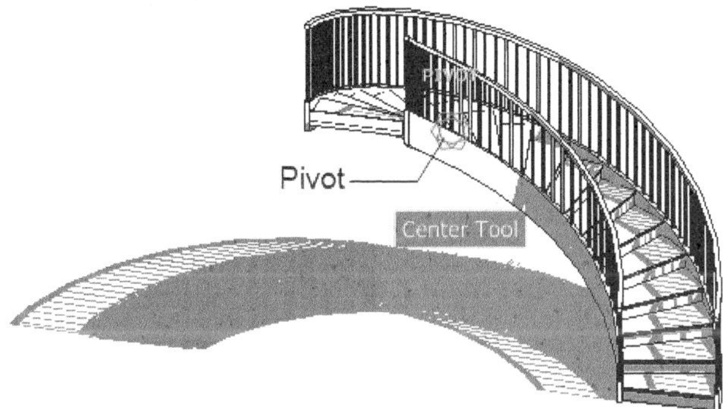

*Figure 14-4 Using the **CENTER** tool of SteeringWheels*

After specifying the new center, you can revert to the original center. To do so, right-click on the **CENTER** button in the SteeringWheels, and then choose the **Restore Original Center** option from the shortcut menu displayed; the original center will be restored.

FORWARD Tool

The **FORWARD** tool is used to navigate a view forward and backward in the current viewport with respect to a pivot point, as shown in Figure 14-5. To invoke the tool, right-click on SteeringWheels and choose **Basic Wheels**; a flyout will be displayed. Choose the **Tour Building Wheel** option from the flyout. Next, you need to fix the pivot point. To fix the pivot point, move the cursor close to the proposed point and then press and hold the left mouse button in such a way that the forward wedge in the SteeringWheels encompasses the proposed pivot point. As a result, the slider will be displayed in the 3D view. This slider is called **Drag Distance Indicator**. It has two marks: **START** and **SURFACE**. The **START** mark shows the starting distance of the navigation from the current viewpoint whereas the **SURFACE** mark shows the end distance from the current viewpoint. When you change the distance using the **Drag Distance Indicator**, the current distance is shown by the bright orange indicator. Move the cursor over the slider up and down to navigate the view. If you release the left mouse button, the slider will disappear.

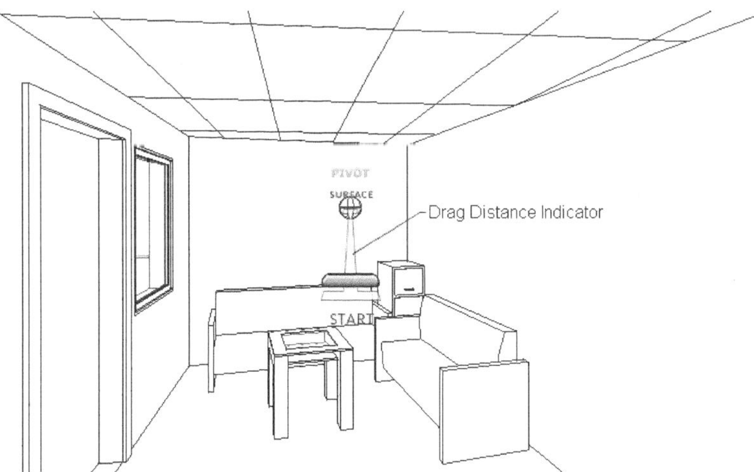

*Figure 14-5 Using the **FORWARD** tool of SteeringWheels*

Note

*When the **FORWARD** tool is clicked once, the model moves forward by 50% of the distance between the current location and the pivot point.*

LOOK Tool

The **LOOK** tool is used to rotate a view horizontally or vertically about a fixed point. The fixed point is defined by the center of the current view.

To invoke the **LOOK** tool, select **Full Navigation Wheel** or **Basic Tour Building Wheel**. Next, choose the **LOOK** option from the wheel and then hold the left mouse button until you notice the look cursor, as shown in Figure 14-6. Drag the look cursor along different directions to view the model.

Figure 14-6 *Using the **LOOK** tool from SteeringWheels*

ORBIT Tool

The **ORBIT** tool is used to orbit or rotate a model about a fixed point. To use the **ORBIT** tool, you need to fix the pivot point that serves as the base point around which the model will rotate. Figure 14-7 shows the pivot point in the model while using the **ORBIT** tool. There are several ways to fix the pivot point for the **ORBIT** tool. One of the ways is to use the **CENTER** tool from SteeringWheels. In this case, the center that you fix up becomes the pivot point of the **ORBIT** tool. Alternatively, set the pivot point by pressing and holding the CTRL key and invoking the **ORBIT** tool from the SteeringWheels. Next, drag the cursor to the proposed pivot point on the model; this will change the cursor to a sphere indicating the new pivot point.

Figure 14-7 *Using the* ***ORBIT*** *tool from SteeringWheels*

You can also set the pivot point by selecting elements about which you want to orbit before using the **ORBIT** tool from SteeringWheels. The pivot point is calculated on the basis of the extent of the selected elements.

If you have not set the pivot point for the **ORBIT** tool by any of these ways, then by default, the target point of the current view will act as the pivot point.

As you invoke the **ORBIT** tool from the SteeringWheels, the cursor will change to the orbit cursor. You can drag the cursor to rotate your model about a pivot point. After dragging the cursor and then fixing a view, you can change the position of the pivot point in various ways.

PAN Tool

The **PAN** tool is used to scroll or move a view along the horizontal and vertical direction in the drawing area. To do so, invoke the **PAN** tool from SteeringWheels and hold the left mouse button; the cursor will take the shape of a four-sided arrow, as shown in Figure 14-8. Drag the arrow in the required direction to scroll the model.

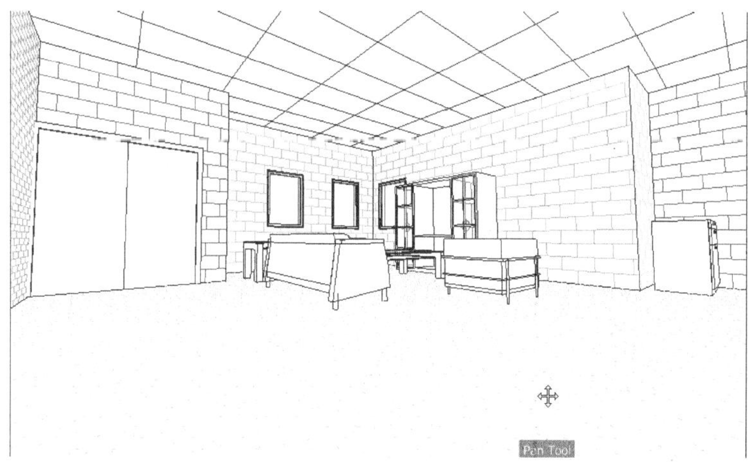

Figure 14-8 *Using the* ***PAN*** *tool from SteeringWheels*

REWIND Tool

The **REWIND** tool holds a collection of previous views that have been navigated using various tools such as **ZOOM**, **PAN**, **LOOK**, **ORBIT**, and so on. The collection of the previous views is temporarily saved in the navigation history. The navigation history contains the representation of the navigated views of a model in the form of thumbnails, as shown in Figure 14-9. The navigation history of the **REWIND** tool is view-specific and has different saving options for different views.

Figure 14-9 *Using the **REWIND** tool from SteeringWheels*

UP/DOWN Tool

Using the **UP/DOWN** tool, you can slide the current view of a model along the vertical axis of the screen. This sliding movement allows the current view plane to move vertically up and down. To invoke this tool, press and hold the **UP/DOWN** tool; a graphical element will be displayed showing the range of the vertical movement. The graphical element, which is called **Vertical Distance indicator**, has **TOP** and **BOTTOM** marked on its two ends, as shown in Figure 14-10. The **TOP** and **BOTTOM** marks show the highest and lowest elevation, respectively, of the view. On changing the elevation of the view with the **Vertical Distance indicator**, the current elevation will be shown by the bright orange indicator whereas the previous elevation will be shown by the dim orange indicator.

WALK Tool

The **WALK** tool helps you virtually walk through the space of a model. Using the **WALK** tool, you can virtually traverse through the space and gain a real time experience of navigating into a virtual 3D environment.

Note

*Using the **WALK** tool, you can navigate only in a 3D perspective view.*

To invoke the **WALK** tool from SteeringWheels, press and hold the left mouse button over it; the cursor will change into a blue circle with a black dot at its center and eight arrows pointing in different directions, as shown in Figure 14-11. These arrows indicate the direction of movement while using the **WALK** tool. Now as you drag the cursor away from the blue circle, a single arrow will replace the cursor, which informs you or indicates the direction of the movement. If you want to change the direction of movement at any time during the navigation, drag the mouse in the specified direction as shown in the arrows.

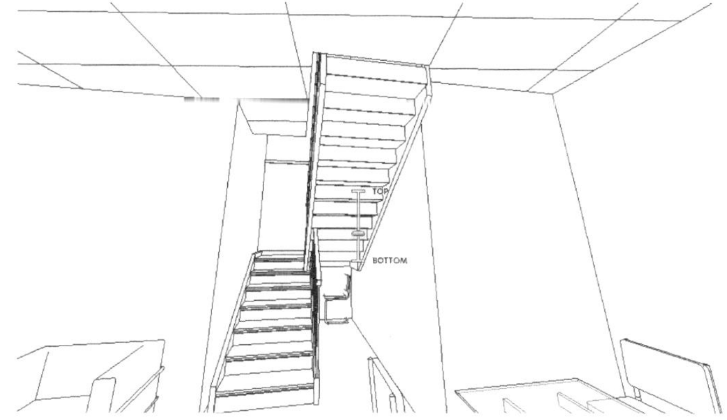

Figure 14-10 *Using the* ***UP/DOWN*** *tool from SteeringWheels*

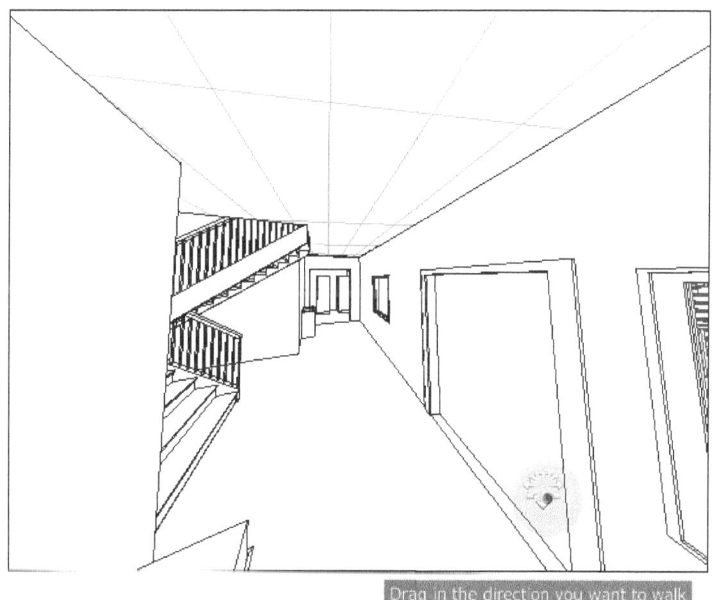

Figure 14-11 *Using the* ***WALK*** *tool from SteeringWheels*

While navigating through the space, you will observe that by default, the viewing plane is fixed to the horizontal plane. You can remove this restriction in order to view the model freely. To do so, right-click on SteeringWheels; a shortcut menu will be displayed. Choose the **Options** option from the shortcut menu; the **Options** dialog box will be displayed with the **Steering Wheels** tab chosen. In the **Walk Tool** area of the **Steering Wheels** tab, clear the **Move parallel to ground plane** check box. Next, choose the **OK** button in the **Options** dialog box to return to the navigation. Now, you can navigate through the space without any restriction of the movement angle.

While you walk or fly through the space in the model, the speed of the movement is controlled by the **Speed Factor** slider that is available in the SteeringWheels tab of the **Options** dialog box. When you move the slider toward right, the value of the **SpeedFactor** increases and when you move toward left, its value decreases. You can enter any value from 0.1 to 10 in the text box displayed next to the **Speed Factor** slider. As you move the slider, you will notice the change in the value of the text box. Alternatively, you can use the period (**.**) and comma (**,**) keys in the keyboard to accelerate and decelerate the movement of navigation while using the **WALK** tool.

Note
*To increase or decrease the speed of navigation while using the **WALK** tool, right-click on the **WALK** option in the SteeringWheels and then choose **Increase Walk Speed** or **Decrease Walk Speed** from the shortcut menu displayed.*

While using the **Walk** tool, you can press and hold the SHIFT key to change the **Up/Down** tool. This tool can, in turn, be used to change the elevation of the viewing plane.

ZOOM Tool

The **ZOOM** tool is used to zoom in and zoom out a view. This tool is controlled by a magnification factor related to the amount of zooming done with respect to the current view scale, as shown in Figure 14-12.

Figure 14-12 *Using the **ZOOM** tool from SteeringWheels*

Tip
*You can use the **ZOOM** tool to zoom in or zoom out the generated 3D perspective view. You can also stretch its extent by dragging the blue dots available in the view box.*

Using the **ZOOM** tool, you can zoom and alter the magnification of your current view in several ways. To zoom out the current view, press and hold the SHIFT key before clicking on the **ZOOM** tool in SteeringWheel; the current view scale of the model will be reduced by

25 percent. Similarly, to increase the view scale of the current view by 25 percent, press and hold the CTRL key before clicking the left mouse button on the **ZOOM** tool. Alternatively, if you simply click the left mouse button once on the **ZOOM** tool, the magnification of the current view will increase by a factor of 25 percent. You can also make the zooming function dynamic by using the **ZOOM** tool. To do so, click the left mouse button on the **ZOOM** tool and drag the cursor up and down until you achieve the desired view on your screen.

Note

*When you are using the **Full Navigation Wheel** for zooming, the single-click zooming option will work, provided the **Zoom in one increment with each mouse click** check box is selected in the **SteeringWheels** tab of the **Options** dialog box.*

Tip

*While using the **ZOOM** tool from the **Full Navigation Wheel** or **View Object Wheel**, the pivot point of the last zoom operation becomes the center point for the future orbit operations unless you use the **CENTER** tool after the zooming function.*

Using the Orient Tool

Autodesk Revit enables you to view the building model from certain predefined orientations such as north, south, east, west, northwest, southeast, and so on. These orientations are created by a camera placed in the respective directions and at a certain elevation. You can easily view the building model from these orientations using the **Orient** tool. To invoke this tool, right-click on the ViewCube; a shortcut menu will be displayed. Next, choose the **Orient to View**, **Orient to a Direction**, or **Orient to a Plane** option from the shortcut menu. You can choose the **Orient to View** option from the shortcut menu to transform the current view of the project to any of the views of floor plans or elevations. You can use the **Orient to a Direction** option from the shortcut menu to change the direction of the current project view to any of the orthographic or isometric view directions such as **North**, **South**, and **Northeast Isometric**. Similarly, you can use the **Orient to a Plane** option from the shortcut menu to change the orientation of the current project view to any of the specified workplanes in the project.

Note

*By default, a building plan is oriented in the north direction toward the top of the screen. You can, however, choose the **Location** tool from the **Project Location** panel in the **Manage** tab to modify the orientation.*

Orienting the 3D View to a Direction

To use the **Orient to a Direction** option, first you need to invoke the ViewCube. To do so, open the 3D view of the model; the ViewCube will be displayed. Next, right-click on the ViewCube to display a shortcut menu. Choose the **Orient to a Direction** option from the shortcut menu and then choose the required direction from the cascading menu, as shown in Figure 14-13.

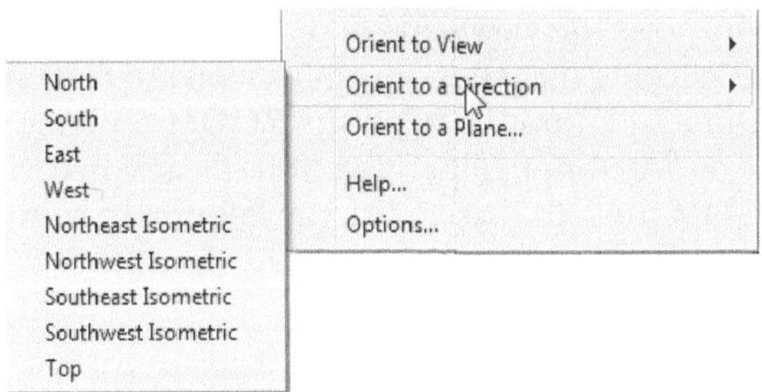

*Figure 14-13 Choosing the **Orient to a Direction** option to open a 3D View*

Note

*You can display the top view of a building model by right-clicking on the ViewCube and then choosing **Orient to a Direction > Top** from the shortcut menu displayed.*

Orienting the 3D View to a View

In Autodesk Revit, you can orient your current project view to a specified saved floor plan or elevation. To do so, open the 3D view to display ViewCube. Next, right-click on it and then choose **Orient to View** from the shortcut menu; a cascading menu will be displayed, as shown in Figure 14-14. You can choose the required Floor Plan/Elevation from the cascading menu.

*Figure 14-14 Choosing the **Orient to View** option from the shortcut menu*

You can also orient the 3D view to a desired view using SteeringWheels. To do so, right-click on SteeringWheels, and then choose **Orient to View** from the shortcut menu; a cascading menu will be displayed. You can select the required Floor Plan/Elevation from this cascading menu.

Orienting the 3D View to a Plane

You can orient your current project view to a specified work plane. To do so, invoke the SteeringWheels by pressing the F8 key and then right-click on SteeringWheels; a shortcut menu will be displayed. In the shortcut menu, choose the **Orient to a Plane** option; the **Select Orientation Plane** dialog box will be displayed, as shown in Figure 14-15. Next, select the required radio button from this dialog box to specify the orientation plane.

Generating Perspective Views

Perspective views provide a realistic view of the exterior or interior space of a building model. Whenever you see an exterior or an interior view of a building with naked eye, it appears as the perspective view with the wall edges of the building converging at imaginary points. Using Autodesk Revit, you can easily create perspective views of a building model by defining the camera location and the target point. In most building projects, you will find it easier to use the floor plan view to define these points (camera location and camera target). You can then modify the view parameters to achieve the desired result.

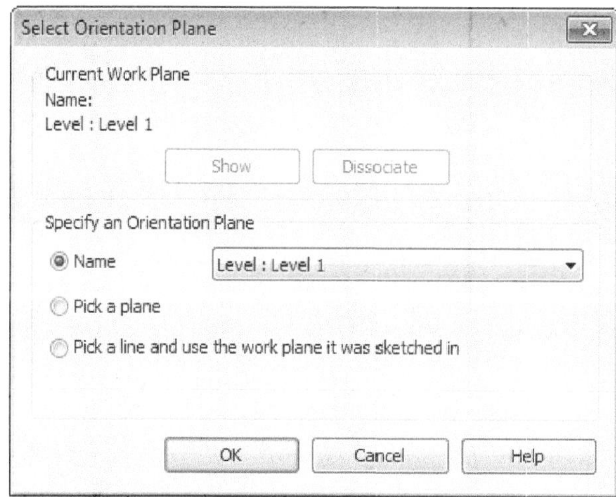

Figure 14-15 *Specifying the orientation plane in the* ***Select Orientation Plane*** *dialog box*

Generating Exterior Perspective Views

Ribbon: View > Create > 3D View drop-down> Camera

The **Camera** tool is used to create both exterior and interior perspective views of a building model. To create a perspective view, first open the floor plan or the ceiling plan view of the building model. Next, in the floor plan or in the ceiling plan view, invoke the **Camera** tool from the **Create** panel. On invoking the **Camera** tool, the **Options Bar** will display various related options for the camera to be placed in the view. Ensure that the **Perspective** check box is selected. The level of the eye point can be selected from the **From** drop-down list in the **Options Bar**. The **Offset** edit box can be used to enter the value of the offset level of the eye point from the selected level. For example, to generate a 3D perspective view from an eye point located at **5'0"** above level 1, you need to select **Level 1** from the **From** drop-down list and enter the value **5'0"** in the **Offset** edit box in **Options Bar**. This process should be followed before selecting the eye point.

As you move the cursor in the drawing window, a camera will be attached to it. Autodesk Revit will prompt you to specify the location of the eye point or the point from where you want to view the model. Next, click to specify location, as shown in Figure 14-16. In order to generate the exterior 3D views, the eye point must be placed outside the building model. Next, you need to specify the target point. To do so, move the cursor away from the camera location; you will notice that three rays are generated from the location point, as shown in Figure 14-17. These rays depict the field of the view for the selected camera point. You can use the **Offset** and **From** options in the **Options Bar** to specify the level and the offset elevation of the target point. Move the cursor and specify its location. The target point must be placed inside or beyond the building model for the camera to capture the model. Once you have selected the target point, Autodesk Revit will automatically generate the 3D perspective view of the building model and display it in the drawing window, as shown in Figure 14-18. The generated view will be added to the **3D Views** subhead of the **Project Browser**. Autodesk Revit will name the generated 3D views as **3D View 1**, **3D View 2**, and so on. You can, however, rename them using the **Rename** option from the shortcut menu that is displayed on right-clicking on the newly created 3D view in the **Project Browser**.

Tip

The locations of the eye point and the target point define the amount of distortion in the perspective view. The closer the eye point to the building, the more is the distortion. To generate a realistic perspective view with minimum distortions, ideally, a building model or the portion of a building model to be viewed must fall within the field of view of the camera.

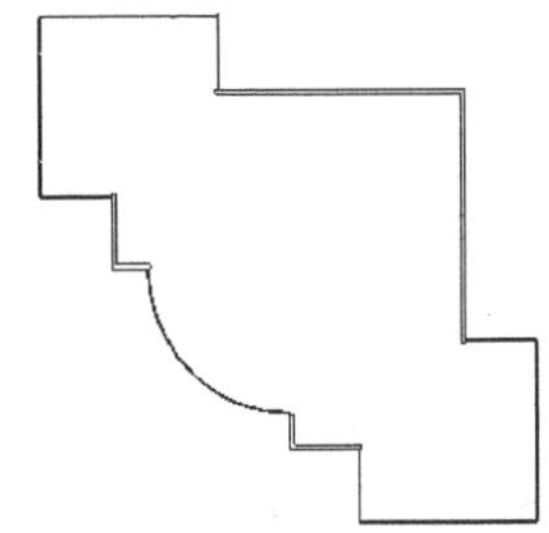

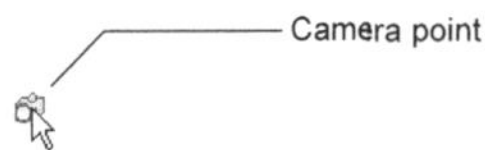

Figure 14-16 *Specifying the camera point to create a perspective view*

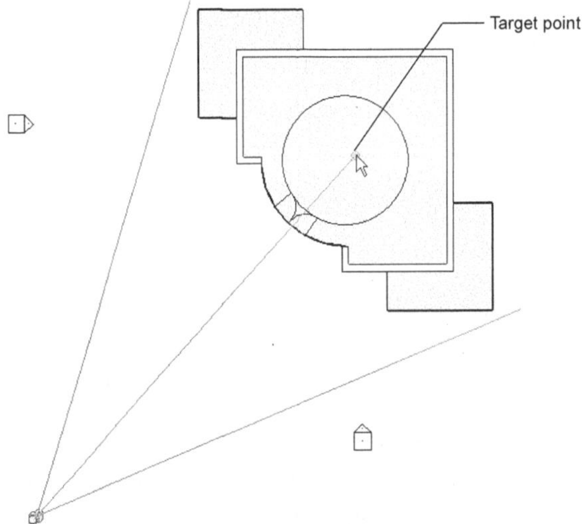

Figure 14-17 *Specifying the target point to create a perspective view*

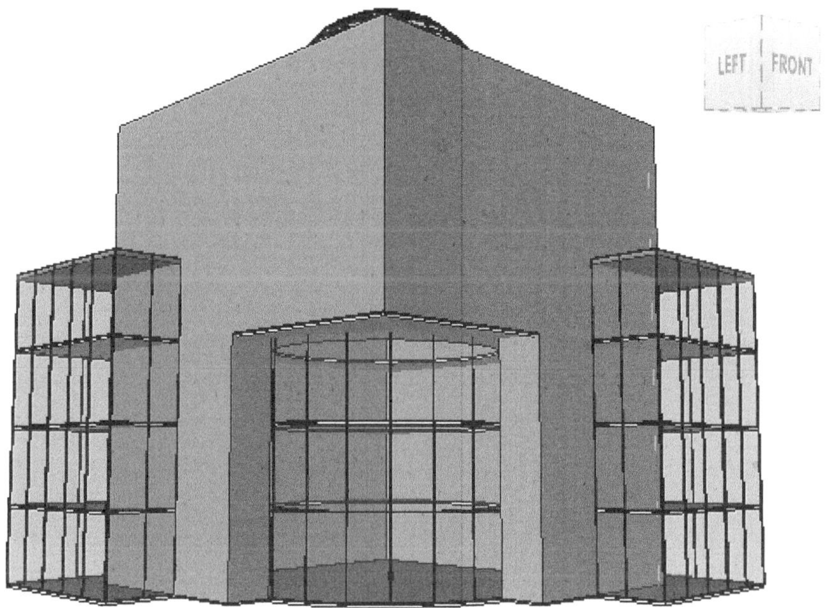

*Figure 14-18 3D perspective view generated using the **Camera** tool*

You can also create orthographic views using the **Camera** tool. To do so, clear the **Perspective** check box in the **Options Bar** and then select the eye and the target points. Next, from the **Scale** drop-down list, select an option to specify the scale of the view. On doing so, an orthographic 3D view will be displayed with a specified scale.

Generating Interior Perspective Views

The procedure of creating an interior perspective view is similar to that of creating an exterior view. The **Camera** tool is also used to generate an interior view. However, in the case of an interior view, the eye point and the target point must be specified within the building model. Figure 14-19 shows the example of the eye point and the target point being specified for generating an interior perspective view.

Note

If you select two different levels for the eye point and the target point, Autodesk Revit will display four lines indicating the field of view for both levels.

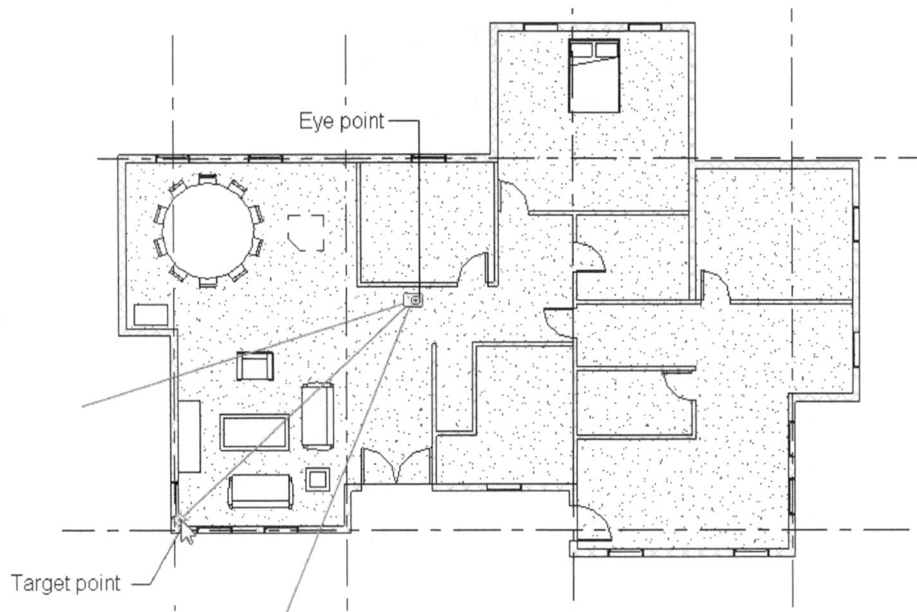

Figure 14-19 Specifying the eye point and the target point to generate an interior view

Autodesk Revit generates the interior perspective view and displays it in the drawing window, as shown in Figure 14-20. To increase its extent, you can select any one of the blue dots at the four edges of the view box and drag them to the desired extent. This modifies the field of view for the camera. An example of the extended interior view is shown in Figure 14-21.

Figure 14-20 The interior perspective view generated

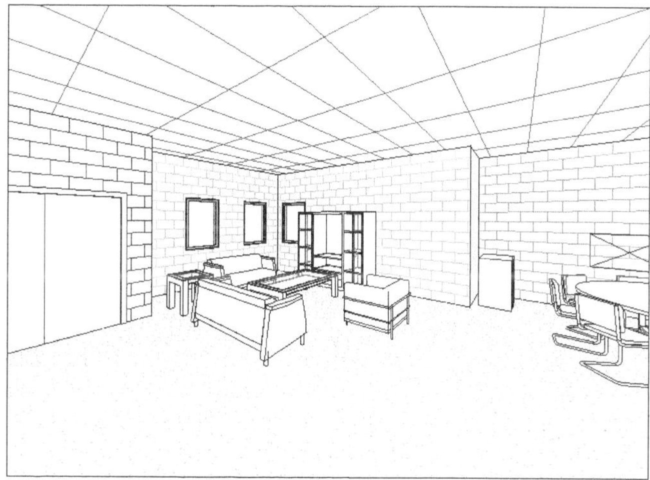

Figure 14-21 Modified extent of the perspective view using the drag controls

Modifying Perspective View Properties

After creating the perspective view, you can modify its properties to achieve the desired effect. To do so, select the perspective view displayed and modify the desired instance properties in the **Properties** palette. The instance properties of the 3D view displayed in the **Properties** palette are described next.

In the **Properties** palette, the **View Name** instance parameter under the **Identity Data** head is used to rename a view. The **Detail Level** instance parameter is used to set the level of details desired in a view. The **Edit** button in the value column of the **Visibility/Graphics Overrides** instance parameter is used to set the visibility of models and annotations. On choosing this button, the **Visibility/Graphics Overrides <view name>** dialog box will be displayed. In this dialog box, you can set the visibility parameters of the model. Autodesk Revit generates a perspective view using the value **5'6"** as the default elevation of the eye and also the target points from their respective specified levels. To modify the elevation of the eye point, enter the new value in the value column of the **Eye Elevation** instance parameter. Similarly, you can enter a new value for the **Target Elevation** instance parameter in its corresponding value column. As soon as you choose the **Apply** button, the perspective view is modified in the drawing window.

Locking and Unlocking 3D Views

In Revit, you can lock, unlock, and save the orientation of a 3D view. By locking a 3D view, you can add annotations and element tags to it. To view the options for locking, unlocking, and saving the 3D views, choose the **Unlocked 3D View** option from the **View Control Bar**. Note that the **Unlocked 3D View** option will be displayed in the 3D and camera views only. On choosing the **Unlocked 3D View** option, a flyout will be displayed, as shown in Figure 14-22. In the flyout, the following options are displayed: **Save Orientation and Lock View**, **Restore Orientation and Lock View**, and **Unlock View**. Note that the **Restore Orientation and Lock View** and **Unlock View** options are inactive by default.

***Figure 14-22** Flyout displayed on choosing the **Unlocked 3D View** option*

On choosing the **Save Orientation and Lock View** option, the **Rename Default 3D View To Lock** dialog box will be displayed. In this dialog box, enter a name in the **Name** edit box and choose the **OK** button; the current view will be renamed, saved, and locked. After you save and lock the orientation of the 3D view, you can also tag the elements. After tagging the elements you can unlock the view. To do so, choose the **Unlock View** option from the flyout; the tags added will disappear and you can re-orient the 3D view. After re-orienting the view, you can restore the previous locked view that was saved. To do so, choose the **Restore Orientation and Lock View** option from the flyout.

Note

*In the Camera view, on choosing the **Save Orientation and Lock View** option from the **View Control Bar**, the **Rename Default 3D View To Lock** dialog box will not be displayed.*

Using the Section Box

A section box is used to limit the model geometry in a file that you want to export to other program such as Autodesk 3ds Max or Autodesk 3ds Max Design. It helps you clip unwanted content in a file. By adjusting the extent of a section box using drag controls, you can clip the unwanted portion of a model in the 3D view, thereby reducing the file size. This helps in easy and fast export of heavy files. Note that a section box can be enabled in a 3D view only.

To enable a section box, open the required 3D view and in the **Properties** palette, select the check box in the **Value** column corresponding to the **Section Box** parameter. Now, choose the **Apply** button in the **Properties** palette; a section box will be displayed in the 3D view as shown in Figure 14-23. Select the section box to display the blue color arrow controls. Drag the blue arrow controls and modify the extent of the section box to clip the unwanted portion of the model. Note that the section box option is available in the **Properties** palette for camera view also.

Note

*To hide the section box, clear the check box for the **Section Box** parameter in the **Properties** palette.*

Autodesk Revit allows you to modify the extents of a section box from the views other than the 3D view such as a plan view or elevation view. To do so, select the section box in a 3D view and then open the required plan or the elevation view. The blue arrow controls will be displayed in the respective view as well. Modify the extent of the section box and then open the 3D view again to see the change. If required, you can modify the extent of the scope box again in the 3D view. To hide the scope box, select the scope box and right-click; a shortcut menu will be displayed. Choose **Hide in view > Elements** from the shortcut menu; the scope box will be visible in the view. To save the view, duplicate the view and rename it.

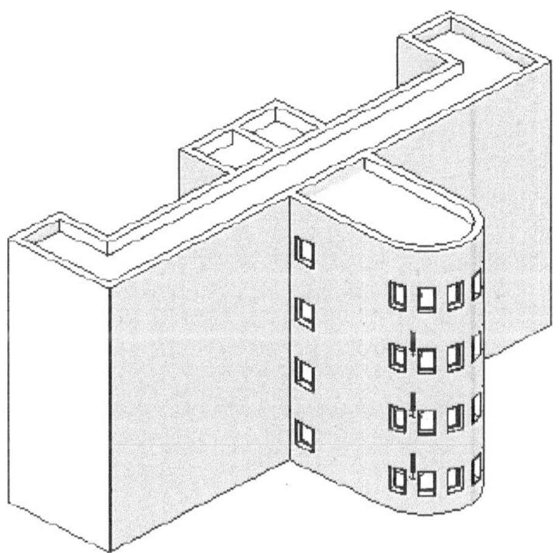

Figure 14-23 *Section Box generated for the 3D view*

Tip

To modify the camera and target locations, open the view in which the camera was placed. Right-click on the ***3D view*** *name in the* ***Project Browser*** *that was created by using the camera. Choose the* ***Show Camera*** *option from the shortcut menu to display the location of the camera and the target points in the drawing window. The camera and target points can now be dragged to a new location. Autodesk Revit immediately regenerates the 3D view for the new location.*

Note

The extents of a section box are not affected by the crop regions.

TUTORIALS

Tutorial 1 Apartment 1

In this tutorial, you will create two interior perspective views for the first floor of the *Apartment 1* project created in Chapter 13 of this textbook, refer to Figures 14-24 and 14-25. The first figure shows the living room and the second figure shows the view of the lobby area from the living room. The exact view angle and height are not important for this tutorial.

(Expected time: 20 min)

Figure 14-24 *3D view of the living room for the Apartment 1 project*

Figure 14-25 *3D view of the lobby area for the Apartment 1 project*

The following steps are required to complete this tutorial:

a. Open the project file and the ground floor plan view.
b. Generate the interior perspective view of the living room using the camera tool, refer to Figure 14-26.
c. Generate the interior perspective view of the lobby room, refer to Figures 14-28 and 14-29.
d. Save the project using the **Save As** tool.
   For Imperial *c14_Apartment1_tut1.rvt*
   For Metric *M_c14_Apartment1_tut1.rvt*
e. Close the project.

Opening the Project File and Invoking the Camera Tool

1. Choose **Open > Project** from the **File** menu and open the *c13_ Apartment 1_tut1.rvt* file created in Tutorial 1 of Chapter 13. You can also download this file from *http://www.cadcim.com*.

The path of the file is as follows: *Textbooks > Civil/GIS > Revit Architecture > Exploring Autodesk Revit 2018 for Architecture.*

2. Double-click on **First Floor** in the **Floor Plans** head of the **Project Browser** to open the corresponding floor plan in the drawing window.

3. Invoke the **Camera** tool from **View > Create > 3D View** drop-down; the **Options Bar** is displayed.

Generating the Interior Perspective View of the Living Room

In this section of the tutorial, you will specify the camera and the target points for the camera. You will use the default value **5'6"** (eye level) for both these points.

1. Select the **Perspective** check box in the **Options Bar**, if it is not selected by default.

2. Move the cursor to the lower right corner of the living room and click to specify the camera point.

3. Now, move the cursor toward the diagonally opposite ends of the living room and click when the field of view resembles the graphic shown in Figure 14-26. The drawing window shows the 3D interior view, as shown in Figure 14-27.

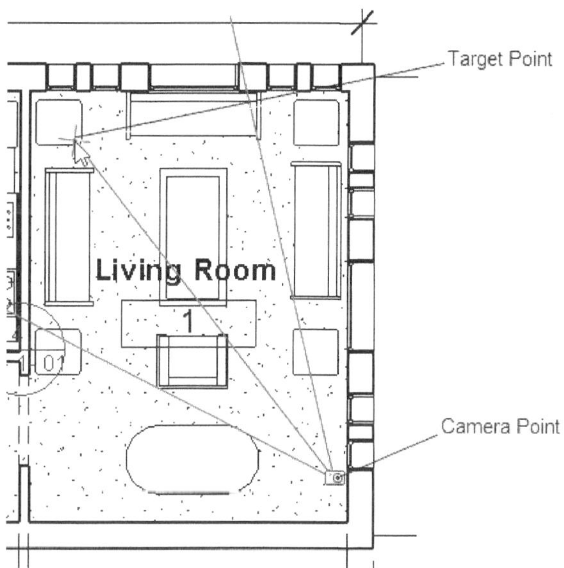

Figure 14-26 *Specifying the camera point and the target point of the interior view*

Figure 14-27 The 3D interior view of the living room

4. The selected 3D view shows the drag controls (blue dots at the midpoint of the four sides of the rectangle). Right-click in the drawing window and then choose **Zoom Out (2x)** from the shortcut menu.

5. Use the drag controls to increase the view extents based on the 3D view given for the living room. Next, press ESC to exit the **Modify | Cameras** tab.

6. In the **Project Browser**, right-click on **3D View 1** under **3D Views**; a shortcut menu is displayed. From the shortcut menu, choose the **Rename** option; the **Rename View** dialog box is displayed. In the **Name** edit box of the dialog box, enter **Living Area** and choose the **OK** button; the **3D View 1** view is renamed as **Living Area**.

Generating the Interior Perspective View of the Lobby

You can use similar steps to generate the 3D interior view of the lobby area.

1. Right-click on the **First Floor** view in the **Floor Plans** head in the **Project Browser** and choose **Open** from the shortcut menu to open the view.

2. Invoke the **Camera** tool from **View > Create > 3D View** drop-down. Ensure that the **Perspective** check box is selected in the **Options Bar** (default setting).

3. Move the cursor near the center of the opening between the lobby area and the living room, refer to Figure 14-28, and click to specify the camera point.

4. Move the cursor horizontally toward the left and click when the field of view resembles the graphic shown in Figure 14-28. The drawing window shows the 3D interior view of the lobby area, as shown in Figure 14-29.

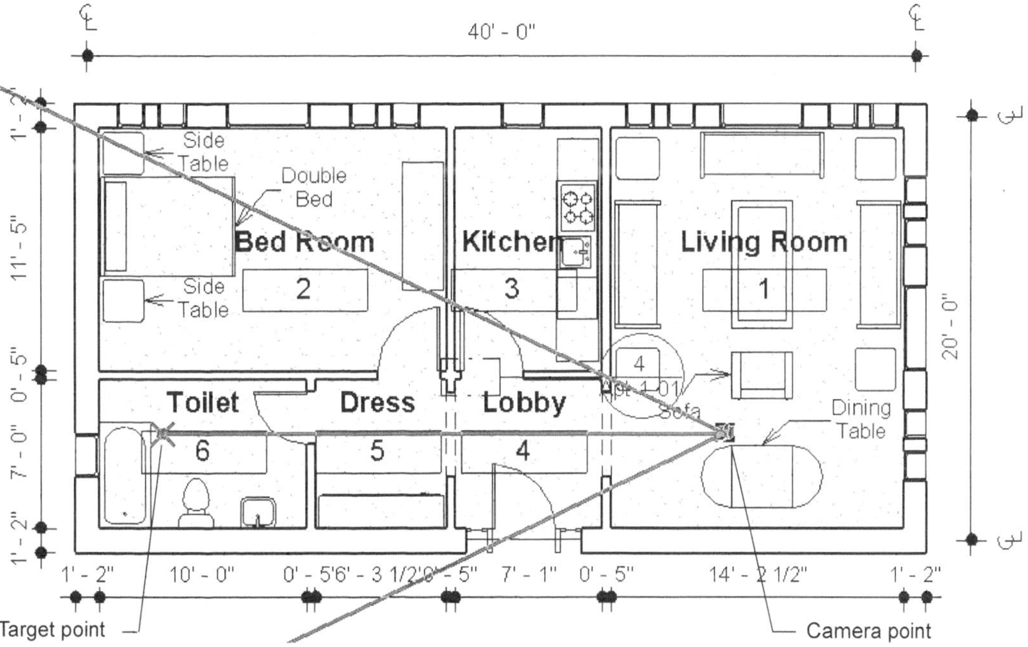

Figure 14-28 Specifying the camera point and the target point for generating the lobby interior view

5. Right-click in the drawing window and then choose **Zoom Out (2x)** from the shortcut menu displayed. Use the drag controls to increase the view extents.

6. Now, choose **Visual Style > Shaded** from the **View Control Bar**; the current view is shaded.

7. Use the drag controls to increase the view extents based on the 3D view given for the lobby area, refer to Figure 14-29.

8. Right-click on **3D View 1** in the **Project Browser** under **3D Views** and rename it as **Lobby Area** by using the **Rename** option from the shortcut menu.

Saving the Project

In this section, you will save the project file using the **Save As** tool.

1. Now, choose **Save As > Project** from the **File** menu; the **Save As** dialog box is displayed. Enter **c14_Apartment1_tut1** in the **File name** edit box and choose **Save**; the project file is saved.

2. Choose **Close** from the **File** menu to close the project file.

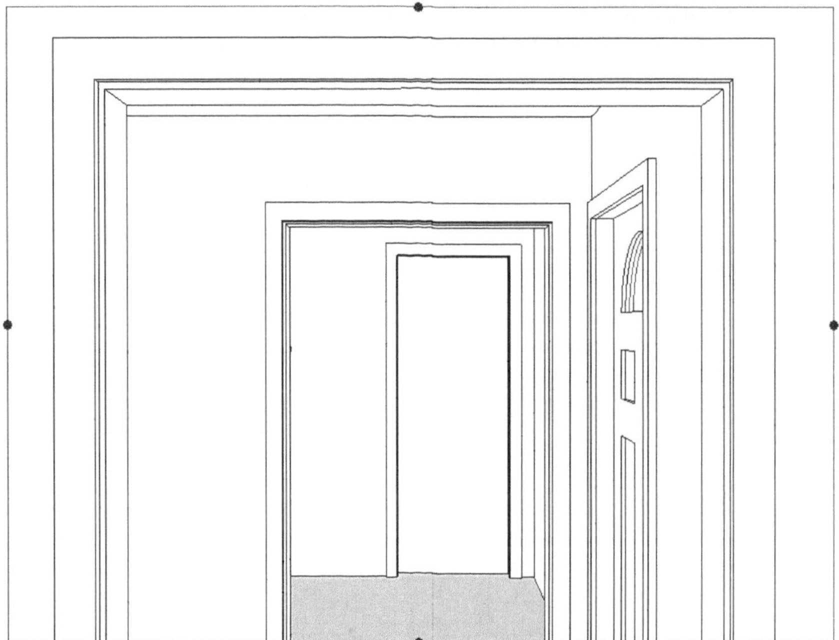

Figure 14-29 The 3D interior view of the lobby area

Tutorial 2 Club

Create an exterior 3D perspective view and an orthographic view for the *Club* project created in Exercise 1 of Chapter 13, refer to Figures 14-30 and 14-31. Note that the exterior 3D perspective view is from the main entrance. The exact view and height are not important for this tutorial.

(Expected time: 20 min)

The following steps are required to complete this tutorial:

a. Open the project file and the ground floor plan view.
b. Invoke the **Camera** tool to generate the exterior 3D view.
c. Generate the exterior perspective view of the Main Entrance, refer to Figure 14-32.
d. Generate the orthographic view of the building, refer to Figure 14-34.
e. Use the SteeringWheels and the **ORBIT** tool to display the orthographic view.
f. Save the project using the **Save As** tool.
   For Imperial *c14_Club_tut2.rvt*
   For Metric *M_c14_Club_tut2.rvt*
g. Close the project.

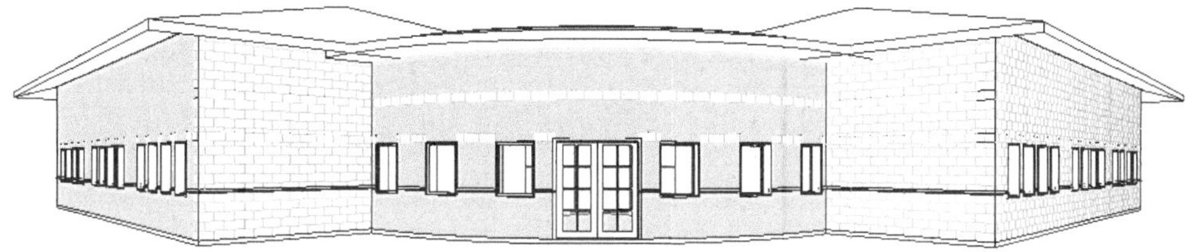

Figure 14-30 3D exterior view of the main entrance of the club building

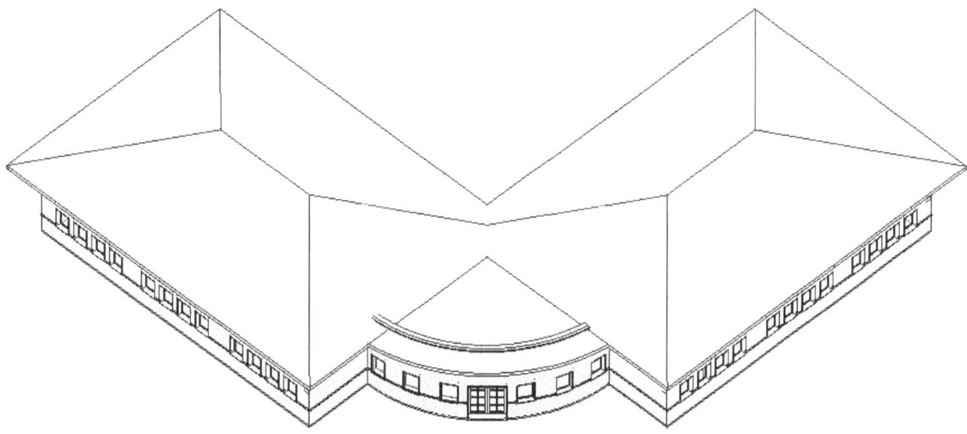

Figure 14-31 Orthographic view of the Club building

Opening the Project File and Invoking the Camera Tool

1. Choose **Open > Project** from the **File** menu and open the *c13_Club_ex1.rvt* file created in Exercise 1 of Chapter 13. You can also download this file from *http://www.cadcim.com*. The path of the file is as follows: *Textbooks > Civil/GIS > Revit Architecture > Exploring Autodesk Revit 2018 for Architecture*.

2. Double-click on **First Floor** in the **Floor Plans** head of the **Project Browser** to open the corresponding floor plan in the drawing window.

3. Invoke the **Camera** tool from **View > Create > 3D View** drop-down; the options for inserting the camera are displayed in the **Options Bar**.

Generating the Exterior Perspective View of the Main Entrance

You need to specify the camera and target points. Also, you will use the default value **5'6"** (**1650** mm) (eye level) for both these points.

1. Select the **Perspective** check box in the **Options** Bar if not selected by default.

2. Move the cursor vertically above the main entrance door and click to specify the camera point, as shown in Figure 14-32.

3. Move the cursor vertically downward and click when the field of view resembles the graphic shown in Figure 14-32; the drawing window shows the 3D exterior view of the main entrance, as shown in Figure 14-33.

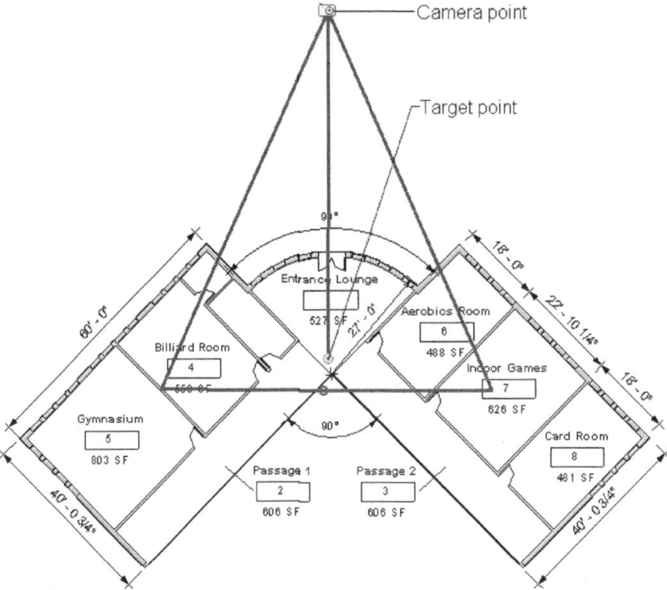

Figure 14-32 *Specifying the camera and the target points for the exterior view*

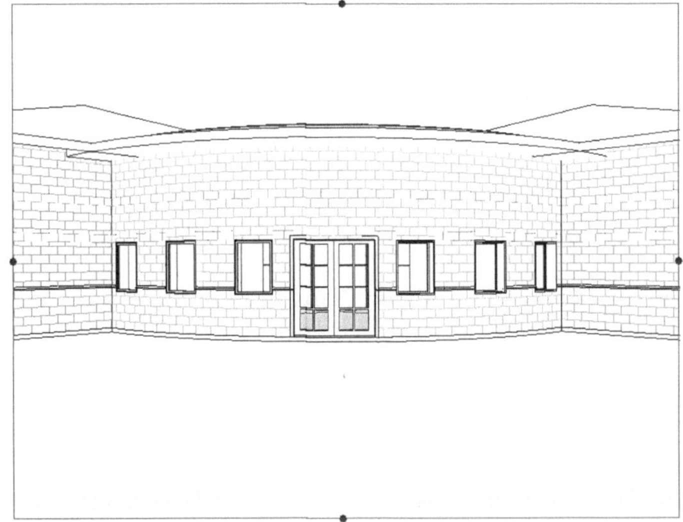

Figure 14-33 *3D exterior view of the main entrance*

4. Right-click in the drawing window and choose **Zoom Out (2x)** from the shortcut menu.

5. Ensure that the crop region of the 3D view is selected in the drawing and it displays the drag controls (blue dots at the midpoint of the four sides of the rectangle).

6. Use the drag controls to increase the view extents based on the 3D view given for the entrance view. Press ESC to exit the **Camera** tool.

7. Rename **3D View 1** to **Entrance View** by using the **Rename** option from the shortcut menu displayed on right-clicking in the view name in the **Project Browser**.

Generating the Orthographic View of the Club Building

You need to display the orthographic view of the club building using the SteeringWheels.

1. Invoke the **Default 3D View** tool from **View > Create > 3D View** drop-down.

2. Move the cursor toward the ViewCube and right-click on it; a shortcut menu is displayed.

3. Choose **Orient to a Direction > Northeast Isometric** from the shortcut menu; the northeast isometric view is displayed, as shown in Figure 14-34.

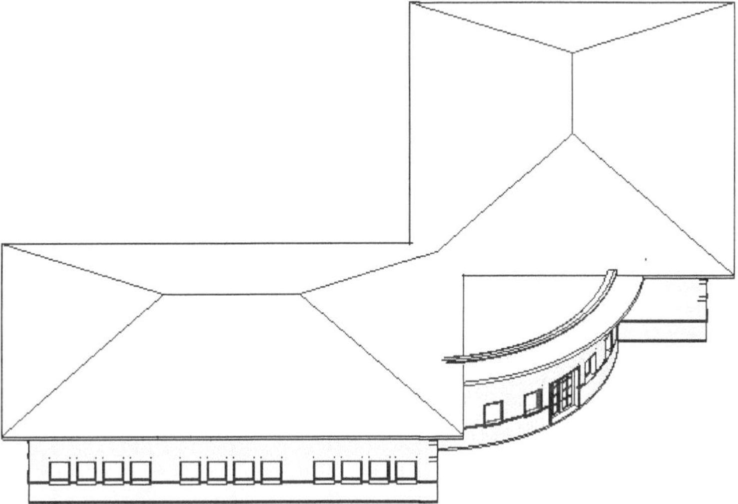

Figure 14-34 *Northeast isometric view of the Club building*

4. Press the F8 key to display SteeringWheels.

5. Next, press and hold the **ORBIT** tool in SteeringWheels and drag the cursor to display a view similar to the one specified for the project. Release the mouse button when the appropriate view is displayed, refer to Figure 14-35. Press ESC to exit.

6. In the **Project Browser**, right-click on **{3D}** under **3D Views** and rename **{3D}** to **Orthographic View** by using the **Rename** option from the shortcut menu displayed.

7. Double-click on **First Floor** in the **Floor Plans** head of the **Project Browser** to open corresponding floor plan in the drawing window.

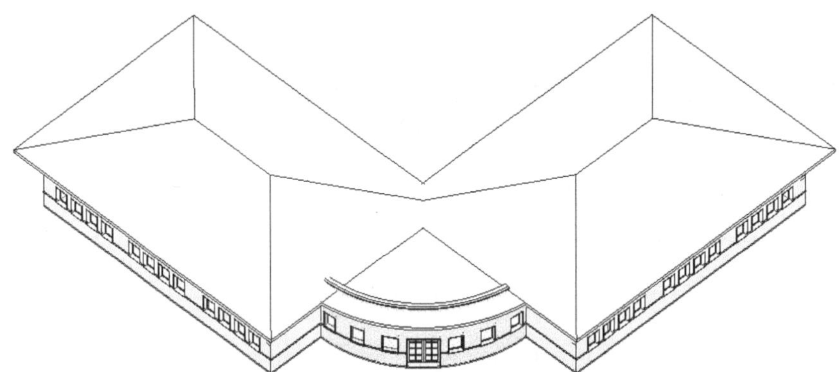

Figure 14-35 Orthographic view of the Club project

Saving the Project

In this section, you will save the project file using the **Save As** tool.

1. Choose **Save As > Project** from the **File** menu; the **Save As** dialog box is displayed.
2. Enter **c14_Club_tut2** in the **File name** edit box and choose **Save** to save the project file.
3. Choose **Close** from the **File** menu to close the project file.

Self-Evaluation Test

Answer the following questions and then compare them to those given at the end of this chapter:

1. The _________ tool is used to orient a 3D view to a plane.
2. To create an orthographic view using the **Camera** tool, the _________ check box in the **Options Bar** must be cleared.
3. The _________ tool can be used to display a 3D perspective view.
4. The _________ instance parameter indicates the height of the camera from the selected level.
5. You can choose the **Unlock View** option from the _________ to unlock a 3D View.
6. The 3D views created in Revit are added under the **Floor Plans** head in the **Project Browser**. (T/F)
7. The last change made in the orientation of a view can be undone using the **Undo view orientation changes** tool. (T/F)

8. The **Save View** tool can be used to save the 3D view within a project file. (T/F)

9. A building model can be viewed in 3D from the predefined camera locations using the **Orient** tool. (T/F)

10. While using the **Camera** tool, the **Offset** edit box can be used to specify the height of the camera from the selected level. (T/F)

11. Once a 3D perspective view has been created, its camera location cannot be modified. (T/F)

12. You can save the current view displayed as the **Home** view of the ViewCube. (T/F)

Review Questions

Answer the following questions:

1. Which of the following tools can be used to view a 3D view with shading and edges?

   (a) **Shading** (b) **Shaded with edges**
   (c) **Wireframe** (d) **Hidden**

2. Which of the following SteeringWheels types has the **Look** tool available in it?

   (a) **Full Navigation Wheel** (b) **View Object Wheel**
   (c) **Mini Full Navigation Wheel** (d) **Tour Building Wheel**

3. Which of the following tools can be used to magnify a view?

   (a) **Orient** (b) **Zoom**
   (c) **Scroll** (d) **Spin**

4. Which of the following tools is used to move the camera point keeping the target point intact?

   (a) **Pan** (b) **Look**
   (c) **Forward** (d) **Slide**

5. The field of view can be modified after creating a 3D view. (T/F)

6. The height of the target point of the camera from the selected level is specified by the **Target Elevation** instance parameter. (T/F)

7. The **Visibility/Graphics** tool can be used to modify the visibility of elements in the 3D view generated. (T/F)

8. The **Perspective** check box in the **Options Bar** needs to be cleared in order to display a perspective view. (T/F)

9. A 3D perspective view can be created by using two different levels for the camera and target points. (T/F)

10. The **Display Model** tool can be used to set the level of detail in a project view. (T/F)

EXERCISES

Exercise 1 Apartment 1

In this exercise, display the 3D exterior views using the file *c14-revit-2018-exr01.rvt* (for Metric *M_c14-revit-2018-exr01.rvt*) after downloading it from the CADCIM website *www.cadcim.com*. Create two exterior perspective views, one from the front and the other from the side of the building model, as shown in Figures 14-36 and 14-37, respectively. Use an appropriate camera location, target point, eye elevation, and target elevation to achieve the given perspective view.

(Expected time: 30 min)

Save the file as *c14_Apartment-1_ex1.rvt* (for Metric *M_c14_Apartment-1_ex1.rvt*)

Figure 14-36 *3D exterior front view for Exercise 1*

Figure 14-37 *3D exterior side view for Exercise 1*

Exercise 2 Office Building 1

In this exercise, display a 3D exterior front view using the file *c14-revit-2018-exr02.rvt* (for Metric *M_c14-revit-2018-exr02.rvt*) after downloading it from the CADCIM website *www.cadcim.com*, as shown in Figure 14-38. Use an appropriate camera location, target point, eye elevation, and target elevation to achieve the given perspective view. **(Expected time: 15 min)**

Save the file as *c14_Office-1_ex2.rvt* (for Metric *M_c14_Office-1_ex2.rvt*)

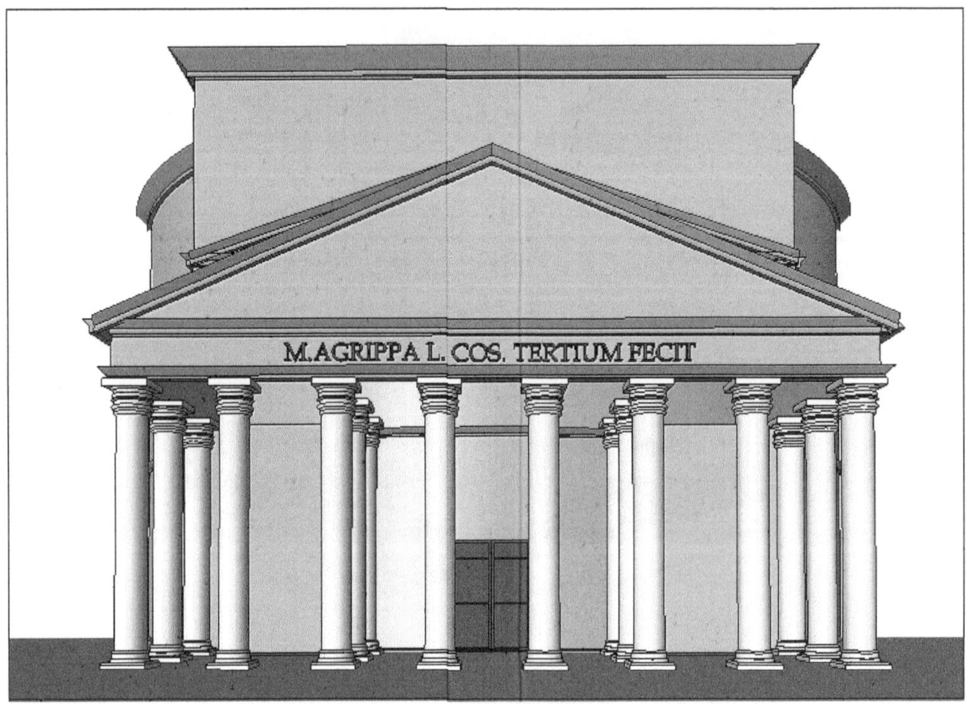

Figure 14-38 *3D exterior front view for Exercise 2*

Exercise 3 — Office Building 2

In this exercise, display an exterior 3D view using the *c10_Office-2_tut1.rvt* (for Metric *M_c10_Office-2_tut1.rvt*) project created in Tutorial 1 of Chapter10, as shown in Figure 14-39. Use an appropriate camera location and target point. The eye elevation and target elevation for the view are 15'0" and 35'0", respectively. **(Expected time: 15 min)**

Save the file as *c14_Office-2_ex3.rvt* (for Metric *M_c14_Office-2_ex3.rvt*)

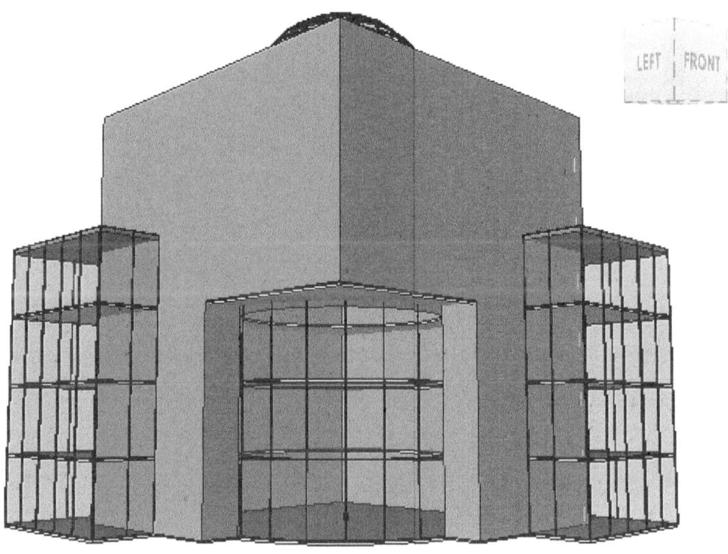

Figure 14-39 *3D exterior view for Exercise 3*

Exercise 4 Hotel Building

In this exercise, display the 3D exterior views using the file *c14-revit-2018-exr04.rvt* (for Metric *M_c14-revit-2018-exr04.rvt*) after downloading it from the CADCIM website *www.cadcim.com*, refer to Figures 14-40 through 14-42. Use an appropriate camera location, target point, eye elevation, and target elevation to achieve the given perspective views.

(Expected time: 25 min)

Save the file as *c14_Hotel_ex4.rvt* (for Metric *M_c14_Hotel_ex4.rvt*)

Figure 14-40 *Camera view 1 of the hotel building*

Figure 14-41 Camera view 2 of the hotel building

Figure 14-42 Camera view 3 of the hotel building

Answers to Self-Evaluation Test

1. **Orient to a Plane**, **2**. **Perspective**, **3**. **Camera**, **4**. **Eye Elevation**, **5**. **View Control Bar**, **6**. F, **7**. T, **8**. T, **9**. T, **10**. T, **11**. F, **12**. T

Chapter 15

Rendering Views and Creating Walkthroughs

Learning Objectives

After completing this chapter, you will be able to:

- *Create a rendered scene*
- *Set natural and artificial lighting*
- *Use different materials and textures*
- *Create and render a walkthrough*
- *Add people and vehicles to a building model*
- *Use the Decal tool*
- *Know about Autodesk 360 / Rendering*

RENDERING IN REVIT

Rendering is an art and a process of generating digital image from a three-dimensional model containing geometry, texture, light, and shading information through a computer program.

The rendering process helps you give a clear picture of the final outcome of an architectural project that you are working on. It bridges the gap between the final outcome and the two-dimensional working drawing, thereby giving you and your client the freedom to select the final finish with reduced cycle time for the approval and finalization of the design. Also, rendering with its rich photorealistic images helps you generate the actual bill of material for a project.

As described in the previous chapter, creating three-dimensional views of a building model enables you to visualize the interior and exterior of a building. However, to give a realistic effect to the view, it is necessary to apply materials to the building elements and render the view. The rendered exterior views of a building not only depict its overall scale, shape, and volume, but also represent the proposed exterior finish as envisaged by the architect. Similarly, a rendered interior three-dimensional view can be used to represent various interior elements such as interior partitions, furniture, plants, and interior finishes.

Revit, with its powerful drafting tool and Building Information Modeling, is capable of generating rich photorealistic images of a three-dimensional model. You can add texture, color, light, and various realistic elements to add life to your three-dimensional models.

In Revit, the mental ray rendering engine is used for rendering views. Mental ray is one of the most popular rendering engines that are used by Autodesk products such as AutoCAD, Autodesk Maya, and Autodesk 3dsMax.

The mental ray was developed by mental images (Berlin, Germany) for the production of quality rendering File. It supports the ray tracing technique to deliver rich photorealistic images.

The inclusion of mental ray in Autodesk Revit has made it more powerful for generating high quality rendering images with improved lighting effects and more accurate render appearances for materials.

In Autodesk Revit, the user-interface for rendering images has been designed to accommodate fewer dialog boxes and a simplified workflow with specified defaults. It helps you generate presentations with high quality images with a little effort and less experience. You can also improve and refine the quality of the output by controlling several advanced settings that are discussed later in this chapter.

Rendering Workflow

In this chapter, you will learn about various methods and techniques used in a rendering workflow. A rendering workflow is a process chart that shows the flow of the rendering process to achieve the end result in the form of high quality rendered image, refer to Figure 15-1.

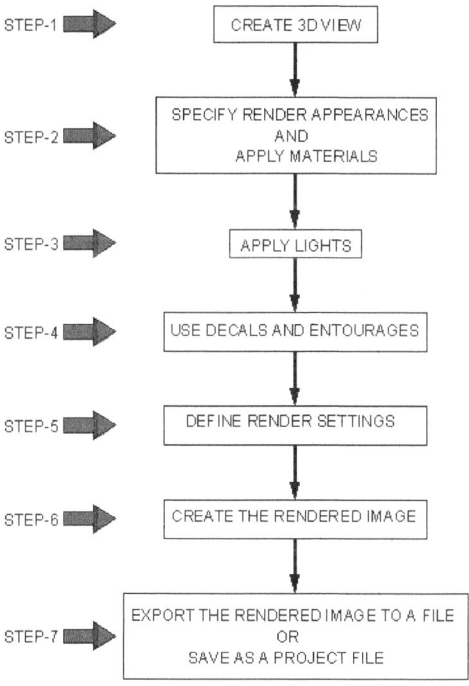

Figure 15-1 *The rendering workflow chart*

Note

In the Rendering workflow, you can alter the order of steps from step1 to step 4.

The steps mentioned above are briefly discussed next.

Step 1 - Creating a Three-Dimensional View

To start with the rendering process, the first step is to generate a three-dimensional view of the exterior or interior of the building model that you have created. You have already learned the methods of creating three-dimensional views of a building model in Chapter 14.

Step 2 - Specifying Render Appearance and Applying Material

A material defines the exact look and finish of elements present in a building model. In Revit, you can create your own material or use in-built materials from the **Render Appearance Library** to apply to specific element. The Revit material defines the texture, color, and exact appearance of an element and also allows you to control various parameters required to define specific material. For example, to define a glass, you can define its transparency, reflection, color, and so on.

The materials provided in Autodesk Revit have been assigned the mental ray material properties, and therefore, they appear more realistic than the standard materials in the previous version. The materials and their applications are discussed later in this chapter.

Step 3 - Applying Lights

You can light a three-dimensional model by using natural illumination from daylight or using artificial light sources such as electric lights, gas lights, lamps, candles, or oil lamps.

While placing artificial lights in a three-dimensional model, you can define lighting fixtures and their light sources to attain the best effect. As you render, Autodesk Revit provides you the facility to control the visibility of these lights in a particular rendered image while defining the setting for rendering the scene. Details about lighting in Revit are discussed later.

Step 4 - Using Entourages and Decals

In Revit, you can use entourages to add additional features such as trees, people, cars, and so on. These features do not represent the main model but contribute toward making the rendered image more realistic. The entourage objects are defined as families and include Archvision's RPC (Rich Photorealistic Contents) objects that can add more realism, when added in a model and rendered.

Similarly, you can use decals to place images on the surfaces of a building model. Decals are generally used to depict signage, paintings, and signboards in a rendered image. In Revit, you can place decals only on a flat or cylindrical surface.

Step 5 - Defining Render Settings

After applying materials, lights, entourages, and creating a three-dimensional view, you need to start the rendering process. To do so, choose the **Show Rendering Dialog** button from the **View Control Bar** or type RR; the **Rendering** dialog box will be displayed. In this dialog box, you can specify the view area for rendering, lighting controls, background, render quality specifications, and size of the rendered image.

Step 6 - Creating the Rendered Image

After specifying all parameters for the rendering, you need to run the render engine using the **Rendering** dialog box to create a rendered image. To do so, choose the **Render** button from the **Rendering** dialog box. You will learn the process of rendering an image using the options in this dialog box later in this chapter.

Step 7 - Exporting the Rendered Image

After finishing the rendering process, you can save it in a file or as a project view. To export the rendered image to a file, choose the **Export** button from the **Image** area in the **Rendering** dialog box; the **Save Image** dialog box will be displayed. You can save the image file to the required location using the appropriate file format. Alternatively, if you want to save the rendered image in your project view, choose the **Save to Project** button from the **Image** area in the **Rendering** dialog box; the **Save To Project** dialog box will be displayed, where you can specify the name of the rendered image by entering a name in the **Name** edit box. Next, choose the **OK** button to save the image and exit the **Save To Project** dialog box. To open the rendered image in the project, you need to select the image by choosing **Views (all) > Renderings** in the **Project Browser**.

Introduction to Materials

In Revit, managing material, which is an important part of rendering process, includes creating and adding of various materials. Material specifies the actual look of the model elements as they appear in the rendered images. Materials convey the structural and descriptive information of model elements. In Revit, you can apply materials to individual elements in a building model or apply materials to elements at the time of defining their families.

Before you learn how to assign materials to the elements, you should be familiar with some of the concepts that are discussed next.

Color in Shaded View

You can define the color of an element in a shaded project view.

Pattern and Color on the Surface

You can specify the pattern and color of the surface of an element while defining a material.

Color and Fill Pattern when the Element is Cut

You can also specify the color and the pattern of a material that appears in the sectioned surface of an element when it is cut and viewed in a sectional view.

Render Appearance for Rendering

You can define materials by assigning textures and properties as the render appearance, which appears in the rendered image.

Description about Manufacturer, Cost, and Keynotes

Descriptive information such as details of manufacturer, cost of the material, and keynotes can also be added while defining a material.

Structural Information

While defining a material, you can add information about various properties. For example, you can define physical properties such as Young's modulus, Shear modulus, Poisson ratio and others, which may be required at the time of structural analysis.

Now, after learning the concept about material, you will now learn how to assign materials to the building elements. You can create, edit, and assign material by using the **Material Browser** dialog box and the **Material Editor** pane, as shown in Figure 15-2, that are discussed next.

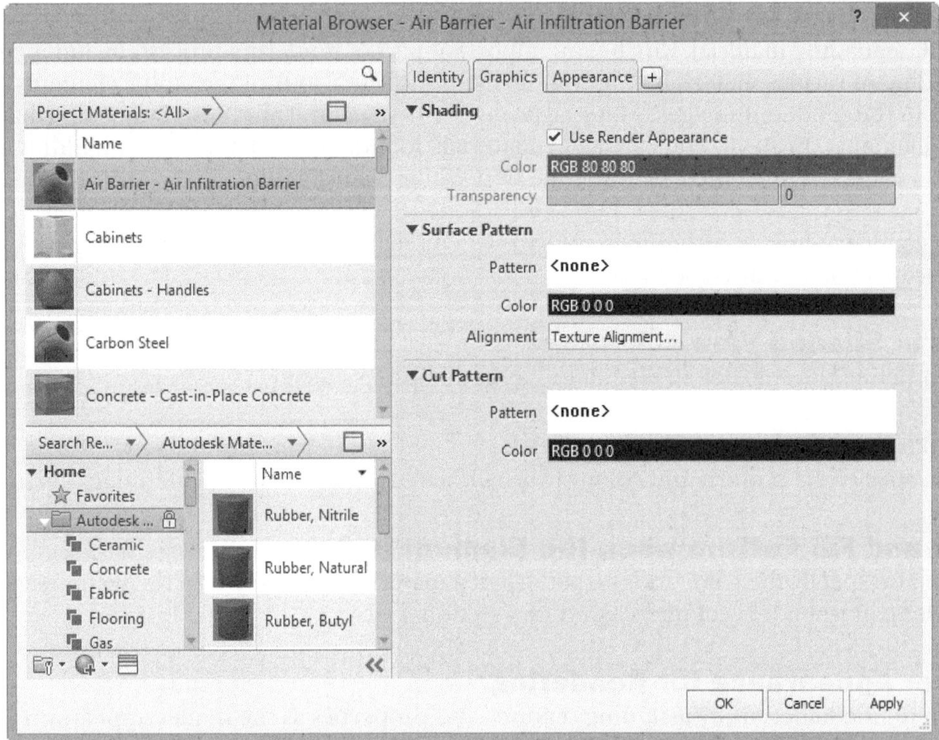

Figure 15-2 The ***Material Browser*** *dialog box along with the* ***Material Editor*** *pane*

Material Browser Dialog Box

The **Material Browser** dialog box can be used to organize materials into separate groups so that they can be easily edited as per the requirement of the project. In this dialog box, you can add new material, create libraries, and edit the properties of the existing materials. To invoke the **Material Browser** dialog box, choose the **Materials** tool from the **Settings** panel of the **Manage** tab.

Materials available in the current project are whether applied to the objects or not will displayed in the **Project Materials: All** area of the **Material Browser** dialog box. From this area, select a material and right-click; a shortcut menu will be displayed. You can choose an option from the shortcut menu to rename or duplicate the selected material, or to add the selected material to the desired library.

In the **Project Materials: All** area, you can also customize the display of materials. To do so, click on the double arrow placed at the bottom right corner of the **Project Materials: All** area. Next, click on the down arrow in the menu displayed; a flyout will be displayed. In this flyout, there are following sections: **Document Materials**, **View Type**, **Sort**, and **Thumbnail Size**. You can choose any option from these sections. For example, you can choose the **Show In Use** option from the **Document Materials** section to display only those elements that have been used in the project.

In the **Material Browser** dialog box, you can customize the **Autodesk Material** list. To do so, choose the **Shows/Hides library panel** button located at the top right of the **Project Materials: All** areas; the **Autodesk Materials** area will be displayed. In this area, there are three material libraries: **Autodesk Materials**, **Favorites**, and **AEC Materials**. Notice that lock icons appear next to the **Autodesk** and **AEC** libraries, which indicate that these libraries are protected and therefore, you cannot modify, add, or delete materials from their content. In the **Autodesk Materials** area, click on the arrow displayed on the left of any of the libraries; the categories of the materials will be displayed. Select a category; various materials belonging to the selected category will be displayed on the right. For example, if you choose **Concrete** from the **Autodesk Materials** library, you will find various materials such as GFRC (Glass Fibre Reinforced Concrete), Concrete Precast Panels, Concrete Panels, Concrete Lightweight, and so on. You can add any of the library materials to the **Project Materials: All** area. This can be done either by clicking on the **Adds material to document** button which is displayed after placing the cursor on the material or by dragging and dropping the desired material in the **Project Materials: All** area.

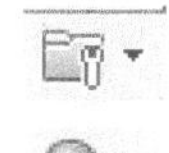

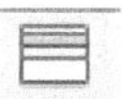

In the material browser toolbar of the **Material Browser** dialog box, refer to Figure 15-2, the **Creates, opens, and edits user-defined libraries** button is used to open or edit an existing library, or to create a new library. The **Creates and duplicates material** button is used to create a new material or to generate a duplicate of the existing material. The **Opens/Closes asset browser** button is used to open or close the **Asset Browser** dialog box. Similarly, the **Opens/closes material editor** button is used to display or hide the **Material Editor** pane.

Material Editor Pane

By default, the **Material Editor** pane is displayed along with the **Material Browser** dialog box. As discussed in the above section, you can choose the **Opens/Closes material editor** button in the **Material Browser** dialog box to display or hide the **Material Editor** pane, refer to Figure 15-3. Alternatively, you can also display the hidden **Material Editor** pane by choosing the **Edits material, including properties and information** button, refer to Figure 15-4. This button will be displayed along with the name of the selected material in the **Project Materials: All** area of the **Material Browser** dialog box.

On selecting a material from the **Material Browser** dialog box, various properties of the selected material will be displayed in the **Material Editor** pane. You can edit these properties by using the options available in the following tabs: **Identity**, **Graphics**, **Appearance**, **Physical**, and **Thermal**. The options in these tabs are discussed next.

Identity Tab

The options in the **Identity** tab help you to define the material, so that whenever you perform a search operation, the material can be recognized by the values specified in this tab.

The **Name** edit box in this tab displays the name of the selected material. You can enter a new name by entering the desired text in this edit box. The other options in this tab are displayed under the following areas: **Descriptive Information**, **Product Information**, and **Revit Annotation Information**. These areas are discussed next.

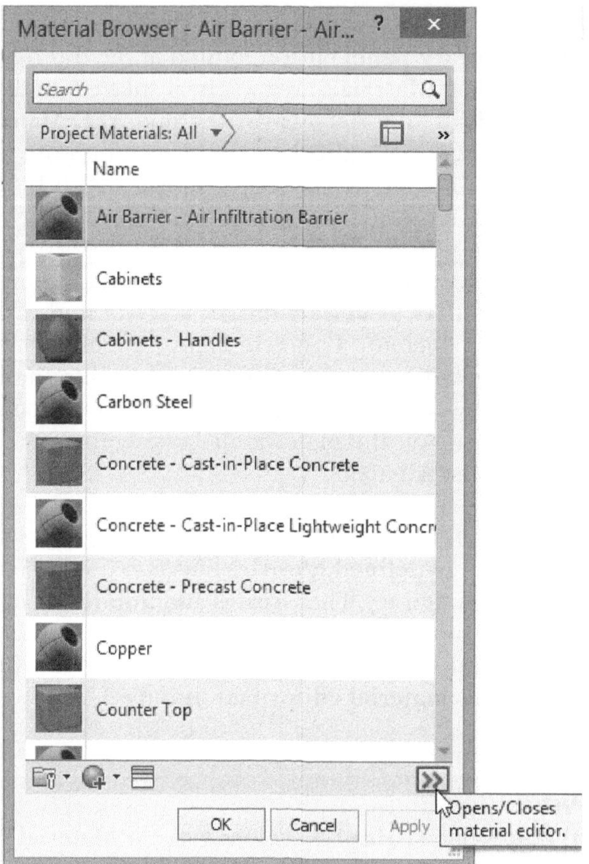

Figure 15-3 *Choosing the* ***Opens/Closes material editor*** *button*

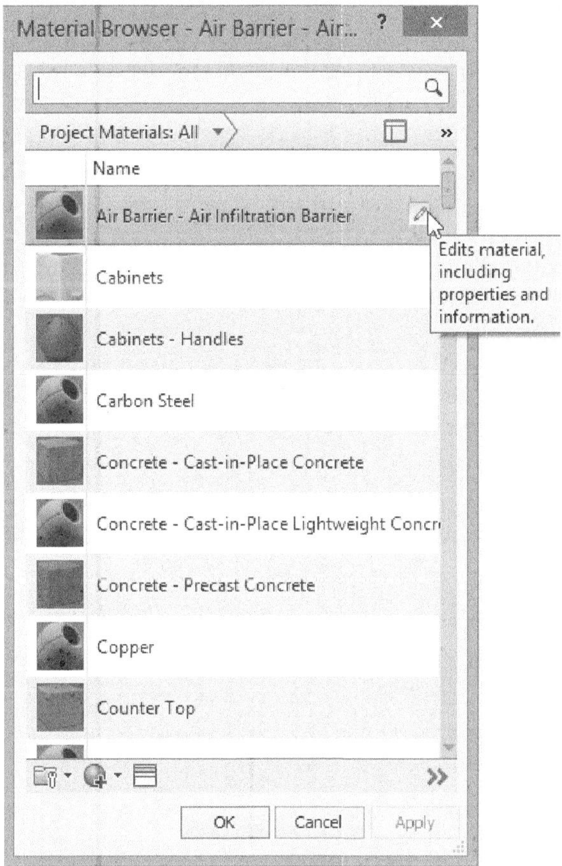

Figure 15-4 Choosing the ***Edits material, including properties and information*** *button*

Descriptive Information. The **Descriptive Information** area contains the **Description**, **Comments**, and **Keywords** edit boxes and the **Class** drop-down list. The **Description** edit box is used to describe the utility and importance of the material. The **Class** drop-down list is used to specify the type of material. The **Comments** edit box is used for entering the general or specific comments regarding the material. The **Keywords** edit box is used for entering specific keywords for the material.

Product Information. The options in the **Product Information** area are used to define the product details such as manufacturer, model, cost, and URL. The **Manufacturer** text box in this area is used to enter the name of the company producing the selected material. Similarly, you can enter price, model number, and important web link of the vendor or manufacturer of the material in the **Cost**, **Model**, and **URL** text boxes, respectively.

Revit Annotation Information. The **Revit Annotation Information** area contains two text boxes: **Keynote** and **Mark**. In the **Keynote** text box, you can enter a specific keynote or choose the browse button next to it to select a standard keynote for the material. Similarly, you can enter a unique identification number for the material in the **Mark** text box.

Graphics Tab

You can use the options in the **Graphics** tab to control the display properties of the material assigned to an object. The **Graphics** tab consists of the following areas: **Shading**, **Surface Pattern**, and **Cut Pattern**, refer to Figure 15-5.

Shading. In the **Shading** area, select the **Use Render Appearance** check box to assign the color of the rendered appearance to the shaded view. In this case, the **Color** edit box and the **Transparency** slider will be deactivated. To assign a color to the shaded view, clear the **Use Render Appearance** check box; the **Color** button and the **Transparency** slider get activated. Choose the **Color** button; the **Color** dialog box will be displayed. From the **Color** dialog box, select the color that you want to assign to the material for its shaded view and then choose the **OK** button to close it. You can also make the shaded element appear opaque, semi-transparent, or transparent. To make the shading completely opaque, move the **Transparency** slider toward the left till it shows 0% in the text box. Similarly, move the slider toward the right to make the material appear transparent.

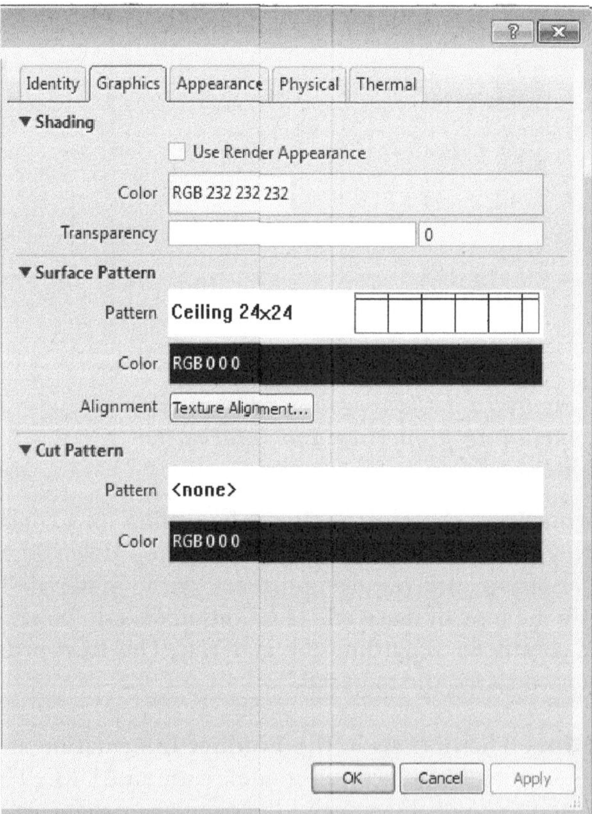

*Figure 15-5 The **Graphics** tab displaying graphical properties of material*

Surface Pattern. Expand the **Surface Pattern** area to display the options in it. The options in the **Surface Pattern** area allow you to assign hatch patterns of different colors to the surface of an element. To assign a hatch pattern, choose the swatch next to the **Pattern** parameter; the **Fill Patterns** dialog box will be displayed. Using the options in this dialog box, you can modify, create, or delete a pattern. After setting the required parameters in the **Fill Patterns** dialog box, choose the **OK** button to close it. Next, to assign a color to the selected hatch pattern, click on the color swatch next to the **Color** parameter; the **Color** dialog box will be displayed. Select the desired color from this dialog box and then choose the **OK** button to close it. You can also align the render appearance relative to the surface pattern using the options in the **Surface Pattern** area. To do so, choose the **Texture Alignment** button corresponding to the **Alignment** parameter in the **Surface Pattern** area; the **Align Render Appearance to Surface Pattern** window will be displayed. In this window, the preview of the render appearance of the material is displayed along with the assigned surface pattern. You can use the four arrows displayed around the preview of the render appearance to align it with the surface pattern. After aligning the surface pattern, choose the **OK** button to close the **Align Render Appearance to Surface Pattern** window.

Cut Pattern. The **Cut Pattern** area displays various options under it. These options help you to edit the view of the cut surface of the material. When you click on the **Pattern** option in the **Cut Pattern** area, the **Fill Pattern** dialog box will appear. You can then assign any fill pattern to the element using the options in this dialog box. You can assign any color to the cut pattern of the element. To do so, click on the **RGB** button corresponding to the **Color** parameter; the **Color** dialog box will be displayed. Select the desired color from this dialog box and then choose the **OK** button to close it.

Appearance Tab

The **Appearance** tab displayed in the **Material Editor** pane, as shown in Figure 15-6, consists of the following area: **Information**, **Generic**, **Reflectivity**, **Transparency**, **Cutouts**, **Self Illumination**, **Bump**, and **Tint**. In these areas, you can assign different textures and colors to the material for changing the appearance of a rendered image, you can also edit existing material, and create a new material using the areas in the tab.

Information. You can use the options in the **Information** area to edit the name and description of the material, and also enter keywords related to the appearance of the material.

Generic. In the **Generic** area, you can change the color of the surface of the material. To do so, click on the **Color** swatch; the **Color** dialog box will appear. To make the elements look realistic, their texture can be edited using the **Texture Editor** dialog box. To invoke this dialog box, choose the drop-down next to the **Image** swatch in the **Generic** area, the **Texture Editor** dialog box will be displayed. The brightness of the image can also be controlled using this dialog box.

The **Image Fade** option in the **Generic** area is used to change the complexity of the appearance of the preview by distinguishing it from its base color. The **Glossiness** option helps you to change the brightness of the preview image. For example, the image can be made dull or bright. You can select the **Metallic** or **Non-metallic** option from the **Highlights** drop-down list to assign the required texture to the material.

Reflectivity. The reflectivity of the element can be changed by using the **Direct** and **Oblique** options in the **Reflectivity** head. On selecting the **Reflectivity** check box, the **Direct** and **Oblique** options get activated and these options help you when light is falling at it directly or at an angle respectively. Similarly, the **Transparency**, **Cutouts**, **Self Illumination**, **Bump**, and **Tint** options in this tab can be used to edit the texture of the image.

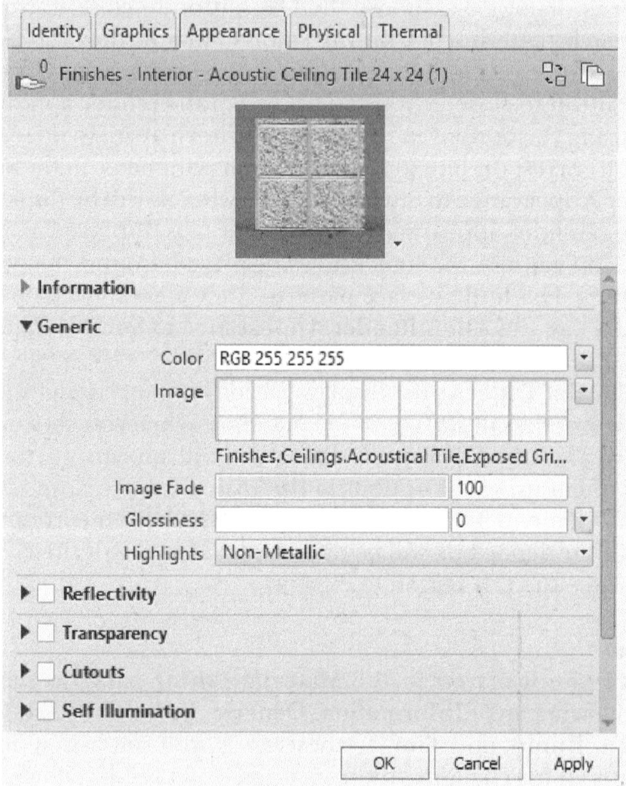

*Figure 15-6 The options displayed under the **Appearance** tab*

Physical Tab

The **Physical** tab in the **Material Editor** pane consists of various options that define the physical state of a material. This tab comprises of the following areas: **Information** and **Mechanical**, refer to Figure 15-7. The options available in these areas are discussed next.

Information. The **Information** area contains the **Name**, **Description**, **Keywords**, **Type**, and **Sub-class** edit boxes. The name of the selected material is displayed in the **Name** edit box of this area. In the **Description** edit box, you can write about the utility and importance of the material. To quicken and refine your search process, you may need to add keywords to the material. You can do so by entering the specific text in the **Keywords** edit box. The **Type** parameter, which is a read-only parameter, displays a value to specify the type of the material in context of its physical properties.

Mechanical. The **Mechanical** area contains the **Density** edit box. You can enter a value in this edit box to specify the density of the selected material.

Thermal Tab

The **Thermal** tab, as shown in Figure 15-8, contains options that describe the material as well define the thermal state and thermal behavior of materials such as thermal conductivity, specific heat, and so on. To edit the parameters, you can click on the **Opens/closes asset browser** button from the **Material Browser** dialog box.

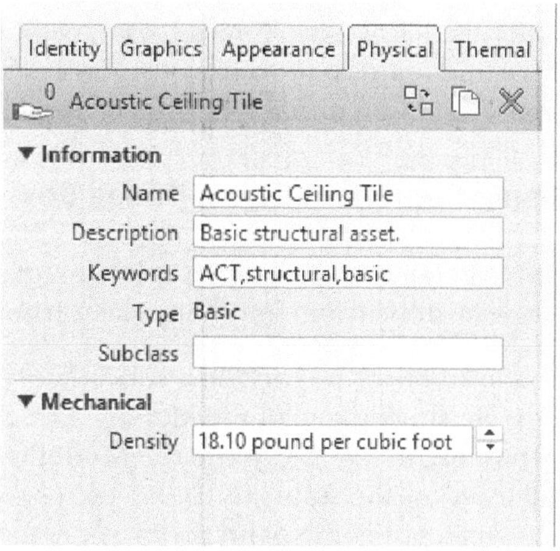

***Figure 15-7** The **Physical** tab displaying physical properties of a material*

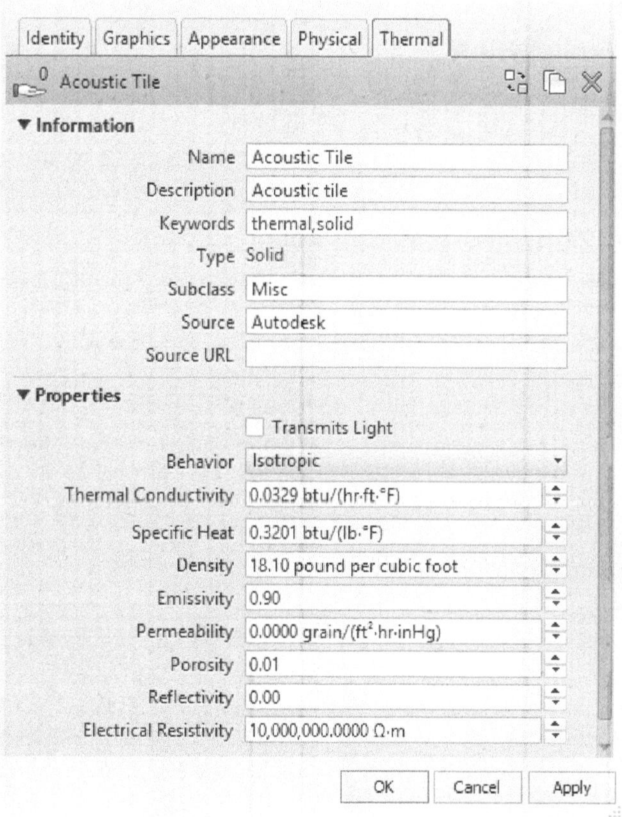

***Figure 15-8** The options under the **Thermal** tab*

Assigning Materials to Elements

After searching and selecting materials in the **Materials Browser** dialog box, you need to assign that material to an element. The materials can be assigned to a category or a subcategory of an element by using the **Object Styles** dialog box. You can also assign material directly to a model element, to the selected face of an element, or to various parts in an element using the family editor. The different methods to assign material in a project are discussed next.

Assigning Materials Using the Object Styles Dialog Box

In Autodesk Revit, you can apply materials to elements based on their categories or subcategories. For example, if you want to assign a material to a window, its category will be window and its subcategories will be frame/mullion, glass, trim, and so on.

To assign the selected material to a category or a subcategory of an element, choose the **Object Styles** tool from the **Settings** panel of the **Manage** tab; the **Object Styles** dialog box will be displayed, as shown in Figure 15-9. Choose the **Model Objects** or **Imported Objects** tab from the dialog box based on the status of the object to which you want to assign the material. Select the required category or expand the category to view its subcategories. Next, click on the cell of the **Material** column corresponding to the subcategory of the expanded category; the browse button will become available on the right of the field. Choose the browse button; the **Material Browser** dialog box will be displayed. Select the appropriate material and choose the **OK** button to exit the **Material Browser** dialog box. Choose **OK** again to close the **Object Styles** dialog box.

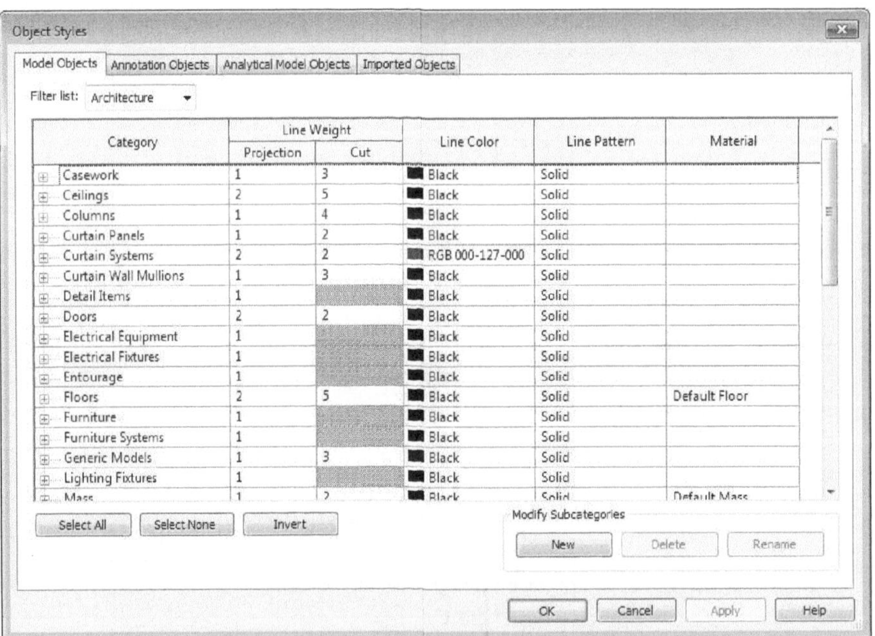

*Figure 15-9 The **Object Styles** dialog box*

Assigning Material Using the Family Editor

Using the family editor, you can assign materials to different parts of an element. To assign material to a particular part of an element, open the family in the family editor. Next, select the part to which you want to apply the material; the properties of the selected part will be displayed in the **Properties** palette. Next, choose the button in the **Value** column corresponding to the **Material** instance parameter under the **Material and Finishes** heading to open the **Associate Family Parameter** dialog box, as shown in Figure 15-10. In this dialog box, you can select or add a parameter.

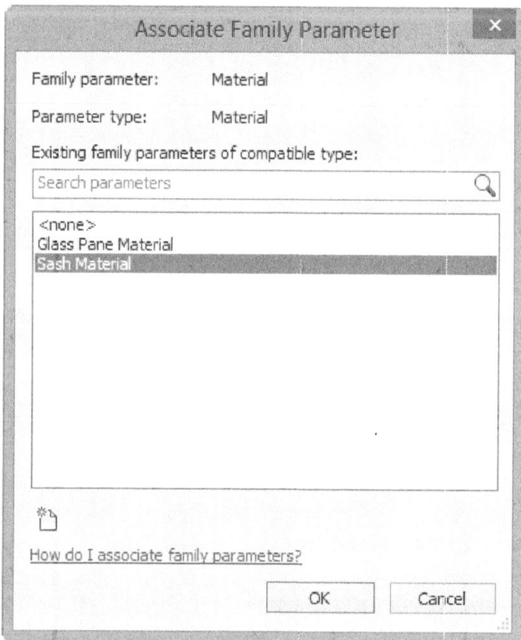

***Figure 15-10** The **Associate Family Parameter** dialog box*

Note

*The parameters displayed in the **Existing family parameters of compatible type** area of the **Associate Family Parameter** dialog box may vary depending on the type of element selected.*

To add a parameter, choose the **New parameter** button in the **Associate Family Parameter** dialog box; the **Parameter Properties** dialog box will be displayed. In this dialog box, select the **Materials and Finishes** option from the **Group parameter under** drop-down list, if it is not selected by default. Next, select the **Instance** or **Type** radio button located on the right of the **Parameter Data** area to define the material of an element as an instance parameter or as a type parameter. In the **Name** edit box, enter the name of the parameter and choose the **OK** button; the created parameter is selected and added to the **Associate Family Parameter** dialog box and the **Parameter Properties** dialog box will be closed. Next, choose the **OK** button twice to exit.

Assigning Materials Directly to Model Elements

In Autodesk Revit, you can assign a material directly to model elements. To do so, select the model element in a view; the properties of the selected element will be displayed in the **Properties** palette. The assignment of material depends on whether the material parameter is defined as instance, type, or structural.

If the material of an element is defined as the instance parameter, click on the value field corresponding to the parameter whose material you need to change in the **Materials and Finishes** area of the **Properties** palette. As you click on the value field, the browse button will appear. Choose this button; the **Material Browser** dialog box will be displayed. Select the material and then choose the **OK** button twice to exit.

If the material of an element is defined as the type parameter, you can change the material in the **Type Properties** dialog box. In this dialog box, click on the **Value** column; the browse button will appear. Choose this button; the **Material Browser** dialog box will be displayed. Select the material and then choose the **OK** button to exit.

If the material of an element is defined as the structural parameter, as in the case of a wall, select the element and choose the **Edit Type** button from the **Properties** palette to invoke the **Type Properties** dialog box. In this dialog box, choose the **Edit** button in the **Value** field corresponding to the **Structural** parameter; the **Edit Assembly** dialog box will be displayed. Click on the **Material** column for the layer whose material you need to change, and then choose the browse button available in the cell to display the **Materials** dialog box. Now, select the appropriate material and choose the **OK** button twice to return to the drawing area.

Assigning Materials to Faces Using the Paint Tool

The **Paint** tool is used to apply a material to the face of an element without modifying its material properties. The elements that can be painted include walls, floor, ceiling, roof, and so on. To apply material to the face of an element, invoke the **Paint** tool from **Modify > Geometry > Paint** drop-down; the **Modify | Paint** tab will be displayed. Select the type of material from the **Material Browser** dialog box and move the cursor to the element to highlight it. Next, click to apply the selected paint to the face of the element. Now, choose the **Done** button in the **Material Browser** dialog box to close it. You can remove the material applied to a face of the element. To do so, choose the **Remove Paint** tool from **Modify > Geometry > Paint** drop-down and click on the desired face of the element.

Note

*The texture of the material assigned to the face of element will be visible only in the **Realistic** visual style.*

Applying Lights

Light is an important factor of the rendering process. It affects the overall appearance of elements and materials in the rendered view. It not only enables you to view the building model, but also helps you express its mood along with its ambience. For example, for the exterior of a shopping mall, a vibrant mood can be created by using bright afternoon lights with sharp shadows. On the contrary, for the exterior of a residential building, soft evening lights can be used to give a relaxing ambience. Similarly, an interior view of a showroom can be brightly lit and a bar interior view can be given an accent lighting. Autodesk Revit enables you to add and control the properties of a variety of artificial lighting fixtures based on the project requirement.

Controlling the Natural Lighting

In Revit, natural light is defined by the direction of sunlight or the location, date, and time of day to achieve a realistic ambience of sunlight on a building model. To set the natural light before the rendering process, choose the **Sun Settings** tool from **Manage > Settings > Additional Settings** drop-down or type **SU**; the **Sun Settings** dialog box will be displayed, as shown in Figure 15-11. In this dialog box, you can select the predefined sunlight settings or define a new setting as per the project requirement.

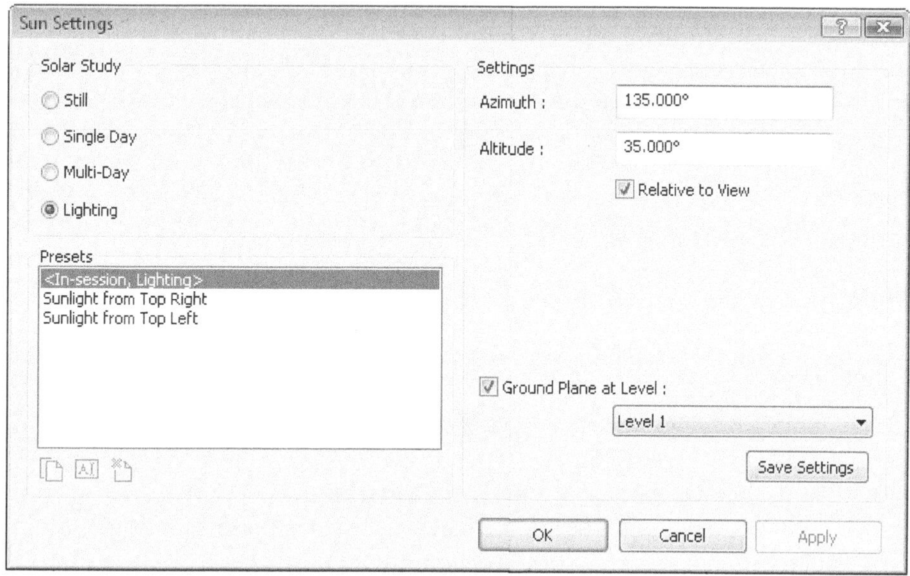

***Figure 15-11** The **Sun Settings** dialog box*

The **Sun Settings** dialog box contains three areas: **Solar Study**, **Presets**, and **Settings**. In the **Solar Study** area, you can select the mode as per your requirement. To specify the sun settings based on a specified geographic location, you can select either **Still**, **Single Day**, or **Multi-Day**. In case you want to define the sun settings based on azimuth and altitude, select the **Lighting** radio button.

From the list box in the **Presets** area, select one of the predefined sun settings (such as a solstice). Next, to define a new sunlight setting, choose the **Duplicate** button in the **Presets** area of the **Sun Settings** dialog box; the **Name** dialog box will be displayed. In this dialog box, enter the desired name for the sunlight settings in the **Name** edit box and choose the **OK** button to exit the **Sun Settings** dialog box. In the **Settings** area of the **Sun Settings** dialog box, you can set the sunlight based on its geographical location or **Azimuth** and **Altitude**.

Next, if you need to cast shadows on a ground plane, select the **Ground Plane at Level** check box and then select the required level from the drop-down list below the check box. Autodesk Revit will cast shadow on the specified level for both the two-dimensional and three-dimensional views. On clearing the **Ground Plane at Level** check box, the shadow casting on levels will be disabled, except on the toposurface. Choose **Apply** and then **OK**; the **Sun Settings** dialog box will be closed.

Note

The options for the shadow, as discussed in the previous section, do not affect the settings of the shadow in the rendered image.

Adding Artificial Lights to a Project

Artificial lights can easily be added to a building model by using light fixture families. To do so, choose the **Place a Component** tool from **Architecture > Build > Component** drop-down; the **Modify | Place Component** tab will be displayed. Now, choose the **Load Family** tool from the **Mode** panel in the **Modify | Place Component** tab; the **Load Family** dialog box will be displayed. You can select various families of lighting fixtures by browsing the **US Imperial > Lighting > Architectural** folder. In the **Architectural** folder, you can select the lighting fixture from the **Internal** or **External** sub-folders. After selecting the desired family of light, choose **Open** to load it into the project file. To select the loaded light fixture and add it to a view, select the desired light type from the **Type Selector** drop-down list and then click at the desired location in the ceiling or floor plan of the required level.

Note

Light fixtures can be added to an appropriate plan only. The exterior floor mounted lighting fixtures such as street lights and bollard lights can be added to the floor plan whereas other ceiling mounted fixtures can be added only to the corresponding ceiling plan (with a false ceiling). Fixtures are visible only when appropriate plan is displayed in the drawing window.

Modifying Properties of the Lighting Fixture

You can modify the properties of a lighting fixture before or after adding them to the project. To modify the lighting fixtures after you add them in the project, select the lighting fixture to be modified; the **Modify | Lighting Fixtures** tab will be displayed. In the **Properties** palette, certain instance parameters such as **Level**, **Phase Created**, and so on can be modified. To modify the type properties of the light fixture, choose the **Edit Type** button; the **Type Properties** dialog box will be displayed. Based on the fixture selected, its type properties are displayed and they can be modified. One of the most important parameter types is the **Initial Intensity** parameter displayed under the **Photometric** head in the **Type Properties** dialog box. Choose the button in its **Value** field; the **Initial Intensity** dialog box will be displayed. In this dialog box, you can set the values of **Wattage**, **Luminous Flux**, **Luminous Intensity**, and **Illuminance** in their respective spinners. After setting the values, choose **OK**; the **Initial Intensity** dialog box will be closed. In the **Type Properties** dialog box, you can also change the other properties associated with the light fixture such as lamp, material of fixture, and so on.

Using Decals and Entourages

The **Decal** tool is used to place an image on the face of a flat or a cylindrical element in the building model. This tool can also be used to represent signals, posters, billboards, and paintings in a rendered view. A decal is an external graphic file that is linked to the project file. The file formats that can be used as decal are *jpeg*, *targa*, *tiff*, and *bmp*. Since the decal files are linked to the project file and are not saved with it, the size of the project file does not increase. It is, however, recommended to save decals along with a project file so that the link is maintained. Entourages are the collection of people, trees, cars, parking elements, and other site components that can be inserted in the model to give a realistic look to the rendered image.

In Revit, entourages are family-based and are available as a library of entourage families. You can add additional entourages to an existing family if you want to use them in your scene. They are displayed in simple line drawings as placeholders in the project views. The photorealistic representations of entourages are displayed only in rendered images.

In a project, the people, plants, vehicles, and office clutters are parts of Archvision's RPC (Rich Photorealistic Content) product family. In Autodesk Revit, you can insert people in floor plans and three-dimensional views, where each people family is displayed as a placeholder.

You cannot place a people family in the elevation and section views. You can see the actual detail of these RPC in a rendered image.

Revit provides two people families: **RPC Male** and **RPC Female**. Each family type provides different render appearances for males and females. The other families of entourages that are available for placing in your project are: **RPC Beetle**, **RPC Chair**, **RPC Notebook Computer**, **RPC Picture Frame**, and **Semi Truck**.

The families of plant in Revit can be placed in the surrounding of a model. The plant family in Revit uses a RPC file to specify the render appearance. In Autodesk Revit, you are provided with several RPC families for trees and plants. Different species of trees and plants are available as types in each family.

Creating Decal Type

Before placing a decal in a view, you need to create a new decal type. To do so, choose the **Decal Types** tool from **Insert > Link > Decal** drop-down; the **Decal Types** dialog box will be displayed. Now, choose the **Create new decal** button at the bottom left corner of the **Decal Types** dialog box; the **New Decal** dialog box will be displayed. Enter a suitable name in the **Name** edit box for the new decal type and choose the **OK** button to exit. On doing so, a decal will be added to the **Decal Types in Project** area of the **Decal Types** dialog box, as shown in Figure 15-12. Next, you need to add an image and the associated attributes to the new decal type by using the options in the **Settings** area of the **Decal Types** dialog box. To add an image, choose the Browse button next to the **Source** text box; the **Select File** dialog box will be displayed. Select an image file from this dialog box and choose the **Open** button. You can preview it in the preview area. Next, set the desired values in the corresponding lists for various attributes. After selecting various attributes, choose the **OK** button to return to the drawing area. Various attributes for **Decal Types** are described in the table given next.

Attributes	Definition
Brightness	Defines the brightness or darkness of the decal
Reflectivity	Measures the quantity of light reflected from the surface of a decal. Enter a value between 0 and 99 to define reflection
Transparency	Measures the quantity of light passing through a decal. Enter a value between 0 (completely opaque) and 1 (completely transparent)

Finish	Defines the finished condition of decal surfaces. Select the **Matte**, **Semi-gloss**, **Gloss**, **High Gloss**, or **Custom** option from the **Finish** drop-down list. If you select the **Custom** option, enter a value between 0 and 1 in the text box available next to it
Luminance (cd/ m ^ 2)	Defines the light emitted by a decal surface. It is measured in candela per meter square. Select various options from the **Luminance** drop-down list or select **Custom** to enter a value
Bump Pattern	Defines a texture that is added in addition to the texture applied to a decal. This texture is placed on the top of the texture that is already applied to the decal
Bump Amount	Reflects the amount of irregularities that can be created on the decal surface due to the **Bump Pattern** parameter. Enter any value between 0 and 100%
Cutouts	Defines the shapes cut on the surface of the decal. Select an image file to define the cut-outs

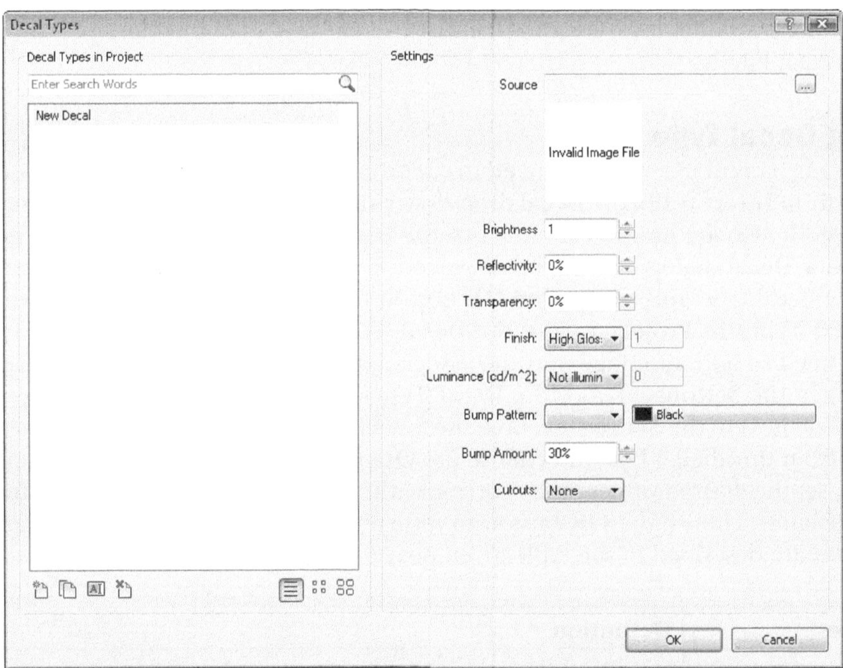

*Figure 15-12 The decal added to the **Decal Types** dialog box*

Placing a Decal

To place a decal in your scene, choose the **Place Decal** tool from the **Link** panel; the **Modify | Decal** tab will be displayed. Now, select the appropriate decal type from the **Type Selector** drop-down list and set the size of the decal in the **Width** and **Height** text boxes in the **Options Bar**. By default, the **Lock Proportions** check box is selected in the **Options Bar** which indicates that the width to height ratio is set to one. You can clear this check box to remove the restriction, so that the width and height are independent of each other. Now, move the cursor near the surface over which the decal is to be placed. After the desired surface or the edge is highlighted, click to place the decal. The decal will appear as a rectangle with two diagonal lines in all views, except the rendered view.

Note

*If no decal is loaded in the **Decal Types** dialog box, then on choosing the **Place Decal** tool, the **Decal Types** dialog box will be displayed and will prompt you to insert a decal.*

Editing a Decal

To edit a decal, select it from the drawing. On doing so, the **Modify | Generic Models** tab along with the **Options Bar** will be displayed. Now, modify its size using the **Width** and **Height** edit boxes in the **Options Bar**. Alternatively, you can also use the drag controls at the four corners of the decal. The **Lock Proportions** check box in the **Options Bar** can be cleared to resize the decal to a different aspect ratio. Choose the **Reset** button in the **Options Bar** to reset the size of the decal to the original size. In the **Properties** palette, you can change the instance parameters such as **Height**, **Width**, and **Lock Proportions** from their corresponding **Value** fields. From the **Properties** palette, choose the **Edit Type** button to invoke the **Type Properties** dialog box. In this dialog box, you can modify the type properties of the decal such as **Decal Attributes**, **Keynotes**, and others. To modify the attributes of the decal such as image, brightness, reflectivity, transparency, and others, choose the **Edit** button in the **Value** field of the **Decal Attributes** parameter; the **Decal Types** dialog box will be displayed. In this dialog box, you can change the attributes of the decal by specifying values in the spinners, edit boxes, buttons and drop-down lists that will be displayed for various parameters in this dialog box.

Placing Entourages

To place entourages and plants in a building model, first you need to load the entourage family types in the drawing. To do so, choose the **Place a Component** tool from **Architecture > Build > Component** drop-down; the **Modify | Place Component** tab will be displayed. In this tab, choose the **Load Family** tool from the **Mode** panel; the **Load Family** dialog box will be displayed. In this dialog box, browse to the folder location **US Imperial > Entourage**. The **Entourage** folder contains the families of the people and vehicles. Alternatively, browse to the **US Imperial > Planting** folder location that contains the families of plants, trees, and shrubs. Select the desired family to be loaded into the **Load Family** dialog box and then choose the **Open** button to load it into the project file.

Next, in the **Modify | Place Component** tab, select the desired entourage from the **Type Selector** drop-down list and select the **Rotate after placement** check box from the **Options Bar**, if you need to rotate the element at the time of insertion. Select the desired floor level for the entourage from the drop-down list displayed next to the **Rotate after placement** check box. Next, move the cursor to the drawing window and click to add the selected element to the appropriate floor plan or the 3D view.

Rendering Settings

After creating three-dimensional view for rendering, applying lights and materials to elements, and placing entourages and decals, you need to do render settings before the final rendering. To render and create the presets for the rendering process, choose the **Show Rendering Dialog** button from **View Control Bar** or type RR; the **Rendering** dialog box will be displayed, as shown in Figure 15-13.

In the **Rendering** dialog box, you can define the view area for rendering, specify the quality of output, specify the light settings, set the background of the rendered image, adjust the rendered image exposure quality, and save the rendered image to a project view or export it as an external image file. Various settings are discussed next.

Setting the View Area

After creating the three-dimensional view and invoking the **Rendering** dialog box, you need to set the view area to be rendered by any one of the following methods, Render region, Crop region, Section Box, and Camera clipping plane. To set the view area by using the Render region method, select the **Region** check box in the **Rendering** dialog box; a red colored rectangular region boundary will be displayed in the drawing area. This boundary is called the render region boundary and is used to determine the enclosed area within which the elements displayed will be rendered. On selecting the render region boundary, the blue colored dots will be visible on all four edges of the rectangle. These dots are called control grips. Click on any one of the control grips and drag to the extent to resize the rectangular area. Similarly, you can use other methods such as Crop region, Section box, and Camera Clipping plane to determine the view area for rendering. These methods have already been discussed in the previous chapters.

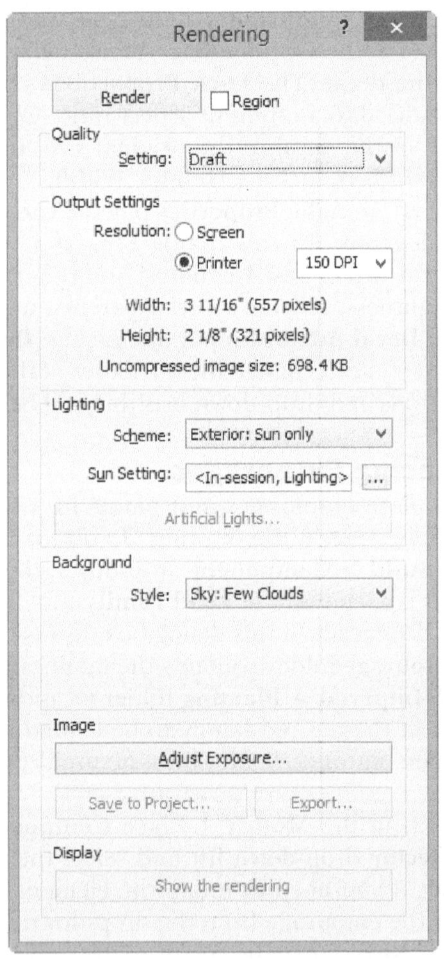

*Figure 15-13 The **Rendering** dialog box*

Specifying Output Settings

After selecting the view area, now you need to set the resolution or the image size of the output image.

You can use various options from the **Output Settings** area of the **Rendering** dialog box to set the image size and the pixel quality of the output image. In the **Output Settings** area, there are two radio buttons, **Screen** and **Printer**. These radio buttons can be used to set the resolution or the image quality of the rendered image. On selecting the **Screen** radio button, you can set the final rendered image size in accordance with the screen display. In this case, you can use various methods as discussed in the previous topic to adjust the size of the final rendered image.

Similarly, you can also set the resolution of the output image in accordance with printer. To do so, select the **Printer** radio button in the **Output Settings** area of the **Rendering** dialog box. For setting the resolution of the output image, you need to set the printing quality in dots per inches (DPI). This is the standard unit of printing for all applications. Higher value of DPI determines better quality of the image and increases the render time. You can set the quality of the rendered image to 75 DPI, 150 DPI, 300 DPI, and 600 DPI by selecting the option from the drop-down list in the **Output Settings** area of the **Rendering** dialog box.

Controlling Lights

While specifying the settings for rendering, it is important to control the lights in a scene externally or internally. To make the lighting process easy, Autodesk Revit has provided you with an integrated control of lights in the scene. The lighting control appears in the **Lighting** area of the **Rendering** dialog box in the form of schemes, position of Sun, and control of artificial light. To set the light scheme for rendering images, select any of the six options, **Exterior: Sun only**, **Exterior: Sun and Artificial**, **Exterior: Artificial only**, **Interior: Sun only**, **Interior: Sun and Artificial**, and **Interior: Artificial only** from the **Scheme** drop-down list available in the **Lighting** area.

To set the position of the Sun, you can select an option from the **Sun Setting** drop-down list only if you select **Exterior: Sun only**, **Exterior: Sun and Artificial**, **Interior: Sun only**, or **Interior: Sun and Artificial** from the **Scheme** drop-down list. To set your own sun and shadow, select the **Choose a sun location** button placed next to the **Sun Setting** text box; the **Sun Settings** dialog box will be displayed. In this dialog box, you can use different types of presets that define the position of the sun on the basis of its location, date, and time. You can also set your own presets in the **Sun Settings** dialog box.

You can control the intensity and visibility of light in a view by setting the corresponding parameters in the **Rendering** dialog box. In the **Lightings** area, the **Artificial Lights** button is deactivated by default. To activate this button, select any scheme that contains artificial light from the **Scheme** drop-down list; the button will be activated. Now, choose this button; the **Artificial Lights - {3D}** dialog box will be displayed, as shown in Figure 15-14. This dialog box contains a list that displays the name of all the lighting fixtures that are placed in a building model. This list of lighting fixtures is divided into **Grouped Lights** and **Ungrouped Lights**. You can create a new group or edit an existing group to add or remove an individual light fixture from the group. In the **Artificial Lights - {3D}** dialog box, you can also set the intensity of individual or group lights by setting the dimming value in the **Dimming (0-1)** column between **0** and **1**. Similarly, you can turn on or off the visibility of the individual light or grouped light fixtures by selecting or clearing the corresponding check boxes in the **On/Off** column of the **Artificial Lights - {3D}** dialog box. A light group is an essential tool in the rendering process which helps you control the light fixtures in a scene collectively as well as individually. To create a new group of lights, choose the **New** button in the **Group Options** area of the **Artificial Lights-{3D}** dialog box. On doing so, the **New Light Group** dialog box will be displayed. Enter the name of the light group in **Name** edit box and choose the **OK** button to return to the **Artificial Lights - {3D}** dialog box. You will notice that a new group has been added under **Grouped Lights** with a default dimming value of 1. Next, you need to add light fixtures to the group. There are several methods by which you can add light fixtures to the group. Some of these methods are discussed next.

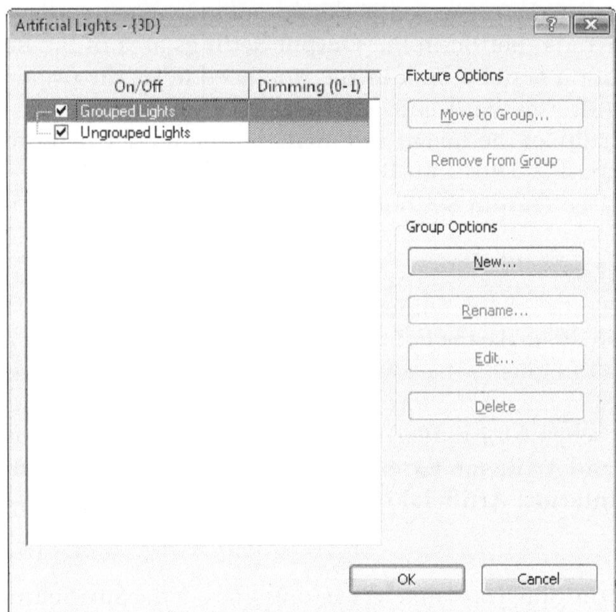

*Figure 15-14 The **Artificial Lights - {3D}** dialog box*

In the **Artificial Lights - {3D}** dialog box, select the group name to which you want to add light fixtures. After selecting the desired group, choose the **Edit** button in the **Group Options** area to display the **Light Group** panel in the **Architecture** tab. You will notice that all the model elements and the lighting fixtures belonging to another light group are displayed in halftone, the lighting fixtures belonging to the selected light group are displayed in green, and lighting fixtures that are not currently assigned to any light group are displayed normally in the drawing area. To add a light fixture to the group, choose the **Add** button, select a light fixture from the drawing area, and then choose the **Finish** button. To remove a light fixture from the group using the **Light Group** toolbar, choose the **Remove** button and select the light fixture from the group, and then choose the **Finish** button.

Alternatively, you can add a light fixture to the group using the **Artificial Lights - {3D}** dialog box. To do so, first select the required light fixtures from the **Ungrouped Lights** hierarchy. Then, choose the **Move to Group** button; the **Light Groups** dialog box will be displayed. In this dialog box, select various light groups from the **Light Group** drop-down list to assign the selected light fixture to the light group. To remove a light from a group, select the name of the light fixture that you want to remove from the **Artificial Lights - {3D}** dialog box and then choose the **Remove from Group** button. This will result in the transition of the light fixture from the **Grouped Lights** to **Ungrouped Lights** area.

Adding a Background to a Scene

You can add a suitable background to the rendered scene using the **Rendering** dialog box. The background that you specify can be of a solid color or a combination of sky and clouds.

Setting the Background of the Rendered Image

To set the background of a rendered image, select an option from the **Style** drop-down list in the **Background** area of the **Rendering** dialog box. After setting the background, you can use the **Haze** slider in the **Background** area to control the haziness of the rendered image. Note that the **Haze** slider will not be displayed in the **Background** area if you select the **Color** or **Image** option from the **Style** drop-down list. You can select the **Color** option from this drop-down list to assign a color to the background. On doing so, the **Color Swatch** button will be activated. Choose this button to display the **Color** window from where you can select the desired color for the background. Alternatively, you can select the **Image** option from the **Style** drop-down list to display an image in the background of the rendered scene. On doing so, the **Background Image** dialog box will be displayed. By default, no image file is assigned in the dialog box. As a result, all the options are disabled. To assign an image file for the background, choose the **Image** button; the **Import Image** dialog box will be displayed. You can use this dialog box to import an image to be used as a background for the rendered scene.

Note

In an interior view, natural light and the sky and cloud background can affect the quality of illumination on the rendered image. It is recommended to use more clouds for better diffuse lighting.

Creating the Rendered Image

After creating 3D view, applying lights, and assigning desired materials to elements, you need to view them in the final rendered image. To start the rendering process, choose the **Render** tool from the **Graphics** panel of the **View** tab; the **Rendering** dialog box will be displayed. Choose the **Render** button from the dialog box; the **Rendering Progress** dialog box will be displayed and Autodesk Revit will begin the rendering process using the mental ray rendering engine that renders one block of an image at a time. While rendering, the **Rendering Progress** dialog box displays information about the progress of the rendering process along with the number of daylight portals and artificial lights used.

If the **Close dialog when Rendering is complete** check box is selected in the **Rendering Progress** dialog box, the dialog box will automatically be closed after the completion of the rendering process and the final rendered image will be displayed on the screen.

Adjusting the Exposure

You can improve the quality of a rendered image before saving it. To do so, choose the **Adjust Exposure** button in the **Image** area of the **Rendering** dialog box; the **Exposure Control** dialog box will be displayed, as shown in Figure 15-15.

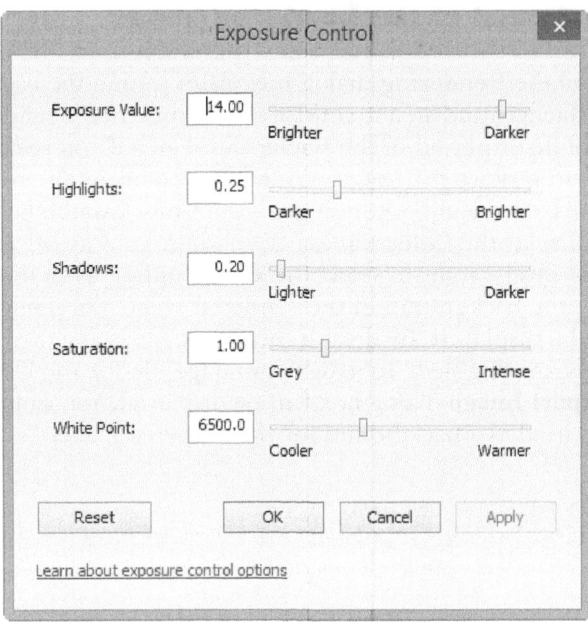

*Figure 15-15 The **Exposure Control** dialog box*

Various settings for the exposure control of an image are discussed in the table given next.

Settings	Description
Exposure Value	Enter a value between –6 and 16. The lesser value results in a brighter image and the higher value results in a darker image.
Highlights	Controls the level of the brightest area of the rendered image. You can enter a value between 0 (darkest) and 1 (brightest) highlights. The default value is 0.25.
Shadows	Controls the level of the darkest area of the rendered image. You can enter a value between 0.1 (lightest) and 4 (darkest) for the shadows. The default value is 0.2.
Saturation	Defines the intensity of colors in the rendered image. Enter a value between 0 (gray/black/white) and 5 (more intense colors) The default value is 1.
White Point	Defines the color temperature of light sources that display white color in the rendered images. Reduce the value if the rendered image looks orange. Increase its value if it looks blue. Use the value of 6500 for the scene illuminated with daylight.

Choose the **Apply** button each time you change the settings in the **Exposure Control** dialog box to see the updated image on your screen.

CREATING A WALKTHROUGH

A well rendered walkthrough can make a project presentation impressive. Using the **Walkthrough** tool, you can easily generate a walkthrough for a building model by rendering a series of 3D views defined by camera frames. The process of generating a walkthrough involves specifying a walkthrough path, editing it, and finally recording the walkthrough.

Creating the Walkthrough Path

Ribbon: View > Create > 3D View drop-down > Walkthrough

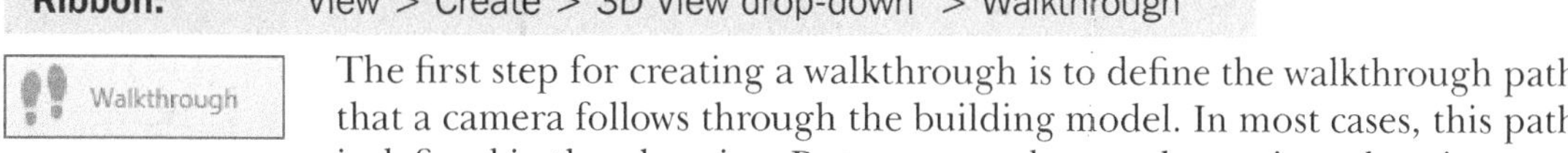

The first step for creating a walkthrough is to define the walkthrough path that a camera follows through the building model. In most cases, this path is defined in the plan view. But, you can also use the section, elevation, and 3D views to define the path.

The walkthrough path is defined by specifying the points that form a spline in the project view. The specified points become key frames in the walkthrough. Autodesk Revit automatically generates additional intermediate frames between these key frames.

To create a walkthrough path, first open the view in which it is to be defined. Next, invoke the **Walkthrough** tool from **View > Create> 3D View** drop-down; the **Modify | Walkthrough** tab will be displayed and the options related to the path creation will be displayed in the **Options Bar**, as shown in Figure 15-16.

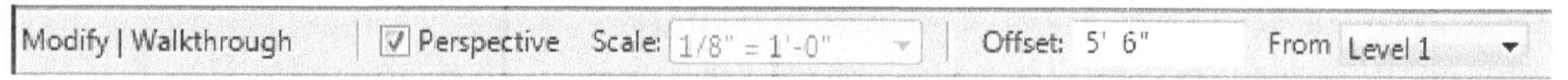

***Figure 15-16** The **Options Bar** displaying the options for creating a walkthrough*

By default, the **Perspective** check box is selected to create walkthrough using perspective views from the camera positions. You can clear the **Perspective** check box to create walkthroughs as orthographic 3D views. Additionally, you can select the required view scale from the **Scale** drop-down list. The **Offset** edit box in the **Options Bar** is used to specify the height of the camera from the selected level. Using this edit box, you can move the camera upward or downward while specifying the key frames along the walkthrough path. For example, by setting higher values for the **Offset** parameter, you can move the camera upward along a ramp or a flight of stairs. The **From** drop-down list displays all the defined levels in the project. You can select the level from which the offset camera height is specified. This parameter can be effectively used while creating an interior walkthrough at multiple levels.

To create the walkthrough path, click at the first point of the camera location; the point will define the first key frame of the walkthrough. As you move the cursor in the drawing area, Autodesk Revit will display three lines indicating the direction of the camera. Click to specify other points to create a spline to define the path of the camera. You can use the **Offset** and **From** options from **Options Bar** to modify the camera height, if required. After specifying the last point, choose the **Finish Walkthrough** button in the **Walkthrough** panel of the **Modify Walkthrough** tab; the **Modify | Cameras** tab will be displayed and the path of the camera for the walkthrough will be completed. The walkthrough path will be displayed in a different color in the drawing window. An example of the walkthrough path is shown in Figure 15-17.

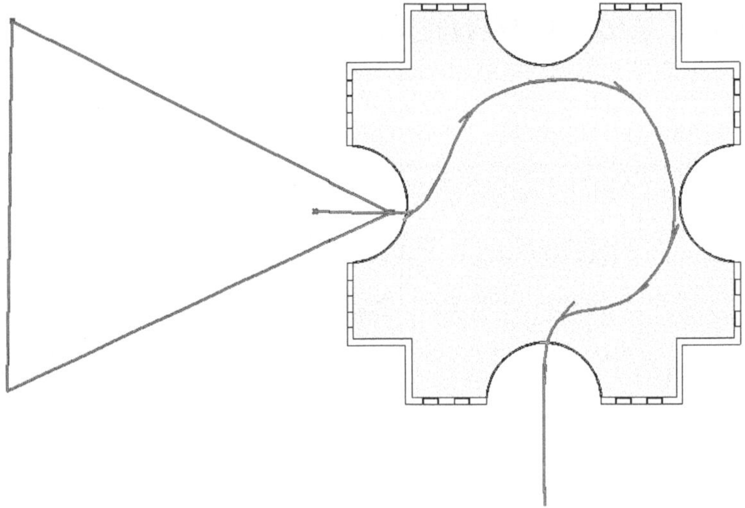

Figure 15-17 *An example showing the walkthrough path*

Note

After creating a complete walkthrough path, you must first create the complete path and then edit it as per your requirement.

Editing and Playing the Walkthrough

When you create a walkthrough path, Autodesk Revit assigns **Walkthrough 1** as its name by default and then it is added to the **Project Browser** under the **Walkthroughs** heading.

To view the created walkthrough, double-click on its name in the **Project Browser** or right-click over the name and then choose **Open** from the shortcut menu; the drawing window will display the 3D view of the last frame. Select the frame from the drawing window; the **Modify | Cameras** tab will be displayed and the crop boundary with the grips will also be displayed. You can use the grips to resize the crop region. Alternatively, if you choose the **Size Crop** button in the **Crop** panel of the **Modify |Cameras** tab, the **Crop Region Size** dialog box will be displayed. In this dialog box, enter the new values for the **Width** and **Height** parameters of the crop region. The **Field of view** radio button in this dialog box is selected to modify the aspect ratio of the crop region. The **Scale** radio button is selected to scale the crop region by locking its aspect ratio. Note that while scaling the crop region, you can modify its width and height without affecting the field of view of the scene. After specifying the desired values, choose **OK**; the **Crop Region Size** dialog box will be closed and the crop region will be resized according to the parameters specified.

Now, to display the walkthrough path, double-click on the level name in which the path was created. While the walkthrough path is displayed in the drawing area, choose the **Edit Walkthrough** button in the **Modify | Cameras** tab; the **Edit Walkthrough** tab will be displayed, as shown in Figure 15-18. The options in the **Edit Walkthrough** tab are used to play or edit a walkthrough. The key frames specified to create the path are highlighted with dots in the drawing.

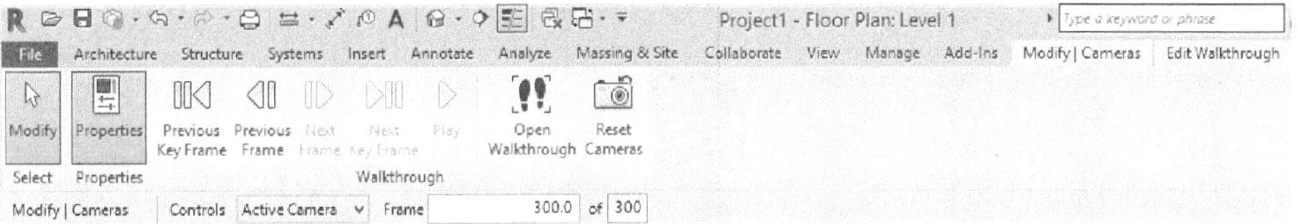

*Figure 15-18 The options for editing and playing a walkthrough in the **Edit Walkthrough** tab*

In the **Options Bar**, the options in the **Controls** drop-down list are used to select the type of editing for the walkthrough. It has four options: **Active Camera**, **Path**, **Add Key Frame**, and **Remove Key Frame**. These options are discussed next.

The **Active Camera** option is used to drag a camera along a path to the desired frame or key frame. As you move the camera, it snaps to the key frame. While using this option, you can also drag the target point and the far clip plane of the camera at the key frames. At other additional frames, you can only modify the far clip plane.

Tip

*After creating the walkthrough path if you press the ESC key or click anywhere in the drawing area, it no longer remains visible. To display the path again, right-click on the name of the walkthrough and then choose the **Show Camera** option from the shortcut menu; the walkthrough path will be displayed in the current view. You can edit this path using the tools such as **Move**, **Copy**, **Mirror**, and so on.*

The **Path** option in the **Controls** drop-down list is used to edit a walkthrough path. When you select this option, key frames get converted into drag controls. You can drag them to modify the walkthrough path.

Select the **Add Key Frame** option to add key frames to the created path. Move the cursor over the path and click at the desired locations to add them. The **Remove Key Frame** option is used to remove the corresponding key frames by clicking over them.

The **Frame** edit box in the **Options Bar** displays the frame for the current location of the camera. You can enter a new frame number in this edit box to view the location of the camera at that frame. The **Frame Settings** button displayed next to the **Frame** edit box is used to set the properties of the frames. When you choose this button, the **Walkthrough Frames** dialog box will be displayed, as shown in Figure 15-19. The options in this dialog box are discussed next.

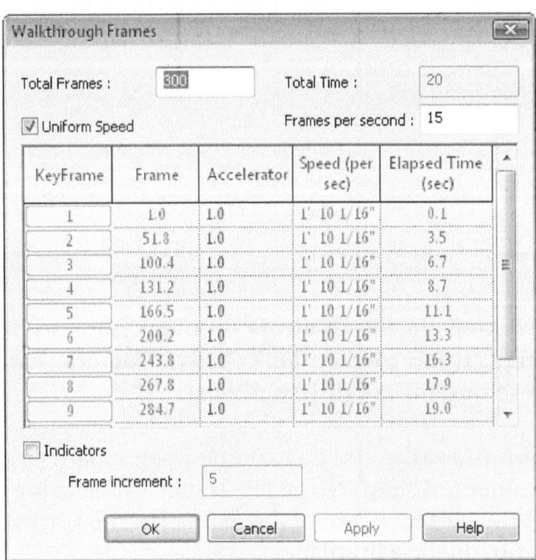

KeyFrame	Frame	Accelerator	Speed (per sec)	Elapsed Time (sec)
1	1.0	1.0	1' 10 1/16"	0.1
2	51.8	1.0	1' 10 1/16"	3.5
3	100.4	1.0	1' 10 1/16"	6.7
4	131.2	1.0	1' 10 1/16"	8.7
5	166.5	1.0	1' 10 1/16"	11.1
6	200.2	1.0	1' 10 1/16"	13.3
7	243.8	1.0	1' 10 1/16"	16.3
8	267.8	1.0	1' 10 1/16"	17.9
9	284.7	1.0	1' 10 1/16"	19.0

*Figure 15-19 The **Walkthrough Frames** dialog box*

The total number of frames in a walkthrough can be set by entering the value in the **Total Frames** edit box. Based on the values entered in this edit box, Autodesk Revit automatically divides frames along the created walkthrough path.

The **Uniform Speed** check box is selected by default. As a result, the camera traverses the walkthrough path at a uniform speed. You can change the speed of the walkthrough by entering a new value in the **Frames per second** edit box. Its default value is **15**. Lower the value in this edit box, slower will be the walkthrough. You can also vary the speed of the walkthrough by clearing the **Uniform Speed** check box in the **Walkthrough Frames** dialog box. This dialog box displays a table that contains five columns. These columns display the frame properties that are automatically generated based on the parameters specified for the walkthrough. When you clear the **Uniform Speed** check box, the **Accelerator** column in the table becomes editable. The **Accelerator** column displays the numerical values that change the speed of the walkthrough at specific key frames. You can enter values in the range of 0.1 and 10 to vary the speed of walkthrough. You can click on the **Key Frame** column to trace the key frame on the walkthrough path. A camera icon is also displayed at the selected key frame.

The **Indicators** check box is used to display the intermediate camera indicators along the walkthrough path. This helps in visualizing the distribution of frames along the path. The increment at which indicators are displayed can be set in the **Frame Increment** edit box.

After setting the required parameters in the **Walkthrough Frames** dialog box, you can play the walkthrough using the buttons in the **Edit Walkthrough** tab, refer to Figure 15-18. In the **Frame** edit box in the **Options Bar**, enter the frame number for the frame you wish to view in the drawing window. Next, in the **Edit Walkthrough** tab, choose the **Open Walkthrough** button to display the perspective view for the specified frame. To select the view type, choose the **Visual Style** button from **View Control Bar**; a cascading menu will be displayed. Now, select an option from this menu. Finally, choose the **Play** button from the **Edit Walkthrough** tab to play the walkthrough in the drawing window; the walkthrough starts playing based on the view type selected and the walkthrough parameters specified.

Note

When you create a walkthrough, it becomes a part of the project file and is not saved to the disk as a separate file. To save it to a disk, you need to record the walkthrough.

Tip

*The value specified in the **Frames per second** edit box indicates the speed of the walkthrough. You can enter a value in this edit box based on the total number of frames in the walkthrough. The **Total Time** edit box displays the total walkthrough time based on the total frames and the frames per second. Lower values of the **Frames per second** parameter may result in a jerky walkthrough.*

Recording a Walkthrough

Autodesk Revit enables you to record the walkthrough as **AVI** files and to export these files to a disk. The **AVI** files can be used to export the walkthrough. To export these files, open the walkthrough and choose **Export > Images and Animations > Walkthrough** from the **File** menu; the **Length/Format** dialog box will be displayed providing you with various options for exporting the walkthrough. The **Output Length** area of this dialog box enables you to select the frames to be exported. The **All frames** radio button in this area can be selected to export all the frames in the walkthrough. Alternatively, you can select the **Frame range** radio button and specify the number of frames to be exported by entering suitable values in the **Start** and **End** edit boxes. The **Frames/second** edit box is used to specify the speed at which the frames will be recorded.

The **Format** area of the **Length/Format** dialog box provides you with the options to specify the type and quality for the recording of the walkthrough. You can select the view type to be used for generating and recording the walkthrough from the **Visual Style** drop-down list. To record the rendered view of frames, select the **Rendering** option from this drop-down list. You can also specify the quality for the recording by setting the **Dimensions** and **Zoom to** spinners. Next, choose the **OK** button to invoke the **Export Walkthrough** dialog box, as shown in Figure 15-20. This dialog box is used to save a walkthrough. Enter a suitable name in the **File name** edit box and select the **AVI Files** option from the **Files of type** drop-down list. Next, choose the **Save** button from the **Export Walkthrough** dialog box to start recording the walkthrough. Now, Autodesk Revit will display the **Video Compression** dialog box that enables you to select a video compressor from a list of compressors installed on your computer. When you choose the **OK** button, the dialog box will be closed and Autodesk Revit will start recording the walkthrough. The progress indicator and **Status Bar** at the bottom of the screen will display the progress of the processes being executed.

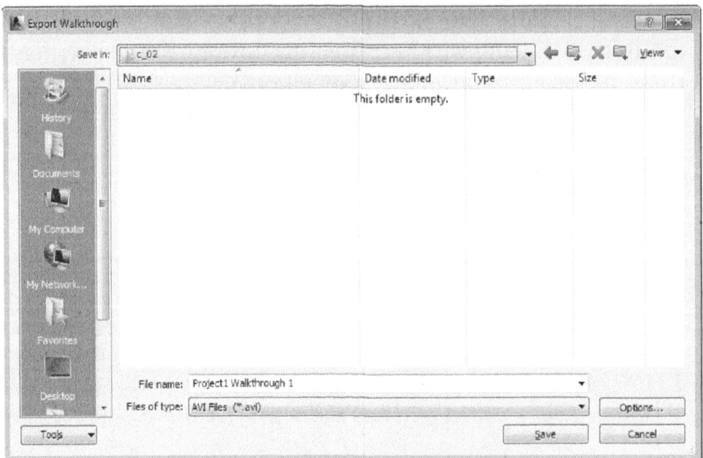

*Figure 15-20 The **Export Walkthrough** dialog box*

Note

The recorded file can be viewed using any of the media players. Note that this animation can now be viewed even without opening Autodesk Revit.

AUTODESK 360 | RENDERING

Autodesk 360 | Rendering is a cloud based rendering service that helps you to create photorealistic images and panoramic views for your project. It is a user interactive platform that provides a broad set of features including online cloud services, and related products.

The main features of the **Autodesk 360 | Rendering** service are:

1. Using the **Autodesk 360 | Rendering** service, you can render your Revit projects from any computer. Note that in Revit 2018, you can have direct access to the **Autodesk 360 | Rendering** rendering service while in Revit 2012 you had to load latest version of the **Autodesk Cloud Rendering** add-on, which had to be downloaded from the **Autodesk 360 | Rendering** service.

2. Using the **Autodesk 360 | Rendering** service, you can access multiple versions of your renderings, render images as panoramas, change rendering quality, and apply background environments to rendered scenes.

3. Using this service, the design files can be reviewed even without the Revit software by accessing the **Autodesk @ 360** account online or even on mobile applications. The design files can be shared among users and the file updates and e-mail notifications reach the users whenever the file is edited.

4. The rendered views generated by the **Autodesk 360 | Rendering** application are grouped as collection in the render gallery. You can also create and view panoramic views. Panoramic views can be accessed from the render gallery.

5. Using the **Autodesk 360 | Rendering** service, you can adjust the exposure of the rendered image directly without having to re-render from the original desktop application.

6. The **Autodesk 360 | Rendering** service helps you to preview the rendered image of a single day or multi-day solar studies.

Rendering in Cloud

To render an image in the cloud, open a view in Revit interface. Next, choose the **Render in Cloud** tool from the **Graphics** panel of the **View** tab; the **Render in Cloud** dialog box will be displayed, as shown in Figure 15-21. Choose the **Continue** button; the **Render in Cloud** dialog box will be displayed again with the rendering options, as shown in Figure 15-22. In this dialog box, the 3D view to be rendered is to be chosen from the **3D View** swatch. You can specify the image type to be displayed, still or panoramic, from the **Output Type** drop-down list. You can specify the quality of rendered image as draft, standard, high, or best by selecting from the **Render Quality** drop-down list. You can specify image size for rendering by selecting an option from the **Image Size** drop-down list. From the **Exposure** drop-down list, you can select an option to specify whether the exposure being adjusted for the rendered image will be in advanced or native mode. After setting the required parameters, you can choose the **Start Rendering** button to render the image in the cloud. The estimated wait time to render a view is displayed at the right corner of this dialog box.

Note

*If a project is not saved in Revit, and the **Render in Cloud** tool is used to render the image, then the **Render in Cloud** message box will be displayed, prompting you to save the project and proceed.*

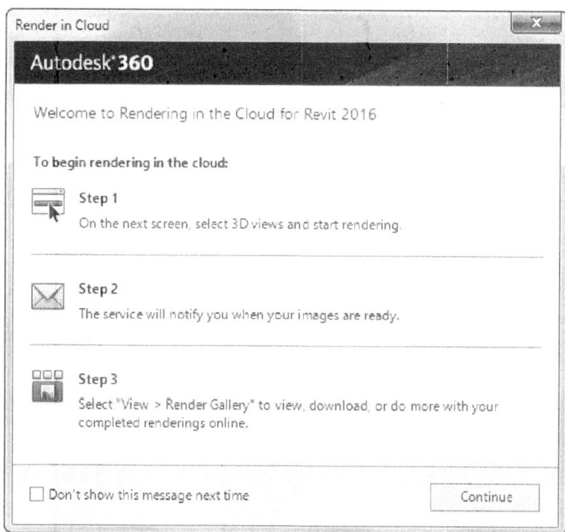

*Figure 15-21 The **Render in Cloud** dialog box*

*Figure 15-22 The **Render in Cloud** dialog box with rendering options*

Tip

*The **Autodesk 360 / Energy Analysis** and **Autodesk 360 / Structural Analysis** cloud based services are available on subscription. The **Autodesk 360 / Energy Analysis** service helps in checking the energy efficiency of a building project whereas the **Autodesk 360 / Structural Analysis** service helps in performing structural analysis of the building elements.*

Accessing Render Gallery

The rendered images and the images being rendered are available online on **Render Gallery** page. The images are arranged in such a way that the newest image is displayed first. The grouping of images is done on the basis of file extension such as *.rvt* or *.dwg*. To access the Render gallery from Revit, choose the **Render Gallery** tool from the **Graphics** panel of the **View** tab; the **Autodesk 360 | Rendering** page will be opened. You need to sign in to your account to access the Render gallery from the **Autodesk 360 | Rendering** page.

TUTORIALS

Tutorial 1 — Apartment 1

Using the project file *c14_Apartment1_tut1.rvt,* created in Tutorial 1 of Chapter 14, render the interior view of the living room at first floor, as shown in Figure 15-23. Replace the existing finish of materials assigned to the floor, wall, ceiling, and chair with new materials/textures (given with their path). Also, create a 200-frame interior walkthrough at eye level using the path shown in Figure 15-24. **(Expected time: 1 hr)**

The rendered image can be downloaded from *http://www.cadcim.com*. The path of the file is as follows: *Textbooks > Civil/GIS > Revit Architecture> Exploring Autodesk Revit 2018 for Architecture*

Note

The expected time of completing the tutorial does not include the rendering time. The rendering time will depend upon the system configuration.

Figure 15-23 *The interior view of the living room after rendering*

The materials used for rendering the scene are as follows:

1. New material for walls: **Finishes - Interior - Gypsum Wall Board** with **Wall-Paint Matte** render appearance.
2. New material for ceiling: **Finishes - Interior - Gypsum Wall Board - Ceiling**
3. New material for floor: **Vinyl Composition Tile**
4. New cushion material for **Chair Corbu: Textile - Brown Leather**

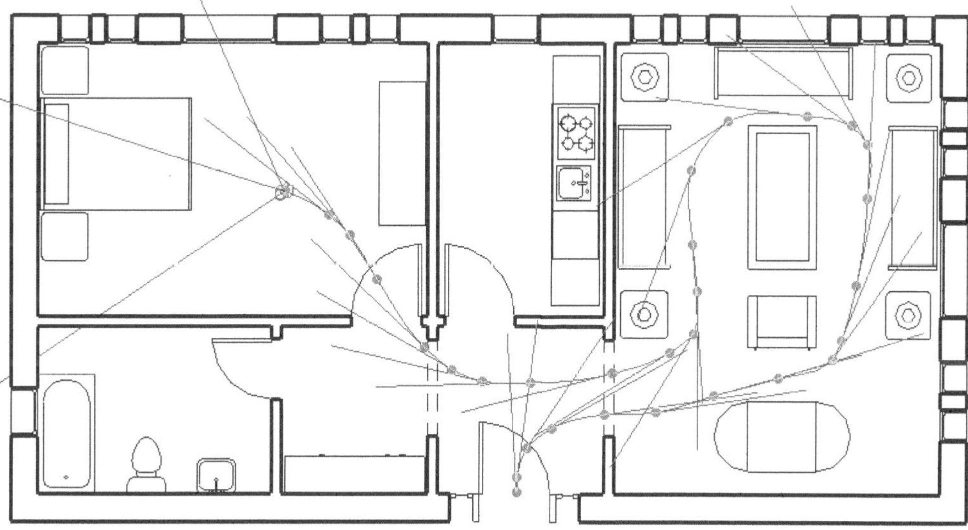

Figure 15-24 *Sketch plan showing the walkthrough path for the Apartment 1 project*

Add lights based on the parameters given below, as shown in Figures 15-25 and 15-26. Their exact location is not important in this tutorial.

1. Light Fixtures to be loaded and used from the **US Imperial > Lighting Fixture** folder:
   Table Lamp - Standard
   Pendant Light - Disk

The following steps are required to complete this tutorial:

a. Open the specified project file and the first floor plan view.
b. Apply materials to the floor using the **Paint** tool.
c. Change the finish of the ceiling, walls, and textile of the chair using the **Material Browser** dialog box.
d. Load lighting fixtures and add them to the floor and ceiling plan, refer to Figures 15-27 through 15-30.
e. Add RPC to the view, refer to Figures 15-31 and 15-32.
f. Set the rendering scene and generate the rendered image, refer to Figure 15-33.
g. Specify the walkthrough path and create a walkthrough, refer to Figures 15-34 through 15-36.
h. Save the project using the **Save As** tool.
   For Imperial *c15_Apartment1_tut1.rvt*
   For Metric *M_c15_Apartment1_tut1.rvt*
i. Close the project.

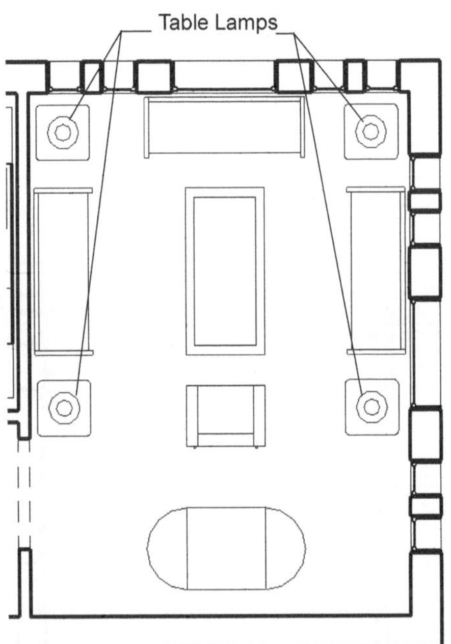

Figure 15-25 *Sketch floor plan for adding table lamps to the living room*

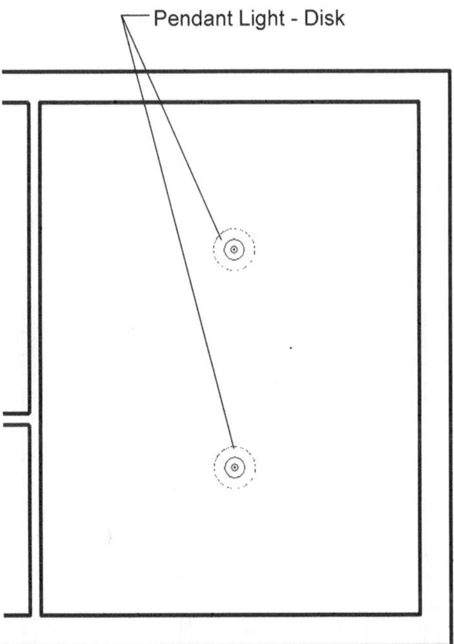

Figure 15-26 *Sketch ceiling plan for adding ceiling lights to the living room*

Opening the Project File and the First Floor Plan View

1. Choose **Open > Project** from the **File** menu and then open the *c14_Apartment1_tut1.rvt* file created in Tutorial 1 of Chapter 14. You can also download this file from *http://www.cadcim.com*. The path of the file is as follows: *Textbooks > Civil/GIS > Revit Architecture > Exploring Autodesk Revit 2018 for Architecture.*

2. Now, double-click on **First Floor** in the **Floor Plans** head of the **Project Browser** to open the corresponding floor plan in the drawing window.

   As dimensions and tags are not required for this tutorial, you can turn off their visibility by using the **Visibility/Graphics** tool.

3. Choose the **Visibility/Graphics** tool from the **Graphics** panel of the **View** tab; the **Visibility/Graphic Overrides for Floor Plan: First Floor** dialog box is displayed. Choose the **Annotation Categories** tab and clear the check boxes for **Callouts**, **Dimensions**, **Furniture Tags**, and **Room Tags**.

4. Next, choose the **Apply** button and then the **OK** button to view the changes in the drawing area and to close the dialog box, respectively.

Modifying the Floor Material Using the Paint Tool

In this section of the tutorial, you will modify the finishes of the materials used in the building model. Also, you will use the **Paint** tool to apply the material to the floor in the section view.

1. Double-click on **Section X** under the **Sections (Building Section)** head in the **Project Browser** to display the section in the drawing window.

2. Choose the **Paint** tool from **Modify > Geometry > Paint** drop-down; the **Material Browser <default material name>** dialog box is displayed.

3. In the **Search** edit box of the **Material Browser** dialog box, type the **Vinyl Composition Tile** text; the **Vinyl Composition Tile** is displayed in the area.

4. Select the **Vinyl Composition Tile** material.

5. Now, in the drawing area, move the cursor near the top of the floor at the **First Floor** level in the section view and click when it is highlighted; the selected material is applied to the floor top. Choose the **Done** button in the **Material Browser** dialog box to close the dialog box.

Modifying the Finish of the Materials Using the Material Editor

In this section, you will modify the finish of other elements by using the **Material Browser** dialog box.

1. Choose the **Modify** button from the **Select** panel and then move the cursor over the left exterior wall. Next, click to select the wall when it is highlighted.

2. Now, choose the **Type Properties** button in the **Properties** panel of the **Modify | Walls** tab; the **Type Properties** dialog box is displayed.

3. Next, choose the **Edit** button in the **Value** column for the **Structure** parameter to display the **Edit Assembly** dialog box, refer to Figure 15-27.

   The finishes and structure of the selected wall type are displayed in the **Layers** area and are arranged with the exterior finish as the first and the interior finish as the last layer, refer to Figure 15-27. As the material properties of the interior finish need to be modified, you will modify the last layer (**Finish 2 [5]**).

4. Click in the **Material** column for the **Finish 2 [5]** layer and choose the browse button; the **Material Browser** dialog box along with the **Material Editor** pane is displayed.

5. In the **Material Browser** dialog box, ensure that the **Gypsum Wall Board** option is selected in the **Project Materials: All** area and its parameters are displayed in the **Material Editor** pane.

6. Choose the **Appearance** tab; the preview of the selected material and its properties are displayed. Now, choose the **Replaces this asset** button from this tab; the **Asset Browser** dialog box is displayed, as shown in Figure 15-28.

7. In the **Asset Browser** dialog box, choose **Favorite > Appearance Library > Wall Paint > Matte > Biege** option from **Appearance Library**; a double arrow button is displayed.

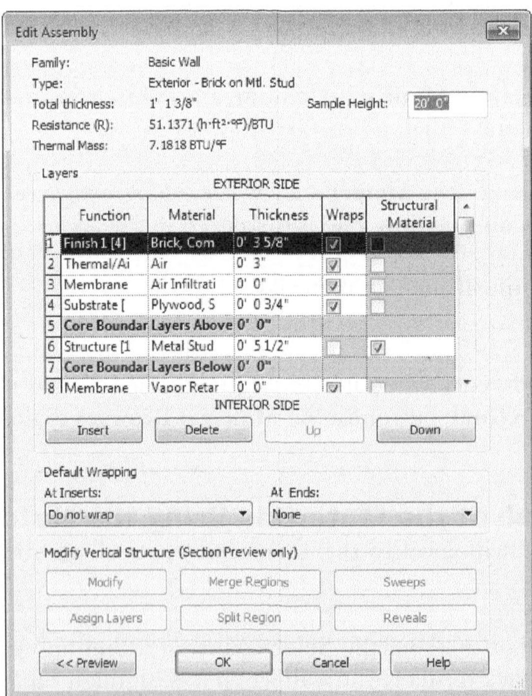

*Figure 15-27 The **Edit Assembly** dialog box for the exterior wall type*

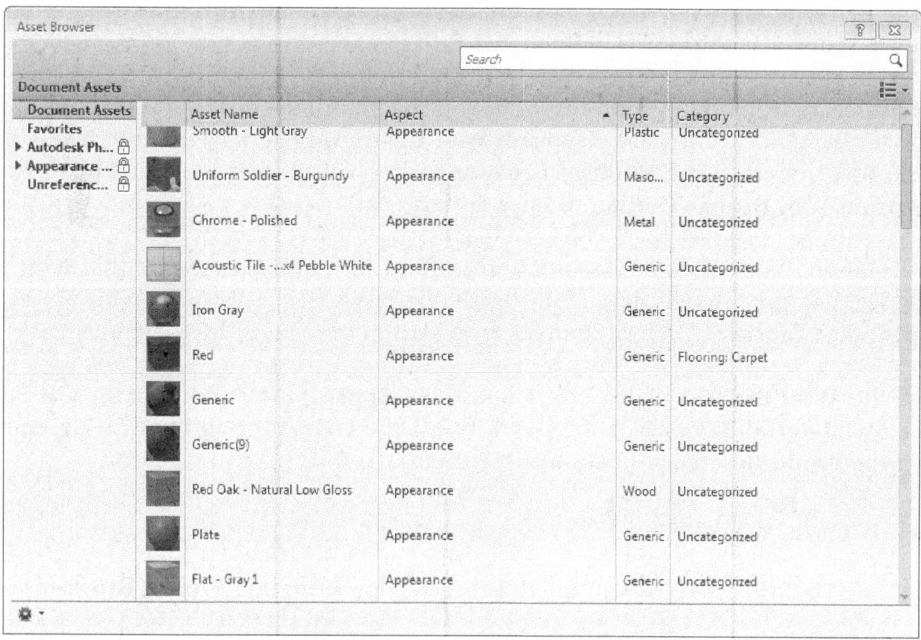

*Figure 15-28 The **Asset Browser** dialog box*

8. Choose the **Replaces the current asset in the editor with this asset** button to replace the current asset from the selected option. Close the **Asset Browser** dialog box and then choose the **OK** button in the **Material Browser** dialog box; the **Material Browser** dialog box along with the **Material Editor** pane is closed.

9. Close all the dialog boxes and return to the drawing window. Now, press ESC to exit the selection.

   Next, modify the appearance of the ceiling material.

10. Open the first floor ceiling plan and select it; the **Modify | Multi-Select** tab is displayed. Choose the **Filter** tool from the **Selection** panel of this contextual tab; the **Filter** dialog box is displayed. By default, all the check boxes are selected. Clear all the check boxes except the check box corresponding to the **Ceilings** parameter.

11. Choose the **OK** button; the **Filter** dialog box is closed; the **Modify | Ceiling** contextual tab is displayed.

12. Now, choose the **Type Properties** tool from the **Properties** panel of the **Modify | Ceilings** tab; the **Type Properties** dialog box is displayed.

13. Choose the **Edit** button in the **Value** field of the **Structure** parameter; the **Edit Assembly** dialog box is displayed with different layers of the selected ceiling.

14. Next, click in the **Material** column for the **Finish 2 [5]** layer and then choose the browse button to display the **Material Browser** dialog box.

15. In the **Material Browser** dialog box, the **Gypsum Wall Board** option is selected in the **Project Materials: All** area. The **Material Editor** pane displays the properties of material. Choose the **Duplicate Selected Material** option from the **Creates and duplicates material** drop-down list located at the lower left corner of the **Material Browser** dialog box; the name **Gypsum Wall Board(1)** is displayed in the **Name** edit box of the **Identity** tab in the **Material Browser** dialog box. Enter the name **Finish - Interior - Gypsum Wall Board - Ceiling** in this edit box.

16. Now, choose the **Replaces this asset** button from the **Appearance** tab; the **Asset Browser** dialog box is displayed. In this dialog box, choose **Paint > White** from **Appearance Library**. Click on double-arrow button to replace the current asset.

17. Close the **Asset Browser** dialog box. Choose the **Apply** button and then the **OK** button to close the **Material Browser** dialog box. Choose the **OK** button in the **Edit Assembly** and the **Type Properties** dialog boxes to close them.

    Next, you will modify the texture of the chair textile.

18. Open the first floor plan view in the drawing window using the **Project Browser**.

19. Select the **Chair-Corbu** in the living room and then choose the **Edit Type** button from the **Properties** palette; the **Type Properties** dialog box is displayed.

20. In this dialog box, click in the **Value** column for the **Cushion Material** type parameter and choose the browse button; the **Material Browser** dialog box is displayed.

21. In the **Material Browser** dialog box, choose the **Duplicate Selected Material** option from the **Creates and Duplicates Material** drop-down at the lower left corner of the **Material Browser** dialog box. Enter the name **Textile - Brown Leather** in the **Name** edit box and press ENTER.

22. Choose the **Replaces this asset** button from the **Appearance** tab in the **Material Editor** pane; the **Asset Browser** dialog box is displayed. In the **Asset Browser** dialog box, choose **Fabric > Leather** option from the **Appearance Library**.

23. Next, select the **Brown** material in the right pane of the **Appearance Library** area and click on the double arrow button to replace the current asset.

24. Now, close the **Asset Browser** dialog box and choose the **Graphics** tab from the **Materials Browser** dialog box; the **Graphic Properties** will be displayed in the **Material Editor** pane. Select the **Use Render Appearance** check box in the **Shading** area and then choose the **OK** button in the **Material Browser** and the **Type Properties** dialog boxes to close them. Now, press ESC to exit the selection of the chair. The **Leather** material is assigned to the cushion.

Loading and Adding Light Fixtures to the Building Model

In this section of the tutorial, you will load the light fixtures and then add them to the floor and ceiling plan.

1. Choose the **Place a Component** tool from **Architecture > Build > Component** drop-down; the **Modify | Place Component** tab is displayed.

2. Now, choose the **Load Family** tool from the **Mode** panel; the **Load Family** dialog box is displayed.

3. Navigate through the **US Imperial > Lighting > Architectural > Internal** folder and load the **Table Lamp - Standard** and **Pendant Light - Disk** fixtures using the CTRL key. Choose the **Open** button to return to the drawing area.

4. From the **Type Selector** drop-down list, select the **Table Lamp-Standard : 60W - 120V** fixture.

5. Move the cursor near the center of the side table placed at the lower right of the living room and click when the **Midpoint and Midpoint** object snap is displayed, as shown in Figure 15-29. Now, choose the **Modify** button to exit the selection mode.

6. Next, select the added table lamp; instance parameters for the component are displayed in the **Properties** palette.

7. Enter the value **1'3"** in the value column for the **Offset** instance parameter and then choose the **Apply** button.

8. Use the **Copy** tool in the **Modify** panel to copy the added lamp to the other three side tables, as shown in Figure 15-30 (Select the **Multiple** check box in the **Options Bar**). Now, press ESC twice to exit the current selection.

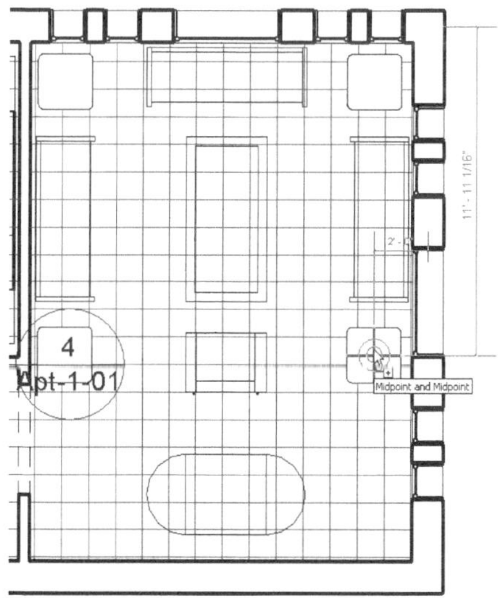

Figure 15-29 *Adding lamp to the side table*

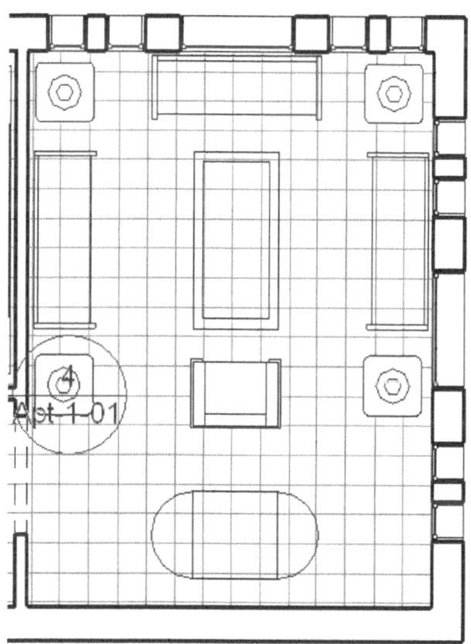

Figure 15-30 *Creating multiple copies of the table lamp component*

9. Double-click on **First Floor** under the **Ceiling Plans** head in the **Project Browser** to display the ceiling plan view.

10. Next, choose the **Place a Component** tool from the **Architecture > Build > Component** drop-down; the **Modify | Place Component** tab is displayed. Select the **Pendant Light - Disk: 100W - 120V** fixture from the **Type Selector** drop-down list.

11. Move the cursor over the sitting area in the living room and click to add the light fixture at the approximate location, as shown in Figure 15-31.

12. Similarly, add the same fixture to the other side of the living room, as shown in Figure 15-32 and then press ESC twice to exit the **Modify | Place Component** tab.

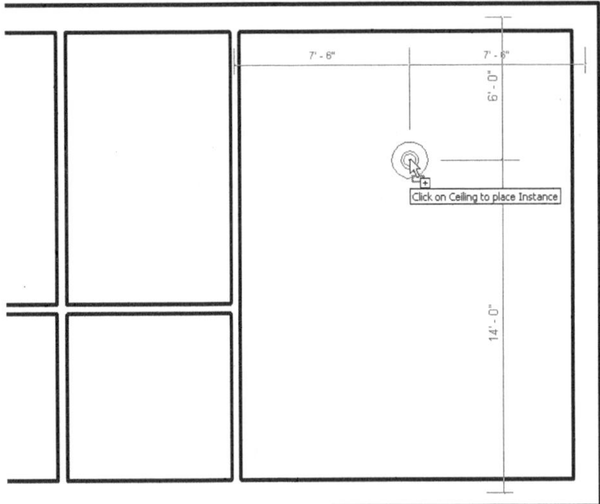

Figure 15-31 Adding the first light fixture in the ceiling plan

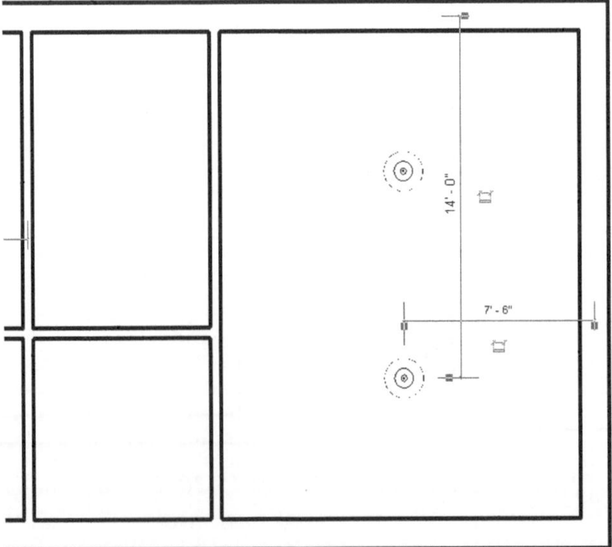

Figure 15-32 Adding the second light fixture in the ceiling plan

Adding RPC to the Interior Scene

In this section of the tutorial, you will use the **Place a Component** tool to load and add the specified RPC to the interior scene. The specified RPC (Rich Photorealistic Content) can be added at the location shown in Figure 15-33.

1. Open the first floor plan view from the **Floor Plans** heading in the drawing window using the **Project Browser**.

2. Now, choose the **Place a Component** tool from the **Architecture > Build > Component** drop-down; the **Modify | Place Component** tab is displayed.

3. Choose the **Load Family** tool from the **Mode** panel; the **Load Family** dialog box is displayed.

4. Navigate through the **US Imperial > Entourage** folder, select the **RPC Female** family file and then choose **Open**; the selected family file is now loaded.

5. Next, select the **RPC Female : Cynthia** option from the **Type Selector** drop-down list.

6. Now, select the **Rotate after placement** check box from the **Options Bar** and then click on the sofa and move the cursor counterclockwise. Next, click to place and align the RPC in the view, as shown in Figure 15-33.

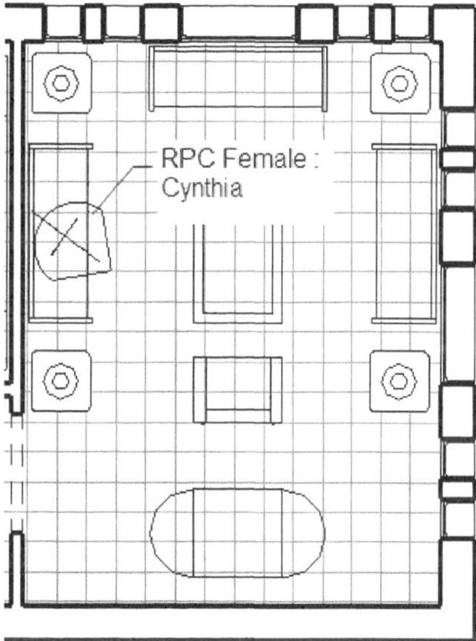

Figure 15-33 *RPC added to the view*

7. Press the ESC key twice to exit the insertion process. Double-click on **Living Area** under the **3D Views** head in the **Project Browser** to view the 3D view after adding the lighting fixtures and RPC, refer to Figure 15-34.

8. Choose **Visual Style > Shaded** from **View Control Bar**; the current view will be shaded.

Note

*You can set the position of the RPCs by selecting the required elevation or section views from the **Project Browser**.*

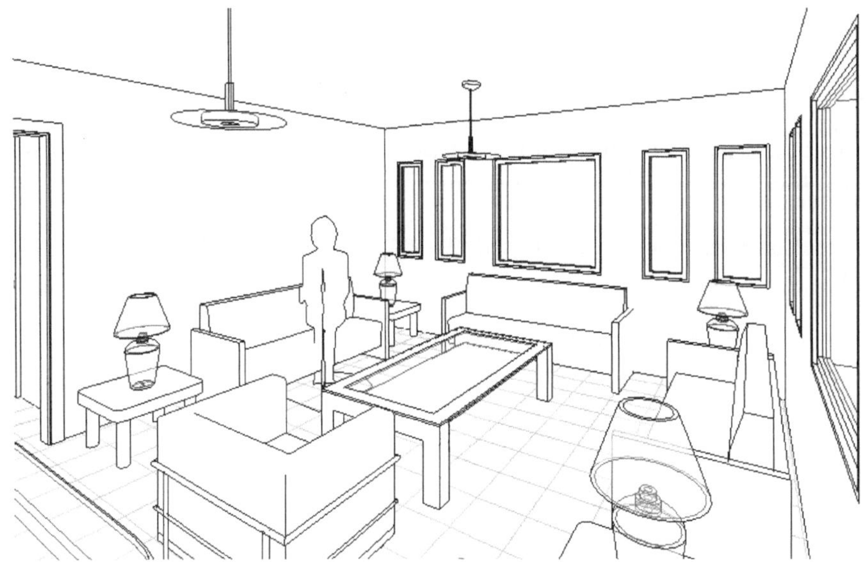

Figure 15-34 *The interior 3D view of the living room with the added lighting fixtures and RPC*

Setting Up the Interior Rendering Scene

In this section of the tutorial, you will invoke the **Rendering** dialog box and specify the settings to render the interior scene.

1. Invoke the **Rendering** dialog box by choosing the **Show Rendering Dialog** button from **View Control Bar**. Alternatively, you can press RR to display the **Rendering** dialog box.

2. In the **Engine** area, ensure that the **Autodesk Raytrace** option is selected in the **Option** drop-down list. In the **Quality** area of the **Rendering** dialog box, select the **Best** option from the **Setting** drop-down list.

3. In the **Lighting** area, select the **Interior : Sun and Artificial** option from the **Scheme** drop-down list.

4. Choose the Browse button displayed next to the **Sun Setting** text box; the **Sun Settings** dialog box is displayed.

5. Select the **Still** radio button in the **Solar Study** area.

6. Choose the button next to the **Location** parameter in the **Settings** area to invoke the **Location Weather and Site** dialog box.

7. In the **Location** tab, select the **Default City List** option from the **Define Location by** drop-down list. Select **Chicago, IL** from the **City** drop-down list and choose the **OK** button.

8. Set the date **14/06/2018** in the **Date** drop-down list and then set the time to **10:00 PM** in the **Time** spinner.

Note

*After specifying settings in the **Sun Settings** dialog box; the **Autodesk Revit 2018** message box is displayed. Choose the **Disable Updater** and then choose the **OK** button; the dialog box is closed and you can make further settings.*

9. Clear the **Ground Plane at Level** check box, if selected.

10. Choose **Apply** and **OK**; the specified settings are applied to the scene and the **Sun Settings** dialog box is closed.

11. Next, in the **Image** area of the **Rendering** dialog box, choose the **Adjust Exposure** button to invoke the **Exposure Control** dialog box.

12. In the **Exposure Control** dialog box, set the values of the parameters as given below:

Exposure Value: **6.5**	Highlights: **0.45**
Mid Tones: **1**	Shadows: **0.2**
White Point: **4000**	

13. Choose **Apply** and **OK**; the specified settings are applied to the scene and the **Exposure Control** dialog box is closed.

14. In the **Rendering** dialog box, choose the **Render** button; Autodesk Revit starts the rendering process using the mental ray rendering engine for the interior view. The **Rendering Progress** dialog box is displayed on your screen. On completion of the process, the rendered image is displayed in the drawing area, as shown in Figure 15-35.

15. After the rendering process is complete, choose the **Save to Project** button in the **Image** area; the **Save to Project** dialog box is displayed. Enter **Living Area** in the **Name** edit box and choose the **OK** button. This will add the rendered image under the **Renderings** head in the **Project Browser**. Now, close the **Rendering** dialog box.

    The rendered image can be downloaded from *http://www.cadcim.com*. The path of the file is as follows: *Textbooks > Civil/GIS > Revit Architecture > Exploring Autodesk Revit 2018 for Architecture*.

Note

*Depending on the hardware configuration of the system, it might take considerable time to render. To do a quick render, select **Draft** or **Low** from the **Setting** drop-down list in the **Rendering** dialog box.*

Figure 15-35 The interior 3D view of the living room rendered using mental ray

Generating the Walkthrough

In this section, you will specify the walkthrough path in the floor plan view.

1. Double-click on **First Floor** under the **Floor Plans** head in the **Project Browser**.

2. Choose the **Walkthrough** tool from the **View > Create > 3D View** drop-down; the **Modify | Walkthrough** tab is displayed. Note that the cursor changes into a **+** mark and different options related to creating a walkthrough path are displayed in the **Options Bar**.

3. Now, start sketching the walkthrough path by clicking at the first point near the center of the main entrance door of the apartment. Ensure that the first point is specified inside the lobby area and not outside the entrance door. Move the cursor toward the living room and click to specify multiple points in such a manner that they form a counterclockwise loop around the center table in the living room, as shown in Figure 15-36.

4. Similarly, move the cursor across the lobby and inside the bed room. Next, click to specify multiple points of the walkthrough path, refer to Figure 15-36. The exact location of these points is not critical.

5. After specifying the last point, choose the **Finish Walkthrough** button from the **Walkthrough** panel of the **Modify | Walkthrough** tab; walkthrough path is now completed and the **Modify | Cameras** tab is displayed.

Note

The dots indicate the specified points and are shown only for illustration. They are not displayed when the walkthrough path is being specified.

Note that the generated walkthrough is now added to the **Project Browser** as **Walkthrough 1** under the new **Walkthroughs** head. You can now modify the total frames for the walkthrough using the **Edit Walkthrough** button.

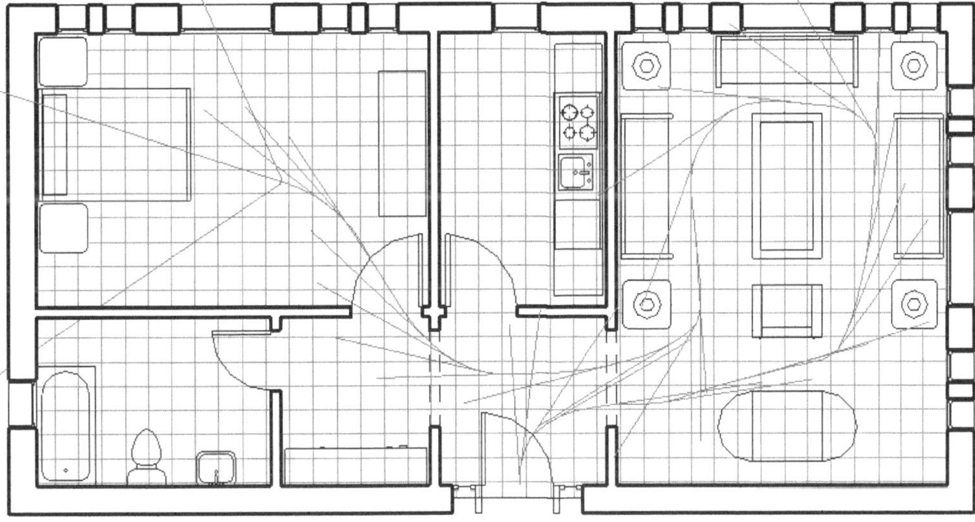

Figure 15-36 *Sketch plan showing the walkthrough path for the Apartment 1 project*

6. Double-click on **Walkthrough 1** under the **Walkthroughs** head in the **Project Browser**. Choose the **Edit Walkthrough** button from the **Walkthrough** panel of the **Modify | Cameras** tab; the **Edit Walkthrough** contextual tab is displayed.

7. Next, in the **Options Bar**, ensure that the **Active Camera** option is selected from the **Controls** drop-down list and **300** is displayed in the **Frame** edit box. Now, choose the **Frame Settings** button next to the **Frame** edit box; the **Walkthrough Frames** dialog box is displayed.

8. In the **Walkthrough Frames** dialog box, enter **200** as the value in the **Total Frames** edit box and choose the **OK** button; the specified settings are now assigned to the walkthrough and the **Walkthrough Frames** dialog box closes. Also the total number of frames in the walkthrough gets modified from **300** to **200** as specified for this tutorial.

Recording the Walkthrough

In this section of the tutorial, you will open the walkthrough, adjust the field of view of the camera and then record it by exporting it using the **AVI** file format.

1. In the **Options Bar**, enter **1** in the **Frame** edit box. Now, choose the **Edit Walkthrough** tab and then choose the **Open Walkthrough** button from the **Walkthrough** panel. The first frame is opened in the drawing window.

2. Right-click inside the drawing window and choose **Zoom Out (2x)** from the shortcut menu displayed.

3. Drag the extents of the rectangle to modify the field of view for the camera such that the view resembles the illustration given in Figure 15-37.

4. Right-click again and choose **Zoom To Fit** to enlarge the view.

5. Next, you will export the walkthrough as an AVI file.

   From the **File** menu, choose **Export > Images and Animations > Walkthrough**; the **Length Format** dialog box is displayed, as shown in Figure 15-38.

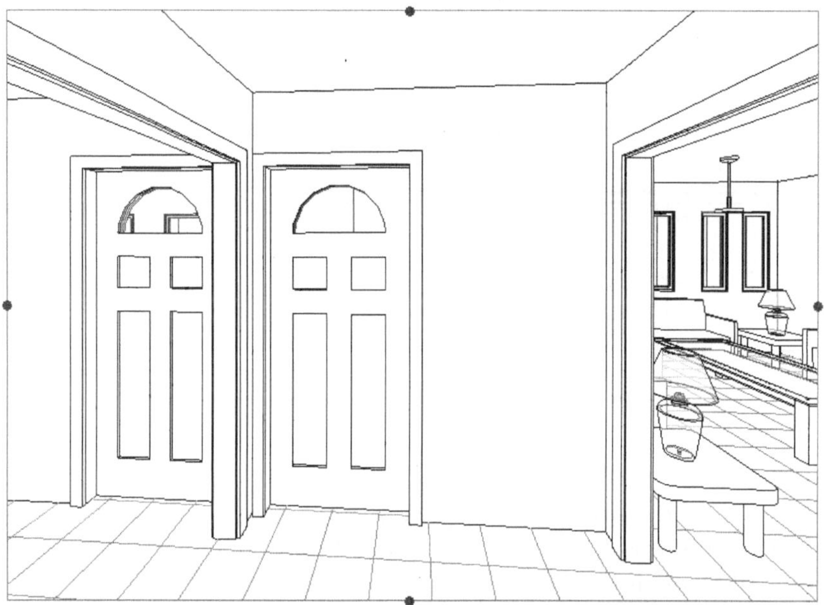

Figure 15-37 *First frame of the walkthrough with the modified field of view*

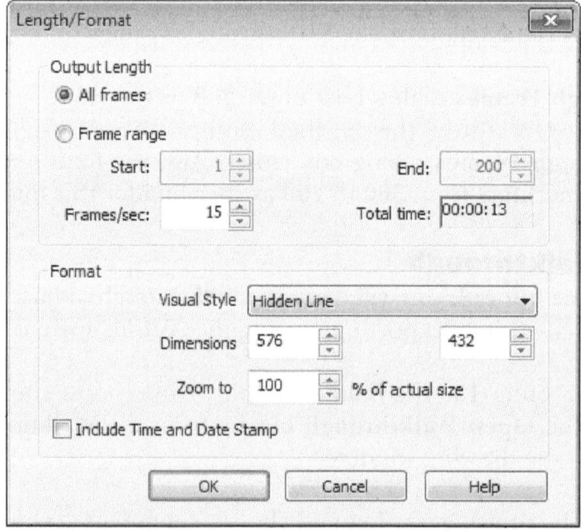

Figure 15-38 *The **Length/Format** dialog box*

6. In the **Length/Format** dialog box, ensure that the **All frames** radio button is selected and then set **10** in the **Frames/sec** spinner.

7. In the **Format** area, select **Rendering** from the **Visual Style** drop-down list.

8. Next, set the value in the **Zoom to** spinner to **43** and choose the **OK** button; the **Length/Format** dialog box closes and the **Export Walkthrough** dialog box is displayed.

9. In the **Export Walkthrough** dialog box, specify an appropriate path, enter **c15_Apartment1_tut1_Walkthrough 1** in the **File name** edit box, and then make sure that **AVI Files** is the default file format selected in the **Files of type** drop-down list. Now, choose the **Save** button; the rendering and recording process starts. After rendering of the first frame, the **Video Compression** dialog box gets displayed. Keep the **Full Frames (Uncompressed)** option selected in the **Compressor** drop-down list and choose the **OK** button to continue.

   Now, the rendering and recording process starts for each frame of the walkthrough and the **Rendering Progress** dialog box is displayed. When the procedure is completed, the file is recorded at the specified location. You can then use any media player to view the walkthrough file.

Saving the Project

In this section, you will save the project file using the **Save As** tool.

1. Choose **Save As > Project** from the **File** menu; the **Save As** dialog box is displayed.

2. Enter **c15_Apartment1_tut1** in the **File name** edit box and then choose **Save**.

3. Choose **Close** from the **File** menu to close the project file.

Tutorial 2 Office Building 2

Render the exterior view of the *Office Building 2* project using the file created in Exercise 3 of Chapter 14. Replace the existing finishes of materials assigned to the exterior walls with the new materials/textures, add trees, and add entourages to the project based on the first floor plan view, as shown in Figure 15-39. Render the 3D view 1 based on the rendered view shown in Figure 15-40. **(Expected time: 30 min)**

The rendered image can be downloaded from *http://www.cadcim.com*. The path of the file is as follows: *Textbooks > Civil/GIS > Revit Architecture > Exploring Autodesk Revit 2018 for Architecture*

1. New material for the exterior wall finish: **Finishes - Exterior- Cladding**
2. New material for toposurface: **Site - Grass**
3. Trees to be loaded and used from **US Imperial\Planting\RPC Tree - Deciduous**

The following steps are required to complete this tutorial:

a. Open the specified project file and the first floor plan view.
b. Apply materials to the exterior walls using the **Paint** tool.

c. Add a toposurface to the building model and assign material to it.
d. Add trees to the exterior view.
e. Add entourages to the building model.
f. Set up the rendering scene and render.
g. Save the project using the **Save As** tool.
   For Imperial *c15_Office-2_tut2.rvt*
   For Metric *M_c15_Office-2_tut2.rvt*
h. Close the project.

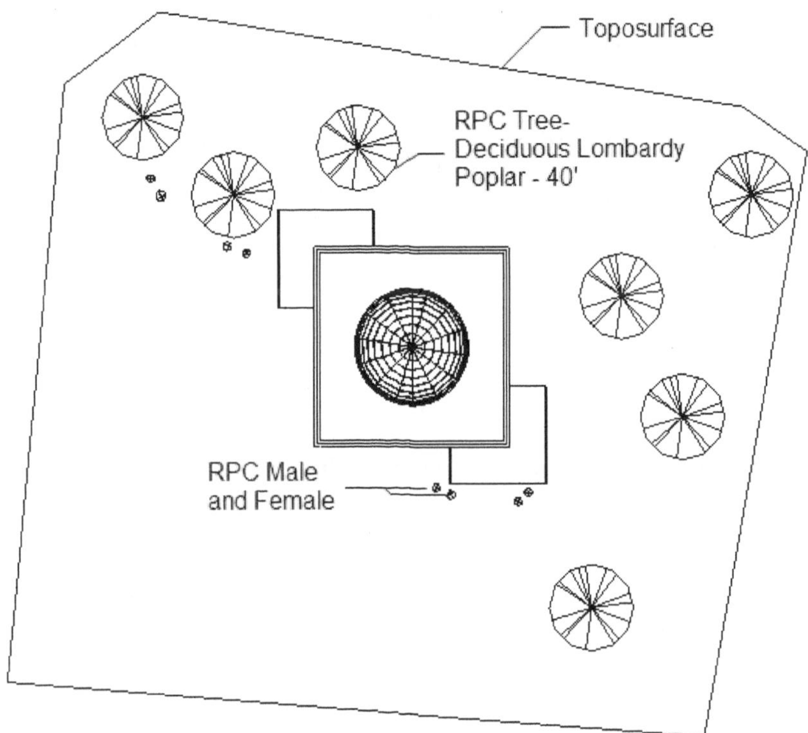

Figure 15-39 *Sketch plan for adding toposurface, trees, and entourages to the Office Building 2*

Figure 15-40 Rendered exterior view for Office Building 2 project

Opening the Project File and the First Floor Plan View

1. To open the specified file

   Choose **Open > Project** from the **File** menu and then open the *c14_Office-2_ex3.rvt* file created in Exercise 3 of Chapter14. You can also download this file from *http://www.cadcim.com*. The path of the file is as follows: *Textbooks > Civil/GIS > Revit Architecture > Exploring Autodesk Revit 2018 for Architecture*

2. Double-click on **First Floor** in the **Floor Plans** head of the **Project Browser** to open the corresponding floor plan in the drawing window.

Modifying the Finishes of the Exterior Wall Using the Paint Tool

In this section of the tutorial, you will first create a new material and then use the **Paint** tool to apply it over the exterior walls.

1. Choose the **Materials** tool from the **Settings** panel of the **Manage** tab; the **Material Browser** dialog box is displayed.

2. In the **Material Browser** dialog box, double-click on the **Metal Deck** from the **Project Materials: All** area; the **Material Editor** pane displays properties of **Metal Deck**. In this dialog box, choose the **Duplicate Selected Material** tool from the **Creates and duplicates a Material** drop-down; a duplicate material name will be displayed in the edit box.

3. In the edit box, enter **Finishes-Exterior-Cladding** and choose the **Appearance** tab in the **Editor** pane. Choose the **Replaces this asset** button; the **Asset Browser** dialog box is displayed.

4. Click on the **Appearance Library** in the **Assets Browser** dialog box and select the **Masonry/ Brick** option from the expanded list.

5. Next, choose the **Non-Uniform Running-Red** material from the material list in the right pane of the **Asset Browser** dialog box and click on the double arrow button to assign the material.

6. Now, close the **Asset Browser** dialog box and you can see the updated preview in the material preview box.

7. Next, choose the **Graphics** tab then select the **Use Render Appearance** check box in the **Shading Area**. Choose the **Apply** and **OK** buttons; the **Material Browser** dialog box is closed.

   You can now use the **Paint** tool to apply the created texture to the exterior walls.

8. Use the **Zoom in Region** tool from the **Navigation Bar** to enlarge the main building in the first floor plan.

9. Now, choose the **Paint** tool from the **Modify > Geometry > Paint** drop-down; the **Modify | Paint** tab and the **Materials Browser** dialog box are displayed.
10. From this dialog box, select the **Finishes - Exterior-Cladding** material.

11. In the drawing area, move the cursor over the exterior face of the wall of the center building; the face gets highlighted. Next, click on the highlighted exterior face; the selected material gets applied to it.

12. Apply the selected texture to the exterior faces of the other exterior walls that are visible in the plan view and then choose the **Done** button in the **Materials Browser** dialog box to close it.

    You can open the 3D view and then choose **Visual Style > Shaded** from the **View Control Bar**, if it is not selected, to display the shaded view of the modified exterior finish. Then, return to the plan view.

Creating a Toposurface and Adding Material to It

In this section of the tutorial, you will create a toposurface to add a base to the building and then add a material to it.

1. Double-click on **Site** in the **Floor Plans** head of the **Project Browser** to open the site plan. Now, hide the elevation symbol by using the **Visibility/Graphics** tool from the **View** tab.

2. Next, choose the **Massing & Site** tab and then choose the **Toposurface** tool from the **Model Site** panel.

3. Now, add points to the drawing area to create the toposurface, refer to Figure 15-39.

Note

The size of the toposurface can vary and is based on the extent of its visibility in the 3D view.

4. Next, choose the **Finish Surface** button from the **Surface** panel of the **Modify | Edit Surface** tab. Next, select the toposurface so that the instance parameters for the surface are displayed in the **Properties** palette.

5. Click on the value field of the **Material** parameter and then choose the browse button to display the **Materials Browser** dialog box.

6. In the dialog box, choose the **Earth** option from the **Project Material: All** list area.

7. Choose the **Duplicate Selected Material** option from the **Creates or duplicates material** drop-down at the lower left corner of the **Material Browser** dialog box; the name **Earth(1)** is displayed in the list under the **Project Material: All** area. Enter the name **Site - Grass** in the **Name** edit box of the **Identity** tab.

8. Choose the **Replaces this asset** button in the **Appearance** tab; the **Asset browser** dialog box is displayed. Now, expand the **Appearance Library** in the left pane of the **Asset Browser** dialog box and select **Sitework** > **Grass-Bermuda**. Next, click on the double arrow button to update the material.

9. Next, close the **Asset Browser** dialog box to return to the **Material Browser** dialog box. Choose the **Graphics** tab from this dialog box; the graphic properties of the material gets displayed. Select the **Use Render Appearance** check box in the **Shading** area and then choose the **Apply** and **OK** buttons in the **Material Browser** dialog box.

10. Now, press ESC to exit the selection.

    You will now use the **Site Component** tool to load and add the specified planting elements and people to the building model. The trees and people can be added to the location given in the sketch plan, refer to Figure 15-39.

11. Next, choose the **Site Component** tool from the **Model Site** panel of the **Massing & Site** tab; the **Modify | Site Component** tab is displayed.

12. Now, choose the **Load Family** tool from the **Mode** panel; the **Load Family** dialog box is displayed.

13. Navigate through the **US Imperial > Planting** folder and select **RPC Tree - Deciduous** and then choose the **Open** button; the selected family type is loaded.

14. Now, from the **Type Selector** drop-down list, select **RPC Tree - Deciduous : Lombardy Poplar - 40'**.

15. Move the cursor near the location shown in the sketch plan for this tutorial and click to add the planting element.

Similarly, click again at the diagonally opposite corners of the office building to add another instance of the planting element based on the given sketch plan. Further add more planting elements, refer to Figure 15-39.

16. Next, to add people to the building model, repeat steps 11 and 12 and invoke the **Load Family** dialog box.

17. Navigate through the **US Imperial > Entourage** folder and load the **RPC Male** and **RPC Female** families.

18. From the **Type Selector** drop-down list, select **RPC Male : Jay**, **RPC Male : Dwayne**, **RPC Male : LaRon**, **RPC Male : Alex**, **RPC Female : Cathy**, **RPC Female : YinYin**, **RPC Female : Tina**, and **RPC Female : Lisa** individually and then add them to the building model as per the site plan, refer to Figure 15-39.

Note

The locations of the RPCs are not fixed. You can change them according to the clarity of view and the requirement of the image.

Setting Up the Exterior Rendering Scene

You will now provide the information required to set up the rendering scene. To make the rendering tools available, open the 3D view of the project.

1. Open the **{3D}** view from the **3D Views** head in the **Project Browser**.

2. Choose the **Show Rendering Dialog** button from the **View Control Bar** to invoke the **Rendering** dialog box.

3. In the **Quality** area of the **Rendering** dialog box, select the **Best** option from the **Setting** drop-down list. Select the **Screen** radio button in the **Resolution** area, if it is not selected.

Note

*The rendering process may take considerable time if you select the **Best** option from the **Settings** drop-down list. To render quickly, select the **Low** or **Draft** option from the **Settings** drop-down list in the **Rendering** dialog box.*

4. Select the **Exterior: Sun only** option from the **Scheme** drop-down list in the **Lighting** area.

5. Next, in this area, choose the Browse button from the **Sun Setting** drop-down list to display the **Sun Settings** dialog box.

Note

*After specifying the settings in the **Sun Settings** dialog box; the **Autodesk Revit 2018** message box is displayed. Choose the **Disable Updater** option and then choose the **OK** button; the dialog box is closed and make other other settings.*

6. In the **Solar Study** area of the **Sun Settings** dialog box, ensure that the **Lighting** radio button is selected.

7. Ensure that **135.00°** is displayed in the **Azimuth** edit box. Next, enter **60.00°** in the **Altitude** edit box and then choose the **OK** button; the **Rendering** dialog box is displayed.

8. In the **Background** area, select the **Sky: Few Clouds** option from the **Style** drop-down list.

Rendering the Exterior View

In this section of the tutorial, you will render the exterior view using the mental ray rendering engine.

1. In the **Rendering** dialog box, choose the **Render** button to start the rendering process.

2. When you finish the rendering process, choose the **Adjust Exposure** button in the **Image** area to invoke the **Exposure Control** dialog box.

3. Enter **13.5** in the **Exposure Value** edit box and **0.3** in the **Shadows** edit box.

4. Choose the **OK** button to return to the **Rendering** dialog box.

5. Choose the **Save to Project** button in the **Image** area; the **Save to Project** dialog box is displayed.

6. Enter the name of the rendered view as **Exterior View 1** in the **Name** edit box and choose the **OK** button to return to the **Rendering** dialog box. Next, close the **Rendering** dialog box. Now, expand the **Renderings** head in the **Project Browser** and double-click on the **Exterior View 1**; the rendered view is displayed in the drawing area.

7. After viewing the rendered image, double-click on **First Floor** under the **Floor Plans** head in the **Project Browser**.

Saving the Project

In this section, you will save the project file using the **Save As** tool.

1. Choose **Save As > Project** from the **File** menu; the **Save As** dialog box is displayed. Enter **c15_Office-2_tut2** in the **File name** edit box and then choose **Save**; the project file is saved.

2. Choose **Close** from the **File** menu; the project file closes.

Self-Evaluation Test

Answer the following questions and then compare them to those given at the end of this chapter:

1. The __________ attribute controls the brightness of the decal.

2. The __________ area of the **Identity** tab is used to specify the manufacturer, model, cost, and URL of the material selected.

3. The __________ tool is used to render only a portion of the 3D view.

4. In a project the people, plants, vehicles, and office clutters are a part of __________ product family.

5. The _________ check box in the **Sun Settings** dialog box controls the visibility of shadows on the toposurface.

6. By choosing the __________ option, you can add keyframes to the path created.

7. In Autodesk Revit, mental ray is used as the rendering engine. (T/F)

8. In the **Graphics** tab, you can assign different colors to the material for its shaded view. (T/F)

9. You cannot modify the predefined materials in the **Autodesk Library**. (T/F)

10. While generating a walkthrough, the height of the camera cannot be modified. (T/F)

Review Questions

Answer the following questions:

1. Which of the following parameters controls the light output of a lighting fixture?

   (a) **Lumen** (b) **Wattage**
   (c) **Light fixture height** (d) **Assembly Code**

2. Which of the following dialog boxes is used to control the Daylight Portals?

   (a) **Render Quality Settings** (b) **Image Quality Settings**
   (c) **Sun Settings** (d) **Manage Place and Locations**

3. Which of the following parameters affects the speed of a walkthrough?

   (a) **Offset** (b) **Indicators**
   (c) **Frames per second** (d) **Total Time**

4. The mental ray rendering is used for quality rendering. (T/F)

5. Each Autodesk Revit building element has a predefined material associated with it. (T/F)

6. The **Decal** tool is used to add 3D text to a plane. (T/F)

7. While generating a walkthrough, Autodesk Revit automatically generates intermediate frames between the specified keyframes. (T/F)

8. You can vary the speed of the camera while creating a walkthrough. (T/F)

9. You can create a new material using the **Material Browser** dialog box. (T/F)

10. The options in the **Style** drop-down list help you to set the background of the rendered image. (T/F)

EXERCISES

Exercise 1 Club

Using the *c14_Club_tut2.rvt* project file created in Tutorial 2 of Chapter 14, render the entrance view, as shown in Figure 15-41. Assume all the information required for this exercise.
Save the file as *c15_Club_ex1.rvt* **(Expected time: 30 min)**

Figure 15-41 *Rendered exterior view of the Club project*

Exercise 2 Apartment 1 - Night View

Using the project file created in Tutorial 1 of this chapter, render the night scene of the living room, as shown in Figure 15-42. You need to modify the time settings to 6:00 A.M.
Save the file as *c15_Apartment-1_ex2.rvt.* **(Expected time: 30 min)**

The rendered image can be downloaded from *http://www.cadcim.com*. The path of the file is as follows: *Textbooks > Civil/GIS > Revit Architecture > Exploring Autodesk Revit 2018 for Architecture*

Figure 15-42 *Rendered interior view of the living room*

Exercise 3 Hotel Building - Walkthrough

Download *c15-revit-2018-ex03.rvt* file from the *CADCIM* website and create a walkthrough of a hotel building project, refer to Figures 15-43 through 15-45. The walkthrough of 1000 frames will be created with 1000 frames and at a frame rate of 15 frames per second. Use the camera at an eye level and move it along the path, as shown in Figure 15-43. Save the file as *c15_Hotel_ex3.rvt.* **(Expected time: 25 min)**

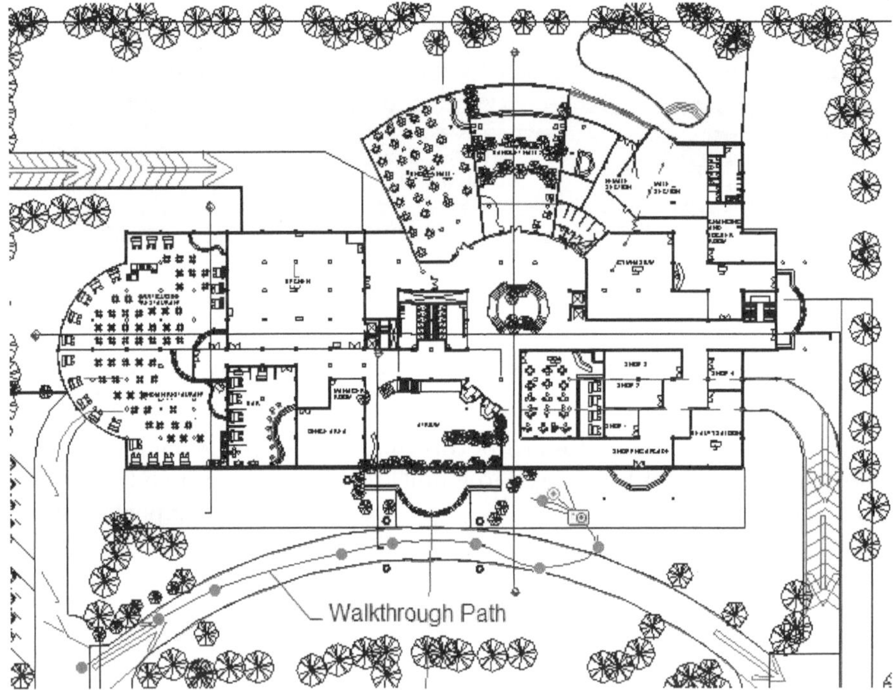

Figure 15-43 The walkthrough path

Figure 15-44 *The walkthrough view at Frame 100*

Figure 15-45 *The walkthrough view at Frame 500*

Answers to Self-Evaluation Test

1. Intensity, **2.** Product Information, **3.** Region, **4.** RPC, **5.** Ground Plane at Level, **6.** Add Key Frames, **7.** T, **8.** T, **9.** F, **10.** F

Chapter 16

Using Advanced Features

Learning Objectives

After completing this chapter, you will be able to:

- *Add structural components to a project*
- *Create multiple design options*
- *Create area schemes and area plans*
- *Create color schemes*
- *Use project phasing tools*
- *Link building models and share coordinates*
- *Share projects using worksets*
- *Purge unused elements from the project file*
- *Organize the Project Browser*
- *Generate solar studies*
- *Understand Point Cloud*
- *Publish views to DWF*

INTRODUCTION

This chapter describes the advanced features of Revit such as adding structural components, creating design options using the phasing tools, and worksharing methodology. With the help of these advanced features, you can easily add structural components to a building model using various tools and in-built components. You can also create various design options based on the project requirement, and also use the area analysis tools to analyze and generate area plans for the building model.

In this chapter, you will learn to represent the phase-wise development of a project, link independently developed projects to each other, and share their coordinates using the project sharing and linking tools. Also, the concept of worksets, which enables multiple users to work on a single project and interoperability of Revit Architecture with other programs such as Autodesk 3ds Max and Autodesk 3ds Max Design, has been discussed in the chapter.

CREATING STRUCTURAL COMPONENTS

Structural components describe the structural system of a building project. The use of some of these elements, such as walls, floors, roof, stairs, and so on has been discussed in the earlier chapters. The structural components may or may not comprise the basic structural support system of a building project. For example, in a multistory building project, steel framing components can form the basic support system and the walls can be non-load bearing. Therefore, it may be necessary to specify and differentiate between the structural and architectural components for some projects.

You can add structural components before or after creating the building model. For example, you can first generate an architectural building model for a multistory building and then add structural components to it, or you can generate the building model over a framework of structural components. The structural property of a wall is represented by its **Structural Usage** instance parameter, and the wall function is represented by its **Wall Function** type parameter. For instance, by default, the **Basic Wall: Generic- 8" Masonry** wall has the value **Non-bearing** for the **Structural Usage** instance parameter. For load bearing structures, you can convert this non-bearing wall into a bearing wall by changing its **Structural Usage** instance parameter to any of the following parameters: **Bearing**, **Shear**, or **Structural combined**.

The structural components that can be created in a Revit building model are broadly classified into the following three categories:

Structural Walls	Walls used for foundation, retaining, or as shear walls
Structural Columns	Structural components for vertical support
Structural Beams and Braces	Components providing connecting ties
Structural Foundations	Components providing support to the superstructure of the building

Figure 16-1 shows the structural components for a project.

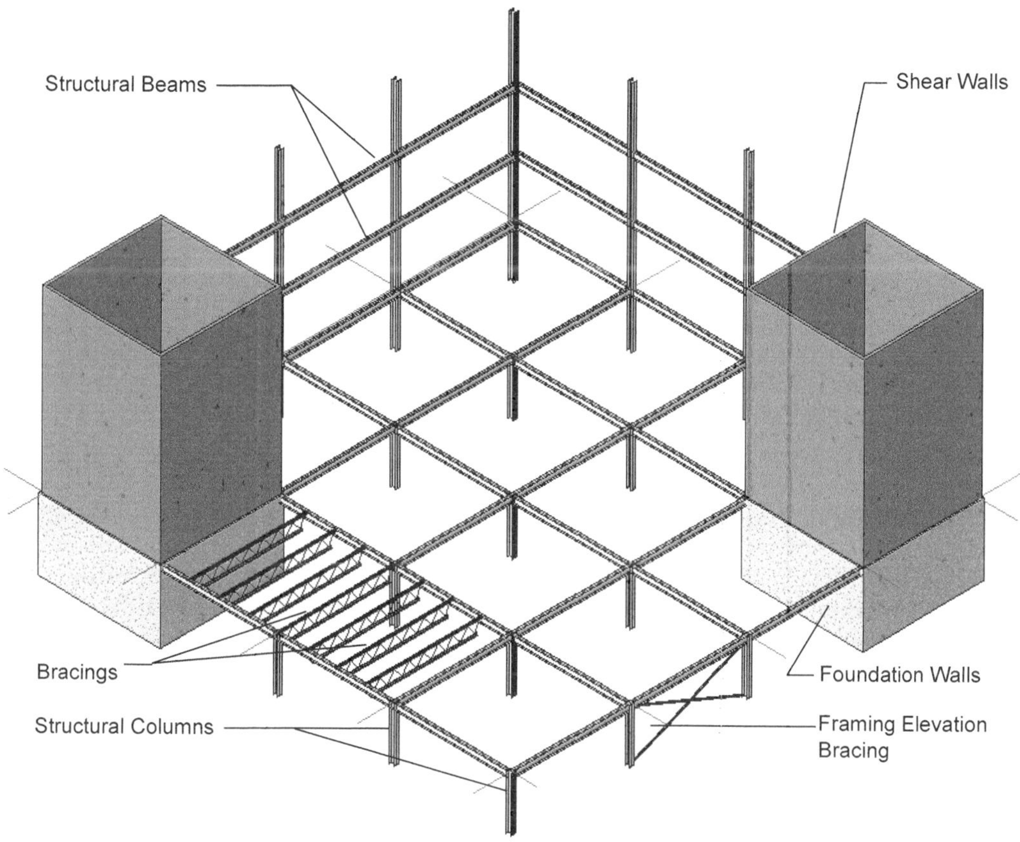

Figure 16-1 The structural elements for a project

Creating Structural Walls

There are four types of functions that can be assigned to a parametric wall. The functions that can be assigned to the wall are interior, exterior, retaining, and foundation. The interior or exterior wall functions have been described in the earlier chapters. A structural wall differs from a non-structural wall only in its structural usage. The four structural usage options are:

Non-bearing Walls supporting only their own weight or are used to divide spaces
Bearing Walls supporting a vertical load in addition to their own weight
Shear Walls supporting a lateral thrust of shear
Structural combined Walls serving more than one purpose

Tip

*While using structural elements, you can choose the **Structural Settings** button (represented by an inclined arrow) from the **Structure** panel of the **Structure** tab; the **Structural Settings** dialog box will be displayed. In this dialog box, you can set the parameters to control the representation of structural elements in a project file. You can also use the Structural-Default.rte template file that contains the view properties and range settings specifically for working with the structural elements.*

Sketching Retaining Walls

To sketch a retaining wall, invoke the **Wall: Structural** tool from **Structure > Structure > Wall** drop-down; the **Modify | Place Structural Wall** tab will be displayed. In the **Properties** palette, select the **Basic Wall: Retaining -12" Concrete** option (for Metric **Basic Wall: Retaining -300mm Concrete**) from the **Type Selector** drop-down list. After selecting the retaining wall option from the **Type Selector** drop-down list, you can sketch a retaining wall in the plan or 3D view. You can also convert a sketched interior, exterior, or foundation wall into a retaining wall. To do so, select the wall and choose the **Edit Type** button in the **Properties** palette; the **Type Properties** dialog box will be displayed. The **Function** type parameter in the **Type Properties** dialog box describes the current function of the wall. Click in the **Value** column of the **Wall Function** type parameter and select the **Retaining** option from the drop-down list. Then choose **Apply** and **OK** buttons, the structural wall is modified to the retaining wall.

Note

When you use a retaining wall or modify the function of a wall to make it a retaining wall, it is automatically set to non-room bounding.

Sketching Foundation Walls

Foundation walls can be sketched by choosing the **Wall : Structural** tool and then selecting the foundation wall type from the **Type Selector** drop-down list. By default, the **Basic Wall: Foundation - 12" Concrete** option is selected from the drop-down list. The foundation wall can be sketched in the plan or 3D view. Note that if the foundation walls are sketched in the plan view, a warning that the foundation walls are not visible in the view in which they were sketched. This warning is displayed because the foundation walls, unlike any other non-structural wall, are created with the current level as the top constraint. This means that they are sketched downward and are not visible in the current level. To view the sketched foundation walls, change the **View Range** instance property of the current view. To do so, click on the view name in the **Project Browser**; the instance properties of the selected view will be displayed in the **Properties** palette. In the **Properties** palette, choose the **Edit** button in the **Value** column of the **View Range** instance parameter; the **View Range** dialog box will be displayed. In the **Primary Range** section of the **View Range** dialog box, change the **Bottom** and **View Depth** parameters to **Level Below** to enable the visibility of the foundation walls in the current view.

Note

*The **Structural Usage** parameter for a sketched foundation wall is automatically set to **Bearing**.*

You can modify the instance and type properties of a foundation wall after you create it. To do so, select the foundation wall from the drawing; the instance properties will be displayed in the **Properties** palette, as shown in Figure 16-2. You can modify the height of the foundation wall by entering a value in the **Base Offset** parameter. The type properties of the foundation wall can be modified by using the **Edit Type** button in the **Properties** palette.

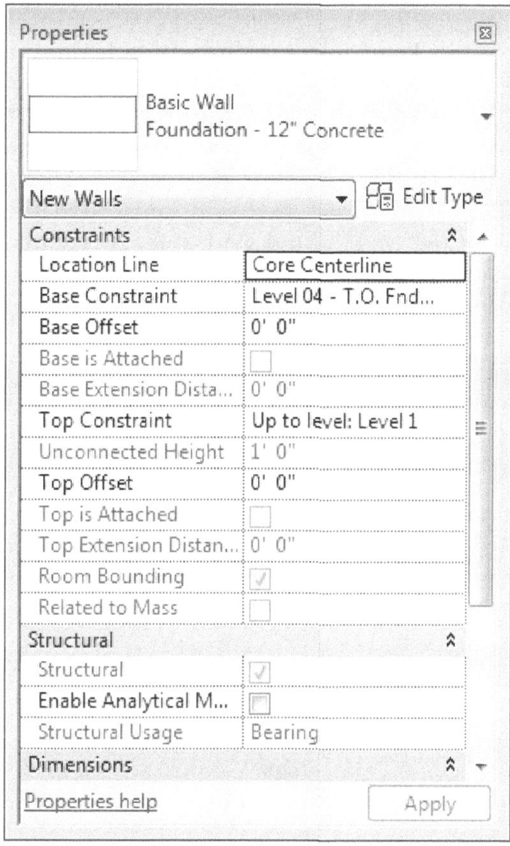

Figure 16-2 The instance properties of a typical foundation wall

Creating Structural Columns

Structural columns can be placed in the plan or 3D view. You can place a single structural column or multiple structural columns by selecting the grid intersection. To add a structural column, invoke the **Column** tool from the **Structure** panel of the **Structure** tab; the **Modify | Place Structural Column** tab will be displayed, as shown in Figure 16-3. In this tab, you can choose the **Load Family** button from the **Mode** panel and then load the additional structural columns from the **Structural Columns** folder in the **US Imperial** folder. Based on the material specification, four subfolders **Concrete**, **Precast Concrete**, **Steel**, and **Wood** have been provided to load the structural columns from the column families.

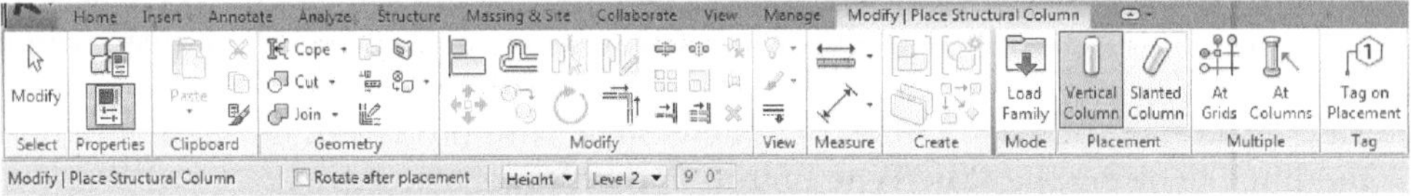

Figure 16-3 *The **Modify / Place Structural Column** tab*

Select the desired type from the **Type Selector** drop-down list in the **Properties** palette and add the structural columns to the building model. Note that before you add the structural columns, you should set up a structural grid. Now, to add a single structural column after setting up the structural grid, move the cursor near the grid intersection; the cursor will snap to the intersection. Click to add the column; the selected structural column will be attached to the cursor. To add a column aligned to an inclined grid, press SPACEBAR; the column toggles parallel and perpendicular to the highlighted grid, refer to Figure 16-4. You can press the SPACEBAR repeatedly until the desired alignment is displayed, and then click to add the column at the desired alignment. You can also select the **Rotate after placement** check box available in **Options Bar** to enable the rotation of the structural column after its placement. You can select the **Height** or **Depth** option from the first drop-down list available in the **Options Bar**. Set the level or constraint for the column height using the other drop-down list. To specify the depth or height of the column based on the project requirement, select the **Unconnected** option from the other drop-down list.

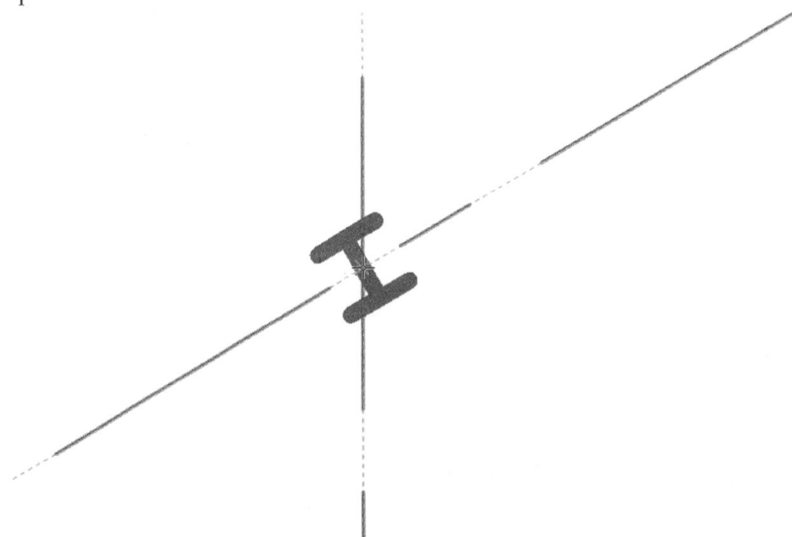

Figure 16-4 *Adding a structural column at an inclined grid intersection*

Note

*Like structural walls, structural columns are also placed from top to bottom. To view them in the current plan view, modify the **Bottom** clip plane setting for the **View Range** parameter.*

Adding Multiple Structural Columns

To add multiple columns at grid intersections, choose the **At Grids** tool from the **Multiple** panel of the **Modify | Place Structural Column** tab; the **Modify | Place Structural Column > At Grid Intersection** tab will be displayed and you will be prompted to select the grid lines to place the structural columns at grid intersections. Select the desired grid lines; the selected grid lines will be highlighted and the columns will be displayed at intersections, as shown in Figure 16-5. Next, choose the **Finish** button from the **Multiple** panel; the multiple structural columns will be added to the selected grid intersections.

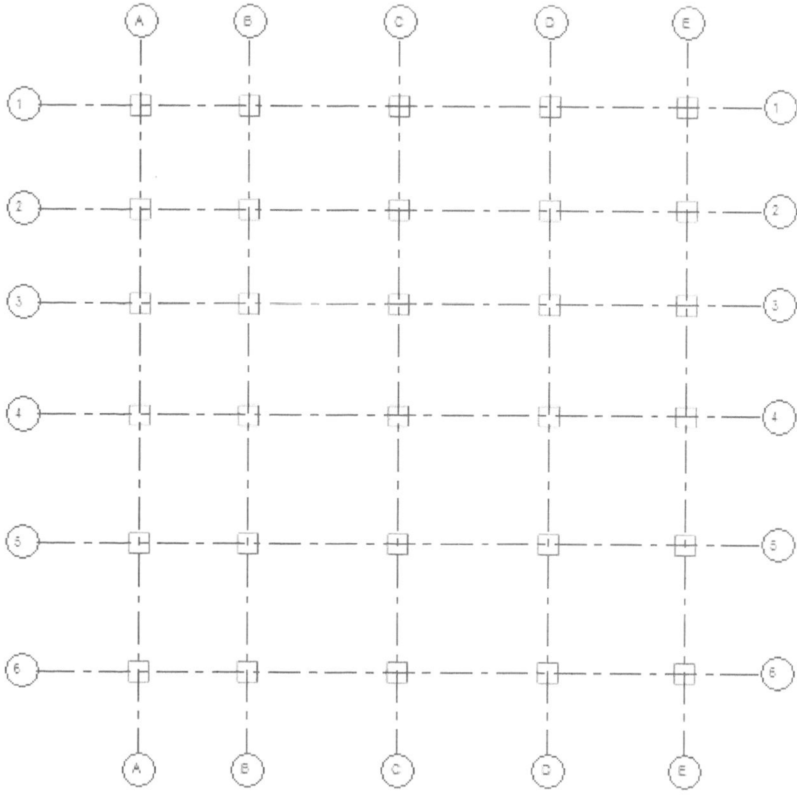

Figure 16-5 *Multiple structural columns added to a grid*

Adding Structural Columns inside Architectural Columns

The **At Columns** tool available in the **Multiple** panel of the **Modify | Place Structural Column** tab enables you to add structural columns inside the existing architectural columns. After invoking this tool, select an individual architectural column or multiple architectural columns; the structural columns automatically snap to the center of the architectural columns. Choose the **Finish** button from the **Multiple** panel of the **Modify | Place Structural Column > At Architectural Columns** tab to complete the process.

Adding Structural Beams and Braces

Beams are structural components that connect the columns or the structural walls. Beams can be joined to the structural bearing walls if their structural usage property is set to bearing or structural combined. You can add beams individually or by selecting the grids along which they are required.

To add a structural beam, invoke the **Beam** tool from the **Structure** panel of the **Structure** tab. After invoking this tool, select the beam type from the **Type Selector** drop-down list in the **Properties** palette. To load additional beams, choose the **Load Family** button from the **Mode** panel of the **Modify | Place Beam** tab; the **Load Family** dialog box will be displayed. In this dialog box, the **Structural Framing** folder will display various files related to various types of concrete, steel, and wooden beam families. Choose the required family and then choose the **Open** button to load the family in the **Type Selector** drop-down list. Now, in the **Modify | Place Beam** tab, you can choose the **On Grids** tool from the **Multiple** panel to select multiple grids along which the required beams can be placed. The **Placement Plane** drop-down list available in the **Options Bar** can be used to select the level for adding beams. The options in the **Structural Usage** drop-down list in the **Options Bar** can be used to select the usage of the beam. By default, **Automatic** is selected in this drop-down list. As a result, Revit determines the usage based on the structural components that the beam connects. The **Chain** check box can be used to add a chain of beams. Select the **3D Snapping** check box to snap to different points in a 3D view. To sketch a beam, specify the start point and the endpoint for the beam in the drawing area.

Braces are diagonal members that connect beams and columns. They can be created by snapping the cursor to the structural components. Usually, braces are placed in framing elevation views. These views show the general arrangement and sizes of structural components as an arrangement of lines and are quite similar to interior views. To create a framing elevation view, invoke the **Framing Elevation** tool from **View > Create > Elevation** drop-down. Now, select a structural grid from the drawing; the framing elevation of that section will be created. You can view the elevation from the **Interior Elevations** head in the **Project Browser**. After opening a framing elevation view from the **Project Browser**, you can add braces to the columns. To do so, invoke the **Brace** tool from the **Structure** panel of the **Structure** tab. Select the brace type from the **Type Selector** drop-down list in the **Properties** palette. You can choose the **Load Family** button from the **Mode** panel of the **Modify |Place Brace** tab to load additional braces from the **Structural Framing** folder. Move the cursor to the desired location in the framing elevation and use the snap options to sketch the braces. The braces are displayed as lines in the framing elevation. You can view the added braces and other structural components in the 3D view.

Tip

*When you load families of structural elements using the **Load Family** button, the **Load Family** dialog box displays a type catalog. This enables you to select and load only specific family types. This decreases the file size, and also reduces the number of entries in the **Type Selector** drop-down list. Also, once the structural elements have been added to a level, you can use the **Copy** and **Paste** tools from the **Clipboard** panel to copy the elements to multiple levels.*

Cutting Openings in Beams, Braces, and Columns

Revit allows you to cut openings in structural members such as beams, braces, and columns. You can cut an opening in a structural member after selecting planes. Every structural member (Beam, Brace, and Column) shows two planes: horizontal and vertical. These planes are perpendicular to each other, as shown in Figures 16-6 and 16-7. You can also lay ducts and pipes passing through the beams and columns by creating the openings of the corresponding shape. You can create different shapes of openings using different sketching tools.

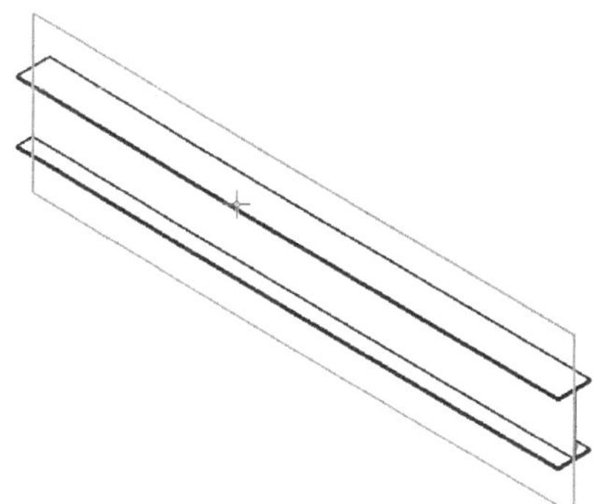

Figure 16-6 *The vertical plane of the beam*

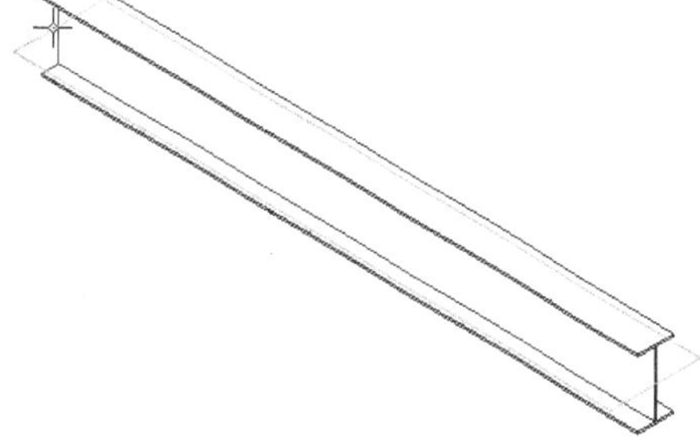

Figure 16-7 *The horizontal plane of the beam*

To cut an opening, choose the **By Face** tool from the **Opening** panel of the **Architecture** tab; you will be prompted to select a planar face of the member. Move your cursor over the member; the planes will be highlighted in green. To select the required plane, click in the drawing when the plane is highlighted; the screen will enter the sketch mode. Draw an opening in the structural member using any sketching tool available in the **Draw** panel of the **Modify | Create Opening Boundary** tab. In Revit, you can also create a rectangular opening with a fillet. To do so, invoke the **Rectangle** sketching tool in the **Draw** panel and select the **Radius** check box from the **Options Bar**. Specify the radius for the fillet in the **Radius** edit box and sketch the opening in the member. Next, choose the **Finish Edit Mode** button from the **Mode** panel. The rectangular openings with a fillet can help reduce the stresses on the structure. Figure 16-8 shows a circular opening and a rectangular opening with a fillet in structural beams.

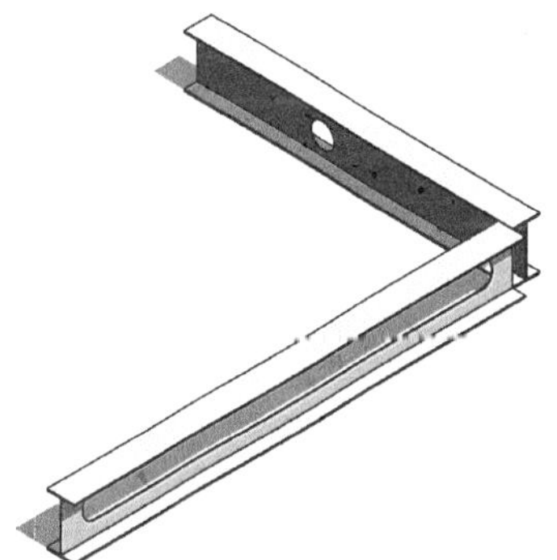

Figure 16-8 *Structural beams with a circular opening and a rectangular opening with a fillet*

GENERATING MULTIPLE DESIGN OPTIONS

In Revit, the **Design Options** tool provides you with the flexibility of choosing several alternatives for your design. As a designer, you need to come up with multiple design ideas, so that you can select the best option that suits the functional, aesthetical, and economical requirement of your project. Therefore, you need to develop and evaluate several design options and then execute the best possible design option for your project.

The **Design Options** tool helps you speed up your project by providing you the options to create and develop several alternatives of a single model. For example, you can use the **Design Options** tool to develop three options of a Kitchen for a residential layout, featuring different materials and space utilization. In such a case, you can create individual details and documentations like drawings, schedules, cost summaries based on the quantity of materials, and so on for these three design options that you have created for the existing kitchen project. These drawings and documentations help you select the best option that meets your project requirement.

To use the **Design Options** tool, first you need to create an option set and then the option in the basic building model. The option set refers to a set of alternatives devised for creating a particular design or subject. For example, if you have three design options for building a kitchen on the first floor of a residential project, then they will form one option set with three different options. You can name the option set as Kitchen_FF and its design options as Island_Kitchen, Closed_L_Shaped Kitchen, and Closed_U_Shaped Kitchen. One of the design options can be made the primary design option in the specified option set. You can have a number of design options in a single design option set.

The purpose of using design options is to enable you to develop and study multiple design alternatives for a single model and pick the best one for the final layout. You can delete or archive the rejected design options once you have picked up the right one.

Generating Design Options for a Project

The **Design Options** tool is used to generate design options for a project. Invoke this tool from the **Design Options** panel in the **Manage** tab; the **Design Options** dialog box will be displayed. To generate a new design option set, choose the **New** button in the **Option Set** section of the **Design Options** dialog box; a new option set will be added to the left pane. Next, to add a new option in this option set, choose the **New** button from the **Option** section. You can also rename an option set by using the **Rename** button in the **Option Set** section. Figure 16-9 shows various design options in the **Design Options** dialog box.

After creating the design option sets and options, you can add building components for each option. To do so, select the design option in the **Design Options** dialog box and then choose the **Edit Selected** button from the **Edit** area. Next, choose the **Close** button to close the **Design Options** dialog box; any element introduced in the building model will be added to the selected option. You can also cut and paste components from the main model to a design option. After editing the building model and completing the design option, you can again choose the **Design Options** tool to view the design. The **Now Editing** text box in the **Design Options** dialog box displays the name of the option to be edited. The **Finish Editing** button is used to complete the editing of a design option. After creating multiple design option sets, you can assign the desired option set as the primary option set by selecting it and choosing the **Accept Primary** button in the **Design Options** dialog box.

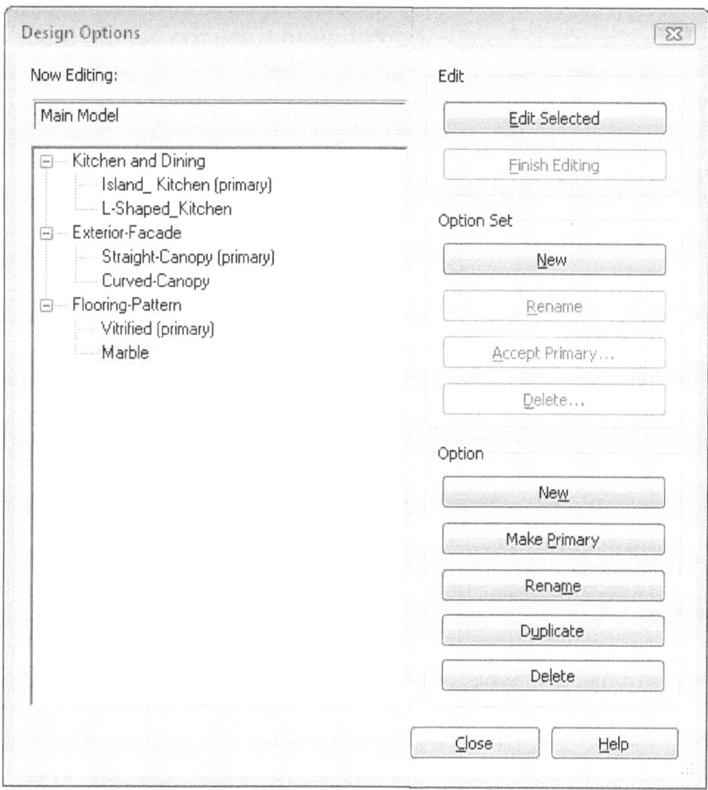

***Figure 16-9** The **Design Options** dialog box with the design option sets and design options created*

Presenting Design Options

After creating the design options, you can compare and present them to clients. To do so, create multiple copies of the view of a design option, and set the visibility setting for each view. You can use the **Visibility/Graphics** tool to control the visibility of a design option in each view. Select the view from the **Project Browser** and right-click. Next, choose **Duplicate View > Duplicate** from the shortcut menu; the copy of the view will be created. You may create a number of copies of the view based on the number of design options generated. Use the shortcut menu to rename each view based on the design option it represents.

Tip

*While using the **Design Options** tool, you need to keep in mind that the view-specific elements such as dimensions and text cannot be added to the design options. Also, you need to be careful in keeping all dependent elements in the same design option.*

Next, choose the **Manage** tab and then select the **Design Option** tool from the **Design Options** panel; the selected design option will be displayed in the view. This process needs to be repeated for each view in which you want to show a different option. You can then add the appropriate views to the sheet and present the design options to the client. You can also use the **Pick to Edit** tool from the **Design Options** panel to select the design option that requires editing.

USING AREA ANALYSIS TOOLS

The area analysis tools are used to analyze and represent different area types. These tools can also be used to create area schemes such as gross building area, rentable area, and area plans. You can access these tools from the **Area** drop-down in the **Room & Area** panel of the **Architecture** tab, as shown in Figure 16-10.

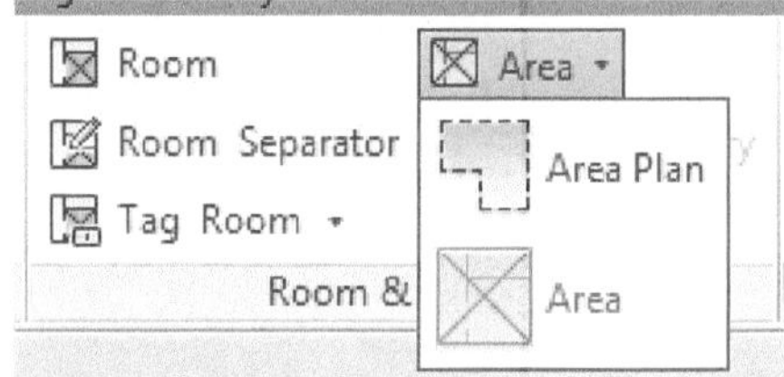

***Figure 16-10** Various tools in the **Area** drop-down*

Note

You can also generate area schemes for the design options developed for a project.

Area Schemes

Area Schemes are the standards that you set to calculate the area of an enclosed boundary with a specific space. You can use the **Area** tool from the **Area** drop-down to differentiate the spaces based on their usage. You can create and implement various types of area schemes in your current project based on the local standards that are followed for the area calculation.

You can create multiple area measurement schemes. To do so, invoke the **Area and Volume Computations** tool from the **Room & Area** panel of the **Architecture** tab; the **Area and Volume Computations** dialog box will be displayed. In this dialog box, choose the **Area Schemes** tab; the options in this tab will be displayed, as shown in Figure 16-11.

By default, the following two areas are created in the **Area Schemes** tab:

Gross Building Total built-up area of the building

Rentable Area measurements based on the calculated floor area using the standard rules

The **Gross Building** area scheme cannot be modified. However, you can modify the **Rentable** area scheme. You can also add a new area scheme by choosing the **New** button then, add description or rename it using the **Description** column. You can then proceed to create its area plan. You can use the **Delete** button in the **Area Schemes** tab of the **Area and Volume Computations** dialog box to delete an existing area scheme.

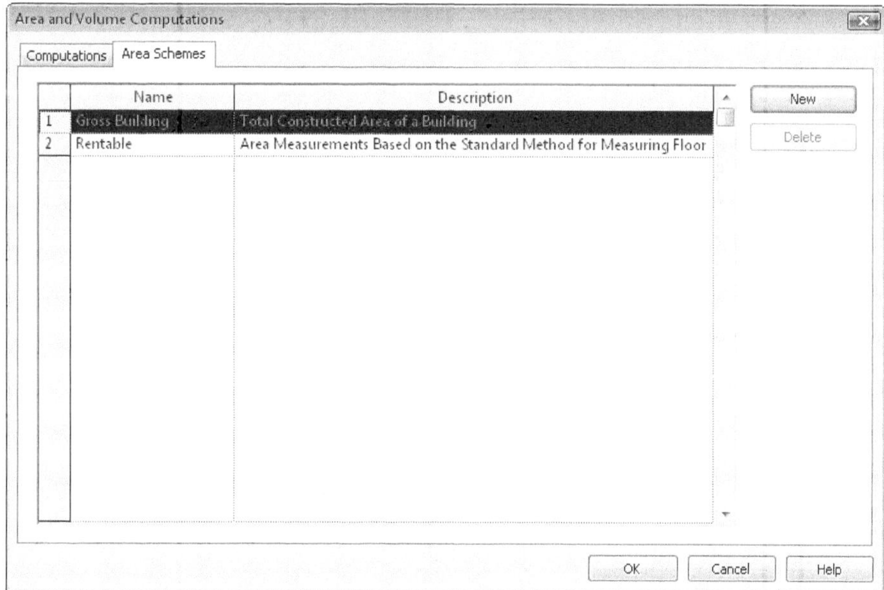

Figure 16-11 *The* ***Area and Volume Computations*** *dialog box*

Area Plans

The **Area Plan** tool is used to create area plans. Area plans are views that describe the subject of the area scheme. You can create a number of area plans for a single area scheme. For example, a rentable area scheme can be created for a commercial project and then you can create the area plans showing the rentable area for each level. Each area plan has distinct area boundaries, tags, and color fills.

To create an area plan, invoke the **Area Plan** tool from **Architecture > Room & Area > Area** drop-down; the **New Area Plan** dialog box will be displayed, as shown in Figure 16-12. In this dialog box, the **Type** drop-down list displays the available area schemes. The **Area Plan views** list box displays the existing levels for which the area plans can be created. To create area plans for more than one level, select multiple levels in this dialog box. When you select multiple levels, Revit creates separate area plans for each level and groups them by the area scheme in the **Project Browser**. If the **Do not duplicate existing views** check box is selected, Revit will use the same views to generate the area plans. If you clear this check box, Revit will create the copies of the views. After specifying all options in the **New Area Plan** dialog box, choose the **OK** button; the **Revit** message box will appear and you will be prompted to choose the method for specifying the area boundary. You can choose the **Yes** button to automatically create an area boundary associated with the external walls or choose the **No** button to manually sketch the area boundary lines. When you choose the **Yes** button, Revit places the boundary lines along the exterior walls of the building model, thus forming a closed loop. In the **Gross Building Area** scheme, the boundary line will be placed on the exterior face of the exterior walls, whereas in case of the **Rentable Area** scheme, the boundary line will be placed on the interior face of the exterior walls. Finally, the created area plan will be added in the **Project Browser** under the **Area Plans** head.

The area scheme is also mentioned along with the area plan title. You can create area boundaries either by picking the walls or by manually sketching the boundary lines. To sketch an area boundary, invoke the **Area Boundary** tool from **Architecture > Room & Area** drop-down; the options to sketch the area boundary will be displayed in the **Draw** panel of the **Modify | Place Area Boundary** tab. In the **Options Bar**, the **Apply Area Rules** check box is selected by default. As a result, the area rules will be applied to the area boundary and Revit Architecture will automatically change the position of the wall boundary when you change the area. On clearing the **Apply Area Rules** check box, the **Offset** edit box and the **Lock** check box will be displayed. You can enter the desired offset distance for the area boundary line in the **Offset** edit box and select the **Lock** check box to lock the position of the area boundary. After creating the area boundary line, you need to create the area for the boundary line. To do so, invoke the **Area** tool from the **Room and Area** panel of the **Architecture** tab; the **Modify | Place Area** tab will be displayed. Move the cursor inside the area boundary line; the area boundary will be displayed along with a tag. In the **Tag on Placement** panel of the **Modify | Place Area** tab, the **Tag on Placement** tool is chosen by default. As a result, the area tag will be displayed along with the area boundary. If you do not need the area tag to be displayed along with the area boundary, do not choose the **Tag on Placement** tool. On choosing the **Tag on Placement** tool, you can set various options in the **Options Bar**. From the drop-down list located at left of the **Options Bar**, you can select the **Horizontal**, **Vertical**, or **Model** option. After selecting the desired option, you can select the **Leader** check box to attach a leader along with the tag. From the **Area** drop-down list, either select an existing area or select the **New** option to create a new area. After selecting the desired options from the **Options Bar**, click inside the area boundary; the area will expand to the extents of the boundaries and the new area will be created.

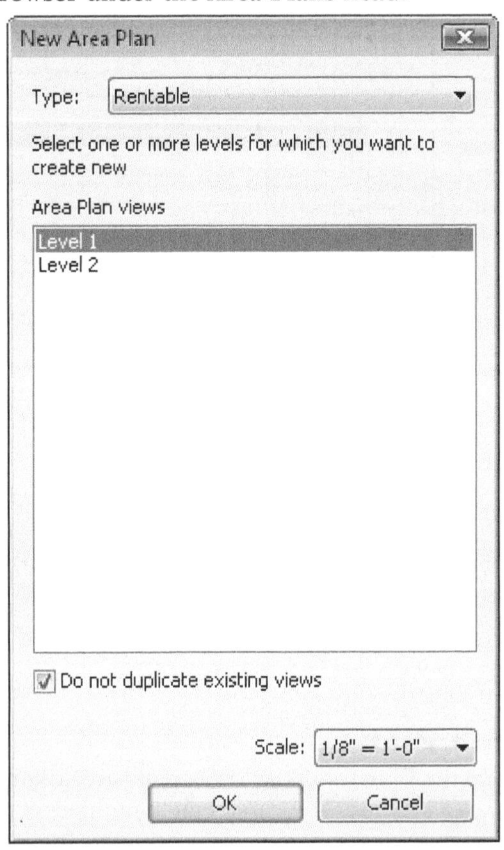

Figure 16-12 *The* ***New Area Plan*** *dialog box*

If you have placed an area without a tag, you can place the tag using the **Tag Area** tool. To do so, invoke the **Tag Area** tool from **Architecture > Room & Area > Tag Area** drop-down. On doing so, the **Modify | Place Area Tag** tab will be displayed. In the **Properties** palette, select the desired area tag type from the **Type Selector** drop-down list and then choose the **Edit Type** button to display the **Type Properties** dialog box. In this dialog box, select a suitable option for the **Leader Arrowhead** parameter from the drop-down list displayed in the **Value** field corresponding to it. Next, choose **OK**; the **Type Properties** dialog box will be closed and the specified parameter will be assigned to the tag. Now, in the **Options Bar**, you can select the **Leader** check box to display the leader line along with the area tag annotation. After specifying the options in the **Modify |Place Area Tag** tab, move the cursor within a closed space in the area boundary, Revit will automatically calculate its area. At this stage, click to add the area tag. Figure 16-13 shows an example of area boundaries and area tags added to a residential project. You can click on the area tag and rename each space.

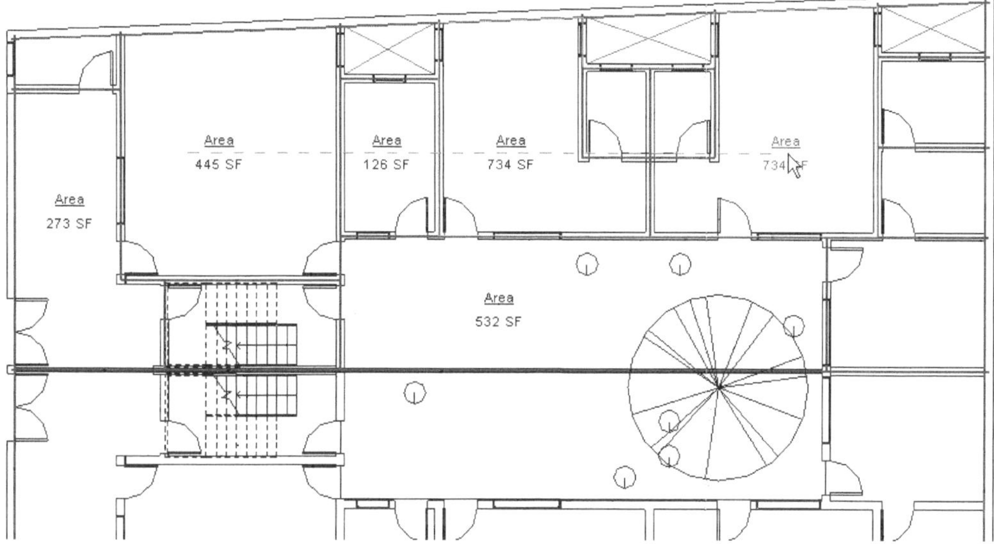

Figure 16-13 *The area boundaries and the area tags added to a residential project*

Number Parameter for Areas

The **Number** parameter is an instance parameter. It can be accessed in the **Properties** palette of the selected area. Whenever you add an area to a project, the area is automatically numbered. This new parameter can also be added to schedules. You can modify the value of the **Number** parameter of any area in the **Properties** palette. If you assign the same values to the **Number** parameter of two rooms, a warning message will be displayed.

Area Schedules

Once you have added area tags to the spaces and renamed them appropriately, you can proceed to create area schedules. To do so, invoke the **Schedule/Quantities** tool from **View > Create > Schedules** drop-down; the **New Schedule** dialog box will be displayed. In this dialog box, the **Category** list box displays the area schemes created in the project. Select the desired area scheme from this list and ensure that the **Schedule building components** radio button is selected. Choose the **OK** button in the **New Schedule** dialog box; the **Schedule Properties** dialog box will be displayed. Select and add the parameters to be included in the scheduled fields from the **Available fields** area, as shown in Figure 16-14.

You can also use the **Fields**, **Filter**, **Sorting/Grouping**, **Formatting**, and **Appearance** tabs available in the **Schedule Properties** dialog box to set the properties of the area schedule. Next, choose the **OK** button; the **Modify Schedule/Quantities** tab will be displayed and the created schedule will be displayed in the drawing area. Add it to the drawing sheet for the presentation of the area schemes. Figure 16-15 shows an example of an area schedule.

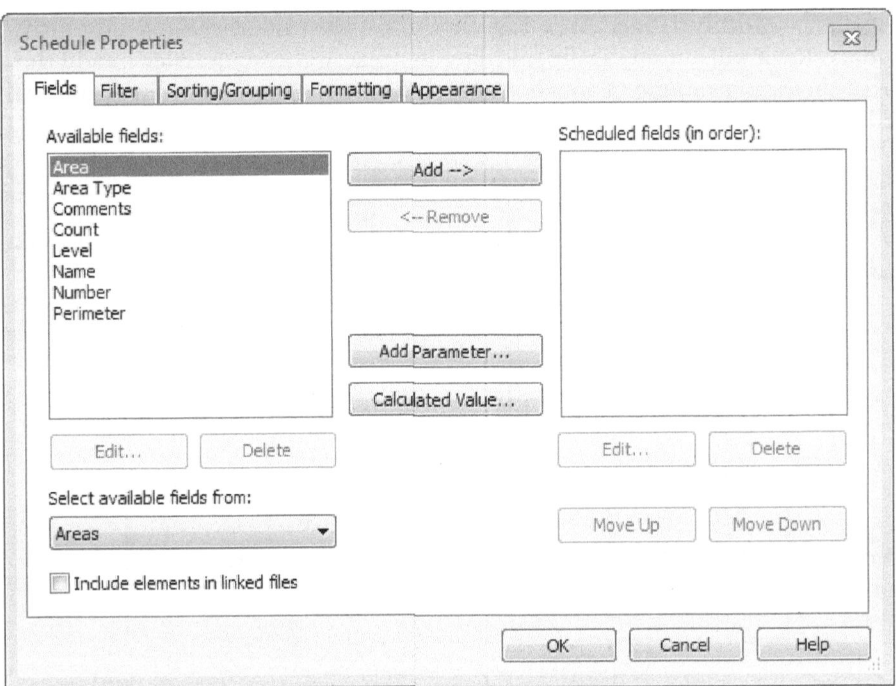

Figure 16-14 *The* ***Schedule Properties*** *dialog box*

Area Schedule (Area Scheme 1)		
Level	Name	Area
Level 1	Living Room	445 SF
Level 1	Kitchen	126 SF
Level 1	Bed Room	734 SF
Level 1	Patio	532 SF
Level 1	Front Open	273 SF
Level 1	Washroom	80 SF
Level 1	Closet	80 SF
Level 1	Bed Room 2	176 SF
Level 1	Shaft 3	47 SF
Level 1	Shaft 2	57 SF
Level 1	Shaft 1	43 SF
Level 1	Utility	45 SF
Level 1	Stairs	128 SF

Figure 16-15 *An example of a created area schedule*

COLOR SCHEMES

Color schemes are used to represent and categorize different areas in the project graphically by using color codes. In other words, color schemes are used to color the rooms and areas in a view. You can create color schemes and then apply them to different plan views. You can create different color schemes for the first and second floors of a building. A color scheme can be created based on a specific category such as Gross area, Rentable area, or an instance property of the room or area such as room perimeter, number, or name. You can also create a color scheme depending on the utilization of different rooms in a building. For example, you can assign different colors to represent areas such as office, storage, or accounts. Then, you can add a color scheme legend to help you identify different areas by the colors assigned to them.

Creating Color Schemes

Before creating a color scheme, the rooms and areas should be defined in the plan view. You can create a color scheme based on any parameter of a room or an area. For example, if you want to create a color scheme for rooms on the basis of room number, room area, or names, make sure that the rooms are numbered and named in the plan view.

To create a color scheme, choose the **Color Schemes** tool from the **Room & Area** panel in the **Architecture** tab; the **Edit Color Scheme** dialog box is invoked, as shown in Figure 16-16. Alternatively, you can display the **Edit Color Scheme** dialog box by choosing the **<none>** button displayed in the value column corresponding to the **Color Scheme** parameter in the **Properties** palette for the current view. Now, in the **Schemes** area of the **Edit Color Scheme** dialog box, select the category for the color scheme from the **Category** drop-down list. Next, choose the **Duplicate** button in the **Schemes** area; the **New color scheme** dialog box will be displayed. Specify the name for the color scheme in the dialog box and choose the **OK** button; the name will be added in the **Schemes** area. Enter a title for the color scheme legend in the **Title** edit box in the **Scheme Definition** area. Next, select the parameter for the color scheme from the **Color** drop-down list; a message prompting you to make a new color scheme will be displayed. Choose the **OK** button to continue. Note that the options in the **Color** drop-down list will vary depending on the category selected.

Note

Make sure you select the correct parameter from the ***Color*** *drop-down list to create a color scheme. The values for the parameters should be predefined. For example, if you select the* ***Area*** *parameter to create a color scheme for a plan view, then the areas must be predefined and tagged in the view.*

In the **Edit Color Scheme** dialog box, the **By value** radio button is selected by default. As a result, the color schemes are created based on the values of the selected parameter. Select the **By range** radio button to create a color scheme based on certain ranges of parameter values. The **By range** radio button will be available only when you select **Area** or **Perimeter** from the **Color** drop-down list in the **Scheme Definition** area. On selecting the **By range** radio button, the **Edit Format** button will be enabled and the unit format used for the parameter will be displayed on the right. Choose the **Edit Format** button; the **Format dialog** box will be displayed. The **Use**

Project Settings check box is selected by default. Clear the **Use project settings** check box in the **Format** dialog box; the options in the dialog box will be enabled. Select the required values for the **Units** and **Rounding** options to set the format of the **Area** and **Perimeter** units. Choose the **OK** button; the scheme definition values will be added in the columns. You can modify the values in the columns as required. The columns displayed in the **Scheme Definition** area are discussed next.

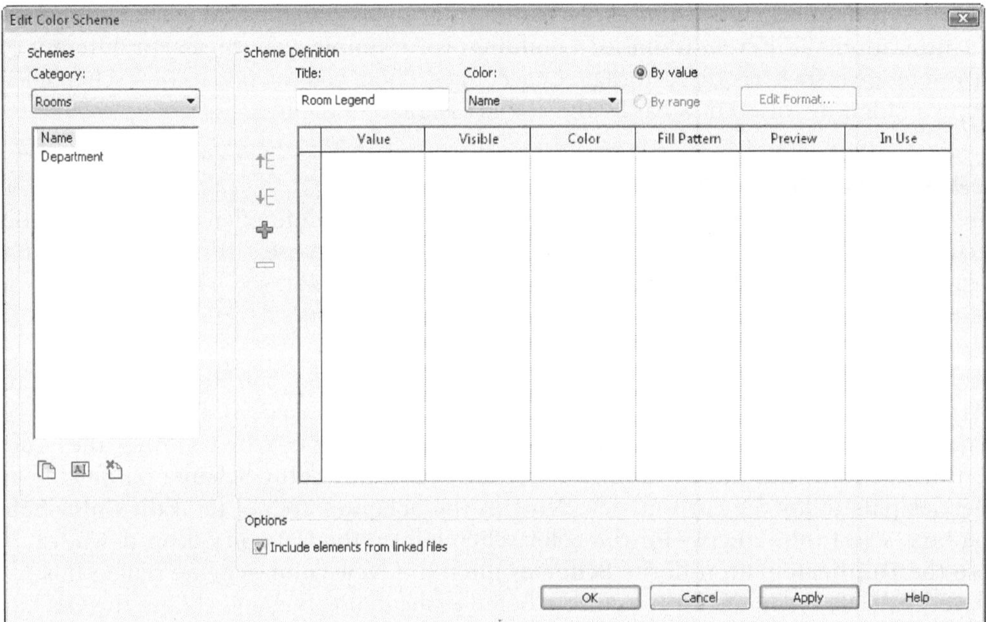

*Figure 16-16 The **Edit Color Scheme** dialog box*

At Least

This column specifies the lowest value of a range.

Less Than

This column specifies the least value of a range and cannot be modified.

Caption

This column specifies the legend text for the range. Click in the column and edit the text.

Visible

This column indicates the visibility of the value in the color scheme legend. By default, the **Visible** check box is selected indicating that the values are visible in the legend. Clear the check box in the column to make the value invisible in the color scheme legend.

Color

This column specifies the color assigned to the range/ class interval. Click on the default color value in the **Color** column; the **Color** dialog box will be displayed. Select the required color and choose the **OK** button; the selected color will be applied to the range/ class interval and displayed in the column.

Fill Pattern

This column specifies the fill pattern assigned to a value by default. Click on the default value in the column and click on the down arrow displayed on the right. Select the suitable fill pattern from the drop-down list displayed.

Preview

This column displays the preview of the color and pattern used for a particular range.

In Use

This column indicates that if a particular value from a range of values is in use in the project, you cannot modify the values in this column.

To move a row up or down in the **Scheme Definition** area, choose the **Move Rows Up/Down** buttons on the left. These buttons will be available only after selecting the **By Value** radio button. To add a new value to the color scheme, choose the **Add Value** button on the left; the **New Color Scheme entry** dialog box will be displayed. In this dialog box, enter a name in the **Name** edit box; a new scheme will be added. By default, the check box displayed in the value column corresponding to this scheme will be selected. As a result, the added color schemes will be applied to rooms. You can clear this check box if you do no want to apply color schemes to rooms and areas from the linked files. Choose the **OK** button after creating the color scheme.

Applying a Color Scheme

To apply a color scheme in the required plan view, you can use the **Properties** palette of the current view. In the **Properties** palette of the current view, choose the **<none >** button in the value column of the **Color Scheme** parameter; the **Edit Color Scheme** dialog box will be displayed. Select the required color scheme and choose the **OK** button in the **Format** dialog box. The colors will be applied to the areas or rooms based on the color scheme selected.

Now, to apply the color scheme in the project view, click on the value field corresponding to the **Color Scheme Location** parameter in the **Properties** palette; a drop-down list will be displayed. You can select any one of the options from **Background** and **Foreground**. On selecting the **Foreground** option, all the elements in the area or room such as furniture or walls, except the columns, will be colored. On selecting the **Background** option only the background or the floor will be colored.

Adding Color Scheme Legends

The color scheme legends help you identify different rooms and areas through different colors assigned to them. The color scheme legends are included in the **Annotation Tag** category. You can place multiple color scheme legends anywhere in the plan view. The color scheme legend belongs to the annotation category and is affected by the Annotation crop region. If you do not want to place the color scheme legend on the view, you can exclude it by adjusting the Annotation crop region of that view.

To add a color fill legend, choose the **Color Fill Legend** tool from the **Color Fill** panel of the **Annotate** tab; the **Modify|Place Color Fill Legend** tab will be displayed. In this tab, select the color scheme from the **Type Selector** drop-down list and then click in the drawing area to place the legend; the color scheme legend will be placed in the drawing view. Figure 16-17 shows a floor plan view with a color scheme and the color scheme legend for the rooms. The color scheme is created based on the area occupied by each room.

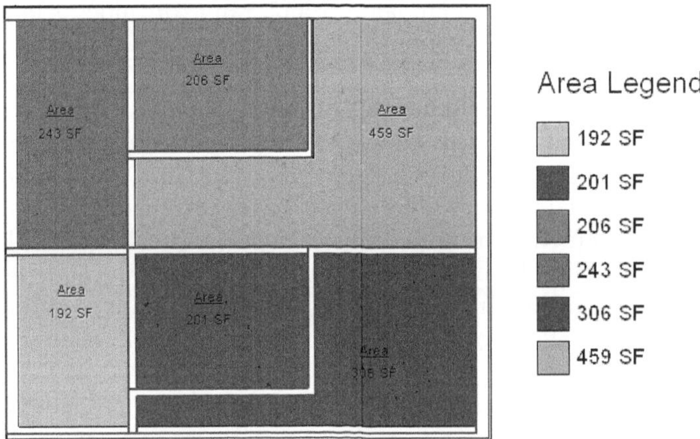

Figure 16-17 *Color scheme with a color scheme legend representing different areas*

You can drag and stretch the color scheme legend by using the drag symbol displayed after selecting the color scheme legend. Figure 16-18 shows an example of using a color fill scheme based on the occupancy of the building.

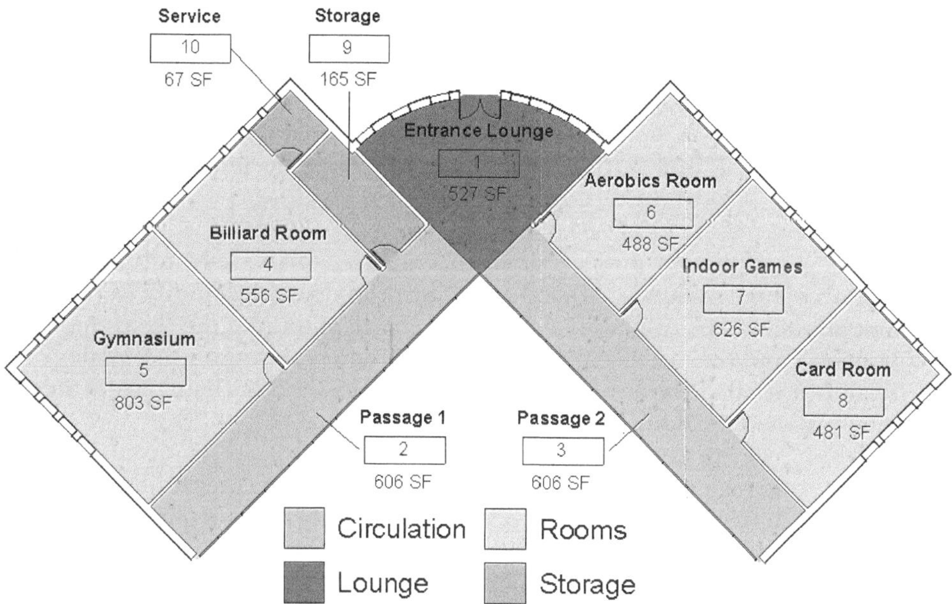

Figure 16-18 An example of color scheme based on the occupancy of the building

Modifying Color Scheme

To modify a color scheme, select the existing color scheme legend and choose **Scheme > Edit Scheme** from the **Modify Color Fill Legends** tab; the **Edit Color Scheme** dialog box will be displayed. Modify the colors, fill patterns, title, parameter, and other values as required and choose the **Apply** button to view the changes. Choose the **OK** button to retain the changes.

Modifying Color Scheme Legends

To modify the color scheme legends, select the existing color scheme legend and drag the blue circular drag control to move the color swatches into new columns. Next, drag the cursor down to move the color swatches into one column. To modify the type properties of the selected color scheme legend, choose the **Edit Type** button in the **Properties** palette; the **Type Properties** dialog box will be displayed. In this dialog box, you can modify various parameters related to the text, swatches, and various elements in the **Color Fill** legend. After modifying the parameters, choose the **OK** button to close the dialog box. You can also hide the title of the color scheme legend by clearing the **Show Title** check box.

MASKING REGIONS

While working in an architectural project, sometimes it becomes difficult to demarcate between different visible elements due to overlapping of lineworks. Therefore, to reduce the congestion of lineworks and interference of unwanted elements in your drawing, it is necessary to hide or obscure them in the view.

You can overcome the problem of overlapping and congestion of lineworks by using the **Masking Region** tool. By using this tool, you can add the masking regions to a project, detail family, or model family. The **Masking Region** tool has an advantage over the **Region** tool in a way that it can help maintain the visual display of Revit family information and maintain the visual accuracy after the files are imported or exported to other AutoCAD based applications. Masking region can be used in 2D model as well as for 2D and 3D Revit families including detail elements and annotations.

To add a masking region to a project, open the required plan view and then invoke the **Masking Region** tool from **Annotate > Detail > Region** drop-down; the **Modify | Create Masking Region Boundary** tab will be displayed and the screen will enter into the sketch mode. Sketch the masking region and then choose the **Finish Edit Mode** button from the **Mode** panel; the **Modify | Detail Items** tab will be displayed. In this tab, you can edit the boundary of the masking region by choosing the **Edit Boundary** tool from the **Mode** panel.

You can add a masking region to a detail family or a model family in the family editor. To do so, open the detail family or the model family in the family editor and then choose the **Masking Region** tool from the **Detail** panel of the **Annotate** tab; the **Modify | Create Masking Region Boundary** tab will be displayed. You can use various sketching tools from the **Draw** panel of this tab to sketch the masking region. Note that the masking region should be a closed loop geometry. After sketching the masking region, you can control its visibility in any model family when the model family is loaded into the project and placed in the drawing. To do so, you can use the instance properties of the masking region displayed in the **Properties** palette. In this palette, clear the **Visible** parameter check box to hide the masking region in a view or select the check box to make it visible in the project. To set the detail level at which the masking region will be displayed, choose the **Edit** button in the **Value** column for the **Visibility/Graphical Overrides** parameter; the **Family element visibility settings** dialog box will be displayed. Set the detail level for the masking region in the **Detail Levels** area of the dialog box and then choose the **OK** button. To set the masking region at the detail plane of the view, select the **Draw in Foreground** check box in the **Properties** palette. To draw the masking region on the work plane on which it is sketched, clear the **Draw in Foreground** check box.

Adding Masking Regions to a Project

To mask or obscure any element in a project, open the floor plan view and choose the **Masking Region** tool from **Annotate > Detail > Region** drop-down; the screen will enter the sketch mode. Choose the required sketching tool from the **Draw** panel, select the line type from the **Line Style** drop-down list, and then sketch the masking regions in the closed loops. After sketching the masking regions, choose the **Finish Edit Mode** button from the **Mode** panel of the **Modify |Create Masking Region Boundary** tab. Figure 16-19 shows the plumbing fixtures such as tub and sink masked in the drawing.

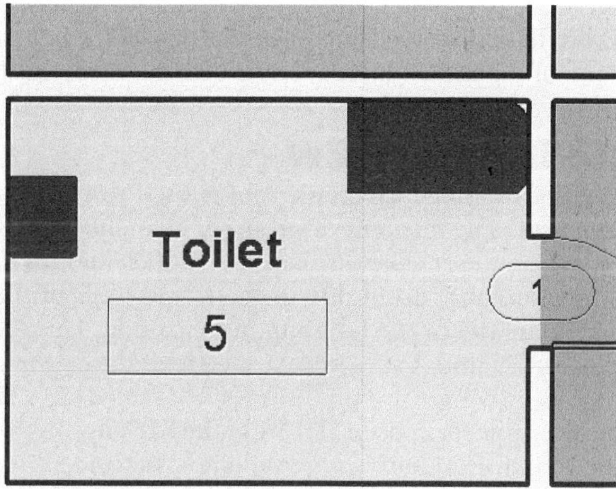

Figure 16-19 Masking regions added to tub and sink

Adding Masking Regions to a Detail Family

While creating and defining a detail family, you can add a masking region to it so that when you load it into a project, it can obscure or hide the elements which are interfering with it. To add a masking region to a detail family, open the floor plan view and choose the **Masking Region** tool from the **Detail** panel of the **Architecture** tab, while you are working in the **Revit Family Editor**. On doing so, the **Modify | Create Masking Region Boundary** tab will be displayed for sketching and editing the masking region. Next, choose the required sketching tool from the **Draw** panel. Select the specific line type from the **Line Style** drop-down list in the **Element** panel and then sketch the masking region over the detail family in a closed loop. Next, in the **Properties** palette, you can clear the check box in the **Value** column for the **Visible** instance parameter to disable the masking region boundaries. As a result, when you load the family into the project, the masking region will not be visible.

Masking regions help in improving the visibility of the detail family in a project. For example, if you are creating a detail family elevation for a display unit, you can add a masking region to it. The shape of the masking region needs to fit the geometry of the model over which it is being used, in such a way that it obscures the visibility of other elements like walls and fixtures behind it, when the detail family is placed in the elevation of your project.

Adding Masking Regions to a Model Family

You can create and define a masking region for a model family in the same way as you do for the detail family. While creating a masking region for a model family, you can control the position of the plane where it is drawn by using the **Draw in Foreground** instance parameter in the **Properties** palette of the masking region. If you clear the check box in the value column of the

Draw in Foreground instance parameter, then you can draw the masking region at the work plane where the model family was created. If you select this check box, then you can draw the masking region at a plane of the model family that is nearest to you in the view.

CREATING DISPLACED VIEW

In Autodesk Revit 2018, the **Displace Elements** tool is used to create a displaced view of an element or group of elements. The element or group of elements of which a displaced view is created is called the displacement set. The displaced view of element is used to see the internal parts of the building which are obstructed due to roofs, and walls of the building. This helps the designer to view the 3D model of the building more closely. This tool is used to move the displacement set along the X, Y, and Z axes upto a specified distance away from a model.

To create displace views in a project choose **{3D}** from the **3D View** in the **Project Browser** and then use the **View Cube** tool from the drawing and align the current view to front view. After aligning, select all the elements above the ground floor; the **Multi | Select** tab will be displayed. In this tab, choose the **Displace Elements** tool from the **View** panel as shown in Figure 16-20; the **Modify | Displacement** tab will be displayed. Also, in the drawing area, the xyz icon will be displayed on the top of the building. The xyz icon help drag the selected elements in X, Y, or Z directions. On doing so, the element will get displaced to the desired direction. Alternatively, in the **Properties** palette**,** you can enter desired value in the value field corresponding to the X, Y, or Z instance parameter. Now, choose the **Modify** button in the **Select** panel to clear the selection. After displacing element, trace the path of the displaced element. To do so, choose the **Path** tool from the **Displacement Sets** panel; the cursor will change its shape. Move the cursor on the building element in the displacement sets, a dotted line will appear. Click to add the path. Figure 16-21 shows the path of the building added in the displacement sets. Now, you can modify the inside elements if required. After modifying, the inside elements of a building, you can reset the building model. To do so, choose the **Reset** button from the **Displacement Sets** panel; the building will reset to its original position.

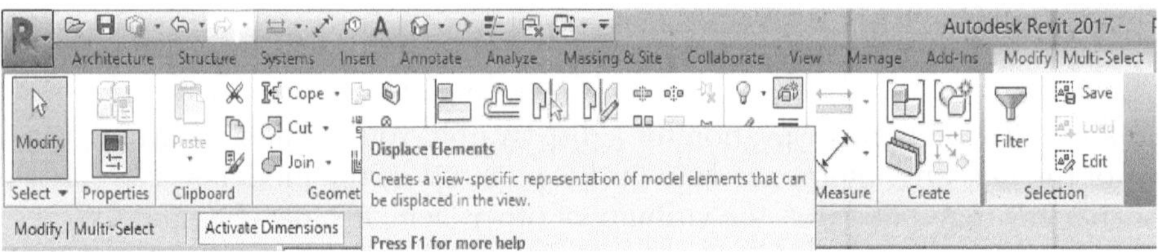

*Figure 16-20 The **Displace Elements** tool in the **Modify / Multi Select** tab*

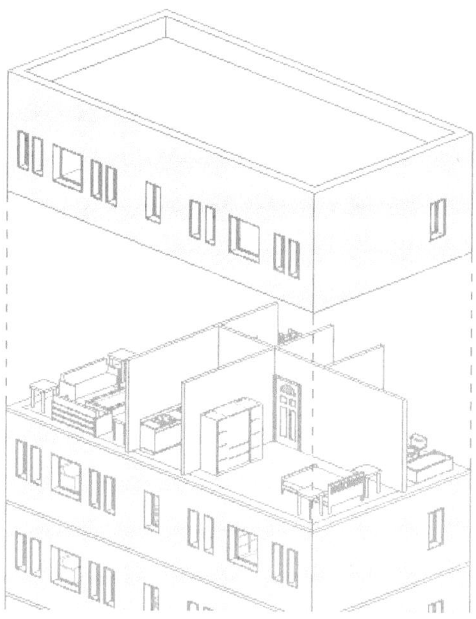

Figure 16-21 The highlighted path added in a building model

USING PROJECT PHASING TOOLS

In some architectural projects, building works need to be carried out in phases. Phases represent the time periods over which a project is to be executed. One of the examples of such a project is building a large institutional complex that requires the construction work of different buildings within the stipulated time. Another example can be an interior renovation project, in which certain building components may need to be constructed and demolished over a number of stages or phases. Revit enables the architects and the interior designers to represent phases in the views of a building model. Using the phasing tools, you can generate 3D views that show the phase-wise addition or demolition of building components and the resulting building model as well.

Understanding Phasing Concepts

To use the phasing tools in Revit, you first need to understand the basic concepts of the working of these tools and their usage. You can create any number of phases for a project and specify them for the building elements. Revit allows you to specify phasing for views and also for the building components. Each new building component added to a project has the **Phase Created** and **Phase Demolished** instance parameters associated with it. These instance properties can be modified. The **Phase Created** instance parameter indicates the phase during which the element will be added and the **Phase Demolished** instance parameter shows the phase in which it will be demolished. By default, you can assign one of the following values for these instance parameters in a building element:

New	Element created in the current phase
Existing	Element created in an earlier phase and continues to exist in the current phase
Demolished	Element created in an earlier phase and demolished in the current phase
Temporary	Element created and demolished in the current phase

Creating Phases and Setting Phase Filters

When you open a new project, by default, it has two predefined phases, **Existing** and **New Construction**. You can specify any number of additional phases in a project. To do so, choose the **Phases** tool from the **Phasing** panel of the **Manage** tab; the **Phasing** dialog box will be displayed, as shown in Figure 16-22. This dialog box displays two predefined phases. You can rename these phases by clicking in the **Name** column and then entering a new name.

The **Before** and **After** buttons in the **Insert** area of the **Phasing** dialog box are used to add new phases before and after a selected phase. The new phases added can suitably be renamed and arranged according to their time period, from the past to the future.

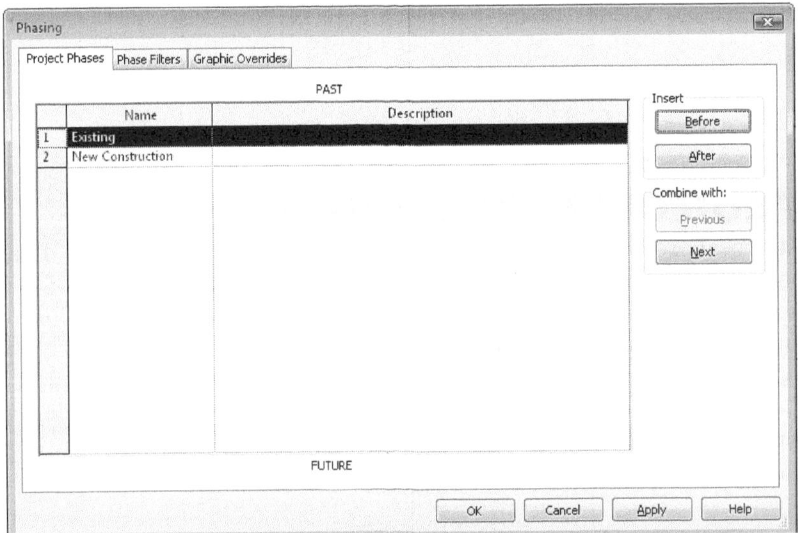

*Figure 16-22 The **Phasing** dialog box*

You can choose the **Previous** or **Next** button from the **Combine with** area of the **Phasing** dialog box to combine the selected phase with the previous or next phase in the **Project Phases** list. The phases cannot be rearranged after they have been created. The appearance of building components in various phases can be controlled by setting phase filters. A phase filter is a tool that determines the visibility of a building element in a view, based on its phase condition. The **Phase Filters** tab in the **Phasing** dialog box displays the preloaded phase filters. The description of these filters is given next.

Show All	Shows the new, existing, demolished, and temporary components in that particular phase. Components demolished in the earlier phases are not displayed
Show Complete	Shows the components in the last phase
Show Demo+New	Shows the demolished and new components
Show New	Shows the elements added to a particular phase
Show Previous+Demo	Shows the existing and demolished components
Show Previous+New	Shows the existing and new components
Show Previous Phase	Shows all components from the previous phase

You can use the **New** button to add new phase filters and set the parameters for the same. Set the parameters for the display of components in different phases using the **Graphic Overrides** tab.

Specifying Phases for Project Views

To create project views for different phases, you need to create the copies of the project view. Right-click on the name of the project view in the **Project Browser**, and then choose **Duplicate View > Duplicate** from the shortcut menu to create a duplicate view. Open each project view and set its phasing parameters. Click on the project view and then from the **Properties** palette select appropriate options from the drop-down lists corresponding to the **Phase Filter** and **Phase** parameters. Revit applies the rules for the specified phase filter and displays the components that belong to the selected phase, in the current project view. This procedure can be adopted for all copies of the project view. You can display components for each phase of a project.

Using the Demolish Tool to Specify Phases for Building Elements

Choose the **Demolish** tool from the **Phasing** panel of the **Manage** tab to demolish components. When you demolish a component, it appears as a dashed line in the view in which it was demolished. Set the appropriate phase filter to display the demolished components in other project views. When you select an element from the drawing area, the value for the **Phase Demolished** parameter in the **Properties** palette indicates the phase in which the component was demolished. You can prepare demolition plans for the building elements in each phase.

LINKING BUILDING MODELS AND SHARING COORDINATES

Some large projects may require you to develop independent building models and later combine them into a comprehensive project. For example, in a large educational campus project, you may need to independently develop the building models of the administrative building, academic complex, faculty residences, student accommodation, and so on, and later add them into a single host project file. You can do so by using Revit's linking and sharing coordinates tools that enable you to link models and share their coordinates within a single host project file. These tools also enable you to work on building models in other project files. When you link projects, you need to share the coordinates of the host model with the linked model so that the linked files retain their positions. To do so, invoke the **Acquire Coordinates** tool from **Manage > Project Locations > Coordinates** drop-down and then select the linked project in your drawing. On selecting the linked project, the origin of the linked project's shared coordinate becomes the origin of the host project's shared coordinates. Revit Architecture provides the flexibility and easy management of the linked models by enhancing the linking of the models and organizing the linked files in the **Project Browser**. You can easily access the linked files, the nested link files, and the Link Manager from the **Project Browser**. The nested Revit links are also listed under the **Revit Links** head with the host link in the **Project Browser**.

Linking or Importing Models

To link or import one project to the other, open the host project file and choose the **Insert** tab, options in this tab will be displayed, as shown in Figure 16-23. You can choose the options from the **Import** or **Link** panel of the **Insert** tab depending upon the file format to be imported or linked. Before you import or link any file, make sure that the file contains the data and geometry that are compatible with Revit Architecture. To link *.dwg, .dwf, .skp, .dgn,* and other files, choose the **Link CAD** tool from the **Link** panel of the **Insert** tab; the **Link CAD Formats** dialog box will be displayed, as shown in Figure 16-24. In this dialog box, select the file type from the **Files of type** drop-down list. Next, browse to the required location and select the file. The options in this dialog box are discussed next.

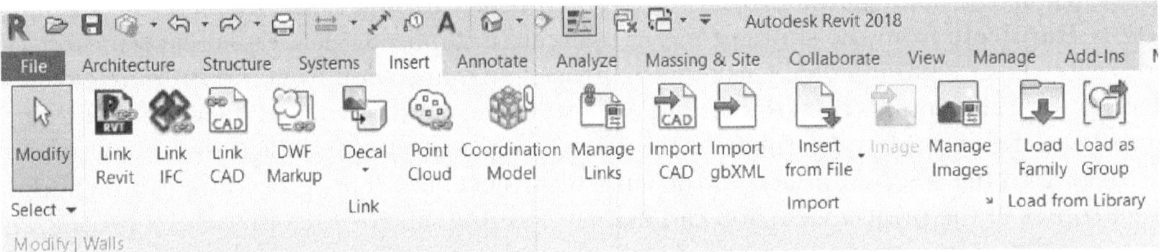

*Figure 16-23 The linking and the importing options in the **Insert** tab*

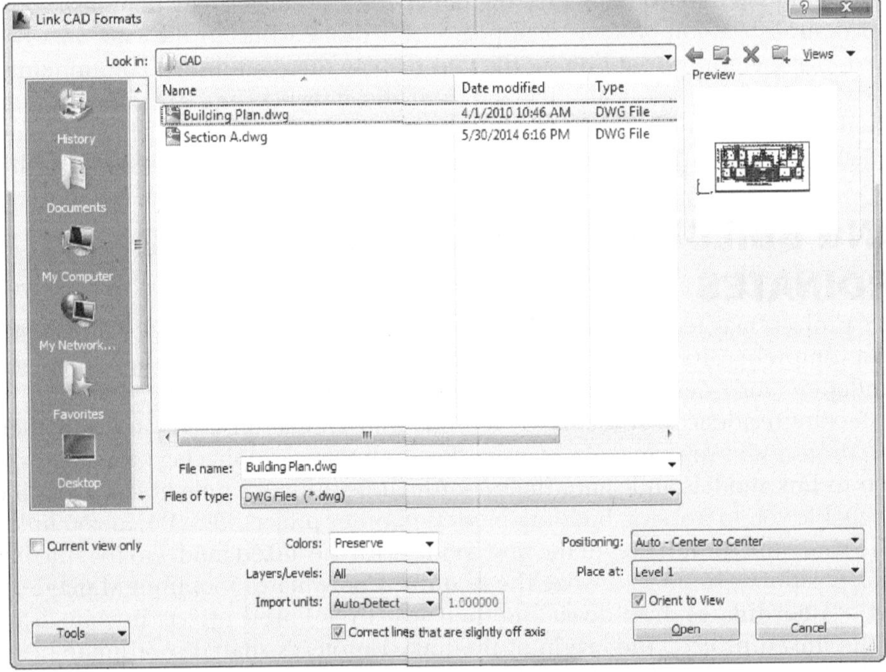

*Figure 16-24 The **Link CAD Formats** dialog box*

Linking or Importing Files

In Revit Architecture, you can link or import the CAD files to the current project. If a CAD file is linked to a project, all changes made in it will simultaneously be updated in the project. However, if you import a file in a project, it will remain unchanged, irrespective of any changes made in the file linked to the project.

To link a CAD file to a project, choose the **Link CAD** tool from the **Link** panel of the **Insert** tab of the ribbon; the **Link CAD Formats** dialog box will be displayed. Select the desired CAD file and then choose **Open**; the selected CAD file will be displayed and linked to the Revit project file. Similarly, you can import a CAD file to a project. To do so, choose the **Import CAD** tool from the **Import** panel of the **Insert** tab; the **Import CAD Formats** dialog box will be displayed. Select the desired CAD file and choose **Open**; the selected file will be imported to the Revit file.

While importing or linking a CAD file to your project, you can control its availability either in all views or only in the current view. If you select the **Current view only** check box in the **Import CAD Formats** or **Link CAD Formats** dialog box, you can import or link the drawing in the CAD format only in the active Revit Architecture view. However, if you clear the check box, you can import the drawing in the CAD format in all views of Revit Architecture. In this case, the lines and geometries of the drawing will be imported without the text.

The **Layers** drop-down list in the **Import CAD Formats** or **Link CAD Formats** dialog box allows you to specify the layers to be imported from the linked file. On selecting **All** from the **Layers** drop-down list, all layers will be imported or linked. The **Visible** options in this list allow you to import or link the visible layers in the view. The **Specify** option allows you to import the specified layers and levels in the project.

Note

If you need to display layers of the linked files that were not selected or visible initially, you can get them by deleting the present link and relinking the file.

Assigning Colors to Imported or Linked Files

In Revit Architecture, you can import or link files in various colors. The **Color** drop-down list in the **Import CAD Formats** or **Link CAD Formats** dialog box allows you to link various colors to the displayed files. The options in this drop-down list are discussed next.

Black and white

If this option is selected, the file will be imported in black and white.

Preserve colors

If this option is selected, you can retain the original colors of the file.

Invert colors

If this option is selected, the color of the objects will be inverted. As a result, the dark colored objects will be converted to light colored objects and vice-versa. This option is useful for improving the clarity of lines and texts of the imported files to make them reader-friendly.

Positioning Imported Files

While importing or linking files to Revit Architecture, it is important that the imported geometries and texts are placed at correct position. Revit allows you to align the imported or linked files to the current geometry by providing various options in the **Positioning** drop-down list of the **Import CAD Formats** or **Link CAD Formats** dialog box. Depending on the project requirement, you can position the imported or linked files automatically or manually in the host project. Various positioning options that can be used to position the imported file automatically are given next.

Auto - Center to Center Revit will place the center of the footprint of the imported model geometry at the center of the model.

Auto - Origin to Origin The world origin of the imported model geometry will be aligned to the internal origin of the host model.

To place the linked model manually, select any of the following options from the **Positioning** drop-down list:

Manual - Origin The origin of the linked or imported project will be attached to the cursor.

Manual - Base point The base point of the linked or imported project will be attached to the cursor.

Manual - Center The center of the linked project will be attached to the cursor.

You can place the origin or the base point of the imported or linked files at the selected level by selecting the options from the **Place at** drop-down list. You can also select the **Orient to View** check box to place the linked or imported file at the same orientation as that of the current view.

Note

Revit uses the coordinate system for its project, but this system is not visible to users. The center of the linked project is the geometric center of its footprint and may change with the change in the model geometry.

Setting Units for Imported or Linked Files

You can set the measurement unit of the imported geometry using the **Import units** drop-down list available in the **Import CAD Formats** or **Link CAD Formats** dialog box. If you select the **Auto-Detect** option, the imported or linked files will be inserted in the unit in which they were created. For example, if you import a file that has been created in AutoCAD using **Imperial(English)** as its default unit, Revit will automatically adopt feet and inches as the units for the imported geometry in the current project. Similarly, you can select other units from the **Import-units** drop-down list as per your project requirement.

Linking Revit Models

To link or import the Revit files, choose the **Link Revit** tool from the **Link** panel of the **Insert** tab; the **Import/Link RVT** dialog box will be displayed, as shown in Figure 16-25. In this dialog box, navigate to the desired folder and select the file to be linked to the host project; the preview image of the selected project file will be displayed in the **Preview** pane. Choose the **Open** button to open the file. Select the appropriate positioning option from the **Positioning** area to position the model automatically or manually in the host project.

Linked Revit Models in the Project Browser

The linked Revit models are listed in the **Project Browser** under the **Revit Links** head. You can access the linked model files from the **Project Browser**. You can also link a new file from the **Project Browser**. To do so, select **Revit Links** sub-node in the **Project Browser** and right-click; a shortcut menu will be displayed. Choose **New Link** from the shortcut menu; the **Import/Link RVT** dialog box will be displayed. Select the file to be linked from this dialog box. Similarly, you can access the link manager by choosing **Manage Links** from the shortcut menu and manage the links. You can also open the linked model in the project by dragging it from the **Project Browser** and dropping it in the project view.

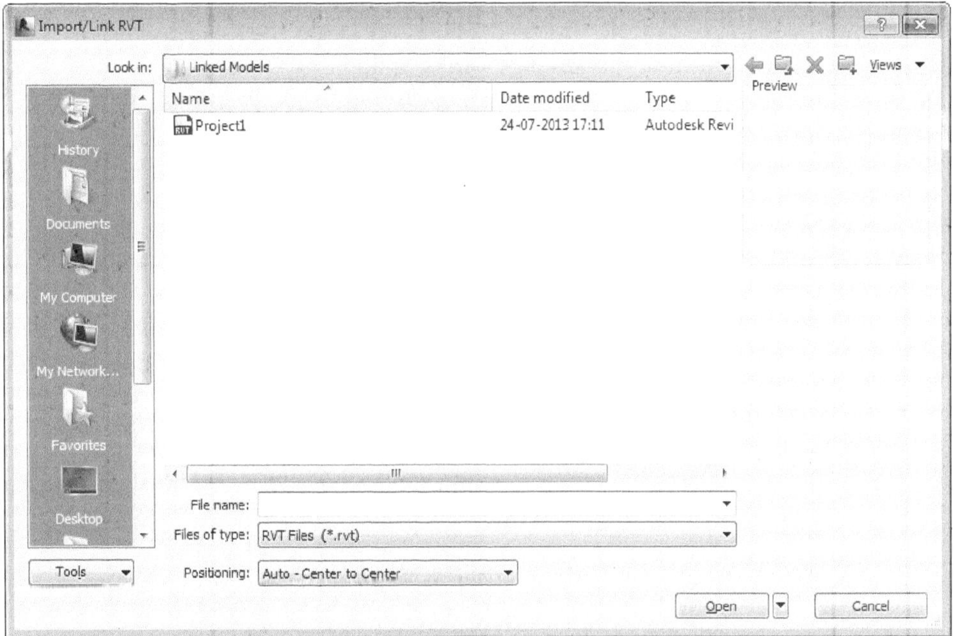

*Figure 16-25 The **Import/Link RVT** dialog box*

Nested Linked Models

If you import a Revit model that already contains a linked file, the linked file becomes a nested link file. You can control the visibility of the nested linked models in the host project file. When you link a file, by default, the nested link model will not be displayed in the host project file and the **Nested Links Invisible** message box will be displayed, as shown in Figure 16-26, indicating that the elements in the linked model will not be visible in the project view. This message is displayed because by default the **Overlay** value is set for the **Reference Type** option in the **Manage Links** dialog box. To display the nested link model in the host model, open the parent link view in which the file is linked and choose the **Manage Links** tool in the **Import** panel of **Insert** tab; the **Manage Links** dialog box will be displayed. Choose the **Revit** tab from the dialog box; the name of the linked file will be displayed in the **Linked File** column. Click in the **Reference Type** column and change the value in this column to **Attachment**. Now, link the parent model file to the host project; the nested linked model will be displayed in the project. If you do not want to display the nested model elements in the host project, accept the default **Overlay** option. When you select the **Overlay** option, Revit does not load the linked model when its host is linked to another model. The following example explains the use of the **Overlay** and **Attachment** options in linking models. Example: Project A consists of a single horizontal wall, as shown in Figure 16-27. The project A is imported and linked to the project B that consists of a single vertical wall. Figure 16-28 shows the Project B and Figure 16-29 shows the project A linked to the project B. The project B becomes a host for project A and project A becomes a link for project B. Now, the project B along with the linked project A (consisting of both horizontal and vertical walls) is imported to another project, Project C, which consists of a single inclined wall. In this case, the project A (consisting of a horizontal wall) becomes a nested link. Figure 16-30 shows the project C after linking with the project B. You will notice that the horizontal wall of project A will not be displayed in the project C. This is because the **Overlay** option is selected in the **Reference Type** column of the **Manage Links** dialog box. To display the horizontal wall of the project A (nested model) in the project C, open the project B parent view, consisting of vertical and horizontal walls. Next, choose the **Manage Links** tool from the **Link** panel in the **Insert** tab; the **Manage Links** dialog box will be displayed. Choose the **Revit** tab in the dialog box; the project A will be displayed in the **Linked File** column. Select the **Attachment** option for the linked project A in the **Reference Type** column and choose the **OK** button. Close the parent view and import the project B into the project C. Now, the horizontal wall of the project A (nested link) will be displayed in the project C, as shown in Figure 16-31. The project A will also be added in the **Project Browser** as the nested link under the parent project B, as shown in Figure 16-32.

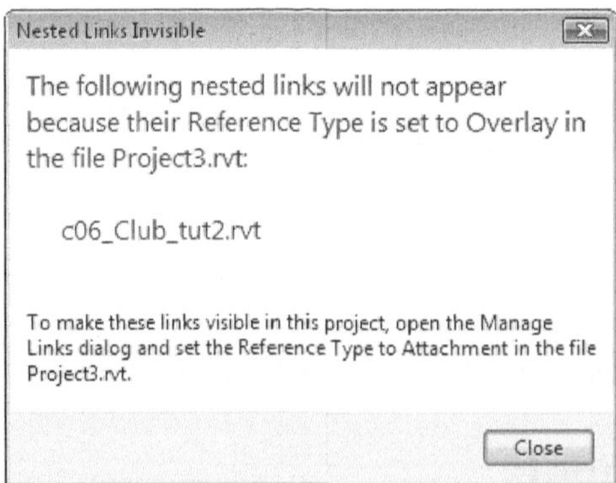

***Figure 16-26** The **Nested Links Invisible** message box*

__Figure 16-27__ Project A consisting of a horizontal wall

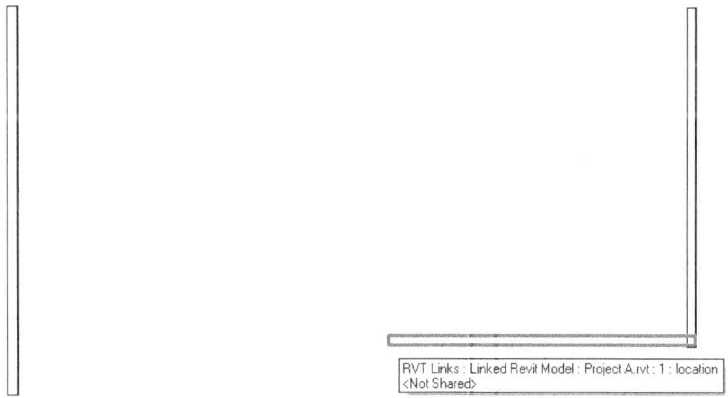

__Figure 16-28__ Project B consisting of a vertical wall

__Figure 16-29__ Project A linked to project B

__Figure 16-30__ The host project B linked to project C with the __Overlay__ option selected

__Figure 16-31__ Project B linked to Project C after selecting the __Attachment__ option for project A

__Figure 16-32__ Project A added as a nested link with parent project B in the __Project Browser__

Converting Linked Models to Groups - Binding Links

You can convert the linked Revit models into groups in the host project. You can do so by binding the linked model with the host project, thereby making it a part of the host project. After binding the linked model, the model geometry will be transformed into a group, and therefore making changes in the host project will be easier for you. To bind and group a linked model, select the linked model in the drawing; the **Modify | RVT Links** tab will be displayed. Choose the **Bind Link** tool from the **Link** panel; the **Bind Link Options** dialog box will be displayed, as shown in Figure 16-33. In the dialog box, select the **Attached Details**, **Levels**, and **Grids** check boxes to include them in the group and then choose the **OK** button; the linked model will be converted into a group. If there is any group in the project with the same name as that of the linked Revit model, a dialog box with a message will be displayed prompting you to replace the group. Choose **Yes** to replace the existing group or choose **No** to rename the group. On choosing **Yes**, another dialog box with a message to remove the link will be displayed, as shown in Figure 16-34. Choose the **Remove** button in the dialog box to remove the link or choose the **OK** button to remove it later; the linked model will be transformed into a group and listed in the **Project Browser** under the **Groups** head.

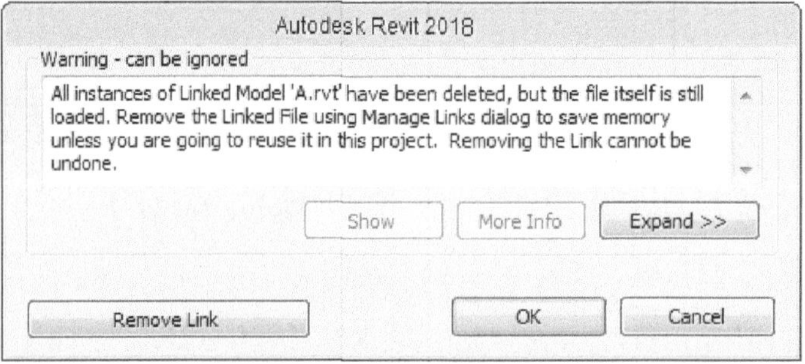

***Figure 16-34** The message box displayed on binding the link*

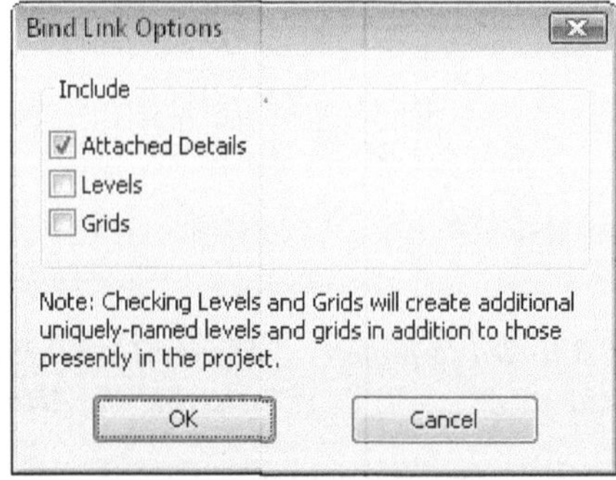

***Figure 16-33** The **Bind Link Options** dialog box*

Controlling the Visibility of Linked and Nested Linked Models

You can control the visibility of the linked and nested Revit linked models in the host project file. Also, you can control the visibility settings, detail level, and display settings of the building elements in the linked project. To modify the visibility settings in the host project, open the view in which the visibility settings are to be modified. Choose the **Visibility/Graphics** tool from the **Graphics** panel in the **View** tab; the **Visibility/Graphic Overrides** dialog box will be displayed. The **Revit Links** tab in this dialog box displays the linked projects, as shown in Figure 16-35. This tab will be displayed only when the files are linked in your project. Click on the project name to display the categories of components in the building model. Use the **Halftone** and **Display Settings** columns to modify the visibility settings and filters of the components of each linked project. The **By Host View** button in the **Display Settings** column can be used to control the visibility of the nested links, phases, and phase filters.

Click in the **Display Settings** column; the **RVT Link Display Settings** dialog box will be displayed. Choose the **Basics** tab from the dialog box. If you select the **By host view** radio button in this tab, the nested linked model will be able to use the same visibility and graphics settings as in the host view. On selecting the **By linked view** radio button, the nested linked model adopt the visibility settings of the parent model to which it was linked originally. On selecting this radio button, the **Linked view** drop-down list will be enabled. You can select the view in which you want to display the linked model from this list.

On selecting the **Custom** radio button, all the options in the **Basics** tab will be enabled. From the **Nested links** drop-down list, select the **By parent link** option to apply the visibility settings of the parent model to the nested link model. If you select **By linked view** from the drop-down list, the visibility and graphics override settings of the top level nested model will be applied to the linked model. The top level model is the first nested linked model. In the example explained earlier, project A will be the top-level nested model. Choose the **Apply** button to view the changes in the project and then choose the **OK** button.

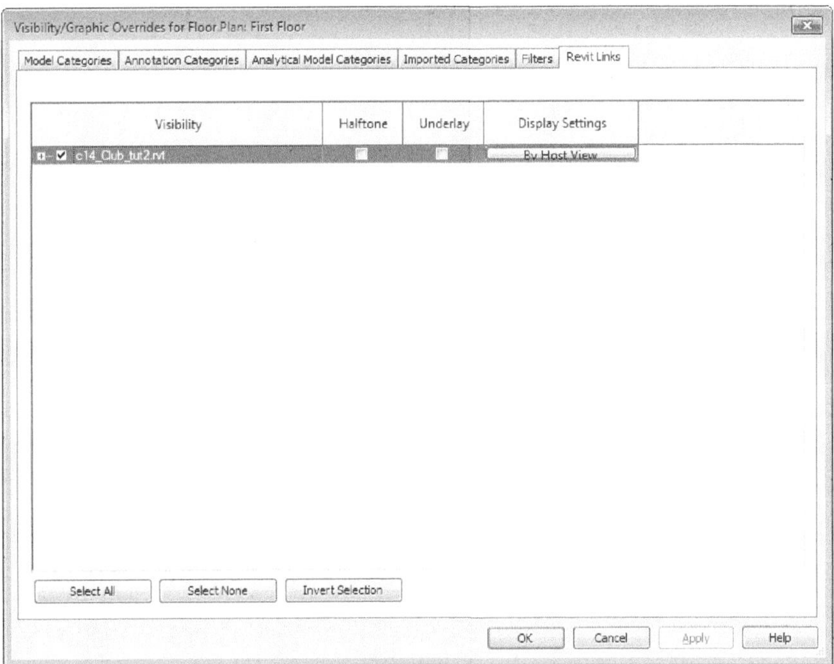

*Figure 16-35 The **Revit Links** tab of the **Visibility/Graphic Overrides** dialog box*

Managing Links

Revit enables you to manage links between the host and the linked projects. To do so, choose the **Manage Links** tool from the **Link** panel of the **Insert** tab; the **Manage Links** dialog box will be displayed with a list of linked projects, as shown in Figure 16-36.

The **Status** column in the **Manage Links** dialog box informs whether the linked project file is loaded in the host project. The **Reference Type** column in the dialog box provides you with the options to display or hide the nested linked Revit models. The default **Overlay** value in the **Reference Type** column restricts the loading and display of the nested linked models in the host project. The **Positions Not Saved** column of the dialog box indicates whether the linked models location is saved in its shared coordinate system or not. The shared coordinates take care of the mutual positions of multiple interlinked files. The **Saved Path** column shows the path of the linked file on your computer. The **Path Type** column is used to specify whether the saved path of the linked file is relative or absolute. It is recommended to keep the linked path relative because it enables Revit to trace and re-establish the link, in case the host and linked projects are moved to a different folder.

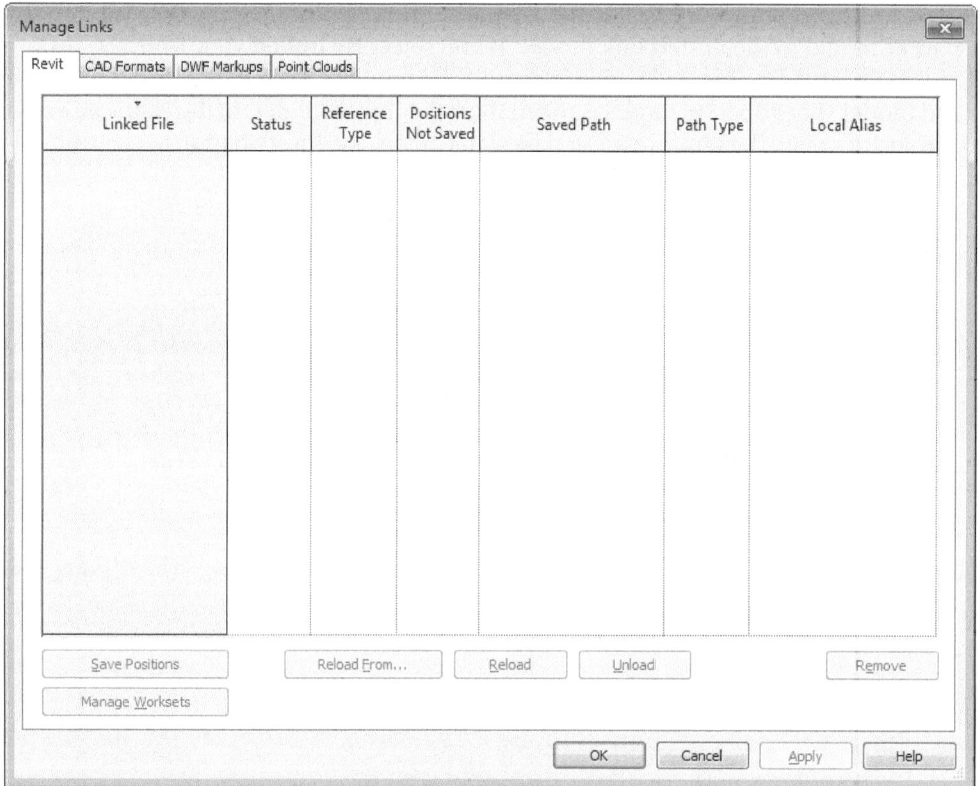

***Figure 16-36** The **Manage Links** dialog box*

Including Elements of Linked Models in Schedules

In Autodesk Revit, you can include different model elements from a linked file such as walls, doors, windows, and so on into a schedule. To do so, select the existing schedule of the current project from the **Schedules/Quantities** head in the **Project Browser**; the instance properties of the selected schedule will be displayed in the **Properties** palette. In the value column of the palette, choose **Edit** in the **Fields** parameter; the **Schedule Properties** dialog box will be displayed. Select the **Include elements in Linked files** check box to include the elements from a linked file, if required. To include project information from a linked file, select **Project Information** from the **Select available fields from** drop-down list. Select the example explained earlier, project A will be the top-level nested model. Choose the **Apply** button to view the changes in the project and then choose the **OK** button.

Applying the Color Schemes of the Host Model to Rooms and Areas of the Linked Models

In Autodesk Revit, you can apply the color scheme assigned to the rooms and areas in the host file to the rooms and areas in the linked file. To do so, choose the **Color Schemes** tool from the **Room & Area** panel of the **Architecture** tab; the **Edit Color Scheme** dialog box will be displayed. In this dialog box, make sure that the **Include Elements from linked files** check box is selected in the **Options** area. Choose the **OK** button to close the dialog box. Next, choose the **Visibility/ Graphics** tool from the **Graphics** panel of the **View** tab; the **Visibility/Graphic Override** dialog box will be displayed for the current view. Next, choose the **Revit Links** tab from the dialog box. Select the linked model to which you want to apply the color scheme of the host file. Choose the default **By Host View** button in the **Display Settings** column; the **RVT Links Display Settings** dialog box will be displayed. You can select the **By host view** or **Custom** radio button in this dialog box if the linked model consists of rooms. However, if the linked model consists of only areas, select the **Custom** radio button. On selecting the **Custom** radio button, all options in the **Basics** tab will be enabled. From the **Linked view** drop-down list, select the view of the linked model to which you want to apply the color scheme. Next, from the **Color Fill** drop-down list, select the **By host view** option. Choose the **Apply** button to apply the changes. Next, choose the **OK** button to close the dialog box.

You can also display the room areas and the area boundary of the linked file in the host project. To do so, open the parent view that contains the linked model and select the **By linked view** radio button in the **RVT Links Display Settings** dialog box. Select the required plan view from the **Linked View** drop-down list and choose the **OK** button; the room areas and the area boundaries in the linked model will be displayed in the host file.

Copying Linked Model Elements

You can copy the elements of the linked model to the host model. To do so, move the cursor over the linked model and press TAB to highlight the required elements, in case the file has a nested link. Click on the element when it is highlighted and choose the **Copy to Clipboard** tool from the **Clipboard** panel of the **Modify | RVT Links** tab. Next, open the host file in which you want to paste the element and choose the **Paste from Clipboard** tool from the **Clipboard** panel; the linked model file from which you have selected the element will be displayed in the **Project Browser** under the **Revit Links** head. You can place the element either by clicking at the required location in the drawing area or by dragging the linked model from the **Project Browser** and dropping it in the drawing area.

WORKSHARING CONCEPTS

Worksharing is a method of distributing work among people involved in a project, and accomplishing it within the stipulated period of time. In Worksharing, each person involved in the project is assigned a task that has to be accomplished through proper planning and by coordinating with the other members of the team.

In a large scale building project, worksharing is the most important method to finish the project in time and meet the quality requirements that are set during the process. Generally, in a large-scale building project, worksharing is based on the specialization of work. For example, professionals like Structural Engineers, Architects, Interior Architects, Electrical Engineers, and Plumbing Engineers can be involved in their respective fields to accomplish the project. So, the distribution of work at the primary stage is made on the basis of the area of specialization. Each professional has his own set of work to perform for the accomplishment of the project. Therefore, worksharing is an important process that is needed to be implemented efficiently to complete the project in time.

Worksharing Using Workset Tools

In Autodesk Revit, you work in an integrated single file model. This implies that all the construction related information and documents are available in a single model file and this forms the basis of the worksharing process.

The process of worksharing can be implemented using the **Worksets** tool. Worksets are a collection of building elements such as walls, doors, windows, and others that define the domain and ownership of the user in a project. For example, a project may contain building elements like beams, columns, furniture, walls, doors, and so on. In a worksharing environment, you can assign each element to a workset, which defines its ownership to the user, thereby restricting other users to change or modify it in the project without prior permission. Therefore, only one user can edit a workset at a time.

When you start a new Revit Architecture project, the worksharing is not activated by default because the software assumes that you are working in a single user environment. When you transform your project from a single user to a multi-tasking environment, you need to understand the concept of central file system and the utility of using the worksets. A central file is a master file of the project and stores the entire building information of the building and its model. This file is connected and shared by all other files representing individual users and it monitors the progress of the entire project. The files that are shared and connected to the central file are called local files. These files are the copy of the central file and are saved on the individual users workstation locally. These files can also be saved in a specified network location, thereby differentiating them from the central file. These local files act as an interfacing mechanism for working on the central file.

Process of Worksharing

With the start of the new project, you start creating the basic building geometry like the shell of the model with basic detailing. But as the project progresses, you underscore the need of sharing the project with multiple users for which you need to speed up the process of work toward completion. To invite multiple users to work in your project, you save the file that you have worked as a central file in a network location and make copies of it in the local hard drives of individual team members. By doing so, you divide the work into different parts. Everybody will start working with the copied central file from his or her individual workstation. Before starting with the file, each member working in the project is instructed to rename the copied central file in their individual hard drive location and then open it in Revit Architecture to proceed further. The flow diagram in Figure 16-37 explains in brief the process of worksharing in brief.

Elements in each separate file are tied to the ownership rule linked to the central file. This restricts individual team members to edit an element in his or her local file, which is owned by someone in local files. In the worksharing process, the central file behaves as the controller of all elements that are shared by members.

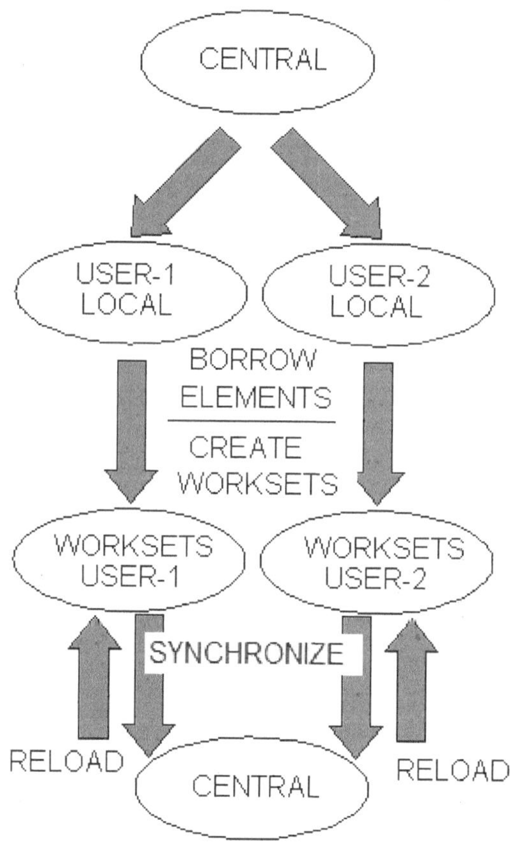

Figure 16-37 *Flow diagram explaining the Worksharing process*

Using Worksets Tool

To enable the process of worksharing choose the **Worksets** tool from the **Worksets** panel of the **Collaborate** tab. Autodesk Revit displays the **Worksharing** dialog box, as shown in Figure 16-38. This dialog box informs you that you are enabling the worksharing process. Once it is enabled, the process cannot be undone. The **Worksharing** dialog box contains two edit boxes: **Move Levels and Grids to Workset** and **Move remaining elements to Workset**. These two edit boxes show two default worksets: **Shared Levels and Grids** and **Workset1**, respectively. You can rename the Worksets, if you need, in the respective edit boxes. To continue with the worksharing process, choose the **OK** button to display the **Worksets** dialog box.

In the **Worksets** dialog box, there are five different columns, **Name**, **Editable**, **Owner**, **Borrowers**, and **Opened**, as shown in Figure 16-39. The **Name** column displays the worksets that are defined or predefined in the project. The **Editable** column shows the status of the modification of elements and components of the workset in the project. The **Owner** column specifies the ownership of the particular workset in the project. The ownership of the workset refers to the name of the user who had created it. This name refers to the user of the master file or the user of the local file. By default, Revit Architecture denotes the name of the user, which is determined by the log-on name of the operating system. In Revit, before enabling the workset, you can change the username. To do so, choose the **Options** button from the **File** menu; the **Options** dialog box will be displayed. In this dialog box, choose the **General** tab and specify a new name in the **Username** edit box.

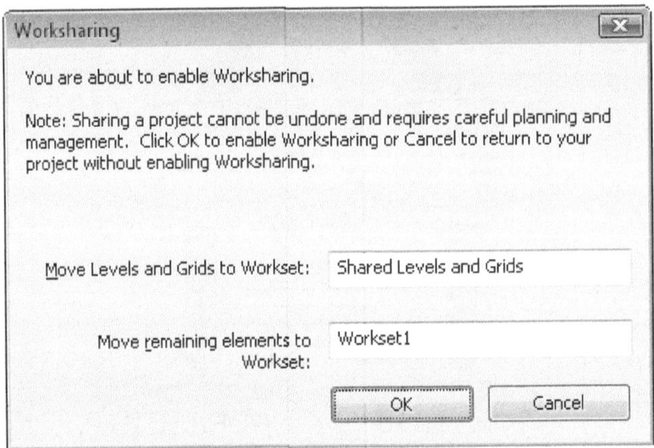

*Figure 16-38 The **Worksharing** dialog box*

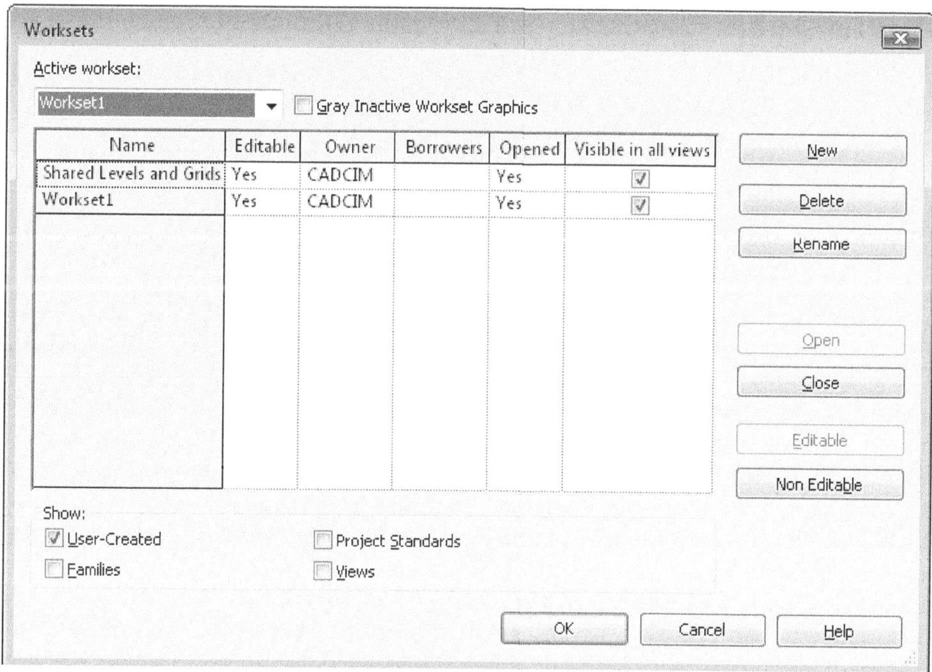

*Figure 16-39 The **Worksets** dialog box displaying different columns*

The **Borrowers** column in the **Worksets** dialog box displays the name of the user currently using the elements of the worksets that do not belong to him or her. In this process, the owner or any other user can only use the borrowed worksets, if the borrower allows to do so.

The **Opened** column is used to select a workset definition. There are two options in this column: **Yes** and **No**. These options can be used to control the visibility of elements in a group. By default, all worksets in the **Worksets** dialog box are assigned the **Yes** option. It means all elements and components of these worksets are visible in the file. But, if you choose the **No** option, the visibility of elements and components of worksets will be disabled.

The **Visible in View** column allows you to show workset in all views. This column carries checkboxes corresponding to the **Shared Level and Grids** and **Workset 1 Name** parameters. These check boxes are selected by default. On clearing these check boxes, the workset will not be displayed in any view.

You can select various options from the **Active workset** drop-down list located at the top in the **Worksets** dialog box. This drop-down list is used to select those worksets that are user defined and have the status **Yes** in the **Opened** column of the **Worksets** dialog box. Select the appropriate workset available in the drop-down list to make it current. If you select the **Gray Inactive Workset Graphics** check box, the elements that do not belong to the active workset will turn gray in the drawing area and the active elements will be displayed in black. If you clear this check box, all elements in the drawing area, irrespective of whether they are active or inactive, will turn black.

To create a new workset definition, choose the **New** button in the **Worksets** dialog box; the **New Workset** dialog box will be displayed, as shown in Figure 16-40. Enter the name of the workset in the **Enter new workset name** edit box and choose the **OK** button to return to the **Worksets** dialog box.

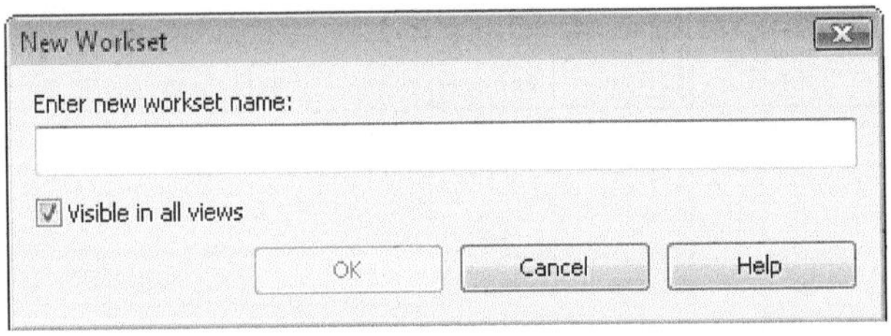

*Figure 16-40 The **New Workset** dialog box*

The **Delete** button in the **Worksets** dialog box is used to completely remove the selected workset. You can delete only that workset definition which is editable. When you choose the **Delete** button, the **Delete Workset** dialog box will be displayed, as shown in Figure 16-41. This dialog box can be used to delete the elements belonging to the deleted workset or to move these elements to a different workset definition. If you select the **Deleted** radio button in this dialog box, elements that belong to the workset being deleted, will be deleted. Similarly, if you want to move these elements to a different workset, select the **Moved to** radio button and then select the appropriate workset from the **Moved to** drop-down list. Choose the **OK** button to return to the **Worksets** dialog box. You can rename the editable worksets. To do so, select the workset in the **Name** column and choose the **Rename** button; the **Rename** dialog box will be displayed. Specify a name in the **New** edit box to change the name of the selected workset. The **Open** and **Close** buttons in the **Worksets** dialog box are used to change the status of the selected workset in the **Opened** column to **Yes** and **No**, respectively. Similarly, the **Editable** and **Non Editable** buttons can also be used to change the status of the selected workset in the **Editable** column to **Yes** and **No**, respectively. While using the Workset for the first time , if you choose the **Non Editable** button before saving the file to the central file, the **Revit** warning message box will be displayed. This message box warns you to save your file to central file.

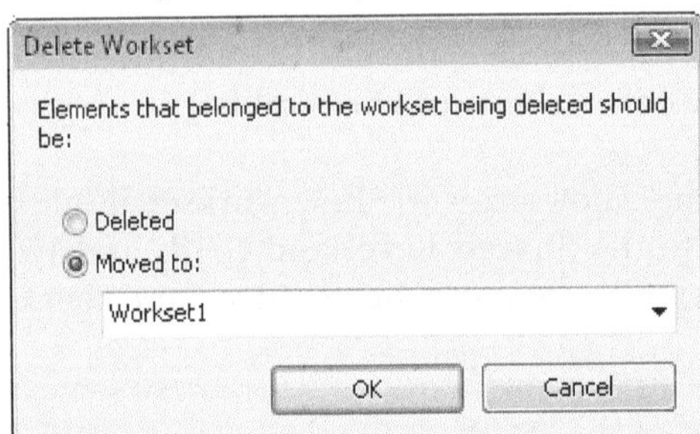

*Figure 16-41 The **Delete Workset** dialog box*

In Autodesk Revit, you can define four different types of worksets. These worksets are **User-Created**, **Family**, **Project Standards**, and **View** worksets. These Worksets are explained next in detail.

User-Created Workset

A user can define and modify this workset as per the requirements. As a user, you can create your own workset and assign different elements and components to it. When you invoke the **Worksets** dialog box, two worksets, **Shared Levels and Grids** and **Workset1** are created by default. The **Shared Levels and Grids** workset is automatically defined for the existing levels and grids in your drawing and the **Workset1** workset is defined for all elements and components created by you.

View Workset

In Revit Architecture, each view has a dedicated view workset that contains a dedicated view property and view-specific elements like dimensions, tags, text, and others. To display view worksets in the **Worksets** dialog box, you need to select the **Views** check box in the **Show** area of this dialog box.

The view-specific elements cannot be moved to other worksets. To own a view in a workset, select the view from the **Project Browser** and click the right mouse button over it; a cascading menu will be displayed. Choose the **Make Workset Editable** option from it to own the view in the workset.

Family Workset

When you load a family into your project, a workset is automatically created for it. You can view the family workset by selecting the **Families** check box in the **Show** area of the **Worksets** dialog box. To own a family, select it in the **Worksets** dialog box and change the default option **No** in the **Editable** column to **Yes** from the available drop-down list.

Project Standards Workset

The project standards worksets are used to set projects. You can view these worksets by selecting the **Project Standards** check box in the **Worksets** dialog box. In the **Worksets** dialog box, you can own a particular workset by changing the default option **No** in the **Editable** column to **Yes** from the available drop-down list for the selected workset. **Materials**, **Line Styles**, and **Callout Tags** are good examples of these worksets.

Once you have created and edited your workset, you can exit the **Worksets** dialog box by choosing the **OK** button from it. You can disable the worksharing in the project by choosing the **Disable Worksharing** tool from the expanded **Workset** panel of the **Collaborate** tab.

Synchronizing with Central

If you choose **Save** from the **File** menu after enabling the worksets for the first time, the **Save File as Central** message box will be displayed. On choosing the **Yes** button from this message box, the current project file will become the central file. If you choose the **No** button, a message box will be displayed informing that the file is not saved. Choose the **Close** button from this message box to close it. To save the file as a central file, choose **Save As > Project** from the **File** menu; the **Save As** dialog box will be displayed. Browse to a different location, specify a name in the **File name** edit box, and then choose **Save**; the file will be saved as a central file. Now, you can synchronize a project with the central file. To do so, choose the **Synchronize Now** tool from **Collaborate > Synchronize > Synchronize with Central** drop-down, as shown in Figure 16-42; the current project will be synchronized with the central file. As a result, all changes made to the current file will reflect in the central file as well.

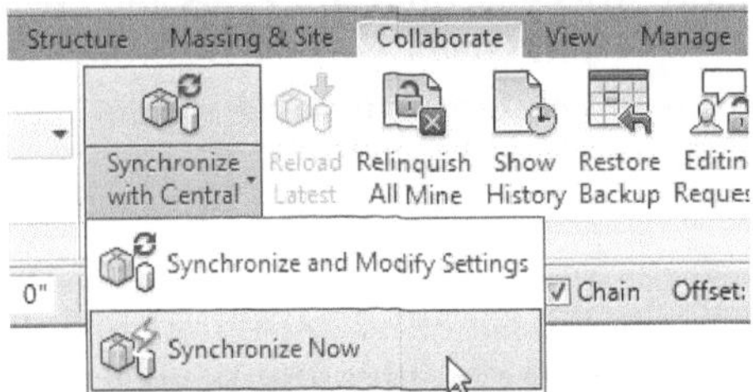

*Figure 16-42 Choosing the **Synchronize Now** tool from the **Collaborate** tab*

Note

A central file is a master project file that stores the information about the ownership of all worksets in a project. The central file should not be used for working when there is only one user.

Creating a Local File

While using a workset, you do not need to be connected to the system network to save the changes. For this, Autodesk Revit allows you to work on a local file of the portion of the building model file. A local file can be created by opening the central file and using the **Save As** tool to create a project file. This local file is only accessible to the user. The team member can work on the file and save it to the central file at regular intervals. The changes made to the workset are then propagated to all team members through the central file.

Saving Methodology in Worksharing

While working in a worksharing environment, it is important to learn the methods of saving your files. There are two methods of saving a file and sharing your files with others by saving a local file and synchronizing with the central file. You can save your file as a local file by choosing **Save** from the **File** menu. The **Save** option is generally used to save the local file. Using this method, you can just secure the work that you have done without affecting the worksharing process. The other method is to synchronize the file with central. The **Synchronize with Central** option is used to publish the work in the central file. The moment you synchronize your file to central, you acquire the changes made by other team members to their local models, provided they had also saved their files to the central file at that particular interval.

In Revit Architecture, you can synchronize a local file with the central file by choosing the **Synchronize Now** tool or the **Synchronize and Modify Settings** tool from the **Synchronize** panel. If you choose the **Synchronize Now** tool, the current project file will be saved to central. On choosing the **Synchronize and Modify Settings** tool, the **Synchronize with Central** dialog box will be displayed. This dialog box allows you to customize the way you save your file to central. In the **Synchronize with Central** dialog box, the **Central Model Location** text box shows the path for the central file in the network. You can use the **Browse** button to change the path, if required. After synchronizing the required file with central, you can use various check boxes to relinquish borrowed elements and various worksets, if required. The **Comment** text box in the **Synchronize with Central** dialog box allows you to publish the message throughout the team members regarding the changes you made in the particular session.

Reloading Files

In a worksharing environment, it is necessary to update your model corresponding to the changes made and saved to the central file by other team members. To do so, choose the **Reload Latest** tool from the **Synchronize** panel of the **Collaborate** tab. Alternatively, press RL in the keyboard to reload the file with the latest changes made in it.

Element Ownership Concepts

In a worksharing environment, you need to know about the status of ownership of a particular element or workset in the project. To check the status of ownership of an element, select it and check whether you can modify or reposition it. If you own the element, it will be highlighted in blue and can be modified and repositioned. In case, you do not own the element that you have selected, it will be highlighted in red, but with a blue icon attached to it indicating it cannot be modified.

In Autodesk Revit, you can use color to visualize the status of workshared elements. To do so, choose the **Worksharing Display Off** option from the **View Control Bar** and then select various options from the flyout displayed. You can use these options to customize the display modes to visually distinguish the following in a view: borrowed elements, current element owners, model updates, and element checkout status.

In Revit Architecture, it is easy to retain the ownership status of a particular element or a component. There are several methods to get the ownership of a particular element or a workset and that discussed next. One of the common methods of owning an element or a component is by trying to move or edit it. If you do so, Autodesk Revit facilitates you to own it, provided it is not owned by anyone else in the worksharing environment. You can also get the ownership of an element by clicking the left mouse button over the blue icon that is displayed along with it. Next, to modify or edit an element, select it and click on the right mouse button and then choose the **Make Elements Editable** option from the shortcut menu displayed. In context to ownership, you need to know other concepts like Borrowing Elements, Placing Requests, and Granting Requests. These concepts are discussed next. Sometimes, you or your team member may need to take the ownership of some of the elements within a particular workset rather than the entire workset. In such a situation, you can borrow elements from other users. To do so, select the element to be borrowed and click on the blue icon displayed with the element; the **Revit 2018** dialog box will be displayed with a warning message regarding the ownership of the element. This message box also informs you to place request to the owner to use it in your file. Choose the **Place Request** button in the dialog box to request the owner to grant permission for using the element. On doing so, the **Check Editability Grants** dialog box will be invoked. Choose the **Check Now** button from the dialog box to check the status of the request made and choose the **Continue** button to resume the work.

Autodesk Revit also provides you with the flexibility to borrow components from worksets that are not editable by a team member. This is possible by getting permission from the user of the component, and then, the borrowed elements or components can be edited, saved to central, and relinquished. In this release, the process of granting or denying permission to borrow an element or a component for editing it has been made more fast and interactive.

PURGING UNUSED ELEMENT FAMILIES

The **Purge Unused** tool enables you to unload families and family types from the project file. This reduces the file size to a considerable extent. However, in case the worksets have been enabled, they must be opened to use this tool.

Invoke the **Purge Unused** tool from the **Settings** panel of the **Manage** tab; the **Purged unused** dialog box will be displayed, as shown in Figure 16-43. It displays the list of element categories that can be unloaded. You can select the families, groups, or annotation types and choose the **OK** button to purge them. You can also use the **Check All** and **Check None** buttons for the selection. In Autodesk Revit, you can also purge unused materials.

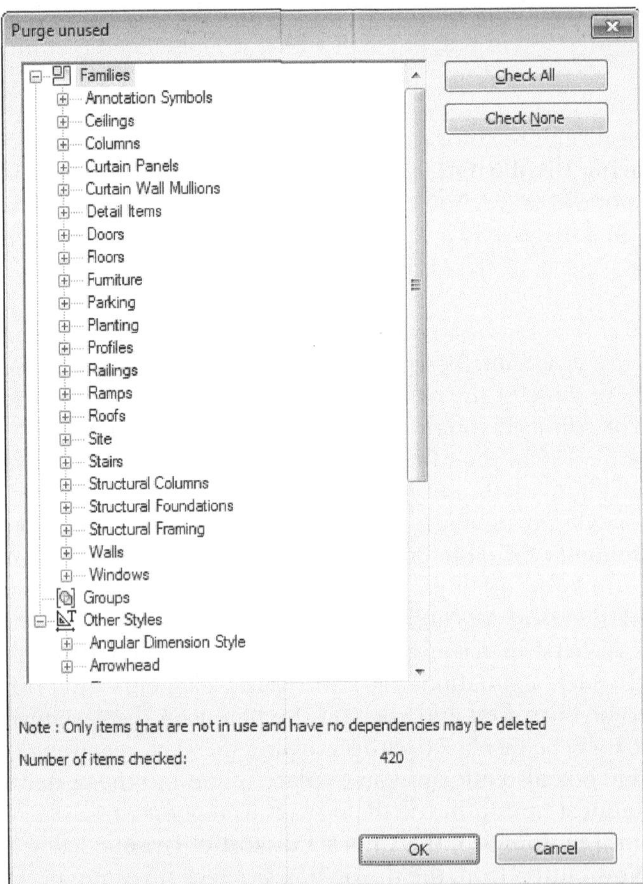

*Figure 16-43 The **Purge unused** dialog box*

TRANSFERRING PROJECT STANDARDS

The **Transfer Project Standards** tool allows you to copy and paste project standards from one project to another. The project standards that can be transferred include family types, materials, view templates, and object types.

To transfer project standards, you first need to open the source and target projects. In the target project, choose the **Transfer Project Standards** tool from the **Settings** panel of the **Manage** tab. On doing so, the **Select Items To Copy** dialog box will be displayed, as shown in Figure 16-44. Select the source project from the **Copy from** drop-down list. From the list box in the dialog box, select the required project standards to be copied. Now, choose the **OK** button; the selected project standards of the source project will be copied to the target project.

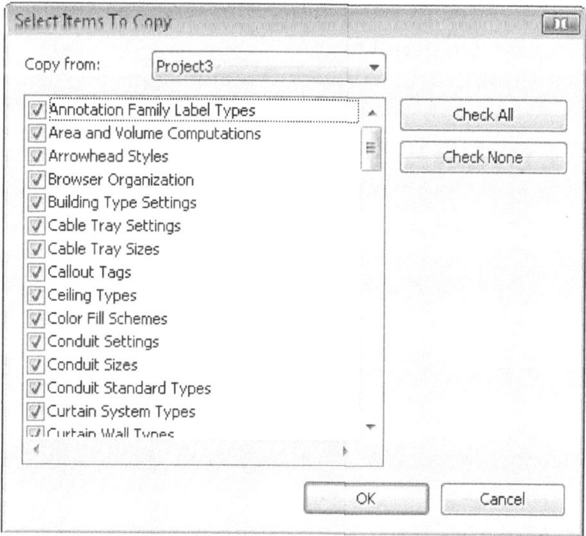

Figure 16-44 The ***Select Items To Copy*** *dialog box*

ORGANIZING THE PROJECT BROWSER

Autodesk Revit also enables you to organize the **Project Browser** based on the documents to be prepared for the project. Invoke the **Browser Organization** tool from **View > Windows > User Interface** drop-down; the **Browser Organization** dialog box is displayed. The **Views** tab of this dialog box displays the parameters that can be selected for organizing the browser.

The **Sheets** tab can be used to view the sheets created for a project in the **Project Browser**. You can select an option to display the sheets. For example, you can rename the sheets created for a construction document package based on their sheet numbers. You can also select the **Sheet Prefix** check box in the **Sheets** tab to arrange the sheet display in the **Project Browser**. Figure 16-45 shows the **Project Browser** with such an arrangement.

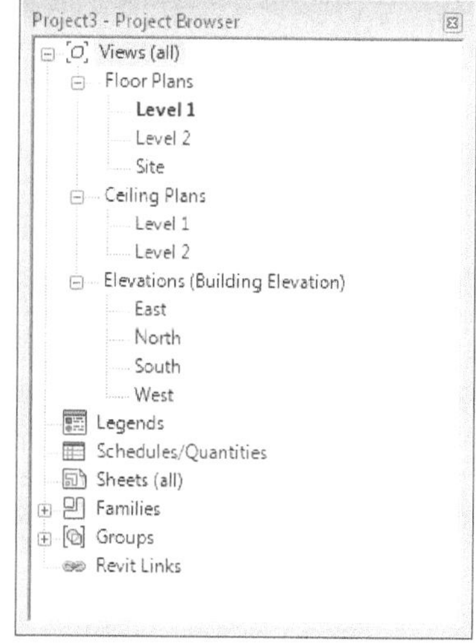

Figure 16-45 An example of organised ***Project Browser***

GENERATING SHADOWS

Another powerful feature provided in Autodesk Revit is the automatic generation of shadows based on the location of the sun with respect to the building. Shadows can be generated in the plan, elevation, section, or 3D view. To use this feature, open the view and click on the inclined arrow symbol (Graphic Display Options) in the **Graphics** panel of the **View** tab. On doing so, the **Graphic Display Options** dialog box will be displayed. In this dialog box, select the **Cast Shadows** check box. The intensity and direction of the shadow can also be controlled by using various options from **Graphic Display Options** dialog box. You can also choose the **Shadow On** button from the **View Control Bar** to generate shadows in the view.

REVIT ARCHITECTURE SOLAR STUDIES

Revit Architecture's solar study helps you visualize and analyze the position of Sun and solar effects on buildings and sites in the real world at a specified time, date, duration, and location. You can analyze the effect of the Sun on the same building at different locations, such as Boston or Melbourne, by changing the location of the building from Boston to Melbourne. The **Solar Study** tools in Revit Architecture provide you with a wide range of locations to view the Sun and shadow effects on the same building or site but at different locations by generating the solar studies. Revit Architecture allows you to generate a still solar study in a single frame depicting the shadows at a specified date and time. It can also generate an animated three-dimensional solar study consisting of multiple frames depicting the shadow movements for a specified duration of time.

These solar studies help you analyze the amount and impact of the natural sunlight and shadows on the building and the site at a particular time in a day and at a particular location. It also helps you study the amount of lighting inside the building during different times of a day and year, at a particular location.

Generating Still Solar Study

You can generate a still solar study to see the shadow patterns based on the location of the building, or the azimuth and altitude of the Sun from the horizontal surface. To generate a still solar study, open the floor plan view or the site plan view. In the **Properties** palette of the opened view, set the value of the **Orientation** parameter to **True North** and choose the **Apply** button. Next, choose the **Rotate True North** tool from **Manage > Project Location > Position** drop-down; a rotation symbol will be displayed in the drawing area. In the **Options Bar**, specify the rotation angle in the **Angle from Project to True North** edit box. This angle specified in the edit box will be the angle difference of the building from the Project North direction to the **True North** direction. You can rotate the building to the **East** or **West** of the **True North** direction. Open the 3D view of the building and adjust the view of the building as required. Choose the **View** tab and then choose the inclined arrow symbol in the **Graphics** panel; the **Graphic Display Options** dialog box will be displayed, as shown in Figure 16-46.

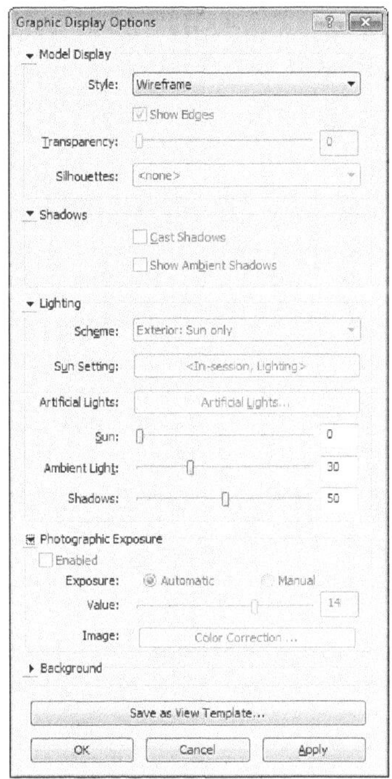

Figure 16-46 *The* ***Graphic Display Options*** *dialog box*

In the **Model Display** area of this dialog box, you can select an option from the **Style** drop-down list to specify the visual style of the model in the drawing area. In this drop-down list the **Hidden Line** option will be selected by default. The other options in this drop-down list are: **Wireframe**, **Hidden Line**, **Shaded**, **Consistent Colors**, and **Realistic**. The **Show Edges** check box will be disabled if you select **Wireframe**, **Hidden Line**, or **Consistent Colors** in the **Style** drop-down list. If this check box is active and selected then the edges of the model will be displayed in the **Shaded** or **Realistic** view style. The transparency of the surfaces of the model in the **Shaded** or **Realistic** view style, can be changed by the **Transparency** slider. The **Silhouettes** drop-down list is used to specify a line style that will help create a silhouette in the model. In the **Shadows** area, you can select the **Cast Shadows** check box to display shadows of a building model in a 3D view. You can select the **Show Ambient Shadows** check box to display shadow in the building model due to ambient light. In the **Lighting** area of the **Graphic Display Options** dialog box, choose the button on the right of the **Sun Setting** text; the **Sun Settings** dialog box will be displayed. By default, the **Lighting** radio button is selected in this dialog box. Select the **Still** radio button and in the **Settings** area and then set the time and date for the solar study in the **Date** and **Time** edit boxes. To specify the location for the solar study, choose the button on the right of the **Location** edit box; the **Location Weather and Site** dialog box will be displayed. In the **Location** tab of the dialog box, select the **Default City List** option from the **Define Location by** drop-down list. On doing so, the options to set the locations will be displayed below this drop-down list. Specify the latitude and longitude in the **Latitude** and **Longitude** edit boxes for a precise solar study or select a city from the **City** drop-down list. Next, choose the **OK** button to close the **Location Weather and Site** dialog box. In the **Sun Settings** dialog box, clear the **Ground Plane at Level** check box to view the shadow pattern on the terrain. If you want the shadows to fall at a particular level or at the entry level, select the **Ground Plane at Level** check box and then select a level from the drop-down list displayed below it. Next, choose the **OK** button to return to the **Graphic Display Options** dialog box.

If you want to create a solar study based on the azimuth and altitude of the Sun from the horizontal surface, select the **Lighting** radio button in the **Sun Settings** dialog box and specify the azimuth and altitude for the solar study. After you have specified the settings for the solar study, choose the **OK** button.

Tip

You can invoke the ***Graphic Display Options*** *dialog box and control the display of shadows from the* ***View Control Bar*** *at the lower left corner of the screen.*

Next, in the **Lighting** area of the **Graphic Display Options** dialog box, set the intensity of the sun, ambient light, and shadows by using the **Sun**, **Ambient Light**, and **Shadows** sliders, respectively. You can save the settings in the **Graphic Display Options** dialog box as a template. To do so, choose the **Save as View Template** button; the **New View Template** dialog box will be displayed. In this dialog box, enter a name for the settings in the **Name** edit box and choose the **OK** button; the **View Templates** dialog box will be displayed. In the **View Properties** area of this dialog box, you can use various options to edit the view properties of the current setting. Now, choose the **OK** button in the **View Templates** dialog box to close it. In the **Graphic Display Options** dialog box, choose the **OK** button to notice the shadows based on the specified date, time, and location. The shadow pattern generated in a Still solar study at the same location at different time during a day is shown in Figures 16-47 through 16-51. The options in the **Photographic Exposure** area helps you to create realistic appearances of objects in **Realistic** and **Raytrace** view style. On selecting the **Realistic** view style from the **Style** drop-down list, the **Enabled** check box is activated. Select the **Enable** check box; the options in the **Exposure** section are enabled. In the **Exposure** section, you can either select the **Automatic** radio button to enable automatic exposure of the model. Alternatively, you can select the **Manual** radio button. On doing so, the **Value** slider will be enabled where you can adjust exposure needed in the model. To improve the appearance of the model and make it more realistic, you can choose the **Color Correction** button corresponding to the **Image** parameter. On doing so, the **Color Correction** dialog box will be displayed. In this dialog box, you can adjust the values of **Highlights**, **Shadow Intensity**, **Color Saturation**, and **White Point** parameters by using their respective sliders. After setting the parameters, choose **OK** to close the **Color Correction** dialog box and return to **Graphic Display Options** dialog box.

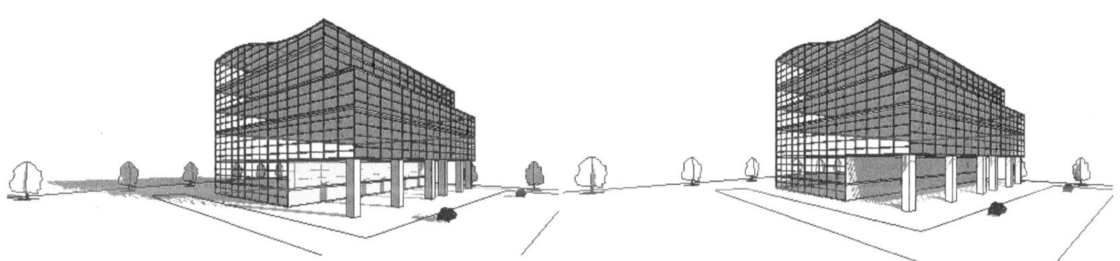

Figure 16-47 *After sunrise at around 6 AM* ***Figure 16-48*** *In the morning at 10.25 AM*

Figure 16-49 *In the afternoon at 1.25 PM* ***Figure 16-50*** *In the evening at 4.30 PM*

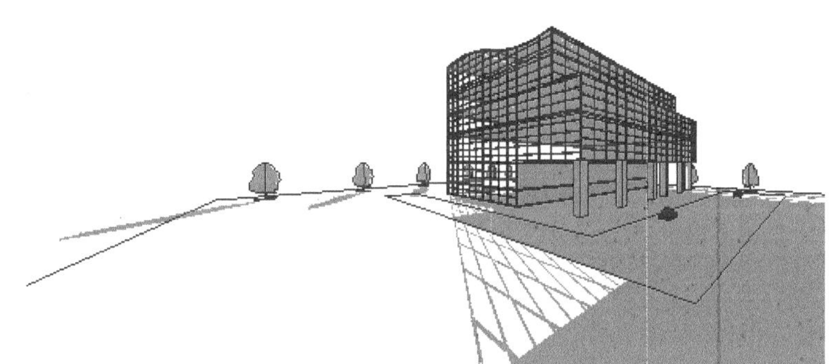

Figure 16-51 *During sunset at 6.55 PM*

In the **Graphic Display Options** dialog box, you can use the options in the **Background** area to set the background of the displayed view. In the **Background** area, you can select any of the four options from the **Background** drop-down list: **Sky, Gradient, Image**, and **None**. On selecting the **Sky** option from the **Background** drop-down list, the **Ground Colo**r parameter will be displayed under it. Choose the swatch corresponding to the **Ground Color** parameter; the **Color** dialog box will be displayed. Select a desired color from this dialog box and choose **OK**. The color of the sky will be set as per your selection and will be applied in the project view. On selecting the **Gradient** option from the **Background** drop-down list, three parameters: **Sky Color**, **Horizon Color,** and **Ground Color** are displayed under it. For each of these, you can choose different colors by using the **Color** dialog box. On selecting the **Image** option from the **Background** drop-down list, the **Customize Image** button will be displayed under it. Choose this button; the **Background Image** dialog box will be displayed. You can use this dialog box to apply an image to the background. After selecting an image and specifying the settings, choose **OK**; the **Background Image** dialog box will be closed and the **Graphic Display Options** dialog box will be displayed. In this dialog box, choose **Apply** and **OK** buttons to apply the display settings to the view.

Creating an Animated Solar Study

In Revit Architecture, you can also create an animated single-day or multi-day solar study. The single-day solar study generates the animation of shadow movements for a specified period of time in a single day and at a particular location. For example, you can create a solar study from 6 AM to 7 PM on August 15 in Boston. The multi-day solar study helps you create an animation of shadow movements at a fixed time of a day, but for specified number of days at a particular location. For example, you can create a solar study at 2 PM from August 15 to August 20, 2012 in Boston.

To generate a single-day solar study, open the 3D view of the building model and click on the inclined arrow symbol in the **Graphics** panel of the **View** tab; the **Graphic Display Options** dialog box will be displayed. Make sure the **Cast Shadows** check box is selected in the dialog box. Choose the button on the right of the **Sun Setting** text; the **Sun Settings** dialog box will be displayed, as shown in Figure 16-52. Select the **Single Day** radio button; the options of sun settings for single day will be displayed in the **Sun Settings** dialog box. Select any of the predefined sun and shadow settings from the **Presets** list box. You can also define your own sun and shadow settings and name them by choosing the **Duplicate** button. The name of the setting will be listed in the list box. Specify the settings for the solar study in the **Settings** area as explained earlier and choose the **OK** button in the **Sun Settings** dialog box. Now, choose the **OK** button from the **Graphic Display Options** dialog box to apply the settings to the project view.

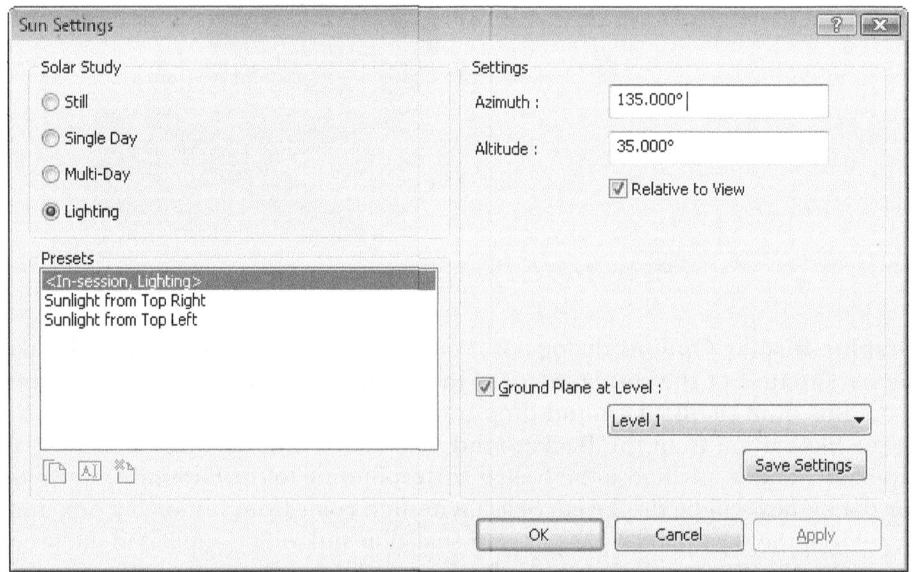

*Figure 16-52 The **Sun Settings** dialog box*

Animation Preview

To preview the solar study animation, choose the **Shadows On** button from the **View Control Bar**. Now, choose the **Preview Solar Study** option from the flyout displayed. Choose the **Play** button from **Options Bar** to play the animation. You will notice the shadow movements in multiple frames at a specified time. You can use the **Previous Key Frame** and **Next Key Frame** buttons from the **Options Bar** to move the animation back or forward by 10 frames. To view a particular frame of the animation, enter the frame number in the **Frame** edit box. Choose the **Next Frame** or **Previous Frame** button to view the previous or the next frame. Similarly, you can create the multi-day animation by selecting the **Multi-Day** radio button from the **Sun Settings** dialog box. In this dialog box, specify the time, location, and dates for the days for which you need to generate the solar study.

Exporting the Solar Study Animation

You can save and export the solar study animation and share it with clients and owners. To export the solar study animation, choose **Export > Images and Animations > Solar Study** from the **File** menu; the **Length/Format** dialog box will be displayed, as shown in Figure 16-53. Select the **Frame range** radio button and set the number of frames to be exported by setting the suitable values in the **Start** and **End** spinners in the **Output Length** area. The animation in that particular range of frames will be exported. You can also set the speed of the animation by setting suitable value in the **Frames/sec** spinner. The **All frames** radio button is selected to export the complete animation. In the **Format** area, select the graphics style from the **Visual Style** drop-down list. Specify the dimensions in pixels or zoom percentage to specify the frame size in the exported file. Choose the **OK** button to display the **Export Animated Solar Study** dialog box, as shown in Figure 16-54.

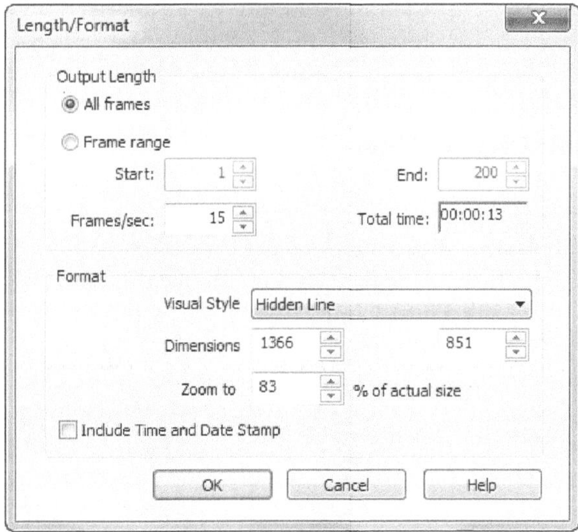

*Figure 16-53 The **Length/Format** dialog box*

In the **Save in** drop-down list, navigate to the required location to save the file. Enter the file name of the file in the **File name** edit box. Select the file format from the **Files of type** drop-down list to save the file.

Next, choose the **Save** button. If you have saved the file using the AVI file format, the **Video Compression** dialog box will be displayed on choosing the **Save** button. Choose the **OK** button to accept the default option in the dialog box; the animation file will be processed frame by frame and finally it will be saved as an AVI format at the specified location.

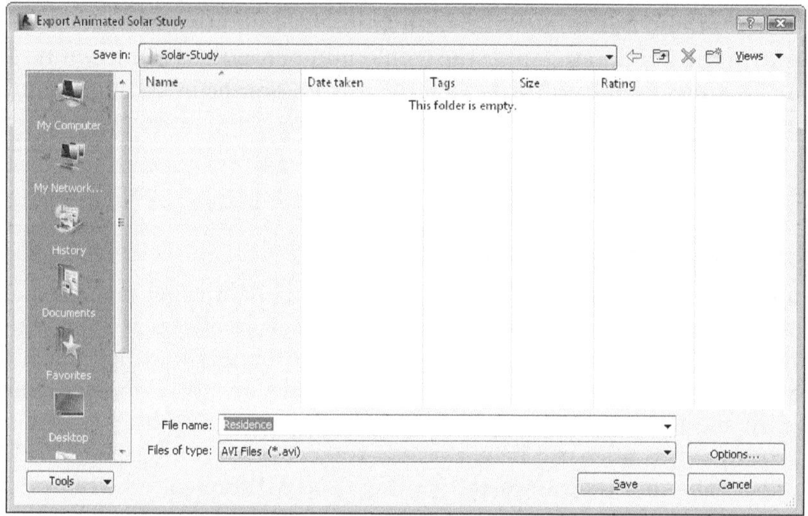

*Figure 16-54 The **Export Animated Solar Study** dialog box*

POINT CLOUD

Point Cloud is a collection of point data in X, Y, and Z ordinates. This data is collected by 3D scanners. These 3D scanned point clouds are then used to create 3D revit models. These point cloud files are inserted in the Revit project to modify the existing condition of a building.

Inserting a Point Cloud File

Point cloud files are .rcp and .rcs type format files. If the file is in raw format such as .pcg or .las format, then you will be prompted to index the data. The .rcp and .rcs format files are indexed point cloud files which are inserted in a Revit project.

To directly use the .rcp or .rcs format file in a project, invoke the **Point Cloud** tool from the **Link** panel of the **Insert** tab; the **Link Point Cloud** dialog box will be displayed. In the **Link Point Cloud** dialog box, navigate to the location of files from the **Look in** drop-down list. Select the desired type of file format from the **Files of Type** drop-down list. After selecting the type of file from the list, select the desired position of file from the **Positioning** drop-down list located at the lower right corner of the **Link Point Cloud** dialog box. Now, choose the **Open** button; Revit retrives the current version of the point cloud file and links the .rcp and .rcs format files in the project.

If the files are in raw format, you will be prompted to index the data. To do so, choose the **Point Cloud** tool from the **Link** panel of the **Insert** tab; the **Link Point Cloud** dialog box will be displayed. In this dialog box, insert the raw format file type and then choose the **Open** button; the **File Not Indexed** window will be displayed prompting you to create the new .rcp or .rcs format file. Choose the **Yes** button in this dialog box; the **Point Cloud File Indexing** dialog box will be displayed. Now, to convert the raw data into the .rcs or .rcp format, choose the **Start Indexing** button; the file will be converted. As the indexing process finishes, choose the **Close** button; the dialog box will be closed. Now, the file is converted into an .rcp format. Choose the **Point Cloud** tool again to insert the new indexed file in the project.

Point Cloud Visibility

To view a point cloud in a project, invoke the **Visibility/Graphic** tool from the **Graphics** panel of the **View** tab; the **Visibility/Graphics Overrides for <current view>** dialog box will be displayed. In this dialog box, choose the **Point Cloud** tab. Next, in the **Visibility** column of this tab, you can select or clear the checkbox corresponding to the selected point cloud file to show or hide the point cloud in the view, respectively. You can also assign the color for each point cloud in the model. To do so, choose the **RGB** button; the **Point Cloud Color Mode** dialog box will be displayed. In the **Point display** area of this dialog box, by default, the **RGB** option is selected in the **Color Mode** drop-down list. On selecting any other color option in the drop-down list, the **Settings** area, and the **Clear Overrides** button at the bottom of the dialog box will be activated. Specify the required settings in the **Settings** area. You can also choose the **Clear Overrides** button to restore the previous settings. Next, choose the **OK** button; the dialog box will be closed.

Using Point Cloud File in a Project

In Autodesk Revit, after inserting the point cloud file, you will use that file in the project. This file helps the user to provide a higher level of visual appearance of existing condition of a building. To capture the existing building, laser scanners are used to sample point from the surface of the existing building and saves that data as point cloud.The data collected by the laser scanner is huge. Thus, Revit links a point cloud as a reference rather than embedding the complete file. Now, you can modify the existing building condition easily and the work performance will be also be improved due to better visibility.

REVIT INTEROPERABILITY

Autodesk Revit is quite compatible with CAD-based programs. You can create your own designs in Revit Architecture and then export them into other programs for visualization and creating photorealistic renderings of your designs. Revit is user-friendly, parametric, flexible, and compatible features help you create and implement your designs better and faster. Revit Architecture supports a wide range of file formats, thereby enabling the files to be imported and exported to other programs such as Autodesk 3ds Max, Autodesk 3ds Max Design, Autodesk Inventor, Revit Structures, Revit MEP, SketchUp, Microstation, and so on.

Interoperability with Autodesk 3ds Max and Autodesk 3ds Max Design

You can export a 3D view from Revit to Autodesk 3ds Max and 3ds Max Design through DWG format to create photorealistic renderings and visualizations. The interoperability of Revit with 3ds Max and 3ds Max Design has improved in the following ways:

1. Before exporting the views, you can use the section box to restrict the unwanted content in the file to be exported to Autodesk 3ds Max and Autodesk 3ds Max Design. The section box has been enhanced to enable you to switch to 2D view while modifying the section box size for the 3D view. Reducing the amount of data from the file reduces the size, thus making the importing and exporting of data faster and easier.

2. The objects that have different materials assigned to different surfaces in Revit Architecture and the objects that have a complex geometry are exported in 3D view as ACIS solids. When such objects are imported in 3ds Max and Autodesk 3ds Max Design, they display different materials assigned to different surfaces unlike the previous releases that showed only one material for the entire ACIS solid.

3. The files exported from Revit and imported into 3ds Max and Autodesk 3ds Max Design show the Revit Material Names, unlike the Material names that used to be displayed for the materials in the previous releases.

4. To export drawings from Revit to 3ds Max and Autodesk 3ds Max Design, you do not need to use the plug-in anymore, as this functionality has been incorporated in Autodesk 3ds Max Design and 3ds Max.

Revit - 3ds Max Workflow

The main steps followed to export a Revit project to 3ds Max are discussed next.

Create a 3D view for the project to be exported to 3ds Max. Choose **Export > CAD Formats > DWG** files /**DXF** files /**DGN** files / **ACIS (SAT)** files from the **File** menu; the **DWG Export** dialog box will be displayed. Export the file using the DWG format in the **DWG Export** dialog box.

In Autodesk 3ds Max, import or link the DWG file using the **File Link Manager** option by choosing **References > Manage Links** from the **File** menu. Linking the file will allow you to make changes in the project design in Revit and then update it in 3ds Max automatically, without making the same changes again in 3ds Max. If you do not want to update the design, then just import the file. Make the final adjustments in the materials for rendering and then render the view. Before you export the project from Revit to 3ds Max, limit the model geometry using the section box and turn off the visibility of the elements or the element categories that will not be used for rendering. For example, while rendering the exterior view, you should turn off the visibility of the elements in the interior of the building. Also, set the detail level for the view. By reducing the detail in a Revit view, the number of objects and the size of the DWG file will be reduced. After you have reduced the unwanted content of the file, you can export the file to 3ds Max or Autodesk 3ds Max Design as DWG file, ACIS solids or by creating a layer mapping template.

Interoperability with Google SketchUp

Revit Architecture supports SKP files. You can create your design in Revit and then export it to Google SketchUp. Similarly, you can import the design from Google SketchUp and link it to Revit. Google SketchUp is best suited for modeling and visualization. You can work on your designs using both Revit and SketchUp. If you want to quickly create a model of your design, assign materials and visualize it, then you can use SketchUp and then Revit Architecture to modify the designs. If you want to create a design, and at the same time, want to analyze and document the results, you should start your design in Revit and then use SketchUp at a later stage when you need to add materials and visualization. Google SketchUp along with Google Earth helps you place your models on the web using the real world coordinates and share it with world using the **3D Ware house** feature of SketchUp that helps you to search, share and store 3D models.

Exporting a Drawing from Revit to SketchUp

Before you export the drawing from Revit to SketchUp, reduce the unwanted drawing file by using the section box, turn off the visibility of the elements, and set the detail levels for the elements. Next, create an export template or a layer mapping file to save the layer settings for the drawing to be exported. These settings are customized to be used with SketchUp. After creating the template, choose **Export > CAD Formats > DWG files** from the **File** menu; the **DWG Export** dialog box will be displayed, as shown in Figure 16-55. On selecting the **Modify Export Setup** option from the **Select Export Setup** drop-down list in this dialog box; the **Modify DWG/DXF Export Setup** dialog box will be displayed. After setting the required views and other options, choose the **OK** button in this dialog box, and then choose the **Next** button in the **DWG Export** dialog box, the **Export CAD Formats - Save to Target Folder** dialog box will be displayed. In this dialog box, navigate to the required location to save the file, and select the DWG format. Next, enter the name of the file in the **File name/prefix** edit box and choose the **OK** button; the file will be exported to the specified location in the DWG format. Now, you can transfer and import the DWG file in SketchUp.

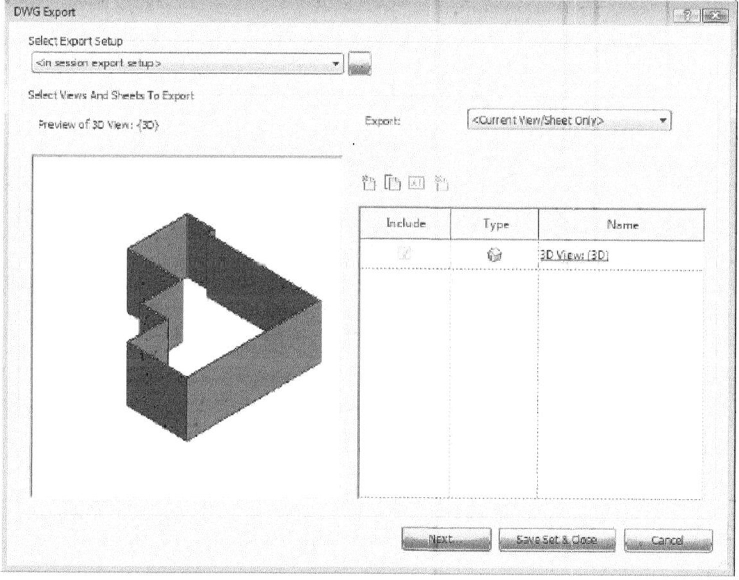

***Figure 16-55** The **DWG Export** dialog box*

Creating a Layer Mapping File for Layer Settings

Creating a layer mapping file or template file helps you to save the layer settings. These settings are customized for the drawing to be exported to SketchUp. To create a layer mapping file, choose **Export > CAD Formats > DWG files** from the **File** menu; the **DWG Export** dialog box will be displayed, refer to Figure 16-55. In this dialog box, choose the **Modify Export Setup** button; the **Modify DWG/DXF Export Setup** dialog box will be displayed, as shown in Figure 16-56. In this dialog box, ensure that the **Layers** tab is chosen and then select an option from the **Export layer options** drop-down list to set the layer mapping for the file to be exported. After selecting an option from the **Export layer options** drop-down list, you can select an option from the **Load layers from standards** drop-down list to specify the standard to be followed for the layer mapping set. Now, choose the OK button; the dialog box will be closed and the layer mapping for the exported file will be set.

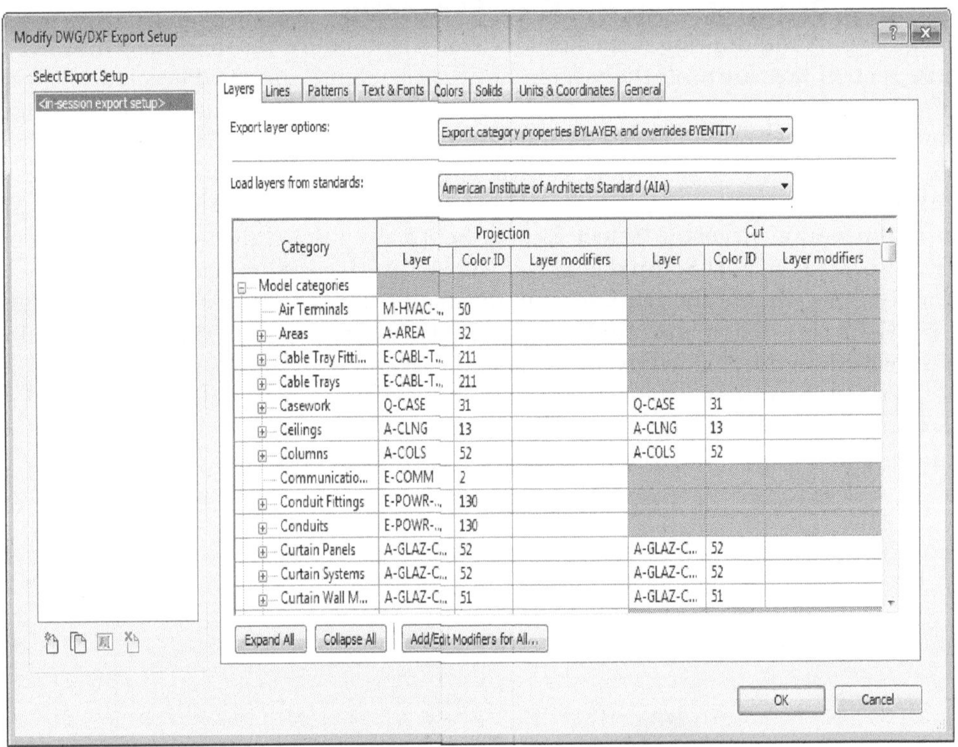

*Figure 16-56 The **Modify DWG/DXF Export Setup** dialog box for creating a layer mapping file*

Publishing Tips in Revit 2018

Revit Architecture allows you to export the 2D and 3D project views to Design Web Format (DWF). DWF provides you with an alternative of Portable Drawing Format (PDF) to publish your project views. The advantages of using the DWF are given below:

1. You can print the same DWF file using any printer since the DWF file is not device specific.

2. You can share the DWF files electronically through emails because of their smaller size.

3. The DWF files are generally one-twentieth the size of the original DWG files.

4. You can publish all your data in one DWF file instead of multiple DWG files.

5. You can place your designs on web using the Google search engine.

6. You can share your files irrespective of the versions of AutoCAD.

7. You can decide what to publish in DWF file and avoid the sharing of the original files.

8. You can see models clearly in a DWF file by zooming in the DWF files.

9. You can use a 3D viewer to view designs in DWF files.

10. Using the DWF files, you can share your designs in a much secure and easy way. You can share your designs even with people who do not use Revit Architecture.

Revit Architecture has the functionality of setting the default zoom option to **Fit To Page** in the **Print SetUp** dialog box. Therefore, you can avoid inclusion of a cropped portion of a 2D view into the DWF file. Also, you can publish rooms, areas, and room boundaries along with walls and other elements.

TUTORIALS

In the following two tutorials, you will combine the projects created in this book. In the first tutorial, you will create two facade options for the *Apartment 1* project. In the second tutorial, you will combine the *Elevator and Stair Lobby* and the *Apartment 2* project to create a cluster of apartments. You will then link the cluster to the *Site Layout* project created earlier in Chapter 9.

Tutorial 1 Apartment 1

In this tutorial, you will create two design options for the exterior facade. The first option uses 18" x 18" (for Metric 450 x 450 mm) square structural columns and beams, as shown in Figure 16-57. The distance between these members is shown in Figure 16-58 and Figure 16-59. The second design option is created using 12" X 12" (for Metric 300 x 300mm) square concrete columns and 12" X 24" rectangular concrete beams, as shown in Figure 16-60. The distances between the structural members and some other dimensions are shown in Figures 16-61 and 16-62. You can assume the missing dimensions for this tutorial.

(Expected time: 45 min)

Note

In this tutorial, the usage of structural elements has been given only as an example for creating the design options for a facade. Their general usage in a project should, however, depend on their placement.

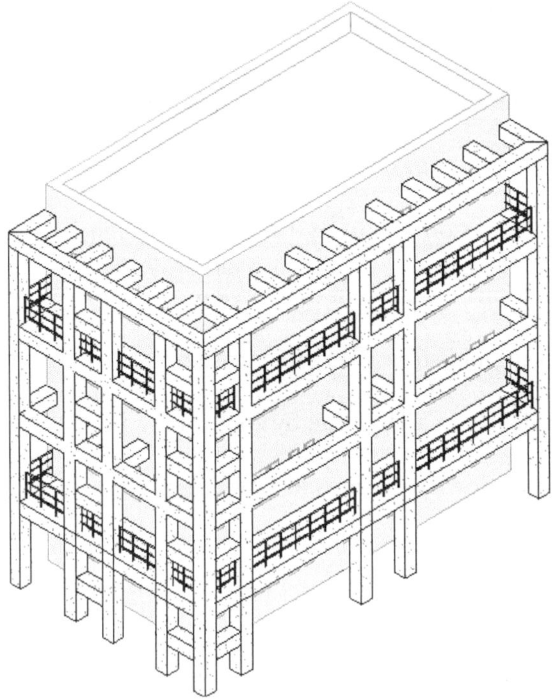

Figure 16-57 The 3D view for creating structural elements for Design Option 1

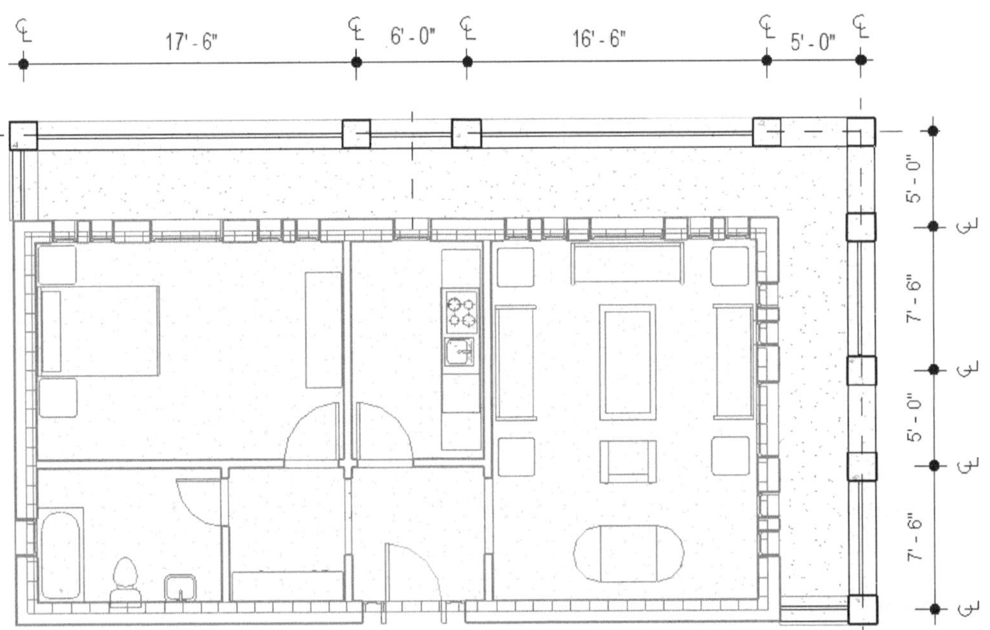

Figure 16-58 The sketch plan for creating structural elements for Design Option 1

The following steps are required to complete this tutorial:

a. Create the design options in the *Apartment 1* project.
b. Add structural elements to the Design Option 1, refer to Figures 16-57 through 16-59.
c. Add structural elements to the Design Option 2.
d. Save the project using the **Save As** tool.
   For Imperial *c16_Apartment1_tut1.rvt*
   For Metric *M_c16_Apartment1_tut1.rvt*
e. Close the project using the **Close** tool.

Creating Design Options

In this section of the tutorial, you will first create the two design options and then add elements to each of them.

1. Choose **Open > Project** from the **File** menu and open the *c15_Apartment1_tut1.rvt* file (for Metric *M_c15_Apartment1_tut1.rvt* file) created in Tutorial 1 of Chapter 15. You can also download this file from *http://www.cadcim.com*. The path of the file is as follows: *Textbooks > Civil/GIS > Revit Architecture > Exploring Autodesk Revit 2018 for Architecture.*

2. Double-click on **First Floor** in the **Floor Plans** head of the **Project Browser** to open the corresponding floor plan in the drawing window.

3. Choose the **Manage** tab and then choose the **Design Options** tool from the **Design Options** panel; the **Design Options** dialog box is displayed.

4. In the **Design Options** dialog box, choose the **New** button from the **Option Set** area; the **Option 1** node with **Option 1(primary)** subhead is displayed in the left side pane of **Design Option** dialog box.

Note

*The headings for the **Option Set**, **Edit**, and **Option** areas in the **Design Options** dialog box will disappear on creating a new option set. To locate these areas in the dialog box, refer to Figure 16-9 in this chapter.*

5. In the **Option** area, choose the **New** button to create **Option 2** under the **Option Set 1**.

6. Select **Option Set 1** and choose the **Rename** button in the **Option Set** area; the **Rename** dialog box is displayed. Enter **Facade Options** in the **New** edit box and choose **OK**; the **Option Set 1** node is renamed to **Facade Options**.

7. Similarly, rename **Option 1(primary)** as **18"X18" columns** (**450 x 450 mm**) and **Option 2** as **12"X12"** (**300 x 300 mm**) **columns**.

8. Select the option **18"X18" columns (primary)** and choose the **Edit Selected** button from the **Edit** area; the drawing area turns into edit mode for the selected design option.

9. Now, choose the **Close** button to close the **Design Options** dialog box.

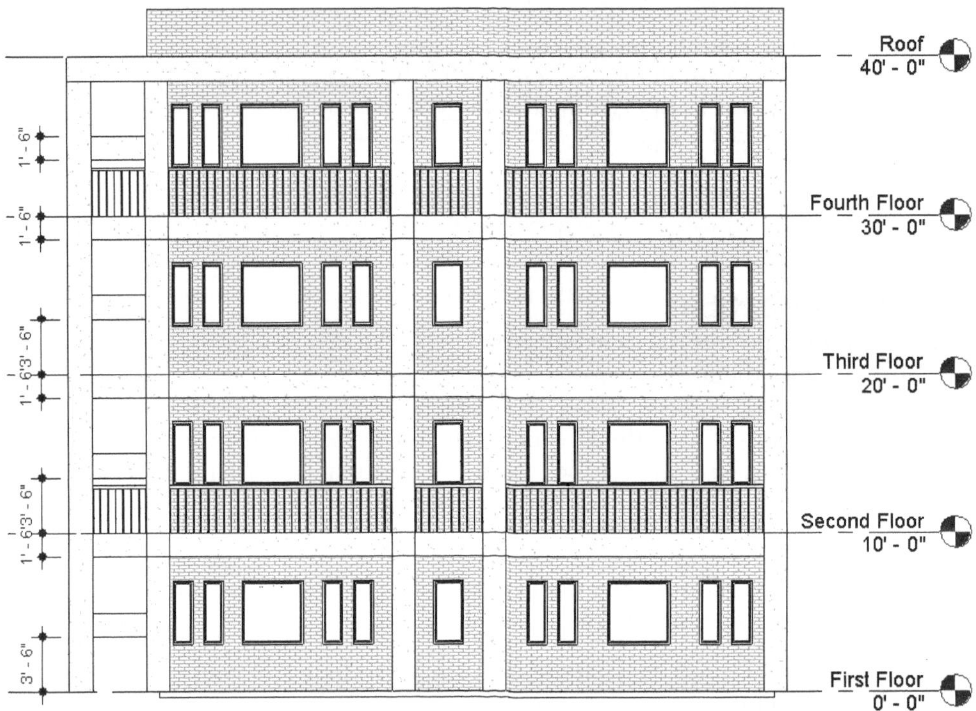

Figure 16-59 *The north elevation view for creating structural elements for Design Option 1*

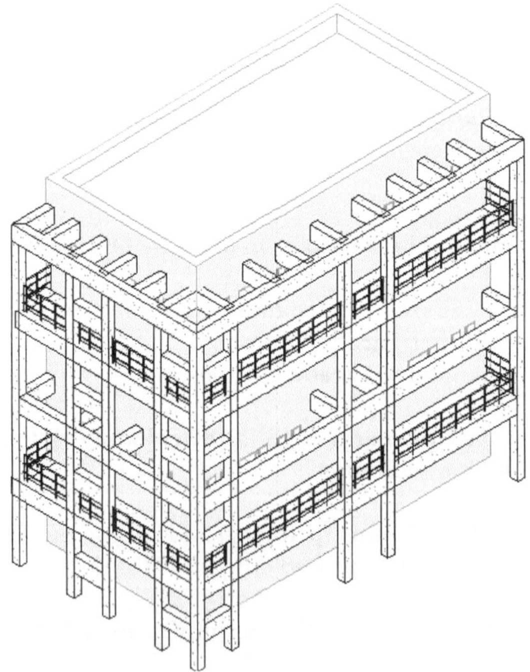

Figure 16-60 *The 3D view for creating structural elements for Design Option 2*

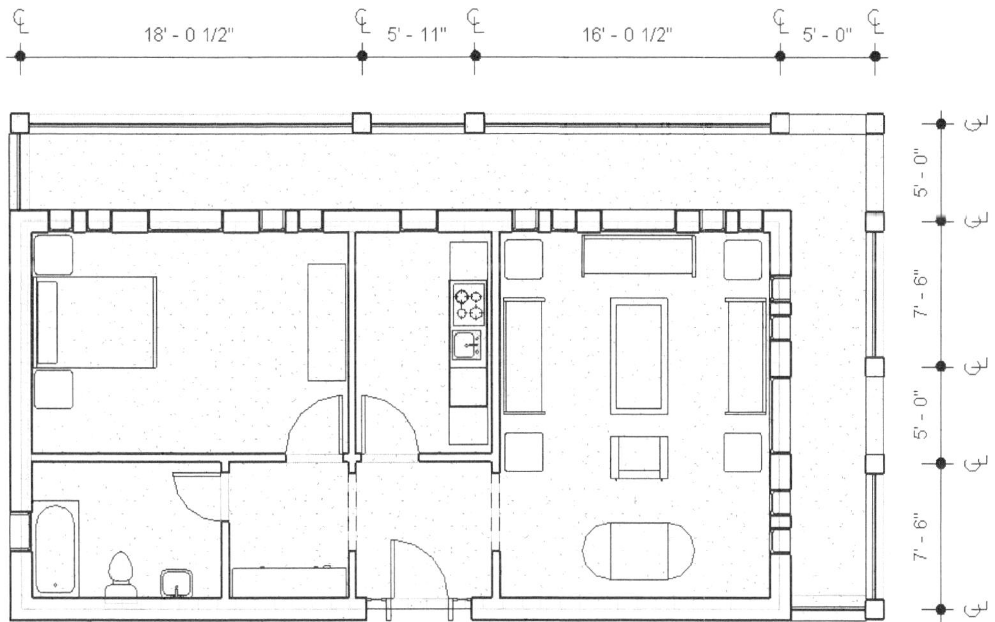

Figure 16-61 *The sketch plan for creating structural elements for Design Option 2*

Adding Structural Components to Design Option 1

In this section of the tutorial, you will load and add structural columns in Design Option 1.

1. You need to add the structural columns to the drawing. To do so, choose the **Structural Column** tool from **Architecture > Build > Column** drop-down; the **Modify | Place Structural Column** tab is displayed.

2. From the **Mode** panel, choose the **Load Family** tool; the **Load Family** dialog box is displayed.

3. In the **Load Family** dialog box, choose **US Imperial > Structural Columns > Concrete** folder (for Metric **US Metric > Structural Columns > Concrete** folder) and select the *Concrete-Square-Column.rfa* file (for Metric *M_Concrete-Square-Column.rfa* file). Next, choose **Open**; the **Concrete-Square-Column** family (for Metric **M_Concrete-Square-Column** family) is loaded into the project file.

4. From the **Type Selector** drop-down list in the **Properties** palette, select **Concrete-Square-Column: 18 x 18** (for Metric **M_Concrete-Square-Column: 450 x 450mm**).

5. Move the cursor near the top right corner of the floor plan and click when the vertical dimension in the upward direction displays **5'-0"** (1500 mm) and the wall centerline is displayed, as shown in Figure 16-63. Now, exit from the **Modify | Place Structural Column** tab by choosing the **Modify** button from the **Select** panel.

6. In the **3D Views** head in the **Project Browser**, double-click on **{3D}**.

7. Select the added structural column to display its instance properties in the **Properties** palette. In the **Properties** palette, click in the value field of the **Base Level** instance parameter and select the **First Floor** option from the drop-down list displayed, if it is not selected by default.

8. Click on the value field of the **Top Level** instance parameter and select **Roof** from the drop-down list displayed. In the value fields of the **Base Offset** and **Top Offset** instance parameters, enter **0'0"** (**0 mm**) and **-6"** (**-150 mm**), respectively.

9. Choose the **Apply** button from the **Properties** palette; the specified instance parameters are assigned to the selected column.

10. Open the **First Floor** plan view. Select the structural column and make its copies, refer to Figure 16-58. To make copies, choose the **Copy** tool from the **Modify** panel of the **Modify | Structural Columns** tab and select the **Multiple** checkbox from the **Options Bar** and create copies in the horizontal direction at the specified dimension, refer to Figure 16-58.

11. Now, choose the **Modify** button from the **Select** panel to clear the selection.

12. Repeat the procedure followed in step 10 to draw the column in vertical direction, refer to Figure 16-58. After adding all columns as per the sketch plan, choose the **Modify** button from the **Select** panel.

13. To add beams to the columns, choose the **Beam** tool from the **Structure** panel of the **Structure** tab; the **No Tag Loaded** window is displayed. Choose the **No** button from the window.

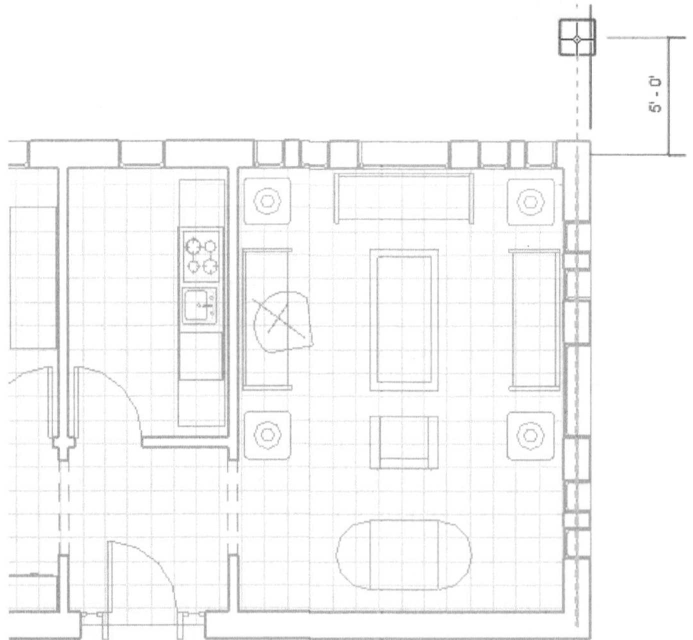

Figure 16-63 *Adding structural elements to the Design Option 1*

14. On invoking the **Beam** tool, the **Modify | Place Beam** tab is displayed. In this tab, choose the **Load Family** tool from the **Mode** panel; the **Load Family** dialog box is displayed.

15. In this dialog box, choose **US Imperial > Structural > Framing > Concrete** folder (for Metric **US Metric > Structural > Framing > Concrete** folder) and then select the *Concrete-Rectangular Beam.rfa* file (for Metric *M_Concrete-Rectangular Beam.rfa* file), and then choose **Open**; the **Concrete - Rectangular Beam** family (for Metric **M_Concrete - Rectangular Beam**) is loaded in the project.

16. In the **Properties** palette, notice that the **Concrete-Rectangular Beam 16 x 32** type (for Metric **M_Concrete-Rectangular Beam 400 x 800mm**) is selected by default in the **Type Selector** drop-down list. Next, choose the **Edit Type** button; the **Type Properties** dialog box for the selected beam type is displayed.

17. Choose the **Duplicate** button; the **Name** dialog box is displayed. Enter **18 x 18** (for Metric **450 x 450mm**) in the **Name** edit box and choose **OK**; the **Name** dialog box closes.

18. In the **Type Properties** dialog box, modify the values for **b** and **h** type parameters to **1' 6"** (**450 mm**) respectively and choose the **OK** button to assign the specified value to the new type and close the **Type Properties** box.

19. In the **Options Bar**, select the **Level: Second Floor** option from the **Placement Plane** drop-down list.

20. Sketch the horizontal beam between the two columns, as shown in Figure 16-64. Ignore the warning displayed.

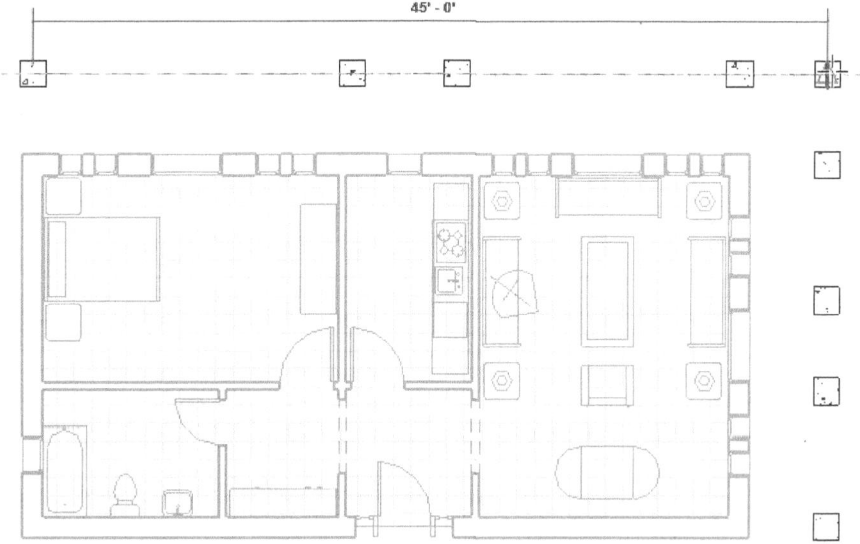

Figure 16-64 *Adding the horizontal structural beam to the Design Option 1*

21. Similarly, sketch the vertical beam between the two columns. Again, ignore the warning. After sketching the vertical beam, choose the **Modify** button; the current selection is cleared.

22. In the **Project Browser**, double-click on **{3D}** under the **3D Views** head; the default 3D view of the project is displayed in the drawing area.

23. Right-click on the **ViewCube** tool; a shortcut menu is displayed. Choose **Orient to a Direction > Northeast Isometric** from the shortcut menu; the current view reorients toward the northeast isometric view, as shown in Figure 16-65.

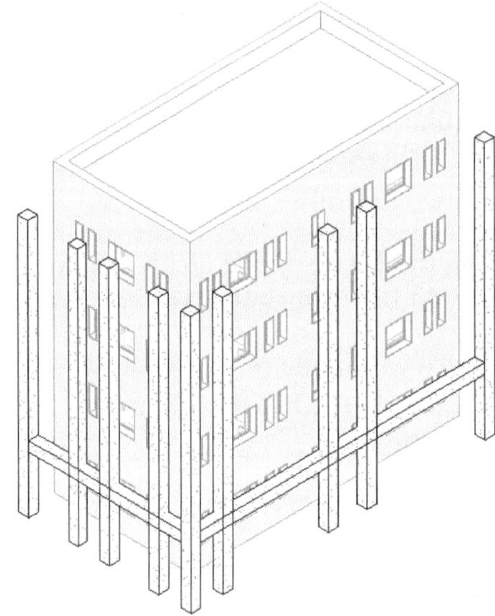

Figure 16-65 *The 3D view of the added structural elements*

24. Select the two beams using the CTRL key; the **Modify | Structural Framing** tab is displayed. Now, choose the **Copy to Clipboard** tool from the **Clipboard** panel; the selected beams are copied to the clipboard.

25. To paste the copied beams, choose the **Aligned to Selected Levels** tool from the **Paste** drop-down in the **Clipboard** panel; the **Select Levels** dialog box is displayed.

26. In this dialog box, select the **Third Floor**, **Fourth Floor**, and **Roof** options using the CTRL key and then choose the **OK** button to paste the beams at the selected levels. Now, choose the **Modify** button to exit the current selection.

27. Select the beams at the roof level and use the drag controls to complete the beam. You will use the **East** and **North Elevation** views to drag and extend the beams. After this step, the 3D view should appear similar to the illustration shown in Figure 16-66.

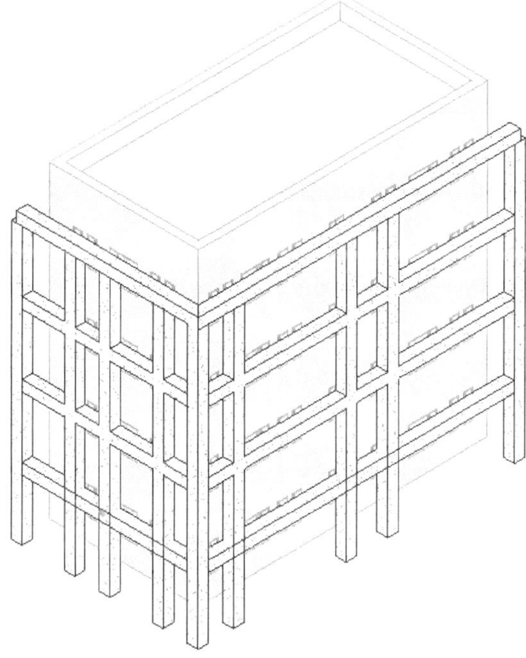

Figure 16-66 *The 3D view of the copied structural beams*

Similarly, you can add other smaller beams between the levels and the beams perpendicular to the walls, based on the given sketch plan and 3D View for Option 1. You may need to convert the exterior wall to bearing.

28. In the **Project Browser**, double-click on the **Second Floor**; to display the corresponding view.

29. Invoke the **Floor: Architectural** tool from **Architecture >Build > Floor** drop-down and add the floor slab between the exterior wall and the columns on the two sides at the second floor level, as shown in Figure 16-67. After you create the floor, Autodesk Revit displays a prompt box. Choose the **No** button to keep the walls detached from the slabs created in this design option.

30. Choose the **Railing** tool from the **Circulation** panel in the **Architecture** tab, create the default railing on the second floor between the structural columns, as shown in the 3D view for Design Option 1, refer to Figure 16-57.

31. After creating the railing and the floor, select them; the **Modify | Multi-Select** tab is displayed. Choose the **Copy to Clipboard** tool from the **Clipboard** panel of the **Modify | Multi-Select** tab; the selected elements are copied to the clipboard.

32. Choose the **Aligned to Selected Levels** tool from the **Modify | Multi-Select > Clipboard > Paste** drop-down; the **Select Levels** dialog box is displayed. From this dialog box, select the **Fourth Floor** option and then choose **OK**; the **Select Levels** dialog box closes and the selected element gets pasted. Choose the **Modify** button to exit the current selection.

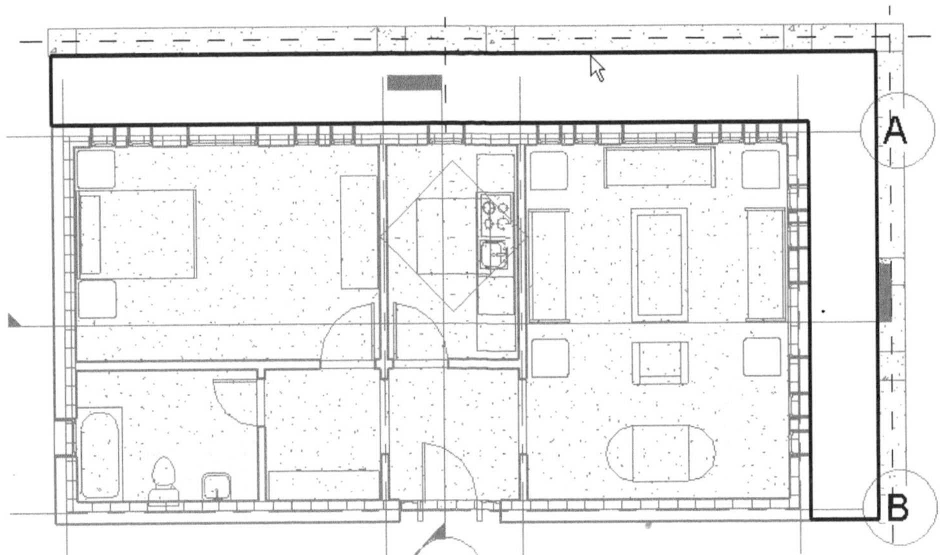

*Figure 16-67 A foor slab added using the **Floor** tool*

33. Choose the **Manage** tab and then choose the **Design Options** tool from the **Design Options** panel; the **Design Options** dialog box is displayed.

34. In this dialog box, choose the **Finish Editing** button from the **Edit** area and then choose the **Close** button; the **Design Options** dialog box closes and the 3D view appears similar to the view given for Option 1, refer to Figure 16-66. Notice that the **Main Model** option is selected in the **Active Design Option** drop-down list that is displayed below the **Pick to Edit** button in the **Design Options** panel of the **Manage** tab.

Adding Structural Components to Design Option 2

In this section of the tutorial, you will create elements to Design Option 2. In general, you can use two methods to create elements to a design option. The first method is to create the elements as they were created in the previous option. The second method is to copy elements from Option 1 to Option 2 and then modify them based on the given project parameters. You will use the second method in this tutorial.

1. To start adding element to the design option, choose the **Design Options** tool from the **Design Options** panel of the **Manage** tab; the **Design Options** dialog box is displayed. In this dialog box, select the **18" X 18" columns(primary)** (for Metric **450 x 450 mm columns(primary)**) choose the **Edit Selected** button. Next, choose the **Close** button; the **Design Option** dialog box is closed.

2. Select all elements created in Design Option 1, including columns, beams, floors, and railings and choose the **Copy to Clipboard** tool from the **Clipboard** panel of the **Modify | Multi-Select** tab and then choose the **Manage** tab.

3. In this tab, select the **12"X 12" columns** (for Metric **300 x 300mm columns**) option from the **Active Design Option** drop-down list in the **Design Options** panel. Notice that from the current view, the elements of the previous design option disappear.

4. Choose the **Modify** tab and then choose the **Aligned to Same Place** tool from the **Paste** drop-down in the **Clipboard** panel. Notice that the copied elements of Design Option 1 are pasted in Design Option 2.

5. Select all the column and by using the **Type Selector** drop-down list in the **Properties** palette, replace all **Concrete-Square-Column 18" X 18"** (for Metric **M_Concrete-Square-Column 450 x 450mm**) types with **Concrete-Square-Column 12" X 12"**types (for Metric **Concrete-Square-Column 300 x 300mm** type). Similarly, select all the beams and replace all **Concrete-Rectangular Beam : 18" X 18"** beams with **Concrete-Rectangular Beam : 12" X 24"** beams.

6. Use the drag control to extend the beams, wherever necessary, such that they completely lie over the column. You may need to work in various views to select and extend the beams based on the given 3D view for Design Option 2.

7. Similarly, select the railings and edit them such that they span between the columns. Also, modify their properties to match the given railing profile. Assume the dimensions for the railing and baluster placement.

8. Select and extend the floor slabs at the second and fourth floors up to the beams. Now, the 3D view of the project should resemble the views given for creating Design Option 2, refer to Figures 16-60 through 16-62.

9. Choose the **Design Options** tool from the **Design Options** panel in the **Manage** tab to invoke the **Design Options** dialog box. Choose the **Finish Editing** button from this dialog box. Ensure that **18" X 18" columns** (for Metric **450 x 450 mm columns(primary)**) is the primary option. Choose the **Close** button to close the dialog box.

Saving the Project

In this section, you will save the project file using the **Save As** tool.

1. Now, choose **Save As > Project** from the **File** menu; the **Save As** dialog box is displayed. Enter **c16_Apartment1_tut1.rvt** (for Metric **M_c16_Apartment1_tut1.rvt**) in the **File name** edit box of the **Save As** dialog box.

2. Choose **Save**; the **Save As** dialog closes and the file is saved.

Note

You will not close the project file for Apartment 1 project at this stage as this file will be required for the next tutorial for building the Apartment Complex.

Tutorial 2 Apartment Complex

In this tutorial, you will generate the Apartment Complex project by copying and pasting the elements of the *Elevator and Stair Lobby* and *Apartment 2* projects into the *Apartment* project. Edit them to attach to the *Apartment* project. Group them into an apartment cluster, as shown in Figure 16-68. Save the project file as *Apartment Cluster.rvt*. Use all latest project files for this tutorial.

In the *Site Plan* file created in Exercise 1 of Chapter 9, link the *Apartment Cluster* and the *Club* project based on Figure 16-69. Save the project file as *Apartment Complex.rvt*.

(Expected time: 45 min)

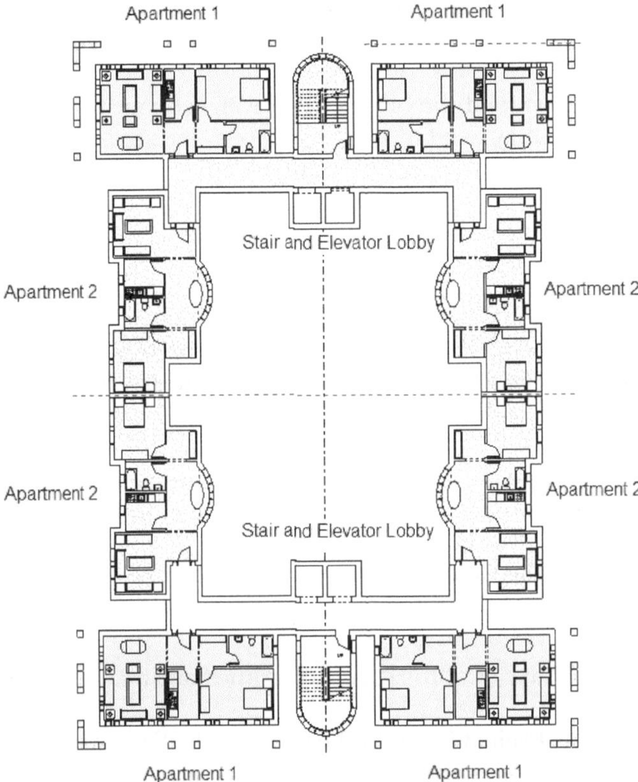

Figure 16-68 *The sketch plan showing the cluster of apartments*

Note

The tools used to copy/paste and link projects have been given to describe their general usage in a project. These tools should, however, be used based on the project parameters and intent.

The following steps are required to complete this tutorial

a. Copy and paste elements of the *Elevator and Stair Lobby* project and the *Apartment 2* project to the base file, refer to Figures 16-70 through 16-72.
b. Group the projects and use the modifying tools to create the *Apartment Cluster* project, refer to Figure 16-73.

c. Open the *Site Plan* project and link the *Apartment Cluster* and the *Club* project using the **Import/Link** tool, refer to Figures 16-74 and 16-75.

d. Save the project using the **Save As** tool.
   For Imperial *c16_ApartmentComplex_tut2.rvt*
   For Metric *M_c16_ApartmentComplex_tut2.rvt*

e. Close the project using the **Close** tool.

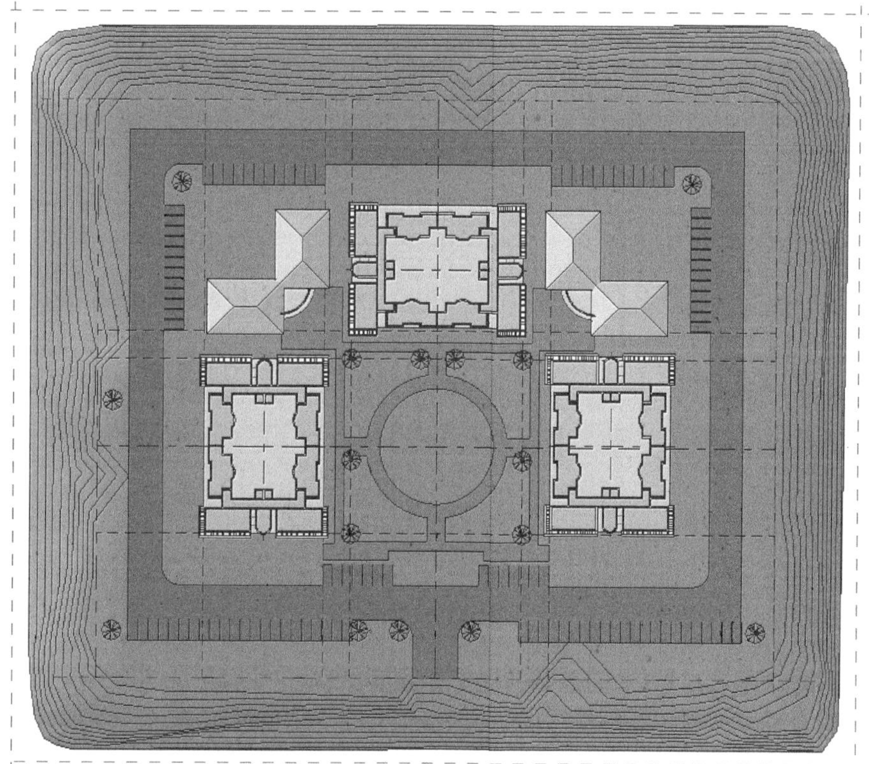

Figure 16-69 *The sketch plan for linking Apartment Cluster and Club project to the Site Plan project*

Copying the Elements of the Elevator and Stair Lobby and Apartment 2 and Pasting in a New Project

In this section of the tutorial, you will first copy and paste the elements of the *Elevator and Stair Lobby* and the *Apartment 2* projects into the *Apartment 1* project. For this, you need to group all the elements in each project before inserting them into the base file. You will also edit the walls of the former project in order to attach them to the latter, based on the layout plan given for the apartment cluster.

1. Choose **Open > Project** from the **File** menu and open the *c11_ElevatorandStairLobby_ex2.rvt* file (for Metric *M_c11_ElevatorandStairLobby_ex2.rvt)* created in Exercise 2 of Chapter 11. You can also download this file from *http://www.cadcim.com*. The path of the file is as follows: *Textbooks > Civil/GIS > Revit Architecture > Autodesk Revit 2018 for Architects and Designers*

2. Open the **{3D}** view from the **Project Browser** and select all elements created in the project. Now, choose the **Create Group** tool from the **Create** panel of the **Modify | Multi-Select** tab; the **Autodesk Revit 2018** message box is displayed.

3. In this message box, choose **OK**; the **Create Model Group** dialog box is displayed. In this dialog box, ensure that **Group 1** is entered in the **Name** edit box and then choose the **OK** button; the **Create Model Group** dialog box closes and the selected elements are highlighted in a group.

4. Next, you need to copy the created group to the clipboard. To do so, ensure that the new group is selected and then choose the **Copy to Clipboard** tool from the **Clipboard** panel of the **Modify | Model Groups** tab; the selected group is copied to the clipboard.

5. Open the *c16_Apartment1_tut1.rvt* file (for Metric *M_c16_Apartment1_tut1.rvt* file) and double-click on the **First Floor** plan view; the corresponding view is displayed. Next, choose the **Modify** tab. In this tab, choose the **Paste from Clipboard** tool from the **Clipboard** panel; the **Duplicate Types** dialog box is displayed. Choose the **OK** button from the dialog box; the copied elements of the *Elevator and Stair Lobby* project are displayed in the drawing area.

6. Zoom out the current view and place the elements of the *Elevator and Stair Lobby* project anywhere outside the *Apartment 1* project profile.

7. Choose the **Move** tool from the **Modify** panel of the **Modify | Model Groups** tab and move the selected elements using the object snaps, as shown in Figure 16-70. Ignore any warning message at this stage. Now, choose the **Finish** button from the **Edit Pasted** panel to clear the current selection.

8. Open the *c08_Apartment2_ex1.rvt* project file (For Metric *M_c08_Apartment2_ex1.rvt* project file) and choose **Site** from the **Project Browser**. Now, select all elements (except the annotations) displayed in the view and choose the **Create Group** tool from the **Create** panel of the **Modify | Model Groups** tab. Then group the selected elements with the default name. Now, ensure that the group is selected and then choose the **Copy to Clipboard** tool from the **Clipboard** panel of the **Modify | Model Groups** tab.

9. Choose the **c16_ Apartment1_tut1-Floor Plan: First Floor** option (for Metric **M_c16_ Apartment1_tut1-Floor Plan: First Floor**) from **View > Windows > Switch Windows** drop-down; the *Apartment 1* project is displayed.

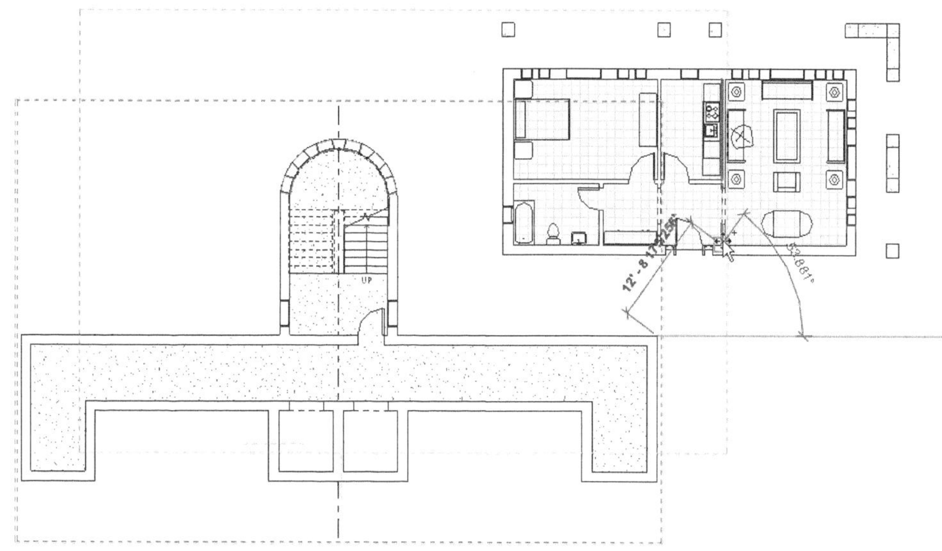

Figure 16-70 Moving the elements of the Elevator and Stair Lobby project

10. In the *Apartment 1* project, choose the **Modify** tab and then choose the **Paste from Clipboard** tool from the **Clipboard** panel of the **Modify | Model Groups** tab; the copied elements of the *Apartment 2* project are displayed in the drawing. Also, the **Duplicate Types** dialog box is displayed. Choose **OK**; the dialog box closes. Now, place the *Apartment 2* elements anywhere outside the profile of the existing project.

11. Next, you need to change the orientation of the pasted elements of the *Apartment 2* project. To do so, ensure that the elements of the *Apartment 2* project are selected and then choose the **Rotate** tool from the **Modify** panel of the **Modify | Model Groups** tab.

12. Use the **Rotate** tool to rotate the elements of the *Apartment 2* project clockwise by 90 degrees, refer to Figure 16-71.

13. Ensure that the elements of the *Apartment 2* project are selected, and then choose the **Mirror - Draw Axis** tool from the **Modify** panel of the **Modify| Model Groups** tab. In the **Options Bar**, ensure that the **Copy** check box is cleared. Now, draw the axis of reflection along the horizontal axis that passes through the centre of the *Apartment 2* project. On doing so, the *Apartment 2* project gets mirrored in its own central horizontal axis.

14. Ensure that the elements of the *Apartment 2* project are selected. Then, choose the **Move** tool from the **Modify** panel of the **Modify | Model Groups** tab and move the elements, as shown in Figure 16-71. Ignore any warning message at this stage. Next, choose the **Modify** button from the **Select** panel.

15. Now, you need to ungroup the elements of the *Elevator and Stair Lobby* project. To do so, select the elements of the *Elevator and Stair Lobby* project from the drawing and then choose the **Ungroup** tool from the **Group** panel of the **Modify| Model Groups** tab; the selected

group is ungrouped and you will notice that the **Modify | Model Groups** tab is replaced by the **Modify | Multi-Select** tab.

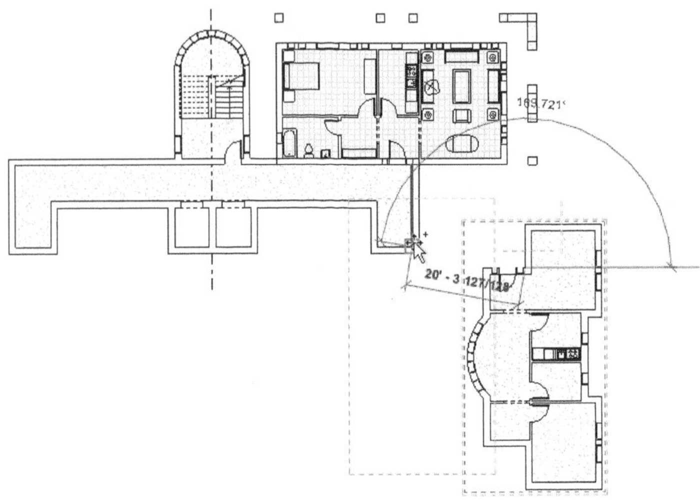

Figure 16-71 *Moving the elements of the Apartment 2 project*

16. Choose the **Modify** button from the **Select** panel and zoom into the area that shows the overlapping walls, refer to Figure 16-72. Next, select the wall of the *Elevator and Stair Lobby* project that overlaps with the wall of the *Apartment 1* project and use the drag control to stretch the walls to their intersection. Similarly, select the other wall of the *Elevator and Stair Lobby* project that intersects with the wall of *Apartment 2* project and use the drag control to stretch it to the intersection point. Use the **Split Element** tool to create a split in the wall that is common to the *Elevator and Stair Lobby* project and the *Apartment 1* project, as shown in Figure 16-73.

17. Next, select the overlapping wall of the *Elevator and Stair Lobby* project near the entrance of the *Apartment 2* project, refer to Figure 16-70 and choose the **Delete** tool from the **Modify** panel of the **Modify | Walls** tab; the selected walls are deleted.

18. Now, you need to save the project file. To do so, choose **Save As > Project**; the **Save As** dialog box is displayed. Enter **c16_Apartment_Cluster_tut2** (for Metric **M_c16_Apartment_Cluster_tut2**) in the **File name** edit box and then choose **Save**; the **Save As** dialog box closes and the project file is saved with the specified name.

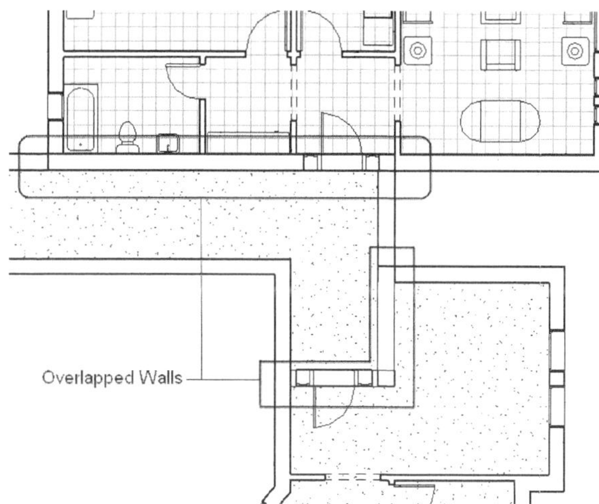

Figure 16-72 The overlapping walls

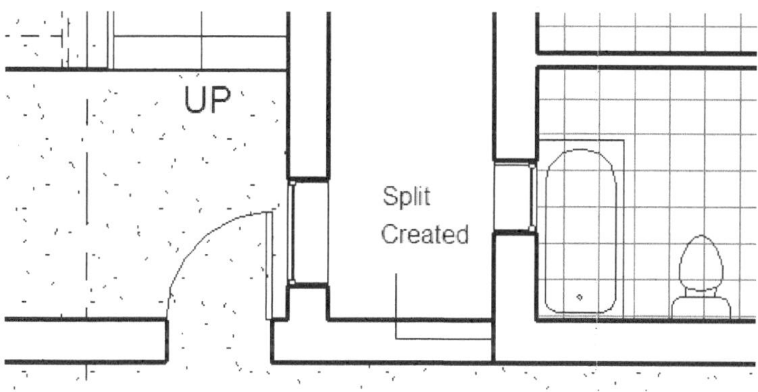

Figure 16-73 The split created to separate the walls

Creating the Apartment Cluster

1. Choose **Site** from the **Floor Plans** head in the **Project Browser** and then select all elements (except annotations) of the *Apartment 1* project. Next, choose the **Create Group** tool from the **Create** panel of the **Modify | Multi-Select** tab; the **Create Model Group** dialog box is displayed.

2. In the **Create Model Group** dialog box, enter **Apartment 1** in the **Name** edit box and choose **OK**; the selected elements of *Apartment 1* project are highlighted as a group. Choose the **Modify** button from the **Select** panel to clear the current selection.

3. Similarly, select the grouped elements of the *Apartment 2* project and rename the group as **Apartment 2**.

4. Choose **First Floor** from the **Floor Plans** head of the **Project Browser** and then select the *Apartment 1* group along with the *Apartment 2* group; the **Modify | Model Groups** tab is displayed.

5. Choose the **Mirror - Pick Axis** tool from the **Modify** panel and mirror the selected groups along the vertical reference line of the center of the *Elevator and Stair Lobby* project. Alternatively, you can choose the **Mirror - Draw Axis** tool and mirror the selected group by drawing a vertical axis along the center of the circular wall. Ignore any warning message at this stage. Choose the **Modify** button from the **Select** panel to clear the current selection.

Note

After mirroring the Apartment 1 and Apartment 2 projects, you will use the drag controls to remove the overlapping of walls, if created.

6. Next, you need to mirror the Design Option 1 of the *Apartment 1* project. To do so, choose **Site** from the **Floor Plans** head in the **Project Browser** and choose the **Manage** tab. Next, select the **18"x18" columns** option from the **Active Design Options** drop-down list in the **Design Options** panel; the elements of the selected Design Option are highlighted.

7. Select the elements created in the **18" X 18" columns** option (for Metric **450 X 450mm columns**). Invoke the **Mirror - Pick Axis** tool from the **Modify | Multi-Select** tab and then mirror the selected elements along the same vertical axis as selected in Step 5. Choose the **Modify** button from the **Select** panel to clear the current selection.

8. Now, choose **First Floor** from the **Floor Plans** head in the **Project Browser** and then select the **Main Model** option from the **Active Design Option** drop-down list in the **Design Options** panel of the **Manage** tab. Next, select all elements of the project and mirror them along the horizontal axis. The horizontal axis should be defined by the wall centerlines of the south walls of the *Apartment 2* project, as shown in the cluster plan of this tutorial, refer to Figure 16-68. Ignore any warning message during the mirroring process. After mirroring the selected elements, choose the **Modify** button from the **Select** panel to clear the current selection.

9. You may need to ungroup the windows of the circular stair wall to mirror the wall separately. You will also mirror the elements created for Design Option 1, separately in the Site view. Use the drag control to complete the overlapping walls. After completing this step, the northeast 3D view should appear similar to the illustration shown in Figure 16-74.

10. Next, select the **Main Model** option from the **Active Design Option** drop-down list in the **Manage** tab and then choose the **Purge Unused** tool from the **Settings** panel of the **Manage** tab. Then, choose the **OK** button from the **Purge unused** dialog box to purge all the unused elements and annotations.

11. Choose **Save** from the **File** menu and save the *Apartment_Cluster* project (for Metric *M_Apartment_Cluster* project).

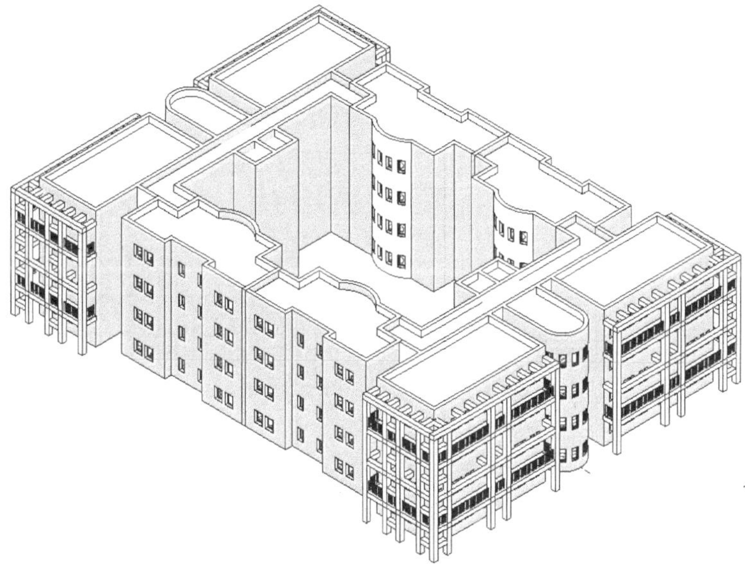

Figure 16-74 *The northeast 3D view for the apartment cluster*

Linking the Apartment Cluster and the Club Projects to the Site

1. Open the *Site Plan* project created in Tutorial 1 of Chapter 9.

2. Choose the **Manage** tab and then choose the **Transfer Project Standards** tool from the **Settings** panel; the **Select Items To Copy** dialog box is displayed. Ensure that the **c16_Apartment _Cluster_tut2** option is selected in the **Copy from** drop-down list. Choose the **OK** button; the **Duplicate Types** message box is displayed. This message box displays the list of element types that are duplicated in the projects.

3. Choose the **New Only** button to return to the *Site Plan* project.

4. Navigate to the *Apartment _Cluster* project and choose **Close** from the **File** menu; the *Apartment Cluster* project is closed.

5. In the *Site Plan* project, choose the **Insert** tab and then choose the **Link Revit** tool from the **Link** panel; the **Import/Link RVT** dialog box is displayed.

6. Select the *c16_Apartment_ Cluster_tut2.rvt* project file (for Metric *M_c16_Apartment_ Cluster_ tut2.rvt* project file)and then select the **Manual - Base point** option from the **Positioning** drop-down list. Choose the **Open** button; the **Import/Link RVT** dialog box closes and the selected file is displayed in the drawing area.

7. Place the *Apartment Cluster* project over the building pad at the location shown in Figure 16-75. You may need to use the **Move** tool to align the linked model. The exact location is not important for this tutorial.

8. Select the linked model and choose the **Array** tool from the **Modify** panel of the **Modify | RVT Links** tab. Create two more copies of the model using the **Radial** tool with center of the model as the center of the site.

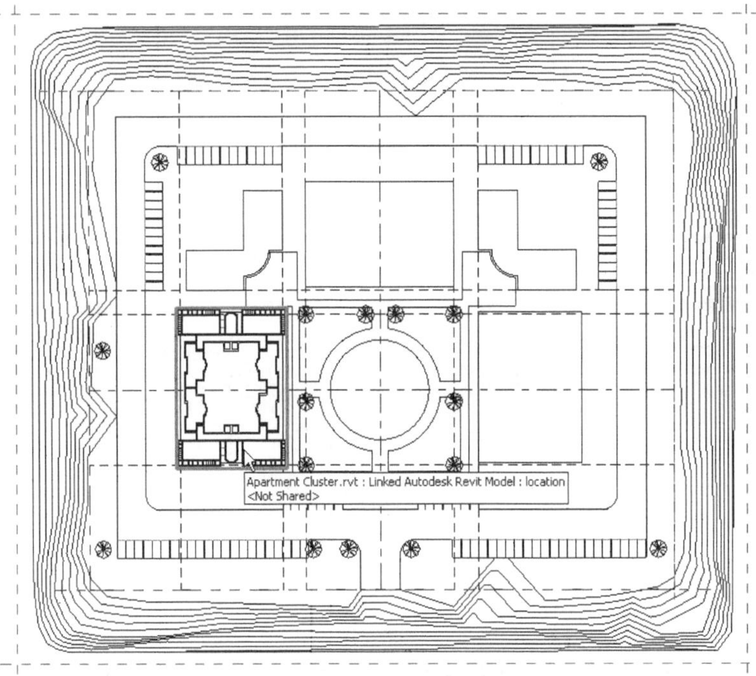

Figure 16-75 *Placing the linked Apartment 1 project over the building pad*

9. Similarly, link and place the *c14_Club_tut2.rvt* file (for Metric *M_c14_Club_tut2.rvt* file)and place it into the *Site Plan* project, as shown in Figure 16-76.

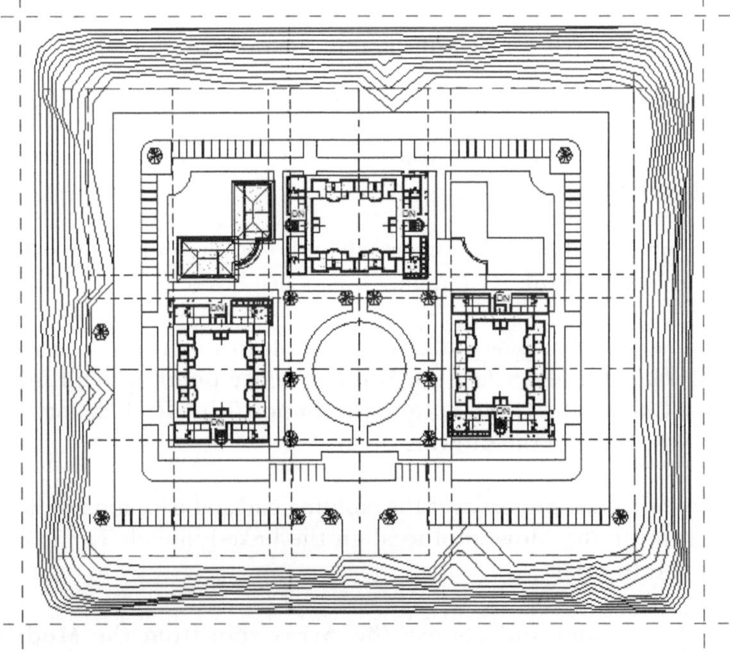

Figure 16-76 *Placing the linked Club project over the building pad*

10. Create a mirror copy of the *Club* project along the vertical axis.

11. You will notice that all the linked projects have been placed at the base level, **Level 1**. Select all the linked models and move them vertically upward by 10'0"(3000mm) using the elevation views. The site plan of the completed project appears similar to the sketch view given for the site plan of this tutorial. The 3D view of the project looks similar to the illustration given in Figure 16-77.

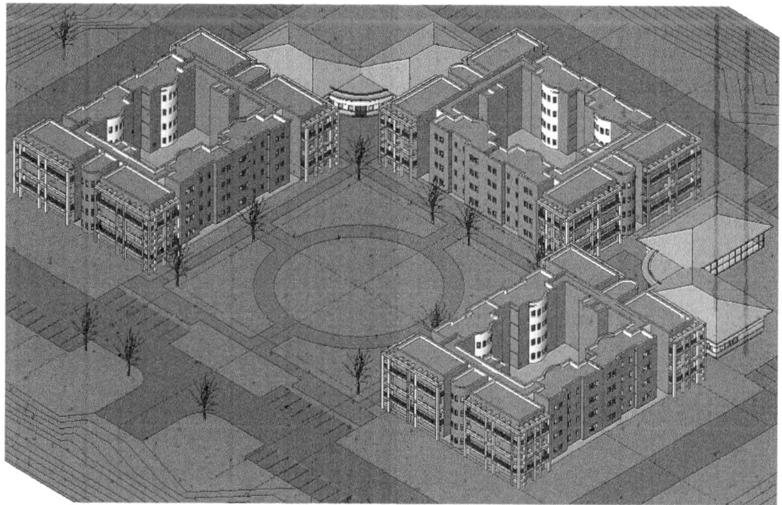

Figure 16-77 *The 3D view of the completed Apartment Complex project*

Saving the Project

In this section, you will save the project file using the **Save As** tool.

1. Choose **Save As > Project** from the **File** menu and save the file as *Apartment Complex* (for Metric *M_Apartment Complex*).

2. Choose **Close** from the **File** menu to close the project file.

Self-Evaluation Test

Answer the following questions and then compare them to those given at the end of this chapter:

1. Structural columns can be aligned along the inclined grid lines using the SPACEBAR. (T/F)
2. You can add structural columns to the multiple grid intersection by using the **At Grids** tool. (T/F)
3. You cannot create multiple design options in the same Autodesk Revit project. (T/F)
4. When a project is linked, its elements can be edited in the base project. (T/F)
5. You cannot control the visibility of elements of a linked project. (T/F)
6. The __________ tool is used to create area schemes.
7. The __________ tool is used to link revit projects.
8. You can use the __________ tool to purge or remove unused elements from an Autodesk Revit project.
9. The __________ tool is used to enable worksets in a project file.
10. The __________ tool can be used to organize the **Project Browser**.

Review Questions

Answer the following questions:

1. The **Transfer Project Standards** tool can be used to link project files. (T/F)

2. The **Manage Links** tool can be used to reload a linked project. (T/F)

3. You can create a number of option sets under each design option. (T/F)

4. Structural columns are created downward from the specified level. (T/F)

5. The **Workset** tool can be used to subdivide and share a large project into smaller projects. (T/F)

6. You can use the **Color Fill** tool to create color plans describing their spatial usage in a building plan. (T/F)

7. The **Phasing** tool enables you to divide a project into various development phases. (T/F)

8. Which of the following tools is used to share projects between project teams?

   a) **Link Revit** b) **Worksets**
   c) **Export** d) **Purge Unused**

9. Which of the following tools is used to create a structural column?

   a) **Wall** b) **Stairs**
   c) **Railing** d) **Structural Column**

10. Which of the following tools is used to remove unused elements and annotations from a project file?

    a) **Purged Unused** b) **Delete**
    c) **Demolish** d) **Cut**

EXERCISES

Exercise 1 Apartment 2

Modify the *Apartment Cluster* project (for Metric *M_Apartment_Cluster* project) created in the Tutorial 1 of this chapter. Add structural elements for the *Apartment 2* exterior wall, based on the sketch plan shown in Figure 16-78 and the sketch elevation, as shown in Figure 16-79. Use 18"x18" columns to generate the facade. The 3D view should appear similar to the illustration given in Figure 16-80. Modify the *Apartment 2* project file and reinsert the elements into the *Apartment Cluster* file. **(Expected time: 45 min)**

Save the file as-

For Imperial *c16_apartment_cluster_ex1.rvt*
For Metric *M_c16_apartment_cluster_ex1.rvt)*

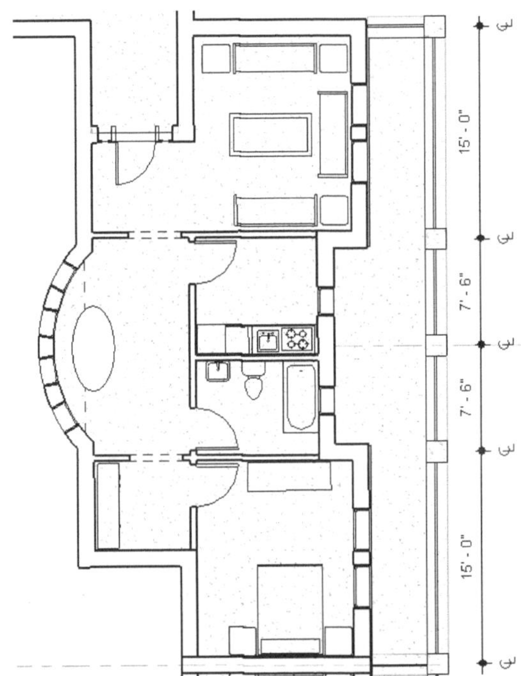

Figure 16-78 *The sketch plan view for adding structural elements to the Apartment 2 project*

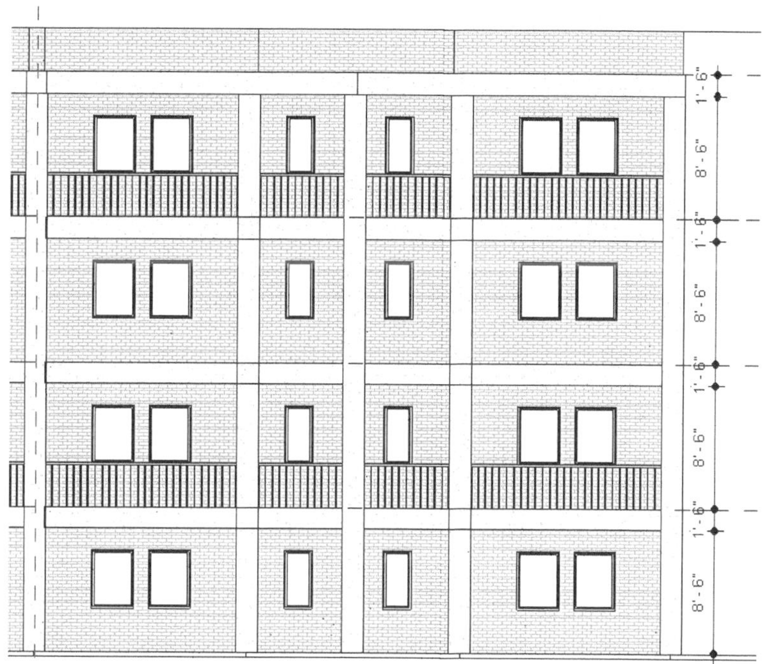

Figure 16-79 *Sketch elevation for adding structural elements to the Apartment 2 project*

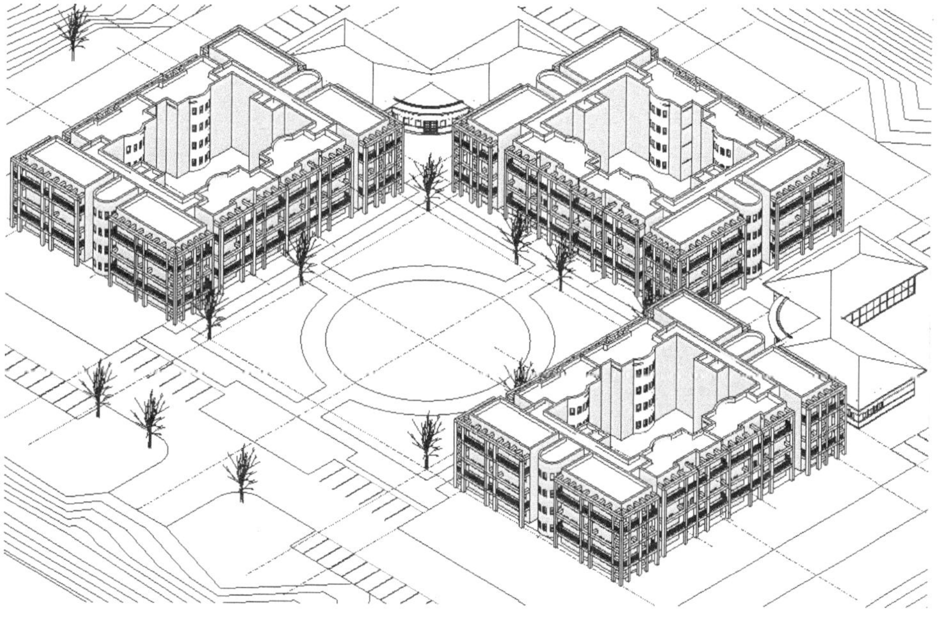

Figure 16-80 *The 3D view of the completed Apartment Complex project*

Exercise 2 Apartment Complex

Create the 3D perspective views of the *Apartment Complex* project, based on the view shown in Figures 16-81 and 16-82. Also, render the perspective views.

(Expected time: 30 min)

Save the file as *exercise1_apartment_cluster.rvt* (for Metric *M_exercise1_apartment_cluster.rvt*)

Figure 16-81 *First 3D perspective view of the Apartment Complex project*

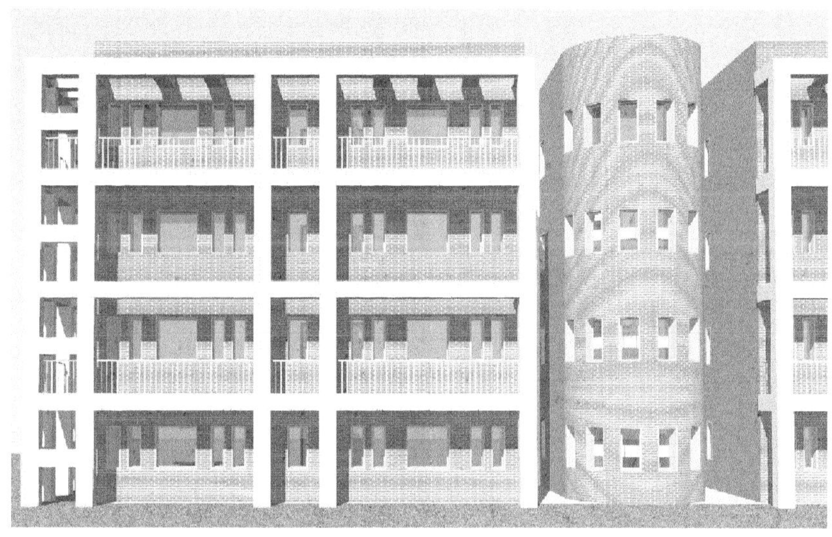

Figure 16-82 *Partial 3D perspective view of the Apartment Complex project*

Answers to Self-Evaluation Test

1. T, **2.** T, **3.** F, **4.** F, **5.** F, **6. Area and Volume Computations**, **7. Link Revit**, **8. Purge Unused**, **9. Worksets**, **10. Browser Organization**

Index

A

B

C

D

E

F

P

R

S

T

U

V

W

CAD/CAM/CIM/ANIMATION/CIVIL BOOKS

by Prof. Sham Tickoo (Purdue University, USA and Autodesk Authorised Author)

Autodesk 3ds Max 2017
A Comprehensive Guide
ISBN: 9789386551139
Price: 999 /-

Autodesk 3ds Max 2017
for **Beginners**
A Tutorial Approach
ISBN: 9789386551122
Price: 999 /-

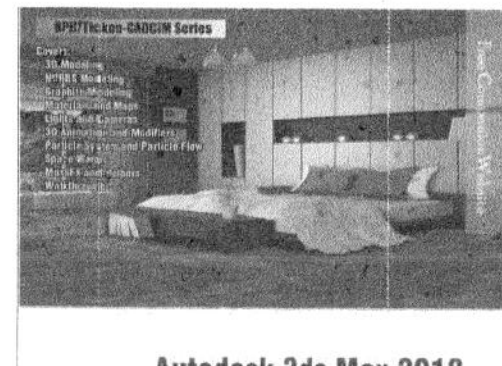

Autodesk 3ds Max 2018
A Comprehensive Guide
ISBN: 9789386551689
Price: 999 /-

Autodesk 3ds Max 2018
for **Beginners**
A Tutorial Approach
ISBN: 9789386551672
Price: 899 /-

Autodesk 3ds Max 2019
A Comprehensive Guide
ISBN: 9789388176279
Price: 999 /-

Autodesk 3ds Max 2019
A Beginners Guide
ISBN: 9789388511186
Price: 899 /-

Blender
for **Digital Artists**
ISBN: 9789388176262
Price: 599 /-

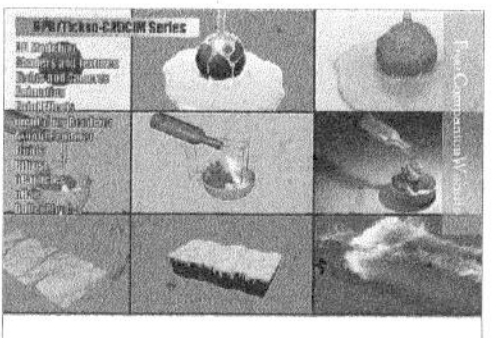

Autodesk Maya 2017
A Comprehensive Guide
ISBN: 9789386551146
Price: 899 /-

Autodesk Maya 2018
A Comprehensive Guide
ISBN: 9789386551702
Price: 899 /-

Autodesk Maya 2019
for **3D Artists**
ISBN: 9789389423181
Price: 899 /-

Autodesk Maya 2019
Workbook
ISBN: 9789389423068
Price: 360/-

Pixologic ZBrush 4R7
A Comprehensive Guide
ISBN: 9789386551153
Price: 899 /-

CAD/CAM/CIM/ANIMATION/CIVIL BOOKS

by Prof. Sham Tickoo (Purdue University, USA and Autodesk Authorised Author)

Creo Parametric 6.0
for **Engineer and Designer**
ISBN: 9789389423136
Price: 1299 /-

Creo Parametric 6.0
Workbook
ISBN: 9789389423075
Price: 360/-

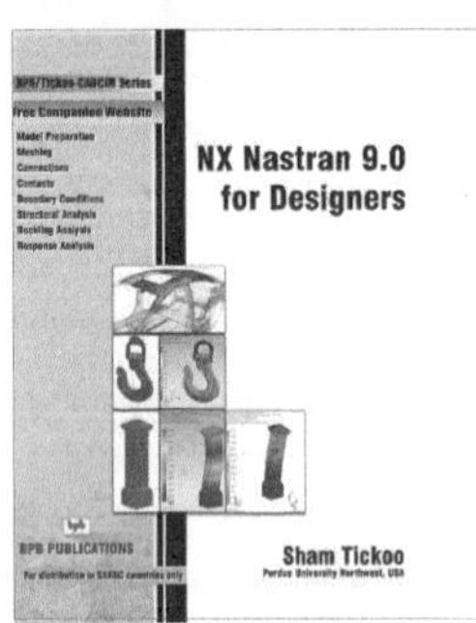

NX Nastran 9.0
for **Designers**
ISBN: 9789386551221
Price: 899 /-

NX 11.0
for **Designers**
ISBN: 9789386551245
Price: 1099 /-

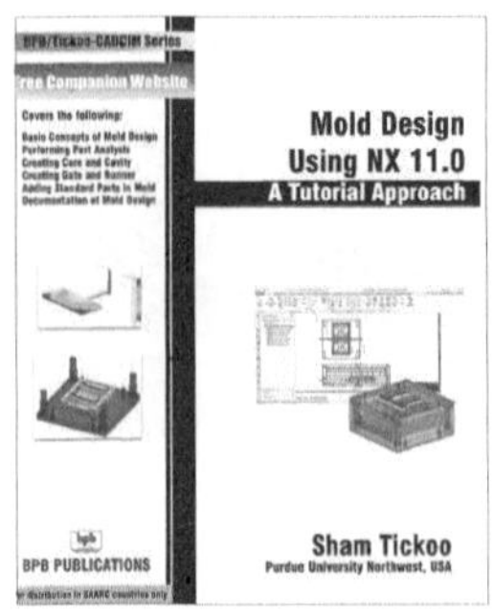

Mold Design Using NX 11.0
A Tutorial Approach
ISBN: 9789387284067
Price: 599 /-

Siemens NX 12.0
for **Designers**
ISBN: 9789387284074
Price: 1099 /-

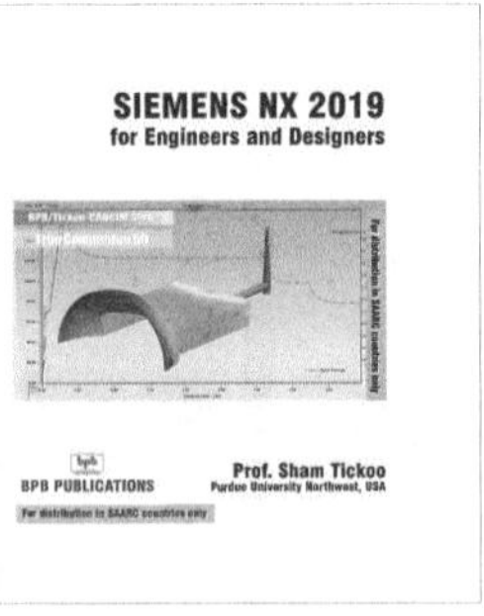

Siemens NX 2019
for **Engineers and Designers**
ISBN: 9789389423112
Price: 1299 /-

Siemens NX 2019
Workbook
ISBN: 9789389423051
Price: 360/-

Autodesk Inventor
Professional 2017
for **Designers**
ISBN: 9789386551269
Price: 1299 /-

Autodesk Inventor
Professional 2018
for **Designers**
ISBN: 9789386551641
Price: 1199 /-

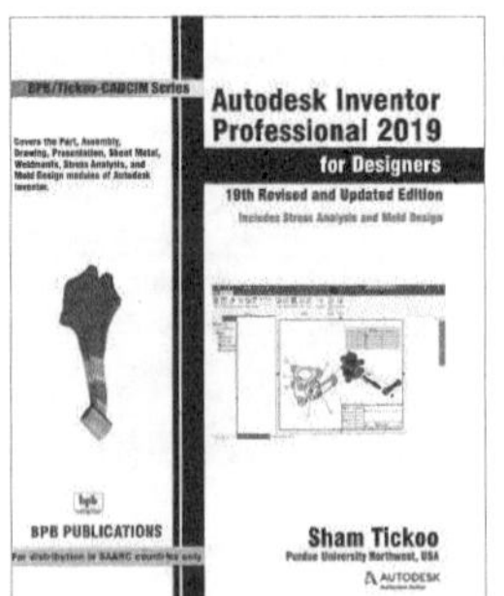

Autodesk Inventor
Professional 2019
for **Designers**
ISBN: 9789388176293
Price: 1299 /-

Autodesk Inventor
Professional 2020
for **Engineers and Designers**
ISBN: 9789389423105
Price: 1299 /-